MiniAtlas
London

Contents

II	**Key to map pages**
IV	Administrative and Postcode boundaries
VI	**Map symbols**
1	**Street maps**
77	**Key to Central London maps, symbols**
78	**Central London enlarged maps**
174	**Index**
288	**List of numbered locations**
312	London Underground
314	Central London theatres and cinemas

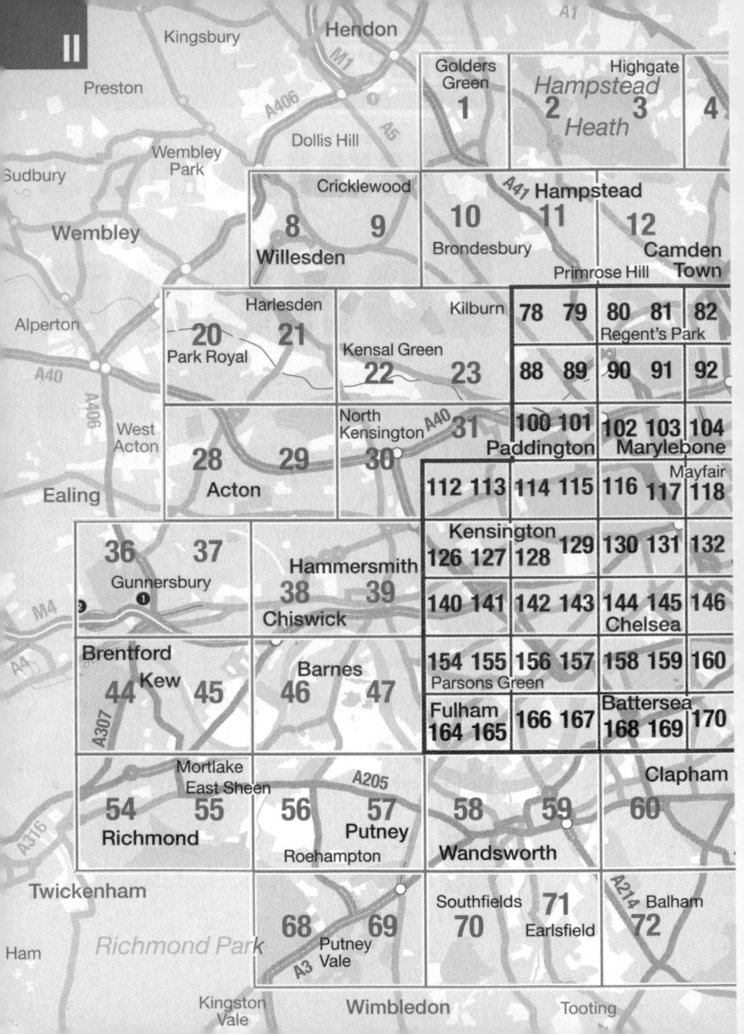

Kingsbury
Hendon
A1

Preston

Golders
Green
1

Highgate

Hampstead

2 *Heath* **3** **4**

A406

M1

Dollis Hill

A5

Sudbury

Wembley
Park

Cricklewood

A41 **Hampstead**

8 **9** **10** **11**

12

Wembley

Brondesbury

Primrose Hill

Camden
Town

Willesden

Alperton

Harlesden

Kilburn

78 **79** **80** **81** **82**

West
Acton

20 **21**

Park Royal

Kensal Green
22 **23**

Regent's Park

A40

88 **89** **90** **91** **92**

A406

North
Kensington A40

100 **101** **102** **103** **104**

28 **29** **30** **31**

Paddington **Marylebone**

Acton

Mayfair

112 **113** **114** **115** **116** **117** **118**

Ealing

36 **37**

Gunnersbury

Hammersmith

38 **39**

Kensington

126 **127** **128** **129** **130** **131** **132**

Chiswick

M4

140 **141** **142** **143** **144** **145** **146**

Chelsea

Brentford

Barnes

154 **155** **156** **157** **158** **159** **160**

44 **Kew**

45 **46** **47**

Parsons Green

Fulham

Battersea

A4

A307

164 **165** **166** **167** **168** **169** **170**

Mortlake
East Sheen

A205

Clapham

A316

54 **55** **56** **57** **58** **59** **60**

Richmond

Putney

Roehampton

Wandsworth

Twickenham

Southfields **71**

A214 Balham

Ham

Richmond Park

68 **69** **70** Earlsfield **72**

Putney
Vale

A3

Kingston
Vale

Wimbledon

Tooting

Key to map pages

Atlas pages at 3½ inches to 1 mile are shown in blue

Central London atlas pages at 7 inches to 1 mile are shown in red
(See page 77)

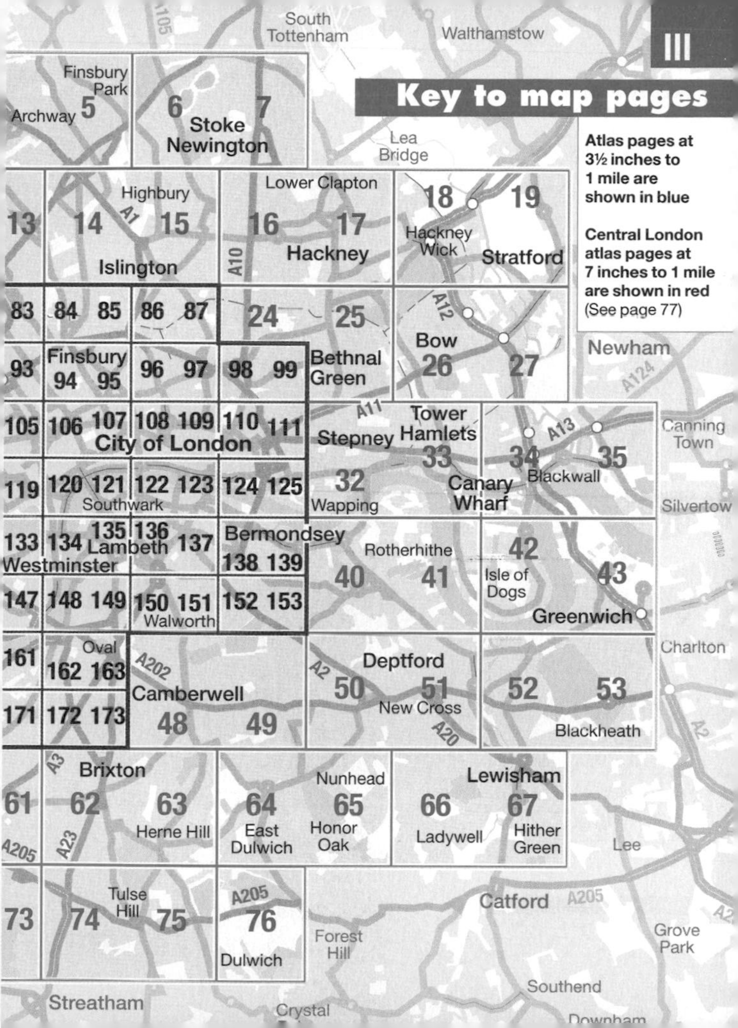

South Tottenham
Walthamstow
Finsbury Park
Archway 5
6
7
Stoke Newington
Lea Bridge
Highbury
13
14
A1
15
Islington
Lower Clapton
16
17
A10
Hackney
18
19
Hackney Wick
Stratford
83
84
85
86
87
24
25
A12
Bow
26
27
Newham
A124
93
Finsbury
94
95
96
97
98
99
Bethnal Green
A11
105
106
107
108
109
110
111
City of London
Stepney
Tower Hamlets
33
34
A13
35
Canning Town
Blackwall
119
120
121
122
123
124
125
Southwark
32
Wapping
Canary Wharf
Silvertow
133
134
135
136
Lambeth
137
Westminster
Bermondsey
138
139
Rotherhithe
40
41
42
Isle of Dogs
43
147
148
149
150
151
Walworth
152
153
Greenwich
161
Oval
162
163
A202
Camberwell
A2
Deptford
50
51
New Cross
A20
52
53
Charlton
171
172
173
48
49
Blackheath
A3
Brixton
61
62
63
Herne Hill
A23
A205
64
East Dulwich
Nunhead
65
Honor Oak
66
Ladywell
Lewisham
67
Hither Green
Lee
73
74
Tulse Hill
75
A205
76
Dulwich
Forest Hill
Catford
A205
Grove Park
Southend
Streatham
Crystal
Downham

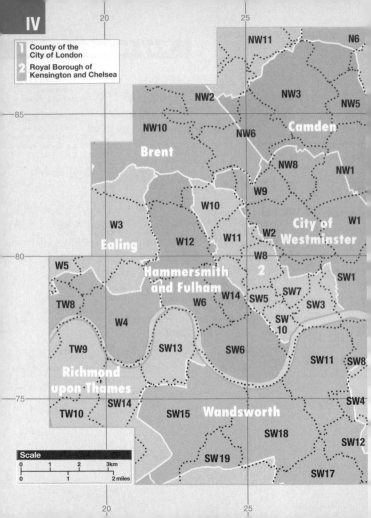

IV

1 County of the
City of London

2 Royal Borough of
Kensington and Chelsea

Scale
0   1   2   3km
0   1   2 miles

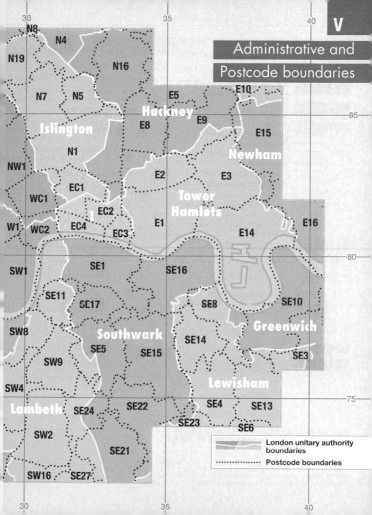

N8
N4
N19
N16
N7
N5
Islington
E5
E10
Hackney
E8
E9
E15
Newham
N1
E2
E3
NW1
EC1
WC1
Tower
Hamlets
W1
WC2
EC4
EC2
E1
E16
EC3
E14
SW1
SE1
SE16
SE11
SE8
SE10
SE17
SW8
SW9
SE5
SE14
Greenwich
SW4
SE15
SE3
Lambeth
SE24
SE22
SE4
SE13
Lewisham
SW2
SE23
SE6
SE21
SW16
SE27

London unitary authority
boundaries
Postcode boundaries

VI

Key to map symbols

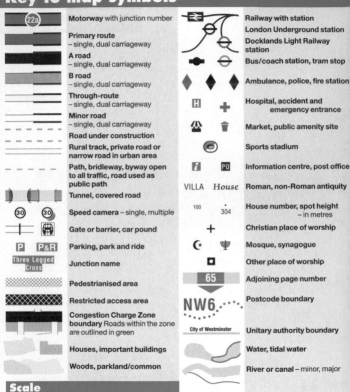

Motorway with junction number	Railway with station
Primary route – single, dual carriageway	London Underground station
A road – single, dual carriageway	Docklands Light Railway station
B road – single, dual carriageway	Bus/coach station, tram stop
Through-route – single, dual carriageway	Ambulance, police, fire station
Minor road – single, dual carriageway	Hospital, accident and emergency entrance
Road under construction	Market, public amenity site
Rural track, private road or narrow road in urban area	Sports stadium
Path, bridleway, byway open to all traffic, road used as public path	Information centre, post office
Tunnel, covered road	Roman, non-Roman antiquity
Speed camera – single, multiple	House number, spot height – in metres
Gate or barrier, car pound	Christian place of worship
Parking, park and ride	Mosque, synagogue
Junction name	Other place of worship
Pedestrianised area	Adjoining page number
Restricted access area	Postcode boundary
Congestion Charge Zone boundary Roads within the zone are outlined in green	Unitary authority boundary
Houses, important buildings	Water, tidal water
Woods, parkland/common	River or canal – minor, major

VILLA *House*

100 304

65

NW6

City of Westminster

Scale

3½ inches to 1 mile   1:18103

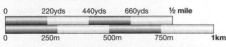

0   220yds   440yds   660yds   ½ mile

0   250m   500m   750m   1km

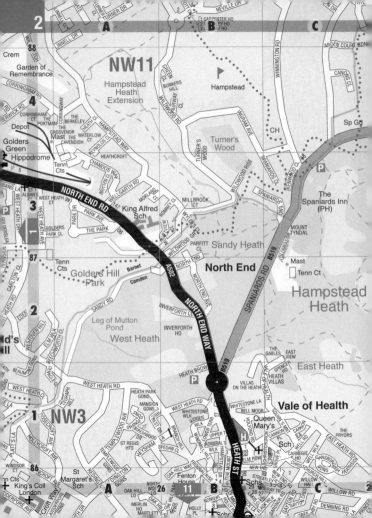

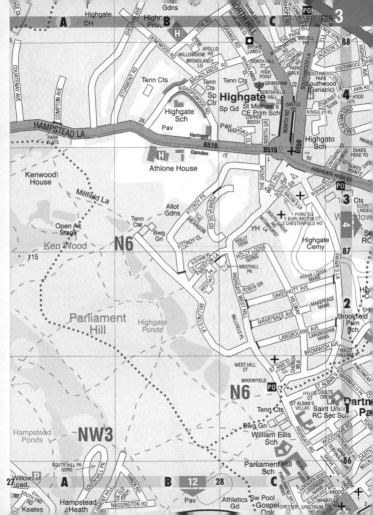

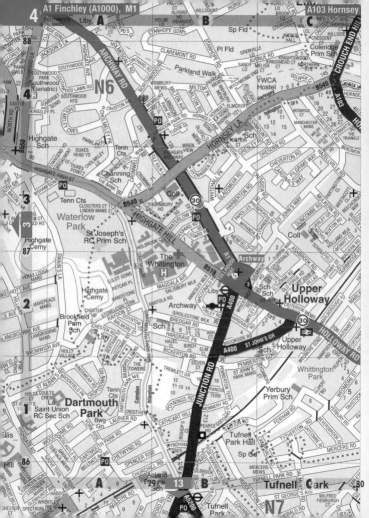

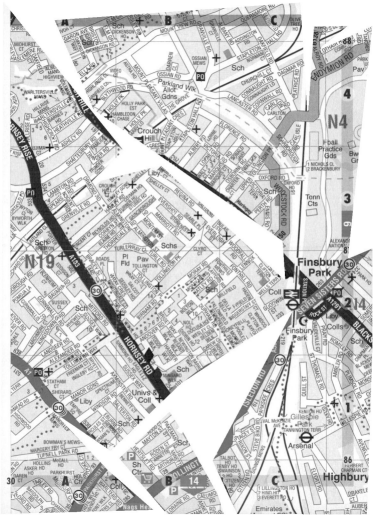

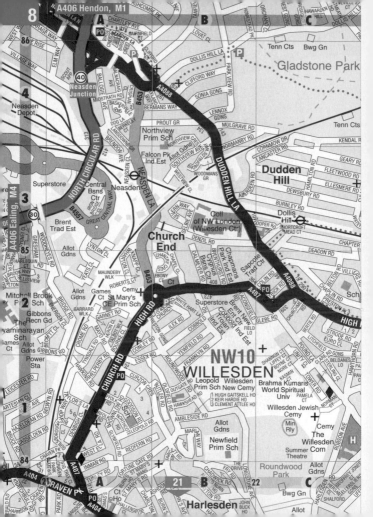

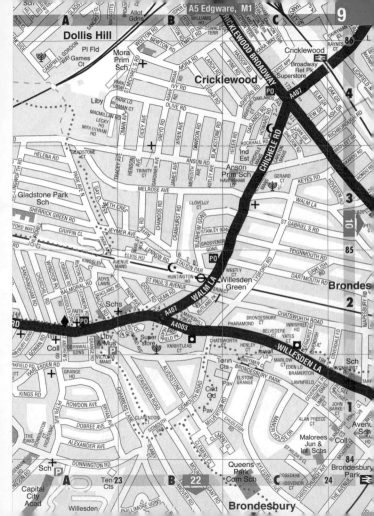

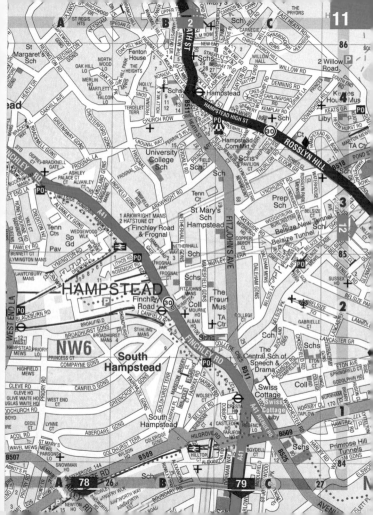

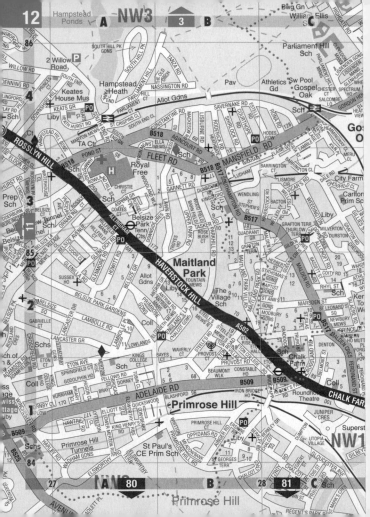

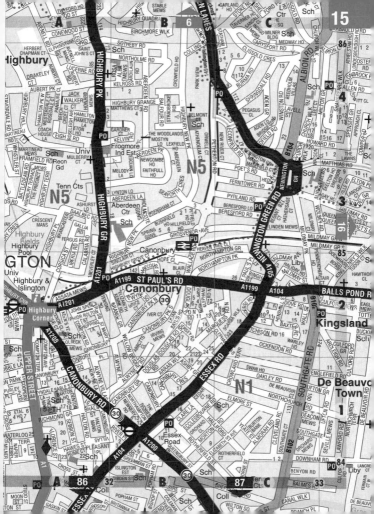

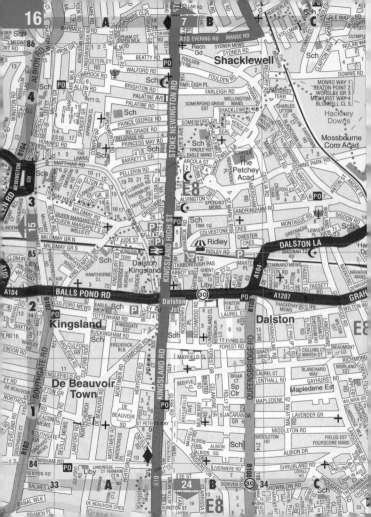

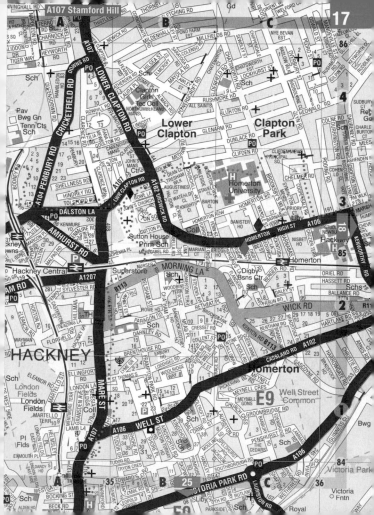

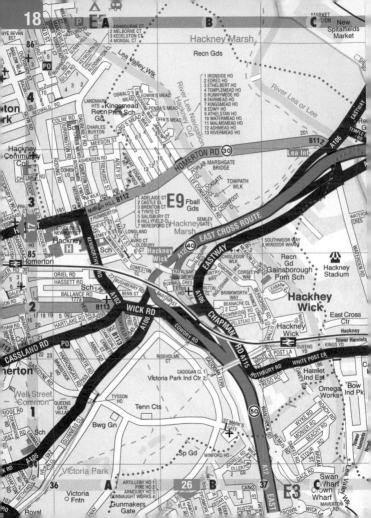

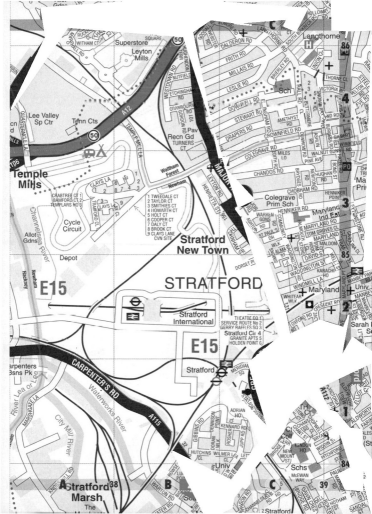

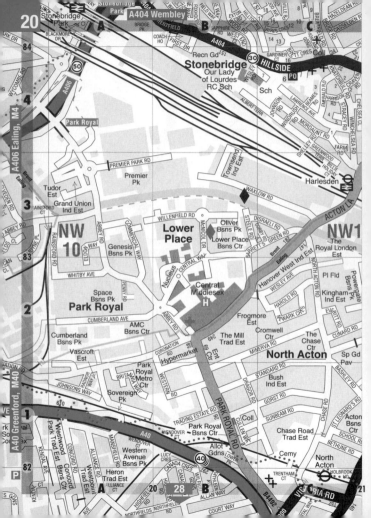

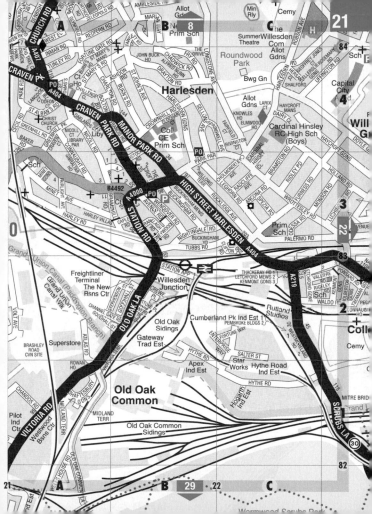

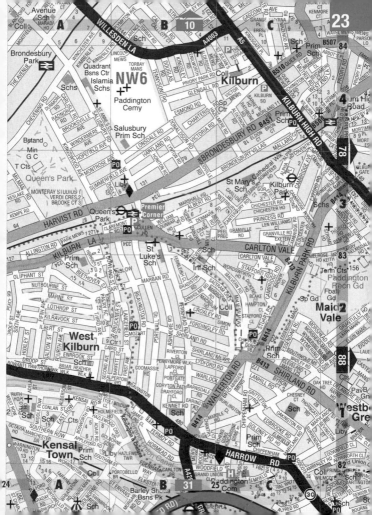

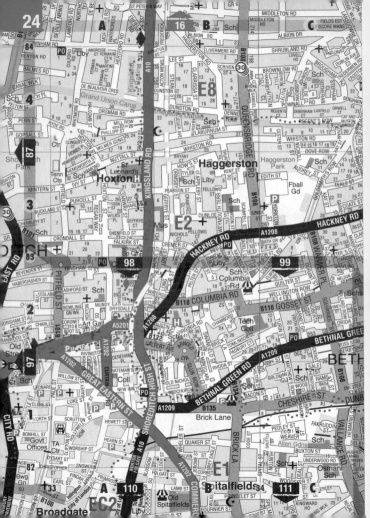

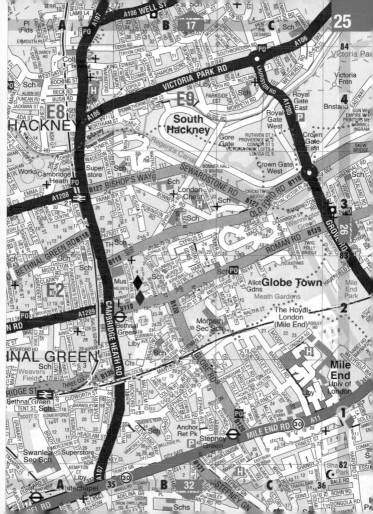

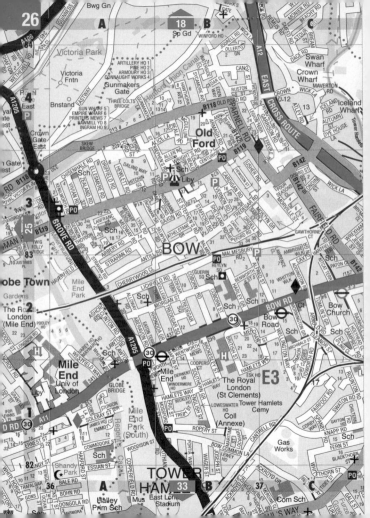

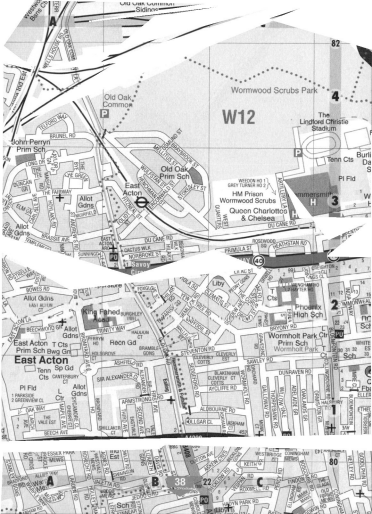

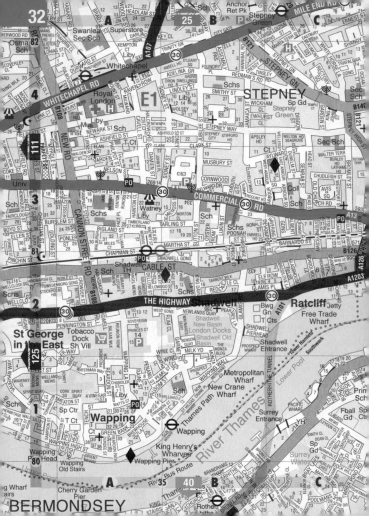

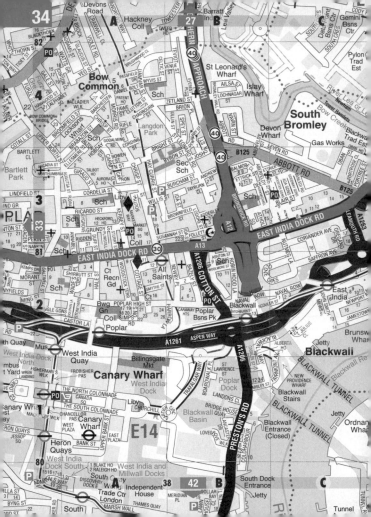

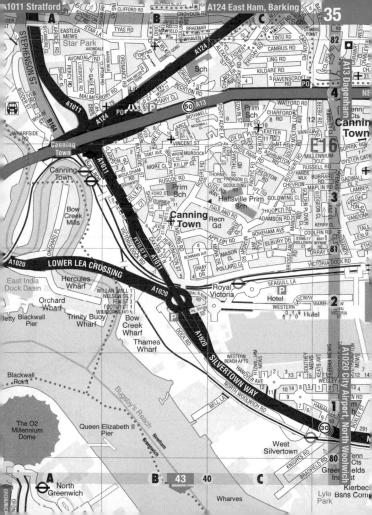

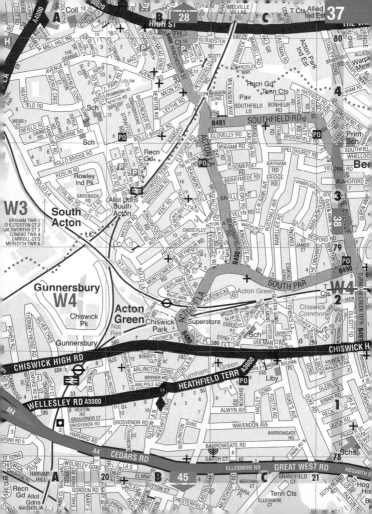

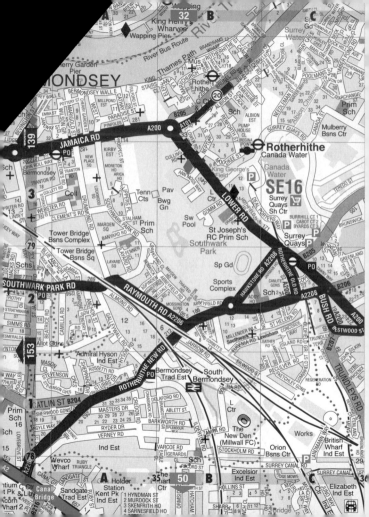

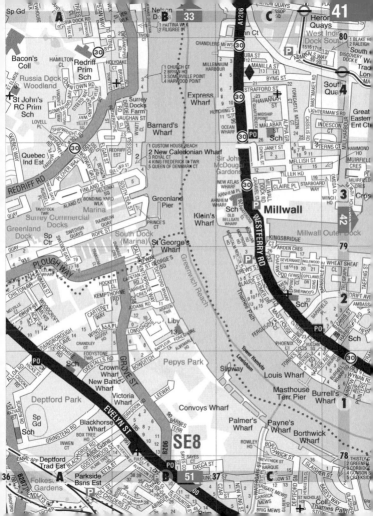

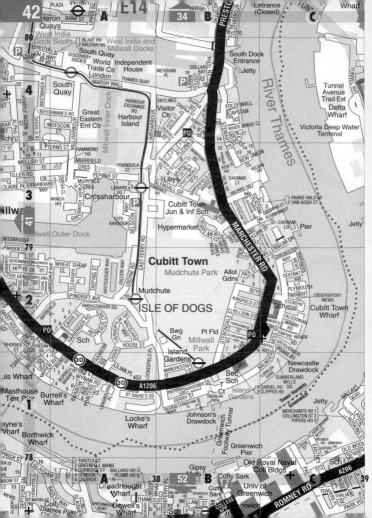

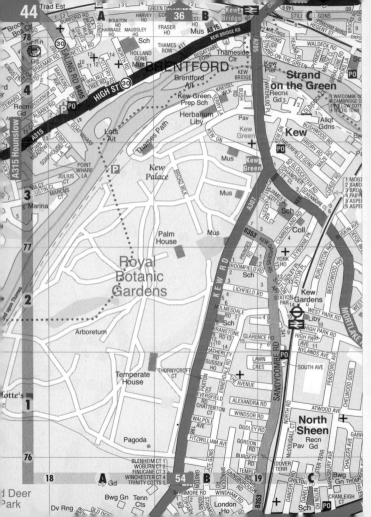

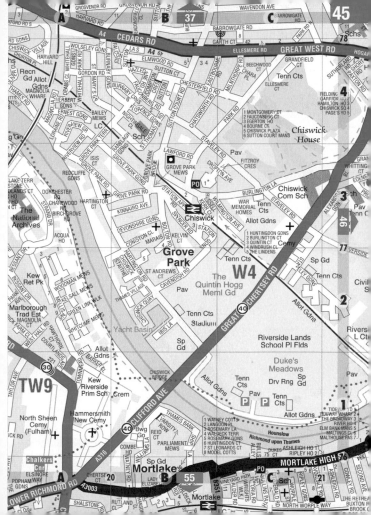

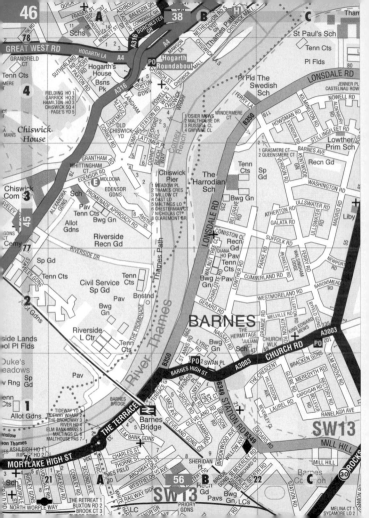

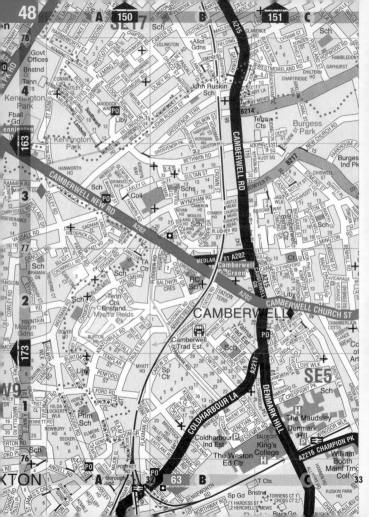

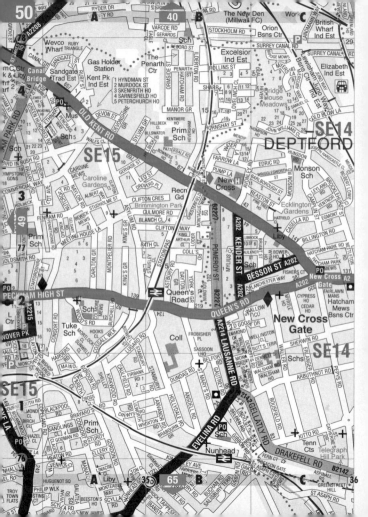

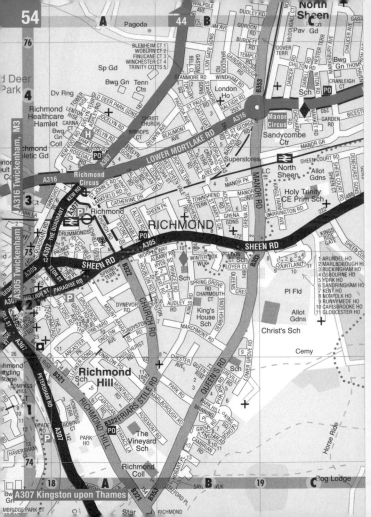

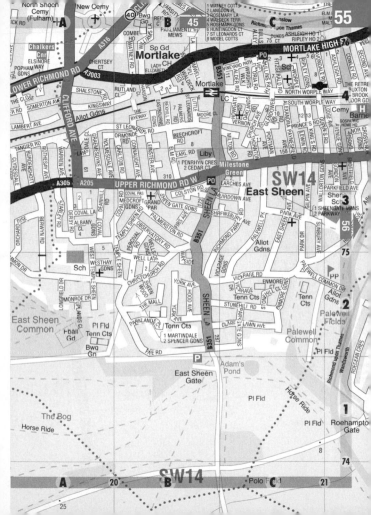

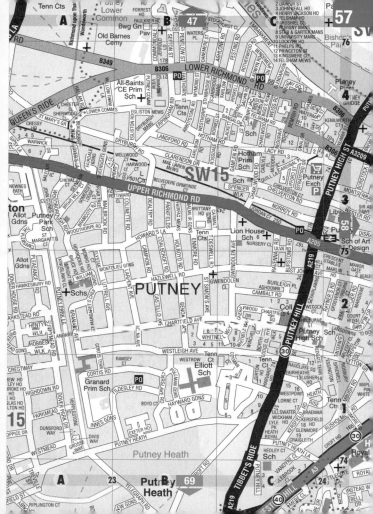

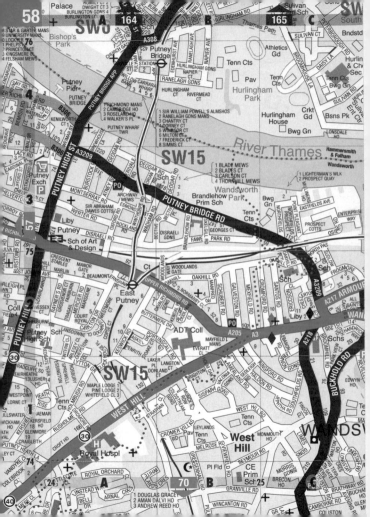

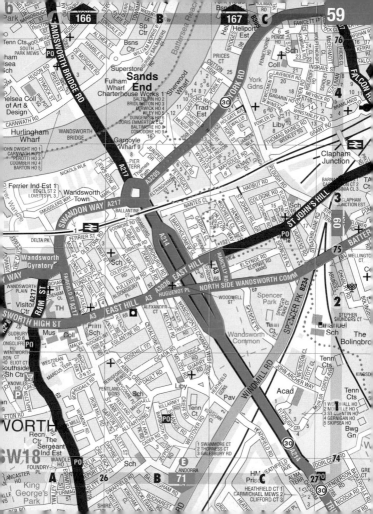

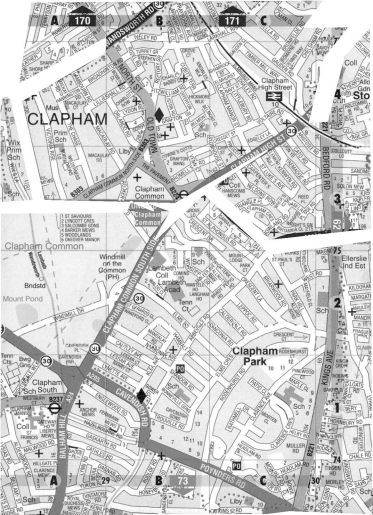

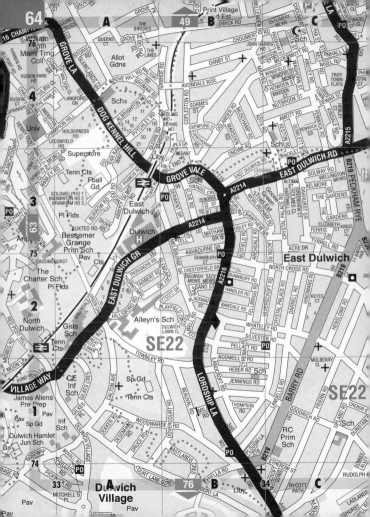

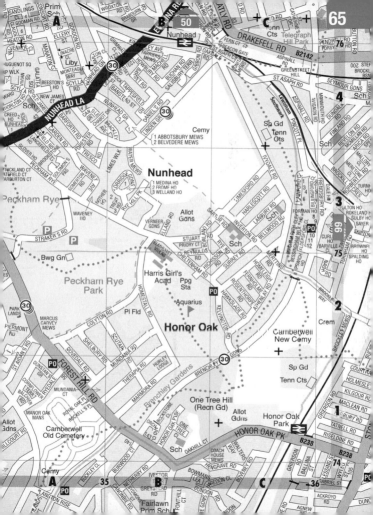

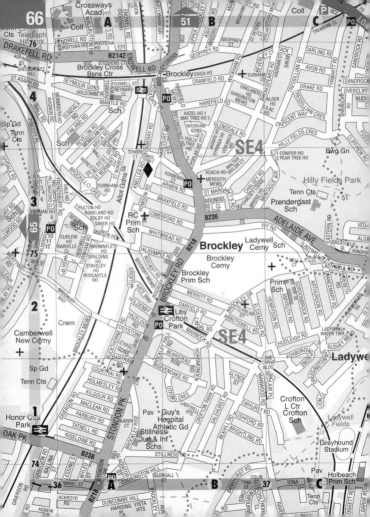

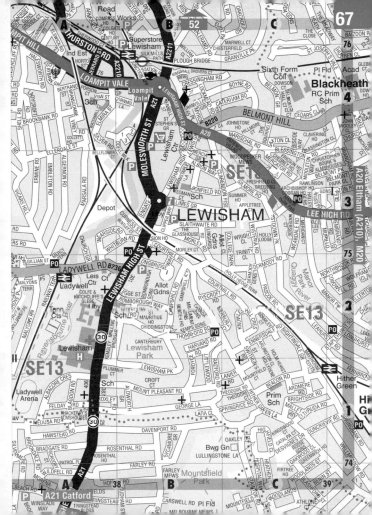

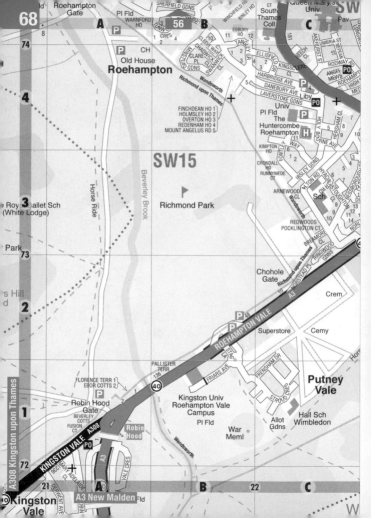

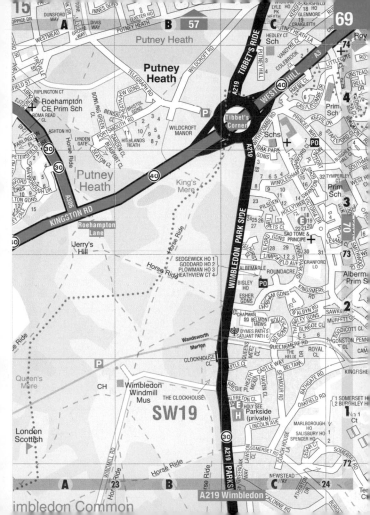

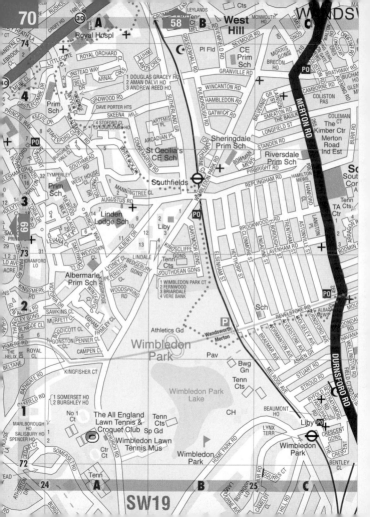

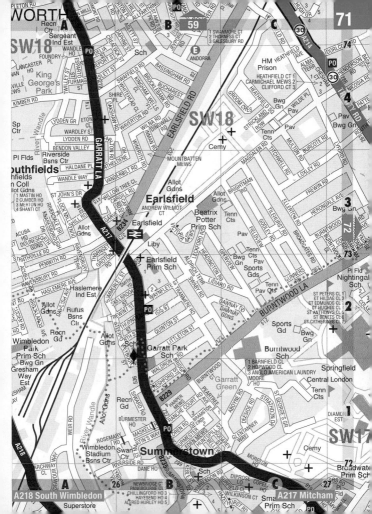

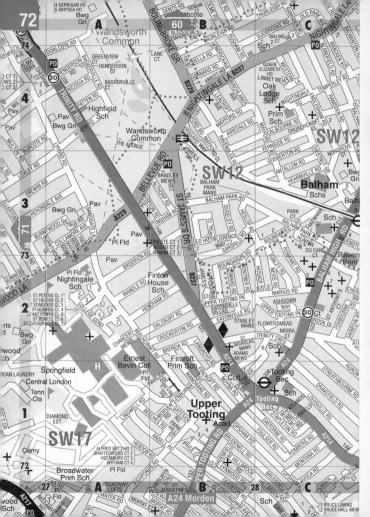

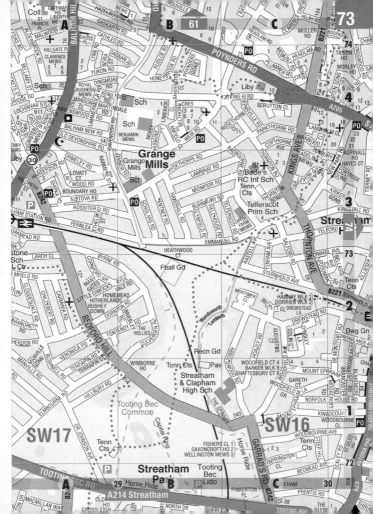

Key to enlarged map pages

78 79 St John's Wood	Primrose Hill 80 81 Regent's Park	82 83 Somers Town	Islington 84 85 King's Cross	86 87	A10
Maida Vale 88 89 Westbourne Green	Lisson Grove 90 91	St Pancras Finsbury Shoreditch 92 93 Bloomsbury	Holborn 94 95	96 97	Bethnal 98 99 Green
Paddington 100 101	Marylebone 102 103	Fitzrovia 104 105	106 107 St Giles	108 109 City	Spitalfields 110 111 Whitechapel A11
Notting Hill 112 113	Bayswater 114 115 Kensington Gardens	Mayfair 116 117 Hyde Park	Strand 118 119 St James	120 121 South Bank	A13 124 125 St George in the East
Kensington Holland Pk 126 127 West Kensington	Knightsbridge 128 129 Brompton	Green Park 130 131	Waterloo 132 133	The Borough 134 135	138 139 Bermondsey
140 141 Earl's Ct	South Kensington 142 143 Westminster	Victoria 144 145 Belgravia Pimlico	Lambeth 146 147 Vauxhall Kennington	Newington 148 149 150 151 Walworth	152 153
West Brompton Chelsea 154 155 Parsons Green	156 157 Walham Green	Battersea Park 158 159 Nine Elms	160 161	South Lambeth 162 163	A2
Fulham 164 165	Battersea 166 167	168 169	170 171	172 173 Stockwell	A202

Congestion
Charge Zone

Additional symbols on enlarged maps

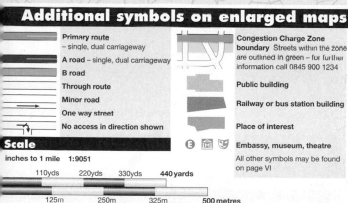

Primary route
– single, dual carriageway

A road – single, dual carriageway

B road

Through route

Minor road

One way street

No access in direction shown

Congestion Charge Zone boundary Streets within the zone are outlined in green – for further information call 0845 900 1234

Public building

Railway or bus station building

Place of interest

Ⓔ 🏛 🎭   Embassy, museum, theatre

All other symbols may be found on page VI

Scale

inches to 1 mile 1:9051

110yds	220yds	330yds	**440 yards**

125m	250m	325m	**500 metres**

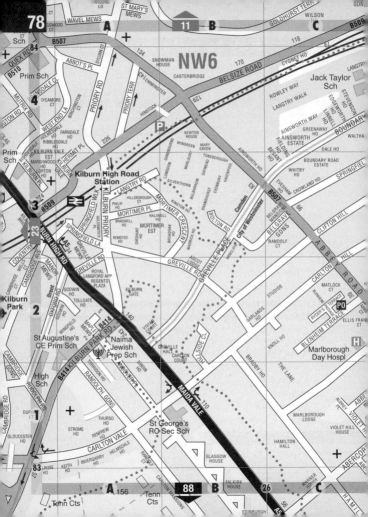

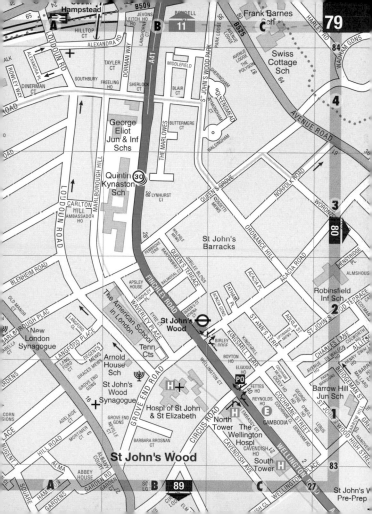

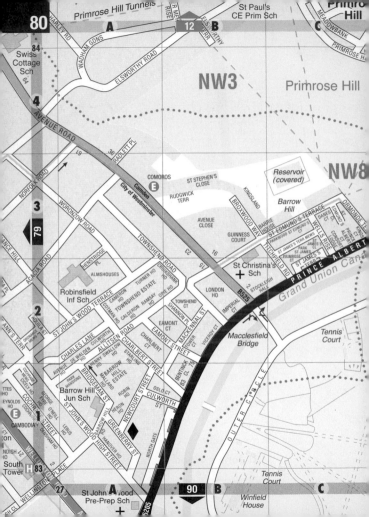

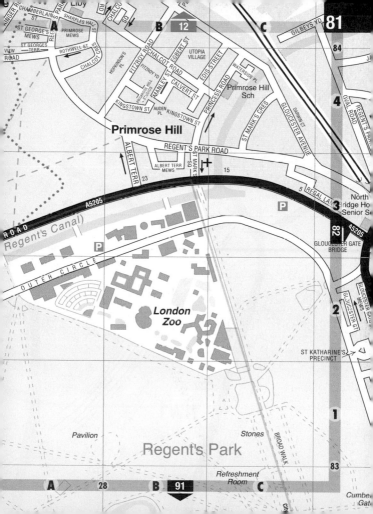

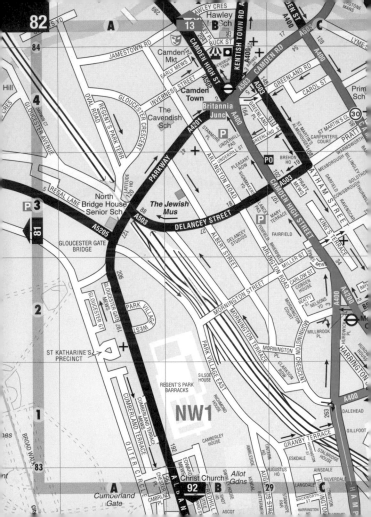

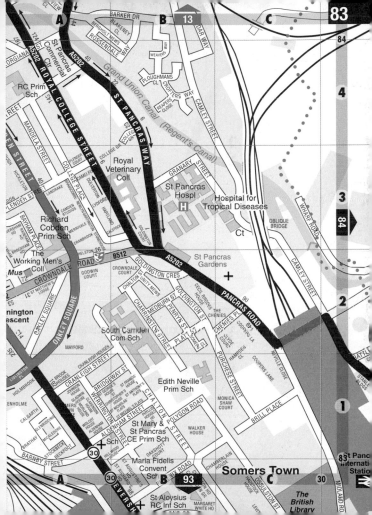

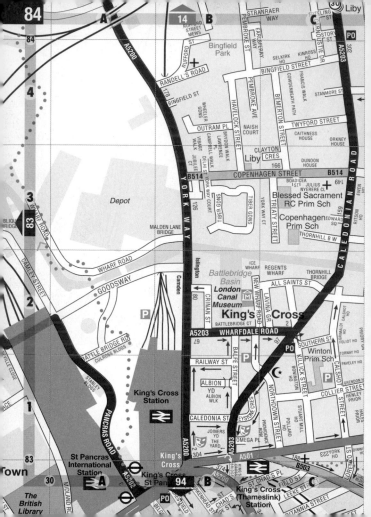

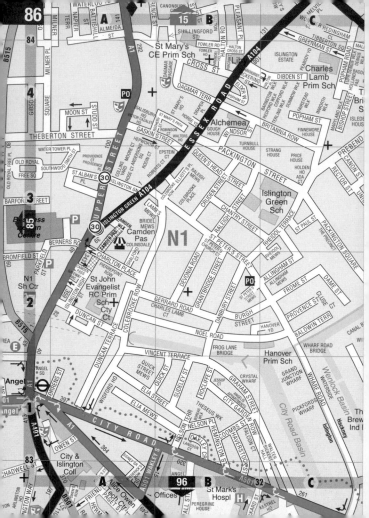

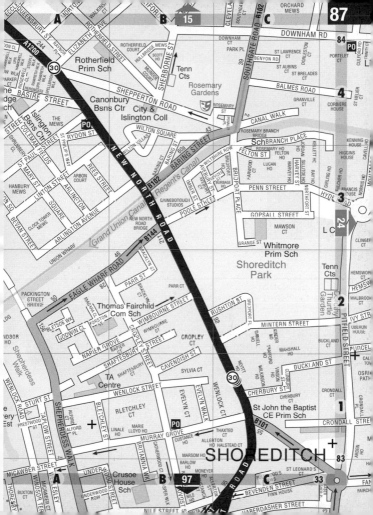

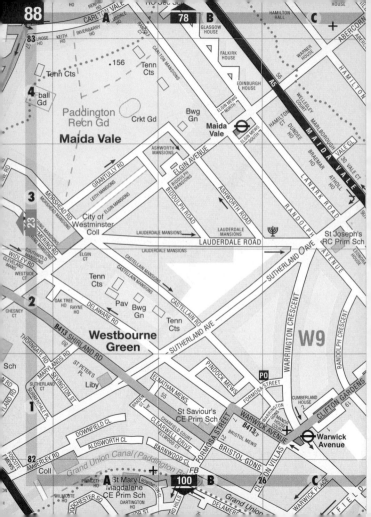

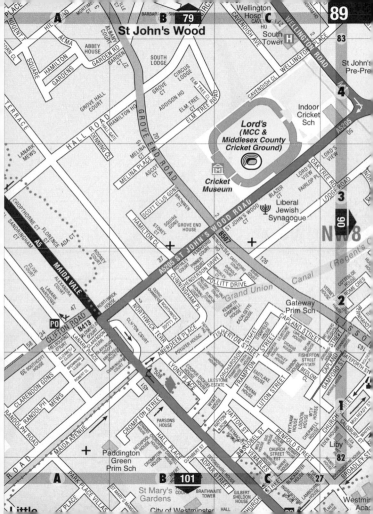

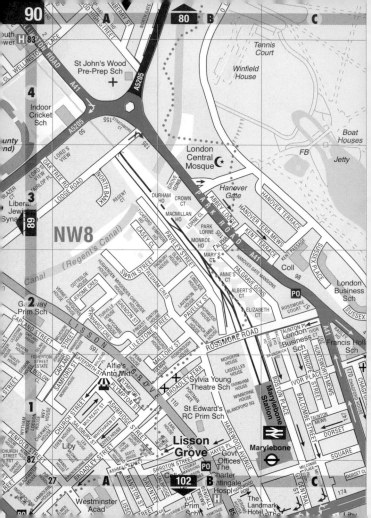

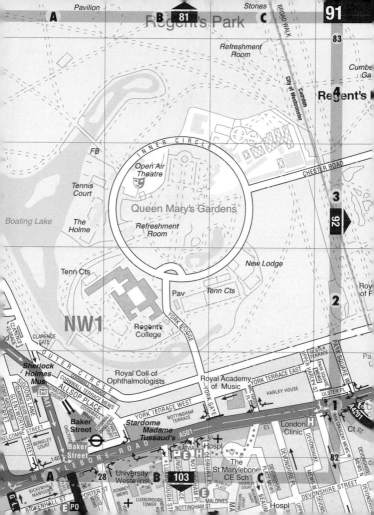

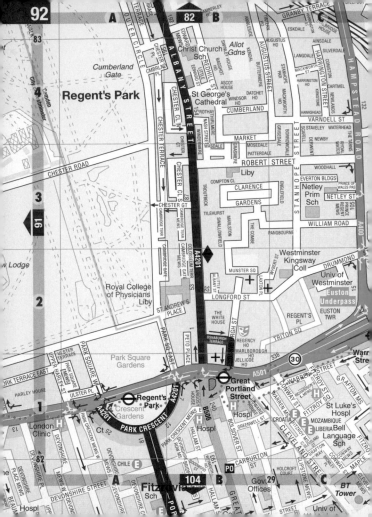

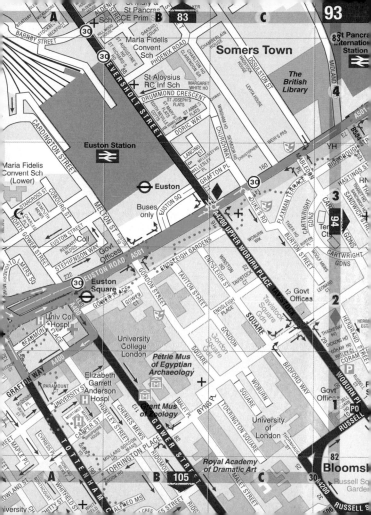

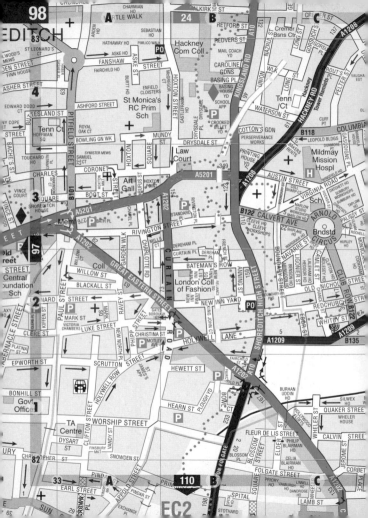

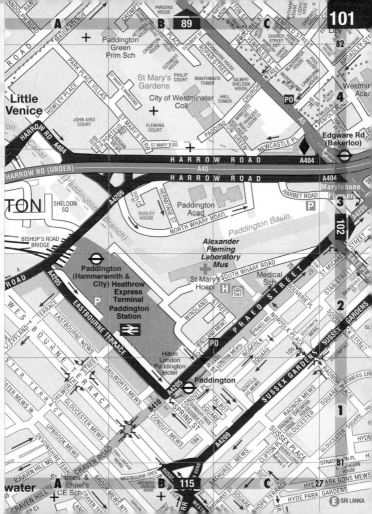

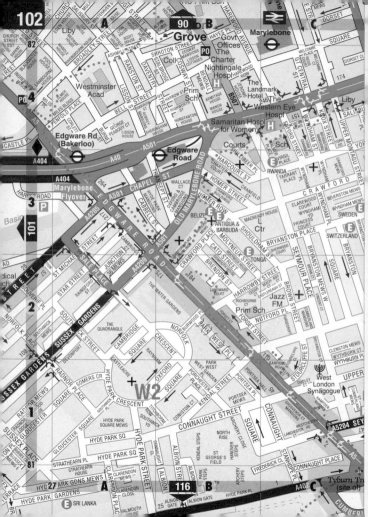

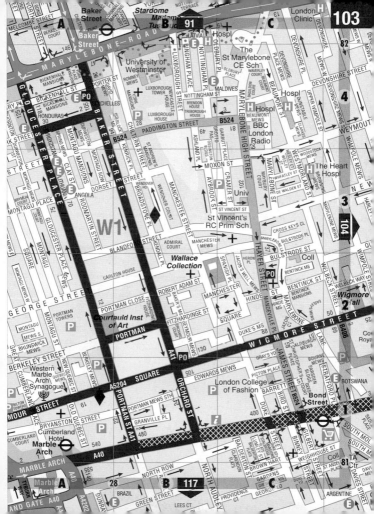

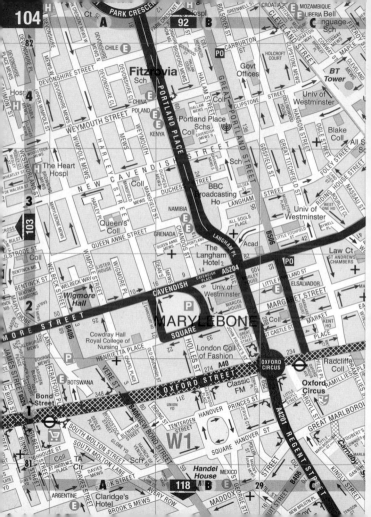

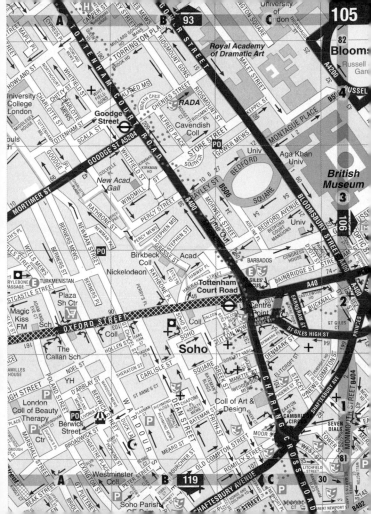

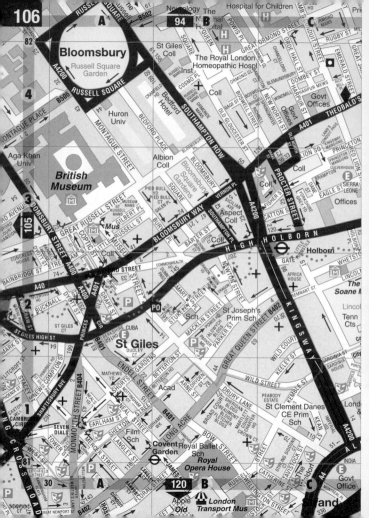

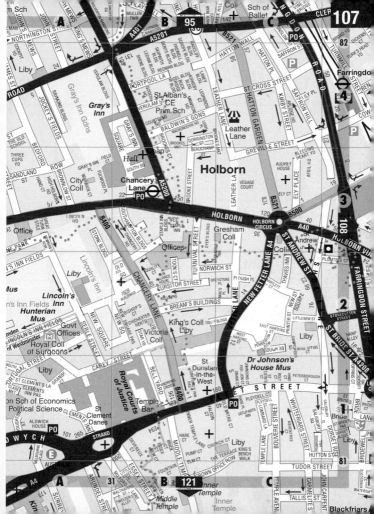

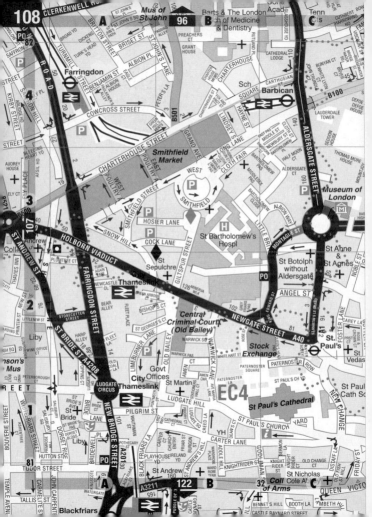

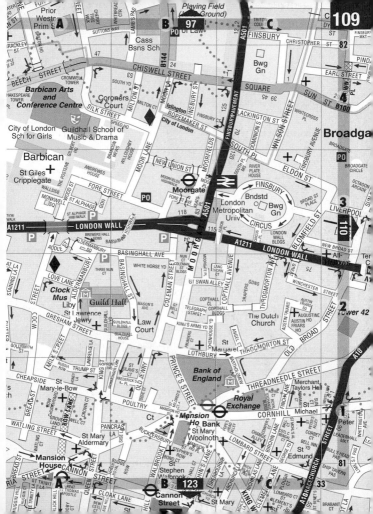

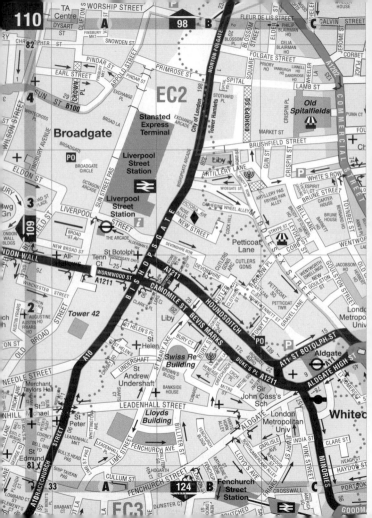

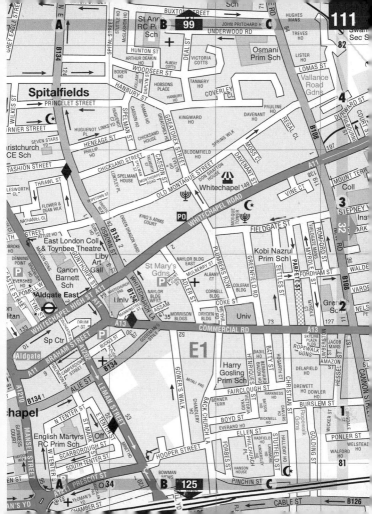

Spitalfields

E1

Whitechapel

Aldgate East

Aldgate

Osmani Prim Sch

East London Coll & Toynbee Theatre

Kobi Nazrul Prim Sch

St Mary's Gdns

Harry Gosling Prim Sch

English Martyrs RC Prim Sch

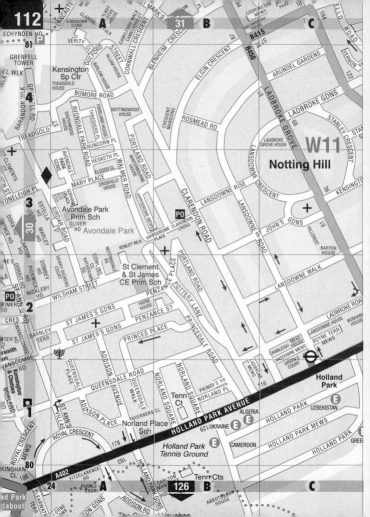

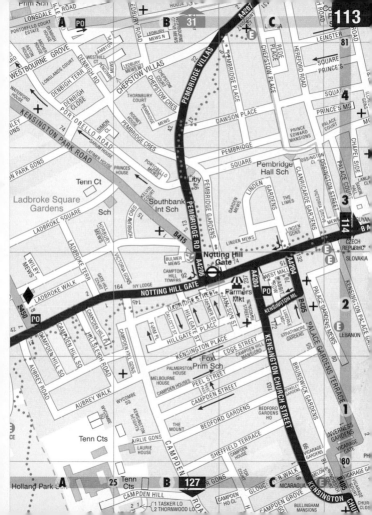

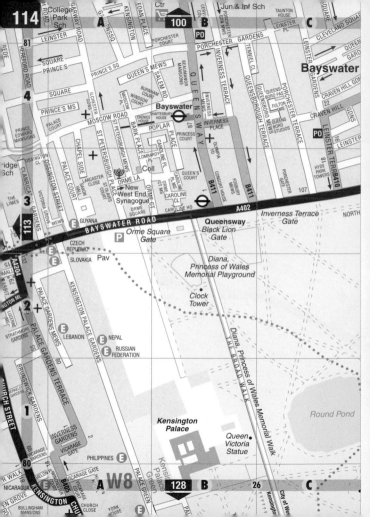

DEVONSHIRE TERR
CRAVEN ROAD
A
CRAVEN ROAD
MEWS
B
101
SUSSEX PLACE
C
SUSSEX PLACE

CRAVEN HILL MS
SMALLBROOK MEWS
STRATH ST
81
N PY
STRATHEARN HOUSE

St James's &
St Michael's CE Prim Sch
Westbourne Cres
A209
SUSSEX GDNS
BATHURST MEWS
CLIFTON PL
SUSSEX
HYDE PARK GDNS MEW

CRAVEN HILL
CRAVEN HILL
LODGE
BROOK MEWS NTH
WESTBOURNE
CRESCENT
MEWS
LANCASTER TERR
GARSON HO
GILRAY HO
A209
BATHURST
SUSSEX
SQUARE
ST
SUSSEX
V 23
STANHOPE TERRACE
HYDE PARK GDNS
HYDE PARK GARDENS
E SRI LANKA

LANCASTER
MEWS
LANCASTER TERRACE
MAITLAND
COURT
ROW
HYDE PARK GDNS
BROOK ST
4

SPIRE
HOUSE
CARROLL HOUSE
ELMS MEWS
Royal
Lancaster
Hotel
A402
Victoria
Gate

COSTA RICA **E**
LANCASTER
GATE
LANCASTER
COURT
30
Westbourne
Gate

MEWS
BARRIE
HOUSE
BAYSWATER ROAD
**Lancaster
Gate**

NORTH FLOWER WALK
Marlborough
Gate
St Agnes' Well

**Lancaster
Gate**
The
Fountains

Bayswater Road
Mkt
Bayard's
Watering Place
(site of)
W2
3

WALK
116 West Carr
NORTH SIDE
BRIAGE DRIVE

• Speke's
Monument
BUDGE'S WALK
LANCASTER WALK
Peter Pan
• Statue
The Long Water
BUCK HILL WALK
2

Diana, Princess of Wales Memorial Walk
Serpentine
Bridge
P

• Physical Engery
Statue
Temple
Lodge
1

**Kensington
Gardens**
P
80

Bandstand
A
LANCASTER WALK
B
129
Serpentine
Gallery
Diana,
Princess of Wales
Memorial Fountain
Diana, Pri
27

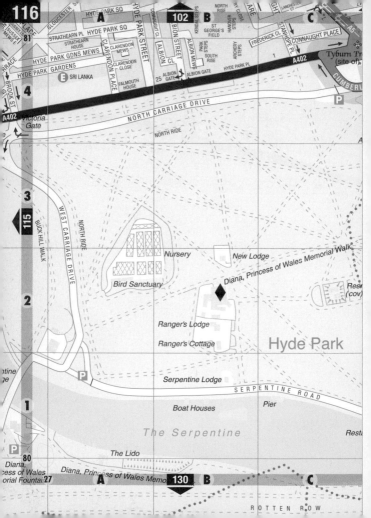

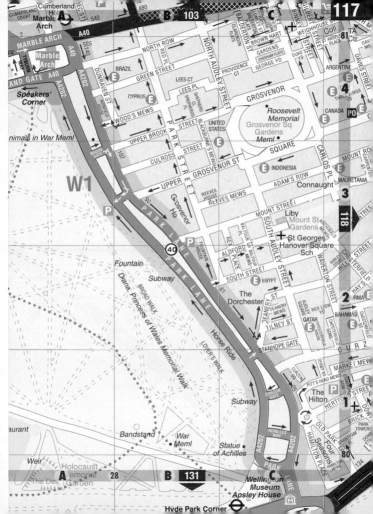

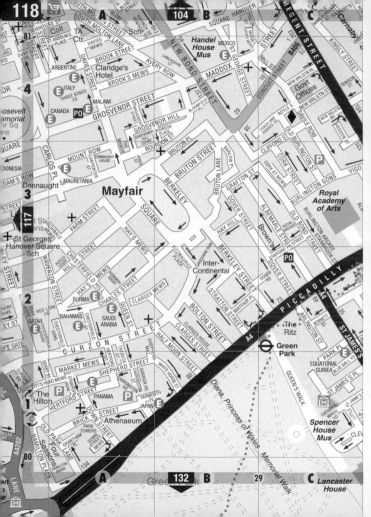

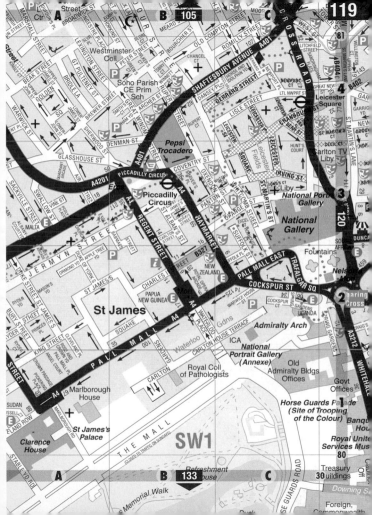

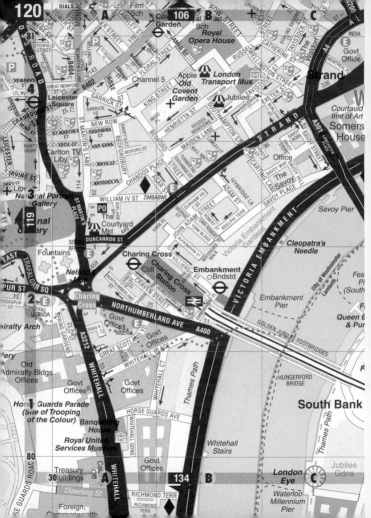

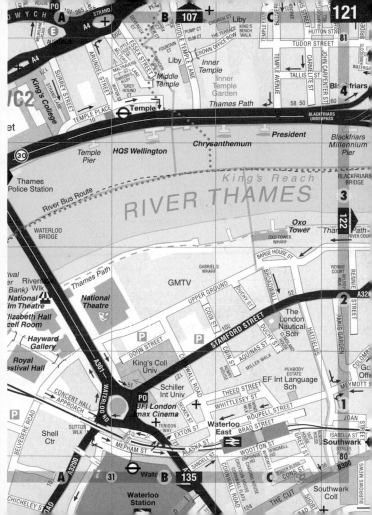

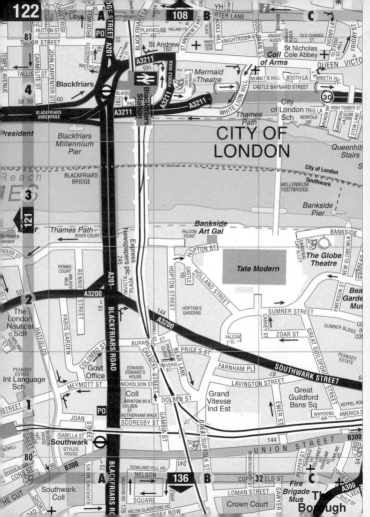

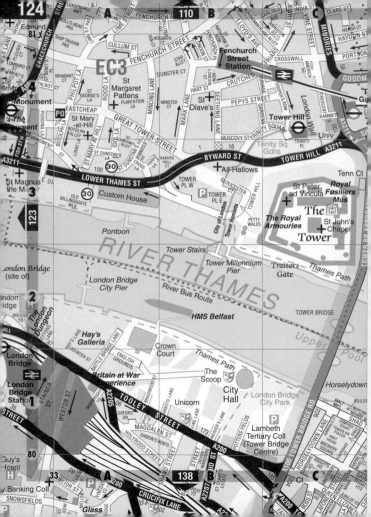

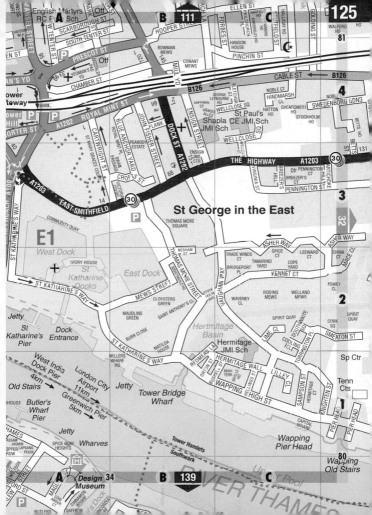

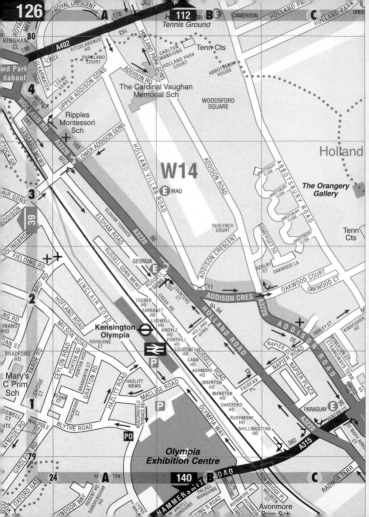

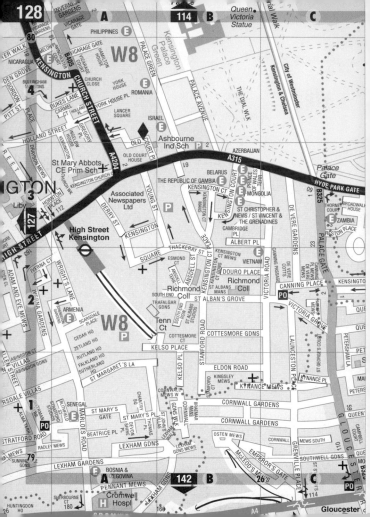

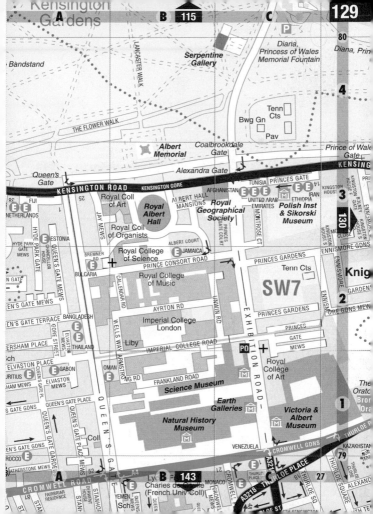

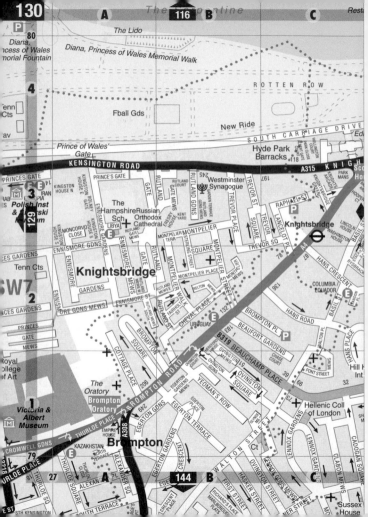

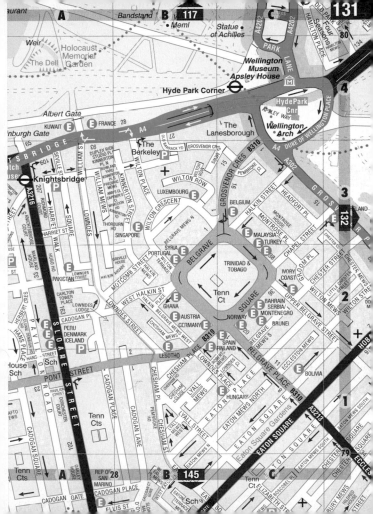

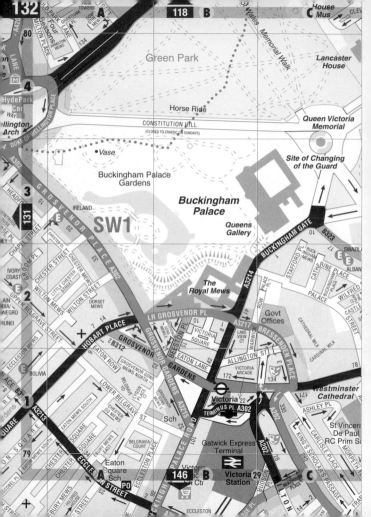

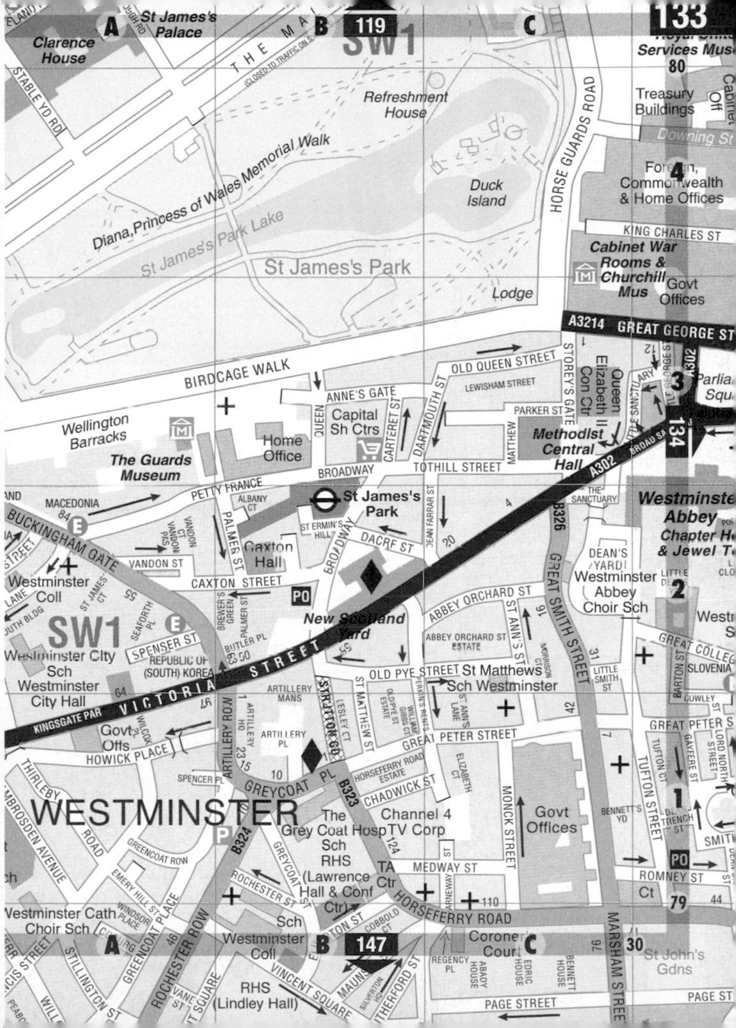
A
B
C
119
SW1
St James's Palace
Clarence House
THE MALL
(CLOSED TO TRAFFIC ON S...)
STABLE YD RD
Royal United Services Mus
80
Treasury Buildings
Cabinet Off
Downing St
Refreshment House
Diana, Princess of Wales Memorial Walk
St James's Park Lake
St James's Park
Duck Island
Lodge
HORSE GUARDS ROAD
Foreign, Commonwealth & Home Offices
4
KING CHARLES ST
Cabinet War Rooms & Churchill Mus
Govt Offices
A3214
GREAT GEORGE ST
A302
Parliament Square
BIRDCAGE WALK
OLD QUEEN STREET
LEWISHAM STREET
STOREY'S GATE
Queen Elizabeth II Con Ctr
LITTLE SANCTUARY
3
ANNE'S GATE
QUEEN
Capital Sh Ctrs
CARTERET ST
DARTMOUTH ST
PARKER ST
MATTHEW
Methodist Central Hall
BROAD SANCTUARY
134
Wellington Barracks
The Guards Museum
Home Office
BROADWAY
TOTHILL STREET
A302
PETTY FRANCE
MACEDONIA
84
ALBANY CT
St James's Park
THE SANCTUARY
Westminster Abbey
Chapter House & Jewel Tower
E
BUCKINGHAM GATE
VANDON CT
VANDON PAS
VANDON ST
PALMER ST
ST ERMIN'S HILL
BROADWAY
Caxton Hall
DACRE ST
DEAN FARRAR ST
20
4
B326
GREAT SMITH STREET
DEAN'S YARD
Westminster Abbey Choir Sch
2
Westminster Coll
CAXTON STREET
PO
ST JAMES'S CT
55
SW1
SEAFORTH PL
E
BREWER'S GREEN
PALMER ST
BUTLER PL
New Scotland Yard
ABBEY ORCHARD ST
ST ANN'S ST
16
ABBEY ORCHARD ST ESTATE
MORRISON CT
31
LITTLE SMITH ST
GREAT COLLEGE ST
BARTON ST
SLOVENIA
SPENSER ST
Westminster City Sch
REPUBLIC OF (SOUTH) KOREA
50
63
VICTORIA STREET
OLD PYE STREET
St Matthews Sch Westminster
Westminster City Hall
64
KINGSGATE PAR
ARTILLERY MANS
STRUTTON GD
LESLEY CT
ST MATTHEW ST
OLD PYE ST ESTATE
WILLIAM GIBBS CT
PERKIN'S RENTS
ST ANN'S LANE
42
COWLEY ST
Govt Offs
WILCOX PL
HOWICK PLACE
ARTILLERY ROW
ARTILLERY HO
ARTILLERY PL
23
15
GREAT PETER STREET
TUFTON CT
TUFTON STREET
GAYFERE ST
LORD NORTH STREET
7
SPENCER PL
10
GREYCOAT PL
HORSEFERRY ROAD ESTATE
ELIZABETH CT
THIRLEBY ROAD
B323
CHADWICK ST
MONCK STREET
1
DEAN TRENCH ST
BENNETT'S YD
WESTMINSTER
The Grey Coat Hosp Sch
Channel 4 TV Corp
Govt Offices
SMITH
AMBROSDEN AVENUE
P
B324
124
GREENCOAT ROW
RHS (Lawrence Hall & Conf Ctr)
TA Ctr
MEDWAY ST
PO
ROMNEY ST
EMERY HILL ST
ROCHESTER ST
GREYCOAT ST
Ct
79
44
WINDSOR PLACE
GREENCOAT PLACE
Sch
HORSEFERRY ROAD
110
Westminster Cath Choir Sch
ROCHESTER ROW
46
Westminster Coll
147
Coroner's Court
MARSHAM STREET
30
76
St John's Gdns
STILLINGTON ST
VANE ST
VINCENT SQUARE
RHS (Lindley Hall)
REGENCY PL
ABADY HOUSE
EDRIC HOUSE
BENNETT HOUSE
PAGE STREET
PAGE ST

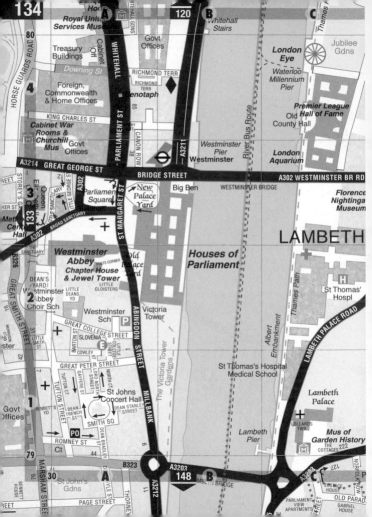

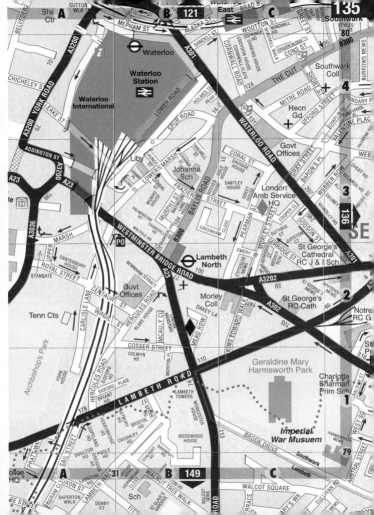

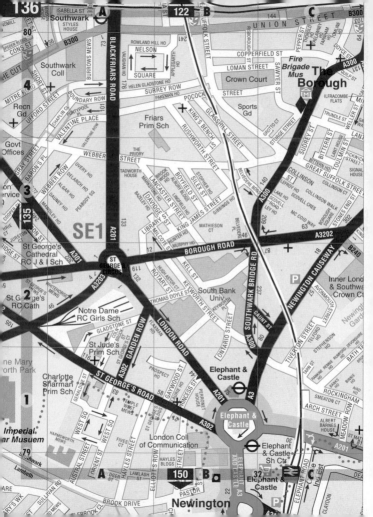

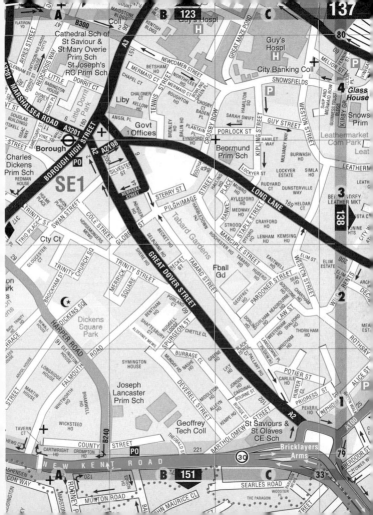

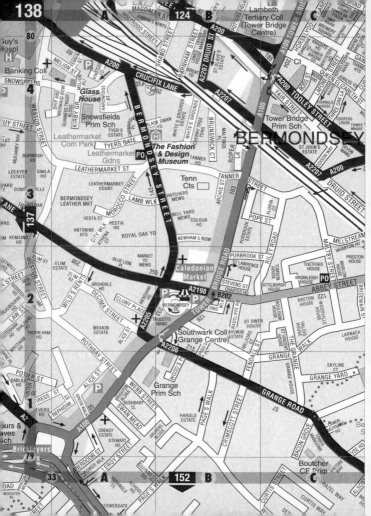

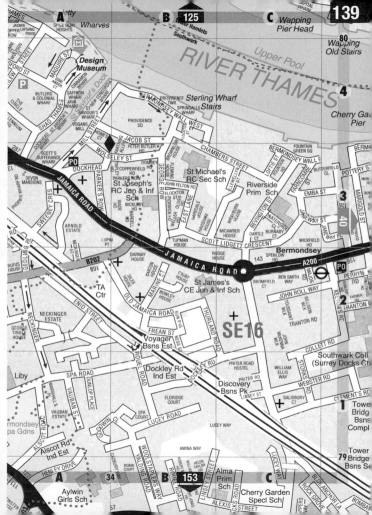

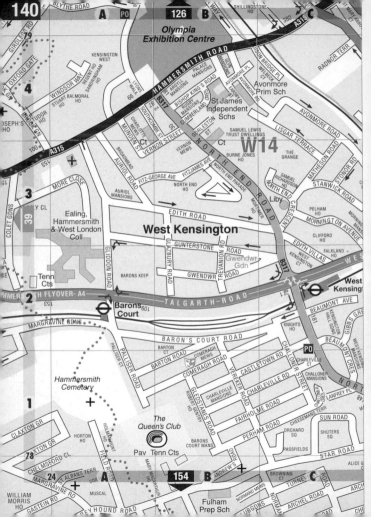

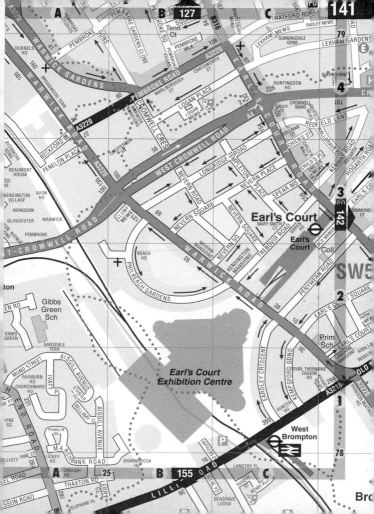

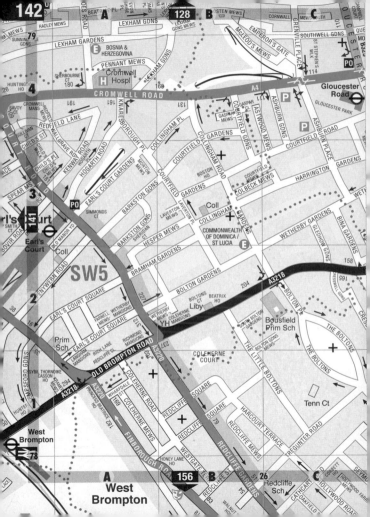

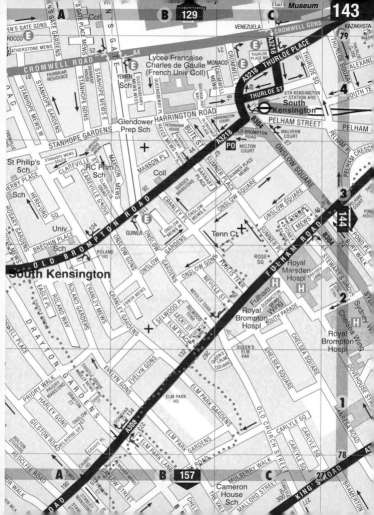

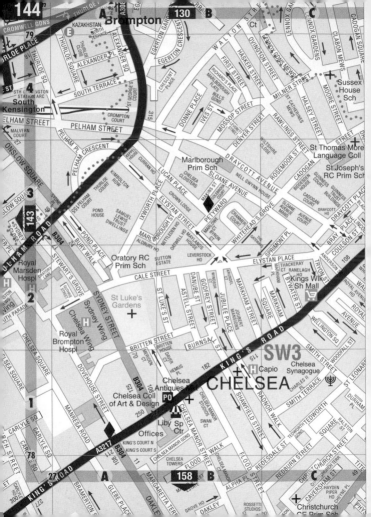

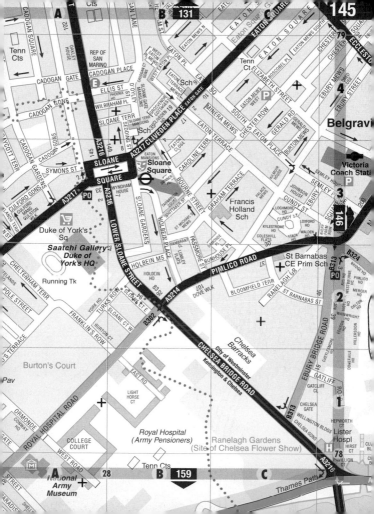

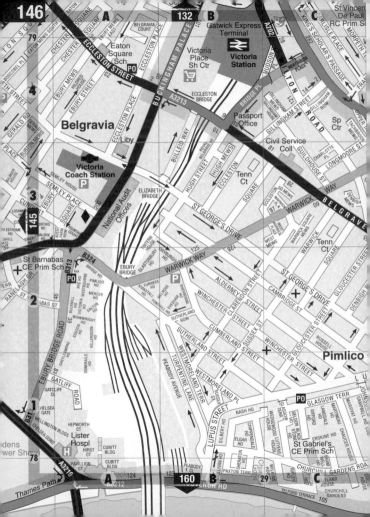

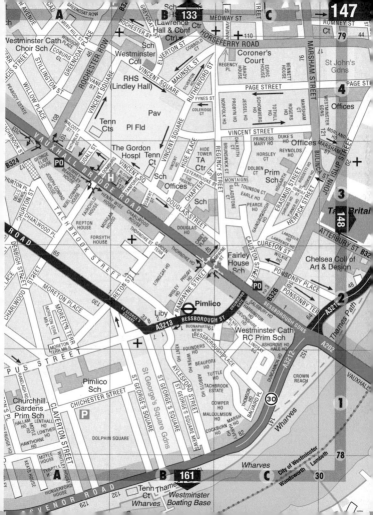

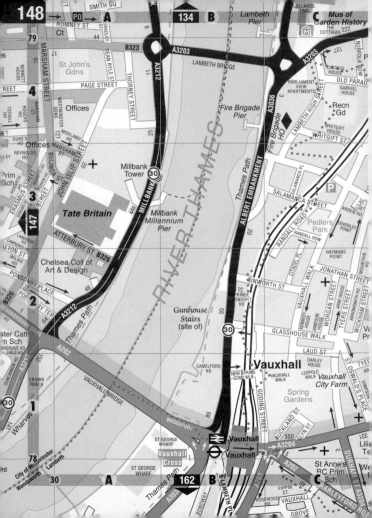

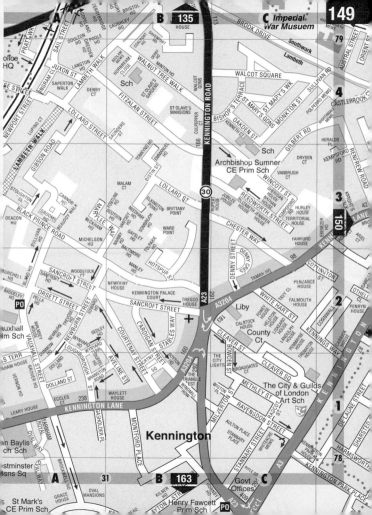

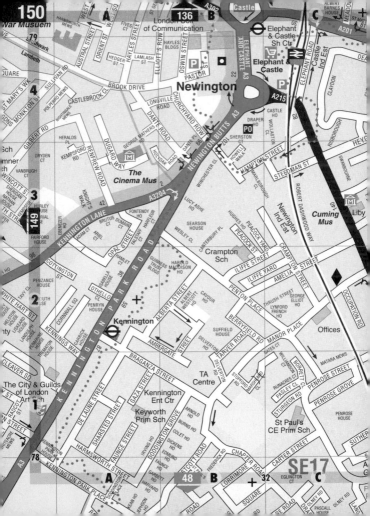

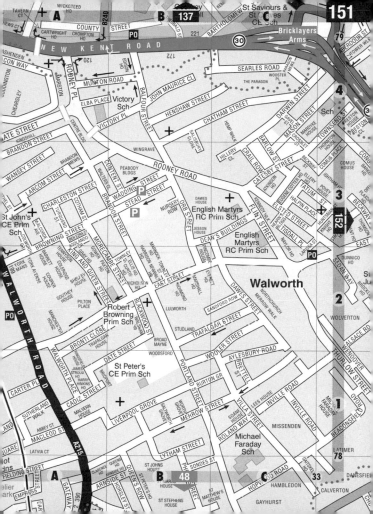

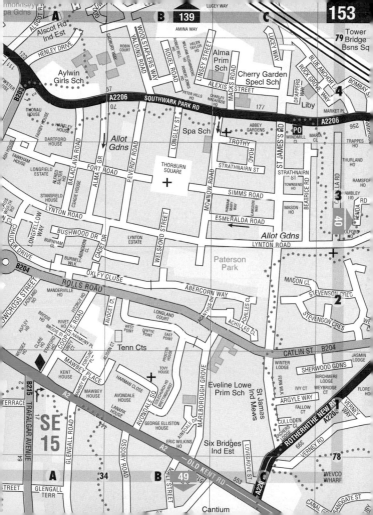

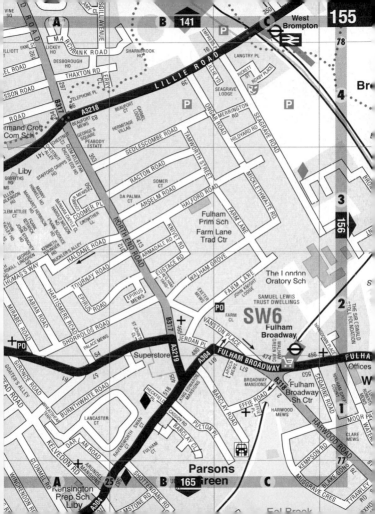

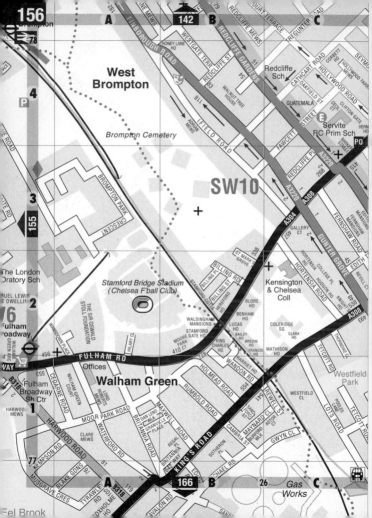

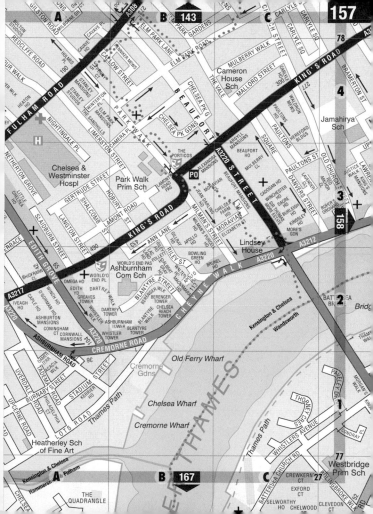

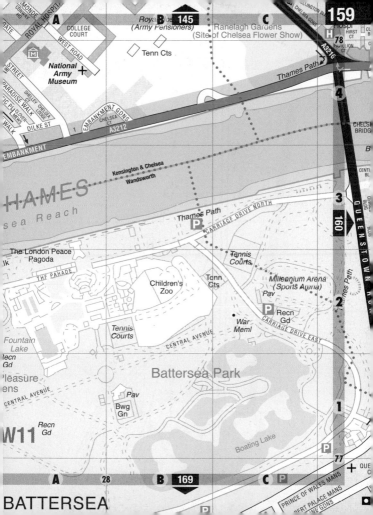

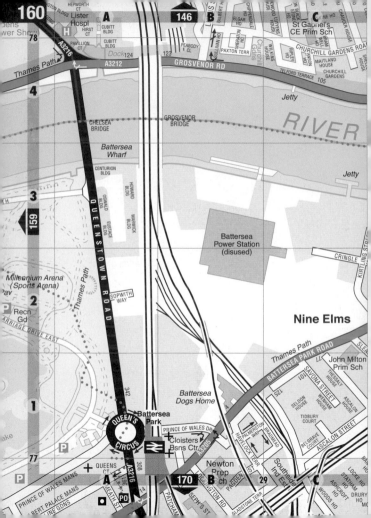

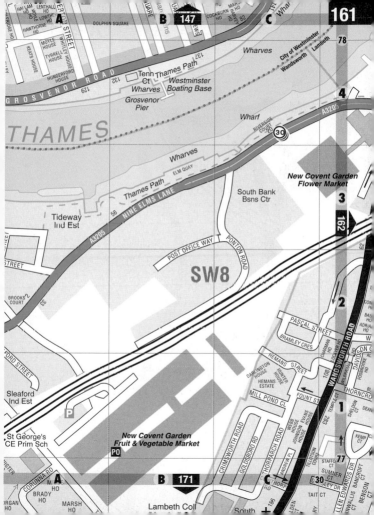

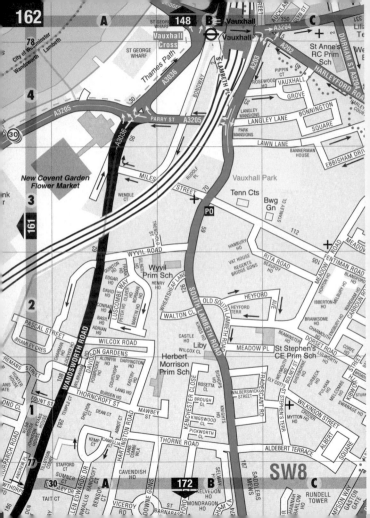

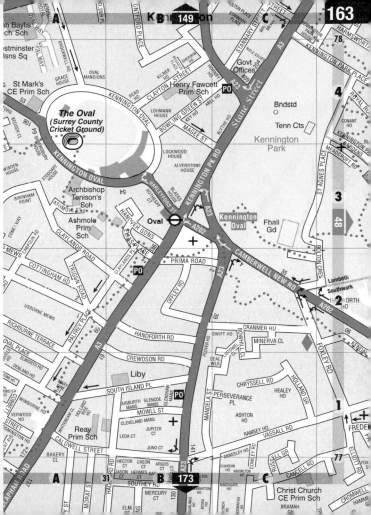

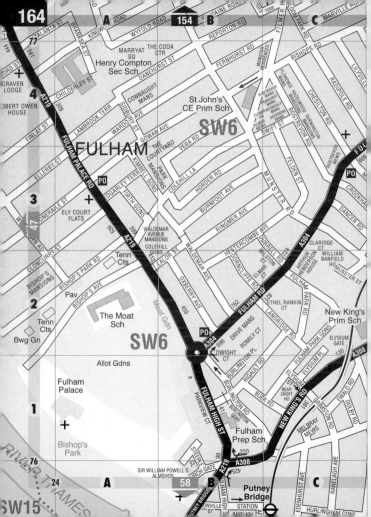

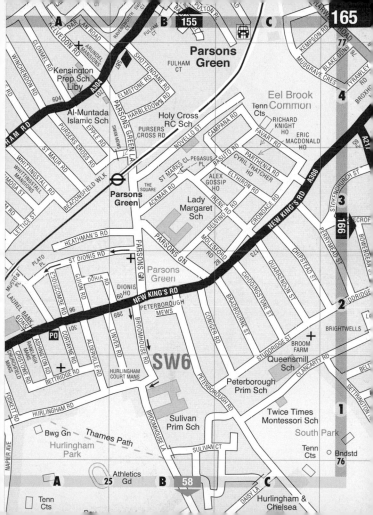

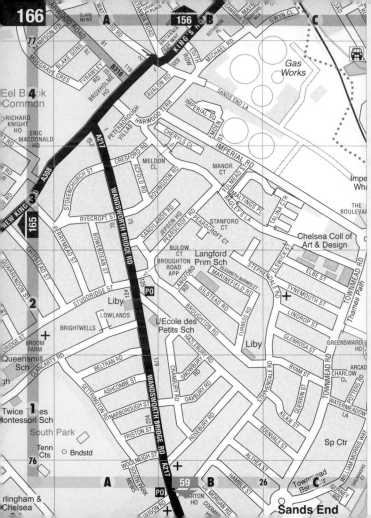

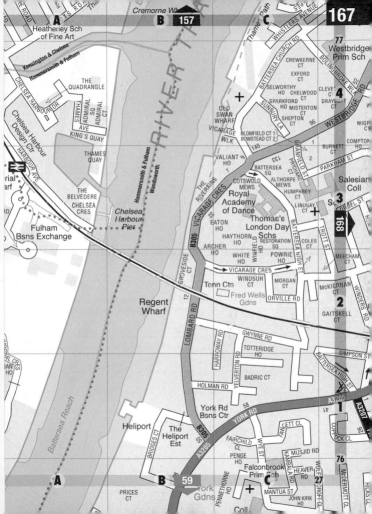

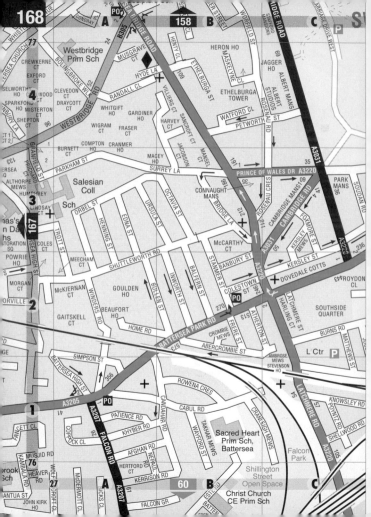

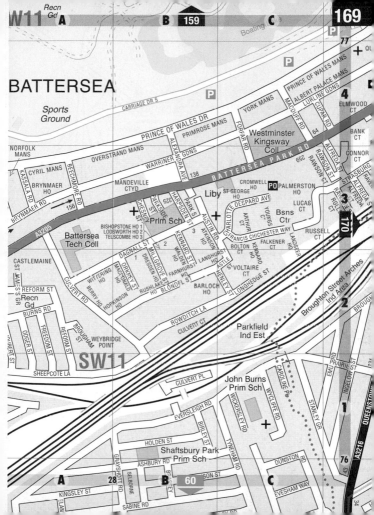

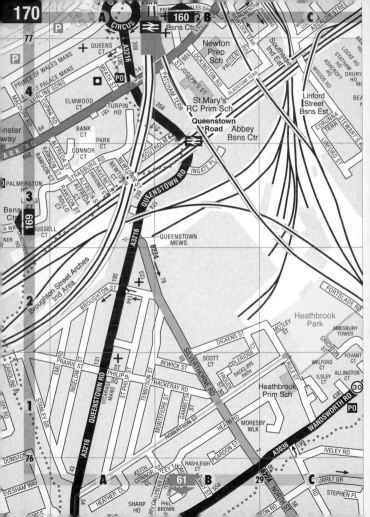

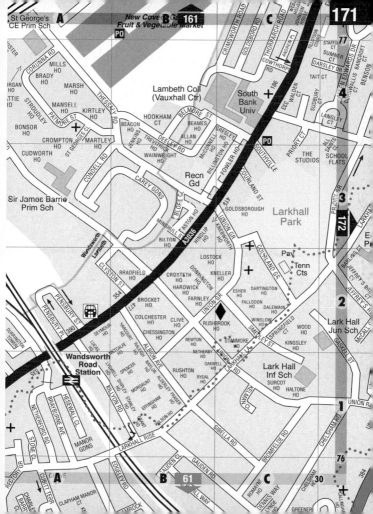

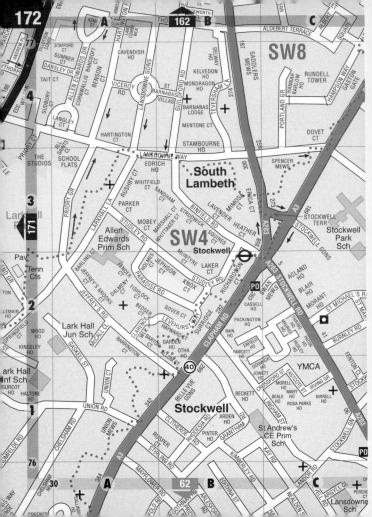

Index

Church Rd 6 Beckenham BR2.........**53** C6 **228** C6

| **Place name** May be abbreviated on the map | **Location number** Present when a number indicates the place's position in a crowded area of mapping | **Locality, town or village** Shown when more than one place (outside London postal districts) has the same name | **Postcode district** District for the indexed place | **Standard scale reference** Page number and grid reference for the standard mapping | **Enlarged scale reference** Page number and grid reference for the central London enlarged mapping, underlined in red |

Public and commercial buildings are highlighted in **magenta**
Places of interest are highlighted in blue with a star*
Cities, towns and villages are listed in CAPITAL LETTERS

Abbreviations used in the index

Acad	Academy	Ct	Court	Int	International	Prom	Promenade
App	Approach	Ctr	Centre	Intc	Interchange	RC	Roman Catholic
Arc	Arcade	Crkt	Cricket	Jun	Junior	Rd	Road
Art Gall	Art Gallery	Ctry Pk	Country Park	Junc	Junction	Rdbt	Roundabout
Ave	Avenue	Cty	County	La	Lane	Ret Pk	Retail Park
Bglws	Bungalows	Ctyd	Courtyard	L Ctr	Leisure Centre	Sch	School
Bldgs	Buildings	Dr	Drive	Liby	Library	Sec	Secondary
Bsns Ctr	Business Centre	Ent Ctr	Enterprise Centre	Mans	Mansions	Sh Ctr	Shopping Centre
Bsns Pk	Business Park	Ent Pk	Enterprise Park	Mdw/s	Meadow/s	Sp	Sports
Bvd	Boulevard	Est	Estate	Meml	Memorial	Specl	Special
Cath	Cathedral, Catholic	Ex Ctr	Exhibition Centre	Mid	Middle	Sports Ctr	Sports Centre
CE	Church of England	Ex Hall	Exhibition Hall	Mix	Mixed	Sq	Square
Cemy	Cemetery	Fst	First	Mkt	Market	St	Street, Saint
Cir	Circus	Gdn	Garden	Mon	Monument	Sta	Station
Circ	Circle	Gdns	Gardens	Mus	Museum	Stad	Stadium
Cl	Close	Gn	Green	Obsy	Observatory	Tech	Technical Technology
Cnr	Corner	Gr	Grove	Orch	Orchard	Terr	Terrace
Coll	College	Gram	Grammar	Par	Parade	Trad Est	Trading Estate
Com	Community	Her Ctr	Heritage Centre	Pas	Passage	Twr/s	Tower/s
Comm	Common	Ho	House	Pav	Pavilion	Univ	University
Comp	Comprehensive	Hospl	Hospital	Pk	Park	Wlk	Walk
Con Ctr	Conference Centre	Hts	Heights	Pl	Place	Yd	Yard
Cotts	Cottages	Ind Est	Industrial Estate	Prec	Precinct		
Cres	Crescent	Inf	Infant	Prep	Preparatory		
Cswy	Causeway	Inst	Institute	Prim	Primary		

Abady Ho SW1 . . . . **147** C4
Abberley Mews 🟦
SW8 . . . . .61 A4
Abbess Cl SW2 . . . . .75 A3
Abbeville Mews 🟦
SW4 . . . . .61 C3
Abbeville Rd SW4 . .61 B2
Abbey Bsns Ctr
SW8 . . . . **170** B4
Abbey Ct
🟦 Bedford Pk
W12 . . . . .38 A3
Camberwell SE17 . **151** A1
St John's Wood
NW8 . . . . .79 A3
Abbeyfield Rd
SE16 . . . . .40 B2
Abbey Gdns
Bermondsey SE16 . **153** C4
St John's Wood
NW8 . . . . .79 A1
West Kensington
W6 . . . . **154** A3
Abbey Ho NW8 . . . .89 A4
Abbey La F15 . . . . .27 C3
Abbey Orchard St
SW1 . . . .**133** B2
Abbey Orchard Street
Est SW1 . . . . **133** C2
Abbey Rd
St John's Wood
NW8 . . . . .78 C2
Wembley NW10 . . . .20 A3
Abbey Rd Motorist Ctr
NW6 . . . . .78 A4
Abbey St SE1 . . . . **138** C2
Abbot Cl SW8 . . . .**162** A1
Abbot Ho 🟦 E14 . . .34 A2
Abbotsbury Cl
Kensington W14 . . .**126** C3
Mill Meads E15 . . . .27 B3
Abbotsbury Ho
W14 . . . .**126** B4
Abbotsbury Mews
SE15 . . . . .65 B4
Abbotsbury Rd
W14 . . . .**126** C3
Abbotshade Rd 🟦
SE16 . . . . .32 C1
Abbots Ho
Kensington W14 . . .**126** C1
Pimlico SW1 . . . . . .**147** B1
Abbots La SE1 . . . .**124** B1
Abbots Pk SW2 . . . .74 C3
Abbot's Pl NW6 . . . .78 A4
Abbot St E8 . . . . . . .16 B2
Abbotstone Ho 🟦
E5 . . . . .7 C2
Abbotstone Rd
SW15 . . . . .57 B4
Abbotswell Rd
SE4 . . . . .66 B2
Abbotswood Rd
London SE22 . . . . . .64 A3
Streatham SW16 . . .73 C1
Abbott Ho SW12 . . .72 B4
Abbott Rd E14 . . . .34 C3
Abbotts Cl N1 . . . . .15 B2
Abbotts Wharf 🟦
E14 . . . . .33 C3
Abchurch La EC2,
EC4 . . . .**123** C4
Abchurch Yd EC4 . .**123** B4

Abdale Rd W12 . . . .30 A1
Abel Ho SE11 . . . . .**163** B4
Aberavon Rd E3 . . . .26 A2
Abercorn Cl NW8 . .**88** C4
Abercorn Mans
NW8 . . . . .79 A1
Abercorn Mews 🟦
TW10 . . . . .54 B3
Abercorn Pl NW8 . .**78** C1
Abercorn Way
SE1 . . . .**153** B2
Abercrombie Ho 🟦
W12 . . . . .30 A2
Abercrombie St
SW11 . . . . **168** B2
Aberdale Ct 🟦
SE16 . . . . .40 C4
Aberdare Gdns
NW6 . . . . .11 A1
Aberdeen Ct
Canonbury N5 . . . . .15 B3
Paddington W2 . . . .**89** B1
Aberdeen Ctr N5 . . .15 B3
Aberdeen La N5 . . . .15 B3
Aberdeen Mans
WC1 . . . .**94** A2
Aberdeen Pk N5 . . .15 B3
Aberdeen Pl NW8 . .**89** B2
Aberdeen Rd
Canonbury N5 . . . . .15 B4
Dudden Hill NW10 . .**8** B3
Aberdeen Terr
SE3 . . . . .52 C1
Aberdour St SE1 . .**152** A4
Aberfeldy Ho SE5 . .48 A3
Aberfeldy St E14 . . .34 B3
Aberford Rd E8 . . . .16 C3
Ability Plaza 🟦
E8 . . . . .16 B1
Ability Twrs EC1 . . . .96 C4
Abingdon Cl
Fulham SE1 . . . .**153** A2
Kentish Town NW1 . .13 C2
Abingdon Ct W8 . . .**127** C1
Abingdon Gdns
W8 . . . .**127** C1
Abingdon Ho
E2 . . . . .24 B1 **98** C2
Abingdon Mans
W8 . . . .**127** B2
Abingdon Rd W8 . . **127** C1
Abingdon St SW1 . .**134** A2
Abingdon Villas
W8 . . . .**127** C1
Abinger Gr SE8 . . . .51 B4
Abinger Ho 🟦 SE1 . **137** B3
Abinger Mews
W9 . . . . .23 C1
Abinger Rd W4 . . . .38 A3
Ablett St SE16 . . . . .40 B1
Abney Gdns 🟦 N16 . .7 B2
Abney Park
Cemetery★
N16 . . . . .7 A2
Aborfield 🟦 NW5 . . .13 B3
Aboyne Rd SW17 . . .71 C1
Abyssinia Cl SW11 .60 A3
Abyssinia Rd
SW11 . . . . .60 A3
Acacia Cl SE8 . . . . .41 A2
Acacia Gdns NW8 . .79 C1
Acacia Gr SE21 . . . .75 C2
Acacia Ho
Brockley SE4 . . . . . .66 B3
Stoke Newington N16 .6 C2

Acacia Pl NW8 . . . . .**79** C2
Acacia Rd
Acton W3 . . . . .28 B2
St John's Wood
NW8 . . . .**79** C2
Acacia Wlk SW10 . .**157** A1
Acad at Peckham The
SE15 . . . . .49 B2
Academy Ct 🟦 E2 . .25 B2
Academy Gdns
W8 . . . .**127** B4
Academy Sch The
NW3 . . . . .11 C4
Academy The 🟦
N19 . . . . .4 C3
Acad of Live &
Recorded Arts The
SW18 . . . . .59 C1
Acanthus Dr SE1 . .**153** B2
Acanthus Rd
SW11 . . . . .60 C4
Accommodation Rd
NW11 . . . . .1 B3
Acer Ct 🟦 NW2 . . . .9 C4
Acfold Rd SW6 . . . **166** A3
Achilles Cl SE1 . . . .**153** C2
Achilles Ho 🟦 E2 . .25 A3
Achilles Rd NW6 . . .10 C3
Achilles St SE14 . . .51 A3
Achilles Way W1 . . **117** C1
Acklam Rd W10 . . . .**31** B4
Ackmar Rd SW6 . . .**165** B3
Ackroyd Dr E3 . . . . .33 C4
Acland Burghley Sch
NW5 . . . . .13 A4
Acland Cres SE5 . . .63 C4
Acland Ho SW9 . . . **172** C2
Acland Rd NW2 . . . . .9 A2
Acol Ct 🟦 NW6 . . . .10 C1
Acol Rd NW6 . . . . . .11 A1
Acorn Ct 🟦 E3 . . . .26 C3
Acorn Gdns W3 . . . .28 C4
Acorn Par 🟦 SE15 . .50 A3
Acorn Production Ctr
N7 . . . . .14 A1
Acorns The 🟦
SE13 . . . . .67 C1
Acorn Wharf SE15 . .49 C4
Acorn Wlk SE16 . . . .33 A1
Acqua Ho TW9 . . . .44 C3
Acre Dr SE22 . . . . . .64 C3
Acre La SW2 . . . . . .62 B3
Acris St SW18 . . . . .59 B2
ACTON 28 C1
Acton Bsns Ctr
NW10 . . . . .20 C1
Acton Central Ind Est
🟦 W3 . . . . .28 A1
Acton Central Sta
W3 . . . . .28 B1
ACTON GREEN . . .37 B2
Acton High Sch
W3 . . . . .36 C4
Acton Hill Mews
W3 . . . . .28 A1
Acton Ho
🟦 Acton W3 . . . . . .28 B3
🟦 Haggerston E8 . . .24 B4
Acton Hospl W3 . . . .36 C4
Acton La
Acton Green W4 . . . .37 B2
Harlesden NW10 . . . .21 A3
Acton Main Line Sta
W3 . . . . .28 B3
Acton Mews E8 . . . .24 B4

Acton Park Ind Est
W3 . . . . .37 C4
Acton St WC1 . . . . . .**94** C3
Acton Town Sta
W3 . . . . .36 C4
Acton Vale Ind Pk
W3 . . . . .29 B1
Acuba Ho SW18 . . . .71 A3
Acuba Rd SW18 . . . .71 A2
Acton St 🟦 NW10 . .21 C3
Ada Gdns E14 . . . . . .34 C3
Ada Ho 🟦 E2 . . . . . .24 C4
Adair Ho SW3 . . . . **158** B4
Adair Rd W10 . . . . . .23 A1
Adair Twr 🟦 W10 . . .23 A1
Ada Kennedy Ct 🟦
SE10 . . . . .52 B3
Adam Ct SE11 . . . . **150** A3
Adam & Eve Ct
W1 . . . .**105** A2
Adam & Eve Mews
W8 . . . .**127** C2
Adamfields 🟦 NW3 . .11 C1
Adams Gardens Est 🟦
SE16 . . . . .40 B4
Adams Ho 🟦 E14 . . .34 C3
Adams Mews
SW17 . . . . .72 B2
Adamson Rd
Hampstead NW3 . . . .11 C1
Newham E16 . . . . . .35 C3
Adams Pl N7 . . . . . . .14 B3
Adam's Row W1 . . . **117** C3
Adam St WC2 . . . . .**120** B3
Adare Ctr The
SW16 . . . . .74 A1
Adare Wlk SW16,
SW2 . . . . .74 A1
Ada St E8 . . . . .25 A4
Adderley Gr SW11 . .60 C2
Adderley Rd E14 . . . .34 B3
Adderley St E14 . . . .34 B3
Addey Ho SE8 . . . . . .51 B3
Addey & Stanhope
Sch SE14 . . . . .51 C2
Addington Ct 🟦
SW14 . . . . .55 C4
Addington Ho
SW9 . . . . **173** A1
Addington Rd E3 . . . .26 C2
Addington Sq SE5 . .48 C3
Addington St SE1 . .**135** A3
Addis Ho 🟦 E1 . . . . .32 B4
Addison Ave
W11 . . . . .31 A1 **112** A1
Addison Bridge Pl
W14 . . . .**140** C4
Addison Cres
W14 . . . .**126** B2
Addison Gdns
W14 . . . . .39 C3
Addison Gr W4 . . . . .38 A3
Addison Ho NW8 . . .**89** B4
Addison Park Mans 🟦
W14 . . . . .39 C4
Addison Pl
W11 . . . . .31 A1 **112** A1
Addison Prim Sch
W14 . . . . .39 C3
Addison Rd W14 . . .**126** C2
Addle Hill EC4 . . . . **108** B1
Addle St EC2 . . . . . **109** A3
Addlestone Ho 🟦
W10 . . . . .30 B4

Addy Ho SE16 . . . . . .40 B2
Adela Ho 🟦 W6 . . . .39 B1
Adelaide Ave SE4 . .66 C3
Adelaide Cl SW9 . . .62 C3
Adelaide Ct
Hackney E5 . . . . .18 A3
St John's Wood
NW8 . . . .**79** A1
Adelaide Gr W12 . . .29 C1
Adelaide Rd
Primrose Hill NW3 . .12 A1
Richmond TW9 . . . . .54 B3
🟦 Wandsworth
SW18 . . . . .58 C2
Adelaide St WC2 . .**120** A3
Adela St W10 . . . . . .23 A1
Adelina Gr E1 . . . . . .32 B4
Adelina Mews
SW12 . . . . .73 C3
Adeline Pl WC1 . . . **105** C3
Adelphi Ct 🟦
SE16 . . . . .40 C4
Adelphi Terr WC2 . .**120** B3
Adeney Cl W6 . . . . . .47 C4
Aden Gr N16 . . . . . . .15 C4
Aden Ho 🟦 E1 . . . . .32 C4
Aden Lo N16 . . . . . . .15 C4
Adeyfield Ho EC1 . . .**97** C3
Adie Rd W6 . . . . .39 B3
Adisham Ho 🟦 E5 . . .17 A3
Adler St E1 . . . . **111** B2
Adley St E5 . . . . .18 A3
Admiral Ct
Chelsea SW10 . . . . .**167** A4
Marylebone W1 . . . **103** B3
Admiral Hyson Ind Est
SE16 . . . . .40 A1
Admiral Mews
W10 . . . . .22 C1
Admiral Pl SE16 . . . .33 A1
Admirals Ct
Bermondsey SE1 . . .**124** C1
🟦 Putney SW19 . . . .69 C3
Admirals Gate
SE10 . . . . .52 A2
Admiral Sq SW10 . .**167** A4
Admiral St SE8 . . . . .51 C2
Admirals Way E14 . .41 C4
Admiral's Wlk NW3 . .2 B1
Admiralty Arch★
SW1 . . . . **119** C2
Admiralty Cl 🟦
SE8 . . . . .51 C2
Admiral Wlk W9 . . . .23 C1
Adolphus Rd N4 . . . . .6 A3
Adolphus St SE8 . . .51 B3
Adpar St W2 . . . . . . **101** B4
Adrian Bolt Ho 🟦
E2 . . . . .25 A2
Adrian Ho
Islington N1 . . . .**85** A3
South Lambeth
SW8 . . . . **162** A1
Stratford E15 . . . . . .19 C1
Adrian Mews
SW10 . . . . **156** B4
Adriatic Bldg 🟦
E14 . . . . .33 A2
Adriatic Ho 🟦 E1 . . .25 C1
Adron Ho 🟦 SE16 . . .40 B2
Adstock Ho 🟦 N1 . . .15 A1
ADT Coll SW15 . . . . .58 B2
Adventurers Ct 🟦
E14 . . . . .34 C2
Adys Lawn NW2 . . . . .9 A2

Adys Rd SE15 . . . . 64 B4
Aegean Apts 7
E16 . . . . 35 C2
Aegon Ho B14 . . . . 42 A3
Affleck St N1 . . . . 85 A1
Afghan Rd SW11 . . . 168 A1
Africa Ho WC2 . . . . . . 106 C2
Afsil Ho EC1 . . . . 107 C3
Aga Khan Univ
WC1 . . . . 105 C3
Agamemnon Rd
NW6 . . . . 10 B3
Agar Gr NW1 . . . . 13 C1
Agar Pl NW1 . . . . 13 B1
Agar St WC2 . . . . 120 B3
Agate Ho W6 . . . . 39 B3
Agatha Cl E1 . . . . 32 B1
Agave Rd NW2 . . . . 9 B4
Agdon St EC1 . . . . 96 A2
Agincourt Rd
NW3 . . . . 12 B4
Agnes Ct 18 SW18 . . 59 C3
Agnes Ho 19 W11 . . 30 C2
Agnes Rd W3 . . . . 38 B4
Agnes St E14 . . . . 33 B3
Aigburth Mans
SW9 . . . . 163 B1
Ailsa St E14 . . . . 34 B4
Ainger Rd NW3 . . . . . . 12 B1
Ainsdale NW1 . . . . 92 C4
Ainsdale Dr SE1 . . . . 153 B1
Ainsley St E2 . . . . 25 A2
Ainslie Wlk 8
SW12 . . . . 73 A4
Ainsty St 20 SE16 . . . . 40 B4
Ainsworth Cl SE5 . . . . 49 A1
Ainsworth Est
NW8 . . . . 78 C4
Ainsworth Ho
NW8 . . . . 78 B4
Ainsworth Rd E9 . . . . 17 B1
Ainsworth Way
NW8 . . . . 78 C4
Aintree St SW6 . . . . . 154 B2
Aird Ho SE1 . . . . 136 C1
Airdrie Cl N1 . . . . 14 B1
Airedale Ave W4 . . . . . 38 B1
Airedale Ave S
W4 . . . . 38 B1
Airedale Rd SW12 . . 72 B4
Airlie Gdns
W8 . . . . 31 C1 113 B1
Air St W1 . . . . 119 A3
Aisgill Ave SW5 . . . . 141 A1
Aiten Pl W6 . . . . 38 C2
Aithan Ho 15 E14 . . 33 B3
Aitken Cl E8 . . . . 24 C4
Ajax Ho 15 E2 . . . . . . 25 A3
Ajax Rd NW6 . . . . 10 C3
Akbar Ho 7 E14 . . . . 42 A2
Akehurst St SW15 . . 68 C4
Akenside Ct 8
NW3 . . . . 11 C3
Akenside Rd NW3 . . . 11 C3
Akerman Rd SW9 . . . 48 A2
Akintaro Ho 7
SE8 . . . . 51 B4
Alamaro Lo 5
SE10 . . . . 43 B3
Aland Ct SE16 . . . . 41 A3
Alan Preece Ct
NW6 . . . . 9 C1
Alaska Bldg 12
SE13 . . . . 52 A2
Alaska St SE1 . . . . . . 121 B1

Alastor Ho 10 E14 . . 42 B3
Albacore Cres
SE13 . . . . 67 A1
Alba Mews SW18,
SW19 . . . . 70 C2
Alban Ho
Hampstead NW3 . . . . . . 11 B2
New Cross SE14 . . . . . . 51 B2
Richmond TW10 . . . . . . 54 B2
Albany W1 . . . . 118 C3
Albany Cl SW14 . . . . . 55 A3
Albany Ct
College Pk NW10 . . . . . 22 A2
NW8 . . . . 79 B1
Westminster SW1 . . . 133 B2
Whitechapel E1 . . . . . 111 B2
Albany Ctyd W1 . . . 119 A3
Albany Mans
SW11 . . . . 158 B1
Albany Par 4
TW8 . . . . 44 A4
Albany Pas 12
TW10 . . . . 54 A2
Albany Rd
Camberwell SE5 . . . . . . 49 A4
Richmond TW10 . . . . . . 54 A2
Albany St NW1 . . . . . . 92 B4
Albany Terr 6
TW10 . . . . 54 A2
Alba 10 W11 . . . . 31 B3
Albemarle SW19 . . . . 69 C2
Albemarle Ho
2 Brixton SW2 . . . . . . 62 C4
Rotherhithe SE16 . . . . . 41 B2
Albemarle Mans
NW3 . . . . 11 A4
Albemarle Prim Sch
SW19 . . . . 70 A2
Albemarle Way
EC1 . . . . 96 A1
Alberta Ct 1
TW10 . . . . 54 B2
Alberta Ho E14 . . . . . 34 B1
Alberta St SE17 . . . . 150 B2
Albert Ave SW8 . . . . 162 C1
Albert Barnes Ho
SE1 . . . . 136 C1
Albert Bigg Point
E15 . . . . 27 B4
Albert Bridge Rd
SW11 . . . . 158 C1
Albert Cl 9 E9 . . . . . . 25 A4
Albert Cotts E1 . . . . 111 B4
Albert Ct
Knightsbridge
SW7 . . . . 129 B3
9 Putney SW19 . . . . . 70 A3
Albert Emb SE1 . . . . 148 B3
Albert Gate Ct
SW1 . . . . 130 C3
Albert Gdns E1 . . . . . 32 C3
Albert Gray Ho
SW10 . . . . 157 B2
Albert Hall Mans
SW7 . . . . 129 B3
Albert Mans
Battersea SW11 . . . . . 168 C4
Hornsey N8 . . . . 5 A4
Albert Meml ∗
SW7 . . . . 129 B3
Albert Mews W8 . . . 128 C2

Albert Palace Mans
SW11 . . . . 169 C4
Albert Pl W8 . . . 128 B3
Albert Rd
Finsbury Pk N4 . . . . 5 B4
Kilburn NW6 . . . . 23 B3
Richmond TW10 . . . . . . 54 B2
Albert's Ct NW1 . . . . 90 B2
Albert Sq SW8 . . . . . 162 C1
Albert St NW1 . . . . . . 82 B3
Albert Starr Ho 1
SE8 . . . . 40 C2
Albert Studios
SW11 . . . . 168 C4
Albert Terr
Camden Town
NW1 . . . . 81 B3
Stonebridge NW10 . . . 20 B4
Albert Terr Mews
NW1 . . . . 81 B3
Albert Way SE15 . . . . 50 A3
Albion Ave SW8 . . . . 171 B1
Albion Cl W2 . . . . 116 B4
Albion Coll WC1 . . . 106 B3
Albion Ct 6 W6 . . . . 39 A2
Albion Dr E8 . . . . 16 C1
Albion Est SE16 . . . . . 40 B4
Albion Gate W2 . . . . 116 B4
Albion Gdns 1
W6 . . . . 39 A2
Albion Ho 1
17 Deptford SE8 . . . . 51 C3
EC1 . . . . 108 A4
Albion Mews
Bayswater W2 . . . . 116 B4
6 Hammersmith
W6 . . . . 39 A2
Islington N1 . . . . 85 B4
Albion Pl
Broadgate EC2 . . . . . . 109 C3
Clerkenwell EC1 . . . . . 108 A4
Hammersmith W6 . . . 39 A2
Albion Prim Sch
SE16 . . . . 40 B4
Albion Rd N16 . . . . 15 C4
Albion Riverside
SW11 . . . . 158 A2
Albion Sq E8 . . . . 16 B1
Albion St
Bayswater W2 . . . . 116 B4
Rotherhithe SE16 . . . . . 40 B4
Albion Terr E8 . . . . 16 B1
Albion Way
Barbican EC1 . . . . 108 C3
Lewisham SE13 . . . . 67 B3
Albion Wlk N1 . . . . . . 84 B1
Albion Works Studios
14 E8 . . . . 16 C3
Albion Yd N1 . . . . 84 B1
Albon Ho SW18 . . . . . 59 A1
Albrighton Rd SE5,
SE22 . . . . 64 A4
Albury Bldgs SE1 . . 136 B3
Albury Ct SE8 . . . . 51 C4
Albury Lo 7 SW2 . . 74 B4
Albury St SE8 . . . . 51 C4
Albyn Rd SE8 . . . . 51 C2
Alchemea Coll of
Audio Engineering
N1 . . . . 86 B4
Alconbury Rd E5 . . . . 7 C2
Aldbourne Rd
W12 . . . . 29 C1

Aldbridge St
SE17 . . . . 152 B2
Aldburgh Mews
W1 . . . . 103 C2
Aldbury Ho SW3 . . . 144 A3
Aldebert Terr
SW8 . . . . 162 C1
Aldeburgh Pl
SE10 . . . . 43 C2
Aldeburgh St
SE10 . . . . 43 C1
Aldenham Ho
NW1 . . . . 83 A1
Aldenham St NW1 . . 83 B1
Alden Ho E8 . . . . 25 A4
Aldensley Rd W6 . . . 39 A3
Alderbrook Prim Sch
SW12 . . . . 73 A4
Alderbrook Rd
SW12 . . . . 61 A1
Alderbury Rd
SW13 . . . . 46 C4
Aldergrove Ho 3
E5 . . . . 7 C2
Alder Ho
Camberwell SE15 . . . . . 49 B4
1 Maitland Pk
NW3 . . . . 12 B2
St Johns SE4 . . . . 66 C4
Alderley Ho 8 SW8 . 171 B1
Alder Lo SW6 . . . . 47 C2
Aldermanbury
EC2 . . . . 109 A2
Aldermanbury Sq
EC2 . . . . 109 A3
Alderman's Wlk
EC2 . . . . 110 A3
Alder Mews 12 N19 . 4 B2
Alderney Ho 20
N1 . . . . 15 B2
Alderney Mews
SE1 . . . . 137 B2
Alderney Rd E1 . . . . . . 25 C1
Alderney St SW1 . . . 146 B2
Alder St E1 . . . . 111 B2
Aldersford Cl SE4 . . 65 C3
Aldersgate Ct
EC1 . . . . 108 C3
Aldersgate St
EC1 . . . . 108 C3
Aldershot Rd NW6 . . 23 B4
Alderson St W10 . . . . 23 A1
Alderton Rd SE24 . . . 63 B4
Alderville Rd
SW6 . . . . 165 A2
Alderwick Ct N7 . . . . 14 B2
Aldford St W1 . . . . . . 117 C2
Aldgate EC3 . . . . 110 B1
Aldgate East Sta
E1 . . . . 111 A2
Aldgate High St
EC3 . . . . 110 C1
Aldgate Sta EC3 . . . 110 C1
Aldham Ho SE4 . . . . . 51 B2
Aldine Ct W12 . . . . 30 B1
Aldine St W12 . . . . 39 B4
Aldington Ct 11
E8 . . . . 16 C1
Aldred Rd NW6 . . . . . . 10 C3
Aldren Rd SW17 . . . . . 71 B1
Aldrich Terr SW18 . . 71 B2
Aldrick Ho N1 . . . . 85 A2
Aldridge Ct W11 . . . . 31 B4
Aldridge Rd Villas
W11 . . . . 31 B4
Aldsworth Cl W9 . . . 88 A1
Aldwich Ho WC2 . . . 107 A1

Aldworth Gr SE13 . . 67 B1
Aldwych WC2 . . . . . . 107 A1
Aldwych Bldgs
WC2 . . . . 106 B2
Aldwyn Ho SW8 . . . . 162 A1
Alexander Ave
NW10 . . . . 9 A1
Alexander Ct
SW18 . . . . 59 B2
Alexander Fleming
Laboratory Mus ∗
W2 . . . . 101 C2
Alexander Ho 15
E14 . . . . 41 C3
Alexander Mews
W2 . . . . 100 A2
Alexander Pl
SW7 . . . . 144 A4
Alexander Rd N19 . . 5 A2
Alexander Sq
SW3 . . . . 144 A4
Alexander St W2 . . . 31 C3
Alexandra Ave
SW11 . . . . 169 B3
Alexandra Cl SE8 . . . 51 B4
Alexandra Cotts
SE14 . . . . 51 B2
Alexandra Ct
Paddington W9 . . . . 89 A2
5 Shacklewell N16 . . 16 B4
7 Shepherd's Bush
W12 . . . . 30 B3
Alexandra Gdns
W4 . . . . 46 A3
Alexandra Gr N4 . . . 6 A3
Alexandra Ho 18
W6 . . . . 39 B1
Alexandra Mans
Chelsea SW3 . . . . 157 B3
Cricklewood NW2 . . . . . 9 C3
6 Hampstead
NW6 . . . . 10 C3
8 Shepherd's Bush
W12 . . . . 30 B1
Alexandra National
Ho N4 . . . . 6 A2
Alexandra Pl NW8 . . 79 A4
Alexandra Rd
Acton W4 . . . . 37 C4
Hampstead NW8 . . . . . 11 C1
Mortlake SW14 . . . . . . 55 C4
Richmond TW9 . . . . . . 44 B1
Alexandra St
6 Deptford SE14 . . . . 51 A3
Newham E16 . . . . 35 C4
Alex Gossip Ho
SW6 . . . . 165 B3
Alexis St SE16 . . . . . . 153 C4
Alfearn Rd E5 . . . . 17 B4
Alford Ct N1 . . . . 87 A1
Alford Pl N1 . . . . 87 A1
Alfreda Ct SW11 . . . 170 A3
Alfreda St SW11 . . . . 170 A3
Alfred Butt Ho
SW17 . . . . 72 B1
Alfred Cl W4 . . . . 37 C2
Alfred Ho E9 . . . . 18 A3
Alfred Mews W1,
WC1 . . . . 105 B4
Alfred Nunn Ho
NW10 . . . . 21 B4
Alfred Pl WC1 . . . . . . 105 B4
Alfred Rd
Acton W3 . . . . 28 B1
Paddington W2 . . . . 31 C4
Alfred Salter Ho
SE1 . . . . 153 A3

Alfred Salter Prim Sch SE16 ...... 40 C4
Alfred St E3 .... 26 B2
Alfreton Cl SW19 .... 69 C1
Alfriston Rd SW11 ... 60 B2
Algar Ho E1 .... 136 A3
Algarve Rd SW18 .... 71 A3
Algernon Rd
 Kilburn NW6 .... 23 C4
 Lewisham SE13 ..... 67 A3
Algiers Rd SE13 ..... 66 C3
Alice Gilliott Ct W14 .... 155 A4
Alice La E3 .... 26 B4
Alice Owen Tech Ctr EC1 .... 96 A4
Alice Shepherd Ho 10 E14 .... 42 B4
Alice St SE1 .... 138 A1
Alice Walker Cl 8 SE24 .... 63 A3
Alie St E1 .... 111 A1
Aliwal Rd SW11 ..... 60 A3
Alkerden Rd W4 ..... 38 A1
Alkham Rd N16 ...... 7 B2
Allam Ho W11 .... 31 A2 112 A4
Allanbridge N16..... 7 A4
Allan Ho SW8 ..... 171 B4
Allan Way W3 ...... 28 B4
Allard Gdns SW4 ... 61 C2
Allardyce St SW9 .... 62 B3
Allbrook Ho 4 SW15 .... 68 C4
Allcroft Rd NW5..... 12 C2
Allendale Cl SE5 .... 48 C2
Allen Edwards Dr SW8 .... 172 A4
Allen Edwards Prim Sch SW4 .... 172 A3
Allenford Ho SW15 .... 56 B1
All England Lawn Tennis & Croquet Club The SW19 ..70 A1
Allen Ho W8 ...... 127 C2
Allen Mans W8 .... 127 C2
Allen Rd
 Old Ford E3........ 26 B3
 Stoke Newington N16 .... 16 A4
Allensbury Pl
 7 Camden Town NW1 .... 13 C1
 Camden Town NW1 .. 14 A1
Allen St W8 .... 127 C1
Allenswood 2 SW19 .... 70 A3
Allerdale Ho 11 N4 .. 6 C4
Allerton Ho 11 ..... 87 C1
Allerton Rd N16 .... 6 B2
Allerton St N1 ..... 97 C4
Allerton Wlk 11 N7 .. 5 B2
Allestree Rd SW6 . 154 A1
Alleyn Cres SE21 ... 75 C2
Alleyn Ho
 Bermondsey SE1 .. 137 B1
 St Luke's EC1 ..... 97 A1
Alleyn Pk SE21 ..... 76 A1
Alleyn Rd SE21 ..... 76 A1
Alleyn's Sch SE22 . 64 A2
Allfarthing La SW18 .... 59 B1
Allfarthing Prim Sch SW18 .... 59 B1
Allgood St 10 E2 ... 24 B3

Allhallows La EC4 . 123 B3
Alliance Ct W3 ..... 28 A4
Alliance Rd W3 ..... 20 A1
Allied Ind Est W3 .. 37 A3
Allied Way W3 ...... 38 A4
Allingham Ct SE13 .. 67 C3
Allingham Mews N1 .... 86 C2
Allingham St N1 .... 86 C2
Allington Ct SW8 . 170 C1
Allington Rd W10 .. 23 A3
Allington St SW1 .. 132 B1
Allison Cl SE10 .... 52 B2
Allison Gr SE21 .... 76 A3
Allison Rd W3 ...... 28 B2
Alliston Ho E2 .... 24 B2 99 A3
Allitsen Rd NW8 ... 80 A2
All Nations Ho 10 E8 .... 17 A1
Allnutt Way SW4 ... 61 C2
Allom Ct SW4 ..... 172 B1
Allonby Ho E14 .... 33 A4
Alloway Rd E3 ...... 26 A2
Allport Ho SE5 ..... 63 C4
Allport Mews 44 E1 .... 25 B1
All Saints CE Prim Sch SW15 .... 57 B4
All Saints' CE Prim Sch
 Blackheath Vale SE3 .... 53 A1
 Child's Hill NW2 ... 1 B1
All Saints Church N19 .... 4 C1
All Saints Ct
 Lower Clapton E5 ... 17 B4
 10 Shadwell E1 .... 32 B2
All Saints Dr SE3 .. 53 B1
All Saints Ho 2 W11 .... 31 B4
All Saints Pas SW18 .... 58 C2
All Saints Rd W11 . 31 B3
All Saints' Rd W3 .. 37 B3
All Saints Rd N1 ... 84 C2
All Saints Sta E14 . 34 A2
Allsop Pl NW1 ..... 91 A1
All Souls CE Prim Sch W1 .... 104 C4
All Souls Pl W1 ... 104 B3
Alma Birk Ho 1 NW6 .... 10 B1
Almack Rd E5 ...... 17 B4
Alma Gr SE1 ...... 153 A3
Alma Ho 7 TW8 ... 44 A4
Alma Pl NW10 ...... 22 A2
Alma Prim Sch SE16 .... 153 C4
Alma Rd SW18 ..... 59 B2
Alma Sq NW8 ...... 89 A4
Alma St
 Camden Town NW5 .... 13 A2
 Stratford New Town E15 .... 19 C2
Alma Terr
 Earl's Ct W8 ..... 127 C1
 Wandsworth SW18 . 71 C4
Almeida St 10 N1 .. 15 A1
Almeric Rd SW11 .. 60 B3
Almington St N4 .... 5 B3
Almond Ave W5 .... 36 A3

Almond Cl SE15 .... 49 C1
Almond Ho SE4 .... 51 B1
Almond Rd SE16 ... 40 A2
Almorah Rd N1 ..... 15 C1
Al-Muntada Islamic Sch SW6 .... 165 B1
Alperton St W10 .. 23 B1
Alphabet Sq E3 .... 33 C4
Alpha Cl NW8 ...... 90 B3
Alpha Ct 7 NW5 .... 13 A2
Alpha Gr E14 ...... 41 C4
Alpha Ho
 6 Brixton SW4 .... 62 A3
 Kilburn NW6 ...... 23 C3
 Lisson Gr NW8 .... 90 B1
Alpha Pl
 Chelsea SW3 ..... 158 B4
 Kilburn NW6 ...... 23 C3
Alpha Rd SE14 .... 51 B2
Alpha St SE15 ..... 49 C1
Alpine Gr 37 E9 ... 17 B1
Alpine Rd SE16 .... 40 C1
Alroy Rd N4 .... 5 C4
Alsace Rd SE17 .. 152 A2
Al Sadiq & Al Zahra Schs NW6 .... 23 A4
Alscot Rd SE1 .... 139 A1
Alscot Road Ind Est SE1 .... 139 A1
Alscot Way SE1 .. 152 C4
Altair Ct N1 .... 15 C2
Altenburg Gdns SW11 .... 60 B3
Althea St SW6 ..... 59 A4
Althorpe Mews SW11 .... 167 C3
Althorp Rd SW17 .. 72 B3
Altima Ct SE22 .... 64 C3
Alton Ho 3 E3 ..... 27 A2
Alton Rd
 Richmond TW10, TW9 .... 54 A3
 Roehampton SW15 .. 68 C3
Alton St E14 .... 34 A4
Alumni Ct SE1 .... 139 A4
Alvanley Ct NW3 ... 11 A3
Alvanley Gdns NW6 .... 11 A3
Alverstone Ho SE11 173 B4
Alverstone Rd NW2 . 9 B1
Alverton St SE8 ... 51 B4
Alvey St SE17 .... 152 A2
Alvington Cres E8 .. 16 B3
Alwyn Ave W4 ...... 37 C1
Alwyne La N1 ...... 15 A1
Alwyne Pl N1 ...... 15 B1
Alwyne Rd N1 ...... 15 B1
Alwyne Sq N1 ...... 15 B2
Alwyne Villas N1 ... 15 A1
Alwyn Gdns W3 .... 28 A3
Alzette Ho 11 E2 ... 25 C3
Aman Dalvi Ho SW18 .... 70 A4
Amazonas E1 ..... 152 B3
Amazon St E1 ...... 32 A3
Ambassador Ct 9 NW6 .... 10 C3
Ambassador Ho NW8 .... 79 A3
Ambassador Sq E14 .... 42 A2
Amber Ct N7 .... 14 C2

Ambergate St SE17 .... 150 B2
Amberley Ct 2 SW9 .... 62 C4
Amberley Rd W9 ... 31 C4
Amber Wharf 29 E2 .... 24 B4
Ambler Prim Sch N4 .... 6 A2
Ambler Rd N4 .... 6 A1
Ambleside
 13 Putney SW19 ... 70 A3
 Putney SW19 ..... 82 B1
Ambleside Cl E9 ... 17 B3
Ambleside Point 4 SE15 .... 50 B3
Ambleside Rd NW10 .... 8 B1
Ambrosden Ave SW1 .... 133 A1
Ambrose Ho 9 E14 .... 33 C4
Ambrose Mews SW11 .... 168 C2
Ambrose St SE16 .. 40 A2
Ambrose Wlk 8 E3 . 26 C3
AMC Bsns Ctr NW10 .... 20 A2
Amelia Cl W3 ...... 37 A4
Amelia Ho 5 W6 ... 39 B1
Amelia St SE17 ... 150 C2
Amen Cnr EC4 .... 108 B1
Amen Ct EC4 ..... 108 B1
American Intercontinental Univ 103 C3
American Sch in London The NW8 . 79 B2
American Univ in London The N7 .... 5 A1
America Sq EC3 .. 124 C4
America St SE1 ... 122 C1
Ameriand Rd SW18 .... 58 B1
Amersham Gr SE14 .... 51 B3
Amersham Rd SE14 .... 51 B3
Amersham Vale SE14, SE8 .... 51 B3
Amery Gdns NW10 .... 22 A4
Amery Ho SE17 ... 152 B2
Amesbury Ave SW2 .... 74 B2
Amesbury Twr 8 SW8 .... 170 C2
Ames Cotts 12 E3 .. 33 A4
Ames Ho 10 E2 .... 25 C3
Amethyst Rd E15 ... 19 C4
Amhurst Ct N4 ...... 6 C4
Amhurst Par N16 ... 7 B4
Amhurst Pk N4, N16 . 7 A4
Amhurst Rd E8, N16 .... 16 C4
Amhurst Terr E8 ... 16 C4
Amias Ho EC1 ..... 96 C2
Amiel St 18 E1 ..... 25 B1
Amies St SW11 ..... 60 B4
Amigo Ho SE1 .... 135 C2
Amina Way SE16 . 139 B1
Amner Rd SW11 .... 60 C1
Amor Rd W6 .... 39 B3
Amory Ho N1 ...... 85 A2
Amott Rd SE15 .... 64 C4
Amoy Pl E14 .... 33 C2
Ampton Pl WC1 .... 94 C3

Ampton St WC1 .... 94 C3
Amstel Ct 15 SE15 . 49 B3
Amsterdam Rd E14 .... 42 B3
Amundsen Ct 7 E14 .... 41 C1
Amwell St EC1 ..... 95 B4
Amyruth Rd SE4 ... 66 C2
Anatola Rd N19 .... 4 B2
Anchorage Point 1 E14 .... 41 C4
Anchor Ho SE16 ... 96 C2
Anchor Mews SW12 .... 61 A1
Anchor Ret Pk E1 .. 25 B1
Anchor St SE16 .... 40 A2
Anchor Terr SE1 .. 123 A2
Anchor Yd EC1 ..... 97 A2
Ancill Cl W6 ...... 154 A3
Ancona Rd NW10 .. 21 C3
Andalus Rd SW9 ... 62 A4
Andaman Ho 10 E1 .... 33 A4
Andersens Wharf 9 E14 .... 33 B3
Anderson Cl W3 ... 28 C3
Anderson Ho
 14 Poplar E14 .... 34 B2
 Vauxhall SW11 .. 163 A2
Anderson Rd E9 ... 17 C2
Andersons Sq N1 .. 86 A3
Anderson St SW3 . 144 C2
Andover Ho 5 N7 ... 5 B2
Andover Pl NW6 ... 78 A1
Andover Rd N7 ...... 5 B2
Andoversford Ct 6 SE15 .... 49 A4
Andre St E8 .... 16 C3
Andrew Borde St WC2 .... 105 C2
Andrew Ho
 New Cross SE4 .... 51 B1
 Putney SW15 ...... 56 C2
Andrew Logan's Glass Ho* SE1 .... 138 A4
Andrew Marvell Ho 11 N16 .... 16 A4
Andrew PI SW8 ... 171 C4
Andrew Reed Ho SW18 .... 70 A4
Andrews Crosse WC2 .... 107 B1
Andrew's Rd E8 .... 25 A4
Andrew St E14 ..... 34 B3
Andrews Wharf 14 E8 .... 25 A4
Andrews Wlk SE17 .... 48 A4
Andrew Wilmot Ct SW18 .... 71 B3
Anfield Cl SW12 ... 73 B4
Angel EC1 .... 86 A1
Angela Davis Ind Est 20 SW9 .... 63 A3
Angel Ct
 Broadgate EC2 ... 109 C2
 St James SW1 ... 119 A1
 11 Willesden NW2 .. 9 A2
Angel Gate EC1 .... 96 B4
Angel Ho N1 .... 85 C1
Angelina Ho 2 SE15 .... 49 C2

Angelis Appartments
N1 . . . . 86 B1
Angel La E15 . . . . 19 C2
Angell Park Gdns
SW9 . . . . 62 C4
Angell Rd SW9 . . . 63 A4
Angel Mews
Finsbury N1 . . . . 85 C1
Putney SW15 . . . . 68 C4
Stepney E1 . . . . . 32 A2
Angel Pas EC4 . . . 123 B3
Angel Pl SE1 . . . . 137 B4
Angel Sq N1 . . . . 85 C1
Angel St EC1 . . . . 108 C2
Angel Sta EC1 . . . 85 C1
Angel Wlk W6 . . . . 39 B2
Angerstein Bsns Pk
SE10 . . . . 43 B2
Angerstein La SE3 . 53 B2
Anglebury ⑤ W2 . . 31 C3
Anglers La NW5 . . 13 A2
Anglesey Ho ⑬
E14 . . . . 33 C3
Anglia Ho E14 . . . 33 A3
Anglo American
Laundry SW17 . . 71 B1
Anglo Rd ⑩ E3 . . . 26 B3
Angrave Ct ⑧ E8 . . 24 B4
Angrave Pas ⑨ E8 . 24 B4
Angus Ho ⑫
SW12 . . . . 73 C4
Angus St SE14 . . . 51 A3
Anhalt Rd SW11 . . 158 B2
Animals in War
Meml* 117 A4
Anley Rd W14 . . . 39 C4
Annabel Ct E14 . . 34 A3
Anna Cl E8 . . . . . 24 B4
Annandale Rd
Chiswick W4 . . . . 38 A1
Greenwich SE10 . . 43 B1
Anne Goodman Ho
E1 . . . . 32 B3
Anne Kerr Ct ⑱
SW15 . . . . 57 C1
Anne's Ct NW8 . . . 90 B2
Annesley Ho SW9 . 173 B4
Annesley Wlk ⑲ N19 . 4 B2
Annette Cres ④
N1 . . . . 15 B1
Annette Ct N7 . . . 5 B1
Annette Rd N7 . . . 14 B4
Anne Besant Cl
E3 . . . . 26 B4
Anning St
E2 . . . . . . 24 A1 98 B2
Annis Rd E9 . . . . 18 A2
Ann La SW10 . . . . 157 B3
Ann Moss Way
SE16 . . . . 40 B3
Ann's Cl SW1 . . . . 131 B3
Ann's Pl E1 . . . . . 110 C3
Ansdell Rd SE15 . . 50 B1
Ansdell St W8 . . . 128 B2
Ansdell Terr W8 . . 128 B2
Ansell Ho ⑩ E1 . . . 32 B4
Ansell Rd SW17 . . 72 B1
Anselm Rd SW6 . . 155 B3
Ansleigh Pl W11 . . 30 C2
Anson Ho
Pimlico SW1 . . . . 160 C4
⑥ Tower Hamlets
E1 . . . . 26 A1

Anson Prim Sch
NW2 . . . . 9 C3
Anson Rd
Cricklewood NW2 . 9 B3
Tufnell Pk N7 . . . 13 C4
Anstey Ct ⑥ W3 . . 37 A4
Anstey Ho ⑦ E9 . . 25 B4
Anstey Rd SE15 . . 64 C4
Anstice Cl W4 . . . 46 A3
Antenor Ho ⑫ E2 . . 25 A3
Anthony Cope Ct
N1 . . . . 97 C4
Anthony Ho NW8 . 90 A1
Anthony St E1 . . . 32 A3
Antilles Bay ⑫
E14 . . . . 42 B4
Antill Ho ⑤ E1 . . . 25 B1
Antill Rd E3 . . . . 26 A2
Antill Terr ⑤ E1 . . 32 C3
Antoine Mews SE1 138 A3
Anton St E8 . . . . 16 C3
Antony Ho
② Deptford SE14 . 50 C3
② Rotherhithe
SE16 . . . . 40 B2
Antrim Gr NW3 . . 12 B2
Antrim Ho SW11 . . 60 C4
Antrim Mans NW3 . 12 B2
Antrim Rd NW3 . . 12 B2
Antrobus Rd W4 . . 37 B3
Apex Ind Est
NW10 . . . . 21 B1
Aphrodite Ct ⑪
E14 . . . . 41 C2
Apollo Bldg ②
E14 . . . . 41 C2
Apollo Ho
Chelsea SW10 . . 157 B3
④ Hackney E2 . . 25 A3
④ Highgate N6 . . 3 B4
Apollo Ind Bsns Ctr ㉙
SE8 . . . . 50 C4
Apollo Pl SW10 . . 157 B2
Apollo Studios ⑱
NW5 . . . . 13 C3
Apothecary St
EC4 . . . . 108 A1
Appach Rd SW2 . . 62 C1
Appleby Ct ⑥ W3 . 37 B4
Appleby Rd
Hackney E8 . . . . 16 C1
Newham E16 . . . 35 C3
Appleby St E2 . . . 24 B3
Appledore Cl SW12,
SW17 . . . . 72 B2
Appleford ⑥ NW5 . 13 B3
Appleford Ho ⑥
W10 . . . . 23 A1
Appleford Rd W10 . 23 A1
Applegarth Ho
Borough The SE1 . 136 B4
⑨ Camberwell
SE15 . . . . 49 C3
Applegarth Rd
W14 . . . . 39 C3
Apple Mkt WC2 . . 120 B4
Appleshaw Ho ⑥
SE5 . . . . 64 A4
Appleton Ct ㉘ SE8 . 17 A3
Appletree Ct SE13 . 67 C3
Apple Tree Yd
SW1 . . . . 119 A2
Appold St EC2 . . . 110 A4
Apollo Ho SW18 . . 173 B4
Apprentice Way ⑤
E5 . . . . 17 A4
Approach Cl N16 . . 16 A4

Approach Rd E2 . . 25 B3
Approach The W3 . 28 C3
April Ct ⑳ E2 . . . 24 C3
April St E8 . . . . . 16 B4
Apsley Ho
Stepney E1 . . . . 32 B4
St John's Wood
NW8 . . . . 79 B2
Apsley Way N1 . . 131 C4
Aquila St NW8 . . . 79 C2
Aquinas St SE1 . . 121 C1
Arabella Ct NW8 . . 79 A2
Arabella Dr SW15 . 56 A3
Arabian Ho ⑧ E1 . . 26 A1
Arabin Rd SE4 . . . 66 B3
Aragon Twr SE8 . . 41 B2
Arakan Ho ④ N16 . 15 C4
Aral Ho ④ E1 . . . . 25 C1
Arapiles Ho ⑥
E14 . . . . 34 C3
Arbery Rd E3 . . . . 26 A3
Arbon Ct N1 . . . . 87 A3
Arbor Ct N16 . . . . 6 C2
Arborfield Cl SW2 . 74 B3
Arborfield Ho ⑦
E14 . . . . 33 C2
Arbour Ho ⑤ E1 . . 32 C3
Arbour Sq E1 . . . . 32 C3
Arbuthnot Rd
SE14 . . . . 50 C1
Arbutus St E8 . . . 24 B4
Arcade The
Broadgate EC2 . . 110 A3
① Tufnell Pk N7 . . 14 A4
Arcadian Ho SE6 . 167 A1
Arcadian Pl SW18 . 70 A4
Arcadia St E14 . . . 33 C3
Archangel St SE16 . 40 C4
Archbishop Coggan
Ho SE13 . . . . . . 67 C2
Archbishop Michael
Ramsey Tech Coll
SE5 . . . . 48 A3
Archbishop's Pl ⑥
SW2 . . . . 74 B4
Archbishop Sumner
CE Prim Sch
SE11 . . . . 149 C3
Archbishop Tenison's
Sch SE11 . . . . . 163 A3
Archdale Ct W12 . 30 A1
Archdale Ho ㉒
SE1 . . . . 138 A2
Archdale Rd SE22 . 64 B3
Archel Rd W14 . . . 154 C4
Archer Ho
Battersea SW11 . . 167 C2
㉔ Hoxton N1 . . . 24 A4
① New Cross SE14 . 51 A2
Notting Hill
W11 . . . . . 31 B2 113 A4
Archers Lo SE16 . . 153 C1
Archer Sq SE14 . . 51 A4
Archer St W1 . . . . 119 B4
Archery Cl W2 . . . 102 B1
Archery Fields Ho
WC1 . . . . 95 B4
Archery Stps W2 . . 116 B4
Arches The W2 . . . 22 C1
Archibald Mews
W1 . . . . 118 A3
Archibald Rd N7 . . 13 C4
Archibald St E3 . . 26 C2
Archie St SE1 . . . 138 B3
Arch St SE1 . . . . 136 C1
Archway N6 . . . . . 4 A4
Archway Bsns Ctr ⑤
N19 . . . . 4 C1

Archway Cl
North Kensington
W10 . . . . 30 C4
② Upper Holloway
N19 . . . . 4 B2
Archway Hts ⑤
N19 . . . . 4 B3
Archway Mews
SW15 . . . . 58 A3
Archway Rd N6 . . 4 A4
Archway St SW13,
SW14 . . . . 56 A4
Archway Sta N19 . 4 B2
Arcola St E8 . . . . 16 B3
Arctic St NW5 . . . 13 A3
Ardbeg Rd SE24 . . 63 C2
Arden ⑩ SW19 . . . 69 C3
Arden Cres E14 . . 41 C2
Arden Ho
㉑ Hoxton N1 . . . 24 A3
Stockwell SW9 . . 172 B1
Vauxhall SE11 . . . 148 C3
Ardent Ho ⑩ E3 . . 26 A3
Ardilaun Rd N5 . . 15 B4
Ardleigh Rd N1 . . 16 A2
Ardlui Rd SE27 . . . 75 B2
Ardmere Rd SE13 . 67 C1
Ardshiel Cl SW15 . 57 C4
Ardwell Rd SW2 . . 74 A2
Ardwick Rd NW2 . 10 C4
Ares Ct ⑬ E14 . . . 41 C2
Arethusa Ho ⑧
E14 . . . . 42 A2
Argo Bsns Ctr ⑦
NW6 . . . . 23 C2
Argon Mews SW6 . 155 C1
Argos Ct ⑤ SW9 . . 173 B4
Argos Ho ⑫ E2 . . . 25 A3
Argosy Ho
Fitzrovia W1 . . . 92 B1
Rotherhithe SE8 . 41 A2
Argyle Ho E14 . . . 42 B3
Argyle Mans ④
NW2 . . . . 9 C4
Argyle Pl W6 . . . . 39 A2
Argyle Prim Sch
WC1 . . . . 94 A4
Argyle Rd E1 . . . . 25 C1
Argyle Sq WC1 . . . 94 B4
Argyle St WC1 . . . 94 B4
Argyle Way SE16 . 153 C1
Argyle Wlk WC1 . . 94 B3
Argyll Cl SW9 . . . 62 B4
Argyll Ct ㊀ SW2 . . 74 A4
Argyll Mans
Chelsea SW10 . . 157 C4
West Kensington
W14 . . . . 140 B4
Argyll Rd W8 . . . . 127 C3
Argyll St W1 . . . . 104 C1
Arica Ho SE16 . . . 40 A3
Arica Rd SE4 . . . . 66 A4
Ariel Ct
⑤ Hammersmith
W12 . . . . 38 C3
Newington SE11 . . 150 A3
Ariel Rd NW6 . . . . 10 C2
Ariel Way W12 . . . 30 B1
Aristotle Rd SW4 . 61 C4
Arizona Bldg ⑩
SE13 . . . . 52 A2
Arkansas Ho ㉑
N19 . . . . 4 C4
Arklow Ho SE17 . . 48 C4
Arklow Rd SE14 . . 51 B4

Arklow Road Trad Est
SE14 . . . . 51 B4
Arkwright Ho ㉓
SW2 . . . . 74 A4
Arkwright Mans
NW3 . . . . 11 B3
Arkwright Rd
NW3 . . . . 11 B3
Arlesey Cl SW15 . . 58 A2
Arlesford Rd SW9 . 62 A4
Arlidge Ho EC1 . . 107 C4
Arlingford Rd
SW2 . . . . 62 C1
Arlington Ave N1 . 87 A3
Arlington Cl SE13 . 67 C2
Arlington Ct ⑬
W3 . . . . 28 A1
Arlington Gdns
W4 . . . . 37 B1
Arlington Ho
③ Deptford SE8 . . 51 B4
Finsbury EC1 . . . 95 C4
① Shepherd's Bush
W12 . . . . 30 A1
Arlington Lo SW2 . 62 B3
Arlington Park Mans
③ W4 . . . . 37 B1
Arlington Rd NW1 . 82 B3
Arlington Sq N1 . . 87 A3
Arlington St SW1 . 118 C2
Arlington Way EC1 . 95 C4
Armada Ct
SE8 . . . . 51 C4
Armada St ⑩ SE8 . 51 C4
Armagh Rd E3 . . . 26 B4
Arminger Rd W12 . 30 A1
Armitage Ho
NW1 . . . . 102 B4
Armitage Rd
Golders Green
NW11 . . . . 1 B3
Greenwich SE10 . 43 B1
Armour Cl N7 . . . 14 B2
Armoury Ho E3 . . 26 A4
Armoury Rd SE8 . . 52 A1
Armoury Way
SW18 . . . . 58 C2
Armsby Ho ⑰ E1 . . 32 B4
Armstrong Ho ⑧
SW15 . . . . 58 A1
Armstrong Rd
East Acton W3 . . 29 B1
Knightsbridge SW7 129 B1
Arncliffe NW6 . . . 78 B3
Arndale Wlk ⑧
SW18 . . . . 59 A2
Arne Ho SE11 . . . 148 C2
Arne St WC2 . . . . 106 B1
Arneway St SW1 . . 133 C1
Arnewood Cl
SW15 . . . . 68 C3
Arnhem Pl E14 . . . 41 C3
Arnhem Way ③
SE22 . . . . 64 A2
Arnhem Wharf
E14 . . . . 41 C3
Arnhem Wharf Prim
Sch E14 . . . . . . 41 C3
Arnold Cir
E2 . . . . . . 24 B2 98 C3
Arnold Est SE1 . . 139 A3
Arnold Ho
Newington SE17 . . 150 B1

Arnold Ho continued
9 Stoke Newington
N16 .... 7 A1
Arnold House Sch
NW8 .... 79 B1
Arnold Rd E3 .... 26 C2
Arnold Ho 27 SE5 ... 48 B3
Arnott Cl W4 .... 37 C2
Arnould Ave E5 ...... 63 C3
Arnside Ho 2
SE17 .... 48 C4
Arnside St SE17 ...... 48 B4
Arodene Rd SW2 ..... 62 B1
Arragon Rd SW18 ... 70 C3
Arran Ho
6 Canary Wharf
E14 .... 34 B1
Stoke Newington N16 .. 7 B2
Arran Wlk N1 .... 15 B1
Arrol Ho SE1 .... 137 A1
Arrowe Ct 6 E5 ..... 17 A4
Arrow Ho 21 N1 ..... 24 A4
Arrow Rd E3 .... 27 A2
Arrowsmith Ho
SE11 .... 148 C2
Arsenal Sta N5 .... 5 C1
Arta Ho 28 E1 .... 32 B3
Artemis Ct 14 E14 .. 41 C2
Artemis Pl SW18 ..... 70 B4
Artesian Rd W2 ...... 31 C3
Arthur Ct
Battersea SW11 ...... 169 C3
10 North Kensington
W10 .... 30 C3
Paddington W2 ...... 100 A2
Arthur Deakin Ho
E1 .... 111 B4
Arthurdon Rd SE4 ... 66 C2
Arthur Henderson Ho
8 Crouch End N19 .... 4 C4
Fulham SW6 .... 164 C2
Arthur Newton 20
SW11 .... 59 C4
Arthur Rd N7 .... 14 B4
Arthur St EC4 .... 123 C4
Arthur Wade Ho
E2 .... 24 B2 99 A4
Artichoke Hill 8
E1 .... 32 A2
Artichoke Mews 5
SE5 .... 48 C2
Artichoke Pl SE5 ..... 48 C2
Artillery Ho
Bow E3 .... 26 A4
Westminster SW1 ... 133 B1
Artillery La
Broadgate E1 .... 110 B3
North Kensington
W12 .... 29 C3
Artillery Pas E1 ..... 110 B3
Artillery Pl SW1 ..... 133 B1
Artillery Row
SW1 .... 133 B1
Artisan Ct E8 .... 16 C2
Artisan Mews 9
NW10 .... 22 C2
Artisan Quarter 10
NW10 .... 22 C2
Arton Wilson Ho 12
SW15 .... 56 C2
Arts Educational Sch
The W4 .... 38 A2
Arundel Bldgs
SE1 .... 138 B1
Arundel Cl SW11 ..... 60 A2

Arundel Ct
Barnes SW13 .... 47 A4
Chelsea SW3 .... 144 B2
Putney SW15 .... 57 C2
Arundel Gdns
W11 .... 31 B2 112 C4
Arundel Gr N16 ...... 16 A3
Arundel Ho
Islington N1 .... 86 B4
Richmond TW10 ..... 54 C2
3 South Acton W3 .. 37 A4
Arundel Lo 9 N19 ... 5 A2
Arundel Mans
Fulham SW6 .... 165 A4
Arundel Pl N1, N7 ... 14 C2
Arundel Sq N7 ...... 14 C2
Arundel St WC2 .... 121 A4
Arundel Terr
SW13 .... 47 A4
Arvon Rd N5 .... 14 C3
Asaph Ho SE14 ..... 51 B2
Ascalon Ct 16
SW2 .... 74 B4
Ascalon Ho SW8 ... 160 C1
Ascalon St SW8 .... 160 C1
Ascham St NW5 ..... 13 B3
Ascot Ct
8 Brixton SW4 ...... 62 A3
St John's Wood
NW8 .... 89 B3
Ascot Ho
6 Acton Green
W4 .... 37 B1
1 Regent's Pk NW1 .. 92 B4
Regent's Pk NW1 ... 92 B4
Ascot Par 9 SW4 ... 62 A3
Ascot Ave SW5 ...... 36 A4
Ashbourne Ct E5 .... 18 A4
Ashbourne Gr
Chiswick W4 .... 38 A1
East Dulwich SE22 .. 64 B3
Ashbourne Ind Sch
W8 .... 128 A3
Ashbridge Ct 8
W6 .... 39 A3
Ashbridge St NW8 .. 90 A1
Ashbrook Rd N19 ... 5 A3
Ashburn Gdns
SW7 .... 142 C4
Ashburnham Com Sch
SW10 .... 157 B2
Ashburnham Gr
SE10 .... 52 A3
Ashburnham Pl
SE10 .... 52 A3
Ashburnham Rd
Chelsea SW10 ...... 157 A1
Kensal Rise NW10 .. 22 B3
Ashburnham Retreat
4 SE10 .... 52 A3
Ashburnham Twr
SW10 .... 157 B2
Ashburn Pl SW7 .... 142 C3
Ashburton Mans
SW10 .... 157 A2
Ashburton Rd E16 .. 35 C3
Ashbury Rd SW11 .. 60 C4
Ashby Ct NW8 ...... 89 C2
Ashby Gr N1 .... 15 B1
Ashby Ho
8 Brixton SW9 ...... 48 A1
1 Islington N1 .... 15 B1
Ashby Mews
4 Clapham Park
SW2 .... 62 A2

Ashby Mews continued
New Cross SE4 .... 51 B1
Ashby Rd SE4 .... 51 B1
Ashby St EC1 .... 96 B3
Ashchurch Ct 2
W12 .... 38 C3
Ashchurch Gr
W12 .... 38 C3
Ashchurch Park Villas
W12 .... 38 C3
Ashchurch Terr
W12 .... 38 C3
Ashcombe Ct 4
SW15 .... 58 A2
Ashcombe Ho 39
E3 .... 27 A2
Ashcombe St
SW6 .... 166 A1
Ashcroft Ho 170
E3 .... 26 A2
Ashcroft Sq 8
W6 .... 39 B2
Ash Ct
Clapham SW11 ...... 60 C2
Marylebone W1 ..... 102 C2
6 Rotherhithe
SE16 .... 33 A1
Upper Holloway N19 .. 4 B2
Ashdale Ho N4 ...... 6 B4
Ashdene 6 SE15 ... 50 A3
Ashdon Ho NW10 .. 30 B4
Ashdown SW15 ..... 57 C2
Ashdown Cres
NW5 .... 12 C3
Ashdown Ct SE22 .. 76 C3
Ashdown Ho 7 E5 .. 7 C2
Ashdown Wlk 20
E14 .... 41 C2
Ashenden SE17 .... 151 A4
Ashenden Rd E5 .... 18 A3
Ashentree Ct EC4 .. 107 C1
Asher Way E1 ...... 125 C3
Ashfield Ho 5 N5 .. 15 B3
Ashfield Rd W3 ..... 38 B4
Ashfield St E1 ...... 32 B4
Ashfield Yd 21 E1 .. 32 B4
Ashford Ct NW2 .... 9 C4
Ashford Ho
1 Brixton SW9 ..... 63 A3
11 Deptford SE8 ... 51 B4
Ashford Rd NW2 ... 9 C4
Ashford St
N1 .... 24 A2 98 A4
Ash Gr
Cricklewood NW2 .. 10 A4
Ealing W5 .... 36 A3
Hackney E8 .... 25 A4
Ashgrove Ct 9
W9 .... 31 C4
Ashgrove Ho
SW1 .... 147 C2
Ash Ho
4 Canary Wharf
E14 .... 42 B4
Fulham SE1 .... 153 A3
Ashington 1 NW5 .. 13 A2
Ashington Ho 18
E1 .... 25 A1
Ashington Rd
SW6 .... 165 A1
Ashland Pl W1 ..... 103 B4
Ashleigh Ho SW14 .. 56 A4
Ashleigh Rd SW14 .. 56 A4
Ashley Cres SW11 .. 60 C4

Ashley Ct
Hampstead NW3 ..... 11 A3
18 Kingsland N16 ... 16 A3
Ashley Pl SW1 ...... 132 C1
Ashley Rd
Hornsey N19 .... 5 A4
Richmond TW9 .... 54 A4
Ashlin Rd E15 .... 19 C4
Ash Lo SW6 .... 47 C2
Ashlone Rd SW15 .. 57 B4
Ashmead Bsns Ctr 2
E16 .... 27 C1
Ashmead Ho E9 .... 18 A3
Ashmead Prim Sch
SE8 .... 51 C1
Ashmead Rd SE8 ... 51 C1
Ashmere Gr 11 SW2,
SW4 .... 62 A3
Ashmere Ho 10
SW2 .... 62 A3
Ashmill St NW8 .... 102 A4
Ashmole Prim Sch
SE11 .... 163 A3
Ashmole St SW8 ... 163 A3
Ashmore NW1 ...... 13 C1
Ashmore Cl SE15 .. 49 B3
Ashmore Ho W14 .. 126 B1
Ashmore Rd W9 ... 23 B2
Ashmount Prim Sch
N19 .... 4 B4
Ashmount Rd N19 .. 4 B4
Ashness Rd SW11 .. 60 B2
Ashpark Ho 4
E14 .... 33 B3
Ashtead Ct 15
SW19 .... 69 C3
Ashted Rd E5 .... 7 C4
Ashton Ho
Kennington SW9 ... 163 C1
Roehampton SW15 .. 69 A4
Ashton Rd E15 ...... 19 C3
Ashton St E14 ...... 34 B2
Ashurst Lo 4 N5 ... 15 A3
Ashwin St E8 .... 16 B2
Ashworth Cl SE5 ... 48 C1
Ashworth Mans
W9 .... 88 B3
Ashworth Rd W9 ... 88 B3
Aske Ho N1 .. 24 A2 98 A4
Asker Ho N7 .... 14 A4
Aske St N1 .. 24 A2 98 A4
Askew Cres W12 ... 38 C4
Askew Mans 14
W12 .... 38 C4
Askew Rd W12 ..... 38 C4
Askham Ct W12 .... 29 C1
Askham Rd W12 ... 29 C1
Askill Dr SW15 ..... 58 A2
Asland Rd E15 ...... 27 C4
Aslett St SW18 ..... 71 B4
Asmara Rd NW2 ... 10 A3
Asolando Dr SE17 .. 151 A3
Aspect Ho 7 E14 .. 42 B4
Aspen Cl Ealing W5 .. 36 B4
13 Upper Holloway
N19 .... 4 B2
Aspen Ct
10 Acton W3 .... 28 B3
12 Hackney E5 ...... 16 C3
Richmond TW9 ...... 44 C3
Aspen Gdns 2
W6 .... 39 A1
Aspen Ho
4 Deptford SE15 ... 50 B4
7 Maitland Pk
NW3 .... 12 B2

Aspen Ho continued
Richmond TW9 .... 44 C3
Asplenia Rd W6 .... 47 C3
Aspen Way E14 ..... 34 B2
Aspern Gr NW3 ..... 12 A3
Aspinall Ho SW12 .. 74 A3
Aspinall Rd SE4 .... 65 C4
Aspinden Rd SE16 .. 40 A2
Aspire Bld 10
SW15 .... 58 B2
Aspley Ho SW18 ... 59 B2
Assam SE1 .... 125 A1
Assam St E1 .... 111 B2
Assata Mews N1 ... 15 A2
Assembly Pas E1 .. 32 B4
Assisi Ct SW12 ..... 72 B3
Astbury Bsns Pk 9
SE15 .... 50 B2
Astbury Ho SE11 .. 135 B1
Astbury Rd SE15 ... 50 B2
Astell St SW3 ...... 144 B2
Aster Ho 3 SE13 .. 52 B1
Aste St E14 .... 42 B4
Astey's Row 1 N1 .. 15 B1
Astle St SW11 ..... 169 C2
Astley Ave NW2 ..... 9 B3
Astley Ho
Fulham SE1 .... 153 A2
30 Paddington W2 .. 31 C4
Aston Ct N4 .... 6 B2
Aston Ho
Notting Hill
W11 .... 31 B2 113 A4
South Lambeth
SW8 .... 171 B3
Aston St E14 .... 33 A4
Astonville St
SW18 .... 70 C3
Astor Ct SW6 .... 156 C1
Astoria Mans 18
SW16 .... 74 A1
Astoria Par SW16 .. 74 A1
Astoria Wlk SW9 ... 62 C4
Astra Ho
8 Bow E3 .... 26 B2
Hornsey N4 .... 5 B4
Astrop Mews W6 .. 39 B3
Astrop Terr W6 ..... 39 B3
Astwood Mews
SW7 .... 142 C4
Asylum Rd SE15 .. 50 A3
Atalanta St
SW6 .... 47 C3 154 A1
Atheldene Rd
SW18 .... 71 B3
Athelstan Gr 2 E3 .. 26 B3
Athelstane Mews
N4 .... 5 C3
Athelstane Gdns 8
NW6 .... 10 A1
Athelstan Ho
Hackney Wick E9 ... 18 B3
Stoke Newington
N16 .... 16 A4
Athena Ct
Bermondsey SE1 ... 138 A3
St John's Wood
NW8 .... 79 B2
Athenia Ho 7 E14 .. 33 A3
Athenlay Rd SE15 .. 65 C2
Athenaeum Ct N5 .. 15 B4
Athens Gdns W9 .. 23 C1
Atherden Rd E5 .... 17 B4
Atherfield Ct
SW18 .... 59 A1

Atherfold Rd SW9 . . . .62 A4
Atherstone Ct
  W2 . . . . .100 B4
Atherstone Mews
  SW7 . . . . .143 A4
Atherton Rd SW13 . .46 C3
Atherton St SW11 .168 B2
Athlone Cl E5 . . . . . . .17 A3
Athlone Ho
  16 Camden Town
  NW5 . . . . .12 C2
  9 Stepney E1 . . . . . .32 B3
Athlone House N6 . . . .3 B3
Athlone Rd SW2 . . . .74 C4
Athlone St NW5 . . . . .12 C2
Athol Ct **18** N4 . . . . . . .5 B2
Atholl Ho W9 . . . . . . .88 C3
Athol Sq E14 . . . . . . .34 B3
Atkins Ct **13** E3 . . . . . .26 B4
Atkins Lo W8 . . . . . .127 B4
Atkinson Ho
  Battersea SW11 . . . .169 B3
  15 Hackney E2 . . . . .24 C3
  Walworth SE17 . . . .151 C3
Atkinson Rd SW4,
  SW2 . . . . .73 C4
Atlanta Bldg **8**
  SE13 . . . . .52 A2
Atlantic Ct **19** E14 . .34 C2
Atlantic Ho
  1 Putney SW15 . . . .58 B2
  4 Tower Hamlets
  E1 . . . . .33 A4
Atlantic Rd SW2, SW9,
  SE24 . . . . .62 C3
Atlas Mews
  Dalston E8 . . . . .16 B2
  Islington N7 . . . . . . .14 B2
Atlas Rd NW10 . . . . . .21 A2
Atley Rd E3 . . . . .26 C4
Atney Rd SW15 . . . . .58 A3
Atterbury St SW1 .148 A3
Attilburgh Ho
  SE1 . . . . .138 C2
Attlee Ho **1** 111 A3
Attneave St WC1 . . . .95 B3
Atwater Cl SW2 . . . . .74 C3
Atwell Rd **2** SE15 . . .49 C1
Atwood Ave TW9 . . . .44 C1
Atwood Ho SE21 . . . .76 A1
Atwood Rd W6 . . . . . .39 A2
Aubert Ct N5 . . . . . . .15 A4
Aubert Pk N5 . . . . . . .15 A4
Aubert Rd N5 . . . . . . .15 A4
Auber Beardsley Ho
  SW1 . . . . .147 A3
Aubrey Mans
  NW1 . . . . .102 A4
Aubrey Moore Point
  E15 . . . . .27 B3
Aubrey Pl NW8 . . . . . .78 C1
Aubrey Rd
  W14 . . . . .31 B1 113 A1
Aubrey Wlk
  W14 . . . . .31 B1 113 A1
Auburn Cl SE14 . . . . .51 A3
Aubyn Sq SW15 . . . . .56 C2
Auckland Ho **11**
  W12 . . . . .30 A2
Auckland Rd
  SW11 . . . . .60 A3
Auckland St SE11 .148 C1
Auden Pl NW1 . . . . . .81 B4
Audley Cl **8**
  SW11 . . . . .60 C4

Audley Ct W1 . . . . .118 A2
Audley Rd TW10 . . . .54 B2
Audley Sq W1 . . . . .117 C2
Audrey Ho EC1 . . . .107 C3
Audrey St E2 . . . . . . .24 C3
Augustas La E4 . . . . . .4 A3
Augustine Ho
  Broadgate EC2 . . . .109 C2
  New Cross SE4 . . . . .51 B2
Augustine Rd
  W14 . . . . .39 C3
Augustines Ct E9 . . . .17 B3
Augustus Cl W12 . . . .39 A3
Augustus Ct
  8 Putney SW19 . . .70 A3
  Streatham SW16 . . .73 C2
Augustus Ho NW1 . .92 C4
Augustus Rd
  SW19 . . . . .70 A3
Augustus St NW1 . . .92 B4
Aulton Pl SE11 . . . .149 C1
Aura Ho **3** TW9 . . . . .45 A2
Auriga Mews N1 . . . .15 C3
Auriol Mans W14 . .140 A3
Auriol Rd W14 . . . . .140 A3
Aurora Bldg **4**
  E14 . . . . .34 B1
Aurora Ho E14 . . . . . .34 A3
Austen Ho **5**
  NW6 . . . . .23 C2
Austin Ct E2 . . . . . .109 C2
Austin Friars Ho
  EC2 . . . . .109 C2
Austin Friars Sq
  EC2 . . . . .109 C2
Austin Ho
  5 Brixton SW2 . . . .62 B2
  1 New Cross SE14 . .51 B3
Austin Rd SW11 . . . .169 B3
Austins Ct SE15 . . . . .64 C4
Austin St E2 . . .24 B2 98 C3
Australia Rd W12 . . .30 A2
Austral St SE11 . . . .150 A4
Autumn Rise **2**
  W4 . . . . .37 C1
Autumn St E3 . . . . . .26 C4
Avalon Rd SW6 . . . .166 A4
Avebury Ct N1 . . . . . .87 B3
Avebury St N1 . . . . . .87 B3
Aveline St SE11 . . . .149 B1
Aveling Ho **12** N19 . .4 B1
Ave Maria La EC4 . .108 B1
Avenell Mans N5 . . . .15 A4
Avenell Rd N5 . . . . . . .6 A1
Avenfield Ho W1 . . .117 A4
Avening Rd SW18 . . .70 C4
Avening Terr
  SW18 . . . . .70 C4
Avenue Cl NW8 . . . . .80 B3
Avenue Cres W3 . . . .37 A4
Avenue Ct
  Chelsea SW3 . . . .144 C3
  Cricklewood NW2 . . .1 A1
Avenue Gdns
  Mortlake SW14 . . . .56 A4
  South Acton W3 . . . .37 A4
Avenue Ho
  St John's Wood
  NW8 . . . . .80 A1
  Upper Clapton N16 . .7 C2
  Willesden Green
  NW10 . . . . .22 A3
Avenue Lo **12**
  NW8 . . . . .11 C1
Avenue Mans
  Clapham SW11 . . . .60 C3
  Hampstead NW3 . . .11 A3

Avenue Mans continued
  Willesden NW2 . . . . . .9 A2
Avenue Park Rd SE21,
  SE27 . . . . .75 A2
Avenue Rd
  Crouch End N8 . . . . . .5 A4
  Harlesden NW10 . . . .21 B3
  Primrose Hill NW8 . .80 A4
  South Acton W3 . . . .37 A4
Avenue Sch The
  NW6 . . . . .10 A1
Avenue The
  Bedford Pk W4 . . . . .38 A3
  Brondesbury Pk
  NW6 . . . . .23 A4
  Clapham SW4 . . . . . .60 C2
  Greenwich SE10 . . . .52 C3
  Richmond TW9 . . . . .44 B1
  Wandsworth SW18,
  SW12 . . . . .72 A4
Averill St W6 . . . . . . .47 C4
Avery Farm Row
  SW1 . . . . .146 A3
Avery Hill Coll (Mile
  End Annexe) E3 . . . .26 B1
Avery Row W1 . . . . .118 B4
Aviary Ct E16 . . . . . . .35 B4
Avignon Rd SE4 . . . . .65 C4
Avingdon Ct **10**
  W3 . . . . .28 B1
Avington Ct SE1 . . . .152 B3
Avis Sq E1 . . . . .32 C3
Avocet Cl SE1 . . . . .153 B2
Avon Ct
  1 Acton W3 . . . . . . .28 B3
  1 Putney SW15 . . . .58 A2
Avondale Ct E16 . . . . .35 B4
Avondale Ho
  Bermondsey SE1 . . .153 B1
  6 Mortlake SW14 . .55 C4
Avondale Mans
  SW6 . . . . .164 C4
Avondale Park Gdns
  W11 . . . . .31 A2 112 A3
Avondale Park Prim
  Sch W11 . .31 A2 112 A3
Avondale Park Rd
  W11 . . . . .31 A2 112 A4
Avondale Rd
  Mortlake SW14 . . . .55 C4
  Newham E16 . . . . . . .35 A4
Avondale Rise
  SE15 . . . . .64 B4
Avondale Sq SE1 . . .153 B1
Avon Ho
  2 Islington N1 . . . .14 C1
  8 Stoke Newington
  N16 . . . . .7 A1
  West Kensington
  W14 . . . . .141 A3
Avonhurst Ho
  NW6 . . . . .10 A1
Avonley Rd SE14 . . . .50 B3
Avonmore Gdns
  W14 . . . . .141 A3
Avonmore Pl
  W14 . . . . .140 B4
Avonmore Prim Sch
  W14 . . . . .140 B4
Avonmore Rd
  W14 . . . . .140 C4
Avonmouth St
  SE1 . . . . .136 C2
Avon Pl SE1 . . . . . . .137 A3
Avon Rd SE4 . . . . . . .66 C4
Avriol Ho W12 . . . . . .30 A1
Avro Ct E9 . . . . .18 A3

Axford Ho SW2 . . . . .75 A3
Axis Bsns Ctr E15 . . .27 A4
Axis Ct SE10 . . . . .53 A4
Axminster Rd N7 . . . . .5 B1
Aybrook St W1 . . . . .103 B3
Aycliffe Rd W12 . . . . .29 C1
Aylesbury Ho **10**
  SE15 . . . . .49 C4
Aylesbury Rd
  SE17 . . . . .151 C1
Aylesbury St E1 . . . . .96 A1
Aylesford Ho SE1 . .137 C3
Aylesford St SW1 . .147 B1
Aylesham Sh Ctr
  SE15 . . . . .49 C2
Aylestone Ave
  NW6 . . . . .22 C4
Aylmer Ho SE10 . . . . .42 C1
Aylmer Rd W12 . . . . .38 B4
Aylton Est **23** SE16 . .40 B4
Aylward St E1 . . . . . .32 C3
Aylwin Est SE1 . . . .138 B2
Aylwin Girls Sch
  SE1 . . . . .153 A4
Aynhoe Mans
  W14 . . . . .39 C2
Aynhoe Rd W14 . . . . .39 C3
Ayres St SE1 . . . . . .137 A4
Ayrsome Rd N16 . . . . .7 A1
Ayrton Gould Ho **9**
  E2 . . . . .25 C2
Ayrton Rd SW7 . . . .129 B2
Aysgarth Rd SE21 . . .76 A4
Ayshford Ho E2 . . . . .25 A2
Ayston Ho **10** SE8 . . .40 C2
Aytoun Ct SW9 . . . .173 A1
Aytoun Pl SW9 . . . . .173 A1
Aytoun Rd SW9 . . . .173 A1
Azalea Ho SE14 . . . . .51 B3
Azania Mews
  NW5 . . . . .13 A2
Azenby Rd SE15 . . . . .49 B1
Azof St SE10 . . . . .43 A2
Azov Ho **10** E1 . . . . . .26 A1
Aztec Ct **8** N16 . . . . .16 A2
Azure Ho E2 . .24 C2 99 B3

B

Baalbec Rd N5 . . . . . .15 A3
Babington Ct
  WC1 . . . . .106 B3
Babington Ho
  SE1 . . . . .137 A4
Babmaes St SW1 . .119 B3
Bacchus Wlk **2**
  N1 . . . . .24 A3
Bache's St N1 . . . . . . .97 C3
Back Church La
  E1 . . . . .111 B1
Back Hill EC1 . . . . . . .95 C1
Backhouse Pl
  SE1 . . . . .152 B3
Back La NW3 . . . . . . .11 B4
Bacon Gr SE1 . . . . .138 C1
Bacon's Coll SE16 . . .41 A4
Bacon's La N6 . . . . . . .3 C3
Bacon St E2 .24 B1 99 A2
Bacton NW5 . . . . .12 C3
Bacton St E2 . . . . . . .25 B2
Baddeley Ho
  SE11 . . . . .149 A2
Baddow Wlk N1 . . . . .86 C4
Baden Pl SE1 . . . . . .137 B4
Badminton Ct **9**
  N4 . . . . .6 B4

Badminton Ho
  SE22 . . . . .64 A3
Badminton Mews **9**
  E16 . . . . .35 C1
Badminton Rd
  SW12 . . . . .60 C1
Badric Ct SW11 . . . .167 C1
Badsworth Rd
  SE5 . . . . .48 B2
Bagley's La SW6 . . .166 B3
Bagnigge Ho WC1 . . .95 B3
Bagshot Ho NW1 . . . .92 B4
Bagshot St SE17 . . . .152 B1
Baildon **27** E2 . . . . . .25 B3
Baildon St SE8 . . . . . .51 B3
Bailey Ct **9** W12 . . . . .38 C4
Bailey Ho W10 . . . . .156 B2
Bailey Mews
  Brixton SW2 . . . . . . .62 C2
  Chiswick W4 . . . . . . .45 A4
Bainbridge St
  WC1 . . . . .105 C2
Bain Ho SW9 . . . . . .172 B2
Baird Ho **20** W12 . . . .30 A2
Baird St EC1 . . . . . . .97 A2
Baizdon Rd SE3 . . . . .53 A1
Baker Ho **8** E3 . . . . . .26 C2
Baker Rd NW10 . . . . .21 A4
Bakers Field N7 . . . . .14 A4
Bakers Hall Ct
  EC3 . . . . .124 B3
Baker's Mews W1 . .103 B2
Bakers Pas **2**
  NW3 . . . . .11 B4
Baker's Rents **1**
  E2 . . . . . .24 B2 98 C3
Baker's Row EC1 . . . .95 B1
Baker St W1 . . . . . . .103 A4
Baker Street W1 . . .103 A4
Baker Street Sta
  NW1 . . . . .91 A1
Baker's Yd EC1 . . . . . .95 B1
Bakery Cl SW9 . . . . .163 A1
Balaclava Rd SE1 . . .153 A3
Balchier Rd SE22 . . . .65 A1
Balcombe Ho
  Lisson Gr NW1 . . . . .90 C2
  3 Streatham SW2 . .74 B3
Balcombe St NW1 . . .90 C1
Balcorne St E9 . . . . . .17 B1
Balderton Flats
  W1 . . . . .103 C1
Balderton St W1 . . .103 C1
Baldock Ho **31**
  SE5 . . . . .48 B1
Baldock St E3 . . . . . . .27 A3
Baldrey Ho **3**
  SE10 . . . . .43 B1
Baldwin Cres SE5 . . .48 B2
Baldwin Ho **15**
  SW2 . . . . .74 C3
Baldwin's Gdns
  EC1 . . . . .107 B4
Baldwin St EC1 . . . . .97 B3
Baldwin Terr N1 . . . . .86 C2
Baldwin Gdns SW3 . .28 C2
Balearic Apts **3**
  E16 . . . . .35 C2
Bale Rd E1 . . . . .33 A4
Balearic Gr SW4 . . . .38 A1
Balfern St SW11 . . . .168 B2
Balfe St N1 . . . . .84 B1
Balfour Ho W10 . . . . .30 C1
Balfour Mews
  W1 . . . . .117 C2

Balfour Pl
Mayfair W1 . . . . . . 117 C3
Putney SW15 . . . . . . 57 A3
Balfour Rd
Highbury N5 . . . . . . 15 B4
North Acton W3 . . . . 28 B4
Balfour St SE17 151 B4
Balfron Twr 4
E14 . . . . 34 B3
BALHAM 72 C3
Balham Gr SW12 . . 72 C4
Balham High Rd SW12,
SW17 . . . . 72 C3
Balham Hill SW12 . . 61 A1
Balham New Rd
SW12 . . . . 73 A4
Balham Park Mans
SW12 . . . . 72 B3
Balham Park Rd SW12,
SW17 . . . . 72 C3
Balham Sta SW12 . 73 A3
Balham Station Rd
SW12 . . . . 73 A3
Balin Ho SE1 . . . 137 B4
Balkan Wlk E1 . . . 32 A2
Balladier Wlk E14 . 34 A4
Ballance Rd E9. . . . 18 A2
Ballantine St
SW18 . . . . 59 B3
Ballantrae Ho
NW2 . . . . 10 B4
Ballard Ho SE10 . . 52 A4
Ballast Quay SE10 . 42 C1
Ballater Rd SW2,
SW4 . . . . 62 A3
Ball Ct EC3 . . . . 109 C1
Ballin Ct E14 . . . . 42 B4
Ballingdon
SW11 . . . . 60 C1
Ballinger Point 18
E3 . . . . 27 A2
Balliol Ho 11
SW15 . . . . 57 C1
Balliol Rd W10 . . . 30 C3
Balloge Ave NW10 . 8 A4
Ballow Cl 5 SE5 . . 49 A3
Ball's Pond Pl 3
N1 . . . . 15 C2
Ball's Pond Rd N1 . 16 A2
Balman Ho 3
SE16 . . . . 40 C2
Balmer Rd E3 . . . . 26 B3
Balmes Rd N1 . . . . 87 C4
Balmoral Cl 1
SW15 . . . . 57 C1
Balmoral Ct
11 Rotherhithe
SE16 . . . . 32 C1
St John's Wood
NW8 . . . . 79 B2
Balmoral Gr N7 . . 14 B2
Balmoral Ho
2 Isle of Dogs
E14 . . . . 42 A3
Stoke Newington N4 . 6 B3
West Kensington
W14 . . . . 140 A4
Balmoral Mews
W12 . . . . 38 B3
Balmoral Rd NW2 . 9 A2
Balmore Cl E14 . . 34 B3
Balmore St N19 . . . 4 A2
Balmuir Gdns
SW15 . . . . 57 B3
Balnacraig Ave
NW10 . . . . 8 A4
Balniel Gate SW1 147 C2

Balsam Ho 9 E14 . .34 A2
Baltic Apts 5 E16. .35 C2
Baltic Ho 7 SE5 . . .48 B1
Baltic St E EC1 . . . 96 C1
Baltic St W EC1 . . . 96 C1
Baltimore Ho
Clapham SW18. . . . .59 B3
Kennington SE11 . . 149 B2
Balvaird Pl SW1 . . 147 C1
Balvernie Gr
SW18 . . . . 70 C4
Bamber Rd 5
SE15. . . . . 49 B2
Bamborough Gdns 12
W12 . . . . 39 B4
Bamford Ct E15 . . . 19 A3
Banbury Ct WC2. . 120 A4
Banbury Ho 9 E9 . . 17 C1
Banbury Ho E9 . . . 17 C1
Banbury St SW11 . 168 B2
Bancroft Ct SW8 . 172 A4
Bancroft Ho 11 E1. .25 B1
Bancroft Rd E1 . . . 25 C1
Banff Ho 11 NW3 . . 12 B2
Banfield Rd SE15 . . 65 A4
Bangabandhu Prim
Sch E2 . . . . 25 B2
Bangalore St
SW15 . . . . 57 C4
Banim St W6. . . . . 39 A2
Banister Ho
Hackney E9. . . . . . 17 C3
Nine Elms SW8 . . . 171 A4
3 West Kilburn
W10 . . . . 23 A2
Banister Rd W10 . . 22 C2
Bank Ct SW11 . . . 170 A4
Bank End SE1 . . . 123 A2
Bank La SW15 . . . 56 A2
Bank of England★
EC2. . . . . 109 B1
Bank of England
Mus★ EC2 . . . . . 109 B1
Bankside
Borough The SE1 . . 123 C1
Borough The SE1 . . 123 A2
Bankside Art Gal★
SE1. . . . . 122 C3
Bankside Ave 1
SE13 . . . . 67 B4
Bankside Ho EC3 . 110 B1
Bankside Pier
SE1 . . . . 122 C3
Bank St E14 . . . . . 34 A1
Bank Sta EC3 . . . 109 C1
Bank The N6 . . . . . 4 A3
Bankton Rd SW2 . . 62 C3
Banner Ct 5 SE16. .40 B2
Banner Ho EC1 . . . 97 A1
Bannerman Ho
SW8 . . . . 162 C3
Banner St EC1. . . . 97 A2
Banning Ho 4
SW19 . . . . 69 C3
Banning St SE10. . . 43 A1
Bannister Cl SW2 . 74 C3
Bannister Ho 28
SE14 . . . . 50 C4
Banqueting Ho★
SW1 . . . . 120 A1
Banstead Ct N4 . . . 6 B3
Banstead St SE15. . .65 B4
Bantock Ho 8
W10 . . . . 23 A2
Bantry Ho 18 E1 . . .25 C1
Bantry St SE5 . . . . 48 C3

Banville Ho SW8 . 163 A1
Banyan Ho 8
NW3 . . . . 11 A2
Banyard Rd SE16 . . 40 A3
Baptist Gdns NW5. .12 C2
Barandon Wlk 9
W11 . . . . 30 C2
Barbanel Ho 3
E1. . . . . 25 B1
Barbara Brosnan Ct
NW8 . . . . 79 B1
Barbara Castle Cl
SW6 . . . . 155 A3
Barbara Rudolph Ct
5 N19 . . . . 5 A4
Barbauld Rd N16 . . 7 A1
Barber Beaumont Ho
21 E1 . . . . 25 C2
Barbers Rd E15 . . . 27 A3
BARBICAN 109 A3
Barbican★ EC2. . . 109 A3
Barbican Arts & Con
Ctr★ EC2. . . . . . 109 A4
Barbican Sta EC1 . 108 C4
Barb Mews W6. . . . 39 B3
Barbon Cl WC1 . . . 106 C4
Barbrook Ho 2 E9 . .17 B2
Barchard St SW18 . .59 A2
Barchester St E14 . .34 A4
Barclay Cl SW6. . . 155 B1
Barclay Ho 22 E9 . .17 B1
Barclay Rd SW6 . . 155 C1
Barcombe Ave
SW2 . . . . 74 B2
Bardell Ho 1 . . . 139 B3
Bardolph Rd
Richmond TW9 . . . . 54 B4
Tufnell Pk N7 . . . . . 14 A4
Bard Rd W10 . . . . . 30 C2
Bardsey Pl 41 E1 . . 25 B1
Bardsey Wlk 7
N1 . . . . 15 B2
Bardsley Ho 8
SE10 . . . . 52 B4
Bardsley La SE10 . .52 B4
Barents Ho 10 E1 . .25 C1
Barfett St W10 . . . 23 B1
Barfleur La SE8 . . . 41 B2
Barford Ho 23 E3 . .26 B3
Barford St N1 . . . . 85 C3
Barforth Rd SE15 . .65 A4
Barge House St
SE1 . . . . 121 C2
Barge La 18 E3 . . . .26 B4
Barham Ho SE17 . . 152 B2
Baring Ct N1 . . . . . 87 B3
Baring Ho 16 E14. .33 C3
Baring St N1 . . . . . 87 B3
Barker Cl TW9 . . . .45 A1
Barker Dr NW1 . . . 13 C1
Barker Ho
Dulwich SE21. . . . . 76 A1
Walworth SE17 . . . 152 A3
Barker St SW10 . . 156 C4
Barker Wlk SW16 . .73 C1
Bark Pl W2 . . . . . 114 A4
Barkston Gdns
SW5 . . . . 142 A3
Barkway Ct N4 . . . . 6 B2
Barkwith Ho 27
SE14 . . . . 50 C4
Barkworth Rd
SE16 . . . . 40 B1
Barlborough St
SE14 . . . . 50 C3
Barlby Gdns W10 . .22 C1

Barlby Prim Sch
W10 . . . . 22 C1
Barlby Rd W10 . . . 30 C4
Barleycorn Way
E14 . . . . 33 B2
Barley Mow Pas
Chiswick W4 . . . . . 37 C1
Clerkenwell EC1 . . 108 B3
Barley Shotts Bsns Pk
W10 . . . . 31 B4
Barling 6 NW1 . . . 13 A1
Barling Ct SW4. . . 172 A2
Barlings Ho 2
SE4 . . . . 65 C3
Barloch Ho SW11. . 169 B2
Barlow Ho
16 Bermondsey
SE16 . . . . 40 A2
Notting Hill
W11 . . . . 31 A2 112 A4
Shoreditch N1 . . . . 97 B4
Barlow Pl W1 . . . 118 B3
Barlow Rd
Acton W3 . . . . . . 28 A1
Brondesbury NW6 . . 10 B2
Barlow St SE17 . . . 151 C3
Barmouth Ho 6
N7 . . . . 5 B2
Barmouth Rd
SW18 . . . . 59 B1
Barnabas Ho EC1 . . 96 C3
Barnabas Lo SW8 172 B4
Barnabas Rd E9 . . 17 C3
Barnaby Pl SW7 . . 143 B3
Barnard Ct SW16 . . 74 B1
Barnard Ho 17 E2 . .25 A2
Barnard Lo 10 W9. .31 C4
Barnard Mews
SW11 . . . . 60 A3
Barnardo Gdns 1
E1 . . . . 32 C2
Barnardo St E1. . . . 32 C3
Barnard Rd SW11 . .60 A3
Barnard's Inn EC4 107 C2
Barnborough NW1 . 82 C3
Barnby St NW1 . . . 93 A4
Barn Cl 18 NW5 . . . 13 C3
Barnersbury Ho
N7. . . . . 14 A4
BARNES 46 B2
Barnes Ave SW13. . 46 C3
Barnes Bridge Sta
SW13 . . . . 46 A1
Barnes Common★
SW13 . . . . 56 C4
Barnes Ct N1 . . . . 14 C1
Barnes High St
SW13 . . . . 46 B1
Barnes Ho
16 Bethnal Green
E2 . . . . 25 B3
Camden Town NW1 . 82 B4
20 Deptford SE14 . . 50 C4
Hornsey N19 . . . . . 5 A4
Barnes Hospl
SW14 . . . . 56 A4
Barnes Prim Sch
SW13 . . . . 56 B4
Barnes St E14 . . . . 33 A3
Barnes Sta SW13 . . 56 C4
Barnes Terr SE8 . . . 41 B1
Barnet Gr
E2 . . . . 24 C2 99 B3
Barnet Ho SE5. . . . 48 B1
Barnett St 6 E1. . . 32 A3
Barnett St E1 . . . . 110 C2
Barn Field NW3. . . . 12 B3

Barnfield Cl
London N4 . . . . . . 5 A4
Wandsworth SW17 . .71 B1
Barnfield Pl E14. . . 41 C2
Barnham St SE1. . . 138 B4
BARNSBURY 14 A1
Barnsbury Gr N7 . . 14 B1
Barnsbury Ho 12
SW4 . . . . 61 C1
Barnsbury Pk N1. . 14 C1
Barnsbury Rd N1. . 85 B3
Barnsbury Sq N1 . . 14 C1
Barnsbury St N1 . . 14 C1
Barnsbury Terr
N1. . . . . 14 B1
Barnsdale Ave
E14 . . . . 41 C2
Barnsdale Rd W9 . . 23 B1
Barnsley St E1 . . . 25 A1
Barn St N16 . . . . . 7 A2
Barnstaple La
SE13 . . . . 67 B3
Barnston Wlk N1 . . 86 C4
Barnwell Ho 1
SE5 . . . . 49 A2
Barnwell Rd SW2 . .62 C2
Barnwood Cl W9 . . 88 B1
Baron Cl N1. . . . . . 85 B2
Baroness Rd
E2 . . . . 24 B2 99 A4
Barons Court Mans
W14 . . . . 140 B1
Baron's Court Rd
W14 . . . . 140 B2
Barons Court Sta
W14 . . . . 140 A2
Barons Gate 13
W4 . . . . 37 B3
Barons Keep
W14 . . . . 140 A2
Barons Lo 9 E14. . .42 B2
Baronsmead Rd
SW13 . . . . 46 C2
Baronsmede W5 . . 36 A4
Baron's Pl SE1 . . . 135 C3
Baron St N1. . . . . . 85 B2
Baron Wlk E16 . . . 35 B4
Barque Mews SE8 . 51 C4
Barradell Ho 16
W14 . . . . 39 C3
Barratt Ho 3 N1. . . 15 A1
Barratt Ind Pk 5
E3 . . . . 27 B1
Barratt Ho for NW6 . 23 C4
Barrett Ct
NW10 . . . . 21 A3
Barrett's Gr N16. . . 16 A3
Barrett's Green Rd
NW10 . . . . 20 C3
Barrett St W1 . . . 103 C1
Barrhill Rd SW2 . . 74 A2
Barriedale SE14 . . 51 A1
Barrie Ho
Acton W3 . . . . . . 37 B4
Bayswater W2 . . . 115 A3
Primrose Hill NW8 . 80 B3
8 Stoke Newington
N16. . . . . 7 A1
Barrington Cl
NW5 . . . . 12 C3
Barrington Ct
9 Acton W3 . . . . . 37 A4
Kentish Town NW5 . .12 C3
South Lambeth
SW9 . . . . 172 B1

Barrington Rd
SW9 . . . . **63** A4
Barrowgate Ho
W4 . . . . **37** C1
Barrowgate Rd
W4 . . . . **37** C1
Barrow Hill Est
NW8 . . . . **80** A1
Barrow Hill Jun Sch
NW8 . . . . **80** A1
Barrow Hill Rd
NW8 . . . . **80** A1
Barry Ct SW4 . . . . **61** B1
Barry Lo N4 . . . . **5** B4
Barry Par SE22 . . . . **64** C3
Barry Rd SE22 . . . . **64** C2
Barset Rd SE15 . . . . **65** B4
Barstow Cres SW2 . . . . **74** B3
Bartell Ho SW2 . . . . **62** C1
Barter St WC1 . . . . **106** B3
Bartholomew Cl
Barbican EC1 . . . . **108** C3
Wandsworth SW18 . . . . **59** B3
Bartholomew Ct
16 Blackwall E14 . . . . . **34** C2
St Luke's EC1 . . . . **97** A2
Bartholomew Ho 22
SE5 . . . . **48** B1
Bartholomew La
EC2 . . . . **109** C1
Bartholomew Pas
EC1 . . . . **108** B3
Bartholomew Pl
EC1 . . . . **108** C3
Bartholomew Rd
NW5 . . . . **13** B2
Bartholomew Sq
18 Bethnal Green
E1 . . . . **25** A1
St Luke's EC1 . . . . **97** A2
Bartholomew St
SE1 . . . . **137** C1
Bartholomew Villas
NW5 . . . . **13** B2
Bartle Rd W11 . . . . **31** A3
Bartlett Cl E14 . . . . **33** C3
Bartlett Ct EC4 . . . . . . **107** C2
Bartok Ho
W11 . . . . . . **31** B2 **112** B3
Barton Cl
Hackney E9 . . . . **17** B3
Peckham SE15 . . . . **65** A4
Barton Ct
South Lambeth
SW4 . . . . **172** A2
West Kensington
W14 . . . . **140** B2
Barton Ho
8 Bromley E3 . . . . **27** A2
Islington N1 . . . . **15** A1
Sands End SW6 . . . . . . **59** A4
Barton Rd W14 . . . . . . **140** B1
Bartonway NW8 . . . . . . **79** B2
Bartram Rd SE4 . . . . . . **66** A1
Bartrip St E9 . . . . **18** B2
Barts & The London
Sch of Medicine &
Dentistry EC1 . . . . . . **96** B1
Barville Cl SE4 . . . . **66** A3
Barwell Ho
E2 . . . . **24** C1 **99** C2
Barwick Ho 7 W3 . . . **37** B4

Bascome St SW2 . . . . . **62** C1
Base Apartments 8
N1 . . . . **15** B1
Baseline Business
Studios SW8 W11 . . . **30** C2
Basevi Way SE8 . . . . . . **52** A4
Bashley Rd NW10 . . . . **20** C1
Basildon Ct W1 . . . . . **103** C4
Basil Ho
South Lambeth
SW8 . . . . **162** A2
Whitechapel E1 . . . . . **111** C2
Basil Mans SW1 . . . . . **130** C3
Basil St
Knightsbridge
SW1 . . . . **130** C3
Knightsbridge SW1,
SW3 . . . . **130** C2
Basin App 20 E14 . . . . . **33** A3
Basing Ct 5 SE15 . . . . **49** B2
Basingdon Way
SE5 . . . . **63** C3
Basinghall Ave
EC2 . . . . **109** B3
Basinghall St EC2 . . . . **109** B2
Basing Hill NW11 . . . . . . **1** B3
Basing House Yd
E2 . . . . **24** A2 **98** B4
Basing Pl
E2 . . . . **24** A2 **98** B4
Basing St W11 . . . . **31** B3
Basire St N1 . . . . **87** A4
Baskerville Ct
SW18 . . . . **72** A4
Baskerville Gdns
NW10 . . . . **8** A4
Baskerville Rd
SW18 . . . . **72** A4
Baslow Wlk E5 . . . . **17** C4
Basnett Rd 8
SW11 . . . . **60** C4
Basque Ct 21 SE16 . . . **40** C4
Bassano St SE22 . . . . . **64** B2
Bassein Park Rd
W12 . . . . **38** B4
Bassett Rd W10 . . . . . . **30** C3
Bassett St NW5 . . . . . . **12** C2
Bassingbourn Ho 1
N1 . . . . **15** A1
Bassingham Rd
SW18 . . . . **71** B4
Bassishaw Highwalk
EC2 . . . . **109** B3
Basswood Cl 5
SE15 . . . . **65** A4
Basterfield Ho EC1 **96** C1
Bastion Highwalk
EC2 . . . . **108** C3
Bastwick St EC1 . . . . . . **96** C2
Basuto Rd SW6 . . . . . . **165** C3
Batavia Ho 1
SE14 . . . . **51** A3
Batavia Mews 3
SE14 . . . . **51** A3
Batavia Rd SE14 . . . . . . **51** A3
Batchelor St N1 . . . . . . **85** C3
Bateman Ho 8
SE17 . . . . **48** A4
Bateman's Bldgs
W1 . . . . **105** B1
Bateman's Row
EC2 . . . . **24** A1 **98** B2
Bateman St W1 . . . . . . **105** B1
Bate St 10 E14 . . . . **33** B2
Bath Cl SW15 . . . . **50** A1

Bath Ct
Finsbury EC1 . . . . **97** B3
3 Forest Hill SE26 . . . . **76** C1
Holborn EC1 . . . . **95** B1
Bathgate Ho 6
SW9 . . . . **48** A2
Bathgate Rd
SW19 . . . . **69** C1
Bath Gr E2 . . . . **24** C3
Bath Ho
Bethnal Green
E2 . . . . **24** C1 **99** C2
Borough The SE1 . . . . **137** A2
Bath Pl
14 Hammersmith
W6 . . . . **39** B1
Shoreditch
EC2 . . . . **24** A2 **98** A3
Bath Rd W4 . . . . **38** A2
Bath St EC1 . . . . **97** B3
Bath Terr SE1 . . . . **136** C2
Bathurst Gdns
NW10 . . . . **22** A3
Bathurst Ho 2
W12 . . . . **30** A2
Bathurst Mews
W2 . . . . **115** C4
Bathurst St W2 . . . . . . **115** C4
Batley Pl 3 N16 . . . . **7** B1
Batley Rd N16 . . . . **7** B1
Batman Cl W12 . . . . **30** A1
Batoum Gdns W6 . . . . . **39** B3
Batson Ho 1 E1 . . . . . **111** C1
Batson St W12 . . . . **38** C4
Batten Ho
7 London SW4 . . . . . . **61** B2
10 West Kilburn
W10 . . . . **23** A2
Batten St SW11 . . . . **60** A4
BATTERSEA **169** A4
Battersea Bridge Rd
SW11 . . . . **158** A1
Battersea Bsns Ctr 6
SW11 . . . . **60** C4
Battersea Church Rd
SW11 . . . . **167** C4
Battersea Dogs Home
SW8 . . . . **160** B1
Battersea High St
SW11 . . . . **167** B1
Battersea Hts 5
SW11 . . . . **60** B4
Battersea Park★
SW11 . . . . **159** B1
Battersea Park Rd
SW11, SW8 . . . . **169** A3
Battersea Park Sta
SW8 . . . . **160** A1
Battersea Power
Station(dis)
SW8 . . . . **160** B4
Battersea Rise
SW11 . . . . **60** A3
Battersea Sq
SW11 . . . . **167** C3
Battishill St 9 N1 . . . **15** A1
Battlebridge Ct
NW1 . . . . **84** B2
Battle Bridge La
SE1 . . . . **124** A1
Battle Bridge Rd
NW1 . . . . **84** A2
Battledean Rd N5 . . . . . **15** A3
Battle Ho 6 SE15 . . . . . **49** C4
Batty St E1 . . . . **111** C2
Baty Ho SW2 . . . . **74** B3
Baulk The SW18 . . . . . . **70** C4

Bavaria Rd N19 . . . . **5** A2
Bavent Rd SE5 . . . . **48** B1
Bawdale Rd SE22 . . . . . **64** B2
Bawtree Rd SE14 . . . . . **51** A3
Baxendale St
E2 . . . . **24** C2 **99** B4
Baxter Ho 11 E3 . . . . **27** A2
Baxter Rd N1 . . . . **15** C2
Baycliffe Ho 2 E9 . . . . . **17** C2
Bay Ct Ealing W5 . . . . . **36** A3
7 Stepney E1 . . . . **25** C1
Bayer Ho EC1 . . . . **96** C1
Bayes Ct NW3 . . . . **12** B1
Bayfield Ho 8
SE4 . . . . **65** C3
Bayford Rd NW10 . . . . **22** C2
Bayford St Ind Ctr 8
E8 . . . . **17** A1
Bayford St 8 E8 . . . . **17** A1
Bayham Pl NW1 . . . . **83** A3
Bayham Rd W4 . . . . **37** C3
Bayham St NW1 . . . . **82** C3
Bayhurst Ho N4 . . . . **6** B4
Bayley St WC1 . . . . **105** B3
Baylis Rd SE1 . . . . **135** B3
Baynes Mews 2
NW3 . . . . **11** C2
Baynes St NW1 . . . . **13** B1
Bayon Ho 20 N19 . . . . **4** C4
Bayonne Rd W6 . . . . . . **154** A3
Bayston Rd N16 . . . . **7** B1
BAYSWATER **114** C4
Bayswater Rd W2 . . . . **115** B3
Bayswater Sta
W2 . . . . **114** B4
Bayton Ct 2 E8 . . . . **16** C1
Baytree Rd SW2 . . . . . . **62** B3
Bazalgette Ho
NW8 . . . . **89** C2
Bazeley Ho SE1 . . . . . **136** A3
Bazely St E14 . . . . **34** B2
BBC Television Ctr
W12 . . . . **30** B1
Beach Ho SW5 . . . . . . **141** B2
Beachy Rd E3 . . . . **18** C1
Beaconfield Terrace
Rd W14 . . . . **126** A1
Beacon Gate SE14 . . . . **65** C4
Beacon Hill N7 . . . . **14** A3
Beacon Ho
11 Camberwell
SE5 . . . . **49** A3
7 Isle of Dogs E14 . . . **42** A1
South Lambeth
SW8 . . . . **171** B4
Beacon Rd SE13 . . . . . . **67** C1
Beaconsfield Cl
Acton Green W4 . . . . . . **37** B1
Greenwich SE3 . . . . **53** C4
Beaconsfield Rd
Acton W4 . . . . **37** B3
Greenwich SE3 . . . . **53** C4
Walworth SE17 . . . . . . **152** A1
Willesden NW10 . . . . . . **8** B2
Beaconsfield Wlk
SW6 . . . . **165** A3
Beadon Rd W6 . . . . **39** B2
Beak St W1 . . . . **119** A4
Beale Ho SW9 . . . . **172** C1
Beale Pl E3 . . . . **26** B3
Beale Rd E3 . . . . **26** B4
Beames Ho 8 SW8 . . . **171** B4
Beames Rd NW10 . . . . . **20** C4
Beaminster Ho
SW8 . . . . **162** C2
Beamish Ho 7
SE16 . . . . **40** B2

Beanacre Cl E9 . . . . **18** B2
Bear Alley EC4 . . . . . . **108** A2
Bear Croft Ho
SW6 . . . . **164** C1
Beardsley Way
W3 . . . . **37** C4
Bear Gardens Mus★
SE1 . . . . **122** C2
Bear Gdns SE1 . . . . . . **122** C2
Bear La SE1 . . . . **122** B1
Bear St WC2 . . . . **119** C4
Bearstead Rise
SE4 . . . . **66** B2
Beaton Cl SE15 . . . . . . **49** B2
Beatrice Ho
1 Brixton SW2 . . . . **62** B2
4 Hammersmith
W6 . . . . **39** B1
2 Stepney E1 . . . . **32** C4
Beatrice Pl W8 . . . . . . **128** A1
Beatrice Rd
Bermondsey SE1 . . . . **153** C3
Finsbury Pk N4 . . . . **5** C4
2 Richmond TW10 . . . **54** B2
Beatrice Tate Sch
E2 . . . . **25** A2
Beatrice Webb Ho 3
E3 . . . . **26** A3
Beatrix Ho SW5 . . . . . **142** B2
Beatrix Potter Prim
Sch SW18 . . . . **71** B3
Beatson Wlk 23
SE16 . . . . **32** C1
Beattie Ho SW8 . . . . . **171** A4
Beatty Ho 10 E14 . . . . . **41** C4
Beatty Rd N16 . . . . **16** A4
Beatty St NW1 . . . . **82** C2
Beauchamp Cl 1
W4 . . . . **37** B3
Beauchamp Pl
SW3 . . . . **130** B1
Beauchamp Rd
SW11 . . . . **60** B3
Beauchamp St
EC1 . . . . **107** B3
Beauchamp Terr
SW15 . . . . **57** A4
Beauclerc Rd W6 . . . . . **39** A3
Beauclerk Ho 10
SW16 . . . . **74** A1
Beaufort Cl SW19 . . . . **69** A4
Beaufort Ct SW6 . . . . . **155** B4
Beaufort Gdns
SW3 . . . . **130** B2
Beaufort Ho
Battersea SW11 . . . . . **168** A2
Chelsea SW3 . . . . **157** C3
22 Millwall E14 . . . . **41** C4
Pimlico SW1 . . . . **147** B1
Beaufort Mans
SW3 . . . . **157** C3
Beaufort Mews
SW6 . . . . **155** A4
Beaufort St SW3 . . . . . **157** B4
Beaufoy Ho
South Lambeth
SW8 . . . . **162** C2
3 West Norwood
SE27 . . . . **75** A1
Beaufoy Rd 10
SW8 . . . . **161** A3
Beaufoy Wlk
SE11 . . . . **149** A3
Beaulieu Cl SE5 . . . . . . **63** C4
Beaulieu Pl W4 . . . . **37** B3
Beaumanor Mans
W2 . . . . **114** A4

Beaumaris Twr **2**
W3 ....37 A4
Beaumont SW15 ......58 A2
Beaumont Ave
 Richmond TW9 ....54 B4
 West Kensington
 W14 ....**140** C2
Beaumont Bldgs
 WC2 ....**106** B1
Beaumont Cres
 W14 ....**140** C2
Beaumont Ct
 10 Acton Green
 W4 ....37 B1
 Marylebone W1 ...**103** C4
 7 Mile End E1 .....26 A2
Beaumont Gdns
 NW3 ....1 C1
Beaumont Gr E1 ......25 C1
Beaumont Ho
 1 Streatham
 SW2 ....74 A3
 West Kensington
 W14 ....**141** A3
 Wimbledon SW19 ...70 C1
Beaumont Lo E8 .....16 C2
Beaumont Pl NW1,
 WC1, W1 ....**93** A2
Beaumont Rd
 Putney SW15,
 SW19 ....70 A4
 South Acton W4 ....37 B3
Beaumont Rise
 N19 ....4 C3
Beaumont Sq E1 .....32 C4
Beaumont St W1 ....**103** C4
Beaumont Wlk
 NW3 ....12 B1
Beauvale E1 ....12 C1
Beauval Rd SE22 ....64 B1
Beavis Ho N16 ....7 A1
Beavor La W6 ....38 C1
Beccles St E14 ......33 B2
Beck Cl E13 ....52 A2
Beckers The Ho 16 C4
Becket Ho SE1 ......**137** B3
Becket St SE1 ....**137** B2
Beckett Cl
 Streatham SW16 ...73 C2
 Willesden NW10 .....8 A2
Beckett Ho
 London SW9 ....**172** B1
 15 Stepney E1 .....32 B4
Beckfoot NW1 ......**83** A1
Beckford Cl W14 ...**141** A3
Beckford Ho **18**
 N16 ....16 A3
Beckford Prim Sch
 NW6 ....10 B3
Beckham Ho
 SE11 ....**149** A3
Beck Ho N16 ....7 A1
Beckington **18**
 NW5 ....12 C2
Beckley Ho E3 ....26 B1
Becklow Gdns
 Chiswick W12 .....38 B4
 1 Shepherd's Bush
 W12 ....38 C4
Becklow Mews **7**
 W12 ....38 B4
Becklow Rd W12 ....38 C4
Beck Rd E8 ....25 A4
Beckton Rd E16 ....35 B4
Beckway St SE17 ..**152** A3
Beckwith Ho **27**
 E2 ....25 A3

Beckwith Rd SE24 ...63 C2
Bective Pl SW15 ....58 B3
Bective Rd SW15 ...58 B3
Bedale St SE1 ......**123** B1
Bedefield WC1 ....**94** B3
Bede Ho
 London SE14 ....51 B2
 9 Putney SW15 .....57 C1
Bedford Ave NW10 .**105** C3
Bedfordbury WC2 ..**120** A3
Bedford Cnr **3**
 W4 ....38 A2
Bedford Court Mans
 WC1 ....**105** C4
Bedford Ct
 8 Richmond TW9 ...54 B3
 St James WC2 .....**120** A3
Bedford Gardens Ho
 W8 ....31 C1 **113** C1
Bedford Gdns
 2 Acton Green ...38 A2
 Stockwell SW4 ....62 A3
 Kensington W8 ....31 C1 **113** C1
Bedford Ho
 2 Acton Green ...38 A2
 4 Stockwell Pk 62 A3
Bedford Park Cnr **3**
 W4 ....38 A2
Bedford Park Mans **4**
 W4 ....37 C2
Bedford Pas SW6 ..**154** B2
Bedford Pl WC1 ....**106** A4
Bedford Rd
 Acton W4 ....38 A3
 Stockwell SW2,
 SW4 ....62 A3
Bedford Row
 WC1 ....**107** A3
Bedford Sq WC1 ...**105** C3
Bedford St WC2 ....**120** B3
Bedford Way WC1 ...**93** C1
Bedgebury Gdns
 SW19 ....70 A2
Bedlam Mews
 SE11 ....**149** B4
Bedlow Cl NW8 .....**89** C1
Bedser Cl SE11 ....**163** A4
Bedser Ct SW4 ....**172** A2
Bedwell Ho SW9 ...**173** B1
Beech Ave W3 .....38 A4
Beech Cl
 Deptford SE8 .....51 B4
 Putney SW15 ......68 C4
Beechcroft Ave
 NW11 ....1 B4
Beechcroft Ct
 3 Golders Green
 NW11 ....1 B4
 Greenwich SE3 ....53 C2
Beech Croft Ct N5 ..15 A4
Beechcroft Rd
 Mortlake SW14 ....55 B4
 Upper Tooting
 SW17 ....72 A2
Beechcroft Way
 N19 ....4 C3
Beech Ct
 Child's Hill NW2 ....1 B2
 Marylebone W1 ...**102** C2
 49 Notting Hill W2 ...31 C4
 2 Rotherhithe
 SE16 ....33 A1
Beechdale Rd
 SW2 ....62 B1
Beechdene **4**
 SE15 ....50 A2

Beeches Rd SW17 ...72 B1
Beeches The **1**
 N19 ....5 A3
Beechey Ho **30** E1 ..32 A1
Beech Gdns W5 ....36 A3
Beech Ho
 6 Maitland Pk
 NW3 ....12 B2
 22 Rotherhithe
 SE16 ....40 B4
 5 Stoke Newington
 N16 ....6 C2
Beechmore Rd
 SW11 ....**169** A3
Beech St EC2 ......**109** A4
Beech Tree Cl N1 ...14 C1
Beechwood Ave
 TW9 ....44 C2
Beechwood Ct
 Chiswick W4 ......45 C4
 Stamford Hill N16 ...7 A4
Beechwood Gr
 W3 ....29 A2
Beechwood Ho **23**
 E2 ....24 C3
Beechwood Rd E8 ..16 B2
Beechworth Cl
 NW3 ....1 C2
Beecroft La SE4 ...66 A2
Beecroft Mews
 SE4 ....66 A2
Beecroft Rd SE4 ...66 A2
Beehive Cl E8 ....16 B1
Beehive Pl SW9 ....62 C4
Beemans Row **1**
 SW18 ....71 B2
Beeston Cl **8** E8 ..16 C3
Beeston Pl SW1 ...**132** B2
Beeston's Ho SE15 .65 A4
Beethoven St
 W10 ....23 A2
Begbie Ho SW9 ....**173** A2
Begonia Wlk W12 ..29 B3
Beira St SW12 ....73 A4
Beis Chinuch Lebonos
 Girls Sch N4 ....6 B4
Beis Rachel d'Satmar
 Girls Sch N16 ....7 A4
Bekesbourne St **17**
 E14 ....33 A3
Beldanes Lo NW10 ...8 C1
Belenoyd Ct SW16 ..74 B1
Belfast Rd N16 ....7 B2
Belfont Wlk N7 .....14 A4
Belford Ho **21** E8 ..24 B4
Belfort Rd SE15 .....50 B1
Belfry Cl **5** SF16 ..40 A1
Belgrade Ho N16 ...16 A4
Belgrade Rd N16 ...16 A4
Belgrave Cl **1** W3 ..37 B4
 8 Acton Green
 W3 ....37 B1
 Limehouse E14 ....33 B2
 Nine Elms SW8 ...**160** C1
Belgrave Gdns
 Kilburn NW8 ......**78** C3
 St John's Wood
 NW8 ....**78** C3
Belgrave Mans
 NW8 ....**78** C3
Belgrave Mews N
 SW1 ....**131** C3
Belgrave Mews S
 SW1 ....**131** C2
Belgrave Mews W
 SW1 ....**131** B2

Belgrave Pl SW1 ...**131** C1
Belgrave Rd
 Barnes SW13 ......46 B3
 Westminster SW1 .**146** C3
Belgrave Sq SW1 ..**131** B2
Belgrave St E1 .....32 C3
Belgrave Yd SW1 ..**132** A1
Belgravia Ho **11**
 SW4 ....61 C1
Belgravia Ct SW1 .**132** A1
BELGRAVIA **146** A4
Belgravia Ho **11**
 SW4 ....61 C1
Belgrove St WC1 ...**94** B4
Belham Wlk **13**
 SE5 ....48 C2
Belinda Rd **3**
 SW9 ....63 A4
Belitha Villas N1 ...14 C1
Bellamy Cl
 18 Millwall E14 .....41 C4
 West Kensington
 SW5 ....**141** A1
Bellamy Ho
 8 Streatham
 SW17 ....73 C2
 Wandsworth
 SW18 ....59 C3
Bellamy's Ct **16**
 SE16 ....32 C1
Bellasis Ave SW2 ..74 A2
Bell Cl SE13 ....66 C2
Bell Dr SW18 ....70 A4
Bellefields Rd
 SW9 ....62 B4
Bellenden Prim Sch
 SE15 ....49 C1
Bellenden Rd
 SE15 ....49 C1
Bellenden Rd Ret Pk
 SE15 ....49 C2
Bellenden Road Bsns
 Ctr SE15 ....49 B1
Bellerbys Coll SE8 .51 C4
Belleville Prim Sch
 SW11 ....60 B2
Belleville Rd
 SW11 ....60 B2
Belle Vue Gdns
 SW9 ....**172** B1
Bellevue Pl E1 ......25 B1
Bellevue Rd
 Barnes SW13 .....46 C1
 Upper Tooting
 SW17 ....72 A3
Bellew St SW17 ....71 B1
Bell Flats **4** NW2 ...8 C2
Bellflower Ct
 SE13 ....67 A3
Bellgate Mews
 NW5 ....4 A1
Bellgrave Lo **8**
 W4 ....37 A1
Bell Ho
 Greenwich SE10 ..52 B4
 18 Streatham SW2 ..74 C4
Bellina Mews
 NW5 ....13 B4
Bell Ind Est **2** W4 ..37 B2
Bell Inn Yd EC3 ...**109** C1
Bell La
 Newham E16 ......35 C1
 Spitalfields E1 ....**110** C3
Bellmaker Ct **18**
 E3 ....33 C4
Bell Moor NW3 .....2 B1
Bello Ct SE24, SW2 .75 A3
Bellot Gdns **1**
 SE10 ....43 A1
Bellot St SE10 .....43 A1

Bell Wharf La
 EC4 ....**123** A4
Bellwood Rd SE15 ..65 C3
Bell Yard Mews
 SE1 ....**138** B3
Bell Yd WC2 ....**107** B1
Belmont Cl SW4 ...61 B4
Belmont Ct
 Highbury N5 ....7 A1
 6 Stamford Hill N16 ..7 A3
Belmont Gr
 Chiswick W4 ......37 C2
 Lewisham SE13 ...67 C4
Belmont Hall Ct
 SE13 ....67 C4
Belmont Hill SE13 ..67 C4
Belmont Mews
 SW19 ....69 C2
Belmont Prim Sch
 W4 ....37 C2
Belmont Rd
 Clapham SW4 .....61 B4
 London W4 ....37 C2
Belmont St NW1 ...12 C1
Belmont Terr W4 ...37 C2
Belmore Ho N7 ....13 C3
Belmore La N7 .....13 C3
Belmore St SW8 ..**171** B4
Beloe Cl SW15 .....56 C3
Belper Ct **11** E5 ...17 C4
Belsham St E9 .....17 B2
Belsize Ave NW3 ..12 A3
Belsize Court Garages
 NW3 ....11 C3
Belsize Cres NW3 ..11 C3
Belsize Ct NW3 ....11 C3
Belsize Gr NW3 ....12 A3
Belsize La NW3 ....11 C3
Belsize Mews
 NW3 ....11 C3
Belsize Park Gdns
 NW3 ....12 A2
Belsize Park Mews **1**
 NW3 ....11 C2
Belsize Park Sta
 NW3 ....12 A3
Belsize Pk NW3 ....11 C3
Belsize Pl NW3 ....11 C3
Belsize Rd NW6 ...**78** B4
Belsize Sq NW3 ...11 C3
Belsize Terr NW3 ..11 C3
Beltane Dr SW19 ..69 C1
Belthorn Cres
 SW12 ....73 B4
Belton Rd NW2 .....8 C2
Belton Way E3 .....33 C4
Beltran Rd SW6 ...**166** A4
Belvedere Bldgs
 SE1 ....**136** B3
Belvedere Ct
 Brondesbury NW2 ...9 C2
 7 Clapham Pk
 SW4 ....61 C1
 Putney SW15 ......57 B3
 23 Shoreditch N1 ...24 A4
Belvedere Htss
 NW8 ....**90** A2
Belvedere Mews
 SE15 ....65 B4
Belvedere Pl
 Brixton SW2 ......62 B3
 Lambeth SE1 .....**136** B3
Belvedere Rd SE1 **121** A1
Belvedere The
 SW10 ....**167** A3

Belvoir Lo SE22 . . . . . .76 C4
Belvoir Rd SE22 . . . . . .76 C4
Bembridge Cl
NW6 . . . . .10 A1
Bembridge Ho
🔟 Deptford SE8 . . . . .41 B2
Wandsworth SW18 . .59 A1
Bemerton St N1 . . . . . .84 C4
Bemish Rd SW15 . . . . .57 C4
Benabo Ct 🐠 E8 . . . . .16 C3
Benbow Ct W6 . . . . . . .39 A3
Benbow Ho 🔢
SE8 . . . . .51 C4
Benbow Rd W6 . . . . . .39 A3
Benbow St SE8 . . . . . . .51 C4
Bence Ho 🕄 SE8 . . . . .41 A2
Bendall Mews
NW1 . . . . .102 B4
Bendemeer Rd
SW15 . . . . .57 C4
Benden Ho SE13 . . . . .67 B2
Bendon Valley
SW18 . . . . .71 A4
Benedict Rd SW9 . .62 B4
Benenden Ho
SE17 . . . . .152 B2
Ben Ezra Ct 🐠 SE17 151 A3
Benfleet Ct 🕅 E8 . . .24 B4
Bengal Ct EC3 . . . . . .109 C1
Bengal Ho E1 . . . . .32 C4
Bengeworth Rd
SE5 . . . . .63 B4
Benham Cl 🐠
SW11 . . . . .59 C4
Benham Ho
SW10 . . . . .156 B2
Benham's Pl 🕦
NW3 . . . . .11 B4
Benhill Rd SE5 . . . . . .48 C2
Benington Ct N4 . . . . . .6 B2
Benjamin Cl 🕤 E8 . . .24 C4
Benjamin Ho 🕦
E2 . . . . .28 A1
Benjamin Mews
SW12 . . . . .73 B4
Benjamin St EC1 . . . .108 A4
Ben Jonson Ct 🕥
N1 . . . . .24 A3
Ben Jonson Prim Sch
E1 . . . . .26 A1
Ben Jonson Rd E1 . . .33 A4
Benledi E14 . . . . .34 C3
Bennelong Cl
W12 . . . . .30 A3
Bennerley Rd
SW11 . . . . .60 B2
Bennet's Hill EC4 . . .122 B4
Bennett Ct
Hampstead NW6 . . . .11 A2
Lower Holloway N7 . . .5 B1
🔼 South Acton W3 . . .37 A4
Bennett Gr SE13 . . . . .52 A2
Bennett Ho
🔁 Streatham
SW4 . . . . .73 A4
Westminster SW1 . . .147 C4
Bennett St
Chiswick W4 . . . . .38 A1
St James SW1 . . . . . .118 C2
Bennett's Yd SW1 . .133 C1
Benn Ho E2 . . .24 C2 99 B3
Benn St E9 . . . . .18 A2
Benns Wlk 🔢
TW9 . . . . .54 A3
Bensbury Cl SW15 . .69 B4

Ben Smith Way
SE16 . . . . .139 C2
Benson Ct
South Lambeth
SW8 . . . . .172 A4
🔟 Tufnell Pk N19 . . .13 B4
Benson Ho
Lambeth SE1 . . . . . . .121 C1
Shoreditch
E2 . . . . .24 B1 98 C2
Benson Quay E1 . . . . .32 B2
Benthal Ct N16 . . . . . . .7 C1
Benthal Prim Sch
N16 . . . . .7 C1
Benthal Rd N16 . . . . . . .7 C1
Bentham Ct 🐦 N1 . .15 B1
Bentham Ho SE1 . . . .137 B2
Bentham Rd E9 . . . . . .17 C2
Bentinck Cl NW8 . . . .80 B1
Bentinck Ho 🕄
W12 . . . . .30 A2
Bentinck Mans
W1 . . . . .103 C2
Bentinck Mews
W1 . . . . .103 C2
Bentinck St W1 . . . . .103 C2
Bentley Cl SW19 . . . . .70 C1
Bentley Ct SE13 . . . . . .67 B3
Bentley Ho
🔂 Bow E3 . . . . .26 C1
🕝 Camberwell SE5 . .49 A2
Bentley Rd N1 . . . . .16 A2
Bentworth Ct
E2 . . . . .24 C1 99 B2
Bentworth Prim Sch
W12 . . . . .30 A3
Bentworth Rd
W12 . . . . .30 A3
Benwell Rd N7 . . . . . . .14 C3
Benwick Cl SE16 . . . . .40 A2
Benworth St E3 . . . . . .26 B2
Benyon Ho EC1 . . . . . .95 C4
Benyon Rd N1 . . . . . . .87 C4
Benyon Wharf 🕘
E8 . . . . .24 A4
Beormund Prim Sch
SE1 . . . . .137 C3
Bequerel Ct 🕅 SE10 .43 B3
Berberis Ho 🔞 E3 . . .33 C4
Berber Pl 🕝 E14 . . . . .33 C2
Berber Rd SW11 . . . . .60 B2
Berebinder Ho 🕥
E3 . . . . .26 B3
Berenger Twr
SW10 . . . . .157 B2
Berenger Wlk
SW10 . . . . .157 B2
Berens Rd NW10 . . . . .22 C2
Beresford Ct E9 . . . . . .18 A3
Beresford Ho
Dulwich SE21 . . . . . . .76 A1
🔟 Stockwell SW4 . . .62 A3
Beresford Rd N4 . . . . .15 C3
Beresford Rd N5 . . . . .15 C3
Beresford Terr 🕄
N5 . . . . .15 B3
Bere St E1 . . . . .32 C2
Berestede Rd 🐠
W6 . . . . .38 B1
Bergen Ho 🔢 SE5 . . .48 B1
Bergen Sq SE16 . . . . . .41 A3
Berger Prim Sch
E9 . . . . .17 C2
Berger Rd E9 . . . . .17 C2
Berghem Mews
W14 . . . . .39 C3
Bergholt Cres N16 . .7 A4

Bergholt Mews 🐠
NW1 . . . . .13 C1
Berglen Ct E14 . . . . . . .33 A2
Bering Sq E14 . . . . .41 C1
Berisford Mews
SW18 . . . . .59 B1
Berkeley Ct
🔟 Golders Green
NW11 . . . . .1 B4
Marylebone NW1 . . . .91 A1
Willesden NW10 . . . . .9 A4
Berkeley Gdns
W8 . . . . .31 C1 113 C1
Berkeley Ho
🕄 Bow E3 . . . . .26 C2
🕝 Deptford SE8 . . . .41 B1
Berkeley Mews
W1 . . . . .103 A1
Berkeley Rd SW13 . . .46 C2
Berkeley Sq W1 . . . . .118 B3
Berkeley Sq W1 . . . . .118 B2
Berkeley The 🕦 N7 .5 B2
Berkeley Wlk 🕦 N7 . .5 B2
Berkley Gr NW1 . . . . . .12 C1
Berkley Rd NW1 . . . . . .12 C1
Berkshire Ho
WC2 . . . . .106 A2
Berkshire Rd E9 . . . . . .18 B2
Bermans Way
NW10 . . . . .8 B4
BERMONDSEY 40 A4
Bermondsey Leather
Mkt E1 . . . . .138 A3
Bermondsey Mkt*
SE1 . . . . .138 B2
Bermondsey Sq
SE1 . . . . .138 B2
Bermondsey St
SE1 . . . . .138 A3
Bermondsey Trad Est
SE16 . . . . .40 B1
Bermondsey Wall E
SE16 . . . . .40 A4
Bermondsey Wall W
SE1, SE16 . . . . .139 B4
Bernard Angell Ho 🕄
SE10 . . . . .52 C4
Bernard Cassidy St 🕄
E16 . . . . .35 B4
Bernard Ho E1 . . . . . .110 C3
Bernard Shaw Ct 🕤
N1 . . . . .13 B1
Bernard Shaw Ho 🕤
NW10 . . . . .20 C4
Bernard St WC1 . . . . . .94 B1
Bernay's Gr SW9 . . . .62 B3
Berners Ho N1 . . . . . . .85 B2
Berners Mews
W1 . . . . .105 A3
Berners Pl W1 . . . . . .105 A2
Berners Rd N1 . . . . . . .86 A3
Berners St W1 . . . . . .105 A2
Berner Terr 🔢 E1 . . .111 C1
Bernhard Baron Ho
E1 . . . . .111 C1
Bernhardt Cres
NW8 . . . . .90 A2
Bernie Grant Ho 🕤
E9 . . . . .17 B1
Benwood Ho 🕧
N4 . . . . .6 C4
Berridge Mews
NW6 . . . . .10 C3
Berriman Rd N7 . . . . . .5 B1
Berry Cotts 🔢
E14 . . . . .33 A3

Berryfield Rd
SE17 . . . . .150 B2
Berry Ho
Battersea SW11 . . . .169 A2
🕂 Bethnal Green
E1 . . . . .25 A1
Berrymede Gdns
W3 . . . . .37 B4
Berrymede Inf Sch
W3 . . . . .37 A4
Berrymede Jun Sch
W3 . . . . .37 A4
Berrymede Rd W4 . .37 C3
Berry Pl EC1 . . . . .96 B3
Berry St EC1 . . . . .96 B1
Berry Way W5 . . . . . . .36 A3
Bertha Neubergh Ho
🔟 SE5 . . . . .48 B2
Berthon St SE8 . . . . . . .51 C4
Bertie Rd NW10 . . . . . .8 C2
Bertram St N19 . . . . . . .4 A2
Bertrand Ho 🕦
SW16 . . . . .74 A1
Bertrand St SE13 . . . . .67 A4
Bertrum House Sch
SW17 . . . . .72 A2
Berwick St W1 . . . . . .105 A1
Berwyn Ho 🕄 N16 . . .7 B3
Berwyn Rd
Mortlake SW14,
TW10 . . . . .55 A3
Streatham SE24 . . . . .75 A3
Beryl Rd W6 . . . . .39 C1
Besant Cl NW2 . . . . . . .1 A1
Besant Ct N1 . . . . .15 C3
Besant Ho NW8 . . . . .78 C3
Besant Pl SE22 . . . . . . .64 B3
Besant Rd NW2 . . . . . .10 A4
Besant Wlk N7 . . . . . . .5 B2
Besford Ho 🕘 E2 . . . .24 C3
Bessant Dr TW9 . . . . . .45 A2
Bessborough Gdns
SW1 . . . . .147 C2
Bessborough Pl
SW1 . . . . .147 C2
Bessborough Rd
SW15 . . . . .68 C3
Bessborough St
SW1 . . . . .147 B2
Bessemer Ct 🕂
NW1 . . . . .13 B1
Bessemer Grange
Prim Sch SE5 . . . . . . .64 A3
Bessemer Park Ind
Est 🕂 SE24 . . . . .63 A3
Bessemer Rd SE5 . . .48 B1
Bessingham Wlk
SE4 . . . . .65 C3
Besson St SE14 . . . . . .50 C2
Bessy St E2 . . . . .25 B2
Bestwood St SE8 . . . .40 C2
Beswick Mews 🔢
NW6 . . . . .11 A2
Beta Pl 🔟 SW4 . . . . . .62 A3
Betchworth Ho 🕅
N7 . . . . .13 C3
Bethersden Ho
SE17 . . . . .152 B2
Bethlehem Ho 🔢
E14 . . . . .33 B2
BETHNAL GREEN .25 A2
Bethnal Green
E2 . . . . .24 C2 99 B3
Shoreditch E1 . . . . . . .24 B1 99 A2
Bethnal Green Sta
Bethnal Green E1 . .25 A1
Bethnal Green E2 . .25 B2
Bethnal Green Tech
Coll E2 . . . . .24 B2 99 A3
Bethune Rd
North Acton NW10 . .20 C1
Stamford Hill N16 . . . .7 A4
Bethwin Rd SE5 . . . . .48 B3
Betsham Ho SE1 . . . .137 B4
Betterton Ho
WC2 . . . . .106 B1
Betterton St WC2 . . .106 B1
Bettridge Rd
SW6 . . . . .165 A1
Betts Ho E1 . . . . .32 A2
Betts St E1 . . . . .32 A2
Betty Layward Prim
Sch N16 . . . . .6 C1
Betty May Gray Ho 🔁
E14 . . . . .42 B2
Bevan St N1 . . . . .87 A3
Bev Callender Cl 🔢
SW8 . . . . .61 A4
Bevenden St N1 . . . . .97 C4
Beveridge Rd 🕦
NW10 . . . . .8 A1
Beverley Cl
Barnes SW13 . . . . . . .46 C1
🕕 Wandsworth
SW11 . . . . .59 C3
Beverley Cotts
SW15 . . . . .68 A1
Beverley Ct
🕄 Acton Green
W4 . . . . .37 B1
🔟 Acton W12 . . . . . .38 A4
Brockley SE4 . . . . .66 A4
Islington N5 . . . . .15 C2
Beverley Gdns
Barnes SW13 . . . . . . .56 B4
Hendon NW11 . . . . .1 A4
Beverley Lo 🕔
TW10 . . . . .54 A2
Beverley Path 🕘
SW13 . . . . .46 B1
Beverley Rd
Barnes SW13 . . . . . . .56 B4
Chiswick W4 . . . . .38 B1
Beversbrook Rd
N19 . . . . .4 C1
Beverstone Rd
SW2 . . . . .62 B2
Beverston Mews
NW1 . . . . .102 C3
Bevin Cl SE16 . . . . . . .33 A1
Bevin Ct WC1 . . . . . . .95 A4
Bevington Prim Sch
W10 . . . . .31 A4
Bevington Rd
W10 . . . . .31 A4
Bevington St
SE16 . . . . .139 C2
Bevin Ho
🕕 Bethnal Green
E2 . . . . .25 B2
🔟 Bow E3 . . . . .26 C2
Bevin Sq SW17 . . . . . .72 B1
Bevin Way WC1 . . . . . .95 B4
Bevis Marks EC3 . . . .110 B2
Bew Ct SE21 . . . . .76 C4
Bewdley Ho N4 . . . . . . .6 B4
Bewdley St N1 . . . . . . .14 C1
Bewick Mews
SE15 . . . . .50 A3
Bewick St SW8 . . . . .170 B1
Bewley Ct SW2 . . . . . .74 B4

Bewley Ho **7** E1 . . . . . . .32 A2
Bewley St E1 . . . . .32 A2
Bexhill Rd
　Catford SE4 . . . . .66 B1
　Mortlake SW14 . . . . . . .55 B4
Bexley Ho SE4 . . . . .66 A3
BFI London Imax
　Cinema SE1 . . . . 121 B1
Bianca Rd SE1,
SE15 . . . . .49 C4
Bicester Rd TW9 . . . . . . .55 A4
Bickenhall Mans
　W1 . . . . 103 A4
Bickenhall St W1 . . . . . 103 A4
Bickerton Rd N19 . . . .4 B2
Bicknell Ho **1** 111 C1
Bicknell Rd SE5 . . . . .63 B4
Bicknor Ho **2** E5 . .17 A3
Bidborough Ho N1,
WC1 . . . . .94 A3
Biddenham Ho **10**
SE16 . . . . .40 C2
Bidder St E16 . . . . .35 A4
Biddesden Ho
SW3 . . . . 144 C3
Biddestone Ho N7 . . .14 B4
Biddulph Mans
W9 . . . . .88 B3
Biddulph Rd W9 . . . . . . .88 B3
Big Ben* SW1 . . . 134 B3
Biggerstaff Rd
E15 . . . . .27 B4
Biggerstaff St N4 . . . .5 C2
Bigg's Row SW15 . . . . . .57 C4
Bigland Green Prim
　Sch E1 . . . . .32 A3
Bigland St E1 . . . . .32 A3
Bilberry Ho **10** E3 . . .33 C4
Billie Holiday Ct
W10 . . . . .20 C3
Billingford Ct SE4 . . .65 C3
Billing Ho **7** E1 . . . . . . .32 C3
Billingley N1 . . . . .82 C3
Billing Pl SW10 . . . . . 156 B2
Billing Rd SW10 . . . . . 156 B2
Billingsgate Mkt
E14 . . . . .34 A1
Billing St SW10 . . . . . 156 B2
Billington Ho
SW8 . . . . 171 C3
Billington Rd
SE14 . . . . .50 C3
Billiter Sq EC3 . . . . . . 110 B1
Billiter St EC3 . . . . . . 110 B1
Billson St E14 . . . . .42 B2
Bilton Ho **5** SW8 . . . . 171 B3
Bilton Twrs W1 . . . . . 103 A1
Bina Gdns SW5 . . . . . . 142 C3
Binbrook Ho **13**
W10 . . . . .30 B4
Binden Rd W12 . . . . . . .38 B3
Binfield Ct SE5 . . . . .48 B1
Binfield Rd SW4 . . . . 172 B3
Bingfield St N1 . . . . . . 84 C4
Bingham Pl W1 . . . . . 103 B4
Bingham St N1 . . . . . . .15 C2
Binley Ho SW15 . . . . . . .56 B1
Binney St W1 . . . . 103 C1
Binnie Ct SE10 . . . . .52 A3
Binnie Ho SE1 . . . . . . 136 C1
Binns Rd W4 . . . . .38 A1
Binns Terr **3** W4 . . .38 A1
Binstead Ho SW18 . .59 A1
Binyon Ho **8** N16 . . .16 A4
Birbeck Ho **4** N19 . .4 C3
Bircham Path SE4 . . .65 C3

Birch Cl
　Newham E16 . . . . .35 A4
　Peckham SE15 . . . . .49 C1
　Upper Holloway N19 . . .4 B2
Birchdown Ho **32**
E3 . . . . .27 A2
Birches The SE5 . . . . . . .49 A1
Birchfield Ho **3**
E14 . . . . .33 C2
Birchfield St E14 . . . . . .33 C2
Birchgrove Ho
TW9 . . . . .45 A3
Birch Ho
　New Cross Gate
　SE14 . . . . .51 B2
　6 Tulse Hill SW2 . . .62 C1
Birchington Ct
NW6 . . . . .78 A4
Birchington Ho **1**
E5 . . . . .17 A3
Birchin La EC3 . . . . . 109 C1
Birchlands Ave
SW12 . . . . .72 B4
Birchmere Lo **18**
SE16 . . . . .40 A1
Birchmere Row
SE3 . . . . .53 B1
Birchmore Wlk N5 . .6 B1
Birch Vale Ct NW8 . .89 C2
Birchwood Dr NW3 . .2 A1
Birdcage Wlk
SW1 . . . . 133 B3
Birdhurst Rd
SW18 . . . . .59 B2
Bird In Bush Rd
SE15 . . . . .49 C3
Bird In Hand Yd **24**
NW3 . . . . .11 B4
Birdsall Ho **5** SE5 . .64 A4
Birdsfield La **12**
E3 . . . . .26 B4
Bird St W1 . . . . 103 C1
Birkbeck Ave W3 . . . . . .28 B2
Birkbeck Coll W1 . . 105 B2
Birkbeck Ct W3 . . . . . . .28 C1
Birkbeck Gr W3 . . . . . . .37 C4
Birkbeck Hill SE21 . . . . .75 A3
Birkbeck Mews **5**
E8 . . . . .16 B3
Birkbeck Pl SE21 . . . . . .75 B2
Birkbeck Rd
　Acton W3 . . . . .28 C1
　Dalston E8 . . . . .16 B3
Birkbeck St E2 . . . . .25 A2
Birkdale Cl **30**
SE16 . . . . .40 A1
Birkenhead Ho **11**
N7 . . . . .14 C3
Birkenhead St
WC1 . . . . .94 B4
Birkwood Cl SW12 . . .73 C4
Birley Lo NW8 . . . . . .79 C2
Birley St SW11 . . . . . 169 B1
Birnam Rd N4 . . . . .5 B2
Birrell Ho SW9 . . . . . 172 C1
Birse Cres NW10 . . . . .8 A4
Birtwhistle Ho **5**
E3 . . . . .26 B4
Biscay Ho **11** E1 . . . .25 C1
Biscay Rd W6 . . . . .39 C1
Biscoe Way SE13 . . . . . .67 C4
Biscott Ho **3** E3 . . . . .27 A1
Bisham Gdns N6 . . . . . .3 C3

Bishop Challoner
　Collegiate Sch
　E1 . . . . .32 B3
Bishop Ct **23** SW2 . .62 C1
Bishop Duppa's
　Almshouses **7**
　TW10 . . . . .54 A2
Bishop King's Rd
　W14 . . . . 140 B4
Bishop's Ave SW6 . . 164 A2
Bishop's Bridge Rd
　W2 . . . . 100 C2
Bishops Cl W4 . . . . . . .37 B1
Bishop's Cl N19 . . . . . . .4 B1
Bishops Ct
　Bayswater W2 . . . . . 100 B2
　Richmond TW9 . . . . . . .54 A4
Bishop's Ct
　Holborn EC4 . . . . . . 108 A2
　Holborn WC2 . . . . . . 107 B2
Bishopsgate EC2 . . . 110 A2
Bishopsgate Arc
　E1 . . . . 110 B3
Bishopsgate
　Churchyard EC2 . . . 110 A2
Bishops Ho SW8 . . . 162 B1
Bishop's Mans
　SW6 . . . . .47 C1
Bishops Mead SE5 . .48 B3
Bishop's Park Rd
　SW6 . . . . .47 C1
Bishops Rd SW6 . . . 164 C4
Bishops Sq E1 . . . . . 110 B4
Bishop St N1 . . . . 86 C4
Bishop's Terr
　SE11 . . . . 149 C4
Bishopstone Ho
　SW11 . . . . 169 B2
Bishop's Way E2 . . . .25 B3
Bishopswood Rd
　N6 . . . . .3 B4
Bishop Way NW10 . . . .8 A1
Bishop Wilfred Wood
　Cl SE15 . . . . .49 C1
Bisley Ho SW19 . . . . . .69 C2
Bissextile Ho SE13 . .52 A1
Bisson Rd E15 . . . . .27 B3
Bittern Ct **4** SE8 . . .51 C4
Bittern Ho SE1 . . . . . 136 C3
Bittern St SE1 . . . . . . 136 C3
Blackall St
　EC2 . . . . .24 A1 98 A2
Blackburn Ct **21**
　SW2 . . . . .62 C1
Blackburne's Mews
　W1 . . . . 117 B3
Blackdown Ho E8 . .16 C4
Blackett St SW15 . . . . . .57 C4
Blackfriars Bridge
　EC4 . . . . 122 A3
Blackfriars Ct
　EC4 . . . . 122 A4
Black Friars La
　EC4 . . . . 108 A1
Blackfriars Pas
　EC4 . . . . 122 A4
Blackfriars Pier
　EC4 . . . . 122 A4
Blackfriars Rd
　SE1 . . . . 122 A4
Blackfriars Sta
　EC4 . . . . 122 A4

Blackfriars Underpass
　EC4 . . . . 121 C2
Blackheath* SE3 . . .53 C4
Blackheath Ave
　SE3 . . . . .53 A3
Blackheath Bsns Est
　SE10 . . . . .52 B2
Blackheath Gr
　SE3 . . . . .53 B1
Blackheath High Sch
　Blackheath SE3 . . . . . .53 C1
　Greenwich SE3 . . . . . .53 C3
Blackheath Hill
　SE10 . . . . .52 B2
Blackheath Prep Sch
　SE3 . . . . .53 C2
Blackheath Rd
　SE10 . . . . .52 A2
Blackheath Rise
　SE13 . . . . .52 B1
BLACKHEATH VALE
　SE3 . . . . .53 B1
Blackheath Vale
　SE3 . . . . .53 A1
Blackheath Village
　SE3 . . . . .53 B1
Black Horse Ct
　SE1 . . . . 137 C2
Blackhorse Rd
　SE8 . . . . .51 A4
Blacklands Terr
　SW3 . . . . 144 C3
Black Lion La W6 . . .38 C2
Black Lion Mews **4**
　W6 . . . . .38 C2
Blackmore Ho
　Islington N1 . . . . .85 A3
　2 Wandsworth
　SW18 . . . . .59 A2
Blackmore Twr **1**
　W3 . . . . .37 B3
Blackpool Rd
　SE15 . . . . .50 A1
Black Prince Rd SE1,
　SE11 . . . . 149 A3
Black Roof Ho **3**
　SE5 . . . . .48 A2
Black's Rd W6 . . . . .39 B2
Blackstock Ho **3**
　N5 . . . . .6 A1
Blackstock Mews
　N4 . . . . .6 A1
Blackstock Rd N4,
　N5 . . . . .6 A2
Blackstone Ho
　Dulwich SE21 . . . . . . .76 A1
　Pimlico SW1 . . . . . . 146 C1
Blackstone Rd NW2 . .9 B4
Black Swan Yd
　SE1 . . . . 138 A4
Blackthorn Ct
　20 Camberwell
　SE5 . . . . .48 B3
　2 Leyton E15 . . . . . . .19 C4
Blackthorn St E3 . . . . . .26 C1
Blacktree Mews **11**
　SW9 . . . . .62 C4
BLACKWALL 34 C2
Blackwall Sta E14 . . . . .34 C2
Blackwall Trad Est
　E14 . . . . .34 C4
Blackwall Tunnel E14,
　SE10 . . . . .34 C1
Blackwall Tunnel App
　SE10 . . . . .43 A4

Blackwall Tunnel
　Northern Approach
　E14, E3 . . . . .27 B1
Blackwall Way
　E14 . . . . .34 B2
Blackwater Ho
　NW8 . . . . 101 C4
Blackwater St
　SE22 . . . . .64 B2
Blackwell Cl **10**
　E5 . . . . .17 C4
Blackwell Ho **3**
　SW4 . . . . .61 C1
Blackwood Ho **11**
　E1 . . . . .25 A1
Blackwood St
　SE17 . . . . 151 B2
Blade Mews SW15 . .58 B3
Bladen Ho **4** E1 . . .32 C3
Blades Ct
　4 Hammersmith
　W6 . . . . .39 A1
　Putney SW15 . . . . .58 B3
Blades Ho SE11 . . . . 163 B3
Blades Lo **15** SW2 . .62 C1
Blagdon Rd SE13 . . . . . .67 A1
Blagrove Rd **1**
　W10 . . . . .31 A4
Blair Ho N1 . . . . .15 B2
Blair Ct NW8 . . . . . . .79 B4
Blairderry Rd
　SW2 . . . . .74 A2
Blairgowrie Ct **13**
　E14 . . . . .34 C3
Blair Ho SW9 . . . . . . 172 C2
Blair St E14 . . . . .34 C3
Blake Coll W1 . . . . . 104 C4
Blake Ct
　3 Bermondsey
　SE16 . . . . .40 A1
　Kilburn NW6 . . . . .23 C2
Blake Gdns SW6 . . . 166 A4
Blake Ho
　4 Deptford SE8 . . .51 C4
　Isle of Dogs E14 . . . . .42 A4
　3 Kentish Town
　N19 . . . . .13 C3
　Lambeth SE1 . . . . . . 135 B2
　4 Stoke Newington
　N16 . . . . .16 A4
Blake Mews **15**
　TW9 . . . . .44 C2
Blakemore Rd
　SW16 . . . . .74 A1
Blakeney Cl
　5 Camden Town
　NW1 . . . . .13 C1
　4 Dalston E8 . . . . . .16 C3
Blakenham Ct
　W12 . . . . .29 C1
Blaker Rd E15 . . . . .27 B4
Blakes Cl W10 . . . . .30 B4
Blake's Rd SE15 . . . . . .49 A3
Blanca Ho **18** N1 . .24 A3
Blanchard Way
　E8 . . . . .16 C2
Blanch Cl SE15 . . . . . . .50 B3
Blanchedowne
　SE5 . . . . .63 C3
Blandfield Rd
　SW12 . . . . .72 C4
Blandford Ct
　Brondesbury Pk
　NW6 . . . . .10 A1

Blandford Ct *continued*
6 De Beauvoir Town
N1 ....16 A1

Blandford Ho
SW8 ....162 C2
Blandford Rd W4 ..38 A3
Blandford Sq NW1. 90 B1
Blandford St W1 ..103 B3
Bland Ho SE11 ....149 A2
Blantyre St SW10. 157 B2
Blantyre Twr
SW10 ....157 B2
Blantyre Wlk
SW10 ....157 B2
Blashford St SE13 .12 B1
Blasker Wlk **8**
E14 ....42 A1
Blaxland Ho **12**
W12 ....30 A2
Blazer Ct NW8 ....89 C3
Blechynden Ho **17**
W10 ....30 C3
Blechynden St
W10 ....30 C2
Bleeding Heart Yd
EC1 ....107 C3
Blemundsbury
WC1 ....106 B4
Blendworth Point **4**
SW15 ....69 A3
Blenheim **26**
SW19 ....69 C3
Blenheim Cres
Notting Hill W11 ..31 A3
Notting Hill
W11 ....31 A2 112 B4
Blenheim Ct
Barnsbury N7 ......14 A2
Richmond TW9 ....54 B4
7 Rotherhithe
SE16 ....32 C1
Upper Holloway N19 .5 A2
Blenheim Gdns
Clapham Pk SW2 ..62 B1
Dollis Hill NW2 .....9 B3
Blenheim Gr SE15 .49 C1
Blenheim Pas
NW8 ....78 C2
Blenheim Rd
Acton W4 ....38 A3
St John's Wood
NW8 ....79 A2
Blenheim St W1. 104 A1
Blenheim Terr
NW8 ....78 C2
Blenkarne Rd
SW11 ....60 B1
Blessed Sacrament
RC Prim Sch N1.. 84 C3
Blessington Cl
SE13 ....67 C4
Blessington Rd
SE13 ....67 C3
Bletchley St N1. 87 B1
Bletchley St N1. 87 A1
Bletsoe Wlk N1 .. 87 A2
Blick Ho **1** SE16 .. 40 B3
Blincoe Cl SW19... 69 C2
Blissett St SE10 ...52 B2
Bliss Mews **14**
W10 ....23 A2
Blisworth Ho **12**
E2 ....24 C4
Blithfield St W8.. 128 A1

Bloemfontein Ave
W12 ....30 A1
Bloemfontein Rd
W12 ....30 A2
Blomfield Ct
Battersea SW11 .. 167 C4
Paddington W9 .... 89 A2
Blomfield Ho **4**
E14 ....34 A2
Blomfield Mans **3**
W12 ....30 B1
Blomfield Rd W9 100 C4
Blomfield St EC2. 109 C3
Blomfield Villas
W9 ....100 C4
Blondel St SW11. 169 B2
Blondin St E3 ......26 C3
Bloomburg St
SW1 ....147 A3
Bloomfield Ho **1** 111 B3
Bloomfield Pl W1 118 B4
Bloomfield Terr
SW1 ....145 C2
Bloom Gr SE27 ....75 A1
Bloom Park Rd
SW6 ....154 C1
BLOOMSBURY 106 A4
Bloomsbury Ct
WC1 ....106 B3
Bloomsbury Ho **10**
SW4 ....61 C1
Bloomsbury Pl
London SW18 ......59 B2
St Giles WC1 ...... 106 B3
Bloomsbury Sq
WC1 ....106 B3
Bloomsbury St
WC1 ....105 C3
Bloomsbury Way
WC1 ....106 B3
Blore Cl SW8.. 171 B3
Blore Ct W1 ...... 119 B4
Blore Ho SW10 .. 156 B2
Blossom Cl W4 ....36 A4
Blossom Pl
E1 ....24 A1 98 B1
Blossom St
E1 ....24 A1 98 B1
Blount St E14 ......33 A3
Blucher Rd SE5 ...48 B3
Blue Anchor Alley **1**
TW9 ....54 A3
Blue Anchor La
SE16 ....40 A2
Blue Anchor Yd
E1 ....125 B4
Blue Ball Yd SW1 118 C1
Blue Gate Fields Jun
& Inf Schs E1 ......32 B2
Bluegate Mews
E1 ....32 A2
Blue Lion Pl SE1 138 A2
Blueprint Apartments
18 SW12 ....73 A4
Blundell Cl E8......16 C4
Blundell St N7 ....14 A2
Blurton Rd E5 .....17 C4
Blythe Ho SE11 .. 163 C4
Blythe Mews **2**
W14 ....39 C3
Blythendale Ho **34**
E2 ....24 C3
Blythe Rd W14 .. 126 A1
Blythe St E2 ....25 A2
Blyth's Wharf E14 .33 A2

Blythwood Rd N4 ...5 A4
Bnois Jerusalem Sch
N16 ....6 C4
Boades Mews **1**
NW3 ....11 C4
Boadicea St N1 .. 84 C3
Boardwalk Pl E14 .34 B1
Boarley Ho SE17 . 152 A3
Boathouse Ctr The
W10 ....22 B1
Boathouse Wlk **24**
SE15 ....49 B3
Boat Lifter Way **19**
SE16 ....41 A2
Bobbin Cl SW4 ....61 B4
Bob Marley Way **1**
SE24 ....62 C3
Bocking St E8 .....25 A4
Boddicott Cl
SW19 ....70 A2
Boddington Gdns
W3 ....36 C4
Boddington Ho **2**
SE14 ....50 B2
Bodeney Ho **10**
SE5 ....49 A2
Boden Ho E1..... 111 B4
Bodington Ct **2**
W12 ....39 C4
Bodley Manor Way
SE24 ....74 C4
Bodmin St SW18 ..70 C3
Bodney Rd E5, E8. 17 A3
Bogart Ct **8** E14 ..33 C2
Bohemia Pl **1** E8 .17 A2
Bohn Rd E1 ....26 A1
Boileau Rd SW13 ..47 A4
Boilerhouse **1**
SE1 ....124 C1
Boisseau Ho **31**
E1 ....32 B4
Bolden St SE8 .....52 A1
Boldero Pl NW8 .. 90 A1
Boleyn Rd N16 ....16 A3
Bolina Rd SE16 ....40 B1
Bolingbroke
SW11 ....60 B1
Bolingbroke Hospl
The SW11 ....59 C3
Bolingbroke Rd
W14 ....39 C3
Bolingbroke Wlk
SW11 .... 168 A4
Bollo Bridge Rd
W3 ....37 B4
Bollo Ct **2** W3 ....37 B3
Bollo La W3 ....37 A3
Bolney Gate SW7 130 A3
Bolney St SW8 ... 162 C1
Bolsover St W1 .... 92 B1
Bolt Ct EC4.........107 C1
Bolton Cres SE5 ...48 A3
Bolton Ct SW11 .. 169 C3
Bolton Gdns
Kensal Rise NW10..22 C3
South Kensington
SW5 ....142 B2
Bolton Gdns Mews
SW10 ....142 C2
Bolton Ho **4** SE10. 43 A1
Bolton Pl SW5 ... 142 C2
Bolton Rd
Chiswick W4 ....45 B3
Harlesden NW10 ..21 A4
Kilburn NW8 ....78 B3
Boltons Cl SW5 .. 142 B2

Boltons The
SW10 ....142 C2
Bolton Studios
SW10 ....143 A1
Bolton Wlk N7 ....5 B2
Bombay Ct **8**
SE16 ....40 B4
Bombay St SE16 ..40 A2
Bomore Rd
W11 ....31 A2 112 A4
Bonar Rd SE15 ....49 C3
Bonchurch Rd
W10 ....31 A4
Bond Ct EC4...... 109 B1
Bond Ho **4** NW6 ..23 B3
Bonding Yard Wlk
SE16 ....41 A3
Bond St W4 ....37 C2
Bond Street Sta
W1 ....103 C1
Bondway SW8 ....162 B4
Bonfield Rd SE13 . 67 B3
Bonham Ho
W11 ....31 B1 112 C2
Bonham Rd SW2 ..62 B2
Bonheur Rd W4 ...37 C4
Bonhill St EC2.... 97 C1
Bonington Ho **1** 84 C1
Bonita Mews SE15. 65 C4
Bonner Ho **3**
SW15 ....56 C2
Bonner Prim Sch
E2 ....25 B2
Bonner Rd E2 .....25 B3
Bonner St E2 ....25 B3
Bonneville Gdns
SW4 ....61 B1
Bonneville Prim Sch
SW4 ....61 B1
Bonnington Sq
SW8 ....162 C4
Bonny St NW1 .... 13 B1
Bonsor Ho SW8 . 171 A4
Bonsor St SE5 .....49 A3
Bonthron Ho
SW15 ....47 B1
Booker Cl **11** E3 ..33 B4
Boord St SE10 .....43 A3
Boothby Rd N19 ...4 C2
Booth Cl **10** E9 ...25 A4
Booth Ho **2** SW2 ..74 C4
Booth La EC4 ...... 122 C4
Booth's Pl W1 .... 105 A3
Boot St N1........... 24 A2 98 A3
Boreas Wlk N1 ... 86 B1
Boreham Ave E16 ..35 C3
Boreman Ho **11**
SE10 ....52 B4
Borland Rd SE15 ..65 B3
Borneo St SW15 ..57 B4
Borough High St
SE1 ....123 B2
Borough Mkt*
SE1 ....123 B1
Borough Rd SE1 136 B2
Borough Sq SE1 . 136 C3
Borough Sta SE1 137 A3
BOROUGH THE . 137 A4
Borrett Cl SE17.. 150 C1
Borrodaile Rd
SW18 ....59 A1
Borrowdale NW1. 92 C3
Borthwick St SE8 . 41 C1
Boscastle Rd NW5 ..4 A1

Boscobel Ho **4**
E8 ....17 A2
Boscobel Pl SW1 145 C4
Boscobel St NW8.. 89 C1
Boscombe Cl E5 ...18 A3
Boscombe Rd
W12 ....38 C4
Boss Ho SE1 ...... 138 C4
Boss St SE1 .... 138 C4
Boston Gdns W4 ..46 A4
Boston Ho
24 Camberwell
SE5 ....48 B1
Earl's Ct SW5 .... 142 B3
Lisson Gr NW1 ... 90 C2
Boston Pl NW1 ... 90 C1
Bosun Ct **22** E14 ..41 C4
Boswell Ct
Bloomsbury WC1 . 106 B4
9 Hammersmith
W6 ....39 C3
Boswell Ho WC1 . 106 B4
Boswell St WC1 .. 106 B4
Bosworth Ho **4**
W10 ....23 A1
Bosworth Rd W10 .23 A1
Bothwell Cl E16 .. 35 B4
Bothwell St **4**
W6 ....47 C4
Botolph Alley
EC3 ....124 A4
Botolph La EC3 .. 124 A4
Bott's Mews W2... 31 C3
Boughton Ho SE1 137 B4
Boulcott St E1 .... 32 C3
Boulevard The
Chelsea SW6 ..... 167 A3
4 Upper Tooting
SW17 ....72 C2
Boulogne Ho SE1 138 C2
Boulter Ho **4**
SE14 ....50 B2
Boulton Ho TW8 .. 36 A1
Boundaries Mans **3**
SW12 ....72 C3
Boundaries Rd
SW12 ....72 C3
Boundary Ho
Balham SW12 ......73 A3
1 Camberwell SE5 .. 48 B3
15 Notting Hill W11 .30 C1
Boundary La SE17.. 48 B4
Boundary Pas
E2 ....24 B1 98 C2
Boundary Rd NW8. 79 A4
Boundary Road Est
NW8 ....78 C3
Boundary Row
SE1 ....136 A4
Boundary St
E2 ....24 B1 98 C2
Bourchier St W1 . 119 B4
Bourdon Pl W1 .. 118 B3
Bourdon St W1 .. 118 B3
Bourke Cl
London SW4 ....62 A1
Willesden NW10 ..8 A2
Bourlet Cl W1 .... 104 C3
Bourne Ct W4 .....45 B4
Bourne Ho **5**
SW4 ....61 B3
Bourne Mews
W1 ....103 C1
Bournemouth Cl
SE15 ....49 C1
Bournemouth Rd
SE15 ....49 C1

Bourne Pl W4 ... 37 C1
Bourne St SW1 ... 145 B3
Bourne Terr W2 ... 100 B4
Bousfield Prim Sch SW10 ... 142 C2
Bousfield Rd SE14 ... 50 C1
Boutcher CE Prim Sch SE1 ... 152 C4
Boutflower Rd SW11 ... 60 A3
Bouverie Mews N16 ... 7 A2
Bouverie Pl W2 ... 101 C2
Bouverie Rd N16 ... 7 A2
Bouverie St EC4 ... 107 C1
Bovingdon Cl 4 N19 ... 4 B2
Bovingdon Rd SW6 ... 166 B3
BOW ... 26 B3
Bowater Cl SW2 ... 62 A1
Bowater Ho EC1 ... 97 A1
Bow Brook The 20 E2 ... 25 C3
Bow Church Sta E3 ... 26 C2
BOW COMMON ... 34 A4
Bow Common La E3 ... 26 B1
Bowden Ho 29 E3 ... 27 A2
Bowden St SE11 ... 149 C1
Bowditch SE8 ... 41 B1
Bowen St E14 N5 ... 15 A4
Bower Dr SF21 ... 76 A1
Bower St E14 ... 34 A3
Bower Ave SE3 ... 53 A3
Bowerdean St SW6 ... 166 A3
Bower Ho SE14 ... 50 C2
Bowerman Ave SE14 ... 51 A4
Bowerman Ct 1 N19 ... 4 C2
Bower St E1 ... 32 C3
Bowes-Lyon Hall 3 E16 ... 35 C1
Bowes Rd W3 ... 29 A2
Bowfell Rd W6 ... 47 B4
Bowhill Cl SW9 ... 163 C2
Bow Ho 1 E3 ... 26 C2
Bowie Cl SW4 ... 73 C4
Bow Ind Pk E15 ... 18 C1
Bow La EC2, EC4 ... 109 A1
Bowland Ho N4 ... 6 B4
Bowland Rd SW4 ... 61 C3
Bowland Yd SW1 ... 131 A3
Bowles Rd 1 SE1 ... 49 C4
Bowley Ho SE16 ... 139 B2
Bowling Green Cl SW15 ... 69 A4
Bowling Green Ho SW10 ... 157 B2
Bowling Green La EC1 ... 95 C2
Bowling Green Pl SE1 ... 137 B4
Bowling Green St SE11 ... 163 B4
Bowling Green Wlk N1 ... 24 A2 98 A4
Bowman Ave E16 ... 35 B2
Bowman Mews
St George in t East
E1 ... 125 B4
Wandsworth SW18 ... 70 B3

Bowman's Mews N7 ... 5 A1
Bowman's Pl N7 ... 5 A1
Bowmore Wlk NW1 ... 13 C1
Bowness Cl 5 E8 ... 16 B2
Bowness Ho SE15 ... 50 B3
Bowood Rd SW11 ... 60 C2
Bow Rd E3 ... 26 C2
Bow Road Sta E3 ... 26 C2
Bowry Ho 14 E14 ... 33 B4
Bow Sch E3 ... 26 C2
Bowsprit Point 1 E14 ... 41 C3
Bow St WC2 ... 106 B1
Bowstead Ct SW11 ... 167 C3
Bow Triangle Bsns Ctr 17 E3 ... 26 C1
Bowyer Ho
27 Shoreditch N1 ... 24 A4
Wandsworth SW18 ... 59 A1
Bowyer Pl SE5 ... 48 B3
Bowyer St 16 SE5 ... 48 B3
Boxall Rd SE21 ... 64 A1
Boxley Ho 3 E5 ... 17 A3
Boxmoor Ho
16 Hackney E2 ... 24 C4
3 Shepherd's Bush
W11 ... 30 C1
Box Tree Ho SE8 ... 41 A1
Boxworth Gr N1 ... 85 A4
Boyce Ho 6 W10 ... 23 B2
Boyd Ct SW15 ... 57 B1
Boydell Ct NW8 ... 11 C1
Boyd St E1 ... 111 C1
Boyfield St SE1 ... 136 B3
Boyle St W1 ... 118 C4
Boyne Ct NW10 ... 8 C1
Boyne Rd SE13 ... 67 C4
Boyson Rd 3 SE17 ... 48 C4
Boyton Cl E1 ... 25 C1
Boyton Ho
Kennington SE11 ... 149 B1
St John's Wood NW8 ... 79 C2
Brabant Ct EC3 ... 124 A4
Brabazon St E14 ... 34 A3
Brabner Ho
E2 ... 24 C2 99 B4
Braborn Gr SE15 ... 50 B1
Bracer Ho 1 N1 ... 24 A3
Bracewell Rd W10 ... 30 B4
Bracey Mews 1
N4 ... 5 A2
Bracey St N4 ... 5 A2
Bracken Ave SW12 ... 72 C4
Brackenbury N4 ... 5 B3
Brackenbury Gdns W6 ... 39 A3
Brackenbury Prim Sch W6 ... 39 A3
Brackenbury Rd W6 ... 39 A3
Bracken Gdns SW13 ... 46 C1
Bracken Ho 5 E3 ... 33 C4
Brackley Ave SE15 ... 65 B4
Brackley Ct NW8 ... 89 C2
Brackley Rd W4 ... 38 A1
Brackley St EC1 ... 109 A4
Brackley Terr 6 W4 ... 38 A1

Bracklyn Ct N1 ... 87 B2
Bracklyn St N1 ... 87 B2
Bracknell Gate NW3 ... 11 A3
Bracknell Gdns NW3 ... 11 A4
Bracknell Way NW3 ... 11 A4
Bradbeer Ho 24 E2 ... 25 B2
Bradbourne St SW6 ... 165 C2
Bradbury Ct 2 SE3 ... 53 C3
Bradbury Ho 1 E1 ... 111 A2
Bradbury St 28 N16 ... 16 A3
Bradby Ho NW8 ... 78 B1
Braddon Rd TW9 ... 54 B4
Braddyll St SE10 ... 43 A1
Bradenham 11 SE17 ... 48 C4
Bradenham Cl SE17 ... 48 C4
Braden St W9 ... 88 A1
Bradfield Ct 14 NW1 ... 13 A1
Bradfield Ho 2 SW8 ... 171 B2
Bradford Ho 4 W14 ... 39 C3
Bradford Rd W3 ... 38 A4
Bradgate Rd SE6 ... 67 A1
Brading Rd SW2 ... 74 B4
Brading Terr W12 ... 38 C3
Bradiston Rd W9 ... 23 B2
Bradley Cl N7 ... 14 B2
Bradley Ho
Bermondsey SE16 ... 40 A2
2 Bromley E3 ... 27 A2
Bradley Mews SW12 ... 72 B3
Bradley's Cl N1 ... 85 C2
Bradlord Ho SE21 ... 76 A1
Bradmead SW8 ... 160 C1
Bradmore Park Rd W6 ... 39 A2
Brad St SE1 ... 121 C1
Bradstock Ho E9 ... 18 A1
Bradstock Rd E9 ... 17 C2
Bradwell Ho NW6 ... 78 A3
Brady Ho
London SW8 ... 171 A4
South Lambeth SW8 ... 61 C4
Brady St E1 ... 25 A1
Braefoot Ct SW15 ... 57 C2
Braemar SW15 ... 57 C2
Braemar Ave SW19, SW19 ... 70 C2
Braemar Ho W9 ... 88 C3
Braes St N1 ... 15 A1
Braganza St SE17 ... 150 A1
Braham St E1 ... 111 A2
Brahma Kumaris World Spiritual Univ NW10 ... 8 C1
Braid Ave W3 ... 29 A3
Braid Ho SE10 ... 52 B2
Braidwood St SE1 ... 124 A1
Brailsford Rd SW2 ... 62 C1
Braintree Ho 6 E1 ... 25 B1

Braintree St E2 ... 25 A2
Braithwaite Ho EC1 ... 97 B2
Braithwaite Twr W2 ... 101 B4
Bramah Gn SW9 ... 173 C4
Bramah Mus of Tea & Coffee* SE1 ... 123 A1
Bramall Ct N4 ... 12 B2
Bramber WC1 ... 94 A3
Bramber Ct TW8 ... 36 A2
Bramber Rd W14 ... 154 C4
Brambledown 1 ...
Bramble Gdns W12 ... 29 B2
Bramble Ho 10 E3 ... 33 C4
Brambling Ct 25 SE8 ...
Bramcote Gr SE16 ... 40 B1
Bramcote Rd SW15 ... 57 A3
Bramerton NW6 ... 9 C1
Bramerton St SW3 ... 158 A4
Bramfield Ct N4 ... 6 B2
Bramfield Rd SW11 ... 60 B2
Bramford Rd SW18 ... 59 B3
Bramham Gdns SW5 ... 142 B2
Bramham Ho SE22 ... 64 A3
Bramlands Cl SW11 ... 60 A4
Bramley Cres SW8 ... 161 C2
Bramley Ho 13 SE13 ... 67 C2
Bramley Ho
11 North Kensington
W10 ... 30 C3
Roehampton SW15 ... 56 B1
Bramley Rd W10 ... 30 C3
Brampton WC1 ... 106 C3
Bramshaw Rd E9 ... 17 C2
Bramshill Gdns NW5 ... 4 A1
Bramshill Rd NW10 ... 21 B3
Bramshurst NW8 ... 78 B3
Bramston Rd
Harlesden NW10 ... 21 C3
Wandsworth SW17 ... 71 B1
Bramwell Ho
Borough The SE1 ... 137 A1
Chelsea SW1 ... 160 C4
Bramwell Mews N1 ... 85 A4
Brancaster Ho
2 Globe Town E1 ... 25 C2
Islington N5 ... 15 A3
Brancaster Rd SE16 ... 74 B1
Branch Hill NW3 ... 2 B1
Branch Pl N1 ... 87 C4
Branch Rd E14 ... 33 A2
Branch St SE15 ... 49 A3
Brand Cl N4 ... 6 A3
Branden Lo 13 W4 ... 37 B1
Brandlehow Rd SW15 ... 58 B3
Brandon Mews
Barbican EC2 ... 109 B4
Walworth SE17 ... 151 A3
Brandon Rd N7 ... 14 A1
Brandon St SE17 ... 151 A3

Brandrams Wharf SE16 ... 40 B4
Brandreth Rd SW17 ... 73 A2
Brand St SE10 ... 52 B3
Brangton Rd SE11 ... 149 A1
Brangwyn Ct W14 ... 126 A3
Branksea St SW6 ... 154 A1
Branksome Ho SW8 ... 162 C2
Branksome Rd SW2 ... 62 A2
Bransby Ct 4 N16 ... 16 A4
Branscombe NW1 ... 83 A3
Branscombe St SE13 ... 67 A4
Bransdale Cl NW6 ... 23 C4
Branstone Ct 9 TW9 ... 44 B2
Branstone Rd TW9 ... 44 B2
Branston Ho N7 ... 14 C3
Brantwood Ho 9 SE5 ... 48 B3
Brantwood Rd SE24 ... 63 B2
Brasenose Dr SW13 ... 47 B4
Brashley Road Cvn Site NW10 ... 21 A2
Brassey Ho 1 E14 ... 42 A2
Brassey Rd NW6 ... 10 B2
Brassey Sq SW11 ... 60 C4
Brassie Ave W3 ... 29 A3
Brass Talley Alley 3 SE16 ... 40 C4
Brathay NW1 ... 83 A1
Brathway Rd SW18 ... 70 C4
Bratley St E1 ... 24 C1 99 B1
Bravington Pl W9 ... 23 B1
Bravington Rd W9 ... 23 B2
Brawne Ho 12 SE17 ... 48 A4
Braxfield Rd SE4 ... 66 B3
Bray NW3 ... 12 A1
Brayard's Rd SE15 ... 50 A1
Braybrook St W12 ... 29 B3
Brayburne Ave SW4 ... 171 A1
Bray Cres SE16 ... 40 C4
Braydon Rd N16 ... 7 C3
Bray Dr E16 ... 35 B2
Brayfield Terr N1 ... 14 C1
Brayford Sq 12 E1 ... 32 B3
Bray Pl SW3 ... 144 C3
Bread St EC2, EC4 ... 109 A1
Breakspeare SE21 ... 76 A1
Breakspears Mews SE4 ... 51 C1
Breakspears Rd SE4 ... 66 C4
Breakwell Ct 18 W10 ... 23 A1
Breamore Cl SW15 ... 68 C3
Breamore Ho 21 SE15 ... 49 C3
Bream's Bldgs EC4 ... 107 B2
Bream St E3 ... 18 C1
Breasley Cl SW15 ... 57 A3

Brechin Pl SW7 .... **143** A3
Brecknock Prim Sch
  N7.................................**13** C2
Brecknock Rd
  N19..............................**13** C3
Brecon Ho
  Stamford Hill N16........7 B3
  Wandsworth SW18 .....**70** C4
Brecon Rd W6 ..... **154** B3
Bredel Ho ❶ E14 ....**33** C4
Bredgar SE13 ....**67** A2
Bredgar Rd N19.......**4** B2
Bredinghurst
  SE22...........................**76** C4
Bredinghurst Sch
  SE15...........................**65** C3
Bredin Ho SW10 . **156** B2
Breer St SW6 ....**59** A4
Breezer's Ct E1 .... **125** C3
Breezer's Hill E1 .. **125** C3
Brehon Ho NW1.....**82** C3
Bremner Rd SW7 **129** B2
Brenchley Gdns SE15,
  SE22, SE23............**65** C1
Brenda Rd SW17 .....**72** B2
Brendon Ave NW10...8 A4
Brendon Ho NW1 ...**103** B4
Brendon St W1 ....**102** B2
Brenley Ho SE1.... **137** B4
Brennands Ct ❶
  N19................................**4** B1
Brent Adult Comm
  Education Service
  Coll NW10.................**20** C4
Brent Ct ❺ W12.....**38** A3
Brent Ho ❷ E9........**17** B2
Brenthouse Rd E9 ..**17** B2
Brenthurst Rd
  NW10............................**8** B2
Brent Mews * NW10 ..9 A2
Brent New Ent Ctr
  NW10............................**8** B2
Brenton Ct E9..........**18** A3
Brenton St E14........**33** A3
Brent Rd E16 ....**35** C4
Brent Trad Est
  NW10............................**8** A3
Brentwick Gdns
  TW8...........................**36** A2
Brereton Ho ❹
  SW2............................**74** C4
Bressenden Pl
  SW1..........................**132** C2
Breton Ho
  Bermondsey SE1 .. **138** C2
  St Luke's EC2 ....**97** A1
Brett Cl N16................**7** A2
Brett Cres NW10 .....**20** C4
Brettell St SE17 .. **151** C1
Brett Ho ❶ SW15 ...**69** C4
Brett House Cl ❷
  SW15...........................**69** C4
Brettinghurst SE1 **153** B1
Bretton Ho N19 ....**5** A3
Brett Pas ❷❽ E8 ...**17** A3
Brett Rd E8 ....**17** A3
Brewers Bldgs
  EC1.............................**96** A4
Brewers Ct W2 ..... **100** C2
Brewer's Gn SW1 **133** B2
Brewers Hall Gdns
  EC2...........................**109** A3
Brewer St W1 ..... **119** A4

Brewery Ind Est
  N1...............................**87** A1
Brewery Rd N7........**14** A2
Brewery Sq
  Bermondsey SE1 .. **124** C1
  Clerkenwell EC1 ......**96** B2
Brewhouse La
  Putney SW15 ....**58** A4
  Wapping E1................**32** A1
Brewhouse Wlk
  SE16............................**33** A1
Brewhouse Yd
  EC1.............................**96** A2
Brewster Gdns
  W10.............................**30** B4
Brewster Ho
  Bermondsey SE1 .. **153** A4
  Poplar E14 ....**33** B2
Briant Ho SE1 ...... **135** A1
Briant St SE14 ....**50** C3
Briar Ct ❼ Bow E3 ..**26** C3
  Dalston E8..................**16** C3
Briardale SW19 ......**70** B3
Briardale Gdns
  NW3...............................**1** C1
Briarsdale Ho ❻
  N16................................**7** A3
Briar Rd NW2 ....**9** C3
Briar Wlk
  Putney SW15 ....**57** A3
  West Kilburn W10 ....**23** A1
Briarwood Rd
  SW4..............................**61** C2
Briary Cl NW3..........**12** A1
Briary Ct ❿ E16 .....**35** B3
Brickbarn Cl
  SW10..........................**157** A2
Brick Ct EC4 .... **107** B1
Brick Farm Cl
  TW9...............................**45** A2
Brick La
  Shoreditch
  E2................**24** B2 **99** A4
  Spitalfields
  E1................**24** B1 **99** A1
Bricklayers Arms
  SE1.............................**137** C1
Brick St W1 .... **118** A1
Brickworth Ho ❼
  SW9...........................**173** C4
Brideale Cl SE15 ...**49** B4
Bride La EC4 .... **108** A1
Bridel Mews N1 .....**86** A3
Bride St N7 ....**14** B2
Bridewain St SE1 **138** C2
Bridewell Pl
  Holborn EC4........... **108** A1
  ❹ Wapping E1.........**32** A1
Bridford Mews
  W1..............................**104** B4
Bridge App NW1 .....**81** B3
Bridge Ave W6.........**39** B1
Bridge Avenue Mans
  ❷ W6.........................**39** B1
Bridge Cl ❸ W10 ...**30** C3
Bridge Ct ❾
  ❷ Blackwall E14...**34** C2
  ❹ Willesden NW10...**8** A1
Bridge Field Ho
  W2..............................**100** A2
Bridgefoot SE1.... **148** B1
Bridge Gdns N16 ...**15** C4
Bridge Ho
  Brockley SE4 ....**66** B3
  ❶ Camden Town
  NW1............................**12** C1

Bridge Ho continued
  Homerton E9 ....**17** C2
Bridge House Quay
  E14..............................**34** B1
Bridge La SW11 ... **168** B3
Bridgeland Rd
  E16..............................**35** C2
Bridgeman Ho ⓲
  E9................................**17** B1
Bridgeman Rd N1 ...**14** B1
Bridgeman St
  NW8..............................**80** A1
Bridge Meadows
  SE14............................**50** C4
Bridgend Rd
  SW18............................**59** B3
Bridgen Ho ❾ E1 ...**32** A3
Bridge Pk ❼
  SW18............................**58** C2
Bridgepoint Pl ❶
  N6..................................**4** B4
Bridge Pl SW1 .... **146** B4
Bridgeport Pl ❶
  E1................................**32** A1
Bridge Rd
  Stratford Marsh
  E15..............................**27** B4
  Willesden NW10 ....**8** A2
Bridge Sch The
  Clerkenwell EC1........**96** A2
  ❷ Shoreditch N1 .....**87** A4
Bridges Ct SW11 . **167** B1
Bridges Ho ❻ SE5 ..**48** C3
Bridge St
  Chiswick W4...............**37** C2
  Westminster SW1 .. **134** B3
Bridge Terr E15 ......**19** C1
Bridgeview ❷ W6...**39** B1
Bridgewater Rd
  E15..............................**27** C4
Bridgewater Sq
  EC2.............................**108** C4
Bridgewater St
  EC2.............................**108** C4
Bridgeway St NW1 **83** A1
Bridge Wharf ⓲
  E2................................**25** C3
Bridge Yd SE1 .... **123** C2
Bridgford St SW17,
  SW18............................**71** B1
Bridgman Rd W4 ....**37** B3
Bridgnorth Ho ❶
  SE15............................**49** C4
Bridgwater Ho
  W2..............................**100** C2
Bridle La W1 .... **119** A4
Bridlington Ho ❶
  SW18............................**59** B3
Bridport SE17 ...... **151** A1
Bridport Ho N1 ......**87** C3
Bridport Pl N1 ....**87** C3
Bridstow Pl ❼ W2 ..**31** C3
Brief St SE5 ....**48** A2
Brierfield NW1 ....**82** C3
Brierley Rd
  Leyton E11.................**19** C4
  Upper Tooting
  SW12............................**73** B2
Brierly Gdns ❷ E2 ..**25** B3
Brigade St SE3 ....**53** B1
Briggeford Cl ❺
  E5..................................**7** C2
Briggs Ho
  E2................**24** B2 **99** A4
Brightling Rd SE4 ..**66** B1
Brightlingsea Pl ❺
  E14..............................**33** B2
Brightman Rd
  SW18............................**71** C3

Brighton Bldgs
  SE1.............................**138** A1
Brighton Ct SW15 ..**58** B1
Brighton Gr SE14 ...**51** A2
Brighton Ho ❼
  SE5..............................**48** C2
Brighton Rd N16 ....**16** A4
Brighton Terr
  SW9..............................**62** B3
Brightside The
  SE13..............................**67** C1
Bright St E14..........**34** A4
Brightwell Ct N7 ....**14** B3
Brightwells Rd SW6 **166** A2
Brig Mews SE8 ....**51** C4
Brigstock Ho SE5....**48** B1
Brill Pl NW1............**83** C1
Brimsdown Ho ❸ E3 **27** B1
Brindley Ho
  ❽ Notting Hill W2 ...**31** C4
  ❷ Streatham
  SW12............................**74** A4
Brindley St SE14 ....**51** B2
Brine Ho ❶ E3 ....**26** A3
Brinklow Ho W2 ... **100** A3
Brinkworth Way
  E9................................**18** B2
Brinsley Ho ❼ E1 ...**32** B3
Brinsley St ❷ E1 ....**32** A3
Brinton Wlk SE1 .. **122** A1
Brion Pl E14 ....**34** B4
Brisbane Ho ❸
  W12..............................**30** A2
Brisbane St SE5 .....**48** C3
Briset St EC1 ....**96** A1
Briset Way N7...........**5** B2
Bristol Gdns
  Putney SW15 ....**69** B4
  Westbourne Green
  W9................................**88** B1
Bristol Ho SE11 ... **135** B1
Bristol Mews W9....**88** B1
Bristowe Cl ⓴
  SW2..............................**62** C1
Britain at War
  Experience *
  SE1.............................**124** A1
Britannia Building
  N1................................**97** B4
Britannia Cl SW4 ...**61** C3
Britannia Gate ⓫
  E16..............................**35** C1
Britannia Junc
  NW1..............................**82** B4
Britannia Rd
  ⓳ Millwall E14.........**41** C2
  Walham Green
  SW6...........................**156** A1
Britannia Row N1 ...**86** C4
Britannia St WC1....**94** C4
Britannia Way
  NW10............................**20** A1
Britannia Wlk N1.....**97** B4
British Coll of
  Osteopathic
  Medicine NW3.........**11** B2
British Gr W4 ....**38** B1
British Grove Pas ❷
  W4................................**38** B1
British Grove S ❸
  W4................................**38** B1
British Library The *
  WC1..............................**93** C4
British Mus *
  WC1.............................**106** A3
British St E3 ....**26** B2

British Wharf Ind Est
  SE14............................**50** C4
Britley Ho ⓰ E14...**33** B3
Brittany Ho SW15 ...**57** B3
Brittany Point
  SE11...........................**149** B3
Britten Cl NW11.......**2** A3
Britten Ho SW3 ... **144** B2
Britten St SW3 .... **144** A2
Britton St EC1 ....**96** A1
BRIXTON **62** C4
Brixton Day Coll
  SW9..............................**62** A4
Brixton Hill SW2 .....**62** B1
Brixton Hill Ct ❺
  SW2..............................**62** B2
Brixton Hill Pl
  SW2..............................**74** A4
Brixton Mkt SW9 ...**62** C3
Brixton Oval ❼
  SW2..............................**62** C3
Brixton Rd SW9 ... **173** B2
Brixton Sta SW9 ....**62** C3
Brixton Station Rd
  SW9..............................**62** C4
Brixton Water La
  SW2..............................**62** B2
Broadbent Cl N6......**4** A3
Broadbent St W1 . **118** A4
Broadbridge Cl
  SE3..............................**53** C3
Broad Common Est
  N16..............................**16** C3
Broad Ct WC2 ...... **106** B1
Broadfield NW6 .....**11** A2
Broadfield La
  NW1..............................**14** A1
Broadfields Way
  NW10............................**8** B3
Broadford Ho ⓲
  E1................................**26** A1
BROADGATE **110** A4
Broadgate EC2 .... **110** A4
Broadgate Circ
  EC2.............................**110** A3
Broadgates Ct
  SE11...........................**149** C1
Broadgates Rd
  SW18............................**71** C3
Broadhinton Rd
  SW4..............................**61** B4
Broadhurst Cl
  Hampstead NW6 .....**11** B2
  ❸ Richmond TW10 .**54** B2
Broadhurst Gdns
  NW6..............................**11** A2
Broadhurst Mans
  NW6..............................**11** A2
Broad La EC2 .... **110** A4
Broadlands N6 ....**3** C4
Broadlands Ave
  SW16............................**74** A2
Broadlands Cl
  Highgate N6 ....**3** C4
  Streatham SW16 .....**74** A2
Broadlands Ct
  TW9...............................**44** C3
Broadlands Lo N6 ....**3** B4
Broadlands Mans ❷
  SW16............................**74** B1
Broadlands Rd N6 ....**3** B4
Broadley St NW8 .. **102** A4
Broadley Terr
  NW1..............................**90** B1
Broadmayne
  SE17...........................**151** B2
Broadmead W14 .. **140** A3

Broadoak Ct 8
  SW9 . . . . 62 C4
Broadoak Ho NW6 . 78 B3
Broad St Ave EC2 . 110 A3
Broad Sanctuary
  SW1 . . . . 134 A3
Broadstone Ho
  SW8 . . . . 162 C1
Broadstone Pl
  W1 . . . . 103 B3
Broad Street Pl
  EC2 . . . . 109 C3
Broadwalk Ho
  SW7 . . . . 128 C3
Broadwalk La
  NW11 . . . . 1 B4
Broadwall SE1 . . 121 C2
Broadway
  Stratford E15 . . . . 19 C1
  Westminster SW1 . 133 B2
Broadway Arc 3
  W6 . . . . 39 B2
Broadway Ctr The 6
  W6 . . . . 39 B2
Broadway Ho 2
  E8 . . . . 25 A4
Broadway Mans
  SW6 . . . . 155 C1
Broadway Market
  E8 . . . . 25 A4
Broadway Market
  Mews 1 E8 . . . . 24 C4
Broadway Mews 5 . 7 B4
Broadway Ret Pk
  NW2 . . . . 9 C4
Broadway The
  Barnes SW13 . . . . 46 A1
  South Acton W3 . . . 36 C4
Broadway Wlk 1
  E14 . . . . 41 C3
Broadwick St W1 . 105 A1
Broad Wlk
  Mayfair W1 . . . . . 117 B2
  Regent's Pk NW1 . . 81 C1
  Richmond TW9 . . . 44 B3
Broad Wlk The
  W8 . . . . 114 B1
Broadwood Terr
  W14 . . . . 141 A4
Broad Yd EC1 . . . 96 A1
Brocas Cl NW3 . . . 12 A1
Brockbridge Ho
  SW15 . . . . 56 B1
Brocket Ho 1 SW8 . 171 B2
Brockham Dr SW2 . 74 B4
Brockham Ho
  Camden Town
  NW1 . . . . 82 C4
  11 Streatham SW2 . 74 B4
Brockham St SE1 . 137 A2
Brockhurst Ho N4 . 6 C4
Brockill Cres SE4 . 66 A3
Brocklebank Rd
  SW18 . . . . 71 A4
Brocklebank Road Ind
  Est SE7 . . . . . . 43 C2
Brocklehurst St
  SE14 . . . . 50 C3
BROCKLEY 66 B3
Brockley Cross
  SE4 . . . . 66 B4
Brockley Cross Bsns
  Ctr SE4 . . . . . . 66 A4
Brockley Gdns
  SE4 . . . . 51 B1
Brockley Gr SE4 . . 66 B2

Brockley Hall Rd
  SE4 . . . . 66 A2
Brockley Ho SE17 . 152 A2
Brockley Mews
  SE4 . . . . 66 A2
Brockley Prim Sch
  SE4 . . . . 66 B2
Brockley Rd SE4 . 153 A2
Brockley Sta SE4 . 66 A4
Brockley Way SE4 . 66 A2
Brockmer Ho 5
  E1 . . . . 32 A2
Brock Pl E3 . . . . 27 A1
Brock St SE15 . . . 65 B4
Brockweir 2 E2 . . 25 B3
Brockwell Ct 2
  SW2 . . . . 62 C2
Brockwell Ho
  SE11 . . . . 163 A4
Brockwell Park★
  SE24 . . . . 63 A1
Brockwell Park Gdns
  SE24 . . . . 75 A4
Brockwell Park Row
  SW2 . . . . 62 C1
Broderick St
  SE21 . . . . 76 A1
Brodia Rd N16 . . . 7 A1
Brodick Ho 12 E3 . 26 B3
Brodie Ho 1
  SE1 . . . . 153 A2
Brodie St SE1 . . . 153 A2
Brodlove La E1 . . 32 C2
Brodrick Rd SW17 . 72 A2
Brody Ho E1 . . . 110 C3
Broken Wharf
  EC4 . . . . 122 C4
Brokesley St E3 . . 26 B2
Broke Wlk
  Hackney E8 . . . . . 24 B4
  1 Hackney E8 . . . 24 C4
Bromar Rd SE5 . . 64 A4
Bromehead St 8
  E1 . . . . 32 B3
Bromell's Rd SW4 . 61 B3
Bromfelde Rd
  SW4 . . . . 171 C1
Bromfield Ct
  SE16 . . . . 139 C2
Bromfield St N1 . . 85 C2
Bromleigh Ho
  SE1 . . . . 138 C2
BROMLEY 27 A2
Bromley-by-Bow Sta
  E3 . . . . 98 A3
Bromley Hall Rd
  E14 . . . . 34 B4
Bromley High St
  E3 . . . . 27 A2
Bromley Lo 2 W3 . 28 B3
Bromley Pl W1 . . 104 C4
Bromley St E1 . . . 32 C3
BROMPTON 130 A1
Brompton Arc
  SW1 . . . . 131 A3
Brompton Oratory
  SW3 . . . . 130 A1
Brompton Park Cres
  SW6 . . . . 156 A3
Brompton Pl
  SW3 . . . . 130 B2
Brompton Rd
  SW3 . . . . 130 A1
Brompton Sq
  SW3 . . . . 130 A2
Bromstone Ho
  SW9 . . . . 173 B3
Bromwich Ave N6 . 3 C2

Bromwich Ho 3
  TW10 . . . . 54 A1
Bromyard Ave W3 . 29 A2
Bromyard Ho
  Acton W3 . . . . . . 29 A1
  3 Peckham SE15 . 50 A3
Bron Ct NW6 . . . 23 C4
BRONDESBURY . . 10 A1
Brondesbury Coll for
  Boys NW6 . . . . . 10 B2
Brondesbury Ct
  NW2 . . . . 9 C2
Brondesbury Mews 1
  NW6 . . . . 10 C1
BRONDESBURY PARK
  . . . . 22 C4
Brondesbury Park Sta
  NW6 . . . . 23 A4
Brondesbury Pk
  NW2 . . . . 9 C1
Brondesbury Rd
  NW6 . . . . 23 C3
Brondesbury Sta
  NW6 . . . . 10 B1
Brondesbury Villas
  NW6 . . . . 23 C3
Bronsart Rd SW6 . 154 A1
Bronte Ct 3 W14 . 39 C3
Bronte Ho
  Kilburn NW6 . . . . . 23 C2
  2 Stoke Newington
  N16 . . . . 16 A3
Bronti Cl SE17 . . 151 A2
Bronwen Ct NW8 . 89 B3
Bronze St SE8 . . . 51 C3
Brookbank Rd
  SE13 . . . . 67 A4
Brook Cl SW17 . . 72 C2
Brook Com Prim Sch
  E8 . . . . 16 C3
Brook Ct
  Mortlake SW14 . . 56 A4
  Stratford New Town
  E15 . . . . 19 B3
Brookdale Rd SE6 . 67 A1
Brook Dr SE11 . . 150 A4
Brooke Ct W10 . . 23 A2
Brooke Ho 6
  SE14 . . . . 51 A2
Brooke Rd E5, N16 . 7 C1
Brookes Ct EC1 . . 107 B4
Brooke's Mkt EC1 . 107 B4
Brooke St EC1 . . 107 B3
Brookfield
  Dartmouth Pk N6 . 3 C1
  1 Finsbury Pk N4 . 5 C2
Brookfield Ho 23
  E2 . . . . 25 A3
Brookfield Pk NW5 . 4 A1
Brookfield Prim Sch
  N19 . . . . 4 A2
Brookfield Rd
  Acton W4 . . . . . . 37 C4
  Homerton E9 . . . . 18 A2
Brookgate N16 . . . 6 C2
Brook Gate W1 . . 117 B3
Brook Gdns SW13 . 56 A4
Brook Gn W6 . . . 39 C2
BROOK GREEN . . 39 C2
Brook Green Flats 11
  W14 . . . . 39 C3
Brook Ho
  3 Clapham Pk
  SW4 . . . . 61 B3
  Ealing W3 . . . . . 36 C4
  4 Hammersmith
  W6 . . . . 39 B2

Brook Ho continued
  Marylebone WC1 . 105 B4
Brook Hos NW1 . . 83 A1
Brooklands Ave
  SW18 . . . . 71 A2
Brooklands Court
  Apartments 1
  NW6 . . . . 10 B1
Brooklands Ct 2
  NW6 . . . . 10 B1
Brooklyn Ct W12 . 30 B1
Brookmarsh Ind Est
  SE10 . . . . 52 A3
Brook Mews N
  W2 . . . . 115 A4
Brookmill Rd SE8 . 51 C2
Brooksbank Ho 7
  E9 . . . . 17 B2
Brooksbank St 9
  E9 . . . . 17 B2
Brooksby Ho 9
  N1 . . . . 14 C1
Brooksby Mews
  N1 . . . . 14 C1
Brooksby St N1 . . 14 C1
Brooksby's Wlk
  E9 . . . . 17 C3
Brooks Ct
  London SW4 . . . . 172 A2
  Nine Elms SW8 . . 161 A2
Brooks Ho 6
  SW2 . . . . 74 C3
Brookside Rd N19 . 4 B2
Brooks La W4 . . . 44 C4
Brook's Mews
  W1 . . . . 118 A4
Brooks Rd W4 . . . 36 C1
Brook St
  Bayswater W2 . . 115 A4
  Mayfair W1 . . . . 118 A4
Brookstone Ct
  SE15 . . . . 65 A3
Brooksville Ave
  NW6 . . . . 23 A4
Brookville Rd
  SW6 . . . . 154 C1
Brookwood Ave
  SW13 . . . . 46 B1
Brookwood Ho
  SE1 . . . . 136 B3
Brookwood Rd
  SW18 . . . . 70 C3
Broome Ct 3
  TW9 . . . . 44 C2
Broome Ho 7 E5 . 17 A3
Broome Way SE5 . 48 C3
Broom Farm SW6 . 165 C2
Broomfield 7
  NW1 . . . . 12 C1
Broomfield Ho
  SE17 . . . . 152 A3
Broomfield House
  Sch TW9 . . . . . 44 B2
Broomfield Rd
  TW9 . . . . 44 B2
Broomfield St E14 . 34 A4
Broomgrove Rd
  SW9 . . . . 173 A1
Broomhill Rd
  SW18 . . . . 58 C2
Broomhouse La
  SW6 . . . . 58 C4
Broomhouse Rd
  SW6 . . . . 165 B2
Broomsleigh St
  NW6 . . . . 10 B3

Broomwood Hall Sch
  SW12 . . . . 72 C4
Broomwood Rd
  SW11 . . . . 60 C2
Brougham Rd
  Acton W3 . . . . . . 28 B3
  Hackney E8 . . . . . 24 C4
Brougham St
  SW11 . . . . 169 A2
Brough Cl SW8 . . 162 A2
Broughton Dr 10
  SW9 . . . . 63 A3
Broughton Rd
  SW6 . . . . 166 B2
Broughton Road App
  SW6 . . . . 166 A2
Broughton St
  SW8 . . . . 170 A2
Brouncker Rd W3 . 37 B4
Browne Ho 18 SE8 . 51 C3
Brownfield St E14 . 34 B3
Brownflete Ho
  SE4 . . . . 66 A3
Brown Hart Gdns
  W1 . . . . 117 C4
Browning Cl W9 . 89 A1
Browning Ct W14 . 154 C4
Browning Ho
  18 London SE14 . . 51 A2
  7 Shepherd's Bush
  W12 . . . . 30 B3
  10 Stoke Newington
  N16 . . . . 16 A4
Browning Mews
  W1 . . . . 103 C3
Browning St SE17 . 151 A3
Brownlow Ho
  SE16 . . . . 139 B3
Brownlow Mews
  WC1 . . . . 95 A1
Brownlow Rd
  Hackney E8 . . . . . 24 C4
  Willesden NW10 . . 8 A1
Brownlow St
  WC1 . . . . 107 A3
Brown's Bldgs
  EC3 . . . . 110 B1
Brown St W1 . . . 102 C2
Brownswood Rd
  N4 . . . . 6 B2
Broxash Rd SW11 . 60 C1
Broxbourne Ho 1
  E3 . . . . 27 A1
Broxholme Ho
  SW6 . . . . 166 A4
Broxholm Rd SE27,
  SW16 . . . . 74 C1
Broxwood Way
  NW8 . . . . 80 B3
Bruce Cl W10 . . . 30 C4
Bruce Glasier Ho 13
  N19 . . . . 4 C1
Bruce Ho
  4 Clapham Pk
  SW4 . . . . 61 C1
  North Kensington
  W10 . . . . 30 C4
  Putney SW15 . . . . 57 A2
Bruce Rd E3 . . . . 27 A2
Bruckner St W10 . 23 B2
Bruges Pl 16 NW1 . 13 B1
Brune Ho E1 . . . 110 C3
Brunel Ct 8 SW13 . 46 B1

Brunel Engine House Rotherhithe★
SE16 . . . . 40 B4
Brunel Est E2 . . . . 31 C4
Brunel Ho
Chelsea SW3 . . . . . **157** C2
 4 Gospel Oak
NW5 . . . . 13 A4
Millwall E14 . . . . 42 A1
New Cross SE8 . . . . . 51 B3
 25 Streatham SW2 . . 74 A4
Brunel Mews
NW10 . . . . 22 C2
Brunel Rd
Acton W3 . . . . 29 A4
Wapping SE16 . . . . . . 32 B1
Brunel St E16 . . . . 35 B3
Brune St E1 . . . . **110** C3
Brunlees Ho SE1 . . . . **137** A1
Bruno St **5** E8 . . . . 16 C2
Brunswick Ct
Bermondsey SE1 . . **138** B4
Finsbury EC1 . . . . . . **96** A3
Westminster SW1 . . **147** C3
Brunswick Gdns
W8 . . . . . . 31 C1 **113** C1
Brunswick Ho
 6 Haggerston E2 . . 24 B3
Lisson Gr NW1 . . . . **90** C2
Brunswick Mews
W1 . . . . **103** A2
Brunswick Park Prim Sch SE5 . . . . 49 A3
Brunswick Pk SE5 . . . . 49 A2
Brunswick Pl N1 . . . . . **97** C3
Brunswick Quay
SE16 . . . . 40 C3
Brunswick Rd E14 . . 34 B3
Brunswick Sh Ctr
WC1 . . . . **94** B2
Brunswick Sq
WC1 . . . . **94** B2
Brunswick Villas **2**
SE5 . . . . 49 A2
Brunton Pl **5** E14 . . . 33 A3
Brushfield St E1 . . . . **110** C4
Brussels Rd SW11 . . . . 59 C3
Bruton La W1 . . . . . . **118** B3
Bruton Pl W1 . . . . . . **118** B3
Bruton St W1 . . . . . . **118** B3
Brutus Ct SE11 . . . . . **150** A3
Bryan Ave NW10 . . . . . 9 A1
Bryan Ct W1 . . . . . . **102** C2
Bryan Ho SE16 . . . . . . 41 B4
Bryan Rd SE16 . . . . . . 41 B4
Bryanston Ct W1 . . . **102** C2
Bryanston Ho **12**
SE15 . . . . 49 B2
Bryanston Mans
W1 . . . . **102** C4
Bryanston Mews E
W1 . . . . **102** C3
Bryanston Mews W
W1 . . . . **102** C2
Bryanston Pl W1 . . . **102** C3
Bryanston Sq W1 . . . **102** C2
Bryanston St W1 . . . **103** A1
Bryant Ct
Acton W3 . . . . 28 C1
Haggerston E2 . . . . . 24 B3
Bryantwood Rd N5,
N7 . . . . 14 C3
Bryce Ho **5** SE14 . . 50 C4
Brydale Ho **2**
SE16 . . . . 40 C2

Brydges Pl WC2 . . . **120** A3
Brydges Rd E15 . . . . . 19 C3
Brydon Wlk N1 . . . . . **84** B4
Bryer Ct EC2 . . . . **108** C4
Bryett Rd N7 . . . . 5 A1
Bryher Ho W4 . . . . 37 B1
Brymay Cl E3 . . . . 26 C3
Brymon Ct W1 . . . . . **103** A3
Brynmaer Ho
SW11 . . . . **169** A3
Brynmaer Rd
SW11 . . . . **169** A3
Brynmawr Rd W12 . . 29 C2
BT Telecom Twr★
W1 . . . . **104** C3
Buccleuch Ho **5** E5 . . . . 7 C4
Buchanan Ct **16**
SE16 . . . . 40 C2
Buchanan Gdns
NW10 . . . . 22 A3
Buchanan Ho
Dulwich SE21 . . . . . 76 A1
Wandsworth SW18 . . 70 C4
Buchan Ho W3 . . . . . . 37 A4
Buchan Rd SE15 . . . . 65 B4
Bucharest Rd
SW18 . . . . 71 B4
Buckfast St
E2 . . . . 24 C2 **99** C3
Buck Hill Wlk W2 **115** C3
Buckhold Rd
SW18 . . . . 58 C1
Buckhurst Ho **15**
N7 . . . . 13 C3
Buckhurst St E1 . . . . . 25 A1
Buckingham Gate
SW1 . . . . **133** A2
Buckingham Ho
Finsbury Pk N4 . . . . . 6 B3
Richmond TW10 . . . . 54 C2
Buckingham Mans
NW6 . . . . 11 A3
Buckingham Mews
Harlesden NW10 . . . 21 B3
 7 Kingsland N1 . . . 16 A2
Westminster SW1 . . **132** C2
Buckingham Pal★
SW1 . . . . **132** C2
Buckingham Palace
Rd SW1 . . . . **146** B4
Buckingham Pl
SW1 . . . . **132** C2
Buckingham Rd
Harlesden NW10 . . . 21 B3
Kingsland N1 . . . . . . 16 A2
Buckingham St
WC2 . . . . **120** B3
Buckingham Yd
NW10 . . . . 21 B3
Buckland Cres
NW3 . . . . 11 C2
Buckland Ct **6**
N1 . . . . 24 A3
Buckland Ho **3**
N1 . . . . 14 C1
Buckland St N1 . . . . . **87** C1
Buckland Wlk **2**
W3 . . . . 37 B4
Buckler's Alley
SW6 . . . . **155** A2
Bucklersbury EC2,
EC4 . . . . **109** B1
Buckle St
Whitechapel E1 . . . **111** A2
Whitechapel E1 . . . **111** B2
Buckley Ct **5**
NW6 . . . . 10 B1

Buckley Rd NW6 . . . . 10 B1
Buckmaster Cl **1**
SW9 . . . . 62 C4
Buckmaster Ho **1**
N7 . . . . 14 B4
Buckmaster Rd
SW11 . . . . 60 A3
Bucknall St WC1 . . . **106** A2
Bucknell Cl SW2 . . . . 62 B3
Buckner Rd SW2 . . . . 62 B3
Buckridge Bldg
EC1 . . . . **107** B4
Buckshead Ho **10**
W2 . . . . 31 C4
Buck St NW1 . . . . 13 A1
Buckstone Cl
SE23 . . . . 65 B1
Buckters Rents
SE16 . . . . 33 A1
Buckthorne Rd
SE4 . . . . 66 A2
Budge Row EC4 . . . **109** B1
Budge's Wlk W2 . . **115** A2
Budleigh Ho **18**
SE15 . . . . 49 C3
Buer Rd SW6 . . . . . . **164** B1
Bugsby's Way
SE10 . . . . 43 B2
Buick Ho **4** E3 . . . . . 26 C1
Bulbarrow NW8 . . . . . 78 B3
Bulinca St **1**
SW1 . . . . **147** C3
Bullace Row SE5 . . . . 48 C2
Bullards Pl **8** E2 . . . 25 C2
Bulleid Way SW1 . . **146** B3
Bullen Ho **18** E1 . . . 25 A1
Bullen St SW11 . . . . **168** B2
Buller Cl SE15 . . . . . . 49 C3
Buller Rd NW10 . . . . 22 C2
Bullfinch Ct **1**
SE21 . . . . 75 C2
Bullingham Mans
W8 . . . . **127** C4
Bull Inn Ct WC2 . . . **120** B3
Bullivant St **9**
E14 . . . . 34 B2
Bulls Gdns SW3 . . . **144** B4
Bull's Head Pas
EC3 . . . . **110** A1
Bull Yd SE15 . . . . 49 C2
Bulmer Mews
W11 . . . . . . 31 C1 **113** B2
Bulow Ct SW6 . . . . . **166** B2
Bulstrode Pl W1 . . . **103** C3
Bulstrode St W1 . . . **103** C2
Bulwer St W12 . . . . . 30 B1
Bunbury Ho SE15 . . . 49 C3
Bunhill Row EC1 . . . **97** B1
Bunhouse Pl SW1 . . **145** C2
Bunkers Hill NW11 . . 2 A4
Bunning Ho **7** N7 . . . 14 A4
Bunning Way **7** N7 . 14 B1
Bunsen Ho **2** E3 . . . 26 A3
Bunsen St **3** E3 . . . 26 A3
Bunyan Ct EC2 . . . . **108** C4
Buonaparte Mews
SW1 . . . . **147** B2
Burbage Cl SE1 . . . . **137** B1
Burbage Ho
 16 Deptford SE14 . . 50 C4
Shoreditch N1 . . . . . **87** C3
Burbage Rd SE21,
SE24 . . . . 75 C4
Burbage Sch N1 . . . . 24 A3
Burcham St E14 . . . . 34 B3
Burchell Ho SE11 . . **149** A2
Burchell Rd SE15 . . . 50 A2

Burcher Gale Gr **5**
SE15 . . . . 49 B3
Burcote Rd SW18 . . . 71 C4
Burden Ho SW8 . . . **162** A1
Burdenshott Ave
TW10 . . . . 55 A3
Burder Cl N1 . . . . 16 A2
Burder Rd N1 . . . . . . 16 A2
Burdett Coutts &
Townshend CE Prim
Sch SW1 . . . . **147** C3
Burdett Mews
W2 . . . . **100** A2
Burdett Rd
Richmond TW9 . . . . . 54 B4
Tower Hamlets E3 . . 33 B4
Burdon Ct **3** E8 . . . 16 C2
Burford Cl SE8 . . . . . **51** C4
Burford Ho
 1 Brentford TW8 . . 36 A1
South Lambeth
SW9 . . . . **173** A1
Burford Rd
Brentford TW8 . . . . . 36 A1
 5 Stratford Marsh
E15 . . . . 27 C4
Burford Wlk SW6 . **156** B1
Burgate Ct **9**
SW9 . . . . 62 C4
Burges Gr SW13 . . . . 47 A3
Burgess Hill NW2 . . . 10 C4
Burgess Ho **5**
SE5 . . . . 48 B3
Burgess Ind Pk
SE5 . . . . 48 C3
Burgess Park Mans
NW6 . . . . 10 C4
Burgess St E14 . . . . . 33 C4
Burge St SE1 . . . . . . **137** C1
Burghley Hall Cl
SW19 . . . . 70 A3
Burghley Ho
SW19 . . . . 70 A1
Burghley Rd NW5 . . 13 A4
Burghley Twr W3 . . . 29 B2
Burgh St N1 . . . . **86** B2
Burgon St EC4 . . . . **108** B1
Burgos Gr SE10 . . . . . 52 A2
Burgoyne Rd SW9 . . 62 B4
Burhan Uddin Ho
E1 . . . . 24 B1 **98** C1
Buriton Ho **9**
SW15 . . . . 69 A3
Burke Cl SW15 . . . . . 56 A3
Burke Ho **1** SW11 . . 59 C3
Burke St E16 . . . . 35 B4
Burland Rd SW11 . . . 60 B2
Burleigh Ho
Chelsea SW3 . . . . . **157** C3
North Kensington
W10 . . . . 30 C4
Burleigh Pl SW15 . . . 57 C2
Burleigh St WC2 . . . **120** C4
Burley Ho E1 . . . . 32 C3
Burlington Arc
W1 . . . . **118** C3
Burlington Ave
TW9 . . . . 44 C2
Burlington Cl W9 . . . 23 C1
Burlington Ct
Chiswick W4 . . . . . . 45 B3
Highgate N6 . . . . 3 C3
Burlington Danes Sch
W12 . . . . 30 A3
Burlington Gdns
Acton Green W4 . . . 37 B1
Acton W3 . . . . 28 B1

Burlington Gdns
continued
Fulham SW6 . . . . . **164** B1
Marylebone W1 . . . **118** C3
Burlington Ho
NW3 . . . . 11 C3
Burlington La W4 . . . 45 C3
Burlington Mews
Acton W3 . . . . 28 B1
 2 Putney SW15 . . **58** B2
Burlington Pl
SW6 . . . . **164** B1
Burlington Rd
Acton Green W4 . . . 37 B1
Fulham SW6 . . . . . **164** B1
Burma Rd N16 . . . . . 15 C4
Burmarsh **6** NW5 . . 12 C2
Burmester Ho
SW17 . . . . 71 B1
Burmester Rd
SW17 . . . . 71 B1
Burnaby Cres **4** W4 . 45 B4
Burnaby Ct SE16 . . **139** C3
Burnaby Gdns W4 . . 45 A4
Burnaby St SW10 . . **157** A1
Burnand Ho **3**
W14 . . . . 39 C3
Burnbury Rd
SW12 . . . . 73 B3
Burne Jones Ho
W14 . . . . **140** B3
Burnell Ho **3**
SW2 . . . . 74 C3
Burnell Wlk SE1 . . . **153** A2
Burness Cl N7 . . . . . 14 B2
Burne St NW1 . . . . . **102** A4
Burnett Cl E9 . . . . . . 17 B3
Burnett Ho **6**
SE13 . . . . 52 B1
Burnett St SE10 . . . . 52 B3
Burnfoot Ave
SW6 . . . . **164** B3
Burnham NW3 . . . . . 12 A1
Burnham Cl SE1 . . . **153** A3
Burnham Ct W2 . . . **114** B4
Burnham Est **8**
E2 . . . . 25 B2
Burnham St E2 . . . . . 25 B2
Burnhill Ho EC1 . . . . **96** C3
Burnley Rd
London SW9 . . . . . **172** C2
Willesden NW10 . . . . 8 B3
Burnsall St SW3 . . . **144** B2
Burns Ho
 16 Bethnal Green
E2 . . . . 25 B2
 4 Islington N7 . . . 14 B2
Kennington SE17 . . **150** B1
 11 Stoke Newington
N16 . . . . 15 B4
Burn's Ho NW10 . . . . 20 C4
Burnside Cl SE16 . . . 32 C1
Burns Rd SW11 . . . . **168** C2
Burn's Rd NW10 . . . . 21 B4
Burnthwaite Rd
SW6 . . . . **155** A1
Burntwood Cl
SW18 . . . . 72 A3
Burntwood Ct
SW17 . . . . 71 B1
Burntwood Grange Rd
SW18 . . . . 72 A3
Burntwood La
SW17 . . . . 71 C2
Burntwood Sch
SW17 . . . . 71 C1

Buross St E1 . . . . . . 32 A1
Burrage Ct 17
  SE16 . . . . 40 C2
Burrard Ho 11 E2 . . 25 B3
Burrard Rd SW6 . . . 10 C4
Burr Cl E1 . . . . . . 125 B2
Burrell St SE1 . . . . 122 A2
Burrell's Wharf Sq
  E14 . . . . 42 A1
Burrhill Ct SE16 . . . 40 C3
Burrow Ho SW9 . . . 173 A1
Burrow Rd SE22 . . . 64 A3
Burrows Mews
  SE1 . . . . 136 A4
Burrows Rd NW10 . . 22 B2
Burrow Wlk SE21 . . 75 B4
Burr Rd SW18 . . . . 70 C4
Bursar St SE1 . . . . 124 A1
Burslem St E1 . . . . 111 C1
Burstock Rd SW15 . . 58 A3
Burston Rd SW15 . . 57 C2
Burtley Ct N4 . . . . . 6 B3
Burton Bank N1 . . . 15 C1
Burton Ct SW3 . . . 145 A2
Burton Gr SE17 . . . 151 B1
Burton Ho
  8 Bermondsey
  SE16 . . . . 40 A4
  Brixton SE5 . . . . . 48 A2
Burton Lo 6
  SW15 . . . . 58 B2
Burton Pl WC1 . . . . 93 C3
Burton Rd
  Brixton SW9 . . . . . 48 A1
  Brixton SW9 . . . . 173 B2
  Brondesbury NW6 . 10 B1
Burtons Ct E15 . . . . 19 C1
Burton St WC1 . . . . 93 C2
Burtonwood Ho N4 . . 6 C4
Burtt Ho N1 . . 24 A2 98 A4
Burwash Ho SE1 . . 137 C3
Burwell Cl E1 . . . . . 32 A3
Burwell Wlk E3 . . . . 26 C1
Burwood Ho 11
  SW9 . . . . 63 A3
Burwood Pl W2 . . . 102 B2
Bury Cl SE16 . . . . . 32 C1
Bury Ct EC3 . . . . . 110 B2
Buryfield Ct
  SE8 . . . . 40 C2
Bury Pl WC1 . . . . . 106 B3
Bury St
  St James SW1 . . . 119 A2
  Whitechapel EC3 . . 110 B2
Bury Wlk SW3 . . . . 144 A2
Busbridge Ho 24
  E14 . . . . 33 C4
Busby Mews 5
  NW1 . . . . 13 C2
Busby Pl NW5 . . . . 13 C2
Bushbaby Cl SE1 . . 138 A1
Bushberry Rd E9 . . . 18 A2
Bush Cotts 12
  SW18 . . . . 58 C2
Bush Ct 7 W12 . . . . 39 C4
Bushell St SW2 . . . 74 B2
Bushey Down
  SW12 . . . . 73 A2
Bushey Hall SE5 . . . 48 B2
Bushey Hill Rd
  SE5 . . . . 49 B2
Bushfield Ho N5 . . . 15 B3
Bush Ind Est
  N19 . . . . 20 C1
Bush La EC4 . . . . . 123 B4

Bushnell Rd SW17 . . 73 A1
Bush Rd
  Bermondsey SE8 . . 40 C2
  Hackney E8 . . . . . 25 A4
  Richmond TW9 . . . 44 B4
Bushwood Dr
  SE1 . . . . 153 A3
Bushwood Rd
  TW9 . . . . 44 C4
Business Design Ctr*
  N1 . . . . 85 C3
Butcher Row E1 . . . 32 C3
Butchers Rd E16 . . . 35 C3
Bute Gdns W6 . . . . 39 C2
Bute House Prep Sch
  W6 . . . . 39 C2
Bute St SW7 . . . . . 143 B4
Bute Wlk 18 N1 . . . 15 C2
Butfield Ho 9 E9 . . . 17 B2
Butler Ho
  2 Bethnal Green
  E2 . . . . 25 B2
  5 Brixton SW9 . . . 48 A2
  11 Poplar E14 . . . 33 B3
Butler Pl SW1 . . . . 133 B2
Butler St 22 E2 . . . 25 B2
Butley Ct 8 E3 . . . . 26 A3
Butler's Wharf W
  SE1 . . . . 124 C1
Butterfield Cl 1
  N1 . . . . 40 A4
Butterfly Wlk 2
  SE5 . . . . 48 C2
Buttermere NW1 . . . 92 B4
Buttermere Cl
  Bermondsey SE1 . . 152 C3
  Leyton E11 . . . . . 19 C4
Buttermere Ct
  NW8 . . . . 79 B4
Buttermere Dr
  SW15 . . . . 58 A2
Buttermere Wlk 9
  E8 . . . . 16 B2
Butterwick W6 . . . . 39 B2
Butterworth Ct
  SW16 . . . . 74 A1
Buttesland St N1 . . . 97 C4
Buxhall Cres E9 . . . 18 B2
Buxted Rd
  Camberwell SE22 . . 64 A3
  Dalston E8 . . . . . . 16 B1
Buxton Ct N1 . . . . . 97 A4
Buxton Gdns W3 . . . 28 A2
Buxton Ho 3
  SW11 . . . . 59 C3
Buxton Rd
  Mortlake SW14 . . . 56 A4
  Upper Holloway N19 . 4 C3
  Willesden NW2 . . . . 9 A2
Buxton St
  E1 . . . . . . 24 B1 99 A1
Byam Shaw Sch of Art
  N19 . . . . 4 C2
Byam St SW6 . . . . 166 C1
Byards Ct SE16 . . . 40 C3
Byas Ho 3 E3 . . . . . 26 B2
Byefield Cl SE16 . . . 41 A4
Byelands Cl 12
  SE16 . . . . 32 C1
Bye The W3 . . . . . . 29 A3

Byeway The SW14 . . 55 B4
Byfeld Gdns SW13 . . 46 C2
Bygrove Prim Sch
  E14 . . . . 34 A3
Bygrove St E14 . . . . 34 A3
Byng Pl WC1 . . . . . 93 B1
Byng St E14 . . . . . . 41 C4
Byrne Ho 11 SW2 . . 62 B2
Byrne Rd SW12 . . . 73 A2
Byron Ct E24 . . . . . 24 C4
Byron Ct
  Chelsea SW3 . . . . 144 B3
  Dulwich SE21 . . . . 76 C3
  3 Hampstead NW6 . 11 B1
  Paddington W9 . . . 23 C1
  St Pancras WC1 . . 94 C2
Byron Mews
  Hampstead NW3 . . 12 A4
  2 Maida Vale W9 . . 23 C1
Byron St E14 . . . . . 34 B3
Bythorn St SW9 . . . 62 B3
Byward St EC3 . . . 124 B3
Bywater Pl SE16 . . . 33 A1
Bywater St SW3 . . . 144 C2
Bywell Pl W1 . . . . . 104 C3
Byworth Wlk N19 . . . 5 A3

C

Cabbell St NW1 . . . 102 A3
Cabinet Off SW1 . . 134 A4
Cabinet War Rooms &
  Churchill Mus*
  SW1 . . . . 133 C4
Cable Ho WC1 . . . . 95 B4
Cable Pl SE10 . . . . . 52 B2
Cable St E1 . . . . . . 32 A2
Cabot Ct SE16 . . . . 40 C3
Cabot Sq E14 . . . . . 33 C1
Cabul Rd SW11 . . . 168 B1
Cactus Cl SE5 . . . . 49 A1
Cactus Wlk W12 . . . 29 B3
Cadbury Way
  SE1 . . . . 153 A4
Caddington Rd
  NW2 . . . . 1 A1
Cadell Cl E2 . . . . . . 24 B3
Cadell Ho 12 E2 . . . 24 B3
Cade Rd SE10 . . . . . 52 C2
Cader Rd SW18 . . . . 59 B1
Cadet Dr SE1 . . . . . 153 A2
Cade Tyler Ho 10
  SE10 . . . . 52 B2
Cadiz St SE17 . . . . 151 A1
Cadman Cl SW9 . . . 48 A3
Cadmore Ho 4
  N1 . . . . 15 A1
Cadmus Cl 9
  SW4 . . . . 61 C4
Cadmus Ct 3
  SW9 . . . . 173 B4
Cadnam Point 15
  SW15 . . . . 69 A3
Cadogan Cl E9 . . . . 18 B1
Cadogan Ct SW3 . . 144 C3
Cadogan Ct Gdns
  SW1 . . . . 145 B4
Cadogan Gate
  SW1 . . . . 145 A4
Cadogan Gdns
  SW3 . . . . 145 A3
Cadogan Ho SW3 . . 157 C3
Cadogan La SW1 . . 131 B1
Cadogan Pl SW1 . . 131 A1
Cadogan Sq SW1 . . 131 A1
Cadogan St SW3 . . 144 C3

Cadogan Terr E9 . . . 18 B1
Caedmon Rd N7 . . . 14 B4
Caernarvon Ho
  W2 . . . . 100 C2
Caesar Ct 2 E2 . . . . 25 C3
Cahill St EC1 . . . . . 97 A1
Cahir St E14 . . . . . . 42 A2
Caine Ho 9 . . . . 37 A4
Caird St W10 . . . . . 23 B2
Cairns Ho 3 N7 . . . . 14 B4
Cairns Rd SW11 . . . 60 A2
Caister Ho N7 . . . . . 14 B2
Caister Ho
  SW12 . . . . 73 A4
Caistor Mews
  SW12 . . . . 73 A4
Caistor Rd SW12 . . . 73 A4
Caithness Ho N1 . . . 84 C4
Caithness Rd W14 . . 39 C3
Calabria Rd N5 . . . . 15 A3
Calais Gate SE5 . . . 48 A2
Calais St SE5 . . . . . 48 A2
Calbourne Rd
  SW12 . . . . 72 C4
Calcraft Ho 2 E2 . . . 25 B3
Caldecot Ct SE5 . . . 48 B1
Caldecot Rd SE5 . . . 48 B1
Calder Ct SE16 . . . . 33 B1
Calderon Ho 8
  NW8 . . . . 80 A2
Calderon Pl 20
  W10 . . . . 30 B4
Caldervale Rd
  SW4 . . . . 61 C2
Caldew St SE5 . . . . 48 C3
Caldwell St SW9 . . . 163 A1
Caldy Rd 18 N1 . . . . 15 C2
Caleb St SE1 . . . . . 137 A4
Caledonia Ho 13
  E14 . . . . 33 A3
Caledonian Market
  SE1 . . . . 138 B2
Caledonian Rd
  Islington N1 . . . . . 84 C3
  Lower Holloway N7 . 14 B2
Caledonian Road &
  Barnsbury Sta
  N7 . . . . 14 B1
Caledonian Road Sta
  N7 . . . . 14 B2
Caledonian Sq 6
  NW1 . . . . 13 C2
Caledonian Wharf Rd
  E14 . . . . 42 C2
Caledonia St N1 . . . 84 B1
Cale St SW3 . . . . . 144 A2
Caletock Way
  SE10 . . . . 43 B1
Calgarth NW1 . . . . . 83 A1
Calgary Ct 30
  SE16 . . . . 40 B4
Caliban Twr 9
  N1 . . . . 24 A3
Calico Ho 15
  SW11 . . . . 59 B4
Calico Row 5
  SW11 . . . . 59 B4
Calidore Cl SW2 . . . 62 B1
California Bldg 2
  SE13 . . . . 52 A2
Callaby Terr 11
  N1 . . . . 15 C2
Callahan Cotts 3
  E1 . . . . 32 B4
Callan Sch The
  W1 . . . . 105 A2
Callcott Ct NW6 . . . 10 B1
Callcott Rd NW6 . . . 10 B1

Callcott St
  W8 . . . . . . 31 C1 113 B2
Callendar Rd
  SW7 . . . . 129 B2
Callingham Cl 13
  E14 . . . . 33 B4
Callingham Ho 1
  SW4 . . . . 62 A4
Callow St SW3 . . . . 157 B3
Calmington Rd
  SE5 . . . . 49 A4
Calshot Ho N1 . . . . 84 C2
Calshot St N1 . . . . . 84 C1
Calstock NW1 . . . . . 83 B1
Calstock Ho SE11 . . 149 C2
Calthorpe St WC1 . . 95 A3
Calton Ave SE21 . . . 64 A4
Calver 13 NW5 . . . . 13 A4
Calverley Gr N19 . . . 4 C3
Calvert Ave
  E2 . . . . . . 24 B2 98 C3
Calvert Ct
  1 London N19 . . . . 4 B3
  5 Richmond TW9 . . 54 B3
Calvert Ho 9
  W12 . . . . 30 A2
Calverton SE5 . . . . 49 A4
Calvert Rd SE10 . . . 43 B1
Calvert's Bldgs
  SE1 . . . . 123 B1
Calvert St NW1 . . . . 81 B4
Calvin St E1 . . 24 B1 98 C1
Calypso Cres 6
  SE15 . . . . 49 B3
Calypso Way SE8,
  SE16 . . . . 41 B3
Cambalt Ho 3
  SW15 . . . . 57 C2
Cambalt Rd SW15 . . 57 C2
Cambay Ho 7 E1 . . . 26 A1
Camber Ho 4
  SE15 . . . . 50 B4
Camberley Ho
  NW1 . . . . 82 B1
CAMBERWELL 48 B2
Camberwell Bsns Ctr
  SE5 . . . . 48 C3
Camberwell Church
  St SE5 . . . . 48 C2
Camberwell Coll of
  Arts
  Camberwell SE5 . . 49 A2
  Camberwell SE15 . . 49 A3
Camberwell Glebe
  SE5 . . . . 49 A2
Camberwell Gn
  SE5 . . . . 48 C2
Camberwell Gr
  SE5 . . . . 49 A1
Camberwell Green
  SE5 . . . . 48 B2
Camberwell New Rd
  SW9 . . . . 48 A3
Camberwell Rd
  SE5 . . . . 48 B3
Camberwell Station
  Rd SE5 . . . . 48 B2
Camberwell Trad Est
  SE5 . . . . 48 B2
Camborne Rd
  SW18 . . . . 70 C4
Cambourne Mews 2
  W11 . . . . 31 A3
Cambray Rd SW12 . . 73 B3

Cambria Ho 14
E14 . . . . .33 A3
Cambria Lo 3
SW15 . . . . .78 B2
Cambrian Cl SE27 . .75 A1
Cambrian Rd
TW10 . . . . .54 B1
Cambria Rd SE5 . . . .63 B4
Cambria St SW6 . .156 B1
Cambridge Ave
NW6 . . . . .23 C3
Cambridge Cir
WC2 . . . . .105 C1
Cambridge Cotts
TW9 . . . . .44 C4
Cambridge Cres 20
E2 . . . . .25 A3
Cambridge Ct
20 Bethnal Green
E2 . . . . .25 A3
7 Hammersmith
W6 . . . . .39 B2
2 Kilburn NW6 . . . .23 C3
Marylebone W2 . .102 A3
Stamford Hill N16. .7 A4
Cambridge Gate
NW1 . . . . .92 A2
Cambridge Gate
Mews NW1 . . . . . . .92 B2
Cambridge Gdns
Kilburn NW6 . . . . . .23 C3
North Kensington
W10 . . . . .31 A3
Cambridge Gr W6. .39 A2
Cambridge Heath Rd
E1, E2 . . . . .25 A2
Cambridge Heath Sta
E2 . . . . .25 A3
Cambridge Ho
SW6 . . . . .58 A4
Cambridge Mans
SW11 . . . . .168 C3
Cambridge Pas 9
E9 . . . . .17 B1
Cambridge Pl W8 .128 B3
Cambridge Rd
Barnes SW13 . . . . . .46 B1
Battersea SW11 . . .168 C3
Kilburn NW6 . . . . . .23 C2
Kilburn NW6 . . . . . .23 C3
Richmond TW9 . . . .44 C3
Cambridge Rd N
W4 . . . . .37 A1
Cambridge Rd S 3
W4 . . . . .37 A1
Cambridge Sch
W6 . . . . .39 A2
Cambridge Sq
W2 . . . . .102 A2
Cambridge St
SW1 . . . . .146 C2
Cambridge Terr
NW1 . . . . .92 A3
Cambridge Terr Mews
NW1 . . . . .92 B3
Cambus Rd E16 . . . .35 C4
Cam Ct 2 SE15 . . .49 B4
Camden Coll of
English NW1 . . . . . .12 C1
Camden Gdns
NW1 . . . . .13 A1
Camden High St
NW1 . . . . .82 C3
Camden Ho 6
SE8 . . . . .41 B1

Camdenhurst St
E14 . . . . .33 A3
Camden Lock Pl
NW1 . . . . .13 A1
Camden Mews
NW1 . . . . .13 C2
Camden Mkt *
NW1 . . . . .82 B4
Camden Park Rd
NW1 . . . . .13 C2
Camden Pas N1. . . .86 A3
Camden Rd NW1 . . .82 B4
Camden Road Sta
NW1 . . . . .13 B1
Camden Row SE3 . .53 A1
Camden Sch for Girls
The NW5. . . . . .13 B2
Camden Sq NW1 . . .13 C2
Camden St NW1. . . .83 A3
Camden Studios
NW1 . . . . .83 A3
Camden Terr 17
NW1 . . . . .13 C2
CAMDEN TOWN . . .13 A1
Camden Town Sta
NW1 . . . . .82 B4
Camden Wlk N1 . . . .86 A3
Cameford Ct 20
SW12 . . . . .74 A4
Camelford Ct 15
W11 . . . . .31 A3
Camelford Ho
SE1 . . . . .148 B1
Camelford Wlk 13
W11 . . . . .31 A3
Camellia Ho SE8 . . .51 B3
Camellia St SW8 . .162 A1
Camelot Ho 19
NW1 . . . . .13 C2
Camera Prim Sch
SE15 . . . . .49 C2
Camera Pl SW10 . .157 B4
Cameret Ct 6
W11 . . . . .39 C4
Cameron Ct 3
SW19 . . . . .70 A3
Cameron Ho
Camberwell SE5. . . .48 B3
St John's Wood
NW8 . . . . .80 A2
Cameron House Sch
SW10 . . . . .157 C4
Cameron Pl SW16 . .74 C2
Camerton Cl 8
E8 . . . . .16 B2
Camilla Rd SE16. . . .40 A2
Camlet St
E2 . . . . .24 B1 98 C2
Camley St NW1 . . . .83 C2
Camomile St EC3 .110 B2
Campaign Ct W9 . . .23 C1
Campana Rd SW6 .165 C4
Campbell Ct
Dulwich SE21 . . . . . .76 C3
South Kensington
SW7 . . . . .128 C1
Campbell Gordon
Way NW2 . . . . .9 A4
Campbell Ho
Paddington W2 . . . .89 B1
1 Shepherd's Bush
W12 . . . . .30 A2
Campbell Rd E3 . . . .26 C2
Campbell Wlk N1 . . .84 B4
Campdale Rd N7. . . .4 C1

Campden Gr W8 . .127 C4
Campden Hill W8 . .127 B4
Campden Hill Ct
W8 . . . . .127 C4
Campden Hill Gate
W8 . . . . .127 B4
Campden Hill Gdns
W8 . . . . .31 C1 113 C2
Campden Hill Mans
W8 . . . . .31 C1 113 C2
Campden Hill Pl 7
W14 . . . . .31 B1 113 A2
Campden Hill Rd
W8 . . . . .127 B4
Campden Hill Sq
W14 . . . . .31 B1 113 A2
Campden Ho 4
NW6 . . . . .11 C1
Campden Hos
W8 . . . . .31 C1 113 B1
Campden House Cl
W8 . . . . .127 C4
Campden St
W8 . . . . .31 C1 113 B1
Campen Cl SW19 . . .70 A2
Camperdown St
E1 . . . . .111 A1
Campion Ho 13
N16. . . . . .16 A3
Campion Rd SW15 .57 B2
Camplin St SE14. . . .50 C3
Campshill Pl SE13 . .67 B2
Campshill Rd
SE13 . . . . .67 B2
Campton Hill Twrs
W8 . . . . .31 C1 113 B2
Cam Rd E15. . . . . . .27 C4
Camsey Ho 8
SW2 . . . . .62 B2
Canada Cres W3 . . .20 B1
Canada Gdns SE13 .67 B2
Canada Rd W3 . . . . .28 B4
Canada Sq E14. . . . .34 A1
Canada St SE16 . . . .40 C4
Canada Water Sta
SE16 . . . . .40 C3
Canada Way W12. . .30 A2
Canal App SE8 . . . . .51 A4
Canal Bldg N1 . . . . .86 C2
Canal Bridge SE15 . .49 C4
Canal Byd 7 NW1 . .13 C2
Canal Cl
Mile End E1. . . . . . . .26 A1
North Kensington
W10 . . . . .22 C1
Canal Gr SE15 . . . . .50 A4
Canal Head Public Sq
1 SE15 . . . . .49 C2
Canal Path 22 E2 . .24 B4
Canalside Studios 24
N1 . . . . .24 A4
Canal St SE5 . . . . . .48 C4
Canal Way W10 . . . .22 C1
Canal Wlk N1 . . . . . .87 C4
CANARY WHARF . . .34 A1
Canary Wharf *
E14 . . . . .34 A1
Canary Wharf Pier
(River Bus) E14 . . . .33 B1
Canary Wharf Sta
E14 . . . . .34 A1
Canary Wharf Sta
(DLR) E14 . . . . .33 C1
Canberra Prim Sch
W12 . . . . .30 A2
Canbury Mews
SE26 . . . . .76 C1

Cancell Rd SW9 . . .173 C4
Candahar Rd
SW11 . . . . .168 B1
Candida Ct 9
NW1 . . . . .13 A1
Candishe Ho SE1 . .138 C4
Candle Gr SE15. . . . .65 A4
Candlemakers 25
SW11 . . . . .59 C3
Candover St W1 . . .104 C3
Candy St E3 . . . . . . .26 B4
Canfield Gdns
NW6 . . . . .11 A1
Canfield Pl NW6. . . .11 B2
Canford Rd SW11. . .60 C2
Canham Rd W3 . . . . .38 A4
Cann Ho W14 . . . . .126 B1
Canning Cross
SE5 . . . . .49 A1
Canning Pas W8 . . .128 C2
Canning Pl W8 . . . .128 C2
Canning Pl Mews
W8 . . . . .128 C2
Canning Rd N5 . . . . .6 A1
Cannington 14
NW5 . . . . .12 C2
CANNING TOWN . . .35 B3
Canning Town
E16 . . . . .35 A3
Canning Town Sta
E16 . . . . .35 A3
Cannock Ho N4 . . . . .6 C4
Cannon Dr 21 E14 . .33 C2
Cannon Hill NW6 . . .10 C3
Cannon Ho SE11 . .149 A3
Cannon La NW3 . . . .2 C1
Cannon Pl NW3 . . . . .2 C1
Cannon St EC4 . . . .123 A4
Cannon Street Rd
E1 . . . . .32 A3
Cannon Street Sta
EC4 . . . . .123 B4
Cannon Wharf Bsns
Ctr 22 SE8 . . . . .41 A2
Canon Barnett Prim
Sch E1 . . . . .111 A2
Canon Beck Rd
SE16 . . . . .40 B4
CANONBURY 15 B2
Canonbury Bsns Ctr
N1 . . . . .87 A4
Canonbury Cres
N1 . . . . .15 B1
Canonbury Ct 21
N1 . . . . .15 A1
Canonbury Gr N1 . . .15 B1
Canonbury Hts 6
N1 . . . . .15 C2
Canonbury La N1. . .15 A1
Canonbury Pk N
N1 . . . . .15 B2
Canonbury Pk S
N1 . . . . .15 B2
Canonbury Pl N1 . . .15 A2
Canonbury Prim Sch
N1 . . . . .15 A2
Canonbury Rd N1 . . .15 A1
Canonbury Sq N1 . . .15 A1
Canonbury Sta N1. .15 B3
Canonbury Sta N1. .15 B3
Canonbury Villas
N1 . . . . .15 B3
Canon Murnane Rd
SE1 . . . . .138 C1

Canon Row SW1 . .134 A3
Canons Cl N2 . . . . . . .2 C4
Canon St N1 . . . . . . .86 C3
Canrobert St E2 . . . .25 A2
Cantelowes Rd
NW1 . . . . .13 C2
Canterbury Cl 16
SE5 . . . . .48 B1
Canterbury Cres
SW9 . . . . .62 C4
Canterbury Ct
Acton W3 . . . . .29 A1
Kilburn NW6 . . . . . .23 C3
Canterbury Gr SE27,
SW16 . . . . .74 C1
Canterbury Ho
6 Bromley E3. . . . . .27 A2
Lambeth SE1 . . . . .135 A2
Canterbury Ind Pk 15
SE15 . . . . .50 B4
Canterbury Mans
NW6 . . . . .11 A2
Canterbury Pl
SE17 . . . . .150 B3
Canterbury Rd
NW6 . . . . .23 C2
Canterbury Terr
NW6 . . . . .23 C3
Cantium Ret Pk
SE1 . . . . .49 B4
Canton St E14. . . . . .33 C3
Cantrell Rd E3 . . . . .26 C1
Canute Ct SW16 . . . .74 C1
Canute Gdns SE16 . .40 C2
Canvey St SE1 . . . .122 C2
Cape Henry Ct 18
E14 . . . . .34 C2
Capel Ho 6 E9 . . . . .17 B1
Capel Lo
8 Richmond TW9 . . .44 B2
12 Streatham SW2 .74 B4
Capener's Cl SW1 .131 B3
Capern Rd SW18 . . .71 B3
Capio Nightingale
Hospl SW4 . . . . . . .144 B1
Capital City Acad
NW10 . . . . .22 A4
Capital East Apts 8
E16 . . . . .35 C2
Capital Interchange
Way TW8 . . . . .36 C1
Capital Sh Ctrs
SW1 . . . . .133 B3
Capital Wharf E1 . .125 C1
Capland Ho NW8 . . .89 C2
Capland St NW8 . . . .89 C2
Caple Ho SW10 . . . .157 A2
Caple Rd NW10. . . . .21 B3
Capper St WC1 . . . . .93 A1
Capstan Ho 6
E14 . . . . .42 B2
Capstan Rd SE8 . . . .41 B2
Capstan Sq E14 . . . .42 B4
Capstan Way SE16 . .33 A1
Capulet Mews 1
E16 . . . . .35 C1
Caradoc Cl W2. . . . . .31 C3
Caradoc St SE10 . . . .43 A1
Cara Ho N1 . . . . .14 C1
Caranday Villas 3
W11 . . . . .30 C1
Caravel Cl E14 . . . . . .41 C3
Caravel Mews 14
SE8 . . . . .51 C4
Caraway Hts E14 . . .34 B2
Carbery Ave W3 . . . .36 B4

Carbis Rd E14.....33 B3
Carbroke Ho 9
 E9.....25 B4
Carburton St W1.....92 B1
Cardale St 1 E14.....42 B3
Carden Rd SE15.....65 A4
Cardiff Ho 9
 SE15.....49 C4
Cardigan Rd
 Barnes SW13.....46 C1
 Bow E3.....26 C3
 Richmond TW10.....54 A1
Cardigan St SE11.....149 B2
Cardigan Wlk 19
 N1.....15 B1
Cardinal Bourne St
 SE1.....137 C1
Cardinal Cap Alley
 SE1.....122 C3
Cardinal Hinsey Cl
 NW10.....21 C3
Cardinal Hinsley RC
 High Sch (Boys)
 NW10.....21 C3
Cardinal Pl SW15.....57 C3
Cardinal Pole RC Sch
 London E9.....17 C1
 London E9.....18 A3
Cardinals Way N19.....4 C3
Cardinal Vaughan
 Meml Sch The
 W14.....126 A4
Cardinal Wlk
 SW1.....132 C1
Cardine Mews
 SE15.....50 A3
Cardington St
 NW1.....93 A3
Cardozo Rd N7.....14 A3
Cardross St W6.....39 A3
Cardwell Rd 3
 N7.....14 A4

Carlisle Pl SW1.....132 C1
Carlisle Rd
 Finsbury Pk N4.....5 C4
 Kilburn NW6.....23 A4
Carlisle St W1.....105 B1
Carlisle Wlk 6 E8.....16 B2
Carlos Pl W1.....118 A3
Carlow St NW1.....82 C4
Carlson Ct SW15.....58 B3
Carlton Cl
 Brixton SW9.....62 C3
 Kilburn NW6.....78 B2
Carlton Ct
 Brixton SW9.....48 A2
 Kilburn NW6.....78 B2
 8 Willesden NW2.....9 B2
Carlton Dr SW15.....58 A2
Carlton Gdns
 SW1.....119 B1
Carlton Gr SE15.....50 A2
Carlton Hill NW8.....78 C2
Carlton Ho
 4 Kilburn NW6.....23 B3
 Kilburn NW6.....23 C3
 Marylebone W1.....103 A2
Carlton House Terr
 SW1.....119 C2
Carlton Lo N4.....5 C4
Carlton Mans
 Brixton SW9.....62 C3
 Cricklewood NW2.....9 C3
 Kensington W14.....126 B4
 Maida Vale W9.....88 C4
 7 South Hampstead
 NW6.....10 C1
 Stamford Hill N16.....7 A4
Carlton Prim Sch
 NW5.....12 C3
Carlton Rd
 Acton W4.....37 C4
 Finsbury Pk N4.....5 C4
 Mortlake SW14.....55 B3
Carlton Sq 1 E1.....25 C1
Carlton St SW1.....119 B3
Carltons The 5
 SW15.....58 A2
Carlton Tower Pl
 SW1.....131 A2
Carlton Vale NW6.....23 C3
Carlton Vale Inf Sch
 NW6.....23 B2
Carlyle Ho
 4 Camberwell
 SE5.....48 B3
 Chelsea SW3.....157 C3
 12 Stoke Newington
 N16.....7 A1
Carlyle Mans
 SW3.....158 A3
Carlyle Mews 24
 E1.....25 C1
Carlyle Pl SW15.....57 C3
Carlyle Rd 1
 NW10.....20 C4
Carlyle's Ho★
 SW3.....158 A3
Carlyle Sq SW3.....143 C1
Carmalt Gdns
 SW15.....57 B3
Carmarthen Ho 8
 SW15.....69 B4
Carmarthen Pl
 SE1.....138 A4
Carmelite Ct EC4.....121 C4
Carmel Lo SW6.....155 C4
Carmen St E14.....34 A3
Carmichael Cl 8
 SW11.....59 C4

Carmichael Ct 5
 SW13.....46 B1
Carmichael Ho 5
 E14.....34 B2
Carmichael Mews
 SW18.....71 C4
Carminia Rd
 SW17.....73 A2
Carnaby St★ W1.....104 C1
Carnac St SE21,
 SE27.....75 C1
Carna St TW9.....54 A3
Carnegie Ho NW3.....2 C1
Carnegie Pl SW19.....69 C1
Carnegie St N1.....85 A3
Carnicot Ho 2
 SE15.....50 A2
Carnoustie Dr N1.....14 B1
Carnwath Ho SW6.....59 A4
Carnwath Rd SW6.....59 A4
Caroline Cl
 Bayswater W2.....114 B3
 Streatham SW16.....74 A1
Caroline Gdns
 E2.....24 A2 98 B4
Caroline Ho
 Bayswater W2.....114 B3
 20 Hammersmith
 W6.....39 B1
Caroline Martyn Ho 3
 N19.....5 A4
Caroline Pl
 Bayswater W2.....114 B3
 Clapham SW11.....169 C1
Caroline Pl Mews
 W2.....114 B3
Caroline St E1.....32 C3
Caroline Terr
 SW1.....145 B3
Caroline Wlk W6.....154 A3
Carol St NW1.....82 C4
Caronia Ct 4
 SE16.....41 A2
Carpenter Ho
 11 Tower Hamlets
 E14.....33 C4
 5 Tufnell Pk N19.....13 C4
Carpenters Bsns Pk
 E15.....19 A1
Carpenter's Pl
 SW4.....61 C3
Carpenters Prim Sch
 E15.....27 B4
Carpenter's Rd
 E15.....19 A1
Carpenter St W1.....118 A3
Carradale Ho 2
 E14.....34 B3
Carrara Cl 18 SW9.....63 A3
Carrara Wharf
 SW6.....58 A4
Carriage Dr E
 SW11.....159 C2
Carriage Drive E
 SW11.....159 C2
Carriage Drive N SW11,
 SW8.....159 C3
Carriage Dr N
 Battersea SW8,
 SW11.....158 C2
 Battersea SW11.....159 C2
Carriage Dr S
 SW11.....169 A2

Carriage Dr W
 SW11.....158 C1
Carrick Ho
 Islington N7.....14 B2
 Kennington SE11.....150 A2
Carrick Mews SE8.....51 C4
Carrington Ct
 SW11.....60 A3
Carrington Ho
 W1.....118 A1
Carrington Lo 3
 TW10.....54 A2
Carrington Rd
 TW10.....54 C3
Carrington St W1.....118 A1
Carrol Cl NW5.....13 A4
Carroll Ct
 Acton W3.....37 A3
 4 Shacklewell E5.....7 C3
Carroll Ho W2.....115 B4
Carron Cl E14.....34 A3
Carroun Rd SW8.....162 C2
Carr St 8 E14.....33 A3
Carslake Rd SW15.....57 B1
Carson Rd
 Dulwich SE21.....75 C2
 Newham E16.....35 C4
Carter Ct EC4.....108 B1
Carteret Ho 3
 W12.....30 A2
Carteret St SW1.....133 B3
Carteret Way SE8.....41 A2
Carter Ho
 11 London SW2.....62 C2
 Spitalfields E1.....110 C3
Carter La EC4.....108 B1
Carter Pl SE17.....151 A1
Carter St SE17.....150 C1
Carter's Yd SW18.....58 C2
Carthew Rd W6.....39 A3
Carthew Villas
 W6.....39 A3
Carthusian St
 EC1.....108 C4
Cartier Circ E14.....34 B1
Carting La WC2.....120 B3
Cartmel NW1.....92 C4
Carton Ho
 Bermondsey SE16.....139 B2
 12 Shepherd's Bush
 W11.....30 C2
Cartoon Mus The★
 WC1.....106 A3
Cartwright Gdns
 WC1.....94 A3
Cartwright Ho
 SE1.....137 A1
Cartwright St E1.....125 A3
Cartwright Way
 SW13.....47 A3
Carvel Ho E14.....42 B1
Carver Cl 15 W4.....37 B3
Carver Rd SE24.....63 B1
Carville Cres TW8.....36 A2
Caryl Ho SW9.....173 C4
Carysfort Rd N16.....15 C4
Casby Ho SE16.....139 B2
Casella Rd SE14.....50 C3
Casey Cl NW8.....90 B3
Casino Ave SE24.....63 C2
Caspian Ho 10 E1.....32 C4
Caspian St SE5.....48 C3
Cassandra Ct 7
 NW2.....9 B2
Cass Bsns Sch EC1.....97 B1
Cassell Ho SW9.....172 B2

Casserley Ho W4.....37 C3
Cass Ho 28 E9.....17 C2
Cassidy Rd SW6.....155 B1
Cassilis Rd E14.....41 C4
Cassinghurst SE24.....63 C2
Cassland Rd E9.....17 C2
Casson Ho E1.....111 B4
Casson St E1.....111 B3
Castalia Sq 6 E14.....42 B4
Castellain Mans
 W9.....88 A2
Castellain Rd W9.....88 B2
Castell Ho 11 SE8.....51 C3
Castello Ave SW15.....57 B2
Castelnau SW13.....47 A3
Castelnau Gdns
 SW13.....47 A4
Castelnau Mans
 SW13.....47 A4
Castelnau Row
 SW13.....47 A4
Casterbridge
 Kilburn NW6.....78 B4
 3 Notting Hill W11.....31 C3
Casterton St E8.....17 A2
Castleacre W2.....102 A1
Castle Baynard St
 EC4.....122 C4
Castlebrook Cl
 SE11.....150 A4
Castle Cl
 12 Acton W3.....37 B4
 Homerton E9.....18 A3
 South Acton W3.....37 A4
 Wimbledon SW19.....69 C1
Castlecombe Dr
 SW19.....69 C4
Castle Ct EC3.....109 C1
Castleden Ho
 NW6.....11 C1
Castleford Ct NW8.....89 C2
Castlefrank Ho
 N1.....24 A2 98 B4
Castlegate TW9.....54 B4
Castlehaven Rd
 NW1.....13 A1
Castle Ho
 Newington SE1.....150 C4
 South Lambeth
 SW8.....162 B2
Castle Ind Est
 SE17.....150 C4
Castle La SW1.....132 C2
Castlemaine
 SW11.....169 A2
Castlemaine St
 E1.....32 A4
Castle Mead SE5.....48 B3
Castle Mews NW1.....13 A2
Castle Pl
 8 Acton W4.....38 A2
 Camden Town NW1.....13 A2
Castle Rd NW1.....13 A2
Castlereagh St
 W1.....102 C2
Castleton Ho 3
 E14.....42 B2
Castletown Rd
 W14.....140 B1
Castleview Cl N4.....6 B2
Castle Way SW19.....69 C1
Castlewood Rd
 WC1.....105 C2
Castle Yd
 Highgate N6.....3 C4

Castle Yd continued
Lambeth SE1 . . . . . **122** B2
Castor La E14. . . . . . .**34** A2
Catalpa Ct SE13 . . . .**67** C1

Caterham Rd
SE13. . . . .**67** C4
Catesby Ho 25 E9 . .**17** B1
Catesby St SE17 . . .**151** C3
Cathay Ho SE16 . . . . .**40** A4
Cathay St 9 SE16. . . .**40** A4
Cathcart Hill N19. . . . .**4** B1
Cathcart Rd
SW10 . . . .**156** C4
Cathcart St NW5 . . . .**13** A2
Cathedral Ct E4. . . .**108** B1
Cathedral Lo EC1 . .**108** C4
**Cathedral Sch of St
Saviour & St Mary
Overie Prim Sch**
SE1. . . . .**137** A4
Cathedral St SE1. . .**123** B2
Cathedral Wlk
SW1. . . . .**132** C2
Catherall Rd N5,
N16. . . . .**6** B1
Catherine Baird Ct 12
SW12 . . . .**73** A4
Catherine Dr TW9 . .**54** A3
Catherine Gr SE10 . .**52** A2
Catherine Griffiths Ct
EC1. . . . .**95** C2
Catherine Ho 16
N1. . . . .**24** A4
Catherine Pl SW1 . .**132** C2
Catherine St WC2 . .**120** C4
Catherine Wheel Alley
E1 . . . .**110** B3
Catherine Wheel Yd
SW1 . . . .**118** C1
Catherwood Ct N1 . .**87** B1
Cathies Rd SW12 . . .**61** A1
Cathnor Rd W12 . . . .**39** A4
Catlin St SE16. . . . . . .**40** A1
Catman Ho N4 . . . .**5** B3
Cato Rd SW4. . . . .**61** C3
Cator St
Camberwell SE15. . . .**49** B3
Camberwell SE15. . . .**49** B4
Cato St W1 . . . .**102** B2
Catton St WC1 . . . .**106** C3
Caughley Ho
SE11 . . . .**135** B1
Caulfield Ct 15
NW1 . . . .**13** B1
Caulfield Rd SE15 . . .**50** A1
Causeway The
SW18 . . . .**59** A2
Causton Cotts 3
E14. . . . .**33** A3
Causton Ho SE5 . . . .**48** B3
Causton Rd N6. . . . . . .**4** A4
Causton St SW1 . . . .**147** C2
Cautley Ave SW4 . . .**61** B2
Cavalry Gdns
SW15 . . . .**58** B2
Cavaye Ho SW10 . . .**157** A4
Cavaye Pl SW10 . . . .**143** A1
Cavell Ct 5 N19. . . . . .**4** B2
Cavell Ho 8 N1. . . . . .**24** A4
Cavell St E1. . . . .**32** A4
Cavendish Ave
NW8 . . . .**79** C1
Cavendish Cl
Brondesbury NW6 . . .**10** B2
3 Putney SW15 . . . . .**58** A2

Cavendish Cl continued
St John's Wood
NW8. . . . .**89** C4
Cavendish Coll
WC1 . . . .**105** A4
Cavendish Ct EC2 . .**110** B2
Cavendish Gdns
SW4 . . . .**61** B1
Cavendish Ho
South Lambeth
8 SW8 . . . .**172** A4
St John's Wood
NW8. . . . .**79** C1
Cavendish Mans
2 Clapham Pk
SW12 . . . .**61** B1
Hackney E5. . . . .**17** B3
Holborn EC1. . . . .**95** B1
8 West Hampstead
NW6 . . . .**10** C3
Cavendish Mews N
W1 . . . .**104** B4
Cavendish Mews S
W1 . . . .**104** B3
Cavendish Par
SW4 . . . .**61** A1
Cavendish Pl
Balham SW4 . . . .**61** A1
Brondesbury NW2 . . . .**9** C2
Marylebone W1 . . . . .**104** B2
Cavendish Prim Sch
W4 . . . .**46** A3
Cavendish Rd
Brondesbury NW6 . . .**10** B1
Chiswick W4 . . . .**45** B2
Clapham Pk SW12 . . .**61** B1
Cavendish Sch The
NW1 . . . .**82** B4
Cavendish Sq W1 . .**104** B2
Cavendish St N1 . . . .**87** B1
Cavendish Terr 11
E3. . . . .**26** B2
Cavendish The
NW11 . . . .**2** A4
Caversham Ho 7
SE15 . . . .**49** C4
Caversham Rd
NW5 . . . .**13** B2
Caversham St
SW3 . . . .**158** C4
Caverswall St
W12 . . . .**30** B3
Cavour Ho SE17 . . .**150** B2
Caxton Gr E3. . . . . . .**26** C2
Caxton Hall ★
SW1 . . . .**133** B2
Caxton Rd W12. . . . . .**39** C4
Caxton St N E16. . . . .**35** B3
Caxton St SW1 . . . .**133** B2
Caxton Wlk WC2 . . .**105** C1
Cazenove Mans 1
N16. . . . .**7** C2
Cazenove Rd N16 . . . .**7** C2
Cecil Cl
Chelsea SW10 . . . . .**156** C4
South Hampstead
NW6 . . . .**11** A1
St James NW2 . . . . .**120** A3
Cecilia Rd E8 . . . .**16** C3
Cecil Mans 2
SW17 . . . .**72** C2

Cecil Rd Acton W3 . .**28** A4
Harlesden NW10 . . . .**21** A4
Cecil Rhodes Ho
NW1 . . . .**83** B2
Cedar Cl
Old Ford E3. . . . .**26** B4
West Norwood
SE21 . . . .**75** B2
Cedar Ct
Islington N1. . . . .**15** B1
Marylebone W1 . . . .**102** B2
Mortlake SW14 . . . . .**55** B3
Wimbledon SW19 . . . .**69** C1
Cedar Gr W5 . . . .**36** A3
Cedar Ho
5 Cubitt Town
E14. . . . .**42** B4
Kensington W8 . . . .**128** A2
New Cross Gate
SE14 . . . .**50** C2
8 Richmond TW9 . . .**45** A2
16 Rotherhithe
SE16 . . . .**40** C4
Cedar La
Brondesbury NW2 . . .**10** B2
Fulham SW6 . . . .**47** C2
Cedarne Rd SW6 . . .**156** A1
Cedar Rd NW2 . . . .**9** B4
Cedars Cl SE13 . . . . .**67** C4
Cedars Ct SW15 . . . .**56** C1
Cedars Ho 26 SW2. . .**62** B3
Cedars Mews
SW4 . . . .**61** A3
Cedars Rd
Barnes SW13 . . . .**46** C1
Clapham SW4 . . . . . .**61** A3
Cedars The E9 . . . . . .**17** C1
Cedar Terr TW9 . . . . .**54** A3
Cedar Way NW1 . . . . .**83** B4
Cedra Ct N16. . . . .**7** C3
Celandine Cl E3,
E14. . . . .**33** C4
Celandine Dr E8 . . . .**16** B1
Celbridge Mews
W2 . . . .**100** B2
Celestial Gdns
SE13 . . . .**67** C3
Celia Blairman Ho
E1 . . . .**110** C4
Celia Ho 10 TW9 . . .**44** B2
Celia Ho 10 N1 . . . . . .**24** A3
Celia St E14 . . . .**34** A4
Celtic St E14 . . . .**34** A4
Cenacle Cl NW3 . . . . . .**1** C1
Cenotaph ★ SW1 . . .**134** A4
Centaur Ct 3
TW8 . . . .**36** A1
Centaur St SE11 . . . .**135** A2
Central Ave SW11 . .**159** A3
Central Bsns Ctr
NW10 . . . .**8** A3
**Central Criminal
Court (Old Bailey) ★**
EC4. . . . .**108** B2
**Central Foundation
Boys' Sch** EC2 . . . . .**97** C2
**Central Foundation
Lower Girls Sch The**
E3. . . . .**26** A2
**Central Foundation
Upper Girls Sch The**
E3. . . . .**26** B2
Central Ho E15. . . . . .**27** B3
**Central Middlesex
Hospl** NW10. . . . .**20** B2

Central Par W3 . . . .**37** A4
**Central St Martins
Coll** EC1 . . . .**95** C1
**Central St Martin's
Coll of Art & Design**
W1 . . . .**105** C1
**Central St Martins
Coll of Art & Design
(The London Inst)**
WC1 . . . .**106** C3
Central Sch of Ballet
EC1. . . . .**95** C1
**Central Sch of Speech
& Drama The**
NW3 . . . .**11** C1
Central St EC1 . . . . . .**96** C3
Central Way
NW10 . . . .**20** B2
Centre Ave W3 . . . . . .**28** B1
Centre Bldg SE17 . .**151** A4
Centre Hts 2
NW3 . . . .**11** C1
Centre Point SE1 . . .**153** B2
Centre Point Ho
WC2 . . . .**105** C2
Centre St E2 . . . .**25** A3
Centurion Bldg
SW8 . . . .**160** A3
Centurion Cl N7. . . . .**14** B1
Centurion La E3 . . . . .**26** B3
Century Ho SE13 . . . .**52** A1
Cephas Ave E1 . . . . . .**25** B1
Cephas Ho 9 E1 . . . . .**25** B1
Cephas St E1 . . . .**25** B1
Cerise Rd SE15 . . . . .**49** C2
Cerney Mews W2 . .**115** B4
Cervantes Ct W2 . . .**100** B1
Cester St E2 . . . .**24** C4
Ceylon Rd
8 Hammersmith
W14 . . . .**39** C3
Kensington W14 . . . .**126** A1
Chabot Dr SE15 . . . . .**65** A4
Chadacre Ho 10
SW9 . . . .**63** A3
Chadbourn St E14. .**34** A4
Chadston Ho 17
N1. . . . .**15** A1
Chadswell WC1 . . . . .**94** B3
Chadwick Cl EC1 . . . .**95** C4
Chadwick Cl
SW15 . . . .**68** B4
Chadwick Rd
Harlesden NW10 . . . .**21** B4
Peckham SE15 . . . . . .**49** B1
Chadwick St SW1 . .**133** B1
Chadworth Ho
Finsbury EC1 . . . .**96** C3
Finsbury Pk N4 . . . .**6** B3
Chagford Ho
31 Bromley E3 . . . . . .**27** A2
Marylebone NW1 . . . .**90** C1
Chagford St NW1 . . .**91** A1
Chalbury Ho 8
SW9 . . . .**62** B3
Chalbury Wlk N1. . . .**85** B2
Chalcot Cres NW1 .**81** A4
Chalcot Gdns
NW3 . . . .**12** B2
Chalcot Mews
SW16 . . . .**74** A1
Chalcot Rd NW1. . . . .**81** B4
Chalcot Sch NW1 . . .**13** A1
Chalcot Sq NW1 . . . .**12** C1
Chaldon Rd SW6 . . .**154** B2
Chale Rd SW2 . . . .**62** A1
Chalfont Ct NW1 . . . .**91** A1

Chalfont Ho 2
SE16 . . . .**40** A3
Chalford 7 NW3 . . . .**11** B2
Chalford Ct 15
SW15 . . . .**57** C1
Chalkers Cnr TW9 . .**55** A4
Chalk Farm Rd
NW1 . . . .**71** A1
Chalk Farm Sta
NW3 . . . .**12** C1
Chalk Hill Rd W6 . . . .**39** C2
Chalkwell Ho 10
E1 . . . .**32** C3
Challenge Cl NW10 **21** A4
Challenger Ho 7
E14. . . . .**33** A2
Challice Way SW2 . .**74** B3
Challoner Cres
W14 . . . .**140** C1
Challoner Mans
W14 . . . .**140** C1
Challoner St W14 . .**140** C1
Chalmers Ho 13
SW11 . . . .**59** B4
Chalmer's Wlk 14
SE17 . . . .**48** A4
Chalner Ho SW2 . . . .**74** C3
Chaloner Ct SE1 . . .**137** B4
Chalsey Lodge
SE4 . . . .**66** B3
Chalsey Rd SE4 . . . . .**66** B3
Chalton St NW1 . . . . .**83** B1
Chamberlain Cotts
SE5 . . . .**48** C2
Chamberlain Ho 6
E1 . . . .**32** B2
Chamberlain St 7
NW1 . . . .**12** B1
Chamberlayne Mans
8 NW10 . . . .**22** C2
Chamberlayne Rd
NW10 . . . .**22** B5
Chambers La NW10 . .**9** B1
Chambers Rd N7. . . .**14** A4
Chambers St
SE16 . . . .**139** C3
Chamber St E1. . . . .**125** A4
Chambon Pl 7
W6 . . . .**38** C2
Chambord Ho
E2 . . . . **24** B2 **99** A3
Chambord St
E2 . . . . **24** B2 **99** A3
Champion Gr SE5 . .**63** C4
Champion Hill
SE5 . . . .**63** C4
Champion Pk SE5 . .**48** C1
Champlain Ho 26
W12 . . . .**30** A2
Chancel Ct W1. . . .**119** B4
Chancellor Gr
SE21 . . . .**75** B1
Chancellor Ho
South Kensington
SW7 . . . .**129** A2
29 Wapping E1. . . . .**32** A1
Chancellor Pas
E14. . . . .**33** C1
Chancellors' Ct
WC1 . . . .**106** C4
Chancellor's Rd
W6 . . . .**39** B1
Chancellors St
W6 . . . .**39** B1
Chancellors Wharf 21
W6 . . . .**39** B1
Chancel St SE1. . . . .**122** A1

Chancery Bldgs 14
E1 . . . . .32 B2
Chancery Ho
WC2 . . . . **107** B3
Chancery La EC4 . **107** B2
Chancery Lane Sta
WC1 . . . . **107** B3
Chancery Mews
SW17 . . . . .72 A2
Chance St
E2 . . . . **98** C2
Chandler Ave E16 . .35 C4
Chandlers Mews
E14 . . . . .41 C4
Chandler St E1 . . . .32 A1
Chandlers Way 11
SE24 . . . . .74 C4
Chandler Way
SE15 . . . . 49 B3
Chandlery Ho E1 . **111** B1
Chandos Pl WC2 . **120** A3
Chandos Rd
Cricklewood NW2 . 9 B3
Old Oak Comm
NW10 . . . . .21 A1
Stratford New Town
E15 . . . . .19 C3
Chandos Way
NW11 . . . . .2 A3
Change Alley EC3 **109** C1
Channel Gate Rd
NW10 . . . . .21 A2
Channel Ho E14 . . . .33 A4
Channelsea Bsns Ctr
E15 . . . . .27 C3
Channelsea Rd
E15 . . . . .27 C4
Channing Sch N6 . . 4 A3
Chantrey Rd SW9 . .62 B4
Chantry Cl W9 . . . .23 B1
Chantry Cres NW10 . 8 B2
Chantry Ct SW6 . . .58 A4
Chantry Sq W8 . . .**128** A1
Chantry St N1 . . . .**86** B3
Chant Sq E15 . . . . .19 C1
Chant St E15 . . . . .19 C1
Chapel Cl NW10 . . . 8 B2
Chapel Ct SE1 . . . **137** B4
Chapel House St
E14 . . . . .42 A2
Chapel Market N1 . **85** B2
Chapel Pl
Islington N1 . . . . .**85** C2
Marylebone W1 . . **104** A1
Shoreditch
EC2 . . . . . .24 A2 **98** A3
Chapel Side W2 . . **114** A3
Chapel St
Paddington NW1 . **102** A3
Westminster SW1 . **131** C3
Chapleton Ho
SW2 . . . . .62 C2
Chaplin Cl SE1 . . . **136** A4
Chaplin Ho 6
SW9 . . . . .62 C3
Chaplin Rd NW2 . . . 8 C2
Chaplow Cl SW6 . . **166** C1
Chapman Ho
26 Stepney E1 . . . .32 A3
2 West Norwood
SE27 . . . . .75 A1
Chapman Rd E9 . . .18 B2
Chapmans Park Ind
Est NW10 . . . . 8 B2
Chapman Sq
SW19 . . . . .69 C2

Chapman St E1 . . . .32 A2
Chapone Pl W1 . . . **105** B1
Chapter Cl 16 W4 . .37 B3
Chapter House &
Jewel Twr★
SW1 . . . . **134** A2
Chapter Rd
Kennington SE17 . **150** B1
Willesden NW2 . . . . 9 A3
Chapter St SW1 . . **147** B3
Chara Pl W4 . . . . .45 C4
Charcot Ho SW15 . .56 B1
Charcroft Ct 11
W14 . . . . .39 C4
Chard Ho 7 N7 . . . . 5 B2
Chardin Ho SW9 . . **173** C4
Chardin Rd 11 W4 . .38 A2
Chardmore Rd N16 . 7 C3
Charecroft Way
W12 . . . . .39 C4
Charfield Ct W9 . . .88 B1
Charford Rd E16 . . .35 C4
Chargrove Cl 24
SE16 . . . . .40 C4
Charing Cross
SW1 . . . . **120** A2
Charing Cross Hospl
W6 . . . . .39 C1
Charing Cross Rd
WC2 . . . . **105** C1
Charing Cross Sta
WC2 . . . . **120** B2
Charing Ho SE1 . . **135** C4
Chariot Cl 7 E3 . . .26 C4
Charlbert Ct NW8 . **80** A2
Charlbert St NW8 . **80** A2
Charles Allen Ho
EC1 . . . . 5 B2
Charles Auffray Ho 10
E1 . . . . .32 B4
Charles Barry Cl
SW4 . . . . .61 B4
Charles Burton Ct
E5 . . . . .18 A4
Charles Coveney Rd
12 SE15 . . . . .49 B2
Charles Darwin Ho 8
E2 . . . . .25 A2
Charles Dickens Ho
1 E2 . . . . .25 A2
Charles Dickens Prim
Sch SE1 . . . . . . **136** C3
Charles Edward
Brooke Sch SW9 . 48 A2
Charles Edward
Brooke Sch (Dennen
Site) SE5 . . . . . . 48 A2
Charles Flemwell
Mews 4 E16 . . . . .35 C1
Charles Haller St 23
SW2 . . . . .74 C4
Charles Harrod Ct
SW13 . . . . .47 B4
Charles Hobson Ho 8
NW10 . . . . 8 A1
Charles Hocking Ho
3 W3 . . . . .37 B4
Charles II Pl SW3 . **144** C1
Charles II St SW1 . **119** B2
Charles La NW8 . . . **80** A2
Charles Lamb Ct
N1 . . . .**86** B2
Charles Lamb Prim
Sch N1 . . . .**86** C4
Charles Mackenzie Ho
SE16 . . . . **153** C4
Charles Pl NW1 . . .**93** A3

Charles Rowan Ho
WC1 . . . . **95** B3
Charles Sq N1 . . . . **97** C3
Charles St
Barnes SW13 . . . . .46 A1
Mayfair W1 . . . . . **118** A2
Charleston St
SE17 . . . . **151** A3
Charles Townsend Ho
EC1 . . . .**96** A2
Charles Utton Ct
E8 . . . . .16 C4
Charlesworth Ho 6
E14 . . . . .33 C3
Charleville Ct
SW5 . . . . **140** C1
Charleville Mans
W14 . . . . **140** B1
Charleville Rd
W14 . . . . **140** C1
Charlotte Ct 10
W6 . . . . .38 C2
Charlotte Despard
Ave SW11 . . . . . **169** C3
Charlotte Ho 12
W6 . . . . .39 B1
Charlotte Mews
Marylebone W1 . . **105** A4
North Kensington
W10 . . . . .30 C3
West Kensington
W14 . . . . **140** A4
Charlotte Pl
Marylebone W1 . . **105** A3
Westminster SW1 . **146** C3
Charlotte Rd
Barnes SW13 . . . . .46 B2
Shoreditch
EC2 . . . . .24 A1 **98** A2
Charlotte Row
SW4 . . . . .61 B4
Charlotte Sharman
Prim Sch SE11 . . **136** A1
Charlotte Sq 6
TW10 . . . . .54 B1
Charlotte St W1 . . **105** A4
Charlotte Terr N1 . .85 A3
Charlton Ct
25 Hackney E2 . . . .24 B4
6 Kentish Town
N7 . . . . .13 C3
Charlton Ho
5 Brentford TW8 . . .44 A4
Somers Town NW1 . .93 B4
Charlton King's Rd
NW5 . . . . .13 C3
Charlton Pl N1 . . . .**86** A2
Charlton Rd NW10 . .21 A4
Charlton Way SE10,
SE3 . . . . .53 A3
Charlwood Ho
1 Streatham SW2 . .74 B3
Westminster SW1 . **147** B3
Charlwood Pl
SW1 . . . . **147** A3
Charlwood St
SW1 . . . . **147** A2
Charlwood Terr 5
SW15 . . . . .57 C3
Charman Ho
10 London SW2 . . .62 C1
South Lambeth
SW8 . . . . **162** A2

Charmian Ho 19
N1 . . . . .24 A3
Charmouth Ct
TW10 . . . . .54 B2
Charmouth Ho
SW8 . . . . **162** C2
Charnock Ho 22
W12 . . . . .30 A2
Charnwood Gdns
E14 . . . . .41 C2
Charrington Ho 6
E1 . . . . .25 B1
Charrington St
NW1 . . . .**83** B2
Charter Bldgs 14
SE10 . . . . .52 A2
Charter Ct
Finsbury Pk N4 . . . . 5 C3
Marylebone W1 . . **102** B3
Charter Ho 4
WC2 . . . . **106** B1
Charterhouse Bldgs
EC1 . . . .**96** C1
Charterhouse Mews
EC1 . . . . **108** B4
Charterhouse Rd
E8 . . . . .16 C3
Charterhouse Sq
EC1 . . . . **108** B4
Charterhouse Square
Sch EC1 . . . . **108** B4
Charterhouse St
EC1 . . . . **108** A3
Charterhouse Works
SW18 . . . . .59 B3
Charteris Rd
Finsbury Pk N4 . . . . 5 C3
Kilburn NW6 . . . . .23 B4
Charter Nightingale
Hospl TW1 NW1 . . **102** B3
Charter Sch The
SE24 . . . . .63 C2
Chartes Ho SE1 . . **138** B2
Chartfield Ave
SW15 . . . . .57 B2
Chartfield Sch
SW15 . . . . .57 A2
Chartfield Sq
SW15 . . . . .57 C2
Chartham Ct 12
SW9 . . . . .62 C4
Chartham Gr SE27 . .75 A1
Chartham Ho SE1 . **137** C2
Chart House The 5
E14 . . . . .42 A1
Chartridge SE17 . . .48 C4
Chart St N1 . . . . . . **97** C4
Chartwell 28
SW19 . . . . .69 C3
Chase Ct SW3 . . . **130** C1
Chase Ctr The
NW10 . . . . .20 C2
Chaseley Ct W4 . . .37 A1
Chaseley St E14 . . .33 A3
Chasemore Ho
SW6 . . . . **154** B2
Chase Road Trad Est
NW10 . . . . .20 C1
Chase The SW4 . . . .61 A4
Chater Ho 6 E2 . . .25 C2
Chatfield Rd
SW11 . . . . .59 B4
Chatham Ct SW11 . .60 B2
Chatham Ho 7
SE5 . . . . .49 A1
Chatham Pl E9 . . . .17 B2
Chatham Rd SW11 . .60 B1

Chatham St SE17 . **151** C4
Chatsworth Ct
Brondesbury NW2 . . 9 C2
Clapton Pk E5 . . . .17 C4
Earl's Ct W8 . . . . **141** B4
Chatsworth Est
E5 . . . . .17 C4
Chatsworth Gdns
W3 . . . . .28 A1
Chatsworth Lo 6
W4 . . . . .37 C1
Chatsworth Rd
Brondesbury NW2 . . 9 C2
Chiswick W4 . . . . .45 B4
Clapton Pk E5 . . . .17 C4
Chatsworth Way
SE27 . . . . .75 B1
Chattenden Ho 8
N4 . . . . 6 B4
Chatterton Ct
TW9 . . . . .44 B1
Chatterton Rd N4 . . 6 A1
Chatto Rd SW11 . . .60 B2
Chaucer Ave TW9 . .44 C1
Chaucer Ct 17
N16 . . . . .16 A4
Chaucer Dr SE1 . . **153** A3
Chaucer Ho SW1 . **146** C1
Chaucer Rd
Acton W3 . . . . . . .28 B1
Herne Hill SE24 . . .63 A2
Chauldon Ho EC1 . .**97** C3
Cheadle Ct NW8 . . **89** C2
Cheadle Ho 17
E14 . . . . .33 B3
Cheam St 8 SE15 . .65 B4
Cheapside EC2 . . . **109** A1
Chearsley SE17 . . . **151** A4
Cheddington Ho 2
E2 . . . . .24 C4
Chedworth Cl E16 . .35 B3
Chedworth Ho
E5 . . . . 7 C2
Cheesemans Terr
W14 . . . . **140** C1
Chelmer Rd E9 . . . .17 C3
Chelmsford Cl W6 . .47 C4
Chelmsford Ho 5
N7 . . . . .14 B4
Chelmsford Sq
NW10 . . . . .22 B4
CHELSEA **144** B3
Chelsea Barracks★
Chelsea Bridge
SW1 . . . . **160** A4
Chelsea Bridge Rd
SW1 . . . . **145** C1
Chelsea Cl NW10 . .20 C4
Chelsea Cloisters
SW3 . . . . **144** B3
Chelsea Coll of Art &
Design
Chelsea SW3 . . . . **144** A1
Pimlico SW1 . . . . **148** A2
Chelsea Cres
Brondesbury NW2 . 10 B2
Chelsea SW10 . . . **167** A3
Chelsea Ct SW3 . . **159** B4
Chelsea Emb
SW3 . . . . **158** A3
Chelsea Est SW3 . **158** A3
Chelsea Farm Ho
SW10 . . . . **157** C3

Chelsea Gate
SW1 . . . . **145** C1
Chelsea Gdns
SW1 . . . . **145** C1
Chelsea Harbour
Design Ctr SW10 **167** A4
Chelsea Harbour Dr
SW10 . . . . **167** A4
Chelsea Harbour Pier
SW10 . . . . **167** B3
Chelsea Lo SW3 . . **159** A4
Chelsea Manor Ct
SW3 . . . . **158** B4
Chelsea Manor Gdns
SW3 . . . . **144** B1
Chelsea Manor St
SW3 . . . . **144** B1
Chelsea Manor
Studios SW3 . . **144** B1
Chelsea Park Gdns
SW3 . . . . **157** B4
Chelsea Physic Gdn* ⌖
SW1 . . . . **158** C4
Chelsea Reach Twr
SW10 . . . . **157** B2
Chelsea Sq SW3 . . **143** C1
Chelsea Twrs
SW3 . . . . **158** B4
Chelsea &
Westminster Hospl
SW10 . . . . **157** A3
Chelsfield Ho
SE17 . . . . **152** A3
Chelsfield Point ❸
E9 . . . . **17** C1
Chelsham Ho ❶
SW4 . . . . **61** C4
Chelsham Rd SW4 . . **61** C4
Cheltenham Pl
⓾ Acton W3 . . . . . . **28** A1
Acton W3 . . . . **37** B4
❸ South Acton W3 **37** A4
Cheltenham Rd
SE15 . . . . **65** B2
Cheltenham Terr
SW3 . . . . **145** A2
Chelverton Ct
SW15 . . . . **57** C3
Chelverton Rd
SW15 . . . . **57** C3
Chelwood NW5 . . . . **12** C3
Chelwood Ct
SW11 . . . . **167** C4
Chelwood Gdns
TW9 . . . . **44** C1
Chelwood Ho W2 **101** C1
Chenies Ho W2 . . . **114** A4
Chenies Mews
WC1 . . . . **93** B1
Chenies Pl NW1 . . . **83** C2
Chenies St WC1 . . **105** B4
Chenies The NW1 . . **83** C2
Cheniston Gdns
W8 . . . . **128** A2
Chepstow Cl
SW15 . . . . **58** A2
Chepstow Cres
W11 . . . . . . **31** C2 **113** B4
Chepstow Ct
W11 . . . . . . **31** C2 **113** B4
Chepstow Pl
W2 . . . . **31** C2 **113** C4
Chepstow Rd W2 . . **31** C3
Chepstow Villas
W11 . . . . . . **31** C2 **113** B4

Chequers Ct EC1 . . . **97** B1
Chequers Ho NW8 . . **90** A2
Chequer St EC1 . . . . **97** A1
Cherbury Ct N1 . . . . **87** C1
Cherbury St N1 . . . . **87** C1
Cheriton Ho ❾ E5 . . **17** A3
Cheriton Sq SW17 . . **72** C2
Cherry Ct ❼ SW2 . . **74** C4
Cherry Cl
Acton W3 . . . . **29** A1
❺ Rotherhithe
SE16 . . . . **33** A1
Cherry Garden Ho ❼
SE16 . . . . **40** A4
Cherry Garden Sch
SE16 . . . . **153** C4
Cherry Garden St
SE16 . . . . **40** A4
Cherry Laurel Wlk
SW2 . . . . **62** B1
Cherry Tree Cl ❶⓿
E9 . . . . **25** B4
Cherry Tree Ct
❶ Camden Town
NW1 . . . . **13** B1
❶❶ Peckham SE15 . . **50** A2
Cherry Tree Dr
SW16 . . . . **74** A1
Cherry Tree Ho
W10 . . . . **22** C2
Cherry Tree Ho
SE14 . . . . **51** B1
Cherry Trees Sch The
E3 . . . . **26** C2
Cherry Tree Terr
SE1 . . . . **138** B4
Cherry Tree Wlk
EC1 . . . . **97** A1
Cherrywood Cl E3 . . **26** A2
Cherrywood Dr
SW15 . . . . **57** C2
Chertsey Ct SW14 . . **55** A4
Chertsey Ho ❷
E2 . . . . **24** B2 **98** C3
Cherwell Ho NW8 . . **89** C1
Cheryls Cl SW6 . . . **166** B4
Chesham Cl SW1 . **131** B1
Chesham Ct SW18 . . **71** C4
Chesham Flats
W1 . . . . **117** C4
Chesham Ho
SW1 . . . . **131** B1
Chesham Mews
SW1 . . . . **131** B2
Chesham Pl SW1 . **131** B1
Chesham St SW1 . **131** B1
Cheshire Cl ❷
SE4 . . . . **24** B1 **99** A2
Chesholm Rd N16 . . **7** A1
Chesholm Rd NW6 . . **78** A3
Chesil Ct
❶❼ Bethnal Green
E2 . . . . **25** B3
Chelsea SW3 . . . . . **158** B4
Chesilton Rd
SW6 . . . . **164** C4
Chesney Ct W9 . . . . **23** C1
Chesney Ho SE13 . . **67** C3
Chesney St SW11 . **169** B3
Chessington Ho
SW8 . . . . **171** B2
Chesson Rd W14 . **155** A4
Chessum Ho E8 . . . . **16** C2
Chester Ave TW10 . . **54** B1
Chester Cl
Barnes SW13 . . . . . **57** A4
Knightsbridge SW1 **132** A3

Chester Cl continued
❶ Richmond TW10 . . **54** B1
Chester Close N
NW1 . . . . **92** B4
Chester Close S
NW1 . . . . **92** B3
Chester Cres E8 . . . . **16** B3
Chester Ct
Bermondsey SE8 . . **40** C1
❹ Camberwell SE5 . . **48** C3
Gospel Oak NW5 . . **12** C4
Regent's Pk NW1 . . **92** B3
Chesterfield Ct
SE13 . . . . **67** B4
Chesterfield Gdns
Greenwich SE10 . . **52** C3
Mayfair W1 . . . . . . **118** A2
Chesterfield Gr
SE22 . . . . **64** B2
Chesterfield Hill
W1 . . . . **118** A2
Chesterfield Ho
Highgate N6 . . . . **3** C3
Mayfair W1 . . . . . . **117** C2
Chesterfield Rd
W4 . . . . **45** B4
Chesterfield St
W1 . . . . **118** A2
Chesterfield Way
SE15 . . . . **50** B3
Chesterford Gdns
NW3 . . . . **11** A4
Chester Gate NW1 . **92** B3
Chester Ho
Dartmouth Pk N19 . . **4** A2
❷ Deptford SE8 . . . . **51** B4
Chesterman Ct
W4 . . . . **46** A3
Chester Mews
SW1 . . . . **132** A2
Chester Pl NW1 . . . . **92** A4
Chester Rd
Dartmouth Pk N19 . . **4** A2
Regent's Pk NW1 . . **92** A4
Chester Row
SW1 . . . . **145** C4
Chester Sq SW1 . . **146** A4
Chester Sq Mews
SW1 . . . . **132** A1
Chester Terr NW1 . . **92** A4
Chesterton Cl
SW18 . . . . **58** C2
Chesterton Ct W3 . . **37** A3
Chesterton Ho
❷❶ Battersea
SW11 . . . . **59** C4
❺ Kensal Town
W10 . . . . **31** A4
Chesterton Prim Sch
SW11 . . . . **169** B3
Chesterton Rd
W10 . . . . **31** A4
Chesterton Sq
W8 . . . . **141** B3
Chester Way
SE11 . . . . **149** C3
Chestnut Alley
SW6 . . . . **155** A3
Chestnut Ave ❶❶
SW14 . . . . **55** C4
Chestnut Cl
New Cross Gate
SE14 . . . . **51** B2

Chestnut Cl continued
❶ Stoke Newington
N16 . . . . **6** C2
Chestnut Ct SW6 . . **155** A4
Chestnut Gr SW12 . . **72** C3
Chestnut Grove Sch
SW12 . . . . **72** C3
Chestnut Ho
❶ Acton W4 . . . . . . **38** A2
Brockley SE4 . . . . . . **66** B4
❹ Maitland Pk
NW3 . . . . **12** B2
West Norwood
SE27 . . . . **75** B1
Chestnut Rd SE21,
SE27 . . . . **75** B1
Chestnuts The ❶
N5 . . . . **15** A4
Chettle Cl SE1 . . . **137** B2
Chetwode Ho
NW8 . . . . **90** A2
Chetwynd Rd NW5 . . **4** A1
Cheval Ct SW15 . . . . **57** A3
Cheval Pl SW7 . . . . **130** B2
Cheval St E14 . . . . . . **41** C3
Chevening Rd
Cubitt Town SE10 . . **43** B1
Kilburn NW6 . . . . . . **23** A4
Cheverell Ho ❸
E2 . . . . **24** C3
Cheverton Rd N19 . . **4** C3
Chevet St E9 . . . . **18** A3
Chevington NW2 . . . **10** B2
Cheviot Ct ❶❻
SE14 . . . . **50** B3
Cheviot Gate NW2 . . . **1** A2
Cheviot Ho N16 . . . . . **7** B3
Chevron Cl E16 . . . . **35** C3
Cheylesmore Ho
SW1 . . . . **146** A2
Cheyne Ct SW3 . . . **158** C4
Cheyne Gdns
SW3 . . . . **158** B3
Cheyne Mews
SW3 . . . . **158** B3
Cheyne Pl SW3 . . . **158** C4
Cheyne Row SW3 . **158** B3
Cheyne Wlk
SW10 . . . . **157** B2
Cheyney Ho ❷ E9 . . **17** C2
Chichele Mans
NW2 . . . . **9** C3
Chichele Rd NW2 . . . **9** C3
Chicheley St SE1 . . **135** A4
Chichester Ct ❷
NW1 . . . . **13** B1
Chichester Ho
NW6 . . . . **23** C3
Chichester Rd
Bayswater W2 . . . . **100** B4
Kilburn NW6 . . . . . . **23** C3
Chichester Rents
WC2 . . . . **107** B2
Chichester St
SW1 . . . . **147** A1
Chichester Way
E14 . . . . **42** C2
Chicksand Ho E1 . **111** B4
Chicksand St E1 . . **111** A3
Chicksand Street
E1 . . . . **111** B3
Chiddingstone
SE13 . . . . **67** B2

Chiddingstone St
SW6 . . . . **165** C2
Chigwell Ct ❶ E9 . . **18** A2
Chigwell Hill E1 . . . . **32** A2
Chiham Ho ❺
SE15 . . . . **50** B4
Chilcombe Ho ❻
SW15 . . . . **68** C4
Chilcot Cl ❶❸ E14 . . **34** A3
Childebert Rd
SW17 . . . . **73** A2
Childeric Prim Sch
SE14 . . . . **51** A3
Childeric Rd SE14 . . **51** A3
Childerley St
SW6 . . . . **164** A4
Childers St SE8 . . . . **51** B4
Child La SE10 . . . . . . **43** B3
CHILD'S HILL **1** C2
Child's Hill Prim Sch
NW2 . . . . **11** A3
Child's Mews
SW5 . . . . **141** C3
Child's Pl SW5 . . . **141** C3
Child's St SW5 . . . **141** C3
Child's Wlk SW5 . . **141** C3
Chilham Ct ❶❸
SW9 . . . . **62** C4
Chilham Ho SE1 . . **137** C2
Chillingford Dr
SW11 . . . . **59** C3
Chillingworth Rd
N7 . . . . **14** C3
Chiltern Ct
❶❺ Deptford SE14 . **50** B3
Marylebone NW1 . . **91** A1
Chiltern Ho
Camberwell SE17 . **48** C4
❹ Kensal Town
W10 . . . . **31** A4
❺ Stamford Hill N16 . . **7** B3
Chiltern Rd E3 . . . . . **26** C1
Chiltern St W1 . . . **103** B4
Chilton Gr SE8 . . . . . **41** A2
Chilton Rd TW9 . . . . **54** C4
Chilton St
E2 . . . . **24** B1 **99** A2
Chilver St SE10 . . . . **43** B1
Chilworth Ct ❽
SW19 . . . . **69** C3
Chilworth Mews
W2 . . . . **101** B1
Chilworth St W2 . . **101** A1
Chimney Ct ❷❸ E1 . **32** A1
China Ct ❶ E1 . . . . . **32** A1
China Hall Mews ❻
SE16 . . . . **40** B3
China Mews ❶❼
SW2 . . . . **74** B4
Chindit Ho ❶ N16 . . **15** C4
Ching Ct WC2 . . . . **106** A1
Chinnocks Wharf
E14 . . . . **33** A2
Chipka St E14 . . . . . **42** B4
Chipley St SE14 . . . . **51** A4
Chippendale Ho
SW1 . . . . **146** B1
Chippenham Gdns
NW6 . . . . **23** C2
Chippenham Mews
W9 . . . . **23** C1
Chippenham Rd
W9 . . . . **23** C1
Chip St SW4 . . . . **61** C3
Chipstead Ho ❹
SW2 . . . . **74** A3

Chipstead St
SW6 . . . . **165** C2
Chirk Ct SE4 . . . . 51 B1
Chisenhale Prim Sch
E3 . . . . 26 A3
Chisenhale Rd E3 . . 26 A3
Chisholm Ct 1
W6 . . . . 38 C1
Chisholm Rd 6
TW10 . . . . 54 B1
Chisledon Wlk E9 . . 18 B2
Chislehurst Rd
TW10 . . . . 54 A2
Chislet 5 NW5 . . . . . 12 C2
Chiswell St
Barbican EC1 . . . **109** B4
Camberwell SE5 . . . 48 C3
CHISWICK 38 B1
Chiswick & Bedford
Park Prep Sch
W4 . . . . 38 A2
Chiswick Common Rd
W4 . . . . 37 C2
Chiswick Com Sch
W4 . . . . 45 C3
Chiswick Green
Studios 1 W4 . . . 37 B2
Chiswick High Rd
W4 . . . . 38 A2
Chiswick High Road
(North Circular Rd)
W4 . . . . 36 C1
Chiswick High* W4 . . 45 C4
Chiswick La W4 . . . . 38 A1
Chiswick La S W4 . . 46 B4
Chiswick Mall W4 . . 38 B1
Chiswick Maternity
Hospl W4 . . . . 38 B1
Chiswick Park Sta
W4 . . . . 37 B2
Chiswick Pier W4 . . 46 B3
Chiswick Pk W4 . . . 37 A2
Chiswick Plaza
W4 . . . . 45 B4
Chiswick Quay
W4 . . . . 45 B2
Chiswick Rd W4 . . . . 37 B2
Chiswick Rdbt W4 . . 36 C1
Chiswick Sq W4 . . . . 46 A4
Chiswick Sta W4 . . . 45 B3
Chiswick Staithe
W4 . . . . 45 B2
Chiswick Terr 6
W4 . . . . 37 B2
Chiswick Village
W4 . . . . 45 A4
Chiswick Wharf
W4 . . . . 46 B4
Chitty St W1 . . . . . . **105** A4
Chivalry Rd SW11 . . 60 A2
Chivelston 27
SW19 . . . . 69 C3
Chobham Gdns
SW19 . . . . 69 C2
Chobham Rd E15 . . 19 C3
Cholmeley Cres N6 . . 4 A4
Cholmeley Lo N6 . . . . 4 A3
Cholmeley Pk N6 . . . 4 A3
Cholmeley Gdns
NW6 . . . . 10 C3
Cholmondeley Ave
NW10 . . . . 21 C3
Chopin's Ct 13 E1 . . 32 A1
Chopwell Cl E15 . . . 19 C1
Choumert Gr SE15 . . 49 C1
Choumert Mews
SE15 . . . . 49 C1

Choumert Rd
SE15 . . . . 49 B1
Choumert Sq 4
SE15 . . . . 49 C1
Chow Sq 2 E8 . . . . 16 B3
Chrisp Ho SE10 . . . . 53 A4
Chrisp St E14 . . . . . . 34 A3
Christ Church
TW9 . . . . 54 A4
Christchurch Ave
NW6 . . . . 10 A1
Christ Church
Bentinck CE Prim
Sch NW1 . . . . **102** B4
Christchurch CE Prim
Sch SW3 . . . . **158** C4
Christ Church CE
Prim Sch
Battersea SW11 . . . 60 A4
Brondesbury NW6 . . 10 B1
Cubitt Town SE10 . . 43 A1
Christchurch CE Sch
E1 . . . . **111** A3
Christ Church
Hampstead NW6 . . . 9 C1
London SE4 . . . . 66 A3
Chudleigh St E1 . . . 32 C3
Chumleigh Gdns
SE5 . . . . 49 A4
Chumleigh St SE5 . . 49 A4
Church App SE21 . . 75 C1
Church Ave
Camden Town
NW1 . . . . 13 A2
Mortlake SW14 . . . . 55 C4
Church Cl W8 . . . . **128** A4
Church Cres E9 . . . . 17 C1
Churchcroft Cl
SW12 . . . . 72 C4
Church Ct
Holborn EC4 . . . . **107** C1
Rotherhithe SE16 . . 41 B4
Churchdale Ct 1
W4 . . . . 37 A1
CHURCH END 8 B3
Church Entry EC4 . **108** B1
Church Estate
Almshouses 8
TW9 . . . . 54 B3
Churchfield Ho
W2 . . . . 89 B1
Churchfield Mans 6
SW6 . . . . **165** A1
Churchfield Rd
W3 . . . . 28 B1
Churchfields SE10 . . 52 B4
Church Garth 4
N19 . . . . 4 C2
Church Gate SW6 . . 58 A4
Church Gn SW9 . . **173** C2
Church Gr SE13 . . . . 67 A2
Churchhill Gardens
Prim Sch SW1 . . . **147** A1
Church Ho EC1 . . . . 96 B2
Church Ct
Finsbury Pk N5 . . . . 5 C4
Peckham SE15 . . . . 49 C1
Wimbledon NW2 . . . 9 A3
Churchill Gdns
SW1 . . . . **160** C4

Christopher Pl
NW1 . . . . **93** C3
Christopher St
EC2 . . . . **97** C1
Christ's Sch TW10 . . 54 C2
Christ the King RC
Prim Sch N4 . . . . . . 5 B2
Christ the King Sixth
Form Coll SE13 . . **67** C4
Chryssell Rd SW9 **163** C2
Chubworthy 5
SE14 . . . . 51 A4
Chudleigh Rd
Hampstead NW6 . . . 9 C1
London SE4 . . . . 66 C2
Chudleigh St E1 . . . 32 C3
Chumleigh Gdns
SE5 . . . . 49 A4
Church Ave
Camden Town
NW1 . . . . 13 A2
Mortlake SW14 . . . . 55 C4
Church Cl W8 . . . . **128** A4
Church Cres E9 . . . . 17 C1
Churchcroft Cl
SW12 . . . . 72 C4
Church Ct
Holborn EC4 . . . . **107** C1
Rotherhithe SE16 . . 41 B4
Churchdale Ct 1
W4 . . . . 37 A1
CHURCH END 8 B3
Church Entry EC4 . **108** B1
Church Estate
Almshouses 8
TW9 . . . . 54 B3
Churchfield Ho
W2 . . . . 89 B1
Churchfield Mans 6
SW6 . . . . **165** A1
Churchfield Rd
W3 . . . . 28 B1
Churchfields SE10 . . 52 B4
Church Garth 4
N19 . . . . 4 C2
Church Gate SW6 . . 58 A4
Church Gn SW9 . . **173** C2
Church Gr SE13 . . . . 67 A2
Churchhill Gardens
Prim Sch SW1 . . . **147** A1
Church Ho EC1 . . . . 96 B2
Church Hill Rd E17 . 30 C1
Church Mead SE5 . . 48 B3
Churchmead Rd
NW10 . . . . 8 C2
Church Path W4 . . . 37 B3
Church Pl SW1 . . . **119** A3
Church Rd
Acton W3 . . . . 37 B4
Barnes SW13 . . . . . 46 C2
24 Canonbury N1 . . 15 B2
Richmond TW10,
TW9 . . . . 54 A2

Church Rd continued
Willesden NW10 . . . 8 A1
Church Row NW3 . . 11 B4
Church St
Chiswick W4 . . . . . 46 B4
Lisson Gr NW8 . . . . **90** A1
Church Street Est
NW8 . . . . 89 C1
Church Studios 16
NW1 . . . . 13 C2
Churchward Ho
Camberwell SE17 . . 48 A4
West Kensington
SW5 . . . . **141** A1
Churchway NW1 . . **93** C4
Church Wlk
Barnes SW13 . . . . . 46 C2
Canonbury N16 . . . 15 C4
Child's Hill NW2 . . . . 1 B1
Stoke Newington
N16 . . . . 6 C1
Churchyard Row
SE11 . . . . **150** B4
Churnfield 2 N4 . . . 5 C2
Churston Cl 16
SW2 . . . . 74 C3
Churston Mans
WC1 . . . . 95 A1
Churton Pl
Brentford W4 . . . . . 45 A4
Pimlico SW1 . . . . **147** A3
Churton St SW1 . . **147** A3
Chute Ho SW9 . . . **173** B1
Chuter Ede Ho
SW6 . . . . **155** A3
Cicada Rd SW18 . . . 59 B2
Cicely Ho NW8 . . . . 79 C1
Cicely Rd SE15 . . . . 49 C2
Cinema Mus The*
SE11 . . . . **150** A3
Cinnamon Cl
SE15 . . . . 49 B3
Cinnamon Row 3
SW11 . . . . 59 B4
Cinnamon St E1 . . . 32 A1
Cinnamon Wharf
SE1 . . . . **139** A4
Circle Ho 14 E14 . . 34 C3
Circle The SE1 . . . **139** A4
Circus Ho NW1 . . . . 92 B1
Circus Mews W1 . . **102** C4
Circus Pl EC2 . . . . 109 C3
Circus Rd SE18 . . . . 79 B1
Circus St SE10 . . . . 52 B3
Cirencester St
W2 . . . . **100** A4
Cissbury Ho 6
SE26 . . . . 76 C1
Citadel Pl SE11 . . **148** C2
Citizen Ho N7 . . . . . 14 C4
Citizen Rd N7 . . . . . 14 C4
Citron Terr 4
SE15 . . . . 65 A4
Citrus Ho 14 SE8 . . 41 B1
City Banking Coll
SE1 . . . . **137** C4
City Bsns Ctr 33
SE16 . . . . 40 B4
City Central Est
EC1 . . . . 96 C3
City Coll N1 . . . . . . **97** B4

City Coll of London
The WC1 . . . . . . **107** A3
City Forum EC1 . . . **96** C4
City Garden Row
N1 . . . . **86** B1
City Gate E1 . . . . . . 25 B1
City & Guilds of
London Art Sch
SE11 . . . . **149** C1
City Harbour E14 . **42** A3
City & Islington 6th
Form Coll EC1 . . . **96** A4
City & Islington Coll
Finsbury Pk N4 . . . . 5 C1
Lower Holloway N7 . 14 A4
Lower Holloway N7 . 14 B4
Shoreditch EC1 . . . **97** A3
Shoreditch N1 . . . . **87** B4
City Lights
SE11 . . . . **149** C1
CITY OF LONDON
. . . . 122 B4
City of London Sch
EC4 . . . . **122** C4
City of London Sch
for Girls EC2 . . . **109** A4
City of Westminster
Coll
Paddington NW1 . **102** B4
Paddington W2 . . **101** B4
City of Westminster
Cull, Maida Vale Ctr
W9 . . . . **88** A3
City of Westminster
Cull, Queens Park
Ctr W9 . . . . 23 C2
City Rd EC1 . . . . **97** C4
City Thameslink Sta
EC4 . . . . **108** A1
City University
. . . . **96** A3
City Wlk SE1 . . . . **138** A3
Civil Service Coll
SW1 . . . . **146** C3
Clabon Mews
SW1 . . . . **144** C4
Clack St SE16 . . . . . 40 B4
Claire Ct SW2 . . . . 10 A2
Claire Pl E14 . . . . . . 41 C3
Clancarty Rd
SW6 . . . . **165** C2
Clandon Cl W3 . . . . 37 A4
Clandon St SE8 . . . 51 C1
Clanfield Ho 12
SW15 . . . . 68 C3
Clanricarde Gdns
W2 . . . . 2 **113** C3
CLAPHAM **61** A4
Clapham Common*
SW4 . . . . 61 A3
Clapham Common
North Side SW4 . . 60 C3
Clapham Common
South Side SW4 . . 61 B2
Clapham Common Sta
SW4 . . . . **61** B2
Clapham Common
West Side
Clapham SW4,
SW11 . . . . 60 B3
Clapham SW11 . . . 60 C2

Clapham Computer &
Secretarial Coll
SW11 .... 60 B2
Clapham Court Terr
2 SW4 .... 62 A2
Clapham Cres
SW4 .... 61 C3
Clapham Ct 3
SW4 .... 62 A2
Clapham High St
SW4 .... 61 C4
Clapham High Street
Sta SW4 .... 61 C4
Clapham Junction Est
SW11 .... 60 A3
Clapham Junction Sta
SW11 .... 60 A3
Clapham Manor Ct 4
SW4 .... 61 B4
Clapham Manor Prim
Sch SW4 .... 61 B4
Clapham Manor St
SW4 .... 61 C4
Clapham Mans
SW4 .... 61 A1
Clapham North Bsns
Ctr 10 SW4 .... 61 C4
Clapham North Sta
SW4 .... 62 A4
CLAPHAM PARK 61 C2
Clapham Park Rd
SW4 .... 61 C3
Clapham Park Terr 4
SW2 .... 62 A2
Clapham South Sta
SW4 .... 61 A1
Clapton Comm E5 .... 7 C4
Clapton Girls Tec Coll
E5 .... 17 B4
CLAPTON PARK 17 C4
Clapton Pas E5 ...... 17 B3
Clapton Sq E5 .... 17 B3
Clapton Terr E5 ...... 7 C2
Clapton Way E5 ..... 16 C4
Clara Grant Ho 10
E14 .... 41 C3
Clara Grant Prim Sch
The E3 .... 26 C1
Clare Ct WC1 .... 94 B3
Claredale Ho 3
E2 .... 25 A3
Claredale St 5
E2 .... 25 A3
Clare Gdns W11 ..... 31 A3
Clare Ho
Bermondsey SE1 ... 153 A2
8 Old Ford E3 .... 26 B4
Clare La N1 .... 15 B1
Clare Lawn Ave
SW14 .... 55 C2
Clare Mews SW6 .... 156 A1
Clare Mkt WC2 ...... 107 A1
Claremont
SW15 .... 58 A2
Claremont Cl
Finsbury N1 .... 85 C1
8 Streatham SW2 ... 74 B3
Claremont Ct 1
W9 .... 23 B2
Claremont Gr W4 .... 46 A3
Claremont Rd
Highgate N6 .... 4 B4
West Kilburn W9 ...... 23 B3
Claremont Sq N1 .... 85 B1

Claremont St
SE10 .... 52 A4
Clarence Ave SW4 ... 61 C1
Clarence Cres
SW4 .... 61 C1
Clarence Ct 10
W6 .... 39 A2
Clarence Gate
NW1 .... 91 A2
Clarence Gate Gdns
NW1 .... 91 A1
Clarence Gdns
NW1 .... 92 B3
Clarence Ho SE17 ... 48 B4
Clarence Ho*
SW1 .... 119 A1
Clarence La SW15 ... 56 B1
Clarence Mews
Balham SW12 .... 73 A4
Hackney E5 .... 17 A3
1 Rotherhithe
SE16 .... 32 C1
Clarence Pl 25 E5 .. 17 A3
Clarence Rd
Brentford W4 .... 36 C1
Brondesbury NW6 .... 10 B2
Lower Clapton E5 .... 17 A4
Richmond TW9 .... 44 C2
Clarence St 5
TW9 .... 54 A3
Clarence Terr
NW1 .... 91 A2
Clarence Way
NW1 .... 13 A1
Clarence Wlk
SW4 .... 172 A2
Clarendon Cl
Bayswater W2 ...... 116 A4
5 Hackney E9 .... 17 B1
Clarendon Cross
W11 .... 31 A2 112 B3
Clarendon Ct
Paddington W9 .... 89 A2
1 Richmond TW9 ... 44 C2
Willesden NW2 .... 9 B1
Clarendon Dr
SW15 .... 57 B3
Clarendon Flats
W1 .... 103 C1
Clarendon Gdns
W9 .... 89 A2
Clarendon Gr NW1 .. 93 B4
Clarendon Ho
NW1 .... 83 A1
Clarendon Mews
W2 .... 116 A4
Clarendon Pl W2 ... 116 A4
Clarendon Rd
W11 .... 31 A2 112 B3
Clarendon Rise
SE13 .... 67 B3
Clarendon St
SW1 .... 146 B2
Clarendon Terr
W9 .... 89 A2
Clarendon Wlk 11
W11 .... 31 A3
Clare Rd
New Cross Gate
SE14 .... 51 B2
Willesden NW10 .... 8 C1
Clare St E2 .... 25 A3
Clareville Grove Mews
SW7 .... 143 A3

Clareville St SW7 .. 143 A3
Clarewood Ct W1 ... 102 C3
Clarewood Wlk
SW9 .... 62 C3
Clarges Ho 1 W1 .. 118 B2
Clarges Mews
W1 .... 118 A2
Clarges St 1 W1 ... 118 B2
Clariat Ct W3 .... 36 C4
Claribel Rd SW9 .... 48 A1
Claridge Ct SW6 ... 164 C3
Clarissa Ho 7
E14 .... 34 A3
Clarissa St E8 .... 24 B4
Clarke Ho 2 SW4 ... 61 B4
Clarke Path N16 ...... 7 C3
Clarkes Mews
W1 .... 103 C4
Clark Ho SW10 ..... 156 C2
Clark Lawrence Ct
SW11 .... 59 C4
Clarkson Rd E16 .... 35 B3
Clarkson Row
NW1 .... 82 C1
Clarkson St E2 ...... 25 A2
Clark's Pl EC2 ..... 110 A2
Clark St E1 .... 32 B4
Classic Mans 3
E9 .... 17 B1
Classinghall Ho 14
SW15 .... 57 C1
Claude Rd SE15 ..... 50 A1
Claude St E14 .... 41 C2
Claudia Jones Way
SW2 .... 62 A1
Claudia Pl SW19 .... 70 A3
Clavell St 8 SE10 ... 52 B4
Claverdale Rd
SW2 .... 74 C4
Clavering Ave
SW13 .... 47 A4
Clavering Ho SE13 .. 67 C3
Claverton St SW1 .. 147 A1
Clave St E1 .... 32 B1
Claxton Gr
W6 .... 39 C1 140 A1
Claybank Gr SE13 ... 67 A4
Claybrook Rd W6 ... 47 C4
Claydon SE17 ...... 150 C4
Clayhall Ct 20 E3 ... 26 B3
Claylands Pl SW8 .. 163 B2
Claylands Rd
SW8 .... 163 A3
Claypole Rd E15 .... 27 B3
Claypole Ave
TW8 .... 36 A2
Claypole Hospl &
Day Treatment Ctr
TW8 .... 36 A2
Claypole La TW8 .... 36 A1
Clays Ct N16 .... 7 B3
Clays La E15 .... 19 A3
Clays Lane Cl E15 .. 19 A3
Clays Lane Cvn Site
E15 .... 19 B3
Clay St W1 .... 103 A3
Clayton Cres N1 .... 84 C3
Clayton Ho 2 E9 .... 17 C4
Clayton Mews
SE10 .... 52 C2
Clayton Rd SE15 .... 49 C2
Clayton St SE11 ... 163 B4
Clearbrook Way 3
E1 .... 32 B3
Clear Water Ho 9
TW10 .... 54 A2

Clearwater Terr 4
W11 .... 39 C4
Clearwell Dr W9 ..... 88 B1
Cleaver Ho 6
NW3 .... 12 B1
Cleaver Sq SE11 ... 149 C2
Cleaver St SE11 ... 149 C2
Cleeve Ho
E2 .... 24 A2 98 B3
Cleeve Way SW15 ... 68 B4
Cleeve Workshops
E2 .... 24 A2 98 B3
Clegg St 16 E1 ...... 32 A1
Cleland Ho 7 E2 ..... 25 B3
Clematis St W12 ..... 29 C2
Clem Atlee Par
SW6 .... 155 A3
Clem Attlee Ct
SW6 .... 155 A3
Clemence St E14 .... 33 B4
Clement Attlee Ho
NW10 .... 8 B1
Clement Ave SW4 ... 61 C3
Clement Cl
Acton W4 .... 37 C2
Hampstead NW6 ...... 9 C1
Clement Danes Ho 2
W12 .... 30 A3
Clement Ho
14 Deptford SE8 ..... 41 A2
17 North Kensington
W10 .... 30 B4
Clements Ave 1
E16 .... 35 C2
Clements Inn
WC2 .... 107 A1
Clements Inn Pas
WC2 .... 107 A1
Clement's La 2
EC4 .... 123 C4
Clement's Rd
SE16 .... 40 A3
Clemson Ho 8 E8 ... 24 B4
Clennam St SE1 ... 137 A4
Clenston Mews
W1 .... 102 C2
Clephane Rd 13
N1 .... 15 B2
Clephane Rd N N1 .. 15 B2
Clephane Rd S N1 .. 15 C2
Clere Pl EC2 .... 97 C2
Clere St EC2 .... 97 C2
CLERKENWELL 96 A1
Clerkenwell Cl
EC1 .... 95 C1
Clerkenwell Gn
EC1 .... 96 A1
Clerkenwell Parochial
CE Prim Sch EC1 .. 95 B3
Clerkenwell Rd
EC1 .... 96 A1
Clermont Rd E9 ..... 25 B4
Clevedon Cl
Battersea SW11 ..... 168 A4
Dulwich SE21 .... 75 C2
Clevedon Mans
NW5 .... 12 C4
Cleve Ho NW6 ...... 11 A1
Cleveland Ave W4 ... 38 B2
Cleveland Ct 1 W1 .. 93 A1
Cleveland Gdns
Barnes SW13 .... 46 B1
Paddington W2 ..... 100 C1

Cleveland Gr 39
E1 .... 25 B1
Cleveland Mans
Brixton SW9 .... 163 B1
4 Brondesbury
NW6 .... 10 B1
Paddington W9 ...... 23 C1
Cleveland Mews
W1 .... 104 C4
Cleveland Pl SW1 .. 119 A2
Cleveland Rd
Barnes SW13 .... 46 B1
Islington N1 .... 15 C1
14 South Acton W4 ... 37 B3
Cleveland Row
SW1 .... 119 A1
Cleveland Sq W2 ... 100 C1
Cleveland St W1 .... 92 C1
Cleveland Terr
W2 .... 101 A2
Cleveland Way E1 .. 25 B1
Clevedon Cl N16 ..... 7 A1
Cleve Rd NW6 .... 11 A1
Cleverly Cotts
W12 .... 29 B1
Cleverly Est W12 .... 29 C2
Cley Ho SE4 .... 65 C3
Clichy Ho 32 E1 .... 32 B4
Clifden Mews E5 .... 17 C3
Clifden Rd E5 .... 17 C3
Cliff Ct 14 NW1 ..... 13 C2
Cliffe Ho 4 SE10 .... 43 B1
Clifford Ave
Mortlake SW14 .... 45 B1
Mortlake SW14,
TW9 .... 55 A4
Clifford Ct
Bayswater W2 ...... 100 A3
Wandsworth SW18 ... 71 C4
Willesden NW10 ...... 8 A4
Clifford Dr SW9 ..... 63 A3
Clifford Gdns
NW10 .... 22 B3
Clifford Haigh Ho
SW6 .... 47 C3
Clifford Ho W14 ... 140 C3
Clifford's Inn Pas
EC4 .... 107 B1
Clifford St W1 ...... 118 C3
Clifford Way NW10 ... 8 B4
Cliff Rd NW1 .... 13 C2
Cliff Road Studios 13
NW1 .... 13 C2
Cliffsend Ho SW9 .. 173 C3
Cliff Terr SE8 .... 51 C1
Cliffview Rd SE13 ... 66 C4
Cliff Villas NW1 ..... 13 C2
Cliff Wlk E16 .... 35 B4
Clifton Ave W12 ..... 29 B1
Clifton Cres SE15 ... 50 A3
Clifton Ct
Finsbury Pk N4 .... 5 C2
Paddington NW8 ..... 89 B2
Peckham SE15 .... 50 A3
Putney SW15 .... 57 C2
Clifton Gate
SW10 .... 156 C4
Clifton Gdns
Chiswick W4 .... 37 C2
Paddington W9 ...... 88 C1
Clifton Gr E8 .... 16 C2
Clifton Hill NW8 ..... 78 C3
Clifton Ho
E2 .... 24 B1 98 C2
Clifton Mans 4
SW9 .... 62 C3

Clifton Pl
Paddington W2 . . . . . . **101** C1
Rotherhithe SE16 . . . . . 40 B4

Clifton Rd
Harlesden NW10 . . . . . 21 C3
Newham E16 . . . . 35 A4
Paddington W9 . . . . . . 89 A2

Clifton Rise SE14 . . . 51 A3

Clifton St
EC2 . . . . 24 A1 98 A1

Clifton Terr N4 . . . . . . 5 C2
Clifton Villas W9 . . . **100** C4
Clifton Way SE15 . . . . 50 B3

Climsland Ho SE1 **121** C2
Clinch Cl E11 E16 . . . 35 C4
Clinger Ct N1 . . . . . . 24 A4
Clink St SE1 . . . . . . **123** B2
Clipper Cl SE16 . . . . . 40 C4
Clipper Ho E14 . . . . . 42 B1
Clipper Way SE13 . . . 67 B3

Clipstone Ho 10
SW15 . . . . 56 C2

Clipstone Mews
W1 . . . . **104** C4
Clipstone St W1 . . . **104** C4
Clissold Cres N16 . . . . 6 B1
Clissold Ct N4 . . . . . . 6 B2
Clissold Ho 4 N16 . . . 6 C2
Clissold Rd N16 . . . . . 6 C1
Clitheroe Rd SW9 **172** B1
Clive Ct W9 . . . . 89 A2
Cliveden Ho SW1 **145** B4
Cliveden Pl SW1 **145** B4

Clive Ho
Clapham SW8 . . . . **171** B2
Greenwich SE10 . . . . . 52 B4

Clive Rd SE21 . . . . 76 A4

Cloak La EC4 . . . . . . **123** B4
Clochar Ct NW10 . . . . 21 B4
Clock Ho N16 . . . . 7 B4

Clockhouse Cl
SW19 . . . . 69 B2
Clockhouse Pl
SW15 . . . . 58 A1
Clockhouse The
SW19 . . . . 69 B2
Clock Mus★ EC2 **109** A2
Clock Tower Mews
N1 . . . . 87 A3
Clock Tower Pl
N7 . . . . 14 A2

Cloister Rd
Acton W3 . . . . 28 B4
Child's Hill NW2 . . . . . . 1 B2
Cloisters Ct N6 . . . . 4 A4
Cloisters The 6
SW9 . . . . **173** C3
Clonbrock Rd N16 . . . 16 A4
Cloncurry St SW6 **47** C2
Clone Ct 4 W12 . . . . . 38 A3
Clonmel Rd SW6 **165** A4
Clonmore St
SW18 . . . . 70 B3
Clorane Gdns NW3 . . . 1 C1

Close The
Lewisham SE3 . . . . 52 C1
Mortlake TW9 . . . . 55 A4
Cloth Ct EC1 . . . . . **108** B3
Cloth Fair EC1 . . . . **108** B3
Clothier St E1 . . . . . . **110** B2
Cloth St EC1 . . . . . . **108** C4

Cloudesdale Rd
SW17 . . . . 73 A2

Cloudesley Mans
N1 . . . . **85** C3
Cloudesley Pl N1 . . **85** C3
Cloudesley Rd N1 . . **85** B3
Cloudesley Sq N1 . . **85** C3
Clove Cres E14 . . . . . 34 C2

Clovelly Ho
W2 . . . . **100** C2
Clovelly Rd W4 . . . . . . 37 C4
Clovelly Way E1 . . . . 32 B3
Clover Mews
SW3 . . . . **159** A4
Clowes Ho 8
SW4 . . . . 62 A3
Cloysters Gn E1 . . **125** B2
Club Row
E2 . . . . 24 B1 98 C2
Clunbury St N1 . . . . **87** C1
Clunie Ho SW1 **131** A2
Cluny Mews SW5 **141** B3
Cluny Pl SE1 . . . . . . **138** A2
Cluse Ct N1 . . . . **86** C2
Clutton St E14 . . . . . 34 A4
Clyde Ct NW1 . . . . . **83** C2
Clyde Flats SW6 **154** C2
Clyde Gdns
TW10 . . . . 55 A3

Clydesdale Ho 6
W11 . . . . 31 B3
Clydesdale Rd
W11 . . . . 31 B3
Clyde St SE8 . . . . 51 B4
Clynes Ho 3 E2 . . . 25 C2
Clyro Ct N4 . . . . 5 B3
Clyston St SW8 **171** A2

Coach & Horses Yd
W1 . . . . **118** C4
Coach House La
Highbury N5 . . . . 15 A4
Wimbledon SW19 . . . . 69 C1
Coach House Mews
SE23 . . . . 65 C1
Coach House Yd 6
NW3 . . . . **11** C4
Coachmaker Mews 5
SW9 . . . . 62 A4
Coalbrook Mans 3
SW12 . . . . 73 A3
Coaldale Wlk
SE21 . . . . 75 B4
Coalecroft Rd
SW15 . . . . 57 B2
Coalport Ho SE11 **149** B4
Coatbridge Ho 8
N1 . . . . 14 B1
Coates Ave SW18 . . . 60 A1
Coates Ct NW3 . . . . . 12 A3
Coate St E2 . . . . 24 C3
Coates Wlk TW8 . . . . . 36 A1
Cobbett St SW8 **163** A1
Cobble La N1 . . . . 15 A1
Cobble Mews N4,
N5 . . . . 6 B4
Cobbold Ct SW1 **147** B4
Cobbold Ind Est
NW10 . . . . 8 B2
Cobbold Mews
W12 . . . . 38 B4
Cobbold Rd
Bedford Pk W12 . . . . . 38 B4
Willesden NW10 . . . . . . 8 B2
Cobb's Hall 1
SW6 . . . . 47 C4
Cobb St E1 . . . . **110** C3

Cobden Bldgs
WC1 . . . . **94** C4
Cobden Ho
Bethnal Green
E2 . . . . 24 C2 **99** C4
Regent's Pk NW1 . . **82** C2
Cobham Cl SW11 . . . 60 A1
Cobham Mews 3
NW1 . . . . 13 C1
Coborn Mews 9
E3 . . . . 26 B2
Coborn Rd E3 . . . . . . 26 B2
Coborn St E3 . . . . . . 26 B2
Cobourg Prim Sch
SE5 . . . . 49 B4
Cobourg Rd SE5 . . . . 49 B4
Cobourg St NW1 . . . **93** A3
Coburg Cl SW1 **147** A4
Coburg Cres SW2 . . . 74 C3
Coburg Dwellings 1
E1 . . . . 32 B2
Cochrane Cl NW8 **79** C1
Cochrane Ho 19
E14 . . . . 41 C4
Cochrane Mews
NW8 . . . . **79** C1
Cochrane St NW8 **79** C1
Coci Ho W14 . . . . . **141** A3
Cockburn Ho
SW1 . . . . **147** C1
Cock Hill E1 . . . . . . **110** B3
Cock La EC1 . . . . . . **108** B3
Cockpit Yd WC1 **107** A4
Cocksure La SW1 **119** C2
Cockspur St SW1 **119** C2
Coda Ctr The
SW6 . . . . **164** B4
Code St E1 . . 24 B1 **99** A1
Codicote Ho 2
SE8 . . . . 40 C2
Codicote Terr N4 . . . . . 6 B2
Codling Cl E1 **125** C2
Codrington Ct 3
SE16 . . . . 33 A1
Codrington Ho 7
E1 . . . . 25 A1
Codrington Mews
W11 . . . . 31 A3
Cody Rd E16 . . . . 27 C1
Coffey St SE8 . . . . . . 51 C3
Cohen Lo E5 . . . . 18 A3
Coin St SE1 . . . . **121** B2
Coity Rd NW5 . . . . . . 12 C2
Cokers La SE21 . . . . . 75 C3
Coke St E1 . . . . **111** C2
Colas Mews 7
NW6 . . . . 23 C4
Colbeck Mews
SW5 . . . . **142** B3
Colberg Pl N16 . . . . . . 7 B4
Colbert 1 SE5 . . . . . 49 B2
Colborne Ho 8
E14 . . . . 33 C2
Colchester Ho
SW8 . . . . **171** B2
Colchester St E1 **111** A2
Coldbath Sq EC1 . . **95** B2
Coldbath St SE13 . . . 52 A1
Cold Blow La
SE14 . . . . 50 C4
Coldharbour E14 . . . . 34 B1
Coldharbour Ind Est
SE5 . . . . 48 B1
Coldharbour La
SW9 . . . . 63 A4
Coldharbour Pl
SE5 . . . . 48 C1

Coldstream Gdns
SW18 . . . . 58 B1
Colebeck Mews
N1 . . . . 15 A2
Colebert Ave E1 . . . . 25 B1
Colebert Ho 21 E1 . . 25 B1
Colebrook Cl
SW19 . . . . 69 C4
Colebrook Ct
SW3 . . . . **144** B3
Colebrooke Pl N1 . . **86** B3
Colebrooke Row
Islington N1 . . . . **86** B3
Islington N1 . . . . **86** A2
Colebrook Ho 1
E14 . . . . 34 A3
Coleby Path 21
SE5 . . . . 48 C3
Colechurch Ho 1
SE1 . . . . **153** B1
Coleford Rd SW18 . . . 59 B2
Colegrave Prim Sch
E15 . . . . 19 C3
Colegrave Rd E15 . . . 19 C3
Colegrove Rd
SE15 . . . . 49 B4
Coleherne Ct
SW10 . . . . **142** B1
Coleherne Mans
SW5 . . . . **142** B2
Coleherne Mews
SW10 . . . . **142** A1
Coleherne Rd
SW10 . . . . **142** A1
Colehill Gdns
SW6 . . . . **164** A3
Colehill La SW6 **164** A3
Cole Ho SE1 . . . . . . **135** C3
Coleman Ct SW18 . . . 70 C4
Coleman Fields
N1 . . . . **87** A4
Coleman Mans N19 . . . 5 A4
Coleman Rd SE5 . . . . 49 A3
Coleman St EC2 **109** B2
Coleman Street Bldgs
EC2 . . . . **109** B2
Colenso Rd E5 . . . . . . 17 B4
Coleraine Rd SE3 . . . 53 B4
Coleridge Cl SW8 **170** B1
Coleridge Ct W14 . . . 39 C3
Coleridge Gdns
NW6 . . . . 11 B1
Coleridge Ho
Pimlico SW1 . . . . . **147** A1
Walworth SE17 . . . . **151** A2
Coleridge Prim Sch
N8 . . . . 5 A4
Coleridge Rd N4,
N7 . . . . 5 C2
Coleridge Sq
SW10 . . . . **156** C2
Coles Ct SW11 . . . . **167** C3
Coleshill Flats
SW1 . . . . **145** C3
Cole St SE1 . . . . . . **137** A3
Colestown St
SW11 . . . . **168** B2
Colet Gdns W14 . . . . . 39 C2
Colet Ho SE17 . . . . . **150** B1
Colette Ct 5 SE16 . . 40 C4
Coley St WC1 . . . . . **95** A1

Colin Ct SW16 . . . . . . 73 C2
Colinette Rd
SW15 . . . . 57 B3
Colin Rd NW10 . . . . . . 8 C2
Colinsdale N1 . . . . . **86** A3
Colin Winter Ho 45
E1 . . . . 25 B1

Coliston Pas
SW18 . . . . 70 C4
Coliston Rd SW18 . . . 70 C4
Collamore Ave
SW18 . . . . 72 A3
Collard Pl NW1 . . . . . 13 A1
Collcutt Lo SW4 . . . . 62 A3
College App SE10 . . . 52 B4
College Cl E5 . . . . . . 17 B3
College Cross N1 . . . 14 C1
College Cross N1 . . . 14 C1

College Ct
Chelsea SW3 . . . . . **145** A1
3 Hammersmith
W6 . . . . 39 B1
Hampstead NW3 . . . 11 C1
College Gdns
Dulwich SE21 . . . . . . 76 A3
Upper Tooting
SW17 . . . . 72 A2
College Gr NW1 . . . **83** B4
College Green Ct
SW9 . . . . 63 A4
College Hill EC4 **123** A4
College La NW5 . . . 13 A4
College Mews 6
SW18 . . . . 59 A2
COLLEGE PARK . . . 22 A2
College Park Cl
SE13 . . . . 67 C3
College Park Sch
W2 . . . . **100** A3
College Pl
Camden Town
NW1 . . . . **83** B3
Chelsea SW10 . . . . . **156** C2
College Rd
Dulwich SE21,
SE19 . . . . 76 A2
Kensal Green NW10 . . 22 B3
College St EC4 **123** A4
College Terr E3 . . . . . 26 B2
Collent Ho 12 E9 . . . 17 B2
Collent St E9 . . . . . . 17 B2
Collerston Ho
SE10 . . . . 43 B1
Collett Ho N16 . . . . . . 7 A3
Collett Rd SE16 . . . . **139** C2
Colley Ho 16 N7 . . . 13 C3
Collier St N1 . . . . . . **84** C1
Collingbourne Rd
W12 . . . . 30 A1
Collingham Gdns
SW5 . . . . **142** B3
Collingham Pl
SW5 . . . . **142** B4
Collingham Rd
SW5 . . . . **142** B3
Collingham Sixth
Form Coll SW5 . . **142** B3
Collington St
SE10 . . . . 42 C1
Collingwood Ho
27 Bethnal Green
E1 . . . . 25 A1
Marylebone W1 . . . **104** C4

Collingwood St
E1 . . . . **25** A1
Collins Ct E8 . . . . . . **16** C2
Collins Ho
6 Cubitt Town
SE10 . . . . **43** B1
4 Poplar E14 . . . . **34** B2
Collinson Ct SE1 . . **136** C3
Collinson Ho 16
SE15 . . . . **49** C3
Collinson St SE1 . . **136** C3
Collinson Wlk
SE1 . . . . **136** C3
Collins Rd N5, N16 . . **15** B4
Collins Sq SE3 . . . . **53** B1
Collins St SE3 . . . . **53** A1
Collins Yd N1 . . . . . **86** A3
Collison Pl N16 . . . . . **7** A3
Coll of Arms*
EC4 . . . . **122** C4
**Coll of Central
London The**
EC2 . . . . **24** A1 **98** A2
Coll of Law The
EC1 . . . . **97** B1
Coll of NW London
NW6 . . . . **23** C4
**Coll of NW London
(Willesden Centre)**
NW10 . . . . **8** B3
**Coll of Optometrists
The** SW1 . . . . **120** A2
Coll Sharp Ct
E2 . . . . **24** B2 **98** C3
Coll's Rd SE15 . . . . . **50** B2
Collyer Pl SE15 . . . . **49** C2
Colmans Wharf 5
E14 . . . . **34** A4
Colmar Ct 3 E1 . . . . **25** C1
Colmore Mews
SE15 . . . . **50** A2
Colnbrook St SE1 **136** A2
Colne Ho NW8 . . . . **89** C1
Colne Rd E5 . . . . **18** A4
Cologne Rd SW11 . . **59** C3
Colombo St SE1 . . **122** A1
Colomb St SE10 . . . **43** A1
Colonades The 4
SE5 . . . . **48** C2
Colonial Dr W4 . . . . **37** B2
Colonnade WC1 . . . **94** B1
Colonnade Ho
SE3 . . . . **53** B1
Colonnades The 6
E8 . . . . **17** A2
Colonnade The 12
SE8 . . . . **41** B2
Colorado Bldg 9
SE13 . . . . **52** A2
Colosseum Terr
NW1 . . . . **92** B2
Colour Ho SE1 . . . . **138** B3
Colstead Ho 22 E1 . . **32** A3
Colston Rd SW14 . . **55** B3
Colthurst Cres N4 . . . **6** B2
Coltman Ho SE10 . . **52** B4
Coltman St E14 . . . . **33** A4
Columba Ho SE14 . . **51** B2
Columbas Dr NW3 . . **2** C3
Columbia Ho 18
E3 . . . . **26** C2
Columbia Point 7
SE16 . . . . **40** B3
Columbia Prim Sch
E2 . . . . **24** B2 **99** A4

Columbia Rd
9 Hackney E2 . . . . . **24** C3
Shoreditch
E2 . . . . **24** B2 **98** C4
Columbia Road Mkt
E2 . . . . **24** B2 **99** A4
Colverson Ho 14
E1 . . . . **32** B4
Colvestone Cres
E8 . . . . **16** B3
Colvestone Prim Sch
E8 . . . . **16** B3
Colville Ho
32 Bethnal Green
E2 . . . . **25** B3
Notting Hill W11 . . **31** B3
Colville Mews
W11 . . . . **31** B3
Colville Ho 17 W11 **105** A3
Colville Prim Sch
W11 . . . . **31** B3
Colville Rd
Notting Hill W11 . . **31** B3
South Acton W3 . . . **37** A3
Colville Sq W11 . . . **31** B3
Colville Terr W11 . . **31** B3
Colwall Ho W9 . . . . **173** A1
Colwall Rd SE22 . . **64** B2
Colwick Cl N6 . . . . . . **4** C4
Colwith Rd W6 . . . . **47** B4
Colworth Gr SE17 . **151** A3
Colwyn Ho SE1 . . . **135** B1
Colyton Rd SE22 . . . **65** A2
Combe Ave SE3 . . . . **53** B3
Combedale Rd
SE10 . . . . **43** C1
Combe Ho
Mortlake SW14 . . . **45** B1
20 Paddington W2 . **31** C4
Combemartin Rd
SW18 . . . . **70** A3
Combe Mews 4
SE3 . . . . **53** B3
Comber Gr SE5 . . . . **48** B3
**Comber Grove Prim
Sch** SE5 . . . . **48** B3
Comber Ho SE5 . . . . **48** B3
Combermere Rd
SW9 . . . . **62** B4
Combe The NW1 . . . **92** B3
**Com Coll Hackney
The** E8 . . . . **25** A4
Comeragh Mews
W14 . . . . **140** B1
Comeragh Rd
W14 . . . . **140** B1
Comerford Rd SE4 **66** B3
Comet Pl SE8 . . . . . **51** C3
Comet St SE8 . . . . . **51** C3
Comins Ho SW4 . . . **61** B2
Commercial Rd
Stepney E1 . . . . . . **32** B3
Whitechapel E1 . . **111** C2
Commercial St
E1 . . . . **110** C4
Commercial Way
Peckham SE15 . . . **49** C3
Wembley NW10 . . . **20** A3
Commerell Pl
SE10 . . . . **43** B1
Commerell St
SE10 . . . . **43** B1
Commodity Quay
E1 . . . . **125** A3
Commodore Ct
SE8 . . . . **51** C2

Commodore Ho 7
E14 . . . . **34** B2
Commodore St E1 . . **26** A1
Commondale
SW15 . . . . **57** B4
Common Rd
SW13 . . . . **56** C4
Common View
SW15 . . . . **57** B4
Commonwealth Ave
21 Shepherd's Bush
W12 . . . . **30** A2
22 Shepherd's Bush
W12 . . . . **30** A2
Commonwealth Ho
WC1 . . . . **106** B2
Community Rd
E15 . . . . **19** C3
Commodore Ho
SW18 . . . . **59** B3
Compania Bldg 12
E1 . . . . **32** C2
Compass Ct SE1 . . **124** C1
Compass Ho
Bayswater W2 . . . **100** A1
London SE8 . . . . . **52** A1
Compass Point 10
E14 . . . . **33** C2
Compayne Gdns
NW6 . . . . **11** A1
Compton Ave
Islington N1 . . . . . **15** A2
London N6 . . . . **3** A4
Compton Cl
Camberwell SE15 . . **49** B3
Regent's Pk NW1 . . **92** B3
Compton Cres W4 . . **45** B4
Compton Ho
SW11 . . . . **168** A4
Compton Pas EC1 . . **96** B2
Compton Pl WC1 . . **94** A2
Compton Rd
Islington N1 . . . . . **15** A2
Kensal Green W10 . **22** C2
Compton St EC1 . . . **96** B2
Compton Terr N1 . . . **15** A2
Comus Ho SE17 . . **152** A3
Comus Pl SE17 . . . **152** A3
Comyn Rd SW11 . . . **60** A3
Comyns Cl E16 . . . . **35** B4
Conant Ho SE11 . . . **48** A4
Conant Mews E1 . . **125** B4
Concanon Rd SW2,
SW4 . . . . **62** B3
Concert Hall App
SE1 . . . . **121** A2
Concord Bsns Ctr
W3 . . . . **28** A4
Concorde Way
SE16 . . . . **40** C2
Concordia Wharf 10
E14 . . . . **34** B1
Concord Rd W3 . . . . **20** A1
Condell Rd SW11 . . **59** C4
Conder St E14 . . . . . **33** A3
Condray Pl SW11 . . **158** A1
Conduit Ct WC2 . . **120** A4
Conduit Ho SE10 . . **52** C2
Conduit Mews
W2 . . . . **101** B1
Conduit Pas W2 . . **101** B1
Conduit Pl W2 . . . . **101** B1
Conduit St W1 . . . . **118** C4
Conewood St N5 . . . **6** A1
Coney Acre SE21 . . **75** B3
Coney Way SW8 . . **163** A3

Congers Ho SE8 . . . **51** C3
Congress Ho
WC1 . . . . **105** C2
Congreve Ho 10
N16 . . . . **16** A3
Congreve St SE17 . **152** A3
Conifer Ct 2
SW19 . . . . **69** C3
Conifer Gdns
SW16 . . . . **74** B1
Conifer Ho SE4 . . . . **66** B3
Coniger Rd SW6 . . **165** B2
Coningham Ct
SW10 . . . . **157** A2
Coningham Mews
W12 . . . . **29** C1
Coningham Rd
W12 . . . . **39** A4
Coningsby Rd N4 . . . **6** A4
Conington Rd
SE13 . . . . **52** B1
Conisbrough NW1 . . **82** C3
Coniston NW1 . . . . . **92** C4
Coniston Cl
Barnes SW13 . . . . . **46** B3
Chiswick W4 . . . . . . **45** B3
Coniston Ct
Marylebone W2 . . **102** B1
6 Rotherhithe
SE16 . . . . **40** C4
Conistone Way
N7 . . . . **14** A1
Coniston Ho
13 Bow E3 . . . . **26** B2
18 Camberwell SE5 . **48** B3
Coniston Wlk E9 . . . **17** B3
Conlan St W10 . . . . **23** A1
Conley Rd NW10 . . . **8** A2
Conley St SE10 . . . . **43** A1
Connaught Ave
SW14 . . . . **55** B3
Connaught Cl W2 **102** B1
Connaught Ho
College Pk NW10 . . **22** A2
Mayfair W1 . . . . . **118** A3
Connaught Lo N4 . . . **5** C4
Connaught Mans
Battersea SW11 . . **168** B3
4 Brixton SW9 . . . **62** C3
Canonbury N16 . . . **15** C4
Fulham SW6 . . . . . **164** A4
Connaught Pl W2 **102** C1
Connaught Rd
Finsbury Pk N4 . . . . **5** C4
Harlesden NW10 . . **21** A3
5 Richmond TW10 . **54** B2
Connaught Sq
W2 . . . . **102** C1
Connaught St W2 **102** B1
Connaught Works
E3 . . . . **26** A4
Connell Ct 6
SE14 . . . . **50** C4
Connor Ct SW11 . . **170** A3
Connor St E9 . . . . . . **25** C4
Conrad Ho
2 Limehouse
SE16 . . . . **33** A2
South Lambeth
SW8 . . . . **162** A2
15 Stoke Newington
N16 . . . . **16** A3
Conrad Twr W3 . . . . **37** A3
Consort Ho W2 . . . **114** B3
Consort Lo NW8 . . . **80** C3
Consort Rd SE15 . . . **50** A1
Cons St SE1 . . . . . . **135** C4

Constable Ct 11
SE16 . . . . **40** A1
Constable Ho
25 Millwall E14 . . . **41** C4
Primrose Hill NW3 . **12** B1
Constable Wlk
SE21 . . . . **76** A1
Constant Ho 28
E14 . . . . **34** A2
Constantine Ho
SW2 . . . . **75** A3
Constantine Rd
NW3 . . . . **12** A4
Constitution Hill SW1,
W1 . . . . **132** B4
Consul Ho 5 E3 . . . . **26** C1
Content St SE17 . . . **151** B3
Convent Gdns
W11 . . . . **31** B3
**Convent of Jesus &
Mary Language Coll**
NW10 . . . . **21** C4
**Convent of Jesus &
Mary RC Inf Sch**
NW2 . . . . **9** B2
Conway Gr W3 . . . . **28** C4
Conway Ho
Chelsea SW3 . . . . **145** A1
4 Millwall E14 . . . **42** A2
6 Streatham SW2 . **74** A3
Conway Mews W1 . . **92** C1
Conway St W1 . . . . . **92** C1
Conybeare NW3 . . . **12** A1
Conyer St 21 E3 . . . **26** A3
Cookham Cres
SE16 . . . . **40** C4
Cookham Ho
E2 . . . . **24** B1 **98** C2
Cook's Rd
Camberwell SE17 . . **48** A4
Stratford Marsh
E15 . . . . **27** A3
Coomassie Rd W9 . . **23** B1
Coombe Ho 13 N7 . . **13** C3
Coombe Rd W4 . . . . **38** A1
Coomber Ho SW6 . . **59** A4
Coombs St N1 . . . . . **86** B1
Coomer Mews
SW6 . . . . **155** A3
Coomer Pl SW6 . . . **155** A3
Cooperage The
SE1 . . . . **124** C1
Cooper Cl SE1 . . . . **135** C3
Cooper Ct E15 . . . . . **19** B3
Cooper Ho NW8 . . . **89** B1
Cooper Rd NW10 . . . **8** C3
Coopersale Rd E9 . . **17** C3
Coopers Cl E1 . . . . . **25** B1
Coopers Ct
9 Acton W3 . . . . . **28** B1
Tower Hamlets E3 . . **26** B1
Coopers La NW1 . . . **83** C1
Coopers Rd SE1 . . **153** A2
Cooper's Row
EC3 . . . . **124** C4
Cooper St 10 E16 . . **35** B4
Coopers Yd N1 . . . . . **15** A1
Cope Ho EC1 . . . . . . **97** A3
Copeland Dr E14 . . . **41** C2
Copeland Ho
SE11 . . . . **135** A1
Copeland Rd SE15 . . **50** A1
Copenhagen Gdns
W4 . . . . **37** C4
Copenhagen Ho
N1 . . . . **85** B3

Copenhagen Pl
E14 . . . . .33 B3
Copenhagen Prim Sch
N1. . . . . .84 C3
Copenhagen St
N1. . . . . .84 C3
Cope Pl W8 . . . . .127 B1
Cope St SE16. . . . . . . .40 C2
Copford Wlk N1. . . . . .86 C4
Copleston Rd
SE15 . . . . .139 B3
Copley Cl 15 SE17 . . . .48 A4
Coppedhall 2
SE21 . . . . .75 C2
Copperas St SE8 . . . . .52 A4
Copper Beech N6 . . . . . .3 C4
Copperbeech Cl
NW3 . . . . .11 C3
Copperfield Ho
SE1 . . . . .139 B3
Copperfield Rd
E3 . . . . .33 A4
Copperfields Ct
W3 . . . . .36 C4
Copperfield St
SE1 . . . . .136 C4
Copper Mews 19
W4 . . . . .37 B3
Coppice Dr SW15. . . . .57 A2
Coppin Ho SW2 . . . . . .75 A3
Coppock Cl SW11 . . . .168 A1
Copse Ct SW15 . . . . . .58 A2
Copthall Ave EC2 . . . .109 C2
Copthall Bldgs
EC2. . . . . .109 C2
Copthall Cl EC2 . . . . .109 B2
Copthorne Ave
SW12 . . . . .73 C4
Coptic St WC1 . . . . . .106 A3
Copton Cl E3. . . . . . . .33 C4
Coral Apts 8 E16 . . . . .35 C2
Coral Ho 6 E1 . . . . . . .26 A1
Coral Row 14
SW11 . . . . .59 B4
Coral St SE1 . . . . .135 C3
Coram Ho
Bloomsbury WC1 . . . . .94 A2
8 Chiswick W4 . . . . . . .38 A1
Coram St WC1 . . . . . . .94 A1
Corbden Cl SE15 . . . . .49 B2
Corbet Ct EC3 . . . . . .109 C1
Corbet Ho 1 . . . . .85 B3
Corbet Ho E1 . . . . . . .110 C2
Corbett Ho SW10 . . . .156 C4
Corbett's La SE16 . . . .40 B2
Corbetts Pas 8
SE16 . . . . .40 B2
Corbidge Ct SE8. . . . . .52 A4
Corbiere Ho 6
N1. . . . . .24 A4
Corbin Ho 7 E3. . . . . . .27 A2
Corbridge Cres
E2 . . . . .25 A3
Corbyn St N4, N19 . . . . .5 A3
Corby Rd NW10 . . . . . .20 C3
Corby Way E3 . . . . . . .26 C1
Cordelia Cl SE24 . . . . .63 A3
Cordelia Ho 26 N1 . . . .24 A3
Cordelia St E14 . . . . . .34 A3
Cording St E14 . . . . . .34 A4
Cordwainers Ct 18
E1 . . . . .17 B1
Corfe Ho SW8 . . . . . .162 C2
Corfe Lodge 4
SE21 . . . . .75 C2

Corfe Twr 6 W3 . . . . . .37 B4
Corfield St E2 . . . . .25 A2
Coriander Ave
E14 . . . . .34 C3
Coriander Ct SE1 . . . .139 A4
Corinne Rd N19 . . . . . .13 B4
Cork St Mews
W1 . . . . .118 C3
Cork Sq E1. . . . . .32 A1
Cork St W1 . . . . .118 C3
Corlett St NW1 . . . . . .102 A4
Cormont Rd SE5 . . . . .48 A2
Cormorant Ct
28 Deptford SE8 . . . . . .51 B4
13 Dulwich SE21 . . . . .75 C2
Cornbury Ho 5
SE8 . . . . .51 B4
Cornelia St N7 . . . . . . .14 B2
Cornell Bldg 1 . . . . . .111 B2
Corner Fielde
SW2 . . . . .74 B3
Corner Gn SE3 . . . . . . .53 C1
Corner House St
WC2 . . . . .120 A2
Cornerstone Ct
E1 . . . . .24 C1 99 C1
Cornerways SW15 . . . .56 C3
Corney Rd W4 . . . . . . .46 A4
Corney Reach Way
W4 . . . . .46 A3
Cornflower Terr
SE22 . . . . .65 A1
Cornford Gr SW12 . . . .73 A2
Cornhill EC3 . . . . .109 C1
Cornick Ho 7
SE16 . . . . .40 A3
Cornish Ho
Brentford TW8 . . . . . . .36 B1
3 Camberwell
SE17 . . . . .48 A4
Cornmill La SE13 . . . . .67 B4
Cornmow Dr NW10 . . .8 C3
Cornwall Ave E2 . . . . .25 B2
Cornwall Cres
W11 . . . . .31 A3
Cornwall Flats
SE1 . . . . .135 C4
Cornwall Gdns
Kensington SW7 . . . . .128 B1
Willesden NW10 . . . . . .9 A2
Cornwall Gdns Wlk
SW7 . . . . .128 B1
Cornwall Gr W4 . . . . . .38 A1
Cornwall Ho
Marylebone NW1 . . . . .91 A1
1 Putney SW15 . . . . . .69 B4
Cornwallis Ct
SW8 . . . . .172 A4
Cornwallis Ho
12 W12 . . . . .30 A2
Cornwallis Rd N19 . . . .5 A3
Cornwallis Sq N19 . . . .5 A3
Cornwall Mans
Chelsea SW10 . . . . . . .157 A2
Marylebone NW1 . . . . .91 A1
Cornwall Mews S
SW7 . . . . .128 C1
Cornwall Mews W
SW7 . . . . .128 B1
Cornwall Rd
Finsbury Pk N4 . . . . . . .5 C4
Lambeth SE1 . . . . .135 C4
Cornwall Sq SE11 . . . .150 A2
Cornwall St 4 E1 . . . . .32 A2
Cornwall Terr
NW1 . . . . .91 A1

Cornwall Terrace
Mews NW1. . . . . .91 A1
Cornwood Dr E1 . . . . . .32 B3
Coronation Ct 11
N16 . . . . .16 A4
Coronation Ct 19
W10 . . . . .30 B4
Coronet St
N1 . . . . .24 A2 98 A3
Corporation Row
EC1 . . . . .95 C2
Corporation St N7 . . . .14 A3
Corpus Christi RC
Prim Sch SW2 . . . . . . .62 B2
Corrance Rd SW2,
SW4 . . . . .62 A3
Corringham Ct
NW11 . . . . .1 C4
Corringham Ho 11
E1 . . . . .32 C3
Corringham Rd
NW11 . . . . .1 C4
Corringway NW11 . . . . .2 A4
Corry Dr SW9 . . . . . . .63 A3
Corry Ho 2 E14 . . . . . .34 A2
Corsham St N1 . . . . . . .97 C3
Corsica St N5 . . . . .15 A2
Corsley Way 17 E9 . . . .18 B2
Cortayne Rd SW6 . . . .165 A2
Cortis Rd SW15 . . . . . .57 A1
Cortis Terr SW15 . . . . .57 A1
Corunna Rd SW8 . . . .170 C4
Corunna Terr
SW8 . . . . .170 C4
Corvette Sq 5
SE10 . . . . .52 C4
Coryton Path W9 . . . . .23 B1
Cosbycote Ave
SE24 . . . . .63 B2
Cosgrove Ho 11
E2 . . . . .24 C4
Cosmo Pl WC1 . . . . . .106 B4
Cosmur Cl W12 . . . . . .38 B3
Cossall Wlk SE15 . . . . .50 A2
Cossar Mews 17
SW2 . . . . .62 C2
Cosser St SE1 . . . . . . .135 B2
Costa St SE15 . . . . . . .49 C1
Coston Wlk 4
SE4 . . . . .65 C3
Cosway Mans
NW1 . . . . .102 B4
Cosway St NW1 . . . . . .102 B4
Cotall St E14 . . . . .33 C4
Cotes Ho NW8 . . . . . . .90 A1
Cotham St SE17 . . . . .151 A3
Cotherstone Rd
SW2 . . . . .74 B3
Cotleigh Rd NW6 . . . . .10 C1
Cotman Cl SW15 . . . . .57 C2
Cotman Ho NW8 . . . . .80 A2
Cotrill Gdns E8 . . . . . .17 A2
Cotswold Ct EC1 . . . . .96 C2
Cotswold Gate
NW2 . . . . .1 A3
Cotswold Ho N16. . . . .7 B3
Cotswold Mews
SW11 . . . . .167 C3
Cottage Gn SE5 . . . . . .48 C3
Cottage Gr SW9 . . . . .62 A4
Cottage Pl SW3 . . . . .130 A1
Cottage St E14 . . . . . . .34 A2
Cottages The SE1 . . . .134 C1
Cottage Wlk 2 N16 . . .7 B1
Cottenham Ho 6
N19 . . . . .5 A2

Cottesbrook St 11
SE14 . . . . .51 A3
Cottesloe Ho NW8. . . .90 A2
Cottesloe Mews
SE1 . . . . .135 C2
Cottesmore Ct
W8 . . . . .128 B2
Cottesmore Gdns
W8 . . . . .128 B2
Cottingham Rd
SW8 . . . . .163 A2
Cottington St
SE11 . . . . .150 A2
Cotton Ave W3 . . . . . .28 C3
Cotton Ho
Bedford Pk W12 . . . . . .38 B3
18 Streatham
SW12 . . . . .74 A4
Cotton Row SW11 . . . .59 C4
Cotton's Gdns
E2 . . . . .24 A2 98 B4
Cottons La SE1 . . . . . .123 C2
Cotton St E14 . . . . . . .34 B2
Cottrell Ct SE10 . . . . . .43 B2
Couchman Ho 8
SW4 . . . . .61 B1
Coulgate St SE4 . . . . . .66 A4
Coulsdon Ho 5
SW2 . . . . .74 A3
Coulson St SW3 . . . . .144 C2
Coulter Rd W6 . . . . . . .39 A3
Coults Cres NW5 . . . . . .3 C1
Councillor St SE5 . . . . .48 B3
Counters Ct W14 . . . .126 B2
Counter St SE1 . . . . . .124 A1
Countess Rd NW5 . . . .13 B3
Countisbury Ho
SE26 . . . . .76 C1
County Gr SE5 . . . . . . .48 B2
County Ho
3 Herne Hill SE24 . . . .63 A3
South Lambeth
SW9 . . . . .173 B4
County St SE1 . . . . . . .137 A1
Courier Ho 17
SW2 . . . . .74 C4
Courland Gr SW8 . . . .171 C3
Courland St SW8 . . . .171 C3
Courtauld Ho 12
E2 . . . . .24 C3
Courtauld Inst of
Art *
Marylebone W1 . . . . . .103 A2
Strand WC2 . . . . .120 C4
Courtauld Rd N19 . . . .5 A3
Courtenay Ave N6 . . . .3 A4
Courtenay Sq
SE11 . . . . .149 B1
Courtenay St
SE11 . . . . .149 B2
Courtfield Gdns
SW5 . . . . .142 B3
Courtfield Ho
EC1 . . . . .107 B4
Courtfield Mews
SW7 . . . . .142 B3
Courtfield Rd
SW7 . . . . .142 C3
Court Gdns N7 . . . . . .14 C2
Courthill Rd SE13 . . . .67 B3
Courthope Ho
8 Rotherhithe
SE16 . . . . .40 B3
South Lambeth
SW8 . . . . .162 A1

Courthouse Rd
NW3 . . . . .12 B4
Court La SE21 . . . . . . .76 B4
Courtlands TW10 . . . . .54 C2
Courtlands Ave
TW9 . . . . .45 A1
Court Lane Gdns
SE21 . . . . .76 A4
Court Mans 8
W6 . . . . .38 C2
Courtmead Cl
SE24 . . . . .63 B1
Courtnell St W2 . . . . . .31 C3
Courtney Ho W14 . . . .126 B2
Courtney Rd N7 . . . . . .14 C3
Courtrai Rd SE23 . . . . .66 A1
Court Royal SW15 . . . .58 A2
Court Sq 5 E1 . . . . . . .32 B3
Courtville Ho 13
W10 . . . . .23 A2
Court Way W3 . . . . . . .28 B4
Courtyard The
Fulham SW6 . . . . .164 A3
Islington N1 . . . . .14 B1
13 Wandsworth
SW18 . . . . .59 C3
Cousin La EC4 . . . . . .123 B3
Couzens Ho 13 E3 . . . .33 B4
Coval Gdns SW14 . . . .55 A3
Coval La SW14 . . . . . .55 A3
Coval Pas SW14 . . . . .55 A3
Coval Rd SW14 . . . . . .55 A3
Covell Ct 16 SE8 . . . . .51 C3
Covent Garden Sta
WC2 . . . . .106 B1
Covent Gdn *
WC2 . . . . .120 B4
Coventry Cl NW6 . . . . .23 C4
Coventry Rd E1 . . . . . .25 A1
Coventry St W1 . . . . . .119 B3
Coverdale Rd
Brondesbury NW2 . . . .10 A2
Hammersmith W12 . . .39 A4
Hampstead NW6 . . . . . .9 C1
Coverham Ho 6
SE4 . . . . .65 C3
Coverley Cl E1 . . . . . .111 C4
Coverley Point
SE11 . . . . .148 C3
Cowcross St EC1 . . . .108 A4
Cowdenbeath Path
N1 . . . . .84 C4
Cowdray Hall Royal
Coll of Nursing
W1 . . . . .104 A2
Cowdray Ho 22
SE22 . . . . .64 A4
Cowdry Rd E9 . . . . . . .18 B2
Cowley Rd
Brixton SW9 . . . . .173 C4
East Acton W3 . . . . . . .29 B1
Mortlake SW14 . . . . . . .56 A4
Cowley St SW1 . . . . . .134 A1
Cowling Cl
W11 . . . . .31 A1 112 A2
Cowper Ho
Pimlico SW1 . . . . .147 C1
Walworth SE17 . . . . . .151 A2
Cowper Rd
Acton W3 . . . . .28 C1
Stoke Newington
N16. . . . . .16 A4
Cowper's Ct EC3 . . . .109 C1

Cowper St EC1,
EC2 .... **97** C2
Cowper Terr W10 ...**30** C4
Cowthorpe Rd
SW8 .... **171** C4
Cox Ho W6 .... **154** A4
Coxson Way SE1 **138** C3
Coysh Ct SW15 ..**58** A2
Crabtree Ct SW3 **24** B2
Crabtree Ct E15 ..**19** A3
Crabtree Hall SW6 **47** B3
Crabtree La SW6 ..**47** C3
Craddock St NW5 ..**12** C2
Cragie Ho SE1 ....**153** A3
Craigleith SW15 ..**57** C1
Craignair Rd SW2 ..**74** C4
Craig's Ct SW1 ....**120** A2
Craik Ct NW6 ......**23** B3
Crail Row SE17 ..**151** C3
Cramer St W1 ....**103** C3
Crammond Cl
W6 ....**154** A3
Crampton Sch
SE17 .... **150** B2
Crampton St
SE17 .... **150** C2
Cranbourn Alley
WC2 .... **119** C4
Cranbourne Ct
SW11 .... **158** B2
Cranbourne Rd
E15 ....**19** B4
Cranbourn Ho [6]
SE16 ....**40** A4
Cranbourn Pas [5]
SE16 ....**40** A4
Cranbourn St
WC2 .... **119** C4
Cranbrook NW1 ..**83** A3
Cranbrook Ho [5]
E5 ....**17** A3
Cranbrook Rd
Chiswick W4 ....**38** A1
St Johns SE8 ....**51** C2
Cranbrook St E2 ..**25** C3
Cranbury Rd SW6 **166** B1
Crandale Ho [8]
E5 ....**17** A3
Crandley Ct SE8 ..**41** A2
Crane Ave W3 ....**28** B2
Crane Ct
[7] Acton W12 ......**38** A4
Holborn EC4 .... **107** C1
Crane Gr N7 ......**14** C2
Crane Ho
[24] Bow E3 ....**26** A3
[10] Peckham SE15 ..**49** B2
Crane Mead SE16 **40** C2
Crane St
Greenwich SE10 .....**42** C1
[5] Peckham SE15 ..**49** B2
Cranfield Ct NW1 **102** B3
Cranfield Ho
WC1 .... **106** B4
Cranfield Rd SE4 ..**66** B4
Cranford Cotts [8]
E1 ....**32** C2
Cranford Lo SW19 **69** C2
Cranford St E1 ....**32** C2
Cranhurst Rd NW2 **9** B3
Cranleigh
W11 ....**31** B1 **112** C2
Cranleigh Ct
Richmond TW9 ......**54** C4
[4] Stamford Hill N16 **7** A3

Cranleigh Hos
NW1 .... **83** A1
Cranleigh Mews
SW11 .... **168** C1
Cranleigh St NW1 **83** A1
Cranley Gdns
SW7 .... **143** B2
Cranley Mews
SW7 .... **143** A2
Cranley Pl SW7 ..**143** B3
Cranmer Ct SW3 **144** B3
Cranmer Ho
SW11 .... **168** A4
Cranmer Rd SW9 **163** C2
Cranswick Rd
SE16 ....**40** A1
Cranwell Cl E3 ....**27** A1
Cranwich Rd N16 ..**7** A4
Cranwood Ct EC1 **97** C3
Cranwood St EC1 **97** C3
Cranworth Gdns
SW9 .... **173** B4
Cranworth Ho [8]
N7 ....**14** B4
Craster Rd SW2 ..**74** B4
Craston Ho [2]
SE5 ....**49** A1
Craven Cl N16 ....**7** C4
Craven Cottage
(Fulham FC)
SW6 ....**47** C2
Craven Ct NW10 ..**21** A4
Craven Hill W2 ..**115** A4
Craven Hill Gdns
W2 .... **114** C4
Craven Hill Mews
W2 .... **115** A4
Craven Ho [2]
SW14 ....**55** C4
Craven Lo
Bayswater W2 ....**115** A4
Fulham SW6 ....**47** C2
Craven Mews [6]
SW11 ....**60** C4
Craven Park Mews
NW10 ....**21** A4
Craven Park Rd
NW10 ....**21** A4
Craven Pas WC2 **120** A2
Craven Pk NW10 ..**21** A4
Craven Rd
Paddington W2 ....**101** A1
Stonebridge NW10 ..**20** C4
Craven St WC2 ..**120** A2
Craven Terr W2 ..**115** A4
Craven Wlk E5, N16 ..**7** C4
Crawford Bldgs
NW1 .... **102** B3
Crawford Mews
W1 .... **102** C3
Crawford Pas EC1 ..**95** C1
Crawford Pl W1 **102** B3
Crawford Place
Dwellings** NW1 **102** B3
Crawford Point [4]
E16 ....**35** B3
Crawford Prim Sch
SE5 ....**48** B2
Crawford Rd SE5 ..**48** B1
Crawford St W1 **102** C3
Crawshay Ct SW9 **173** C4
Crawshay Ho [3]
N16 ....**15** C4
Crawthew Gr SE22 **64** B3
Crayford Ho
Bermondsey SE1 ..**137** C3

Crayford Ho continued
[5] Lower Holloway
N7 ....**14** A4
Crayford Rd N7 ....**14** A4
Crayle Ho EC1 ....**96** B2
Crealock St SW18 **59** A1
Creasy Est SE1 ..**138** A1
Crebor St SE22 ....**64** C1
Credenhill Ho [2]
SE15 ....**50** A3
Crediton Hill NW6 **11** A3
Crediton Rd
Brondesbury Pk
NW10 ....**22** C4
Newham E16 ....**35** C3
Credon Rd SE16 ..**40** A1
Creechurch La
EC3 .... **110** B1
Creechurch Pl
EC3 .... **110** B1
Creed Ct [5] E1 ..**26** A2
Creed Ho SE15 ....**65** A4
Creed La EC4 ....**108** B1
Creek Ho W14 ..**126** B2
Creek Rd SE10,
SE8 ....**52** A4
Creek Road Ind Est
SE8 ....**52** A4
Creekside SE8 ....**52** A3
Creekside Foyer
SE8 ....**52** A4
Crefeld Cl W6 ..**154** A3
Creighton Cl W12 **30** A2
Creighton Rd
NW6 ....**23** A3
Cremer Bsns Ctr [8]
E2 ....**24** B3
Cremer Ho [9] SE8 **51** C3
Cremer St E2 ....**24** B3
Cremorne Rd
SW10 .... **157** B2
Creon Ct SW9 ..**173** B4
Crescent EC3 ....**124** C1
Crescent Arc [1]
SE10 ....**52** B4
Crescent Court Bsns
Ctr** [1] E16 ....**27** C1
Crescent Ct SW4 **61** C2
Crescent Gdns
SW19 ....**70** C1
Crescent Gr SW4 **61** B3
Crescent Ho SE13 **52** A1
Crescent La SW4 ..**61** C2
Crescent Mans
Islington N5 ....**15** A3
Notting Hill
W11 ....**31** A2 **112** B4
Crescent Pl SW3 **144** B4
Crescent Row EC1 ..**96** C1
Crescent St N1 ....**14** B1
Crescent Stables
SW15 ....**58** A2
Crescent The
Acton W3 ....**29** A3
Barnes SW13 ....**46** C1
Wimbledon SW19 ..**70** C1
Crescent Way SE4 **66** C4
Crescent Wood Rd
SE21, SE26 ....**76** C1
Cresford Rd SW6 **166** A3
Cressage Ho [2]
TW8 ....**44** A4
Cressall Ho [14]
E14 ....**41** C3
Cresset Ho [8] E9 ..**17** B2
Cresset Rd E9 ....**17** B2

Cresset St SW4 ....**61** C4
Cressfield Cl NW5 ..**12** C3
Cressida Rd N19 ....**4** C3
Cressingham Rd
SE13 ....**67** B4
Cressington Cl [4]
N16 ....**16** A3
Cresswell Gdns
SW5 .... **142** C2
Cresswell Pl
SW10 .... **143** A2
Cressy Ct
Hammersmith W6 ..**39** A3
[6] Stepney E1 ......**32** B4
Cressy Ho SW13 ..**57** A4
Cressy Hos [7] E1 ..**32** B4
Cressy Pl E1 ......**32** B4
Cressy Rd NW3 ....**12** B4
Cresta Ho
[3] Bow E3 ....**26** C1
Hampstead NW6 ....**11** C1
Crestfield St N1,
WC1 ....**94** B4
Crestview NW5 ....**4** A1
Crestway SW15 ..**57** A1
Creswick Ct W3 ..**28** A2
Creswick Rd W3 ..**28** A2
Creswick Wlk [7]
E3 ....**26** C2
Crewdson Rd
SW9 .... **163** B1
Crewe Pl NW10 ..**21** B2
Crewkerne Ct
SW11 .... **167** C4
Crews St E14 ......**41** C2
Crewys Rd
Child's Hill NW2 ......**1** B2
London SE15 ....**50** A1
Crichton St SW8 **171** C3
Cricketers Mews [4]
SW18 ....**59** A2
Cricketfield Rd E5 **17** A4
Cricklade Ave
SW2 ....**74** B2
CRICKLEWOOD **9** B4
Cricklewood
Broadway** NW2 ....**9** C4
Cricklewood La
NW2 ....**1** B1
Cricklewood Sta
NW2 ....**9** C4
Crieff Rd SW18 ....**59** B1
Criffel Ave SW2 ..**73** C3
Crimscott St SE1 **138** B1
Crimsworth Rd
SW8 .... **161** C1
Crinan St N1 ......**84** B2
Cringle St SW8 ..**160** C2
Cripplegate St
EC1 .... **109** A4
Crispe Ho N1 ....**85** A3
Crispian Cl NW10 ..**8** A4
Crispin Cl SE17 ..**152** A3
Crispin Pl E1 ....**110** C4
Crispin St E1 ....**110** C3
Crisp Rd W6 ......**39** B1
Cristowe Rd SW6 **165** A1
Criterion Mews
N19 ....**4** C2
Crockerton Rd
SW17 ....**72** B2
Croft Ct SE13 ....**67** B1
Croftdown Rd NW5 ..**4** A1
Crofters Ct [9] SE8 **41** A2
Crofters Way NW1 **83** B4
Croft Ho
Putney SW15 ......**58** A1

Croft Ho continued
[11] West Kilburn
W10 ....**23** A2
Crofton Ave W4 ..**45** C3
Crofton Gate Way
SE4 ....**66** A2
Crofton L Ctr SE4 **66** C1
Crofton Park Rd
SE4 ....**66** B1
Crofton Park Sta
SE4 ....**66** B1
Crofton Rd SE5 ..**49** A1
Crofton Sch SE4 ..**66** C1
Crofton Terr
Homerton E5 ....**18** A3
Richmond TW9 .....**54** B3
Crofts Ho [7] E2 ..**24** C3
Crofts St E1 ....**125** B3
Croft St SE8 ......**41** A2
Croft The W10 ....**21** B3
Crogsland Rd
NW1 ....**12** C1
Cromartie Rd N19 ..**4** C4
Cromarty Ho [8]
E1 ....**33** A4
Crombie Mews
SW11 .... **168** B2
Cromdale Ct N16 ..**7** B4
Crome Ct
Streatham SW16 ....**74** A1
Wandsworth SW18 **58** B1
Crome Rd NW10 ..**8** A2
Cromer St WC1 ..**94** B3
Cromer Terr [8] E8 **16** C3
Cromer Villas Rd
SW18 ....**58** B1
Cromford Path [1]
E5 ....**17** C4
Cromford Rd
SW18 ....**58** C2
Crompton Ct
SW3 .... **144** A4
Crompton Ho
Borough The SE1 ..**137** A1
Paddington W2 ......**89** B1
South Lambeth
SW8 .... **171** A3
Crompton St W2 ..**89** B1
Cromwell Ave
Hammersmith W6 ..**39** A2
Highgate N6 ....**4** A3
Cromwell Cl
Acton W3 ....**28** B1
[2] Gunnersbury
W4 ....**37** C1
Cromwell Cres
SW5 .... **141** B4
Cromwell Ctr
NW10 ....**20** C2
Cromwell Gdns
SW7 .... **129** C1
Cromwell Gr W6 ..**39** B3
Cromwell Ho
Battersea SW11 ..**169** C3
Putney SW15 ....**56** C3
Cromwell Hospl
SW5 .... **142** A4
Cromwell Lo [10]
E1 ....**25** B1
Cromwell Mans
SW5 .... **141** C4
Cromwell Mews
SW7 .... **143** C4
Cromwell Pl
[8] Acton W3 ....**28** B1
Highgate N6 ....**4** A3
Mortlake SW14 .....**55** A4

Cromwell PI *continued*
South Kensington
SW7 . . . . **143** C4
Cromwell Rd
Brixton SW9 . . . . .48 A2
South Kensington
SW7 . . . . **143** A4
Cromwell Twr
EC2 . . . . **109** A4
Crondace Rd
SW6 . . . . **165** C3
Crondall Ct **7** N1 . .24 A3
Crondall Ho SW15 . .68 C3
Crondall PI **15** N1 . . .24 A3
Crondall St N1 . . . . . .24 A3
Crone Ct **5** NW6 . . . .23 B3
Cronin St SE15 . . . . .49 B3
Crooked Billet Yd
E2 . . . . .24 A2 **98** B4
Crooke Rd SE8 . . . . .41 A1
Crookham Rd
SW6 . . . . **164** C3
Croom's Hill SE10 . .52 C3
Croom's Hill Gr
SE10 . . . . .52 B3
Cropley Ct N1 . . . . . . **87** B2
Cropley St N1 . . . . . . **87** B2
Cropthorne Ct W9 . . **89** A3
Crosby Ct SE1 . . . . . **137** B4
Crosby Ho **3** E14 . . .42 B3
Crosby Row SE1 . . . **137** B4
Crosby Sq EC3 . . . . **110** A2
Crosby Wlk
5 Dalston E8 . . . .16 B2
Streatham SE24 . . .74 C4
Crosfield Ct **3**
W10 . . . . .30 C3
Crosfield Ho
W11 . . . . .31 A2 **112** A3
Crosland PI **5**
SW11 . . . . .60 C4
Crossbow Ho **15**
N1 . . . . .24 A4
Cross CI SE15 . . . . . .50 A1
Cross Ct SE5 . . . . . . .63 C4
Crossfield Rd
NW3 . . . . .11 C2
Crossfield St SE8 . . .51 C3
Crossford St SW9 **172** C1
Crossharbour Sta
E14 . . . . .42 A3
Cross Keys CI W1 **103** C3
Cross La EC3 . . . . . **124** A3
Crossleigh Ct **3**
SE14 . . . . .51 B3
Crosslet St SE17 . . . **151** C4
Crosslet Vale
SE10 . . . . .52 A2
Crossley St N7 . . . . . .14 C2
Crossman Hos **15**
SW12 . . . . .74 A4
Crossmount Ho **13**
SE5 . . . . .48 B3
Cross Rd SE5 . . . . . .49 A1
Cross St
Islington N1 . . . . . . **86** B4
Mortlake SW13 . . . .56 A4
Crossthwaite Ave
SE24 . . . . .63 C3
Crosstrees Ho **7**
E14 . . . . .41 C3
Crosswall EC3 . . . . **124** C4
Crossway E8, N16 . . .16 A3
Crossway Ct **4**
SE4 . . . . .51 A1
Crossways Acad
SE4 . . . . .51 A1
Croston St E8 . . . . . .24 C4

Crouch End Hill N8 . . .4 C4
Crouch Hall Ct N19 . . .5 A3
Crouch Hill N4, N8,
N19 . . . . .5 A4
Crouch Hill Sta N4 . . .5 B4
Crouchmans CI SE21,
SE26 . . . . .76 C1
Crowder St E1 . . . . .32 A2
Crowfield Ho N5 . . . .15 B3
Crowfoot CI E9 . . . . .18 B3
Crowhurst Ct
SW9 . . . . **173** C2
Crowhurst Ho **2**
SW9 . . . . **173** A1
Crowland Ho NW8 . . **78** C3
Crowland Terr N1 . . .15 C1
Crowline Wlk **1**
N1 . . . . .15 B2
Crown CI Bow E3 . . .26 C4
Hampstead NW6 . . . .11 A2
Crown Close Bsns Ctr
12 E3 . . . . .26 C4
Crown Ct
City of London
EC4 . . . . **109** A1
4 Putney SW15 . .57 C3
St Giles WC2 . . . . . **106** B1
St John's Wood
NW8 . . . . **90** B3
Crowndale Ct
NW1 . . . . **83** B2
Crowndale Rd
NW1 . . . . **83** A2
Crownfield Rd
E15 . . . . .19 C4
Crowngate Ho **23**
E3 . . . . .26 B3
Crownhill Rd
NW10 . . . . .21 B4
Crownleigh Ct
SW2 . . . . .62 C2
Crown Lo SW3 . . . . **144** B3
Crown Mews **9**
E1 . . . . .32 C4
Crown Office Row
EC4 . . . . **121** B4
Crown Pas SW1 . . . **119** A1
Crown Pl
Broadgate EC2 . . . **110** A4
Kentish Town NW5 . .13 A2
Crown Reach
SW1 . . . . **147** C1
Crown St
Acton W3 . . . . .28 B1
Camberwell SE5 . . . .48 B3
Crownstone Ct **1**
SW2 . . . . .62 C2
Crownstone Rd
SW2 . . . . .62 C2
Crows Rd E15 . . . . . .27 C2
Crowther Ave
TW8 . . . . .36 A2
Crowther CI SW6 **155** A3
Crowthorne CI
SW18 . . . . .70 B3
Crowthorne Rd
W10 . . . . .30 C3
Croxley Rd W9 . . . . .23 B2
Croxted CI SE21 . . . .75 B4
Croxted Rd SE21,
SE24 . . . . .75 C3
Croxteth Ho SW8 . **171** B2
Croydon Ho SE1 . . . **135** C4
Crozier Ho SW8 . . . **162** C1
Crozier Terr E9 . . . . . .17 C3

Crucifix La SE1 . . . **138** A4
Cruden Ho
15 Bow E3 . . . . . .26 B3
11 Camberwell
SE17 . . . . .48 A4
Cruden St N1 . . . . . . **86** B3
Cruickshank St
WC1 . . . . **95** A4
Cruikshank Ho
NW8 . . . . **80** B2
Crusader Ho EC1 . . . **96** A1
Crusoe House Sch
N1 . . . . **97** B4
Crusoe Mews N16 . . .6 C2
Crutched Friars
EC3 . . . . **124** B4
Crystal Palace Rd
SE22 . . . . .64 C2
Crystal Wharf N1 . . . **86** B1
Cuba St E14 . . . . . . .41 C4
Cubitt Bldg SW1 . . . **146** A1
Cubitt Ho **2** SW4 . .61 B1
Cubitt St WC1 . . . . . **95** A3
Cubitt Terr SW4 . . . .61 B4
CUBITT TOWN 42 B2
Cubitt Town Jun & Inf
Sch E14 . . . . .42 B3
Cuddington SE17 . . **151** A4
Cudworth Ho
SW8 . . . . **171** A3
Cudworth St **1**
E1 . . . . .25 A1
Cuff Cres SE9 . . . . . .14 C2
Cuffley Ho **8** W10 . .30 B4
Cuff Point
E2 . . . . .24 B2 **98** C4
Culand Ho SE17 . . . **152** A3
Culford Gdns
SW3 . . . . **145** A3
Culford Gr N1 . . . . . .16 A2
Culford Mans
SW3 . . . . **145** A3
Culford Mews N1 . . .16 A2
Culford Rd
Kingsland N1 . . . . . .16 A2
Shoreditch N1 . . . . .24 A4
Culham Ho
21 Paddington W2 . .31 C4
Shoreditch
E2 . . . . .24 B2 **98** C3
Cullen Ho W9 . . . . . .23 B3
Cullen Way NW10 . . .20 B1
Culling Rd SE16 . . . .40 B3
Cullingworth Rd
NW10 . . . . .9 A3
Culloden CI SE16 . . **153** C1
Culloden Prim Sch
E14 . . . . .34 B3
Cullum St EC3 . . . . **124** A4
Culmore Rd SE15 . . .50 B3
Culmstock Rd
SW11 . . . . .60 C2
Culpepper Ct
SE11 . . . . **149** B4
Culross Bldgs
NW1 . . . . **84** A2
Culross St W1 . . . . . **117** B3
Culver Ct SW18 . . . .59 A1
Culverden Rd
SW12 . . . . .73 B2
Culverhouse WC1 **106** C3
Culverhouse Gdns
SW16 . . . . .74 B1
Culverin Ct **1** N7 . .14 B3
Culvert Ct SW11 . . . **169** B2
Culvert PI SW11 . . . **169** B1
Culvert Rd SW11 . . **169** A2
Culworth Ho NW8 . . **80** A2
Culworth St NW8 . . **80** A1

Cumber Ho SW18 . . .70 C3
Cumberland Ave
NW10 . . . . .20 A1
Cumberland Bsns Pk
NW10 . . . . .20 A2
Cumberland CI E8 . . .16 B2
Cumberland Cres
W14 . . . . **140** B4
Cumberland Ct
W1 . . . . **103** A1
Cumberland Gate
W1 . . . . **117** A4
Cumberland Gdns
WC1 . . . . **95** B4
Cumberland Ho
Paddington W9 . . . . **88** C1
1 Putney SW15 . . .69 B4
Cumberland Mans
Marylebone W1 . . . **102** C2
7 West Hampstead
NW6 . . . . .10 C3
Cumberland Market
NW1 . . . . **92** C4
Cumberland Mills Sq
E14 . . . . .42 C1
Cumberland Park Ind
Est NW10 . . . . .21 C2
Cumberland Pk
W3 . . . . .28 B2
Cumberland Pl
Acton W3 . . . . .28 B2
Barnes SW13 . . . . . .46 C2
Richmond TW9 . . . . .44 C3
Cumberland St
SW1 . . . . **146** B2
Cumberland Terr
NW1 . . . . **82** A1
Cumberland Terrace
Mews NW1 . . . . . . **82** A1
Cumberland Villas
W3 . . . . .28 B2
Cumberland Wharf **6**
SE16 . . . . .40 B4
Cumbrian Gdns
NW2 . . . . .1 A2
Cuming Mus* **150** C3
Cumming St N1 . . . . **85** A1
Cumnor CI SW9 . . . **173** A2
Cunard PI EC3 . . . . **110** B1
Cunard Rd NW10 . . .20 C2
Cunard Wlk **3**
SE16 . . . . .41 A2
Cundy Rd E16 . . . . . .35 C3
Cundy St SW1 . . . . **145** C2
Cunningham Ct
W2 . . . . **89** B1
Cunningham Ho **5**
SE5 . . . . .48 C3
Cunningham Pl
NW8 . . . . **89** B2
Cupar Rd SW11 . . . **169** C4
Cureton St SW1 . . . **147** C3
Curlew Ho
Brockley SE4 . . . . . .66 A3
7 Peckham SE15 . .49 B2
Curlew St SE1 . . . . **139** A4
Curness St SE13 . . . .67 B3
Curran Ho SW3 . . . **144** A3
Curricle St W3 . . . . . .29 A1
Currie Ho **13**
SW12 . . . . .73 C4
Cursitor St EC4 . . . . **107** B2
Curtain Pl
EC2 . . . . .24 A1 **98** B2

Curtain Rd
EC2 . . . . .24 A1 **98** B2
Curtis Dr W3 . . . . . . .28 C3
Curtis Ho SE17 . . . . **151** B2
Curtis St SE1 . . . . . **152** C4
Curtis Way SE1 . . . **152** C4
Curve Bldg The
SE4 . . . . .66 B2
Curve The W12 . . . . .29 C2
Curwen & New Acad
Gall* W1 . . . . **105** B3
Curwen Rd W12 . . . .38 C4
Curzon Cres NW10 . . .8 A1
Curzon Gate W1 . . . **117** C1
Curzon Sq W1 . . . . **117** C1
Curzon St W1 . . . . . **118** A2
Custance Ho N1 . . . . **87** B1
Custance St N1 . . . . **97** B4
Custom House
E16 . . . . **124** A3
Custom House Reach
SE16 . . . . .41 B3
Cutbush Ho N7 . . . . .13 C3
Cutcombe Rd SE5 . . .48 B1
Cuthbert Harrowing
Ho EC1 . . . . **96** C1
Cuthbert Ho W2 . . . **101** B4
Cuthbert St W2 . . . . **89** B1
Cuthill Wlk **3** SE5 . .48 C2
Cutlers Gdns EC2 . . **110** B2
Cutlers Sq E14 . . . . .41 C2
Cutlers Sq E14 . . . . .41 C2
Cutler St EC2 . . . . . **110** B2
Cut The SE1 . . . . . . **135** C4
Cutty Sark* SE10 . . .52 B4
Cutty Sark Ho **12**
E14 . . . . .42 A2
Cutty Sark Ret
Development
SE10 . . . . .52 B4
Cutty Sark Sta
SE10 . . . . .52 B4
Cuxton Ho SE17 . . . **152** B2
Cyclops Mews **12**
E14 . . . . .41 C2
Cygnet Ho NW8 . . . . **78** C4
Cygnet House N **18**
E14 . . . . .34 A3
Cygnet House S **19**
E14 . . . . .34 A3
Cygnet St
E1 . . . . .24 B1 **99** A2
Cygnus Bsns Ctr
NW10 . . . . .8 B3
Cynthia St N1 . . . . . **85** A1
Cyntra PI **8** E8 . . . .17 A1
Cypress CI **5** E5 . . .7 C2
Cypress Ct **6** E11 . .19 C4
Cypress Gdns SE4 . .66 A2
Cypress Ho SE14 . . .50 C2
Cypress PI W1 . . . . . **93** A1
Cyprus PI **2** E2 . . .25 B3
Cyprus St E2 . . . . . . .25 B3
Cyrena Rd SE22 . . . .64 B2
Cyril Jackson Prim
Sch (North Bldg)
E14 . . . . .33 B2
Cyril Jackson Prim
Sch (South Bldg)
E14 . . . . .33 B2
Cyril Mans SW11 . . **169** A3
Cyril Thatcher Ho
SW6 . . . . **165** B3
Cyrus Ho EC1 . . . . . . **96** B2

Cyrus St EC1 .... 96 B2
Czar St SE8 .... 51 C4

D

Dabb's La EC1 .... 95 C1
Dabin Cres SE10 .. 52 B2
Dacca St SE8 .... 51 B4
Dace Rd E3 .... 26 C4
Dacre Ho SW3 .... 157 C3
Dacre St SW1 .... 133 B2
Daffodil St W12 .... 29 B2
Dafforne Rd SW17 .72 C1
Dagmar Ct E14 .... 42 B3
Dagmar Gdns
  NW10 .... 22 C3
Dagmar Pas N1 .. 86 B4
Dagmar Rd
  Camberwell SE5 ...49 A2
  Finsbury Pk N4 ... 5 C4
Dagmar Terr N1 .. 86 B4
Dagnall St SW11 169 B3
Dagnan Rd SW12 .73 B4
Dagobert Ho 27
  E1 .... 32 B4
Daimler Ho 8 3 .26 C1
Dainton Ho 22 .... 31 C4
Daintry Way 19 .... 18 B2
Dairy Cl NW10 .... 21 C4
Dairyman Cl NW2 ..1 A1
Daisy Dormer Ct 11
  SW9 .... 62 B3
Daisy La SW6 .... 58 C4
Dakin Pl 9 E1 .... 33 A4
Dakota bldg 6
  SE13 .... 52 A2
Dalberg Rd SW2 ..62 C2
Dalbury Ho 6
  SW9 .... 62 B3
Dalby Rd SW18 ...59 B3
Dalby St NW5 .... 13 A2
Daley Ho 6 W12 ..30 A3
Daley St E9 .... 17 C2
Daley Thompson Way
  7 SW8 .... 61 A4
Dalgarno Gdns
  W10 .... 30 B4
Dalgarno Way
  W10 .... 22 B1
Daling Way E3 .... 26 A3
Dalkeith Ct SW1 . 147 C3
Dalkeith Ho 6
  SW9 .... 48 A2
Dalkeith Rd SE21 .75 B4

Dalling Rd W6 .... 39 A2
Dallington Sch
  EC1 .... 96 B2
Dallington St EC1 . 96 B2
Dalmeny Ave N7 ..13 C4
Dalmeny Avenue Est
  3 N7 .... 13 C4
Dalmeny Ct 4
  SW4 .... 172 A2
Dalmeny Rd N7 .. 13 C4
Dalmeyer Rd NW10 .8 B2
Dalmore Rd SE21 .75 B2
Dalrymple Rd SE4 .66 A3
DALSTON 16 C2
Dalston Jct E8 .... 16 B2
Dalston Kingsland Sta
  .... 16 B3
Dalston La E8 .... 16 C3
Dalton Ho
  3 Balham SW12 .73 A4
  10 Bow E3 .... 26 A3
  18 Deptford SE14 .50 C4
Dalton St SE27 .. 75 A1
Dalwood St SE5 ..49 A2
Daly Ct E15 .... 19 B3
Dalyell Rd SW9 ..62 B4
Damascene Wlk
  SE21 .... 75 B3
Damer Ho 9
  TW10 .... 54 B1
Damer Terr SW10 157 A1
Dame St N1 .... 86 C2
Damien Ct 12 E1 ..32 A3
Damien St E1 .... 32 A3
Damory Ho 1
  SE16 .... 40 B2
Dan Bryant Ho 5
  SW12 .... 73 B4
Danbury St N1 .. 86 B2
Danby Ho
  23 Hackney E9 ...17 B1
  3 West Kilburn
  W10 .... 23 B2
Dancer Rd
  Fulham SW6 .... 164 C3
  Richmond TW9 ...54 C4
Dandridge Cl
  SE10 .... 43 B1
Dandridge Ho 110 C4
Danebury 3 W10 .30 B4
Danebury Ave
  SW15 .... 56 B1
Danecroft Rd
  SE24 .... 63 C2
Dane Ho 15 SE5 ..48 B1
Danehurst St
  SW6 .... 164 A4
Danemere St
  SW15 .... 57 B4
Dane Pl E3 .... 26 B3
Danes Ct NW8 .. 80 C3
Danesdale Rd E9 .18 A2
Danesfield SE5 ...49 A4
Danes Ho 10 W10 .30 B4
Dane St WC1 .... 106 C3
Daneville Rd SE5 ..48 C2
Daniel Bolt Cl E14 .34 A4
Daniel Ct W3 .... 29 A2
Daniel Gdns SE15 .49 B3
Daniell Ho N1 .... 87 C2
Daniel's Rd SE15 .65 B4
Dan Leno Wlk
  SW6 .... 156 A1
Dansey Pl W1 .... 119 B4
Dante Pl SE11 .. 150 B3
Dante Rd SE11 .. 150 A4

Danube Ct 13
  SE15 .... 49 B3
Danube St SW3 . 144 B2
Danvers Ho 11 .. 111 C1
Danvers St SW3 . 157 C3
Da Palma Ct SW6 155 B3
Daphne St SW18 ..59 B1
Daplyn St 1 .... 111 B4
D'arblay St 1 .... 105 A1
Darcy Ho E8 .... 25 A4
Darell Prim Sch
  TW9 .... 54 C4
Darell Rd TW9 .. 54 C4
Daren Ct N7 .... 14 A4
Darent Ho NW8 .. 101 C4
Darenth Rd N16 ...7 B3
Darfield NW1 .... 82 C3
Darfield Way W10 .30 C3
Darfur St SW15 ..57 C4
Darien Ho
  11 London SW11 ..59 C4
  10 Stepney E1 .. 32 C4
Darien Rd SW11 ..59 C4
Daring Ho 23 E3 ..26 A3
Darlan Rd SW6 .. 155 A1
Darley Ho SE11 . 148 C1
Darley Rd SW11 ..60 B1
Darling Rd SE4 ..66 C4
Darling Row E1 ..25 A1
Darlington Ho
  SW8 .... 161 C1
Darnall Ho 9
  SE10 .... 52 B2
Darnay Ho 3 SE16 139 B2
Darnell Ho 9
  SE10 .... 52 B2
Darnley Ho 7 E14 .33 A3
Darnley Rd E9 ...17 B2
Darnley Terr 12
  W11 .... 30 C1
Darrell Rd SE22 ..64 C2
Darsley Dr SW8 . 172 A4
Dartford Ho SE1 . 153 A4
Dartford St SE17 ..48 B4
Dartington NW1 .. 83 A3
Dartington Ho
  Bayswater W2 .. 100 A4
  London SW8 .. 171 C2
Dartle Ct 16 .... 139 C3
Dartmoor Wlk 18
  E14 .... 41 C2
Dartmouth Cl
  W11 .... 31 C3
Dartmouth Ct
  SE10 .... 52 B2
Dartmouth Gr
  SE10 .... 52 B2
Dartmouth Hill
  SE10 .... 52 B2
Dartmouth Ho
  N19 .... 4 A2
  Lewisham SE10 ..52 B1
DARTMOUTH PARK
  .... 4 A1
Dartmouth Park Ave
  NW5 .... 4 A1
Dartmouth Park Hill
  N19 .... 4 A2
Dartmouth Park Rd
  NW5 .... 4 A1
Dartmouth Pl W4 ..46 A4
Dartmouth Rd NW2 .9 C2
Dartmouth Row
  SE10 .... 52 B1

Dartmouth St
  SW1 .... 133 C3
Dartmouth Terr
  SE10 .... 52 C2
Darton Ct W3 .... 28 B1
Dartrey Twr
  SW10 .... 157 B2
Dartrey Wlk
  SW10 .... 157 A2
Darville Rd N16 ...7 B1
Darwen Pl E2 .... 25 A4
Darwin Ct NW1 .. 81 C4
Darwin Ho 8
  SE13 .... 52 B1
Darwin St SE17 .. 151 C4
Dashwood Ho
  SE21 .... 76 B1
Data Point Bsns Ctr
  E16 .... 27 C1
Datchelor Pl 2
  SE5 .... 48 C2
Datchet Ho 14 .. 92 B4
Datchett Ho
  4 E2 .... 98 C3
Datchwood St N4 ..6 B1
Datchworth Ho 8
  N1 .... 15 A1
Date St SE17 .... 151 B1
Daubeney Prim Sch
  E5 .... 18 A4
Daubeney Rd E5 .18 A4
Daubeney Twr 2
  SE8 .... 41 B1
Dault Rd SW18 .. 59 B1
Dauney Ho SE1 .. 136 A3
Dave Adams Ho 8
  E3 .... 26 B3
Davenant Ho 11 . 111 C4
Davenant Rd N19 ..4 C2
Davenant St E1 . 111 C3
Davenport Ho
  SE11 .... 135 B1
Davenport Mews 8
  W12 .... 30 A1
Davenport Rd SE6 .67 B1
Daventry St NW1 102 A4
Dave Porter Hts
  SW19 .... 70 A4
Davern Cl SE10 .. 43 B2
Davey Cl N7 .... 14 B2
Davey Rd E9 .... 18 C1
Davey's Ct WC2 . 120 A4
Davey St SE15 ...49 B4
David Beckham Acad
  The SE10 .... 43 C4
David Devine Ho 2
  E8 .... 16 C3
David Game Coll
  SW7 .... 143 B3
Davidge Ho SE1 . 135 C3
Davidge St SE1 .. 136 B3
David Hewitt Ho 2
  E3 .... 34 A4
David Ho
  11 Putney SW15 ..56 C2
  South Lambeth
  SW8 .... 162 A2
David Mews W1 .. 103 A4
Davidson Gdns
  SW8 .... 162 A2
Davidson Ho 7
  N19 .... 13 B4
David St E15 .... 19 C3

Davies Laing & Dick
  Coll W1 .... 103 C2
Davies Mews W1 . 118 A4
Davies St W1 .... 118 A4
Davina Ho
  Brondesbury NW2 ..10 B2
  14 Hackney E5 ...17 A3
Da Vinci Ct 12
  SE16 .... 40 A1
Davis Ho 15 W12 ..30 A2
Davis Rd W3 .... 38 B4
Davisville Rd W12 .38 C4
Dawes Ho SE17 . 151 B3
Dawes Rd SW6 .. 154 C2
Dawes St SE17 .. 151 C2
Dawlish Ave SW18 .71 A2
Dawlish Rd NW2 ..9 C2
Dawnay Gdns
  SW18 .... 71 C2
Dawnay Rd SW17,
  SW18 .... 71 C2
Dawn Cres E15 .. 27 C4
Dawson Ho
  22 Bethnal Green
  E2 .... 25 B2
  5 Camberwell SE5 .49 A2
Dawson Pl
  W2 .... 31 C2 113 C4
Dawson Rd NW2 ..9 B4
Dawson St E2 .... 24 B3
Day Ho 2 SE5 .... 48 B3
Daylesford Ave
  SW15 .... 56 C3
Daynor Ho 4
  NW6 .... 23 C4
Daysbrook Rd
  SW2 .... 74 B2
Dayton Gr SE15 ..50 B2
Deacon Ho SE11 . 149 A3
Deacon Mews N1 .15 C1
Deacon Rd NW2 ..8 C2
Deacon Way
  SE17 .... 151 A4
Deal Ho
  Deptford SE15 ...50 C4
  Walworth SE17 .. 152 B2
Deal Porters Way
  SE16 .... 40 C3
Deal St E1 .... 111 B4
Dealtry Rd SW15 .57 B3
Deal Wlk SW9 .. 163 C1
Dean Bradley St
  SW1 .... 134 A1
Dean Cl
  Hackney E9 .... 17 B3
  Rotherhithe SE16 .32 C1
Dean Coll of London
  N7 .... 5 B1
Deancross St E1 .32 B3
Dean Ct Acton W3 .28 C3
  South Lambeth
  SW8 .... 162 A1
Deanery Mews
  W1 .... 117 C2
Deanery St W1 .. 117 C2
Dean Farrar St
  SW1 .... 133 C2
Deanhill Ct 2
  SW14 .... 55 A3
Deanhill Rd SW14 .55 A3
Dean Ho London N4 ..6 B4
  New Cross SE14 ..51 B3
  Stamford Hill N16..7 A3
  18 Stepney E1 ...32 B3
Dean Rd NW2 .... 9 B2
Dean Ryle St
  SW1 .... 148 A4

Dean's Bldgs
SE17 .... 151 C2
Deans Cl W4 .... 45 A4
Dean's Ct E C4 ..... 108 B1
Deanshanger Ho 21
SE8 .... 40 C2
Dean's Mews W1 .. 104 B2
Dean St W1 .... 105 B1
Dean Stanley St
SW1 .... 134 A1
Dean's Yd SW1 ... 133 C2
Dean Trench St
SW1 .... 134 A1
Dearmer Ho 4
SW2 .... 74 C4
Deason St E15 ...... 27 B4
Deauville Ct
14 London SW4 .. 61 B1
4 Rotherhithe
SE16 .... 40 C4
Deauville Mans 13
SW4 .... 61 B1
De Barowe Mews 1
N5 .... 15 A3
Debdale Ho 20 E2 . 24 C4
De Beauvoir Cres
.... 24 A4
De Beauvoir Ct
N1 .... 15 C1
De Beauvoir Pl 5
N1 .... 16 A2
De Beauvoir Prim Sch
N1 .... 16 A2
De Beauvoir Sq
N1 .... 16 A1
DE BEAUVOIR TOWN
.... 16 A1
Debenham Ct E8 .. 24 C4
Debnams Rd SE16 . 40 B2
Decima St 1 .... 138 A2
Deck Cl SE16 .... 32 C1
De Crespigny Pk
SE5 .... 48 C1
Deeley Rd SW8 .. 171 B4
Deepdale Ho 6 .. A1
Deepdene Gdns
SW2 .... 74 B4
Deepdene Ho N16 .. 6 C4
Deepdene Lo 5
SW2 .... 74 B4
Deepdene Mans
SW6 .... 164 C4
Deepdene Rd SE5,
SE24 .... 63 C3
Deerbrook Rd SE24,
SW2 .... 75 A3
Dee Rd TW9 .... 54 B3
Deerdale Rd SE24 . 63 B3
Deerhurst Ho 6
SE15 .... 49 C4
Deerhurst Rd NW2 . 9 C2
Deer Lo SW6 .... 58 A4
Deeside Rd SW17 .. 71 C1
Dee St E14 .... 34 B3
Defoe Av TW9 ..... 44 C3
Defoe Ho
Barbican EC2 ... 108 C4
5 Stoke Newington
N16 .... 7 A1
Defoe Pl EC2 ..... 108 C4
Defoe Rd
Rotherhithe SE16 . 41 B4
Stoke Newington N16 . 7 A1
De Gama Pl 3
E14 .... 41 C1

Dekker Ho 19 SE5 . 48 C3
Dekker Rd SE21 .... 64 A1
Delafield Ho 1 ... 111 C1
Delaford Rd SE16 .. 40 A1
Delaford St SW6 .. 154 B3
Delamere Ho 4 N4 . 6 C4
Delamere Rd W5 .. 36 A4
Delamere St W2 .. 100 C3
Delamere Terr
W2 .... 100 B3
Delancey Pas NW1 . 82 B3
Delancey St NW1 .. 82 B3
Delancey Studios
NW1 .... 82 B3
Delany Ho SF10 .... 52 B4
Delarch Rd SE1 .. 136 A3
De Laune St SE17 . 150 A1
Delaware Rd W9 ... 88 A2
Delawyk Cres
SE24 .... 63 C1
Delft Way 2 .... 64 A2
Delhi St N1 .... 84 B3
Delia St SW18 ...... 71 A4
Delius Gr E15 .... 27 B3
Dellafield N4 .... 5 C2
Dell Cl E15 .... 27 C4
Dellow Ho 6 E1 .. 32 A2
Dellow St E1 .... 32 A2
Dell's Mews SW1 . 147 A3
Deloraine Ho 8 .. 51 C2
Deloraine St SE8 .. 51 C2
Delorme St W6 ..... 47 C4
Delta Bldg 7 E14 . 34 B3
Delta Ho N1 .... 97 B4
Delta Pk SW18 .... 59 A3
Delta Point
E2 .... 24 C2 99 B4
Delta St E2 .. 24 C2 99 B4
Delverton Ho
SE17 .... 150 B2
Delverton Rd
SE17 .... 150 B2
Delvino Rd SW6 .. 165 C3
De Montfort Ct 1
SW16 .... 74 A1
De Montfort Rd
SW16 .... 74 A2
De Morgan Rd
SW6 .... 59 A4
Dempster Rd
SW18 .... 59 B2
Denbigh Cl
Notting Hill
W11 .... 31 B2 113 A4
Willesden NW10 .. 8 A1
Denbigh Gdns
TW10 .... 54 B2
Denbigh Ho
Knightsbridge
SW1 .... 131 A2
7 Notting Hill W11 . 31 B3
Notting Hill
W11 .... 31 B2 113 A4
Denbigh Mews
SW1 .... 146 C3
Denbigh Pl SW1 . 146 C2
Denbigh Rd
W11 .... 31 B2 113 A4
Denbigh St SW1 . 147 A2
Denbigh Terr
W11 .... 31 B2 113 A4
Denbury Ho 48 E3 . 27 A2
Denby Ct SE11 .... 149 A4
Dence Ho
E2 .... 24 C2 99 B3
Denchworth Ho
SW9 .... 173 B1

Dene Cl SE4 .... 66 A3
Denehurst Gdns
Acton W3 .... 28 A1
Richmond TW10 .. 54 C3
Dene Mans 1
NW6 .... 10 C2
Denesmead SE24 .. 63 B2
Denewood Rd N6 .. 3 B4
Dengie Wlk N1 .... 86 C4
Denham Ho 22
W12 .... 30 A2
Denham St SE10 .. 43 C1
Denholme Rd W9 . 23 B2
Denland Ho SW8 . 163 A1
Denman Ho N16 ... 7 A2
Denman Rd SE15 . 49 B1
Denman St W1 ... 119 B3
Denmark Gr N1 .... 85 B2
Denmark Hill SE5 . 48 C1
Denmark Hill Sta
SE5 .... 48 C1
Denmark Mans 14
SE5 .... 48 B1
Denmark Pl
2 Bromley E3 ..... 26 C2
Soho WC2 .... 105 C2
Denmark Rd
Camberwell SE5 .. 48 B1
Kilburn NW6 ...... 23 B3
Denmark St WC2 . 105 C2
Denmead Ho
SW15 .... 56 B1
Denne Terr E8 ..... 24 B4
Dennett's Gr SE14 . 50 C1
Dennett's Rd SE14 . 50 B2
Denning Cl NW8 .. 89 A3
Denning Point E1 . 111 A2
Denning Rd NW3 .. 11 C4
Dennington Park
Mansions 1
NW6 .... 10 C2
Dennington Park Rd
NW6 .... 10 C2
Dennis Ct SE10 ... 52 B2
Dennis Ho 6 E3 .. 26 B3
Dennison Point
E15 .... 19 B1
Dennis Way SW4 .. 61 C4
Denny Cres SE11 . 149 C2
Denny St SE11 ... 149 C2
Densham Ho NW8 . 79 C1
Denstone Ho 5
SE15 .... 49 C4
Dent Ho SE17 .... 152 A3
Denton NW1 .... 12 C2
Denton Ho N1 ..... 15 A1
Denton St SW18 .. 59 A1
Dents Rd SW11 ... 60 B1
Denver Rd N16 .... 7 A4
Denyer Ho 1
NW5 .... 13 A4
Denyer St SW3 .. 144 B3
Denys Bldg EC1 .. 107 B4
Denzil Rd NW10 ... 8 B3
Deodar Rd SW15 .. 58 A3
Depot App NW2 ... 9 C4
Depot Rd W12 ..... 30 B2
Depot St SE5 ...... 48 C4
DEPTFORD 50 C3
Deptford Bridge
SE8 .... 51 C2
Deptford Bridge Sta
SE8 .... 51 C2
Deptford Broadway
SE8, SE14 .... 51 C2
Deptford Church St
SE8 .... 51 C3

Deptford Ferry Rd 24
E14 .... 41 C2
Deptford Gn 1 SE8 . 51 C4
Deptford Green Sch
SE14 .... 51 B3
Deptford Green Sch
(Annex) SE14 .... 51 A3
Deptford High St
SE8 .... 51 C3
Deptford Park Prim
Sch SE8 .... 41 A1
Deptford Sta SE8 . 51 C3
Deptford Trad Est
SE8 .... 51 A4
Dept of Transport &
Environment
SW1 .... 133 C1
De Quincey Mews 3
E16 .... 35 C1
Derby Ct 3 E5 ..... 17 C4
Derby Gate SW1 . 134 A4
Derby Ho SE11 ... 149 B4
Derby Rd
Mortlake SW14 ... 55 A3
South Hackney E9 . 25 C4
Derbyshire St
E2 .... 24 C2 99 C3
Derby St W1 ...... 117 C1
Dereham Ho 7
SE4 .... 65 C3
Dereham Pl
EC2 .... 24 A1 98 B2
Derek Walcott Cl
SE24 .... 63 A2
Dericote St E8 ..... 25 A4
Dering St W1 .... 104 B1
Dermody Gdns
SE13 .... 67 C2
Dermody Rd SE13 . 67 C2
Deronda Rd SE24,
SW2 .... 75 A3
Derrick Ho 13
SE13 .... 74 C3
Derrycombe Ho 18
W2 .... 31 C4
Derry St W8 ...... 128 A3
Dersingham Rd
NW2 .... 1 A1
Derwent NW1 ..... 92 C3
Derwent Ct
South Kensington
SW7 .... 143 A4
Tower Hamlets E3 . 26 B1
Derwent St SE10 .. 43 A1
Derwentwater Mans
2 W3 .... 28 B1
Derwentwater Prim
Sch W3 .... 28 B1
Derwentwater Rd
W3 .... 28 B1
Desborough Cl
W2 .... 100 B4
Desborough Ho
W14 .... 155 A4
Desenfans Rd
SE21 .... 64 A1
Desmond St SE14 . 51 A4
Despard Ho SW2 . 74 C2
Despard Rd N19 ... 4 B3

Desvignes Dr
SE13 .... 67 C1
Dethick Ct E3 ...... 26 A4
Detling Ho SE17 . 152 A3
Devas St E3 .... 27 A1
Deventer Cres 8
SE22 .... 64 A2
De Vere Cotts
W8 .... 128 C2
De Vere Gdns W8 128 C3
Deverell St SE1 .. 137 B1
De Vere Mews
W8 .... 128 C2
Devereux Ct WC2 107 B1
Devereux Ho 7
SW15 .... 56 C2
Devereux La
SW13 .... 47 A3
Devereux Rd
SW11 .... 60 B1
Devitt Ho 5 E14 .. 34 A2
Devizes St N1 ..... 87 C3
Devonhurst Pl 4
W4 .... 37 C1
Devonia Rd N1 .... 86 B2
Devon Mans SE1 138 B4
Devonport W2 ..... 102 A2
Devonport Ho
Greenwich SE10 .. 52 B4
23 Paddington W2 . 31 C4
Devonport Rd
W12 .... 39 A4
Devonport St E1 .. 32 B3
Devonshire Cl
W1 .... 104 A4
Devonshire Dr
SE10 .... 52 A2
Devonshire Gdns
W4 .... 45 B3
Devonshire Gr
SE15 .... 50 A4
Devonshire Hall 1
E9 .... 17 B2
Devonshire Ho
Brondesbury NW6 . 10 B2
Newington SE1 .. 136 C2
Paddington W2 .. 101 C4
2 Putney SW15 .. 69 B4
Westminster SW1 147 C2
Devonshire Hospl
W1 .... 103 C4
Devonshire House
Prep Sch NW3 ... 11 C3
Devonshire House
Sch NW3 .... 11 B3
Devonshire Mews 2
W4 .... 38 A1
Devonshire Mews N
W1 .... 104 A4
Devonshire Mews S
W1 .... 104 A4
Devonshire Mews W
W1 .... 103 C4
Devonshire Pl
Child's Hill NW2 .... 1 C1
Kensington W8 .. 128 A1
Marylebone W1 .. 103 C4
Devonshire Place
Mews W1 .... 103 C4
Devonshire Rd
W4 .... 38 A1

Devonshire Row
EC2 . . . . 110 B3
Devonshire Row
Mews W1 . . . . . . 92 B1
Devonshire Sq
EC2 . . . . 110 B2
Devonshire St
Chiswick W4 . . . . . . 38 A1
Marylebone W1 . . . . 104 A4
Devonshire Terr
W2 . . . . 101 A1
Devons Rd E3 . . . . . 27 A1
Devons Road Sta
E3 . . . . 27 A1
Devon St SE15 . . . . 50 A4
De Walden Ho
NW8 . . . . 80 A2
De Walden St W1 . 103 C3
Dewar St SE15 . . . . 64 C4
Dewberry St E14 . . 34 B4
Dewey Rd N1 . . . . . 85 B2
Dewhurst Rd W14 . 39 C3
Dewsbury Ct 5
W4 . . . . 37 B2
Dewsbury Rd NW10 . 8 C3
Dewsbury Terr
NW1 . . . . 82 B4
D'eynsford Rd SE5 . 48 C2
Dhonau Ho SE16 . 153 A4
Diadem Ct W1 . . . 105 B2
Dial Wlk The W8 . 128 B4
Diamond Est
SW17 . . . . 72 A1
Diamond Ho 22
E3 . . . . 27 A2
Diamond St SE15 . . 49 A3
Diamond Terr
SE10 . . . . 52 B2
Diana Cl 2 SE8 . . . . 51 B4
Diana Ho
Barnes SW13 . . . . . . 46 B2
4 Brixton SW2 . . . . . 62 B2
Diana, Princess of
Wales Mml Wlk
W2 . . . . 114 C1
Dibden Ho 8 SE5 . . 49 A3
Dibden St N1 . . . . . 86 C4
Dibdin Ho W9 . . . . . 78 A1
Dicey Ave NW2 . . . . . 9 B4
Dickens Ct EC1 . . . . 96 A1
Dickens Ho
Bloomsbury WC1 . . . 94 A2
Kennington SE17 . . 150 B1
Kilburn NW6 . . . . . . 23 C2
Paddington NW8 . . . 89 C2
Dickens House Mus★
WC1 . . . . 94 C1
Dickenson Rd N8 . . . 5 A4
Dickens Sq SE1 . . . 137 A2
Dickens St SW8 . . 170 B2
Dickinson Ho
E2 . . . . 24 C2 99 B3
Dicksee Ho NW8 . . . 89 B1
Dick Shepherd Ct 7
SW2 . . . . 62 C1
Dickson Ho 4 E1 . . 32 A3
Didbin Ho N7 . . . . . . 5 B2
Digby Bsns Ctr E9 . . 17 C2
Digby Cres N4 . . . . . 6 B2
Digby Mans W6 . . . . 39 B1
Digby Rd E9 . . . . . . 17 C2
Digby St E2 . . . . 25 B2
Diggon St E1 . . . . . . 32 C4
Dighton Ct SE17 . . . 48 B4
Dighton Rd SW18 . . 59 B3

Dignum St N1 . . . . . 85 B2
Digswell St N7 . . . . 14 C2
Dilke St SW3 . . . . . 159 A4
Dilston Gr SE16 . . . 40 B2
Dilton Gdns SW15 . . 69 A3
Dimes Pl 3 W6 . . . . . 39 A2
Dimson Cres E3 . . . . 26 C2
Dinerman Ct NW8 . . 79 A4
Dingle Gdns E14 . . . 33 C2
Dingley La SW16 . . . 73 C2
Dingley Pl EC1 . . . . . 97 A3
Dingley Rd EC1 . . . . 96 C3
Dingwall Rd SW18 . . 71 B4
Dinmont Ho 27 E2 . . 24 C3
Dinmont St 1 E2 . . . 25 A3
Dinmore Ho 6 E9 . . 25 B4
Dinnington Ho 17
E1 . . . . 25 A1
Dinsdale Rd SE3 . . . 53 B4
Dinsmore Rd
SW12 . . . . 73 A4
Dinton Ho NW8 . . . . 90 A2
Dinwiddy Ho N1 . . . 84 C1
Dionis Ho SW6 . . . 165 B2
Disbrowe Rd W6 . . 154 B3
Discovery Bsns Pk
SE16 . . . . 139 C1
Discovery Dock E
E14 . . . . 42 A4
Discovery Ho 1
E14 . . . . 34 B2
Disney Pl SE1 . . . . . 137 B4
Disney St SE1 . . . . 137 B4
Disraeli Cl 1 W4 . . . 37 C2
Disraeli Gdns
SW15 . . . . 58 B3
Disraeli Rd
Acton NW10 . . . . . . 20 C3
Putney SW15 . . . . . . 58 A3
2 Stratford E15 . . . . 27 C4
Diss St E2 . . . . 24 B2 98 C4
Distaff La EC4 . . . . 122 C4
Distillery La W6 . . . 39 B1
Distillery Rd W6 . . . 39 B1
Distillery Wlk 14
TW8 . . . . 44 A4
Distin St SE11 . . . . 149 B3
Ditchburn St E14 . . 34 B2
Ditton Ho 10 E5 . . . 17 A3
Divis Way SW15 . . . 57 A1
Dixon Clark Ct N1 . . 15 A2
Dixon Ho 2 NW10 . . 30 C3
Dixon Rd SE14 . . . . 51 A2
Dixon's Alley 16
SE16 . . . . 40 A4
Dobree Ave NW10 . . . 9 A1
Dobson Cl NW6 . . . . 11 C1
Dobson Ho 18
SE14 . . . . 50 C4
Doby Ct EC4 . . . . . 123 A4
Dockers Tanner Rd 6
E14 . . . . 41 C2
Dockhead SE1 . . . . 139 A3
Dockhead Wharf
SE1 . . . . 139 B4
Dock Hill Ave
SE16 . . . . 40 C4
Docklands Ct 20
E14 . . . . 33 B3
Docklands Heritage
Mus★
SE16 . . . . 139 B1
Dock Offices 12
SE16 . . . . 40 B3
Dock St E1 . . . . 125 B4

Doctor Spurstowe
Almshouses 9
E8 . . . . 17 A2
Docura Ho N7 . . . . . . 5 B2
Docwras Bldgs
N1 . . . . 15 C2
Dodbrooke Rd
SE27 . . . . 75 A1
Dodd Ho 18 SE16 . . 40 A2
Doddington Gr
SE17 . . . . 150 B1
Doddington Pl 4
SE17 . . . . 48 A4
Dodson St SE1 . . . 135 C3
Dod St E14 . . . . 33 C3
Dog Kennel Hill
SE22 . . . . 64 A4
Dog Kennel Hill Sch
SE22 . . . . 64 A4
Dog La NW10 . . . . . . 8 A4
Dolben Ct SW1 . . . 147 C3
Dolben St SE1 . . . . 122 B1
Dolby Rd SW6 . . . . 164 C1
Doleman Ho 19
SE10 . . . . 52 A2
Dolland Ho SE11 . . 149 A1
Dolland St SE11 . . . 149 A1
Dollar Bay E14 . . . . 42 B4
DOLLIS HILL 9 A4
Dollis Hill Sta NW2 . . 8 C3
Dolman Rd W4 . . . . 37 C2
Dolman St SW4 . . . 62 B3
Dolphin Cl 2
SE16 . . . . 40 C4
Dolphin Ct N7 . . . . 13 C4
Dolphin La E14 . . . . 34 A2
Dolphin Sch SW11 . . 60 B2
Dolphin Sq SW1 . . 147 A1
Dolphin Twr 21
SE8 . . . . 51 B4
Dombey Ho
Bermondsey SE1 . . 139 B3
4 Shepherd's Bush
W11 . . . . 30 C1
Dombey St WC1 . . 106 C4
Domelton Ho
SW18 . . . . 59 A1
Domett Cl SE5 . . . . 63 C3
Domfe Pl E5 . . . . . . 17 C4
Domingo St EC1 . . . 96 C1
Dominion St EC2 . 109 C4
Donaghue Cotts 11
E14 . . . . 33 A4
Donaldson Rd
NW6 . . . . 23 B4
Donegal Ho 2 N1 . . 25 B1
Donegal St N1 . . . . 85 A1
Doneraile Ho
SW1 . . . . 146 A1
Doneraile St SW6 . . 47 C2
Dongola Rd E1 . . . . 33 A4
Don Gratton Ho
E1 . . . . 111 B3
Donkey Alley
SE22 . . . . 64 C1
Donkin Ho 15
SE16 . . . . 40 A2
Donne Ct SE24 . . . . 63 B1
Donne Ho
10 Canonbury N16 . 15 C4
16 Deptford SE14 . . 50 C4
2 Poplar E14 . . . . . . 33 C3
Donnelly Ct SW6 . . 154 B2
Donne Pl SW3 . . . . 144 B4
Donnington Ct
11 Camden Town
NW1 . . . . 13 A1

Donnington Ct
continued
Willesden NW10 . . . . 9 A1
Donnington Ho
SW8 . . . . 171 B2
Donnington Prim Sch
NW10 . . . . 22 A4
Donnington Rd
NW10 . . . . 22 A4
Donovan Ct SW7 . . 143 B1
Donovan Ho 4 E1 . . 32 B2
Don Phelan Cl
SE5 . . . . 48 C2
Doon St SE1 . . . . . 121 B2
Doradus Ct 20
SW19 . . . . 69 C3
Dora Ho
11 Shepherd's Bush
W11 . . . . 30 C2
1 Tower Hamlets
E14 . . . . 33 B3
Dorando Cl W12 . . . 30 A2
Doran Wlk
Stratford E15 . . . . . . 19 B1
Stratford Marsh E15 . 27 B4
Dora St E14 . . . . 33 B3
Dorcas Ct 9
SW18 . . . . 59 C3
Dorchester Ct
De Beauvoir Town
N1 . . . . 16 A1
Herne Hill SE24 . . . . 63 B2
Knightsbridge SW1 . 131 A1
5 Streatham
SW16 . . . . 74 A2
Dorchester Dr
SE24 . . . . 63 B2
Dorchester Gr W4 . . 38 B1
Dorchester Ho
TW9 . . . . 45 A3
Dorcis Ave SW19 . . 69 C2
Dorking Cl SE8 . . . . 51 B4
Dorking Ho SE1 . . . 137 C2
Dorland Ct SW15 . . 58 B1
Dorlcote Rd SW18 . . 72 A4
Dorleston Ct N1 . . . 87 C4
Dorman Way NW8 . . 79 B4
Dormay St SW18 . . . 59 A2
Dormstone Ho
SE17 . . . . 152 A3
Dornberg Cl SE3 . . . 53 C3
Dorncliffe Rd
SW6 . . . . 164 B2
Dorney Ho NW3 . . . 12 B1
Dorney Ct SW6 . . . . 58 A4
Dornfell St NW6 . . . 10 B3
Dornoch Ho 3 E3 . . 26 B3
Dornton Rd SW12,
SW17 . . . . 73 B2
Dorothy Charrington
Ho 1 SE22 . . . . . . 64 C2
Dorothy Rd SW11 . . 60 B4
Dorrien Wlk SW16 . . 73 C2
Dorrington Point 20
E3 . . . . 27 A2
Dorrington St
EC1 . . . . 107 B4
Dorrit Ho 2 W11 . . . 30 C1
Dorrit St SE1 . . . . . 137 A4
Dorset Bldgs EC4 . 108 A1
Dorset Cl NW1 . . . . 102 C4
Dorset St 3 N1 . . . . 16 A1

Dorset Mans 2
W6 . . . . 47 C4
Dorset Mews
SW1 . . . . 132 A2
Dorset Pl E15 . . . . . 19 C2
Dorset Rd SW8 . . . 162 C2
Dorset Rise EC4 . . . 108 A1
Dorset Sq NW1 . . . . 90 C1
Dorset St W1 . . . . . 103 A3
Dorton Cl 6 SE15 . . 49 A3
Dorville Cres W6 . . . 39 A3
Doughty Ct 11 E1 . . 32 A1
Doughty Mews
WC1 . . . . 94 C1
Doughty St WC1 . . . 94 C1
Douglas Bldgs
SE1 . . . . 137 A4
Douglas Ct 5
NW6 . . . . 10 C1
Douglas Gracey Ho
SW18 . . . . 70 A4
Douglas Ho
Putney SW15 . . . . . . 56 C1
Westminster SW1 . . 147 B3
Douglas Johnstone
Ho SW6 . . . . 154 C3
Douglas Mews
NW2 . . . . 1 A1
Douglas Path E14 . . 42 B1
Douglas Rd
Islington N1 . . . . . . 15 B1
Kilburn NW6 . . . . . . 23 B4
5 Newham E16 . . . . 35 C4
Douglas Rd N N1 . . 15 B2
Douglas Rd S N1 . . 15 B2
Douglas St SW1 . . . 147 B3
Douglas Waite Ho
NW6 . . . . 11 A1
Douglas Way SE8 . . 51 B3
Doulton Ho SE11 . . 149 A4
Doulton Mews 4
NW6 . . . . 11 A2
Dounesforth Gdns
SW18 . . . . 71 A3
Douro Pl W8 . . . . . 128 B2
Douro St E3 . . . . . . 26 C3
Douthwaite Sq
E1 . . . . 125 C2
Dovecote Gdns 8
SW14 . . . . 55 C4
Dove Ct EC2 . . . . . 109 B1
Dovedale Cotts
SW11 . . . . 168 C2
Dovedale Ho N16 . . . 6 C4
Dovedale Rd SE22 . . 65 A1
Dovehouse St
SW3 . . . . 144 A1
Dove Mews SW7 . . 143 A2
Dovercourt Rd
SE22 . . . . 64 B1
Dover Ct
Clerkenwell EC1 . . . 96 A2
17 Greenwich SE10 . 52 A2
Dove Rd N1 . . . . . . 15 C2
Doverfield Rd
SW2 . . . . 74 A4
Dover Flats SE1 . . . 152 B3
Dover Ho
Brixton SE5 . . . . . . 48 A2
13 Deptford SE15 . . 50 B4
Dover House Rd
SW15 . . . . 57 A2
Dover Mans 18
SW9 . . . . 62 C4
Dove Row E2 . . . . . 24 C4
Dover Park Dr
SW15 . . . . 57 A1

Dover St W1.... 118 C2
Dover Terr TW9 .. 44 C1
Dover Yd W1 .... 118 C2
Doves Cl W8 .... 85 B3
Dovet Ct SW8 .. 172 C4
Doveton St E1 .. 25 B1
Doveton St E1.. 25 B1
Dove Wlk SW1 .. 145 B2
Dovey Lo 4 N1 .. 14 C1
Dowdeny Cl 12
NW5 ....12 C3
Dowdeswell Cl
SW15 ....56 A3
Dowding Ho N6 .. 3 C4
Dowell Ho SF21 .. 76 B1
Dowes Ho 13
SW16 ....74 A1
Dowgate Hill EC4. 123 B4
Dowland St W10 .. 23 A2
Dowlas St E5 .... 18 A2
Dowlen Ct 14 E14 .41 C4
Dowler Ho 16 E1 ... 111 C1
Downbarton Ho
SW9 ....173 B4
Downbury Mews 13
SW18 ....58 C2
Downend Ct 1
SE15 ....49 A4
Downer's Cotts
SW4 ....61 B3
Downey Ho 6 E1 ... 26 A1
Downfield Cl W9 . 88 A1
Downham Ct 1
N1................15 C1
Downham Rd N1 .15 C1
Downing Ho
2 North Kensington
W10..............30 C3
4 Putney SW15 ..56 C2
Downing St*
SW1 ....134 A4
Down Pl W6 .....39 A1
Down St Mews
W1 ....118 A1
Downs Ct 16 E8 .. 17 A3
Downsell Prim Sch
E15 ....19 C4
Downsell Rd E15 .19 C4
Downshire Hill
NW3 ....11 C4
Downside 6
SW15 ....58 A2
Downside Cres
NW3 ....12 A3
Downs La 2 E5 ...17 A4
Downs Park Rd E5,
E8................16 C3
Downs Rd E5, N16 .16 C4
Down St W1 .... 118 A1
Downsview Sch
E5................17 A4
Downton Ave SW2 .74 B2
Downtown Rd
SE16.............41 A4
Dowrey St N1 .. 85 B4
Dowson Cl SE5 .. 63 C3
Dowson Ct SE13 .67 C4
Dowson Ho 8 E1 .. 32 C3
Doyce St SE1 .. 136 C4
Doyle Gdns NW10 .22 A4
Doyle Ho W3 .....37 A4
D'Oyley St SW1 . 145 B4
Doynton St N19 ..4 A2
Draco St SE17 .. 48 B4
Dragon Ct WC2 . 106 B2
Dragon Rd SE15.. 49 A4
Dragon Yd WC1 . 106 B2

Dragoon Rd SE8....41 B1
Dragor Rd NW10 ..20 B1
Drake Cl 50 SE16 .40 C4
Drake Croft N16... 6 C2
Drake Ct 5 W12 .. 39 A4
Drakefield Rd
SE14 ....65 C4
Drakefield Rd
SW17 ....72 C1
Drake Ho
2 Limehouse E14 ..33 A2
20 Stepney E1 .....32 B4
Drakeley Ct N5 ...15 A4
Drake Rd SE4 .....66 C4
Drakes Ctyd NW6 ..10 B1
Drake St WC1 .. 150 B4
Draper Pl N1 ... 86 B4
Drapers Almshouses
6 E3................27 A2
Drapers Gdns
EC2 ....109 C2
Drapers Rd E15 ..19 C4
Drapers Way
SE16 ....153 C4
Draycott Ave
SW3 ....144 B3
Draycott Ct SW11 .48 C3
Draycott Ho SW3 .144 C3
Draycott Pl SW3 .144 C3
Draycott Terr
SW3 ....145 A3
Drayford Cl W9 ..23 B1
Dray Gdns SW2 ..62 B2
Draymans Ct 4
SW9 ....62 B4
Drayson Mews
W8 ....127 C3
Drayton Ct SW10 .143 A1
Drayton Gdns
SW10 ....143 A1
Drayton Ho 14
N5.................15 C4
Drayton Park Mews
2 N5 ....14 C3
Drayton Park Prim
Sch N5 ....14 C3
Drayton Park Sta
N5.................14 C3
Drayton Pk N5, N7 .14 C1
Drayton Rd NW10 .21 B4
Dreadnought St
SE10..............43 B3
Dresden Cl NW6 ..11 A2
Dresden Ho
Clapham SW11 ...169 B2
Lambeth SE11 ....149 A4
Dresden Rd N19...4 C3
Dressington Ave
SE4 ....66 C1
Drewett Ho 6 E1 .. 111 C1
Drew Ho 11 SW16 ..74 A1
Drewstead La
SW16 ....73 C2
Drewstead Rd
SW16 ....73 C2
Driffield Rd E3 ...26 A3
Driftway Ho 18 E3 .26 B3
Drinkwater Ho 11
SE5 ....48 C3
Drive Mans SW6 . 164 B2
Drive The
Acton W3 ....28 B3
Harlesden NW10 ..21 B4
Hendon NW11 .....1 A4
Islington N7 ......14 B2

Dr Johnson Ave
SW17.............73 A1
Dr Johnson's House
Mus* EC4 ....107 C1
Droitwich Cl SE26 .76 C1
Dromore Rd SW15.58 A1
Dron Ho 1 E1 ....32 B4
Droop St W10 .....23 A1
Drovers Ct SE13 .67 B4
Drovers Pl SE15 ..50 A3
Druce Rd SE21 ...64 A1
Druid St SE1 ... 138 C3
Drummer Lo N7 .. 5 B1
Drummond Cres
NW1 ....93 B4
Drummond Gate
SW1 ....147 C2
Drummond Ho 13
E2.................24 C3
Drummond Rd
SE16..............40 A3
Drummonds Pl
TW9 ....54 A3
Drummond St
NW1 ....92 C2
Drum St E1 .... 111 A2
Drury Ho SW8 ...170 C4
Drury La WC2 .. 106 B1
Dryad St SW15 ...57 C4
Dryburgh Ho
SW1 ....146 B2
Dryburgh Mans
SW15 ....57 B4
Dryburgh Rd
SW15 ....57 B4
Dryden Bldg 1 E1 .111 B2
Dryden Ct SE11 .149 C3
Dryden Ho
6 Camberwell
SE5 ....48 C3
16 Stoke Newington
N16.................7 A1
Dryden St WC2 .106 B1
Dryfield Wlk 8
SE8 ....51 C4
Drysdale Flats 3
E8.................16 B3
Drysdale Ho
E2 ....24 A2 98 B4
Drysdale Pl
N1 ....24 A2 98 B4
Drysdale St
N1 ....24 A2 98 B4
Dublin Ave E8 ....24 C4
Ducal St E2 ..24 B2 99 A3
Ducane Cl 6 W12 .30 B3
Du Cane Ct SW12 .72 C3
Du Cane Rd W12 ..29 C3
Ducavel Ho SW2 ..74 B3
Duchess Mews
W1 ....104 B3
Duchess of Bedford
Ho W8 ....127 B3
Duchess of Bedford's
Wlk W8 ....127 B3
Duchess St W1 .104 B3
Duchy St SE1 ...121 C2
Ducie Ho 7 SW15 .57 B2
Ducie St SW4 ....62 B3
Duckett St E1 ....33 A4
Duck La W1 .... 105 B1
Du Cros Rd W3 ..29 A1
DUDDEN HILL 8 C3
Dudden Hill La
NW10 .... 8 B3
Dudley Ct
Marylebone W1 ..102 C1

Dudley Ct continued
St Giles WC2.....106 A2
Dudley Ho
Brixton SW9 ....173 B2
Paddington W2 ..101 B3
Dudley Mews 14
SW2 ....62 C1
Dudley Rd
Kilburn NW6 .....23 B3
Richmond TW9 ...44 B1
Dudley St W2 ...101 B3
Dudmaston Mews
SW3 ....143 C2
Duffell Ho SE11 .149 A1
Dufferin Ave EC1 .97 B1
Dufferin Ct EC1 ..97 B1
Dufferin St EC1 ..97 B1
Duffield Ho N4 ....6 B4
Duff St E14 ......34 A3
Dufour's Pl W1 ..105 A1
Dugard Way SE11 .150 A3
Dugdale Ho 10 N7 .13 C3
Duke Humphrey Rd
SE3 ....53 A1
Duke of Wellington Pl
SW1, W1 ....131 C3
Duke of York's Sq
SW3 ....145 A3
Duke of York St
SW1 ....119 A2
Duke Rd W4 ......37 C1
Duke Shin St SE1 .123 C2
Duke St St James's
SW1 ....119 A2
Duke's Ave W4 ...37 C1
Dukes Ct
Dulwich SE22 ....76 C3
East Dulwich SE22 ..64 C3
Lewisham SE13 ..52 B1
Mortlake SW14 ...45 C1
Dukes Gate 4 W4 .37 B2
Dukes Head Yd N6 .4 A3
Duke Shore Wharf
E14 ....33 B2
Duke's La W8 ...128 A4
Duke's Mews W1 .103 C2
Duke's Pl EC3 ...110 B1
Dukes Point N6 ...4 A3
Duke's Rd WC1 ..93 C3
Duke St W1 ....103 C1
Duke Street Mans
W1 ....103 C1
Duke's Yd 2 SW15 .57 B2
Dulas St N4 ......5 B3
Dulford St
W11 .....31 A2 112 A4
Dulka Rd SW11 ..60 B2
Dulverton NW1 ..83 A3
Dulverton Mans
WC1 ....95 A1
DULWICH 76 C3
Dulwich Coll SE21.76 A2
Dulwich Coll Picture
Gall SE21 ....76 A4
Dulwich Coll Prep
Sch SE21 ....76 A1
Dulwich Comm
SE21 ....64 A1
Dulwich Hamlet Jun
Sch SE21 ....63 C1
Dulwich Hospl
SE22 ....64 A3
Dulwich Lawn Cl
SE22 ....64 B2
Dulwich Mead
SE24 ....63 B1

Dulwich Mews
East Dulwich SE22 ..64 B2
1 East Dulwich
SE22...............64 B3
Dulwich Oaks The
SE21...............76 B1
Dulwich Rd SE24 .63 A1
DULWICH VILLAGE ..76 A4
Dulwich Village
SE21...............64 A1
Dulwich Village CE Inf
Sch SE21 ....64 A3
Dumain Ct SE11 .150 A3
Du Maurier Ho 2
NW3 ....12 B3
Dumbarton Ct 18
SW2 ....74 A4
Dumbarton Rd
SW2 ....62 A1
Dumont Rd N16 ..7 A1
Dumphreys Ho 5
SW4 ....73 C4
Dumpton Pl NW1 .12 C1
Dunbar St SE27 ..75 B1
Dunbar Wharf 20
E14 ....33 B2
Dunboyne Rd
NW3 ....12 B3
Dunbridge Ho 12
SW15 ....56 B1
Dunbridge St
Bethnal Green E2 .25 A1
21 Bethnal Green
E2 ....24 C1 99 C2
Duncan Ct 8 E14 .34 B4
Duncan Gr W3 ...29 A3
Duncan Ho 5
NW3 ....12 B1
Duncannon Ho
SW1 ....147 C1
Duncannon St
WC2 ....120 A3
Duncan Rd
Hackney E8 ......25 A4
Richmond TW9 ...54 A3
Duncan St N1 ...86 A2
Duncan Terr N1 ..86 A2
Dunch St 33 E1 ...32 A3
Duncombe Ho 7
SW19 ....69 C3
Duncombe Prim Sch
N19 ....5 A3
Duncombe Rd N19 .4 C3
Duncrievie Rd
SE13 ....67 C1
Dundalk Ho 2 E1 .32 B3
Dundalk Rd SE4 .66 A4
Dundas Ho 12 E2 .25 B3
Dundas Rd SE15 .50 B1
Dundee Ct 28 E1 ..32 A1
Dundee Ho W9 ...88 C4
Dundee St E1 ....32 A1
Dundee Wharf
E14 ....33 B2
Dundonald Rd
NW10 ....22 C4
Dundry Ho 5
SE26 ....76 C1
Dunelm Gr SE27 .75 B1
Dunelm St E1 ....32 C3
Dunford Rd N7 ...14 B4
Dungarvan Ave
SW15 ....56 C3

Dungeness Ho SW18 . . . . 59 B3
Dunhill Point 12 SW15 . . . . 69 A3
Dunkeld Ho 15 E14 . . . . 34 C3
Dunlace Rd E5 . . . . 17 C4
Dunlin Ct 16 SE21 . . . . 75 C2
Dunlin Ho 18 SE16 . . . . 40 C2
Dunloe Ct 7 E2 . . . . 24 B3
Dunloe St E2 . . . . 24 B3
Dunlop Pl SE16 . . . . 139 A1
Dunmore Point E2 . . . . 24 B2 98 C3
Dunmore Rd NW6 . . . . 23 A4
Dunmow Rd SE11 . . . . 149 A2
Dunmow Rd E15 . . . . 19 C4
Dunmow Wlk N1 . . . . 86 C4
Dunnage Cres SE16 . . . . 41 A2
Dunne Mews 11 NW5 . . . . 13 B3
Dunnet Ho 27 E3 . . . . 26 B3
Dunnico Ho SE17 . . . . 152 A2
Dunnock Ct 1 SE21 . . . . 75 C2
Dunn's Pas WC1 . . . . 106 B2
Dun St E8 . . . . 16 B3
Dunollie Pl NW5 . . . . 13 B3
Dunollie Rd NW5 . . . . 13 B3
Dunoon Ho N1 . . . . 84 C3
Dunraven Ho 12 TW9 . . . . 44 B2
Dunraven Rd W12 . . . . 29 C1
Dunraven Sch SW16 . . . . 74 B1
Dunraven St W1 . . . . 117 A4
Dunrobin Ct NW3 . . . . 11 A3
Dunsany Rd W14 . . . . 39 C3
Dunsfold Ho 4 SW2 . . . . 74 B4
Dunsford Way SW15 . . . . 57 A1
Dunsmure Rd N16 . . . . 7 A3
Dunstable Ct 3 SE3 . . . . 53 C3
Dunstable Mews W1 . . . . 103 C4
Dunstable Rd TW10, TW9 . . . . 54 A3
Dunstall Ho 9 SE15 . . . . 49 C2
Dunstan Ho SE4 . . . . 51 B1
Dunstan Hos 5 E1 . . . . 32 B4
Dunstan Rd NW11 . . . . 1 C3
Dunstan's Gr SE22 . . . . 65 A1
Dunstan's Rd SE22 . . . . 64 C1
Dunster Ct EC3 . . . . 124 B4
Dunster Gdns NW6 . . . . 10 B1
Dunsterville Way SE1 . . . . 137 C3
Dunston Rd
  Clapham SW11 . . . . 169 C1
  Hackney E8 . . . . 24 B4
Dunston St E8 . . . . 24 B4
Dunton Ho 16 SW16 . . . . 74 A1
Dunton Rd SE1 . . . . 152 C3
Dunworth Mews W11 . . . . 31 B3
Duplex Ride SW1 . . . . 131 A3

Durand Gdns SW9 . . . . 173 A3
Durand Prim Sch SW9 . . . . 173 A4
Durant St E2 . . . . 24 C2 99 B4
Durban Ho 28 W12 . . . . 30 A2
Durdans Ho 3 NW1 . . . . 13 B1
Durfey Pl SE5 . . . . 48 C3
Durford Cres SW15 . . . . 69 A3
Durham Ct
  Brockley SE4 . . . . 66 C4
  Kilburn NW6 . . . . 23 C3
Durham Ho
  1 Dartmouth Pk NW5 . . . . 4 B1
  Lisson Gr NW8 . . . . 90 B3
Durham House St WC2 . . . . 120 B3
Durham Pl SW3 . . . . 144 C1
Durham Rd N4, N7 . . . . 5 B2
Durham Row E1 . . . . 33 A4
Durham St SE11 . . . . 162 C4
Durham Terr W2 . . . . 100 A2
Durley Rd N16 . . . . 7 A4
Durlock Ho SW9 . . . . 173 B4
Durlston Rd E5 . . . . 7 C2
Durnford St SE10 . . . . 52 B4
Durnsford Ave SW18, SW19 . . . . 70 C2
Durnsford Rd SW18, SW19 . . . . 70 C1
Durrell Rd SW6 . . . . 164 C3
Durrels Ho W14 . . . . 141 A4
Durrington Rd E5 . . . . 18 A4
Durrington Twr SW8 . . . . 171 A2
Durrisdeer Ho NW2 . . . . 10 B4
Durston Ho SE5 . . . . 12 C3
Durward St E1 . . . . 32 A4
Durweston Mews W1 . . . . 103 A4
Durweston St W1 . . . . 103 A3
Dutch Yd SW18 . . . . 58 C2
Dutton Ho SW2 . . . . 75 A3
Dutton St SE10 . . . . 52 B2
Dwight Ct SW6 . . . . 164 B2
Dycer Ho 19 E9 . . . . 17 C2
Dye House La E3 . . . . 26 C4
Dyer Ho SE4 . . . . 51 A1
Dyer's Bldgs EC1 . . . . 107 B3
Dyer's La SW15 . . . . 57 A3
Dykes Ct 11 SW2 . . . . 74 B3
Dylan Rd 2 SE24 . . . . 63 A3
Dylways SE5 . . . . 63 C3
Dymchurch Ho 12 E5 . . . . 17 A3
Dymes Path SW19 . . . . 69 C2
Dymock St SW6 . . . . 59 A4
Dyne Rd NW6 . . . . 10 B1
Dynevor Rd
  Richmond TW10 . . . . 54 A2
  Shacklewell N16 . . . . 7 B1
Dynham Rd NW6 . . . . 10 C1
Dyott St
  Soho WC1 . . . . 105 C2
  St Giles WC1, WC2 . . . . 106 A2
Dysart St EC2 . . . . 24 A1 98 A1
Dyson Ho 3 SE10 . . . . 43 B1

E

Eade Rd N4 . . . . 6 B4
Eagle Cl SE16 . . . . 40 B1
Eagle Ct
  1 Dulwich SE21 . . . . 75 C2
  Holborn EC1 . . . . 108 A4
Eagle Dwellings EC1 . . . . 97 A4
Eagle Ho
  22 Bethnal Green E1 . . . . 25 A1
  Finsbury Pk N7 . . . . 5 B1
Eagle Hts 10 SW11 . . . . 60 A4
Eagle Lo NW11 . . . . 1 B4
Eagle Mans N16 . . . . 16 B3
Eagle Pl
  South Kensington SW7 . . . . 143 A2
  St James SW1 . . . . 119 A3
Eagle St WC1 . . . . 106 C3
Eagle Wharf SE1 . . . . 138 C4
Eagle Wharf Rd N1 . . . . 87 A2
Eagle Works E1 . . . . 24 B1 99 A1
Eagling Cl E3 . . . . 26 C2
Ealing, Hammersmith & West London Coll W14 . . . . 140 A2
Ealing Tertiary Coll W3 . . . . 28 A1
Eamann Casey Ho SW9 . . . . 173 C3
Eamont Ct NW8 . . . . 80 B2
Eamont St NW8 . . . . 80 B2
Eardley Cres SW5 . . . . 141 C1
Eardlom Rd SW17 . . . . 57 B3
Earldom Rd SW15 . . . . 57 B3
Earle Ho SW1 . . . . 147 C3
Earlham Gr E7 . . . . 19 B1
Earlham St WC2 . . . . 106 A1
Earl Ho NW1 . . . . 90 B1
Earlom Ho WC1 . . . . 95 B3
Earl Rd SW14 . . . . 55 B3
EARL'S COURT SW5 . . . . 141 C3
Earl's Court Ex Ctr* SW5 . . . . 141 B1
Earl's Court Gdns SW5 . . . . 142 A3
Earl's Court Rd SW5, W8 . . . . 141 C4
Earl's Court Sq SW5 . . . . 142 A2
Earl's Court Sta SW5 . . . . 141 C3
Earlsferry Way N1 . . . . 14 A1
EARLSFIELD 71 B3
Earlsfield Prim Sch SW18 . . . . 71 B2
Earlsfield Rd SW18 . . . . 71 B3
Earlsfield Sta SW18 . . . . 71 B3
Earlsmead Rd NW10 . . . . 22 B2
Earl St EC2 . . . . 110 A4
Earls Terr W8 . . . . 127 B1
Earlsthorpe Mews 3 SW12 . . . . 60 C1
Earlstoke St EC1 . . . . 96 A4
Earlston Gr E9 . . . . 25 A4
Earls Wlk W8 . . . . 127 B1
Earlswood Cl 10 SE10 . . . . 43 A1

Earlswood Ho 2 SW2 . . . . 74 B3
Earlswood St SE10 . . . . 43 A1
Early Mews NW1 . . . . 82 B4
Earnshaw Ho EC1 . . . . 96 B3
Earnshaw St WC1, WC2 . . . . 105 C2
Earsby St W14 . . . . 140 B4
Earth Galleries* SW7 . . . . 129 C1
Eashing Point 5 SW15 . . . . 69 A3
Easleys Mews W1 . . . . 103 C2
EAST ACTON 29 A1
East Acton Arc W3 . . . . 29 B3
East Acton Ct W3 . . . . 29 A2
East Acton La W3 . . . . 29 A1
East Acton Prim Sch W3 . . . . 29 A2
East Acton Sta W3 . . . . 29 B3
East Arbour St E1 . . . . 32 C3
East Bank N16 . . . . 7 A4
East Block 5 E1 . . . . 32 C2
Eastbourne Ave W3 . . . . 28 C3
Eastbourne Gdns SW14 . . . . 55 B4
Eastbourne Mews W2 . . . . 101 A2
Eastbourne Rd W4 . . . . 45 B4
Eastbourne Terr W2 . . . . 101 A2
Eastbury Gr W4 . . . . 38 A1
Eastbury Terr E1 . . . . 25 C1
Eastcastle St W1 . . . . 105 A2
Eastcheap EC3 . . . . 124 A4
East Churchfield Rd W3 . . . . 28 C1
Eastcote St SW9 . . . . 172 C1
East Cross Ctr E15 . . . . 18 C3
East Cross Route
  Bow E3 . . . . 26 C4
  Hackney Wick E9 . . . . 18 B3
Eastdown Ho E8 . . . . 16 C4
Eastdown Pk SE13 . . . . 67 C3
EAST DULWICH 64 C2
East Dulwich Gr SE22 . . . . 64 A2
East Dulwich Rd SE15, SE22 . . . . 64 C3
Eastern Rd SE4 . . . . 66 C3
East Ferry Rd E14 . . . . 42 A2
Eastfields Ave SW18 . . . . 58 C3
Eastfields Rd W3 . . . . 28 B4
Eastfield St E14 . . . . 33 A4
East Harding St EC4 . . . . 107 C2
East Heath Rd NW3 . . . . 2 C1
East Hill SW18 . . . . 59 B2
East India Bldgs 9 E14 . . . . 33 C2
East India Ct 7 SE16 . . . . 40 B4
East India Dock Basin* E14 . . . . 35 A2
East India Dock Rd E14 . . . . 34 A2

East India Dock Road Tunnel 18 E14 . . . . 34 C2
East India Sta E14 . . . . 34 C2
East La SE16 . . . . 139 C3
Eastlake Ho NW8 . . . . 89 C1
Eastlake Rd SE5 . . . . 48 B1
Eastlands Cres SE21 . . . . 64 B1
Eastleigh Wlk 9 SW15 . . . . 68 C4
East London Coll & Toynbee Theatre E1 . . . . 111 A3
East London Stad E3 . . . . 33 B4
Eastman Dental Hospl WC1 . . . . 94 C2
Eastman Ho 7 SW4 . . . . 61 B1
Eastman Rd W3 . . . . 37 C4
Eastmearn Rd SE21, SE27 . . . . 75 B2
East Mount St E1 . . . . 32 A4
Eastney St SE10 . . . . 42 C1
Easton Ho 4 SE27 . . . . 75 A1
Easton St WC1 . . . . 95 B2
East Parkside SE10 . . . . 43 B4
East Pas EC1 . . . . 108 C4
East Plaza E14 . . . . 34 A1
East Point 1 SE1 . . . . 153 B2
East Poultry Ave EC1 . . . . 108 A3
East Putney Sta SW15 . . . . 58 B2
East Rd
  Chelsea SW1 . . . . 145 B1
  Shoreditch N1 . . . . 97 C4
East Row W10 . . . . 23 A1
Eastry Ho 9 SW8 . . . . 162 A1
EAST SHEEN 55 C3
East Sheen Ave SW14 . . . . 55 C3
East Sheen Prim Sch SW14 . . . . 56 A3
East Smithfield E1 . . . . 125 A3
East St SE17 . . . . 151 B2
East Surrey Gr SE15 . . . . 49 B3
East Tenter St E1 . . . . 111 A1
Eastvale W3 . . . . 29 B1
East View NW3 . . . . 2 C2
Eastway
  South Hackney E3, E9 . . . . 26 A4
  Temple Mills E9, E10 . . . . 18 C4
Eastwell Ho SE1 . . . . 137 C2
Eastwick Ct 2 SW19 . . . . 69 C3
Eastwood Cl 2 N7 . . . . 14 C3
Eaton Cl SW1 . . . . 145 B3
Eaton Dr SW9 . . . . 63 A3
Eaton Gate SW1 . . . . 145 B4
Eaton Ho
  Battersea SW11 . . . . 167 C3
  2 Limehouse E14 . . . . 33 B2
Eaton House Sch SW1 . . . . 145 B4
Eaton House The Manor SW4 . . . . 61 A3
Eaton La SW1 . . . . 132 B1
Eaton Mans SW1 . . . . 145 B3

Eaton Mews N SW1 ... 131 C1
Eaton Mews S SW1 ... 132 A1
Eaton Mews W SW1 ... 145 C4
Eaton Pl SW1 ... 131 C1
Eaton Row SW1 ... 132 A1
Eaton Sq SW1 ... 131 C1
Eaton Square Sch SW1 ... 146 A4
Eaton Terr Belgravia SW1 ... 145 C4
Bow E3 ... 26 A2
Eaton Terr Mews SW1 ... 145 B4
Eatonville Rd SW17 ... 72 B2
Eatonville Villas SW17 ... 72 B2
Ebbisham Dr SW8 ...
Ebbsfleet Rd NW2 ... 10 A4
Ebenezer Ho SE11 ... 150 A3
Ebenezer Mussel Ho ■ E2 ... 25 B3
Ebenezer St N1 ... 97 B4
Ebley Cl SE15 ... 49 B4
Ebner St SW18 ... 59 A2
Ebony Cl NW10 ... 8 B2
Ebony Ho Bethnal Green E2 ... 24 C2 99 B3
■ West Hampstead NW3 ... 11 A2
Ebor Cotts SW15 ... 68 A1
Ebor St E1, ...
Eburne Rd N7 ... 5 A1
Ebury Bridge Rd SW1 ... 145 C1
Ebury Mews Belgravia SW1 ... 146 A4
West Norwood SE27 ... 75 A1
Ebury Mews E SW1 ... 132 A1
Ebury Sq SW1 ... 145 C3
Ebury St SW1 ... 146 A4
Ecclesbourne Rd N1 ... 15 B1
Eccles Rd SW11 ... 60 B3
Eccleston Ho ■ SW2 ... 62 C1
Eccleston Mews SW1 ... 131 C1
Eccleston Pl SW1 ... 146 A4
Eccleston Sq SW1 ... 146 A2
Eccleston Sq Mews SW1 ... 146 A4
Eccleston St SW1 ... 146 A4
Eckford St N1 ... 85 02
Eckstein Rd SW11 ... 60 A3
Edans Ct W12 ... 38 B4
Edbrooke Rd W9 ... 23 C1
Eddisbury Ho ■ SE26 ... 76 C1
Eddiscombe Rd SW6 ... 165 A2
Eddison Ct N19 ... 5 A2
Eddystone Rd SE4 ... 66 A2
Eddystone Twr SE8 ... 41 A1

Edenbridge Cl 26 SE16 ... 40 A1
Edenbridge Rd E9 ... 17 C1
Eden Cl Child's Hill NW3 ... 1 C2
Kensington W8 ... 127 C2
Edendale W3 ... 28 A2
Eden Gr N7 ... 14 B3
Edenham Way W10 ... 31 B4
Eden Ho ■ Battersea SW11 ... 60 A4
Lisson Gr NW8 ... 90 A1
Edenhurst Ave SW6 ... 58 B4
Eden Lodge NW6 ... 9 C1
Eden Mews SW17 ... 71 B1
Edensmuir Ct SE3 ... 53 C3
Edensor Gdns W4 ... 46 A3
Edensor Rd W4 ... 46 A3
Edenvale St SW6 ... 166 C1
Eden Way E3 ... 26 B4
Edgar Ho Homerton E9 ... 18 A3
South Lambeth SW8 ... 162 A2
Edgar Kail Way SE22 ... 64 A3
Edgarley Terr SW6 ... 164 A3
Edgar Rd E3 ... 27 A2
Edgar Wallace Cl 4 SE15 ... 49 A3
Edgcott Ho 2 W10 ... 30 B4
Edgecombe Ho ■ London SE5 ... 49 A1
Putney SW19 ... 70 A4
Edgecote Cl 7 W3 ... 28 B1
Edgehill Ho 4 SW9 ... 48 A1
Edgeley La SW4 ... 61 C4
Edgeley Rd SW4 ... 61 C4
Edge St W8 ... 31 C1 113 C2
Edgeworth Ho NW8 ... 78 C4
Edgson Ho ■ SW1 ... 146 A2
Edgware Acad WC2 ... 106 B1
Edgware Rd W1, W2, NW1, NW8 ... 102 A3
Edgware Road Sta (Bakerloo) NW1 ... 102 A3
Edgware Road Sta (Met, Distr, Circle) NW1 ... 102 B3
Edinburgh Cl 7 E2 ... 25 B3
Edinburgh Ct 10 SE16 ... 32 C1
Edinburgh Ho ■ Acton W3 ... 28 C3
Maida Vale W9 ... 88 B4
Edington 20 NW5 ... 12 C2
Edison Bldg 7 E14 ... 41 C4
Edison Ct SE10 ... 43 B3
Edison Ho ■ SE1 ... 151 B4
Edis St NW1 ... 81 C4
Editha Mans SW10 ... 156 C3
Edith Cavell Cl 2 N19 ... 5 A4

Edith Gr SW10 ... 157 A2
Edith Ho 6 W6 ... 39 B1
Edithna St SW9 ... 62 A4
Edith Neville Cotts NW1 ... 93 B4
Edith Neville Prim Sch NW1 ... 83 B1
Edith Ramsay Ho 2 E1 ... 33 A4
Edith Rd Stratford New Town E15 ... 19 C3
West Kensington W14 ... 140 B3
Edith Row SW6 ... 166 B4
Edith St E2 ... 24 C3
Edith Summerskill Ho SW6 ... 154 C2
Edith Terr SW10 ... 156 C2
Edith Villas W14 ... 140 C2
Edith Yd SW10 ... 157 A2
Edmeston Cl E9 ... 18 A2
Edmond Ct SE14 ... 50 B2
Edmonton Ct 5 SE16 ... 40 B3
Edmund Halley Way SE10 ... 43 A4
Edmund Ho Kennington SE17 ... 150 B1
New Cross Gate SE14 ... 51 B2
Edmundsbury Ct Est 16 SW9 ... 62 B3
Edmund St SE5 ... 48 C3
Edmund Waller Prim Sch SE14 ... 50 C1
Edna St SW11 ... 168 A3
Edred Ho E9 ... 18 A4
Edrich Ho SW4 ... 172 A3
Edric Ho ■ SW1 ... 147 C4
Edric Rd SE14 ... 50 C3
Edridge Ho 9 SE27 ... 75 A1
Edward Alleyn Ho SE21 ... 76 A4
Edward Ct 2 E16 ... 35 C4
Edward Dodd Ct N1 ... 97 C4
Edward Edward's Ho SE1 ... 122 A1
Edwardes Pl W8 ... 127 A1
Edwardes Sq W8 ... 127 A1
Edward Friend Ho N16 ... 7 A1
Edward Ho Paddington W2 ... 89 B1
Vauxhall SE11 ... 149 A2
Edward Kennedy Ho 18 W10 ... 23 A1
Edward Mann Cl 13 E1 ... 32 C3
Edward Mews NW1 ... 82 B1
Edward Pl SE8 ... 51 B4
Edward Robinson Ho 3 SE14 ... 50 C3
Edward's Cotts 11 N1 ... 15 A1
Edward's La N16 ... 7 A2
Edward Sq Islington N1 ... 84 C3
■ Rotherhithe SE16 ... 33 A1

Edward St SE14 ... 51 B3
Edward VII Mans NW10 ... 22 C2
Edward Wilson Prim Sch W2 ... 100 A4
Edwin Ho SE15 ... 49 C3
Edwin's Mead E9 ... 18 A4
Edwin St Bethnal Green E1 ... 25 B1
Newham E16 ... 35 C4
Edwy Ho E9 ... 18 B4
Edwyn Ho SW18 ... 59 A1
Effie Pl SW6 ... 155 C1
Effie Rd SW6 ... 155 C1
Effingham Ho SW8 ... 171 B1
Effra Ct SW2 ... 62 B2
Effra Mans SW2 ... 62 C2
Effra Par SW2 ... 62 C2
Effra Rd SW2 ... 62 C2
Effra Road Ret Pk SW2 ... 62 C2
Egbert Ho E9 ... 18 A3
Egbert St NW1 ... 81 B4
Egbury Ho SW15 ... 56 B1
Egerton Cres SW3 ... 144 B4
Egerton Ct 5 TW10 ... 54 A2
Egerton Dr SE10 ... 52 A2
Egerton Gdns Knightsbridge SW3 ... 130 A1
Willesden NW10 ... 22 C2
Egerton Gdns Mews SW3 ... 130 B1
Egerton Ho W4 ... 45 B4
Egerton Pl SW3 ... 130 B1
Egerton Rd N16 ... 7 B4
Egerton Terr SW3 ... 130 B1
Egham Cl SW19 ... 70 A2
Eglantine Rd SW18 ... 59 B2
Eglington Ct SE17 ... 48 B4
Egliston Mews SW15 ... 57 B4
Egliston Rd SW15 ... 57 B4
Egmont St SE14 ... 50 C3
Egremont Ho SE13 ... 52 A1
Egremont Rd SE27 ... 74 C1
Eider Ct 38 SE8 ... 51 B4
Elaine Ct 13 NW3 ... 12 B2
Elaine Gr NW5 ... 12 C3
Elam Cl SE5 ... 48 A1
Elam St SE5 ... 48 A1
Elan Ct E1 ... 32 A4
Fland Rd SW11 ... 60 B4
Elba Pl SE17 ... 151 A4
Elbe St SW6 ... 166 C2
Elborough St SW18 ... 70 C3
Elbury Dr E16 ... 35 C3
Elcho St SW11 ... 158 B1
Elcot Ave SE15 ... 50 A3
Elderberry Rd W5 ... 36 A4
Elderfield Ho 4 E14 ... 33 C2
Elderfield Rd E5 ... 17 B4
Elder St E1 ... 24 B1 98 C1

Elder Wlk Islington N1 ... 86 B4
■ Lewisham SE13 ... 67 B4
Eldon Ct NW6 ... 23 C4
Eldon Gr NW3 ... 11 C3
Eldon Ho SW9 ... 63 A4
Eldon Rd W8 ... 128 B1
Eldon St EC2 ... 109 C3
Eldon Way NW10 ... 20 A3
Eldridge Ct SE16 ... 139 B1
Eleanor Cl SE16 ... 40 C4
Eleanor Ct 13 E2 ... 24 C4
Eleanor Gr SW13 ... 56 A4
Eleanor Ho ■ Hammersmith W6 ... 39 B1
■ Kentish Town NW5 ... 13 B3
Eleanor Palmer Prim Sch NW5 ... 13 B4
Eleanor Rathbone Ho ■ N6 ... 4 C4
Eleanor Rd E8 ... 17 A1
Eleanor St E3 ... 26 C2
Electra Ct 6 NW2 ... 9 B2
Electric Ave SW9 ... 62 C3
Electric Ho ■ E3 ... 26 C2
Electric La 2 SW9 ... 62 C3
Electric Mans ■ SW9 ... 62 C3
Elephant & Castle Newington SE1 ... 150 B4
Newington SE1 ... 136 B1
Elephant & Castle Sh Ctr SE1 ... 150 C4
Elephant & Castle Sta Lambeth SE1 ... 136 B1
Newington SE1 ... 150 C4
Elephant La SE16 ... 40 B4
Elephant Rd SE17 ... 150 C4
Elfindale Rd SE24 ... 63 B2
Elf Row E1 ... 32 B2
Elgar Ave W5 ... 36 A4
Elgar Cl SE8 ... 51 C3
Elgar Ct W14 ... 126 A1
Elgar Ho Pimlico SW1 ... 146 B1
South Hampstead NW6 ... 11 B1
Elgar St SE16 ... 41 A3
Elgin Ave Hammersmith W12 ... 39 A3
Westbourne Green W9 ... 88 B4
Elgin Cl W12 ... 39 A4
Elgin Cres W11 ... 31 A2 112 B4
Elgin Ct W9 ... 88 A2
Elgin Ho 8 E14 ... 34 A3
Elgin Mans W9 ... 88 A3
Elgin Mews W11 ... 31 A3
Elgin Mews N W9 ... 88 B4
Elgin Mews S W9 ... 88 B4
Elgood Cl W11 ... 31 A1 112 A2
Elgood Ho NW8 ... 79 C1
Elham Ho 19 E5 ... 17 A3
Elia Mews N1 ... 86 A1
Elias Pl SW8 ... 163 B3
Elia St N1 ... 86 A1
Elim Est SE1 ... 138 A2

Elim St SE1 . . . . **138** A2
Eliot Cotts SE3 . . . . . . 53 A1
Eliot Ct SW18 . . . . 59 A1
Eliot Gdns SW15 . . . . 56 C2
Eliot Hill SE13 . . . . . . 67 B4
Eliot Ho IO SW10 . . . . 54 B1
Eliot Mews NW8 . . . . . 78 C1
Eliot Pk SE13 . . . . 67 B4
Eliot Rd SE3 . . . . 53 A1
Eliot Vale SE3 . . . . . . 52 C1
Elizabeth Ave
 Islington N1 . . . . 15 C1
 Shoreditch N1 . . . . . 87 A4
Elizabeth Barnes Ct I
SW6 . . . . **166** B2
Elizabeth Blount Ct 4
E14 . . . . 33 A3
Elizabeth Cl
 Paddington W9 . . . . . **89** A1
 IO Poplar E14 . . . . . 34 A3
Elizabeth Cooper Lo
SW12 . . . . 60 C1
Elizabeth Cotts I
TW9 . . . . 44 C2
Elizabeth Ct
 Chelsea SW10 . . . . . **157** C3
 East Dulwich SE22 . . 64 C3
 Marylebone NW8 . . . **90** B2
 Westminster SW1 . . **133** C1
Elizabeth Finn Ho I
W12 . . . . 38 C3
Elizabeth Garrett
 Anderson Hospl
NW1 . . . . **93** A1
Elizabeth Garrett
 Anderson Language
 Coll N1 . . . . **85** A1
Elizabeth Gdns
W3 . . . . 29 B1
Elizabeth Ho
 IO Hammersmith
 W6 . . . . 39 B1
 Lambeth SE11 . . . . . **149** C3
Elizabeth Ind Est
SE14 . . . . 50 C4
Elizabeth Kenny Ho
N1 . . . . 15 B2
Elizabeth Mews
 28 Hackney E2 . . . . . 25 A3
 Maitland Pk NW3 . . . 12 B2
Elizabeth Selby Inf
 Sch E2 . . . . 24 C2 **99** C4
Elizabeth Sq I
SE16 . . . . 33 A2
Elizabeth St SW1 **145** C4
Elkington Point
SE11 . . . . **149** B3
Elkstone Rd W10 . . 31 B4
Ellacombe Ho I
SW2 . . . . 74 B4
Ellaline Rd W6 . . . . . . 47 C4
Ella Mews NW3 . . . . . 12 B3
Elland Ho IO E14 . . . 33 B3
Elland Rd SE15 . . . . . 65 B3
Ella Rd N4, N8 . . . . . . 5 A4
Ellenborough Ho I
W12 . . . . 30 A2
Ellenborough Pl
SW15 . . . . 56 C3
Ellen St E1 . . . . **111** C1
Ellen Wilkinson Ho
 7 Globe Town E2 . . 25 C2
 West Brompton
 SW6 . . . . **155** A3
Ellerby St SW6 . . . . . 47 C2

Ellerdale Cl I
NW3 . . . . 11 B4
Ellerdale Rd NW3 . . 11 B3
Ellerdale St SE13 . . 67 A3
Ellerker Gdns
TW10 . . . . 54 A1
Ellerslie Gdns
NW10 . . . . 21 C4
Ellerslie Ind Est
SW2 . . . . 62 A2
Ellerslie Rd W12 . . 30 A1
Ellerton Rd SW13 . . 47 A4
Ellerton Rd
 Barnes SW13 . . . . . . 46 C2
 Wandsworth SW17,
 SW18 . . . . 71 C3
Ellery Cl I SW13 . . 22 B1
Ellery Ho SE17 . . . . **151** C3
Ellery St SE15 . . . . . . 50 A1
Ellesmere Ct W4 . . 45 C4
Ellesmere Rd
 Bow E3 . . . . 26 A3
 Chiswick W4 . . . . 45 C4
 Willesden NW10 . . . . 8 A3
Ellesmere St E14 . . 34 A3
Ellingfort Rd E8 . . 17 A1
Ellingham Rd
 Leyton E15 . . . . 19 C4
 Shepherd's Bush
 W12 . . . . 38 C4
Ellington Ho SE1 . . **137** A1
Ellington St N7 . . . . . 14 C2
Elliott Rd
 Acton W4 . . . . 38 A2
 Brixton SW9 . . . . 48 A2
 Camberwell SW9 . . . 48 A2
Elliott's Pl N1 . . . . . **86** B3
Elliott Sq NW3 . . . . . 12 A1
Elliott's Row SE11 . **150** B4
Ellis Cl NW10 . . . . . . 9 B1
Ellisfield Dr SW15 . 68 C4
Ellis Franklin Ct
NW8 . . . . **78** C2
Ellis Ho SE17 . . . . . **151** B2
Ellison Ho I SE13 . 52 B1
Ellison Rd SW13 . . 46 B1
Ellis St SW1 . . . . **145** B4
Ellsworth St E2 . . . . 25 A2
Ellwood Ct I W9 . . **88** B1
Elmar Ct SW6 . . . . . **164** B2
Elm Bank Gdns
SW13 . . . . 46 A1
Elm Bank Mans
SW13 . . . . 46 A1
Elmbourne Rd
SW17 . . . . 73 A1
Elmbridge Wlk E8 . 16 C1
Elm Cl N19 . . . . 4 B2
Elmcourt Rd SE21,
SE27 . . . . 75 A2
Elm Court Sch
SE27 . . . . 75 A2
Elm Cres W5 . . . . . . 36 A4
Elmcroft N6 . . . . 4 B4
Elmcroft Ave NW11 . 1 B4
Elmcroft Cres
NW11 . . . . 1 A4
Elmcroft St E5 . . . . 17 B4
Elm Ct
 Brixton SW9 . . . . . . **173** B4
 Lewisham SE13 . . . . 67 C4
 42 Notting Hill W2 . 31 C4
 Strand EC4 . . . . **121** B4
Elmer Ho NW1 . . . . **102** A4
Elmfield Ho
 6 Canonbury N5 . . 15 B3

Elmfield Ho continued
 Paddington W9 . . . . 23 C1
Elmfield Mans I
SW17 . . . . 72 C2
Elmfield Rd SW17 . . 73 A2
Elmfield Way W9 . . 31 C4
Elm Friars Wlk
NW1 . . . . 13 C1
Elm Gn W3 . . . . 29 A3
Elm Gr
 Cricklewood NW2 . . . 9 C4
 Peckham SE15 . . . . . 49 C1
Elm Grove Rd
 Barnes SW13 . . . . . . 46 C1
 Ealing W5 . . . . 36 A4
Elm Ho 4 E14 . . . . 42 B4
Elmhurst Mans
SW4 . . . . 61 C4
Elmhurst St SW4 . . 61 C4
Elmhurst Villas
SE15 . . . . 65 B3
Elmington Rd SE5 . 48 C3
Elmira St SE13 . . . . 67 A4
Elm Lo SW6 . . . . 47 C2
Elmore Ho SW9 . . . 48 A1
Elmore St N1 . . . . . . 15 C1
Elm Park Gdns
SW10 . . . . **143** B1
Elm Park Ho
SW10 . . . . **143** B1
Elm Park La SW3 . **143** B1
Elm Park Mans
SW10 . . . . **157** A4
Elm Park Rd SW3 . **157** B4
Elm Pk SW2 . . . . 74 B4
Elm Pl SW7 . . . . **143** B2
Elm Quay SW8 . . . . **161** B4
Elm Rd SW14 . . . . . . 55 B3
Elm Row NW3 . . . . . . 2 B1
Elms Cres SW4 . . . . 61 C1
Elmshaw Rd SW15 . 56 C2
Elmslie Point 2
E3 . . . . 33 B4
Elms Mews W2 . . . **115** B4
Elms Rd SW4 . . . . . . 61 B2
Elm St WC1 . . . . 95 A1
Elm The
 Barnes SW13 . . . . . . 56 B4
 3 Harlesden
 NW10 . . . . 21 A3
Elmstone Rd SW6 **165** B4
Elm Terr NW2 . . . . 1 C1
Elmton Ct NW8 . . . **89** B2
Elm Tree Cl NW8 . . **89** B4
Elm Tree Ct
 5 Camberwell
 SE5 . . . . 48 B2
 St John's Wood
 NW8 . . . . **89** B4
Elm Tree Rd NW8 . . **89** B4
Elm Way NW10 . . . . . 8 A4
Elm Wlk NW3 . . . . 1 C2
Elmwood Ct
SW11 . . . . **170** A4
Elm Wood Prim Sch
SE27 . . . . 75 C1
Elmwood Rd
 Chiswick W4 . . . . 45 B4
 Herne Hill SE24 . . . 63 C2
Elmworth Gr SE21 . 75 C2
Elnathan Mews
W9 . . . . **88** B1
Elphinstone St N5 . 15 A4
Elrington Rd E8 . . 16 C2
Elsa St E1 . . . . 33 A4
Elsdale Ho IO E9 . . 17 B1
Elsdale St E9 . . . . . . 17 B1

Elsden Mews E2 . . 25 B3
Elsenham St SW18,
SW19 . . . . 70 B2
Elsfield NW5 . . . . . . 13 A3
Elsham Rd W14 . . . **126** A3
Elsham Terr W14 . . **126** A3
Elsie Lane Ct W2 . **100** A3
Elsiemaud Rd SE4 . 66 B2
Elsie Rd SE22 . . . . . . 64 B3
Elsinore Gdns NW2 . 1 A1
Elsinore Ho
 12 Camberwell
 SE5 . . . . 48 B1
 Islington N1 . . . . . . **85** B3
Elsinore Way TW9 . 55 A4
Elsley Rd SW11 . . . . 60 C4
Elspeth Rd SW11 . . 60 B3
Elstead Ho I
SW2 . . . . 74 B4
Elsted St SE17 . . . . **151** C3
Elstow Grange
NW6 . . . . 9 C1
Elswick Rd SE13 . . 52 A1
Elswick St SW6 . . . **166** C2
Elsworthy Rd NW3 . 80 A4
Elsworthy Rise
NW3 . . . . 12 A1
Elsworthy Terr
NW3 . . . . 12 A1
Elsynge Rd SW18 . . 59 C2
Elsynge Road Mans
SW18 . . . . 59 C2
Elthiron Rd SW6 . . **165** C3
Elthorne Rd N19 . . . . 4 C2
Elthruda Rd SE13 . . 67 C1
Elton Ho 3 E3 . . . . 26 B3
Elton Pl N16 . . . . 16 A3
Elton St 10 N16 . . 16 A3
Eltringham St
SW18 . . . . 59 B3
Elvaston Mews
SW7 . . . . **129** A2
Elvaston Pl SW7 . . **129** A1
Elveden Ho IO
SW9 . . . . 63 A3
Elver Gdns
E2 . . . . 24 C2 **99** C4
Elverson Rd SE8 . . 52 A1
Elverson Rd Sta
SE8 . . . . 52 A1
Elverton St SW1 . . **147** B4
Elvin Ho 2 E9 . . . . 17 B2
Elvis Rd NW2 . . . . 9 B2
Elwin St E2 . . . 24 C2 **99** B4
Elwood St N5, N4 . . . 6 A1
Elworth Ho SW8 . . **163** A1
Ely Cotts SW8 . . . . **162** C1
Ely Court Flats
SW6 . . . . **164** B4
Ely Ct Holborn EC1 **107** C3
 3 Maida Vale NW6 . 23 C3
Ely Ho 22 SE15 . . . 49 C3
Ely Pl EC1 . . . . **107** C3
Elysium Gate
SW6 . . . . **164** C2
Elysium Pl SW6 . . **164** C1
Elysium St 6 SW6 **164** C1
Elystan Ct SW15 . . 57 A2
Elystan Pl SW3 . . . **144** B2
Elystan St SW3 . . . **144** B3
Elystan Wlk N1 . . . **85** B3
Emanuel Ave W3 . . 28 B3
Emanuel Sch
SW11 . . . . 60 A2

Embankment
SW15 . . . . 47 C1
Embankment Gdns
SW3 . . . . **159** A4
Embankment Pier
WC2 . . . . **120** B2
Embankment Pl
WC2 . . . . **120** B2
Embankment Sta
WC2 . . . . **120** B2
Embassy Ct NW8 . . **79** C1
Embassy Ho 2
NW6 . . . . 10 C1
Emba St SE16 . . . . **139** C3
Ember Ct 2 W12 . . 38 A3
Emberton SE5 . . . . . 49 A4
Emberton Ct EC1 . **96** A3
Embleton Rd SE13 . 67 A3
Emden St SW6 . . . . **166** B4
Emerald Rd NW10 . 20 C4
Emerald St WC1 . . **106** C4
Emerson Ho N16 . . 16 A3
Emerson St SE1 . . **122** C2
Emery Hill St
SW1 . . . . **133** A1
Emery St SE1 . . . . . **135** C2
Emily St 2 E16 . . . 35 B3
Emirates Stad
 (Arsenal FC) N7 . . . 14 C4
Emlyn Gdns 3
W12 . . . . 38 A3
Emlyn Rd W12 . . . . . 38 B3
Emmanuel CE Prim
 Sch NW6 . . . . 10 C3
Emmanuel Ho
 Dulwich SE21 . . . . . 75 C1
 Lambeth SE11 . . . . **149** B3
Emmanuel Rd
SW12 . . . . 73 C3
Emma St 2 E2 . . . . 25 A3
Emminster NW6 . . 78 A4
Emmott Cl E1 . . . . . 26 A1
Emperor's Gate
SW7 . . . . **142** C4
Empingham Ho 20
SE8 . . . . 40 C2
Empire Ho SW3 . . **130** A1
Empire Sq N19 . . . . . 5 A1
Empire Wharf E3 . . 26 A4
Empire Wharf Rd
E14 . . . . 42 C2
Empress Mews 30
SE5 . . . . 48 B1
Empress Pl SW5 . . **141** B1
Empress St SE17 . . 48 B4
Empson St E3 . . . . . 27 A1
Emsworth St SW2 . 74 B2
Emu Rd SW8 . . . . . **170** A1
Enard Ho 28 E3 . . . 26 B3
Enbrook St W10 . . . 23 A2
Endell St WC2 . . . . **106** A1
Enclave Ct EC1 . . . **96** B2
Enderby St SE10 . . 43 A1
Endlesham Ct 2
SW12 . . . . 72 C4
Endlesham Rd
SW12 . . . . 72 C4
Endsleigh Gdns
WC1 . . . . **93** B2
Endsleigh Mans 4
SW16 . . . . 74 A1
Endsleigh Pl WC1 . **93** C2
Endsleigh St WC1 . **93** C2
Endwell Rd SE4 . . . 51 A1
Endymion Rd
 Harringay N4 . . . . 6 A4
 Tulse Hill SW2 . . . . . 62 B1

nergen Cl NW10....... 8 A2
nfield Cloisters
  N1...........24 A2 98 A4
nfield Ho SW9..... 172 B2
nfield Rd
  De Beauvoir Town E8......
  ....16 A1
  South Acton W3......37 A4
nford St W1......102 C4
ngadine St SW18...70 C3
ngate St SE3.......67 B3
ngland's La NW3...12 B2
nglefield N1.......92 C3
nglefield Rd N1....16 A1
nglewood Rd
  SW12..............61 B3
nglish Gardening
  Sch The SW3......158 C4
nglish Grounds
  SE1.............124 A1
nglish Martyrs RC
  Prim Sch E1......111 A1
nglish St E3.......26 B1
nid St SE16.......139 A2
nid Stacy Ho 11
  N19...............4 C4
nmore Ct SW14....55 C4
nmore Gdns
  SW14.............55 C2
nmore Rd SW15...57 B2
nnerdale Ho 11
  N4................6 C4
nnerdale Rd
  TW9..............44 B1
nnersdale Rd
  SE13.............67 C2
nnis Ho 11 E14....34 A3
nnis Rd N4.........5 C3
nsbury Ho SW8...162 C2
nsign Ct E1......125 C3
nsign Ho 12 E14..41 C4
nsign Pl E1.......25 B4
nsor Mews SW7...143 B2
nterprise Ho 38
  E9................17 B1
nterprise Way
  College Pk NW10...21 C2
  Wandsworth SW18..58 C3
nterprise Way
  SE8...............41 B2
pirus Mews
  SW6.............155 B2
pirus Rd SW6.....155 A3
pping Cl E14......41 C2
pping Ho 8 E5.....7 C2
pping Pl N1.......15 A2
pple Rd SW6......165 A4
pstein Ct N1......86 B3
pworth St EC2.....97 C1
quity Sq
  E2..........24 B2 99 A3
rasmus St SW1...147 C3
rconwald St W12..29 B3
resby Ho SW7....130 A3
resby Ho NW6.....10 C1
rica Ct SW4......172 B3
rica Ho SE4.......66 B4

Erica St W12......29 C2
Ericcson Cl SW18..58 C2
Eric Fletcher Ct 15
  N1................15 B1
Eric Macdonald Ho
  W6..............165 C3
Ericson Ho
  London SE13......67 C3
  Stamford Hill N16...7 B3
Eric St E3.........26 B1
Eric Wilkins Ho
  SE1.............153 B1
Eridge Ho SE22....64 B4
Eridge Rd W4......37 C3
Frin Ct NW2........9 B2
Erlanger Rd SE14..50 C1
Ermine Rd SE13...67 A3
Ernest Bevin Coll
  SW17.............72 A2
Ernest Gdns W4...45 A4
Ernest Simmonds
  Ho SE14...........50 B1
Ernest St E1.......25 C1
  SE14.............50 B1
Ernshaw Pl SW15..58 A2
Erpingham Rd
  SW15.............57 B4
Errington Rd W9...23 B1
Errol St EC1.......97 A1
Erskine Ho SW1..146 C1
Erskine Mews 11
  NW3.............12 B1
Escuan Lo N5......15 B3
Esher Gdns SW19..69 C2
Esher Ho 4 SW8..171 C2
Eskdale NW1......82 C1
Esk Ho E3..........26 B1
Esme Ho SW15.....56 B3
Esmeralda Rd
  SE1.............153 C3
Esmond Cl 11 W8..128 B2
Esmond Gdns W4..37 C2
Esmond Rd
  Acton W4..........37 C3
  Kilburn NW6......23 B4
Esmond St SW15...58 A3
Esparto St SW18..71 A4
Espirit Ct E1......110 C3
Espirit Ho 6
  SW15.............58 A2
Essendine Mans
  W9...............23 C2
Essendine Prim Sch
  W9...............23 C2
Essendine Rd W9...23 C2
Essex Ct
  Barnes SW13......46 B1
  Hammersmith W6..39 B3
  Holborn EC4.....107 B1
Essex Ho 2 E14...34 A3
Essex Park Mews
  W3...............29 A1
Essex Rd Acton W3..28 B2
  Chiswick W4......37 C2
  Islington N1......86 B4
  Willesden NW10....8 A1
Essex Road Sta
  N1...............15 B1
Essex St WC2.....121 B4
Essex Villas W8...127 B3
Essian St E1.......33 A4
Essington SW15...58 A1
Estcourt Rd SW6..154 C2

Estella Ho 18 W11..30 C2
Estelle Ho 11
  SW11.............12 B4
Esterbrooke St
  SW1.............147 B3
Este Rd SW11......60 A4
Estoria Cl 22 SW2..74 C4
Etal Ho N1.........15 A1
Etchingham Rd
  E15...............19 B4
Eternit Wlk SW6...47 C2
Ethelbert Ho E9...18 A4
Ethelbert St SW12..73 A3
Ethelburga St
  SW11.............168 B4
Ethelburga Twr
  SW11.............168 B4
Ethelden Rd W12...30 A1
Ethel Rankin Ct 1
  SW6.............164 C2
Ethel St SE17.....151 A3
Ethelworth Ct 5
  SW2...............74 C3
Etherow St SE22...76 C4
Ethnard Rd SE15...50 A4
Etloe Ho 5 E10....19 A4
Eton Ave NW3.....12 A1
Eton Cl SW18......71 A4
Eton College Rd
  NW3..............12 B2
Eton Ct NW3........11 C1
Eton Garages 11
  NW3..............12 B2
Eton Hall NW3.....12 B2
Eton Ho
  Hackney E9........18 A3
  Highbury N5.......15 A4
Eton Pl NW1.......12 C1
Eton Rd NW3......12 B2
Eton Rise NW3....12 B2
Eton St TW10......54 A2
Eton Villas NW3...12 B2
Etta St SE8.........51 A4
Ettrick St E14.....34 B3
Eugene Cotter Ho
  SE17.............151 C3
Eugenia Rd SE16..40 B2
Euro Cl NW10.......8 C2
Eurolink Bsns Ctr
  SW2...............62 C2
Europa Pl EC1......96 C3
Eustace Bldg
  SW8.............160 A3
Eustace Ho SE11..148 C4
Eustace Rd SW6..155 B2
Euston Rd NW1....93 A2
Euston Sq NW1....93 B3
Euston Square Sta
  WC1..............93 A2
Euston St NW1.....93 A3
Euston Sta NW1...93 B3
Euston Underpass
  NW1..............92 C2
Evandale Rd SW9.173 C2
Evangelist Rd
  NW5...............13 A4
Evans Cl E8........16 B2
Evans Ho
  24 Shepherd's Bush
    W12............30 A2
  South Lambeth
    SW8...........161 C1
Evelina Mans 9
  SE5...............48 C3
Evelina Rd SE15...50 B1
Eveline Lowe Prim
  Sch SE1.........153 C3
Evelyn Ct
  Marylebone W1...102 C1

Evelyn Ct continued
  Shacklewell E8....16 C4
  Shoreditch N1.....87 B1
Evelyn Denington Ct
  2 N1..............15 A1
Evelyn Fox Ct
  W10...............30 B4
Evelyn Gdns
  Richmond TW9.....54 A3
  South Kensington
    SW7...........143 B1
Evelyn Ho
  Bedford Pk W12....38 B4
  3 Brixton SW2.....62 B2
  Spitalfields E1....111 B3
Evelyn Rd
  Acton W4..........37 C3
  Richmond TW9.....54 A4
Evelyn St SE8......41 A1
Evelyn Terr TW9...54 A4
Evelyn Wlk N1.....87 B1
Evelyn Yd W1.....105 B2
Evenwood Cl
  SW15.............58 A2
Everard Ho 1 E1...111 C1
Everatt Cl SW18...58 B2
Everdon Rd SW13..46 C4
Everest Pl E14.....34 B4
Evergreen Sq 3
  E8................16 B1
Everilda St N1......85 A3
Evering Rd E5, N16..7 C1
Everington St W6..47 C4
Everitt Rd NW10...20 C2
Everleigh St N4....5 B3
Eversfield Rd TW9.44 B1
Evershed Ho 11 E1.111 A2
Evershed Wlk 4 W4.37 C2
Eversholt St NW1..93 B4
Evershot Rd N4....5 B3
Eversleigh Rd
  SW11.............169 B1
Eversley Ho
  E2..........24 C2 99 B3
Everthorpe Rd
  SE15.............64 B4
Everton Bldgs
  NW1..............92 C3
Evesham Ho
  1 Bethnal Green
    E2..............25 B3
  St John's Wood
    NW8............78 C3
Evesham St W11...30 C2
Evesham Way
  SW11.............60 C4
Evesham Wlk
  Brixton SW9.....173 B2
  Camberwell SE5...48 C1
Ewald Rd SW6....164 C1
Ewart Pl 18 E3.....26 B3
Ewe Cl N7.........14 A2
Ewen Cres SW2....74 C4
Ewen Henderson Ct
  10 SE14..........51 A3
Ewen Ho N1........84 C3
Ewer St SE1......122 C1
Ewhurst 19 SW15..57 C1
Ewhurst Cl E1.....32 B4
Ewhurst Rd SE4...66 B1

Exbury Ho
  Hackney E9........17 B2
  4 London SW9.....62 B3
Excel Ct WC2.....119 C3
Excelsior Gdns
  SE13.............52 B1
Excelsior Ind Est
  SE16.............50 B4
Exchange Arc
  EC2.............110 B4
Exchange Ct WC2.120 B3
Exchange Mans 2
  NW11.............1 B4
Exchange Pl EC2..110 A4
Exeter Ct NW6.....23 C3
Exeter Ho
  Paddington W2...100 C2
  14 Peckham SE15..49 C4
  Putney SW15......57 B1
Exeter Mans NW2..10 A2
Exeter Mews
  Fulham SW6......155 B2
  12 Hampstead
    NW6............11 A2
Exeter Rd
  Brondesbury NW2..10 A2
  Newham E16......35 C4
Exeter St WC2....120 C4
Exeter Way 2
  SE14.............51 B3
Exford Ct SW11...167 C4
Exhibition Cl W12..30 B2
Exhibition Rd
  SW7.............129 C2
Exmoor Ho 22 E3..26 A3
Exmoor St W10....30 C4
Exmouth Ho
  Clerkenwell EC1...95 C2
  6 Millwall E14....42 A2
Exmouth Market
  EC1...............95 C2
Exmouth Mews
  NW1..............93 A3
Exmouth Pl E8.....17 A1
Exmouth St E1.....32 B3
Exonbury NW8.....78 B3
Exon St SE17.....152 A3
Explorers Ct 6
  E14...............34 C2
Express Wharf 10
  E14...............41 C4
Exton St SE1.....121 B1
Eynella Rd SE21...76 B3
Eynham Rd W12...30 B3
Eynsford Ho
  Borough The SE1...137 B4
  15 Deptford SE15..50 B4
  Walworth SE17...152 A3
Eyot Gdns W6......38 B1
Eyot Gn W4........38 B1
Eyre Ct NW8.......79 B2
Eyre St Hill EC1.....95 B1
Eythorne Rd SW9.173 C3
Ezra St E2....24 B2 99 A4

F
Fabian Rd SW6....155 A2
Fabyc Ho TW9......44 C3
Faircares SW11....56 C3
Fairbairn Gn 1
  SW9...............48 A2
Fairbriar Residence
  SW7.............143 A4

Fairbridge Rd N19....4 C2
Fairburn Ct SW15 ..58 A2
Fairburn Ho
 9 Stamford Hill
  ....7 A3
 West Kensington
  SW5 ....141 A1
Fairby Ho SE1....153 A4
Faircharm Trad Est
  SE8 ....52 A3
Fairchild Cl SW11..167 C4
Fairchild Ho
 13 Hackney E9...17 B1
 Pimlico SW1 .....147 A3
 Shoredtich
  N1 ....24 A2 98 A4
Fairchild Pl
  EC2 .....24 A1 98 B1
Fairchild St
  EC2 .....24 A1 98 B1
Fairclough St E1...111 C1
Faircourt N4 NW3 ..12 B2
Faircroft N16.......6 C3
Fairdale Gdns
  N7..............14 A4
Fairdene Ct N7....14 A3
Fairfax Ho
 Brixton SW9.....173 C1
 6 Putney SW15 ..56 C2
Fairfax Mews
  SW15 ....57 B3
Fairfax Pl
 Kensington W14..126 B1
 South Hampstead
  NW6 ....11 B1
Fairfax Rd
 Acton W4........38 A3
 South Hampstead
  NW6 ....11 B1
Fairfield
 Camden Town
  NW1 ....82 C3
 4 Stepney E1....32 B4
Fairfield Ct
 Harlesden NW10 ..21 C4
 1 London SW18..59 A2
Fairfield Dr SW18 ..59 A2
Fairfield Rd E3....26 C3
Fairfield St SW18..59 A2
Fairfoot Rd E3....26 C1
Fairford Ho SE11 ..149 C3
Fairhazel Gdns
  NW6 ....11 B1
Fairheathe SW15 ..57 C1
Fairholme Rd
  W14 ....140 B1
Fairholt Cl N16....7 A3
Fairholt Rd N16 ...6 C3
Fairholt St SW7 ..130 B2
Fairhurst **4** NW6...11 B2
Fairlawn Ave W4 ..37 B2
Fairlawn Cl **3** W4 ..37 B2
Fairlawn Gr W4 ...37 B2
Fairlawn Mans
  SE14 ....50 C2
Fairlawns SW15 ..57 C2
Fairlead Ho 6
  E14 ....41 C3
Fairley House Sch
  SW1 ....147 C2
Fairlie Ct
 22 Bromley E3...27 A2
 1 Tufnell Pk N7..13 C4
Fairlight Ave
  NW10 ....21 A3

Fairlight Ct **4**
  NW10 ....21 A3
Fairlop Pl NW8....89 C3
Fairmead Ho E9....18 A4
Fairmead Rd N7,
  N19 ....5 A1
Fairmont Ave E14 ..34 C1
Fairmont Ho 1
  E3 ....26 C1
Fairmount Rd
  SW2 ....62 B1
Fair St SE1.......138 C4
Fairstead Wlk N1 ..86 C4
Fairthorn Rd SE7,
  SE10 ....43 C1
Fairview Ho **14**
  SW2 ....74 B4
Fairview Pl SW2 ..74 B4
Fairwall Ho 9
  SE5 ....49 A2
Fairway Cl NW11 ..2 B4
Fairway Ct **13**
  SE16 ....40 C4
Fairway The W3 ..29 A3
Fairweather Ho
  N7............14 A4
Faith Ct NW2 .....9 A2
Faithfull Ho N5 ...15 B3
Fakruddin St
  E1 ......24 C1 99 C1
Falconberg Ct
  W1 ....105 C2
Falconberg Mews
  W1 ....105 C2
Falconbrook Prim Sch
  SW11 ....59 C4
Falcon Cl
 Chiswick W4 ....45 B4
 Lambeth SE1 ...122 B2
Falcon Ct
 9 Dulwich SE21 ..75 C2
 Holborn EC4 ....107 B1
 Islington N1 .....86 B3
Falcon Gr SW11...60 A4
Falcon Ho **11** SE15..49 B2
Falcon La SW11 ..60 A4
Falcon Lo
 11 Paddington W9 ..31 C4
 West Hampstead
  NW3 ....11 A4
Falcon Pk Ind Est
  NW10 ....8 A3
Falcon Point SE1 ..122 B3
Falcon Rd SW11...60 A4
Falcon Terr SW11 ..60 A4
Falcon Way E14 ...42 A2
Falconwood Ct
  SE3 ....53 B1
Falkener Ct SW11 ..170 A3
Falkirk Ct **11** SE16...32 C1
Falkirk Ho W9 ....88 B4
Falkirk St N1 .....24 A3
Falkland Ho
 Kensington W8...128 A1
 West Kensington
  W14 ....140 C2
Falkland Pl **2**
  NW5 ....13 B3
Falkland Rd NW5...13 B3
Falkner House Sch
  SW7 ....143 A2
Fallodon Ho
 London SW8 ....171 C2
 Paddington W11...31 B4
Fallow Ct SE16 ...153 C1
Fallowfield N4 ....5 B2

Falmouth Ho
 Bayswater W2...116 A4
 Kennington SE11..149 C2
Falmouth Rd SE1 ..137 A1
Falmouth St E15 ..19 C3
Falstaff Ct SE11 ..150 A3
Falstaff Ho **10** N1...24 A3
Fane St W14 ....155 A4
Fann St EC1 .....97 A1
Fanshaw St
  N1 .....24 A2 98 A4
Fanthorpe St
  SW15 ....57 B4
Faraday Cl N7....14 B2
Faraday Ho
 2 Balham SW12...73 A4
 6 Gospel Oak
  NW5 ....12 C2
 Kensal Town W10...31 A4
 6 Poplar E14 ....33 B2
Faraday Rd
 Acton W3.......28 B2
 Kensal Town W10...31 A4
Fareham Ho **13**
  SW15 ....68 C3
Fareham St W1...105 B2
Farjeon Ho NW6 ..11 C1
Farleigh Pl N16 ...16 B4
Farleigh Rd N16 ..16 B4
Farley Ct
 Kensington W14..126 C2
 Marylebone NW1 ..91 B1
Farlington Pl
  SW15 ....69 A4
Farlow Rd SW15 ..57 C4
Farlton Rd SW18 ..71 A4
Farm Ave NW2 ...1 B1
Farm Cl SW6 ....155 C2
Farmdale Rd SE10..43 C1
Farmer Ho **4**
  SE16 ....40 A3
Farmer Rd SE5 ...48 A3
Farmer St
  W8 .....31 C1 113 B2
Farm La SW6 ....155 C2
Farm Lane Trad City
  SW6 ....155 C3
Farmleigh Ho
  SW9 ....63 A2
Farm Pl
  W8 .....31 C1 113 B2
Farm Rd NW10 ...20 C4
Farm St W1 .....118 A3
Farnaby Ho **2**
  W10 ....23 B2
Farnborough Ho **6**
  SW15 ....68 C3
Farncombe St
  SE16 ....139 C3
Farndale Ho NW6...78 A4
Farnell Mews
  SW5 ....142 A2
Farnell Pl W3 ....28 A2
Farnfield Ho **12**
  SW2 ....62 B2
Farnham Ho
 Borough The SE1..122 C1
 Marylebone NW1...90 B1
Farnham Pl SE1 ..122 B1
Farnham Royal
  SE11 ....149 A1
Farnhurst Ho **5**
  SW11 ....169 B2
Farningham Ho **9**
  N4.............6 C4

Farnley Ho SW8...171 B2
Farnsworth Ct
  SE10 ....43 B3
Farnworth Ho **5**
  E14 ....42 C2
Faroe Rd W14 ....39 C3
Farquhar Rd
  SW19 ....70 C1
Farrance St E14 ..33 C3
Farrant Ho **19**
  SW11 ....59 C4
Farrell Ho E1 ....32 B3
Farrer Ho SE8 ....51 C3
Farriers Mews
  SE15 ....65 B4
Farrier St NW1 ...13 B1
Farrier Wlk SW10 ..156 C4
Farringdon La EC1 ..95 C1
Farringdon Rd
  EC1 ....95 C1
Farringdon Sta
  EC1 ....108 A2
Farrington Rd
  EC4 ....108 A2
Farrins Rents
  SE16 ....33 A1
Farrow La SE14 ..50 B3
Farrow Pl SE16 ...41 A3
Farthing Alley
  SE1 ....139 B3
Farthing Fields **8**
  E1 ....32 A1
Fashion & Design Mus
  The★ SE1 .....138 A4
Fashion Retail Acad
  The W1 ....105 A2
Fashion St E1 ...111 A3
Fassett Rd E8 ....16 C2
Fassett Sq E8 ....16 C2
Fauconberg Ct
  W4 ....45 B4
Fauconberg Rd
  W4 ....45 B4
Faulkner Ho SW15..47 B1
Faulkner's Alley
  EC1 ....108 A4
Faulkner St SE14 ..50 B2
Faunce Ho **1**
  SE17 ....48 A4
Faunce St SE17 ..150 A1
Favart Rd SW6 ..165 C3
Faversham Ho
 Camden Town
  NW1 ....83 A3
 Walworth SE17...152 A1
Fawcett Cl SW11 ..167 C1
Fawcett Est E5 ...7 C3
Fawcett Ho SW9 ..172 B2
Fawcett Rd NW10..8 B1
Fawcett St SW10 ..156 C4
Fawe Park Rd
  SW15 ....58 B3
Fawe St E14 .....34 A4
Fawkham Ho SE1 ..153 A3
Fawley Ct SE27 ..75 A2
Fawley Lo **2** E14 ..42 C2
Fawley Rd NW6 ..11 A3
Fawnbrake Ave
  SE24 ....63 B2
Fayetville Ho **26**
  N19 ....5 A4
Fazerley Ct **49** W2..31 C4
Fearnley Ho SE5 ..49 A1
Fearon St SE10 ...43 C1

Feathers Pl SE10 ..52 C4
Featherstone St
  EC1 ....97 B2
Featley Rd SW9 ..63 A4
Felbridge Ho **21**
  SE22 ....64 A4
Felday Rd SE13 ..67 A1
Felden St SW6 ...164 C3
Feldman Cl N16 ...7 C3
Felgate Mews **4**
  W6 ....39 A2
Felix St **19** E2 ....25 A3
Felixstowe Rd
  NW10 ....22 A2
Fellbrigg Rd SE22 ..64 B2
Fellbrigg St **21** E1 ..25 A1
Fell Ho **18** N19 ...4 B1
Fellows Ct E2 ....24 B3
Fellows Rd NW3 ..12 A1
Fells Haugh **6**
  W3 ....28 B3
Felltram Way SE7 ..43 C1
Felmersham Cl **2**
  SW4 ....61 C3
Felsberg Rd SW2 ..74 A4
Felsham Ho SW15 ..57 C4
Felsham Mews
  SW15 ....57 C4
Felsham Rd SW15 ..57 C4
Felstead St E9 ...18 B2
Felstead Wharf
  E14 ....42 B1
Felton Ho N1 ....87 C3
Felton St N1 .....87 C3
Fenchurch Ave
  EC3 ....110 A1
Fenchurch Bldgs
  EC3 ....110 B1
Fenchurch Pl
  EC3 ....124 B4
Fenchurch St
  EC3 ....124 B4
Fenchurch Street Sta
  EC3 ....124 B4
Fen Ct EC3 ......124 A4
Fendall St SE1 ...138 B1
Fender Ct SW4 ...172 A2
Fendt Cl **8** E16 ...35 B3
Fenelon Pl W14 ..141 A3
Fenham Rd SE15 ..50 A3
Fenner Cl SE16 ...40 A2
Fenner Ho **25** E1 ..32 A1
Fenner Sq **10**
  SW11 ....59 C4
Fenning St SE1 ..138 A4
Fenn St E9 ......17 B3
Fenstanton **31** N4 ..5 B3
Fenstanton Prim Sch
  SW2 ....74 C3
Fentiman Rd
  SW8 ....162 C2
Fenton Cl
 Dalston E8 .....16 B2
 South Lambeth
  SW9 ....172 C2
Fenton Ho SE14 ..51 A3
Fenton House★
  NW3 ....2 B1
Fentons SE3 .....53 B3
Fenton St E1 .....32 A3
Fenwick Gr SE15 ..64 C4
Fenwick Pl SW9 ..62 A4
Fenwick Rd SE15 ..64 C4
Ferdinand Ho **1**
  NW1 ....13 A1
Ferdinand Pl NW1 ..12 C1

Ferdinand St NW1 . . . 12 C1
Ferguson Dr W3 . . . . 28 C3
Ferguson Ho SE10 . . 52 B2
Ferguson's Cl E14 . . 41 C2
Fergus Rd N5 . . . . . . 15 A3
Fermain Ct E N1 . . . . 24 A4
Fermain Ct N N1 . . . . 24 A4
Fermain Ct W N1 . . . 24 A4
Fermoy Rd W9 . . . . . 23 B1
Fernbank Mews
 . . . . 61 B1
Fern Cl 3 N1 . . . . . . 24 A3
Ferncliff Rd E8 . . . . . 16 C3
Ferncroft Ave
 NW3 . . . . 10 C4
Fern Ct SE14 . . . . . . 50 C1
Ferndale Ct 2
 SE3 . . . . 53 B3
Ferndale Ho N16 . . . 6 C3
Ferndale Rd SW4, . . .
 SW9 . . . . 62 B3
Ferndene Rd SE24 . . 63 B3
Ferndown Lo 17
 E14 . . . . 42 B3
Fernhead Rd W9 . . . 23 B2
Fernhill Ho E5 . . . . . 7 C2
Fernholme Rd
 SE15 . . . . 65 C2
Fernhurst Rd
 SW6 . . . . 164 B4
Fernie Ho SE22 . . . . 64 B4
Fernlea Rd SW12 . . 73 A3
Fernleigh Cl W9 . . . 23 B2
Fernsbury St WC1 . . 95 B3
Fernshaw Mans
 SW10 . . . . 156 C3
Fernshaw Rd
 SW10 . . . . 156 C3
Fernside NW11 . . . . 1 C3
Fernside Rd SW12 . 72 C4
Fern St E3 . . . . 26 C1
Ferntower Rd N5 . . 15 C3
Fernwood Wlk SE16 153 C1
Fernwood SW19 . . . 70 B3
Ferrey Mews
 SW9 . . . . 173 B1
Ferriby Cl N1 . . . . . . 14 C1
Ferrier Ind Est
 SW18 . . . . 59 A3
Ferrier Point 6
 E16 . . . . 35 C4
Ferrier St SW18 . . . 59 A3
Ferrings SE21 . . . . . 76 A1
Ferris Rd SE22 . . . . 64 C3
Ferrybridge Ho
 SE11 . . . . 135 A1
Ferry La
 Barnes SW13 . . . . 46 B4
 Brentford TW8 . . . 44 A4
 Richmond TW9 . . . 44 B4
Ferry Rd SW13 . . . . 46 C2
Ferry Sq 1 TW8 . . . 44 A4
Ferry St E14 . . . . . . 42 B1
Festing Rd SW15 . . 57 C4
Festival St 5 E8 . . . 16 B1
Festival Pier SE1 . . 120 C2
Festival Pleasure
 Gdns SW11 . . . . . 158 C1
Fetter La EC4 . . . . . 107 C2
Fettes Ho NW8 . . . . 79 C1
Ffinch St SE8 . . . . . 51 C3
Field Ct
 Hampstead NW3 . . 11 B3
 Holborn WC1 . . . . 107 A3
 Lower Holloway N7 . . 14 A3
 Wimbledon SW19 . 70 C1

Fieldgate Mans
 E1 . . . . 111 C3
Fieldgate St E1 . . . . 111 C3
Field Ho NW10 . . . . 22 C2
Fieldhouse Rd
 SW12 . . . . 73 B3
Fielding Ho
 Chiswick W4 . . . . . 46 A4
 St John's Wood
 NW6 . . . . 23 C2
 St John's Wood
 NW8 . . . . 78 C4
Fielding Mews
 SW13 . . . . 47 A4
Fielding Rd
 Acton W4 . . . . 38 A3
 Hammersmith W14 . 39 C3
Field Rd W6 . . . . . . 154 A4
Fieldside Sq SE10 . 6 C3
Field St WC1 . . . . . . 94 C4
Fieldsway Ho N5 . . 14 C3
Fieldview SW17,
 SW18 . . . . 71 C3
Fieldview Ct 2
 N5 . . . . 15 A3
Fieldway Cres N5,
 N7 . . . . 14 C3
Fieldwick Ho 14
 E9 . . . . 17 C2
Fife Rd
 Mortlake SW14 . . . 55 B2
 Newham E16 . . . . 35 C4
Fife Terr N1 . . . . . . 85 A2
Fifth Ave W10 . . . . 23 A2
Fig Tree Cl NW10 . . 21 A4
Filey Ave N16 . . . . 7 C3
Filey Ho SW18 . . . . 59 B3
Filigree Ct SE16 . . 33 B1
Filmer Ho SW6 . . . 164 B4
Filmer Mews
 SW6 . . . . 164 B4
Filmer Rd SW6 . . . 154 C1
Filton Ct 14 SE14 . 50 B3
Finborough Rd
 SW10 . . . . 156 B4
Finchdean Ho
 SW15 . . . . 68 B4
Finch Ho 1 SE8 . . 52 A3
Finch La EC2, EC3 . 109 C1
Finchley Pl NW8 . . 79 B2
Finch Mews 3
 SE15 . . . . 49 B2
Finch's Ct 10 E14 . 34 A2
Findhorn St 8
 E14 . . . . 34 B3
Findon Cl SW18 . . 58 C1
Findon Rd W12 . . . 38 C4
Fineran Ct 16
 SW11 . . . . 59 C3
Fingal St SE10 . . . 43 B1
Fingest Ho NW8 . . 90 A2
Finland Rd SE4 . . . 66 A4
Finland St SE16 . . 41 A3
Finlay St SW6 . . . 47 C2
Finley Ct 21 SE5 . 48 B3
Finmere Ho 21 N4 . 6 B4
Finnemore Ho N1 . 86 C4

Finn Ho N1 . . . . . . 97 C4
Finnis St E2 . . . . . 25 A1
FINSBURY 95 C4
Finsbury Ave EC2 . 109 C3
Finsbury Cir EC2 . 109 C3
Finsbury Coll 14 . 109 B3
Finsbury Ct EC2 . . 109 B3
Finsbury Market
 EC2 . . . . 110 A4
Finsbury Mkt
 EC2 . . . . 24 A1 98 A1
FINSBURY PARK . . 5 C2
Finsbury Park Rd N4,
 N5 . . . . 6 A2
Finsbury Park Sta
 N4 . . . . 5 C2
Finsbury Pavement
 EC2 . . . . 109 C4
Finsbury Sq EC2 . . 109 C4
Finsbury St EC2 . . 109 B4
Finsen Rd SE5 . . . 63 B4
Finstock Rd W10 . . 30 C3
Finton House Sch
 SW17 . . . . 72 B2
Finucane Ct TW9 . 54 B4
Finwhale Ho E14 . 42 A3
Fiona Ct 9 NW6 . 23 B3
Firbank Rd SE15 . 50 A1
Fircroft N1 . . . . . 86 B4
Fircroft Prim Sch
 SW17 . . . . 72 B1
Fircroft Rd SW17 . 72 B1
Fire Brigade Pier
 SE1 . . . . 148 B2
Firecrest Dr NW3 . 2 A1
Firle Ho 7 W10 . . 30 B4
Firmston Ho 8
 SW14 . . . . 55 C4
Firs Ave SW14 . . 55 B3
Firsby Rd N16 . . . 7 C3
First Ave
 East Acton W3 . . 29 B1
 Mortlake SW14 . . 56 A4
 West Kilburn W10 23 B1
First St SW3 . . . . 144 B4
Firth Gdns SW6 . 164 A3
Fir Tree Ho 11
 SE14 . . . . 50 B3
Fir Trees Cl SE16 33 A1
Fisher Ho
 Islington N1 . . . 85 B3
 2 Shadwell E1 . 32 B2
 2 Tufnell Pk N19 . 4 B1
Fishermans Dr
 SE16 . . . . 40 C4
Fisherman's Wlk
 E14 . . . . 33 C1
Fishers Cl SW16 . 73 C1
Fishers Ct SE14 . 50 C2
Fisher's La W4 . . 37 C2
Fisher St
 Holborn WC1 . . 106 C3
 Newham E16 . . 35 C4
Fisherton St NW8 89 C2
Fisherton Street Est
 NW8 . . . . 89 C1
Fishlock Ct SW4 . 172 A2
Fish St Hill EC3 . 123 C3
Fitch Ct SW2 . . . 62 C2
Fitzalan St SE11 . 149 B4
Fitzclarence Ho
 W11 . . . . 126 A4
Fitz-George Ave
 W14 . . . . 140 A3
Fitzgerald Ave
 SW14 . . . . 56 A4

Fitzgerald Ho
 Brixton SW9 . . . 173 B1
 16 Poplar E14 . . 34 A3
Fitzgerald Rd
 SW14 . . . . 55 C4
Fitzhardinge Ho
 W1 . . . . 103 B2
Fitzhardinge St
 W1 . . . . 103 B2
Fitzherbert Ho 11
 TW10 . . . . 54 B1
Fitzhugh Gr SW18 59 C1
Fitzjames Ave
 W14 . . . . 140 B3
Fitzjohn's Ave
 NW3 . . . . 11 C3
Fitzjohns Mans
 NW3 . . . . 11 B2
Fitzjohns Prim Sch
 NW3 . . . . 11 C3
Fitzmaurice Ho 7
 SE16 . . . . 40 A2
Fitzmaurice Pl
 W1 . . . . 118 B2
Fitzneal St W12 . 29 B3
FITZROVIA 104 A4
Fitzroy Cl N6 . . . 3 B3
Fitzroy Cres W4 . 45 C3
Fitzroy Ct W1 . . 93 A1
Fitzroy Ho
 Bermondsey SE1 . 153 A2
 12 Tower Hamlets
 . . . . 33 B3
Fitzroy Mews W1 . 92 C1
Fitzroy Pk N6 . . . 3 B3
Fitzroy Rd NW1 . 81 B4
Fitzroy Sq W1 . . 92 C1
Fitzroy St W1 . . . 92 C1
Fitzroy St NW1 . . 92 C1
Fitzwarren Gdns
 N19 . . . . 4 B3
Fitzwilliam Ave
 TW9 . . . . 44 B1
Fitzwilliam Mews
 E16 . . . . 35 C1
Fitzwilliam Rd
 SW4 . . . . 61 B4
Fives Ct SE11 . . 136 A1
Fiveways Rd SW9 173 C1
Flamborough Ho 12
 SE15 . . . . 49 C2
Flamborough St
 E14 . . . . 33 A3
Flamingo Ct 2
 SE8 . . . . 51 C3
Flamsteed Ct 18
 SE13 . . . . 52 A2
Flamsteed Ho*
 SE10 . . . . 52 C3
Flanchford Rd
 W12 . . . . 38 B3
Flanders Ho N16 . 7 A1
Flanders Mans 1
 W4 . . . . 38 A2
Flanders Rd W4 . 38 A2
Flanders Way E9 . 17 C2
Flank St E1 . . . 125 B4
Flansham Ho 2
 E14 . . . . 33 B3
Flask Cotts 4
 NW3 . . . . 11 C4
Flask Wlk NW3 . . 11 C4
Flatiron Sq SE1 . 123 A1
Flatiron Yd SE1 . 123 A1
Flavell Mews SE10 . 43 A1
Flaxman Ct W1 . 105 B1

Flaxman Ho
 10 Chiswick W4 . . 38 A1
 Newington SE1 . . 136 B2
Flaxman Rd SE5 . . 48 A1
Flaxman Terr WC1 . 93 C3
Flecker Ho 8 SE5 . 48 C3
Fleece Wlk N7 . . . 14 A2
Fleet Ct 1 W12 . . 38 A3
Fleetfield WC1 . . . 94 B4
Fleet Ho
 6 Brixton SW2 . . 62 C2
 4 Limehouse E14 . 33 A2
Fleet PI EC4 . . . . 108 A2
Fleet Prim Sch
 NW3 . . . . 12 B3
Fleet Rd NW3 . . . 12 B3
Fleet Sq WC1 . . . 95 A3
Fleet St EC4 . . . . 107 C1
Fleet Street Hill
 E1 . . . . 24 C1 99 B1
Fleetway WC1 . . . 94 B4
Fleet Wood 6 N16 . 7 B2
Fleetwood Rd
 NW10 . . . . 8 C3
Fleetwood St N16 . 7 A2
Fleming Cl 1 W9 . 23 C1
Fleming Ct W2 . . 101 B4
Fleming Ho
 Bermondsey SE16 139 B3
 Finsbury Pk N4 . . 6 B3
Fleming Rd SE17 . 48 A4
Fletcher Bldgs
 WC2 . . . . 106 B1
Fletcher Ct 9
 NW5 . . . . 13 A4
Fletcher Ho 18
 . . . . 16 A4
Fletcher Path 7
 SE8 . . . . 51 C3
Fletcher Rd W4 . 37 B3
Fletcher St E1 . . 125 C4
Fleur De Lis St
 E1 . . . . 24 B1 98 C1
Fleur Gates 5
 SW19 . . . . . . 69 C4
Flinders Ho 28 E1 . 32 A1
Flinton St SE17 . 152 B2
Flint St SE17 . . 151 C3
Flitcroft St WC2 . 105 C1
Flitton Ho 5 N1 . 15 A1
Flock Mill PI
 SW18 . . . . . . 71 A3
Flodden Rd SE5 . 48 B2
Flood St SW3 . . 158 B4
Flood Wlk SW3 . 158 B4
Flora Cl E14 . . . 34 A3
Flora Gardens Prim
 Sch W6 . . . . . 39 A2
Flora Gdns 2 W6 . 39 A2
Floral St WC2 . . 120 A4
Florence Ct W9 . 89 A3
Florence Gdns
 W4 . . . . 45 B4
Florence Ho
 2 Bermondsey
 SE16 . . . . . . 40 A1
 3 Brixton SW2 . 62 B2
 10 Shepherd's Bush
 W11 . . . . . . 30 C2
 7 Wandsworth
 SW18 . . . . . . 59 C3
Florence Mans
 SW6 . . . . . . 164 C4
Florence Nightingale
 Ho 14 N1 . . . 15 B2

Florence Nightingale
Mus* SE1 .... **135** A3
Florence Rd
 Acton W4 .... 37 C3
 Finsbury Pk N4 .... 5 C4
 New Cross Gate
 SE14 .... 51 B2
Florence St N1 .... 15 A1
Florence Terr
 Kingston u T SW15 .... 68 A1
 New Cross Gate
 SE14 .... 51 B2
Florence Way
 SW12 .... 72 B3
Flores Ho 15 E1 .... 32 C4
Florfield Rd E8 .... 17 A2
Florian SE5 .... 49 A2
Florian Rd SW15 .... 58 A3
Florida St
 E2 .... 24 C2 99 C3
Florida State Univ
 WC1 .... **105** C3
Florin Ct SE1 .... **138** C3
Floris Pl 7 SW4 .... 61 B4
Florys Ct 7 SW19 .... 70 A3
Floss St SW15 .... 47 B1
Flower & Dean Wlk
 E1 .... **111** A3
Flowersmead
 SW17 .... 72 C2
Flowers Mews 1
 N19 .... 4 B2
Flower Wlk The
 SW7 .... **129** A4
Floyer Cl TW10 .... 54 B2
Flynn Ct 19 E14 .... 33 C2
Foley Ho 6 E1 .... 32 B3
Foley St W1 .... **104** C3
Folgate St E1 .... **110** C4
Foliot Ho N1 .... **84** C2
Foliot St W12 .... 29 B3
Follett Ho SW10 .... **157** B2
Follett St E14 .... 34 B3
Folly Wall E14 .... 42 B4
Fonda Ct 14 E14 .... 33 C2
Fontarabia Rd
 SW11 .... 60 C3
Fontenelle SE5 .... 49 A2
Fontenoy Ho
 SE11 .... **150** A3
Fontenoy Rd SW12,
 SW17 .... 73 B2
Fonthill Ho
 Kensington W14 .... **126** B2
 Pimlico SW1 .... **146** B2
Fonthill Mews N4 .... 5 B2
Fonthill Rd N4 .... 5 C2
Fontley Way
 SW15 .... 68 C4
Footpath The
 SW15 .... 56 C2
Forber Ho 25 E2 .... 25 B2
Forbes Ho 2 W4 .... 36 C1
Forbes St E1 .... **111** C1
Forburg Rd N16 .... 7 C3
Ford Cl 12 E3 .... 26 A3
Fordcombe 15
 NW5 .... 12 C2
Fordham Ho 13
 SE14 .... 51 A3
Fordham St E1 .... **111** C2
Fordingley Rd W9 .... 23 B2
Ford Rd E3 .... 26 B3
Fords Park Rd
 E16 .... 35 C3

Ford Sq E1 .... 32 A4
Ford St Bow E3 .... 26 A3
 Canning Town E16 .... 35 B3
Fordwych Ct NW2 .... 10 A2
Fordwych Rd
 NW2 .... 10 A3
Fordyce Rd SE13 .... 67 B2
Forecastle Ct E14 .... 41 C4
Foreign,
 Commonwealth &
 Home Offices
 SW1 .... **134** A4
Foreland Ho
 W11 .... 31 A2 **112** A4
Foreshore SE8 .... 41 B2
Fore St EC2 .... **109** A3
Forest Cl NW6 .... 10 A1
Forester Rd SE15 .... 65 A4
Forester Ho 6 E8 .... 22 B2
Forest Hill Rd
 SE22 .... 65 A1
Forest Rd
 Dalston E8 .... 16 B2
 Richmond TW9 .... 44 C3
Fore Street Ave
 EC2 .... **109** B3
Forest Way 9 N19 .... 4 B2
Forfar Rd SW11 .... **169** C4
Forge Pl NW1 .... 12 C2
Forman Ho SE4 .... 65 C3
Forman Pl N16 .... 16 B4
Formby Ct 8 N7 .... 14 C3
Formosa Ho 1 E1 .... 26 A1
Formosa St W9 .... **88** B1
Formunt Cl E16 .... 35 B4
Forrest Ct N7 .... 14 C2
Forrest Ho SW15 .... 47 B1
Forset Ct W1 .... **102** B2
Forset St W1 .... **102** B2
Forster Rd SW2 .... 74 A4
Forston St N1 .... **87** A2
Forsyth Gdns
 SE17 .... 48 A4
Forsyth Ho
 14 Hackney E9 .... 17 B1
 Pimlico SW1 .... **147** A3
Forsythia Ho SE4 .... 66 A4
Fortescue Ave 1
 E8 .... 17 A1
Fortess Gr NW5 .... 13 B3
Fortess Rd NW5 .... 13 B3
Fortess Wlk NW5 .... 13 A3
Forthbridge Rd
 SW11 .... 60 C3
Forth Ho 30 E3 .... 26 B3
Forties The 9
 NW5 .... 13 B3
Fortior Ct N6 .... 4 B4
Fortnam Rd N19 .... 4 C2
Fort Rd SE1 .... **153** A3
Fortrose Cl E14 .... 34 C3
Fortrose Gdns SW12,
 SW2 .... 74 A3
Fort St E1 .... **110** B3
Fortuna Cl N7 .... 14 B2
Fortune Ct 6 E8 .... 16 B4
Fortune Gate Rd
 NW10 .... 21 A4
Fortune Green Rd
 NW6 .... 10 C4
Fortune Ho
 Lambeth SE11 .... **149** B3
 St Luke's EC1 .... **97** A1
Fortune St EC1 .... **97** A1
Fortune Way
 NW10 .... 21 C2
Forty Acre La E16 .... 35 C4

Forum Cl 7 E3 .... 26 C4
Forward Bsns Ctr The
 3 E16 .... 27 C1
Fosbrooke Ho
 SW8 .... **162** A1
Fosbury Ho 7
 SW9 .... 62 B3
Fosbury Mews
 W2 .... **114** B3
Foscote Mews W9 .... 31 C4
Foskett Rd SW6 .... **165** A1
Fossil Rd SE13 .... 66 C4
Foster Ct
 6 Camden Town
 NW1 .... 13 B1
 Canning Town E16 .... 35 B2
Foster Ho SE14 .... 51 B2
Foster La EC2 .... **108** C2
Foster Rd
 Acton W3 .... 29 A2
 Chiswick W4 .... 37 C1
Foubert's Pl W1 .... **104** C1
Foulden Rd N16 .... 16 B4
Foulden Terr N16 .... 16 B4
Foulis Terr SW7 .... **143** C2
Foulser Rd SW17 .... 72 C1
Foundary Ho 4
 E14 .... 34 A4
Founders Ct EC2 .... **109** B2
Founders Ho
 SW1 .... **147** B2
Foundling Ct WC1 .... **94** A2
Foundling Mus The*
 WC1 .... **94** B2
Foundry Cl SE16 .... 33 A1
Foundry Mews
 NW1 .... **93** A2
Foundry Pl
 Stepney E1 .... 32 B4
 Wandsworth SW18 .... 71 A4
Fountain Ct
 Belgravia SW1 .... **146** A3
 3 Shepherd's Bush
 W11 .... 39 C4
 Strand EC4 .... **121** B4
Fountain Green Sq
 SE16 .... **139** C3
Fountain Ho
 Bermondsey SE16 .... **139** C3
 3 Brondesbury Pk
 NW6 .... 10 A1
 Mayfair W1 .... **117** B2
Fountain Mews
 5 Highbury N5 .... 15 B4
 Maitland Pk NW3 .... 12 B2
Fountain Pl SW9 .... **173** C3
Fountayne Rd N16 .... 7 C2
Fount St SW8 .... **161** C1
Fournier St E1 .... **111** A4
Fourscore Mews
 E8 .... 16 C1
Four Seasons Cl
 E3 .... 26 C3
Fourth Ave W10 .... 23 A2
Fovant Ct SW8 .... **170** C1
Fowey Cl E1 .... 32 A1
Fowey Ho SE11 .... **149** C2
Fowler Cl SW11 .... 59 C4
Fowler Ho
 5 Camberwell
 SE5 .... 49 A1
 Islington N1 .... **86** B4
 South Lambeth
 SW8 .... **171** C3
Fowler Rd N1 .... **86** B4
Fownes St SW11 .... 60 A4

Fox and Knot St
 EC1 .... **108** B4
Foxberry Ct SE4 .... 66 B3
Foxberry Rd SE4 .... 66 A4
Foxborough Gdns
 SE4 .... 66 C2
Foxbourne Rd
 SW17 .... 72 C2
Fox Cl
 Bethnal Green E1 .... 25 B1
 Newham E16 .... 35 C4
Foxcombe Rd 6
 SW15 .... 68 C3
Foxcote SE5 .... **152** B1
Foxcroft N1 .... **85** A1
Foxfield NW1 .... **82** B3
Foxglove St W12 .... 29 B2
Foxham Rd N19 .... 4 C1
Fox Ho 2 SW11 .... 59 C3
Foxley Cl E8 .... 16 C3
Foxley Ho 4 E3 .... 27 A2
Foxley Rd SW9 .... 48 A3
Foxley Sq 3 SW9 .... 48 A2
Foxmore St SW11 .... **168** C3
Fox Prim Sch
 W8 .... 31 C1 **113** B1
Fox Rd E16 .... 35 B4
Fox's Yd E2 .... 24 B1 99 A2
Foxwell Mews
 SE4 .... 66 A4
Foxwell St SE4 .... 66 A4
Foyle Rd SE3 .... 53 B4
Fradel Lo N16 .... 6 C3
Framfield Rd N5 .... 15 A3
Frampton N1 .... **83** A3
Frampton Ct 3
 W3 .... 37 B4
Frampton Ho NW8 .... **89** C1
Frampton Park Rd
 E9 .... 17 B1
Frampton St NW8 .... **89** C1
Francemary Rd
 SE4 .... 66 C2
Franche Court Rd
 SW17 .... 71 B1
Francis Chichester
 Way SW11 .... **169** C3
Francis Cl 2 E14 .... 42 C2
Francis Ct 12 SE14 .... 50 C4
Francis Ho
 Harlesden NW10 .... 21 B4
 11 Shoreditch N1 .... 24 A4
 Walham Green
 SW10 .... **156** B2
Francis Holland Sch
 Belgravia SW1 .... **145** C3
 Marylebone NW1 .... **90** C2
Francis Snary Lo 1
 SW18 .... 58 C2
Francis St SW1 .... **147** A4
Francis Terr N19 .... 4 B1
Francis Terrace Mews
 15 N19 .... 4 B1
Francis Wlk N1 .... **84** C4
Franconia Rd
 SW4 .... 61 C2
Frank Barnes Sch
 NW3 .... 11 C1
Frank Beswick Ho
 SW6 .... **155** A3
Frank Dixon Cl
 SE21 .... 76 A3
Frank Dixon Way
 SE21 .... 76 A3
Frankfurt Rd SE24 .... 63 B2
Frankham Ho 8
 SE8 .... 51 C3

Frankham St SE8 .... 51 C3
Frank Ho SW8 .... **162** A2
Frankland Cl SE16 .... 40 A2
Frankland Ho 4
 SW12 .... 73 A4
Frankland Rd
 SW7 .... **129** B1
Franklin Bldg 5
 E14 .... 41 C4
Franklin Cl
 Greenwich SE13 .... 52 A2
 West Norwood
 SE27 .... 75 A1
Franklin Ho
 New Cross SE14 .... 51 A1
 28 Wapping E1 .... 32 A1
Franklin Pl SE13 .... 52 A2
Franklin Sq SW5 .... **141** A1
Franklin's Row
 SW3 .... **145** A2
Franklin St 13 E3 .... 27 A2
Franklyn Rd NW10 .... 8 B2
Frank Soskice Ho
 SW6 .... **155** A3
Frank Whymark Ho 4
 SE16 .... 40 B4
Frans Hals Ct E14 .... 42 C3
Fraserburgh Ho 29
 E3 .... 26 B3
Fraser Ct SW11 .... **168** A4
Fraser Ho
 Brentford TW8 .... 36 B1
 Clapham SW8 .... **171** B1
Fraser Regnart Ct 12
 NW5 .... 12 B3
Fraser St W4 .... 38 A1
Frazier St SE1 .... **135** B3
Frean St SE16 .... **139** B2
Freda Corbett Cl 5
 SE15 .... 49 C3
Frederica St 4
 N7 .... 14 B1
Frederick Blg N1 .... 16 A2
Frederick Charrington
 Ho 2 E1 .... 25 B1
Frederick Cl W2 .... **116** C4
Frederick Cres
 SW9 .... 48 A3
Frederick Ct SW6 .... 58 A4
Frederick's Pl
 EC2 .... **109** B1
Frederick Sq 11
 SE16 .... 33 A2
Frederick's Row
 EC1 .... **96** A4
Frederick St WC1 .... **94** C3
Frederick Terr 8
 E8 .... 16 B1
Frederic Mews
 SW1 .... **131** B3
Freedom St
 SW11 .... **169** A2
Freegrove Rd N7 .... 14 A3
Freeling Ho NW8 .... **79** B4
Freeling St 7 N1 .... 14 B1
Freeman Ho 13
 SW2 .... 74 A4
Freemantle St
 SE17 .... **152** A2
Freemens Hos 1
 SW9 .... 62 B3
Freke Rd SW11 .... 60 C4
Fremantle Ho 14
 E1 .... 25 A1
Fremont St E9 .... 25 B4
French Pl
 E1 .... 24 A1 **98** B2

Frendsbury Rd
SE4 . . . . 66 A3
Frensham Ct N5 . . 15 B3
Frensham Dr
SW15 . . . . 68 C2
Frensham St SE15 . 49 C4
Frere St SW11 . . . 168 A1
Freshfield Ave E8 . 16 B1
Freshfield Cl SE13 . 67 C3
Freshford St SW17,
SW18 . . . . 71 B1
Freston Rd W10,
W11 . . . . 30 C2
Freswick Ho 8
SE8 . . . . 41 A2
Freud Mus The*
NW3 . . . . 11 B2
Frewell Bldg EC1 . 107 B4
Frewin Rd SW18 . . 71 C3
Friar Mews SE27 . . 75 A1
Friars Ave SW15 . . 68 B1
Friars Cl SE1 . . . . 122 B1
Friars Gdns W3 . . . 28 C3
Friars Mead E14 . . 42 B3
Friars Place La
W3 . . . . 28 C2
Friars Prim Sch
SE1 . . . . 136 B3
Friars Stile Pl 9
TW10 . . . . 54 A1
Friars Stile Rd
TW10 . . . . 54 A1
Friar St EC4 . . . . 108 B1
Friars Way W3 . . . 28 C3
Friary Park Ct 12
W3 . . . . 28 B3
Friary Rd
Acton W3 . . . . . . 28 C3
Peckham SE15 . . . 49 C3
Friday Grove Mews 11
SW12 . . . . 73 B4
Friday St EC4 . . . 122 C4
Frideswide Pl
NW5 . . . . 13 B3
Friendly Pl 16
SE13 . . . . 52 A2
Friendly St SE8 . . . 51 C2
Friendly Street Mews
SE8 . . . . 51 C1
Friendship Way
E15 . . . . 27 B4
Friend St EC1 . . . . 96 A4
Friern Rd SE22 . . . 64 C1
Frigate Ho 7 E14 . 42 B2
Frigate Mews SE8 . 51 C4
Frimley Cl SW19 . . 70 A2
Frimley Way E1 . . . 25 C1
Frinstead Ho 1
W10 . . . . 30 C2
Friston St SW6 . . . 166 A1
Frith Ho
Bethnal Green
E2 . . . . 24 C2 99 B3
Paddington NW8 . . 89 C1
Frith Rd E11 . . . . . 19 C4
Frith St W1 . . . . . 105 B1
Frithville Ct 2
W12 . . . . 30 B1
Frithville Gdns
W12 . . . . 30 B1
Frobisher Ct 1
Greenwich
SE10 . . . . 52 C4
3 Shepherd's Bush
W12 . . . . 39 B4
Frobisher Ho 27
E1 . . . . 32 A1

Frobisher Pas E14 . 33 C1
Frobisher Pl SE14 . 50 B2
Frobisher St SE10 . 53 A4
Frogley Rd SE22 . . 64 B3
Frogmore SW18 . . 58 C2
Frogmore Est
NW10 . . . . 20 B2
Frogmore Ind Est
N5 . . . . 15 B4
Frognal NW3 . . . . 11 B3
Frognal Cl NW3 . . 11 B3
Frognal Ct NW3 . . 11 B2
Frognal Gdns
NW3 . . . . 11 B4
Frognal La NW3 . . 11 A3
Frognal Par NW3 . . 11 B2
Frognal Rise NW3 . 11 B4
Frognal Way NW3 . 11 B4
Fromow's Cnr 10
W4 . . . . 37 B1
Frontenac NW10 . . 9 A1
Frostic Wlk E1 . . . 111 A3
Froude St SW8 . . . 170 B1
Frye Ct 5 E3 . . . . . 26 B2
Frying Pan Alley
E1 . . . . 110 C3
Fry Rd NW10 . . . . 21 B4
Fulbeck Ho N7 . . . 14 B2
Fulbourne St E1 . . 32 A4
Fulbrook Rd N19 . . 13 B4
Fulcher Ct 5 SE8 . . 51 B4
Fulcher Ho
9 Deptford SE8 . . . 41 B1
10 Shoreditch N1 . . 24 A4
Fulford Mans 3
N19 . . . . 5 A1
Fulford St SE16 . . . 40 A4
FULHAM 47 C1
Fulham Broadway
SW6 . . . . 155 C1
Fulham Broadway Sh
Ctr SW6 . . . . . . 155 C1
Fulham Broadway Sta
SW6 . . . . 155 C2
Fulham Bsns
Exchange SW6 . . 167 A3
Fulham Cross Sec Sch
SW6 . . . . 154 A1
Fulham Ct 5 SW6 . 165 B4
Fulham High St
SW6 . . . . 164 B1
Fulham Pal*
SW6 . . . . 164 A1
Fulham Palace Rd
SW6,W6 . . . . . . 47 C4
Fulham Park Gdns
SW6 . . . . 164 C2
Fulham Park Rd
SW6 . . . . 164 C2
Fulham Prep Sch
Fulham SW6 . . . . 164 B1
Fulham W14 . . . . 154 B4
Fulham Prim Sch
SW6 . . . . 155 B3
Fulham Rd
Chelsea SW10 . . . 157 A4
Fulham SW6 . . . . 165 A4
Fuller Cl E2 . . 24 C1 99 B2
Fullers Ho 6
SW18 . . . . 58 C2
Fullerton Rd
SW18 . . . . 59 B2
Fullwood's Mews
N1 . . . . 97 C4
Fulmar Ct 6 SE21 . 75 C2

Fulmar Ho
12 Bermondsey
SE16 . . . . 40 C2
Marylebone NW8 . . 90 B1
Fulmead St SW6 . . 166 B3
Fulneck 1 E1 . . . . . 32 B4
Fulthorp Rd SE3 . . 53 C1
Fulton Mews W2 . 114 C4
Fulwood Pl WC1 . . 107 A3
Fulwood Wlk
SW19 . . . . 70 A3
Furber St W6 . . . . 39 A3
Furley Ho 7 SE15 . 49 C3
Furley Rd SE15 . . . 49 C3
Furlong Rd N7 . . . 14 C2
Furmage St SW18 . 71 A4
Furness Ho SW1 . . 146 A2
Furness Lo 4
SW14 . . . . 55 A3
Furness Prim Sch The
NW10 . . . . 21 C3
Furness Rd
Harlesden NW10 . . 21 C3
Sands End SW6 . . 166 B2
Furnival St EC4 . . 107 B2
Furrow La E9 . . . . 17 B3
Fursecroft W1 . . . 102 C2
Furze St E3 . . . . . . 33 C4
Fusion Ct SW15 . . 68 A1
Futters Ct 1
NW10 . . . . 21 A3
Fyfield N4 . . . . 5 C2
Fyfield Rd 8 SW9 . 62 C4
Fynes St SW1 . . . 147 B4

G

Gable Ho 12 W4 . . 38 A2
Gables Cl SE5 . . . . 49 A2
Gables The
1 Clapham SW4 . . 61 B4
Hampstead NW3 . . 2 C2
Gabriel Ho SE11 . . 148 C4
Gabrielle Ct NW3 . 11 C2
Gabriel Mews NW2 . 1 B2
Gabriel's Wharf
SE1 . . . . 121 B2
Gaddesden Ho
EC1 . . . . 97 C3
Gadsden Ho
8 Homerton E9 . . . 17 C2
13 Kensal Town
W10 . . . . 23 A1
Gagarin Ho SW11 . 59 C4
Gage Rd E16 . . . . 35 A4
Gage St WC1 . . . . 106 B4
Gainford Ho 8 E2 . 25 A2
Gainford St N1 . . . 85 B4
Gainsborough Ct
6 Bermondsey
SE16 . . . . 40 A1
Dulwich SE21 . . . . 76 A2
Shepherd's Bush
W12 . . . . 39 B4
Gainsborough Gdns
Golders Green
NW11 . . . . 1 B4
Hampstead NW3 . . 2 C1
Gainsborough Ho
Finsbury Pk N4 . . . 5 B3
3 Hampstead NW3 . 11 C4
4 Limehouse E14 . . 33 A2
Westminster SW1 . 147 C3
Gainsborough Prim
Sch E9 . . . . 18 C2

Gainsborough Rd
Bedford Pk W4 . . . 38 B2
Richmond TW9 . . . 54 B4
Gainsborough St 3
E9 . . . . 18 B2
Gainsborough Studios
N1 . . . . 87 B3
Gainsford St SE1 . 139 A4
Gairloch Ho 2
NW1 . . . . 13 C1
Gairloch Rd SE5 . . 49 A1
Gaisford St NW5 . . 13 B2
Gaitskell Ct SW11 . 168 A2
Gaitskell Ho SE17 . 48 C4
Gaitskell Way
SE1 . . . . 136 C4
Galata Rd SW13 . . 46 C3
Galatea Sq SE15 . . 65 A4
Galaxy Bldg 8
E14 . . . . 41 C2
Galaxy Ho EC2 . . . 97 C2
Galbraith St E14 . . 42 B3
Gale Ho 10 SW2 . . 62 B2
Galena Ho 5 W6 . . 39 A2
Galena Rd W6 . . . 39 A2
Galen Pl WC1 . . . 106 B3
Galesbury Rd
SW18 . . . . 59 B1
Gales Gdns E2 . . . 25 A2
Gale St E3 . . . . . . 33 C4
Galgate Cl 4
SW19 . . . . 70 A3
Galleon Cl 6 SE16 . 40 C4
Galleon Ho 8 E14 . 42 B2
Galleria Ct 5 SE15 . 49 B4
Gallery Ct SW10 . . 156 C3
Gallery Rd SE21 . . 75 C3
Galleywall Rd
SE16 . . . . 40 A2
Galleywall Road Trad
Est 12 SE16 . . . . 40 A2
Galleywood Ho 1
W10 . . . . 30 B4
Gallia Rd N5 . . . . . 15 A3
Galloway Rd W12 . 29 C1
Galsworthy Ave
E14 . . . . 33 A4
Galsworthy Ct W3 . 37 A3
Galsworthy Ho 2
W11 . . . . 31 A3
Galsworthy Rd
NW2 . . . . 10 A4
Galton St W10 . . . 23 A2
Galveston Ho 2
E1 . . . . 26 A1
Galveston Rd
SW15 . . . . 58 B2
Galway Cl 23 SE16 . 40 A1
Galway Ho
Finsbury EC1 . . . . 97 A3
1 Stepney E1 . . . . 32 C4
Galway St EC1 . . . 97 A3
Gambetta St SW8 . 170 B1
Gambia St SE1 . . . 122 B1
Gambier Ho 6 EC1 . 97 A3
Gamlen Rd SW15 . 57 C3
Gandolfi St 5
SE15 . . . . 49 A4
Ganley Ct 16
SW11 . . . . 59 C4
Gannet Ct 5 SE21 . 75 C2
Gannet Ho SE15 . . 49 B2
Ganton St W1 . . . 105 A1
Garand Ct 2 N7 . . 14 B3
Garbett Ho 2
SE17 . . . . 48 A4
Garbutt Pl W1 . . . 103 C3
Garden Cl SW15 . . 69 A4

Garden Ct
4 Richmond TW9 . . 44 B2
12 South Acton W4 . 37 B3
St John's Wood
NW8 . . . . 89 B4
Strand EC4 . . . . 121 B4
Garden Flats
SW6 . . . . 74 A1
Garden Ho SW9 . . 172 B2
Garden La SW2 . . . 74 B3
Garden Mews
W2 . . . . . . 31 C2 113 C3
Garden Pl 78 E2 . . . 24 B4
Garden Rd
Richmond TW9 . . . 54 C4
St John's Wood
NW8 . . . . 89 A4
Garden Row SE1 . 136 A2
Garden Royal 6
SW15 . . . . 57 C1
Garden St E1 . . . . 32 C4
Gardens The
East Dulwich SE22 . 64 C3
Stamford Hill N16 . . 7 B4
Garden Terr
Knightsbridge
SW1 . . . . 130 B3
Pimlico SW1 . . . . 147 B2
Garden Wlk
EC2 . . . . . . 24 A1 98 A2
Gardiner Ave NW2 . 9 B3
Gardiner Ct NW10 . 20 C4
Gardiner Ho
SW11 . . . . 168 A1
Gardner Ct N5 . . . 15 B4
Gardners La EC4 . 122 C4
Gardnor Mans 14
NW3 . . . . 11 B4
Gardnor Rd NW3 . . 11 C4
Gard St EC1 . . . . . 96 B4
Gareth Ct SW16 . . 73 C1
Garfield Ho W2 . . 102 C1
Garfield Mews 7
SW11 . . . . 60 C4
Garfield Rd SW11 . 60 C4
Garford St E14 . . . 33 C2
Garland Ct 12 E14 . 33 C2
Garland Ho N16 . . . 6 C1
Garlands Ho NW8 . 78 B2
Garlick Hill EC4 . . 123 A4
Garlinge Ho SW9 . 173 B4
Garlinge Rd NW2 . 10 B2
Garnault Mews
EC1 . . . . 95 C3
Garnault Pl EC1 . . 95 C3
Garner St E2 . . . . . 24 C3
Garnet Rd NW10 . . 8 A2
Garnet St E1 . . . . . 32 B2
Garnett Ho 5
NW3 . . . . 12 B3
Garnett Rd NW3 . . 12 B3
Garnham St 1 N16 . 7 B2
Garnies Cl SE15 . . 49 B3
Garrad's Rd SW16 . 73 C1
Garrard Wlk NW10 . 8 A2
Garratt Ho 8 N16 . . 7 A3
Garratt La SW18 . . 71 A3
Garratt Park Sch
SW18 . . . . 71 B1
Garraway Ct SW13 . 47 B3
Garraway Ho SE21 . 76 B1
Garrett Cl W3 . . . . 28 C4
Garrett Ho
W12 . . . . 30 A3

Garrett St EC1 . . . .**97 A2**
Garrick Cl SW18 . . . . . .**59 B3**
Garrick Ho
  Chiswick W4 . . . .**46 A4**
  Mayfair W1 . . . .**118 A1**
Garrick Rd TW9 . . . .**44 C1**
Garrick St WC2 . . . .**120 A4**
Garrick Yd WC2 . . . .**120 A4**
Garsdale Terr
  SW5 . . . .**141 A2**
Garsington Mews
  SE4 . . . .**66 B4**
Garson Ho W2 . . . .**116 B4**
Garston Ho 6 N1 . . . .**15 A1**
Garter Way SE16 . . . . . .**40 C4**
Garth Ct W4 . . . .**45 C4**
Garth Ho NW2 . . . .**1 B2**
Garth Rd
  Child's Hill NW2 . . . .**1 B2**
  8 Kentish Town W4 . . .**37 C1**
Gartmoor Gdns
  SW19 . . . .**70 B3**
Garton Ho 6 N6 . . . . . .**4 C4**
Garton Pl SW18 . . . .**59 B1**
Gartons Way . . . .
  SW11 . . . .**59 B4**
Garway Rd W2 . . . .**100 A1**
Gascony Pl
  E2 . . . .**24 B2 98 C3**
Gascony Ave NW6 . . . . .**10 C1**
Gascoyne Ho 2
  E9 . . . .**17 C1**
Gascoyne Rd E9 . . . .**17 C1**
Gaselee St E14 . . . .**34 B2**
Gasholder Pl
  SE11 . . . .**149 A1**
Gaskarth Rd SW12 . . . . .**61 A1**
Gaskell St SW4 . . . .**172 A2**
Gaskin Ho N16 . . . .**6 C1**
Gaskin St N1 . . . .**86 A4**
Gaspar Cl SW7 . . . .**142 B4**
Gaspar Mews
  SW5 . . . .**142 B4**
Gasson Ho 24
  SE14 . . . .**50 C4**
Gaston Bell Cl
  TW9 . . . .**54 B4**
Gaston Gate SW8 . . . . .**172 C4**
Gataker Ho 5
  SE16 . . . .**40 A3**
Gataker St 5
  SE16 . . . .**40 A3**
Gatcliff Cl SW1 . . . .**145 C1**
Gatcombe Ho 20 . . . .
  SE22 . . . .**64 A4**
Gatcombe Rd
  8 Newham E16 . . . . . .**35 C1**
  Tufnell Pk N19 . . . .**4 C1**
Gatefield Ct SE15 . . . . . .**64 C4**
Gateforth St NW8 . . . . . .**90 A1**
Gate Hill Ct
  W11 . . . . . .**31 B1 113 A2**
Gatehouse Sch 2 . . . .
  E2 . . . .**25 C3**
Gatehouse Sq
  SE1 . . . .**123 A2**
Gateley Ho 6 . . . .
  SE4 . . . .**65 C3**
Gateley Rd SW9 . . . .**62 B4**
Gate Mews SW7 . . . . . .**130 B3**
Gatesborough St . . . .
  EC2 . . . .**24 A1 98 A2**
Gates Ct SE17 . . . .**150 C2**
Gatesden WC1 . . . .**94 B3**
Gateside Rd SW17 . . . . .**72 B1**

Gate St WC2 . . . .**106 C2**
Gateway SE17 . . . .**48 B4**
Gateway Arc N1 . . . .**86 A2**
Gateway Ho SW12 . . . . .**61 A1**
Gateway Mews 4 . . . .
  E8 . . . .**16 B3**
Gateway Prim Sch . . . .
  NW8 . . . .**89 C2**
Gateways The . . . .
  SW3 . . . .**144 B3**
Gateway Trad Est . . . .
  NW10 . . . .**21 B2**
Gathorne St 19 E2 . . . .**25 C3**
Gatliff Rd SW1 . . . .**146 A1**
Gatonby St SE15 . . . . . .**49 B2**
Gatwick Ho 8 . . . .
  E14 . . . .**33 B3**
Gatwick Rd SW18 . . . . . .**70 B4**
Gauden Cl SW4 . . . .**61 C4**
Gauden Rd SW4 . . . .**61 C1**
Gaugin Ho 13 SE16 . . . .**40 A1**
Gaunt St SE1 . . . .**136 C2**
Gautrey Rd SE15 . . . . . .**50 B1**
Gavel St SE17 . . . .**151 C4**
Gaverick Mews 3 . . . .
  E14 . . . .**41 C2**
Gaviller Pl 8 E5 . . . . . .**17 A4**
Gawber St 2 E2 . . . . . .**25 B2**
Gawthorne Ct E3 . . . . . .**26 C3**
Gay Cl NW2 . . . .**9 A3**
Gaydon Ho W2 . . . .**100 A4**
Gayfere St SW1 . . . .**134 A1**
Gayford Rd W12 . . . . . .**38 B4**
Gay Ho N16 . . . .**16 A3**
Gayhurst SE17 . . . .**48 C4**
Gayhurst Ho NW8 . . . . . .**90 B2**
Gayhurst Prim Sch . . . .
  E8 . . . .**16 C1**
Gayhurst Rd E8 . . . .**16 C1**
Gaymead NW8 . . . .**78 B3**
Gay Rd E15 . . . .**27 C3**
Gaysley Ho SE11 . . . . . .**149 B3**
Gay St SW15 . . . .**57 C4**
Gayton Cres NW3 . . . . . .**11 C4**
Gayton Ho E3 . . . .**26 C1**
Gayton Rd NW3 . . . .**11 C4**
Gayville Rd SW11 . . . . . .**60 B1**
Gaywood Cl SW2 . . . . . .**74 C3**
Gaywood St SE1 . . . . . .**136 B1**
Gaza St SE17 . . . .**150 A1**
Gaze Ho 11 E14 . . . .**34 C3**
Gean Ct 3 E11 . . . .**19 C4**
Geary Ho N7 . . . .**14 B3**
Geary Rd NW10 . . . .**8 C3**
Geary St N7 . . . .**14 B3**
Gedling Ho SE22 . . . . . .**64 B4**
Gedling Pl SE1 . . . .**139 A2**
Gees Ct W1 . . . .**103 C1**
Gee St EC1 . . . .**96 C2**
Geffrye Ct 1 N1 . . . .**24 A3**
Geffrye Mus * 1 N1 . . . .
Geffrye St E2 . . . .**24 B3**
Geldart Rd SE15 . . . .**50 A3**
Geldeston Rd E5 . . . .**7 C2**
Gellatly Rd SE14 . . . .**50 C1**
Gemini Bsns Ctr . . . .
  E16 . . . .**27 C1**
Gemini Ho 11 E3 . . . .**26 C4**
General Wolfe Rd . . . .
  SE10 . . . .**52 C2**
Genesis Bsns Pk . . . .
  NW10 . . . .**20 A3**
Geneva Ct . . . .
  1 Putney SW15 . . . . . .**57 C2**
  Stoke Newington N16 . . .**6 C3**
Geneva Dr SW9 . . . .**62 C3**
Genoa Ave SW15 . . . . . .**57 B2**

Genoa Ho 19 E1 . . . . . .**25 C1**
Geoffrey Chaucer . . . .
  Tech Coll SE1 . . . .**137 C1**
Geoffrey Cl SE5 . . . .**48 B1**
Geoffrey Ct SE4 . . . .**66 B4**
Geoffrey Ho SE1 . . . . . .**137 C2**
Geoffrey Jones Ct . . . .
  NW10 . . . .**21 C4**
Geoffrey Rd SE4 . . . .**66 B4**
George Beard Rd 11 . . . .
  SE8 . . . .**41 B2**
George Beare Lo 9 . . . .
  SW4 . . . .**61 B2**
George Belt Ho 8 . . . .
  E2 . . . .**25 C2**
George Ct WC2 . . . .**120 B3**
George Downing Est . . . .
  N16 . . . .**7 B2**
George Eliot Ho . . . .
  SW1 . . . .**147 A3**
George Eliot Jun & Inf . . . . . .
  Schs NW8 . . . .**79 B4**
George Elliot Ho . . . .
  SE17 . . . .**150 C2**
George Elliston Ho . . . .
  SE1 . . . .**153 B1**
George Eyre Ho . . . .
  NW8 . . . .**79 C1**
George Green's Sec . . . .
  Sch E14 . . . .**42 B1**
George Inn Yd . . . .
  SE1 . . . .**123 B1**
George La SE13 . . . .**67 B1**
George Lansbury Ho . . . .
  7 Bow E3 . . . .**26 B2**
  3 Willesden NW10 . . . . .**8 B1**
George Lashwood Ct . . . .
  12 SW9 . . . .**62 B3**
George Leybourne Ho . . . .
  E1 . . . .**125 C4**
George Lindgren Ho . . . .
  SE15 . . . .**49 C3**
George Loveless Ho . . . .
  E2 . . . .**24 B2 99 A4**
George Mathers Rd . . . .
  SE11 . . . .**150 A4**
George Mews . . . .
  NW1 . . . .**92 C3**
George Peabody Ct . . . .
  NW1 . . . .**102 A4**
George Row SE16 . . . . .**139 B3**
George's Rd N7 . . . .**14 B3**
George's Sq SW6 . . . . .**155 A4**
George St . . . .
  6 Canning Town . . . .
  E16 . . . .**35 B3**
  Marylebone W1 . . . . . .**103 A2**
George Tingle Ho . . . .
  SE1 . . . .**139 A2**
Georgette Pl SE10 . . . . . .**52 B3**
George Vale Ho 15 . . . .
  E2 . . . .**24 C3**
George Walter Ho . . . .
  SE16 . . . .**40 B2**
George Wyver Cl . . . .
  SW18 . . . .**70 A4**
George Yd . . . .
  City of London . . . .
  EC3 . . . .**109 C1**
  Mayfair W1 . . . .**117 C4**
Georgiana St NW1 . . . . . .**83 A4**
Georgian Ct 12 E9 . . . . .**25 B4**
Georgina Gdns . . . .
  E2 . . . .**24 B2 99 A4**
Geraldine Rd . . . .
  Brentford W4 . . . .**44 C4**
  Wandsworth SW18 . . . . .**59 B2**

Geraldine St . . . .
  SE11 . . . .**136 A1**
Gerald Mews . . . .
  SW1 . . . .**145 C4**
Gerald Rd SW1 . . . .**145 C4**
Gerard Ct NW2 . . . .**9 C3**
Gerard Rd SW13 . . . . . .**46 B2**
Gerards Cl SE16 . . . .**40 B1**
Gernigan Ho . . . .
  SW18 . . . .**59 C1**
Gernon Rd E3 . . . .**26 A3**
Gerrard Ho 5 . . . .
  SE14 . . . .**50 C3**
Gerrard Pl W1 . . . .**119 C4**
Gerrard Rd N1 . . . .**86 B2**
Gerrard St W1 . . . .**119 C4**
Gerridge Ct SE1 . . . . . .**135 C2**
Gerridge St SE1 . . . . . .**135 C2**
Gerry Raffles Sq . . . .
  E15 . . . .**19 C2**
Gertrude St . . . .
  SW10 . . . .**157 A3**
Gervase St SE15 . . . .**50 A3**
Getters Talmud Torah . . . .
  N16 . . . .**7 B3**
Ghent Way 8 E8 . . . .**16 B2**
Giant Arches Rd . . . .
  SE24 . . . .**63 B1**
Gibbings Ho SE1 . . . . . .**136 B3**
Gibbins Rd E15 . . . .**19 B1**
Gibbon Ho NW8 . . . .**89 C1**
Gibbon Rd . . . .
  Acton W3 . . . .**29 A2**
  Nunhead SE15 . . . .**50 B1**
Gibbons Rd NW10 . . . . . .**8 A2**
Gibbon's Rents . . . .
  SE1 . . . .**124 A1**
Gibbon Wlk SW15 . . . . .**56 C3**
Gibbs Green Cl . . . .
  W14 . . . .**140 C2**
Gibbs Green Sch . . . .
  W14 . . . .**141 A2**
Gibbs Ho 5 SW12 . . . . . .**73 A4**
Gibraltar Ho . . . .
  NW10 . . . .**21 A3**
Gibraltar Wlk . . . .
  E2 . . . .**24 B2 99 A3**
Gibson Cl E1 . . . .**25 B1**
Gibson Gdns N16 . . . .**7 B2**
Gibson Rd SE11 . . . .**149 A3**
Gibson Sq N1 . . . .**85 C3**
Gibson St SE10 . . . .**43 A1**
Gideon Rd SW11 . . . .**60 C4**
Giesbach Rd N19 . . . .**4 C2**
Giffen Square Mkt . . . .
  SE8 . . . .**51 C3**
Giffin St SE8 . . . .**51 C3**
Gifford Ho . . . .
  8 Clapham SW4 . . . . . .**61 C3**
  Pimlico SW1 . . . .**146 C1**
Gifford St N1 . . . .**84 B4**
Gilbert Ho . . . .
  Barbican EC2 . . . .**109 A3**
  Deptford SE8 . . . .**51 C4**
  5 Globe Town E2 . . . . .**25 C2**
  Pimlico SW1 . . . .**146 B1**
  South Lambeth . . . .
  SW8 . . . .**162 A2**
Gilbert Pl WC1 . . . .**106 A3**
Gilbert Rd SE11 . . . .**149 C4**
Gilbert Sheldon Ho . . . .
  W2 . . . .**101 C4**
Gilbertson Ho 11 . . . .
  E14 . . . .**41 C3**
Gilbert St W1 . . . .**103 C1**

Gilbeys Yd NW1 . . . .**12 C1**
Gilby Ho 5 E9 . . . .**17 C2**
Gilda Cres N16 . . . .**7 C3**
Gildea St W1 . . . .**104 B3**
Gilden Cres NW5 . . . . . .**12 C3**
Giles Ho . . . .
  Bermondsey SE16 . . . .**139 B2**
  Notting Hill W11 . . . . . .**31 C3**
Gilesmead SE5 . . . .**48 C2**
Gilkes Cres SE21 . . . .**64 A4**
Gilkes Pl SE21 . . . .**64 A4**
Gillam Ho 9 SE16 . . . . . .**40 B2**
Gill Ave E16 . . . .**35 C3**
Gillender St E3 . . . .**27 B1**
Gillespie Prim Sch . . . .
  N5 . . . .**6 A1**
Gillespie Rd N4,N5 . . . . . .**6 A1**
Gillett Pl 21 E8 . . . .**16 A4**
Gillett St E8,N16 . . . .**16 A4**
Gillfoot NW1 . . . .**82 C1**
Gillian St SE13 . . . .**67 A2**
Gillies Ho 7 NW5 . . . . . .**12 C3**
Gilling Ct 5 NW3 . . . . . .**12 A2**
Gillingham Ho . . . .
  SW1 . . . .**146 C4**
Gillingham Mews . . . .
  SW1 . . . .**146 C4**
Gillingham Row 2 . . . .
  SW1 . . . .**146 C4**
Gillingham St . . . .
  SW1 . . . .**146 C4**
Gillison Wlk SE16 . . . . .**139 C2**
Gillman Ho 24 E2 . . . . . .**24 C3**
Gillray Ho SW10 . . . . . .**157 B3**
Gill St E14 . . . .**33 B2**
Gilmore Ho SW4 . . . .**60 B3**
Gilmore Rd SE13 . . . .**67 C3**
Gilpin Ave SW14 . . . .**55 C3**
Gilpin Cl W2 . . . .**101 A4**
Gilpin Rd E5 . . . .**18 A4**
Gilray Ho W2 . . . .**115 B4**
Gilstead Ho SW6 . . . . . .**166 B2**
Gilston Rd SW10 . . . . . .**143 A1**
Giltspur St EC1 . . . .**108 B2**
Gilwell Ct 7 E5 . . . .**17 A4**
Gipsy Cnr W3 . . . .**28 C4**
Gipsy La SW15 . . . .**57 A4**
Gipsy Moth IV * . . . .
  SE10 . . . .**52 B4**
Giraud St E14 . . . .**34 A3**
Girdlers Rd W14 . . . .**39 C3**
Girdlestone Wlk . . . .
  N19 . . . .**4 B2**
Girdwood Rd SW18 . . . .
  SW19 . . . .**70 A4**
Girling Ho 9 N1 . . . .**24 A4**
Gironde Rd SW6 . . . . . .**155 A1**
Girton Ho SW15 . . . .**57 C1**
Girton Villas 6 . . . .
  W10 . . . .**30 C3**
Gisburn Ho 22 . . . .
  SE15 . . . .**49 C3**
Gissing Wlk N1 . . . .**14 C1**
Glade The W12 . . . .**39 A4**
Glading Terr N16 . . . .**7 B1**
Gladsmuir Rd N19 . . . . . .**4 B3**
Gladstone Ct . . . .
  Westminster SW1 . . . . .**147 C3**
  Willesden NW2 . . . .**9 A3**
Gladstone Ho 16 . . . .
  E14 . . . .**33 C3**
Gladstone Park Sch . . . .
  NW10 . . . .**9 A4**
Gladstone St SE1 . . . . .**136 A2**
Gladstone Terr . . . .

Gladstone Terr
SW8 . . . . **170 B4**
Gladwin Ho NW1 . . . **83 A1**
Gladwyn Rd SW15 . **57 C4**
Gladys Rd NW6 . . . . . . **10 C1**
Glaisher St SE8 . . . . **52 A4**
Glamis Ct W3 . . . . . . **37 A4**
Glamis Est **8** E1 . . **32 B2**
Glamis Pl E1 . . . . . . **32 B2**
Glamis Rd E1 . . . . . . **32 B2**
Glanville Ho **4**
SW12 . . . . **73 B4**
Glanville Rd SW2 . **62 A2**
Glasbury Ho **5**
SW9 . . . . **62 B3**
Glaserton Rd N16 . . **7 A4**
Glasgow Ho W9 . . . **78 B1**
Glasgow Terr
SW1 . . . . **146 C1**
Glasshill St SE1 . . **136 B3**
Glasshouse Fields
E1 . . . . **32 C2**
Glasshouse St
W1 . . . . **119 A3**
Glasshouse The
SE13 . . . . **67 B3**
Glasshouse Wlk
SE11 . . . . **148 C2**
Glasshouse Yd
EC1 . . . . **96 C1**
Glass St **4** E2 . . . . **25 A1**
Glastonbury Ct **12**
SE14 . . . . **50 B3**
Glastonbury Ho
SW1 . . . . **146 A2**
Glastonbury Pl **22**
E1 . . . . **32 B3**
Glastonbury St
NW6 . . . . **10 B3**
Glaucus St E3 . . . . . **34 A4**
Glazbury Rd W14 . **140 B2**
Glazebrook Cl
SE21 . . . . **75 C2**
Glebe Cl **1** W4 . . . **38 A1**
Glebe Ct **13** E3 . . . . **27 A2**
Glebelands Cl SE16 . **40 A3**
Glebelands SE15 . . **64 A4**
Glebe Pl SW3 . . . **158 A4**
Glebe Rd
Barnes SW13 . . . . . **46 C1**
Dalston E8 . . . . **16 B1**
Willesden NW10 . . . **8 C2**
Glebe St W4 . . . . . . **38 A1**
Gledhow Gdns
SW5 . . . . **142 C3**
Gledstanes Rd
W14 . . . . **140 B1**
Glegg Pl **3** SW15 **57 C3**
Glenaffric Ave
E14 . . . . **42 C2**
Glen Albyn Rd
SW19 . . . . **69 C2**
Glenalmond Ho **2**
SW15 . . . . **57 C1**
Glenarm Rd E5 . . . **17 C4**
Glenbrook Prim Sch
OW4 . . . . **61 C1**
Glenbrook Rd
NW6 . . . . **10 C3**
Glenburnie Rd
SW17 . . . . **72 B1**
Glencoe Mans
SW9 . . . . **163 B1**
Glendall St SW9 . . **62 B3**
Glendarvon St
SW15 . . . . **57 C4**

Glendower Gdns **10**
SW14 . . . . **55 C4**
Glendower Pl
SW7 . . . . **143 B4**
Glendower Prep Sch
SW7 . . . . **143 B4**
Glendower Rd
SW14 . . . . **55 C4**
Glendown Ho **2**
E8 . . . . **16 C3**
Glendun Ct W3 . . . **29 A2**
Glendun Rd W3 . . . **29 A2**
Gleneagles Cl **21**
SE16 . . . . **40 A1**
Glenelg Rd SW2 . . **62 A2**
Glenfield Rd
SW12 . . . . **73 B3**
Glenfinlas Way
SE5 . . . . **48 A3**
Glenforth St SE10 . **43 B1**
Glengall Gr E14 . . **42 B3**
Glengall Pass **2**
NW6 . . . . **23 C4**
Glengall Rd
Camberwell SE15 . **49 B4**
Kilburn NW6 . . . . . **23 B4**
Glengall Terr
SE15 . . . . **49 B4**
Glengarnock Ave
E14 . . . . **42 B2**
Glengarry Rd
SE22 . . . . **64 B2**
Glenhurst Ave
NW5 . . . . **12 C4**
Glenilla Rd NW3 . . **12 A2**
Glenister Rd SE10 . **43 B1**
Glenkerry Ho **1**
E14 . . . . **34 B3**
Glenloch Ct **2**
NW3 . . . . **12 A2**
Glenloch Rd NW3 . **12 A3**
Glenluce Rd SE3 . . **53 C4**
Glenmore SW15 . . . **57 C1**
Glenmore Ho **6**
TW10 . . . . **54 A1**
Glenmore Rd
NW3 . . . . **12 A2**
Glennie Ho SE10 . . **52 B2**
Glennie Rd SE27 . . . .
SW16 . . . . **74 C1**
Glenridding NW1 . **83 A1**
Glenrosa St SW6 . **166 C2**
Glenroy St W12 . . . **30 B3**
Glensdale Rd SE4 . **66 B4**
Glenshaw Mans
SW9 . . . . **163 B1**
Glentanner Way
SW17 . . . . **71 C1**
Glen Terr E14 . . . . **42 B4**
Glentham Gdns
SW13 . . . . **47 A4**
Glentham Rd
SW13 . . . . **47 A4**
Glenthorne Mews
W6 . . . . **39 A2**
Glenthorne Rd
W6 . . . . **39 A2**
Glenthorpe SW15 . **56 C3**
Glentworth St
NW1 . . . . **91 A1**
Glenville Gr SE8 . **51 B3**
Glenville Mews
SW18 . . . . **70 C4**
Glenworth Ave
E14 . . . . **42 C2**
Gliddon Dr E5 . . . . **17 A4**

Gliddon Rd W14 . . **140 A2**
Globe Pond Rd
SE16 . . . . **33 A1**
Globe Prim Sch
E2 . . . . **25 B2**
Globe Rd SE1, E2 . **25 B2**
Globe St SE1 . . . . . **137 B3**
Globe Terr **2** E2 . **25 B2**
Globe Theatre The*
SE1 . . . . **122 C3**
GLOBE TOWN **25 C2**
Globe View EC4 . . **122 C4**
Globe Yd W1 . . . . **104 A1**
Gloucester Ave
NW1 . . . . **81 C4**
Gloucester Cir
SE10 . . . . **52 B3**
Gloucester Cres
NW1 . . . . **82 A4**
Gloucester Ct
Borough The SE1 . **137 B4**
City of London EC3 **124 B3**
Dulwich SE22 . . . **76 C3**
Richmond TW9 . . **44 C3**
Gloucester Dr N4 . . **6 A2**
Gloucester Gate
NW1 . . . . **82 A2**
Gloucester Gate
Mews **2** NW1 . . **82 A2**
Gloucester Gdns
Golders Green
NW11 . . . . **1 B4**
Paddington W2 . . **100 C2**
Gloucester Ho
Kilburn NW6 . . . . . **23 C3**
Richmond TW10 . **54 C2**
Gloucester Mews
W2 . . . . **101 A1**
Gloucester Mews W
W2 . . . . **101 A1**
Gloucester Pk
SW7 . . . . **142 C4**
Gloucester Pl W1 **103 A4**
Gloucester Pl Mews
W1 . . . . **103 A3**
Gloucester Prim Sch
SE15 . . . . **49 A3**
Gloucester Rd
Acton W3 . . . . **37 B4**
Richmond TW9 . . **44 C3**
South Kensington
SW7 . . . . **142 C4**
Gloucester Road Sta
SW7 . . . . **142 C4**
Gloucester Sq
6 Hackney E2 . . **24 C4**
Paddington W2 . . **102 A1**
Gloucester St
SW1 . . . . **146 C2**
Gloucester Terr
W2 . . . . **101 A4**
Gloucester Way
EC1 . . . . **95 C3**
Gloucester Wlk
W8 . . . . **127 C4**
Glover Ho
London SE15 . . . . . **65 A3**
2 South Hampstead
NW6 . . . . **11 B1**
Glycena Rd SW11 . **60 B4**
Glyn Ct SE27 . . . . . **74 C1**
Glynde Mews
SW3 . . . . **130 B1**
Glynde Reach
WC1 . . . . **94 B3**

Glynde St SE4 . . . . **66 B1**
Glynfield Rd NW10 . **8 A1**
Glyn Mans W14 . . **140 B3**
Glyn Rd E5 . . . . . . **17 C4**
Glyn St SE11 . . . . **148 C1**
Goater's Alley
SW6 . . . . **155 A1**
Goat Wharf TW8 . . **44 A4**
Godalming Rd
E14 . . . . **34 A4**
Goddard Ho SW19 . **69 C2**
Goddard Pl N19 . . . **4 B1**
Godfrey Ho EC1 . . . **97 B3**
Godfrey St
Chelsea SW3 . . . . **144 B2**
Mill Meads E15 . . . **27 B3**
Goding St SE11 . . . **148 B1**
Godley Rd SW18 . . **71 C3**
Godliman St EC4 . **122 C4**
Godman Rd SE15 . . **50 A1**
Godolphin Ho
Primrose Hill NW3 . **12 A1**
7 Streatham SW2 . **74 C3**
Godolphin & Latymer
Sch W6 . . . . **39 A1**
Godolphin Pl W3 . . **28 C2**
Godolphin Rd
W12 . . . . **39 A4**
Godson St N1 . . . . . **85 B2**
Godstone Ct **1**
N16 . . . . **6 C3**
Godstone Ho SE1 **137 C2**
Godwin Cl N1 . . . . . **87 A2**
Godwin Ho
8 Haggerston E2 . **24 B3**
Kilburn NW6 . . . . . **23 C2**
Goffers Ho SE3 . . . **53 A1**
Goffers Rd SE3,
SE13 . . . . **53 A1**
Goffton Ho SW9 . . **173 A1**
Golborne Gdns
5 Kensal Town
W10 . . . . **23 A1**
West Kilburn W10 . **23 B1**
Golborne Mews **9**
W10 . . . . **31 A4**
Golborne Rd W10 . **31 A4**
Golden Cross Mews
2 W11 . . . . **31 B3**
Golden Hinde The*
SE1 . . . . **123 B2**
Golden Hind Pl **5**
SE8 . . . . **41 B2**
Golden La EC1 . . . . **97 A1**
Golden Plover Cl
E14 . . . . **34 A3**
Golden Sq W1 . . . **119 A4**
Golders Ct NW11 . . . **1 B4**
Golders Gdns
NW11 . . . . **1 B4**
GOLDERS GREEN . . . **1 C3**
Golders Green Coll
NW11 . . . . **1 C3**
Golders Green Cres
NW11 . . . . **1 C3**
Golders Green Rd
NW11 . . . . **1 A4**
Golders Green Sta
NW11 . . . . **1 C3**
Golders Hill Sch
NW11 . . . . **1 B4**
Golderslea NW11 . . . **1 C3**
Golders Park Cl
NW11 . . . . **1 C3**
Golders Way NW11 . **1 B4**

Goldhawk Ind Est The
W6 . . . . **39 A3**
Goldhawk Mews **2**
W12 . . . . **39 A4**
Goldhawk Rd W12 . **38 C3**
Goldhawk Road Sta
W12 . . . . **39 B4**
Goldhurst Terr
NW6 . . . . **11 B1**
Goldie Ho N19 . . . . . **4 C4**
Golding St E1 . . . . **111 C1**
Goldington Cres
NW1 . . . . **83 B2**
Goldington Ct
NW1 . . . . **83 B3**
Goldington St
NW1 . . . . **83 B2**
Goldman Cl
E2 . . . . **24 C1 99 B2**
Goldney Rd W9 . . . **23 C1**
Goldsboro Rd
SW8 . . . . **161 C1**
Goldsborough Ho
SW8 . . . . **171 C3**
Goldsmith Ave
W3 . . . . **28 C2**
Goldsmith Ct
WC1 . . . . **106 B2**
Goldsmith Ho W3 . **28 C2**
Goldsmith Rd
Acton W3 . . . . **28 C1**
Peckham SE15 . . . **49 C2**
Goldsmith's Bldgs
W3 . . . . **28 C1**
Goldsmiths Coll, Univ
of London SE14 . . **51 A2**
Goldsmith's Pl
NW6 . . . . **78 A3**
Goldsmith's Row
E2 . . . . **24 C3**
Goldsmith's Sq **17**
E2 . . . . **24 C3**
Goldthorpe NW1 . . **82 C3**
Goldwell Ho SE22 . **64 A3**
Goldwin Cl SE14 . . **50 B2**
Goldwing Cl E16 . . **35 C3**
Gomm Rd SE16 . . . **40 B3**
Gondar Gdns NW6 . **10 B3**
Gondar Mans
NW6 . . . . **10 B3**
Gonson St SE8 . . . . **52 A4**
Gonston Cl SW19 . **70 A2**
Gonville Ho **6**
SW15 . . . . **57 C1**
Gonville St SW6 . . **58 A4**
Gooch Ho EC1 . . . **107 B4**
Goodall Ho **10** SE4 . **65 C3**
Goodenough Coll
WC1 . . . . **94 C2**
Goodfaith Ho **18**
E14 . . . . **34 A2**
Goodge Pl W1 . . . **105 A3**
Goodge St W1 . . . **105 A3**
Goodge Street Sta
W1 . . . . **105 B4**
Goodhall St NW10 . **21 B2**
Good Hart Pl E14 . . **33 A2**
Goodhope Ho **17**
E14 . . . . **34 A2**
Gooding Cl N7 . . . . **14 A3**
Goodinge Rd N7 . . **14 A2**
Goodman Cres
SW2 . . . . **73 C2**

Goodman's Stile
E1 . . . . **111** B2
Goodman's Yd E1,
E3 . . . . **124** C4
Goodrich Com Sch
SE22 . . . . .64 C1
Goodrich Ct 9
W10 . . . . .30 C3
Goodrich Ho
20 Bethnal Green
E2 . . . . .25 B3
Stamford Hill N16 . . . .7 A4
Goodrich Rd SE22 . .64 C1
Good Shepherd RC
Prim Sch The
W12 . . . . .38 B4
Goodson Rd NW10 . .8 A1
Goodspeed Ho 20
E14 . . . . .34 A2
Goodsway NW1 . . . .84 A2
Goodway Gdns
E14 . . . . .34 C3
Goodwill Ho 22
E14 . . . . .34 A2
Goodwin Cl SE16 . .139 A1
Goodwin Ho 2
SE15 . . . . .65 A4
Goodwin Rd W12 . .38 C4
Goodwins Ct
WC2 . . . . .120 A4
Goodwin St N4 . . . . .5 C2
Goodwood Ct W1 . .104 B4
Goodwood Ho 3
W4 . . . . .37 B1
Goodwood Mans 1
SW9 . . . . .62 C4
Goodwood Rd
SE14 . . . . .51 A3
Goose Green Prim
Sch SE22 . . . . .64 B3
Goose Green Trad Est
SE22 . . . . .64 C3
Gophir La EC4 . . . . .123 B4
Gopsall St N1 . . . . . .87 C3
Gordon Ave SW14 . .56 A3
Gordonbrook Prim
Sch SE4 . . . . .66 C2
Gordonbrock Rd
SE4 . . . . .66 C2
Gordon Ct 5 W12 . .30 B3
Gordondale Rd SW18,
SW19 . . . . .70 C2
Gordon Gr SE5 . . . . .48 A1
Gordon Ho 17 E1 . . .32 B2
Gordon Hospl The
SW1 . . . . .147 B3
Gordon House Rd
NW5 . . . . .12 C4
Gordon Ho N16 . . . . .6 C3
Gordon Mans W1 . . .93 B1
Gordon Pl W8 . . . . .127 C4
Gordon Rd
Chiswick W4 . . . . . . .45 A4
Leyton E15 . . . . .19 B4
Peckham SE15 . . . . . .50 A1
Richmond TW9 . . . . . .44 B1
Gordon Sq WC1 . . . .93 C2
Gordon St WC1 . . . .93 B2
Gorefield Ho NW6 . .23 C3
Gorefield Pl NW6 . . .23 C3
Gore Rd E9 . . . . .25 B4
Gore Rd SW7 . . . . .129 A2
Gorham Ho 12
SW4 . . . . .61 B1

Gorham Pl
W11 . . . . . .31 A2 112 A3
Goring St EC3 . . . . .110 B2
Gorleston St W14 140 B4
Gorse Cl E16 . . . . . . .35 C3
Gorsefield Ho 6
E14 . . . . .33 C2
Gorst Rd
London SW11 . . . . . .60 B1
North Acton NW10 . . .20 C1
Gorsuch Pl 9
E2 . . . . .24 B2 98 C4
Gorsuch St
E2 . . . . .24 B2 98 C4
Gosberton Rd
SW12 . . . . .72 C3
Gosfield St W1 . . . .104 C3
Gosford St E2 . . . . . .26 B3
Goslett Yd WC2 . . . .105 C2
Gosling Ho 2 E1 . . . .32 B2
Gosling Way SW9 . .173 B4
Gospatric Home Ho
SW14 . . . . .56 A4
GOSPEL OAK 12 C4
Gospel Oak Prim Sch
NW5 . . . . .12 C4
Gospel Oak Sta
NW5 . . . . .12 C4
Gosport Ho 8
SW15 . . . . .68 C3
Gosset St
E2 . . . . .24 C2 99 B4
Gosterwood St
SE8 . . . . .51 A4
Goswell Pl EC1 . . . . .96 B3
Goswell Rd EC1 . . . . .96 B4
Gothic Ct 17 SE5 . . .48 B3
Gottfried Mews
NW5 . . . . .13 B4
Gough Ho N1 . . . . . . .86 B4
Gough Sq EC4 . . . . .107 C2
Gough St WC1 . . . . . .95 A1
Gough Wlk 14 E14 . .33 C3
Goulden Ho
SW11 . . . . .168 A2
Gouldman Ho 33
E1 . . . . .25 B1
Gould Terr 28 E8 . . .17 A3
Goulston St E1 . . . . .110 C2
Goulton Rd E5 . . . . .17 A4
Govan St E2 . . . . . . .24 C4
Gover Ct SW4 . . . . .172 B2
Gowan Ave SW6 . . .164 A4
Gowan Ho
E2 . . . . .24 B2 99 A3
Gowan Rd NW10 . . . .9 A2
Gower Ct SW4 . . . . . .61 B1
Gower Ho SE17 . . . .151 A2
Gower Mews
WC1 . . . . .105 C4
Gower Pl NW1,
WC1 . . . . .93 B2
Gower Sch The
N7 . . . . .14 A2
Gower St WC1 . . . . . .93 B1
Gower's Wlk E1 . . . .111 B1
Gowlett Rd SE15 . . . .64 C4
Gowrie Rd SW11 . . . .60 C4
Gracechurch St EC2,
EC4 . . . . .123 C4
Gracefield Gdns
SW16 . . . . .74 A1
Gracehill 2 E1 . . . . .32 B4
Grace Ho SE11 . . . . .163 A4
Grace Jones Cl
E8 . . . . .16 C2

Grace Pl E3 . . . . .27 A2
Graces Mews NW8 . .79 A1
Grace's Mews SE5 . . .49 A1
Grace's Rd SE5 . . . . .49 A1
Grace St E3 . . . . .27 A2
Graemesdyke Ave
SW14 . . . . .55 A3
Grafton Cres NW1 . .13 A2
Grafton Ct 8 E8 . . . .16 C3
Grafton Ho
10 Bow E3 . . . . .26 C2
2 Deptford SE8 . . . . .41 B1
Grafton Mans
SW4 . . . . .61 B3
Grafton Mews W1 . . .92 C1
Grafton Pl NW1 . . . . .93 C3
Grafton Prim Sch
N7 . . . . .5 A1
Grafton Rd
Acton W3 . . . . .28 B2
Gospel Oak NW5 . . . .12 C3
Grafton Sq SW4 . . . .61 B4
Grafton St W1 . . . . .118 B3
Grafton Terr NW5 . . .12 C3
Grafton Way W1 . . . .93 A1
Grafton Yd NW5 . . . .13 A2
Graham Ct 5
SE14 . . . . .50 C4
Graham Ho
5 Balham SW12 . . . .73 A4
6 Tufnell Pk N19 . . . .13 C4
Graham Mans 2
E8 . . . . .17 A2
Graham Rd
Acton W4 . . . . .37 C3
Dalston E8 . . . . .16 C2
Graham St N1 . . . . . .86 B1
Graham Terr
SW1 . . . . .145 C3
Graham Twr W3 . . . .37 A3
Grainger Ct 27
SE5 . . . . .48 B3
Grampian Gdns
NW2 . . . . .1 A3
Grampians The 10
W14 . . . . .39 C4
Granard Ave
SW15 . . . . .57 A2
Granard Ho 20 E9 . .17 C2
Granard Prim Sch
SW15 . . . . .57 A1
Granard Rd SW11,
SW12 . . . . .59 C3
Granary Rd E1 . . . . . .25 A1
Granary Sq N1 . . . . . .14 C2
Granary St NW1 . . . .83 B3
Granary The SE8 . . . .51 C3
Granby Pl SE1 . . . . .135 B3
Granby St
Bethnal Green
E2 . . . . .24 C1 99 B2
Shoreditch
E2 . . . . .24 B1 99 A2
Granby Terr NW1 . . .82 C1
Grand Ave EC1 . . . . .108 B4
Grandfield Ct W4 . . .45 C4
Grandison Rd
SW11 . . . . .60 B2
Grand Junction Wharf
N1 . . . . .86 C1
Grand Par SW14 . . . .55 B3
Grand Union Cl
W9 . . . . .31 B4
Grand Union Cres
E8 . . . . .24 C4
Grand Union Ind Est
NW10 . . . . .20 A3

Grand Vitesse Ind Est
SE1 . . . . .122 B1
Granfield St
SW11 . . . . .167 C3
Grangecourt Rd
N16 . . . . .7 A3
Grange Ct
Peckham SE15 . . . . . .49 B1
Strand WC2 . . . . . . .107 A1
Grange Gdns NW3 . . .2 A1
Grange Gr N1 . . . . . . .15 B2
Grange Ho
Bermondsey SE1 . . . .138 C1
Willesden NW10 . . . . .9 A1
Grange La SE21 . . . . .76 B2
Grangemill
NW5 . . . . .13 A4
GRANGE MILLS 73 B3
Grange Mills
SW12 . . . . .73 B3
Grange Pl NW6 . . . . .10 C1
Grange Prim Sch
SE1 . . . . .138 A1
Grange Rd
Barnes SW13 . . . . . . .46 C2
Bermondsey SE1 . . . .138 C1
Gunnersbury W4 . . . .37 A1
Willesden NW10 . . . . .9 A2
Grange St N1 . . . . . . .87 C3
Grange The
Bermondsey SE1 . . . .138 C1
7 Gunnersbury
W4 . . . . .37 A1
Hammersmith W12 . .39 A3
19 Maitland Pk
NW3 . . . . .12 B2
South Acton W3 . . . . .37 A4
West Kensington
W14 . . . . .140 C3
Grangeway NW6 . . . .10 C1
Grange Wlk SE1 . . . .138 C1
Grange Yd SE1 . . . . .138 C1
Granite Apts E15 . . . .19 C2
Grannary The 10
SE16 . . . . .40 B4
Gransden Ave E8 . . . .17 A1
Gransden Ho 8
SE8 . . . . .41 B1
Gransden Rd W12 . . .38 B4
Grantbridge St N1 . . .86 B2
Grantham Ct 8
SE16 . . . . .40 C4
Grantham Ho 2
SE15 . . . . .49 C4
Grantham Pl W1 . . . .118 A1
Grantham Rd
Chiswick W4 . . . . . . .46 A3
South Lambeth
SW9 . . . . .172 B1
Grant Ho
Clapham SW8 . . . . . .171 B1
Clerkenwell EC1 . . . .108 B4
Grantley Ho
2 Deptford SE14 . . . .50 C4
5 Putney SW19 . . . . .69 C3
Grantley St E1 . . . . . .25 C1
Grant Mus of Zoology
& Comparative
Anatomy* W1 . . . . . .93 B1
Grant Rd SW11 . . . . .60 A4
Grant St N1 . . . . .85 B2
Grantully Rd W9 . . . .88 A3
Granville Ct
8 Deptford SE14 . . . .51 A3
Shoreditch N1 . . . . . .87 C3

Granville Gr SE13 . . .67 B4
Granville Ho 18
E14 . . . . .33 C3
Granville Ind Est
NW2 . . . . .1 B1
Granville Mans 8
W12 . . . . .39 B4
Granville Pk SE13 . . .67 C4
Granville Pl
Marylebone W1 . . . . .103 B1
Walham Green
SW6 . . . . .156 A1
Granville Point
NW2 . . . . .1 B2
Granville Rd
Child's Hill NW2 . . . . .1 B2
Kilburn NW6 . . . . . . .23 C3
Wandsworth SW18 . . .70 B4
Granville Sq
1 Camberwell
SE15 . . . . .49 A3
Finsbury WC1 . . . . . . .95 A3
Granville St WC1 . . . .95 A3
Grape St WC2 . . . . .106 A2
Grasgarth Cl W3 . . . .28 B2
Grasmere NW1 . . . . .92 B3
Grasmere Ave W3 . . .28 C2
Grasmere Ct
SW13 . . . . .46 C4
Grasmere Ho 20
N16 . . . . .15 C4
Grasmere Point 2
SE15 . . . . .50 B3
Grasmere Prim Sch
N16 . . . . .15 C4
Grateley Ho 10
SW15 . . . . .69 A3
Gratton Rd W14 . . .126 A1
Graveley Ho 7
SE8 . . . . .41 A2
Gravel La E1 . . . . . . .110 C2
Gravesend Rd
W12 . . . . .29 C2
Grayfriars Pas
EC1 . . . . .108 B2
Gray Ho SE17 . . . . .151 A2
Grayland Ct WC1 . . .94 C3
Grayling Rd N16 . . . . .6 C2
Grayling Sq
E2 . . . . .24 C2 99 C4
Grayshott Rd
SW11 . . . . .60 C4
Gray's Inn* WC1 107 A4
Gray's Inn PI WC1 107 A3
Gray's Inn Rd WC1 95 A2
Gray's Inn Sq
WC1 . . . . .107 B4
Grayson Ho EC1 . . . . .97 A3
Gray St SE1 . . . . . . .135 C3
Grayswood Point 14
SW15 . . . . .68 C3
Gray's Yd W1 . . . . . .103 C2
Grazebrook Prim Sch
N16 . . . . .7 A2
Grazebrook Rd N16 . .6 C2
Great Arthur Ho
EC1 . . . . .96 C1
Great Bell Alley
EC2 . . . . .109 B2
Great Castle St
W1 . . . . .104 C2
Great Central St
NW1 . . . . .102 C4
Great Chapel St
W1 . . . . .105 B2
Great Chart St
SW11 . . . . .59 B3

Great Chertsey Rd
SW14, W4.........45 C2
Great Church La
W6.........39 C1
Great College St
SW1.........134 A2
Great Croft WC1.....94 B3
Great Cross Ave
SE3.........53 A3
Great Cumberland
Mews W1.........102 C1
Great Cumberland Pl
W1.........103 A1
Great Dover St
SE1.........137 B2
Great Eastern Bldgs
10 E8.........17 A2
Great Eastern Ent Ctr
E14.........42 A4
Great Eastern Pier
E14.........41 C1
Great Eastern Rd
E15.........19 C2
Great Eastern St
EC2.........24 A1 98 A2
Great Eastern Wharf
SW11.........158 B1
Great Field 7
NW5.........13 B3
Greatfield Cl
London SE4.........66 C3
4 Tufnell Pk N19....13 B4
Great George St
SW1.........134 A3
Great Guildford Bsns
Sq SE1.........122 C1
Great Guildford St
SE1.........122 C1
Greatham Wlk 8
SW15.........68 C3
Great James St
WC1.........106 C4
Great Marlborough St
W1.........104 C1
Great Maze Pond
SE1.........137 C4
Great Newport St
WC2.........120 A4
Greatorex Ho 1 E1..111 B4
Greatorex St 11 E1..111 B4
Great Ormond St
Hospl for Children
WC1.........94 C1
Great Ormond St
WC1.........94 C1
Great Percy St
WC1.........95 B4
Great Peter St
SW1.........133 C1
Great Portland St
W1.........104 B4
Great Portland Street
Sta W1.........92 B1
Great Pulteney St
W1.........119 A4
Great Queen St
WC2.........106 B2
Great Russell Mans
WC1.........106 A3
Great Russell St
WC1.........106 A3
Great St Helen's
EC3.........110 A2
Great St Thomas
Apostle EC4....123 A4
Great Scotland Yard
SW1, WC2.......120 A2

Great Smith St
SW1.........133 C2
Great Spilmans
SE22.........64 A2
Great Suffolk St
SE1.........122 B1
Great Sutton St
EC1.........96 B1
Great Swan Alley
EC2.........109 B2
Great Titchfield St
W1.........104 C3
Great Tower St
EC3.........124 A4
Great Trinity La
EC4.........123 A4
Great Turnstile
WC2.........107 A3
Great Western Rd W2,
W9.........31 B4
Great West Rd W4,
W6.........45 C4
Great West Road
Cedars Rd W4....45 B4
Great West Road
Hogarth La W4....46 A4
Great Winchester St
EC2.........109 C2
Great Windmill St
W1.........119 B4
Great Yd SE1.......138 B4
Greaves Cotts 9
E14.........33 A4
Greaves Twr
SW10.........157 A2
Grebe Ct 16 E14....42 B4
Greek Ct W1........105 C1
Greek St W1........105 C1
Greenacre Ct 8 SE16 C3
Greenacre Sq 26
SE16.........40 C4
Greenaleaf Cl 1
SW2.........74 C4
Green Arbour Ct
EC1.........108 A2
Greenaway Gdns
NW3.........11 A4
Greenaway Ho
Finsbury WC1.....95 B3
St John's Wood
NW8.........78 C4
Green Bank 1 E1....32 A1
Greenberry St
NW8.........80 A1
Green Cl NW11......1 C4
Greencoat Pl
SW1.........147 A4
Greencoat Row
SW1.........133 B1
Greencourt Ho 25
E1.........25 C1
Greencroft Gdns
NW6.........11 B1
Green Ct 2 NW10...8 A4
Green Dale SE22...64 A2
Greendale Cl SE22..64 A2
Green Dragon Ct
SE1.........123 B1
Green Dragon Ho
W4.........106 B2
Green Dragon La
TW8.........36 B1
Green Dragon Prim
Sch TW8.......44 A4
Green Dragon Yd
E1.........111 B3
Greene Ct 20 SE14..50 C4
Greene Ho SE1.....137 B1
Greenend Rd W4...38 A4

Greener Ho 3
SW4.........61 C4
Greenfell Mans
SE8.........52 A4
Greenfield Gdns
NW2.........1 A1
Greenfield Ho 28
SW19.........69 C3
Greenfield Rd E1..111 C2
Greenham Cl SE1..135 B3
Greenham Ho 5
E9.........25 B4
Greenheath Bsns Ctr
3 E2.........25 A1
Greenhill NW3.....11 C4
Greenhill Pk
NW10.........21 A4
Greenhill Rd
NW10.........21 A4
Greenhill's Rents
EC1.........108 A4
Greenhills Terr 18
N1.........15 C2
Green Ho The 5
SW19.........70 A3
Green Hundred Rd
SE15.........49 C4
Greening Ho SE13..67 C3
Greenland Ho
Bermondsey SE8...40 C1
4 Mile End E1.....26 A1
Greenland Mews
SE8.........40 C1
Greenland Pl NW1..82 B4
Greenland Quay
SE16.........40 C2
Greenland Rd
NW1.........82 C4
Greenland St
NW1.........82 C4
Green Lanes N4, N8,
N15.........6 A4
Greenleaf Cl 10
SW2.........74 C4
Green Link Wlk
TW9.........45 A2
Greenman St 1
N1.........86 C4
Greenmead Sch
SW15.........57 A2
Greenock Rd 11
W3.........37 B3
Green Park ★ SW1,
W1.........132 B4
Green Park Sta
W1.........118 C2
Greenroof Way
SE10.........43 B3
Green's Ct 11 W11..31 B1 112 C1
Green's Ct
W11.........31 B1 112 C1
Greenside Prim Sch
W12.........38 C4
Greenside Rd
W12.........38 C4
Green St W1......117 B4
Greenstead Gdns
SW15.........57 A2
Greensward Ho
SW6.........166 C2
Green Terr EC1....95 C3
Green The W3.....29 A1
Greenview Cl W3...29 A1
Greenview Ct
East Dulwich SE22.64 C3
Wandsworth SW18.72 A4
Greenway Cl N4....6 B2

Greenwell St W1..92 B1
GREENWICH.......43 C3
Greenwich Acad
SE10.........52 A3
Greenwich Bsns Ctr
SE10.........52 A3
Greenwich Bsns Pk
SE10.........52 A3
Greenwich Church St
SE10.........52 B4
Greenwich Coll
SE10.........52 B4
Greenwich Ct 11
E1.........32 A3
Greenwich High Rd
SE10.........52 A3
Greenwich Ho
SE13.........67 C1
Greenwich Ind Est
SE10.........52 A3
Greenwich Mkt
SE10.........52 B4
Greenwich Mkt 2
SE10.........52 B4
Greenwich Park ★
SE10.........53 C2
Greenwich Park St
SE10.........52 C4
Greenwich Quay
SE8.........52 A4
Greenwich South St
SE10.........52 B2
Greenwich Sta
SE10.........52 A3
Greenwich View Pl
E14.........42 A3
Green Wlk SE1....138 A1
Green Wood NW5..13 B3
Greenwood 8
SW19.........69 C4
Greenwood Ho
Finsbury WC1.....95 B3
8 Nunhead SE4...65 C3
Greenwood Pl
NW5.........13 A3
Greenwood Rd E8..16 C2
Greenwood Terr
NW10.........20 C3
Green Yd WC1.....95 A2
Green Yd The 5
SW19.........75 C1
Greet St SE1......121 C1
Gregor Mews SE3..53 C3
Gregory Ho 8
SW1.........128 A4
Greig Terr SE17...48 A4
Grenada Ho 18
E14.........33 B2
Grenade St E14....33 B2
Grena Gdns TW9..54 B3
Grena Rd TW10,
TW9.........54 B3
Grenard Cl SE15...49 C3
Grendon Ho
20 Hackney E9....17 B1
Pentonville N1...84 C1
Grendon St NW8..90 A2
Grenfell Ho SE5...48 B3
Grenfell Rd W11...30 C2
Grenfell Twr 5
W11.........30 C2
Grenfell Wlk 4
W11.........30 C2
Grenier Apartments
11 SE15.......50 A3
Grenville Ho
20 Bow E3......26 A3
4 Deptford SE8...51 C4
Grenville Lo N6....4 B4

Grenville Mans
WC1.........94 A2
Grenville Mews
SW7.........142 C3
Grenville Pl SW7..142 C4
Grenville Rd N19...5 A3
Grenville St WC1...94 B3
Gresham Almshouses
3 SW9.........62 B3
Gresham Coll
EC1.........107 C3
Gresham Gdns
NW11.........1 A3
Gresham Pl 2 N19..4 C2
Gresham Rd SW9..62 C4
Gresham St EC2..109 A2
Gresham Way
SW19.........70 C1
Gresham Way Est
SW19.........70 C1
Gresley Ho SW8..171 C4
Gresley Rd N19....4 B4
Gressenhall Rd
SW18.........70 B4
Gresse St W1.....105 B2
Greswell St SW6..47 C2
Greta Ho SE3......53 B4
Gretton Ho 2 E2...25 B2
Greville Hall NW6..78 B2
Greville Ho
Knightsbridge
SW1.........131 B2
Putney SW15.....57 C1
Greville Lo 2
SW1.........100 C2
Greville Mews
NW6.........78 A3
Greville Pl NW9...78 B2
Greville Rd
Richmond TW10..54 B1
Greville St EC1....107 C4
Grey Coat Hospital
Sch (St Michaels)
The SW1.......147 B3
Grey Coat Hospital
Sch The SW1...133 B1
Greycoat Pl SW1..133 B1
Greycoat St SW1..133 B1
Grey Eagle St
E1.........24 B1 99 A1
Greyfriars 15 SE26..76 C1
Greyfriars Ho SE3..53 B4
Grey Ho 2 W12...30 A2
Greyhound Ct
WC2.........121 B4
Greyhound Rd
College Pk NW10..22 A2
Fulham W6.......154 A4
Greyladies Gdns
SE10.........52 B1
Greystoke Ho
SE15.........65 A4
Greystoke Pl EC4..107 C2
Grey Turner Ho
W12.........29 C3
Grice Ct N1.......15 B2
Grierson Rd SE23..66 A1
Griffin Cl NW10....9 A3
Griffin Ct
5 Brentford TW8..44 A4
Chiswick W4.....38 B1
Shepherd's Bush
W12.........30 A1
Griffin Gate SW15..57 C4

Griffon Ho 🅱
SW11 . . . . 60 A4
Grigg's Pl SE1 . . . . . 138 B1
Grimaldi Ho N1 . . . . 84 C2
Grimsby St
Bethnal Green
E2 . . . . 24 C1 99 A2
Shoreditch
E2 . . . . 24 B1 99 A2
Grimsel Path SE5 . . 48 A3
Grimshaw Cl N6 . . . . . 3 C4
Grimston Rd SW6 164 C1
Grimthorpe Ho
EC1 . . . . 96 A2
Grimwade Cl SE15 . 65 B4
Grindall Ho 🔟 E1 . . 25 A1
Grindal St SE1 . . . . 135 B3
Grindley Ho 🗲 E3 . . 33 B4
Grinling Gibbons Prim
Sch SE8 . . . . 51 B4
Grinling Pl SE8 . . . . 51 C4
Grinstead Rd SE8 . . 41 A1
Grisedale Rd NW1 . 92 C4
Grittleton Rd W9 . . . 23 C1
Groombridge Rd
E9 . . . . 18 A1
Groom Cres SW18 . 71 C4
Groome Ho SE11 . 149 A3
Groom Pl SW1 . . . . 131 C2
Grosse Way SW15 . . 57 A1
Grosvenor Ave
Canonbury N5 . . . . . . 15 B3
Mortlake SW14 . . . . . 56 A4
Richmond TW10 . . . . 54 A2
Grosvenor Bridge
SW1 . . . . 160 B4
Grosvenor Cotts
SW1 . . . . 145 B4
Grosvenor Court
Mans W2 . . . . 102 C1
Grosvenor Cres
SW1 . . . . 131 C3
Grosvenor Cres Mews
SW1 . . . . 131 B3
Grosvenor Ct
Brondesbury Pk
NW6 . . . . 22 C4
Gunnersbury W4 . . . . 37 A1
🔳 Poplar E14 . . . . . . 33 B3
Putney SW15 . . . . . . 58 A2
Grosvenor Gdns
Cricklewood NW2 . . . . 9 B3
Mortlake SW14 . . . . . 56 A4
Westminster SW1 . 132 B1
Grosvenor Gdns
Mews E SW1 . . . . 132 B2
Grosvenor Gdns
Mews N SW1 . . . . 132 A1
Grosvenor Gdns
Mews S SW1 . . . . 132 B2
Grosvenor Hill
W1 . . . . 118 A4
Grosvenor Hill Ct
W1 . . . . 118 A4
Grosvenor Ho E5 . . . . 7 C3
Grosvenor Park
SE5 . . . . 48 B3
Grosvenor Pier
SW1 . . . . 161 B4
Grosvenor Pk SE5 . 48 B4
Grosvenor Pl
SW1 . . . . 132 A3
Grosvenor Rd
Acton Green W4 . . . . 37 B1

Grosvenor Rd continued
Pimlico SW1 . . . . . 161 A4
Richmond TW10 . . . . 54 A2
Grosvenor Residences
🔳 W14 . . . . 39 C3
Grosvenor Sq W1 117 C4
Grosvenor Sq W1 118 A4
Grosvenor Terr
SE5 . . . . 48 B4
Grosvenor The
NW11 . . . . 2 A4
Grosvenor Wharf Rd
E14 . . . . 42 C2
Grote's Bldgs SE3 . 53 A1
Grote's Pl SE3 . . . . 53 A1
Groton Rd SW18 . . . 71 A2
Grotto Ct SE1 . . . . 136 C4
Grotto Pas W1 . . . . 103 B4
Grove Crescent Rd
E15 . . . . 19 C2
Grove Ct
Camberwell SE5 . . . . 49 A1
Clapham SW4 . . . . . . 61 B4
South Kensington
SW10 . . . . 143 A1
St John's Wood
NW8 . . . . 89 B4
Grovedale Rd N19 . . 4 C2
Grove Dwellings
E1 . . . . 32 B4
Grove End NW5 . . . . 13 A4
Grove End Gdns
NW8 . . . . 79 A1
Grove End Ho
NW8 . . . . 89 B3
Grove Gdns NW8 . . 90 B3
Grove Hall Ct
Bow E3 . . . . 26 C3
St John's Wood
NW8 . . . . 89 A4
Grove Hill Rd SE5 . 64 A4
Grove Ho
Blackheath SE3 . . . . . 53 B1
Chelsea SW3 . . . . . 158 B4
Grove La SE5 . . . . . . 64 A4
Groveland Ct EC4 109 B1
Grovelands Cl SE5 . 49 A1
Grove Lane Terr
SE5 . . . . 48 C1
Grove Lo SW4 . . . . . 61 B3
Grove Mans
London SW6 . . . . . . 60 B3
🔳 Shepherd's Bush
W6 . . . . 39 B4
🔳 Stamford Hill N16 . 7 C3
Grove Mews W6 . . . 39 B3
GROVE PARK 45 B3
Grove Park Bridge
W4 . . . . 45 B3
Grove Park Gdns
W4 . . . . 45 A3
Grove Park Mews
W4 . . . . 45 B3
Grove Park Prim Sch
W4 . . . . 45 B3
Grove Park Rd
W4 . . . . 45 A3
Grove Park Terr
W4 . . . . 45 A3
Grove Pk SE5 . . . . . . 49 A1
Grove Pl Acton W3 . 28 B1
Balham SW12 . . . . . . 61 A3
Hampstead NW3 . . . . 2 C1
Grover Ct SE13 . . . . 52 A1

Grove Rd Acton W3 . 28 B1
Barnes SW13 . . . . . . 46 B1
Bow E3 . . . . 26 A3
Richmond TW10 . . . . 54 B1
Willesden NW2 . . . . . . 9 B2
Grover Ho
🔳 London SW4 . . . . 61 B2
Vauxhall SE11 . . . . 149 A1
Groveside Ct
SW11 . . . . 167 B2
Grove St SE8 . . . . . . 41 B1
Grove Terr NW5 . . . . 13 A4
Grove Terrace Mews
NW5 . . . . 4 A1
Grove The
Dulwich SE22 . . . . . . 76 C3
Hendon NW11 . . . . . . 1 A4
Highgate N6 . . . . 3 C3
Stroud Green N4 . . . . 5 B4
Grove Vale SE22 . . . 64 B3
Groveway SW9 . . . 173 A3
Grovewood 🔳
TW9 . . . . 44 C2
Grovewood Ho
NW2 . . . . 1 B2
Grummant Rd
SE15 . . . . 49 B2
Grundy St E14 . . . . . 34 A3
Guardian Angels RC
Prim Sch E3 . . . . . . 26 A2
Guards Mus The★
SW1 . . . . 133 A3
Gubyon Ave SE24 . . 63 A2
Guerin Sq E3 . . . . . . 26 B2
Guernsey Gr SE24 . 75 B4
Guernsey Ho 🔟
N1 . . . . 15 B2
Guernsey Rd 🔟
N1 . . . . 15 B2
Guildford Gr SE10 . 52 A2
Guildford Ho 🐉
SE5 . . . . 48 B1
Guildford Rd
SW9 . . . . 173 B2
Guildhall★ EC2 . . . 109 A2
Guildhall Bldgs
EC2 . . . . 109 B2
Guildhall Ho EC2 . 109 B2
Guildhall Sch Music &
Drama EC2 . . . . . 109 A2
Guildhall Yd EC2 . 109 A2
Guildhouse St
SW1 . . . . 146 C3
Guildpl House St
Guilford Pl WC1 . . . 94 C1
Guilford St WC1 . . . 94 B1
Guillemot Ct 🐉
SE8 . . . . 51 B4
Guilsborough Cl
NW10 . . . . 8 A1
Guinness Cl E9 . . . . 18 A1
Guinness Ct
Chelsea SW3 . . . . . 144 C3
Finsbury EC1 . . . . . . 97 A3
Primrose Hill NW8 . . 80 B3
Whitechapel E1 . . . 111 A1
Guinness Sq SE1 . 152 A4
Guinness Trust Bldgs★
Bermondsey SE1 . . 138 A4
🔳 Bethnal Green
E2 . . . . 24 C3
Chelsea SW3 . . . . . 144 C3
Hammersmith W6 . . 39 B1
Kennington SE11 . . 150 A2
Guion Rd SW6 . . . . 165 A2
Gujarat Ho 🔟 N16 . . 7 A1

Gulland Wlk 🔳
N1 . . . . 15 B2
Gullane Ho 🔟 E3 . . 26 B3
Gulliver St SE16 . . . 41 B3
Gulston Wlk SW3 145 A3
Gunmakers La E3 . . 26 A4
GUNNERSBURY . . 37 A2
Gunnersbury Avenue
(North Circular Rd)
W3 . . . . 36 C3
Gunnersbury Cl 🐉
W4 . . . . 37 A1
Gunnersbury Cres
W3 . . . . 36 C4
Gunnersbury Ct 🔳
W3 . . . . 37 A4
Gunnersbury Dr
W5 . . . . 36 B4
Gunnersbury Gdns
W3 . . . . 36 C4
Gunnersbury La
W3 . . . . 36 C4
Gunnersbury Mews 🔳
W4 . . . . 37 A1
Gunnersbury Park
W3 . . . . 36 B3
Gunnersbury Park
Mus★ W3 . . . . 36 B3
Gunnersbury Sta
W4 . . . . 37 A1
Gunners Rd SW18 . 71 C2
Gunpowder Sq
EC4 . . . . 107 C2
Gun St E1 . . . . 110 C3
Gunstor Rd N16 . . . 16 A4
Gunter Gr SW6 . . . 156 C2
Gunterstone Rd
W14 . . . . 140 B2
Gunthorpe St E1 . . 111 A2
Gunwhale Cl SE16 . 32 C1
Gun Wharf
Old Ford E3 . . . . 26 A4
Wapping E1 . . . . 32 B1
Gurdon Ho 🔳 E14 . 33 C3
Gurdon Rd SE7 . . . . 43 C1
Gurney Ho
Bayswater W2 . . . . 100 A2
🔳 Bethnal Green
E2 . . . . 24 C3
Gurney Rd SW6 . . . 59 B4
Guthrie St SE1 . . . 135 C3
Guthrie St SW3 . . . 144 A2
Gutter La EC2 . . . . 108 C2
Guyscliff Rd SE13 . 67 B2
Guy's Hospl SE1 . . 137 C4
Guy's Hospl Sch
SE1 . . . . 123 C1
Guy St SE1 . . . . . . 137 C4
Gwalior Rd SW15 . . 57 C4
Gwendolen Ave
SW15 . . . . 57 C3
Gwendolen Cl
SW15 . . . . 57 C2
Gwendwr Rd
W14 . . . . 140 B2
Gwent Ct 🔳 SE16 . 32 C1
Gwilym Maries Ho 🔳
E2 . . . . 25 A2
Gwyn Cl SW6 . . . . 156 C1
Gwynne Cl W4 . . . . 46 A4
Gwynne Ho
Finsbury WC1 . . . . . . 95 B3
🔳 Streatham SW2 . . 74 B3
Whitechapel E1 . . . . 25 C1
Gwynne Pl WC1 . . . 95 A3
Gwynne Rd SW11 . 167 C2

Gye Ho 🔳 SW4 . . . . 62 A3
Gylcote Cl SE5 . . . . 63 C3

H

Haarlem Rd 🔟
W14 . . . . 39 C3
Haberdasher Pl
N1 . . . . 24 A2 98 A4
Haberdashers' Aske's
Hatcham Coll
SE4 . . . . 51 A1
Haberdasher St
N1 . . . . 97 C4
Hackford Rd SW9 173 A4
Hackford Wlk
SW9 . . . . 173 B3
HACKNEY 17 A2
Hackney Central Sta
E8 . . . . 17 A2
Hackney Coll (Poplar
Ctr) E3 . . . . 27 A1
Hackney Com Coll
N1 . . . . 24 A2 98 A4
Hackney Downs Sta
E8 . . . . 17 A3
Hackney Free &
Parochial CE Sec
Sch E9 . . . . 17 A2
Hackney Gr E8 . . . . 17 A2
Hackney Hospl E9 . 18 A3
Hackney Rd E2 . . . . 24 C3
Hackney Stadium
Mkt★ E15 . . . . 18 C2
HACKNEY WICK . . . 18 C2
Hackney Wick E9 . . 18 B2
Hackney Wick Sta
E9 . . . . 18 C2
Hackworth Point 🔳
E3 . . . . 27 A2
Haddo Ho
Gospel Oak NW5 . . . 13 A4
Greenwich SE10 . . . 52 A4
Haddon Ct W3 . . . . 29 B2
Haddo St SE10 . . . . 52 B4
Haden Ct N4 . . . . 5 C2
Hadfield Ho 🔳
E1 . . . . 111 C1
Hadleigh Cl 🔳 E1 . 25 B1
Hadleigh Ho 🔳
E1 . . . . 25 B1
Hadleigh St E2 . . . . 25 B2
Hadley Cl N16 . . . . . 7 C3
Hadley Gdns W4 . . 37 C1
Hadley St NW1 . . . . 13 A2
Hadlow Ho SE17 . . 152 B2
Hadrian Cl 🔳 E3 . . 26 C4
Hadrian Ct SE4 . . . . 66 C4
Hadrian Est 🔳 E2 . 24 C3
Hadrian St SE10 . . . 43 A1
Hadstock Ho NW1 . 93 C4
Hadyn Park Ct 🔳
W12 . . . . 38 C4
Hadyn Park Rd
W12 . . . . 38 C4
Hafer Rd SW11 . . . . 60 B3
HAGGERSTON . . . 24 B3
Haggerston Rd E8 . 24 B4
Haggerston Sch
E2 . . . . 24 B3
Haggerston Studios
🔳 E8 . . . . 24 B4
Hague Prim Sch
E2 . . . . 25 A1
Hague St 🔳 E2 . . . 24 C2 99 A3
Haig Ho 🔳 E2 . . . . 24 C3

Heilsham Ave
SW2 .... 74 B2
Hainford Cl SE4 ....65 C3
Haining Cl 3 W4 ...36 C1
Hainton Cl E1 ....32 A3
Halcomb St N1 .....24 A4
Halcrow St E1 ....32 A4
Halcyon Wharf
E1 .... 125 C2
Haldane Pl SW18 ..71 A3
Haldane Rd SW6 .155 A3
Haldon Rd SW18 ..58 B1
Hale Ho SW1 ......147 C2
Hales Ho 3 SW12 .73 A4
Hales Prior N1 ....84 C1
Hales St SF8 ....51 C3
Hale St E14 ....34 A2
Halesworth Rd
SE13 ....67 A4
Half Moon Cres
N1 .... 85 A2
Half Moon Ct EC1 108 C3
Half Moon La
SE24 ....63 B1
Halfmoon Pas E1 111 A1
Half Moon St W1 118 B1
Halford Ho 9
SW15 ....57 C2
Halford Rd
Richmond TW10 ...54 A2
West Brompton
SW6 .... 155 B3
Haliday Ho N1 .....15 C2
Haliday Wlk 4 N1 .15 C2
Halidon Cl 7 E9 .....17 B3
Haliwell Ho NW6 ..78 A3
Halkett Ho 3 E2 ...25 B4
Halkin Arc SW1 ...131 A2
Halkin Mews
SW1 .... 131 B2
Halkin Pl SW1 .....131 B2
Halkin St SW1 .....131 C3
Hallam Ct W1 .....104 B4
Hallam Ho
London SW9 ....173 B4
Pimlico SW1 ......147 A1
Hallam Mews W1 104 B4
Hallam Rd SW13 ...57 A4
Hallam St W1 ......104 B4
Halley Gdns SE13 ..67 C3
Halley Ho
16 Bethnal Green
E2 ....24 C3
3 Cubitt Town
SE10 ....43 B1
Halley Prim Sch
E14 ....33 A4
Halley St E14 ....33 A4
Hallfield Jun & Inf
Schs W2 ....100 B1
Hall Gate NW8 .....89 A4
Halliday Ho E1 ....111 C1
Halliford St N1 .....15 C1
Halling Ho SE1 ...137 C3
Hallings Wharf
Studios 2 E15 .....27 C4
Halliwell Ct 8
SE22 ....64 C2
Halliwell Rd SW2 ..62 B1
Hall Oak Wlk NW6 10 B2
Hall Pl W2 ....89 B1
Hall Rd Leyton E15 .19 C4
St John's Wood
NW8 ....89 A4
Hall Sch The NW3 ..11 C2
Hall Sch Wimbledon
SW15 ....68 C1

Hall St EC1 ....96 B4
Hallsville Prim Sch
E16 ....35 C3
Hallsville Rd E16 ...35 B3
Hall Twr W2 ....101 C4
Halpin Pl SE17 ....151 C3
Halsbury Ho 4
N7 ....14 B4
Halsbury Rd W12 ..30 A1
Halsey St SW3 ....144 C4
Halsmere Rd SE5 ..48 A2
Halstead Ct N1 ......87 C1
Halston Cl SW11 ...60 B1
Halstow NW5 ....12 C2
Halstow Prim Sch
SE10 ....43 C1
Halstow Rd
Greenwich SE3,
SE10 ....43 C1
Kensal Green NW10 .22 C2
Halton Cross St
N1 ....86 B4
Haltone Ho SW4 .171 C1
Halton Ho 22 N1 ...15 A1
Halton Mans N1 ...15 A1
Halton Pl N1 ....86 C4
Halton Rd N1 ....86 B4
Halyard Ho E14 ....42 B3
Hambalt Rd SW4 ...61 B2
Hambledon SE17 ..48 C4
Hambledon Chase
N4 ....5 A4
Hambledon Ho E5 .17 A4
Hambledon Pl
SE21 ....76 B3
Hambledon Rd
SW18 ....70 B4
Hamble St SW6 .....59 A4
Hambley Ho 5
SE16 ....40 A2
Hamblyn Ct N16 ....7 B4
Hambridge Way
SW2 ....74 C4
Hamilton Cl
St John's Wood
NW8 ....79 B3
Hamilton Ct W9 ....88 C4
Hamilton Gdns
NW8 ....89 A4
Hamilton Hall
NW8 ....78 C1
Hamilton Ho
22 Bow E3 ....26 B2
Chiswick W4 ....46 A4
Kensington W8 ...128 A4
1 Poplar E14 ....33 B2
10 Richmond TW9 ..54 A3
St John's Wood
NW8 ....89 B4
Hamilton La N5 ....15 A4
Hamilton Lo 37 E1 .25 B1
Hamilton Mews
W1 ....132 A4
Hamilton Pk N5 ....15 A4
Hamilton Pk W
N5 ....15 A4
Hamilton Rd SW19 117 C1
Hamilton Rd
Acton W4 ....38 A4
Hendon NW11 ....1 A4
Willesden NW10 ...9 A3

Hamilton Sq SE1 .137 C4
Hamilton St SW8 ..51 C4
Hamilton Terr
NW8 ....89 A4
Hamlet Ct
1 Hammersmith
W6 ....38 C2
Kennington SE11 .150 A2
Hamlet Gdns W6 ...38 C2
Hamlet Ind Est E9 .18 C1
Hamlet Sq NW2 .....1 A1
Hamlets Way E3 ...26 B1
Hamlet The SE5 ....63 C4
Hamlet Way SE1 ..137 C4
Hammelton Gn 2
SW9 ....48 A2
Hammersley Ho 8
SE14 ....50 B3
HAMMERSMITH .39 B2
Hammersmith Bridge
W6, SW13 ....39 B1
Hammersmith
Broadway
Hammersmith W6 .39 B1
5 Hammersmith
W6 ....39 B1
Hammersmith Flyover
W6 ....39 B1
Hammersmith Gr
W6 ....39 B3
Hammersmith Hospl
W12 ....30 A3
Hammersmith Rd
Hammersmith W6 .39 C2
Kensington W14 ..140 B4
Hammersmith Sta
W6 ....39 B2
Hammersmith Terr 6
W6 ....38 C1
Hammett St EC3 ..124 C4
Hammond Ho
10 Deptford SE14 ..50 B3
Millwall E14 ....42 A3
Hammond Lo 6
W9 ....31 C4
Hammond St NW5 .13 B2
Hamond Sq N1 .....24 A3
Hampden Cl NW1 ..83 C2
Hampden Gurney CE
Prim Sch W1 .....102 B2
Hampden Gurney St
W1 ....102 C1
Hampden Rd N19 ...4 C2
Hampshire Ct 6
SW13 ....46 B1
Hampshire Hog La
3 Hammersmith
W6 ....39 A1
4 Hammersmith
W6 ....39 A1
Hampshire Sch The
SW7 ....130 A3
Hampshire St
NW5 ....13 C2
Hampson Way
SW8 ....172 C4
HAMPSTEAD 11 B2
Hampstead Coll of
Fine Arts &
Humanities NW3 ..12 A2
Hampstead Gate
NW3 ....11 B3
Hampstead Gn
NW3 ....12 A3
Hampstead Gr NW3 . 2 B1

Hampstead Heath*
NW3 ....2 C2
Hampstead Heath Sta
NW3 ....12 A4
Hampstead High St
NW3 ....11 C3
Hampstead Hill Gdns
NW3 ....12 A3
Hampstead Hill Sch
NW3 ....12 A3
Hampstead La N6 ...3 A4
Hampstead Parochial
CE Prim Sch
NW3 ....11 B4
Hampstead Rd
NW1 ....92 C4
Hampstead Sch
NW3 ....10 A4
Hampstead Sq 1
NW3 ....2 B1
Hampstead Sta
NW3 ....11 B4
Hampstead West 4
NW6 ....10 C2
Hampton Cl NW6 ..23 C2
Hampton Ct
1 Islington N1 ...15 A2
11 Rotherhithe
SE16 ....32 C1
Hampton St SE1 ..150 B3
Hamstead Gates 5
NW5 ....13 A2
Ham Yd W1 ....119 B4
Hana Mews E5 .....17 A4
Hanbury Ho
Bethnal Green E1 ..111 B4
South Lambeth
SW8 ....162 B3
Hanbury Mews N1 .87 A3
Hanbury Rd W3 ....37 A4
Hanbury St E1 ....111 A4
Hancock Nunn Ho 7
NW3 ....12 B1
Hancock Rd E3 .....27 B2
Handa Wlk 3 N1 ...15 B2
Hand Ct WC1 ....107 A3
Handel Mans
Barnes SW13 ....47 B3
Bloomsbury WC1 ...94 B2
Handel St WC1 .....94 B2
Handforth Rd
SW9 ....163 B2
Handley Rd E9 .....25 B4
Hands Wlk E16 .....35 C3
Hanford Cl SW18 ..70 C3
Hankey Pl SE1 ....137 C3
Hanley Ct N4 ....5 B3
Hanley Gdns N4 ....5 B3
Hanley Rd N4, N19 .5 A3
Hanmer Wlk N7 .....5 B2
Hannah Mary Way
SE1 ....153 C3
Hannay La N8 ....4 C4
Hannay Wlk SW16 .73 C2
Hannell Rd SW6 ..154 B2
Hannen Ho SE5 ....63 C4
Hannen Rd SE27 ...75 A1
Hannibal Rd E1 ....32 B4
Hannington Rd
SW4 ....61 A4
Hanover Ave E16 ..35 C1
Hanover Cl TW9 ...44 C3
Hanover Ct
Shepherd's Bush
W12 ....29 C1

Hanover Ct continued
Stamford Hill N16 ..7 B4
Hanover Gate Mans
NW1 ....90 B2
Hanover Gdns
SE11 ....163 B4
Hanover Ho NW8 ..80 A1
Hanover Mans 5
SW2 ....62 C2
Hanover Pk SE15 ..49 C2
Hanover Pl
3 Bow E3 ....26 B2
St Giles WC2 ......106 B1
Hanover Prim Sch
N1 ....86 C2
Hanover Rd NW10 .22 B4
Hanover Sq W1 ...104 B1
Hanover St W1 ....104 B1
Hanover Stps W2 .102 B1
Hanover Terr NW1 .90 C3
Hanover Terrace
Mews NW1 ....90 B2
Hanover West Ind Est
NW10 ....20 C2
Hanover Yd N1 .....86 C2
Hansard Mews
W14 ....39 C4
Hanscomb Mews
SW4 ....61 B3
Hans Cres SW1 ...130 C2
Hansler Ct 8
SW19 ....70 A3
Hansler Rd SE22 ..64 B2
Hanson Cl
Balham SW12 ....73 A4
Mortlake SW14 .....55 B4
Hanson Ho E1 .....125 C4
Hanson St W1 ....104 C4
Hans Pl SW1 ......130 C2
Hans Rd SW3 .....130 C2
Hans St SW1 ......131 A1
Hanway Ho 7 SW9 173 C4
Hanway Pl W1 ....105 B2
Hanway St W1 ....105 B2
Hanworth Ho SE5 .48 A3
Harben Rd NW6 ...11 B1
Harberson Rd
SW12 ....73 A3
Harberton Rd N19 ..4 B3
Harbet Rd W2 .....101 C3
Harbinger Prim Sch
E14 ....42 A2
Harbinger Rd E14 .42 A2
Harbin Ho 5 SW2 .74 C3
Harbledown Ho
SE1 ....137 B3
Harbledown Rd
SW6 ....165 B4
Harbord Cl SE5 ....48 C1
Harbord Ho 5
SE16 ....40 C2
Harbord St SW6 ...47 C2
Harborough Sch
N19 ....4 C2
Harbour Ave
SW10 ....167 A3
Harbour Exchange Sq
E14 ....42 A4
Harbour Rd SE5 ...63 B4
Harbridge Ave
SW15 ....68 C4
Harbut Rd SW11 ...59 C3
Harcombe Rd N16 ..7 A1
Harcourt Ho
Clapham SW8 ....171 B2

Harcourt Ho continued
Marylebone W1 .... **104** A2
4 Willesden NW10.... 9 B2
Harcourt Ho **6** **66** B4
Harcourt St W1 .. **102** B3
Harcourt Terr
SW10 .... **142** B1
Hardcastle Ho
3 New Cross Gate
SE14 .... 51 A2
3 Peckham SE15 .. 49 C2
Hardel Rise SW2 .. 75 A3
Hardel Wlk SW24,
SW2 .... 74 C4
Harden Ho SE15 .. 50 A1
Harders Rd SE15 .. 50 A1
Hardess St SE24 .. 63 B3
Hardham Ho **5**
SW2 .... 62 C1
Harding Cl SE17 .. 48 B4
Hardinge Rd
NW10 .... 22 B4
Hardinge St E1 .... 32 B3
Harding Ho SW13 .. 47 A4
Hardington **2**
NW1 .... 12 C1
Hardwicke Ho **14**
E3 .... 27 A2
Hardwicke Mews
WC1 .... **95** A3
Hardwicke Rd W4 .. **37** C2
Hardwick Ho
London SW8 .... **171** B2
Marylebone NW8 .. **90** B2
Hardwick St EC1 .. **95** C3
Hardwick's Way
SW18 .... 58 C2
Hardwidge St
SE1 .... **138** A4
Hardy Ave **4** E16.. **35** C1
Hardy Cl SE16 ...... 40 C4
Hardy Cotts **2**
SE10 .... 52 C4
Hardy Ct SE3 ...... 53 B4
Hardy Rd SE3 ...... 53 B4
Hare and Billet Rd
SE3 .... 52 C1
Harecourt Rd N1 .. 15 B2
Hare Ct EC4 .... **107** B1
Haredale Ho
SE16 .... **139** B3
Haredale Rd SE24 .. 63 B3
Harefield Mews
SE4 .... 66 B4
Harefield Rd SE4 .. 66 B4
Hare Marsh
E2 .... 24 C1 **99** B2
Hare Row E2 ...... **25** A3
Hare Wlk N1 ...... 24 A3
Harewood Ave
NW1 .... 90 B1
Harewood Pl W1 **104** B1
Harewood Row
NW1 .... **102** B4
Harfield Gdns **1**
SE5 .... 64 A4
Harfleur Ct SE11 .. **150** A3
Harford Ho
Camberwell SE5.. 48 B4
Notting Hill W11 ..31 B4
Harford Mews **6**
N19 .... 4 C1
Harford St E1 ...... 26 A1

Hargrave Mans **3**
N19.................. 4 C2
Hargrave Park Prim
Sch N19 .... 4 B2
Hargrave Pk N19 .... 4 B2
Hargrave Pl N7 .... 13 C3
Hargrave Rd N19 .. 4 B2
Hargraves Ho **14**
W12 .... 30 A2
Hargwyne St SW9.. 62 B4
Harkness Ho E1 .. **111** C1
Harlech Twr **8**
W3 .... 37 B4
Harlescott Rd
SE15 .... 65 C3
HARLESDEN 21 B4
Harlesden Gdns
NW10 .... 21 B4
Harlesden Plaza **2**
NW10 .... 21 B3
Harlesden Prim Sch
NW10 .... 21 A3
Harlesden Rd
NW10 .... 21 C4
Harlesden Sta
NW10 .... 21 A3
Harleyford Ct
SW8 .... **162** C4
Harleyford Manor **6**
W3 .... 28 B1
Harleyford Rd
SE11 .... **162** C4
Harleyford St
SE11 .... **163** B3
Harley Gdns
SW10 .... **143** A1
Harley Gr E3 ...... 26 B2
Harley Pl W1 .... **104** A3
Harley St W1 .... **104** A3
Harley Villas
NW10 .... 21 A3
Harling Ct SW11 .. **168** C2
Harlowe Ho **13** E8.. 24 B4
Harlynwood **19**
SE5 .... 48 B3
Harman Cl
Bermondsey SE1 .. **153** B1
Cricklewood NW2 ... 1 A2
Harman Dr NW2.... 10 A4
Harmon Ho **7**
SE8 .... 41 B2
Harmood Gr NW1 ..13 A1
Harmood Ho **2**
NW1 .... 13 A1
Harmood St NW1 .. 13 A1
Harmsworth St
SE17 .... **150** A1
Harnage Ho NW8 .. 36 A1
Harney Ct SE14.... 51 A2
Harold Ct SE16 .. **40** C4
Harold Est SE1 .. **138** B1
Harold Ho **15** E2 .. 25 C3
Harold Laski Ho
EC1 .... **96** B3
Harold Maddison Ho
SE17 .... **150** A2
Harold Rd NW10 .. **20** C2
Harold Wilson Ho
SW6 .... **155** A3
Harp Alley EC4 .. **108** A2
Harpenden Rd SE27,
SW16 .... 75 A2

Harpenmead Point
NW2 .... 1 B2
Harper Ho **3** SW9.. **63** A4
Harper Mews
SW17 .... 71 B1
Harper Rd SE1 .. **137** A2
Harp La EC3 ...... **124** A3
Harpley Sq E1 ...... 25 C1
Harpsden St
SW11 .... **169** B3
Harpur Mews
WC1 .... **106** C4
Harpur St WC1 .. **106** C4
Harrier Ho **9**
SW11 .... 60 A4
Harriet Cl **8** E8.... **24** C4
Harriet Ho SW6 .. **156** B1
Harriet St SW1 .. **131** A3
Harriet Tun Cl **20**
SW2 .... 74 C4
Harriet Wlk SW1 .. **131** A3
Harrington Ct
South Kensington
SW7 .... **143** C4
2 West Kilburn W9.. 23 B2
Harrington Gdns
SW7 .... **142** C3
Harrington Ho
Regent's Pk NW1 .. **92** C4
Westminster SW1 . **147** C2
Harrington Rd
SW7 .... **143** B4
Harrington Sq
NW1 .... 82 C1
Harrington St
NW1 .... **92** C4
Harriott Cl SE10.... **43** B2
Harriott Ho **11** E1 .. 32 B3
Harris Girl's Acad
SE15 .... 65 B2
Harris Ho
11 Bow E3 ...... 26 C2
3 Brixton SW9.... 62 C4
Harrison Ho SE17 **151** B2
Harrison Rd NW10 .. 20 C4
Harrisons Ct **1**
SE14 .... 50 C4
Harrison St WC1 .. **94** B3
Harris St SE5 ...... 48 C3
Harrodian Sch The
SW13 .... 46 B3
Harrogate Ct **2**
SE26 .... 76 C1
Harrold Ho **1**
NW3 .... 11 B1
Harroway Rd
SW11 .... **167** C2
Harrowby St W1 .. **102** B2
Harrowgate Ho **22**
E9 .... 17 C2
Harrowgate Rd
E9 .... 18 A1
Harrow La E14 .... 34 B2
Harrow Pl E1 .... **110** B2
Harrow Rd
Little Venice W2 .. **101** A3
Westbourne Green W2,
W9 .... 23 C1
Harrow St NW1 .. **102** A4
Harry Gosling Prim
Sch E1 .... **111** C1
Harry Hinkins Ho
SE17 .... **151** A1
Harry Lambourn Ho
10 SE15 .... 50 A3
Hartfield Terr E3 .. 26 C3
Hartham Cl N7 .... **14** A3

Hartham Rd N7 .... **14** A3
Hart Ho SW2 ...... **74** C3
Hartington Ct
Chiswick W4 ...... 45 A3
South Lambeth
SW8 .... **172** A4
Hartington Rd
Chiswick W4 ...... 45 B2
South Lambeth
SW8 .... **162** A1
Hartismere Rd
SW6 .... **155** A2
Hartlake Rd E9 .... **18** A2
Hartland Rd **1**
NW1 .... **83** A3
Hartland Rd
Camden Town
NW1 .... 13 A1
Kilburn NW6 ...... 23 B4
Hartley Ho
Bermondsey SE1.. **153** A4
Putney SW15 ...... 56 C2
Hartley St E2 ...... 25 B2
Hartnoll Ho **4** N7.. **14** C3
Hartnoll St N7 .... 14 B3
Harton Lodge **2**
SE8 .... 51 C2
Harton St SE8 .... 51 C2
Hartopp Ct **20** N16.. 7 A1
Hartopp Point
SW6 .... **154** B2
Hartshorn Alley
EC3 .... **110** B1
Hart's La SE14.... 51 A2
Hart St EC3 ...... **124** B4
Hartswood Ho **9**
SW2 .... 74 A3
Hartswood Rd
W12 .... 38 B3
Hartwell Cl SE22 .. 64 C3
Hartwell St E8 .... 16 B2
Harvard Ct NW6.... 11 A3
Harvard Hill W4 .... 45 A4
Harvard Ho
3 Camberwell
SE17 .... 48 A4
Putney SW15 ...... 57 C1
Harvard Mans **18**
SW11 .... 59 C3
Harvard Rd
3 Acton Green
W4 .... 37 B1
Gunnersbury W4 .. 37 A1
Lewisham SE13 .. **67** B2
Harvey Ct SW11 .. **168** B4
Harvey Ho
10 Bethnal Green
E1 .... 25 A1
Brentford TW8 .... 36 A1
Pimlico SW1 .... **147** C1
Shoreditch N1 .... **87** C3
Harvey Lo **6** W9 .. **31** C4
Harvey Point **7**
E16 .... 35 C4
Harvey Rd **15** SE5.. **48** C2
Harvey St N1 .... **87** C3
Harvington Wlk
E8 .... 16 C1
Harvist Rd NW6 .. 23 A3
Harwood Ct
Putney SW15 ...... 57 B3
Shoreditch N1 .... **87** C3
Harwood Point
SE16 .... 41 B4
Harwood Rd SW6 .. **156** A1
Harwood Terr
SW6 .... **166** A4

Hascombe Ho **11**
SW15 .... **69** A3
Hascombe Terr **2**
SE5 .... 48 C1
Haselrigge Rd
SW4 .... **61** C3
Hasker St SW3 .. **144** B4
Haslam Cl N1 ...... 14 C1
Haslam Ho **2** N1... 15 B1
Haslam St SE15 .. 49 B2
Haslemere Ave
SW18 .... 71 A2
Haslemere Ct **5**
N16................... 7 A3
Haslemere Ind Est
SW18 .... 71 A2
Haslemere Rd N8 .. 5 A4
Hassard St E2 .... 24 B3
Hassett Rd E9 .... 18 A2
Hassop Rd NW2 .... 9 C4
Hastings Cl **7**
SE15 .... 49 C3
Hastings Ho **18**
W12 .... 30 A2
Hastings Hos WC1 .. **94** A3
Hastings St WC1 .. 94 A3
Hatcham Mews Bsns
Ctr SE14 .... 50 C2
Hatcham Park Mews
SE14 .... 50 C2
Hatcham Park Rd
SE14 .... 50 C2
Hatcham Rd SE15 .. 50 B4
Hatchard Rd N19.. 5 A2
Hatchers Mews
SE1 .... **138** B3
Hatcliffe Almshouses
8 SE10 .... 43 B1
Hatcliffe St SE10 .. 43 B1
Hatfield Cl SE14 .. 50 C3
Hatfield Ct SE3 .. 53 C3
Hatfield Ho EC1 .. **96** C1
Hatfield Rd W4 .... 37 C4
Hatfields SE1 .... **121** C2
Hathaway Ho
N1 .... 24 A2 **98** A4
Hatherley Ct W2 .. **100** A2
Hatherley Gr W2 .. **100** A2
Hatherley Rd TW9.. 44 B2
Hatherley St SW1 **147** A3
Hathersage Ct N1 .. 15 C3
Hathersley Ho **3**
SW2 .... 74 C4
Hathorne Cl **3**
SE15 .... 50 A1
Hathway Ho **3**
SE15 .... 50 B1
Hathway St **4**
SE15 .... 50 B1
Hatley Rd N4, N7 .. 5 B2
Hat & Mitre Ct
EC1 .... **96** B1
Hatstone Ct NW3 .. 11 B3
Hatteraick St **5**
SE16 .... 40 B4
Hatton Gdn EC1 .. **107** C4
Hatton Ho E1 .... **125** C4
Hatton Pl EC1 .... **107** C4
Hatton Row NW8 .. 89 C1
Hatton St NW8 .... 89 C1
Hatton Wall EC1 .. **107** C4
Haunch of Venison Yd
W1 .... **104** A1
Hauteville Court Gdns
2 W6 .... 38 B3
Havana Rd SW18,
SW19 .... **70** C3

Havannah St E14 . . . . .41 C4
Havelock Cl 13
W12 . . . . .30 A2
Havelock Ct 8
SE15 . . . . .50 A3
Havelock St N1 . . . . .84 B4
Havelock Terr
SW8 . . . . .160 B1
Haven Cl SW19 . . . . .69 C1
Havenpool N8 . . . . . .78 B3
Haven St 18 NW1 . . . .13 A1
Haven The TW9 . . . . .54 C4
Havercourt 3
NW3 . . . . .12 A2
Haverfield Gdns
TW9 . . . . .44 C3
Haverfield Rd E3 . . . .26 A2
Haverhill Rd SW12 . .73 B3
Havering 8 NW1 . . . . .13 A1
Havering Ho N1 . . . . . .6 B4
Havering St E1 . . . . . .32 C3
Haversham Cl NW2 . . .9 C3
Haversham Pl N6 . . . .3 B2
Haverstock Hill
NW3 . . . . .12 B2
Haverstock Rd
NW5 . . . . .12 C3
Haverstock Sch
NW1 . . . . .12 C2
Havil St SE5 . . . . .49 A2
Havisham Ho
SE16 . . . . .139 B3
Hawarden Gr
SE24 . . . . .75 B4
Hawberry Lo N7 . . . . .14 A2
Hawes St N1 . . . . .15 A1
Hawgood St E3 . . . . . .33 C4
Hawke Ho 20 E1 . . . . .25 C1
Hawke Pl 22 SE16 . . .40 C4
Hawkesbury Rd
SW15 . . . . .57 A2
Hawkesworth Ho 5
SW4 . . . . .61 B1
Hawke Twr 4
SE14 . . . . .51 A4
Hawk Ho 7 SW11 . . .60 A4
Hawkins Ho 3
SE8 . . . . .51 C4
Hawkins Rd NW10 . . .8 A1
Hawkley Gdns
SE27 . . . . .75 A2
Hawkridge 19
NW5 . . . . .12 C2
Hawkshaw Cl 23
SW2 . . . . .74 A4
Hawkshead Rd
Acton W4 . . . . .38 A4
Willesden NW10 . . . . .8 B1
Hawkslade Rd
SE15 . . . . .65 C2
Hawksley Rd N16 . . . .7 A1
Hawks Mews 10
SE10 . . . . .52 B3
Hawksmoor Mews
E1 . . . . .32 A2
Hawksmoor Pl
E2 . . . . .24 C1 99 B2
Hawksmoor St 5
W6 . . . . .47 C4
Hawkstone Rd
SE16 . . . . .40 B2
Hawkwell Wlk N1 . . .87 A4
Hawley Cres NW1 . . .13 A1
Hawley Inf Sch
NW1 . . . . .13 A1

Hawley Mews 4
NW1 . . . . .13 A1
Hawley Rd 3
NW1 . . . . .13 A1
Hawley St NW1 . . . . .13 A1
Haworth Ho 7
SW2 . . . . .62 C1
Hawstead Rd SE6 . . .67 A1
Hawthorn Ave E3 . . .26 B4
Hawthorn Ct
Putney SW15 . . . . . . .57 A4
Richmond TW9 . . . . . .45 A2
Hawthorn Cl N1 . . . . .16 A2
Hawthorne Ho
SW1 . . . . .147 A1
Hawthorn Ho
SE14 . . . . .51 B2
Hawthorn Rd NW10 . .8 C1
Hawthorn Wlk
W10 . . . . .23 A1
Hawtrey Rd NW3 . . . .12 A1
Haycroft Gdns
NW10 . . . . .22 A4
Haycroft Mans 1
NW10 . . . . .21 C4
Haycroft Rd SW2 . . . .62 A2
Hayday Rd E16 . . . . . .35 C4
Hayden Piper Ho
SW3 . . . . .158 C4
Hayden's Pl W11 . . . .31 B3
Haydon St E1 . . . . . .124 C4
Haydon Way
SW11 . . . . .59 C3
Haydon Wlk E1 . . . .111 A1
Hayes Ct
26 Camberwell
SE5 . . . . .48 B3
Streatham SW2 . . . . .74 A3
Hayes Gr SE15 . . . . . .64 B3
Hayes Pl NW1 . . . . . .90 B1
Hayfield Pas 1 E1 . . .25 B1
Hayfield Yd 13 E1 . . .25 B1
Hay Hill W1 . . . . . . .118 B3
Hayhurst N1 . . . . .86 A4
Hayles Bldgs
SE11 . . . . .150 A4
Hayles St SE11 . . . . .150 A4
Hayling Cl 20 N16 . . .16 A3
Haymans Point
SE11 . . . . .148 C2
Haymarket SW1 . . . .119 B3
Haymarket Ho 6
SE11 . . . . .49 C3
Haymerle Ho 8
SE15 . . . . .49 C4
Haymerle Rd SE15 . . .49 C4
Haymerle Sch
SE15 . . . . .49 C4
Hayne Ho
W11 . . . . .31 A1 112 A2
Haynes Ho 6 E9 . . . .17 C2
Hay's Galleria ★
SE1 . . . . .124 A2
Hay's La SE1 . . . . . .124 A2
Hay's Mews W1 . . . .118 A2
Hay St E2 . . . . .24 C4
Hayter Ho W12 . . . . .29 C2
Hayter Rd SW2 . . . . .62 B2
Haythorn Ho
SW11 . . . . .167 C3
Hayton Cl 11 E8 . . . .16 B2
Hayward Ct 34 SW4 .172 B2
Hayward Gallery ★
SE1 . . . . .121 A2
Hayward Gdns
SW15 . . . . .57 B1

Hayward Ho N1 . . . .85 B2
Haywards Pl EC1 . . . .96 A2
Hayward's Pl EC1 . . . .96 A2
Haywood Lo 28
N7 . . . . .13 C3
Hazelbourne Rd
SW12 . . . . .61 A1
Hazel Cl
Peckham SE15 . . . . . .49 C1
Upper Holloway N19 . .4 B2
Hazel Ct 13 SE16 . . . .33 A1
Hazeldon Rd SE4 . . . .66 A2
Hazel Ho
London SE4 . . . . .66 B4
12 Maitland Pk
NW3 . . . . .12 B2
Hazellville Rd N19 . . . .4 C3
Hazelmere Ct 10
SW2 . . . . .74 B3
Hazelmere Rd
NW6 . . . . .23 B4
Hazel Rd NW10 . . . . .22 B2
Hazelwood Ho 11
SE8 . . . . .41 A2
Hazelwood Mans
SW6 . . . . .164 C4
Hazlebury Rd
SW6 . . . . .166 B2
Hazledene Rd W4 . . .45 B4
Hazlewell Rd
SW15 . . . . .57 B2
Hazlewood Cres
W10 . . . . .23 A1
Hazlewood Twr
W10 . . . . .23 B1
Hazlitt Mews
W14 . . . . .126 A1
Hazlitt Rd W14 . . . .126 A1
Headbourne Ho
SE1 . . . . .137 C2
Headcorn 10 NW5 . .12 C2
Headfort Pl SW1 . . .131 C3
Headington Rd
SW18 . . . . .71 B2
Headlam Rd SW4 . . . .73 C4
Headlam St E1 . . . . . .25 A1
Heads Mews W11 . . . .31 C3
Head St E1 . . . . .32 C3
Heald St SE8, SE14 . . .51 C2
Healey St NW1 . . . . . .13 A2
Healy Ho 8 E3 . . . . . .26 C1
Heanor Ct 4 E5 . . . . .17 C4
Hearne Rd W4 . . . . . .44 C4
Hearn's Bldgs
SE17 . . . . .151 C3
Hearnshaw St 1
E14 . . . . .33 A3
Hearn St
EC2 . . . . .24 A1 98 B1
Hearnville Rd
SW12 . . . . .72 C3
Heart Hospl The
W1 . . . . .103 C3
Heart Raido W1 . . . .30 C2
Heathbrook Prim Sch
SW8 . . . . .170 B1
Heathcote Point 25
E9 . . . . .17 C2
Heathcote St WC1 . . .94 C3
Heathcroft NW11 . . . .2 A3
Heath Ct
2 Hampstead
NW3 . . . . .11 B2

Heath Ct continued
Stoke Newington N16 . .6 C3
Heather Cl SW8 . . . . .61 A4
Heather Ct SW4 . . . .172 B3
Heather Ho 11
E14 . . . . .34 B3
Heatherley Ct N16 . . . .7 C1
Heatherley Sch of
Fine Art SW10 . . . .157 A1
Heather Lo N16 . . . . . .7 A3
Heather Wlk W10 . . . .23 A1
Heathfield Ave
SW18 . . . . .71 C4
Heathfield Ct
1 Bow E3 . . . . .26 C3
5 Chiswick W4 . . . . . .37 C1
Wandsworth SW18 . . .71 C4
Heathfield Gdns
Acton Green W4 . . . . .37 B1
Blackheath SE3 . . . . .53 A1
Wandsworth SW18 . . .71 C4
Heathfield Ho SE3 . . .53 A1
Heathfield Pk NW2 . . .9 B2
Heathfield Rd
South Acton W3 . . . . .37 A4
Wandsworth SW18 . . .71 C4
Heathfield Sq
SW18 . . . . .71 C4
Heathfield Terr
W4 . . . . .37 C1
Heathgate Pl NW3 . .12 B4
Heath Hurst Rd
NW3 . . . . .12 A4
Heath La SE3 . . . . . . .52 C1
Heathland Rd N16 . . . .7 A3
Heath Mans
5 Hampstead
NW3 . . . . .11 B4
Putney SW15 . . . . . . .57 C1
Heathman's Rd
SW6 . . . . .165 A3
Heath Mead SW19 . . .69 C1
Heathmere Prim Sch
SW15 . . . . .68 C3
Heath Park Gdns
NW3 . . . . .2 A1
Heathpool Ct 8
E1 . . . . .25 A1
Heath Rd SW8 . . . . .170 B1
Heath Rise SW15 . . . .57 C1
Heath Royal SW15 . . .57 C1
Heathshott 8
TW10 . . . . .54 A1
Heathside NW3 . . . . .11 C4
Heathside Prep Sch
NW3 . . . . .11 B4
Heath Side NW3 . . . . .2 B1
Heathstan Rd
W12 . . . . .29 C3
Heath View NW5 . . . .12 C4
Heathview Ct
SW19 . . . . .69 C2
Heathview Gdns
SW15 . . . . .69 B4
Hoath Villas NW3 . . . .2 C1
Heathville Rd N4, ...5 A4
Heathwall St
SW11 . . . . .60 B4
Heathway SE3 . . . . . .53 C3
Heathway Ct NW3 . . . .1 C2
Heathwood Ct
SW12 . . . . .73 B3
Heaton Ho
Chelsea SW10 . . . . .157 A4
6 Peckham SE15 . . .50 A1
Heaton Rd SE15 . . . . .50 A1

Heaven Tree Cl
N1 . . . . .15 B3
Heaver Rd 24
SW11 . . . . .59 C4
Hebden Ct 24 E2 . . . .24 B4
Hebdon Rd SW17 . . . .72 A1
Heber Prim Sch
SE22 . . . . .64 B1
Heber Rd
Cricklewood NW2 . . . .9 C3
East Dulwich SE22 . . .64 B1
Hebron Rd W6 . . . . . .39 A3
Heckfield Pl SW6 . . .155 B1
Heckford Ho E14 . . . .34 A3
Heckford St E1 . . . . . .32 C2
Hector Ct
London SW9 . . . . . .173 B4
Putney SW15 . . . . . . .57 C2
Hector Ho 10 E2 . . . .25 A3
Heddington Gr N7 . . .14 B3
Heddon St W1 . . . . .118 C4
Hedger's Gr E9 . . . . . .18 A2
Hedger St SE11 . . . .150 A4
Hedingham Cl 6
N1 . . . . .15 B1
Hedley Ct SW15 . . . . .57 C1
Hedley Ho E14 . . . . . .42 B3
Hedley Row N5,
N16 . . . . .15 C3
Hedsor Ho
E2 . . . . .24 B1 98 C2
Heidegger Cres
SW13 . . . . .47 A3
Heights The SW11 . . . .11 B4
Heiron St SE17 . . . . . .48 A4
Helby Rd SW4 . . . . . .61 C1
Heldar Ct SE1 . . . . . .137 C3
Helena Pl 8 E9 . . . . . .25 B4
Helena Rd NW10 . . . . .9 A3
Helena Sq 12
SE16 . . . . .33 A2
Helen Gladstone Ho
SE1 . . . . .136 A4
Helen Ho 9 E2 . . . . . .25 A3
Helen Mackay Ho 7
E14 . . . . .34 C3
Helen Peele Cotts 10
SE16 . . . . .40 B3
Helensiea Ave
NW11 . . . . .1 C3
Helen's Pl E2 . . . . .25 B2
Helen Taylor Ho 9
SE16 . . . . .153 B4
Heliport Est The
SW11 . . . . .167 B1
Helix Ct 17 W11 . . . .30 C1
Helix Gdns SW2 . . . . .62 B1
Helix Rd SW2 . . . . . . .62 B1
Helix The SW19 . . . . .69 C2
Hellenic Coll of
London 130 C1
Hellings St E1 . . . . . .125 C1
Helmet Row EC1 . . . . .97 A2
Helmsdale Ho
NW6 . . . . .78 A1
Helmsley Pl E8 . . . . . .17 A1
Helmsley St 7 E8 . . . .17 A1
Helperby Rd NW10 . . .8 A1
Helsby Ct NW8 . . . . . .89 B2
Helsinki Sq SE16 . . . .41 A3
Helston Ho SE11 . . . .149 C2
Helston NW1 . . . . .83 A2
Helston Ho SE11 . . . .149 C2
Hemans St SW8 . . . .161 C1
Hemans St SW8 . . . .161 C1

Hemberton Rd
SW9 ....62 A4

Hemingford Rd
N1...........................85 A4

Hemlock Rd W12..29 B2

Hemming St
E1............24 C1 99 C1

Hemmingway Cl
NW5........................12 C4

Hemp Wlk SE17...151 C4
Hemstal Rd NW6...10 C1
Hemsworth Ct N1 ..24 A3
Hemsworth St N1 ..24 A3
Hemus Pl SW3 ....144 B1
Henchman St W12 ..29 B3
Henderson Ct
  8 Deptford SE14 ....50 C4
  Hampstead NW3 .....11 C3
  Wandsworth SW18 ...72 A4

Henderson Rd
NW8.......................89 B2

Henderson Rd
SW18 ....72 A4

Hendham Rd
SW17 ....72 B2
Hendre Ho SE1....152 B3
Hendre Rd SE1....152 B3
Hendrick Ave
SW12 ....72 B4
Heneage La EC3 ..110 B1
Heneage Pl EC3 ..110 B1
Heneage St E1......111 A4
Henfield Cl N19 .....4 B3
Henley Cl SE16 .....40 B4
Henley Ct
  Brondesbury NW2 .....9 C2
  Peckham SE15.......64 C4
Henley Dr SE1 ....153 A4
Henley Ho
E2.................24 B1 99 A2
Henley Prior N1 ...84 C1
Henley Rd NW10 ..22 B4
Henley St SW11 ..169 C2

Henniker Mews
SW3 ....157 A4
Henniker Rd E15 ..19 C3
Henning St SW11 168 A3
Henrietta Cl SE8 ...51 C4
Henrietta Ho **11**
W6.........................39 B1

Henrietta Mews
WC1 ....94 B2
Henrietta Pl W1...104 A2
Henrietta St
  Strand WC2 ....120 B4
  Stratford New Town
  E15 ....19 B3
Henriques St E1...111 C1

Henry Cavendish Prim
  Sch SW12 ....73 B3
Henry Compton Sec
  Sch SW6.................164 A4
Henry Dent Cl SE5..63 C4
Henry Dickens Ct
W11...........31 A1 112 A2
Henry Fawcett Prim
  Sch SE11................163 B4
Henry Ho
  Lambeth SE1 ....121 C1
  South Lambeth
  SW8 ....162 A2
  St John's Wood
  NW8 ....80 A2
Henry Jackson Ho
SW15 ....57 C4

Henry Jackson Rd
SW15 ....57 C4
Henry Rd N4 ....6 B3
Henryson Rd SE4 ..66 C2
Henry Wise Ho
SW1 ....147 A3

Henshall Point **19**
E3...........................27 A2
Henshall St N1......15 C2
Henshaw St SE17 .151 B4
Hensley Point **28**
E9...........................17 C2

Henslowe Rd
SE22 ....64 C2
Henslow Ho **12**
SE15 ....49 C3
Henson Ave NW2 ....9 B3
Henson Ct **3** N5 ...15 B4
Henstridge Pl
NW8.......................80 A3
Henty Cl SW11 ....168 B4
Henty Wlk SW15 ...57 A2
Hepburn Mews
SW11 ....60 B2
Hepplestone Cl
SW15 ....57 A1
Hepscott Rd E9 ....18 C1
Hepworth Ct
  Chelsea SW1 ....146 A1
  Islington N1 ....86 A4
Hera Ct **11** E14 .....41 C2
Heralds Pl SE11 ...150 A4
Herald St **5** E2 ......25 A1
Herbal Hill EC1 .....95 C1
Herbert Chapman Ct
N5...........................15 A4
Herbert Cres
SW1 ....131 A2
Herbert Gdns
  Chiswick W4...........45 A4
  Willesden Green
  NW10 ....22 A3
Herbert Ho E1 .....110 C2
Herbert Mews **15**
SW2 ....62 C1
Herbert Morrison Ho
SW6 ....154 C3
Herbert Morrison
  Prim Sch SW8...162 A1
Herbert St NW5 .....12 C2
Herbrand Est WC1..94 A2
Herbrand St WC1...94 A2
Hercules Ct **7**
SE14 ....51 A4
Hercules Pl N7 ....5 A1
Hercules Rd SE1 ..135 A1
Hercules St N7 ....5 A1
Hereford Bldgs
SW3 ....157 C4
Hereford Ho
  4 Brixton SW2 .....62 C3
  25 Camberwell SE5...48 B1
  Knightsbridge SW3 130 B2
  Walham Green
  SW10 ....156 B2
Hereford Mans **10**
W2...........................31 C3
Hereford Mews **11**
W2...........................31 C3
Hereford Pl SE14...51 B3
Hereford Rd
  Acton W3................28 B2
  Bayswater
  W2............31 C2 113 C4
Hereford Retreat **9**
SE15 ....49 C3
Hereford Sq SW7 143 A3

Hereford St
E2.................24 C1 99 B2
Hereward House Sch
NW3.........................11 C3
Heritage Cl SW9 ...63 A4
Heritage Cl SE8.....51 A4
Heritage Ho **22**
SW19 ....69 C3
Hermes Cl **11** W9...23 C1
Hermes Ct **11** SW9...173 B4
Hermes St N1 ....85 B1
Hermitage Ct
  2 Child's Hill NW2 ...1 C1
  Wapping E1 ....125 C1
Hermitage Gdns
NW2..........................1 C1
Hermitage La NW2..1 C1
Hermitage Prim Sch
E1...........................125 C2
Hermitage Row **4**
E8............................16 C3
Hermitage St W2 .101 B3
Hermitage The
  Barnes SW13 ....46 B2
  Richmond TW10 .....54 A2
Hermitage Villas
SW6 ....155 B4
Hermitage Wall
E1...........................125 C1
Hermit Pl NW6 ......78 A3
Hermit St EC1 ....96 A4
Herndon Rd SW18..59 B2
HERNE HILL.............63 B2
Herne Hill SE24 ....63 B3
Herne Hill Ho
SE24 ....63 A1
Herne Hill Mans
SE24 ....63 B3
Herne Hill Rd
SE24 ....63 B3
Herne Hill Sch
SE24 ....63 B2
Herne Hill Sta
SE24 ....63 A1
Herne Hill Stad
SE24 ....63 C1
Herne Pl SE24.......63 A2
Heron Cl NW10 ......8 A2
Heron Ct
  16 Cubitt Town
  E14 ....42 B3
  7 Dulwich SE21......75 C2
Herondale Ave
SW18 ....72 A3
Heron Dr N4 ....6 B2
Herongate N1 ....87 A4
Heron Ho
  Battersea SW11 ....168 B4
  Peckham SE15 ....49 B2
  St John's Wood
  NW8 ....80 A1
Heron Ind Est E15 .27 A3
Heron Pl
  Marylebone W1 .....103 C2
  Rotherhithe SE16 ...33 A1
Heron Quays E14 ..33 C1
Heron Quays Sta
E14 ....33 C1
Heron Rd SE24......63 B3
Heron Trad Est
W3...........................28 A4
Herrick Ho
  18 Camberwell
  SE5 ....48 C3
  17 Canonbury N1...15 C4
Herrick Rd N5 ....6 B1
Herrick St SW1....147 C3

Herries St W10 ......23 A3
Hersant Cl NW10 ...21 C4
Herschell's Mews
SE5 ....63 B4
Hersham Cl SW15 ..68 C4
Hershell Ct **1**
SW14 ....55 A3
Hertford Ave
SW14 ....56 A3
Hertford Ct **10**
SW11 ....60 A4
Hertford Lo **10**
SW19 ....70 A3
Hertford Pl W1 ......93 A1
Hertford Rd N1 .....24 A4
Hertford St W1 ....118 A1
Hertmitage The **5**
SE13 ....52 B1
Hertslet Rd N7 ....5 B1
Hertsmere Rd E14..33 C2
Hesewall Cl SW4 .171 A1
Hesketh Pl
W11............31 A2 112 A3
Heslop Ct **1**
SW12 ....72 C3
Heslop Rd SW12...72 B3
Hesper Mews
SW5 ....142 A3
Hesperus Cres
E14 ....42 A2
Hessel St E1 ....32 A3
Hestercombe Ave
SW6 ....164 B3
Hester Rd SW11 ..158 A1
Hester Terr TW9 ...54 C4
Hestia Ho **5**
SE1 ....138 A3
Heston Ho
  Gunnersbury W4 ....37 A1
  5 St Johns SE8 ....51 C2
Heston St SE14 .....51 C2
Hetherington Rd SW2,
SW4 ....62 A3
Hethpool Ho W2 ...89 B1
Hetley Rd W12 ......39 A4
Hetty Rees Ct **1**
N19.............................5 A4
Hevelius Cl SE10 ..43 B1
Hever Ho SE15 .....50 C4
Heversham Ho
SE15 ....50 B4
Heward Ct SE13 ....52 B1
Hewer Ho **6** SW4..61 B2
Hewer St W10........30 C4
Hewett Ho SW15 ..47 B1
Hewett St
EC2..............24 A1 98 B1
Hewison St E3 ......26 B3
Hewlett Rd E3 ....26 A3
Hewling Ho **1**
N16.........................16 A3
Hexagon The N6 ....3 B3
Hexham Rd SE27...75 B2
Hexton Ct N4 ....6 B2
Heybridge **9**
NW1.........................13 A2
Heydon Ho **3**
SE14 ....50 B2
Heyford Ave SW8 162 A2
Heyford Terr
SW8 ....162 B2
Heygate St SE17 ..151 A4
Heylyn Sq E3.........26 B2
Heysham La NW3 ...2 A1
Heythorp St SW18 ..70 B2
Heywood Ho
  11 Deptford SE14 ..50 C4
  6 Tulse Hill SW2...62 C1

Heyworth Rd E5....17 A4
Hibbert Ho **13** E14 ..41 C3
Hibbert St SW11 ...59 C4
Hichisson Rd SE15 .65 B2
Hickes Ho **6** NW6 ..11 C1
Hickey's Almshouses
  7 TW9 ....54 B3
Hickin St **2** E14 ....42 B3
Hickleton NW1 ......83 A3
Hickling Ho **10**
SE16 ....40 A3
Hickmore Wlk
SW4 ....61 B4
Hicks Cl SW11 ......60 A4
Hicks St SE8 ....41 A1
Hide Pl SW1 ....147 B3
Hide Twr SW1 ......147 B3
Hieover SE21 ....75 B2
Higgins Ho **7** N1...24 A4
Higginson Ho **2**
NW3...........................12 B1
Higgs Ind Est **9**
SE24 ....63 A4
Highbridge Ct **13**
SE14 ....50 B3
High Bridge Wharf
SE10 ....42 C1
Highbury Mans **24**
N1...........................15 A2
HIGHBURY..............15 A4
Highbury Cnr N5 ...15 A2
Highbury Corner
N5...........................15 A2
Highbury Cres N5 .14 C2
Highbury Fields Sch
N5...........................15 A3
Highbury Gr N5 ....15 A3
Highbury Grange
N5...........................15 A4
Highbury Grove Ct
N5...........................15 A2
Highbury Grove Sch
N5...........................15 B4
Highbury Hill N5 ...15 A4
Highbury & Islington
  Sta N1 ....15 A1
Highbury New Pk
N5...........................15 B4
Highbury Pk N5 ....15 A4
Highbury Pl N5 .....15 A3
Highbury Quadrant
N5.............................6 B1
Highbury Quadrant
  Prim Sch N5 ....15 B4
Highbury Station Rd
N1...........................14 C1
Highbury Terr N5 ..15 A3
Highbury Terrace
  Mews N5 ....15 A3
Highcliffe Dr
SW15 ....56 B1
Highcroft Rd N19 ....5 A4
Highcross Way **4**
SW15 ....68 C3
Highdown Rd
SW15 ....57 A4
Highfield Ave
NW11 ....1 A4
Highfield Cl SE13 .67 C1
Highfield Mews
NW6........................11 A4
Highfield Rd W3 ..28 B4
Highfield Sch
SW18 ....72 A4
Highfields Gr N6 ....3 B3
HIGHGATE..................3 C1

Highgate Archway
  N6...................4 B3
Highgate Ave N6...4 B4
Highgate Cemetery★
  N19.....................4 A3
Highgate CI N6......3 C4
Highgate High St
  N6....................4 A3
Highgate Ho ■
  SE26................76 C1
Highgate Rd NW5..13 A4
Highgate Sch
  Highgate N6...........3 B4
  Highgate N6...........3 C4
Highgate West Hill
  N6.....................3 C2
Highgrove Point ■
  NW3..............11 B4
High Holborn
  WC1..............106 C3
High Holborn Ho
  WC1..............107 A3
Highlands Ave W3..28 B2
Highlands CI N4.....5 A4
Highlands Heath
  SW15................69 B4
Highlever Rd W10..30 B4
High London ■ N6..4 C4
Highmore Rd SE3..53 A3
High Mount ■ N4...5 A4
High Park Ave
  TW9................44 C2
High Park Rd TW9..44 C2
High Par The
  SW16................74 A1
High Point N6........3 C4
High Rd NW10......8 C2
Highshore Rd
  SE15................49 B1
Highshore Sch
  SE15................49 B1
High St Acton W3...28 A1
  Brentford TW8.........44 A4
  Stratford Marsh E15 27 B4
High Street Harlesden
  NW10................21 B3
High Street
  Kensington Sta
  W8................128 A3
High The SW16.....74 A1
High Timber St
  EC4................122 C4
High Trees SW2....74 C3
Hightrees Ho
  SW12................60 C1
Highview N8..........5 A4
Highview ■
  SW19................70 A3
High View Prim Sch
  SW11................59 C3
Highway Bsns Pk The
  ■ E1................32 C2
Highway The ■ E1..32 B2
Highway Trad Ctr The
  ■ E1................32 C2
Highwood CI SE22..76 C3
Highwood Rd N19...5 A1
Highworth St
  NW1................102 B4
Hilary CI SW6......156 A2
Hilary Rd W12.......29 B2
Hilborough Ct ■
  E8...................24 B4
Hilborough Rd ■
  E8...................16 B1

Hilda Lockert Wlk
  SW9...................48 A1
Hilda Terr ■ SW9..173 C2
Hildith Ho ■
  TW10................54 B1
Hildred Ho SW1...146 A4
Hildreth St SW12..73 A3
Hildreth Street Mews
  ■ SW12..............73 A3
Hildyard Rd SW6..155 C4
Hiley Rd NW10.....22 B2
Hilgrove Rd NW6...11 B1
Hillary Ct ■ W12..39 B4
Hillbeck CI
  Deptford SE15.......50 B3
  Deptford SE15.......50 B4
Hillbrow ■ TW10..54 A1
Hillbury Rd SW17..73 A1
Hillcourt Rd SE22..65 A1
Hillcrest
  Camberwell SE24...63 C3
  Highgate N6...........3 C4
  Notting Hill
  W11...........31 B2 112 C3
Hillcrest CI SE26..76 B1
Hillcrest Rd W3.....28 A1
Hill Ct
  Hampstead NW3.....12 A4
  Putney SW15...........57 C2
Hilldrop Cres N7...13 C3
Hilldrop La N7.......13 C3
Hilldrop Rd N7......13 C3
Hillersdon Ave
  SW13................46 C1
Hillersdon Ho
  SW1................146 A2
Hillery Cl SE17....151 C3
Hill Farm Rd W10..30 C4
Hillfield Ct NW3....12 A3
Hillfield Ho N5.....15 B3
Hillfield Mans
  NW3................11 B4
Hillfield Rd NW6...10 C3
Hillgate Pl
  Balham SW12.........73 A4
  Kensington
  W8............31 C1 113 B2
Hillgate St
  W8............31 C1 113 B2
Hill House Sch
  SW1................131 A1
Hilliard Ho ■ E1...32 A1
Hilliard's Ct ■ E1..32 B1
Hillier Ho ■ NW1..13 C1
Hillier Rd SW11....60 B1
Hillingdon St
  SE17................48 A4
Hill Lo SW11........59 C3
Hillman Dr ■
  NW10................22 B1
Hillman St E8.......17 A2
Hillmarton Rd N7..14 A3
Hillmead Dr SW9..63 A3
Hill Mead Prim Sch
  SW9.................63 A3
Hillmore Ct SE13..67 C4
Hill Rd NW8.........79 A1
Hillrise Mans N19..5 A4
Hillrise Rd N19......5 A4
Hillsboro Rd SE22..64 A2
Hillsborough Ct
  NW6.................78 A3
Hillside
  Greenwich SE10...52 C3
  Stonebridge NW10..20 C4
Hillside Ct NW8....78 B2
Hillside Ct NW3....11 A3

Hillside Gdns SW2..74 C2
Hillside Rd SW2....74 C2
Hillsleigh Rd
  W14..........31 B1 113 A2
Hills Pl W1.........104 C1
Hill St W1...........118 A2
Hillstone Ct ■ E3..27 A1
Hilltop Ct
  London SW18.......59 C3
  South Hampstead
  NW8................11 B1
Hilltop Ho ■ N6....4 C4
Hilltop Rd NW6....10 C1
Hill View NW1......81 A4
Hillway N6............4 A2
Hill Wood Ho NW1..83 B1
Hillworth Rd SW2..74 C4
Hillyard St SW9...173 B3
Hillyfield Cl E9......18 A3
Hilly Fields Cres
  SE4..................66 C4
Hilsea Point ■
  SW15................69 A3
Hilsea St E5..........17 B4
Hilton Ho
  Lower Holloway
  N7...................14 A4
  ■ Nunhead SE4....65 C3
Hilversum Cres ■
  SE22................64 A2
Hinckley Rd SE15..64 C3
Hind Ct EC4.......107 C1
Hinde Mews W1...103 C2
Hinde St W1........103 C2
Hind Gr E14.........33 C3
Hindhead Point ■
  SW15................69 A3
Hind Ho
  ■ Deptford SE14..50 C4
  Islington N7...........14 C4
Hindle Ho E8........16 B3
Hindley Ho N7......5 B1
Hindlip Ho SW8...171 B3
Hindmans Rd
  SE22................64 C2
Hindmarsh CI E1..125 C4
Hindrey Rd E5......17 A3
Hinstock NW6......78 A4
Hinton Rd SE24....63 A4
Hippodrome Mews
  W11.........31 A2 112 A3
Hippodrome Pl
  W11.........31 A2 112 A3
Hirst Ct SW1.......146 A1
Hitchin Sq E3.......26 A3
Hither Gr ■ SE16..40 B3
Hitherfield Prim Sch
  SW16................74 C1
Hitherfield Rd SW16,
  SW27................74 C1
Hither Green La
  SE13................67 C1
Hither Green Prim
  Sch SE13............67 C1
Hitherlands SW12..73 A2
HM Prison
  Wormwood Scrubs
  W12.................29 C3
HMS Belfast★
  SE1................124 B2
Hoadly Rd SW16...73 C2
Hobart Pl SW1.....132 A2
Hobbes Wlk SW15..57 A2
Hobb's Ct SE1.....139 A4
Hobbs' Pl N1........24 A4
Hobday St E14......34 A3

Hobhouse Ct
  SW1................119 C3
Hobsons Pl E1.....111 B4
Hobury St SW10...157 B3
Hocker St
  E2.............24 B2 98 C3
Hockett Cl SE8.....41 B2
Hockley Ho ■ E9..17 B2
Hockliffe Ho ■
  W10.................30 B4
Hockney Ct ■
  SE16................40 A1
Hockworth Ho ■
  N16....................7 A3
Hocroft Ave NW2..1 B1
Hocroft Ct NW2....1 B1
Hocroft Rd NW2...1 B1
Hocroft Wlk NW2..1 B1
Hodford Lo NW11..1 C2
Hodford Rd NW11..1 B3
Hodister Cl SE5...48 B3
Hoffman Sq N1....97 C4
Hofland Rd W14..126 A2
Hogan Mews ■ W2.101 B4
Hogan Way E5.......7 C2
Hogarth Bsns Pk
  W4...................46 A4
Hogarth Ct
  ■ Camden Town
  NW1................13 B1
  City of London EC3..124 B4
  ■ Whitechapel E1..111 C1
Hogarth Ho SW1..147 C3
Hogarth Ind Est
  NW10................21 C1
Hogarth La W4.....46 A4
Hogarth Pl SW5...142 A3
Hogarth Rd SW5..142 A3
Hogarth Roundabout
  W4...................46 A4
Hogarth's House★
  W4...................46 A4
Holbeach Mews ■
  SW12................73 A3
Holbeck Row
  SE15................49 C3
Holbein Ho ■ SW1.145 B2
Holbein Mews
  SW1................145 B2
Holbein Pl SW1...145 B3
Holberton Gdns
  NW10................22 A2
HOLBORN............107 C3
Holborn EC1.......107 C3
Holborn Cir EC1...107 C2
Holborn Ho ■
  W12..................30 A2
Holborn Pl WC1...106 C3
Holborn Sta WC1..106 C3
Holborn Viaduct
  EC1................108 A3
Holbrooke Cl N7...14 A4
Holbrooke Ct N7...14 A4
Holbrook Ho
  Acton W3...........28 C4
  ■ Streatham SW2 74 B3
Holcombe Ho
  SW9..................62 A4
Holcombe Pl SE4..66 A4
Holcombe St W6..39 A2
Holcroft Ct W1....104 C4
Holcroft Ho
  Battersea SW11....59 C4
  Lewisham SE13....52 B2
Holcroft Rd E9......17 B1
Holdenby Rd SE4..66 A2

Hig–Hol   225

Holden Ho
  ■ Deptford SE8...51 C3
  Islington N1.........86 C3
Holden Point E15..19 C2
Holden St SW11...169 B1
Holdernesse Rd ■
  SW17................72 C2
Holderness Ho
  SE5..................64 A4
Holdsworth Ho ■
  SW2..................74 C4
Holford Ho
  ■ Bermondsey
  SE16................40 A2
  Finsbury WC1.......95 A4
Holford Pl WC1....95 A4
Holford Rd NW3....2 B1
Holford Yd WC1....95 B4
Holgate Ave SW11..59 C4
Holland Gdns
  Brentford TW8......44 A4
  Kensington W14..126 B2
Holland Gr SW9...163 C1
Holland Park
  W11..........31 B1 112 C1
Holland Park Ave
  W11..........31 A1 112 B1
Holland Park Gdns
  W14................126 A4
Holland Park Mews
  W11..........31 B1 112 C1
Holland Park Rd
  W14................127 A1
Holland Park Rdbt
  W12..................39 C4
Holland Park Sch
  W8................127 A4
Holland Park Sta
  W11..........31 B1 112 C1
Holland Pas N1.....86 C4
Holland Pl W8.....128 A4
Holland Rd
  West Kensington
  W14................126 B2
  Willesden Green
  NW10................22 A3
Holland Rise Ho
  SW9................163 A1
Holland St
  Kensington W8...127 C4
  Lambeth SE1.....122 B2
Holland Villas Rd
  W14................126 A3
Holland Wlk
  Kensington W14..127 A3
  Upper Holloway N19 4 C3
Hollar Rd N16........7 B1
Hollen St W1......105 B2
Holles Ho SW9....173 B2
Holles St W1.......104 B2
Holley Rd W3.......38 A4
Holliday Sq ■
  SW11................59 C4
Hollies The SW12..73 B2
Hollies Way ■
  SW12..................72 C4
Hollingbourne Rd
  SE24................63 B2
Hollins Ho N7.......14 A4
Hollisfield WC1.....94 B3

Holloway Rd
Lower Holloway
N7 . . . . 14 B4
Upper Holloway N19 . . 4 C2
Holloway Road Sta
N7 . . . . 14 B4
Holloway Sch N7 . . . 13 C3
Holly Berry La 8
NW3 . . . . 11 B4
Hollybush Gdns
E2 . . . . 25 A2
Holly Bush Hill 4
NW3 . . . . 11 B4
Hollybush Ho 23
E2 . . . . 25 A2
Holly Bush Pl E2 . . 25 A2
Holly Bush Steps 6
NW3 . . . . 11 B4
Holly Bush Vale 10
NW3 . . . . 11 B4
Hollycroft Ave NW3 . 1 C1
Hollydale Prim Sch
SE15 . . . . 50 B1
Hollydale Rd SE15 . 50 B1
Hollydene
Hither Green SE13 . . 67 C1
7 Peckham SE15 . . . 50 A2
Holly Gr SE15 . . . . 49 C1
Hollyhedge Ho
SE3 . . . . 52 C1
Holly Hedge Terr
SE13 . . . . 67 C2
Holly Hill NW3 . . . 11 B4
Holly Lo W8 . . . . . 127 B4
Holly Lodge SE13 . . 67 C3
Holly Lodge Gdns
N6 . . . . 3 C3
Holly Lodge Mans
N6 . . . . 3 C2
Holly Mews SW10 143 A1
Holly Mount NW3 . 11 B4
Hollymount Cl 9
SE10 . . . . 52 B2
Holly Park Est N4 . . 5 B4
Holly Pk N4 . . . . 5 B4
Holly Pl NW3 . . . . . 11 B4
Holly Rd 6 W4 . . . 37 C2
Holly St E8 . . . . . . 16 B1
Holly Terr N6 . . . . . . 3 C3
Hollytree Cl SW19 . 69 C3
Holly Tree Ho SE4 . 66 B4
Holly Village N6 . . . . 4 A2
Holly Wlk NW3 . . . 11 B4
Hollywood Lofts
E1 . . . . 24 B1 98 C1
Hollywood Mews
SW10 . . . . 156 C4
Hollywood Rd
SW10 . . . . 156 C4
Holman Ho 2 E2 . . 25 C2
Holman Hunt Ho
W14 . . . . 140 A1
Holman Rd SW11 . 167 B1
Holmbrook NW1 . . 83 A1
Holmbury Ct
SW17 . . . . 72 B2
Holmbury Ho SW9 . 63 A2
Holmbush Rd
SW15 . . . . 58 A1
Holmcote Gdns
N5 . . . . 15 B3
Holmdale Rd NW6 . 10 C3
Holmdene Ave
SE24 . . . . 63 B2
Holmead Rd SW6 156 B1

Holmefield Ct 4
NW3 . . . . 12 A2
Holmefield Ho
W10 . . . . 23 A1
Holmes Cl SE22 . . 64 C3
Holmes Ct
18 South Acton
W4 . . . . 37 B3
South Lambeth
SW4 . . . . 172 A2
Holmesdale Ave
SW14 . . . . 55 A3
Holmesdale Ho 12
NW6 . . . . 23 C4
Holmesdale Rd
Highgate N6 . . . . 4 A4
Richmond TW9 . . . . 44 B2
Holmesley Rd
SE23 . . . . 66 A1
Holmes Pl SW10 . 157 A4
Holmes Rd NW5 . . 13 A3
Holmes Terr SE1 . 135 B4
Holmewood Gdns
SW2 . . . . 74 B4
Holmewood Rd
SW2 . . . . 74 B4
Holmhurst SE13 . . 67 C1
Holmleigh Prim Sch
N16 . . . . 7 A3
Holmleigh Rd N16 . . 7 A3
Holm Oak Cl
SW15 . . . . 58 B1
Holmsbury Ho 6
N7 . . . . 13 C3
Holmsdale Ho 24
E14 . . . . 34 A2
Holmside Ct SW12 . 60 C1
Holmside Rd
SW12 . . . . 60 C1
Holmsley Ho
SW15 . . . . 68 B4
Holm Wlk SE3 . . . 53 C1
Holmwood Ct 3
N16 . . . . 7 B4
Holocaust Meml
Gdn★ W2 . . . . 131 A4
Holroyd Rd SW15 . 57 B2
Holsgrove Ct W3 . . 29 A1
Holst Mans SW13 . 47 B3
Holsworthy Ho 49
E3 . . . . 27 A2
Holsworthy Sq
WC1 . . . . 95 A1
Holt Ct
Greenwich SE10 . . . 52 B4
Stratford New Town
E15 . . . . 19 B3
Holt Ho SW2 . . . . . 62 C1
Holton St E1 . . . . . . 25 C1
Holwood Pl 7
SW4 . . . . 61 C3
Holybourne Ave
SW15 . . . . 68 C4
Holy Cross RC Sch
SW6 . . . . 165 B4
Holy Family RC Prim
Sch E14 . . . . 33 C2
Holy Ghost RC Prim
Sch SW12 . . . . 72 C4
Holyhead Cl E3 . . . 26 C2
Holyoake Ct SE16 . 41 B4
Holyoak Rd SE11 . 150 B3
Holyport Rd SW6 . . 47 C3
Holyrood Ho N4 . . . 6 B3
Holyrood Mews 10
E16 . . . . 35 C1
Holyrood St SE1 . . 124 A1

Holy Trinity CE Prim
Sch
Belgravia SW1 . . . . 145 B4
Dalston E8 . . . . 16 B2
Hampstead NW3 . . . 11 B2
Richmond TW10 . . . 54 C3
Streatham SW2 . . . 74 B4
Holy Trinity & St
Silas CE Prim Sch
NW1 . . . . 13 A1
Holywell Cl
38 Bermondsey
SE16 . . . . 40 A1
2 Greenwich SE3 . . 53 C4
Holywell La
EC2 . . . . 24 A1 98 B2
Holywell Row
EC2 . . . . 24 A1 98 A1
Homan Ho 6
SW4 . . . . 73 C4
Homecross Ho 7
W4 . . . . 37 C1
Homefield Ho W4 . 38 B1
Homefield St 14
N1 . . . . 24 A3
Homeleigh Ct 3
SW16 . . . . 74 A1
Homeleigh Rd
SE15 . . . . 65 C2
Homemead SW12 . 73 A2
Home Office SW1 133 B3
Home Park Rd
SW19 . . . . 70 B1
Home Rd SW11 . . 168 A2
Homer Dr E14 . . . . 41 C2
Homer Rd E9 . . . . . 18 A2
Homer Row W1 . . 102 B3
Homer St W1 . . . . 102 B3
HOMERTON 17 C2
Homerton Coll of
Technology E9 . . . 17 B3
Homerton Gr E9 . . 17 C3
Homerton High St
E9 . . . . 17 B3
Homerton Rd E9 . . 18 B3
Homerton Row E9 . 17 B3
Homerton Sta E9 . . 17 C2
Homerton Terr E9 . 17 B2
Homerton University
Hosp E9 . . . . 17 C3
Homestall Rd
SE22 . . . . 65 B2
Homestead Rd
SW6 . . . . 155 A1
Homewoods 3
SW12 . . . . 73 B4
Homildon Ho 10
SE26 . . . . 76 C1
Honduras St EC1 . . 96 C2
Honeybourne Rd
NW6 . . . . 11 A3
Honeybrook Rd SW12,
SW4 . . . . 73 B4
Honeyfield N4 . . . . . 5 C2
Honey La EC2 . . . . 109 A1
Honey Lane Ho
SW10 . . . . 156 B4
Honeyman Cl NW6 . 9 C1
Honeywell Jun & Inf
Schs SW11 . . . . . . 60 B1
Honeywell Rd
SW11 . . . . 60 B1
Honeywood Ho 6
SE15 . . . . 49 C2
Honeywood Rd
NW10 . . . . 21 B3

Honiton Gdns 1
SE15 . . . . 50 B1
Honiton Ho 26
SE5 . . . . 48 B1
Honiton Rd NW6 . . 23 B3
HONOR OAK 65 B2
Honor Oak Park Sta
SE23 . . . . 65 C1
Honor Oak Pk
SE23 . . . . 65 C1
Honor Oak Rise
SE23 . . . . 65 B1
Honwell Ho 24
W2 . . . . 31 C4
Hood Ave SW14 . . 55 B2
Hood Ct N7 . . . . 5 B1
Hood Ho 17 SE5 . . 48 C3
Hooke Ct SE10 . . . 52 B2
Hooke Ho 23 E3 . . 26 A3
Hookham Ct SW8 171 B4
Hooks Cl SE15 . . . 50 A2
Hooper Ho 9
SW18 . . . . 58 B2
Hooper Rd E16 . . . 35 C3
Hooper's Ct SW1 . 130 C3
Hooper's Mews 4
W3 . . . . 28 B1
Hooper St E1 . . . . 111 B1
Hoop La NW11 . . . . 1 C4
Hope 2
Brentford TW8 . . 36 A1
Canonbury N1 . . . . . 15 B2
Hopefield Ave
NW6 . . . . 23 A3
Hope Gdns 19 W3 . 37 A4
Hope St SW11 . . . . 59 C4
Hopetown St E1 . . 111 A3
Hopewell St SE5 . . 48 C3
Hop Gdns WC2 . . . 120 A3
Hopgood St 8
W12 . . . . 30 B1
Hopkins Ho 17
E14 . . . . 33 C3
Hopkinson Ho
SW11 . . . . 169 B2
Hopkins's Pl
NW1 . . . . 81 B4
Hopkins St W1 . . . 105 B1
Hopping La N1 . . . . 15 A2
Hopton Ho 9
SW9 . . . . 48 A1
Hopton's Gdns
SE1 . . . . 122 B2
Hopton St SE1 . . . 122 B2
Hopwood Cl SW17 . 71 B1
Hopwood Rd SE17 . 48 C4
Hopwood Wlk E8 . . 16 C1
Horatio Ho 21 E2 . . 24 B3
Horatio Pl 9 E14 . . 34 B1
Horatio St 1 E2 . . . 24 B3
Horbury Cres
W11 . . . . 31 C2 113 B3
Horbury Mews
W11 . . . . 31 B2 113 A3
Horder Rd SW6 . . 164 B3
Hordle Prom E 18
SE15 . . . . 49 B3
Hordle Prom N 4
SE15 . . . . 49 B3
Hordle Prom S 7
SE15 . . . . 49 B3
Horizon Bldg 22
E14 . . . . 33 C2
Horizon Sch N16 . . 16 A4
Horle Wlk SE5 . . . . 48 A1
Hormead Rd W9 . . 23 B1

Hornbeam Cl
SE11 . . . . 149 B4
Hornbeam Ho 2
NW3 . . . . 12 B2
Hornbeam Sq 3
E3 . . . . 26 B4
Hornblower Cl 2
SE16 . . . . 41 A2
Hornby Ho 2 SE11 . 163 B3
Hornby Ho 5 SE11 . 163 C3
Horndean Cl 3
SW15 . . . . 68 C3
Horner Hos 51 N1 . . 24 A4
Horne Way SW15 . . 47 B1
Horn La Acton W3 . 28 B3
Greenwich SE10 . . . 43 C2
Horn Link Way
SE10 . . . . 43 C2
Hornsby House Sch
SW12 . . . . 72 C3
Hornsey La N6 . . . . 4 B4
Hornsey Lane Gdns
N6 . . . . 4 B4
Hornsey Rd N7, N19 . 5 B2
Hornsey Rise Gdns
N19 . . . . 5 A4
Hornsey St N7 . . . . 14 B3
Hornshay St SE15 . 50 B4
Hornton Ct W8 . . . 127 C3
Hornton Pl W8 . . . 127 C3
Hornton St W8 . . . 127 C4
Horrocks Ho
SW15 . . . . 68 C4
Horse & Dolphin Yd
W1 . . . . 119 C4
Horseferry Pl
SE10 . . . . 52 B4
Horseferry Rd
Limehouse E14 . . . . 33 A2
Westminster SW1 . 147 C4
Horseferry Rd Est
SW1 . . . . 133 B1
Horse Guards Ave
SW1 . . . . 120 A1
Horse Guards Par★
SW1 . . . . 119 C1
Horse Guards Rd
SW1 . . . . 133 C4
Horsell Rd N5 . . . . 14 C3
Horselydown La
SE1 . . . . 124 C1
Horselydown Mans
SE1 . . . . 138 C4
Horsemongers Mews
SE1 . . . . 137 A3
Horsendon Ho 11
N7 . . . . 13 C3
Horseshoe Cl E14 . 42 B1
Horse Yd N1 . . . . . 86 B4
Horsfield Ho 13
N1 . . . . 15 B1
Horsford Rd SW2 . . 62 B2
Horsley Ct SW1 . . 147 C3
Horsley Ho 11 SE4 . 65 C3
Horsley St 3
SE17 . . . . 48 C4
Horsman Ho SE5 . . 48 B4
Horsman St SE5 . . 48 B4
Horsmonden Rd
SE4 . . . . 66 B1
Horston Ho N4 . . . . 6 B4
Hortensia Ho
SW10 . . . . 156 C2
Hortensia Rd
SW10 . . . . 156 C2
Horticultural Pl 6
W4 . . . . 37 C1

Horton Ave NW2 ...10 A4
Horton Ho
13 Deptford SE15 ...50 B4
South Lambeth
SW8 ......162 C2
West Kensington
W14 ....140 A1
Horton Rd E8 ...17 A2
Horton St SE13 ...67 A4
Horwood Ho
24 Bethnal Green
E2 ....25 A2
Marylebone NW8... 90 B2
Hosack Rd SW17 ...72 C2
Hosier La EC1 ...108 B3
Hoskins St SE10 ...42 C1
Hospl for Tropical
Diseases
Fitzrovia NW1 ......93 A1
Somers Town NW1 ..83 C3
Hospl of St John & St
Elizabeth NW8 ...79 B1
Hotham Prim Sch
SW15 ......57 C3
Hotham Rd SW15...57 B4
Hothfield PI SE16...40 B3
Hotspur St SE11 ...149 B2
Houblon Rd TW10 ..54 A2
Houghton Cl 7
E8 ....16 B2
Houghton Sq SW9..62 A4
Houghton St
WC2 ......107 A1
Houndsditch EC3...110 B2
House of Detention★
EC1 ....95 C2
Houseman Way 3
SE5 ....48 C3
Houses of
Parliament★
SW1 ....134 B2
Hoveden Rd NW2 ...10 A3
Howard Bldg
SW8 ....160 A3
Howard Cl
Acton W3 .....28 A3
Cricklewood NW2 ..10 A4
Howard Ct
Lewisham SE10 ...52 B2
Peckham SE15 ....64 C4
Howard Ho
8 Brixton SW9 ...62 C4
14 Deptford SE8 ...51 B4
Fitzrovia W1 ......92 B1
Howard Mews N5..15 A4
Howard's La SW15 ...57 B3
Howarth Ct E15 ...19 B3
Howbury Rd SE15 ...65 B4
Howcroft Ho 3
E3 ....26 B2
Howden St SE15...64 C4
Howell Ho 5 N7...13 C3
Howell Wlk SE1 ...150 B3
Howgate Rd SW14...55 C4
Howick PI SW1 ...133 A1
Howie St SW11 ...158 A1
Howitt Cl
5 Maitland Pk
NW3 ....12 A2
Stoke Newington
N16.............16 A4
Howitt Rd NW3 ...12 A2

Howland Ho 9
SW16 ....74 A1
Howland Mews E
W1 ....105 A4
Howland St W1 ...105 A4
Howland Way
SE16 ....41 A4
Howletts Rd SE24...63 B1
Howley PI W2 ...101 A4
Howsman Rd
SW13.........46 B4
Howson Rd SE4 ...66 A3
Howson Terr
TW10 ....54 A1
How's St E2 ....24 B3
HOXTON 24 A3
Hoxton Mkt
N1........24 A2 98 A3
Hoxton Point
EC1 ....98 A3
Hoxton Sq
N1.......24 A2 98 A3
Hoxton St N1 ...24 A3
Hoylake Rd W3...29 A3
Hoyland Cl 4
SE15 ....50 A3
Hoy St E16 ......35 B3
Hub Buildings The 4
SW12 ....73 A3
Huberd Ho SE1 ...137 C2
Hubert Gr SW9 ...62 A4
Hubert Ho NW8 ...90 A1
Hucknall Ct NW8...89 B2
Huddart St 5 E3 ...33 B4
Huddleston Cl E2 ...25 B3
Huddlestone Rd
NW2 ....9 A2
Huddleston Rd N7...13 A4
Hudson Cl 15 W12...30 A2
Hudson Ct 1 E14...41 C1
Hudson Ho
Chelsea SW10 ...156 C2
5 Notting Hill W11...31 A3
Hudsons Ho N1 ...97 C3
Hudson's PI SW1 ...146 C4
Huggin Ct EC4 ...123 A4
Huggin Hill EC4 ...123 A4
Huggins Ho 5 E3...26 C2
Huggins PI SW2 ...74 B3
Hughan Rd E15 ...19 C3
Hugh Astor Ct
SE1 ....136 B3
Hugh Dalton Ave
SW6 ....154 C3
Hughenden Ho
NW8 ....90 A2
Hughendon Terr
F15 ....19 B4
Hughes Ho
26 Bethnal Green
E2 ....25 B2
Camberwell SE5 ...48 B2
3 Deptford SE8 ...51 C4
Newington SE17 ...150 B3
Hughes Mans E1 ....99 C1
Hughes Terr 6
E16 ....35 B4
Hugh Gaitskell Cl
SW6 ....154 C3
Hugh Gaitskell Ho
Stoke Newington
N16..........7 B2
Willesden NW10 ...8 B1
Hugh Mews SW1 ...146 B3
Hugh Morgan Ho 3
SW4 ....61 C4

Hugh Myddelton Prim
Sch EC1 .....95 C3
Hugh Platt Ho 20
E2 ....25 A3
Hugh St SW1 ...146 B3
Hugo Ho SW1 ...131 A2
Hugon Rd SW6 ...59 A4
Hugo Rd N19 ...13 B4
Huguenot Ct E1 ...111 B4
Huguenot PI
London SW18 ...59 B2
Spitalfields E1 ...111 A4
Huguenot Sq
SE15 ....65 A4
Hullbridge Mews
N1 ....87 B4
Hull Cl SE16 ......32 C1
Hull Ct SE15 .....48 C1
Hull St EC1 ......96 C3
Hulme PI 3 SE1 ...137 A3
Humber Dr W10 ...22 C1
Humber Rd SE3 ...53 B4
Humberton Cl E9...18 A3
Humbolt Rd W6 ...154 A3
Hume Ct 11 N1 ...15 A1
Hume Ho 13 W11...30 C1
Humphrey Ct
SW11 ....167 C3
Humphry Ho 10
SW15 ....57 C2
Hungerford Bridge
WC2 ....120 C2
Hungerford Ho
SW1 ....161 A4
Hungerford La
WC2 ....120 B2
Hungerford Prim Sch
N7 ....13 C2
Hungerford Rd
12 Camden Town
N7 ....13 C2
Lower Holloway N7 ...14 A3
Hungerford St 12
E1 ....32 A3
Hunsdon Rd SE14...50 C3
Hunslett St 28 E2 ...25 B3
Hunstanton Ho
NW1 ....102 A4
Hunt Cl W11 .....30 C1
Hunter Cl
Borough The SE1 ...137 C1
Upper Tooting
SW12 ....72 C3
Hunter Ct
8 London SE5 ...63 C3
27 Streatham SW2 ...74 C4
Hunter Ho
Bloomsbury WC1 ...94 B2
Lambeth SE1 ...136 B3
South Lambeth
SW8 ....161 C1
6 Tufnell Pk N19...4 B1
West Brompton
SW5 ....141 C1
Hunterian Mus★
WC2 ....107 A2
Hunter Lo 9 W9...31 C4
Hunter St WC1 ...94 B2
Huntingdon Ct
SW14 ....55 B4
Huntingdon Gdns
W4 ....45 B3

Huntingdon Ho
SW5 ....141 C2
Huntingdon St
Canning Town E16 ...35 B3
Islington N1 ...14 B1
Huntingfield Rd
SW15 ....56 C2
Huntingford Ho
SW15 ....47 B1
Huntington Ho
NW2 ....9 B2
Huntley St WC1 ...93 B1
Hunton St E1 ...111 B4
Hunts Cl SE3 ...53 C1
Hunt's Ct WC2 ...119 C3
Huntshaw Ho 37
E3 ....27 A2
Hunt's La E15 ...27 B3
Huntsman St
SE17 ....152 A3
Huntspill St SW17...71 B1
Hunts Slip Rd
SE21 ....76 A2
Huntsworth Mews
NW1 ....90 C1
Hurdwick Ho NW1 ...82 C2
Hurdwick PI NW1 ...82 C2
Hurleston Ho 10
SE8 ....41 B1
Hurley Cres SE16...40 C4
Hurley Ho
Lambeth SE11 ...149 C3
Shoreditch
E2 ......24 B2 98 C3
Hurley Lo SE22 ...64 B3
Hurlingham Bsns Pk
SW6 ....58 C4
Hurlingham &
Chelsea Sec Sch
SW6 ....58 C4
Hurlingham Court
Mans SW6 ...165 B1
Hurlingham Ct
SW6 ....58 B4
Hurlingham Gdns
SW6 ....58 B4
Hurlingham Rd
SW6 ....165 A1
Hurlingham Sch
SW15 ....58 B3
Hurlingham Sq
SW6 ....59 A4
Hurlock Ho 1 N5...6 A1
Hurlock St N5 ...6 A1
Huron Rd SW17 ...72 C1
Huron Univ WC1 ...106 A4
Hurstbourne Ho
SW15 ....56 B1
Hurstdene Gdns
N15 ....7 A4
Hurst Ho N1 .....85 A1
Hurst St SE24 ...63 A1
Hurstway Wlk 2
W11 ....30 C2
Husbourne Ho 8
SE8 ....41 A2
Huson Cl NW3 ...12 A1
Hutching's St E14...41 C4
Hutching's Wharf 11
E14...........41 C4
Hutchins Cl E15...19 B1
Hutchins Ho 3
SW4 ....73 C4
Hutchinson Ho 9
SE14 ....50 B3
Hutton Ct 4 N4...5 B3

Hutton Ho
E2 ......24 C2 99 B3
Hutton St EC4 ...107 C1
Huxbear St SE4 ...66 B2
Huxley Ho
London SW9 ...172 C2
Paddington NW8 ...89 C1
Huxley St W10 ...23 A2
Hyacinth Rd SW15...68 C3
Hyde Farm Mews
SW12 ....73 C3
Hyde La SW11 ...168 A4
Hyde Park★ W2 ...116 C1
Hyde Park Cnr
SW1 ....131 C4
Hyde Park Corner Sta
SW1 ....131 C4
Hyde Park Cres
W2 ....102 A3
Hyde Park Gate Mews
SW7 ....129 A3
Hyde Park Gdns
W2 ....115 C4
Hyde Park Gdns Mews
W2 ....116 A4
Hyde Park Mans
NW1 ....102 A3
Hyde Park PI W2 ...116 A4
Hyde Park Sq W2 ...102 A1
Hyde Park Square
Mews W2 .....102 A1
Hyde Park St W2 ...102 A1
Hyde Park Twrs
W2 ....114 C3
Hyde Rd
Richmond TW10 ...54 B2
Shoreditch N1 ...24 A4
Hyde's PI 12 N1 ...15 A1
Hyde St SE8 .....51 C4
Hydethorpe Rd
SW12 ....73 B3
Hyde Vale SE10...52 B3
Hylda Ct NW5 ...3 C1
Hyndman Ho 4
N19...........4 C4
Hyndman St SE15...50 A4
Hyperion Ho
27 Bow E3 ......26 A3
Streatham SW2 ...74 B4
Hyson Rd SE16 ...40 A1
Hythe Ho 14 SE16...40 B4
Hythe Rd NW10 ...21 C1
Hythe Road Ind Est
NW10 ....21 C2

I

Ian Hamilton Ho
NW1 ....93 B4
Ian Mikardo Sch
E3 ....27 A2
Ibberton Ho
Kensington W14 ...126 B1
South Lambeth
SW8 ....162 C2
Ibbotson Ave E16...35 B3
Ibbott St 22 E1 ...25 B1
Iberia Ho 17 N19...4 C4
Ibis Ct 18 SE8 ...51 B4
Ibis La W4 ......45 B2
Ibsley Gdns SW15...68 C3
Ibstock Place Sch
SW15 ....56 A1
Icarus 21 E3 ...26 B2

Iceland Rd E3 .....26 C4
Iceland Wharf
  SE16 .... 41 A2
Iceni Ct 28 E2 ....26 C1
Ice Wharf NW1 .... 84 B2
Idaho Bldg 7
SE13 .... 52 A2
Ida St E14 .... 34 B3
Idmiston Rd SE21,
  SE27 .... 75 B2
Idol La EC3 ...... 124 A3
Idonia St SE8 ..... 51 C3
Iffley Rd E2 ..24 B2 98 C3
Iffley Rd W6 ..... 39 B2
Ifield Ho SE17 ... 152 B2
Ifield Rd SW10 .. 156 B4
Ifor Evans Pl E1 .. 25 C1
Ightham Ho
SE17 .... 152 A3
ikon ho E17 ...... 32 C2
Ikra Prim Sch N16 .16 B4
Ilbert St W10 ...... 23 A2
Ilchester Gdns
  W2 .... 114 A4
Ilchester Mans
W8 .... 127 B2
Ilchester Pl W14 . 127 A2
Ildersly Gr SE21 ...75 C2
Ilderton Prim Sch
SE16 .... 40 B1
Ilderton Rd SE15,
SE16 .... 50 B4
Ilex Rd NW10 ...... 8 B2
Ilford Ho N1 ...... 15 C2
Ilfracombe Flats
SE1 .... 137 A4
Iliffe St SE17 .... 150 B2
Iliffe Yd SE17 .... 150 B2
Ilkeston Ct 7 E5 ..17 C4
Ilminster Gdns
SW11 .... 60 A3
Ilsley Ct SW8 .... 170 C1
Ilsmer St N1 ...... 87 B3
Imperial Ave 5
N16 .... 16 A4
Imperial College Rd
SW7 .... 129 B2
Imperial College
  London SW7 .... 129 B2
Imperial Cres
SW6 .... 167 A1
Imperial Ho
  1 Bow E3 ...... 26 A2
  2 Poplar E14 ... 33 B2
  Strand WC2 .... 106 C1
Imperial Rd SW6 . 166 B3
Imperial Sq SW6 . 166 B4
Imperial St E3 ..... 27 B2
Imperial Twrs 3
NW3 .... 11 B2
Imperial War Mus *
SE1, SE11 ...... 135 C1
Imperial Wharf Sta
SW10 .... 167 A3
Imre Cl W12 ...... 30 A1
Independent Pl
E8 .... 16 B3
Indescon Ct E14 .. 42 A4
Indiana Bldg 7
SE8 .... 51 C2
India St EC3 ...... 110 C1
India Way W12 .... 30 A2
Indigo Mews N16 .. 6 C1
Indus Ct 18 SE15 .. 49 B3

Ingate Pl SW8 .... 170 B3
Ingelow Ho W8 ... 128 A4
Ingersoll Rd W12 ..30 A1
Ingestre Pl W1 ... 105 A1
Ingestre Rd NW5 .. 13 A4
Ingham Rd NW6 .. 10 C4
Inglebert St EC1 .. 95 B4
Ingleborough St
SW9 .... 173 B2
Ingleby Rd N7 ..... 5 A1
Inglefield Sq 12
E1 .... 32 A1
Ingle Ho 3 SW12 .73 C3
Inglesham Wlk E9 .18 B2
Ingleside Gr SE3 .. 53 B4
Inglethorpe Ho 6
E5 .... 7 C2
Inglethorpe St
SW6 .... 47 C2
Ingleton St SW9 . 173 B2
Inglewood Cl E14 . 41 C2
Inglewood Mans 11
NW6 .... 10 C3
Inglewood Rd
NW6 .... 10 C3
Inglis Ho 1 SW15 . 57 B2
Inglis St SE5 ..... 48 A2
Ingram Ave NW11 .. 2 B4
Ingram Cl SE11 .. 149 A4
Ingram Ho 3 E3 .. 26 A4
Ingram Lo 5 SW4 . 61 C1
Ingrave St SW11 .. 60 A4
Ingrebourne Ho
NW8 .... 101 C4
Ingress St 8 W4 .. 38 A1
Inigo Pl WC2 .... 120 A4
Inkerman Rd NW5 . 13 A2
Inkerman Terr
W8 .... 127 C1
Inkster Ho 9
SW11 .... 60 A4
Inman Rd
Harlesden NW10 ..21 A4
Wandsworth SW18 ..71 B4
Inner Circ NW1 ... 91 B4
Inner Park Rd
SW19 .... 69 C2
Inner Temple *
EC4 .... 121 B4
Inner Temple La
EC4 .... 107 B1
Innes Gdns SW15 . 57 A1
Innisfree Ho NW2 .. 9 C2
Innis Ho SE17 .... 152 A2
Inst for Child Health
WC1 .... 94 C1
Institute Pl 8 E8 ..17 A3
Instituto Espanol
Vicente Canada
Blanch W10 ..... 31 A4
Inst of Neurology
Bloomsbury WC1 . 106 B4
St Pancras WC1 .. 94 B1
Int Coll of
  Accountancy The
SW17 .... 72 B1
Interchange The
NW5 .... 13 A3
International House
Language Sch
WC2 .... 106 B2
International Sch of
London W3 .... 36 C2
Inver Ct
Bayswater W2 ... 100 B1

Inver Ct continued
  4 Hammersmith
  W6 .... 38 C3
Inverforth Cl NW3 . 2 B2
Inverforth Ho NW3 . 2 B2
Invergarry Ho
NW6 .... 78 A1
Invermead Cl W6 . 38 C2
Inverness Gdns
W8 .... 114 A1
Inverness Mews
W2 .... 114 B4
Inverness Pl W2 .. 114 B4
Inverness St NW1 . 82 B4
Inverness Terr
W2 .... 114 B4
Inverton Rd SE15 . 65 C3
Invicta Cl 2 E3 .. 33 C4
Invicta Plaza SE1 122 A2
Invicta Prim Sch
SE3 .... 53 C3
Invicta Rd SE3,
SE7 .... 53 C4
Inville Rd SE17 .. 151 C1
Inwen Ct SE8 ..... 41 A1
Inwood Ho 12 NW1. 13 B1
Inwood Ho 17
SE22 .... 64 A4
Inworth St SW11 . 168 B2
Inworth Wlk N1 .. 86 C4
Ion Ct 8 E2 ...... 24 C3
Ionian Bldg 19
E14 .... 33 A2
Ionian Ho 22 E1 .. 25 C1
Ipsden Bldgs SE1 135 C4
Ipswich Ho SE4 .. 65 C2
Irby Ho SW2 ..... 62 C1
Ireland Yd EC4 ... 108 B1
Irene Rd SW6 .... 165 C3
Ireton Ho SW9 ... 173 C1
Ireton St 13 E3 .. 26 C1
Iris Ct 8 SE15 ... 65 A4
Iroko Ho 7 NW3 .. 11 A2
Iron Bridge Cl
NW10 .... 8 A3
Iron Bridge Ho
NW3 .... 12 B1
Irongate Ho EC3 . 110 B2
Iron Mill Pl SW18 . 59 A1
Iron Mill Rd SW18 . 59 A1
Ironmonger La
EC2 .... 109 B1
Ironmonger Pas
EC1 .... 97 A3
Ironmonger Row
EC1 .... 97 A3
Ironmonger's Pl 2
E14 .... 41 C2
Ironside Cl SE16 .. 40 C4
Ironside Ho E9 .... 18 A4
Ironworks 1 E3 .. 26 C4
Irvine Ct N1 ...... 93 A1
Irvine Ho N7 ...... 14 B2
Irving Gr SW9 ... 172 C1
Irving Ho SE17 .. 150 A1
Irving Mews N1 .. 15 B2
Irving Rd W14 .... 39 C3
Irving St WC2 .... 119 C3
Irwell Est 33 SE16 . 40 B4
Irwin Gdns NW10 . 22 A4
Isabella Ct 8
TW10 .... 54 B1
Isabella Ho
  19 Hammersmith
  W6 .... 39 B1
  Kennington SE11 . 150 A2
Isabella Rd E9 .... 17 B3

Isabella St SE1 .. 122 A1
Isabel St SW9 ... 173 A4
Isambard Mews
E14 .... 42 B3
Isambard Pl SE16 . 32 B1
Iseldon Ct N7 ..... 14 A4
Isel Way 4 SE22 . 64 A2
Isis Cl SW15 ...... 57 B3
Isis Ct W4 .... 45 A3
Isis Ho NW8 ...... 89 C1
Isis St SW18 ...... 71 B2
Islamia Girls' High
Sch NW6 .... 23 A4
Islamia Prim Sch
NW6 .... 23 C4
Islamic Coll for
  Advanced Studies
NW10 .... 9 A2
Island Gardens Sta
E14 .... 42 B1
Island Ho E14 .... 27 B2
Island Rd SE16 ... 40 C2
Island Row E14 ... 33 B3
Islay Wlk 17 N1 .. 15 B2
Isleden Ho N1 .... 86 C4
Isledon Rd N4,N7 . 5 C1
ISLE OF DOGS ... 42 B2
ISLINGTON 14 C2
Islington Arts &
  Media Sch N4 .... 5 B3
Islington Bsns Ctr
N1 .... 87 A4
Islington Est N1 .. 86 C4
Islington Gn N1 .. 86 A3
Islington Green Sch
N1 .... 86 C3
Islington High St
N1 .... 86 A2
Islington Park Mews
  1 N1 .... 15 A1
Islington Park St
N1 .... 14 C1
Islington Sixth Form
  Ctr N7 .... 14 C4
Islip St NW5 ...... 13 B3
Isokon Flats 3
NW3 .... 12 B3
Issac Way SE1 ... 137 A4
Italia Conti Acad of
  Theatre Arts 1 . 96 C1
Ivanhoe Ho
  11 Balham SW12 .73 A4
  24 Bow E3 ...... 26 A3
Ivanhoe Rd SE5 .. 64 B4
Ivatt Pl W14 ..... 141 A1
Iveagh Cl E9 ..... 25 C4
Iveagh Ct EC3 ... 110 C1
Iveagh Ho
  2 Brixton SW9 .. 48 A1
  Chelsea SW10 .. 157 A2
Ivebury Ct 9 W10 . 30 B3
Iveley Rd SW4 ... 170 C1
Iver Ct N1 .... 15 B2
Iverna Ct W8 .... 127 C2
Iverna Gdns W8 .. 127 C2
Ives Rd E16 ...... 35 A4
Ives St SW3 ..... 144 B4
Ivimey St E2 ..C2 99 C4
Ivinghoe Ho 14
N7 .... 13 C3
Ivor Ct NW1 ...... 90 C2
Ivories The N1 ... 15 B1
Ivor Mayor Lo
SW12 .... 60 C1
Ivor Pl NW1 ...... 90 C1
Ivor St NW1 ...... 13 B1

Ivory Ho
  1 London SW11 ..59 B4
  St George in I East
E1 .... 125 A2
Ivory Sq 15 SW18 . 59 B4
Ivybridge Ho 8
SE22 .... 64 A4
Ivybridge La WC2 120 B3
Ivy Church La SE1,
SE17 .... 152 C2
Ivy Cres W4 ...... 37 B2
Ivy Ct 12 SE16 ... 153 C1
Ivydale Prim Sch
SE15 .... 65 C3
Ivydale Rd SE15 .. 65 C3
Ivyday Gr SW16 .. 74 B1
Ivy Lo W8 ..31 C1 113 B2
Ivymount Rd SE27 . 74 C1
Ivy Rd Brockley SE4 . 66 C3
  Cricklewood NW2 .. 9 B4
  Newham E16 ..... 35 C3
Ivy St N1 .... 24 A3
Ixworth Pl SW3 .. 144 A3

J

Jacaranda Gr E8 . 16 B1
Jackman Ho 24
E1 .... 32 A1
Jackman St E8 ... 25 A4
Jackson Cl E9 .... 17 C1
Jackson Ho 16
SW11 .... 59 C4
Jackson Rd N7 ... 14 B4
Jackson's La N6 ... 4 A4
Jack Taylor Sch
NW8 .... 78 C4
Jack Tizard Sch
W12 .... 30 A1
Jack Walker Ct
N5 .... 15 A4
Jacobin Lo N7 ... 14 A3
Jacob Mans 15 E1 . 32 A3
Jacobson Ct
SW11 .... 168 B3
Jacobson Ho E1 . 110 C2
Jacob St SE1....7, 139 B4
Jacob's Well Mews
W1 .... 103 C2
Jacotts Ho W10 .. 22 B1
Jacqueline Ho 8
E1 .... 32 C4
Jaggard Way
SW12 .... 72 B4
Jagger Ho SW11 . 168 C4
Jago Wlk SE5 .... 48 C3
Jamahirya Sch
SW3 .... 158 A4
Jamaica Rd
  Bermondsey SE1 . 139 A3
  Bermondsey SE16 . 40 A3
Jamaica St E1 .... 32 B4
James Allen's Girls'
  Sch SE22 .... 64 A2
James Allens Pre-
  Prep Sch SE21 .. 63 C1
James Anderson Ct 2
E2 .... 24 A3
James Ave NW2 ... 9 B3
James Brine Ho
E2 ....24 B2 99 A4
James Campbell Ho
2 E2 .... 25 B3
James Collins Cl
W9 .... 23 B1

James Docherty Ho
◨ E2 .... 25 B3
James Hammett Ho
◨ E2 .... 24 B3
James Ho
Mile End E1 .... 26 A1
☒ Rotherhithe
SE16 .... 40 C4
James Joyce Wlk ◨
SE24 .... 63 A3
James Leicester Hall
of Residence N7 ... 14 A2
James Lind Ho ◨
SE8 .... 41 B2
James Middleton Ho
◨ E2 .... 25 A2
Jameson Cl ◨ .. 25 B3
Jameson Ho
SE11 .... 148 C2
Jameson Pl ⓫
W3 .... 37 B3
Jameson St
W8 .... 31 C1 113 C2
Jamestown
TW9 .... 44 C3
James's Cotts
TW9 .... 44 C3
James St
Marylebone W1 ... 103 C1
Strand WC2 ...... 120 B4
James Stewart Ho
NW6 .... 10 B1
James Stroud Ho
SC17 .... 151 A2
Jamestown Rd
NW1 .... 82 A4
Jamestown Way
E14 .... 34 C2
Janeway Pl ◪
SE16 .... 40 A4
Janeway St SE16 139 C3
Janson Ho
W15 .... 56 C2
Jansen Wlk SW11 59 C3
Japan Cres N4 .... 5 B3
Jardine Rd E1 .... 32 C2
Jarman Ho
Bermondsey SE16 .. 40 C2
◨ Stepney E1 ..... 32 B4
Jarrett Cl SW2 ... 75 A3
Jarrow Rd SE16 .... 40 B1
Jarrow Way E9 .... 18 A4
Jarvis Ho ◨ SE15 . 49 C2
Jarvis Rd SE22 .... 64 A3
Jasmin ◨ SE1 .... 125 A1
Jasmine Sq ⓭ E3 26 B4
Jasmine St E44 .. 36 B4
Jasmin Lo ⓱
SE16 .... 40 A1
Jason Ct
London SW9 ...... 173 A4
Marylebone W1 ... 103 C2
Jasper Wlk N1 .... 97 B4
Java Wharf SE1 .. 139 A4
Jay Ho SW15 ...... 47 B1
Jay Mews SW7 ... 129 A3
Jean Darling Ho
SW10 .... 157 B3
Jean Pardies Ho ⓯
E1 .... 32 B4
Jebb Ave SW2 .... 62 A1
Jebb St E3 .... 26 C3
Jedburgh St
SW11 .... 60 C3

Jeddo Mews W12 .. 38 B4
Jeddo Rd W12 ..... 38 B4
Jefferson Bldg ◨
E14 .... 41 C4
Jeffrey's Ct SW4 172 A2
Jeffrey's Pl NW1 .. 13 B1
Jeffrey's Rd SW4 172 A2
Jeffrey's St NW1 .. 13 B1
Jeff Wooller Coll
WC1 .... 106 B3
Jeger Ave ◨ E2 .. 24 B4
Jelf Rd SW2 ...... 62 C2
Jellicoe Ho
◪ Bethnal Green
E2 ◪ FITZ70V(А HALL) . 92 B1
⓫ Putney SW15 .. 57 C2
Jemotts Ct ◨
SE14 .... 50 C4
Jenkins Ho SW8 .. 171 B4
Jenkinson Ho ⓬
E2 .... 25 C2
Jenner Ave W3 ... 28 C4
Jenner Ho SE3 .... 53 A4
Jenner Pl SW13 .. 47 A4
Jenner Rd N16 .... 7 B1
Jennifer Ho SE11 149 C3
Jennings Ho SE10 42 C1
Jennings Rd SE22 64 B1
Jensen Ho ⓯ E13 26 C1
Jephson Ct SW4 172 B1
Jephson Ho ⓬
SE17 .... 48 A4
Jephtha Rd SW18 58 C1
Jephson St SE5 .. 48 C2
Jephtha Rd SW18 58 C1
Jeremiah St ⓫
E14 .... 34 A3
Jeremy Bentham Ho
E2 .... 24 C2 99 C3
Jermyn St SW1 .. 119 A2
Jerningham Ct
SE14 .... 51 A2
Jerningham Rd
SC14 .... 51 A2
Jerome Cres NW8 . 90 A2
Jerome Ho NW1 .. 102 B4
Jerome St ◨
E1 .... 24 B1 98 C1
Jerome Twr ⓪
W3 .... 37 A4
Jerrard St SE13 .. 67 A4
Jerrold Lo SW15 . 57 B4
Jerrold St ◨ N1 .. 24 A3
Jersey Ho ⓯ N1 .. 15 B2
Jersey Rd N1 .... 15 B2
Jersey St E2 ...... 25 A2
Jerusalem Pas
EC1 .... 96 A1
Jervis Bay Ho ◪
E14 .... 34 C3
Jervis Ct
☒ Greenwich
SE10 .... 52 B2
Marylebone W1 .. 104 B1
Jessel Ho
St Pancras WC1 ... 94 A3
Westminster SW1 147 C4
Jessica Rd SW18 . 59 B2
Jessie Blythe La ◪
N19 .... 5 A4
Jessie Duffett Ho ◨
SE5 .... 48 B3
Jessop Ct N1 .... 86 B1
Jessop Ho ◩ W4 . 37 C2

Jessop Prim Sch
SE24 .... 63 B3
Jessop Sq E14 .... 33 C1
Jeston Ho ◨ SE27 .75 A1
Jethou Ho ◩ N1 .. 15 B2
Jevons Ho ◪
NW3 .... 11 C1
Jewell Ho ◪
SE22 .... 73 B4
Jewish Mus The*
NW1 .... 82 B3
Jewry St EC3 .... 110 C1
Jewry Row SW18 .. 59 B3
Jeymer Ave NW2 .. 9 B3
Jeypore Rd SW18 59 B1
Jim Griffiths Ho
SW6 .... 155 A3
Joanna Ho ◩ W6 . 39 B1
Joan St SE1 ...... 122 A1
Jocelin Ho N1 .... 85 A3
Jocelyn Rd TW9 .. 54 A4
Jocelyn St SE15 .. 49 C2
Jockey's Fields
WC1 .... 107 A4
Jodane Rd SE8 .... 41 B2
Jodrell Rd E3 .... 26 B4
Johanna Prim Sch
SE1 .... 135 B3
Johanna St SE1 .. 135 B3
John Adam St
WC2 .... 120 B3
John Aird Ct W2 . 101 A4
John Archer Way
SW18 .... 59 C1
John Ashby Cl
SW2 .... 62 A1
John Ball Prim Sch
SE3 .... 53 B1
John Barker Ct
NW6 .... 10 A1
John Betts' Ho
W12 .... 38 C3
John Betts Prim Sch
W6 .... 39 A3
John Bond Ho ◨
E3 .... 26 B3
John Brent Ho ◨
SE8 .... 40 C2
John Buck Ho
NW10 .... 21 B4
John Burns Prim Sch
SW11 .... 169 C1
John Campbell Rd ◨
N16 .... 16 A3
John Carpenter St
EC4 .... 122 A4
John Cartwright Ho
◱ E2 .... 25 A2
John Clynes Ct
SW15 .... 57 A3
John Conwey Ho ⓬
SW2 .... 62 C1
John Dee Ho ◨
SW14 .... 55 C4
John Donne Prim Sch
SE15 .... 50 A2
John Dwight Ho
SW6 .... 59 A4
John Fearon Wlk ◪
W10 .... 23 A2
John Felton Rd
SE16 .... 139 B3
John Fielden Ho ◩
E2 .... 25 A2
John Fisher St
E1 .... 125 B4

John F. Kennedy
Specl Sch SE15 .... 27 C4
John Harris Ho
SE15 .... 64 C4
John Harrison Way
SE10 .... 43 B3
John Islip St SW1 148 A3
John Keall Ho
SW15 .... 57 C4
John Keble CE Prim
Sch NW10 .... 21 B4
John Kennedy Ho ◨
N1 .... 15 B2
John Kennedy Lo ◨
N1 .... 15 C2
John King Ct ◪
N19 .... 4 C2
John Kirk Ho
SW11 .... 59 C4
◪ Streatham
SW16 .... 74 A1
John Knight Lo
SW6 .... 155 C2
John McDonald Ho
E14 .... 42 B3
John McKenna Wlk
SE16 .... 139 C2
John & Mary Sch
NW5 .... 13 C3
John Maurice Cl
SE17 .... 151 B4
John Milton Prim Sch
SW8 .... 160 C1
John Nettleford Ho
E2 .... 25 A2
John Orwell Sports
Ctr E1 .... 32 A1
John Parker Sq ◪
SW11 .... 59 C4
John Parry Ct ⓴
N1 .... 24 A3
John Paul II Sch
SW19 .... 69 C4
John Penn Ho
SE8 .... 51 B3
John Penn St
SE13 .... 52 A2
John Perryn Prim Sch
W3 .... 29 A3
John Prince's St
W1 .... 104 B2
John Pritchard Ho
E1 .... 24 C1 99 C1
John Ratcliffe Ho ◨
NW6 .... 23 C2
John Rennie Wlk ◪
E1 .... 32 B1
John Roan Sch The
SE3 .... 53 A3
John Roll Way
SE16 .... 139 C2
John Ruskin Prim Sch
SE5 .... 48 A4
John Ruskin St
SE5 .... 48 B4
John Scurr Ho ⓲
E14 .... 33 A3
John Scurr Prim Sch
E1 .... 25 B1
John Silkin La
SE8 .... 40 C1
John's Mews WC1 . 95 A1
John Smith Ave
SW6 .... 154 C2

John Smith Mews
E14 .... 34 C2
John Cl E8 .... 24 C4
Johnson Ct ⓾
SW18 .... 59 C3
Johnson Ho
Belgravia SW1 ... 145 C3
Bethnal Green
E2 .... 24 C2 99 C3
Somers Town NW1 . 83 A1
South Lambeth
SW8 .... 161 C1
Johnson Lo ⓬
W9 .... 31 C4
Johnson Rd NW10 . 20 C4
Johnsons Ct EC4 . 107 C1
Johnson's Pl SW1 146 C1
Johnson St E1 .... 32 B3
Johnsons Way
NW10 .... 20 A1
John Spencer Sq
N1 .... 15 A2
John's Pl E1 ...... 32 A3
John St WC1 ...... 95 A1
John Stainer Com
Prim Sch SE4 .... 66 A4
Johnston Cl SW9 173 A3
Johnstone Ho
SE13 .... 67 C4
John Strachey Ho
SW6 .... 155 A3
John Trundle Ct
EC2 .... 108 C4
John Tucker Ho ◨
E14 .... 41 C3
John Wesley's House
& Mus* EC1 ...... 97 C2
John Wheatley Ho
⓮ London N19 ..... 4 C4
West Brompton
SW6 .... 155 A3
John Williams Cl
SE14 .... 50 C4
Joiners Arms Yd ◪
SE5 .... 48 C2
Joiner St SE1 .... 123 C1
Joiners Yd N1 .... 84 B1
Jolles Ho ◪ E3 .. 27 A2
Jonathan Ct ◪
W4 .... 38 A2
Jonathan St SE11 148 C2
Jones Ho
☒ South Bromley
E14 .... 34 C3
Stamford Hill N16 . 7 C3
Jones St W1 ...... 118 A3
Jones Wlk ⓬
TW10 .... 54 B1
Jonson Ho
Borough The SE1 . 137 C2
☒ Canonbury N16 . 15 C4
Jordan Ct SW15 .. 57 C3
Jordan Ho
⓬ London SE4 .... 65 C3
Shoreditch N1 .... 87 C3
Jordans Ho NW8 . 90 A1
Joscoyne Ho ◪
E1 .... 32 A3
Joseph Ave W3 .. 28 C3
Joseph Conrad Ho
SW1 .... 147 A3
Joseph Ct N16 .... 7 A4
Joseph Hardcastle Cl
SE14 .... 50 C3

Josephine Ave
SW2 . . . . 62 B2
Joseph Irwin Ho 11
E14 . . . . 33 C2
Joseph Lancaster
Prim Sch SE1 . . . . 137 B1
Joseph Powell Cl 4
SW12 . . . . 61 B1
Joseph Priestley Ho
12 E2 . . . . 25 A2
Joseph St E3 . . . . 26 B1
Joseph Trotter Cl
EC1 . . . . 95 C3
Joshua St E14 . . . . 34 B3
Joslings Cl W12 . . . . . . 29 C2
Josseline Ct 9 E3 . . 26 A3
Joubert Mans
SW3 . . . . 144 B2
Joubert St SW3 . . . . 169 A2
Jowett Ho SW9 . . . . 172 B1
Jowett St SE15 . . . . . 49 B3
Jubet Ho 9 N16 . . . . 15 C4

Jubilee Bldgs
NW8 . . . . 79 B2
Jubilee Cl
NW10 . . . . 21 B3
Jubilee Cres E14 . . . . 42 B3
Jubilee Ct N1 . . . . 84 B4
Jubilee Ho SE11 . . . . 149 C3
Jubilee Hts NW2 . . . . 10 B2
Jubilee Mans 10
E1 . . . . 32 B3
Jubilee Mkt WC2 . . 120 B4
Jubilee Pl SW3 . . . . 144 B2
Jubilee Prim Sch
London SW2 . . . . 62 C1
Stamford Hill N16 . . . . 7 C3
Jubilee St E1 . . . . 32 B4
Jubilee The 2
SE10 . . . . 52 A3
Jubilee Yd SE1 . . . . 138 C4
Judd St WC1 . . . . 94 A3
Jude St E16 . . . . 35 B3
Judges' Wlk NW3 . . . 2 B1
Juer St SW11 . . . . . . 158 B1
Julian Ave W3 . . . . . . 28 A2
Julian Ct SW13 . . . . . 46 B2
Julian Pl E14 . . . . 42 A1
Julia St NW5 . . . . 12 C3
Juliet Ho 11 N1 . . . . 24 A3
Julius Ct TW8 . . . . . . 44 A3
Julius Ho 8 E14 . . . . 34 C3
Julius Nyerere Cl
N1 . . . . 84 C3
Junction App
Battersea SW11 . . . . . . 60 A4
Lewisham SE13 . . . . . . 67 B4
Junction Mews
W2 . . . . 102 A2
Junction Pl W2 . . . . 101 C2
Junction Rd N19 . . . . 4 B1
Juniper Cres NW1 . . 12 C1
Juniper Ct N16 . . . . . . 6 C2
Juniper Dr SW18 . . . . 59 B3
Juniper Ho
6 Peckham SE14,
SE15 . . . . 50 B3
9 Richmond TW9 . . . . 45 A2
Juniper St 18 E1 . . . 32 B2
Juno Ct SW9 . . . . 163 B1
Juno Ho 2 E3 . . . . . . 26 C4
Juno Way SE14 . . . . . 50 C4
Juno Way Ind Est
SE14 . . . . 50 C4
Jupiter Ct SW9 . . . . 163 B1

Jupiter Way N7 . . . . 14 B2
Jupp Rd E15 . . . . 19 C1
Jupp Rd W E15 . . . . . 27 C4
Jura Ho SE16 . . . . 41 A2
Justice Wlk SW3 . . . 158 A3
Justines Pl E2 . . . . . . 25 C2
Justice Wlk SW3 . . . 158 A3
Justines Pl E2 . . . . . . 25 C2
Jutland Cl N19 . . . . . . 5 A3
Jutland Ho 4 SE5 . . 48 B1
Juxon St SE11 . . . . . 149 A4

K

Kambala Rd SW11 . . 59 C4
Kara Way NW2 . . . . . . 9 C4
Karen Ct
2 Camberwell
SE5 . . . . 48 B3
Forest Hill SE23 . . . . . 66 A1
Karen Ho 7 N16 . . . . 15 C4
Kasmin Ct NW10 . . . . 8 C1
Kassala Rd SW11 . . 169 A3
Katherine Cl 3
SE16 . . . . 32 C1
Katherine Ho 18
W10 . . . . 23 A1
Katherine Sq
W11 . . . . 31 A1 112 A2
Kathleen Ave W3 . . . . 28 B4
Kathleen Rd SW11 . . 60 B4
Kay Rd SW9 . . . . 172 C1
Kay St E2 . . . . 24 C3
Kean Ho 5 SE17 . . . . 48 A4
Kean St WC2 . . . . . . 106 C1
Keates Est N16 . . . . . . 7 B2
Keats Cl
Bermondsey SE1 . . . . 152 C3
Hampstead NW3 . . . . . 12 A4
Keats Gr NW3 . . . . 12 A4
Keats Ho
22 Bethnal Green
E2 . . . . 25 B2
30 Camberwell SE5 . . 48 B3
Keats House Mus★
NW3 . . . . 12 A4
Keats Ho EC2 . . . . . . 109 B3
Keble Ho 4 SW15 . . 57 C1
Keble Pl SW13 . . . . . . 47 A4
Kedelston Ct E5 . . . . 18 A4
Kedge Ho 16 E14 . . . 41 C3
Kedleston Wlk 21
E2 . . . . 25 A2
Keel Cl SE16 . . . . 32 C1
Keel Ct 8 E14 . . . . . . 34 C2
Keeley St WC2 . . . . . 106 C1
Keeling Ho 4 E2 . . . . 25 A3
Keelson Ho 9
E14 . . . . 41 C3
Keen's Yd N1 . . . . 15 A2
Keeper Wharf E1 . . . 32 C2
Keepier Wharf 18
E1 . . . . 32 C2
Keep The SE3 . . . . . . 53 C1
Keeton's Rd SE16 . . 40 A3
Keevil Dr SW19 . . . . . 70 A4
Keighley Cl N7 . . . . . 14 A4
Keildon Rd SW11 . . . 60 B3
Keir Hardie Ho
Fulham W6 . . . . 47 C4
15 Upper Holloway
N19 . . . . 4 C4
Willesden NW10 . . . . . 9 A2
Keir Hardy Prim Sch
E16 . . . . 35 C4

Keith Connor Cl 5
SW8 . . . . 61 A4
Keith Gr W12 . . . . 29 C1
Keith Ho NW6 . . . . . . 78 A1
Kelby Ho N7 . . . . 14 B2
Kelfield Ct 1
W10 . . . . 30 C3
Kelfield Gdns
W10 . . . . 30 C3
Kelfield Mews
W10 . . . . 30 C3
Kellett Ho N1 . . . . 87 C3
Kellett Rd SW2 . . . . . 62 C3
Kellow Ho SE1 . . . . . 137 B4
Kell St SE1 . . . . 136 B2
Kelly Ave SE15 . . . . . . 49 B2
Kelly Mews 8 W9 . . 23 B1
Kelly St NW1 . . . . 13 A2
Kelman Cl SW4 . . . . 171 C1
Kelmore Gr SE22 . . . 64 C3
Kelmscott Gdns
W12 . . . . 38 C3
Kelmscott Rd
SW11 . . . . 60 B2
Kelross Rd N5 . . . . . . 15 B4
Kelsall Mews TW9 . . 45 A2
Kelsey St E2 . . . . 24 C1 99 C2
Kelshall Ct N4 . . . . 6 B2
Kelson Ho E14 . . . . . . 42 B3
Kelso Pl W8 . . . . 128 B2
Kelvedon Ho
SW8 . . . . 172 B4
Kelvedon Rd SW6 . . 155 A1
Kelvin Ct
Chiswick W4 . . . . 45 B3
Notting Hill
W11 . . . . 31 C2 113 B3
Kelvington Rd
SE15 . . . . 65 C2
Kelvin Rd N5 . . . . 15 A4
Kelway Ho 20
SW2 . . . . 74 C4
Kember St N1 . . . . 14 B1
Kemble Ho SW9 . . . . 63 A4
Kemble St WC2 . . . . 106 C1
Kemerton Rd SE5 . . . 63 B4
Kemey's St E9 . . . . . . 18 A3
Kemp Ct SW8 . . . . . . 162 A1
Kempe Ho SE1 . . . . . 137 C1
Kempe Rd NW6 . . . . . 22 C3
Kemp Ho
Finsbury EC1 . . . . 97 B3
1 Globe Town E2 . . . . 25 C3
Kempis Way 5
SE22 . . . . 64 A2
Kemplay Rd NW3 . . . 11 C4
Kemp's Ct W1 . . . . . . 105 B1
Kemps Dr E14 . . . . . . 33 C2
Kempsford Gdns
SW5 . . . . 141 C1
Kempsford Rd
Lambeth SE11 . . . . . . 149 C3
Newington SE11 . . . . 150 A3
Kemps Gdns SE13 . . 67 B2
Kempson Rd SW6 . . 155 C1
Kempthorne Rd
SE8 . . . . 41 B2
Kempton Ct E1 . . . . . 32 A4
Kempton Ho 13
N1 . . . . 24 A4
Kemsing Ho SE1 . . . 137 C3
Kemsing Rd SE10 . . . 43 C1
Kemsley SE13 . . . . . . 67 A2
Kenbrook Ho
Kensington W14 . . . . 127 A1

Kenbrook Ho continued
5 Kentish Town
NW5 . . . . 13 B3
Kenbury Gdns 10
SE5 . . . . 48 B1
Kenbury Mans 8
SE5 . . . . 48 B1
Kenbury St SE5 . . . . . 48 B1
Kenchester Cl
SW8 . . . . 162 B1
Kendal NW1 . . . . 92 B4
Kendal Ave W3 . . . . . 28 A4
Kendal Cl SE5 . . . . . . 48 A3
Kendal Ct NW2 . . . . . 10 A3
Kendall Ct 3
SW16 . . . . 74 C1
Kendall Pl W1 . . . . . 103 B3
Kendal Ho
2 Hackney E9 . . . . . . 17 B1
Islington N1 . . . . 85 A2
Kendall Ct 3
SE22 . . . . 64 C2
Kendall Pl W1 . . . . . 103 B3
Kendall Pl SW15 . . . 58 B2
Kendal Rd NW10 . . . . 8 C4
Kendal St W2 . . . . . . 102 B1
Kendal Stps W2 . . . 102 B1
Kender Prim Sch
SE14 . . . . 50 B2
Kender St SE14 . . . . . 50 B2
Kendoa Rd 1
SW4 . . . . 61 C3
Kendon Ho E15 . . . . . 19 C1
Kendrick Ct 12
SE15 . . . . 50 A2
Kendrick Mews
SW7 . . . . 143 B3
Kendrick Pl SW7 . . . 143 B3
Kenilford Rd
SW12 . . . . 73 A4
Kenilworth Ct
SW6 . . . . 58 A4
Kenilworth Rd
Bow E3 . . . . 26 A3
Kilburn NW6 . . . . 23 B4
Kenley Wlk
W11 . . . . 31 A2 112 A2
Kenmont Gdns
NW10 . . . . 22 A2
Kenmont Prim Sch
NW10 . . . . 22 A2
Kenmore Cl TW9 . . . 44 C3
Kenmore Ct NW6 . . . 10 C1
Kenmore Rd E8 . . . . . 17 A3
Kenmure Rd E8 . . . . . 17 A3
Kenmure Yd E8 . . . . . 17 A3
Kennacraig Cl 6
E16 . . . . 35 C1
Kennard Ho
SW11 . . . . 169 C3
Kennard Rd E15 . . . . . 19 C1
Kennard St SW11 . . 169 B3
Kennedy Cox Ho 5
E16 . . . . 35 B4
Kennedy Ho SE11 . . 148 C2
Kennedy Wlk
SE17 . . . . 151 C3
Kennet Cl SW11 . . . . 59 C3
Kennet Ct 47 W2 . . . 31 C4
Kenneth Campbell Ho
NW8 . . . . 89 C2
Kenneth Cres NW2 . . 9 A3
Kenneth Ct SE11 . . . 149 C4
Kennet Ho NW8 . . . . 89 C1
Kenneth Younger Ho
SW6 . . . . 155 A3
Kenneth Rd SW9 . . . 23 B1
Kennet St E1 . . . . 125 C2
Kennett Wharf La
EC4 . . . . 123 A4
Kenning Ho 6 N1 . . . 24 A4

Kenning St 18
SE16 . . . . 40 B4
Kennings Way
SE11 . . . . 149 C2
KENNINGTON 149 B1
Kennington Ent Ctr
SE17 . . . . 150 A1
Kennington La
SE11 . . . . 149 C1
Kennington Oval
SE11 . . . . 163 B1
Kennington Palace Ct
SE11 . . . . 149 B2
Kennington Park
Gdns SE17 . . . . 48 A4
Kennington Park Ho
SE11 . . . . 149 C1
Kennington Park
Pl SE11 . . . . 48 A4
Kennington Park Rd
SE11 . . . . 150 A1
Kennington Rd
SE1 . . . . 135 C2
SE11 . . . . 149 B1
Kennington Sta
SE17 . . . . 150 A2
Kennoldes SE21 . . . . 75 C2
Kenrick Pl W1 . . . . . 103 B3
KENSAL GREEN . . 22 B2
Kensal Green Cemy
(All Souls)★
NW10 . . . . 22 B2
Kensal Green Sta
NW10 . . . . 22 B2
Kensal Ho W10 . . . . . 22 C1
Kensal Rd W10 . . . . . 23 A1
KENSAL RISE 22 C2
Kensal Rise Prim Sch
NW6 . . . . 22 C2
Kensal Rise Sta
NW6 . . . . 22 C2
KENSAL TOWN . . . 23 A1
KENSINGTON 127 C2
Kensington &
Chelsea Coll
Chelsea SW10 . . . . . . 156 C2
Kensal Town W10 . . . 31 A4
Kensington Church St
W8 . . . . 128 A4
Kensington Church St
W8 . . . . 31 C1 113 C2
Kensington Church
Wlk W8 . . . . 128 A3
Kensington Court
Mans W8 . . . . 128 B3
Kensington Court
Mews W8 . . . . 128 B3
Kensington Court Pl
W8 . . . . 128 B2
Kensington Ct
W8 . . . . 128 B3
Kensington Ct Gdns
W8 . . . . 128 B2
Kensington Gardens★
W2 . . . . 115 C2
Kensington Gate
W8 . . . . 128 C2
Kensington Gdns Sq
W2 . . . . 100 A1
Kensington Gore
SW7 . . . . 129 B3
Kensington Hall Gdns
W14 . . . . 140 C2
Kensington High St
W8 . . . . 127 C2
Kensington Ho 3
NW5 . . . . 13 B3

Kensington Hts
W8 . . . . 31 C1 113 B1
Kensington Mall
W8 . . . . 31 C1 113 C2
Kensington Mans
SW5 . . . . 141 C2
Kensington Olympia
Sta W14 . . . . 126 A2
Kensington Pal* . . . .
W8 . . . . 114 B1
Kensington Palace
Gdns W8 . . . . 114 A2
Kensington Park Gdns
W11 . . . . 31 B2 113 A3
Kensington Park
Mews W11 . . . . 31 B3
Kensington Park Rd
W11 . . . . 31 B2 113 A3
Kensington Pl
W8 . . . . 31 C1 113 B2
Kensington Prep Sch
SW6 . . . . 165 A4
Kensington Rd
SW7 . . . . 129 A3
W8 . . . . 31 C1 112 A4
Kensington Sports Ctr
W11 . . . . 31 A2 112 A4
Kensington Sq
W8 . . . . 128 B3
Kensington Village
W14 . . . . 141 A3
Kensington W
W14 . . . . 140 A4
Kensworth Rd EC1 . . 97 C3
Kent St 5 E2 . . . . 24 B3
Kent Ho
Camberwell SE1 . . . 153 A1
13 Chiswick W4 . . . . 38 A1
Marylebone W1 . . . . 104 C2
Pimlico SW1 . . . . . . 147 B1
Richmond TW10 . . . 54 C2
Kentish Bldgs
SE1 . . . . 123 B1
KENTISH TOWN . . 13 B2
Kentish Town CE Prim
Sch NW5 . . . . 13 B3
Kentish Town Rd
NW1 . . . . 13 A2
Kentish Town Sta
NW5 . . . . 13 B3
Kentish Town West
Sta NW5 . . . . 13 A2
Kentmere Ho
SE15 . . . . 50 B4
Kenton Ct W14 . . . . 126 C1
Kenton Ho
20 Globe Town E1 . . 25 B1
Highbury N5 . . . . 5 C1
Kenton Rd E9 . . . . . . 17 C2
Kenton St WC1 . . . . 94 A2
Kent Pas NW1 . . . . . 90 C2
Kent Pk Ind Est
SE15 . . . . 50 A4
Kent Rd
Richmond TW9 . . . . 44 C3
South Acton W3 . . . 37 B3
Kent St 5 E2 . . . . . . 24 B3
Kent Terr NW1 . . . . . 90 B3
Kentwell CE Sch E4 . 66 A3
Kentwode Gn
SW13 . . . . 46 C2
Kenway Rd SW5 . . . 142 A3
Ken Wilson Ho 8
E2 . . . . 24 C3
Kenwood Cl NW3 . . . 2 C3

Kenwood Ho 15
SW9 . . . . 63 A3
Kenwood Ho* . . . .
NW3 . . . . 3 A3
Kenworthy Rd E9 . . . 18 A2
Kenwrick Ho N1 . . . 85 A3
Kenwyn Rd SW4 . . . 61 C3
Kenyon St SW6 . . . . 47 C2
Kepler Ho 9 SE10 . . 43 B1
Kepler Rd SW2,
SW4 . . . . 62 A3
Keppel Ho
Brompton SW3 . . . 144 A3
5 Deptford SE8 . . . 41 B1
Keppel Row SE1 . . . 122 C1
Keppel St WC1 . . . . 105 C4
Kerbela St
E2 . . . . 24 C1 99 B2
Kerbey St E14 . . . . . 34 A3
Kerfield Cres SE5 . . . 48 C2
Kerfield Pl SE5 . . . . 48 C2
Kerridge Ct N1 . . . . . 16 A2
Kerrier Ho SW10 . . . 157 A1
Kerrington Ct 6
W12 . . . . 39 B4
Kerrison Rd
Battersea SW11 . . . . 60 A4
Mill Meads E15 . . . . 27 C4
Kerry N7 . . . . 14 A2
Kerry Ho 1 E1 . . . . . 32 B3
Kerry Path SE8 . . . . 51 B4
Kerry Rd SE8 . . . . . 51 B4
Kerscott Ho 30 E3 . . 27 A2
Kersfield Ho
SW15 . . . . 57 C1
Kersfield Rd
SW15 . . . . 57 C1
Kershaw Cl SW18 . . 59 C1
Kershaw Ho 7
SE27 . . . . 75 A1
Kersley Mews
SW11 . . . . 168 C3
Kersley Rd N16 . . . . . 7 A1
Kersley St SW11 . . . 168 C2
Kerwick Cl 1 N7 . . . 14 B1
Keslake Mans
NW10 . . . . 22 C3
Keslake Rd NW6 . . . 22 C3
Keston Ho SE17 . . . 152 B2
Keston Rd SE15 . . . . 64 C4
Kestrel Ave SE24 . . . 63 B2
Kestrel Ho
4 Battersea
SW11 . . . . 60 A4
Finsbury EC1 . . . . . 96 C4
Keswick Ct SE14 . . . 51 A4
Keswick Broadway 1
SW15 . . . . 58 B2
Keswick Ct 2
SE22 . . . . 64 C2
Keswick Ho 8
SE5 . . . . 48 B2
Keswick Hts 6
SW15 . . . . 58 A2
Keswick Lo E8 . . . . . 16 B2
Keswick Rd SW15 . . 58 A2
Kett Gdns SW2 . . . . 62 B2
Kettleby Ho NW9 . . . 63 A4
Ketton Ho 11 W10 . . 22 B1
Kevan Ho SE5 . . . . . 48 B3
Kew Bridge Ct 8
W4 . . . . 36 C1

Kew Bridge
Distribution Ctr
TW8 . . . . 36 B1
Kew Bridge Rd
TW8 . . . . 36 B1
Kew Bridge Sta
TW8 . . . . 36 B1
Kew Bridge Steam
Mus* TW8 . . . . 36 B1
Kew Coll TW9 . . . . . 44 C3
Kew Foot Rd TW9 . . 54 A4
Kew Gardens Rd
TW9 . . . . 44 C2
Kew Gardens (Royal
Botanic)* TW9 . . . 44 A2
Kew Gardens Sta
TW9 . . . . 44 C2
Kew Gn TW9 . . . . . . 44 B4
Kew Green TW9 . . . . 44 B4
Kew Green Prep Sch
TW9 . . . . 44 B4
Kew Lo 11 TW9 . . . . 44 B2
Kew Montessori Sch
TW9 . . . . 44 C2
Kew Pal* TW9 . . . . . 44 A3
Kew Pier TW9 . . . . . 44 B3
Kew Rd TW9 . . . . . . 44 B4
Kew Ret Pk TW9 . . . 45 A2
Kew Riverside Prim
Sch TW9 . . . . 45 A1
Key Cl E1 . . . . 25 A1
Keyes Ct SE22 . . . . 64 C2
Keyes Rd NW2 . . . . . 9 C3
Keyham Ho 11 W2 . . 31 C4
Key Ho SE11 . . . . . 163 B4
Keymer Rd SW2 . . . . 74 B2
Keynsham Ho 2
N4 . . . . 6 B4
Keynsham Rd SE9 . . 164 A3
Keyse Rd SE1 . . . . 138 C1
Keystone Cres N1 . . 84 B1
Keyworth Cl E5 . . . . 18 A4
Keyworth Pl SE1 . . 136 B2
Keyworth Prim Sch
SE17 . . . . 150 A2
Keyworth St SE1 . . 136 B2
Kezia St SE8 . . . . . 41 A1
Khyber Rd SW11 . . . 168 A1
Kibworth St SW8 . . 162 C1
Kidbrooke Gdns
SE3 . . . . 53 C2
Kidderpore Ave
NW3 . . . . 10 C4
Kidderpore Gdns
NW3 . . . . 10 C4
Kiffen St EC2 . . . . . . 97 C2
Kilbrennan Ho 8
E14 . . . . 34 B3
KILBURN 23 C4
Kilburn Bridge 14
NW6 . . . . 23 C4
Kilburn Gate NW6 . . 78 A2
Kilburn High Rd
NW6 . . . . 78 A3
Kilburn High Road Sta
NW6 . . . . 78 A3
Kilburn Ho 21 W9 . . 23 B2
Kilburn La W10 . . . . 23 A3
Kilburn Park
Foundation Sch The
NW6 . . . . 23 B3
Kilburn Park Rd
NW6 . . . . 23 C2
Kilburn Park Sta
NW6 . . . . 23 C3
Kilburn Pl NW6 . . . . 23 C4
Kilburn Priory
NW6 . . . . 78 A3

Kilburn Sq NW6 . . . . 23 C4
Kilburn Sta NW2 . . . 10 B2
Kilburn Vale NW6 . . 78 A3
Kilburn Vale Est 13
NW6 . . . . 23 C4
Kilby Ct SE10 . . . . . 43 B3
Kildare Ct W2 . . . . . 31 C3
Kildare Gdns W2 . . . 31 C3
Kildare Rd E16 . . . . 35 C4
Kildare Terr W2 . . . . 31 C3
Kildare Wlk E14 . . . 33 C3
Kildoran Rd SW2 . . . 62 A2
Kilgour Rd SE23 . . . 66 A1
Kilkie St SW6 . . . . 166 C1
Killarney Rd SW18 . 59 B1
Killick St N1 . . . . . . 84 C1
Killieser Ave SW2 . . 74 A2
Killip Cl E16 . . . . . . 35 B3
Killoran Ho 8 E14 . . 42 B3
Killowen Rd E9 . . . . 17 C2
Killyon Rd SW8 . . . 171 B1
Kilmaine Rd SW6 . . 154 B1
Kilmarsh Rd W6 . . . 39 B2
Kilmington Rd
SW13 . . . . 46 C4
Kilmore Ho 7
E14 . . . . 34 A3
Kilmuir Ho 1 SW1 . . 145 C3
Kiln Ct E14 . . . . 33 B2
Kilner Ho 5 SE11 . . 163 B4
Kilner St E14 . . . . . 33 C4
Kiloh Ct 1 SW11 . . . 60 A4
Kilpatrick Ct N16 . . . 7 B3
Kilpeck Ho 8 N4 . . . . 6 B4
Kilravock St W10 . . . 23 A2
Kilronan 3 W3 . . . . 28 C3
Kimbell Gdns
SW6 . . . . 164 B3
Kimber Ctr The
SW18 . . . . 70 C4
Kimberley Ave
SE15 . . . . 65 B4
Kimberley Ct NW6 . . 23 A4
Kimberley Ho 8
E14 . . . . 42 B3
Kimberley Rd
Kilburn NW6 . . . . . . 23 A4
Stockwell SW9 . . . . 62 A4
Kimber Rd SW18 . . . 71 A4
Kimble Ho
Lisson Gr NW8 . . . . 90 B2
1 Lower Holloway
N7 . . . . 14 A3
Kimbolton Row
SW3 . . . . 144 A3
Kimpton Ct 12
SE5 . . . . 48 C2
Kimpton Ho SW15 . . 68 C4
Kimpton Rd SE5 . . . 48 C2
Kinburn St SE16 . . . 40 C4
Kincaid Rd SE15 . . . 50 A3
Kincardine Gdns
W9 . . . . 23 C1
Kindell Ho 4
SW14 . . . . 55 C4
Kinder Ho N1 . . . . . 87 C2
Kindersley Ho 1
SE1 . . . . 111 C1
Kinder St 19 E1 . . . 32 A3
Kinefold Ho N7 . . . . 14 A2
Kinfauns Rd SW2 . . 74 C2
King Alfred Sch
NW11 . . . . 2 A3
King Arthur Cl
SE15 . . . . 50 B3
King Charles Ho
SW6 . . . . 156 B2
King Charles St . . . .
SW1 . . . . 134 A4
King Charles Terr 11
E1 . . . . 32 A2
King Charles Wlk 6
SW19 . . . . 70 A3
King David La E1 . . . 32 B2
Kingdom Ho 8
E14 . . . . 42 B3
Kingdon Rd NW6 . . . 10 C2
Kingdown Cl W10 . . 30 C3
King Edward Mans 8
E8 . . . . 25 A4
King Edward Mews
SW13 . . . . 46 C2
King Edwards Mans
SW6 . . . . 155 B1
King Edward's Rd
E9 . . . . 25 B4
King Edward St
EC1 . . . . 108 C2
King Edward The
Third Mews 11
SE16 . . . . 40 A4
King Edward VII Hospl-
Sister Agnes W1 . 103 C4
King Edward Wlk
SE1 . . . . 135 C2
King Fahed Acad
W3 . . . . 29 B2
Kingfield St E14 . . . 42 B2
Kingfisher Ct
8 Battersea
SW11 . . . . 60 A4
11 Cubitt Town E14 . 42 B4
Putney SW19 . . . . . 70 A2
Kingfisher Ho
16 Battersea
SW18 . . . . 59 B4
Peckham SE15 . . . . 49 B2
West Kensington
W14 . . . . 126 C2
Kingfisher Mews
SE13 . . . . 67 A2
Kingfisher Sq 19
SE8 . . . . 51 B4
King Frederick IX Twr
SE16 . . . . 41 B3
King George Sq
TW10 . . . . 54 B1
King George St
SE10 . . . . 52 B3
Kingham Cl
3 Shepherd's Bush
W11 . . . . 39 C3
Wandsworth SW18 . 71 B4
Kingham Ind Est
NW10 . . . . 20 C2
King Henry's Rd
NW3 . . . . 12 A1
King Henry's Reach
W6 . . . . 47 B4
King Henry St
N16 . . . . 16 A3
King Henry's Wlk
N1 . . . . 16 A2
King Henry's Yd 5
N16 . . . . 16 A3
King Ho 5 W12 . . . . 30 A3
Kinghorn St EC1 . . . 108 C3

King James St
SE1 . . . . **136** B3
King John Ct
EC2 . . . . . . .24 A1 **98** B2
King John St E1. . . .32 C4
Kinglake St SE17 . .**152** B2
Kingly Ct W1. . . . . .**119** A4
Kingly St W1. . . . . .**118** C4
King & Queen St
SE17 . . . .**151** A2
King's Arms Ct
E1 . . . .**111** B3
King's Arms Yd
EC2 . . . .**109** B2
Kings Ave SW4 . . . .62 A1
Kings Avenue Sch
SW4 . . . . .62 A2
King's Bench St
SE1 . . . .**136** B4
King's Bench Wlk
EC4 . . . .**107** C1
Kingsbridge N16 . . .6 C3
Kingsbridge Ave
W3 . . . . .36 B4
Kingsbridge Ct
E14 . . . . .41 C2
W10 . . . . .30 B3
Kingsbury Rd N1 . . .16 A2
Kingsbury Terr
N1. . . . . .16 A2
Kingsclere Ct
SW15 . . . . .68 C4
Kingscliffe Gdns
SW19 . . . . .70 B3
King's Coll
Dulwich Village
SE24 . . . . .63 C1
Strand WC2 . . . . .**121** A4
Kings College Ct
NW3 . . . . .12 A1
King's College Hospl
SE5 . . . . .48 C1
Kings College Rd
NW3 . . . . .11 C1
**King's Coll London
(Hampstead)**
NW3 . . . . .10 C4
King's Coll Univ
SE1 . . . .**121** B1
Kingscote NW11. . . .1 B3
Kingscote Rd W4. . .37 C3
Kingscote St EC4 . .**122** A4
King's Court N
SW3 . . . .**144** A1
Kingscourt Rd
SW16 . . . . .74 A1
King's Court S
SW3 . . . .**144** A1
King's Cres N4, N5. . .6 B1
Kingscroft SW4 . . . .62 A1
Kingscroft Rd
NW2 . . . . .10 B2
KING'S CROSS . . .84 C2
King's Cross WC1 . .94 B4
King's Cross Bridge
WC1 . . . . .94 B4
King's Cross Rd
WC1 . . . . .95 A3
**King's Cross, St
Pancras** N1. . . . . .94 A4
King's Cross Sta
N1. . . . . .84 B1
**King's Cross (Thames
Link) Sta** WC1. . . .94 B4

Kings Ct
6 Barnsbury N7 . . .14 B1
Chiswick W6. . . . . .38 C2
East Dulwich SE5 . .64 C3
Primrose Hill NW8. . .80 C3
10 Putney SW15 . . .68 C4
Kingsdale Gdns
W11 . . . . .30 C1
Kingsdale Sec Sch
SE21 . . . . .76 A1
Kingsdown Ave
W3 . . . . .29 A2
Kingsdown Cl
28 Deptford SE16 . . .40 A1
12 Notting Hill W11 . .31 A3
Kingsdown Ct
SW11 . . . . .60 A1
Kingsdown Ho 1
E8 . . . . .16 C3
Kingsdown Rd 4
N19. . . . . .5 A2
Kings Farm Ave
TW10 . . . . .54 C3
Kingsfield Ho 18
N16. . . . . .7 A1
Kingsford St NW5 . .12 B3
Kingsgate Est N1. .16 A2
Kingsgate Ho
SW9 . . . .**173** C4
Kingsgate Par
SW1 . . . .**133** A1
Kingsgate Pl NW6 . .10 C1
Kingsgate Prim Sch
NW6 . . . . .10 C1
Kingsgate Rd
NW6 . . . . .10 C1
King's Gdns 6
NW6 . . . . .1 C1
King's Gr
Peckham SE15 . . . .50 A2
Peckham SE15 . . . .50 A3
Kingshall Mews
SE13 . . . . .67 B4
King's Head Yd
SE1 . . . .**123** B1
Kingshill SE17. . . . .**151** A4
Kings Ho
Richmond TW10,
TW9 . . . . .54 B2
Wallington NW10 . . . .9 A1
King's Rd
Chelsea SW3 . . . . .**144** B1
Chelsea SW10 . . . .**157** B3
Mortlake SW14 . . . .55 C4
Kings Ride Gate
TW10 . . . . .54 C4
Kingsridge SW19 . . .70 A2
King's Scholars' Pas
SW1 . . . .**146** C4
King St Acton W3 . . .28 B1
Hammersmith W6 . .38 D2
St James SW1 . . . .**119** A2
Strand WC2 . . . . .**120** A4
Whitechapel EC2 . .**109** A1
King Stairs Cl
SE16 . . . . .40 A4
King's Terr NW1. . . .82 C3
Kingston Ave 4
SW14 . . . . .55 A4
Kingston Ho 4
NW6 . . . . .10 A1
Kingston Ho E
SW7 . . . .**130** A3
Kingston Ho N
SW7 . . . .**130** A3
Kingston Ho S
SW7 . . . .**130** A3
Kingston Rd SW15,
SW19 . . . . .69 A3
**Kingston Univ
Roehampton Vale
Campus** SW15. . . .68 B1
Kingston Vale
SW15 . . . . .68 A1

Kingsley Mews
Kensington W8 . . . .**128** B1
11 St George in t East
E1 . . . . .32 A2
Kingsley Pl N6 . . . . .3 C4
Kingsley Rd NW6 . . .23 B4
Kingsley St SW11 . .60 B4
Kings Mall Sh Ctr
W6 . . . . .39 B2
King's Mans SW3 . .**158** A3
Kingsmead TW10 . . .54 B1
Kingsmead Ct N6 . . .4 C4
Kingsmead Ho E9 . .18 A4
Kingsmead Prim Sch
E9 . . . . .18 A4
Kingsmead Rd
SW2 . . . . .74 C2
King's Mead Way E5,
E9 . . . . .18 A4
Kingsmere Cl
SW15 . . . . .57 C4
Kingsmere Pl N16 . . .6 C3
Kingsmere Rd
SW19 . . . . .69 C2
King's Mews
1 Clapham Pk
SW4 . . . . .62 A2
Gray's Inn WC1 . . .**95** A1
Kingsmill NW8 . . . .**79** C2
Kingsmill Terr
NW8 . . . .**79** C2
Kingsnorth Ho 12
W10 . . . . .30 C3
King's Par
Hammersmith
W12 . . . . .38 C3
Willesden NW10 . . .22 B4
Kings Pl W4 . . . . . .37 B2
King's Pl SE1 . . . . .**136** C3
King Sq EC1 . . . . . .**96** C3
King's Quay SW10 . .**167** A4
Kings Rd
Richmond TW10,
TW9 . . . . .54 B2
Willesden NW10 . . . .9 A1
King's Rd
Chelsea SW3 . . . . .**144** B1
Chelsea SW10 . . . .**157** B3
Mortlake SW14 . . . .55 C4
Kings Ride Gate
TW10 . . . . .54 C4
Kingsway
Mortlake SW14,
TW9 . . . . .55 A4
St Giles WC2 . . . . .**106** C2
Kingsway Coll
NW5 . . . . .13 A2
Kingsway Mans
WC1 . . . .**106** C4
Kingsway Pl EC1 . . .**96** A2
Kingswear Rd NW5. . .4 A1
Kings Well 28
NW3 . . . . .11 B4
Kings Wlk Sh Mall
SW3 . . . .**144** C2
Kingswood **20** E2 . . .25 B3
Kingswood Ave
NW6 . . . . .23 A3
Kingswood Cl
SW8 . . . .**162** B1
Kingswood Ct
Hither Green SE13 . .67 C1
7 Richmond TW10 . .54 B2
Kings Wood Ct 4
NW6 . . . . .10 C1
Kingswood Rd
South Acton W4 . . . .37 B3
Streatham SW2 . . . .74 A4
Kingswood Terr
W4 . . . . .37 B3
Kings Yd E15 . . . . . .18 C2
Kington Ho NW6 . . .78 B3
Kingward Ho E1. . . .**111** B4
Kingweston Cl
NW2 . . . . .1 A1
King William La 3
SE10 . . . . .43 A1
King William St
EC4 . . . .**123** C4
King William Wlk
SE10 . . . . .52 B4
Kingwood Rd
SW6 . . . .**154** A1
Kinloch St N7. . . . . . .5 B1
Kinnaird Ave W4 . . .45 B3
Kinnear Rd W12. . . .38 B4
Kinnerton Pl N
SW1 . . . .**131** A3
Kinnerton Pl S
SW1 . . . .**131** A3
Kinnerton St
SW1 . . . .**131** B3
Kinnerton Yd
SW1 . . . .**131** B3
Kinnoull Mans 10
E5 . . . . .17 A4
Kinnoul Rd W6 . . . .**154** A4
Kinross Ho N1 . . . . .84 C4
Kinsale Rd SE15 . . .64 C4
Kinsham Ho
E2 . . . . .24 C1 **99** C2
Kintore Way SE1 . .**152** C4
Kintyre Ct **17** SW2. .74 A4
Kintyre Ho **6** E14. .34 B1
Kinver Ho N4. . . . . . .6 C4
Kipling Ho **2** SE5 . .48 B3
Kipling St SE1 . . . .**137** C4
Kipling Twr **3** W3 . .37 B3
Kirby Est SE16. . . . .40 A3
Kirby Gr SE1 . . . . .**138** C4
Kirby St EC1 . . . . . .**107** C4

Kingston St NW1 . .81 B4
King Street Cloisters
8 W6 . . . . .39 A2
King Street Coll
W12 . . . . .39 B4
Kingswater Pl
SW11 . . . .**158** A1
Kingsway
Mortlake SW14,
TW9 . . . . .55 A4
St Giles WC2. . . . .**106** C2
Kingsway Coll
NW5 . . . . .13 A2
Kingsway Mans
WC1 . . . .**106** C4
Kingsway Pl EC1 . . .**96** A2
Kingswear Rd NW5. . .4 A1
Kings Well 28
NW3 . . . . .11 B4
Kings Wlk Sh Mall
SW3 . . . .**144** C2
Kingswood **20** E2 . . .25 B3
Kingswood Ave
NW6 . . . . .23 A3
Kingswood Cl
SW8 . . . .**162** B1
Kingswood Ct
Hither Green SE13 . .67 C1
7 Richmond TW10 . .54 B2
Kings Wood Ct 4
NW6 . . . . .10 C1
Kingswood Rd
South Acton W4 . . . .37 B3
Streatham SW2 . . . .74 A4
Kingswood Terr
W4 . . . . .37 B3
Kings Yd E15 . . . . . .18 C2
Kington Ho NW6 . . .78 B3
Kingward Ho E1. . . .**111** B4
Kingweston Cl
NW2 . . . . .1 A1
King William La 3
SE10 . . . . .43 A1
King William St
EC4 . . . .**123** C4
King William Wlk
SE10 . . . . .52 B4
Kingwood Rd
SW6 . . . .**154** A1
Kinloch St N7. . . . . . .5 B1
Kinnaird Ave W4 . . .45 B3
Kinnear Rd W12. . . .38 B4
Kinnerton Pl N
SW1 . . . .**131** A3
Kinnerton Pl S
SW1 . . . .**131** A3
Kinnerton St
SW1 . . . .**131** B3
Kinnerton Yd
SW1 . . . .**131** B3
Kinnoull Mans 10
E5 . . . . .17 A4
Kinnoul Rd W6 . . . .**154** A4
Kinross Ho N1 . . . . .84 C4
Kinsale Rd SE15 . . .64 C4
Kinsham Ho
E2 . . . . .24 C1 **99** C2
Kintore Way SE1 . .**152** C4
Kintyre Ct **17** SW2. .74 A4
Kintyre Ho **6** E14. .34 B1
Kinver Ho N4. . . . . . .6 C4
Kipling Ho **2** SE5 . .48 B3
Kipling St SE1 . . . .**137** C4
Kipling Twr **3** W3 . .37 B3
Kirby Est SE16. . . . .40 A3
Kirby Gr SE1 . . . . .**138** C4
Kirby St EC1 . . . . . .**107** C4

Kirkeby Bldg EC1. .**107** B4
Kirkland Wlk 4
E8 . . . . .16 B2
Kirkley Ho N16 . . . . .7 A3
Kirkman Ho W1. . . .**105** B3
Kirkman Pl W1. . . .**105** B3
Kirkmichael Rd
E14 . . . . .34 B3
Kirkside Rd SE3 . . .53 C4
Kirkstall Gdns
SW2 . . . . .74 A3
Kirkstall Ho SW1 . .**146** A2
Kirkstall Rd SW2 . . .74 A3
Kirkstead Ct E5 . . . .18 A4
Kirkstone NW1. . . . .**92** C4
Kirkwall Pl E2 . . . . .25 B2
Kirkwood Rd SE15. .50 A1
Kirtley Ho SW8 . . . .**171** A4
Kirtling St SW8. . . .**160** C2
Kirton Cl W4 . . . . . .37 C2
Kirton Gdns
E2 . . . . .24 B2 **99** A3
Kirwin Way SE5. . . .48 A3
Kitcat Terr E3 . . . . .26 C2
Kite Ho **5** SW11 . . .60 A4
Kite Pl E2 . . . .24 C2 **99** C4
Kitson Rd
Barnes SW13 . . . . .46 C2
Camberwell SE5 . . .48 B3
Kittiwake Ct **26**
SE8 . . . . .51 B4
Kitto Rd SE14 . . . . .50 C1
Kiver Rd N19. . . . . . .5 A2
Klea Ave SW4. . . . . .61 B1
Kleffens Ct **2** SE3 . .53 B3
Kleine Wharf 80
N1. . . . . .24 A4
Knapp Cl NW10 . . . . .8 A2
Knapp Rd E3 . . . . . .26 C1
Knaresborough Dr
SW18 . . . . .71 A3
Knaresborough Ho 6
N4. . . . . .6 B4
Knaresborough Pl
SW5 . . . .**142** A4
Knatchbull Rd
Brixton SE5 . . . . . .48 A2
Stonebridge NW10. . .20 C4
Knebworth Ho
South Lambeth
SW8 . . . .**171** C3
2 Stoke Newington
N16. . . . . .16 A4
Knebworth Rd 3
N16. . . . . .16 A4
Kneller Ho SW3 . . .**171** C2
Kneller Rd SE4. . . . .66 A3
Knighten St E1 . . . .32 A1
Knighthead Point 28
E14 . . . . .41 C4
Knight Ho SE17 . . .**152** A3
Knightleas Ct NW2 . .9 B2
Knightrider Ct
EC4 . . . .**122** C4
Knightrider St
EC4 . . . .**122** C4
Knights Arc SW1 . .**130** C3
Knight's Ave W5 . . .36 A4
KNIGHTSBRIDGE . . .
. . . .**130** A2
Knightsbridge SW1,
SW7 . . . .**130** C3
Knightsbridge Ct
SW1 . . . .**131** A3
Knightsbridge Gn
SW1 . . . .**130** C3

Knightsbridge Under
Sch SW7 . . . . **143** A3
Knights CI E9 . . . . .17 B3
Knights Ho
Bermondsey SE1 . . **138** C4
South Lambeth
SW8 . . . . **162** B1
West Kensington
SW5 . . . . .141 A1
Knight's Ho SW10 **156** C2
Knights Rd E16 . . . . . .43 C4
Knight's Wlk
SE11 . . . . **150** A3
Knightswood Ct N6 . .4 C4
Knivet Rd SW6 . . . . **155** B3
Knobs Hill Rd E15 . .27 B4
Knoll Ho NW8 . . . . . . .78 C2
Knoll Rd SW18 . . . . .59 B2
Knolly's CI SE27,
SW16 . . . . .74 C1
Knolly's Rd SE27,
SW16 . . . . .74 C1
Knot Ho SE1 . . . . . **124** C1
Knottisford St E2 . . .25 B2
Knowlden Ho [5]
E1 . . . . .32 B2
Knowle CI SW9 . . . . .62 C4
Knowledge Point Sch
N7 . . . . .14 B2
Knowles Hill Cres
SE13 . . . . .67 C2
Knowles Ho
Wandsworth
SW18 . . . . .59 A1
Willesden Green
NW10 . . . . .21 C4
Knowles Wlk SW4 . .61 B4
Knowlton Ho
SW9 . . . . **173** C4
Knowsley Rd
SW11 . . . . **168** C1
Knox Ct SW4 . . . . . **172** B2
Knox Ho SW15 . . . . .47 B1
Knox St W1 . . . . . . **102** C4
Knoyle Ho W14 . . . **126** B2
Knoyle St SE14 . . . . .51 A4
Kobi Nazrul Prim Sch
E1 . . . . **111** C2
Kossuth St SE10 . . . .43 A1
Kotree Way [3]
SE1 . . . . **153** C4
Kramer Mews
SW5 . . . . **142** A1
Kreedman Wlk [2]
E8 . . . . .16 C3
Kreisel Wlk TW9 . . . .44 B4
Kylemore Ct [4]
W12 . . . . .38 C4
Kylemore Rd NW6 . .10 C1
Kylestrome Ho
SW1 . . . . **145** C3
Kynance Mews
SW7 . . . . **128** B1
Kynance PI SW7 . . . **128** C1
Kynaston Ho [7]
SW2 . . . . .74 B3
Kynaston Rd N16 . . . .7 A1
Kyrle Rd SW11 . . . . .60 C1
Kyverdale Rd N16 . . . .7 B3

L

Laburnum Ct NW2 . .1 B2
Laburnum Ho [5]
SE15 . . . . .50 B3
Laburnum Ho [24]
E2 . . . . .24 B4

Laburnum Ho
New Cross SE4 . . . . .51 B1
[6] Stoke Newington
N16 . . . . .6 C2
Laburnum JMI Sch
E2 . . . . .24 B4
Laburnum St E2 . . . .24 B4
Lacey Ho [7] SE13 . .52 B1
Lacine Ct [12] SE16 . .40 C4
Lackington St
EC2 . . . . **109** C4
Lackland Ho [1]
SE1 . . . . **153** A2
Lacland Ho SW10 . . **157** B2
Lacon Rd SE22 . . . . .64 C3
Lacy Rd SW15 . . . . .57 C3
Ladbroke Cres
W11 . . . . .31 A3
Ladbroke Gdns
W11 . . . .31 B2 **112** C4
Ladbroke Gr
Kensal Town W10 . .31 A4
Notting Hill
W11 . . . .31 B2 **112** C4
Ladbroke Gr Ho
W11 . . . . .31 A3
Ladbroke Grove Sta
W10 . . . . .31 A3
Ladbroke Ho [1]
E1 . . . . **111** A3
Ladbroke Mews
W11 . . . .31 A1 **112** B1
Ladbroke Rd
W11 . . . .31 B1 **112** C3
Ladbroke Sq
W11 . . . .31 B2 **113** A3
Ladbroke Terr
W11 . . . .31 B1 **113** A3
Ladbroke Wlk
W11 . . . .31 B1 **113** A3
Ladlands SE22 . . . . .76 C4
Ladybower Ct [6]
E5 . . . . .17 C4
Ladycroft Rd SE13 . .67 A4
Lady Elizabeth Ho
SW14 . . . . .55 B4
Ladyfern Ho [8]
E3 . . . . .33 C4
Lady Florence Ctyd [6]
SE8 . . . . .51 C3
Lady Margaret Ho
NW5 . . . . .13 A4
Lady Margaret Sch
SW6 . . . . **165** B3
Lady Somerset Rd
NW5 . . . . .13 A4
LADYWELL 66 C1
Ladywell CI SW4 . . . .66 C1
Ladywell Hts SE4 . . .66 B1
Ladywell Rd SE13 . . .67 A2
Ladywell Sta SE13 . .67 A2
Ladywell Water Twr
SE4 . . . . .66 C2
Lafitte Ho [22] N19 . . .4 C4
Lafone Ho [11] SW2 .74 A4
Lafone St SE1 . . . . **138** C4
Lagado Mews
SE16 . . . . .32 C1
Lagonda Ho [3] E3 . .26 C1
Lagonier Ho EC1 . . .97 A3
Laindon Ho [6] N16 . . .7 B3
Laing Ho SE5 . . . . . .48 B3
Lainson St SW18 . . .70 C4
Lairdale CI SE21 . . . .75 B4
Laird Ho SE5 . . . . . .48 B3
Lairs CI N7 . . . . .14 A2
Laitwood Rd
SW12 . . . . .73 A3
Lakanal [14] SE5 . . . .49 A2
Lake Ho SE14 . . . . **136** C3

Laker Ct SW4 . . . . **172** B2
Laker PI SW15 . . . . .58 A1
Lakeside Ct N4 . . . . . .6 B3
Lakeside Rd W14 . . .39 C3
Lakeview [23] E3 . . . .25 C3
Lake View Ho
SW1 . . . . **132** B2
Lakis CI NW3 . . . . . . .11 B4
Laleham Ho
E2 . . . . .24 B1 **98** C2
Lalor St SW6 . . . . . **164** B2
Lambard Ho [4]
SE10 . . . . .52 B3
Lambert Ho
Brixton SW9 . . . . . **173** B1
[19] Crouch End N19 . .4 C4
Lambert Rd SW2 . . .62 B2
Lambert St N1 . . . . .14 C1
LAMBETH **134** C3
Lambeth Acad
SW4 . . . . .61 B2
Lambeth Coll (Brixton
Ctr) SW2 . . . . .62 B2
Lambeth Coll
(Clapham Ctr)
SW4 . . . . .61 B2
Lambeth Coll (Tower
Bridge Ctr) SE1 . . **124** B1
Lambeth Coll
(Vauxhall Ctr)
SW8 . . . . **171** B4
Lambeth High St
SE1 . . . . **148** C4
Lambeth Hill EC4 **122** C4
Lambeth Hospl
SW9 . . . . .62 C4
Lambeth North Sta
SE1 . . . . **135** B2
Lambeth Pal **134** C1
Lambeth Palace Rd
SE1 . . . . **134** C2
Lambeth Pier
SE1 . . . . **134** B1
Lambeth Rd SE1 . . **135** C1
Lambeth Twrs
SE11 . . . . **135** B1
Lambeth Wlk
SE11 . . . . **149** A4
Lambfold Ho N7 . . . .14 A2
Lamb Ho
[28] Camberwell
SE5 . . . . .48 B3
[11] Camberwell SE5 .48 C2
Greenwich SE10 . . . .52 B4
Lamb La E8 . . . . .17 A1
Lamble St NW5 . . . .12 C4
Lambolle PI NW3 . . .12 A2
Lambolle Rd NW3 . .12 A2
Lambourn CI [3]
NW5 . . . . .13 B4
Lambourn Gr
SE16 . . . . .40 C1
Lambourne Ho
NW8 . . . . **101** C4
Lambourn Rd
SW4 . . . . .61 A4
Lambrook Ho [15]
SE15 . . . . .49 C2
Lambrook Terr
SW6 . . . . **164** A4

Lamb's Bldgs EC1 . .97 B1
Lamb's Conduit Pas
WC1 . . . . **106** C4
Lamb's Conduit St
WC1 . . . . .94 C1
Lamb's Mews N1 . . .86 A3
Lamb's Pas EC1 . . . .97 B1
Lamb St E1 . . . . . . **110** C4
Lambton Ct [2] N19 . .5 A3
Lambton Mews
N19 . . . . .5 A3
Lambton PI
W11 . . . .31 B2 **113** A4
Lambton Rd N19 . . . .5 A3
Lamb Wlk SE1 . . . . **138** A3
Lamerton Lo [10]
TW9 . . . . .44 B2
Lamerton St [8]
SE8 . . . . .51 C4
Lamington St [3]
W6 . . . . .39 A2
Lamlash St SE11 . . **150** A4
Lamley Ho SE10 . . . .52 A3
Lammas Rd E9 . . . . .17 C1
Lammermoor Rd
SW12 . . . . .73 A4
Lamont Rd SW10 . . **157** B3
Lamont Rd Pas
SW10 . . . . **157** B3
Lampard Gr N16 . . . . .7 B3
Lampern Sq
E2 . . . . .24 C2 **99** C4
Lampeter Sq W6 . . **154** A3
Lamplighter CI [4]
E1 . . . . .25 B1
Lampson Ho [6]
N19 . . . . .13 B4
Lanark Ho SE1 . . . . **153** B1
Lanark Mans
Paddington W9 . . . .89 A2
[3] Shepherd's Bush
W12 . . . . .39 B4
Lanark Mews NW8 . .89 A3
Lanark PI W9 . . . . . .89 A2
Lanark Rd W9 . . . . . .88 C3
Lanark Sq E14 . . . . .42 A3
Lanbury Rd SE15 . . .65 C3
Lancashire Ct
W1 . . . . **118** B4
Lancaster Ave SE21,
SE27 . . . . .75 B2
Lancaster CI
[1] De Beauvoir Town
N1 . . . . .16 A1
Kensington W2 . . **114** A3
Lancaster Cotts [1]
TW10 . . . . .54 A1
Lancaster Ct
Bayswater W2 . . . **115** A4
Parsons Green
SW6 . . . . **155** A1
West Norwood
SE27 . . . . .75 A2
Lancaster Dr
Canary Wharf E14 . .34 B1
Maitland Pk NW3 . . .12 B2
Lancaster Gate
W2 . . . . **115** A4
Lancaster Gate Sta
W2 . . . . **115** B4
Lancaster hall [14]
E16 . . . . .35 C1
Lancaster Ho
SW15 . . . . .47 B1
Lancaster Lo [2]
W11 . . . . .31 A3

Lancaster Ho
SW18 . . . . .71 A4
Lancaster Lo [2]
W11 . . . . .31 A3
Lancaster Mews
Bayswater W2 . . . **115** A4
[3] Richmond TW10 . .54 A1
[3] Wandsworth
SW18 . . . . .59 A2
Lancaster Pk
TW10 . . . . .54 A2
Lancaster PI WC2 **120** C3
Lancaster Rd
Dudden Hill NW10 . . .8 C3
Finsbury Pk N4 . . . . . .5 C4
Notting Hill W11 . . . .31 A3
Lancaster St SE1 . . **136** B3
Lancaster Stables [10]
NW3 . . . . .12 A2
Lancaster Terr
W2 . . . . **115** A4
Lancaster Wlk
W2 . . . . **115** A2
Lancefield Ho
SE15 . . . . .65 A4
Lancefield St W10 . .23 B2
Lancell St N16 . . . . . .7 A2
Lancelot PI SW7 . . **130** C3
Lancer Sq W8 . . . . **128** A4
Lanchester Ct
W2 . . . . **102** C1
Lanchester Way
SE14 . . . . .50 C2
Lancing St NW1 . . . .93 B3
Lancresse Ct N1 . . . .24 A4
Landale Ct SE16 . . . .52 B2
Landale Ho [13]
SE16 . . . . .40 B3
Landcroft Rd SE22 . .64 B1
Landells Rd SE22 . . .64 C1
Landford Rd SW15 . .57 C4
Landleys Field [2]
N7 . . . . .13 C3
Landmann Ho [16]
SE16 . . . . .40 A2
Landmann Way
SE14 . . . . .40 C1
Landmark Hts E5 . . .18 A4
Landon PI SW1 . . . **130** C2
Landons CI E14 . . . .34 B1
Landon Wlk [6]
E14 . . . . .34 A2
Landor Ct N16 . . . . .16 A3
Landor Ho [7] SE5 . .48 C2
Landor Rd SW9 . . . .62 A4
Landor Wlk [1]
W12 . . . . .38 C4
Landrake NW1 . . . . .83 A3
Landridge Rd
SW6 . . . . **164** C2
Landseer Ct [10]
N19 . . . . .5 A2
Landseer Ho
Battersea SW11 . . **169** C3
Paddington NW8 . . .89 C2
Westminster SW1 **147** C3
Landseer Rd N19 . . . .5 A2
Landulph Ho
SE11 . . . . **149** C2
Landward Ct W1 . . **102** B2
Lane Cl NW2 . . . . .9 A4
Lanercost CI SW2 . .74 C2
Lanercost Rd SW2 . .74 C2
Lane The NW8 . . . . .78 C1
Laneway SW15 . . . . .57 A2

Laney Bldg EC1 . . . **107** B4
Lanfranc Rd E3 . . . . . **26** A3
Lanfrey Pl W14. . . **140** C1
Langbourne Ho
  N6 . . . . 3 C2
Langbourne Ho **7**
SW2. . . . . .62 C2
Langbourne Mans
  N6 . . . . 3 C2
Langbourne Pl
  E14 . . . . .42 A1
Langbourne Prim Sch
  SE21. . . . . .76 A1
Langdale NW1 **1** . .92 C4
Langdale Cl
  Camberwell SE17 . .48 B4
  Mortlake SW14 . . . .55 A3
Langdale Ho SW1 **146** C1
Langdale Rd SE10 . .52 B3
Langdale St **25** E1 . .32 A3
Langdon Ct
  Finsbury EC1 . . . . . **86** B1
  Harlesden NW10 . . .21 A4
Langdon Ho **3**
  E14 . . . . .34 B3
Langdon Park Rd
  N6 . . . . 4 B4
Langdon Park Sec
  Sch E14. . . . . .34 B3
Langdon Sch SW14 . .55 B4
Langdon Way
  SE1 . . . .**153** C3
Langford Cl
  Shacklewell E8 . . . .16 C3
  St John's Wood
  NW8 . . . .**79** A2
Langford Ct NW8 . . .**79** A1
Langford Gn SE5 . . .64 A4
Langford Ho **5**
  SE8 . . . . .51 C4
Langford Pl NW8 . . .**79** A2
Langford Prim Sch
  SW6 . . . .**166** B2
Langford Rd SW6 . .**166** B2
Langham Ct **1**
  SW15 . . . . .57 C2
Langham Ho SW4 . .61 B2
Langham Mans
  SW5 . . . .**142** A1
Langham Pl
  Chiswick W4 . . . . . .46 A4
  Fitzrovia W1 . . . . .**104** B3
Langham St W1 . . .**104** B3
Lang Ho
  South Lambeth
  SW8 . . . .**162** A1
  3 Tufnell Pk N19. . . 4 B1
Langholm Cl
  SW12 . . . . .73 C4
Langhorne Ct **10**
  NW8 . . . . .11 C1
Langhurst Ho
  SW11 . . . .**169** B2
Langland Gdns
  NW3 . . . . .11 A3
Langland Ho **10**
  SE5 . . . . .48 C3
Langland Mans
  NW3 . . . . .11 A3
Langler Rd NW10 . .22 B3
Langley Ct
  South Lambeth
  SW8 . . . .**172** A4
  Strand WC2 . . . . .**120** A4
Langley Dr W3 . . . . .37 A4

Langley Ho
  11 Lower Clapton
  E5 . . . . .17 A3
  36 Paddington W2 . .31 C4
Langley La SW8 . . .**162** B4
Langley Mans
  SW8 . . . .**162** B4
Langley St WC2 . . .**106** A1
Langmead Ho **34**
  E3 . . . . .27 A2
Langmore Ho E1 . .**111** C1
Langport Ho **1**
  SW9 . . . . .48 A1
Langridge **18** NW5 . .12 C2
Langroyd Rd
  SW17 . . . . .72 B2
Langside Ave
  SW15 . . . . .56 C3
La Sng St E1 . . . . . .25 B1
Langston Hughes Cl
  5 SE24 . . . . .63 A3
Langthorn Ct EC2 **109** C2
Langthorne Ho **1**
  SW2 . . . . .74 C4
Langthorne St
  SW6 . . . . .47 C3
Langton Cl WC1 . . .**95** A3
Langton Ct SW15 . .58 B1
Langton Ho SE11 . .**149** A4
Langton Pl SW18 . .70 C3
Langton Rd SW9 . . .48 A3
Langton St SW10 . .**157** A3
Langton Way SE3 . .53 B3
Langtry Pl SW6 . . .**155** C4
Langtry Rd NW8 . . .**78** A3
Langtry Wlk NW8 . .**78** C4
Lanhill Rd W9 . . . . . .23 C1
Lanier Rd SE13 . . . .67 C1
Lanner Ho **2**
  SW11 . . . . .60 A4
Lannoy Point
  SW6 . . . .**154** B2
Lanrick Rd E14 . . . .35 A3
Lansbury Gdns **1**
  E14 . . . . .34 C3
Lansbury Lawrence
  Prim Sch E14 . . . .34 A3
Lanscombe Wlk
  SW8 . . . .**162** A1
Lansdell Ho **9**
  SW2 . . . . .62 C1
Lansdowne Coll
  W2 . . . .**114** A3
Lansdowne Cres
  W11 . . . . 31 A2 **112** B3
Lansdowne Dr E8 . .16 C1
Lansdowne Gdns
  SW8 . . . .**172** A4
Lansdowne Gr
  NW10 . . . . 8 A4
Lansdowne Hill
  SE27 . . . . .75 A1
Lansdowne Ho
  W11 . . . . 31 B1 **112** C2
Lansdowne Int Coll
  Ltd SW7 **1** **143** A4
Lansdowne Mews
  W11 . . . . 31 B1 **112** C2
Lansdowne Pl
  SE1 . . . .**137** C2
Lansdowne Rd
  W11 . . . . 31 A2 **112** B3
Lansdowne Rise
  W11 . . . . 31 A2 **112** B3
Lansdowne Row
  W11 . . . .**118** B2

Lansdowne Sch
  SW9 . . . . .62 B4
Lansdowne Terr
  WC1 . . . .**94** B1
Lansdowne Way
  SW8 . . . .**172** B3
Lansdowne Wlk
  W11 . . . . 31 B1 **112** C2
Lansdowne Wood Cl
  11 SE27 . . . . .75 A1
Lantern Cl SW15 . . .56 C3
Lantern Ho E14 . . . .41 C4
Lanterns Ct E14. . . .41 C3
Lant Ho SE1 . . . . .**136** C3
Lantry Cl **1** W9 . . . .28 A1
Lant St SE1 . . . . . .**137** A3
Lanvanor Rd SE15 . .50 B1
Lanyard Ho **4**
  SE8 . . . . .41 B2
Lapford Cl W9 . . . .23 B1
Lapsang **1** SE1 . .**125** A1
Lapwing Twr **31**
  SE8 . . . . .51 B4
Lapworth **34** W2 . .**100** B4
Lara Cl SE13 . . . . . .67 B1
Larch Ave W3 . . . . .29 A1
Larch Cl
  Balham SW12 . . . . . .73 A2
  18 Deptford SE8 . . .51 B4
  10 Upper Holloway
  N19. . . . . 4 B2
Larch Ct **41** W2. . . .31 C4
Larches Ave SW14 . .55 C3
Larchfield Ho **2**
  N5 . . . . .15 B3
Larch Ho **23** SE16. . .40 B4
Larchmore Ct N19. . . 5 A2
Larch Rd NW2 . . . . . 9 B4
Larcom St SE17 . . .**151** A3
Larden Rd W3 . . . . .38 A4
La Retraite RC Girls
  Sch SW12 . . . . .73 B4
Larissa St SE17. . . .**151** C3
Larix Ct NW10 . . . . .21 C4
Larkfield Rd TW9 . . .54 A3
Larkhall La SW4 . . .**172** A3
Larkhall Rise
  SW4 . . . .**171** B1
Lark Row E2 . . . . . .25 B4
Larmenier & Sacred
  Heart RC Prim Sch
  W6 . . . . .39 C2
Larnaca Ho SE1 . . .**138** C2
Larnach Rd W6 . . . .47 C4
Larpent Ave SW15 . .57 B2
La Sainte Union RC Sec
  Sch NW5. . . . . .13 A4
Lascelles Ho NW1 . .**90** B1
Lassell St SE10 . . . .42 C1
Lasseter Pl SE3 . . . .53 B4
Latchmere Rd
  SW11 . . . .**168** C1
Latchmere St
  SW11 . . . .**168** C2
Latham Ho E1 . . . . .32 C3
Latimer SE17 . . . . .**152** A1
Latimer Ho
  11 Homerton E9. . . . .17 C2
  Notting Hill
  W11 . . . . 31 B2 **113** A3
Latimer Ind Est **1**
  NW10 . . . . .30 B3
Latimer Pl W10 . . . .30 B3
Latimer Rd W10 . . . .30 B3

Latimer Road Sta
  W10 . . . . .30 C2
Latitude Ho NW1 . . .**82** A3
Latona Rd SE15 . . . .49 C4
Latimer Pl W44 . . . .46 A4
Latvia Ct SE17 . . . .**151** A1
Latymer Ct W6 . . . .39 C2
Latymer Upper Sch
  W6 . . . . .38 C1
Lauderdale Mans
  W9 . . . .**88** B3
Lauderdale Rd W9 . .**88** B3
Lauderdale Twr
  EC2 . . . .**108** C4
Laud St SE11 . . . .**148** C2
Laughton Ho **11**
  SW2 . . . . .62 C1
Launcelot St SE1 . .**135** B3
Launceston Pl
  W8 . . . .**128** B1
Launch St E14. . . . .42 B3
Laundress La N16 . . . 7 C1
Laundry La **7** N1 . .15 B1
Laundry Rd W6 . . .**154** A3
Laura Pl E5 . . . . . . .17 B4
Laurel Bank Gdns
  SW6 . . . .**165** A2
Laurel Cl **8** N19 . . . 4 B2
Laurel Ct
  Dalston E8 . . . . .16 B1
  5 Putney SW15 . . . .57 C2
  9 Rotherhithe
  SE16 . . . . .33 A1
Laurel Ho
  8 Deptford SE8 . . .51 B4
  3 Hamstead NW3 . .11 A2
Laurel Rd SW13 . . . .46 C1
Laurel St E8 . . . . . .16 B2
Laurence Mews **12**
  W12 . . . . .38 C4
Laurence Pountney
  Hill EC4 . . . .**123** B4
Laurence Pountney La
  EC4. . . . .**123** C4
Laurie Gr SE14 . . . .51 A2
Laurie Ho
  Newington SE1. . . .**136** B1
  Notting Hill
  W8 . . . . 31 C1 **113** B1
Laurier Rd NW5 . . . 4 A1
Lauriston Ho **6**
  E9 . . . . .17 C1
Lauriston Lo NW6 . . .10 B2
Lauriston Rd E9 . . . .25 C4
Lausanne Rd SE15 . .50 B2
Lavell St N16. . . . . . .15 C4
Lavender Cl SW3 . .**157** C3
Lavender Ct **4**
  SW4 . . . .**172** B3
Lavender Gdns
  SW11 . . . . .60 B3
Lavender Gr E8 . . . .16 C1
Lavender Hill
  SW11 . . . . .60 C4
Lavender Ho
  Battersea SW11 . . . .59 C4
  4 Rotherhithe
  SE16 . . . . .32 C1
Lavender Sweep
  SW11 . . . . .60 B3
Lavender Terr **12**
  SW11 . . . . .60 A4
Lavender Wlk
  SW11 . . . . .60 B3

Lavendon Ho NW8 . .**90** B2
Lavengro Rd SE27 . .75 B2
Lavenham
  SW18 . . . . .70 C3
Laverstoke Gdns
  SW15 . . . . .68 C4
Laverton Mews
  SW5 . . . .**142** B3
Laverton Pl SW5 . .**142** B3
Lavina Gr N1 . . . . . .**84** C2
Lavington Cl E9 . . .**18** B2
Lavington St SE1 . .**122** B1
Lawdale Jun Sch
  E2 . . . . .24 C2 **99** C4
Lawford Rd
  Chiswick W4 . . . . . .45 B3
  De Beauvoir Town
  N1. . . . . .16 A1
  Kentish Town NW5 . .13 B3
Lawfords Wharf **18**
  NW1 . . . . .13 B1
Lawless Ho **5** E14 . .34 B2
Lawless St **12** E14 . .34 A2
Lawley St E5 . . . . . .17 B4
Lawman Ct **2**
  TW9 . . . . .44 B2
Lawn Cres TW9 . . . .44 C1
Lawnfield Ct NW6 . . . 9 C1
Lawn House Cl
  E14 . . . . .42 B4
Lawn La SW8 . . . .**162** C4
Lawn Rd NW3 . . . . . .12 B3
Lawns The N16 . . . .16 A3
Lawrence Ave
  NW10 . . . . .20 C4
Lawrence Bldgs **11**
  N16 . . . . 7 B1
Lawrence Cl
  Bow E3 . . . . .26 C3
  6 Shepherd's Bush
  W12 . . . . .30 A2
Lawrence Ct
  4 South Acton
  W3 . . . . .37 B3
  Stoke Newington N16 . 7 B1
Lawrence Ho
  20 Camden Town
  NW1 . . . . .13 A1
  Westminster SW1 . .**147** C3
Lawrence La EC2 . .**109** A2
Lawrence Mans
  SW3 . . . .**158** A3
Lawrence Pl N1 . . . .**84** B4
Lawrence Rd
  Canning Town E16 . .35 B4
  Chelsea SW3 . . . . .**158** A3
Lawrence Trad Est
  SE10 . . . . .43 A2
Lawrence Univ
  SW7 . . . .**143** A3
Lawson Cl SW19. . . .69 C1
Lawson Ct **1** N4 . . . 5 B3
Lawson Ho **7**
  W12 . . . . .30 A2
Law St SE1 . . . . . .**137** C2
Lawton Rd E3 . . . . .26 A2
Laxfield Ct E8 . . . . .24 C4
Laxley Cl SE5 . . . . .48 A3
Laxton Path **1**
  SE4 . . . . .65 C3
Laxton Pl NW1 . . . .**92** B2
Layard Rd SE16. . . .40 A2
Layard Sq SE16. . . .40 A2
Laybourne Ho **18**
  E14 . . . . .41 C4

Laycock Prim Sch
N1..................15 A2
Laycock St N1 ......14 C2
Layfield Ho **1**
SE10.....................43 C1
Laystall Ct EC1......95 B1
Laystall St EC1 .....95 B1
Layton Pl TW9.......44 C2
Lazar Wlk **2** N1....18 A2
Leabank Sq E9 ......18 C2
Leabourne Rd N16 ..7 C4
Leacroft Ave
SW12....................72 B4
Lea Ct **3** W12........38 A4
Leadenhall Mkt
EC3...................110 A1
Leadenhall Pl
EC3...................110 A1
Leadenhall St
EC3...................110 A1
Leadenham Ct **15**
E3.........................26 C1
Lea Ho NW8..........90 A1
Leahurst Rd SE13 ..67 C1
Lea Int E9...............18 C3
Leake St
Lambeth SE1 ......135 B3
South Bank SE1 ..135 A4
Leamington Ct
4 Forest Hill
SE26....................76 C1
North Acton W3 ....28 C4
Leamington Ho **4**
W11.....................31 B4
Leamington Pk
W3.......................28 C4
Leamington Rd Villas
W11.....................31 B4
Leamore St W6 .....39 B2
Leamouth Rd E14 ..34 C3
Leander Ct
27 Hackney E9.......17 B1
St Johns SE8 ....51 C2
Leander Rd SW2 ...62 C1
Leary Ho SE1 ......149 A1
Lea Sq **22** E3.........26 B4
Leatherdale St
32 Bethnal Green
E1........................25 B1
18 Globe Town E1 ..25 C2
Leatherhead Cl
N16........................7 B3
Leather La EC1 ....107 C4
Leathermarket Ct
SE1....................138 A3
Leathermarket St
SE1....................138 A2
Leather Rd SE16 ...40 C2
Leathwaite Rd
SW11....................60 B2
Leathwell Rd SE8 ..52 A1
Lebanon Gdns
SW18....................58 C1
Lebanon Rd SW18 ..58 C2
Lebus Ho NW8 ......80 A1
Lechmere Rd NW2 ...9 A2
Leckford Rd SW18 ..71 B3
Leckhampton Pl **23**
SW2....................74 C4
Lecky Ho NW2 ....9 A4
Lecky St SW7 .....143 B2
L'Ecole des Petits Sch
SW6..................166 A2
Leconfield Ave SW13,
SW15....................56 C4
Leconfield Ho SE5 ..64 A4
Leconfield Rd N5...15 C4

Lector Ct EC1 ....95 C1
Leda Ct SW9 ....163 B1
Ledam Bldg EC1...107 B4
Ledbury Ho **12**
SE22....................64 A4
Ledbury Mews N
W11.....................31 C2 113 B4
Ledbury Mews W
W11.....................31 C2 113 B4
Ledbury Rd W11 ...31 C3
Ledbury St SE15....50 A3
Ledo Ho **1** N16 .....15 C4
Lee Conservancy Rd
E9........................18 B3
Lee Ct SE13 ....67 C3
Leeds Ct EC1 ....96 A2
Leeds Pl W1 ....117 B4
Lee St E8 ....24 B4
Leeke St WC1 ....94 C4
Leeland Way NW10 ..8 B4
Leerdam Dr E14 ....42 B3
Lees Ct W1 ....117 B4
Lees Ho SE17 .....151 C1
Leeson Rd **12**
SE24....................62 C3
Lees Pl W1 ....117 B4
Lee St E8 ....24 B4
Lee Ct N16 ....15 C4
Lee Valley Sp Ctr
E10......................19 A4
Leeve Ho **7** W9...23 B2
Leeward Ct E1 ....125 C2
Leeway SE8...........41 B1
Leffern Rd W12 ....38 C4
Leff Ho **9** NW6 ....10 A1
Lefroy Ho SE1.....136 C3
Lefroy Rd W12 .....38 B4
Legard Rd N5.........6 A1
Leggatt Rd E15.....27 B3
Legge St SE13......67 B2
Leghorn Rd NW10 .21 C3
Legion Cl N1 ....14 C1
Legion Terr E3 ......26 C4
Leicester Ct
18 Paddington W2 ..31 C4
4 Brixton SW9 ......63 A4
5 Putney SW15 ......57 B4
Leicester Ho
4 Brixton SW9 ......63 A4
5 Putney SW15 ......57 B4
Leicester Pl WC2 ..119 C4
Leicester Sq WC2 ..119 C3
Leicester Sq *
Leicester Square Sta
WC2....................119 C3
Leicester St WC2 ..119 C3
Leigham Ave
SW16....................74 A1
Leigham Hall **3**
SW16....................74 A1
Leigham Hall Par **2**
SW16....................74 A1
Leigham Vale SE27,
SW16, SW2...........74 C2
Leigh Ct **22** SW2 ..62 C2
Leigh Ho **8** SW15 ..56 C2
Leigh Orchard Cl
SW16....................74 B1
Leigh Pl EC1 ....107 B4
Leigh Rd N5 ....15 A4
Leigh St WC1 ....94 A3
Leighton Cres
NW5.....................13 B3
Leighton Gdns
NW10....................22 B3

Leighton Gr NW5...13 B3
Leighton House (Art
Gall & Mus)*
W14....................127 A2
Leighton Pl NW5 ...13 B3
Leighton Rd NW5 ..13 B3
Leinster Ave
SW14....................55 B3
Leinster Gdns
W2.....................114 C4
Leinster Mews
W2.....................114 C4
Leinster Pl W2 .....100 C1
Leinster Sq W2 ....100 A1
Leinster Terr W2 ..114 C4
Leitch Ho **8** NW8 ..11 C1
Leithcote Path
SW16....................74 B1
Leith Ho
7 Kentish Town
N7........................13 C3
3 Streatham SW2 ..74 B4
Leith Mans W9 .....88 A3
Leith Yd **3** NW6 ...23 C4
Lelitia Cl E8 ....24 C4
Leman St E1 ....111 B1
Lemmon Rd SE10 ..53 A4
Le Moal Ho **22** E1 ..32 B4
Lemsford Ct N4.....6 B2
Lena Gardens Prim
Sch W6 ....39 B3
Lena Gdns W6 ......39 B3
Lendal Terr **7**
SW4....................61 C4
Len Freeman Pl
SW6...................154 C3
Lenham NW5 ....12 C2
Lenham Ho SE1 ...137 C3
Lennon Rd NW2....9 B2
Lennox Gdns
Knightsbridge
SW1....................130 C1
Willesden NW10 .....8 B4
Lennox Gdns Mews
SW1....................144 C4
Lennox Ho **10** E9 ..17 B2
Lennox Rd N4, N7 ..5 C2
Lenthall Ho SW1 ..147 A1
Lenthall Rd E8 ......16 C1
Lenthorp Rd SE10 ..43 B2
Lenton Rise TW9 ...54 A4
Len Williams Ct
NW6....................23 C3
Leonard Ct
Bloomsbury WC1 ....94 A2
Kensington W8 ....127 B2
Leonard Day Ho **5**
NW5....................13 A2
Leonard Pl **16** N16 ..16 A4
Leonard St EC2.....97 C2
Leonora Ho W9 ....88 C2
Leontine Cl SE15 ..49 C3
Leopards Ct EC1 ..107 B4
Leopold Bldgs
E2 ....24 B2 98 C4
Leopold Mews E9 ..25 B4
Leopold Prim Sch
NW10....................8 B1
Leopold Rd NW10 ..8 A1
Leopold St E3 ....33 B4
Leopold Wlk
SE11....................148 C1
Leo St SE15 ....50 A3
Leo Yd EC1 ....96 B1
Leppoc Rd SW4 ....61 C2
Leroy St SE1 ....152 A4
Lerry Cl W14 ......155 A4

Lerwick Ho SW18 ..59 B3
Lesley Ct SW1 .....133 B1
Leslie Prince Ct **3**
SE5........................48 C3
Leslie Rd E11 ....19 C4
Lessar Ave SW4 ....61 B1
Lessar Ct SW4 ......61 B1
Lester Ct **3** E3......27 A2
Leswin Pl N16........7 B1
Leswin Rd N16.......7 B1
Letchford Gdns
NW10....................21 C2
Letchford Mews
NW10....................21 C2
Letchmore Ho **7**
W10......................22 B1
Lethaby Ho **13**
SW4......................62 B3
Lethbridge Cl
SE13......................52 B1
Letterstone Rd
SW6...................154 C2
Lettice St SW6 ....165 A3
Lett Rd E15 ....19 C1
Lettsom St SE5 .....49 A1
Levana Cl SW19 ....70 A3
Levant Ho **17** E1 ....25 C1
Levehurst Way SW4,
SW9....................172 B2
Leven Rd E14 ....34 C3
Lever Ct **15** E9 ......17 C2
Leverett St SW3 ..144 B4
Leverington Pl N1 ..97 C3
Lever St EC1 ....97 A3
Leverstock Ho
SW3....................144 B2
Leverton Pl NW5 ..13 B3
Leverton St NW5 ..13 B3
Levison Way **2**
N19......................4 C3
Levita Ho NW1 ......93 C4
Levyne Ct EC1 ....95 B2
Lewesdon Cl **13**
SW19....................69 C3
Lewes Ho
Bermondsey SE1 ..138 B4
Peckham SE15 ......49 C4
Leweston Pl N16.....7 B4
Lewey Ho E3 ....26 B1
Lewin Rd SW14 ....55 C4
Lewis Ct **6** SE16 ...40 A1
Lewis Gr SE13 ....67 B4
LEWISHAM 67 B3
Lewisham Bridge
Prim Sch SE13 .....67 A4
Lewisham Bsns Ctr
SE14......................50 C4
Lewisham Coll
SE4........................51 C1
Lewisham Ctr
SE13......................67 B4
Lewisham High St
SE13......................67 B2
Lewisham Hill
SE13......................52 B1
Lewisham Hospl
SE13......................67 A1
Lewisham Pk
SE13......................67 B1
Lewisham Rd
SE13......................52 B1
Lewisham Sta
SE13......................67 B3
Lewisham Way SE4,
SE14......................51 B2

Lewis Pl E8 ....16 C3
Lewis Silkin Ho **2**
SE15......................50 B4
Lewis St NW1 ....13 A2
Lexden Rd W3 ......28 A1
Lexfield Ho N5 ......15 B4
Lexham Gardens
Mews W8 ....128 B1
Lexham Gdns W8 ..142 A4
Lexham Mews
W8......................141 C4
Lexham Wlk W8...128 B1
Lexington St W1 ...119 A4
Lexton Gdns
SW12....................73 C3
Leybon Pk TW9 ....44 C2
Leybourne Ho **20**
SE15......................50 B4
Leybourne Rd
NW1.....................13 A1
Leybourne St **5**
NW1.....................13 A1
Leyden Mans **7**
N19.......................5 A4
Leyden St E1 ....110 C3
Leydon Cl SE16 ....32 C1
Ley Ho SE1 ....136 C3
Leyland Ho **8** E14 ..34 A2
Leylands SW18 .....58 B1
Leylang Rd SE14 ..50 C3
Leys Ct SW9 ....173 B1
Leysdown **5** NW5 ..12 C2
Leysdown Ho
SE17....................152 B2
Leysfield Rd W12 ..38 C4
Leythe Rd W3 ......37 B4
Leyton Ct SE23 .....65 C1
LEYTON 19 C4
Leyton Mills E10 ...19 B4
Leyton Rd E15 ......19 C3
Liardet St SE14 .....51 A4
Liberia Rd N5 ....15 A2
Liberty Mews
SW12....................61 A1
Liberty St SW9 ....173 A4
Libra Rd **7** E3 .....26 B3
Library Mews
W12......................39 B4
Library Par NW10 ..21 A4
Library Pl E1 ....32 A2
Library St SE1 .....136 B3
Lichfield Ct TW9 ...54 A3
Lichfield Gdns TW10,
TW9......................54 A2
Lichfield Ho **27**
SE5 .... A
Lichfield Rd
Mile End E3 ....26 A2
Richmond TW9 ......44 B2
West Hampstead
NW2.....................10 A4
Lichfield Terr **1**
TW9......................54 A2
Lichport Ct N4 ....6 A3
Lickey Ho W14 ....155 A4
Lidcote Gdns
SW9....................173 A1
Liddell Gdns
NW10....................22 B3
Liddell Rd NW6 ....10 C2
Lidfield Rd N16 .....15 C4
Lidgate Rd **22**
SE15......................49 B3
Lidiard Rd SW18 ...71 B2
Lidlington Pl NW1 ..83 A1
Lidyard Rd N19......4 B3

Liffey Ct NW10 . . . . .8 C1
Liffords Pl SW13 . . . .46 B1
Lifford St SW15 . . . .57 C3
Lighter Cl E16 . . . .E16. .41 A2
Lighterman Mews **15**
E1 . . . . .32 C3
Lighterman's Rd
E14 . . . . .42 A3
Lightermans Wlk
SW18 . . . . .58 C3
Light Horse Ct
SW1 . . . .**145** B1
Ligonier St
E2 . . . . .24 B1 98 C2
Lilac Ave SE4 . . . . . . .66 B4
Lilac Pl SE11 . . . . . .148 C3
Lilac St W12 . . . . .29 C2
Lilestone Est NW8 . .89 C1
Lilestone Ho NW8 . .89 C2
Lilestone St NW8 . . .90 A2
Lilford Ho **21** SE5 . . .48 B1
Lilford Rd SE5 . . . . . .48 A1
Lilian Baylis Ho
N1 . . . . .15 B2
Lilian Baylis Tech Sch
SE11 . . . .**149** A1
Lilley Cl E1 . . . . .125 C1
Lilian Ave W3 . . . . . . .36 C4
Lilian Cl **8** N16 . . . . . .7 A1
Lilian Rd SW13 . . . . .47 A4
Lillie Ho N5 . . . . .14 C3
Lillie Rd SW6 . . . . .154 C3
Lillie Road Mans
SW6 . . . . .154 B3
Lillieshall Rd SW4 . .61 B4
Lillie Yd SW6 . . . . . .155 B4
Lillingston Ho N7 . . . .14 C4
Lily Cl W14 . . . . .39 C2
Lily Pl EC1 . . . . .107 C4
Lilyville Rd SW6 . . .164 C4
Limborough Ho **5**
E14 . . . . .33 C4
Limburg Rd SW11 . .60 A3
Limeburner La
EC4 . . . . .108 A2
Lime Cl E1 . . . . .125 C2
Lime Ct SW15 . . . . . .57 A4
Lime Gr W12 . . . . .39 B4
Limeharbour E14 . . .42 A4
Lime Ho **7** TW9 . . . . .45 A2
LIMEHOUSE 33 A2
Limehouse Cswy
E14 . . . . .33 B2
Limehouse Ct **5**
E14 . . . . .33 C3
Lime House Ct **28**
E14 . . . . .33 B3
Limehouse Cut **4**
E14 . . . . .34 A4
Limehouse Fields Est
14 E14 . . . . .33 A4
Limehouse Link
(Tunnel) E14 . . . . . . .33 B2
Limehouse Sta
E14 . . . . .33 A3
Limekiln Wharf **31**
E14 . . . . .33 B2
Limerick Cl **3**
SW12 . . . . .73 B4
Limerick Ct **1**
SW12 . . . . .73 B4
Limerston St
SW10 . . . . .157 A3
Lime St Pas EC3 . . .124 A4
Limes Ave
Barnes SW13 . . . . . . .46 B1

Limes Ave continued
Golders Green NW11 . .1 A4
Limes Gdns SW18 . . . .9 C1
Limes Field Rd
SW14 . . . . .56 A4
Limesford Rd
SE15 . . . . .65 C3
Limes Gdns SW18 . . .58 C1
Limes Gr SE13 . . . . .67 B3
Lime St EC3 . . . . . . .110 A1
Limes The
Camberwell SE5 . . . . .64 A4
Kensington
W2 . . . . . . .31 C2 **113** C3
Limes Wlk SE15 . . . . .65 B3
Limetree Cl SW2 . . . .74 B3
Lime Tree Ct **14**
E3 . . . . .33 C4
Limpsfield Ave
SW19 . . . . .69 C2
Limscott Ho **3** E3 . . .27 A2
Linacre Cl SE15 . . . . .65 A4
Linacre Ct W6 . . . . . .39 C1
Linacre Rd NW2 . . . . .9 A2
Linale Ho N1 . . . . . . .87 B1
Linberry Wlk **3**
SE8 . . . . .41 B2
Lincoln Ave SW19 . . .69 C1
Lincoln Ct N16 . . . . . . .6 C4
Lincoln Ho
Bloomsbury WC1 . . .**107** A3
9 Dartmouth Pk
NW5 . . . . .4 B1
2 Islington N1 . . . . . .15 B2
Knightsbridge SW1 **130** C3
10 Putney SW15 . . .58 A2
Lincoln Mews
NW6 . . . . .23 B4
Lincoln's Inn★
WC2 . . . . .107 A2
Lincoln's Inn Fields
WC2 . . . . .107 A2
Lindale Sw19 . . . . . . .70 A2
Lindal Rd SE4 . . . . . .66 B2
Linden Ave NW10 . . .22 C3
Linden Ct **8**
Battersea
SW18 . . . . .59 C3
7 Shepherd's Bush
W12 . . . . .30 B1
Linden Gdns
Chiswick W4 . . . . . . .37 C1
Notting Hill
W2 . . . . . . .31 C2 **113** C3
Linden Gr SE15 . . . . .65 B4
Linden Ho **3** SE8 . . .51 B4
Linden Lodge Sch
SW19 . . . . .70 A2
Linden Mans N6 . . . . .4 A3
Linden Mews
Kensington
W2 . . . . . . .31 C2 **113** C3
Stoke Newington
N1 . . . . .15 C3
Lindens The N12 . . . . .1 A4
Lindfield Gdns
NW3 . . . . .11 B3
Lindfield Hts NW3 . . .11 B3
Lindfield St E14 . . . . .33 C3
Lindford Christie
Stadium The
W12 . . . . .30 A4
Lindisfarne Way
E9 . . . . .18 A4

Lindley Ho
1 Peckham SE15 . . .49 C3
3 Stepney E1 . . . . . .32 B4
Lindley Pl TW9 . . . . .44 C2
Lindley St E1 . . . . . . .32 B4
Lindop Ho **3** E1 . . . .26 A1
Lindore Rd SW11 . . .60 B3
Lindo St SE15 . . . . . .50 B1
Lindrop St SW6 . . . .166 C2
Lindsay Ct SW11 . . .167 C3
Lindsay Sq SW1 . . . .147 C2
Lindsell St **6**
SE10 . . . . .52 B2
Lindsey Ho★
SW10 . . . . .157 C2
Lindsey Mews **13**
N1 . . . . .15 B1
Lindsey St EC1 . . . .108 B4
Lind St SE8 . . . . .52 A1
Linfield W1 . . . . .94 C3
Linford Ho **1** E2 . . . .24 C4
Linford St SW8 . . . .170 C3
Linford Street Bsns
Est SW8 . . . . .170 C4
Lingard Ho **11** E14 . .42 B3
Lingards Rd SE13 . . .67 B3
Lingfield Ho
8 Acton Green
W4 . . . . .37 B1
Lambeth SE1 . . . . . .136 B3
Lingham St SW9 . . .172 C1
Ling Rd E16 . . . . .35 C4
Ling's Coppice
SE21 . . . . .75 C2
Lingwell Rd SW17 . . .72 A1
Lingwood Rd E5 . . . . .7 C4
Linhope St NW1 . . . . .90 C1
Linkenholt Mans **6**
W6 . . . . .38 B2
Links Yd E1 . . . . .111 A4
Linkway N4 . . . . .6 B4
Linkwood Wlk
NW1 . . . . .13 C1
Linnell Ho
Spitalfields E1 . . . . .110 C4
St John's Wood
NW8 . . . . .78 C4
Linnell Rd SE5 . . . . . .49 A1
Linnet Mews
SW12 . . . . .72 C4
Linom Rd SW4 . . . . . .62 A3
Linscott Rd E5 . . . . . .17 B4
Linsey St
Bermondsey SE16 . .153 B4
Bermondsey SE16 . .139 C1
Linslade Ho
10 Hackney E2 . . . .24 C4
Marylebone NW8 . . . .90 B2
Linstead St
NW6 . . . . .10 C1
Linstead Way
SW19 . . . . .70 A4
Lintaine Cl W6 . . . . .154 B3
Linthorpe Rd N16 . . . .7 A4
Linton Ho
Lower Holloway
N7 . . . . .14 B4
2 Tower Hamlets
E3 . . . . .33 C4
Linton St N1 . . . . .87 A3
Linver Rd SW6 . . . . .165 B2
Linwood Cl SE5 . . . . .49 B1
Lion Cl SE4 . . . . .66 C1

Lionel Ho **6** W10 . . .31 A4
Lionel Mans **14**
W14 . . . . .39 C3
Lionel Mews **13**
W10 . . . . .31 A4
Lion Gate Gdns
TW9 . . . . .54 B4
Lion Gate Mews
SW18 . . . . .70 C4
Lion House Sch
SW15 . . . . .57 C3
Lion Mills **17** E2 . . .24 C3
Lion Yd SW4 . . . . .61 C3
Lipton Rd **9** E1 . . . . .32 C3
Lisburne Rd NW3 . . .12 B4
Lisford St SE15 . . . . .49 B2
Lisgar Terr W14 . . . .140 C4
Liskeard Gdns
SE3 . . . . .53 C2
Liskeard Ho SE11 . .149 C2
Lisle Ct NW2 . . . . .1 A1
Lisle St W1 . . . . .119 C4
Lismore Cir NW5 . . . .12 C3
Lismore Wlk **4**
N1 . . . . .15 B2
Lissenden Gdns
NW5 . . . . .12 C4
Lissenden Mans
NW5 . . . . .12 C4
Lisson Cotts NW1 . .102 B4
Lisson Gr NW1,
NW8 . . . . .90 A2
LISSON GROVE 90 B1
Lisson Ho NW1 . . . .102 A4
Lisson St NW1 . . . . .102 A4
Lister Cl W3 . . . . .28 C4
Lister Ct N16 . . . . .7 A2
Lister Ho
Greenwich SE3 . . . . .53 A4
Marylebone W1 . . . .104 A2
Spitalfields E1 . . . . .111 C4
Lister Mews N7 . . . . .14 B4
Liston Rd SW4 . . . . . .61 B4
Listowel Cl SW9 . . .163 C2
Listria Lo N16 . . . . . . .7 B2
Listria Pk N16 . . . . . . .7 B2
Litcham Ho **22** E1 . .25 C2
Litchfield Gdns
NW10 . . . . .8 C2
Litchfield St WC2 . .119 C4
Lithos Rd NW3 . . . . . .11 B2
Lithe Albany St
NW1 . . . . .92 B2
Little Argyll St W1 . .104 B1
Little Boltons The
SW10 . . . . .142 B1
Little Britain EC1 . . .108 C3
Littlebury Rd SW4 . . .61 C4
Little Chelsea Ho
SW10 . . . . .157 A3
Little Chester St
SW1 . . . . .132 A2
Little Cloisters
SW1 . . . . .134 A2
Little College St
SW1 . . . . .134 A2
Little Combe Cl **13**
SW15 . . . . .57 C1
Littlecote Cl SW19 . .70 A4

Little Cottage Pl
SE10 . . . . .52 A3
Little Deans Yd
SW1 . . . . .134 A2
Little Dimocks
SW12 . . . . .73 A2
Little Dorrit Ct
SE1 . . . . .137 A4
Little Edward St
NW1 . . . . .92 B4
Little Essex St
WC2 . . . . .121 B4
Littlefield Cl N19 . . .13 B4
Little George St
SW1 . . . . .134 A3
Little Green St
NW5 . . . . .13 A4
Little Marlborough St
W1 . . . . .104 C1
Little Newport St
WC2 . . . . .119 C4
Little New St EC4 . . .107 C2
Little Portland St
W1 . . . . .104 C2
Little Russell St
WC1 . . . . .106 A3
Little St James's St
SW1 . . . . .118 C1
Little St Leonards
SW14 . . . . .55 B4
Little Sanctuary
SW1 . . . . .134 A3
Little Smith St
SW1 . . . . .133 C2
Little Somerset St
E1 . . . . .110 C1
Little Titchfield St
W1 . . . . .104 C3
Littleton St SW18 . . .71 B2
Little Trinity La
EC4 . . . . .123 A4
Little Turnstile
WC1 . . . . .106 C2
LITTLE VENICE 101 A4
Little Venice★ 100 C4
Littlewood SE13 . . . .67 B1
Livermere Ct **8**
E8 . . . . .24 B4
Livermere Rd E8 . . . .24 B4
Liverpool Gr SE17 . .151 B2
Liverpool Ho N7 . . . .14 C2
Liverpool Rd
Islington N1 . . . . . . .85 C3
Islington N1, N7 . . . .14 C1
Newham E16 . . . . . . .35 A4
Liverpool Street Sta
EC2 . . . . .110 A3
Livesey Mus★ 50 A4
Livesey Pl SE15 . . . .49 C4
Livingstone Ho
SE5 . . . . .48 B3
Livingstone Lo **9**
W9 . . . . .31 C4
Livingstone Pl E14 . .42 B1
Livingstone Rd
14 Battersea
SW11 . . . . .59 C4
Mill Meads E15 . . . . .27 A4
Livity Sch The
SW2 . . . . .62 A2
Livonia St W1 . . . . . .105 A1
Lizard St EC1 . . . . . . .97 A3
Llandovery Ho **1**
E14 . . . . .42 B4

Llanelly Rd NW2 . . . 1 B2
Llanvanor Rd NW2 . . . 1 B2
Llewellyn Ho 10
  N19. . . . . 4 B1
Llewellyn St SE16 139 C3
Lloyd Baker St
  WC1. . . . . 95 B3
Lloyd Ct
  Ladywell SE13 . . . . . 67 A2
  6 West Norwood
  SE27. . . . . 75 A1
Lloyd Ho N16 . . . . 6 C1
Lloyd's Ave EC3 . . 110 B1
Lloyd's Bldg★
  EC3. . . . . 110 A1
Lloyd's Pl SE3 . . . . 53 A1
Lloyd Sq WC1 . . . . 95 B4
Lloyd's Row EC1 . . 96 A3
Lloyd St WC1 . . . . . 95 B4
Lloyd Villas SE4 . . 51 C1
Loampit Hill SE13 . 52 A1
Loampit Vale
  SE13. . . . . 67 B4
Loanda Cl 17 E8 . . . 24 B4
Loats Rd SW2 . . . . 62 A1
Locarno Rd 8 W3 . . 28 B1
Lochaline St W6 . . 47 B4
Lochbie 9 N4 . . . . . 5 A4
Lochinvar St
  SW12. . . . . 73 A4
Lochmore Ho
  SW1. . . . . 145 C3
Lochnagar St E14 . . 34 B4
Lockbridge Ct 8
  W9. . . . . 31 C4
Locke Ho
  Nine Elms SW8. . . . 170 C4
  Stamford Hill N16 . . . 7 B3
Lockesfield Pl
  E14. . . . . 42 B1
Lockgate Cl E9 . . . 18 B3
Lockhart Cl N7 . . . 14 B2
Lockhart St E3 . . . 26 B1
Lockhurst St E5 . . 17 C4
Lockington Rd
  SW8. . . . . 170 B4
Lockmead Rd
  SE13. . . . . 67 B4
Lock Mews 9
  NW1. . . . . 13 C2
Lockside 17 E14 . . 33 A2
Locksley St E14 . . 33 B4
Lock View Ct 9
  E14. . . . . 33 A2
Lockwood Ho
  SE11. . . . . 163 B3
Lockwood Sq
  SE16. . . . . 40 A3
Lockyer Est SE1 . . 137 C3
Lockyer Ho
  7 Greenwich
  SE10. . . . . 43 B1
  Putney SW15 . . . . . . 57 C4
  South Lambeth
  SW8 . . . . 162 A2
Lockyer St SE1 . . . 137 C3
Locton Gn 4 E3 . . 26 B4
Loddiges Ho 8
  E9. . . . . 17 B1
Loddiges Rd E9 . . 17 B1
Loddon Ho NW8 . . 89 C1
Loder St SE15. . . . . 50 B3
Lodge Ave SW14 . . 56 A4
Lodge Rd NW8 . . . 90 A3
Lodge The 9 W4 . . 38 A3
Lodore St E14. . . . . 34 B3

Lodsworth Ho
  SW11. . . . . 169 B3
Loftie St SE16 . . . 139 C3
Lofting Ho 8 N1 . . 14 C1
Lofting Rd N1. . . . . 14 C1
Lofts on the Park 2
  E9. . . . . 17 C2
Loftus Rd W12 . . . 30 A1
Loftus Rd (Queens
  Park Rangers FC)
  W12. . . . . 30 A1
Logan Mews W8 . . 141 B4
Logan Pl W8 . . . . . 141 B4
Loggetts SE21. . . . . 76 A2
Lohmann Ho
  SE11. . . . . 163 B4
Loiesworth Cl E1 . 111 A3
Lollard St SE11. . . 149 B3
Lollards Twr SE1 . . 134 C1
Loman St E1 . . . . . 136 B4
Lomas St E1 . . . . . 111 C4
Lombard Ct
  14 Acton W3 . . . . . . 28 A1
  City of London EC3 123 C4
Lombard La EC4. . . 107 C1
Lombard Rd
  SW11. . . . . 167 B2
Lombard St EC3 . . 109 C1
Lombardy Pl W2 . . 114 B3
Lomley Ho 10
  SW2. . . . . 74 C4
Lomond Gr SE5 . . . 48 C3
Lomond Ho 10
  SE5 . . . . 48 C2
Loncroft Rd SE5 . . 49 A4
Londesborough Ho 1
  N16. . . . . 16 A4
Londesborough Rd
  N16. . . . . 16 A4
London Acad of
  Computing &
  Electronics SW17. . 72 B1
London Aquarium★
  SE1 . . . . 134 C3
London Bridge City
  Pier SE1 . . . . 124 A2
London Bridge Hospl
  SE1. . . . . 123 C2
London Bridge St
  SE1 . . . . 123 C1
London Bridge Sta
  SE1 . . . . 123 C1
London Bridge Wlk
  SE1 . . . . 123 C2
London Britannia Coll
  N1. . . . . 97 B4
London Business Sch
  NW1. . . . . 90 C2
London Canal Mus★
  N1 . . . . 84 B2
London Central
  Mosque★ NW8. . . . 90 B3
London Chest Hospl
  E2. . . . . 25 B3
London Clinic
  NW1. . . . . 91 C1
London Coll of
  Advanced Studies
  SE1. . . . . 123 B1
London Coll of Beauty
  Therapy W1. . . . . 105 A1
London Coll of Bsns &
  Computer Studies
  SW4 . . . . 61 C3

London Coll of
  Communication (Sch
  of Printing &
  Publishing)
  SE11. . . . . 136 B1
London Coll of
  Economics &
  Science NW10. . . . 20 B1
London Coll of
  Fashion
  Broadgate
  EC2. . . . . 24 A1 98 B2
  Marylebone W1 . . . 103 C1
  Marylebone W1 . . . 104 B2
  Marylebone W1 . . . 104 A1
  St Luke's EC1 . . . . . 96 C1
London Coll of
  Fashion (Mare St)
  E8. . . . . 17 A1
London Coll of
  International
  Business Studies
  WC1. . . . . 106 B3
London Ct 3
  SW18. . . . . 58 C2
London Docklands
  Visitor Ctr★ E14. . 42 B4
London Dungeon
  The★ SE1 . . . . . . 123 C2
London Electronics
  Coll SW5. . . . . . . 142 A2
London Eye
  (Millennium
  Wheel)★ SE1 . . . 134 C4
London Fields East
  Side SE8 . . . . 17 A1
London Fields Prim
  Sch E8. . . . . 25 A4
London Fields Sta
  E8. . . . . 17 A1
London Fields West
  Side SE8 . . . . 16 C1
London Fire Brigade
  Mus★ SE1 . . . . . . 136 C1
London Gas Mus
  The★ E16 . . . . . . 27 C1
London Ho 10 W6 . . 38 C1
London Ho NW8. . . 80 B2
London Hospital
  Dental Inst E1 . . . 32 A4
London Independent
  Hospl The E1 . . . . 32 C4
London Int Coll N7 . 5 B1
London International
  Film Sch WC2 . . . 106 A1
London La E1 . . . . . 17 A1
London Metropolitan
  Univ
  Islington N7 . . . . . . 14 C4
  Whitechapel E1 . . . 110 C2
  Whitechapel E1 . . . 110 C2
  Whitechapel EC3 . . 124 C4
London Metropolitan
  Univ (Central Ho)
  E1 . . . . 111 B2
London Metropolitan
  Univ (Commercial
  Rd) E1 . . . . 111 C2
London Metropolitan
  Univ (Ladbroke Ho)
  N5. . . . . 15 A3
London Metropolitan
  Univ (Moorgate)
  EC2. . . . . 109 C3

London Metropolitan
  Univ (Spring Ho)
  N7. . . . . 14 C2
London Mews
  W2 . . . . 101 C2
London Nautical Sch
  The SE1 . . . . 121 C2
London Oratory Sch
  The SW6. . . . . 155 C2
London Pavilion
  SW1 . . . . 119 B3
London Peace
  Pagoda★
  SW3 . . . . 159 A2
London Rd SE1 . . . 136 B2
London Sch of
  Economics &
  Political Science
  WC2 . . . . 107 A1
London Stile 5
  W4 . . . . 36 C1
London Stock
  Exchange★ EC2 . 108 C2
London Term 1
  E2 . . . . 24 C3
London Transport
  Mus★ WC2. . . . . 120 B4
London Wall EC2 . 109 C3
London Wall Bldgs
  EC2 . . . . 109 C3
London Wetland Ctr★
  SW13 . . . . 47 A3
London Wetland
  Visitor Ctr★
  SW13 . . . . 47 A2
London Wharf 11
  E2 . . . . 25 A4
London Xtra Tuition
  Coll N4 . . . . 6 A2
London Zoo★
  NW1. . . . . 81 B2
Long Acre WC2 . . 106 B1
Longbeach Rd
  SW11. . . . . 60 B4
Longberrys NW2 . . 1 B1
Longbridge Way
  SE13. . . . . 67 B2
Longcliffe Ho
  SW18. . . . . 59 A2
Long Dr W3 . . . . . . 29 A3
Longfellow Way
  SE1. . . . . 153 A3
Longfield Dr
  SW14 . . . . 55 A2
Longfield Est SE1 . 153 A3
Longfield St SW18. . 70 C4
Longford Ct
  11 Bedford Pk
  W12. . . . . 38 A4
  2 Clapton Pk E5 . . . 17 C4
Longford Ho 8
  E1. . . . . 32 B3
Longford St NW1. . . 92 B2
Longford Wlk 7
  SW2 . . . . 74 C4
Longhope Cl SE15. . 49 A4
Longhurst Ho 8
  W9 . . . . 23 B2
Long La
  Bermondsey SE1 . . . 137 C3
  Holborn EC1 . . . . . 108 B4
Longland Ct
  Bermondsey SE1 . . 153 B2

Longland Ct continued
  Hackney E9. . . . . 18 A3
Longlands Ct
  W11 . . . . 31 B2 113 A4
Longleat Ho SW1. . 147 B2
Longleigh Ho 8
  SE5 . . . . 49 A2
Longlents Ho 3
  NW10. . . . . 20 C4
Longley Ho 5
  N19. . . . . 13 B4
Longley St SE1 . . 153 B4
Longman Ho
  9 Globe Town E2 . . 25 C3
  8 Shoreditch E8 . . . 24 B4
Long Meadow 20
  N7 . . . . 13 C3
Longmoor Point 12
  SW15. . . . . 69 A3
Longmore St
  SW1 . . . . 146 C3
Longnor Rd E1 . . . 25 C2
Long Pond Rd
  SE3 . . . . 53 A2
Long Rd SW4 . . . . . 61 B3
Longridge Ho
  SE1 . . . . 137 A1
Longridge Rd
  SW5 . . . . 141 C3
Longs Ct 2 TW9 . . 54 B3
Long's Ct W1 . . . . 119 C3
Longshore SE8. . . . 41 B2
Long St E2 . . . . 24 B2 98 C4
Longstaff Cres
  SW18 . . . . 70 C4
Longstaff Rd
  SW18 . . . . 58 C1
Longstone Ave
  NW10. . . . . 21 B4
Longthorne Ho 18
  E3 . . . . 26 B2
Longthorpe Ct 9
  W6 . . . . 38 C2
Longville Rd
  SE11. . . . . 150 B4
Longwood Dr
  SW15. . . . . 56 C1
Long Yd WC1 . . . . . 94 C1
Lonsdale Ho
  Fulham SW6. . . . . . . 58 C4
  6 Stoke Newington
  N4 . . . . 6 B4
Lonsdale Mews
  Notting Hill W11 . . . . 31 B3
  4 Richmond TW9 . . 44 C2
Lonsdale Pl N1. . . . 14 C1
Lonsdale Rd
  Barnes SW13 . . . . . . 46 B3
  Chiswick W4 . . . . 38 B2
  Kilburn NW6. . . . . . . 23 B4
  Notting Hill W11 . . . . 31 B3
Lonsdale Sq
  Islington N1 . . . . . . 14 C1
  Islington N1 . . . . . . 85 C4
Lopez Ho 6 SW9. . 62 A4
Loraine Rd
  Chiswick W4 . . . . 45 A4
  Islington N7 . . . . . . 14 B4
Lord David Pitt Ho 8
  SE24 . . . . 62 C3
Lorden Wlk
  E2 . . . . 24 C2 99 B3
Lord Hills Rd W2 . . 100 B4

Lord Holland La
SW9 . . . . **173** C2
Lord Napier Pl
W6 . . . . **38** C1
Lord North St
SW1 . . . . **134** A1
Lord Roberts Mews
SW6 . . . . **156** A1
Lords Cl SE21 . . . . . 75 B2
Lord's Cricket Mus★
NW8 . . . . **89** C3
Lordship Gr N16 . . . . . 6 C2
Lordship Ho 3 N16 . . 6 C2
Lordship La SE22 . . . 64 B1
Lordship Park Mews
N16 . . . . 6 C2
Lordship Pk N16 . . . . . 6 C2
Lordship Pl SW3 . . . **158** A3
Lordship Rd N16 . . . . . 6 C2
Lordship Terr N16 . . . . 6 C2
Lord's Indoor Cricket
Sch NW8 . . . . **90** A4
Lord's (MCC &
Middlesex Cty
Cricket Ground)★
NW8 . . . . **89** C4
Lord's View NW8 . . . **89** C3
Loreburn Ho 3
N7 . . . . 14 B4
Lorenzo St N1,
WC1 . . . . **94** C4
Loris Rd W6 . . . . 39 B3
Lorn Ct SW9 . . . . . **173** B2
Lorne Cl NW8 . . . . . **90** B3
Lorne Ct SW15 . . . . 57 C1
Lorne Gdns 5
W11 . . . . 39 C4
Lorne Ho
Hornsey N4 . . . . 5 B4
7 Tower Hamlets
E1 . . . . 33 A4
Lorne Rd
Finsbury Pk N4 . . . . . 5 B3
3 Richmond TW10 . 54 B2
Lorn Rd SW9 . . . . . **173** B2
Lorraine Ct 10
NW1 . . . . 13 A1
Lorrimore Rd
SE17 . . . . 48 A4
Lorrimore Sq
SE17 . . . . 48 A4
Lorton Ho 9 NW6 . 23 C4
Lostock Ho 5 . . . **171** B2
Lothair Rd S N4 . . . . . 6 A4
Lothbury EC2 . . . . . **109** B2
Lothian Rd SW9 . . . . 48 A2
Lothrop St W10 . . . . 23 A2
Lots Rd SW10 . . . . . **157** A1
Loudoun Rd NW8 . . . **79** A3
Loughborough Ct 7
SW9 . . . . 63 A4
Loughborough
Junction Sta
SW9 . . . . 63 A4
Loughborough Pk
SW9 . . . . 63 A3
Loughborough Prim
Sch SW9 . . . . 48 A1
Loughborough Rd SE5,
SW9 . . . . 48 A1
LOUGHBOROUGH
SE11 . . . . **149** A1
Lough Rd N7 . . . . . . 14 B2
Louisa Cl E9 . . . . . . 25 C4
Louisa Gdns E1 . . . . 25 C1

Louisa Ho SW15 . . 56 B3
Louisa St E1 . . . . . . 25 C1
Louise Bennett Cl 9
SE24 . . . . 63 A3
Louise De Marillac Ho
10 E1 . . . . 32 B4
Louise White Ho 8
N19 . . . . 4 C3
Louisville Rd
SW17 . . . . 72 C1
Louvaine Rd
SW11 . . . . 59 C3
Lovat La EC3 . . . . . **124** A3
Lovatt Ct SW12 . . . . 73 A3
Loveday Ho 2
SW2 . . . . 74 C3
Lovegrove St SE1 . . 49 C4
Lovegrove Wlk
E14 . . . . 34 B1
Love La EC2 . . . . . **109** A2
Lovelace Ho 12 E8 . 24 B4
Lovelace Rd SE21 . . 75 B2
Lovelinch Cl SE15 . . 50 B4
Lovell Ho E8 . . . . . . 24 C4
Lovell Pl SE16 . . . . . 41 A3
Loveridge Mews
NW6 . . . . 10 B2
Loveridge Rd
NW6 . . . . 10 B2
Lovette Ho 3 E3 . . 26 C2
Lovett's Pl SW18 . . 59 A3
Lovick Rd SE5 . . . . . 48 C1
Lowden Rd SE24 . . 63 B3
Lowder Ho 6 E1 . . 32 A1
Lowe Ave E16 . . . . . 35 C4
Lowell Ho 15 SE5 . . 48 B3
Lowell St E14 . . . . . 33 A3
Lower Addison Gdns
W14 . . . . **126** A3
Lower Belgrave St
SW1 . . . . **132** A1
LOWER CLAPTON . . 17 B4
Lower Clapton Rd
E5 . . . . 17 B4
Lower Clarendon Wlk
8 W11 . . . . 31 A3
Lower Comm S
SW15 . . . . 57 A4
Lower Grosvenor Pl
SW1 . . . . **132** B2
Lower Grove Rd
TW10 . . . . 54 B2
LOWER HOLLOWAY . 14 A3
Lower James St
W1 . . . . **119** A4
Lower John St
W1 . . . . **119** A4
Lower Lea Crossing
E14, E16 . . . . 35 A2
Lower Mall W6 . . . 39 A1
Lower Marsh SE1 . **135** B3
Lower Merton Rise
NW3 . . . . 12 A1
Lower Mortlake Rd
TW9 . . . . 54 B4
Lower Pk
Acton W3 . . . . 20 B1
5 Putney SW15 . . 57 C2
LOWER PLACE 20 B3
Lower Place Bsns Ctr
NW10 . . . . 20 B3
Lower Rd SE16 . . . 40 B4

Lower Richmond Rd
Mortlake SW14,
TW9 . . . . 55 A4
Putney SW15 . . . . 57 B4
Lower Robert St
WC2 . . . . **120** B3
Lower Sloane St
SW1 . . . . **145** B2
Lower Terr NW3 . . . . 2 B1
Lower Thames St
EC3 . . . . **124** A3
Lowerwood Ct
W11 . . . . 31 A3
Loweswater Ho
E3 . . . . 26 B1
Lowfield Rd
Dagenham W3 . . . 28 B3
Hampstead NW6 . . 10 C1
Lowlands NW3 . . . 12 A2
Lowman Rd N7 . . . 14 B4
Lowndes Cl SW1 . . **131** C1
Lowndes Ct
Knightsbridge
SW1 . . . . **131** A2
Marylebone W1 . . **104** C1
Lowndes Lo SW1 . . **131** A2
Lowndes Pl SW1 . . **131** B1
Lowndes Sq SW1 . **131** A3
Lowndes St SW1 . . **131** B2
Lowood Ho 1 E1 . . 32 B2
Lowood St E1 . . . . . 32 A2
Lowry Ct 6 SE16 . . 40 A1
Lowth Rd SE5 . . . . . 48 B1
Loxford Ho SW1 . . **145** C3
Loxham St WC1 . . . **94** B3
Loxley Rd SW18 . . 71 C3
LTC Coll London
W1 . . . . **104** C2
Lubavitch House Sch
(Jun Boys) E5 . . . 7 B4
Lubbock Ho 21
E14 . . . . 34 A2
Lubbock St SE14 . . 50 B3
Lucan Ho N1 . . . . **87** C3
Lucan Pl SW3 . . . **144** B3
Lucas Ct SW11 . . . **169** C3
Lucas Ho
Clapham SW8 . . . **171** A2
Walham Green
SW10 . . . . **156** B2
Lucas St SE4, SE8 . . 51 C2
Lucas Vale Prim Sch
SE8 . . . . 51 C2
Lucerne Mews
W8 . . . . 31 C1 **113** C2
Lucerne Rd N5 . . . 15 A4
Lucey Rd SE16 . . . **139** B1
Lucey Way SE16 . . **153** C4
Lucien Rd SW18 . . 71 A2
Lucraft Ho 12
SW2 . . . . 74 A4
Lucy Ashe Ho
SE17 . . . . **150** B3
Lucy Brown Ho
SE1 . . . . **123** A1
Lucy Cres W3 . . . . . 20 B1
Ludgate Broadway
EC4 . . . . **108** B1

Ludgate Cir EC4 . . **108** A1
Ludgate Hill EC4 . . **108** A1
Ludgate Sq EC4 . . **108** B1
Ludham NW5 . . . . 12 B3
Ludlow Ct W3 . . . . . 37 B4
Ludlow St EC1 . . . **96** C2
Ludovick Wlk
SW15 . . . . 56 A3
Ludwell Ho W14 . . **126** B2
Ludwick Mews
SE14 . . . . 51 A3
Lugard Ho 2 W12 . 30 A1
Lugard Rd SE15 . . . 50 A2
Luke Ho 2 E1 . . . . 32 A3
Luke St EC2 . . . . . **98** A2
Lukin St E1 . . . . . . 32 B3
Lullingstone Ho 2
SE15 . . . . 50 B4
Lullingstone La
SE13 . . . . 67 C1
Lulot Gdns N19 . . . 4 A2
Lulworth
Camden Town
NW1 . . . . 13 C1
Walworth SE17 . . . **151** B2
Lulworth Ho SW8 . **162** C1
Lulworth Rd SE15 . . 50 A1
Lumiere Ct 7
SW17 . . . . 72 C2
Lumina Bldg 1
E14 . . . . 34 B1
Lumley Ct WC2 . . **120** B3
Lumley Flats
SW1 . . . . **145** B2
Lumley St W1 . . . **103** C1
Lumsdon NW8 . . . **78** B3
Lunan Ho 8 E3 . . . 26 B3
Lund Point E15 . . . 27 B4
Luntley Pl E1 . . . . . **111** B3
Lupin Cl SW2 . . . . . 75 A2
Lupino Ct SE11 . . . **149** A4
Lupin Point SE1 . . **139** A3
Lupton St NW5 . . . 13 B4
Lupus St SW1 . . . **147** A1
Luralda Gdns E14 . 42 C1
Lurgan Ave W6 . . . 47 C4
Lurline Gdns
SW11 . . . . **169** C4
Luscombe Ho
SW18 . . . . 58 B2
Luscombe Way
SW8 . . . . **162** A2
Lusher Ho SW15 . . 57 C1
Lushington Rd
NW10 . . . . 22 A3
Lushington Terr 11
E8 . . . . 16 C3
Luton Pl SE10 . . . . . 52 B3
Luton St NW8 . . . . **89** C1
Luttrell Ave SW15 . 57 A2
Lutyens Ho 5 SW1 . **146** C1
Luxborough Ho
W1 . . . . **103** B4
Luxborough St
W1 . . . . **103** B4
Luxborough Twr
W1 . . . . **103** B4
Luxemburg Gdns
W6 . . . . 39 C2
Luxford St SE16 . . . 40 C2
Luxmore St SE4 . . . 51 B2
Luxor St SE5 . . . . . 63 B4
Lyall Mews SW1 . . **131** B1
Lyall Mews W
SW1 . . . . **131** B1
Lyall St SW1 . . . . **131** B1

Lyal Rd E3 . . . . . . 26 A3
Lycée Francais
Charles de Gaulle
(French Univ Coll)
SW7 . . . . **143** B4
Lycee Ct N5 . . . . **149** C1
Lycett Ho 10 SW2 . 74 A4
Lycett Pl 3 W12 . . 38 C4
Lydden Gr SW18 . . 71 A4
Lydden Rd SW18 . . 71 A4
Lydford NW1 . . . . **83** A3
Lydford Cl 22 N16 . 16 A3
Lydford Rd
Brondesbury NW2 . . 9 C2
Paddington W9 . . . 23 B1
Lydgate Ho 8
N16 . . . . 16 A3
Lydhurst Ave SW2 . 74 B2
Lydney Cl
Camberwell SE15 . . 49 A3
Putney SW19 . . . . 70 A2
Lydon Rd SW4 . . . 61 B4
Lydwell Ho SW8 . . **171** B1
Lyford Rd SW18 . . 72 A3
Lygoe Ho 10 N6 . . . 4 C4
Lygon Ho
E2 . . . . 24 C2 **99** B4
Lygon Pl SW1 . . . **132** A1
Lyham Cl SW2 . . . 62 A1
Lyham Rd SW2 . . . 62 A1
Lyle Pk SW15 . . . . 57 C1
Lily Ho SW1 . . . . **137** C1
Lyme Gr E9 . . . . . 17 B1
Lyme Grove Ho 2
E9 . . . . 17 B1
Lyme St NW1 . . . . **82** C4
Lyminge Gdns SW17,
SW18 . . . . 72 A3
Lymington Mans
NW6 . . . . 11 A2
Lymington Rd
NW6 . . . . 11 A2
Lympstone Gdns
SE15 . . . . 49 C3
Lynbrook Gr SE15 . 49 A3
Lynch Wlk 2 SE8 . . 51 B4
Lyncott Cres SW4 . 61 A3
Lyncourt SE12 . . . . 52 C1
Lyncroft Gdns
NW6 . . . . 10 C3
Lyncroft Mans 4
NW6 . . . . 10 C3
Lyndale NW2 . . . . 1 B1
Lyndale Ave NW2 . . 1 B1
Lyndale Cl SE3 . . . 53 B4
Lynde Ho 3 SW4 . . 61 C4
Lynden Gate
SW15 . . . . 69 A4
Lyndhurst Gdns
NW3 . . . . 11 C3
Lyndhurst Gr SE5,
SE15 . . . . 49 B1
Lyndhurst Ho 7
SW15 . . . . 68 C4
Lyndhurst House Prep
Sch NW3 . . . . . . 11 C3
Lyndhurst Lo 8
E14 . . . . 42 C2
Lyndhurst Rd
NW3 . . . . 11 C3
Lyndhurst Sch
SE5 . . . . 48 C1
Lyndhurst Sq SE15 . 49 B2
Lyndhurst Terr
NW3 . . . . 11 C3
Lyndhurst Way
SE15 . . . . 49 B1

Lyneham Wlk E5 ....18 A3
Lynette Ave SW4 ....61 B1
Lynford French Ho
SE17 ....150 C2
Lyngham Ct 10 N4 ....5 A4
Lynhurst Ct NW8 ....79 B3
Lyn Mews 10 E3 ....26 B2
Lymouth Rd N16 ....7 B3
Lynne Ct NW6 ......11 A1
Lynnett Ct E9 ......18 A2
Lynn Ho SE15 ......49 C4
Lynn Rd SW12 ......73 A4
Lynton CI NW10 ....8 B3
Lynton Est SE1 ....153 B3
Lynton Ho 2 W2 ....100 B1
Lynton Mans SE1 ..135 B2
Lynton Rd
  Acton W3 ....28 A2
  Bermondsey SE1 ..153 A3
  Paddington NW6 ..23 B3
Lynton Terr 4
  W3 ....28 A2
Lynx Terr SW19 ....70 C1
Lyon Ho NW8 ......90 A1
Lyons PI NW8 ......89 B1
Lyon St N1 ....14 B1
Lyons Wlk W14 ....140 A4
Lyric Rd SW13 ....46 B2
Lysander Gr N19 ....4 C3
Lysander Ho 7
  E2 ....25 A3
Lysia Ct SW6 ......47 C3
Lysias Rd SW12 ....61 A1
Lysia St SW6 ......47 C3
Lysons Wlk SW15 ..56 C2
Lytcott Gr SE22 ....64 B2
Lytham St SE17 ....151 B1
Lyttelton Ct N2 ....2 A1
Lytten Ct 6 W12 ..38 C4
Lysias Rd SW12 ....61 A1
Lyttleton Ho 10 E9 ..17 B1
Lytton Ct WC1 ....106 B3
Lytton Gr SW15 ....58 A1

M

Mabel Thornton Ho 12
  N16 ....15 C4
Mabledon PI NW1,
  WC1 ....93 C3
Mablethorpe Rd
  SW6 ....154 A1
Mabley St E9 ......18 A3
MacArthur Ho 8
  SW2 ....74 A4
Macartney Ho
  SE10 ....52 C3
Macaulay CE Prim
  Sch SW4 ....61 A3
Macaulay Ct SW4 ..61 A4
Macaulay Ho 4
  2 Kensal Town
  W10 ....31 A4
  10 Stoke Newington
  N16 ....7 A1
Macaulay Rd SW4 ..61 A4
Macaulay Sq SW4 ..61 A3
McAuley Ct SE1 ....135 B2
McAuley Mews
  SE13 ....67 B3
McAusland Ho 5
  E3 ....26 B3
Macbeth Ho 4
  N1 ....24 A3
Macbeth St W6 ....39 A1

McBride Ho 6 E3 ..26 B3
McCall CI SW4 ....172 A2
McCall Ho N7 ......14 A4
McCarthy Ct
  SW11 ....168 B3
Macclesfield Rd
  EC1 ....96 C4
Macclesfield St
  W1 ....119 C4
McCoid Way SE1 ..136 C3
McConnell Ho
  SW8 ....171 B3
McCormick Ho 9
  SW2 ....74 C3
McCrone Mews 3
  NW3 ....11 C2
McCullum Rd E3 ..26 B4
McDermott CI
  SW11 ....60 A4
McDermott Rd
  SE15 ....64 C4
MacDonald Ho 8
  SW11 ....169 B2
MacDonald Rd N19 ..4 B2
McDougall Ct
  TW9 ....44 C1
Mcdougall Ho
  E2 ....24 C2 99 B3
McDowall CI E16 ..35 B4
McDowall Rd SE5 ..48 B2
Macduff Rd SW11 ..169 C4
Mace CI E1 ....32 A1
Mace St E2 ....25 C3
McEwan Way E15 ..27 C4
Macey Ho
  Battersea SW11 ..168 A3
  8 Greenwich SE10 ..52 B4
Macfarlane Rd
  W12 ....30 B1
MacFarren Ho 7
  W10 ....23 A2
MacFarren PI
  NW1 ....91 C1
McGlashon Ho 5
  E1 ....24 C1 99 B1
McGregor Ct
  N1 ....24 A2 98 B4
McGregor Ho 2
  SW12 ....73 B4
McGregor Rd W11 ..31 B4
McIndoe Ct N1 ....87 B4
McIntosh Ho 15
  SE16 ....40 B2
McIntyre Ct SW4 ..172 B2
Mackay Ho 15
  W12 ....30 A2
Mackay Rd SW4 ....61 A4
McKenna Ho 3
  E3 ....26 B3
Mackennal St
  NW8 ....80 B2
Mackenzie CI 7
  W12 ....30 A2
Mackenzie Ho 6 N7 ..14 B2
Mackenzie Wlk
  E14 ....33 C1
McKerrell Rd
  SE15 ....49 C2
Mackeson Rd
  NW3 ....12 B4
Mackie Ho 16
  SW2 ....74 C4
Mackie Rd SW2 ....74 C4
McKiernan Ct
  SW11 ....168 A3

McKinnon Wood Ho
  E2 ....24 C2 99 B3
Mackintosh La E9 ..17 C3
Macklin St WC2 ....106 B2
Mackonochie Ho
  EC1 ....107 B4
Mackrow Wlk 1
  E14 ....34 B2
Macks Rd SE16 ....153 C4
Mackworth Ho
  NW1 ....92 C4
Mackworth St
  NW1 ....92 C4
Mac Laren Mews
  SW15 ....57 B3
Maclean Rd SE23 ..66 A1
McLeod Ct SE21 ....76 C3
McLeod's Mews
  SW7 ....142 B4
MacLeod St SE17 ..151 A1
Maclise Rd W14 ..126 A1
McManus Ho 3
  SW11 ....59 C4
McMillan Ho SE4 ..66 A4
Macmillan Ho
  Cricklewood NW4 ..9 A4
  Lisson Gr NW8 ....90 B3
McMillan St SE8 ..51 C4
Mcmorran Ho 4
  N7 ....14 A4
Macnamara Ho
  SW10 ....157 B2
McNeil Rd SE5 ....49 A1
McNicol Dr NW10 ..20 B3
Maconochies Rd 5
  E14 ....42 A1
Macquarie Way
  E14 ....42 A2
Macready Ho 1
  N7 ....14 A4 102 B3
Macready PI 2
  N7 ....14 A4
Macroom Ho W9 ..23 B2
Macroom Rd W9 ..23 B2
Mac's PI EC4 ......107 C2
Madame Tussaud's ★
  NW1 ....91 B1
Maddams St E3 ....27 A1
Maddocks Ho 3
  E1 ....32 A2
Maddock Way
  SE17 ....48 A4
Maddox St W1 ....118 B4
Madinah Rd E8 ....16 C3
Madison Ho E3 ....27 B2
Madras PI N7 ......14 C2
Madrid Rd SW13 ..46 C3
Madron St SE17 ..152 A2
Mafeking Ave
  TW8 ....44 A4
Magdala Ave N19 ..4 B2
Magdalene CI 7
  SE15 ....50 A1
Magdalene Ho 7
  SW15 ....57 C1
Magdalen Pas E1 ..125 A4
Magdalen St SE1 ..124 A1
Magee St SE11 ....163 B4
Magellan Ho 16
  E1 ....25 C1
Magellan PI 26
  E14 ....41 C2
Magnin CI 8 E8 ....24 C4
Magnolia Ct
  Richmond TW9 ....45 A2
  Wandsworth SW11 ..60 B1

Magnolia Ho 13
  SE8 ....51 B4
Magnolia PI SW4 ..62 A2
Magnolia Rd W4 ..45 A4
Magnolia Wharf
  W4 ....45 A4
Magpie CI 12 E3 ..26 B3
Magpie Ho 3 E3 ..26 B4
Magri Wlk 21 E1 ..32 B4
Maguire St SE1 ..139 A4
Mahatma Gandhi Ind
  Est 1 SE24 ......63 A3
Mahogany CI
  SE16 ....33 A1
Maida Ave W2 ....89 A1
Maida Vale Rd W4 ..45 B4
MAIDA VALE 88 A4
Maida Vale W9 ....88 C3
Maida Vale Sta
  W9 ....88 B4
Maiden La
  Borough The SE1 ..123 A2
  Camden Town NW1 ..13 C1
  Strand WC2 ......120 B4
Maidenstone Hill
  SE10 ....52 B2
Maidstone Bldgs
  SE1 ....123 B1
Maidstone Ho 4
  E14 ....34 A3
Mail Coach Yd 1
  E2 ....24 A2 98 B4
Main Yd E9 ......18 C2
Maismore St SE15 ..49 C4
Maitland CI 3
  SE10 ....52 A3
Maitland Ct 4 W2 ..115 B4
Maitland Ho
  Chelsea SW1 ....160 C4
  16 South Hackney
  E2 ....25 B3
MAITLAND PARK ..12 B2
Maitland Park Rd
  NW3 ....12 B2
Maitland Park Villas
  NW3 ....12 B2
Maitland PI E5 ....17 B4
Majestic Ct N4 ....6 A3
Major CI SW9 ......63 A4
Major Rd
  Bermondsey SE1 ..139 A2
  Stratford New Town
  E15 ....19 C3
Makepeace Ave N6 ..3 C2
Makepeace Mans
  N6 ....3 C2
Makins St SW3 ....144 B3
Malabar Ct 20
  W12 ....30 A2
Malabar St E14 ....41 C4
Malam Ct SE11 ....149 B3
Malam Gdns 3
  E14 ....34 A2
Malay Ho 2 E1 ....32 B1
Malbrook Rd
  SW15 ....57 A3
Malcolm Ho 13
  N1 ....24 A3
Malcolm PI E2 ....25 B1
Malcolm Rd E1 ....25 B1
Malcolmson Ho
  SW1 ....147 C1
Malden Cres NW1 ..12 C2
Malden PI NW5 ....12 C3
Malden Rd NW5 ....12 C2
Maldon CI
  Camberwell SE5 ..64 A4
  Shoreditch N1 ....87 A4

Maldon CI continued
  Stratford New Town
  E15 ....19 C3
Maldon Rd W3 ....28 B2
Malet PI WC1 ......93 B1
Malet St WC1 ......105 C4
Maley Ave SE27 ....75 A2
Malfort Rd SE5 ....64 A4
Malins Ct SW12 ....60 C1
Mallams Mews 1
  SW9 ....63 A4
Mallard CI
  1 Hackney E9 ....18 D2
  Kilburn NW6 ......23 C4
Mallard Ho
  6 Camberwell
  SE5 ....49 B2
  St John's Wood
  NW8 ....80 A1
Mallard Point 3
  E3 ....26 C2
Mallet Ho 11
  SW15 ....56 C2
Mallet Rd SE13 ....67 C1
Malling Ho SE13 ..67 A2
Mallinson Rd
  SW11 ....60 B2
Mallon Gdns 1 E1 ..111 A3
Mallord St SW3 ..157 C4
Mallory Bldgs EC1 ..96 A1
Mallory CI SE4 ....66 A3
Mallory St NW8 ....90 B2
Mallow Ct SW13 ..52 B1
Mallow St EC1 ....97 B2
Mall Rd W6 ....39 A1
Mall Studios 3
  NW3 ....12 B3
Mall The
  Mortlake SW14 ....55 B2
  St James SW1 ....119 B1
Malmesbury 30 E2 ..25 B3
Malmesbury Prim Sch
  E3 ....26 B2
Malmesbury Rd
  Bow E3 ....26 B3
  Newham E16 ....35 A4
Malmesbury Terr
  E16 ....35 B4
Malmsey Ho SE11 ..149 A2
Malmsmead Ho
  E9 ....18 A3
Malorees Jun & Inf
  Schs NW6 ....9 C1
Malpas Rd
  Hackney E8 ......17 A2
  New Cross SE4 ....51 B1
Malta St EC1 ......96 B2
Maltby St SE1 ....138 C2
Malthouse Dr W4 ..46 B4
Malthouse Pas
  SW13 ....46 A1
Malting Ho E14 ..33 B2
Maltings W4 ......36 C1
Maltings CI SW13 ..46 A1
Maltings Lo W4 ..46 A3
Maltings PI
  Bermondsey SE1 ..138 B4
  Parsons Green
  SW6 ....166 B3
Malt Mill SE1 ....124 C1
Malton Mews 1
  W10 ....31 A3
Malton Rd W10 ....31 A3
Maltravers St
  WC2 ....121 B4

Malt St SE1 . . . . .49 C4
Malva Cl SW18 . . . . . .59 A2
Malvern Cl W10 . . . .31 B4
Malvern Ct 🆖
🆖 Shepherd's Bush
W12 . . . . .39 A4
South Kensington
SW7 . . . . .143 C3
Malvern Gdns NW2 . .1 A2
Malvern Ho
London N16 . . . . .7 B3
SE17 . . . . .151 A1
Malvern Mews
NW6 . . . . .23 C2
Malvern PI NW6 . . . . .23 B2
Malvern Rd
Dalston E8 . . . . .16 C1
Maida Vale NW6 . . . .23 C2
Upper Holloway N19 . . .4 C3
Malvern Terr N1 . . . .85 B4
Malwood Rd
SW12 . . . . .61 A1
Malyons Rd SE13 . . . .67 A2
Malyons Terr
SE13 . . . . .67 A2
Managers St 🛭
E14 . . . . .34 B1
Manaton Cl SE15 . . . .65 A4
Manbre Rd W6 . . . . .47 B4
Manchester Dr
W10 . . . . .23 A1
Manchester Gr
E14 . . . . .42 B1
Manchester Ho
SE17 . . . . .151 A2
Manchester Mans
N19 . . . . .4 C4
Manchester Mews
W1 . . . . .103 B3
Manchester Rd
E14 . . . . .42 B3
Manchester Sq
W1 . . . . .103 C2
Manchester St
W1 . . . . .103 B3
Manchuria Rd
SW11 . . . . .60 C1
Manciple St SE1 . . . .137 C2
Mandalay Ho 🛭
N16 . . . .
Mandalay Rd SW4 . . .61 B2
Mandarin Ct 🛭
SE8 . . . . .51 C4
Mandela Cl 🛐
W12 . . . . .30 A2
Mandela Ho
E2 . . . . .24 B2 98 C4
Mandela Rd E16 . . . . .35 C3
Mandela St
Camden Town
NW1 . . . . .83 A4
Kennington SW9 . .163 B1
Mandela Way
SE1 . . . . .152 B4
Manderville Ho
SE1 . . . . .152 B4
Mandeville Cl 🛐
SE3 . . . . .53 B3
Mandeville Ct
NW3 . . . . .11 A3
Mandeville Ctyd
SW11 . . . . .169 B3
Mandeville Ho 🛭
SW4 . . . . .61 B2

Mandeville PI W1 . . .103 C2
Mandrake Rd
SW17 . . . . .72 B1
Mandrell Rd SW2 . . . .62 A2
Manette St W1 . . . . .105 C1
Manfred Ct 🛭
SW15 . . . .
Manfred Rd SW15 . . .58 B2
Manger Rd N7 . . . . . .14 A2
Manilla St E14 . . . . . .41 C4
Manitoba Ct 🛭
SE16 . . . . .40 B4
Manley Ho SE16 . . . . .7 B1
Manley Ct SW11 . . . .149 B2
Mannaby Prior N1 . . .85 A1
Manneby Prior N1 . . .85 A1
Manning Ho
W11 . . . . .31 A3
Manning PI TW10 . . . .54 B1
Manningtree Cl
SW19 . . . . .70 A3
Manningtree St
E1 . . . . .111 B2
Manny Shinwell Ho
SW6 . . . . .155 A3
Manor Ave SE4 . . . . . .51 B1
Manor Circus
TW9 . . . . .54 C4
Manor Ct
🛭 Brixton SW2 . . . . .62 B2
Camberwell SE15 . . .49 B2
Gunnersbury W3 . . . .36 C2
Parsons Green
SW6 . . . . .166 B3
Streatham SW16 . . . .74 A1
Manorfield Cl 🛐
N19 . . . . .13 B4
Manorfield Prim Sch
E14 . . . . .34 A4
Manor Gdns
🛭 Chiswick W4 . . . . .38 A1
Clapham SW4 . . . . .171 A1
Gunnersbury W3 . . . .36 C2
Richmond TW10,
TW9 . . . . .54 B3
Upper Holloway N7 . . .5 A1
Manor Gr
Deptford SE15 . . . . . .50 B4
Richmond TW9 . . . . .54 C4
Manor Gt SW15 . . . . .58 A2
Manor Ho NW1 . . . .102 B4
Manor House Ct
W9 . . . . .88 C1
Manor House Dr
NW6 . . . . .9 C1
Manor House Sta
N4 . . . . .6 A3
Manor Lo NW2 . . . . . .9 C2
Manor Mans
🛭 Hampstead
NW3 . . . . .12 A2
Tufnell Pk N7 . . . . . . .5 A1
Manor Mews
New Cross SE14 . . . .51 B1
Paddington NW6 . . . .23 C3
Manor Oak Mans
SE22 . . . . .65 A1
Manor Par N16 . . . . . .7 B2
Manor Park Par
SE13 . . . . .67 C3
Manor Park Rd
NW10 . . . . .21 B4
Manor Pk TW9 . . . . . .54 B3

Manor PI SE17 . . . . .150 C2
Manor Rd
Richmond TW10,
TW9 . . . . .54 B3
Stamford Hill N16 . . . .7 A3
Manor St East
SW3 . . . . .158 B4
Manor The W1 . . . . .118 A3
Manor Way W3 . . . . . .36 C2
Manresa Rd SW3 . . .144 A1
Mansel Ct SW11 . . . .168 B3
Mansell Ho SW8 . . . .171 A4
Mansell Rd W3 . . . . . .37 C4
Mansell St E1 . . . . . .111 A1
Manse Rd N16 . . . . . . .7 B1
Mansfield Ct 🛭
E2 . . . . .24 B4
Mansfield Ho
SW15 . . . . .57 C1
Mansfield Mews
W1 . . . . .104 A3
Mansfield PI 🛭
NW3 . . . . .11 B4
Mansfield Rd
Acton W3 . . . . .20 A1
Maitland Pk NW3 . . .12 B4
Mansfield St W1 . . . .104 A3
Mansford St E2 . . . . .24 C3
Mansion Cl SW9 . . . .173 C4
Mansion Gdns NW3 . . .2 A1
Mansion Ho★
EC4 . . . . .109 B1
Mansion House PI EC3,
EC4 . . . . .109 B1
Mansion House Sta
EC4 . . . . .123 A4
Mansions The
SW7 . . . . .143 A3
Manson Mews
SW7 . . . . .143 B3
Manson PI SW7 . . . .143 B3
Manston NW1 . . . .
NW2 . . . . .10 A3
Mantell Ho SW4 . . . . .61 B2
Mantle Rd SE4 . . . . . .66 A4
Manton Ho N16 . . . . . .6 C1
Mantua St 🛭
SW11 . . . . .59 C4
Mantus Cl
Bethnal Green E1 . . .25 B1
🛭 Stepney E1 . . . . .25 B1
Mantus Rd E1 . . . . . .25 B1
Manville Gdns
SW17 . . . . .73 A1
Manville Rd SW17 . . .73 A1
Manwood SE4 . . . . . . .66 B1
Many Gates SW12 . . .73 A2
Mapesbury Ct
NW2 . . . . .10 A3
Mapesbury Rd
NW2 . . . . .10 A2
Mapeshill PI NW2 . . . .9 B2
Mapes Ho 🛭 NW6 . .10 A1
Mape St E2 . . . . .25 A1
Maple Ave W3 . . . . . .29 A1
Maple Cl SW4 . . . . . . .61 C1
Maple Ct 🛭 NW2 . . . .9 C4

Maple Ho continued
🛭 New Cross SE8 . . .51 B3
🛭 Richmond TW9 . . .45 A2
Maple Leaf Sq 🛃
SE16 . . . . .40 C4
Maple Lo SW15 . . . . .58 A1
Maple Mews NW6 . . .78 A2
Maple PI W1 . . . . .93 A1
Maples PI 🛭 E1 . . . . .32 A4
Maple St
🛭 Bethnal Green
E2 . . . . .25 A3
Fitzrovia W1 . . . . .93 A1
Maplestead Rd
SW2 . . . . .74 B4
Mapleton Cres
SW18 . . . . .59 A1
Mapleton Rd
SW18 . . . . .59 A1
Maple Wlk W10 . . . . .22 C1
Marada Ho NW6 . . . .10 A1
Marais W4 . . . . .45 B3
Marban Rd W9 . . . . . .23 B2
Marble Arch★
W1 . . . . .117 A4
Marble Arch Sta
W1 . . . . .103 A1
Marble Cl W3 . . . . . . .28 A1
Marbleford Ct 🛭
N6 . . . . .4 C4
Marble Ho W9 . . . . . .23 B1
Marcella Rd SW9 . . .173 B1
Marchant Ho 🛭
SW2 . . . . .62 B2
Marchant St SE14 . . .51 A4
Marchbank Rd
W14 . . . . .155 A4
March Ct SW15 . . . . . .57 A3
Marchmont Ho 🛭
TW10 . . . . .54 B2
Marchmont St
WC1 . . . . .94 A2
Marchwood Cl
SE5 . . . . .49 A3
Marcia Rd SE1 . . . . .152 B3
Marcilly Rd SW18 . . .59 C2
Marcol Ho W1 . . . . . .104 B2
Marcon Ct 🛭 E8 . . . .17 A3
Marcon PI E8 . . . . . . .17 A3
Marco Rd W6 . . . . . . .39 B3
Marcus Ct TW8 . . . . . .44 A3
Marcus Garvey Mews
SE22 . . . . .65 A2
Marcus Garvey Way
🛭 SE24 . . . . .62 C3
Marcus Ho 🛭
SE15 . . . . .49 B2
Marcus St SW18 . . . . .59 A1
Marcus Terr
SW18 . . . . .59 A1
Marden Ho 🛭 E8 . . .17 A3
Marden Sq SE16 . . . . .40 A3
Mardyke Ho SE17 . . .151 C4
Maresfield Gdns
NW3 . . . . .11 B2
Mare St E8 . . . . .17 A1
Margaret Bondfield
Ho
🛭 Bow E3 . . . . .26 A3
🛭 Kentish Town
N7 . . . . .13 C3
Margaret Ct W1 . . . .104 C2
Margaret Herbison Ho
SW6 . . . . .155 A3
Margaret Ho 🛭
W6 . . . . .39 B1

Margaret Ingram Cl
SW6 . . . . .154 C3
Margaret Mcmillan
Ho 🛭 N19 . . . . .4 C4
Margaret Rd N16 . . . . .7 B3
Margaret St W1 . . . .104 C2
Margaretta Terr
SW3 . . . . .158 B4
Margaret White Ho
NW1 . . . . .93 B4
Margate Rd SW2 . . . .62 A2
Margery Fry Ct N7 . . .5 A1
Margery St WC1 . . . .95 B3
Margravine Gdns
Hammersmith W6 . . .39 C1
West Kensington
W14 . . . . .140 A2
Margravine Rd
W6 . . . . .154 A4
Marham Gdns SW17,
SW18 . . . . .72 A3
Maria Cl SE1 . . . . . . .153 C4
Maria Fidelis Convent
Sch (Lower) NW1 . .93 A3
Maria Fidelis Convent
Sch (Upper) NW1 . .93 B4
Marian Ct E9 . . . . .17 B3
Marian PI E2 . . . . .25 A3
Marian St 🛭 E2 . . . . .25 A3
Marian Way NW10 . . . .8 B1
Maribor 🛐 SE10 . . . .52 B3
Marie Curie SE5 . . . . .49 A2
Marie Lloyd Ct 🛭
SW9 . . . . .62 B3
Marie Lloyd Gdns 🛭
N19 . . . . .5 A4
Marie Lloyd Ho
N1 . . . . .87 B1
Marie Stopes Ct 🛐
N19 . . . . .5 A4
Marigold St SE16 . . . .40 A4
Marina Ct 🛭 E3 . . . .26 C2
Marina Point 🛭
E14 . . . . .42 A3
Marinefield Rd
SW6 . . . . .166 B2
Marinel Ho 🛂 SE5 . . .48 B3
Mariners Mews
E14 . . . . .42 C2
Marine St SE16 . . . . .139 B2
Marine Twr 🛚
SE8 . . . . .51 B4
Marion Richardson
Prim Sch E1 . . . . . . .32 C3
Marischal Rd
SE13 . . . . .67 C4
Maritime Ho 🛐
SW4 . . . . .61 B4
Maritime Quay 🛅
E14 . . . . .41 C1
Maritime St E3 . . . . . .26 B1
Marius Mans 🛐
SW17 . . . . .72 C2
Marius Rd SW17 . . . . .72 C2
Marjorie Gr SW11 . . .60 B3
Market Ct W1 . . . . . .104 C2
Market La W12 . . . . . .39 B4
Market Mews W1 . . .118 A1
Market PI
🛭 Acton W3 . . . . . . .28 B1
🛭 Bermondsey
SE16 . . . . .40 A2
Marylebone W1 . . . .104 C2
Market Rd
Barnsbury N7 . . . . . . .14 A2

Market Rd continued
Richmond TW9 . . . . . . **54** C4
Market Sq E14 . . . . **34** A3
Market St E1 . . . . **110** C4
Market Studios [14]
W12 . . . . **39** B4
Market Way E14 . . . . . . **34** A3
Market Yd Mews
SE11 . . . . **149** C2
Markham Pl SW3 . . . . **144** C2
Markham Sq SW3 . . . . **144** C2
Markham St SW3 . . . . **144** B2
Mark Ho E3 . . . . **27** A1
Mark La E3 . . . . **124** B4
Markland Ho W10 . . . . . **30** C2
Mark Mans W12 . . . . . . **38** C3
Markbury Ave
TW9 . . . . **54** C4
Mark Sq
EC2 . . . . **24** A1 **98** A2
Mark St EC2 . . . . . **24** A1 **98** A2
Markstone Ho
SE1 . . . . **136** A3
Markyate Ho [6]
W10 . . . . **22** B1
Marland Ho SW1 . . . . . **146** C3
Marlborough
[1] Putney SW19 . . . . . . **69** C3
St John's Wood W9 . . . . **88** C4
Marlborough Ave
E8 . . . . **24** C4
Marlborough Cl
SE17 . . . . **150** B3
Marlborough Cres
W4 . . . . **38** A3
Marlborough Ct
Kensington W8 . . . . . . **141** B4
Marylebone W1 . . . . . . **104** C1
Marlborough Day
Hospl NW8 . . . . **78** C3
Marlborough Flats
SW3 . . . . **144** B4
Marlborough Gr
SE1 . . . . **153** B1
Marlborough Hill
NW8 . . . . **79** A3
Marlborough Ho
Marylebone NW1 . . . . . **92** B3
Richmond TW10 . . . . . . **54** B1
Stoke Newington N4 . . . . **6** B3
Marlborough Ho
SW1 . . . . **119** A1
Marlborough Ho
SW19 . . . . **69** C1
Marlborough Lo
[38] Stepney E1 . . . . **25** B1
St John's Wood
NW8 . . . . **78** C1
Marlborough Mans [5]
NW6 . . . . **10** C3
Marlborough Mews
[18] SW2 . . . . **62** B3
Marlborough Pl
NW8 . . . . **79** A2
Marlborough Prim
Sch SW3 . . . . **144** B3
Marlborough Rd
Acton Green W4 . . . . . . **37** B1
Richmond TW10 . . . . . . **54** B1
St James SW1 . . . . **119** A1
Upper Holloway N19 . . . . **5** A2
Marlborough St
SW3 . . . . **144** B3
Marlborough Trad Est
TW9 . . . . **45** A2
Marlborough Yd
N19 . . . . **4** C2

Marlbury NW8 . . . . . . **78** B3
Marley Ho [3] W11 . . . **30** C2
Marley Wlk NW2 . . . . . **9** B3
Marlin Ho SW15 . . . . . . **58** A2
Marloes Rd W8 . . . . . . **128** A1
Marlow Ct NW6 . . . . **9** C1
Marlow Bsns Ctr [2]
SE14 . . . . **50** B4
Marlowe Ct SW3 . . . . **144** B3
Marlowe Ho [19]
N16 . . . . **16** A4
Marlowes The
NW8 . . . . **79** A4
Marlow Ho
Bermondsey SE1 . . . . . **138** C2
Kensington W2 . . . . **100** B1
Spitalfields
E2 . . . . **24** B2 **98** C3
Marlow Studio
Workshops
E2 . . . . **24** B2 **98** C3
Marlow Way SE16 . . . . **40** C4
Marl Rd SW18 . . . . **59** B3
Marlston NW1 . . . . **92** B3
Marlton St SE10 . . . . . . **43** B1
Marmara Apts [4]
E16 . . . . **35** C2
Marmion Ho [13]
SW12 . . . . **73** A4
Marmion Mews [4]
SW11 . . . . **60** C4
Marmion Rd
SW11 . . . . **60** C3
Marmont Rd SE15 . . . . **49** C3
Marmora Ho E1 . . . . . . **33** A4
Marmora Rd SE22 . . . . **65** B1
Marner Prim Sch
E3 . . . . **27** A1
Marne St W10 . . . . **23** A2
Marney Rd SW11 . . . . . **60** C3
Marnfield Cres
SW2 . . . . **74** B3
Marnham Ave
NW2 . . . . **10** A4
Marnock Ho SE17 . . . . **151** B2
Marnock Rd SE4 . . . . . **66** B2
Maroon St E14 . . . . **33** A4
Marquess Rd N1 . . . . . . **15** C2
Marquess Rd N
N1 . . . . **15** C2
Marquess Rd S [22]
N1 . . . . **15** B2
Marquis Ct N4 . . . . **5** B3
Marquis Rd
Finsbury Pk N4 . . . . **5** C3
Kentish Town NW1 . . . . **13** C2
Marrick Ct SW15 . . . . . **56** C3
Marrick Ho NW6 . . . . . . **78** B3
Marriott Rd N4 . . . . **5** B3
Marryat Ct [12] W6 . . . **39** A2
Marryat Ho SW1 . . . . . **146** C1
Marryat Sq SW6 . . . . . **164** A4
Marsala Rd SE13 . . . . . **67** A3
Marsalis Ho [3] E3 . . . . **26** C2
Marsden Rd SE15 . . . . **64** B4
Marsden St NW5 . . . . . **12** C2
Marshall Cl SW18 . . . . . **59** B1
Marshall Ct SW4 . . . . . **172** B3
Marshall Ho
Paddington NW6 . . . . . . **23** B3
Shoreditch N1 . . . . **87** C2
Walworth SE17 . . . . . . **151** B2
Marshall Rd E10 . . . . . . **19** A4
Marshall's Pl
SE16 . . . . **139** A1
Marshall St W1 . . . . . . **105** A1

Marshalsea Rd
SE1 . . . . **137** A4
Marsham Ct
[19] Putney SW19 . . . . . . **69** C3
Westminster SW1 . . . . **147** C4
Marsham St SW1 . . . . **147** C4
Marsh Ct E8 . . . . **16** C2
Marshfield St E14 . . . . **42** B3
Marsh Gate Bsns Ctr
E15 . . . . **27** B3
Marshgate Ctr The
E15 . . . . **27** A4
Marshgate La E15 . . . . . **19** A1
Marshgate Prim Sch
TW10 . . . . **54** B2
Marsh Hill E9 . . . . **18** A3
Marsh Ho
Nine Elms SW8 . . . . **171** A4
Pimlico SW1 . . . . **147** C1
Marsh St E14 . . . . **42** A2
Marsh Wall E14 . . . . . . **42** A4
Marshwood Ho [10]
NW6 . . . . **23** C4
Marsland Cl SE17 . . . . **150** B1
Marsom Ho N1 . . . . **87** B1
Marston SE17 . . . . **151** A4
Marston Cl NW6 . . . . . . **11** B1
Marston Ho [9] SW9 . . . **173** C1
Marsworth Ho [8]
E2 . . . . **24** C4
Martaban Rd N16 . . . . . . **7** B2
Martello St E8 . . . . **17** A1
Martello Terr E8 . . . . . . **17** A1
Martell Rd SE21 . . . . . . **75** C1
Martel Pl E8 . . . . **16** B2
Martha's Bldgs
EC1 . . . . **97** B2
Martha St E1 . . . . **32** B3
Martin Ct [18] E14 . . . . . **42** B4
Martindale SW14 . . . . . **55** B2
Martindale Ave [2]
E16 . . . . **35** C2
Martindale Ho [21]
E14 . . . . **34** A2
Martindale Rd
SW12 . . . . **73** A4
Martineau Ho
SW1 . . . . **146** C1
Martineau Mews
N5 . . . . **15** A4
Martineau Rd N5 . . . . . . **15** A4
Martin Ho
Newington SE1 . . . . **137** A1
South Lambeth
SW8 . . . . **162** A2
Martin La EC4 . . . . **123** C4
Martlett Ct WC2 . . . . . **106** B1
Martlett Lo NW3 . . . . . . **11** A4
Martley Ho SW8 . . . . . . **171** A4
Martock Ct [10]
SE15 . . . . **50** A2
Marton Rd [2] N16 . . . . . . **7** A1
Marvel Ho [5] SE5 . . . . . **48** C3
Marville Rd SW6 . . . . . **154** C1
Marvin St [8] E8 . . . . . . **17** A2
Marwell Ct SE3 . . . . **52** C1
Mary Adelaide Cl
SW15 . . . . **68** A1
Mary Adelaide Ho
W2 . . . . **101** C4
Mary Ann Bldgs
SE8 . . . . **51** C4
Mary Datchelor Cl
SE5 . . . . **48** C2
Mary Dine Ct
SW8 . . . . **163** A1
Mary Gn NW8 . . . . **78** B4

Mary Ho
[8] Hammersmith
W6 . . . . **39** B1
Stockwell SW9 . . . . **172** C1
Mary James Ho [2]
E2 . . . . **24** C3
Mary Jones Ho [20]
E14 . . . . **33** C2
Maryland Rd
Paddington W9 . . . . **23** C1
Stratford New Town
E15 . . . . **19** C3
Marylands Rd W9 . . . . . **88** A1
Maryland Wlk N1 . . . . . **86** C4
Mary Lawrenson Pl [1]
SE3 . . . . **53** C3
MARYLEBONE **104** B2
Marylebone Flyover
NW1 . . . . **102** A3
Marylebone High St
W1 . . . . **103** C4
Marylebone La
W1 . . . . **103** C1
Marylebone Mews
W1 . . . . **104** A3
Marylebone Pas
W1 . . . . **105** A2
Marylebone Rd
NW1 . . . . **103** A4
Marylebone St
W1 . . . . **103** C3
Marylebone Sta
NW1 . . . . **90** C1
Marylee Way
SE11 . . . . **149** A3
Mary McArthur Ho [12]
E14 . . . . **34** C3
Mary Macarthur Ho
[15] Globe Town E2 . . . . **25** C2
W14 . . . . **154** A4
Maryon Mews
NW3 . . . . **12** A4
Mary Pl
W11 . . . . . **31** A2 **112** A3
Mary Secole Cl [21]
E8 . . . . **24** B4
Mary Smith Ct
SW5 . . . . **141** C3
Mary St
[5] Canning Town
E16 . . . . **35** B4
Shoreditch N1 . . . . **87** A3
Mary Terr NW1 . . . . **82** C3
Mary Wharrie Ho [4]
NW3 . . . . **12** B1
Masbro' Rd W14 . . . . . . **39** C3
Mascotte Rd [2]
SW15 . . . . **57** C3
Masefield Ct SE5 . . . . . **15** C3
Masefield Ho [4]
NW6 . . . . **23** C2
Mashie Rd W3 . . . . **29** A3
Maskall Cl SW2 . . . . . . **74** C3
Maskell Rd SW17 . . . . . **71** B1
Maskelyne Cl
SW11 . . . . **168** B4
Mason Cl
Bermondsey SE16 . . . . **153** C2
Newham E16 . . . . **35** C2
Mason Ho
Bermondsey SE1 . . . . . **153** C3
[16] Hackney E9 . . . . . . **17** B1
Mason's Arms Mews
W1 . . . . **118** A4
Mason's Ave EC2 . . . . . **109** B2
Mason's Pl EC1 . . . . **96** C4

Mason St SE17 . . . . . . **151** C4
Mason's Yd
Finsbury EC1 . . . . **96** B4
St James SW1 . . . . **119** A2
Massie Rd E8 . . . . **16** C2
Massinger St SE1,
SE17 . . . . **152** A3
Massingham St
E1 . . . . **25** C1
Mast Ct [17] SE16 . . . . . **41** A2
Masterman Ho [1]
SE5 . . . . **48** C3
Masters Dr SE16 . . . . . . **40** A1
Masters Lo [24] E1 . . . . **32** B3
Master's St [11] E1 . . . . **32** C4
Mast House Terr
E14 . . . . **41** C2
Mastin Ho SW18 . . . . . . **70** C3
Mastmaker Rd
E14 . . . . **41** C4
Matara Mews
SE17 . . . . **150** C1
Matching Ct [14] E3 . . . **26** C2
Matham Gr SE22 . . . . . . **64** B3
Matheson Lang Ho
SE1 . . . . **135** B3
Matheson Rd
W14 . . . . **140** C3
Mathews Yd WC2 . . . . . **106** A1
Mathieson Ct SE1 . . . . **136** B3
Mathison Ho
SW10 . . . . **156** C2
Matilda Ho E1 . . . . **125** B2
Matilda St N1 . . . . **85** A4
Matlock Cl SE24 . . . . . . **63** B3
Matlock Ct
[7] Herne Hill SE5 . . . . . **63** C3
St John's Wood
NW8 . . . . **78** C2
Matlock St E14 . . . . **33** A3
Maton Ho SW6 . . . . **154** C2
Matson Ho
[7] Bermondsey
SE16 . . . . **40** A3
[10] Homerton E9 . . . . . . **17** C2
Matthew Cl W10 . . . . . . **22** C1
Matthew Parker St
SW1 . . . . **133** C3
Matthews Ct N5 . . . . . . **15** B4
Matthews Ho
E14 . . . . **33** C4
Matthews St
SW11 . . . . **168** C2
Matthias Ct [12]
TW10 . . . . **54** A1
Matthias Ho [2]
N16 . . . . **16** A3
Mattingly Way [3]
SE15 . . . . **49** B3
Maude Ho [3] E2 . . . . . . **24** C3
Maude Rd SE5 . . . . **49** A2
Maudlins Gn E1 . . . . . . **125** B2
Maudsley Ho TW8 . . . . . **36** A1
Maudsley Hospl The
SE5 . . . . **48** C1
Maud St E16 . . . . **35** B4
Maud Wilkes Cl [2]
NW5 . . . . **13** B3
Maugham Ct [8]
W3 . . . . **37** B3
Mauleverer Rd
SW2 . . . . **62** A2
Maundeby Wlk
NW10 . . . . **8** A2

Maunsel St SW1... 147 B4
Maurer Ct SE10. 43 B3
Mauretania Bldg 11
E1 .... 32 C2
Maurice Ct 4 E1 ... 26 A2
Maurice Ho SW9 . 172 C2
Maurice St W12 ... 30 A3
Mauritius Rd 43 A2
Maury Rd N16 .... 7 C1
Maverton Rd E3 ... 26 C4
Mavor Ho N1 ..... 85 A3
Mawbey Ho SE1 . 153 A1
Mawbey Pl SE1 ... 153 A1
Mawbey Rd SE1 .. 153 A1
Mawbey St SW8 .. 162 A1
Mawdley Ho SE1 135 C3
Mawson Ct N1 ... 87 C3
Mawson Ho EC1 .. 107 B4
Mawson La W4 ... 46 B4
Maxden Ct SE15 ... 64 C4
Maxted Rd SE15 .. 64 B4
Maxwell Ct SE21 .. 76 C3
Maxwell Rd SW6 156 B1
Maya Ct SE15 ..... 50 A1
Mayall Rd SE24 ... 63 A2
Maybury Ct W1 ... 103 C3
Maybury Gdns
NW10 .... 9 A2
Maybury Mews N6 . 4 B4
Maydew Ho SE16 .. 40 B2
Maydwell Ho 6
E14 .... 33 C4
MAYFAIR 118 A3
Mayfair Pl W1 ... 118 B2
Mayfield Ave W4 . 38 A2
Mayfield Ho
Clapham Pk SW4 .. 61 C2
Dalston E8 ...... 16 B2
Mayfield Ho
51 Bethnal Green
E2 .... 25 A3
Stamford Hill N16 ... 7 A4
Mayfield Mans
SW15 .... 58 B2
Mayfield Rd
Acton W3 .... 28 A2
Bedford Pk W12 .. 38 A4
Dalston E8 ...... 16 B1
Mayflower Cl
SE16 .... 40 C2
Mayflower Prim Sch
E14 .... 34 A3
Mayflower Rd
SW9 .... 62 A4
Mayflower St 1
SE16 .... 40 B4
Mayford NW1 .... 83 A2
Mayford Cl SW12 . 72 B4
Mayford Rd SW12 . 72 C4
Maygood Ho N1 ... 85 B2
Maygood St N1 ... 85 B2
Maygrove Rd NW6 . 10 B2
Mayhew Ct 2 SE5 .. 63 C3
Maylands Ho
SW3 .... 144 B3
Maylie Ho 8 SE16 .. 40 A4
Maynard Cl SW6 156 B1
Maynard Ho E1 ... 26 A2
Maynards Quay
E1 .... 32 B2
Mayne Ct E8 ..... 16 C4
Mayo Ho 10 E1 ... 32 B4
Mayola Rd E5 .... 17 B4
Mayo Rd NW10 .... 8 A3

May's Buildings Mews
SE10 .... 52 C3
Mays Ct WC2 ..... 120 A3
May's Ct SE10 .... 52 C3
Maysoule Rd
SW11 .... 59 C3
May St W14 ..... 141 A1
Maystone Mews 3
SE10 .... 43 C1
Maythorne Cotts
SE13 .... 67 C1
May Tree Ho SE4 .. 66 B4
Maytree Wlk SW2 . 74 C2
Mayward Ho 7
SE5 .... 49 A2
Maze Hill SE10,
SE3 .... 53 A4
Maze Hill Lodge 7
SE10 .... 52 C1
Maze Hill Sta
SE10 .... 53 A4
Mazenod Ave
NW6 .... 10 C1
Maze Rd TW9 .... 44 C3
Mead Cl 3 N6/ .. 12 C1
Meadcroft Rd
SE17 .... 48 A4
Meade Cl W4 ..... 44 C4
Meader Ct SE14 ... 50 C3
Mead Ho
W11 . 31 B1 112 C2
Mead Lo W4 ...... 37 C4
Meadowbank
NW3 .... 12 B1
Meadow Bank 8
SE13 .... 58 B2
Meadowbank Cl
SW6 .... 47 B3
Meadow Cl E9 .... 18 B3
Meadowcroft 9
W4 .... 36 C1
Meadowgate Sch
SE4 .... 66 A4
Meadow Mews
SW8 .... 162 C2
Meadow Pl
Chiswick W4 .... 46 A3
South Lambeth
SW8 .... 162 B2
Meadow Rd SW8 162 C2
Meadow Row
SE1 .... 136 C1
Mead Pl E9 ...... 17 B2
Mead Row SE1 .. 135 B2
Meadway The SE3 . 52 C1
Meakin Est SE1 .. 138 A2
Meakin Ho N7 .... 14 B3
Meard St W1 ..... 105 B1
Meath Ho SE24 ... 63 A1
Meath St SW11 .. 170 A4
Mecklenburgh Pl
WC1 .... 94 C3
Mecklenburgh Sq
WC1 .... 94 C3
Mecklenburgh St
WC1 .... 94 C2
Medburn St NW1 . 83 B2
Medcroft Gdns
SW14 .... 55 B3
Medfield St SW15 . 69 A4
Medhurst Cl 19
E3 .... 26 A3
Median Rd E5 .... 17 B3
Medina Ct N7 ..... 5 C1
Medina Gr N7 .... 5 C1
Medina Ho SE15 .. 65 B3

Medina Rd N7 ..... 5 C1
Medlar St SE5 .... 48 B2
Medley Rd NW6 .. 10 C2
Medora Rd SW2 .. 74 B4
Medresco Ho
NW3 .... 11 C3
Medusa Ho SE6,
SE13 .... 67 A1
Medway Bldgs 3 E3 26 A3
Medway Ct WC1 .. 94 A3
Medway Ho
Bermondsey SE1 . 137 C3
Paddington NW8 . 102 A4
Stoke Newington
N16 .... 15 C4
Medway Mews 38
E3 .... 26 A3
Medway Rd E3 ... 26 A3
Medway St SW1 . 133 C1
Medwin St SW4 .. 62 B3
Meecham Ct
SW11 .... 168 A2
Meeson St E5 .... 18 A4
Meeting House Alley
7 E1 .... 32 A1
Meeting House La
SE15 .... 50 A3
Mehetabel Rd E9 . 17 B3
Melba Way SE13 ... 52 A2
Melbourne Ct
Hackney E5 ...... 18 A4
Paddington W9 ... 89 A2
Melbourne Gr
SE22 .... 64 B3
Melbourne Ho
W8 . 31 C1 113 B1
Melbourne Mews
SW9 .... 173 B3
Melbourne Pl
WC2 .... 107 A1
Melbourne Sq
SW9 .... 173 B3
Melbray Mews
SW6 .... 164 C1
Melbreak Ho 11
SE22 .... 64 A4
Melbury Ct W8 .. 127 A2
Melbury Dr SE5 ... 49 A3
Melbury Ho SW8 162 C2
Melbury Rd W14 127 A2
Melchester 5
W11 .... 31 B3
Melchester Ho
N19 .... 4 C1
Melcombe Ct
NW1 .... 102 C4
Melcombe Ho
SW8 .... 162 C1
Melcombe Pl
NW1 .... 102 C4
Melcombe Prim Sch
W6 .... 47 C4
Melcombe St NW1 91 A1
Meldon Cl SW6 .. 166 B4
Melford Ct
Bermondsey SE1 . 138 B2
Dulwich SE22 .... 76 C4
Melford Rd SE21,
SE22 .... 76 C4
Melgund Rd N5 .. 14 C3
Melina Ct
Putney SW15 .... 56 C4
St John's Wood
NW8 .... 89 B3
Melina Pl NW8 .. 89 B3
Melina Rd W12 ... 39 A4
Melior Pl SE1 ... 138 A4

Melior St SE1 .... 138 A4
Melisa Ct N6 ...... 4 C4
Mellington 2
N16. .... 7 C1
Mellis Ave TW9 ... 45 A2
Mellish Ho 2 E1 .. 32 A3
Mellish St E14 .... 41 C3
Mellitus St W12 .. 29 B3
Mell St 6 SE10 ... 43 A1
Melody La N5 .... 15 B3
Melody Rd SW18 . 59 B2
Melon Pl W8 .... 127 C4
Melon Rd SE15 ... 49 C2
Melrose Ave
Cricklewood NW2 .. 9 C3
Wimbledon SW19 ... 70 C1
Melrose Cl SW18 .. 58 B1
Melrose Gdns W6 . 39 B3
Melrose Ho
Maida Vale NW6 .. 23 C2
Pimlico SW1 .... 146 B2
Melrose Rd
1 Barnes SW13 .. 46 B1
Wandsworth SW18 58 B1
Melrose Terr W6 . 39 B3
Melton Ct SW7 .. 143 C3
Melton Ho E5 .... 7 C2
Melton St NW1 ... 93 B3
Melville Court Flats
W12 .... 39 A4
Melville Cl
4 Brentford W4 .. 36 C1
Rotherhithe SE8 ... 41 A2
Melville Ho SE10 . 52 B2
Melville Pl 4 N1 .. 15 B1
Melville Rd SW13 . 46 C2
Melville Villas Rd
W3 .... 29 A1
Melvin Ct 1 TW9 . 44 C2
Melwood Ho 23
E1 .... 32 A3
Melyn Cl N7 ..... 13 B4
Memel Ct EC1 .... 96 C1
Memel St EC1 .... 96 C1
Menai Pl 2 E3 ... 26 C3
Menard Ct EC1 ... 97 A3
Mendham Ho
SE1 .... 138 A2
Mendip Ct
1 Battersea
SW11 .... 59 B4
Deptford SE14 ... 50 B4
Mendip Dr NW2, ... 1 A2
Mendip Ho 2 E5 ... 6 C4
Mendip Hos SE12 . 25 B2
Mendip Rd SW11 . 59 C4
Menelik Rd NW2 .. 10 B4
Menorah Prim Sch
NW11 .... 1 A4
Menotti St
E2 ...... 24 C1 99 C2
Menteath Ho 9
E14 .... 33 C3
Mentmore Terr
E8 .... 17 A1
Mentone Ct SW8 172 B4
Meon Rd W3 ..... 37 B4
Mepham St SE1 .. 121 B1
Merbury Cl SE13 .. 67 C2
Mercator Pl 4
E14 .... 41 C1
Mercator Rd SE13 . 67 C3
Merceron Ho 3
E2 .... 25 B2
Merceron St E1 .. 25 A1

Mercers Cl SE10 ... 43 B2
Mercer's Cotts 8
E3 .... 33 A3
Mercers Mews N7 . 13 C4
Mercers Pl W6 ... 39 C2
Mercers Rd N19 ... 4 C1
Mercer St WC2 .. 106 A1
Merchant Cl 1
SE16 .... 32 B1
Merchants Ho
SE10 .... 42 C1
Merchant St E3 .. 26 B2
Merchant Taylors
Hall* EC3. ...... 109 C1
Merchon Ho N7 .. 13 B4
Mercia Gr SE13 .. 67 B3
Mercia Ho 8 SE5 . 48 B1
Mercie Ct SE22 .. 76 C3
Mercier Rd SW15 . 58 A2
Mercury Ct
Brixton SW9 .... 173 B4
10 Millwall E14 .. 41 C2
Mercury Ho 6 E3 . 26 C4
Mercury Way
SE14 .... 50 C4
Mercy Terr SE13 .. 67 A2
Mere Cl SW15, ... 69 C4
SW19
Meredith Ave NW2 . 9 B3
Meredith Ho 17
N16 .... 16 A3
Meredith Mews
SE4 .... 66 B3
Meredith St EC1 .. 96 A3
Meredith Twr W3 . 37 A3
Meredyth Rd
SW13 .... 46 C1
Meretone Cl SE4 .. 66 A3
Mereton Mans 8
SE8 .... 51 C2
Merewood Ho
SE15 .... 50 B4
Merganser Ct 17
SE8 .... 51 B4
Meriden Ct SE13 .. 67 C3
Meriden Ho 1 N1 . 24 A4
Meriden St SW3 . 144 A3
Meridian Ho SE10 52 C3
Meridian Pl E14 .. 42 B4
Meridian Prim Sch
SE10 .... 52 C4
Meridian Sq E15 .. 19 C1
Merivale Rd SW15 58 A3
Merlin Ho
2 Chiswick W4 .. 37 C1
West Hampstead
NW3 .... 11 A4
Merlins Ct WC1 .. 95 B3
Merlin St WC1 ... 95 B3
Mermaid Ct
Bermondsey SE1 . 137 B4
Rotherhithe SE16 . 33 B1
Mermaid Ho 6
E14 .... 34 B2
Mermaid Twr 22
SE8 .... 51 B4
Meroe Ct N16 ..... 7 A2
Merredene St
SW2 .... 62 B1
Merriam Ave 2
E9 .... 18 B2
Merricks Ct 5
SW14 .... 55 A3
Merrick Sq SE1 .. 137 B2

Merrington Rd
SW6 . . . . 155 C4
Merritt Rd SE4 . . . . . . 66 B2
Merrivale NW1 . . . . . . 83 A3
Merrow St SE17 . . . . 151 B1
Merrow Wlk SE17 151 C2
Merryfield SE3 . . . . . . 53 B1
Merryweather Ct 13
N19 . . . . 4 B2
Mersey Ho N7 . . . 14 C3
Merstone Ho
SW18 . . . . 59 A1
Merthyr Terr
SW13 . . . . 47 A4
Merton Ave W4 . . . . 38 B2
Merton Ho SW18 . . 70 C3
Merton La N6 . . . . 3 B2
Merton Rd SW18 . . 70 C4
Merton Rise NW3 . 12 A1
Merton Road Ind Est
SW18 . . . . 70 C4
Merttins Rd SE15 . . 65 C2
Meru Cl NW5 . . . . 12 C3
Mervan Rd SW2 . . . . 62 C3
Messaline Ave W3 . . 28 B3
Messina Ave NW6 . . 10 C1
Messiter Ho N1 . . . . 85 A3
Metcalfe Ho SW8. 171 B2
Meteor St SW11 . . . 60 C3
Methley Ho N7 . . . . 5 B2
Methley St SE11 . . . 149 C1
Methodist Central
Hall * SW1 . . . . 133 C3
Methwold Rd W10. 30 C4
Metropolis
Apartments 5
SW12 . . . . 73 A3
Metropolitan Benefit
Societies
Almshouses 3
N1 . . . . 16 A2
Metropolitan Bsns Ctr
6 N1 . . . . 15 C2
Metropolitan Cl 22
E14 . . . . 33 C4
Mews St E1 . . . . 125 B2
Mews The
Shoreditch N1 . . . . . 87 A4
5 Upper Holloway
N19 . . . . 5 A3
Mexborough NW1 . 82 C3
Mexfield Rd SW15 . 58 B2
Meyer Ho 1
SW12 . . . . 73 A4
Meymott St SE1 . . . 122 A1
Meynell Cres E9 . . . 17 C1
Meynell Gdns E9 . . 17 C1
Meynell Rd E9 . . . . 17 C1
Meyrick Ho 6
E14 . . . . 33 C4
Meyrick Rd
Battersea SW11. . . . 60 A4
Willesden NW10 . . . . 8 C2
Miah Terr 1 E1 . . . . 125 C1
Micawber Ct N1 . . . 97 A4
Micawber Ho
SE16 . . . . 139 C3
Micawber St N1 . . . 97 A4
Michael Cliffe Ho
EC1 . . . . 95 C3
Michael Faraday Ho
SE17 . . . . 151 C1
Michael Faraday Sch
SE17 . . . . 151 C1
Michael Rd SW6 . . 166 B4
Michael Tippet Sch
SE27 . . . . 75 B2

Michael Tippett Sch
The SE11 . . . . 149 C3
Michelangelo Ct 13
SE16 . . . . 40 A1
Michelle Ct 3 W3 . 28 C2
Michels Almshouses
11 TW10 . . . . 54 A2
Michelsdale Dr 3
TW9 . . . . 54 A3
Michelson Ho
SE11 . . . . 149 A3
Michel's Row 3
TW9 . . . . 54 A3
Michigan Ho E14 . . 41 C3
Mickledore NW1 . . . 83 A1
Micklethwaite Rd
SW6 . . . . 155 C3
Mickleton Ho 30
W2 . . . . 31 C4
Middlefield NW8 . . 79 B4
Middle Row W10 . . 23 A1
Middle Row Prim Sch
W10 . . . . 23 A1
Middlesex Ct 5
W4 . . . . 38 B2
Middlesex Ho W1 . 105 A4
Middlesex Pas
EC1 . . . . 108 B3
Middlesex Pl 13
E9 . . . . 17 B2
Middlesex St E1 . . . 110 C2
Middle St EC1 . . . . 108 C4
Middle Temple *
EC4 . . . . 121 B4
Middle Temple La
EC4 . . . . 121 B4
Middleton Dr
SE16 . . . . 40 C4
Middleton Gr N7 . . 14 A3
Middleton Ho
Dalston E8 . . . . 16 B1
Newington SE1 . . . . 137 B1
Middleton Mews
N7 . . . . 14 A3
Middleton Pl W1 . . 104 C3
Middleton Rd
Dalston E8 . . . . 16 B1
Golders Green NW11. 1 C4
Middleton St E2 . . . 25 A2
Middleton Way
SE13 . . . . 67 C3
Midford Pl W1 . . . . 93 A1
Midhope Ho WC1 . 94 B3
Midhope St WC1 . . 94 B3
Midhurst Ct N8 . . . 5 A4
Midhurst Ho 6
E14 . . . . 33 B3
Midhurst Way E5 . . 16 C4
Midland Mainline
Terminal NW1 . . . . 83 C1
Midland Pl E14 . . . 42 B1
Midland Rd NW1 . . 94 A4
Midland Terr
NW10 . . . . 21 A1
Midlothian Ho NW2 . 9 A4
Midlothian Rd E3 . 26 B1
Midmoor Rd
SW12 . . . . 73 B3
Midship Cl SE16 . . 32 C1
Midship Point E14 . 41 C4
Midstrath Rd NW10. 8 A4
Midway Ho EC1 . . . 96 B4
Milborne Gr
SW10 . . . . 143 A1
Milborne Ho 11
E9 . . . . 17 B2
Milborne St E9 . . . 17 B2

Milbrook Ct NW3. . 2 B3
Milcote St SE1 . . . . 136 B3
Mildmay Ave N1 . . 15 C2
Mildmay Gr N N1 . . 15 C3
Mildmay Gr S N1 . . 15 C3
Mildmay Ho 6
SW15 . . . . 57 B2
Mildmay Mission
Hospl E2 . . . 24 B2 98 C3
Mildmay Pk N1 . . . 15 C3
Mildmay Rd N1 . . . 16 A3
Mildmay St N1 . . . 15 C2
MILE END 26 A1
Mile End Pl E1 . . . . 25 C1
Mile End Rd E1,
E3 . . . . 25 C1
Mile End Sta E3 . . . 26 B2
Miles Bldgs NW1 . 102 A4
Miles Coverdale Prim
Sch W12 . . . . 39 B4
Miles Ct 5 SE10 . . 43 A1
Miles Ho 5 SE10 . . 43 A1
Miles Lo E15 . . . . . 19 C3
Miles Pl NW8 . . . . 101 C4
Miles St SW8 . . . . 162 B3
Milestone Green
SW14 . . . . 55 C3
Milfoil St W12 . . . . 29 C2
Milford Ct 3 N16 . . 7 A3
Milford La WC2 . . . 121 B4
Milford Mews
SW16 . . . . 74 B1
Milk St EC2 . . . . . . 109 A2
Milkwell Yd 7
SE5 . . . . 48 B2
Milkwood Rd
SE24 . . . . 63 A3
Milk Yd E1 . . . . 32 B2
Millais Rd E11 . . . . 19 C4
Milland Ho 11
SW15 . . . . 68 C3
Millard Cl 21 N16 . 16 A3
Millbank SW1 . . . . 148 A3
Millbank Prim Sch
SW1 . . . . 147 C3
Millbrooke Ct 7
SW15 . . . . 58 A2
Millbrook Ho 4
SE15 . . . . 49 C4
Millbrook Pl NW1 . 82 C2
Millbrook Rd SW9 . 63 A4
Millender Wlk
SE16 . . . . 40 B2
Millennium Bridge *
SE1, EC4. . . . . 122 C3
Millennium City Acad
W1 . . . . 104 B3
Millennium Dr
E14 . . . . 42 C2
Millennium Harbour
E14 . . . . 41 C4
Millennium Pl 27
E2 . . . . 25 A3
Millennium Prim Sch
SE10 . . . . 43 B3
Millennium Sq
SE1 . . . . 139 A4
Millennium Way
SE10 . . . . 43 A3
Miller Ho 5 SW2 . 74 A4
Miller's Ave E8,
N16. . . . . 16 B3
Miller's Ct 1 W4. . 38 B1
Miller's House Visitor
Ctr * 11 E3 . . . . . . 27 B2
Miller St NW1 . . . . 82 C2

Miller's Terr 1 E8. 16 B3
Miller's Way W6 . . 39 B4
Millers Wharf Ho
E1 . . . . 125 B1
Miller Wlk SE1 . . . 121 C1
Millfield N4 . . . . . . 5 B2
Millfield La N6 . . . 3 B2
Millfield Pl N6 . . . . 3 C2
Millfields Com Sch
E5 . . . . 17 B4
Millgrove St
SW11 . . . . 169 B2
Millharbour E14 . . . 42 A4
Mill Hill SW13 . . . . 56 C4
Mill Hill Gr 11 W3 . 28 A1
Mill Hill Rd
Barnes SW13 . . . . . . 46 C1
South Acton W3 . . . . 37 A4
Mill Hill Terr 9
W3 . . . . 28 A1
Mill Ho 4 SE13 . . . 67 B4
Milligan St E14 . . . 33 B2
Milliners Ho 58 SW18 . . . . 58 C3
Millington Ho N16. . 6 C1
Mill La NW6 . . . . . . 10 B3
Millman Ct WC1 . . . 94 C1
Millman Mews
WC1 . . . . 94 C1
Millman Pl WC1 . . . 95 A1
Millman St WC1 . . . 94 C1
Millmark Gr SE14 . . 51 A1
MILL MEADS 27 C3
Millner Ct SE4 . . . . 51 B1
Mill Pl E14 . . . . 33 A3
Mill Pond Cl SW8 . 161 C1
Millpond Est SE16 . 40 A4
Mill Row N1 . . . . . . 24 A4
Mills Ct EC2 . . . . . . 98 A4
Mills Gr 1 E14 . . . 34 B4
Mills Ho SW8 . . . . 171 A4
Millshott Cl SW6 . . 47 B2
Mills Row W4 . . . . . 37 C2
Mill St
Bermondsey SE1 . . . 139 A4
Mayfair W1 . . . . 118 C4
SE16 . . . . 40 A4
Millstream Ho 14
SE16 . . . . 40 A4
Millstream Rd
SE1 . . . . 138 C2
Mill Trad Est The
NW10 . . . . 20 B2
MILLWALL 41 C3
Millwall Dock Rd
E14 . . . . 41 C3
Millwood St 10
W10 . . . . 31 A4
Mill Yd E1 . . . . 125 B4
Milman Rd NW6 . . 23 A3
Milman's Ho
SW10 . . . . 157 B3
Milman's St SW10 . 157 B3
Milne Gdns SE9 . . . 53 A3
Milner Ho 3
SW11 . . . . 59 C4
Milner Pl N1 . . . . . . 85 C4
Milner Sq N1 . . . . . 15 A1
Milner St SW3 . . . . 144 C4
Milnthorpe Rd
W4 . . . . 45 C4
Milo Rd SE22 . . . . . 64 B1
Milroy Wlk SE1 . . . 122 A2
Milson Rd W14 . . . 126 A2
Milsted Ho 26 E5. . 17 A3
Milton Ave
Becontree NW10 . . . 20 C4
Crouch End N6 . . . . . 4 B4

Milton Cl SE1 . . . . 152 C3
Milton Court Rd
SE14 . . . . 51 A4
Milton Ct
Fulham SW6 . . . . 58 A4
St Luke's EC2 . . . . . 109 B4
SW18 . . . . 58 C2
Milton Gr N16 . . . . 16 A4
Milton Ho
16 Bethnal Green
E2 . . . . 25 B2
2 Camberwell SE5 . 48 C3
Milton House Mans
E8 . . . . 16 B4
Milton Pk N6 . . . . . 4 B4
Milton Pl 3 N7 . . . 14 C3
Milton Rd
Acton W3 . . . . 28 C1
Crouch End N6 . . . . . 4 B4
Mortlake SW14 . . . . 55 C4
Tulse Hill SE24 . . . . 63 A2
Milton St EC1, EC2 109 B4
Milverton NW5 . . . 12 C3
Milverton Rd NW6 . 9 B1
Milverton St SE11 . 149 C1
Milward St E1 . . . . 32 A4
Mimosa St SW4 . . 172 B3
Mimosa St SW6 . . 165 A3
Mina Rd SE17 . . . . 152 B2
Minchin Ho 10
E14 . . . . 33 C3
Mincing La EC3 . . . 124 A4
Minera Mews
SW1 . . . . 145 C4
Minerva Cl SW9 . . 163 C2
Minerva Rd NW10 . 20 C2
Minerva St E2 . . . . 25 A3
Minerva Wlk EC1 . 108 B1
Minet Ave NW10 . . 21 A3
Minet Ct NW10 . . . 21 A3
Minet Gdns NW10 . 21 A3
Minet Ho 1 . . . . . 111 B1
Minet Rd SE5, SW9. 48 A1
Minford Gdns
W14 . . . . 39 C4
Mingard Wlk N7 . . 5 B1
Ming St E14 . . . . . . 33 C2
Minnow Wlk
SE17 . . . . 152 B3
Minories EC3. . . . . 124 C4
Minshull St SW8 . 171 B3
Minson Rd E9 . . . . 25 C4
Minstead Gdns
SW15 . . . . 68 B4
Minster Ct EC3 . . . 124 B4
Minster Rd NW2 . . 10 A3
Mint Bsns Pk 12
E16 . . . . 35 C4
Mintern St N1 . . . . 87 C2
Minton Ho SE11 . . 149 B4
Minton Mews 3
NW6 . . . . 11 A2
Mint St SE1 . . . . . . 137 A4
Mirabel Rd SW6 . . 155 A2
Miranda Cl 1 E1 . . 32 B4
Miranda Ho 17 N1. 24 A3
Miranda Rd N19 . . . 4 B3
Missenden SE17 . . 151 C1
Missenden Ho
NW8 . . . . 90 A2
Mission Pl SE15 . . 49 C2
Mission Sq 18
TW8 . . . . 44 A4

Mission The
🔞 Bermondsey
SE16 ....40 A4
🔞 Poplar E14 ......33 B3

Misterton Ct
SW11 ....167 C4
Mistral SE5 ....49 A2
Mitali Pas E1 ...111 B1
Mitcham Ho 🔟
SE5 ....48 B2

Mitchell Brook Prim
Sch NW10 ....8 A2
Mitchell Ct SW14 ..56 A3
Mitchell Ho
Gunnersbury W4 ...37 A1
🔞 Islington N1 ....14 C1
🔞 Shepherd's Bush
W12 ....39 A4
Mitchell's Pl SE21 .76 A4
Mitchell St EC1 ...97 A2
Mitchison Rd N1 ..15 C2
Mitford Rd N19 .....5 A2
Mitre Bridge Ind Pk
W10 ....22 A1
Mitre Rd SE1 .....135 C4
Mitre Sq EC3 .....110 B1
Mitre St EC3 .....110 B1
Mitre The 🔟 E14 ..33 B2
Mitre Way W10 .....30 A4
Mizzen Ct E14 .....41 C4
Moatfield NW6 .....10 A1
Moat Pl Acton W3 ..28 A3
Stockwell SW9 .....62 B4
Moat Sch The
SW6 ....164 A2
Moberly Rd SW4 ...73 C4
Mobey Ct SW4 ....172 A3
Mocatta Ho 🔟 E1 ..25 A1
Modbury Gdns
NW5 ....12 C2
Modder Pl SW15 ...57 C3
Model Cotts SW14 ..55 B4
Modling Ho 🔞 E2 ..25 C3
Moelwyn Hughes Ct
N7 ....13 C3
Moffat Ho 🔟 SE5 ..48 B3
Mohawk Ho 🔞 E3 ..26 A3
Moira Ct SW17 .....72 C2
Moira Ho SW9 ....173 B4
Molasses Ho 🔟
SW11 ....59 B4
Molasses Row 🔟
SW11 ....59 B4
Mole Ct 🔟 W12 ...38 A4
Mole Ho NW8 ....89 C1
Molesey Ho
E2 ....24 B1 98 C2
Molesford Rd
SW6 ....165 B3
Molesworth Ho 🔟
SE17 ....48 A4
Molesworth St
SE13 ....67 B4
Molly Huggins Cl
SW12 ....73 B4
Molton Ho N1 .....85 A3
Molyneux Ho W1 ..102 B2
Molyneux St W1 ..102 B3
Mona Rd SE15 .....50 B1
Mona St E16 ....35 B4
Monck's Row
SW18 ....58 B1
Monck St SW1 ....133 C1
Monckton Ct
W14 ....126 C2

Monclar Rd SE5 ....63 C3
Moncorvo Cl
SW7 ....130 A3
Moncrieff St SE15 ..49 C1
Mondragon Ho
SW8 ....172 B4
Monet Ct 🔞 SE16 ..40 A1
Moneyer Ho N1 ....97 B4
Monica Shaw Ct
NW1 ....83 C1
Monier Rd E3 ......18 C1
Monkbretton Ho
E2 ....24 C2 99 B3
Monk Ct W12 ....29 C1
Monk Dr E16 ....35 C2
Monkridge 🔞 N8 ....5 C4
Monksfield N4 ......5 C2
Monkswell Ho
E2 ....24 C2 99 B3
Monkton Ho
🔞 Bermondsey
SE16 ....40 C4
🔞 Hackney E5 ......17 A3
Monkton St SE11 ..149 C4
Monkwell Sq EC2 ..109 A3
Monmouth Cl W4 ...37 C3
Monmouth Ho
🔞 Camden Town
NW5 ....13 A2
Wandsworth SW18 ..58 C1
Monmouth Pl W2 ..100 A1
Monmouth Rd W2 ..31 C3
Monmouth St
WC2 ....106 A1
Monnery Rd N19 ....4 B1
Monnow Rd SE1 ...153 B3
Monroe Dr SW14 ..55 A2
Monroe Ho
🔞 Crouch End N19 ...4 C4
Lisson Gr NW8 .....90 B3
Monro Ho
🔞 Hampstead
NW3 ....11 B4
Putney SW15 ....57 A2
Monro Way E5 .....16 C4
Monsal Ct E5 ......18 A4
Monsell Ct 🔟 N4, N5 ...6 A1
Monson Prim Sch
SE14 ....50 C3
Monson Rd
Deptford SE14 .....50 C3
Willesden Green
NW10 ....22 A3
Montagu Ct W1 ...103 A3
Montague Ave
SE4 ....66 C3
Montague Cl SE1 ..123 B2
Montague Pl
WC1 ....105 C4
Montague Rd
Richmond TW10 ....54 A1
Shacklewell E8 ....16 C3
Montague Sq
SE15 ....50 B3
Montague St
Bloomsbury W1 ...106 A4
City of London EC1 ..108 C3
Montagu Mans
W1 ....103 A4
Montagu Mews N
W1 ....103 A3
Montagu Mews S
W1 ....103 A2

Montagu Mews W
W1 ....103 A2
Montagu Pl W1 ...103 A3
Montagu Row
W1 ....103 A3
Montagu Sq W1 ...103 A3
Montagu St W1 ...103 A2
Montaigne Cl
SW1 ....147 C3
Montana Bldg 🔟
SE13 ....52 A2
Montana Rd SW17 ..72 C1
Montcalm Ho E14 ..41 C2
Montclare St
E2 ....24 B1 98 C2
Monteagle Ct 🔞
N1 ....24 A3
Monteagle Way
Nunhead SE15 .....65 A4
Shacklewell E5 ......7 C1
Montefiore Ct 🔞
N16 ....7 B3
Montefiore St
SW8 ....170 C1
Montego Cl 🔟
SW2 ....62 B2
Montem Prim Sch
N7 ....5 B1
Montem St N4 ......5 B3
Monteray Studios
W10 ....23 A3
Montesquieu Terr 🔟
E16 ....35 B3
Montfichet Rd E20 ..19 B1
Montford Pl SE11 ..149 B1
Montfort Ho
🔞 Bethnal Green
E2 ....25 B2
Cubitt Town E14 ...42 B3
Montfort Pl SW19 ..69 C3
Montgomery Ct
W4 ....45 B4
Montgomery Ho 🔟
SW14 ....55 C4
Montgomery Lo 🔞
E1 ....25 B1
Montgomery Rd
W4 ....37 B2
Montholme Rd
SW11 ....60 B1
Monthope Rd E1 ..111 B3
Montolieu Gdns
SW15 ....57 A2
Montpelier Gr
NW5 ....13 B3
Montpelier Mews
SW7 ....130 B2
Montpelier Pl
Knightsbridge
SW7 ....130 B2
🔞 Stepney E1 ......32 B3
Montpelier Rd
SE15 ....50 A2
Montpelier Rise
NW11 ....1 A4
Montpelier Row
SE3 ....53 B1
Montpelier Sq
SW7 ....130 B3
Montpelier St
SW7 ....130 B2
Montpelier Terr
SW7 ....130 B3
Montpelier Vale
SE3 ....53 B1
Montpelier Way
NW11 ....1 A4

Montpelier Wlk
SW7 ....130 B2
Montreal Pl WC2 ..120 C4
Montrell Rd SW2 ...74 A3
Montrose Ave
NW6 ....23 A3
Montrose Ct SW7 ..129 C3
Montrose Ho
Belgravia SW1 ....131 C3
Millwall E14 ....41 C3
Montrose Pl SW1 ..131 C3
Montrose Villas 🔟
W6 ....38 C1
Montserrat Rd
SW15 ....57 C3
Monument Gdns
SE13 ....67 B2
Monument St
EC3 ....123 C4
Monument Sta
EC3 ....123 C4
Monument The★
EC3 ....123 C4
Monza Bldg The
E1 ....32 B2
Monza St E1 ....32 B2
Moodkee St SE16 ..40 B3
Moody Rd SE15 ...49 B2
Moody St E1 ....25 C2
Moon St N1 ....86 A4
Moorcroft Rd
SW16 ....74 A1
Moore Ct SW14 ...55 B4
Moore Ct N1 ....86 A3
Moore Ho
🔟 Bethnal Green
E2 ....25 B2
🔞 Greenwich SE10 ..43 A1
🔞 Shadwell E1 .....32 B2
Wandsworth SW17 ..71 C1
Moore Park Ct
SW6 ....156 B2
Moore Park Rd
SW6 ....156 A1
Moore St SW3 ....144 C4
Moorfields EC2 ...109 B3
Moorfields Eye Hospl
EC1 ....97 B3
Moorfields Highwalk
EC2 ....109 B3
Moorgate EC2 ....109 B3
Moorgate EC2 .....109 C3
Moorgate Sta
EC2 ....109 B3
Moorgreen Ho
EC1 ....96 A4
Moorhouse Rd
W2 ....31 C3
Moor La EC2 .....109 B3
Moorland Rd SW9 ..63 A3
Moor Pl EC2 .....109 B3
Moor St W1 .....105 C1
Morant St E14 .....33 C2
Mora Prim Sch
NW2 ....9 B4
Mora Rd NW2 ......9 B4
Mora St EC1 ....97 A3
Morat St SW9 ....173 A4
Moravian Cl SW3 ..157 C2
Moravian Pl
SW10 ....157 C3
Moravian St 🔟 E2 ..25 B2
Moray Ho 🔟 E1 ...26 A1
Moray Mews N4, N7 ..5 B2
Moray Rd N4, N7 ...5 B2

Mordaunt Ho
🔟 Becontree
NW10 ....20 C4
Clapham SW8 .....171 B1
Mordaunt Rd
NW10 ....20 C4
Mordaunt St SW9 ..62 B4
Morden Hill SE13 ..52 B1
Morden Ho 🔟
SW2 ....62 C1
Morden La SE13 ...52 B2
Morden Mount Prim
Sch SE13 ....52 A1
Morden Rd SE3 ....53 C1
Morden Road Mews
SE3 ....53 C1
Morden St SE13 ....52 A3
Morden Wharf Rd
SE10 ....43 A3
Mordern Ho NW1 ..90 B1
Morecambe Cl 🔟
E1 ....32 C4
Morecambe St
SE17 ....151 A2
More Cl
Canning Town E16 ..35 B3
West Kensington
W14 ....140 A3
Moredown Ho 🔞
E8 ....16 C3
More House Sch
SW1 ....131 A1
Moreland Ct 🔟
NW2 ....1 C1
Moreland Prim Sch
EC1 ....96 B3
Moreland St EC1 ...96 B3
Morella Rd SW11,
SW12 ....72 B4
Morell Ho SW9 ...172 C1
Moresby Wlk
SW8 ....170 B1
More's Gdn SW3 ..157 C3
Moreton Ho SE16 ..40 A3
Moreton Pl SW1 ..147 A2
Moreton St SW1 ..147 B2
Moreton Terr
SW1 ....147 A2
Moreton Terr Mews N
SW1 ....147 A2
Moreton Terr Mews S
SW1 ....147 A2
Moreton Twr 🔟
W3 ....28 A1
Morgan Ct SW11 ..167 C2
Morgan Ho
Nine Elms SW8 ...171 A4
Pimlico SW1 ......147 A3
Morgan Rd
Islington N7 ......14 C3
Notting Hill W10 ...31 B4
Morgan St
Canning Town E16 ..35 B4
Globe Town E3 ....25 C2
Morgan's Wlk
SW11 ....158 A1
Moriatry Cl N7 .....14 A4
Morie St SW18 .....59 A2
Morkyns Wlk
SE21 ....76 A1
Morland Cl NW11 ...2 A3
Morland Ct W12 ...39 A4
Morland Est E8 ....16 C1
Morland Ho
Kilburn NW6 .....23 C4
Notting Hill W11 ...31 A3
Somers Town NW1 ..83 A3

Morland Ho continued
Westminster SW1 . . . 148 A4

Morland Mews
N1 . . . . 14 C1
Morley Coll SE1 . . . 135 C2
Morley Ct SE13 . . . . 67 B3
Morley Ho
Stoke Newington
N16 . . . . 7 C2
Streatham SW2 . . . . 74 A4
W1 . . . . 104 C2
Morley Rd SE13 . . . . 67 B3
Morley St SE1 . . . . 135 C3
Morna Rd SE5 . . . . . 48 B1
Morning La E9 . . . . . 17 B2
Morningside Prim Sch
E9 . . . . 17 B2
Mornington Ave
W14 . . . . 140 C3
Mornington Avenue
Mans W14 . . . . . . 140 C3
Mornington Cres
NW1 . . . . 82 C2
Mornington Crescent
Sta NW1 . . . . 82 C2
Mornington Ct
NW1 . . . . 82 C2
Mornington Gr E3 . . 26 C2
Mornington Mews 2
SE5 . . . . 48 B2
Mornington Pl
1 New Cross SFR 51 B3
Regent's Pk NW1 . . . 82 C2
Mornington Rd SE14,
SE8 . . . . 51 B3
Mornington St
NW1 . . . . 82 B2
Mornington Terr
NW1 . . . . 82 B2
Morocco St SE1 . . . 138 A3
Morpeth Gr E9 . . . . 25 C4
Morpeth Rd E9 . . . . 25 C4
Morpeth Sec Sch
E2 . . . . 25 C2
Morpeth St E2 . . . . 25 C2
Morpeth Terr
SW1 . . . . 146 C3
Morrel Ct 11 E2 . . . . 24 C3
Morris Blitz Ct 2
N16 . . . . 16 B4
Morris Ct 3 SE5 . . . 63 C3
Morris Gdns
SW18 . . . . 70 C4
Morris Ho
17 Bethnal Green
E2 . . . . 25 B2
Lisson Gr NW8 . . . . 90 A1
11 Stockwell SW4 . . . 62 A3
12 Tufnell Pk N19 . . . 13 B4
Morrish Rd SW2 . . . . 74 A4
Morrison Bldgs
E1 . . . . 111 B2
Morrison Ho SW2 . . 74 C3
Morrison St SW11 . . 60 C4
Morris Pl N4 . . . . 5 C2
Morris Rd E14 . . . . . 34 A4
Morriss Ho 8
SE16 . . . . 40 A4
Morris St E1 . . . . . . 32 A3
Morshead Mans
W9 . . . . 23 C2
Morshead Rd W9 . . . 23 C2
Mortain Ho 9
SE16 . . . . 40 A2
Morten Cl SW4 . . . . 61 C1
Mortimer Cl
1 Child's Hill NW2 . . 1 B1

Mortimer Cl continued
Streatham SW16 . . . 73 C2
Mortimer Cres
NW6 . . . . 78 B3
Mortimer Ct NW8 . . 79 A1
Mortimer Est NW6 . 78 A3
Mortimer Ho
7 Shepherd's Bush
W11 . . . . 30 C1
West Kensington
W14 . . . . 140 B3
Mortimer Lo 11
SW19 . . . . 70 A3
Mortimer Market
WC1 . . . . 93 A1
Mortimer Pl NW6 . . 78 A3
Mortimer Rd
De Beauvoir Town
N1 . . . . 16 A1
Kensal Green NW10 . . 22 C2
Mortimer Sq W11 . . 30 C2
Mortimer St W1 . . . 105 A3
Mortimer Terr
NW5 . . . . 13 A4
MORTLAKE 55 B4
Mortlake High St
SW14 . . . . 55 C4
Mortlake Ho 7
W4 . . . . 37 B2
Mortlake Rd SW14,
TW9 . . . . 44 C2
Mortlake Sta
SW14 . . . . 55 B4
Mortlake Terr
TW9 . . . . 44 C3
Mortlock Cl SE15 . . 50 A2
Morton Ho SE17 . . . 48 A4
Morton Mews
SW5 . . . . 142 A3
Morton Pl SE1 . . . . 135 B1
Morton Rd N1 . . . . . 15 B1
Morval Rd SW2 . . . . 62 C2
Morven Rd SW17 . . . 72 B1
Morville Ho SW18 . . 59 C1
Morville St E3 . . . . . 26 C3
Morwell St WC1 . . . 105 C3
Moscow Pl W2 . . . . 114 A4
Moscow Rd W2 . . . . 114 A4
Mosedale NW1 . . . . 92 B3
Moseley Row
SE10 . . . . 43 B2
Mosque Tower
E1 . . . . 111 C3
Mossbourne Com
Acad E8 . . . . 16 C3
Mossbury Rd
SW11 . . . . 60 A4
Moss Cl E1 . . . . . . 111 C4
Mossford St E3 . . . . 26 B1
Mossington Gdns
SE16 . . . . 40 B2
Mossop St SW3 . . . 144 B4
Mostyn Gdns
NW10 . . . . 22 C3
Mostyn Gr E3 . . . . . 26 C3
Mostyn Rd SW9 . . . 173 C3
Motcomb St SW1 . . 131 B2
Mothers Sq The 18
E5 . . . . 17 A4
Motley Ave
EC2 . . . . 24 A1 98 A2
Motley St SW8 . . . 170 C2
Moules Ct SE5 . . . . 48 B3
Moulins Rd E9 . . . . 17 B1

Moulsford Ho
5 Lower Holloway
N7 . . . . 14 A3
22 Paddington W2 . . 31 C4
Mounsey Ho 18
W10 . . . . 23 A2
Mount Adon Pk SE21,
SE22 . . . . 76 A1
Mountague Pl 2
E14 . . . . 34 B2
Mountain Ho
SE11 . . . . 148 C2
Mount Angelus Rd
SW15 . . . . 68 B4
Mount Ararat Rd
TW10 . . . . 54 A2
Mount Carmel 3
N7 . . . . 14 B3
Mount Carmel RC
Tech Coll for Girls
N19 . . . . 4 C3
Mount Ephraim La
SW16 . . . . 73 C1
Mount Ephraim Rd
SW16 . . . . 73 C1
Mountfield NW2 . . . . 1 B2
Mountfield Ct
SE13 . . . . 67 C1
Mount Ford St
E1 . . . . 111 B2
Mountfort Cres
N1 . . . . 14 C1
Mountfort Terr 7
N1 . . . . 14 C1
Mountgrove Rd N5 . . 6 B1
Mountjoy Ho EC2 . 108 C3
Mount Lodge SW4 . 61 C3
Mount Mills EC1 . . . 96 B3
Mount Nod Rd SW16,
SW2 . . . . 74 B1
Mount Pl 7 W3 . . . 28 A1
Mount Pleasant
WC1 . . . . 95 B1
Mount Pleasant Cres
N4 . . . . 5 B4
Mount Pleasant Rd
Lewisham SE13 . . . . 67 B1
Willesden NW10 . . . 22 B4
Mount Pleasant Villas
N4 . . . . 5 B4
Mount Rd SW18,
SW19 . . . . 71 A2
Mount Row W1 . . . 118 A3
Mounts Pond Rd SE3,
SE13 . . . . 52 C1
Mount Sq The 3
NW3 . . . . 2 B1
Mount St W1 . . . . . 117 C3
Mount Terr E1 . . . . 32 A4
Mount The
Hampstead NW3 . . . 2 B1
Kensington
W8 . . . . 31 C1 113 B1
Mount Tyndal NW3 . . 2 C3
Mount Vernon
NW3 . . . . 11 B4
Mountview 5
SW16 . . . . 74 B1
Mountview Cl
NW11 . . . . 2 B3
Mount Villas SE27 . . 75 A1

Mourne Ho NW3 . . 11 B2
Mowatt Cl N19 . . . . 4 C3
Mowbray Rd NW6 . . 10 A1
Mowlem Prim Sch
E2 . . . . 25 B3
Mowlem St E2 . . . . 25 A3
Mowll St SW9 . . . . 163 B1
Moxon St W1 . . . . 103 B3
Moye Cl 10 E2 . . . . 24 C4
Moylan Rd W6 . . . 154 B3
Moyle Ho SW1 . . . . 161 A4
Moyne Ho 16 SW9 . 63 A3
Mozart St W10 . . . . 23 B2
Mudchute Sta E14 . . 42 A2
Mudie Ho 8 SW2 . . 74 A4
Mudlarks Blvd 3
SE10 . . . . 43 B3
Muirdown Ave
SW14 . . . . 55 C3
Muir Dr SW18 . . . . 60 A1
Muirfield W3 . . . . . 29 A3
Muirfield Cl 23
SE16 . . . . 40 A1
Muirfield Cres
E14 . . . . 42 A3
Muir Rd E5 . . . . 7 C1
Mulberry Bsns Ctr
SE16 . . . . 40 C4
Mulberry Cl
Chelsea SW3 . . . . . 157 C3
East Dulwich SE22 . . 64 C1
Hampstead NW3 . . . 11 C4
Mulberry Ct
Finsbury EC1 . . . . . 96 B3
Islington N5 . . . . 15 A3
3 Leyton E11 . . . . . 19 C4
4 Paddington W9 . . 23 B2
Mulberry Ho
3 Bethnal Green
E2 . . . . 25 B2
8 Deptford SE8 . . . 51 B4
Mulberry House Sch
The NW2 . . . . 10 A3
Mulberry Mews
SW5 . . . . 51 B2
Mulberry Pl W6 . . . 38 C1
Mulberry Rd E8 . . . 16 B1
Mulberry Sch for
Girls
Stepney E1 . . . . 32 A3
St George in East
E1 . . . . 32 A2
Mulberry St 1
E1 . . . . 111 B2
Mulberry Wlk
SW3 . . . . 157 C4
Mulgrave Rd
West Kensington
W14 . . . . 154 C4
Willesden NW10 . . . . 8 B4
Mulkern Rd N19 . . . . 4 C3
Mullard Ho WC1 . . 105 B4
Mullens Ho 7
SW15 . . . . 57 B2
Mullen Terr EC1 . . . 95 B4
Muller Rd SW4 . . . . 61 C1
Mullet Gdns
E2 . . . . 24 C2 99
Mulletsfield WC1 . . 94 B3
Mull Ho 17 E3 . . . . 26 B3
Mullins Path
SW14 . . . . 55 C4
Mulready St NW8 . . 90 A1
Multi Way W3 . . . . 38 A4
Multon Ho E9 . . . . 17 B1
Multon Rd SW18 . . 71 C4
Mulvaney Way
SE1 . . . . 137 C3

Mumford Rd SE24 . . 63 A2
Muncaster Rd
SW11 . . . . 60 C2
Mundania Ct SE22 . . 65 A1
Mundania Rd
SE22 . . . . 65 B1
Munday Ho SE1 . . . 137 B1
Munday Rd E16 . . . 35 C2
Munden Ho 5 E3 . . 27 A2
Munden St W14 . . . 140 A4
Mund St W14 . . . . 141 A1
Mundy Ho 6 W10 . . 23 A2
Mundy St
N1 . . . . 24 A2 98 B4
Munro Ho
Bermondsey SE1 . . . 137 C3
Lambeth SE1 . . . . . 135 B3
Munro Mews W10 . . 31 A4
Munster Ct SW6 . . . 164 C2
Munster Rd SW6 . . 154 B2
Munster Residences
SW6 . . . . 164 B4
Munster Sq NW1 . . 92 B2
Munton Rd SE1,
SE17 . . . . 151 A4
Murchison Ho 4
W10 . . . . 31 A4
Murdoch Ho 4
SE16 . . . . 40 B3
Murdock Cl E16 . . . 35 B3
Murdock St SE15 . . 50 A4
Murfett Cl SW19 . . . 70 A2
Muriel St N1 . . . . . 85 A4
Murphy Ho SE1 . . . 136 B2
Murphy St SE1 . . . 135 B3
Murray Gr N1 . . . . . 87 B1
Murray Mews
NW1 . . . . 13 C1
Murray St NW1 . . . 13 C1
Murray Terr NW3 . . 11 C4
Musard Rd W6 . . . 154 B4
Musbury St E1 . . . . 32 B3
Muscal W6 . . . . . . 154 A4
Muscatel Pl SE5 . . . 49 A2
Muschamp Rd
SE15 . . . . 64 B4
Muscott Ho 18 E2 . . 24 C4
Muscovy St EC3 . . 124 B4
Museum Ho 7 E2 . . 25 B2
Museum in
Docklands ★
E14 . . . . 33 C2
Museum Mans
WC1 . . . . 106 A3
Museum of Brands ★
W11 . . . . 31 B3
Museum of London ★
WC1 . . . . 106 A2
Musgrave Cres
SW6 . . . . 165 C4
Musgrave Ct
SW11 . . . . 168 A4
Musgrove Ho 11
E9 . . . . 17 C2
Musgrove Rd
SE14 . . . . 51 A2
Musical Mus The ★
TW8 . . . . 44 A4
Musjid Rd SW11 . . 167 C1
Mus of Childhood
(V&A) ★ E2 . . . . . 25 B2
Mus of Culinary
History &
Alimentation ★
NW1 . . . . 83 A2

Mus of Garden
History★ SE1..... **134** C1
Mus of London★
EC2 .... **108** C3
Mus of the Order of
St John★ EC1 ..... **96** A1
Mustow Ho SW6 **165** A2
Mutrix Rd NW6...**23** C4
Mutton Pl NW1....**12** C2
Myatt Garden Prim
Sch SE4.......... **51** B1
Myatt Ho SE5 .....**48** A1
Myatt Rd SW9.....**48** A2
Myatts Field Ct
SE5 ....**48** B2
Mycenae Rd SE3 ..**53** C4
Myddelton Pas
EC1 ....**95** C4
Myddelton Sq EC1 **95** C4
Myddelton St EC1 ..**95** C3
Myddleton Ave N4..**6** B2
Myers Ho **5** SE5 ...**48** B3
Myers La SE14.....**50** C4
Mylius Cl SE14....**50** B2
Mylne Cl W6.......**38** C1
Mylne St EC1......**85** B1
Mynterne Ct **15**
SW19 ....**69** C3
Myrdle Ct E1 .....**111** C2
Myrdle St E1 .....**111** C2
Myron Pl SE13 ....**67** B4
Myrtle Ho SE14...**50** C2
Myrtle Rd W3 .....**28** B1
Myrtle Wlk **8** N1...**24** A3
Mysore Rd SW11 ..**60** B3
Myton Rd SE21 ....**75** C1
Mytton Ho SW8 ..**162** C1

N

N1 Shopping Ctr
N1................ **85** C2
Nags Head N7 .....**14** B4
Nags Head Ct EC1 **97** A1
Nags Head Sh Ctr The
N7................**14** B4
Naima Jewish Prep
Sch NW6..........**78** A2
Nainby Ho SE11 .**149** B3
Nairne Gr SE5,
SE24..............**63** C3
Nairn St E14 ......**34** B4
Naish Ct N1.......**84** B4
Naldera Gdns SE3 **53** C4
Nalton Ho NW6 ..**11** B1
Nankin St E14.....**33** C3
Nansen Rd SW11..**60** C4
Nant Cc NW2 ....**1** B2
Nantes Cl SW18 ...**59** B3
Nant Rd NW2 ....**1** B2
Nant St E2 ....**25** A2
Naoroji St WC1.....**95** B3
Napier Ave
Deptford E14 .....**41** C1
Fulham SW6......**58** B4
Napier Cl
New Cross SE14,
SE8 ....**51** B3
West Kensington
W14 ....**126** C2
Napier Ct
Fulham SW6......**58** B4
Shoreditch N1 ....**87** B2
Napier Gr N1......**87** A2

Napier Ho SE17...**48** A4
Napier Pl W14 ...**126** C1
Napier Rd
College Pk NW10 .**22** A2
Kensington W14...**126** C1
Napier Terr N1 ...**15** A1
Narbonne Ave
SW4 ....**61** B2
Narborough St
SW6 ....**166** A1
Narcissus Rd NW6.**10** C3
Narford Rd E5 .....**7** C2
Narrow St
6 Acton W3 .....**28** A1
Limehouse E14....**33** A2
Nascot St W12 .....**30** B3
Naseby Cl NW6....**11** B1
Nashe Ho SE1 ....**137** B2
Nash Ho
5 Millwall E14 ...**41** C3
Pimlico SW1 .....**146** B1
Nash Rd SE4 ......**66** A2
Nash St NW1......**92** B4
Nasmyth St W6 ...**39** A3
Nassau Rd SW13 ..**46** B2
Nassau St W1 ....**104** C3
Nassington Rd
NW3 ....**12** B4
Nathan Ho SE11 .**149** C3
Nathaniel Cl E1 ..**111** A3
National Army Mus★
SW3 ....**159** A4
National Fan Mus★
SE10 ....**52** B3
National Film
Theatre★
SE1 ....**121** A2
National Gallery★
W1 ....**119** C3
National Hospl The
WC1 ....**94** B1
National Maritime
Mus★ SE10 ....**52** C4
National Portrait
Gallery★ W1 ....**119** C3
National Portrait
Gallery (Annexe)★
WC2 ....**120** A2
National Theatre★
SE1 ....**121** A2
Natural History Mus★
SW7 ....**129** B1
Nat West Twr★
EC2 ....**110** A2
Nautilus Bldg The
E14 ....**95** C4
Naval Row E14 ....**34** B2
Navarino Gr E8....**16** C2
Navarino Mans E8 .**16** C2
Navarino Rd E8 ...**16** C2
Navarre St
E2 .....**24** B1 **98** C2
Navenby Wlk **13**
E3 ....**26** C1
Navy St SW4 ......**61** C4
Naxos Bldg **11**
E14 ....**41** C4
Naylor Bldg W **1** **111** B2
Naylor Ho
Clapham SW8....**171** B1
Walworth SE17...**151** C2
5 West Kilburn
W10 ....**23** B2
Naylor Rd SE15...**50** A3
Nayor Bldg E E1...**111** B2
Nazareth Cl SE15..**50** A1
Nazrul St E2 .**24** B2 **98** C4

Nealden St SW9...**62** B4
Neal St WC2 .....**106** A1
Neal's Yd WC2 ...**106** A1
Neasden Cl NW10 ..**8** A3
Neasden Junc
NW10 ....**8** A4
Neasden La NW10...**8** A3
Neasden Sta NW10 .**8** A3
Neate St SE5 ......**49** B4
Neathouse Pl
SW1 ....**146** C4
Nebraska Bldg **11**
SE13 .... A1
Nebraska St SE1 .**137** B3
Neckinger SE16 ..**139** A2
Neckinger Est
SE16 ....**139** A2
Neckinger St SE1 **139** A2
Nectarine Way
SE13 ....**52** A1
Nedahall Ct **4**
NW11 ....**1** B4
Needham Ho
SE11 ....**149** B3
Needham Rd W11..**31** C3
Needleman St
SE16 ....**40** C4
Needwood Ho N4 ...**6** B3
Neilson-Terry Ct
SW9 ....**62** B3
Neil Wates Cres **17**
SW2 ....**74** C3
Nella Rd W6 ......**47** C4
Nelldale Rd SE16..**40** B2
Nell Gwynn Ho
SW3 ....**144** B3
Nelson Cl **2** NW6 .**23** C2
Nelson Cl SE16....**33** B1
Nelson Dock Pier
SE16 ....**33** B1
Nelson Gdns
E2 .....**24** C2 **99** C4
Nelson Pas EC1 ...**97** A4
Nelson Pl N1......**86** B1
Nelson Rd SE10 ...**52** B4
Nelson's Monument★
WC2 ....**120** A2
Nelson Sq SE1 ...**136** A4
Nelsons Row SW4 .**61** C3
Nelson St
Canning Town E16 .**35** B2
Stepney E1 ....**32** A3
Nelsons Yd NW1...**82** C2
Nelson Terr N1 ...**86** B1
Nemoure Rd W3 ..**28** B2
Nepaul Rd **17**
SW11 ....**60** A4
Nepean St SW15 ..**68** C4
Neptune Ct **13**
E14 ....**41** C2
Neptune Ho
2 Rotherhithe
SE16 ....**40** B3
14 Stoke Newington
N16...............**16** A3
Neptune St SE16..**40** B3
Nesham Ho N1 ....**24** A4
Nesham St E1 ....**125** B2
Ness St SE16 ....**139** B2
Nestor Ho **19** E2 ...**25** A3
Netheravon Rd
W4 ....**38** B1
Netheravon Rd S
W4 ....**38** B1
Netherby Ho SW8 **171** B1
Nethercombe Ho **1**
SE3 ....**53** C4

Nethercott Ho **27**
E3 ....**27** A2
Netherfield Rd
SW17 ....**72** C1
Netherford Rd
SW4 ....**171** A1
Netherhall Gdns
NW3 ....**11** B3
Netherhall Way
NW3 ....**11** B3
Netherleigh Cl N6 .**4** A3
Netherton Gr
SW10 ....**157** A3
Netherwood Rd
W14 ....**39** C4
Netherwood St
NW6 ....**10** C2
Netley **1** SE5 ....**49** A2
Netley Prim Sch
NW1 ....**92** C3
Netley Rd TW8 ....**44** A4
Netley St NW1 ....**92** C3
Nettlecombe NW1 .**13** C1
Nettleden Ho
SW3 ....**144** B3
Nettlefold Pl SE27 .**75** A1
Nettleton Rd SE14 .**50** C2
Nevada St SE10 ...**52** B4
Nevena Ct **3** SW2 .**62** C2
Nevern Mans
SW5 ....**141** B2
Nevern Pl SW5 ...**141** C3
Nevern Rd SW5 ..**141** B3
Nevern Sq SW5 ..**141** C3
Nevil Ho **7** SW9 ..**48** A1
Nevill Ct SW10 ...**156** C2
Neville Cl
Acton W3 ....**37** B4
Paddington NW6 ..**23** B3
Peckham SE15 ....**49** C2
Somers Town NW1 .**83** C1
Neville Ct **10**
SW12 ....**73** B4
Neville Gill Cl
SW18 ....**59** A1
Neville Rd NW6 ...**23** B3
Neville St SW7 ...**143** B2
Neville Terr SW7 .**143** B2
Nevill Rd N16 .....**7** A1
Nevinson Cl SW18 .**59** C1
Nevis Rd SW17 ...**72** C2
Nevitt Ho N1 .....**87** C1
Newall Ho SE1 ...**137** A2
Newark Cres
NW10 ....**20** C2
Newark Ho **3**
SW9 ....**48** A1
Newark St E1 .....**32** A4
New Atlas Wharf
E14 ....**41** C3
New Bentham Ct **10**
N1................**15** B1
Newbery Ho N1 ...**15** B1
Newbold Cotts **4**
E1 ....**32** B3
New Bond St W1 .**118** B4
New Bridge St
EC4 ....**108** A1
New Broad St
EC2 ....**110** A3
Newburgh Rd W3 .**28** B1
Newburgh St W1 .**105** A1
New Burlington Mews
W1 ....**118** C4

New Burlington Pl
W1 ....**118** C4
New Burlington St
W1 ....**118** C4
Newburn Ho
SE11 ....**149** A2
Newburn St SE11 **149** A2
Newbury Ct E5 ...**18** A3
Newbury Ho
Brixton SW9......**48** A1
Kensington W2...**100** B1
Newbury Mews
NW5 ....**12** C2
Newbury St EC1 .**108** C4
New Butt La SE8 ..**51** C3
Newby NW1........**92** C4
Newby Pl E14 ....**34** B2
Newby St SW8 ....**61** A4
New Caledonian
Wharf SE16 ....**41** B3
New Campden Ct **3**
NW3 ....**11** B4
Newcastle Cl EC4 **108** A2
Newcastle Ct **23**
EC4 ....**123** A4
Newcastle Ho
W1................**103** B4
Newcastle Pl W2 **101** C4
Newcastle Row
EC1 ....**95** C1
New Cavendish St
W1 ....**104** A3
New Change EC4 **108** C1
New Charles St
EC1 ....**96** B4
New Church Rd
32 Camberwell
SE5 ....**48** B3
Camberwell SE5 ..**48** C4
New College Ct **8**
NW3 ....**11** B2
New College Mews **7**
N1................**14** C1
New College Par **1**
NW3 ....**11** C3
Newcombe Ho N5..**15** B3
Newcombe St
W8 .....**31** C1 **113** C2
Newcomen Ho **5**
NW5 ....**13** A4
Newcomen Rd
SW11 ....**59** C4
Newcomen St
SE1 ....**137** B4
New Compton St
WC2 ....**106** A1
New Concordia Wharf
SE1 ....**139** A4
Newcourt Ho **2**
E2 ....**25** A2
Newcourt St NW8 .**80** A1
New Covent Garden
Flower Market
SW8 ....**162** A3
New Covent Garden
Fruit & Vegetable
Mkt SW8 ....**161** B1
New Crane Pl E1 ..**32** B1
New Crescent Yd **1**
NW10 ....**21** B3
NEW CROSS **51** B2
New Cross SE14 ...**51** B3
NEW CROSS GATE **50** C2
New Cross Gate
SE14 ....**50** C2
New Cross Gate Sta
SE14 ....**51** B1

New Cross Hospl
SE14........50 B3
New Cross Rd
SE14........51 A2
New Cross Sta
SE14........51 B3
New Ct
City of London
EC4........107 B1
28 Hampstead NW3 .11 B4
Stoke Newington N16 .6 C3
New Den (Millwall
FC) The SE16....40 B1
Newdigate Ho 5
E14........33 B3
Newell St E14....33 B3
New End NW3.......2 B1
New End Prim Sch
NW3........11 B4
New End Sq NW3 .11 C4
Newent Cl SE15 ...49 A3
New Fetter La
EC4........107 C2
Newfield Prim Sch
NW10........8 B1
Newgate St EC1 .108 B2
New Globe Wlk
SE1........122 C2
New Goulston St
E1........110 C2
Newham Sch of
Nursing E3.......27 A1
Newham Sixth Form
Coll (Stratford Ctr)
E15........19 C1
Newham's Row
SE1........138 B3
Newhaven La 3
E16........35 C4
NEWINGTON ...150 B4
Newington Barrow
Way N7........5 B1
Newington Butts SE1,
SE11........150 B3
Newington Cswy
SE1........136 C2
Newington Gn
N16........15 C3
Newington Green
Mans N16.......15 C3
Newington Green
Prim Sch N16 ...15 C3
Newington Green Rd
N1........15 C3
Newington Ind Est
SE17........150 C3
New Inn Broadway
EC2........24 A1 98 B2
New Inn Sq
EC2........24 A1 98 B2
New Inn St
EC2........24 A1 98 B2
New Inn Yd
EC2........24 A1 98 B2
New James Ct
SE15........65 A4
New Kent Rd SE1 .151 A4
New King's Prim Sch
SW6........165 A2
New King's Rd
SW6........165 A2
New King St SE8 ..51 C4
Newland Cl EC1 ...97 B2
Newland Ho 17
SE14........50 C4
Newlands NW1 ....92 C4

Newlands Quay
E1........32 B2
New London St
EC3........124 B4
Newlyn NW1 .....83 A3
Newman Pas W1 .105 A3
Newman's Ct EC3 109 C1
Newman's Row
WC2........107 A3
Newman St W1 ...105 A3
Newmill Ho E3 ....27 B1
Newmount NW3 ...11 C3
New Mount St
E15........19 C1
Newnes Path
SW15........57 A3
Newnham Terr
SE1........135 B2
New North Com Sch
The N1........125 C1
New North Pl
EC2........24 A1 98 A2
New North Rd N1 .87 B3
New North Road
Bridge N1.......87 B3
New North St
WC1........106 C4
Newnton Cl N4.....6 C4
New Oxford St
WC1........106 A2
New Palace Yd
SW1........134 A3
New Park Ct 28
E2........24 A1 98 B2
New Park Par 18
SW2........74 A4
New Park Rd SW2 .74 A4
New Place Sq
SE16........40 A3
Newport Ave E14 ..34 C2
Newport Ct WC2 .119 C4
Newport Ho 2 E3 ..26 A2
Newport Pl WC2 .119 C4
Newport Rd SW13 .46 C2
Newport St SE11 .149 A4
New Priory Ct 9
NW6........10 C1
New Providence
Wharf 4 E14 ....34 C1
Newquay Ho
SE11........149 B2
New Quebec St
W1........103 A1
New Rd E1........32 A4
New River Ct N5 ...15 C4
New River Way N4 ..6 C4
New Row WC2 ....120 A4
New Sq 5 SE11 ...149 C4
New Scotland Yard *
SW1........133 B2
New Shepherd's Bush
Mkt* 6 W12 ....39 B4
New Spring Gdns Wlk
SE11........148 B1
New Sq WC2 .....107 A2
New Square Pas
WC2........107 A2
New St EC2........110 B3
Newstead Ho N1 ..85 C2
Newton Ave W3 ...37 B4
Newton Gr W4 ....38 A2
Newton Ho
Clapham SW8 ...171 B2
Paddington NW8 ..78 B4
1 Stepney E1 .....32 A3

Newton Pl E14 ....41 C2
Newton Point 1
E16........35 B3
Newton Prep Sch
SW8........170 B1
Newton Rd
Acton W3........37 B4
Kensington W2 ..100 C1
Stratford New Town
E15........19 C3
Newton St WC2 ..106 B2
Newton's Yd 14
SW18........58 C2
New Tower Bldgs 21
E1........32 A1
Newtown Ct
Battersea SW4 ...170 A3
Clapham SW4 ....61 A2
New Union Cl E14 ..42 B3
New Union St
EC2........109 B3
New Wharf Rd N1 ..84 B2
Niagara Cl N1 ....87 A2
Niagara Ct 6
SE16........40 B3
Nicholas Ct
Chiswick W4 .....46 A3
Golders Green NW11 .1 C4
Nicholas Ho 2
SW15........56 C2
Nicholas La EC2,
EC4........123 C4
Nicholas Pas EC3 123 C4
Nicholas Rd E11 ...25 B1
Nicholay Rd N19 ...4 C3
Nicholl Ho 4 N4 ....6 B3
Nicholl St E2.....24 C4
Nichols Cl N4 .....5 C3
Nichols Ct E2 ....24 B3
Nicholson Ho
SE17........151 B2
Nicholson St SE1 .122 A1
Nickleby Ho
Bermondsey SE1 ..139 B3
7 Shepherd's Bush
W11........30 C1
Nickols Wlk SW18 .59 A3
Nicoll Ct NW10 ....21 A4
Nicoll Rd NW10 ...21 A4
Nicosia Rd SW18 ..72 A4
Nigel Bldg EC1 ...107 B4
Nigel Playfair Ave
W6........39 A1
Nigel Rd SE15 ....64 C4
Nightingale Cl W4 .45 B4
Nightingale Ct
1 Cubitt Town
E14........42 B3
Finsbury Pk N4 ....5 B2
Nightingale Ho
21 Hoxton N1 ....24 A4
4 North Kensington
W12........30 B3
St George in t East
E1........125 B2
Nightingale La SW4,
SW12........60 C1
Nightingale Lo 5
W9........31 C4
Nightingale Mans 4
SW12........60 C1
Nightingale Mews
1 Bow E3........26 A3
SE11........150 A4

Nightingale Pl
SW10........157 A4
Nightingale Prim Sch
E5........16 C4
Nightingale Rd
NW10........21 B3
Nightingale Sch
SW17........72 A2
Nightingale Sq
SW12........72 C4
Nightingale Wlk SW8,
SW4........61 A1
Nile Cl N16........7 B1
Nile Ho N1........97 B4
Nile St N1........97 B4
Nile Terr SE1,
SE15........153 A1
Nimegen Way 9
SE22........64 A2
Nimrod Pas 2 N1 .16 A2
NINE ELMS 160 C2
Nine Elms La
SW8........161 B3
Nisbet Ho 9
E9........17 C3
Niton St SW6 .....47 C3
Niton St SW6 .....47 C3
No 2 Willow Rd *
NW3........12 A4
Nobel Ho 8 SE5 ...48 B1
Noble Ct E1......32 A2
Noble St EC2 ....108 C2
Noel Coward Ho
SW1........147 A3
Noël Ho 3 NW3 ...11 C3
Noel Rd Acton W3 .28 A3
Islington N1......86 B2
Noel St W1 .....105 A1
Noko NW10........22 C2
Nolan Way E5 .....16 C4
Noll Ho N7........5 B2
Norbiton Rd E14 ..33 B3
Norbrooke St W12 .29 B2
Norburn St W10 ...31 A4
Norcombe Ho 2
N19........4 C1
Norcott Rd N16 ....7 C1
Norcroft Gdns
SE22........76 C4
Norden Ho 22 E2 ..25 A2
Nore Ct NW10 .....8 C1
Norfolk Cres W2 .102 B2
Norfolk Ho
City of London
EC4........122 C4
Greenwich SE3 ...53 A4
8 Putney SW15 ..69 B4
Richmond TW10 ..54 C2
Shacklewell E8 ...16 B4
St Johns SE8 .....51 C2
Westminster SW1 .147 C4
Norfolk House Rd
SW16........74 A1
Norfolk Mans
Battersea SW11 ..169 A3
13 Wandsworth
SW18........58 C2
Norfolk Mews 12
W10........31 A4
Norfolk Pl W2 ....101 C2
Norfolk Rd
St John's Wood
NW8........79 C3
Willesden NW10 ...8 C1
Norfolk Row SE1,
SE11........148 C4
Norfolk Sq W2 ...101 C2

Norfolk Sq Mews
W2........101 C1
Norgrove St SW12 .72 C4
Norland Ho 19
W11........30 C1
Norland Pl
W11........31 A1 112 B1
Norland Place Sch
W11........31 A1 112 B1
Norland Rd 16
W11........30 C1
Norland Sq
W11........31 A1 112 B1
Norley Vale SW15 .68 C3
Norman Butler Ho 11
W10........23 A1
Normanby Cl
SW15........58 B2
Normanby Rd
NW10........8 B4
Norman Ct
Dulwich SE21 ....76 C4
Finsbury Pk N4 ....5 C4
Willesden NW10 ...8 C1
Normand Croft Com
Sch W14 ......155 A4
Normand Mews
W14........154 B4
Normand Rd W14 154 C4
Normandy Ho 8
E14........42 B4
Normandy Rd
SW9........173 B3
Norman Gr E3 ....26 A3
Norman Ho SW8 .162 A2
Normanhurst Rd
SW2........74 B2
Norman St EC1 ....97 A3
Normanton Ave SW18,
SW19........70 C2
Normanton Ho 6
SW4........61 B1
Norman Way W3 ..28 A3
Norris Ho
12 Hoxton N1 ....24 A4
15 South Hackney
E9........25 B4
Norris St SW1 ...119 B3
Norroy Rd SW15 ...57 C3
Norse Ho 13 SE5 ..48 B1
Norstead Pl SW15 .68 C2
NORTH ACTON 20 C2
North Acton Rd
NW10........20 C2
North Acton Sta
W3........28 C4
Northampton Gr
N1........15 C3
Northampton Pk
N1........15 C3
Northampton Rd
EC1........95 C2
Northampton Sq
EC1........96 A3
Northampton St
N1........15 B1
North Audley St
W1........117 B4
North Ave 8 TW9 ..44 C2
Northaw Ho 4
W10........22 B1
North Bank NW8 ...90 A3
North Block 18 E1 ..32 A2

Northbourne Ho **21**
E5 . . . . .17 A3
Northbourne Rd
SW4 . . . . .61 C2
North Bridge House
Sch NW1 . . . . .79 A4
North Bridge House
Senior Sch NW1 . .82 A3
Northburgh St
EC1 . . . . .96 B2
North Carriage Dr
W2 . . . . .116 B3
Northchurch
SE17 . . . . .151 C2
Northchurch Ho **19**
E2 . . . . .24 C4
Northchurch Rd
N1 . . . . .15 C1
Northchurch Terr
N1 . . . . .16 A1
North Circular Rd NW2,
NW10 . . . . .8 A4
North Colonnade The
E14 . . . . .34 A1
Northcote Lodge Sch
SW11 . . . . .60 B1
Northcote Rd
Wandsworth
SW11 . . . . .60 B2
Willesden NW10 . . . .8 A4
Northcourt W1 . . . .105 A4
North Cres
Marylebone WC1 . .105 B4
Newham E16 . . . . . .27 C1
Northcroft Ct **8**
W12 . . . . .38 C4
North Cross Rd
SE22 . . . . .64 C2
North Ct SW1 . . . .134 A1
Northdown St N1 . .84 C1
North Dulwich Sta
SE21 . . . . .63 C2
NORTH END 2 B2
North End Ho NW3 . .2 B2
North End Ave NW3 . 2 B2
North End Cres
W14 . . . . .140 C3
North End Ho
W14 . . . . .140 B3
North End Par
W14 . . . . .140 B3
North End Rd
Golders Green
NW11 . . . . .2 A3
West Kensington
W14 . . . . .141 A1
North End Way
NW3 . . . . .2 B2
Northern Hts N8 . . .4 C4
Northesk Ho **6**
E1 . . . . .25 A1
North Eyot Gdns **5**
W6 . . . . .38 B1
Northey St E14 . . . .33 A2
Northfield Ho **3**
SE15 . . . . .49 C4
Northfield Rd N16 . .7 A4
Northfields SW18 . .58 C3
Northfields Prospect
SW18 . . . . .58 C3
Northfields Rd
W3 . . . . .28 B4
Northfleet Ho
SE1 . . . . .137 B4

North Flower Wlk
W2 . . . . .115 B3
North Gate NW8 . . .80 A1
Northgate Ct **14**
SW9 . . . . .62 C4
North Gower St
NW1 . . . . .93 A3
North Gr N6 . . . . .3 C4
North Greenwich Sta
SE10 . . . . .43 A4
North Ho **31** SE8 . . .41 B1
Northiam WC1 . . . .94 B3
Northiam St E9 . . . .25 A4
Northington St
WC1 . . . . .95 A1
NORTH KENSINGTON
. . . . .30 C4
Northlands St SE5 . .48 B1
Northleigh Ho **38**
E3 . . . . .27 A2
North Lo E3 . . . . . . .26 C2
North Lodge Cl
SW15 . . . . .57 C2
North Mews WC1 . . .95 A1
Northolme Rd N5 . .15 B4
North Pas SW18 . . .58 C2
Northpoint Sq **8**
NW1 . . . . .13 C2
North Pole Rd
W10 . . . . .30 B4
Northport St N1 . . . .87 C3
North Rd
Barnsbury N7 . . . . . .14 A2
Brentford TW8 . . . . .44 A4
Highgate N6 . . . . .3 C4
Richmond TW9 . . . . .44 C3
North Ride W2 . . . .116 A3
North Rise W2 . . . .102 B1
North Row W1 . . . .117 B4
NORTH SHEEN 44 B1
North Sheen Sta
TW10 . . . . .54 C3
North Side
Wandsworth Comm
SW18 . . . . .59 C2
North St SW4 . . . . .61 B4
Northstead Rd
SW2 . . . . .74 C2
North Tenter St
E1 . . . . .111 A1
Northumberland Alley
EC3 . . . . .110 B1
Northumberland Ave
WC2 . . . . .120 A2
Northumberland Ho
NW5 . . . . .13 B2
Northumberland
Mans E5 . . . . .17 B4
Northumberland Pl
W2 . . . . .31 C3
Northumberland St
WC2 . . . . .120 A2
Northumbria Ct **10**
TW9 . . . . .54 A3
Northumbria St
E14 . . . . .33 C3
North Verbena Gdns
7 W6 . . . . .38 C1
Northview **1** N7 . . . .5 A1
Northview Cres
NW10 . . . . .8 B4
Northview Prim Sch
NW10 . . . . .8 B4
North Villas NW1 . .13 C2
Northway Rd SE5 . .63 B4

Northways Par **2**
NW3 . . . . .11 C1
Northwest Pl N1 . . .85 C2
North Wharf Rd
W2 . . . . .101 B3
Northwick Cl NW8 . .89 B2
Northwick Ho
NW8 . . . . .89 A2
Northwick Terr
NW8 . . . . .89 B2
North Wlk W2 . . . .114 C3
Northwold Prim Sch
E5 . . . . .7 C2
Northwold Rd E5,
N16 . . . . .7 C2
North Wood Lo
NW3 . . . . .11 A4
Northwood Rd N6 . . .4 A4
North Worple Way
SW14 . . . . .55 C4
Norton Folgate
E1 . . . . .110 B4
Norton Ho
14 Globe Town E2 . .25 C3
30 Stepney E1 . . . .32 A3
Stockwell SW9 . . . .173 A1
Norval Gn SW9 . . .173 C2
Norvic Ho **5** SE5 . .48 B1
Norway Gate SE16 . .41 A3
Norway Pl E14 . . . . .33 B3
Norway St SE10 . . . .52 A4
Norwich Ho **6**
E14 . . . . .34 A3
Norwich St EC4 . . .107 B2
Norwood Cl NW2 . . .1 A1
Norwood Ho **25**
E14 . . . . .34 A2
Norwood Rd SE24,
SE27 . . . . .75 A3
Notley St SE5 . . . . .48 C3
Notre Dame RC Girls
Sch SE1 . . . . .136 B1
Notting Barn Rd
W10 . . . . .22 C1
Nottingdale Sq
W11 . . . . . .31 A1 112 A2
Nottingham Ct
WC2 . . . . .106 A1
Nottingham Ho
22 Camberwell
SE5 . . . . .48 B1
Stoke Newington N4 . .6 B3
Nottingham Pl
W1 . . . . .103 B4
Nottingham Rd
SW17 . . . . .72 B3
Nottingham St
W1 . . . . .103 B4
Nottingham Terr
NW1 . . . . .91 B1
NOTTING HILL 31 C3
Notting Hill Gate
W11 . . . . . .31 C1 113 B2
Notting Hill Gate Sta
W11 . . . . .31 C3
Nottingwood Ho
W11 . . . . . .31 A2 112 A4
Nova Bldg **1** E14 . .41 C2
Nova Ct E **3** E14 . . .34 B1
Nova Ct W **4** E14 . .34 B1
Novello St SW6 . . .165 B4
Nowell Rd SW13 . . .46 C4
Noyna Rd SW17 . . .72 B1
Nucleus NW10 . . . . .20 B2
Nuding Cl SE13 . . . .66 C4
Nuffield Lo **14** W9 . .31 C4
Nugent Ct **3** N19 . . .5 A3

Nugent Rd N19 . . . . .5 A3
Nugent Terr NW8 . . .79 A1
Nun Ct EC2 . . . . . . .109 B2
NUNHEAD 65 B3
Nunhead Cres
SE15 . . . . .65 A4
Nunhead Gn SE15 . .65 A4
Nunhead Gr SE15 . .65 A4
Nunhead La SE15 . .65 A4
Nunhead Sta SE15 . .50 B1
Nursery Cl
New Cross SE4 . . . . .51 B1
Putney SW15 . . . . . .57 C3
Nursery La
North Kensington
W10 . . . . .30 B4
Shoreditch E2 . . . . . .24 B4
Nursery Rd
Hackney E9 . . . . .17 B2
Stockwell SW9 . . . . .62 B3
Nursery Row
SE17 . . . . .151 B3
Nutbourne St
W10 . . . . .23 A2
Nutbrook St SE15 . .64 C4
Nutcroft Rd SE15 . .50 A3
Nutfield Rd
East Dulwich SE22 . .64 B3
Leyton E15 . . . . .19 B4
Nutford Pl W1 . . . .102 C2
Nuthurst Ave SW2 . .74 B2
Nutley Terr NW3 . . .11 C2
Nutmeg La E14 . . . .34 C3
Nuttall St N1 . . . . . .24 A3
Nutt St SE15 . . . . . .49 B3
NW London Jewish
Day Sch NW6 . . . .10 A1
Nye Bevan Ho
SW6 . . . . .154 C2
Nye's Wharf SE1,
SE15 . . . . .49 C4
Nylands Ave TW9 . .44 C1
Nynehead St SE14 . .51 A3
Nyton Cl N19 . . . . . . .5 A3

O

O2 Millennium Dome
The* SE10 . . . . .35 A1
Oakbank Gr SE24 . .63 B3
Oakbury Rd SW6 . .166 B1
Oakcourt **17** SE15 . .49 B3
Oak Cres E16 . . . . . .35 A4
Oakcroft Ct SE13 . .53 C2
Oakcroft Rd SE13 . .52 C1
Oakdale Ct N19 . . . . .5 A2
Oakdale Rd SE15 . . .65 B4
Oakdene **3** SE15 . .50 A2
Oakdene Ho **11**
N16 . . . . .7 A4
Oak End Way **10** N4 . .5 C4
Oakeshott Ave N6 . . .3 C2
Oakey La SE1 . . . . .135 B2
Oakfield Ct
Clapham Pk SW4 . . .62 A1
Finsbury Pk N8 . . . . . .5 A4
Oakfield Prep Sch
SE21 . . . . .75 C3
Oakfield Rd
Finsbury Pk N4 . . . . . .5 C4
Wimbledon SW19 . . .69 C1
Oakfield St SW10 . .156 C4

Oakford Rd NW5 . . .13 B4
Oak Gr NW2 . . . . . . .10 A4
Oakham Ho **5**
W10 . . . . .22 B1
Oakhall Ave NW3 . .12 A4
Oakhill Ct
Honor Oak SE23 . . . .65 B1
Putney SW15 . . . . . .58 B2
Oak Hill Lo NW3 . . .11 A4
Oak Hill Park Mews
NW3 . . . . .11 B4
Oak Hill Pk NW3 . . .11 A4
Oakhill Pl SW15 . . .58 C2
Oakhill Rd SW15 . . .58 B2
Oak Hill Way NW3 . .11 B4
Oak Ho
13 Cubitt Town
E14 . . . . .42 B4
8 Maitland Pk
NW3 . . . . .12 B2
2 Richmond TW9 . .45 A2
Stoke Newington
N16 . . . . .7 A1
Oakhurst Gr SE22 . .64 C3
Oakington Rd W9 . .23 C1
Oakington Way N8 . . .5 A4
Oak La E14 . . . . .33 B2
Oaklands
Dagenham NW10 . . .21 A4
5 Shepherd's Bush
W12 . . . . .30 A1
Oaklands Gr W12 . .29 C1
Oaklands Ho SE4 . .66 B4
Oaklands Mews **1**
NW2 . . . . .9 C4
Oaklands Pas NW2 . .9 C4
Oaklands Pl **8**
SW4 . . . . .61 C3
Oaklands Rd
Cricklewood NW2 . . . .9 C4
Mortlake SW14 . . . .55 C4
Oaklands Sec Sch
E2 . . . . .25 A2
Oakley Cres EC1 . . .86 B1
Oakley Dr SE13 . . . .67 C1
Oakley Gdns SW3 .158 B4
Oakley Ho SW1 . . .145 A4
Oakley Pl SE1 . . . .152 C1
Oakley Rd N1 . . . . . .15 C1
Oakley Sq NW1 . . . .83 A2
Oakley St SW3 . . . .158 A4
Oakley Wlk W6 . . . .47 C4
Oak Lodge **14**
SE21 . . . . .75 C2
Oak Lodge Sch
SW12 . . . . .72 C4
Oakman Ho **29**
SW19 . . . . .69 C3
Oakmead Rd
SW12 . . . . .73 A3
Oak Park Gdns
SW19 . . . . .69 C3
Oak Park Mews
N16 . . . . .7 B1
Oakshaw Rd
SW18 . . . . .71 A4
Oakshott Ct NW1 . .83 B1
Oaks Sh Ctr The
W3 . . . . .28 B1
Oaks The
Brondesbury Pk
NW6 . . . . .9 C1
Willesden NW10 . . . . .9 A1
Oak Tree Ct
Acton W3 . . . . .28 A2
8 Clapham Pk
SW4 . . . . .61 B3

Oak Tree Ho W9 . . . . **88** A2
Oak Tree Ho NW8 . . . **90** A3
Oakview Lo NW11 . . . 1 B4
Oak Village NW5 . . . . 12 C4
Oak Way W3 . . . . 29 A1
Oakwell Ho SW8 . . 171 B1
Oakwood CI SE13 . . 67 C1
Oakwood Ct W14 . . **126** C2
Oakwood La W14 . . **126** C2
Oakworth Rd W10 . . 30 C4
Oast Ct SE8 8 . . . . 41 B2
Oast Lo W4 . . . . 46 A3
Oat La EC2 3 . . . . . **109** A2
Oatlands Ct 3
SW19 . . . . 69 C3
Oatwell Ho SW3 . . **144** B3
Oban Ho E14 . . . . 34 C3
Oban St E14 . . . . 34 C3
Oberon Ho 5 N1 . . 24 A3
Oberstein Rd 13
SW11 . . . . 59 C3
Oborne CI SE24 . . . 63 A2
O'Brian Ho 10 E1 . . 25 C1
Observatory Gdns
W8 . . . . **127** C4
Observatory Mews
E14 . . . . 42 C2
Observatory Rd
SW14 . . . . 55 B3
Occupation Rd
SE17 . . . . **150** C2
Ocean St E1 . . . . 32 C4
Ocean Wharf E14 . . 41 C4
Ockbrook 5 E1 . . . . 32 B4
Ockendon Rd N1 . . . 15 C2
Ockley Rd SW16 . . . 74 A1
Octagon Arc EC2 . . **110** A3
Octagon The N1 . . . . 10 C4
Octavia Ho W10 . . . 23 A1
Octavia Mews 1
W9 . . . . 23 B1
Octavia St SW11 . . **168** B3
Octavius St SE8 . . . 51 C3
Odell Wlk SE13 . . . . 67 B4
Odeon Ct
Dagenham NW10 . . 21 A4
1 Newham E16 . . . . 35 C4
Odessa Rd NW10 . . 21 C3
Odessa St SE16 . . . 41 B3
Odette Duval Ho 28
E1 . . . . 32 B4
Odger St SW11 . . . **169** A2
Odhams Wlk
WC2 . . . . **106** B1
Odin Ho 6 SE5 . . . . 48 B1
O'Donnell Ct WC1 . . **94** B2
O'Driscoll Ho 4
W12 . . . . 30 A3
Offa's Mead E9 . . . . 18 A4
Offenbach Ho 12
E2 . . . . 25 C3
Offerton Rd SW4 . . 61 B4
Offham Ho SE17 . . **152** A3
Offley Ho 10 E9 . . . 17 C2
Offley Rd SW9 . . . . **163** B2
Offord Rd N1 . . . . . . 14 B1
Offord St N1 . . . . 14 B1
Ogilvie Ho 11 E1 . . 32 C3
Oglander Rd SE15 . 64 B4
Ogle St W1 . . . . **104** C4
O'Gorman Ho
SW10 . . . . **157** A2
Ohio Bldg 13 SE13 . 52 A2
Oil Mill La W6 . . . . . 38 C1
Okehampton Rd
NW10 . . . . 22 C4

Okeover Manor
SW4 . . . . 61 A3
Olaf St W11 . . . . 30 C2
Old Bailey EC4 . . . **108** B1
Old Barrack Yd
SW1 . . . . **131** B3
Old Bellgate Wharf
E14 . . . . 41 C3
Old Bethnal Green Rd
E2 . . . . 25 A2
Old Billingsgate Wlk
EC3 . . . . **124** A3
Old Bldgs WC2 . . . **107** B2
Old Bond St W1 . . **118** C3
Old Brewery Mews
NW3 . . . . 11 C4
Old Broad St EC2 **109** C2
Old Brompton Rd SW5,
SW7 . . . . **143** A3
Old Burlington St
W1 . . . . **118** C3
Oldbury Ct E9 . . . . . 18 A3
Oldbury PI W1 . . . **103** C4
Old Castle St E1 . . **111** A2
Old Cavendish St
W1 . . . . **104** A1
Old Change Ct
EC4 . . . . **108** C1
Old Chiswick Yd
W4 . . . . 46 A4
Old Church Rd E1 . 32 C3
Old Church St
SW3 . . . . **143** C1
Old Compton St
W1 . . . . **105** B1
Old Court Ho W8 **128** A3
Old Court PI W8 . . **128** A3
Old Covent Garden★
WC2 . . . . **120** B4
Old City Wall 6 E1 **110** C3
Old Dairy Mews
5 Balham SW12 . . 72 C3
4 Camden Town
NW5 . . . . 13 A2
Old Deer Park Gdns
TW9 . . . . 54 A3
Old Devonshire Rd
SW12 . . . . 73 A4
Old Dock Cl TW9 . . 44 C4
Oldfield Gr SE16 . . . 40 C2
Oldfield Ho 4 W4 . . 38 A1
Oldfield Mews N6 . . 4 B4
Oldfield Rd
Bedford Pk W3,
W12 . . . . 38 B4
Stoke Newington N16 . 7 A1
Willesden NW10 . . . 8 B1
Old Fish St Hill
EC4 . . . . **122** C4
Old Fleet La EC4 . **108** A2
Old Ford Prim Sch
E3 . . . . 26 B3
Old Ford Rd E2,E3 . 25 C3
Old Ford Trad Ctr 13
E3 . . . . 26 C4
Old Forge Mews
W12 . . . . 39 A4
Old Forge Rd N19 . . 4 C2
Old Gloucester St
WC1 . . . . **106** B4
Oldham Terr W3 . . . 28 B1
Oldhill St N16 . . . . . . 7 C3
Old Hospital Cl SW12,
SW17 . . . . 72 B3
Olding Ho 6
SW12 . . . . 73 B4

Old Jamaica Bsns Est
SE16 . . . . **139** B1
Old Jamaica Rd
SE16 . . . . **139** B2
Old James St
SE15 . . . . 65 A4
Old Jewry EC2 . . . **109** B1
Old Kent Rd
Deptford SE1, ... 50 A4
Walworth, SE1, . . **152** B2
Old Laundry The 14
SW18 . . . . 59 B3
Old Manor Ct NW8 **79** A2
Old Manor Yd
SW5 . . . . **142** A3
Old Market Sq
E2 . . . . 24 B2 99 A4
Old Marylebone Rd
NW1 . . . . **102** B3
Old Mitre Ct EC4 . **107** C1
Old Montague St
E1 . . . . **111** B3
Old Nichol St
E2 . . . . 24 B1 98 C2
Old North St WC1 **106** C4
OLD OAK COMMON
. . . . 21 B1
Old Oak Common La
NW10 . . . . 21 A2
Old Oak La NW10 . . 21 B2
Old Oak Prim Sch
W12 . . . . 29 B3
Old Oak Rd W3 . . . . 29 B2
Old Orch The
SW11 . . . . 60 C4
Old Palace Prim Sch
E3 . . . . 27 A2
Old Paradise St
SE11 . . . . **148** C4
Old Park Ave
SW12 . . . . 60 C1
Old Park La W1 . . **118** A1
Old Pye St SW1 . . **133** B2
Old Pye Street Est
SW1 . . . . **133** B1
Old Quebec St
W1 . . . . **103** A1
Old Queen St
SW1 . . . . **133** C3
Oldridge Rd SW12 . 73 A4
Old Royal Free PI
N1 . . . . **85** C3
Old Royal Free Sq
N1 . . . . **85** C3
Old School Sq 12
E14 . . . . 33 C3
Old School The
WC1 . . . . **107** A4
Old Seacoal La
EC4 . . . . **108** A2
Old South Lambeth
Rd SW8 . . . . **162** B2
Old Spitalfields Mkt
E1 . . . . **111** A4
Old Sq WC2 . . . . . . **107** A2
Old St EC1 . . . . **97** C2
Old Stable Mews
N5 . . . . 6 B1
Old Street Sta EC1 **97** C2
Old Sun Wharf
E14 . . . . 33 A2
Old Swan Wharf
SW11 . . . . **167** A4
Old Theatre Ct
SE1 . . . . **123** A2
Old Town SW4 . . . . 61 B4

Old Vicarage Sch
TW10 . . . . 54 A1
Old Woolwich Rd
SE10 . . . . 52 C4
Old York Rd SW18 . 59 A2
O'Leary Sq E1 . . . . . 32 B4
Olga Prim Sch E3 . . 26 A3
Olga St 20 E3 . . . . . 26 A3
Oliphant St W10 . . . 23 A2
Olive Blythe Ho 14
W10 . . . . 23 A1
Oliver Bsns Pk
NW10 . . . . 20 B3
Oliver CI W4 . . . . . . 45 A4
Olive Rd NW2 . . . . . . 9 B4
Oliver Goldsmith Prim
Sch SE5 . . . . 48 B2
Oliver Ho
Bermondsey SE16 **139** B3
Notting Hill
W11 . . . . . . 31 A2 **112** A3
South Lambeth
SW8 . . . . **162** A2
Oliver House Prep
Sch SW4 . . . . 61 A1
Oliver Mews SE15 . 49 C1
Oliver's Yd EC1 . . . **97** C2
Olive Tree Ho 7
SE15 . . . . 50 B4
Olive Tree Sch The
SE13 . . . . 67 A1
Olivette St 1
SW15 . . . . 57 C4
Olive Waite Ho
NW6 . . . . 11 A1
Ollerton Gn E3 . . . . 26 B4
Ollgar CI W12 . . . . . 29 B1
Olliffe St E14 . . . . . . 42 B3
Olmar St SE1 . . . . . 49 C4
Olney Ho NW8 . . . . **90** B2
Olney Rd SE17 . . . . **48** B4
Olympia Ex Ctr★
W14 . . . . **126** B1
Olympian Ct 8
E14 . . . . 41 C2
Olympia Way
W14 . . . . **126** B1
Olympia Yd W2 . . **114** B3
Olympic Ho
W10 . . . . 30 B3
Olympus Sq E5 . . . . 7 C1
Oman Ave NW2 . . . . 9 B4
Oman Ct NW4 . . . . . . 9 A4
Ombersley Ho N4 . . 6 B4
Omeara St SE1 . . . **123** A1
Omega CI E14 . . . . . 42 A3
Omega Ho SW10 . . **157** A2
Omega PI N1 . . . . . . **84** B1
Omega St SE14 . . . 51 C2
Omega Works 3 E3 18 C1
Ommaney Rd
SE14 . . . . 51 A2
Omnibus Bsns Ctr
N7 . . . . 14 A3
Ondine Rd SE15 . . . 64 B3
Onedin Point E1 . . **125** C3
Onega Gate SE16 . . 41 A3
O'Neill Ho NW8 . . . **79** C1
One Tree CI SE23 . . 65 B1
Ongar Ho 18 N1 . . . 15 C2
Ongar Rd SW6 . . . **155** C4
Onslow Ave TW10 . 54 A2
Onslow Avenue Mans
10 TW10 . . . . 54 A2
Onslow CI W9 . . . . . 23 B2
Onslow Ct SW10 . . **143** A1

Onslow Gdns
SW7 . . . . **143** B2
Onslow Lo 28
SW2 . . . . 74 C4
Onslow Mews E
SW7 . . . . **143** B3
Onslow Mews W
SW7 . . . . **143** B3
Onslow Sq SW7 . . . 54 A1
Onslow Sq SW7 . . **143** C3
Onslow St EC1 . . . . **95** C1
Ontario St SE1 . . . **136** B2
Ontario Way E14 . . 33 C2
Opal St SE11 . . . . . **150** A2
Open Air Theatre,
Regent's Pk★
NW1 . . . . **91** B3
Openview SW17,
SW18 . . . . 71 C2
Opera Ct 7 N19 . . . . 4 C1
Operating Theatre
Mus & Herb Garret★
SE1 . . . . **123** C2
Ophelia Gdns NW2 . . 1 A1
Ophir Terr SE15 . . . 49 C2
Opie Ho NW8 . . . . . **80** B2
Oppenheim Rd
SE13 . . . . 52 B1
Oppidan Apartments
NW6 . . . . 10 C2
Oppidans Rd NW3 . 12 B1
Orange PI SE16 . . . 40 B3
Orangery Gallery
The★ W8 . . . . **126** C3
Orange St WC2 . . **119** C3
Orange Yd WC2 . . **105** C1
Oransay Rd 21 N1 . 15 B2
Oratory La SW3 . . **143** C2
Oratory RC Prim Sch
SW3 . . . . **144** A3
Oratory The★
SW7 . . . . **130** A1
Orbain Rd SW6 . . **154** B1
Orbel St SW11 . . . **168** A3
Orb St SE17 . . . . . **151** B3
Orchard CI
Honor Oak SE23 . . 65 B1
Islington N1 5 . . . . . 15 B1
Kensal Town W10 . . 31 A4
Orchard Ct
Barnes SW13 . . . . . 56 B4
Marylebone W1 . . . **103** B2
Orchard Dr SE3 . . . 53 A1
Orchard Hill SE13 . 52 A2
Orchard Ho
Camberwell SE5 . . 48 B2
5 Rotherhithe
SE16 . . . . 40 B3
Shepherd's Bush
W12 . . . . 29 C2
Orchard Mead Ho
NW11 . . . . 1 C1
Orchard Mews N1 . 15 C1
Orchard PI E14 . . . . 35 A2
Orchard Prim Sch
E9 . . . . 17 B1
Orchard Rd
Highgate N6 . . . . 4 A4
Richmond TW9 . . . . 54 C4
Orchard Rise
TW10 . . . . 55 A3
Orchardson Ho
NW8 . . . . **89** C1
Orchardson St
NW8 . . . . **89** C1

Orchard Sq W14 . . . **140** C1
Orchard St W1 . . . . **103** C2
Orchard The
  Acton Green W4 . . . .37 C2
  Lewisham SE3 . . . . .52 C1
Orchid St W12 . . . . .29 C2
Orde Hall St WC1 . . **106** C4
Orde Ho ◊ N16 . . . .15 C4
Ordell Ct ◙ E3 . . . .26 B3
Ordell Rd E3 . . . . . .26 B3
Ordnance Cres
  SE10 . . . . .43 A4
Ordnance Hill
  NW8 . . . . **79** C2
Ordnance Mews
  NW8 . . . . .79 C2
Ordnance Rd E16 . . .35 B4
Organana Dr E14 . . .34 C3
Oregon Bldg ◙
  SE13 . . . . .52 A2
Orestes Mews ◙
  NW6 . . . . .10 C3
Orford Ct SE27 . . . .75 A2
Oriana Ho ◙ E14 . . .33 B2
Oriel Ct NW3 . . . . .11 B4
Oriel Dr SW13 . . . . .47 B4
Oriel Rd
  Hackney E9 . . . . . . .18 A2
  Homerton E9 . . . . . .17 C2
Orient St SE11 . . . . **150** A4
Orion Bsns Ctr
  SE14 . . . . .40 C1
Orion Ho ◙ E1 . . . .25 A1
Orion Point ◙
  E14 . . . . .41 C2
Orkney Ho ◙ N1 . . .84 C4
Orkney St SW11 . . **169** B2
Orlando Rd SW4 . . .61 B4
Orleston Mews
  N7 . . . . .14 C2
Orleston Rd N7 . . . .14 C2
Orlop St SE10 . . . . .43 A1
Orme Ct W2 . . . . . **114** A3
Orme Ct Mews
  W2 . . . . **114** A3
Orme Ho ◙ E8 . . . .24 B4
Orme La W2 . . . . . **114** A3
Orme Sq SW12 . . . .73 A3
Ormerod Ho ◙
  SW9 . . . . .62 A4
Orme Sq W2 . . . . . **114** A3
Ormiston Gr W12 . . .30 A1
Ormiston Rd SE10 . .43 C1
Ormond Cl WC1 . . **106** B4
Ormonde Ct SW15 . .57 B3
Ormonde Gate
  SW3 . . . . **145** A1
Ormonde Mans
  WC1 . . . . **106** B4
Ormonde Pl SW1 . . **145** C3
Ormonde Rd
  SW14 . . . . .55 B4
Ormonde Terr
  NW8 . . . . .80 C3
Ormond Ho ◙ N16 . .6 C2
Ormond Mans
  WC1 . . . . .94 C1
Ormond Mews
  WC1 . . . . .94 B1
Ormond Rd N4, N19 . .5 A3
Ormond Yd SW1 . . **119** A2
Ormrod Ct W11 . . . .31 B3
Ormsby Lo ◙ W4 . . .38 A3
Ormsby Pl N16 . . . . .7 B1
Ormsby St E2 . . . . .24 B3

Ormside St SE15 . . .50 B4
Ornan Rd NW3 . . . .12 A3
Orpen Ho SW5 . . . **141** C3
Orpen Wlk N16 . . . . .7 A1
Orpheus Ho ◙ N19 . .4 C4
Orpheus St SE5 . . . .48 C2
Orsett Mews W2 . . **100** C2
Orsett St SE11 . . . . **149** A2
Orsett Terr W2 . . . **100** C2
Orsman Rd N1 . . . . .24 A4
Orton St E1 . . . . . **125** B1
Orville Rd SW11 . . **167** C2
Orwell Ct
  Hackney E8 . . . . . . .24 C4
  Highbury N5 . . . . . .15 B4
Orwell Ho W12 . . . .29 C2
Osbaldeston Rd
  N16 . . . . .7 C3
Osbert St SW1 . . . **147** B3
Osborn Cl E8 . . . . .24 C4
Osborne Rd
  Finsbury Pk N4 . . . . .5 C3
  Hackney E9 . . . . . . .18 B2
  South Acton W3 . . . .37 A4
  Willesden NW2 . . . . .9 A2
Osborn St E1 . . . . **111** A4
Osbourne Ho
  TW10 . . . . .54 C2
Oscar Faber Pl ◙
  N1 . . . . .16 A1
Oscar St SE8 . . . . . .51 C1
Oseney Cres NW5 . .13 C2
Osier Ct ◙ E1 . . . . .25 C1
Osier La SE10 . . . . .43 B3
Osier Mews W4 . . . .46 B4
Osiers Rd SW18 . . . .58 C3
Osier St ◙ E1 . . . . .25 B1
Oslo Ct NW8 . . . . .80 A1
Oslo Ho ◙ SE5 . . . .48 B1
Oslo Sq SE16 . . . . .41 A3
Osman Prim Sch
  E1 . . . . **111** C4
Osman Rd ◙ W6 . . .39 B3
Osmington Ho
  SW8 . . . . **163** A1
Osmund St W12 . . . .29 B4
Osnaburgh St
  NW1 . . . . .92 B2
Osnaburgh Terr
  NW1 . . . . .92 B2
Osprey Ct NW3 . . . .11 A3
Osprey Ho
  Camberwell SE5 . . . .49 A1
  ◙ Limehouse E14 . .33 A2
Ospringe Ho ◙ SE1 . **121** C1
Ospringe Rd NW5 . . .13 B4
Osram Ct W6 . . . . .39 B3
Osric Path ◙ N1 . . .24 A3
Ossian Mews N4 . . . .5 B4
Ossian Rd N4 . . . . . .5 B4
Ossington Bldgs
  W1 . . . . **103** B3
Ossington Cl
  W2 . . . . 31 C2 **113** C3
Ossington St W2 . . **114** A3
Ossory Rd SE1 . . . . .49 C4
Ossulston St NW1 . .83 C2
Ostade Rd SW2 . . . .74 B4
Osten Mews SW7 . . **128** B1
Osterley Ho ◙
  E14 . . . . .34 A3
Osterley Rd N16 . . . .16 A4
Oswald Bldg SW8 . . **160** A3
Oswald's Mead E9 . .18 A4
Oswald Rd SW12,
  SW17 . . . . .72 B2
Oswell Ho ◙ E1 . . . .32 A1

Oswin St SE11 . . . . **150** B4
Oswyth Rd SE5 . . . .49 A1
Otford Cres SE4 . . . .66 B1
Otford Ho
  Bermondsey SE1 . . **137** C3
  ◙ Deptford SE15 . . .50 B4
Otha Ho ◙ SW9 . . . **172** B2
Othello Cl SE11 . . . **150** A2
Otis St E3 . . . . .27 B2
Otley Ho N5 . . . . . . .6 A1
Ottaway St E5 . . . . .7 C1
Ottaway St E5 . . . . .7 C1
Otterburn Ho ◙
  SE5 . . . . .48 B3
Otter Cl E15 . . . . . .27 B4
Otto St SE17 . . . . . .48 A4
Our Lady of Dolours
  RC Prim Sch W2 **100** A4
Our Lady of Lourdes
  RC Prim Sch
  SE13 . . . . .67 C4
Our Lady of Lourdes
  RC Sch NW10 . . . .20 B4
Our Lady of Victories
  RC Prim Sch
  Putney SW15 . . . . .57 C3
  South Kensington
  SW7 . . . . **143** A3
Our Lady Queen of
  Heaven RC Sch
  SW19 . . . . .69 C4
Our Lady RC Prim
  Sch
  Camden Town
  NW1 . . . . .83 A4
  Poplar E14 . . . . . . .33 B3
Our Lady & St Joseph
  RC Prim Sch N1 . . .16 A2
Our Lady's Convent
  RC High Sch N15 . . .7 A4
Ouseley Rd SW12 . . .72 B3
Outer Circ NW8 . . . .81 A1
Outgate Rd NW10 . . .8 B1
Outram Pl N1 . . . . .84 B4
Outwich St EC3 . . . **110** B2
Outwood Ho ◙
  SW2 . . . . .74 B4
Oval PI SW8 . . . . . **163** A2
Oval Prim Sch
  SE11 . . . . **163** B3
Oval Rd NW1 . . . . . .82 A4
Oval Sta SE11 . . . . **163** B3
Oval The E2 . . . . . . .25 A3
Oval The (Surrey Cnty
  Crkt Gd) SE11 . . . **163** A3
Oval Way SE11 . . . **149** A1
Overbury Ho ◙
  E5 . . . . .17 C4
Overbury Rd N15 . . . .7 C4
Overcliff Rd SE13 . . .66 C4
Overhill Rd SE21,
  SE22 . . . . .76 C4
Overlea Rd E5 . . . . . .7 C4
Oversley Ho ◙
  W2 . . . . .31 C4
Overstone Ho ◙
  E14 . . . . .33 C3
Overstone Rd W6 . . .39 B2
Overstrand Mans
  SW11 . . . . **169** B3
Overton Ho SW15 . .68 B4
Overton Rd SW9 . . **173** C1
Overy Ho SE1 . . . . **136** A3
Ovex Cl E14 . . . . . .42 B4
Ovington Ct SW3 . . **130** B1
Ovington Gdns
  SW3 . . . . **130** B1

Ovington Mews
  SW3 . . . . **130** B1
Ovington Sq SW3 . . **130** B1
Ovington St SW3 . . **144** B4
Owen Ho ⑪ N19 . . .5 A1
Owen's Ct EC1 . . . .96 A4
Owen's Row EC1 . . .96 A4
Owen St EC1 . . . . .86 A1
Owgan Cl SE5 . . . . .48 C3
Oxberry Ave SW6 . **164** B2
Oxbridge Ct ◙
  W4 . . . . .37 A1
Oxendon St SW1,
  W1 . . . . **119** B3
Oxenford St SE15 . . .64 B4
Oxenham Ho ◙
  SE8 . . . . .51 C4
Oxenholme NW1 . . .83 A1
Oxestalls Rd SE8 . . .41 A1
Oxford & Cambridge
  Mans NW1 . . . . . **102** B3
Oxford Cir W1 . . . . **104** C1
Oxford Circus Ave
  W1 . . . . **104** C1
Oxford Circus Sta
  W1 . . . . **104** C1
Oxford Ct
  City of London
  EC4 . . . . **123** B4
  Gunnersbury W4 . . .37 A1
  ◙ Paddington W2 . .31 C4
Oxford Dr SE1 . . . . **124** A1
Oxford Gardens Prim
  Sch W10 . . . . .30 C3
Oxford Gate W6 . . .39 C2
Oxford Gdns
  Brentford W4 . . . . . .44 C4
  North Kensington
  W10 . . . . .30 C3
Oxford Ho N4 . . . . . .5 C3
Oxford Rd
  Finsbury Pk N4 . . . . .5 C3
  Paddington NW6 . . .23 C3
  Putney SW15 . . . . .58 A3
  Stratford E15 . . . . .19 C2
Oxford Rd N SW4 . . .37 A1
Oxford Rd S W4 . . . .37 A1
Oxford Sq W2 . . . . **102** B1
Oxford St W1 . . . . **104** B1
Oxley Cl SE1 . . . . . **153** A2
Oxonian St SE22 . . .64 B3
Oxo Tower Wharf
  SE1 . . . . **121** C3
Oxo Twr* SE1 . . . . **121** C3
Oxted Ct N16 . . . . . .7 A3
Oyster Row E1 . . . .32 B3
Ozolins Way E16 . . .35 C3

P

Pablo Neruda Cl ◙
  SE24 . . . . .63 A3
Pace PI E1 . . . . . . .32 A3
Pacific Ho ◙ E1 . . . .25 C1
Pacific Rd E16 . . . . .35 C3
Pacific Wharf
  SE16 . . . . .32 C1
Packenham Ho
  ❷ Crouch End N19 . .4 C4
  ◙ 24 B2 **99** A4
  Spitalfields
Packington Sq N1 . .86 C4
Packington St N1 . . .86 B3
Padbury SE17 . . . . **152** B1
Padbury Ct
  E2 . . . . 24 B2 **99** A3

Padbury Ho NW8 . . .90 B2
Paddenswick Ct ◙
  W6 . . . . .39 A3
Paddenswick Rd
  W6 . . . . .38 C3
PADDINGTON ⑦ . .31 C2
Paddington Acad
  Paddington W9 . . . **101** B3
  Paddington W9 . . . .23 C1
Paddington Com
  Hospl W9 . . . . . . .31 C4
Paddington Gn
  W2 . . . . **101** B4
Paddington Green
  Prim Sch NW8 . . .89 B1
Paddington St
  W1 . . . . **103** B4
Paddington Sta
  W2 . . . . **101** B2
Paddock Cl SE3 . . . .53 C1
Paddock Sch
  SW15 . . . . .56 B3
Padfield Rd SE5 . . . .63 B4
Padstow Ho ◙
  E3 . . . . .27 A2
Padstow Ho ◙
  E14 . . . . .33 B2
Pagden St SW8 . . . **170** B4
Pageant Cres
  SE16 . . . . .33 B1
Pageantmaster Ct
  EC4 . . . . **108** A1
Page Ho ◙ SE10 . . .52 B4
Page's Wlk SE1 . . . **138** B1
Page's Yd W4 . . . . .46 A4
Paget Ho ◙ E2 . . . .25 B3
Paget Rd N16 . . . . . .6 C3
Paget St EC1 . . . . .96 A4
Pagham Ho ◙
  W10 . . . . .22 B1
Pagnell St SE14 . . . .51 B3
Pagoda Ave TW9 . . .54 B4
Pagoda Gdns SE3 . .52 C1
Pagoda Gr SE27 . . .75 B2
Paine Ct SE3 . . . . . .53 B4
Painsthorpe Rd ◙
  N16 . . . . .7 A1
Painswick Ct ◙
  SE15 . . . . .49 B3
Painters Mews
  SE16 . . . . **153** C4
Pakeman Ho SE1 . . **136** B4
Pakeman Prim Sch
  N7 . . . . .5 B1
Pakeman St N7 . . . . .5 B1
Pakenham Cl
  SW12 . . . . .72 C3
Pakenham St WC1 . .95 A2
Palace Ave W8 . . . **128** B4
Palace Ct
  Hampstead NW3 . . .11 A3
  Kensington W2 . . . **114** A3
  Streatham SW2 . . . .74 C2
Palace Garden Mews
  W8 . . . . 31 C1 **113** C2
Palace Gate W8 . . . **128** C3
Palace Gdns Mews
  W8 . . . . **114** A3
Palace Gn W8 . . . . **114** A4
Palace Mans
  W14 . . . . **140** B4
Palace Mews
  Belgravia SW1 . . . **145** C3
  Fulham SW6 . . . . . **155** A2

Palace Pl SW1 ... **132** C2
Palace Rd SE27, SW16,
  SW2 .... **74** C2
Palace St SW1 ... **132** C2
Palatine Ave N16 ...16 A4
Palatine Rd N16 .....16 A4
Palazzo Apartments
  11 N1 ....16 A1
Palemead Cl SW6 ..47 C2
Palermo Rd NW10 ..21 C3
Palewell Common Dr
  SW14 ....55 C2
Palewell Pk SW14 .55 C3
Palfrey Pl SW8 ..**163** A2
Palgrave Gdns
  NW1 ....**90** B2
Palgrave Ho
  7 Camberwell
  SE5 ....48 B3
  4 Maitland Pk
  NW3 ....12 B3
Palgrave Rd W12 ..38 B3
Palissy St
  E2 ....24 B2 **98** C3
Pallant Ho SE1 ..**137** C1
Pallester Ct NW11 ...1 A3
Palliser Ct W14 ..**140** A1
Palliser Ho
  3 Greenwich
  SE10 ....52 C4
  7 Stepney E1 ...25 C1
Palliser Rd W14 .**140** A1
Palliser Terr
  SW15 ....68 B2
Pall Mall SW1 ...**119** B1
Pall Mall E SW1 .**119** C2
Pall Mall Pl SW1 **119** A1
Palm Ct
  18 Camberwell
  SE15 ....49 B3
  Stoke Newington N16 .6 C2
Palmer Ho
  8 Deptford SE14 .50 C3
  8 Kentish Town
  NW5 ....13 B4
  5 Tufnell Pk N19 ...4 B1
Palmer Pl N7 .....14 C3
Palmers Rd
  Globe Town E2 ...25 C3
  Mortlake SW14 ...55 B4
Palmer St SW1 ...**133** B2
Palmerston Ct 22
  E3 ....25 C3
Palmerston Ho
  Battersea SW11 .**169** C3
  Kensington
  W8 ....31 C1 **113** B1
Palmerston Rd
  Acton Green W3 ...37 B3
  Brondesbury NW6 ..10 B1
  Hampstead NW6 ...10 C1
  Mortlake SW14 ...55 B3
Palmerston Way
  SW8 ....**160** B1
Palm Gr W5 ....36 A3
Palm Tree Ho 2
  SE14 ....50 C3
Pamela Ct NW10 ...8 C1
Pamela Ho 8 E8 ..24 B4
Pamlion Ct N4 .....5 A4
Panama Ho 8 E1 ..32 C4
Pancras La EC2 ..**109** B1
Pancras Rd N1 ....**83** C2
Pandian Way 4
  NW5 ....13 C3
Pandora Rd NW6 ..10 C2
Pangbourne NW1 ..**92** C3

Pangbourne Ave
  W10 ....30 B4
Pangbourne Ho 4
  N7 ....14 B3
Pankhurst Cl 7
  SE14 ....50 C3
Pankhurst Ho 2
  NW10 ....30 B3
Panmure Cl N5 ....15 A4
Pansy Gdns W12 ..29 C2
Panton St SW1 ...**119** B3
Panyer Alley EC2 **108** C2
Paper Mill Wharf
  E14 ....33 A2
Papworth Gdns
  N7 ....14 B3
Papworth Way
  SW2 ....74 C4
Parade Mans 19
  SE27 ....48 B1
Parade Mews SE27,
  SW2 ....75 A2
Parade The SW11 **159** A2
Paradise Pas N7 ..14 C3
Paradise Rd
  Richmond TW10 ..54 A2
  South Lambeth
  SW4 ....**172** A2
Paradise Row E2 ..25 A2
Paradise St SE16 ..40 A4
Paradise Wlk
  SW3 ....**159** A4
Paragon Cl E16 ...35 C3
Paragon Ho SE3 ..53 B1
Paragon Mews
  SE1 ....**151** C4
Paragon Pl SE3 ...53 B1
Paragon Rd E9 ....17 B2
Paragon The
  Kidbrooke SE3 ...53 C1
  Walworth SE17 ..**151** C4
Paramount Bldg
  EC1 ....**96** A2
Paramount Ct
  WC1 ....**93** A1
Parbury Rd SE23 ..66 A1
Pardoner St SE1 .**137** C2
Pardon St EC1 .....**96** B2
Parfett St E1 ....**111** C2
Parfitt Cl NW11 ....2 B3
Parfrey St W6 .....47 B4
Paris Gdn SE1 ...**122** A2
Paris Ho 12 E2 ....25 A3
Park Ave
  Golders Green
  NW11 ....2 A3
  Mortlake SW14 ...55 C3
  Willesden NW2 ....9 B2
Park Ave N NW10 ...9 A3
Park Cl
  Kensington W14 .**127** A3
  Knightsbridge SW1 **130** C3
  13 South Hackney
  E9 ....25 B4
Park Cres W1 .....**92** B1
Park Crescent Mews
  E W1 ....**92** B1
Park Crescent Mews
  W W1 ....**92** A1
Park Ct
  Battersea SW11 .**170** A4
  Clapham Pk SW4 ..61 C2
  Dulwich SE21 ....75 C1
  3 Hammersmith
  W6 ....38 C2
  Upper Tooting
  SW12 ....72 C3

Park Dr Acton W3 ..36 C3
  Golders Green NW11 ..2 A3
  Mortlake SW14 ...55 C3
Park Dwellings 7
  NW3 ....12 B3
Park End NW3 .....12 A4
Parker Ct
  Shoreditch N1 ....**87** A4
  South Lambeth
  SW4 ....**172** A3
Parke Rd SW13 ...46 C2
Parker Mews
  WC2 ....**106** B2
Parkers Row
  SE16 ....**139** B3
Parker's Row SE1 **139** A3
Parker St WC2 ...**106** B2
Parkfield Ave
  SW14 ....56 A3
Parkfield Ct SE14 .51 B2
Parkfield Ind Est
  SW11 ....**169** C2
Parkfield Rd
  New Cross SE14 ..51 B2
  Willesden NW10 ...9 A1
Parkfields SW15 ..57 B3
Parkfield St N1 ....**85** C2
Park Flats N6 ......3 A4
Parkgate Gdns
  SW14 ....55 C2
Parkgate House Sch
  SW11 ....60 C3
Parkgate Mews N6 .4 B4
Parkgate Rd
  SW11 ....**158** B1
Park Hall SE10 ....52 C3
Park Hall Rd SE21 .75 C1
Park Hall Road Trad
  Est SE21 ....75 C1
Parkham St
  SW11 ....**168** A3
Park Heights 21
  E14 ....33 B3
Park Hill
  Clapham SW4 ....61 C2
  Richmond TW10 ..54 B2
Park Hill Ct SW17 .72 B1
Parkhill Rd NW3 ..12 B3
Park Hill Wlk 12
  NW3 ....12 B3
Park Ho
  6 Camberwell
  SE5 ....48 C2
  Finsbury Pk N4 ....6 A2
  25 Hackney E9 ...17 B1
Parkholme Rd E8 ..16 C2
Parkhouse St SE5 .48 C3
Parkhurst Ct N7 ..14 A4
Parkhurst Rd N7 ..14 A4
Parkinson Ct
  Finsbury N1 ......**97** B3
  Shoreditch EC1 ...**97** C4
Parkinson Ho 6
  E9 ....25 B4
Park La
  Mayfair W1 .....**117** B3
  Mill Meads E15 ...27 C4
Parkland Ct W14 .**126** A4
Parkland Gdns 12
  SW19 ....69 C3
Parklands
  East Dulwich SE22 .65 A2
  Highgate N6 ......4 A4
Parklands Cl
  SW14 ....55 B2
Park Lea Ct N16 ...7 A4

Park Lo
  11 South Hampstead
  NW8 ....11 C1
  16 Wapping E1 ...32 A1
  Willesden NW2 ....9 B4
Park Lofts 5 SW4 ..62 A2
Park Lorne NW8 ..**90** B3
Park Mans
  Battersea SW11 .**168** C3
  Bedford Pk W6 ...38 B3
  Fulham SW6 ....**164** B3
  Knightsbridge SW1 **130** C3
  St John's Wood
  NW8 ....**80** A1
  Vauxhall SW8 ...**162** C2
Parkmead SW15 ..57 A1
Park Mews
  Greenwich SE10 ..43 B1
  Kensal Rise W10 ..23 A3
Park Par Acton W3 .36 C3
Park Piazza 6
  SE10 ....52 C4
Park Place Villas
  W2 ....**101** A4
Park Rd
  Chiswick W4 .....45 C4
  Dagenham NW10 ..21 A4
  Lisson Gr NW1,
  NW8 ....**90** B2
  Richmond TW10 ..54 B1
Park Rd E W3 ....37 B4
Park Rd N
  Chiswick W4 .....37 C1
  South Acton W3 ..37 A4
Park Road E 11
  W3 ....37 A4
Park Row SE10 ...52 C4
PARK ROYAL 20 A2
Park Royal NW10 ..20 A3
Park Royal Bsns Ctr
  NW10 ....20 B1
Park Royal Metro Ctr
  NW10 ....20 B1
Park Royal Rd NW10,
  W3 ....20 B1
Park S SW11 .....**169** B3
Park St James
  NW8 ....**80** C3
Park Sheen 3
  SW14 ....55 A3
Parkshot TW9 .....54 A3
Parkside
  East Acton W3 ...29 A1
  Greenwich SE3 ...53 B3
Park Side NW2 ....9 A4
Parkside Bsns Est
  SE8 ....51 A4
Parkside Cres N7 ..5 C1
Parkside Est 99 ...25 C4
Parkside (private)
  Hospl SW19 .....69 C1
Park Sq E NW1 ....**92** B2
Park Square Mews
  NW1 ....**92** A1
Park Sq W NW1 ...**92** A1
Park St
  Borough The SE1 .**123** A2
  Mayfair W1 .....**117** B3

Parkstead Rd
  SW15 ....**57** A2
Parkstone Rd 5
  SE15 ....49 C1
Park Stps SW17 ..**116** B4
Park The NW11 ....2 A3
Parkthorne Rd
  SW12 ....73 C4
Park Twrs W1 ....**118** A3
Park View
  Dagenham W3 ...28 B4
  Highbury N5 .....15 B4
  Willesden NW2 ....9 B4
Parkview Ct SW6 **164** B3
Park View Ct
  SW18 ....**58** C1
Park View Ho
  SE24 ....**63** A1
Park View Mews
  N4 ....6 A4
Park View Mews
  SW9 ....**172** C2
Park View Rd
  NW10 ....8 B4
Park Village E
  NW1 ....**82** B1
Park Village W
  NW1 ....**82** A2
Parkville Rd SW6 **154** C1
Park Vista SE10 ...52 C4
Park Walk Prim Sch
  SW10 ....**157** B3
Parkway NW1 .....**82** A3
Park Way N8 ......36 C2
Parkway Ho SW14 .55 C3
Park West W2 ....**102** B1
Park West Pl W1,
  W2 ....**102** B2
Park Wlk
  Chelsea SW10 ...**157** B4
  Highgate N6 ......**3** C4
Parkwood NW8 ...**80** C3
Parkwood Prim Sch
  N4 ....6 A2
Parliament Ct
  NW3 ....12 B4
Parliament Hill
  NW3 ....12 A4
Parliament Hill Mans
  NW5 ....12 C4
Parliament Hill Sch
  NW5 ....12 C4
Parliament Mews
  SW14 ....45 B1
Parliament Sq*
  SW1 ....**134** A3
Parliament St
  SW1 ....**134** A4
Parliament View
  Apartments
  SE11 ....**148** C4
Parma Cres SW11 .60 B3
Parminter Ind Est 24
  E2 ....25 A3
Parmiter St E2 ....25 A3
Parmoor Ct EC1 ...**96** C2
Parnell Cl W12 ....39 A3
Parnell Ho WC1 ..**105** C2
Parnell Rd E3 .....26 B4
Parnham St E14 ..33 A3
Parolles Rd N19 ...4 B3
Parr Ct N1 ....**87** B2
Parrington Ho 1
  SW4 ....61 C1
Parr Pl W4 ....38 B2

Parr St N1 . . . . 87 B2
Parry Ho 52 E1 . . . . 32 A1
Parry Rd W10 . . . . . 23 A2
Parry St SW8 . . . . . 162 B4
Parsifal Coll NW3 . . .10 C4
Parsifal Ho NW3 . . . .10 C4
Parsifal Rd NW3 . . . .10 C4
Parsonage St E14 . . .42 B2
Parsons Gn SW6 . . . 165 B3
PARSONS GREEN
. . . . 165 B4
Parsons Green La
SW6 . . . . 165 B4
Parsons Green Sta
SW6 . . . . 165 B4
Parsons Ho
Paddington W2 . . . . 89 B1
5 Streatham
SW12 . . . . .74 A4
Parsons Lo NW6 . . . .11 A1
Parthenia Rd
SW6 . . . . 165 C3
Partington Cl N19 . . . .4 C3
Parton Lo 114 E8 . . . 16 B2
Partridge Ct EC1 . . . 96 A2
Partridge Ho 2
E3 . . . . 26 B3
Pascall Ho SE17 . . . .48 B4
Pascal St SW8 . . . . 161 C2
Pascoe Rd SE13 . . . .67 C2
Pasley Cl SE17 . . . . 150 C1
Passfield Dr E14 . . . .34 A4
Passfields W14 . . . . 140 C1
Passing Alley EC1 . . . 96 B1
Passmore St SW1 145 B2
Pastor St SE1,
SE11 . . . . 150 B4
Patcham Terr
SW8 . . . . 170 B4
Patent Ho E14 . . . . . 34 A4
Paternoster La
EC4 . . . . 108 B2
Paternoster Row EC2,
EC4 . . . . 108 C1
Paternoster Sq
EC4 . . . . 108 B2
Pater St W8 . . . . . . 127 B1
Patience Rd
SW11 . . . . 168 A1
Patience Villas
SE13 . . . . .67 C4
Patio Cl SW4 . . . . . .61 C1
Patmore Ho 9
N16 . . . . .16 A3
Patmore St SW8 . . . 171 A4
Patmos Rd SW9 . . . .48 A2
Paton Cl E3 . . . . . . .26 C2
Paton Ho SW9 . . . . 172 C2
Paton St EC1 . . . . . . 96 C3
Patrick Coman Ho
EC1 . . . . 96 A3
Patrick Connolly Gdns
41 E3 . . . . .27 A2
Patriot Sq E2 . . . . . .25 A3
Patrol Pl SE6 . . . . . .67 A1
Pat Shaw Ho 2
E1 . . . . .25 C1
Patshull Pl NW5 . . . .13 B2
Patshull Rd NW5 . . . .13 B2
Patten Ho N4 . . . . . . .6 B3
Patten Rd SW18 . . . .72 A4
Patterdale NW1 . . . . 92 B3
Patterdale Rd
SE15 . . . . .50 B3
Pattina Wlk SE16 . . . .33 A1

Pattison Point 10
E16 . . . . .35 C4
Pattison Ho
Borough The SE1 . . 137 A4
1 Stepney E1 . . . . . 32 C3
Pattison Rd NW2 . . . .1 C1
Pat Williams Ho
SE27 . . . . .75 B1
Paul Daisley Ct 2
NW6 . . . . .10 A1
Paulet Rd SE5 . . . . . 48 A2
Paul Ho 18 W10 . . . .23 A1
Pauline Ho E1 . . . . . 111 C4
Paul Julius Cl E14 . . 34 C2
Paul St EC2 . . 24 A1 98 A2
Paultons Sq SW3 . . 157 C4
Paultons Sq SW3 . . 157 C3
Paultons St SW3 . . . 157 C3
Pauntley St 4 N19 . . .4 B3
Pavan Ct 8 E2 . . . . . 25 B2
Paveley Dr SW11 . . . 158 A1
Paveley Ho N1 . . . . . 84 C1
Paveley St NW8 . . . . 90 B2
Pavement The
Brentford W5 . . . . . 36 A3
Clapham SW4 . . . . . 61 B3
Pavilion Ct
1 Hampstead
NW3 . . . . .11 B4
Hampstead NW3 . . . 11 C3
8 Paddington NW6 . . 23 C2
Pavilion Mans 10
SW9 . . . . .62 B3
Pavilion Rd SW1 . . . 131 A1
Pavilion Sq SW17 . . 72 B1
Pavilion St SW1 . . . . 131 A1
Pavilion Terr 8
W12 . . . . .30 B3
Pavillion Ct SW1 . . . 160 A4
Pavitt Ct NW10 . . . . . .8 C1
Paxton Cl TW9 . . . . .44 B1
Paxton Ho SE17 . . . 151 A2
Paxton Rd W4 . . . . . 46 A4
Paxton Terr SW1 . . . 160 B4
Paymal Ho 33 E1 . . . 32 B4
Payne Ho N1 . . . . . . 85 A3
Payne Rd E3 . . . . . . 27 A3
Paynesfield Ave
SW14 . . . . .55 C4
Payne St SE8 . . . . . . 51 B4
Paynes Wlk W6 . . . . 154 A3
Peabody Ave
SW1 . . . . 146 B3
Peabody Bldgs
6 Camberwell
SE5 . . . . 48 C2
Walworth SE17 . . . . 151 B3
Peabody Cl SW1 . . . 160 B4
Peabody Ct
5 Camberwell
SE5 . . . . 48 C2
St Luke's EC1 . . . . . 97 A1
Peabody Est
16 Bethnal Green
E2 . . . . .25 A3
Borough The SE1 . . 122 C1
Fulham SW6 . . . . . . 155 A4
4 Hammersmith
W6 . . . . .39 B1
Holborn EC1 . . . . . . 95 C1
Lambeth SE1 . . . . . 121 C1
North Kensington
W10 . . . . .30 B4
4 Ratcliff E1 . . . . . . 32 C2
St George in East
E1 . . . . 125 B4

Peabody Est continued
St Luke's EC1 . . . . . 97 A1
Strand WC2 . . . . . . 106 C1
Streatham SE24 . . . .75 B4
Westminster SW1 . . 147 A4
Peabody Hill SE21 . . 75 B3
Peabody Sq 1 . . . . 136 A3
Peabody Twr EC1 . . . 97 A1
Peabody Yd N1 . . . . 86 C4
Peach Rd W10 . . . . . 23 A2
Peachum Rd SE3 . . . 53 B4
Peach Walk Mews 24
E3 . . . . .26 A3
Peacock St SE17 . . . 150 B3
Peacock Yd SE17 . . 150 B3
Peak Ho N4 . . . . .6 B3
Pearce Ho
Camden Town N19 . . 4 B1
7 Brentford TW8 . . . 36 B1
College Pk NW10 . . .22 A2
8 Streatham SW2 . . 74 A4
Westminster SW1 . . 147 C3
Pear Cl SE14 . . . . . . 51 A3
Pear Ct 21 SE15 . . . .49 B3
Peardon St SW8 . . . 170 B1
Pearfield Ho 1
N5 . . . . .15 B3
Pearl St E1 . . . . 32 A1
Pearman St SE1 . . . 135 C3
Pear Pl SE1 . . . . . . 135 B4
Pearscroft Ct
SW6 . . . . 166 B3
Pearscroft Rd
SW6 . . . . 166 B3
Pearse St 3 SE5 . . . .49 A4
Pearson Cl 4 SE5 . . .48 B2
Pearson Ho SW15 . . .47 B1
Pearson's Ave SE8,
SE14 . . . . .51 C2
Pearson St E2 . . . . . 24 B3
Peartree Ave
SW17 . . . . .71 B1
Pear Tree Cl 23
E2 . . . . .24 B4
Pear Tree Ct
Holborn EC1 . . . . . . 95 C1
Putney SW15 . . . . . .57 A3
Pear Tree Ho SE4 . . .66 B3
Peartree La E1 . . . . . 32 B2
Peartree St EC1 . . . . 96 C2
Peartree Way
SE10 . . . . .43 C2
Peary Pl E2 . . . . 25 B2
Peckarmans Wood
SE21, SE26 . . . . . . .76 C1
Peckett Sq 3 N5 . . . .15 A4
Peckford Pl SW9 . . . 173 C1
PECKHAM 49 C1
Peckham Gr SE15 . . 49 A3
Peckham High St
SE15 . . . . .49 C2
Peckham Hill St
SE15 . . . . .49 C3
Peckham Park Prim
Sch SE15 . . . . .49 C3
Peckham Park Rd
SE15 . . . . .49 C3
Peckham Rd SE5 . . . 49 A2
Peckham Rye
East Dulwich SE22 . . 64 C3
Peckham SE15,
SE22 . . . . .65 A3
Peckham Rye Sta
SE15 . . . . .49 C1
Peckwater Ho 2
NW5 . . . . .13 C2

Peckwater St
NW5 . . . . .13 B3
Pedlars Wlk N7 . . . . 14 A3
Pedley St
E1 . . . . 24 B1 99 A1
Pedro St E5 . . . . . . .17 C4
Pedworth Gdns 4
SE16 . . . . .40 B2
Peel Gr E2 . . . . 25 B3
Peel Pass
W8 . . . . 31 C1 113 B1
Peel Prec NW6 . . . . .23 C3
Peel St W8 . 31 C1 113 B1
Peerless St EC1 . . . . 97 B3
Pegasus Cl N16 . . . . 15 C4
Pegasus Ct
11 Acton W3 . . . . . .28 B3
Brentford TW8 . . . . .36 B1
College Pk NW10 . . .22 A2
Pegasus Ho 8 E1 . . .25 C1
Pegwell Ho 6 E5 . . . 17 A3
Pekin St E14 . . . . . . 33 C3
Pekoe SE1 . . . . 125 A1
Peldon Ct TW10 . . . .54 B2
Pelham Cl SE5 . . . . . 64 A4
Pelham Cres
SW7 . . . . 144 A3
Pelham Ct SW3 . . . . 144 A3
Pelham Ho W14 . . . 140 C3
Pelham Pl SW7 . . . . 144 A3
Pelham St SW7 . . . . 143 C4
Pelican Ho 8 SE8 . . .41 B2
Pelican Pas 3 E1 . . . 25 B1
Pelier St SE17 . . . . . 48 B4
Pella Ho SE11 . . . . . 149 A2
Pellant Rd SW6 . . . . 154 B2
Pellatt Rd SE22 . . . . 64 B2
Pellerin Rd N16 . . . . 16 A3
Pelling St E14 . . . . . 33 C3
Pelter St E2 . . 24 B2 98 C4
Pelton Rd SE10 . . . . 43 A1
Pember Rd NW10 . . .22 C2
Pemberton Ct 18
E1 . . . . .25 C2
Pemberton Gdns
N19 . . . . .4 B1
Pemberton Pl 2
E8 . . . . .17 A1
Pemberton Row
EC4 . . . . 107 C2
Pemberton Terr
N19 . . . . .4 B1
Pembridge Cres
W2 . . . . 31 C2 113 B4
Pembridge Gdns
W2 . . . . 31 C2 113 B3
Pembridge Hall Sch
W2 . . . . 113 C3
Pembridge Mews
W11 . . . . . . 31 C2 113 B4
Pembridge Pl
Notting Hill
W2 . . . . 31 C2 113 B4
1 Wandsworth
SW15 . . . . .58 C2
Pembridge Rd
W11 . . . . . . 31 C2 113 B3
Pembridge Sq
W2 . . . . 31 C2 113 C3
Pembridge Villas
W11 . . . . . . 31 C2 113 B4
Pembroke W14 . . . . 141 A3
Pembroke Ave N1 . . .84 B4
Pembroke Bldgs
NW10 . . . . .21 C2

Pembroke Cl
SW1 . . . . 131 C3
Pembroke Gdns
W8 . . . . 141 A4
Pembroke Gdns Cl
W8 . . . . 127 B1
Pembroke Ho
Acton W3 . . . . 37 B4
Chelsea SW1 . . . . . 131 B1
8 Clapham Pk
SW2 . . . . .62 A2
Kensington W2 . . . . 100 B1
Putney SW15 . . . . . .56 C2
Pembroke Lo 2
SW16 . . . . .74 B1
Pembroke Mews
8 Bow E3 . . . . 26 A3
Kensington W8 . . . . 127 B1
Pembroke Pl W8 . . . 127 B1
Pembroke Rd W8 . . 141 B4
Pembroke Sq W8 . . 127 B1
Pembroke St N1 . . . . 84 B4
Pembroke Studios
W8 . . . . 127 A1
Pembroke Terr
NW8 . . . . 79 B3
Pembroke Villas
W8 . . . . 141 B4
Pembroke Wlk
W8 . . . . 141 B4
Pembury Cl E5 . . . . . 17 A3
Pembury Ho SE5 . . . 49 A1
Pembury Pl 18 E5,
E8 . . . . .17 A3
Pembury Rd E5 . . . . 17 A3
Pemell Cl 30 E1 . . . . 25 B1
Pemell Ho 31 E1 . . . 25 B1
Penally Pl N1 . . . . . . 87 C4
Penang St E1 . . . . . . 32 A1
Penarth Ctr The
SE15 . . . . .50 B4
Penarth St SE15 . . . 50 B4
Pencombe Mews
W11 . . . . . . 31 B2 113 A4
Pencraig Way
SE15 . . . . .50 A4
Penda's Mead E9 . . .18 A4
Pendennis Ho 15
E8 . . . . .41 A2
Penderyn Way N7 . . .13 C4
Pendle Ho 11
SE26 . . . . .76 C1
Pendley Ho 18 E2 . . 24 C4
Pendrell Ho WC2 . . . 105 C1
Pendrell Rd SE4 . . . .51 A1
Penelope Ho
SW9 . . . . 173 B3
Penfield Lo 6 W9 . . . 31 C4
Penfields Ho N7 . . . .14 A2
Penfold Pl NW1 . . . . 102 A4
Penfold St NW8 . . . . 89 C1
Penford St SE5 . . . . 48 A1
Penhurst Mans
SW6 . . . . 164 C4
Peninsula Ct E14 . . . 42 A3
Peninsular Park Rd
SE7 . . . . .43 C2
Penmayne Ho
SE11 . . . . 149 C2
Pennack Rd SE15 . . 49 B4
Penn Almshouses 7
SE10 . . . . .52 B2
Pennant Mews
W8 . . . . 142 A4
Pennard Mans 5
W12 . . . . 39 B4
Pennard Rd W12 . . . 39 B4

Pennefather Ho
N1 . . . . 15 C2
Penner Cl SW19 . . . . 70 A2
Pennethorne Cl
E9 . . . . 25 B4
Pennethorne Ho
SW11 . . . . 59 C4
Pennethorne Rd
SE15 . . . . 50 A3
Penn Ho NW8 . . . . . 90 A1
Pennine La E14 . . . . 1 A2
Pennine Mans NW2 . . 1 A2
Pennine Par NW2 . . 1 A2
Pennington Ct
4 Rotherhithe
SE16 . . . . 33 A1
St George in t East
E1 . . . . 125 C3
Pennington St E1 . . 32 A2
Penn Rd N7 . . . . 14 A4
Penny St SW10 . . . . 157 A4
Pennyfields E14 . . . 33 C2
Pennyford Ct NW8 . 89 B2
Penny Mews
SW12 . . . . 73 A4
Pennymore Wlk
W9 . . . . 23 B1
Penny Rd NW10 . . . 20 A2
Penpoll Rd E8 . . . . . 17 A2
Penrhyn Cres
SW14 . . . . 55 B3
Penrith Cl SW15 . . . 58 A2
Penrith Pl SE27 . . . . 75 A2
Penrose Gr SE17 . . 150 C1
Penrose Ho SE17 . . 150 C1
Penrose St SE17 . . 150 C1
Penryn Ho SE11 . . 150 A2
Penryn St NW1 . . . . 83 B2
Penry St SE1 . . . . . 152 B3
Pensbury Pl SW8 . . 171 A2
Pensbury St SW8 . . 171 A2
Pensford Ave
TW9 . . . . 44 C1
Penshurst **2** NW5 . 12 C2
Penshurst Ho **10**
SE15 . . . . 50 B4
Penshurst Rd E9 . . . 17 C1
Pentland Cl NW11 . . 1 A2
Pentland Gdns
SW18 . . . . 59 B1
Pentland Ho
17 Camden Town
NW5 . . . . 12 C2
7 Stamford Hill N16 . 7 B3
Pentland Rd **1**
NW6 . . . . 23 C2
Pentland St SW18 . . 59 B1
Pentlow St SW15 . . 57 B4
Pentney Rd SW12 . . 73 B3
Penton Gr N1 . . . . . 85 B1
Penton Ho N1 . . . . . 85 B1
Penton Pl SE17 . . . 150 B2
Penton Rise WC1 . . 95 A4
Penton St N1 . . . . . . 85 B1
PENTONVILLE 85 A1
Pentonville Rd N1 . . 84 C1
Pentridge St SE15 . . 49 B3
Penwith Rd SW18 . . 71 A2
Penwood Ho
SW15 . . . . 56 B1
Penywern Rd
SW5 . . . . 141 C2
Penzance Ho
SE11 . . . . 149 C2
Penzance Pl
W11 . . . . 31 A1 **112** B2

Penzance St
W11 . . . . 31 A1 **112** A2
Peony Gdns W12 . . . 29 C2
Peperfield WC1 . . . . 94 C3
Pepler Ho **17** W10 . . 23 A1
Pepler Mews SE1 . . 152 C1
Peploe Rd NW6 . . . . 22 C3
Peppermead Sq
SE13 . . . . 66 C2
Pepper St
Borough The SE1 . . 136 C4
Millwall E14 . . . . . . 42 A3
Peppie Cl N16 . . . . . . 7 A2
Pepsi Trocadero *
W1 . . . . 119 B4
Pepys Cres **2** E16 . 35 C1
Pepys Ent Ctr **13**
SE8 . . . . 41 B2
Pepys Ho
4 Bethnal Green
E2 . . . . 25 B2
Clapham Pk SW4 . . 61 C2
Pepys Rd SE14 . . . . 50 C1
Pepys St EC3 . . . . 124 B4
Perceval Ave NW3 . 12 A3
Percheron Ct **3**
SW9 . . . . 62 B4
Perch St E8 . . . . 16 B4
Percival Rd SW14 . . 55 B3
Percival St EC1 . . . . 96 B3
Percy Cir WC1 . . . . . 95 A4
Percy Laurie Ho **6**
SW15 . . . . 57 C3
Percy Mews W1 . . . 105 B3
Percy Pas W1 . . . . . 105 B3
Percy Rd
Newham E16 . . . . . 35 A4
Shepherd's Bush
W12 . . . . 38 C4
Percy St W1 . . . . . . 105 B3
Peregrine Ho
6 Battersea
SW11 . . . . 60 A4
Finsbury EC1 . . . . . . 96 B4
Perham Rd W14 . . . 140 B1
Perifield SE21 . . . . . 75 B3
Perkins Ho **15** E14 . 33 B4
Perkins Rents
SW1 . . . . 133 B1
Perkins Sq SE1 . . . 123 A2
Perley Ho **3** E3 . . . . 33 B4
Perotti Ho SW6 . . . . 59 A4
Perran Ct SE24,
SW2 . . . . 75 A2
Perren St NW5 . . . . 13 A2
Perrers Rd W6 . . . . 39 A2
Perring Est E3 . . . . . 33 C4
Perrin's Ct **20**
NW3 . . . . 11 B4
Perrin's La NW3 . . . 11 B4
Perrin's Wlk NW3 . . 11 B4
Perronet Ho SE1 . . 136 B1
Perry Ave W3 . . . . . 28 C3
Perry Ct **6** E14 . . . . 41 C1
Perry Ho **24** SW2 . . 74 A4
Perrymead St
SW6 . . . . 166 A3
Perryn Ho W3 . . . . . 29 A2
Perryn Rd
Acton W3 . . . . 28 C2
1 Bermondsey
SE16 . . . . 40 A3
Perry's Pl W1 . . . . . 105 B2
Perrywood Ho **17**
E5 . . . . 17 A3
Perseverance Works
E2 . . . . 24 A2 **98** A4

Perth Ct **5** SE5 . . . 63 C3
Perth Ho N1 . . . . . . 14 B1
Perth Rd N4 . . . . 5 C3
Petchey Acad The
E8 . . . . 16 B3
Peter Ave NW10 . . . . 9 A1
Peter Best Ho **1**
E1 . . . . 32 B3
Peterboat Cl SE10 . . 43 A2
Peterborough Ct
EC4 . . . . 107 C1
Peterborough Mews
SW6 . . . . 165 B2
Peterborough Prim
Sch SW6 . . . . 165 C1
Peterborough Rd
SW6 . . . . 58 C4
Peterborough Villas
SW6 . . . . 166 A4
Peter Butler Ho
SE1 . . . . 139 B3
Peterchurch Ho
SE15 . . . . 50 A4
Petergate SW11 . . . 59 B3
Peter Heathfield Ho
4 E15 . . . . 27 C4
Peter Hills Ho **6**
SE16 . . . . 153 B4
Peter Hills with St
Mary's & St Paul's CE
Prim Sch SE16 . . . 32 C1
Peter Ho SW8 . . . . 162 A2
Peter James Ent Ctr
NW10 . . . . 20 B2
Peterley Bsns Ctr **21**
E2 . . . . 25 A3
Peters Ct **2** W2 . . 100 B2
Peter's Ct SW4 . . . . 62 A1
Petersfield Rd W3 . . 37 B4
Petersfield Rise
SW15 . . . . 69 A3
Petersham Ho
SW7 . . . . 143 B4
Petersham La
SW7 . . . . 128 C2
Petersham Mews
SW7 . . . . 129 A1
Petersham Pl
SW7 . . . . 129 A2
Peter's La EC1 . . . . 108 B4
Petrarch ST SE21 . . 75 C2
Peterstow Cl
SW19 . . . . 70 A2
Petherton Ct
NW10 . . . . 22 C2
Petherton Ho N4 . . . 6 B3
Petherton Rd N5 . . . 15 B3
Petiver Cl **22** E9 . . . 17 B1
Petley Rd W6 . . . . . . 47 C3
Peto Pl NW1 . . . . . . 92 B2
Peto St N E16 . . . . . 35 B3
Petrel Ct **8** SE21 . . 75 C2
Petrie Cl NW2 . . . . . 10 A2
Petrie Mus of
Egyptian
Archaeology*
WC1 . . . . 93 B1
Petros Gdns **1**
NW3 . . . . 11 B2
Petticoat Lane Mkt*
EC2 . . . . 110 C3
Petticoat Sq E1 . . . 110 C2
Petticoat Twr E1 . . . 110 C2
Pettiward Cl
SW15 . . . . 57 B3
Petty France
SW1 . . . . 133 B2

Petty Wales EC3 . . 124 B3
Petworth Ho **18**
SE22 . . . . 64 A4
Petworth St
SW11 . . . . 168 B3
Petyt Pl SW3 . . . . . 158 A3
Petyward SW3 . . . . 144 B3
Pevensey Ct
4 South Acton
W3 . . . . 37 A4
West Norwood
SW16 . . . . 74 C1
Pevensey Ho **5**
E1 . . . . 33 A4
Peveril Ho SE1 . . . 137 C1
Pewsham Ho N4 . . . 6 B3
Peyton Pl SE10 . . . . 52 B3
Pharamond NW2 . . . 9 C2
Phelps Ho SW15 . . . 57 C4
Phelp St SE17 . . . . . 48 C4
Phene St SW3 . . . . 158 B4
Philadelphia Ct
SW10 . . . . 157 A1
Philbeach Gdns
SW5 . . . . 141 B2
Phil Brown Pl **3**
SW8 . . . . 61 A4
Philchurch Pl E1 . . 111 C1
Philia Ho **4** NW1 . . 13 B1
Philip Ct W2 . . . . . 101 B4
Philip Ho Mews **6**
E9 . . . . 17 B2
Philip Wlk SE15 . . . 64 C4
Phillimore Ct W8 . . 127 B3
Phillimore Gardens Cl
W8 . . . . 127 B2
Phillimore Gdns
Kensington W8 . . . 127 B3
Willesden NW10 . . . 22 B4
Phillimore Pl W8 . . 127 B3
Phillimore Terr
W8 . . . . 127 C2
Phillimore Wlk
W8 . . . . 127 C2
Phillip Ho E1 . . . . . 111 A3
Phillipp St N1 . . . . . 24 A4
Philpot La EC3 . . . . 124 A4
Philpot Sq SW6 . . . 59 A4
Philpot St E1 . . . . . . 32 A3
Philson Mans **18**
E1 . . . . 32 A3
Phipps Ho **10** W12 . 30 A2
Phipp St
EC2 . . . . . . 24 A1 **98** A2
Phoebeth Rd SE4 . . 66 C2
Phoenix Bsns Ctr **29**
E3 . . . . 33 A4
Phoenix Ct
3 Brentford TW8 . 36 A1
2 Deptford SE14 . . 51 A4
Millwall E14 . . . . . . 41 C2
Phoenix High Sch
W12 . . . . 29 C2
Phoenix Ho SW1 . . 145 B4
Phoenix Lodge Mans
1 W6 . . . . 39 B2
Phoenix Pl WC1 . . . 95 A2
Phoenix Rd NW1 . . . 93 B4
Phoenix Sch E3 . . . 26 B2
Phoenix Sch The
NW3 . . . . 11 B2
Phoenix St WC2 . . . 105 C1

Phoenix Wharf Rd
SE1 . . . . 139 A3
Phyllis Hodges Ho
NW1 . . . . 83 B1
Physic Pl SW3 . . . . 158 C4
Piccadilly W1 . . . . . 118 C2
Piccadilly Arc
SW1 . . . . 118 C2
Piccadilly Cir*
W1 . . . . 119 B3
Piccadilly Circus Sta
SW1 . . . . 119 B3
Piccadilly **5**
N7 . . . . 14 B2
Piccadilly Pl W1 . . 119 A3
Pickard St EC1 . . . . 96 B4
Pickering Cl E9 . . . . 17 C1
Pickering Ho
Kensington W2 . . . 100 B1
Stoke Newington N4 . 6 C4
Pickering Mews
W2 . . . . 100 B1
Pickering Pl SW1 . . 119 A1
Pickering St N1 . . . . 86 B4
Pickets St SW12 . . . 73 A4
Pickfords Wharf
N1 . . . . 86 C1
Pickwick Ho
Bermondsey SE16 . 139 B3
3 Shepherd's Bush
W11 . . . . 30 C1
Pickwick Rd SE21 . . 76 A4
Pickwick St SE1 . . 136 C3
Pickworth Cl
SW8 . . . . 162 B1
Picton Ho **1** SW4 . 74 A4
Picton Pl W1 . . . . . 103 C1
Picton St SE5 . . . . . 48 C3
Picture Ho **6**
SW16 . . . . 74 A3
Pied Bull Ct WC1 . . 106 B3
Pied Bull Yd WC1 . . 106 B3
Pier Head E1 . . . . . . 32 A1
Pierhead Wharf **37**
E1 . . . . 32 A1
Pier Ho SW3 . . . . . 158 B3
Piermont Rd SE22 . . 65 A2
Pierpoint Bldg **4**
E14 . . . . 41 C4
Pierrepoint Rd
W3 . . . . 28 A2
Pierrepoint Row
N1 . . . . 86 A2
Pier St E14 . . . . 42 B2
Pier Terr SW18 . . . . 59 B3
Piggott St **2** E14 . . 33 C3
Pigott St E14 . . . . . . 33 C3
Pilgrimage St
SE1 . . . . 137 B3
Pilgrim Ho SE1 . . . 137 C1
Pilgrims Cloisters **1**
SE5 . . . . 49 A3
Pilgrims Ct SE3 . . . 53 C2
Pilgrim's La NW3 . . 11 C4
Pilgrims Mews **12**
E14 . . . . 34 C2
Pilgrim's Pl **6**
NW3 . . . . 11 C4
Pilgrim St EC4 . . . 108 A1
Pilgrims Way N19 . . 4 C3
Pilgrims Way Prim
Sch SE15 . . . . 50 B4
Pilkington Rd **4**
SE15 . . . . 50 A1

Pilot Ind Ctr NW10.....21 A1
Pilsden Cl SW19...69 C3
Pilton Pl SE17...151 A2
PIMLICO...146 C1
Pimlico Rd SW1...145 C2
Pimlico Sch SW1...146 C1
Pimlico Wlk N1...24 A2 98 A4
Pinchin St E1...125 C4
Pincombe Ho SE17...151 B2
Pincott Pl SE4...65 C4
Pindar St EC2...110 A4
Pindock Mews W9...88 B1
Pine Apple Ct SW1...132 C2
Pine Ave E15...19 C3
Pine Cl **11** N19...4 B2
Pinedene **2** SE15...50 A2
Pinefield Cl E14...33 C2
Pine Gr N4, N19...5 B2
Pine Ho Bow E3...26 A4 / **21** Rotherhithe SE16...40 B3
Pinehurst Ct **6** W11...31 B3
Pinelands Cl **7** SE3...53 B3
Pine Lo SW15...58 A1
Pine Rd NW2...9 C4
Pines Ct **14** SW15...69 C3
Pine St EC1...95 B2
Pine Tree Ho SE14...50 C3
Pinewood Ct SW4...61 C1
Pinkham Mans W4...36 C1
Pinnace Ho E14...42 B3
Pinnacle Ho EC3...124 A3
Pinnacle The **7** N1...15 C2
Pinner Ct NW8...89 B2
Pinner Ho **30** SE5...48 B1
Pintail Cl **30** SE8...51 B4
Pinter Ho SW9...172 B1
Pioneer Cl W12...30 A3
Pioneer St SE15...49 C2
Pioneer Way W12...30 B3
Piper Cl N7...14 B3
Pipers Ho SE10...42 C1
Pippin Ho **17** W10...30 C2
Pirbright Rd SW18...70 C3
Pitcairn Ho **1** E9...17 B1
Pitfield Ho N5...15 B3
Pitfield St N1...24 A3
Pitman Ho **2** SE8...51 C2
Pitman St SE5...48 B3
Pitmaston Ho **2** SE13...52 B1
Pitsea Pl E1...32 C3
Pitsea St E1...32 C3
Pitt Ho **4** SW11...59 C3
Pitt's Head Mews W1...117 C1
Pitt St W8...127 C4
Pixley St E14...33 B3
Planetree Ct W6...39 C2
Plane Tree Ho SE8...51 A4
Plantain Pl SE1...137 B4
Plantation La EC4...124 A4

Plantation The SE3...53 C1
Platehouse The **3** E14...42 A1
Platina St EC2...97 C2
Plato Pl SW6...165 A2
Plato Rd SW2...62 A3
Platt's La NW3...1 C1
Platt St NW1...83 B2
Plaxdale Ho SE17...152 A3
Playfair St W6...39 B1
Playfield Cres SE22...64 B2
Playford Rd Finsbury Pk N4...5 B2 / Finsbury Pk N4...5 C2
Playhouse Yd EC4...108 A1
Plaza Sh Ctr W1...105 A2
Pleasance Rd SW15...57 A2
Pleasance The SW15...57 A3
Pleasant Pl N1...15 A1
Pleasant Row NW1...82 B3
Plender Ct NW1...83 A3
Plender St NW1...83 A3
Pleshey Rd N7...13 C4
Plevna St E14...42 B3
Pleydell Ave W6...38 B2
Pleydell Ct EC4...107 C1
Pleydell St EC4...107 C1
Plimsoll Cl E14...34 A3
Plimsoll Rd N4...6 A1
Plough Ct EC3...123 C4
Plough La SE22...64 B1
Ploughmans Cl NW1...83 B4
Plough Mews **19** SW11...59 C3
Plough Pl EC4...107 C2
Plough Rd SW11...59 C3
Plough St **1** E1...111 A2
Plough Terr SW11...59 C3
Plough Way SE16...41 A2
Plough Yd EC2...24 A1 98 B1
Plover Ho SW9...163 B2
Plover Way SE16...41 A3
Plowman Ho SW19...69 C2
Plumbers Row E1...111 C2
Plumbridge St **7** SE10...52 B2
Plume Ho SE10...52 A4
Plummer Ct SE13...67 A1
Plummer Rd SW4...73 C4
Plumtree Ct EC4...108 A2
Plymouth Ho **20** SE10...52 A4
Plymouth Rd E16...35 C4
Plymouth Wharf E14...42 C2
Plympton Ave NW6...10 B1
Plympton Pl NW1...90 A1
Plympton Rd NW6...10 B1
Plympton St NW8...90 A1
Pocklington Ct SW15...68 C3
Pocklington Lo **6** W12...38 C3
Pocock St SE1...136 B4
Podmore Rd SW18...59 B3

Poets Cnr* SW1...134 A2
Poet's Rd N5...15 C3
Point Cl SE10...52 B2
Pointer Sch The SE3...53 C3
Pointers Cl E1...42 A1
Point Hill SE10...52 B2
Point Ho SE10...52 B2
Point Pleasant SW18...58 C3
Point Wharf La TW8...44 A3
Poland Ho **3** E15...27 C4
Poland St W1...105 A1
Polesworth Ho **10** W2...31 C4
Polish Inst & Sikorski Mus* SW7...129 C3
Polish Univ Abroad W6...38 C2
Pollard Cl Islington N7...14 B4 / Newham E16...35 C2
Pollard Ho N1...84 C1
Pollard Row E2...24 C2 99 C4
Pollard St E2...24 C2 99 C4
Pollen St W1...104 B1
Pollitt Dr NW8...89 C2
Pollock Ho W10...23 A1
Polperro Mans **3** NW6...10 C3
Polperro Mews SE11...150 A4
Polygon Rd NW1...83 B1
Polygon The **1** Clapham SW4...61 B3 / St John's Wood NW8...80 A4
Pomell Way E1...111 A2
Pomeroy Ct W11...31 A3
Pomeroy Ho **5** E2...25 C3
Pomeroy St SE14...50 B2
Pomfret Rd SE5...63 A4
Pomoja La N19...5 A2
Pomona Ho SE8...41 A2
Pond Cl SE3...53 C1
Pond Cotts SE21...76 A3
Ponder St **5** N7...14 B1
Pondfield Ho **4** N5...15 B3
Pond Ho SW3...144 A3
Pond Mead SE21...63 C1
Pond Pl SW3...144 A3
Pond Rd SE3...53 B1
Pond Sq N6...3 C3
Pond St NW3...12 A3
Ponler St **5** E1...32 A3
Ponsard Rd NW10...22 A2
Ponsford St E9...17 B2
Ponsonby Ho **13** E2...25 B3
Ponsonby Pl SW1...147 C2
Ponsonby Rd SW15...69 A4
Ponsonby Terr SW1...147 C2
Ponton Rd SW2...74 C3
Ponton Rd SW8...161 C3
Pont St Mews SW1...130 C1
Pont St SW1...131 A1
Pontypool Pl SE1...136 A4
Poole Ct N1...16 A1

Poole Ho SE11...135 A1
Poole Rd E9...17 C2
Pooles Bldgs EC1...95 B1
Pooles La SW10...156 C1
Pooles Park Prim Sch N4...5 B2
Pooles Pk N4...5 B2
Poole St N1...87 B3
Pooley Ho E1...25 C2
Pool Ho NW8...101 C4
Poolmans St SE16...40 C4
Poonah St E1...32 B3
Pope Ho **7** Bermondsey SE16...40 A2 / **3** Camberwell SE5...48 C3
Pope John RC Prim Sch W12...30 A2
Pope's Head Alley EC3...109 C1
Pope's La W5...36 A3
Pope's Rd SW9...62 C4
Pope St SE1...138 B3
Popham Ct N16...7 A1
Popham Gdns TW9...55 A4
Popham Rd N1...86 C4
Popham St Islington N1...86 B4 / Shoreditch N1...86 C4
POPLAR...33 C3
Poplar Bath St **3** E14...34 A2
Poplar Bsns Pk E14...34 B2
Poplar Cl E9...18 B3
Poplar Ct **4** SW16...74 A1
Poplar Gr W6...39 B4
Poplar High St E14...34 A2
Poplar Ho **1** Brockley SE4...66 B3 / **10** Rotherhithe SE16...40 C4
Poplar Mews **4** W12...30 B1
Poplar Pl W2...114 B4
Poplar Rd SE24...63 B3
Poplar Sta E14...34 A2
Poplar The NW5...13 B3
Poplar Wlk SE24...63 B3
Poppins Ct EC4...108 A1
Porchester Ct W2...100 B1
Porchester Gate W2...114 C3
Porchester Gdn Mews **2** W2...100 B1
Porchester Gdns W2...114 B4
Porchester Ho **5** E1...32 A3
Porchester Mews W2...100 B2
Porchester Pl W2...102 B1
Porchester Rd W2...100 B2
Porchester Sq W2...100 B2
Porchester Terr N W2...100 B2
Porchester Terr W2...114 C4
Porden Rd SW2...62 B3
Porland Rd SE17...137 B2

Porlock Ho **5** SE26...76 C1
Porlock St SE1...137 C4
Porson Ct SE13...67 A4
Portal Cl SE27...74 C1
Portal Way W3...28 C4
Portbury Cl **17** SE15...49 C2
Portchester Cl SE24...63 C3
Portelet Ct **1** N1...24 A4
Portelet Rd E1...25 C2
Porten Hos W14...126 A1
Porten Rd W14...126 A1
Porter Sq N19...5 A3
Porter St Borough The SE1...123 A2 / Marylebone W1...103 A4
Porteus Rd W2...101 A4
Portfleet Pl **24** N1...24 A4
Portgate Cl W9...23 B1
Port Ho **8** SW11...59 B4
Port House The **8** E14...42 A1
Portia Way E3...26 B1
Porticos The SW3...157 B3
Portinscale Rd SW15...58 B2
Portishead Ho **23** W2...31 C4
Portland Ave N16...7 B4
Portland Ct **1** De Beauvoir Town N1...16 A1 / **1** Deptford SE14...51 A4
Portland Gr SW8...172 C4
Portland Ho **10** SW2...74 C3
Portland Hospl for Women & Children The W1...92 B1
Portland Mews W1...105 A1
Portland Pl W1...104 B3
Portland Place Sch W1...104 B3
Portland Place Schs W1...104 B4
Portland Rd Notting Hill W11...31 A1 112 B2 / Notting Hill W11...31 A1 112 A3
Portland Rise N4...6 B3
Portland Sq **4** E1...32 A1
Portland St SE17...151 B1
Portland Village W6...39 B3
Portman Ave SW14...55 C4
Portman Cl W1...103 B2
Portman Gate NW1...90 B1
Portman Hts **1** NW3...1 C1
Portman Mews S W1...103 B1
Portman Pl E2...25 B2
Portman Sq W1...103 B1
Portman St W1...103 B1
Portman The NW11...1 C4
Portman Twrs W1...103 A2
Portnall Rd W9...23 B2
Portobello Ct Est W11...31 B3

Portobello Mews
W11 . . . . . . 31 C2 113 B3

Portobello Rd
W11 . . . . . . 31 B2 113 A4

Portobello Road
Mkt★ W10 . . . . . 31 C2

Portpool La EC1 . . . 107 B4

Portree St E14 . . . . 34 C3

Port Royal Pl 3
N16 . . . . 16 A3

Portsea Hall W2 . . 102 B1

Portsea Pl 3
SW15 . . . . 69 A3

Portsea Mews
W2 . . . . 102 B1

Portsea Pl W2 . . . 102 B1

Portslade Rd
SW8 . . . . 170 C2

Portsmouth Rd
SW15 . . . . 69 B4

Portsmouth St
WC2 . . . . 107 A1

Portsoken St E1,
EC3 . . . . 124 C4

Portswood Pl
SW15 . . . . 56 B1

Portugal St WC2 . . 107 A1

Poseidon Ct 9
E14 . . . . 41 C2

Postern The EC2 . . 109 A3

Post Office Way
SW8 . . . . 161 B2

Potier St E1 . . . . . 137 C1

Potterne Cl 5
SW19 . . . . 69 C4

Potters Cl 6 SE15 . 49 A3

Potters Fields
SE1 . . . . 124 B1

Potters Lo E14 . . . 42 B1

Potters Rd SW6 . . 166 C1

Pottery La
W11 . . . . 31 A1 112 B2

Pottery Rd TW8 . . 44 A4

Pottery St SE16 . . 40 A4

Pott St E2 . . . . . . 25 A2

Poullett Ho SW2 . . 75 A3

Poulton Cl E8 . . . . 17 A2

Poultry EC2 . . . . . 109 B1

Pound La NW10 . . . 8 C2

Pountney Rd
SW11 . . . . 60 C4

Povey Ho
Tulse Hill SW2 . . . 62 C1
Walworth SE17 . . . 152 A3

Powell's Wlk W4 . . 46 B4

Powergate Bsns Pk
NW10 . . . . 20 C2

Power Ho 9 TW9 . . 44 C2

Power Ho The W4 . . 38 B2

Power Rd W4 . . . . 36 C2

Powerscroft Rd
E5 . . . . 17 B4

Powis Gdns
Golders Green
NW11 . . . . 1 B4
Notting Hill W11 . . 31 B3

Powis Ho WC2 . . . 106 B2

Powis Mews W11 . . 31 B3

Powis Pl WC1 . . . . 94 B1

Powis Rd E3 . . . . . 27 A2

Powis Sq W11 . . . . 31 B3

Powis Terr W11 . . . 31 B3

Powlesland Ct 21
E14 . . . . 33 A3

Powlett Ho NW1 . . . 13 A2

Powlett Pl NW1 . . . 13 A1

Pownall Rd E8 . . . . 24 C4

Powrie Ho SW11 . . 167 C2

Poynder Ct 3 N7 . . 14 A3

Poynders Ct 9
SW4 . . . . 61 B1

Poynders Gdns
SW4 . . . . 73 B4

Poynders Rd SW12,
SW4 . . . . 73 C4

Poynings Rd N19 . . 4 B1

Poynter Ho
Paddington NW8 . . 89 B2
10 Shepherd's Bush
W11 . . . . 30 C1

Poyntz Rd SW11 . . 168 C1

Poyser St E2 . . . . . 25 A3

Praed Mews W2 . . 101 C2

Praed St W2 . . . . 101 C2

Prague Pl SW2 . . . 62 A2

Prah Rd N4 . . . . . . 5 C2

Prairie St SW8 . . . 170 A1

Pratt Mews NW1 . . 82 C3

Pratt St NW1 . . . . 82 C4

Pratt Wlk SE1 . . . . 149 A4

Preachers Ct 6 EC1 . 96 B1

Prebend Gdns W4,
W6 . . . . 38 B2

Prebend Mans 4
W6 . . . . 38 B2

Prebend St N1 . . . 86 C4

Precinct The 6
Islington N1 . . . . 86 C3
Islington N5 . . . . 15 A3

Premier Corner
NW6 . . . . 23 B2

Premier Ho 25 N1 . . 15 A1

**Premier League Hall
of Fame★** SE1 . . . 134 C4

Premier Park Rd
NW10 . . . . 20 A3

Premier Pk NW10 . . 20 A3

Premier Ho 17 E14 . 33 C2

Prendergast Ho 7
SW4 . . . . 73 C4

Prendergast Sch
SE4 . . . . 66 C3

Prescot St E1 . . . . 125 A4

Prescott Ho 13
SE17 . . . . 48 A4

Prescott Pl SW4 . . 61 C3

Presentation Mews
SW2 . . . . 74 B3

President Dr E1 . . . 32 A1

President Ho 6 EC1 . 96 B3

President St EC1 . . 96 C4

Prestage Way 13
E14 . . . . 34 B2

Prested Rd SW11 . . 60 A3

Preston Cl SE1 . . . 152 A4

Preston Gdns
NW10 . . . . 8 A2

Preston Ho
Bermondsey SE1 . . 138 C2
Walworth SE1 . . . 152 A4

Preston Pl
Richmond TW10 . . . 54 A2
Willesden NW2 . . . 8 C2

Prestwich Terr
SW4 . . . . 61 C2

Prestwood Ho 3
SE16 . . . . 40 A3

Prestwood St N1 . . 87 A1

Priam Ho 17 E2 . . . 25 A3

Price Cl SW17 . . . . 72 B1

Price Ho N1 . . . . . 86 C3

Prices Ct SW11 . . . 59 C4

Price's St SE1 . . . . 122 B2

Price's Yd N1 . . . . 85 A3

Prichard Ct
Battersea SW11 . . 167 C3
Islington N7 . . . . . 14 B3

Prideaux Ho WC1 . . 95 A4

Prideaux Pl
Acton W3 . . . . . . 28 C2
St Pancras WC1 . . 95 A4

Pride Ct N1 . . . . . . 85 C2

Priestley Cl N16 . . . 7 B4

Priestley Ho
2 Camden Town
NW5 . . . . 13 A2
St Luke's EC1 . . . . 97 A2

Priestman Point 25
E3 . . . . 27 A2

Priests Bridge
SW14 . . . . 56 A4

Priest's Ct EC2 . . . 108 C2

Prima Rd SW9 . . . 163 B2

Primrose Ct
2 Child's Hill NW2 . 1 B1
Primrose Hill NW8 . 80 C3
11 Streatham
SW12 . . . . 73 C4

Primrose Gdns
NW3 . . . . 12 A2

PRIMROSE HILL . . . 12 B1

Primrose Hill EC4 . . 107 C1

Primrose Hill Ct
NW3 . . . . 12 B1

Primrose Hill Rd
Primrose Hill NW3,
NW3 . . . . 12 B1
NW3 . . . . 80 C4

Primrose Hill Sch
NW1 . . . . 81 C4

Primrose Hill Studios
NW1 . . . . 81 B4

Primrose Ho 2
7 Peckham SE15 . . 49 C2
11 Richmond TW9 . 44 B2

Primrose Mans
SW11 . . . . 169 B4

Primrose Mews 9
NW1 . . . . 12 B1

Primrose Sq E9 . . . 25 B4

Primrose St EC2 . . 110 B4

Primrose Wlk 6
SE14 . . . . 51 A3

Primula St W12 . . . 29 C3

Prince Albert Ct
NW8 . . . . 80 C3

Prince Albert Rd
NW8 . . . . 80 C3

Prince Arthur Ct 18
NW3 . . . . 11 B4

Prince Arthur Mews
17 NW3 . . . . 11 B4

Prince Arthur Rd
NW3 . . . . 11 B3

Prince Charles Rd
SE3 . . . . 53 B2

Prince Consort Ho
SE1 . . . . 148 B2

Prince Consort Rd
SW7 . . . . 129 B2

Princedale Rd
W11 . . . . 31 A1 112 B2

Prince Edward Mans
W2 . . . . . 31 C2 113 C4

Prince Edward Rd
E9 . . . . 18 B2

Prince George Rd
N16 . . . . 16 A4

Princelet St E1 . . . 111 A4

Prince of Orange La
3 SE10 . . . . 52 B3

Prince of Wales Dr
SW11 . . . . 169 B4

**Prince of Wales
Mans**
Battersea SW11 . . 169 C4
Clapham SW4 . . . . 60 A3

Prince of Wales Pas
NW1 . . . . 92 C3

Prince of Wales Rd
Blackheath Vale
SE3 . . . . 53 B2
Camden Town NW5 . 12 C2

**Prince of Wales
Terr**
Chiswick W4 . . . . 38 A1
Kensington W8 . . . 128 B3

Prince Regent Ct 2
SE16 . . . . 33 A1

Prince Regent Mews
NW1 . . . . 92 C3

Princes Arc SW1 . . 119 A2

Princes Ave W3 . . . 36 C3

Princes Cir WC2 . . 106 A2

Princes Ct E1 . . . . 125 C4

Princes Coll WC1 . . 106 A2

Princes Court Bsns
Ctr 14 E1 . . . . . . 32 A2

Princes Ct
Brondesbury NW2 . 10 A3
Hampstead NW3 . . 11 C4
Stepney NW3 . . . . 32 A2

Prince's Ct SE16 . . 41 B3

Princes Gate
SW7 . . . . 129 C3

Prince's Gate
SW7 . . . . 130 A3

Princes Gate Ct
SW7 . . . . 129 C3

Princes Gate Mews
SW7 . . . . 129 C2

Princes Gdns
SW7 . . . . 129 C2

Princes Ho
W11 . . . . 31 C2 113 B3

Prince's Mews
1 Hammersmith
W6 . . . . 39 A1
Kensington W2 . . . 114 A4

Princes Pl
Notting Hill
W11 . . . . 31 A1 112 A2
St James SW1 . . . 119 A2

Princes Rd
Kew TW9 . . . . 44 B2
Richmond TW10 . . . 54 B2

Prince's Rd SW14 . . 55 C4

Princes Rise SE13 . 52 B1

Princes Riverside Rd
7 SE16 . . . . 32 C1

**Princess Alexandra
School of Nursing
The** E1 . . . . 32 A4

Princess Alice Ho 6
W10 . . . . 22 B1

Princess Beatrice Ho
SW10 . . . . 142 A1

Princess Cres N4 . . 6 A2

Princess Ct
Hampstead NW6 . . 11 A1
Kensington W2 . . . 114 B4

Princess Ct continued
Marylebone W1 . . . 102 C3

**Princess Frederica CE
Prim Sch** NW10 . . 22 B3

**Princess Grace Hospl
The** W1 . . . . 91 B1

Princess Louise Cl
W2 . . . . 101 C4

Princess Louise Hospl
W10 . . . . 30 B4

Princess Mary Ho
SW1 . . . . 147 C3

**Princess May Prim
Sch** N16 . . . . . . 16 B4

Princess May Rd
N16 . . . . 16 A4

Princess Mews
NW3 . . . . 11 C2

Prince's Sq W2 . . . 114 A4

Princess Rd
Camden Town
NW1 . . . . 81 C4
Paddington NW6 . . 23 C3

Princess St SE1 . . 136 B1

Princes St SE1 . . . 104 B1

Prince's St
City of London
EC2 . . . . 109 B1
Richmond TW10,
TW9 . . . . 54 A2

Prince St SE8 . . . . 51 B4

Princes Way
Acton W3 . . . . . . 36 C3
Putney SW15 . . . . 70 A3

Princes Yd
W11 . . . . 31 A1 112 B1

Princethorpe Ho
W2 . . . . 100 A4

Princeton Ct
SW15 . . . . 57 C4

Princeton Mans
WC1 . . . . 106 C3

Princeton St WC1 . . 106 C3

Principal Sq E9 . . . 17 C3

Printers Mews E3 . . 26 A4

Printer St EC4 . . . 107 C2

Printing House Yd
13 E2 . . . . 24 A2 98 B3

Printon Ho 3 E3 . . 33 B4

Print Village Ind Est
SE15 . . . . 49 B1

Prior Bolton St
N1 . . . . 15 A2

Prioress Ho 2 E3 . . 27 A2

Prioress Rd SE27 . . 75 A1

Prioress St SE1 . . . 137 C1

Priors Lo 2 TW10 . . 54 A1

Prior St SE10 . . . . 52 B3

**Prior Weston Prim
Sch**
Broadgate EC1 . . . 97 B1
St Luke's EC1 . . . . 97 A1

Priory Ave W4 . . . . 38 A3

Priory Ct
City of London
EC4 . . . . 108 B1
Homerton E9 . . . . 17 C3
Nunhead SE15 . . . 65 B3
Roehampton SW15 . 56 B3
South Lambeth
SW8 . . . . 171 C3

Priory Gdns
Barnes SW13 . . . . 56 B4
6 Chiswick W4 . . . 38 A2

Priory Gn N1 . . . . 84 C2
Priory Gr SW8 . . . . 172 A3
Priory Ho
Clerkenwell EC1 . . . . . . 96 A2
Pimlico SW1 . . . . 147 B2
Spitalfields E1 . . . . 110 C4
Priory Hospl
SW15 . . . . 56 B3
Priory Htts N1 . . . . 85 A2
Priory La SW15 . . . . 56 B2
Priory Lo 7 W4 . . . . 36 C1
Priory Mans
17 Maitland Pk
NW3 . . . . 12 B2
South Kensington
SW10 . . . . 143 A1
Priory Park Rd
NW6 . . . . 23 B4
Priory Rd
Bedford Pk W4 . . . . 37 C3
Hampstead NW6 . . . . . 11 A1
Richmond TW9 . . . . 44 C3
Priory St 15 E3 . . . . 27 A2
Priory Terr NW6 . . . . 78 A4
Priory The SE1 . . . . 136 A3
Priory Wlk SW10 . . . . . 143 A1
Pritchard Ho 38
Pritchard's Rd E2 . . . . . 24 C3
Priter Rd SE16 . . . . 139 C1
Priter Road Hostel
SE16 . . . . 139 C1
Probert Rd SW2 . . . . 62 C2
Probyn Ho SW1 . . . . . . 147 C4
Probyn Rd SW2 . . . . 75 A2
Procter Ho 12 SE5 . . . . . 48 C3
Procter St WC1 . . . . . . 106 C3
Proctor Ho 5 SE1 . . . . . 153 B1
Prome Ho 3 N16 . . . . . . 15 C4
Promenade Approach
Rd W4 . . . . 46 A3
Promenade The
W4 . . . . 46 A2
Prospect Cotts
SW18 . . . . 58 C3
Prospect Ho
1 Dalston E8 . . . . 16 B2
Islington N1 . . . . 85 B1
Newington SE1 . . . . . 136 B1
14 West Kensington
W10 . . . . 30 C3
Prospect House Sch
SW15 . . . . 69 C4
Prospect Pl
1 Child's Hill NW2 . . . 1 B1
2 Chiswick W4 . . . . . . 37 C1
6 Deptford SE8 . . . . . 51 B4
12 Hampstead NW3 . . 11 B4
7 Lower Holloway
N7 . . . . 14 A4
Wapping E1 . . . . 32 B1
Prospect Quay
SW18 . . . . 58 C3
Prospect Rd NW2 . . . . 1 B1
Prospect St SE16 . . . . . . 40 A4
Prospect Wharf
E1 . . . . 32 B2
Prospero Rd N19 . . . . 4 C3
Prothero Rd SW6 . . . . . 154 C2
Prout Ho 19 E3 . . . . 32 A3
Prout Gr NW10 . . . . 8 B4
Provence St N1 . . . . 86 C2
Providence Ct E9 . . . . . 25 C4
Providence Ct
Islington N1 . . . . 86 A3

Providence Ct
continued
Mayfair W1 . . . . 117 C4
Providence Pl N1 . . . . . . 86 A3
Providence Row
N1 . . . . 84 C1
Providence Row Cl 30
E1 . . . . 25 A2
Providence Sq
SE1 . . . . 139 B4
Providence Yd
E2 . . . . 24 C2 99 B4
Provost Rd NW3 . . . . 12 B1
Provost St N1 . . . . 97 B4
Prowse Pl NW1 . . . . 13 B1
Prudent Pas EC2 . . . . . 109 A1
Prusom's Island 8
E1 . . . . 32 B1
Prusom St E1 . . . . 32 A1
Public Record Office
TW9 . . . . 45 A3
Pudding La EC3 . . . . . . 123 C4
Pudding Mill La
E15 . . . . 27 B4
Pudding Mill Lane Sta
E15 . . . . 27 B4
Puddle Dock EC4 . . . . . 122 B4
Pugin Ct N1 . . . . 14 C1
Pulborough Rd
SW18 . . . . 70 B4
Pulham Ho SW8 . . . . . . 162 C1
Pullman Ct SW2 . . . . 74 B3
Pullman Gdns
SW15 . . . . 57 B1
Pulross Rd SW9 . . . . 62 B4
Pulton Ho SE4 . . . . 66 A3
Pulton Pl SW6 . . . . 155 B1
Puma Ct E1 . . . . 110 C4
Pump Ct EC4 . . . . 107 B1
Pump House Cl
SE16 . . . . 40 B4
Pumphouse
Educational Mus
The★ SE16 . . . . 33 A1
Pumping Ho 8
E14 . . . . 34 C2
Pumping Station Rd
W4 . . . . 46 A4
Pump La SE14 . . . . 50 B3
Punderson's Gdns
E2 . . . . 25 A2
Purbeck Ho SW8 . . . . . 162 C1
Purbrook Est SE1 . . . . . 138 B3
Purbrook Ho 2
SW15 . . . . 69 A3
Purbrook St SE1 . . . . . 138 B2
Purcell Cres SW6 . . . . . 154 A2
Purcell Ho SW10 . . . . . 157 B3
Purcell Mews 2
NW10 . . . . 8 A1
Purcell St N1 . . . . 24 A3
Purchese St NW1 . . . . . . 83 C1
Purday Ho 4 W10 . . . . . . 23 B2
Purdon Ho 11
SE15 . . . . 49 C2
Purdy St E3 . . . . 27 A1
Purley Ave NW2 . . . . 1 A2
Purley Pl N1 . . . . 15 A1
Purser Ho 2 SW2 . . . . . 62 C1
Pursers Cross Rd
SW6 . . . . 165 A4
Purves Rd NW10 . . . . . . 22 B3
Pusey Ho 20 E14 . . . . . 33 C3

Puteaux Ho 2 E2 . . 25 C3
PUTNEY 57 B2
Putney Bridge App
SW6 . . . . 58 A4
Putney Bridge Rd
SW15 . . . . 58 B3
Putney Bridge Sta
SW6 . . . . 58 B3
Putney Comm
SW15 . . . . 57 B4
Putney Exchange
Shopping Ctr
SW15 . . . . 57 C3
PUTNEY HEATH 57 B1
Putney Heath
SW15 . . . . 57 C1
Putney Heath La
SW15 . . . . 57 C1
Putney High Sch
SW15 . . . . 57 C2
Putney High St
SW15 . . . . 58 A3
Putney Hill SW15 . . . . . 57 C2
Putney Park Ave
SW15 . . . . 56 C3
Putney Park La
SW15 . . . . 57 A2
Putney Pier SW15 . . . . . 58 A4
Putney School of Art
& Design SW15 . . . . 58 A3
Putney Sta SW15 . . . . . 58 A2
PUTNEY VALE 68 C1
Putney Wharf Twr
SW15 . . . . 58 A4
Pykewell Lo 11 E18 . . 16 C4
Pylon Trad Est
E16 . . . . 34 C4
Pymers Mead
SE21 . . . . 75 B3
Pynfolds SE16 . . . . 40 A4
Pynnersmead
SE24 . . . . 63 B2
Pyrford Ho 12
SW9 . . . . 63 A3
Pyrland Rd
Richmond TW10 . . . . . 54 B1
Stoke Newington
N5 . . . . 15 C3
Pyrmont Gr SE27 . . . . . . 75 A1
Pyrmont Rd W4 . . . . 44 C4
Pytchley Rd SE22 . . . . . 64 A4

Q

Quadrangle Cl
SE1 . . . . 152 A4
Quadrangle The
Chelsea SW10 . . . . . 167 A4
Fulham SW6 . . . . 154 A1
Herne Hill SE24 . . . . . 63 B2
3 North Kensington
W12 . . . . 30 B3
Paddington W2 . . . . . 102 A2
Quadrant Arc W1 119 A3
Quadrant Bsns Ctr
NW6 . . . . 23 B3
Quadrant Gr NW5 . . . . . 12 B3
Quadrant The
5 Kensal Green
W10 . . . . 22 C2
Richmond TW9 . . . . . 54 A3
Quaker Ct E1 . . . . 97 A2
Quaker St
E1 . . . . 24 B1 98 C1

Quality Ct WC2 . . . 107 B2
Quantock Ho N16 . . 7 B3
Quantock Mews 3
SE15 . . . . 49 C1
Quarrendon St
SW6 . . . . 165 C2
Quarry Rd SW18 . . . 59 B1
Quarterdeck The
E14 . . . . 41 C4
Quartermile La E10 . . . . .
E15 . . . . 19 A4
Quayside Ct 7
SE16 . . . . 32 C1
Quebec & Crown
Wharves E14 . . . . . . 33 B3
Quebec Ind Est
SE16 . . . . 41 A3
Quebec Mews
W1 . . . . 103 A1
Quebec Wharf 22
E8 . . . . 24 A4
Quedgeley Ct 3
SE15 . . . . 49 B4
Queen Alexandra
Mans ★ WC1 . . . . . . 94 A3
Queen Anne Mews
W1 . . . . 104 B3
Queen Anne Rd
E9 . . . . 17 C2
Queen Anne's Gate
SW1 . . . . 133 B3
Queen Anne's Gdns
Bedford Pk W4 . . . . . 38 A3
Ealing W5 . . . . 36 A4
Queen Anne's Gr
Bedford Pk W4 . . . . . 38 A3
Ealing W5 . . . . 36 A4
Queen Anne St
W1 . . . . 104 A3
Queen Anne Terr 9
E1 . . . . 32 A2
Queen Caroline St
W6 . . . . 39 B1
Queen Charlottes &
Chelsea Hospl
W12 . . . . 29 C3
Queen Ct WC1 . . . . . . 94 B1
Queen Elizabeth Ct 3
N1 . . . . 87 C4
Queen Elizabeth Hall
& Purcell Room★
SE1 . . . . 121 A2
Queen Elizabeth Ho
SW12 . . . . 72 C4
Queen Elizabeth II
Con Ctr SW1 . . . . . 133 C3
Queen Elizabeth II
Jubilee Sch W9 . . . 23 B1
Queen Elizabeth II
Pier SE10 . . . . 35 B1
Queen Elizabeth's Coll
15 SE10 . . . . 52 A3
Queen Elizabeth St
SE1 . . . . 138 C4
Queen Elizabeth's Wlk
N16 . . . . 6 C2
Queenhithe EC4 . . . . 123 A4
Queen Margaret Flats
22 E2 . . . . 25 A2
Queen Margarets
N1 . . . . 16 A3

Queen Margaret's Gr
N1 . . . . 16 A3
Queen Mary's Gdns★
NW1 . . . . 91 B3
Queen Mary's Hospl
NW3 . . . . 2 A1
Queen Mary's Univ
Hospl SW15 . . . . 56 C1
Queen Mary, Univ of
London E1 . . . . 26 A1
Queen of Denmark Ct
SE16 . . . . 41 B3
Queen St Pl EC4 . . 123 A4
Queensberry Mews W
SW7 . . . . 143 B4
Queensberry Pl
SW7 . . . . 143 B4
Queensberry Way
SW7 . . . . 143 B4
Queensborough Mews
W2 . . . . 114 C4
Queensborough Pas
W2 . . . . 114 C4
Queensborough Terr
W2 . . . . 114 B4
Queensbridge Ct 1
E2 . . . . 24 B3
Queensbridge Inf Sch
E8 . . . . 16 B1
Queensbridge Rd
Dalston E8 . . . . 16 B1
Shoreditch E2, E8 . . 24 B4
Queensbury St N1 . 15 B1
Queen's CE Prim Sch
The TW9 . . . . 44 C3
Queen's Cir SW11 . . 160 A1
Queen's Club Gdns
W14 . . . . 154 B4
Queen's Club The
W14 . . . . 140 B1
Queen's Coll W1 . . 104 A3
Queens Cres
TW10 . . . . 54 B2
Queen's Cres NW5 . 12 C2
Queens Ct
Battersea SW11 . . . . 170 A4
Camberwell SE5 . . . . 49 A1
4 Limehouse E14 . . . 33 B2
Queen's Ct
Barnes SW13 . . . . . . 56 C4
Kensington W2 . . . . . 114 B3
3 Richmond TW10 . . 54 B1
St John's Wood
NW8 . . . . 79 B2
Queensdale W11 . . 30 C1
Queensdale Cres
W11 . . . . 30 C1
Queensdale Pl
W11 . . . . . . 31 A1 112 A1
Queensdale Rd
Notting Hill W11 . . . . . 30 C1
Notting Hill
W11 . . . . . . 31 A1 112 A1
Queensdale Wlk
W11 . . . . . . 31 A1 112 A1
Queensdown Rd
E5 . . . . 17 A4
Queen's Dr N4 . . . . 6 A2
Queen's Elm Par
SW3 . . . . 143 C2
Queen's Elm Sq
SW3 . . . . 143 C1
Queen's Gallery★
SW1 . . . . 132 B3
Queen's Gate
SW7 . . . . 129 A1

Queensgate Gdns
SW15 .... 57 A3
Queen's Gate Gdns
SW7 .... 129 A1
Queensgate Ho 34
E3 .... 26 B3
Queen's Gate Mews
SW7 .... 129 A2
Queensgate Pl 10
NW6 .... 10 C1
Queen's Gate Pl
SW7 .... 129 A1
Queen's Gate Pl Mews
SW7 .... 129 A1
Queen's Gate Sch
SW7 .... 143 B4
Queen's Gate Terr
SW7 .... 129 A2
Queens Gate Villas
E9 .... 18 B1
Queen's Gdns W2 114 C4
Queen's Gr NW8 . 79 C3
Queen's Head Pas
EC2 .... 108 C2
Queen's Head St
N1 .... 86 B3
Queen's Head Yd
SE1 .... 123 B1
Queens Ho 3
SE17 .... 48 C4
Queen's House The*
SE10 .... 52 C4
Queensland Rd
N7 .... 14 C4
Queens Manor Sch
SW6 .... 47 C3
Queens Mans
NW6 .... 11 A3
Queen's Mans NW6. 39 C2
Queensmead NW8. 79 C4
Queensmere Cl
SW19 .... 69 C2
Queensmere Ct
SW13 .... 46 C4
Queensmere Rd
SW19 .... 69 C2
Queen's Mews
W2 .... 114 A4
Queensmill Rd
SW6 .... 47 C3
Queensmill Sch
SW6 .... 165 C1
Queens Par 3 NW2. 9 B2
Queens Park Com Sch
NW6 .... 22 C4
Queens Park Ct 5
W10 .... 22 C2
Queen's Park Prim
Sch W10 .... 23 A1
Queens Park Sta
NW6 .... 23 B3
Queen Sq WC1 . 106 B4
Queen's Quay
EC4 .... 123 A4
Queen's Rd
Mortlake SW14 ... 55 C4
New Cross Gate SE14,
SE15 .... 50 B2
Richmond TW10 ... 54 B1
Queen's Ride
SW13 .... 57 A4
Queen's Rise
TW10 .... 54 B2
Queen's Road Sta
SE15 .... 50 B2
Queen's Row SE17 .48 C4

Queen St
City of London
EC4 .... 123 A4
Mayfair W1 ...... 118 A2
Queens Terr NW8... 79 B2
Queenstown Mews
SW8 .... 170 A3
Queenstown Rd
SW8 .... 170 B4
Queenstown Road Sta
SW8 .... 170 B4
Queensville Rd SW12,
SW4 .... 73 B4
Queensway W2 .. 114 B4
Queensway Sta
W2 .... 114 B3
Queen's Wlk SW1 118 A2
Queenswood Ct 5
SW4 .... 62 A2
Queens Yd E9 ... 18 C2
Queen's Yd W1 ... 93 A1
Queen Victoria
Meml* SW1 .... 132 C4
Queen Victoria St
EC4 .... 122 C4
Queen Victoria Terr
2 E1 .... 32 A2
Quelch Ho 2 N19 13 C3
Quemerford Rd
N7 .... 14 B3
Quendon Ho 9
W10 .... 22 B1
Quenington Ct 5
SE15 .... 49 B4
Quenington Mans
SW6 .... 164 C4
Quennel Ho 7
SW12 .... 73 B4
Querrin St SW6 .. 166 C1
Quested Ct 27 E8 . 17 A3
Quex Mews NW6 .23 C4
Quex Rd NW6 .... 23 C4
Quick Rd W4 ..... 38 A1
Quick St N1 ..... 86 B1
Quick Street Mews
N1 .... 86 B1
Quickswood NW3 . 12 A1
Quill La SW15 .... 57 C3
Quill St N4 .... 5 C1
Quilp St SE1 .... 136 C4
Quilter St
E2 .... 24 C2 99 B4
Quilting Ct 28
SE16 .... 40 C4
Quince Rd SE13 . 52 A2
Quintin Ct W4 ... 45 B3
Quintin Kynaston Sch
NW8 .... 79 B3
Quintock Ho 2
TW9 .... 44 C2
Quinton Ho 8 SW8 162 A2
Quinton St SW18 . 71 B2
Quixley St 1 E14 .34 C2
Quorn Rd SE22 ... 64 A4

R

Rabbit Row
W8 ...... 31 C1 113 C2
Raby St E14 ...... 33 A3
Racine 15 SE5 .... 49 A2
Racton Rd SW6 .. 155 B3
Radbourne Cl E5 .17 C4
Radbourne Rd
SW12 .... 73 C3
Radcliff Bldg EC1 107 B4

Radcliffe Ave
NW10 .... 21 C3
Radcliffe Coll
Marylebone W1 ... 104 C1
Soho W1 .... 105 B2
Radcliffe Ho 11
SE16 .... 40 A2
Radcliffe Path
SW8 .... 170 B1
Radcliffe Rd SE1 138 B2
Radcliffe Sq SW15 57 C1
Radcot St SE11 .. 149 C1
Raddington Rd
W10 .... 31 A4
Radford Ho
7 Bow Comm E14..34 A4
Islington N7 ...... 14 B3
Radford Rd SE13 . 67 B1
Radipole Rd SW6 164 C4
Radland Rd E16 ..35 C3
Radlett Pl NW8 ... 80 A4
Radley Ct 23 SE16 .40 C4
Radley Ho NW1 .. 90 C2
Radley Lo 30
SW19 .... 69 C3
Radley Mews W8 125 A1
Radley Terr 1
E16 .... 35 B4
Radnor Lo W2 .. 101 C1
Radnor Mews W2 101 C1
Radnor Pl W2 ... 102 A1
Radnor Rd
Kensal Rise NW6 ..23 A4
Peckham SE15 .... 49 C3
Radnor St EC1 ... 97 A3
Radnor Terr W14 140 C4
Radnor Way
NW10 .... 20 A1
Radnor Wlk
Chelsea SW3 ..... 144 C1
21 Millwall E14 ... 41 C2
Radstock St
SW11 .... 158 A1
Radway Ho 38 W2 ..31 C4
Radwell Ho SW2 . 62 C2
Raeburn Ct 6
SW16 .... 74 A1
Raeburn St SW2 . 62 A3
Ragged School Mus
The* E3 .... 33 A4
Raglan Ct SW9 .. 62 C4
Raglan St NW5 .. 13 A2
Ragley Cl W3 .... 37 B4
Rahere Ho EC1 ... 96 C4
Railey Mews NW5 .13 B3
Railton Rd SE24 .. 63 A2
Railway App SE1 123 C2
Railway Ave SE16.. 40 B4
Railway Cotts W6 .39 B4
Railway Gr SE14 .. 51 B3
Railway Rise SE22..64 A3
Railway Side
SW13 .... 56 A4
Railway St N1 .... 84 B1
Railway Terr SE13 .67 A2
Rainbow Ave E14 ..42 A1
Rainbow Ct 4
SE14 .... 51 A4
Rainbow Quay
SE16 .... 41 A3
Rainbow Sch The
SW17 .... 71 B2
Rainbow St SE5 ..49 A3
Raines Ct N16 ..... 7 B2
Raine's Foundation
Lower Sch E2 ...25 A3

Raine's Foundation
Sch E2 .... 25 B3
Raine St E1 ...... 32 A1
Rainford Ho 7 N7 . 5 B2
Rainham Cl SW11 .60 A1
Rainham Ho NW1 . 83 A3
Rainham Rd NW10 22 B2
Rainhill Way E3 ...26 C2
Rainsborough Ave
SE8 .... 41 A2
Rainsford Ct
NW10 .... 20 A3
Rainsford Ho 14
SW2 .... 62 B2
Rainsford Rd
NW10 .... 20 A3
Rainsford St W2.. 102 A2
Rainton Rd SE7 .. 43 C1
Rainville Rd W6 ...47 B4
Raleigh Ct
7 Hammersmith
W12 .... 39 A4
2 Rotherhithe
SE16 .... 32 C1
Raleigh Gdns SW2 .62 B1
Raleigh Ho
Clapham SW8 .... 171 B2
Isle of Dogs E14 ...42 A4
Raleigh Mews N1 . 86 B3
Raleigh Rd TW9 ..54 B4
Raleigh St N1 .... 86 B3
Ralph Ct W2 .... 100 B2
Ralston St SW3 .. 144 C1
Ramar Ho 16 E1 . 111 B4
Ramilles Cl SW2 .. 62 A1
Ramilles Ho W1 . 105 A1
Ramillies Pl W1 .. 104 C1
Ramillies Rd W4 ..37 C3
Ramillies St W1 . 104 C1
Rampart St E1 .... 32 A3
Rampayne St
SW1 .... 147 B2
Ramsay Ho NW8 . 80 A2
Ramsay Rd W3 .. 37 B4
Ramsdean Ho 1
SW15 .... 69 A3
Ramsden Rd
SW12 .... 72 C4
Ramsey Ct
Putney SW15 ..... 57 B1
10 Upper Holloway
N19 .... 4 C2
Ramsey Ho
5 Battersea
SW11 .... 59 C3
Kennington SW9.. 163 C1
Ramsey St
E2 .... 24 C1 99 C2
Ramsfort Ho
SE16 .... 40 A2
Ramsgate St E8 ..16 B2
Ram St SW18 ..... 59 A2
Randal Cremer JMI
Sch E2 .... 24 B3
Randall Cl SW11 . 168 A4
Randall Pl SE10 .. 52 B3
Randall Rd SE11 . 148 C3
Randall Row
SE11 .... 149 A3
Randell's Rd N1 .. 84 B4
Randolf Ct
Paddington NW6 .. 78 A1
St John's Wood
NW8 .... 78 C3
Randolph Ave W9 . 88 C3
Randolph Cres W9 88 C2

Randolph Gdns
NW6 .... 78 A1
Randolph Mews
W9 .... 89 A1
Randolph Rd W9 . 89 A1
Randolph St NW1 . 13 B1
Ranelagh Ave
Barnes SW13 ..... 46 C1
Fulham SW6 ...... 58 B4
Ranelagh Gardens
Mans SW6 ...... 58 A4
Ranelagh Gardens
(site of Chelsea
Flower Show)*
SW1 .... 145 C1
Ranelagh Gdns
8 Bedford Pk W6 ..38 B3
Chiswick W4 ...... 45 B3
Fulham SW6 ...... 58 B4
Ranelagh Gr SW1 145 C2
Ranelagh Ho
SW3 .... 144 C2
Ranelagh Mans
SW6 .... 165 A2
Ranelagh Rd
Dagenham NW10 .. 21 B3
Pimlico SW1 ..... 147 A1
Rangdon St EC3 . 110 C1
Ranger's House (The
Wernher
Collection)*
SE10 .... 52 C2
Rangers Sq SE10 . 52 C2
Rangoon Ho 5
N16 .... 15 C4
Rankine Ho SE1 . 136 C1
Ranmere St SW12 .73 A3
Rann Ho 11 SW14 .55 C4
Rannoch Rd W6 ..47 C4
Ransomes Dock Bsns
Ctr SW11 .... 158 A1
Ransomes Mews
SW11 .... 158 B2
Ranston St NW1 . 102 A4
Ranulf Rd NW2 .. 10 B4
Ranwell Cl 23 E3 .. 26 B4
Ranwell Ho 22 E3 . 26 B4
Raphael Ct 9
SE16 .... 40 A1
Raphael St SW7 . 130 C3
Rapley Ho
E2 .... 24 C2 99 B3
Rashleigh Ct 8
SW8 .... 61 A4
Rashleigh Ho WC1 94 A3
Rastell Ave SW12 .73 C3
RATCLIFF 32 C3
Ratcliffe Cross St
E1 .... 32 C3
Ratcliffe Ho 10
E14 .... 33 A3
Ratcliffe La 16
E14 .... 33 A3
Ratcliffe Orch 5
E1 .... 32 C2
Rathbone Ho
5 Canning Town
E16 .... 35 B3
Kilburn NW6 ...... 23 C4
Rathbone Mkt 3
E16 .... 35 B4
Rathbone Pl W1 . 105 B2
Rathbone St
Canning Town E16 .35 B3
Fitzrovia W1 ..... 105 A3

Rathgar Rd SW9 . . . .**63** A4
Rathmell Dr SW4 . . . . . .**61** C1
Rattray Rd SW2 . . . .**62** C2
Raul Rd SE15 . . . .**49** C2
Raveley St NW5 . . . .**13** B4
Ravenet Ct
  Battersea SW11 . . . . .**170** A3
  Clapham SW4 . . . .**61** A2
Ravenet St SW11 . . . .**170** A3
Ravenfield Rd
  SW17 . . . .**72** B1
Ravenna Rd SW15 . . . .**57** C2
Raven Row E1 . . . .**32** A4
Ravensbourne Ho
  NW8 . . . .**102** A4
Ravensbourne Mans
  [9] SE8 . . . .**51** C4
Ravensbourne Pl
  SE13 . . . .**52** A1
Ravensbury Rd
  SW18 . . . .**71** A2
Ravensbury Terr
  SW18 . . . .**71** A2
Ravenscar NW1 . . . . . .**82** C3
Ravenscourt [1]
  N16 . . . .**7** C1
Ravenscourt Ave
  W6 . . . .**38** C2
Ravenscourt Gdns
  W6 . . . .**38** C2
Ravenscourt Ho [13]
  W6 . . . .**39** A3
Ravenscourt Park
  Mans [1] W6 . . . .**39** A3
Ravenscourt Park
  Prep Sch W6 . . . .**38** C2
Ravenscourt Park Sta
  . . . .**39** A2
Ravenscourt Pl
  W6 . . . .**38** C2
Ravenscourt Rd
  W6 . . . .**38** C2
Ravenscourt Sq
  W6 . . . .**38** C3
Ravenscourt Theatre
  Sch W6 . . . .**39** A2
Ravenscroft Ave
  NW11 . . . .**1** B4
Ravenscroft Cl [4]
  E16 . . . .**35** C4
Ravenscroft Ct
  NW11 . . . .**1** B4
Ravenscroft Point [26]
  E9 . . . .**17** C2
Ravenscroft Rd
  Acton W4 . . . .**37** B2
  Newham E16 . . . .**35** C4
Ravenscroft St
  E2 . . . .**24** B2 **99** A4
Ravensdon St
  SE11 . . . .**149** C1
Ravenshaw St
  NW6 . . . .**10** B3
Ravenslea Rd SW11,
  SW12 . . . .**72** B4
Ravensmede Way
  W4 . . . .**38** B2
Ravenstone SE17 . . . .**152** B1
Ravenstone Prim Sch
  . . . .**72** C3
Ravenstone St
  SW12 . . . .**72** C3

Ravenswood Rd
  SW12 . . . .**73** A4
Ravensworth Ct
  SW6 . . . .**155** B1
Ravensworth Rd
  NW10 . . . .**22** A2
Raven Wharf SE1 . . .**138** C4
Ravey St
  EC2 . . . .**24** A1 **98** A2
Raw Pinter Cl N16 . . . .**7** A4
Rawlings St SW3 . . . .**144** C4
Rawlinson Ho
  SE13 . . . .**67** C3
Rawlinson Point [8]
  E16 . . . .**35** B4
Rawreth Wlk N1 . . . . . .**87** A4
Rawson Ct SW11 . . . .**169** C3
Rawson St SW11 . . . .**170** A3
Rawstone Pl EC1 . . . . .**96** A4
Rawstorne St EC1 . . . .**96** A4
Raydon St N19 . . . .**4** A2
Ray Ho
  [7] North Kensington
    . . . .**30** C3
  Shoreditch N1 . . . .**87** C3
Raymede Twr
  W10 . . . .**30** C4
Raymond Bldgs
  WC1 . . . .**107** A4
Raymouth Rd
  SE16 . . . .**40** A2
Raynald Ho [15]
  SW16 . . . .**74** A1
Rayne Ct SE1 . . . . . .**138** C4
Rayne Ho
  [1] Balham SW12 . . .**60** C1
  Paddington W9 . . . . . .**88** A2
Rayner Ct [10] W12 . . .**39** B4
Rayner's Rd SW15 . . .**58** A2
Raynes Ct NW2 . . . . . .**10** A4
Raynham Ho [1]
  E1 . . . .**25** C1
Raynham Rd W6 . . . . .**39** A2
Raynor Pl N1 . . . .**87** A4
Ray St EC1 . . . .**95** C1
Ray Wlk N7 . . . .**5** B2
Reachview Ct [17]
  NW1 . . . .**13** B1
Reade Ct [6] W3 . . . . .**37** B3
Reade Wlk [5]
  NW10 . . . .**8** A1
Read Ho SE11 . . . . . .**163** B4
Reading Ho
  Paddington W2 . . . . .**100** C1
  Peckham SE15 . . . .**49** C4
Reading La E8 . . . .**17** A2
Reapers Cl NW1 . . . . . .**83** B4
Reardon Ho [5] E1 . . . .**32** A1
Reardon Path [8]
  E1 . . . .**32** A1
Reardon St E1 . . . .**32** A1
Reaston St SE14 . . . . .**50** C3
Reay Prim Sch
  SW9 . . . .**163** A1
Reckitt Rd W4 . . . .**38** A1
Record St SE16 . . . . . .**50** B4
Rector St N1 . . . .**86** C3
Rectory Gdns [8]
  SW4 . . . .**61** B4
Rectory Gr [4] SW4 . .**61** B4
Rectory Rd
  Barnes SW13 . . . .**46** C1
  [1] London W3 . . . . . .**28** B1
  Shacklewell N16 . . . .**7** B1

Rectory Road Sta
  N16 . . . .**7** B1
Rectory Sq E1 . . . .**32** C4
Reculver Ho [2]
  SE15 . . . .**50** B4
Reculver Rd SE16 . . . .**40** C1
Red Anchor Cl
  SW3 . . . .**158** A3
Redan Pl W2 . . . .**100** A1
Redan St W14 . . . .**39** C3
Redan Terr SE5 . . . . . .**48** A1
Redbourne Ho [7]
  E14 . . . .**33** B3
Redbourn Ho [10]
  W10 . . . .**22** B1
Redbridge Gdns
  SE5 . . . .**49** A3
Redburn St SW3 . . . .**158** C4
Redcar St SE5 . . . .**48** B3
Redcastle Cl [1] E1 . . .**32** B2
Redchurch St
  E2 . . . .**24** B1 **98** C2
Redcliffe Cl [5] SW5 .**142** A1
Redcliffe Gdns
  Chiswick W4 . . . .**45** A3
  Fulham SW10 . . . .**156** B4
Redcliffe Mews
  SW10 . . . .**142** B1
Redcliffe Pl
  SW10 . . . .**156** C3
Redcliffe Rd
  SW10 . . . .**157** A4
Redcliffe Sch
  SW10 . . . .**156** C4
Redcliffe Sq
  SW10 . . . .**142** B1
Redcliffe St
  SW10 . . . .**156** B4
Redclyf Ho [3] E1 . . . . .**25** B1
Redcroft [5] NW6 . . . . .**10** C2
Red Cross Cotts
  SE1 . . . .**137** A4
Redcross Way
  SE1 . . . .**123** A1 **137** A4
Reddins Rd SE15 . . . . .**49** C4
Rede Pl
  W2 . . . .**31** C2 **113** C4
Redesdale St
  SW3 . . . .**158** C4
Redfern Rd NW10 . . . . . .**8** A1
Redfield La SW5 . . . .**142** A4
Redfield Mews
  SW5 . . . .**141** C4
Rediff Est SE16 . . . . . .**41** B3
Redford Wlk N1 . . . . . .**86** C4
Redgate Terr
  SW15 . . . .**57** C1
Redgrave Rd
  SW15 . . . .**57** C4
Redhill Ct SW2 . . . . . .**74** C2
Redhill St NW1 . . . .**92** B4
Red House Sq [20]
  N1 . . . .**15** B1
Redington Gdns
  NW3 . . . .**11** A4
Redington Ho N1 . . . . .**85** A2
Redington Rd
  NW3 . . . .**11** A4
Redlands Prim Sch
  E1 . . . .**32** B4
Redlands Way
  SW2 . . . .**74** B4
Red Lion Cl [9]
  SE17 . . . .**48** C4
Red Lion Ct EC4 . . . .**107** C1
Red Lion Row
  SE17 . . . .**48** B4

Red Lion Sq WC1 . . . .**106** C3
Red Lion St WC1 . . . .**106** C3
Red Lion Yd W1 . . . . .**117** C2
Redlynch Ct W14 . . . .**126** B3
Redlynch Ho SW9 . . .**173** C4
Redman Bldg
  EC1 . . . .**107** B4
Redman Ho SE1 . . . . .**137** A3
Redman's Rd E1 . . . . .**32** B4
Redmayne Ho
  SW9 . . . .**173** A2
Redmead La E1 . . . . .**125** B1
Redmill Ho [24] E1 . . .**25** A1
Redmond Ho N1 . . . . .**85** A3
Redmore Rd W6 . . . . .**39** A2
Red Pl W1 . . . .**117** B4
Red Post Hill SE21,
  SE24 . . . .**63** C2
Redriff Prim Sch
  SE16 . . . .**41** A4
Redriff Rd SE16 . . . . . .**41** A3
Red Rover SW14 . . . . .**56** C4
Redrup Ho [21]
  SE14 . . . .**50** C4
Redruth Rd E9 . . . .**25** B4
Red Sq The N16 . . . .**6** C1
Redstart Cl SE14 . . . . .**51** A3
Redvers St
  E2 . . . .**24** A2 **98** B4
Redwald Rd E5 . . . .**17** C4
Redwood Cl
  [4] Bow E3 . . . .**26** C3
  Rotherhithe SE16 . . . . .**33** A1
Redwood Ct
  Brondesbury NW6 . . . . .**10** B1
  Crouch End N19 . . . .**4** C4
Redwood Mews [2]
  SW4 . . . .**61** A4
Redwoods SW15 . . . . .**68** C3
Reece Mews SW7 . . .**143** B4
Reed Cl E16 . . . .**35** C4
Reedham St SE15 . . . . .**64** C4
Reed Ho SW15 . . . .**56** C1
Reedholm Villas
  N16 . . . .**15** C4
Reed Pl SW4 . . . .**61** C3
Reed's Pl NW1 . . . .**13** B1
Reedworth St
  SE11 . . . .**149** C3
Reef Ho E14 . . . .**42** B3
Rees St N1 . . . .**87** A3
Reeves Ho
  Lambeth SE1 . . . .**135** B3
  Mayfair W1 . . . .**117** B3
Reeves Mews W1 . . .**117** C3
Reeves Rd E3 . . . .**27** A1
Reflection Ho
  E2 . . . .**24** C1 **99** B2
Reform St SW11 . . . .**169** A2
Regal Cl E1 . . . .**111** C4
Regal La NW1 . . . .**81** C3
Regal Pl
  [1] Tower Hamlets
    E3 . . . .**26** B2
  Walham Green
    SW6 . . . .**156** B1
Regan Way N1 . . . .**24** A3
Regatta Point
  TW8 . . . .**44** B4
Regency Ct
  [3] Bow E3 . . . .**26** B3
  [4] South Hackney
    E9 . . . .**25** B4
Regency Ho NW1 . . . . .**92** B2
Regency Lo NW3 . . . . .**11** C1
Regency Mews
  Camberwell SW9 . . . . .**48** A3

Regency Mews
  continued
  [1] Willesden NW10 . . .**8** C2
Regency Pl SW1 . . . .**147** C4
Regency St SW1 . . . .**147** C3
Regency Terr
  SW7 . . . .**143** B2
Regency Wlk [6]
  TW10 . . . .**54** A2
Regeneration Rd
  SE16 . . . .**40** C2
Regent Ct
  Lisson Gr NW8 . . . .**90** A3
  [1] Stamford Hill N16 .**7** B4
Regent Ho W14 . . . . .**140** A4
Regent Pl W1 . . . .**119** A4
Regent Rd SE24 . . . . . .**63** A2
Regents Bridge Gdns
  SW8 . . . .**162** B2
Regents Canal Ho
  E14 . . . .**33** B3
Regent's Coll NW1 . . .**91** B2
Regents Ct E8 . . . .**24** C4
Regents Gate Ho [20]
  E14 . . . .**33** A2
Regents Lo [9]
  SW2 . . . .**74** B3
Regents Mews
  NW8 . . . .**79** A2
REGENT'S PARK★ **81** B1
Regent's Park★
  NW1 . . . .**81** B1
Regent's Park
  Barracks NW1 . . . . .**82** B1
Regent's Park Rd
  Camden Town
    NW1 . . . .**81** B4
  Primrose Hill NW3 . . . .**12** C1
Regent's Park Sta
  . . . .**92** A1
Regent's Park Terr
  NW1 . . . .**82** B4
Regent's Pl SE3 . . . . . .**53** C1
Regents Plaza
  NW6 . . . .**78** A2
Regent Sq
  [2] Bromley E3 . . . . .**27** A2
  St Pancras WC1 . . . . . .**94** B3
Regent's Row E8 . . . . .**24** C4
Regent St
  Brentford W4 . . . .**36** C1
  [7] Kensal Green
    NW10 . . . .**22** C2
  Mayfair W1 . . . .**118** C4
Regents Wharf
  [3] Hackney E2 . . . . .**25** A4
  Islington N1 . . . .**84** C2
Reginald Pl [6]
  SE8 . . . .**51** C3
Reginald Rd SE8 . . . . .**51** C3
Reginald Sq SE8 . . . . .**51** C3
Regina Point SE16 . . .**40** B3
Regina Rd N4 . . . .**5** B3
Regis Ct NW1 . . . .**102** C4
Regis Pl [17] SW2 . . . .**62** B3
Regis Rd NW5 . . . .**13** A3
Regnart Bldgs
  NW1 . . . .**93** A3
Reid Ct SW14 . . . .**45** B1
Reighton Rd E5 . . . .**7** C2
Reizel Cl N16 . . . .**7** B3
Relay Rd W12 . . . .**30** B1
Relf Rd SE15 . . . .**64** C4
Reliance Sq
  E2 . . . .**24** A1 **98** B2
Relton Ct SW8 . . . .**36** C4

Relton Mews
SW7 . . . . **130** B2
Rembrandt Cl E14 . .42 C3
Rembrandt Ct █
SE16 . . . . .40 A1
Rembrant Cl SW1 **145** B3
Remington St N1 . . . .86 B1
Remnant St WC2 . **106** C2
Remsted Ho NW6 . .78 A3
Remus Rd E3 . . . . . .18 C1
Renaissance Wlk █
SE10 . . . . .43 B3
Renbold Ho █
SE10 . . . . .52 B2
Rendlesham Ho █ E5,
N16 . . . . .7 C1
kendlesham Rd . .7 C1
Renforth St SE16 . . .40 A4
Renfrew Ho NW6 . . .78 A1
Renfrew Rd SE11 **150** A3
Rennell Ho █ E9 . . .17 C2
Rennell St SE13 . . . .67 B4
Rennie Cotts █
E1 . . . . .25 B1
Rennie Ct SE1 . . . . **122** A2
Rennie Ho SE1 . . . **136** C1
Rennie St SE1 . . . . **122** A2
Renoir Ct █ SE16 . .40 A1
Renton Cl SW2 . . . .62 B1
Rephidim St SE1 . **138** A1
Replingham Rd
SW18 . . . . .70 C3
Reporton Rd SW6 **154** B1
Repton Ho SW1 . . **147** A3
Repton St E14 . . . . .33 A3
Reservoir Rd SE4 . .51 A1
Reservoir Studios █
E1 . . . . .32 C3
Resolution Way █
SE8 . . . . .51 C3
Restell Cl SE3 . . . . .53 A4
Reston Pl SW7 . . . **128** C3
Restoration Sq
SW11 . . . . **167** C3
Retcar Pl N19 . . . . . .4 A2
Retford St E2 . . . . . .24 A3
Retreat Ho █ E9 . . .17 B2
Retreat Pl E9 . . . . . .17 B2
Retreat The SW14 . .56 A4
Reunion Row E1 . . .32 A2
Reveley Sq SE16 . . .41 A4
Revelon Rd SE4 . . .66 A4
Revelstoke Rd SW18,
SW19 . . . . .70 C2
Reverdy Rd SE1 . . **153** B3
Rewell St SW6 . . . **156** C1
Rex Pl W1 . . . . **117** C2
Reynard Cl SE4 . . . .66 A4
Reynard Pl SE14 . . .51 A4
Reynolds Cl NW11 . .2 A4
Reynolds Ho
Finsbury Pk N4 . . . . . .5 A4
█ South Hackney
E2 . . . . .25 B3
St John's Wood
NW8 . . . . .79 C1
Westminster SW1 . **147** C3
Reynolds Pl █
TW10 . . . . .54 B1
Reynolds Rd
Acton Green W4 . . . .37 B3
Nunhead SE15 . . . . . .65 B3
Rheidol Mews █ . .86 C3
Rheidol Terr N1 . . . .86 C3
Rhoda St E2 .24 B1 **99** A2

Rhodes Ho █
Shepherd's Bush
W12 . . . . .30 A1
Shoreditch N1 . . . . . .97 B4
Rhodesia Rd SW9 **172** B1
Rhodeswell Rd
E14 . . . . .33 B3
Rhondda Gr E3 . . . .26 B2
Rhyl Prim Sch
NW5 . . . . .12 C2
Rhyl St NW5 . . . . . .12 C2
Ribblesdale Ho █
NW6 . . . . .23 C4
Ribbon Dance Mews
SE5 . . . . .48 C2
Ribstone Ho █
E9 . . . . .17 C2
Ricardo St E14 . . . .34 A3
Riceyman Ho WC1 . .95 B3
Richard Anderson Ct
█ SE14 . . . . .50 C3
Richard Atkins Prim
Sch SW2 . . . . .74 A4
Richard Burbidge
Mans SW13 . . . . . .47 B4
Richard Cloudesley
Sch EC1 . . . . .96 C1
Richard Cobden Prim
Sch NW1 . . . . .83 A3
Richard Fox Ho N4 .6 B1
Richard Ho █
SE16 . . . . .40 B2
Richard Knight Ho
SW6 . . . . **165** C4
Richard Neale Ho █
E1 . . . . .32 A2
Richardson Cl █
E8 . . . . .24 B4
Richardson Ct
SW4 . . . . **172** B2
Richardson Ho █
E14 . . . . .33 C4
Richardson's Mews
W1 . . . . .92 C1
Richard's Pl SW3 . **144** B4
Richard St █ E1 . . .32 A3
Richbell WC1 . . . . **106** B4
Richbell Pl WC1 . **106** C4
Richborne Terr
SW8 . . . . **163** A2
Richborough Ho
█ Deptford SE15 . . .50 B4
█ Hackney E5 . . . . .17 A4
Richborough Rd
NW2 . . . . .10 A4
Richbourne Ct
W1 . . . . **102** B2
Richford Gate W6 . .39 B3
Richford St W6 . . . .39 B3
Rich La SW5 . . . . . **142** A2
Richland Ho █
SE15 . . . . .49 C2
Richman Ho █
SE8 . . . . .41 B1
RICHMOND 54 B3
Richmond Ave
Islington N1 . . . . .85 A4
Willesden NW10 . . . . .9 B2
Richmond Bldgs
W1 . . . . **105** B1
Richmond Circus
TW9 . . . . .54 A3
Richmond Coll
W8 . . . . **128** B2
Richmond Cres
N1 . . . . .85 A4

Richmond Ct
SW1 . . . . **131** A3
Richmond Gr N1 . . .15 A1
Richmond Healthcare
Hamlet Hospl
TW9 . . . . .54 A4
RICHMOND HILL . . .54 A1
Richmond Hill
TW10 . . . . .54 A1
Richmond Hill Ct █
TW10 . . . . .54 A1
Richmond Ho
█ Forest Hill
SE26 . . . . .76 C1
Regent's Pk NW1 . . . .82 B1
Walworth SE17 . . . . **151** B2
Richmond
International Bsns
Ctr █ TW9 . . . . .54 A4
Richmond Mans
Earl's Ct SW5 . . . . . **142** A2
Putney SW15 . . . . . . .58 A4
Richmond Mews
W1 . . . . **105** B1
Richmond Park Rd
SW14 . . . . .55 C2
Richmond Rd
Dalston E8 . . . . .16 C1
Ealing W5 . . . . .36 A4
Richmond Sta
TW9 . . . . .54 A4
Richmond Terr
SW1 . . . . **134** A4
Richmond Way W12,
W14 . . . . .39 C4
Rich St E14 . . . . . . .33 B2
Rickett St SW6 . . **155** C4
Rickman Ho █ E1 . .25 B1
Rickman St █ E1 . .25 B1
Rick Roberts Way
E15 . . . . .27 C3
Rickthorne Rd █
N19 . . . . .5 A2
Riddell Ct SE1 . . . **152** C2
Ridgdale St E3 . . . .27 A3
Ridge Hill NW11 . . . .1 A3
Ridge Rd NW2 . . . . .1 B1
Ridgeway █
TW10 . . . . .54 A1
Ridgeway Dr W4 . . .36 C3
Ridgeway Gdns N6 . .4 B4
Ridgeway The
Acton W3 . . . . .36 C3
Golders Green NW11 . .1 B3
Ridgewell Cl N1 . . **87** A4
Ridgmount Gdns
WC1 . . . . **105** B4
Ridgmount Pl
WC1 . . . . **105** B4
Ridgmount Rd
SW18 . . . . .59 A2
Ridgmount St
WC1 . . . . **105** B4
Ridgway Rd SW9 . . .63 A4
Riding House St
W1 . . . . **104** C3
Ridings Cl N6 . . . . . .4 B4
Riding The NW11 . . .1 B4
Ridley Ho █
SW11 . . . . .60 A4
Ridley Rd
Dalston E8 . . . . .16 B3
Willesden Green
NW10 . . . . .21 C3
Ridley Road Mkt
E8 . . . . .16 B3

Riffel Rd NW2 . . . . . .9 B3
Rifle Ct SE11 . . . . . **163** C4
Rifle Pl W11 . . . . . . .30 C1
Rifle St E14 . . . . . . .34 A4
Riga Ho █ E1 . . . . . .32 C4
Rigault Rd SW6 . . **164** B1
Rigden St E14 . . . . .34 A3
Rigeley Rd NW10 . . .21 C2
Rigge Pl SW4 . . . . . .61 C3
Rigg Ho █ SW4 . . . .74 A4
Rignold Ho █ SE5 . .49 A1
Riley Ho
█ Bow E3 . . . . .26 C1
Chelsea SW10 . . . . . **157** B3
█ Streatham SW4 . .73 C4
Riley Rd SE1 . . . . . **138** C2
Riley St SW10 . . . . **157** B2
Rill Ho █ SE5 . . . . .49 A3
Rimini Ct SW12 . . . .72 B3
Rinaldo Rd SW12 . . .73 A4
Ringcroft St N7 . . . .14 C3
Ringford Ho SW18 . .58 B2
Ringford Rd SW18 . .58 C1
Ring Ho █ E1 . . . . . .32 B2
Ringmer Ave
SW6 . . . . **164** B3
Ringmer Gdns █
N19 . . . . .5 A2
Ringmer Ho █
SE22 . . . . .64 A4
Ring Rd W12 . . . . . .30 B1
Ringsfield Ho
SE17 . . . . **151** A1
Ringwood Gdns
█ Millwall E14 . . . . . .41 C2
Roehampton SW15 . . .68 C3
Ripley Gdns SW14 . .56 A4
Ripley Ho
Mortlake SW14 . . . . . .56 A4
Nine Elms SW11 . . . **160** C4
Riplington Ct
SW15 . . . . .69 A4
Ripplevale Gr N1 . . .14 B1
Risborough SE17 . **150** C4
Risborough Ho
NW8 . . . . .90 B2
Risborough St
SE1 . . . . **136** B4
Risdon Ho █ SE16 . .40 B4
Risdon St █ SE16 . .40 B4
Risholme Ct E9 . . . .18 B2
Riseholme Ho █
SE22 . . . . .64 A4
Riseldine Rd SE23 . .66 A1
Risinghill St N1 . . . .85 B2
Rising Sun Ct
EC1 . . . . **108** B3
Risley Ho █ E9 . . . .17 C2
Rita Rd SW8 . . . . . **162** C2
Ritchie Ho
Crouch End N19 . . . . .4 C4
█ Rotherhithe
SE16 . . . . .40 B3
█ South Bromley
E14 . . . . .34 C3
Ritchie St N1 . . . . . .85 C2
Ritherdon Rd
SW17 . . . . .73 A2
Ritson Ho N1 . . . . . .84 C3
Ritson Rd E8 . . . . . .16 C2
Rivaz Pl E9 . . . . . . .17 B2
Riven Ct W2 . . . . . **100** B1
Riverains The
SW11 . . . . **167** B3
River Barge Cl
E14 . . . . .42 B4
Rivercourt Rd W6 . .39 A1

River Ct SE1 . . . . . **122** A3
Riverdale Dr
SW18 . . . . .71 A3
Riverfleet WC1 . . . .94 B4
Riverford Ho █
W2 . . . . .31 C4
River Ho SW13 . . . .46 A1
Rivermead Ct
SW6 . . . . .58 B4
Rivermead Ho E9 . .18 A3
River Pl N1 . . . . .15 B1
River Plate Ho
EC2 . . . . **109** C3
Riverside Prim Sch
SE16 . . . . .70 C3
Riverside Rd N15 . . .6 B1
Riversdene N5 . . . . .6 B1
Rivers Ho █ TW8 . . .36 C1
Riverside
Battersea SW11 . . . **158** B2
█ Rotherhithe
SE16 . . . . .40 B4
St Pancras WC1 . . . . .94 B4
Riverside Bsns Ctr
SW18 . . . . .71 A3
Riverside Cl SW8 **161** C4
Riverside Dr W4 . . .46 A2
Riverside Gdns
W6 . . . . .39 A1
Riverside Ho █
N1 . . . . .15 B1
Riverside Mans █
E1 . . . . .32 B1
Riverside Prim Sch
SE16 . . . . **139** C3
Riverside Rd
Mill Meads E15 . . . . .27 B3
Wandsworth SW17,
SW19 . . . . .71 B1
Riverside Workshops
SE1 . . . . **123** A2
River St EC1 . . . . . . .95 B4
River Terr W6 . . . . . .39 B1
Riverton Cl W9 . . . .23 B2
Riverview Gdns
SW13 . . . . .47 A4
Riverview Gr W4 . . .45 A4
Riverview Rd W4 . . .45 A4
River Way SE10 . . . .43 B3
Rivet Ho SE1 . . . . . **153** A2
Rivington Ct
NW10 . . . . .21 C4
Rivington Pl
EC2 . . . . .24 A2 **98** A4
Rivington St
EC2 . . . . .24 A2 **98** A4
Rivington Wlk █
E8 . . . . .24 C4
Rixon St N7 . . . . .5 C1
Roach Rd E3 . . . . . .18 C1
Roads Pl N19 . . . . . .5 A2
Roan St SE10 . . . . . .52 B4
Robert Adam St
W1 . . . . **103** B2
Roberta St
E2 . . . . .24 C2 **99** C3
Robert Bell Ho █
SE16 . . . . **153** B4
Robert Blair Prim Sch
N7 . . . . .14 A2
Robert Browning
Prim Sch SE17 . . **151** B2
Robert Cl W9 . . . . . .89 A1
Robert Dashwood
Way SE17 . . . . **150** C3

Robert Gentry Ho
W14 . . . . **140** B1
Robert Jones Ho
SE16 . . . . **153** B4
Robert Keen Cl 18
SE15 . . . . .49 C2
Robert Lowe Cl
SE14 . . . . .50 C3
Robert Owen Ho
Fulham SW6 . . . . . .47 C2
Spitalfields
E2 . . . . .24 B2 **99** A4
Robert Owen Lo 4
E5 . . . . .17 A4
Roberts Ct
Islington N1 . . . . . .86 B3
Willesden NW10 . . . .8 A2
Roberts Ho 5
SE27 . . . . .75 A1
Roberts Mews
SW1 . . . . **131** B1
Robertson Ho 11
SE10 . . . . .52 B2
Robertson Rd E15 . .27 B4
Robertson St
SW8 . . . . **170** B1
Robert's Pl EC1 . . . **95** C2
Robert St
Regent's Pk NW1 . . . **92** B3
Strand WC2 . . . . . . **120** B3
Robert Sutton Ho 20
E1 . . . . .32 B3
Robeson St 7 E3 . . .33 B4
Robin Cl E14 . . . . .42 B3
Robin Gr N6 . . . . . . .3 C2
Robin Ho 15 E14 . .42 B3
Robin Hood SW15 .68 A4
Robin Hood Gdns 12
E14 . . . . .34 B2
Robin Hood La
E14 . . . . .34 B2
Robinscroft Mews 18
SE10 . . . . .52 A2
Robins Ct 10 SW14 .54 A1
Robin's Ct SW4 . . . .62 A1
Robinsfield Inf Sch
NW8 . . . . .80 A2
Robinson Ct
Islington N1 . . . . . . .86 B4
4 Richmond TW9 . . .54 B3
Robinson Ho
4 North Kensington
W10 . . . . .30 C3
12 Tower Hamlets
E14 . . . . .34 C4
Robinson Rd E2 . . .25 B3
Robinson St SW3 . **158** C4
Robsart St SW9 . . **173** B2
Robson Ave NW10 . . .8 C1
Robson Rd SE21,
SE27 . . . . .75 B1
Roby Ho EC1 . . . . . . **96** C2
Rochdale Way 4
SE8 . . . . .51 C3
Roche Ho 15 E14 . .33 B2
Rochelle Cl SW11 . .59 C3
Rochelle Ct 14 E1 . .32 B3
Rochelle St
E2 . . . . .24 B2 **98** C3
Rochemont Wlk 2
E8 . . . . .24 C4
Roche Sch The
SW18 . . . . .58 C2

Rochester Ct
1 Bethnal Green
E2 . . . . .25 A1
9 Camden Town
NW1 . . . . .13 B1
Rochester Ho
Bermondsey SE1 . . **137** C3
18 Deptford SE15 . . .50 B4
Rochester Mews
NW1 . . . . .13 B1
Rochester Pl NW1 . .13 B1
Rochester Rd
NW1 . . . . .13 B2
Rochester Row
SW1 . . . . **147** A4
Rochester Sq
NW1 . . . . .13 B1
Rochester St
SW1 . . . . **133** B1
Rochester Terr
NW1 . . . . .13 B2
Rochester Wlk
SE1 . . . . **123** B2
Rochford Wlk 3
E8 . . . . .16 C1
Rochfort Ho 4
SE8 . . . . .41 B1
Rock Ave 18 SW14 .55 C4
Rockell's Pl SE22 . .65 A1
Rockfield Ho SE10 . .52 B4
Rock Grove Way
SE16 . . . . **153** C4
Rockhall Rd NW2 . . . .9 C4
Rockingham Cl
SW15 . . . . .56 B3
Rockingham St
SE1 . . . . **136** C1
Rockland Rd
SW15 . . . . .58 A3
Rockley Ct 8
W14 . . . . .39 C4
Rockley Rd W14 . . .39 C4
Rocks La SW13 . . . .56 C4
Rock St N4 . . . . .5 C2
Rockstraw Ho 5
NW3 . . . . .12 B1
Rockwood Ct N16 . . .7 C4
Rocliffe St N1 . . . . .86 B1
Rocque Ho SW6 . . **154** C2
Rodborough Rd
NW11 . . . . .1 C3
Rodenhurst Ct
SW4 . . . . .61 C2
Rodenhurst Rd
SW4 . . . . .61 C1
Roden St N7 . . . . . . .5 B1
Roderick Ho 3
SE16 . . . . .40 B2
Roderick Rd NW3 . .12 B4
Rodgers Ho 4
SW4 . . . . .73 C4
Rodin Ct N1 . . . . . . .86 A3
Roding Ct 12 E14 . .38 A4
Roding Ho N1 . . . . .85 B3
Roding Mews E1 . . **125** C2
Roding Rd E5 . . . . . .18 A3
Rodmarton St
W1 . . . . **103** A3
Rodmell WC1 . . . . . .94 B3
Rodmere St SE10 . . .43 A1
Rodmill La SW2 . . .74 A4
Rodney Ct NW8 . . . .89 A2
Rodney Ho
1 Cubitt Town
E14 . . . . .42 A2
Islington N1 . . . . . . .85 A1

Rodney Ho continued
Notting Hill
W11 . . . . . .31 C2 **113** B4
Rodney Pl SE17 . . . **151** A4
Rodney Rd SE17 . . **151** B3
Rodney St N1 . . . . . .85 A1
Rodway Rd SW15 . . .68 C4
Rodwell Rd SE22 . . .64 B1
Roedean Cres
SW15 . . . . .56 A2
ROEHAMPTON 56 C2
Roehampton CE Prim
Sch SW15 . . . . . . .69 A4
Roehampton Cl
SW15 . . . . .56 C3
Roehampton Ct
SW13 . . . . .56 C4
Roehampton Gate
SW15 . . . . .56 A1
Roehampton High St
SW15 . . . . .68 C4
Roehampton La
Putney SW15 . . . . . .56 C1
Roehampton SW15 . .69 A3
Roehampton Univ
(Digby Stuart Coll)
SW15 . . . . .56 C2
Roehampton Univ
(Froebel Coll)
SW15 . . . . .56 B1
Roehampton Univ
(Southlands Coll)
SW15 . . . . .56 C2
Roehampton Univ
(Whitelands Coll)
SW15 . . . . .68 C4
Roehampton Vale
SW15 . . . . .68 B2
Roffey St E14 . . . . . .42 B4
Rogate Ho E5 . . . . . . .7 C1
Roger Dowley Ct 8
E2 . . . . .25 B3
Roger's Almshouses
2 SW9 . . . . .62 B3
Rogers Ct 16 E14 . .33 C2
Rogers Est 28 E2 . . .25 B2
Rogers Ho Pimlico
SW1 . . . . **147** C4
Rogers Rd E16 . . . . .35 B3
Roger St WC1 . . . . . .95 A1
Rokeby Ho
8 Balham SW12 . . . .73 A4
Bloomsbury WC1 . . .94 C1
Rokeby Rd SE4 . . . . .51 B1
Rokeby St E15 . . . . .19 C1
Rokeland Ho SE4 . . .66 A3
Roland Gdns
SW7 . . . . **143** A2
Roland Ho SW7 . . . **143** A2
Roland Mews 1
E1 . . . . .32 C4
Roland Way
South Kensington
SW7 . . . . **143** A2
Walworth SE17 . . . **151** C1
Rollins St SE15 . . . . .50 B4
Rollit Ho N7 . . . . . . .14 C3
Rollit St N7 . . . . . . .14 C3
Rollo Ct SW11 . . . . .170 A3
Rolls Bldgs EC4 . . . **107** C2
Rollscourt Ave
SE24 . . . . .63 B2
Rolls Pas EC4 . . . . . **107** B2
Rolls Rd SE1 . . . . . **153** A2
Rolt St SE8 . . . . .51 A4
Roman Cl W3 . . . . . .37 A4
Roman Ct N7 . . . . . .14 B2

Romanfield Rd
SW2 . . . . .74 B4
Roman Rd
Chiswick W4 . . . . . .38 B2
Globe Town E2, E3 . .25 C3
25 Old Ford E3 . . . . .26 B3
Roman Square Mkt
1 E3 . . . . .26 B3
Roman Way
Barnsbury N7 . . . . . .14 B2
4 Deptford SE15 . . .50 B4
Roma Read Cl
SW15 . . . . .69 A4
Romayne Ho SW4 . .61 C4
Romberg Rd
SW17 . . . . .72 C1
Romborough Gdns
SE13 . . . . .67 B2
Romborough Way
SE13 . . . . .67 B2
Romer Ho 9 SW2 . .62 B2
Romero Cl SW9 . . . .62 B4
Romeyn Rd SW16 . .74 B1
Romford Ho 17
N1 . . . . .15 C2
Romford St E1 . . . . .32 A4
Romilly Rd N4 . . . . . .6 A2
Romilly St W1 . . . . **119** C4
Romily Ct SW6 . . . **164** B2
Romney Cl
7 Deptford SE14 . . .50 B3
North End NW11 . . . . .2 A3
Romney Ct
9 Hammersmith
W12 . . . . .39 B4
3 Hampstead
NW3 . . . . .12 A2
Romney Ho 2
E14 . . . . .34 C2
Romney Mews
W1 . . . . **103** B4
Romney Rd SE10 . . .52 C4
Romney St SW1 . . . **134** A1
Romola Rd SE24,
SW2 . . . . .75 A3
Ronald Ross Prim Sch
SW19 . . . . .70 A4
Ronaldshay N4 . . . . . .5 C3
Ronalds Rd N5 . . . . .14 C3
Ronald St E1 . . . . . . .32 B3
Rona Rd NW3 . . . . . .12 C4
Rona Wlk 20 N1 . . .15 C2
Rondu Rd NW2 . . . . .10 A3
Rood La EC3 . . . . . . **124** A4
Rookery Rd SW4 . . .61 B3
Rooke Way SE10 . . .43 B1
Rookwood Rd N16 . . .7 C4
Roosevelt Ct 15
SW19 . . . . .70 A3
Rootes Dr W10 . . . . .30 C4
Ropemaker Rd
SE16 . . . . .41 A3
Ropemaker's Fields 7
E14 . . . . .33 B2
Ropemaker St
EC2 . . . . **109** B4
Roper La SE1 . . . . . **138** B3
Roper's Orch
SW3 . . . . **158** A3
Ropers Wlk 18
SE24 . . . . .74 C4
Ropery St E3 . . . . . . .26 B1
Rope St SE16 . . . . . .41 A3
Ropewalk Gdns
E1 . . . . **111** C2
Ropley St 6 E2 . . . . .24 C3

Rosa Alba Mews
N5 . . . . .15 B4
Rosalind Ho 25
N1 . . . . .24 A3
Rosaline Rd SW6 . . **154** B1
Rosaline Terr
SW6 . . . . **154** B1
Rosa Parks Ho
SW9 . . . . **172** C1
Rosary Ct 11 E1 . . . .32 C4
Rosary Gdns SW7 **143** A3
Rosary RC Prim Sch
NW3 . . . . .12 A3
Rosaville Rd SW6 . **154** C1
Rosbury SW15 . . . . .58 A1
Roscastle Rd SE4 . . .66 A2
Roscoe St EC1 . . . . . .97 A1
Roscommon Ho 2
NW3 . . . . .11 C3
Rose Alley
Borough The SE1 . . **123** A2
Broadgate EC2 . . . . **110** B3
Rosebank
2 Dagenham W3 . . .28 C3
Fulham SW6 . . . . . .47 B3
Rosebank Gdns
Bow E3 . . . . .26 B3
1 Dagenham W3 . . .28 C3
Rosebank Way
W3 . . . . .28 C3
Rosebank Wlk
NW1 . . . . .13 C1
Rosebay Ho 20 E3 . .33 C4
Roseberry Pl E8 . . . .16 B2
Roseberry St SE16 . .40 A2
Rosebery Ave EC1 . . **95** C3
Rosebery Ct
Holborn EC1 . . . . . . **95** B2
Mayfair W1 . . . . . . **118** A2
Rosebery Ho 21
E2 . . . . .25 B3
Rosebery Rd SW2 . .62 A1
Rosebery Sq EC1 . . . **95** B1
Rosebury Rd
SW6 . . . . **166** B1
Rose Bush Ct
NW3 . . . . .12 B3
Rosecroft Ave NW3 . .1 C1
Rose & Crown Ct
EC2 . . . . **108** C2
Rose & Crown Yd
SW1 . . . . **119** A1
Rose Ct
7 Dalston E8 . . . . . .16 B1
Islington N1 . . . . . . .86 A3
Spitalfields E1 . . . . **111** A3
Rosedale Ct N5 . . . . .15 A4
Rosedale Ho N16 . . . .6 C3
Rosedale Rd TW9 . . .54 A3
Rosedale Terr W6 . . .39 A3
Rosedene NW6 . . . . .22 C4
Rosedene Ave
SW16 . . . . .74 B1
Rosedew Rd W6 . . . .47 C4
Rosefield Gdns
E14 . . . . .33 C2
Roseford Ct 18
W12 . . . . .39 C4
Rosegate Ho 32
E3 . . . . .26 B3
Rosehart Mews 8
W11 . . . . .31 C3
Rosehill Rd SW18 . .59 B2
Roseland Ho SW6 . .58 A4
Roseleigh Ave N5 . . .15 A4
Rosemary Branch
Bridge N1 . . . . . . .87 C4

Rosemary Ct 🔟	Rossendale Way	Rothsay St SE1 . . . . **138** A1
SE8 . . . . .51 B4	NW1 . . . . **83** A4	Rothsay Wlk 🔟
Rosemary Dr 🔟	Rossetti Ct WC1 . . . . **105** B4	E14 . . . . .41 C2
E14 . . . . .34 C3	Rossetti Gdns Mans	Rothschild Rd W4 . .37 B3
Rosemary Gdns	SW3 . . . . **158** C4	Rothwell St
SW14 . . . . .55 B4	Rossetti Ho SW1 . **147** C3	🔟 Hampstead
Rosemary Ho	Rossetti Mews	NW1 . . . . .12 B1
Shoreditch N1 . . . . **87** C3	NW8 . . . . **79** C3	Primrose Hill NW1 . . .81 A4
Willesden NW10 . . . .22 A4	Rossetti Rd SE16 . .40 A1	Roth Wlk N7 . . . . .5 B2
Rosemary La	Rossetti Studios	Rotten Row SW1 . **130** C4
SW14 . . . . .55 B4	SW3 . . . . **158** B4	Rotterdam Dr E14 . .42 B3
Rosemary Rd	Ross Ho 🔟 E1. . . . . . .32 A1	Rouel Rd
Camberwell SE15 . . . .49 B3	Rossington St E5 . . . .7 C2	Bermondsey SE16 . **139** C2
Wandsworth SW17 . .71 B1	Rossiter Rd SW12 . .73 A3	Bermondsey SE16 . **139** B1
Rosemary St N1 . . . **87** C3	Rosslyn Ave SW13 . .56 B4	Roundacre SW19 . . . .69 C2
Rosemary Works Sch	Rosslyn Ct NW3 . . . .12 A3	Roundel Cl SE4 . . . .66 B3
N1 . . . . **87** C3	Rosslyn Hill NW3 . . .11 C3	Roundwood Rd
Rosemead Prep Sch	Rosslyn Ho 🔟	NW10 . . . . .8 B2
SE27 . . . . .75 B2	TW9 . . . . .44 B2	Rounton Rd E3 . . . .26 C1
Rosemont Mans 🔟	Rosslyn Mans	Roupell Rd SW2 . . . .74 B3
NW3 . . . . .11 A2	🔟 Hampstead	Roupell St SE1 . . . **121** C1
Rosemont Rd	NW3 . . . . .11 B2	Rousden St NW1 . . . .13 B1
Acton W3 . . . . .28 A2	South Hampstead	Routh Rd SW18 . . . .72 A4
Richmond TW10 . . . .54 A1	NW3 . . . . .11 C4	Rover Ho 🔟 N1 . . . .24 A4
South Hampstead	Rosslyn Mews 🔟	Rowallan Rd SW6 . **154** A1
NW3 . . . . .11 B2	NW3 . . . . .11 C4	Rowan Cl W5 . . . . . .36 A4
Rosemont St	Rosslyn Park Mews	Rowan Ct
SW3 . . . . **144** C3	NW3 . . . . .11 C3	🔟 Bow E3 . . . . .26 B4
Rosemount Ct 🔟	Rossmore Cl NW1 . **90** C2	Dagenham NW10 . . . .21 A1
W3 . . . . .28 A1	Rossmore Rd NW1 . **90** B2	🔟 Maitland Pk
Rosemount Lo	Rostrevor Mans	NW5 . . . . .12 B3
W3 . . . . .28 A2	SW6 . . . . **164** C4	Rowan Rd W6 . . . . .39 C2
Rosenau Cres	Rostrevor Mews	Rowan Terr W6 . . . .39 C2
SW11 . . . . **168** C3	SW6 . . . . **164** C4	Rowan Wlk
Rosenau Rd	Rostrevor Rd	🔟 Dartmouth Pk
SW11 . . . . **168** C4	SW6 . . . . **164** C4	N19 . . . . .4 B2
Rosendale Prim Sch	Rotary La SE27 . . . .75 A1	Kensal Town W10 . . .23 A1
SE21 . . . . .75 B4	Rotary St SE1 . . . . **136** B2	Rowberry Cl SW6 . .47 B3
Rosendale Rd SE21,	Rothay NW1 . . . . . . **92** B4	Rowcross St SE1 . **153** A2
SE24 . . . . .75 C3	Rothbury Rd E9 . . . .18 C1	Rowditch La
Roseneath Rd	Rotheley Ho 🔟 E9 . .17 B1	SW11 . . . . **169** B2
SW11 . . . . .60 C1	Rotherfield Ct	Rowdon Ave NW10 . . .9 A1
Rosenthal Ho SE6 . .67 A1	De Beauvoir Town	Rowe Ho E9 . . . . . . .17 B2
Rosenthal Rd SE6 . .67 B1	N1 . . . . .15 C1	Rowe La E9 . . . . . . .17 B3
Rosenthorpe Rd	Shoreditch N1 . . . . **87** B4	Rowena Cres
SE15 . . . . .65 C2	Rotherfield Prim Sch	SW11 . . . . **168** B1
Roserton St E14 . . .42 B4	N1 . . . . **87** A4	Rowfant Rd SW12,
Rose Sq SW7 . . . . **143** C2	Rotherfield St	SW17 . . . . .72 C2
Rose St	Islington N1 . . . . . . .15 B1	Rowhill Mans 🔟
Holborn EC4 . . . . . **108** D2	Shoreditch N1 . . . . **87** A4	E5 . . . . .17 A4
Strand WC2 . . . . . **120** A4	Rotherham Wlk	Rowhill Rd E5 . . . . .17 A4
Rosethorn Cl	SE1 . . . . **122** A1	Rowington Cl W2 . **100** A4
SW12 . . . . .73 C4	ROTHERHITHE 40 C4	Rowland Hill Ho
Rosetta Cl 🔟 SW8 . .162 B1	Rotherhithe Bsns Est	SE1 . . . . **136** A4
Roseway SE21 . . . . .63 C1	🔟 SE16 . . . . .40 B2	Rowland Hill St
Rosewood Ct 🔟	Rotherhithe New Rd	NW3 . . . . .12 A3
E11 . . . . .19 C4	SE16 . . . . .40 A1	Rowley Gdns N4 . . . .6 B4
Rosewood Gdns	Rotherhithe Old Rd	Rowley Ho SE8 . . . .51 C4
SE13 . . . . .52 B1	SE16 . . . . .40 C2	Rowley Ind Pk W3 . .37 A3
Rosewood Ho 🔟	Rotherhithe Prim Sch	Rowley Way NW8 . .78 C4
NW3 . . . . .11 A2	SE16 . . . . .40 C2	Rowntree Cl NW6 . .10 C2
Rosewood Sq	Rotherhithe St	Rowse Cl E15 . . . . . .27 B4
W12 . . . . .29 C3	SE16 . . . . .40 B4	Rowstock 🔟 NW5 . .13 C2
Rosher Cl E15 . . . . .19 C1	Rotherhithe Tunnel	Rowstock Gdns
Rosina St E9 . . . . . .17 C2	SE16 . . . . .32 C1	N7 . . . . .13 C3
Roskell Rd SW15 . .57 C4	Rother Ho SE15 . . . .65 A3	Roxby Pl SW6 . . . **155** C4
Roslin Ho 🔟 E1 . . . .32 C2	Rotherwick Rd	Roxford Ho 🔟 E3 . . .27 A1
Roslin Rd W3 . . . . . .37 A3	NW11 . . . . .1 C4	Roxley Rd SE13 . . . .67 A1
Rosmead Rd	Rotherwood Rd	Roxwell 🔟 NW1 . . . .13 A2
W11 . . . . .31 A2 **112** B4	SW15 . . . . .57 C4	Roxwell Rd W12 . . .38 C4
Rosoman Pl EC1 . . **95** C3	Rotherwood St N1 . . .	Royal Academy of
Rosoman St EC1 . . **95** C3	Rothery St SE11 . . **163** B3	Dramatic Art*
Ross Ct	Rothesay Ave SW14,	WC1 . . . . **105** B4
🔟 Hackney E5 . . . . .17 A4	TW10 . . . . .55 A3	
🔟 Putney SW15 . . . .69 C4	Rothesay Ct SE11 . **163** B3	
Rossdale Rd SW15 . .57 B3	Rothley Ct NW8 . . . **89** B2	
Rosse Gdns SE13 . . .67 C1		

Royal Acad of Arts*	Royal Ct	
W1 . . . . **118** C3	City of London	
Royal Acad of Dance	EC3 . . . . **109** C1	
SW11 . . . . **167** C3	Rotherhithe SE16 . . .41 B3	
Royal Acad of Music	Royal Duchess Mews	
NW1 . . . . **91** C1	SW12 . . . . .73 A4	
Royal Albert Hall*	Royal Exchange*	
SW7 . . . . **129** B3	EC3 . . . . **109** C1	
Royal Arc W1 . . . . **118** C3	Royal Exchange Bldgs	
Royal Armouries	EC3 . . . . **109** C1	
The* E1 . . . . **124** C3	Royal Festival Hall*	
Royal Ave SW3 . . **144** C2	SE1 . . . . **121** A1	
Royal Avenue Ho	Royal Free Hospl	
SW3 . . . . **144** C2	NW3 . . . . .12 A3	
Royal Ballet Sch The	Royal Fusiliers Mus*	
Hammersmith	E1 . . . . **124** C3	
W14 . . . . .39 C1	Royal Geographical	
St Giles WC2 . . . . **106** B1	Society SW7 . . . **129** C3	
Royal Brompton	Royal Hill SE10 . . . .52 B3	
Hospl	Royal Hill Ct 🔟	
Chelsea SW3 . . . . **143** B2	SE10 . . . . .52 B3	
Chelsea SW3 . . . . **144** A2	Royal Horticultural	
Royal Cir SE27 . . . .75 A1	Society (Lawrence	
Royal Cl	Hall & Conf Ctr)	
Deptford SE8 . . . . . .51 B4	SW1 . . . . **133** B1	
Kensington W10 . . **69** C2	Royal Horticultural	
Stamford Hill N16. . . .7 A3	Society (Lindley	
Royal College of	Hall) SW1 . . . . . **147** B4	
Physicians Liby	Royal Hospital (Army	
NW1 . . . . **92** B2	Pensioners)*	
Royal College St	SW1 . . . . **145** B1	
NW1 . . . . **83** A4	Royal Hospital Rd	
Royal Coll of	SW3 . . . . **145** A1	
Anaesthetists	Royal Hospl and	
WC1 . . . . **106** C3	Home SW15 . . . . .58 A1	
Royal Coll of Art	Royal Langford	
SW7 . . . . **129** B3	Apartments NW6 . **78** A2	
Royal Coll of Art	Royal London Est The	
Sculpture Sch	NW10 . . . . .20 C3	
SW11 . . . . **158** A1	Royal London	
Royal Coll of	Homeopathic Hospl	
Midwives W1 . . . **104** A3	The WC1 . . . . . . **106** B4	
Royal Coll of Music	Royal London Hospl	
SW7 . . . . **129** B2	Archives & Mus*	
Royal Coll of	E1 . . . . .32 A4	
Obstetricians &	Royal London Hospl	
Gynaecologists	(Mile End) The	
NW1 . . . . **90** C2	E2 . . . . .25 C2	
Royal Coll of	Royal London Hospl	
Ophthalmologists	(St Clements) The	
NW1 . . . . **91** B1	E3 . . . . .26 B2	
Royal Coll of	Royal London Hospl	
Paediatrics & Child	(Whitechapel) The	
Health W1 . . . . . **104** B4	E1 . . . . .32 A4	
Royal Coll of	Royal Marsden Hospl	
Pathologists	SW3 . . . . **143** C2	
SW1 . . . . **119** B3	Royal Mews The*	
Royal Coll of	SW1 . . . . **132** B2	
Physicians NW1 . . **92** B2	Royal Mint Pl E1 . **125** C4	
Royal Coll of	Royal Mint St E1 . **125** A4	
Radiologists W1 **104** B4	Royal National	
Royal Coll of Science	Orthopaedic Hospl	
SW7 . . . . **129** B2	W1 . . . . **92** B1	
Royal Coll of Speech	Royal National TNE	
Language Therapists	Hospl The WC1 . . **94** C4	
SE1 . . . . **123** B3	Royal Naval Pl	
Royal Coll of	SE14 . . . . .51 B3	
Surgeons WC2 . . **107** A2	Royal Oak Ct	
Royal Courts of	N1 . . . . .24 A2 **98** A4	
Justice WC2 . . . . **107** B1	Royal Oak Pl SE22 . .65 A1	
Royal Cres	Royal Oak Rd 🔟	
W11 . . . . .31 A1 **112** A1	E8 . . . . .17 A2	
Royal Crescent Mews	Royal Oak Sta	
W11 . . . . .30 C1	W2 . . . . **100** B3	
	Royal Oak Yd SE1 . **138** A3	

Royal Obsy The★ SE10 . . . . 52 C3
Royal Opera Arc SW1 . . . . . . 119 B2
Royal Orchard Cl SW18 . . . . 70 A4
Royal Par
  Blackheath Vale SE3 . . . . 53 B1
  Fulham SW6 . . . 154 A2
  12 Penge New Town NW4 . . . . 49 C2
Royal Pl **11** SE10 . . 52 B3
Royal Rd SE17 . . . 48 A4
Royal Sch Hampstead The NW3 . . . . 11 C4
Royal St SE1 . . . . . 135 A2
Royalty Ho **1** . . . 105 B1
Royalty Mews W1 . . . . 105 B1
Royalty Studios W11 . . . . 31 A3
Royal United Services Mus★ SW1 . . . 120 A1
Royal Veterinary Coll NW1 . . . . 83 B3
Royal Victoria Sta E16 . . . . 35 C2
Royal Victor Pl E3 . . 25 C3
Roycroft Cl SW2 . . . 74 C3
Roydon Cl SW1 . . . 168 C2
Roy Ridley Ho **6** SW4 . . . . 61 C4
Roy Sq E14 . . . . . . 33 A2
Royston Cl
  New Cross SE4 . . 51 B1
  3 Richmond TW9 . . 44 B2
Royston Ho SE15 . . . . 49 C4
Royston St **24** E2 . . 25 B3
Rozel Cl **3** N1 . . . . 24 A4
Rozel Rd SW4 . . . . 61 B4
Ruby St SE15 . . . . 50 A4
Ruby Triangle SE15 . . . . 49 C4
Rucklidge Ave NW10 . . . . 21 C3
Rudall Cres **3** NW3 . . 11 C4
Rudbeck Ho **11** SE15 . . . . 49 C3
Ruddington Cl E5 . . 18 A4
Rudge Ho SE16 . . . 139 C2
Rudgwick Terr NW8 . . . . 80 B3
Rudhall Ho **4** SW2 . . . . 62 C1
Rudloe Rd SW12 . . 73 B4
Rudolf Pl SW8 . . . . 162 B3
Rudolph Rd NW6 . . . 23 C3
Rudstone Ho **10** E3 . . . . 27 A2
Rudyard Ct SE1 . . . 137 C3
Rufford St N1 . . . . 84 B4
Rufford Street Mews N1 . . . . 14 A1
Rufford Twr **5** W3 . . . . 28 A1
Rufus Bsns Ctr SW18 . . . . 71 A2
Rufus Ho SE1 . . . . 139 A2
Rufus St N1 . . 24 A2 98 B3
Rugby Mans W14 . . 140 B4
Rugby Rd W4 . . . . 38 A4
Rugby St WC1 . . . . 94 C1
Rugg St E14 . . . . . 33 C2

Rugless Ho **2** E14 . . 42 B4
Rugmere **4** NW1 . . 12 C1
Rumball Ho **14** SE5 . . . . 49 A3
Rumbold Rd SW6 . . 156 B1
Rum Cl E1 . . . . . . 32 B2
Rumford Ho SE1 . . 136 C1
Rumsey Rd SW9 . . . 62 B4
Runacres Ct SE17 . . 150 C1
Runcorn Pl W11 . . . . . . 31 A2 112 A4
Rundell Twr SW8 . . 172 C4
Running Horse Yd **12** TW8 . . . . 44 A4
Runnymede Ct SW15 . . . . 68 C3
Runnymede Ho
  Hackney E9 . . . . 18 A4
  Richmond TW10 . . 54 C2
Rupack St **3** SE16 . . 40 B4
Rupert Ct **1** W1 . . . 119 B4
Rupert Gdns SW9 . . 48 A1
Rupert Ho SE11 . . . 149 C3
  8 Upper Holloway N19 . . . . 4 C1
Rupert St W1 . . . . 119 B4
Rusbridge Cl E8 . . . 16 C3
Ruscoe Rd E16 . . . 35 B3
Rusham Rd SW12 . . 72 B4
Rushbrook Ho SW8 . . . . 171 B2
Rushby Ct SW4 . . . 172 A3
Rush Common Mews **18** SW2 . . . . 74 B4
Rushcroft Rd SW2, SW9 . . . . 62 C3
Rushcutters Ct **18** SE16 . . . . 41 A2
Rushey Mead SE4 . . 66 C2
Rushford Rd SE4 . . . 66 B1
Rush Hill Mews **3** SW11 . . . . 60 C4
Rush Hill Rd SW11 . . . . 60 C4
Rushlake Ho SW11 . . . . 169 B2
Rushmead **6** E2 . . . 25 A2
Rushmere Ho **4** SW15 . . . . 68 C3
Rushmore Cres **9** E5 . . . . 17 C4
Rushmore Ho
  5 Kentish Town N7 . . . . 13 C3
  W14 . . . . 126 B1
Rushmore Prim Sch E5 . . . . 17 C4
Rushmore Rd
  Clapton Pk E5 . . . 17 C4
  Hackney E5 . . . . 18 A4
Rusholme Rd SW15 . . . . 58 A1
Rushton Ho SW8 . . 171 B1
Rushton St N1 . . . . 87 C2
Rushworth St SE1 . . . . 136 B3
Ruskin Ave TW9 . . 44 C3
Ruskin Ct SE5 . . . . 63 C4
Ruskin Ho SW1 . . . 147 C3
Ruskin Park Ho SE5 . . . . 63 C4
Ruskin Wlk SE24 . . 63 B2
Rusper Ct SW9 . . . 172 B1

Russell Cl W4 . . . . 46 B1
Russell Ct
  Battersea SW11 . . 169 C3
  Bloomsbury WC1 . . 94 A1
  5 Peckham SE15 . . 50 A1
  St James SW1 . . . 119 A1
Russell Gdns W14 . . . . 126 A2
Russell Gdns Mews W14 . . . . 126 A2
Russell Gr SW9 . . . 173 C4
Russell Ho
  21 Poplar E14 . . . 33 C3
  SW1 . . . . 146 C2
Russell Kerr Cl W4 . . . . 45 B3
Russell Lo SE1 . . . . 137 B2
Russell Mans WC1 . . . . 106 B3
Russell Pickering Ho **2** SW4 . . . . 62 A4
Russell Pl
  Hampstead NW3 . . 12 A3
  Rotherhithe SE16 . . 41 A3
Russell Rd W14 . . . 126 B1
Russell Sq WC1 . . . 94 A1
Russell Square Ho WC1 . . . . 94 A1
Russell Square Mans WC1 . . . . 106 A2
Russell Square Sta WC1 . . . . 94 A1
Russell St WC2 . . . 120 B4
Russell's Wharf **7** W9 . . . . 23 B1
Russell Wlk **6** TW10 . . . . 54 B1
Russet Cres N7 . . . 14 B3
Russett Way SE13 . . 52 A1
Russia Dock Rd SE16 . . . . 33 A1
Russia La E2 . . . . . 25 B3
Russia Row EC2 . . . 109 A1
Rusthall Ave W4 . . . 37 C3
Rusthall Mans **3** W4 . . . . 37 C2
Ruston Mews W11 . . . . 31 A3
Ruston St **3** E3 . . . 26 B4
Rust Sq SE5 . . . . 48 C3
Ruth Ct **10** E3 . . . 26 A3
Rutherford Ho **12** E1 . . . . 25 A1
Rutherford St SW1 . . . . 147 B4
Ruth Ho W10 . . . . 23 A1
Ruthin Cl NW9 . . . . 1 A2
Ruthin Rd SE3 . . . . 53 C4
Ruthven St E9 . . . . 25 C4
Rutland Cl SW14 . . 55 B4
Rutland Ct
  Herne Hill SE5 . . . 63 C3
  SW7 . . . . 130 B3
Rutland Gate SW7 . . . . 130 B3
Rutland Gate Mews SW7 . . . . 130 A3
Rutland Gdns SW7 . . . . 130 B3
Rutland Gdns Mews SW7 . . . . 130 B3
Rutland Gr W6 . . . 39 A1
Rutland Ho
  10 Putney SW15 . . 69 B4
  W8 . . . . 128 A1
Rutland Mews E SW7 . . . . 130 B2

Rutland Mews S SW7 . . . . 130 A2
Rutland Mews W SW7 . . . . 130 A2
Rutland Park Gdns **1** NW2 . . . . 9 B2
Rutland Park Mans **2** NW2 . . . . 9 B2
Rutland Pl EC1 . . . 108 B4
Rutland Rd E9 . . . 25 C4
Rutland St SW7 . . . 130 B2
Rutland Studios NW10 . . . . 21 C2
Rutley Cl SE11 . . . . 48 A4
Rutt's Terr SE14 . . . 50 C2
Ruvigny Gdns SW15 . . . . 57 C4
Ruvigny Mans SW15 . . . . 57 C4
Rycott Path SE22 . . 76 C4
Rycuff Sq SE3 . . . . 53 B1
Rydal Ho SW8 . . . . 171 B1
Rydal Water NW1 . . 92 C3
Ryde Ho **11** NW6 . . 23 C4
Ryder Cl **10** E14 . . . 119 A2
Ryder Ct SW1 . . . . 119 A2
Ryder Ho **10** E1 . . . 25 B1
Ryder St SW1 . . . . 119 A2
Ryder's Terr NW8 . . 78 C2
Ryder Yd SW1 . . . . 119 A2
Ryde Vale Rd SW12 . . . . 73 B2
Rydon St N1 . . . . 87 A4
Rydston Cl **2** N7 . . . 14 B1
Ryecotes Mead SE21 . . . . 76 A3
Ryecroft Rd SE13 . . 67 B2
Ryecroft St SW6 . . 166 A3
Ryedale SE22 . . . . 65 A1
Ryefield Path **7** SW15 . . . . 68 C3
Ryegates **2** SE15 . . 50 A1
Rye Hill Pk SE15 . . . 65 B3
Rye Ho **17** SE16 . . . 40 B4
Rye La SE15 . . . . 49 C1
Rye Lane Mkt SE15 . . . . 49 C1
Rye Oak Sch SE15 . . 65 A4
Rye Rd SE15 . . . . 65 C3
Rye Wlk SW15 . . . 57 C2
Ryfold Rd SW19 . . . 70 C1
Ryland Rd NW5 . . . 13 A2
Rylett Cres W12 . . . 38 B3
Rylett Rd W12 . . . 38 B3
Rylston Rd SW6 . . . 154 C3
Rymer St SE24 . . . 63 A1
Rysbrack St SW1 . . 130 C2

S

Saatchi Gallery Duke of York's HQ★ SW3 . . . . 145 A2
Sabarton St **9** E16 . . . . 35 B3
Sabella Ct E3 . . . . 26 B3
Sabine Rd SW11 . . 60 C4
Sable St N1 . . . . . 15 A1
Sacketts Ho SW9 . . 173 C4
Sackville Ho **16** SW16 . . . . 74 A1
Sackville St W1 . . . 119 A3
Sacred Heart High Sch W6 . . . . . . 39 B2

Sacred Heart Jun Sch W6 . . . . 39 C2
Sacred Heart Prim Sch, Battersea SW11 . . . . 168 B1
Sacred Heart RC Prim Sch
  Islington N7 . . . 14 B3
  Putney SW15 . . . 56 C2
Sacred Heart RC Sec Sch SE5 . . . . 48 B2
Saddlers Mews SW8 . . . . 172 B4
Sadler Ho
  3 Bromley E3 . . . 27 A2
  EC1 . . . . 96 A4
Saffron Ave E14 . . . 34 C2
Saffron Ct **10** N1 . . 15 B2
Saffron Hill EC1 . . . 107 C4
Saffron Ho **6** TW9 . . . . 45 A2
Saffron St EC1 . . . 107 C4
Saffron Wharf SE1 . . . . 139 A4
Sage Mews SE22 . . 64 B2
Sage St E1 . . . . . 32 B2
Sage Way WC1 . . . 94 C3
Sailacre Ho **10** SE10 . . . . 43 B1
Sail Ct **10** E14 . . . 34 C2
Sailmakers Ct SW6 . . . . 59 B4
Sail St SE11 . . . . 149 A4
Sainfoin Rd SW17 . . 72 C2
St Agnes Cl E9 . . . 25 B4
St Agnes Pl SE11 . . 48 A4
St Agnes RC Prim Sch E3 . . . . 27 A2
St Agnes RC Sch NW2 . . . . 1 A1
St Aidan's Prim Sch N4 . . . . 5 C2
St Aidan's Rd SE22 . . . . 65 A2
St Alban Ave W4 . . 37 C3
St Alban's CE Prim Sch EC1 . . . 107 B4
St Alban's Cl NW11 . . 1 C3
St Alban's Gr W8 . . 128 B2
St Albans La NW11 . . 1 C3
St Albans Mans W8 . . . . 128 B2
St Alban's Pl N1 . . . 86 A3
St Alban's Rd
  Dagenham NW10 . . 21 A4
  4 Dartmouth Pk NW5 . . 4 A1
St Alban's St SW1 . . 119 B3
St Albans Studios W8 . . . . 128 B2
St Albans Terr W6 . . . . 154 A4
St Alban's Villas NW5 . . . . 3 C1
St Alfege Pas SE10 . . . . 52 B4
St Alfege with St Peter's CE Prim Sch SE10 . . . . 52 B4
St Aloysius RC Coll N19 . . . . 4 B3
St Aloysius RC Inf Sch NW1 . . . . 93 B4
St Aloysius RC Jun Sch NW1 . . . 83 B1
St Alphage Gdn EC2 . . . . 109 A3

St Alphage Highwalk EC2.......109 A3
St Alphonsus Rd SW4.......61 C3
St Andrew & St Francis CE Prim Sch NW2.......8 C2
St Andrew's (Barnsley) CE Prim Sch N1.......85 A4
St Andrew's CE Prim Sch SW9.......172 B1
St Andrews Chambers W1.......105 A2
St Andrews Cl 28 SE16.......40 A1
St Andrew's Ct W4.......45 B2
St Andrew's Ct 2 SW18.......71 B2
St Andrew's Gr N16.......6 C3
St Andrew's Greek Sch NW1.......13 C1
St Andrews Hill EC4.......108 B1
St Andrews Ho 11 SE16.......40 A3
St Andrew's Hospl E3.......27 A1
St Andrew's Mans 9 E5.......17 A4
St Andrew's Mans W1.......103 B3
St Andrews Mews Greenwich SE3.......53 C3
St Andrew's Mews 4 Streatham SW12.......73 C3
St Andrew's Mews N16.......7 A3
St Andrew's Pl NW1.......92 B2
St Andrew's Rd Dagenham W3.......29 A3
W14.......154 B4
Willesden NW2.......9 A2
St Andrew's Sq W11.......31 A3
St Andrew St EC4.......107 C3
St Andrews Way E3.......27 A1
St Andrew's Wharf SE1.......139 A4
St Anne RC Prim Sch E1.......24 C1 99 B1
St Anne's CE Prim Sch SW18.......59 A2
St Anne's Cl N6.......3 C1
St Anne's Ct Kensal Rise NW6.......23 A4
W1.......105 B1
St Anne's Flats NW1.......93 B4
St Anne's Pas E14.......33 B3
St Anne's RC Prim Sch SE11.......162 C4
St Anne's Row E14.......33 B3
St Anne St E14.......33 B3
St Anne's Trad Est 25 E14.......33 B3
St Ann's Cres SW18.......59 B1
St Ann's Gdns NW5.......12 C2
St Ann's Hill SW18.......59 B1
St Ann's Ho WC1.......95 B3
St Ann's La SW1.......133 C1

St Ann's Park Rd SW18.......59 B1
St Anns Rd SW13.......46 B2
St Ann's Rd W11.......30 C2
St Ann's St SW1.......133 C2
St Ann's Terr NW8.......79 C2
St Ann's Villas W11.......31 A1 112 A1
St Anselm's Pl W1.......118 A4
St Anselm's RC Prim Sch SW17.......72 C1
St Anthonys Cl E1.......125 B2
St Anthony's Ct 2 Balham SW12.......60 C1
Upper Tooting SW17.......72 A2
St Anthony's Flats NW1.......83 B1
St Anthony's RC Prim Sch SE22.......64 C1
St Asaph Ct SE4.......65 C4
St Asaph Rd SE4.......65 C4
St Aubins Ct N1.......87 C4
St Augustine's CE High Sch NW6.......23 C3
St Augustine's CE Prim Sch NW6.......78 A2
St Augustine's Ho NW1.......93 B1
St Augustine's RC Prim Sch NW1.......13 C1
St Augustine's Rd NW1.......13 C1
St Austell Rd SE13.......52 C1
St Barnabas CE Prim Sch SW1.......145 C2
St Barnabas Cl 11 SE22.......64 A2
St Barnabas & St Philip's CE Prim Sch W8.......127 B1
St Barnabas St SW1.......145 C2
St Barnabas Terr E9.......17 C3
St Barnabas Villas SW8.......172 B4
St Bartholomew's Hospl EC1.......108 B3
St Bede's RC Inf Sch SW12.......73 C3
St Benets Cl SW17.......72 A2
St Benet's Pl EC3.......123 C4
St Bernadette RC Jun Sch SW12.......73 B4
St Bernard Ho 6 E14.......42 B3
St Botolph St E1.......110 C2
St Brelades Ct N1.......87 C4
St Bride's Ave EC4.......108 A1
St Bride's Pas EC4.......108 A1
St Bride St EC4.......108 A2
St Catherines Cl SW17.......71 C1
St Catherine's Ct 8 W4.......38 A3
St Catherine's Dr SE14.......50 C1
St Catherines Mews SW3.......144 C4

St Cecilia's CE Sch SW18.......70 B3
St Chad's Pl WC1.......94 C4
St Chad's St WC1.......94 B4
St Charles' Hospl W10.......30 C4
St Charles Pl W10.......31 A4
St Charles RC Prim Sch W10.......30 C4
St Charles RC Sixth Form Coll W10.......30 C4
St Charles Sq W10.......30 C4
St Christina's Sch NW8.......80 B2
St Christophers Ct 15 N19.......4 C1
St Christopher's Ho NW1.......83 B1
St Christopher's Pl W1.......103 C2
St Christopher's Sch NW3.......11 C3
St Clair Ho 17 E3.......26 C2
St Clare St EC3.......110 C1
St Clement & St James CE Prim Sch W11.......31 A1 112 A1
St Clements Ct Barnsbury N7.......14 B2
7 SE14.......50 C4
6 Shepherd's Bush W11.......30 C2
St Clements Ho E1.......110 C3
St Clement's La WC2.......107 A1
St Clements Mans 7 SW6.......47 C4
St Clements St N7.......14 C1
St Columb's Ho 10 W10.......31 A4
St Crispins Ct E14.......33 A2
St Cross St EC1.......107 C4
St Cuthbert's Ho NW2.......10 B1
St Cuthbert with St Matthias Prim Sch SW5.......142 A2
St Davids Cl 27 SE16.......40 A1
St David's Sq E14.......42 A1
St Dionis Rd SW6.......165 A2
St Dominic RC Prim Sch NW5.......12 B3
St Dominics RC Prim Sch E9.......18 A3
St Donatt's Rd SE14.......51 B2
St Dunstan's Alley EC3.......124 A3
St Dunstan's Ave W3.......28 C2
St Dunstan's Ct EC4.......107 C1
St Dunstan's Gdns W3.......28 C2
St Dunstan's Hill EC3.......124 A3
St Dunstan's La EC3.......124 A3

St Dunstan's Rd W6.......39 C1
St Edmund RC Sch E14.......41 C2
St Edmunds Ct NW8.......80 C3
St Edmund's Cl NW8.......80 C3
St Edmund's Sq SW13.......47 B4
St Edmund's Terr NW8.......80 C3
St Edward's RC Prim Sch NW1.......90 B1
St Elizabeth RC Prim Sch E2.......25 B3
St Elizabeth's RC Prim Sch TW10.......54 B1
St Elmo Rd W12.......38 B4
St Elmos Rd SE16.......41 A4
St Ermin's Hill SW1.......133 B2
St Ervan's Rd W10.......31 B4
St Eugene de Mazenod RC Prim Sch NW6.......10 C1
St Faith's CE Prim Sch SW18.......59 B2
St Faith's Rd SE24.......75 A3
St Francesca Cabrini Prim Sch SE23.......65 B1
St Francis' Ho NW1.......83 B1
St Francis of Assisi RC Prim Sch W11.......30 C1
St Francis Pl SW12.......61 A1
St Francis RC Prim Sch SE15.......49 C3
St Francis Rd SE22.......64 A3
St Francis Xavier Sixth Form Coll SW12.......61 A1
St Fridewides Mews 5 E14.......34 B3
St Gabriel's CE Prim Sch SW1.......146 C1
St Gabriels Cl 3 E14.......34 A4
St Gabriel's Rd NW2.......9 C3
St George Ho SW11.......169 C3
ST GEORGE IN THE EAST.......32 A2
St George's Ave N7.......13 C4
St George's Battersea CE Prim Sch SW8.......161 A1
St George's Bldgs SE11.......136 B1
St George's Cath NW1.......92 B4
St George's Cath RC Jun & Inf Sch SE1.......136 A2
St George's CE Prim Sch SE5.......49 A3
St George's Circ SE1.......136 A2
St George's Cl SW8.......171 A4

St A – St G 263

St Georges Coll N7.......5 C1
St Georges Ct SW15.......58 B3
St George's Ct Brompton SW3.......144 A4
Kensington SW7.......128 C1
Newington SE11.......136 A1
St George's Dr SW1.......146 C2
St George's Field W2.......102 B3
St George's Gr SW17.......71 C1
St Georges Hanover Sq Sch W1.......117 C3
St George's Ho NW1.......83 A1
St George's La EC3.......124 A4
St Georges Mews 11 NW1.......12 B1
St George's Mews 2 Rotherhithe SE8.......41 B2
SE1.......135 C2
St Georges Pl N7.......13 C4
St George's RC Cath SE1.......135 C2
St George's RC Sec Sch W9.......78 B4
St Georges Rd W4.......37 C4
St George's Rd Newington SE1.......136 A1
Richmond TW9.......54 B4
St George's Residences 4 SW2.......62 C2
St George's Ct EC4.......108 A2
St Georges Sq 1 E14.......33 A2
St George's Sq Rotherhithe SE8.......41 B2
SW1.......147 B1
St George's Square Mews SW1.......147 B1
St George St W1.......118 B4
St George's Terr Hampstead NW1.......12 B1
NW1.......82 C4
St George's Way SE15.......49 A4
St George the Martyr CE Prim Sch WC1.......95 A1
St George Wharf SW8.......162 A4
St Gerards Cl SW4.......61 B2
St German's Pl SE3.......53 C2
St Gildas' RC Jun Sch N8.......5 A4
ST GILES.......106 A2
St Giles Cir WC1.......105 C2
St Giles Coll WC1.......106 A4
St Giles High St WC2.......105 C2
St Giles Ho SW16.......74 A1
St Giles Hospl SE5.......49 A2
St Giles Pas WC2.......105 C1
St Giles Rd SE5.......49 A2
St Giles Twr 3 SE5.......49 A2
St Gilles Ho 15 E2.......25 C3

St Helena Ho WC1. **95** B3
St Helena Rd SE16. **40** C2
St Helena St WC1 . **95** B3
St Helen's Gdns
　W10 . . . . **30** C3
St Helen's Pl EC3 . **110** A2
St Helen's RC Sch
　SW9 . . . . **62** C4
St Helier Ct 4 N1 . **24** A4
St Hildas Cl SW17 . **72** A2
St Hilda's Cl NW6 . . **9** C1
St Hilda's Rd
　SW13 . . . . **47** A4
St Hildas Wharf
　E1 . . . . **32** B1
St Hubert's Ho 2
　E14 . . . . **41** C3
St Hughes Cl
　SW17 . . . . **72** A2
St Ives Ct NW2 . . . **10** A2
ST JAMES **119** B2
St James Ct
　Bethnal Green
　E2 . . . . **24** C2 **99** C3
　10 Brentford W4 . . **36** C1
St James' Ct
　Bedford Pk W4 . . . . . **37** C3
　SW1 . . . . **133** A2
St James Ho N5 . . **14** C3
St James Independent
Schs 4 . . . . **140** B4
St James Ind Mews
　SE1 . . . . **153** C2
St James' Mans
　NW6 . . . . **10** C1
St James Mews
　E14 . . . . **42** B3
St James's SE14 . . **51** A2
St James's App
　EC2 . . . . **98** A1
St James's Ave E2 . **25** B3
St James School Flats
　5 N7 . . . . **14** C3
St James's Cl NW8 **80** C3
　Upper Tooting
　SW17 . . . . **72** B2
St James's Cloisters
　2 SE22 . . . . **64** B3
St James's Cres
　SW9 . . . . **62** C4
St James's Dr
　Balham SW12,
　SW17 . . . . **72** B4
　Upper Tooting
　SW17 . . . . **72** B3
St James's Gdns
　W11 . . . . . . **31** A1 **112** A2
St James's Gr
　SW11 . . . . **169** A2
St James's Hatcham
CE Prim Sch
　SE14 . . . . **51** A2
St James's Market
　SW1 . . . . **119** B3
St James's Pal★
　SW1 . . . . **119** A1
St James's Park Sta
　SW1 . . . . **133** B2
St James's Pas
　EC3 . . . . **110** B1
St James's Pk★
　SW1 . . . . **133** B4
St James's Pl
　SW1 . . . . **118** C1

St James's Rd
　Bermondsey SE1,
　SE16 . . . . **153** C4
　Peckham SE16 . . . . **49** C4
St James's & St
Michael's CE Prim
Sch W2 . . . . **115** A4
St James's Sq
　SW1 . . . . **119** A2
St James's St
　SW1 . . . . **118** C2
　SW6 . . . . **39** B1
St James's Terr
　NW8 . . . . **80** C4
　2 Upper Tooting
　SW12 . . . . **72** C3
St James's Terrace
Mews NW8 . . . . . . **80** C3
St James The Great
RC Prim Sch
　SE15 . . . . **49** B2
St James Wlk EC1 . **96** A2
St Joan of Arc RC
Prim Sch N5 . . . . . **15** B4
St John Evangelist RC
Prim Sch N1 . . . . . **86** A2
St John of Jerusalem
CE Prim Sch E9 . . . **17** B1
St John & St James
CE Prim Sch E9 . . . **17** B3
St John's Angell Town
CE Prim Sch
　SW9 . . . . **173** B1
St John's Ave
　Dagenham NW10 . . **21** B4
　Putney SW15 . . . . . **57** C2
St John's CE Prim
Sch
　Fulham SW6. . . . . . **164** B4
　SE17 . . . . **151** A3
　South Hackney E2 . . **25** B3
St John's Church Rd
　E9 . . . . **17** B3
St John's Cl SW6 . **155** B2
St Johns Concert
Hall★ SW1 . . . . . **134** A1
St John's Cres
　SW9 . . . . **62** C4
St Johns Ct 59 E1 . **32** A1
St John's Ct
　Finsbury Pk N4 . . . . **6** A2
　Hammersmith W6 . . **39** A2
　Lewisham SE13 . . . **52** B1
　6 South Hampstead
　NW3 . . . . **11** B2
Saint John's Ct
　N5 . . . . **15** A4
St John's Dr SW18 **71** A3
St John's Est SE1 **138** C3
St John's Gdns
　W11 . . . . . . **31** B2 **112** C2
St John's Gr
　3 Barnes SW13 . . . **46** B1
　1 Richmond TW9 . . **54** A3
St John's Highbury
Vale CE Prim Sch
　N5 . . . . **6** A1
St John's Hill
　SW11 . . . . **59** C3
St John's Hill Gr
　SW11 . . . . **59** C3
St Johns Ho 5
　SE17 . . . . **48** C4

St John's Ho 1
　E14 . . . . **42** B2
St John's La EC1 . **108** B4
St John's Lodge 8
　SE8 . . . . **51** C2
St John's Mans E5 . **17** B3
St John's Park Mews
　N19 . . . . **4** B1
St John's Path EC1 . **96** A1
St John's Pk SE3 . . **53** C3
St John's Pl EC1 . . **96** A1
St John's RC Prim Sch
　SE16 . . . . **41** A4
St John's Rd
　Battersea SW11 . . . . **60** A3
　Canning Town E16 . . **35** C3
　Richmond TW9 . . . . . **54** A3
St John's & St
Clements CE Prim
Sch SE15 . . . . **64** C4
St John's Sq EC1 . . **96** A1
St Johns Sta SE8 . **51** C1
St John St EC1 . . . **96** A2
St John's Terr
　W10 . . . . **22** C1
St John's Upper
Holloway CE Prim
Sch N19 . . . . **4** C2
St John's Vale
　SE8 . . . . **51** C1
St John's Villas
　Upper Holloway N19 . . **4** C2
　W8 . . . . **128** B1
St John's Way N19 . . **4** C3
ST JOHN'S WOOD . . . **79** B1
St John's Wood Ct
　NW8 . . . . **89** C3
St John's Wood High
St NW8 . . . . **80** A1
St John's Wood Park
　NW8 . . . . **79** B4
St John's Wood Pre-
Prep Sch NW8 . . . **90** A4
St John's Wood Rd
　NW8 . . . . **89** C3
St John's Wood Sta
　NW8 . . . . **79** C1
St John's Wood Terr
　NW8 . . . . **80** A2
St John the Baptist
CE Prim Sch N1 . . . **87** C1
St John the Divine CE
Jun & Inf Sch
　SE5 . . . . **48** A3
St Joseph's Cl
　W10 . . . . **31** A4
St Josephs Ct 3
　NW10 . . . . **21** B3
St Joseph's Flats
　NW1 . . . . **93** B4
St Joseph's Ho
　W6 . . . . **39** C2
St Joseph's Hospice
　E9, E8 . . . . **25** A4
St Joseph's RC Inf &
Jun Schs SE5 . . . . **48** B3
St Joseph's RC Prim
Sch
　Chelsea SW3 . . . . . **144** C3
　Deptford SE8 . . . . . **51** A3
　Greenwich SE10 . . . **43** A1
　Paddington NW8 . . . **89** C3
　Rotherhithe SE16 . . . **40** B3
　St Giles WC2 . . . . . **106** B2
　Upper Holloway N19 . . **4** A3
　Wandsworth SW18 . . **58** C2

St Joseph's RC Prim
Sch continued
　Willesden NW10 . . . . **8** A1
St Joseph's St
　SW8 . . . . **170** B4
St Joseph's Vale
　SE3 . . . . **67** C4
St Jude & St Paul's CE
Prim Sch N1 . . . . . . **16** A2
St Jude's CE Prim Sch
　SE24 . . . . **63** A2
St Judes Ho 6
　W10 . . . . **23** B2
St Jude's Prim Sch
　SE1 . . . . **136** A1
St Jude's Rd E2 . . **25** A3
St Jude St N16 . . . **16** A3
St Julian's Rd
　NW6 . . . . **23** C4
St Katharine's Ho
　N1 . . . . **85** B2
St Katharine's Prec
　NW1 . . . . **82** A2
St Katharine's Way
　E1 . . . . **125** A2
St Katherine's Row
　EC3 . . . . **110** B1
St Katharine's Wlk 1
　W11 . . . . **30** C1
St Kilda's Rd N16 . . . **7** A3
St Laurence's Cl
　NW6 . . . . **22** C4
St Lawrence Ct N1 . **87** C4
St Lawrence Ho
　SE1 . . . . **138** B2
St Lawrence St
　E14 . . . . **34** B1
St Lawrence Terr
　W10 . . . . **31** A4
St Lawrence Way
　SW9 . . . . **173** C2
St Leonards Ct
　SW14 . . . . **55** B4
St Leonard's Ct N1 **97** C4
St Leonard's Hospl
　N1 . . . . **24** A3
St Leonards Rd
　SW14 . . . . **55** B4
St Leonard's Rd
　Becontree NW10 . . . **20** C1
　South Bromley E14 . . **34** B4
St Leonard's Sq
　NW5 . . . . **12** C2
St Leonard's St E3 . **27** A2
St Leonard's Terr
　SW3 . . . . **145** A1
St Loo Ave SW3 . . **158** B4
St Loo Ct SW3 . . . **158** C4
St Luke Prim Sch
　E16 . . . . **35** B3
ST LUKE'S **97** A2
St Luke's Ave SW4 . **61** C3
St Luke's CE Prim
Sch
　Cubitt Town E14 . . . **42** C2
　Paddington W9 . . . . **23** B2
　Shoreditch EC1 . . . . **97** A2
St Luke's Cl EC1 . . **97** A2
St Luke's Ct W11 . . **31** B3
St Luke's Hospl
　W1 . . . . **92** C1
St Luke's Mews
　W11 . . . . **31** B3
St Luke's Rd W11 . . **31** B4
St Luke's Sq E16 . . **35** B3
St Luke's St SW3 . . **144** B2

St Margaret's Cres
　SW15 . . . . **57** A2
St Margaret's Ct
　Putney SW15 . . . . . **57** A3
　SE1 . . . . **123** B1
St Margaret's La
　W8 . . . . **128** A1
St Margarets Lo
　W3 . . . . **37** A4
St Margaret's Rd
　Brockley SE4 . . . . . **66** B3
　Kensal Green NW10. . **22** B2
St Margaret's Sch
　NW3 . . . . **11** A4
St Margaret St
　SW1 . . . . **134** A3
St Mark's CE Prim Sch
　SE11 . . . . **163** A4
St Marks Cl 5
　SE10 . . . . **52** B3
St Marks Cres
　NW1 . . . . **81** C4
St Marks Gate E9 . . **18** B1
St Mark's Gr
　SW10 . . . . **156** B2
St Marks Ho 6
　SE17 . . . . **48** C4
St Mark's Hospl
　EC1 . . . . **96** B4
St Mark's Mans 14
　N4 . . . . **5** B2
St Mark's Pl W11 . . **31** A3
St Mark's Prim Sch
　N19 . . . . **5** A2
St Marks Rd 15
　NW10 . . . . **30** C3
St Mark's Rd
　North Kensington
　W10 . . . . **30** C4
　Notting Hill W11 . . . **31** A3
St Mark's Rise E8 . . **16** B3
St Mark's Sq NW1 . **81** B3
St Mark St E1 . . . . **111** A1
St Martin-in-the-
Fields High Sch for
Girls SW2 . . . . **74** C3
St Martin's
Almshouses NW1 . **82** C4
St Martin's Cl NW1 **82** C4
St Martins Ct N1 . . **24** A4
St Martin's Ct
　WC2 . . . . **120** A4
　West Norwood
　SE27 . . . . **75** A2
St Martin's La
　WC2 . . . . **120** A3
St Martin's Le Grand
　EC1 . . . . **108** C2
St Martin's Pl
　WC2 . . . . **120** A3
St Martin's Rd
　SW9 . . . . **172** C2
St Martin's St
　WC2 . . . . **119** C3
St Martin's Way
　SW17 . . . . **71** B1
St Mary Abbots CE
Prim Sch W8 . . . . . **128** A3
St Mary Abbot's Ct
　W14 . . . . **126** C1
St Mary Abbot's Pl
　W8 . . . . **127** A1
St Mary Abbots Terr
　W14 . . . . **127** A1
St Mary at Hill
　EC3 . . . . **124** A3
St Mary Axe EC3 . . **110** B2

St Marychurch St
SE16 . . . . .40 B4
St Mary Graces Ct
E1 . . . . .125 A3
St Marylebone CE Sch
The W1 . . . . .104 C2
St Mary le Bow
Church* EC2 . . . .109 A1
St Mary' le-Park Ct
SW11 . . . . .158 B1
St Mary Magdalene
CE Prim Sch
Islington N7 . . . . .14 C2
Paddington W2 . . .100 A4
Peckham SE15 . . . .50 A1
St Mary Magdalen's
RC Prim Sch
Brockley SE4 . . . . .66 A3
Mortlake SW14 . . .55 C4
St Mary Magdelen's
RC Jun Sch NW2 . . .9 A2
St Mary Newington Cl
SE17 . . . . .152 B2
St Mary of the Angels
RC Prim Sch W2 . .31 C3
St Mary RC Prim Sch
W10 . . . . .23 A1
St Mary & St Michael
Prim Sch E1 . . . .32 B3
St Mary & St Pancras
CE Prim Sch
NW1 . . . . .83 B1
St Mary's Bryanston
Square CE Sch
W1 . . . . .102 C4
St Mary's CE Prim
Sch
Islington N1 . . . . .86 B4
Putney SW15 . . . . .57 C4
Willesden NW10 . . .8 A2
St Mary's Ct W6 . . .38 B3
St Mary's Est 2
SE16 . . . . .40 B4
St Mary's Flats
NW1 . . . . .93 B4
St Mary's Gate
W8 . . . . .128 A1
St Mary's Gdns
SE11 . . . . .149 C4
St Mary's Gr
Barnes SW13 . . . . .57 A4
Chiswick W4 . . . . .45 A4
Islington N1 . . . . . .15 A2
Richmond TW10,
TW9 . . . . .54 B3
St Mary's Ho N1 . . .86 B4
St Mary's Hospl
W2 . . . . .101 C2
St Mary's Hospl
Medical Sch W2 .101 C2
St Mary's Kilburn CE
Prim Sch NW6 . . .23 C4
St Mary's Lewisham
CE Prim Sch
SE13 . . . . .67 A2
St Mary's Mans
Dagenham NW10 . .21 A4
Paddington W2 . . .101 B4
St Mary's Mews
NW6 . . . . .11 A1
St Mary's Path N1 .86 B4
St Mary's RC Prim
Sch
Chiswick W4 . . . . .46 A4

St Mary's RC Prim Sch
continued
Clapham Pk SW4 . . .61 B2
Clapham SW8 . . . .170 B4
Hammersmith W14 . .39 C3
Paddington NW6 . . .23 C3
St Mary's Rd
Dagenham NW10 . .21 A4
Golders Green NW11 . .1 A4
Nunhead SE15 . . . .50 B1
St Mary's Sch
Hampstead NW3 . . .11 C3
St Mary's Sq W2 .101 B4
St Mary's Stoke
Newington CE Prim
Sch N16 . . . . . . .7 A2
St Mary's Terr
W2 . . . . .101 B4
St Mary's Twr EC1 . .97 A1
St Mary's Wlk
SE11 . . . . .149 C4
St Matthews Ct
SE1 . . . . .136 C1
St Matthew's Ho 8
SE17 . . . . .48 C4
St Matthew's Lo
NW1 . . . . .83 A2
St Matthew's Rd
SW2 . . . . .62 B2
St Matthews Row
E2 . . . . .24 C1 99 B2
St Matthews Sch
Westminster
SW1 . . . . .133 C2
St Matthew St
SW1 . . . . .133 B1
St Matthias CE Prim
Sch E2 . . . .24 B1 99 A2
St Matthias's CE Prim
Sch N16 . . . . . . .16 A4
St Mauritius Ho
SE13 . . . . .67 B1
St Maur Rd SW6 . .165 A3
St Michael's Alley
EC3 . . . . .109 C1
St Michael's CE Prim
Sch
Camden Town
NW1 . . . . .82 C4
Highgate N6 . . . . . .3 C4
Wandsworth SW18 . .70 B4
St Michaels Ct 2
E14 . . . . .34 B4
St Michael's Ct
NW11 . . . . .1 C4
St Michael's Flats
NW1 . . . . .83 B1
St Michael's Gdns
W10 . . . . .31 A4
St Michael's Rd
Cricklewood NW2 . . .9 B4
Stockwell SW9 . . . .172 C2
St Michael's
Steiner
W2 . . . . .102 A2
St Michael Steiner
Sch The SW18 . .58 C2
St Mildred's Ct
EC2 . . . . .109 B1
St Monica's RC Prim
Sch N1 . . .24 A2 98 A4
St Nicholas' Flats
NW1 . . . . .83 B1
St Nicholas Ho
SE8 . . . . .51 C4
St Nicholas Mans
SW17 . . . . .72 B2

St Nicholas St
SE8 . . . . .51 C2
St Norbert Gn SE4 .66 A3
St Norbert Rd SE4 .66 A3
St Olaf's Rd SW6 .154 B1
St Olaves Ct W2 . .114 A3
St Olave's Ct EC2 .109 B1
St Olave's Est SE1 .138 B4
St Olave's Gdns
SE11 . . . . .149 B1
St Olave's Mans
SE11 . . . . .149 B1
St Olav's Sq 32
SE16 . . . . .40 B4
St Osmund's RC Prim
Sch SW13 . . . . . .46 B2
St Oswald's Pl
SE11 . . . . .148 C1
St Oswald's Rd SW16 .74 D1
St Owen Ho SE1 . .138 B2
ST PANCRAS 94 B4
St Pancras
Almshouses 13
NW5 . . . . .13 B3
St Pancras
Commercial Ctr
NW1 . . . . .83 A4
St Pancras Hospl
NW1 . . . . .83 B3
St Pancras
International Sta
WC1 . . . . .94 A4
St Pancras Way
NW1 . . . . .83 A4
St Patrick's Coll
W1 . . . . .105 B2
St Patrick's RC Prim
Sch
Wapping SE16 . . . .15 A3
Willesden NW2 . . . .9 A3
St Paul's Cath* . . .
EC4 . . . . .108 C1
St Paul's Cath Sch
EC4 . . . . .108 C1
St Paul's CE Prim
Sch
Hammersmith W6 . .39 B1
Hampstead NW3 . . .11 C4
SE17 . . . . .150 C2
St Paul's Church Yd
EC4 . . . . .108 C1
St Pauls Cl W5 . . . .36 B4
St Pauls Cres
NW1 . . . . .13 C1
St Paul's Ct
11 Upper Holloway
N19 . . . . .5 A2
Clapham SW4 . . . .61 C3
St Paul's Dr E15 . .19 C3
St Paul's Girls' Sch
W6 . . . . .39 C2
St Pauls Mews
NW1 . . . . .13 C1
St Paul's Pl N1 . . . .15 C2
St Pauls Rd NW1 . .54 B4
St Paul's Rd N1 . . . .15 B2
St Paul's Sch
SW13 . . . . .38 C1
St Paul's Sta EC2 . .87 A3
St Paul St N1 . . . . .87 A3
St Paul's Terr
SE17 . . . . .48 A4
St Pauls View
WC1 . . . . .95 B3
St Paul's Way E3 . . .33 B4

St Paul's Way Com
Sch E3 . . . . .33 C4
St Paul's with St
Michael's Prim Sch
E8 . . . . .24 C4
St Paul with St Luke
CE Prim Sch E3 . .33 B4
St Peter & St Paul RC
Prim Sch EC1 . . .96 B2
St Peter's Alley
EC3 . . . . .109 C1
St Peter's Ave 27
E2 . . . . .25 A3
St Petersburgh Mews
W2 . . . . .114 A4
St Petersburgh Pl
W2 . . . . .114 A3
St Peter's CE Prim
Sch
Chiswick W6 . . . . . .38 C1
Paddington W9 . . . .23 C1
SE17 . . . . .151 B1
St Peter's Church Ct
N1 . . . . .86 B3
St Peters Cl SW17 .72 B2
St Peter's Cl E2 . . .24 C3
St Peters Ct
New Cross SE4 . . . .51 B1
28 Stepney E1 . . . .25 B1
St Peter's Eaton
Square CE Prim Sch
SW1 . . . . .132 B1
St Peter's Gdns
SE27 . . . . .74 C1
St Peter's Gr W6 . .38 C2
St Peters Ho WC1 . .94 B3
St Peter's Ho
2 SE17 . . . . .48 C4
Stamford Hill N16 . . .7 A4
St Peter's London
Docks CE Prim Sch
E1 . . . . .32 B1
St Peter's Pl W9 . . .88 A1
St Peter's Rd W6 . .38 C1
St Peter's Sq
Chiswick W6 . . . . . .38 B1
Hackney E2 . . . . . .24 C3
St Peter's St N1 . . .86 B3
St Peter's Street
Mews N1 . . . . . . .86 B2
St Peter's Terr
SW6 . . . . .154 B1
St Peter's Villas 5
W6 . . . . .38 C2
St Peter's Way N1 . .16 A1
St Peter's Wharf 9
W6 . . . . .38 C1
St Philip Ho WC1 . . .95 B3
St Philip Sq SW8 . .170 A1
St Philip's Rd E8 . . .16 C2
St Philip's Sch
SW7 . . . . .143 A3
St Philip St SW8 . .170 A1
St Philip's Way N1 .87 A3
St Quentin Ho
SW18 . . . . .59 C1
St Quintin Ave
W10 . . . . .30 C4
St Quintin Gdns 21
W10 . . . . .30 B4
St Regis Hts NW3 . . .2 A1
St Richard's Ho
NW1 . . . . .93 B4
St Rule St SW8 . . .170 C1
St Saviours SW4 . . .61 A3

St Saviour's CE Prim
Sch
Bow Comm E14 . . . .34 A4
Camberwell SE24 . . .63 B4
Paddington W9 . . . .88 B1
St Saviours Ho
SE1 . . . . .139 B3
St Saviour's RC Prim
Sch SE13 . . . . . . .67 B3
St Saviour's Rd
SW2 . . . . .62 B2
St Saviours & St
Olaves CE Sch
SE1 . . . . .137 C1
St Saviour's Wharf
SE1 . . . . .139 A4
St Silas Pl NW5 . . .12 C2
St Simon's Ave
SW15 . . . . .57 B2
St Stephen's Ave
W12 . . . . .39 A4
St Stephen's CE Prim
Sch
Paddington W2 . . . .31 C4
Shepherd's Bush
W12 . . . . .39 B4
St Johns SE8 . . . . .51 C1
SW8 . . . . .162 C2
St Stephen's Cl
Maitland Pk NW5 . .12 B3
NW8 . . . . .80 B3
St Stephen's Cres
W2 . . . . .31 C3
St Stephen's Gdns
Notting Hill W2 . . . .31 C3
4 Putney SW15 . . .58 B2
St Stephen's Gr
SE13 . . . . .67 B4
St Stephens Ho 7
SE17 . . . . .48 A4
St Stephen's Mews 34
W2 . . . . .31 C4
St Stephen's Rd
E3 . . . . .26 B3
St Stephen's Row
FC4 . . . . .109 B1
St Stephen's Terr
SW8 . . . . .162 C1
St Stephen's Wlk
SW7 . . . . .142 C4
St Swithin's La
EC4 . . . . .123 B4
St Swithun Rd
SE13 . . . . .67 C2
St Thomas' CE Prim
Sch W10 . . . . . . .23 A1
St Thomas Ct 14
NW1 . . . . .13 B1
St Thomas Ho 2
E1 . . . . .32 C3
St Thomas More
Language Coll
SW3 . . . . .144 C3
St Thomas of
Canterbury RC Prim
Sch SW6 . . . . . .154 C2
St Thomas Rd E16 . .35 C3
St Thomas' Rd W4 . .45 B4
St Thomas's Gdns
NW5 . . . . .12 C2

St Thomas's Hospl
SE1 . . . . **134** C2
St Thomas's Hospl Medical Sch SE1 **134** C1
St Thomas's Pl 20
E9 . . . . 17 B1
St Thomas's Rd
Dagenham NW10 . . . . 21 A4
Highbury N4, N5 . . . . . 5 C1
St Thomas's Sq E9 .17 B1
St Thomas St SE1 **123** C1
St Thomas's Way
SW6 . . . . **155** A2
St Thomas the Apostle Coll The
SE15 . . . . 50 B2
St Ursula's Convent Sch SE10 . . . . . . .52 C3
St Vincent De Paul Ho
24 E1 . . . . **132** A4
St Vincent De Paul RC Prim Sch SW1 . **133** A2
St Vincent Ho
SE1 . . . . **138** C2
St Vincent's RC Prim Sch
Acton W3 . . . . 28 A2
Marylebone W1 **103** C3
St Vincent St W1 . **103** C3
Salamanca Pl
SE1 . . . . **148** C3
Salamanca St SE1,
SE11 . . . . **148** C3
Salcombe Gdns
SW4 . . . . 61 A3
Salcombe Rd 19 NW5 . .12 C4
Salcombe Rd 28
N16 . . . . .16 A3
Salcombe Villas 13
TW10 . . . . 54 A2
Salcot N4 . . . . 5 B2
Salcott Rd SW11 . . . .60 B2
Salehurst Rd SE4 . . .66 B1
Salem Ho 19 E9 . . . .17 C2
Salem Rd W2 . . . **114** B4
Sale Pl W2 . . . . . . **102** A2
Salesian Coll
SW11 . . . . **168** A3
Sale St E2 . . .24 C1 99 C2
Salford Ho 5 E14 . .42 B2
Salford Rd SW12,
SW2 . . . . .73 C3
Salisbury Cl SE17 . **151** B4
Salisbury Ct
Bermondsey SE16 **139** C1
Chiswick W4 . . . . . . .38 A2
EC4 . . . . **108** A1
Hackney E9 . . . . .18 A3
Salisbury Ho
2 Islington N1 . . . . .15 A2
Islington N1 . . . . 86 A4
3 Poplar E14 . . . . . . 34 A3
Westminster SW1 . **147** C2
Wimbledon SW19 . . .69 C1
Salisbury Mews
SW6 . . . . **154** C1
Salisbury Pl
Camberwell SW9 . . .48 A3
Marylebone W1 **102** C4
Salisbury Prim Sch
NW6 . . . . .23 B4
Salisbury Rd TW9 . .54 A3
Salisbury Sq EC4 . **107** C1
Salisbury St
10 Acton W3 . . . . . . .37 B4
NW8 . . . . 90 A1

Salisbury Terr
SE15 . . . . 65 B4
Salmon La E14 . . . . .33 A3
Salmon St 13 E14 . .33 B3
Saltcoats Rd W4 . . .38 A4
Saltdene N4 . . . . 5 B3
Salter Rd SE16 . . . . .33 A1
Salters' Hall Ct
EC4 . . . . **123** B4
Salters Rd W10 . . .22 C1
Salter St
College Pk NW10 . . .21 C2
11 Poplar E14 . . . . . .33 C2
Salterton Rd N7 . . . . 5 B1
Saltoun Rd SW2,
SW9 . . . . .62 C3
Saltram Cres W9 . .23 C2
Saltwell St E14 . . . .33 C2
Saltwood Gr SE17 **151** B1
Saltwood Ho 18
SE15 . . . . **50** B4
Salusbury Prim Sch
NW6 . . . . .23 B4
Salusbury Rd
NW6 . . . . .23 B4
Salutation Rd
SE10 . . . . 43 A2
Salvin Rd SW15 . . .57 C4
Salway Rd E15 . . . .19 C2
Salween Ho 2
N16 . . . . .15 C4
Samaritan Hospl for Women W1 . . .**102** C4
Sambrook Ho 28
E1 . . . . .32 B4
Samels Ct W6 . . . . .38 C1
Samford Ho N1 . . . 85 B3
Samford St NW8 . . . 90 A1
Sam Manners Ho 7
SE10 . . . . 43 A1
Sam March Ho 5
E14 . . . . .34 C3
Sampson St E1 . . **125** C1
Samuel Cl SE14 . . .50 C4
Shoreditch E8 . . . . . . 24 B4
Samuel Ct
N1 . . . . .24 A2 98 A3
Samuel Ho 8 E8 . . .24 B4
Samuel Jones Ind Est
7 SE15 . . . . .49 A3
Samuel Lewis Bldgs
N1 . . . . .14 C2
Samuel Lewis Trust Dwellings
6 Camberwell
SE5 . . . . .48 B2
Chelsea SW3 . . . . . **144** A3
Walham Green
SW6 . . . . **155** C2
West Kensington
W14 . . . . **140** B4
Samuel Rhodes Sch
N1 . . . . 85 C4
Samuel Richardson Ho W14 . . . .**140** C3
Samuel's Cl 2 W6 .39 B2
Sancroft Ct SW11 **168** B4
Sancroft Ho SE11 **149** A2
Sancroft St SE11 . **149** A2
Sanctuary Mews
E8 . . . . .16 B2
Sanctuary St SE1 **137** A4
Sanctuary The
35 Wapping E1 . . .**32** A1

Sanctuary The
continued
Westminster SW1 . **133** C2
Sandale SE17 . . . . . .**151** B3
Sandall Ho 7 E3 . . . .26 A3
Sandall Rd NW5 . . . .13 B2
Sandalwood Cl 11
E1 . . . . .26 A1
Sandalwood Ho 5
NW3 . . . . .11 A2
Sandbourne
4 Kensington
W11 . . . . .31 C3
Paddington NW8 . . . 78 B4
Sandbourne Rd
SE4 . . . . .51 A1
Sandbrook Rd N16 . . 7 A1
Sandby Ho
6 Camberwell
SE5 . . . . .49 A2
6 Kilburn NW6 . . . . .23 C4
Sandell St SE1 . . . **135** B4
Sanderling St 20
SE8 . . . . .51 A4
Sanders Ho WC1 . . . 95 B4
Sanderson Cl
NW5 . . . . .13 A4
Sanderson Ho 7
SE8 . . . . .41 B1
Sanderstead Ave
NW2 . . . . 1 A2
Sanderstead Cl
SW12 . . . . .73 B4
Sanders Way 3
N19 . . . . 4 C3
Sandfield WC1 . . . . .94 B3
Sandford Ct N16 . . . 7 A3
Sandford Row
SE17 . . . . **151** C2
Sandford St SW6 . . **156** B1
Sandgate Ho 18
E5 . . . . .17 A4
Sandgate La SW17,
SW18 . . . . .72 A3
Sandgate St SE15 . .50 A4
Sandgate Trad Est
SE15 . . . . 50 A4
Sandham Ct SW4 . **172** B3
Sandhills The
SW10 . . . . **157** A4
Sandhurst Ct SW2 . .62 A3
Sandhurst Ho 12
E1 . . . . .32 B4
Sandilands Rd
SW6 . . . . **166** A3
Sandison St SE15 . .64 C4
Sandland St WC1 . **107** A3
Sandlings SE15 . . . .50 A1
Sandmere Rd
SW4 . . . . .62 A3
Sandon Ho 5
SW2 . . . . .74 A4
Sandown Ho 2
W4 . . . . .37 B1
Sandpiper Ct SE16 . .41 B4
Sandpiper Ct
18 Cubitt Town
E14 . . . . .42 B3
1 SE8 . . . . .51 C3
Sandridge St 3
N19 . . . . 4 B2
Sandringham Cl 1
SW19 . . . . .69 C3
Sandringham Ct
Marylebone W1 . . **105** A1
Putney SW15 . . . . . . .57 C1

Sandringham Ct
continued
18 Rotherhithe
SE16 . . . . .32 C1
St John's Wood W9 . 89 A3
Sandringham Flats
WC2 . . . . **119** C4
Sandringham Ho
Richmond TW9 . . . . .54 C4
W14 . . . . **140** A4
Sandringham Rd
Dalston E8 . . . . .16 B3
Golders Green NW11 . 1 A4
Willesden NW2 . . . . . 9 A2
Sandrock Rd SE13 . .66 C4
SANDS END 59 B4
Sands End La
SW6 . . . . **166** B4
Sandstone TW9 . . . .44 C3
Sandstone Pl N19 . . .4 A2
Sandways 6 TW9 . .44 C2
Sandwell Cres 2
NW6 . . . . .10 C2
Sandwell Mans 3
NW6 . . . . .10 C2
Sandwich Ho
18 Rotherhithe
SE16 . . . . .40 B4
WC1 . . . . 94 A3
Sandwich St WC1 . . 94 A3
Sandycombe Ctr
TW9 . . . . .54 C4
Sandycombe Rd
TW9 . . . . .44 C1
Sandy Lo N6 . . . . 4 B4
Sandy Rd NW3 . . . . . 2 A2
Sandy's Row E1 . . **110** B3
Sanford La 8 N16 . . 7 B2
Sanford St SE14,
SE8 . . . . .51 A4
Sanford Terr N16 . . . 7 B1
Sanford Wlk SE14 . .51 A4
4 Stoke Newington
N16 . . . . 7 B2
Sangora Rd 17
SW11 . . . . 59 C3
San Ho 20 E9 . . . . . .17 C2
Sankey Ho 22 E2 . .25 B3
Sansom St
Camberwell SE5 . . . .48 C2
SE5 . . . . .48 C3
Sans Wlk EC1 . . . . . 96 A2
Santley Ho SE1 . . . **135** C3
Santley St SW4 . . . .62 B3
Santos Rd SW18 . . . .58 C2
Sapcote Trad Ctr
NW10 . . . . 8 B3
Saperton Wlk
SE11 . . . . **149** A4
Sapperton Ct EC1 . . 96 C2
Sapphire Ct 1 E1 **125** B4
Sapphire Rd SE8 . . .41 A2
Saracen St E14 . . . .33 C3
Sarah Ho
Roehampton SW15 . .56 B3
8 Stepney E1 . . . . . .32 A3
Sarah Swift Ho
SE1 . . . . **137** C4
Sara Lane Ct 81
N1 . . . . .24 A3
Saratoga Rd E5 . . . .17 B4
Sardinia Ho WC2 . **106** C1
Sardinia St WC2 . . **106** C2
Sarjant Path
SW19 . . . . .69 C3
Sark Ho 9 N1 . . . . .15 B2

Sarnesfield Ho
SE15 . . . . .50 A4
Sarratt Ho 6 W10 . .30 B4
Sarre Rd NW2 . . . . .10 B3
Sarsden Bldgs
W1 . . . . **103** C1
Sarsfeld Rd SW12,
SW17 . . . . .72 B3
Sartor Rd SE15 . . . . .65 C3
Sarum Hall Sch
NW3 . . . . .12 A1
Sarum Ho
W11 . . . . . .31 B2 **113** A3
Sassoon Ho SE15 . .50 B1
Satchwell Rd
E2 . . . . .24 C2 **99** B3
Saturn Ho 4 E3 . . . .26 C4
Saul Ct 4 SE15 . . . . .49 B4
Saunders Cl 11
E14 . . . . .33 B2
Saunders Ho 11
SW2 . . . . .74 C3
Saunders Ness Rd
E14 . . . . .42 C2
Saunders St SE11 **149** B4
Savage Gdns EC3. **124** B4
Savana N16 . . . . 7 A2
Savannah Cl 9
SE15 . . . . .49 B3
Savernake Ho N4 . . . 6 C4
Savernake Rd
NW3 . . . . .12 B4
Saville Rd W4 . . . . . .37 C3
Saville Row W1 . . **118** C4
Savill Ho 2 SW4 . . . .61 C1
Savona St SW8 . . . **160** C1
Savoy Circus W3 . .29 B2
Savoy Ct
Earl's Ct SW5 . . . . . **141** C4
Strand WC2 . . . . . . **120** B3
Savoy Hill WC2 . . . **120** C3
Savoy Mews SW9 . .62 A4
Savoy Pier WC2 . . **120** C3
Savoy Pl WC2 . . . . **120** C3
Savoy Row WC2 . . **120** C4
Savoy St WC2 . . . . **120** C3
Savoy Stps WC2 . . **120** C3
Savoy Way WC2 . . **120** C3
Sawkins Cl SW19 . .70 A2
Sawley Rd W12 . . . .29 C1
Sawmill Yd E3 . . . . .26 A4
Sawyer St SE1 . . . **136** C4
Saxby Rd SW2 . . . . .74 A4
Saxonbury Ct
16 Kentish Town
N7 . . . . .13 C3
1 Lower Holloway
N7 . . . . .14 A3
Saxoncroft Ho
SW16 . . . . .73 C1
Saxon Dr W3 . . . . . .28 A4
Saxonfield Cl SW2 .74 B4
Saxon Hall W2 . . . **114** A3
Saxon Ho 4 SW4 . .61 C3
Saxon Rd E3 . . . . . . .26 B3
Saxton Cl SE13 . . . .67 C4
Sayer Ho SE4 . . . . . .66 A3
Sayes Court St
SE8 . . . . .51 B4
Sayes Ct SE8 . . . . . .51 B4
Scafell NW1 . . . . 92 C4
Scala St W1 . . . . . . **105** A4
Scampston Mews 5
W10 . . . . .30 C3
Scandrett St 38
E1 . . . . .32 A1
Scarba Wlk N1 . . . .15 C2

Scarborough Rd
N4 . . . . .5 C3
Scarborough St
E1 . . . . .111 A1
Scarlette Manor Wlk
10 SE24 . . . . .74 C4
Scarsbrook Ho 2
SW2 . . . . .62 C1
Scarsdale Ho 8 . 128 A2
Scarsdale Villas
W8 . . . . .127 C1
Scarth Rd SW13 . . .56 B4
Scawen Rd SE8 . . .41 A1
Scawfell St E2 . . . . .24 B3
Sceptre Ho 10 E1 . .25 B1
Sceptre Rd E2 . . . . .25 B2
Schiller International
Univ SE1 . . . . .123 A1
Schofield Wlk SE3 .53 C3
Sch of Pharmacy
WC1 . . . . .94 B2
Scholars St 5
Scholars Rd SW12 .73 B3
Scholefield Rd N19 . .4 C2
Scholey Ho SW11 . .60 A4
Schomberg Ho
SW1 . . . . .147 C4
Schonfeld Sq 16 . . .6 C2
School App
E2 . . . . .24 A2 98 B4
Schoolbank Rd
SE10 . . . . .43 B2
School Bell Cloisters
17 E3 . . . . .26 A3
Schoolhell Mews 18
E3 . . . . .26 A4
School Flats SW8 172 A3
School Ho SE1 . . . .152 A4
Schoolhouse La
E1 . . . . .32 C2
School Rd NW10 . . .20 C1
School Sq SE10 . . .43 B3
Schooner Cl
Cubitt Town E14 . . .42 C4
1 Rotherhithe
SE16 . . . . .40 C4
Schubert Rd
SW15 . . . . .58 B2
Science Mus★
SW7 . . . . .129 B1
Sclater St
E1 . . . . .24 B1 99 A2
Scoles Cres SW2 . .74 C3
Scoresby St SE1 . .122 A1
Scorton Ho 2 N1 . .24 A3
Scotch Ho SW1 . .130 C3
Scoter Ct 23 SE8 . .51 B4
Scotia Bldg 10 E1 . .32 C2
Scotia Ct 3 SE16 . .40 B3
Scotia Rd 24 SW2 . .74 C4
Scotland St 1
SW1 . . . . .120 A1
Scotney Ho E9 . . . .17 B2
Scotson Ho SE11 . .149 B3
Scotswood St EC1 . .95 C2
Scott Ct Acton W4 . .37 C4
Clapham SW11 . . . .170 B1
17 Stoke Newington
N16 . . . . .7 A1
Scott Ellis Gdns
NW8 . . . . .89 B3
Scott Ho
2 Barnsbury N7 . . .14 B2
Islington N1 . . . . . . .87 B4
Lisson Gr NW8 . . . .90 A1
17 Millwall E14 . . . .41 C4

Scotts Ct 6 W12 . . .39 A4
Scott's Rd W12 . . . .39 A4
Scott's Sufferance
Wharf SE1 . . . . . . .139 A3
Scott St 1 . . . . .25 A1
Scott's Yd EC4 . . . .123 B4
Scoulding Ho 7
E14 . . . . .41 C3
Scouler St E16 . . . . .35 C1
Scouler St 34 C2
Scout App NW10 . . . .8 A4
Scout La SW4 . . . . .61 B4
Scovell Cres SE1 . .136 C3
Scovell Rd SE1 . . . .136 C3
Scriven Ct 2 E8 . . . .24 B4
Scriven St 8 . . . . . . .24 B4
Scrooby St SE6 . . . .67 A1
Scrope Bldg EC1 . . .107 B4
Scrubs La NW10, W10,
W12 . . . . .22 B2
Scrutton Cl SW12 . .73 C4
Scrutton St
EC2 . . . . .24 A1 98 A1
Scutari Rd SE22 . . .65 B2
Scylla Rd SE15 . . . .65 A4
Seabright St 27
E2 . . . . .25 A2
Seacole Cl W3 . . . . .28 C4
Seacon Twr 8
E14 . . . . .41 C4
Seaford Ho 18
SE16 . . . . .40 B4
Seaford St WC1 . . . .94 B3
Seaforth Cres N5 . . . .15 B3
Seaforth Lo 2
SW13 . . . . .46 B1
Seaforth Pl SW1 . .133 A2
Seagrave Lo SW6 . .155 C4
Seagrave Rd SW6 .155 C4
Seagrove Cl E1 . . . .32 C4
Seal Ho SE1 . . . . . .137 C2
Seal St E8 . . . . .16 B4
Searle Pl N4 . . . . .5 B3
Searles Cl SW11 . .158 B1
Searles Rd SE1 . . . .151 C4
Searson Ho SE17 . .150 B3
Sears St SE5 . . . . . .48 C3
Seasalter Ho
SW9 . . . . .173 B4
Season St SW15 . . .69 A4
Seaton Point E5 . . .16 C4
Seavington Ho 8
N1 . . . . .24 A4
Sebastian Ho 22
N1 . . . . .24 A3
Sebastian St EC1 . . .96 B3
Sebbon St N1 . . . . . .15 A1
Sebright Ho 22 E2 . .24 C3
Sebright Pas 29
E2 . . . . .24 C3
Sebright Sch 2 E2 . .24 C3
Secker Ho SW9 . . . .48 A1
Secker St SE1 . . . .121 B1
Second Ave
East Acton W3 . . . . .29 B1
Kensal Town W10 . .23 A1
Mortlake SW14 . . . .56 A4
Sedan Way SE17 . .152 A2
Sedding St SW1 . . .145 B4
Seddon Ho EC2 . . .108 C4
Seddon St WC1 . . . .95 A3
Sedgeford Rd
W12 . . . . .29 B1
Sedgewick Ho
SW19 . . . . .69 C2
Sedgley Ho N4 . . . . . .5 B2

Sedgmoor Pl SE5 . .49 A3
Sedgwick St E9 . . . .17 C2
Sedley Ho SW18 . . .58 B1
Sedlescombe Rd
SW6 . . . . .155 B3
Sedley Ho SE11 . . .149 A2
Sedley Pl W1 . . . . . .104 A1
Seething La EC3 . . .124 B4
Sefton St SW15 . . . .57 B4
Sekforde St EC1 . . . .96 A2
Selbie Ave NW10 . . . .8 B3
Selborne 2 SW11 . . .60 C4
Selborne Ho SE1 . .137 B3
Selborne Rd 11
SE5 . . . . .48 C1
Selby Ho 10 SW4 . . .61 B1
Selby Sq 11 W10 . . .23 A2
Selby St E1 . . . .24 C1 99 C1
Selden Ho 2
SE15 . . . . .50 B1
Selden Rd SE15 . . . .50 B1
Selden Wlk N7 . . . . . .5 B2
Seldon Ho
Nine Elms SW8 . . . .160 C1
Pimlico SW1 . . . . . .146 C1
Selhurst Cl SW19 . .69 C3
Selina Ho NW8 . . . .89 C2
Selkirk Ho N1 . . . . . .84 C4
5 Stoke Newington
N16 . . . . .7 A1
Sellons Ave NW10 . .21 B4
Selma Ho 7 W12 . . .30 A3
Selman Ho 8 E9 . . .18 A2
Selsdon Way E14 . . .42 A3
Selsea Pl N16 . . . . .16 A3
Selsey St E14 . . . . . .33 C4
Selway Ho SW8 . . .172 B4
Selwood Ho 9 N4 . . .6 C4
Selwood Pl SW7 . .143 B2
Selwood Terr
SW7 . . . . .143 B2
Selworthy Ho
SW11 . . . . .167 C4
Selwyn Ave TW9 . . .54 B4
Selwyn Ct 8
TW10 . . . . .54 B2
Selwyn Ho 8
SW15 . . . . .57 C1
Selwyn Rd Bow E3 . .26 B3
Willesden NW10 . . . .8 A1
Semley Gate E9 . . . .18 B2
Semley Ho SW1 . . .146 A3
Semley Pl SW1 . . . .146 A3
Senate St SE15 . . . .50 B1
Senators Lo 21 E3 . .26 A3
Sendall Ct 13
SW11 . . . . .59 C4
Senior St W2 . . . . .100 A4
Senrab St E1 . . . . . .32 C3
Seraph Ct EC1 . . . . .96 C4
Serenaders Rd
SW9 . . . . .173 B1
Sergeant Ind Est The
SW18 . . . . .59 A1
Serica Ct 14 SE10 . .52 B3
Serjeants' Inn
EC4 . . . . .107 C1
Serlby Ct W14 . . . .126 C2
Serle St WC2 . . . . .107 A2
Sermon La EC4 . . . .108 C1
Serpentine Ct 10
SE16 . . . . .40 C4
Serpentine Gallery★
W2 . . . . .129 B4
Serpentine Rd
W2 . . . . .116 C1

Serpentine The★
W2 . . . . .116 B1
Service Route No 1
E15 . . . . .19 C1
Service Route No 2 1
E15 . . . . .19 C1
Service Route No 3 2
E15 . . . . .19 C1
Servite RC Prim Sch
SW10 . . . . .156 C4
Setchell Rd SE1 . . .152 C4
Setchell Way SE1 . .152 C4
Seth St SE16 . . . . . .40 B4
Settlers Ct 11 E14 . .34 C2
Settles St E1 . . . . . .111 C2
Settrington Rd
SW6 . . . . .166 A1
Seven Dials WC2 . .106 A1
Seven Mills Prim Sch
E14 . . . . .41 C4
Sevenoaks Rd SE4 . .66 B1
Seven Sisters Rd
Finsbury Pk N4 . . . . .6 A2
Stoke Newington N4, N7,
N15 . . . . .6 B4
Seven Stars Cnr
W12 . . . . .38 C3
Seven Stars Yd
E1 . . . . .111 A4
Severnake Cl E14 . . .41 C2
Severn Ave 2
W10 . . . . .23 A2
Severn Way NW10 . . .8 B3
Severus Rd SW11 . .60 A3
Seville Ho 3 E1 . . . .125 C1
Seville Mews N1 . . .16 A1
Seville St SW1 . . . .131 A3
Sevington St W9 . . . .88 A1
Seward St EC1 . . . . .96 C3
Sewardstone Rd
E2 . . . . .25 B3
Sewell Ho 7 N16 . . .16 A3
Sextant Ave E14 . . .42 C2
Sexton Ct 7 E14 . . .34 C2
Sexton's Ho 5
SE13 . . . . .52 B4
Seymour Ct
Putney SW15 . . . . . .57 A4
Upper Clapton N16 . .7 C3
Seymour Gdns
SE4 . . . . .66 A4
Seymour Ho
Bloomsbury WC1 . . .94 A3
Clapham SW8 . . . . .171 A2
Somers Town NW1 . .93 C4
Seymour Mews
W1 . . . . .103 B2
Seymour Pl W1 . . .102 C2
Seymour Rd
Acton W4 . . . . .37 B2
Wandsworth SW18 . .58 B1
Wimbledon SW19 . . .69 C1
Seymour St W1 . . . .103 A1
Seymour Wlk
SW10 . . . . .156 C4
Seyssel St E14 . . . . .42 B2
Shaa Rd W3 . . . . . . .28 C2
Shabana Ct 3
W12 . . . . .30 A1
Shackleton Ct
3 Dulwich SE21 . . .75 C2
2 Isle of Dogs E14 . .41 C1
4 Shepherd's Bush
W12 . . . . .39 A4
Shackleton Ho 5
E1 . . . . .32 B1

SHACKLEWELL 16 B4
Shacklewell Ho 8
E8 . . . . .16 B4
Shacklewell La E8 . .16 B3
Shacklewell Prim Sch
E8 . . . . .16 B4
Shacklewell Rd
N16 . . . . .16 B4
Shacklewell Row
E8 . . . . .16 B4
Shacklewell St
E2 . . . . .24 B2 99 A3
Shad Thames
SE1 . . . . .139 A4
SHADWELL 32 B2
Shadwell Gdns E1 . .32 B2
Shadwell Pierhead
E1 . . . . .32 B2
Shadwell Pl 3 E1 . . .32 B2
Shadwell Sta E1 . . . .32 A2
Shaftesbury Ave
W1 . . . . .119 C4
Shaftesbury Ct
Borough The SE1 . .137 B2
1 Herne Hill SE5 . . .63 C3
Shoreditch N1 . . . . .87 B1
Streatham SW16 . . .73 C1
Shaftesbury Ctr
NW10 . . . . .22 C1
Shaftesbury Gdns
NW10 . . . . .21 A1
Shaftesbury Ho
1 Canning Town
E16 . . . . .35 B3
5 Stoke Newington
N16 . . . . .7 A1
W2 . . . . .114 B4
Shaftesbury Lo 7
E14 . . . . .34 A3
Shaftesbury Mews
3 Clapham Pk
SW4 . . . . .61 B2
W8 . . . . .127 C1
Shaftesbury Park
Chambers 1
SW11 . . . . .60 C4
Shaftesbury Rd
Finsbury Pk N4, N19 . .5 A3
Richmond TW9 . . . . .54 A4
Shaftesbury St N1 . .87 B1
Shafteswood Ct
SW17 . . . . .72 B1
Shafto Mews
SW1 . . . . .131 A1
Shafton Rd E9 . . . . .25 C4
Shaftsbury Park Prim
Sch SW11 . . . . .169 B1
Shafts Ct EC3 . . . . .110 A1
Shahjalal Ho 18
E2 . . . . .24 C3
Shakespeare Ave
NW10 . . . . .20 C4
Shakespeare Ho 9
E9 . . . . .17 B1
Shakespeare Rd
Acton W3 . . . . .28 B1
Brixton SE24 . . . . . .63 A3
Shakespeare's Globe
Theatre (site of)★
SE1 . . . . .123 A2
Shakespeare Twr
EC2 . . . . .109 A4
Shakspeare Mews 7
N16 . . . . .16 A4

Shakspeare Wlk
  N16 . . . . 16 A4
Shalbourne Sq E9 . .18 B2
Shalcomb St
  SW10 . . . . 157 A3
Shalden Ho SW15 . .56 B1
Shalfleet Dr W10 . .30 C2
Shalford Ho NW10 . .21 C4
Shalford Ct W1 . . .86 A2
Shalford Ho SE1 . .137 C2
Shalimar Gdns
  W3 . . . . .28 B2
Shalimar Lo W3 . . .28 B2
Shalimar Rd W3 . . .28 B2
Shalstone Rd SW14,
  TW9 . . . . .55 A4
Shamrock St SW4 .61 C4
Shandon Ct SE4 . . .51 A1
Shandon Rd SW4 . .61 B1
Shand St SE1 . . . .138 B4
Shandy St E1 . . . . .25 C1
Shan Ho WC1 . . . . .94 C1
Shannon Ct
  11 Peckham SE15 . .49 B3
  Stoke Newington N16 . 7 A1
  Willesden NW10 . . . 8 C2
Shannon Gr SW9 . .62 B3
Shannon Pl NW8 . . .80 B2
Shanti Ct SW18 . . .70 C3
Shapla Prim Sch
  E1 . . . . .125 C3
Shardcroft Ave
  SE24 . . . . .63 A2
Shardeloes Rd
  SE14 . . . . .51 B1
Shard's Sq SE15 . . .49 C4
Sharebourne Ho
  SW2 . . . . .62 C2
Sharman Ho 🔟
  E14 . . . . .34 B3
Sharnbrook Ho
  W6 . . . . .155 B4
Sharon Gdns E9 . . .25 B4
Sharon Rd W4 . . . .37 C1
Sharp Ho SW8 . . . .61 A4
Sharples Hall St 8
  NW1 . . . . .12 B1
Sharpness Ct 2
  SE15 . . . . .49 B3
Sharratt St SE15 . . .50 B4
Sharsted St SE17 .150 A1
Sharwood WC1 . . . .85 A1
Shaver's Pl SW1 . .119 B3
Shawbury Ct SE22 . .64 B2
Shawbury Rd
  SE22 . . . . .64 B2
Shaw Cres 8 E14 . .33 A3
Shaw Ct
  1 Acton Green
  W3 . . . . .37 B3
  2 Battersea SW11 . .59 C4
  Upper Holloway N19 . . 5 A2
Shawfield St SW3 .144 B1
Shawford Ct 8
  SW15 . . . . .68 C4
Shaw Rd SE22 . . . .64 A3
Shearling Way N7 . .14 A2
Shearsmith Ho
  E1 . . . . .125 C4
Shearwater Ct 24
  SE8 . . . . .51 B4
Sheba Pl E1 . . 24 B1 99 A1
Sheen Common Dr
  SW14, TW10 . . . . .54 C2

Sheen Court Rd
  TW10 . . . . .54 C3
Sheen Ct TW10 . . . .54 C3
Sheendale Rd
  TW9 . . . . .54 B3
Sheen Gate Gdns
  SW14 . . . . .55 B3
Sheen La 55 C3
Sheen Gr N1 . . . . .85 B4
Sheen La SW14 . . . .55 B3
Sheen Mount Prim
  Sch SW14 . . . . . . .55 A2
Sheen Pk TW10,
  TW9 . . . . .54 A3
Sheen Rd TW10,
  TW9 . . . . .54 A3
Sheen Wood
  SW14 . . . . .55 B2
Sheepcote La
  SW11 . . . . .169 A1
Sheep La E8 . . . . . .25 A4
Sheffield Ho 15
  SE15 . . . . .49 B2
Sheffield Sq 2 E3 . .26 B2
Sheffield St WC2 . .106 C1
Sheffield Terr
  W8 . . . 31 C1 113 C1
Shelburne Ho 20
  SW15 . . . . .57 C2
Shelburne Rd N7 . . .14 B4
Shelbury Rd SE22 . .65 A2
Sheldon Ct SW8 . .162 A1
Sheldon Ho 6 E9 . .17 C2
Sheldon Pl E2 . . . .25 A3
Sheldon Rd NW2 . . . 9 C4
Sheldon Sq W2 . . .101 A3
Sheldrake Ho 16
  SE16 . . . . .40 C2
Sheldrake Pl W8 . .127 B4
Shelduck Ct 37
  SE8 . . . . .51 B4
Shelford Pl N16 . . . .6 C1
Shelgate Rd SW11 . .60 B2
Shell Ctr SE1 . . . .121 A1
Shelley Cl SE15 . . . .50 A1
Shelley Ct
  Finsbury Pk N4 . . . 5 B3
  SW3 . . . . .159 A4
Shelley Ho
  21 Bethnal Green
  E2 . . . . .25 B2
  Chelsea SW1 . . . .160 C4
  9 Stoke Newington
  N16 . . . . .16 A4
  Walworth SE17 . . .151 A2
Shelley Rd NW10 . .20 C4
Shellgrove Rd
  N16 . . . . .16 A3
Shellness Rd E5 . . .17 A3
Shell Rd SE13 . . . . .67 A4
Shellwood Rd
  SW11 . . . . .168 C1
Shelmerdine Cl
  E3 . . . . .33 C4
Shelton St WC2 . . .106 A1
Shene Bldg EC1 . . .107 B4
Shene Sch SW14 . . .56 A3
Shenfield St N1 . . . .24 A3
Shenley Rd SE5 . . . .49 A2
Shepard Ho 18
  SW11 . . . . .59 C4
Sheperdess Pl N1 . .97 A4
Shepherd Cl W1 . . .117 B4

Shepherdess Wlk
  N1 . . . . .87 A1
Shepherd Ho
  Barnsbury N7 . . . . .14 A2
  10 Poplar E14 . . . . .34 A3
Shepherd Mkt
  W1 . . . . .118 A1
SHEPHERD'S BUSH
  . . . . .30 A1
Shepherd's Bush
  (Central Line) Sta
  W12 . . . . .39 C4
Shepherd's Bush Gn
  W12 . . . . .39 B4
Shepherd's Bush
  (Hamm & City) Sta
  W12 . . . . .30 B1
Shepherd's Bush
  Market W12 . . . . . .39 B4
Shepherd's Bush Pl
  W12 . . . . .39 C4
Shepherd's Bush Rd
  W6 . . . . .39 B3
Shepherds Ct 8
  W12 . . . . .39 C4
Shepherd's La E9 . .17 C2
Shepherds Pl W1 .117 B4
Shepherd St W1 . .118 C1
Shepherd's Wlk
  NW3 . . . . .11 C4
Sheppard Dr SE16 . .40 A1
Sheppard Ho
  31 Hackney E2 . . . .24 C3
  8 Streatham SW2 . .74 C3
Shepperton Rd N1 . .87 B4
Sheppey Ho 16 E5 . .17 A4
Shepton Ct SW11 .167 C4
Shepton Hos 11
  E2 . . . . .25 B2
Sherard Ct N19 . . . .5 A1
Sherard Ho 24 E9 . .17 B1
Sheraton Ho SW1 .160 B4
Sheraton St W1 . . .105 B1
Sherborne Ho
  Pimlico SW1 . . . . .146 B2
  South Lambeth
  SW8 . . . . .162 C1
Sherborne La
  EC4 . . . . .123 C4
Sherborne St N1 . . .87 B4
Sherbourne Ct
  SW5 . . . . .142 A4
Sherbrooke Ho 9
  E2 . . . . .25 B3
Sherbrooke Rd
  SW6 . . . . .154 B1
Sherbrooke Terr
  SW6 . . . . .154 B1
Shere Ho SE1 . . . .137 B2
Sherfield Gdns
  SW15 . . . . .56 B1
Sheridan Bldgs
  WC2 . . . . .106 B1
Sheridan Ct
  Earl's Ct SW5 . . . .142 A3
  South Hampstead
  NW6 . . . . .11 B1
  South Lambeth
  SW9 . . . . .173 A3
Sheridan Ho
  SE11 . . . . .149 C3
  7 Stoke Newington
  N16 . . . . .16 A4
Sheridan Pl SW13 . .56 B4
Sheridan St 34 E1 . .32 A3
Sheringham Prim Sch
  SW18 . . . . .70 B3

Sheringham NW8 . .79 C4
Sheringham Ho
  NW1 . . . . .102 B4
Sheringham Mews 7
  SW18 . . . . .71 B2
Sheringham Rd
  N7 . . . . .14 C2
Sherlock Ct NW8 . . .79 B4
Sherlock Holmes
  Mus* NW1 . . . . . . .91 A1
Sherlock Mews
  W1 . . . . .103 B3
Sherren Ho 35 E1 . .25 B1
Sherrick Green Rd
  NW10 . . . . 9 A3
Sherriff Ct NW6 . . .10 C2
Sherriff Rd NW6 . . .10 C2
Sherrin Rd E10 . . . .19 A4
Sherston Ct
  Finsbury WC1 . . . . .95 B3
  Newington SE1 . . .150 B4
Sherwin Ho SE11 .163 B4
Sherwin Rd SE14 . .50 C2
Sherwood NW6 . . .10 A1
Sherwood Cl
  SW13 . . . . .57 A4
Sherwood Ct
  11 Battersea
  SW11 . . . . .59 B4
  St Johns SE13 . . . . .52 A1
  W1 . . . . .102 C3
Sherwood Gdns
  Bermondsey SE16 . .40 A1
  Millwall E14 . . . . . .41 C2
Sherwood Ho N4 . . . 6 B4
Sherwood St W1 . .119 A4
Shetland Rd E3 . . . .26 B3
Shillaker Ct W3 . . .29 B1
Shillibeer Pl W1 . .102 B3
Shillingford Ho 25
  E3 . . . . .27 A2
Shillingford St 28
  N1 . . . . .15 A1
Shillingstone Ho
  W14 . . . . .126 B1
Shinfield St W12 . . .30 B3
Shipka Rd SW12 . . .73 A3
Shiplake Ho 45
  E2 . . . . 24 B2 98 C3
Shipley Ho SW8 . .171 B1
Ship & Mermaid Row
  SE1 . . . . .138 A4
Ship St SE8 . . . . . .51 C2
Ship Tavern Pas
  EC3 . . . . .124 A4
Shipton Ho
  7 Camden Town
  NW5 . . . . .12 C2
  14 Haggerston E2 . .24 B3
Shipton St
  E2 . . . . 24 B2 99 A4
Shipwright Rd
  SE16 . . . . .41 A4
Shipwright Yd
  SE1 . . . . .124 A1
Shirbutt St E14 . . . .34 A2
Shire Pl SW18 . . . .71 B4
Shirland Mews
  W9 . . . . .23 B2
Shirland Rd W9 . . . .23 C1
Shirley Gr SW11 . . .60 C4
Shirley Ho 13 SE5 . .48 C3
Shirley Rd W4 . . . . .37 C4
Shirley St E16 . . . . .35 B3
Shirlock Rd NW3 . . .12 B4
Shoe La EC4 . . . . .107 C2

Shooters Hill Rd SE3,
  SE10 . . . . .53 A2
Shoot-Up Hill
  NW2 . . . . .10 A2
Shopstop SW11 . . .60 A3
Shore Bsns Ctr 31
  E9 . . . . .17 B1
SHOREDITCH 87 C1
Shoreditch Ct 6
  E8 . . . . .16 B1
Shoreditch High St
  E2 . . . . 24 A1 98 B2
Shoreditch Ho N1 . .97 C3
Shoreham Cl
  SW18 . . . . .59 A2
Shore Ho SW8 . . . .61 A4
Shore Mews 38
  E9 . . . . .17 B1
Shore Pl E9 . . . . . .17 B1
Shore Rd E9 . . . . . .17 B1
Shorncliffe Rd
  SE1 . . . . .152 C2
Shorrolds Rd
  SW6 . . . . .155 A2
Shortcroft Mead Ct
  NW10 . . . . 8 C3
Shorter St EC3 . . . .125 A4
Shortlands W6 . . . .39 C2
Short Rd W4 . . . . . .46 A4
Shorts Gdns WC2 . .106 A1
Short St SE1 . . . . .135 C4
Shottendale Ho
  SW6 . . . . .165 B4
Shottfield Ave
  SW14 . . . . .56 A3
Shottsford 8
  W11 . . . . .31 C3
Shoulder of Mutton
  Alley 16 E14 . . . . . .33 A2
Shouldham St
  W1 . . . . .102 B3
Shreveport Ho 22
  N19 . . . . 4 C4
Shrewsbury Ave
  SW14 . . . . .55 C3
Shrewsbury Ho
  Chelsea SW3 . . . .158 A3
  Kennington SE11 . .163 A3
Shrewsbury Mews 33
  W2 . . . . .31 C3
Shrewsbury Rd
  W2 . . . . .31 C3
Shrewsbury St
  W10 . . . . .22 B1
Shropshire Ho
  WC1 . . . . .93 A1
Shroton St NW1 . . .102 B4
Shrubbery Cl N1 . . .87 A3
Shrubland Rd E8 . . .24 C4
Shrubs Ho SW1 . . .147 C3
Shurland Gdns
  SE15 . . . . .49 B3
Shuters Sq W14 . . .140 C1
Shuttle St
  E1 . . . . 24 C1 99 B1
Shuttleworth Rd
  SW11 . . . . .168 A2
Sibella Rd SW4 . . .171 C1
Sicilian Ave WC1 . .106 B3
Sidbury St SW6 . . .164 A4
Siddons Ct WC2 . . .106 C1
Siddons Ho 13
  NW3 . . . . .12 B3
Siddons La NW1 . . .91 A1
Sidford Ho SE1 . . .135 A1
Sidford Pl SE1 . . . .135 A1
Sidgwick Ho SW9 .172 B1

Sidings Mews N7 ...14 C4
Sidlaw Ho N16 ....7 B3
Sidmouth Ho
18 Camberwell
SE15 ....49 C3
Marylebone W1 **A** .102 B2
20 Streatham SW2 .74 C4
Sidmouth Mews
WC1 ....94 C3
Sidmouth Par NW2 ...9 A3
Sidmouth Rd NW2 ....9 A3
Sidmouth St WC1 ..94 C3
Sidney Boyd Ct
NW6 ....10 C1
Sidney Godley (VC)
Ho **31** E2 ....25 C2
Sidney Gr EC1 ......86 A1
Sidney Ho **4** E2 ...25 C3
Sidney Miller Ct **8**
W3 ....28 A1
Sidney Rd SW9 ....173 A1
Sidney Sq E1 ....32 B4
Sidney St E1 ....32 B4
Sidworth St **6** E8 .17 A1
Siebert Rd SE3 ....53 C4
Siege Ho **40** E1 ....32 A3
Sigdon Rd E8 ......16 C3
Signal Ho
9 London E8 ......17 A1
SE1 ....136 C3
Signmakers Yd
NW1 ....82 B3
Silbury Ho **9**
SE26 ....76 C1
Silbury St N1 ....97 B4
Silchester Rd
W10 ....30 C3
Silesia Bldgs E8 ...17 A1
Silex St SE1 ......136 B3
Silk Mills Path
SE13 ....67 B4
Silk Mills Sq E9 ...18 B2
Silk St EC2 ....109 A4
Sillitoe Ho N1 ......87 C3
Silsoe Ho NW1 .....82 B1
Silverbirch Wlk **1**
NW3 ....12 C2
Silverburn Ho **4**
SW9 ....48 A2
Silver Cl SE14 .....51 A3
Silver Court **45** 37 A8
Silver Ct N19 ....4 B1
Silverdale NW1 .....92 C4
Silverdale Ct EC1 ..96 B2
Silvermere Ho
SE6 ....67 A1
Silver Pl W1 ......119 A4
Silver Rd
Shepherd's Bush
W12 ....30 C2
St Johns SE13 .....67 A4
Silverthorne NW6 ..78 B3
Silverthorne Rd
SW8 ....170 B1
Silverton Rd W6 ...47 C4
Silvertown Way
E16 ....35 C4
Silver Wlk SE16 ...33 B1
Silvester Ho
47 Bethnal Green
E2 ....25 B2
1 Notting Hill W11 .31 B3
6 Stepney E1 .....32 A3
Silvester SE22 ....64 B3
Silvester St SE1 ..137 B3
Silwex Ho
E1 ....24 B1 98 C1

Silwood St SE16 ....40 B1
Simla Ho SE1 .....137 C3
Simmonds Ct
SW5 ....142 A3
Simmons Ho
Bethnal Green
E2 ....24 C2 99 B3
Finsbury Pk N7 .....5 B2
Simms Ct SW6 ....154 A1
Simms Rd SE1 ....153 C3
Simon Cl
W11 ....31 B2 113 A4
Simon Ct SW9 .....23 C2
Simon Lo **31**
SW19 ....69 C3
Simon Marks Jewish
Prim Sch N16 .....7 B2
Simons Wlk E15 ...19 C3
Simpson Dr W3 ....28 C3
Simpson Ho
Lisson Gr NW8 ....90 A3
Vauxhall SE11 ....148 C1
Simpson's Rd E14 .34 A2
Simpson St SW11 .168 A1
Sinclair Ct N5 .....15 B2
Sinclair Gdns
W14 ....39 C4
Sinclair Ho **1**
SW12 ....73 C3
Sinclair Mans **13**
W12 ....39 C4
Sinclair Pl SE4 ....66 C1
Sinclair Rd W14 ..126 A2
Sinclairs Ho **18** E3 .26 B3
Singer St EC2 .....97 C3
Sion Ho SE13 ......67 B3
Sion-Manning RC
Sch for Girls
Kensal Town W10 ..31 A4
North Kensington
W10 ....30 C4
Sir Abraham Dawes
Cotts SW15 ....58 A3
Sir Alexander Cl
W3 ....29 B1
Sir Alexander Rd
W3 ....29 B1
Sirdar Rd
W11 ....31 A2 112 A3
Sir Francis Drake
Prim Sch SE8 .....41 A1
Sirinham Point
SW8 ....163 A3
Sirius Bldg **21** E14 ..34 C2
Sir James Barrie Prim
Sch SW8 ....171 A3
Sir John Cass
Foundation &
Redcoat CE Sec Sch
E1 ....25 C1
Sir John Cass's
Foundation Prim Sch
EC3 ....110 B1
Sir John Kirk Cl **38**
SE5 ....48 B3
Sir John Lillie Prim
Sch SW6 ....154 B3
Sir Oswald Stoll
Foundation The
SW6 ....156 A2
Sir Thomas Abney
Sch N16 ....6 C3
Sir Thomas More Est
SW3 ....157 C3
Sir William Burrough
Prim Sch E14 .....33 A3

Sir William Powell's
Almshos SW6 ......58 A4
Sise La EC4 ......109 B1
Siskin Ho **37** SE16 ..40 C2
Sispara Gdns
SW18 ....58 B1
Sissinghurst Ho **7**
SE15 ....50 B4
Sister Mabel's Way **18**
SE15 ....49 C3
Sisters Ave SW11 .60 B3
Sistova Rd SW12 ..73 A3
Sisulu Pl SW9 .....62 C4
Sitarey Ct **4** W12 .30 A1
Site of Changing of
the Guard*
SW1 ....132 C3
Sivill Ho E2 ...24 B2 99 A4
Siward Rd SW17....71 B1
Six Bridges Ind Est
SE1 ....153 C1
Sixth Ave W10 .....23 A2
Skardu Rd NW2 ....10 A3
Skeena Hill SW18,
SW19 ....70 A4
Skegness Ho **3**
N7 ....14 B1
Skelbrook St
SW18 ....71 B2
Skelgill Rd SW15 ..58 B3
Skelton Cl **7** E8 ...16 B2
Skelton Ho N16 ...16 A3
Skelwith Rd W6 ...47 B4
Skenfrith Ho SE15 .50 A4
Sketchley Gdns
SE16 ....40 C1
Skiffington Cl
SW2 ....74 C3
Skinner Pl SW1 ...145 B3
Skinners Company
Sch (Upper) N16 ...7 B4
Skinners La EC4 ..123 A4
Skinner St EC1 ....95 C2
Skipsea Ho SW18 .59 C1
Skipton Ho SE4 ...66 A3
Skipwith Bldg
EC1 ....107 B4
Skipworth Rd E9 ..25 B4
Skua Ct **24** SE8 ....51 B4
Skyline Ct SE1 ...138 C1
Skyline Plaza Bldg
E1 ....111 C2
Skylines E14 ......42 B4
Slade Ct NW2 .....10 A3
Sladen Pl **12** E5 ...17 A4
Slagrove Pl SE13 ..67 A2
Slaidburn St
SW10 ....157 A3
Slaithwaite Rd
SE13 ....67 B3
Slaney Ct NW10 ....9 B1
Slaney Pl **1** N7 ...14 C3
Sleaford Ho **18** E3 .26 C1
Sleaford Ind Est
SW8 ....161 A1
Sleaford St SW8 ..161 A1
Sleat Ho **11** E3 ...26 B3
Slievemore Cl **8**
SW4 ....61 C4
Sligo Ho **8** E1 ...25 C1
Slingsby Pl WC2 ..120 A4
Slippers Pl SE16 ..40 A3
Slipway Ho **1** E14 .42 A1
Sloane Ave SW3 ..144 B3
Sloane Avenue Mans
SW3 ....144 C3

Sloane Ct E SW3 .145 B2
Sloane Ct W SW3 .145 B2
Sloane Gate Mans
SW1 ....145 B4
Sloane Gdns SW1 .145 B3
Sloane Ho **7** E9 ...17 B1
Sloane St SW1 ....131 A1
Sloane Square **8**
SW1 ....145 B3
Sloane St SW1 ....131 A1
Sloane Terr SW1 ..145 B4
Sloane Terr Mans
SW1 ....145 B4
Sly St **17** E1 ......32 A3
Smallbrook Mews
W2 ....101 B1
Smalley Cl N16 .....7 B1
Smart's Pl WC1,
WC2 ....106 B2
Smart St E2 ....25 C2
Smeaton Ct SE1 ..136 C1
Smeaton Rd SW18 .70 C4
Smeaton St E1 ....32 A1
Smedley St SW4 ..171 C2
Smeed Rd E3 ......18 C1
Smiles Pl SE13 ....52 B1
Smith Cl SE16 .....32 C1
Smithfield Mkt
EC1 ....108 B3
Smithfield St EC1 .108 A3
Smithies Ct E15 ...19 B3
Smith's Ct W1 ....119 B4
Smith Sq SW1 ....134 A1
Smith St SW3 .....144 C1
Smith's Yd SW18 ..71 B2
Smith Terr SW3 ...144 C1
Smithwood Cl
SW19 ....70 A2
Smithy St E1 ......32 B4
Smithy Street Sch
E1 ....32 B4
Smugglers Way
SW18 ....59 A3
Smyrk's Rd SE17 ..152 B1
Smyrna Mans **8**
NW6 ....10 C1
Smyrna Rd NW6 ...10 C1
Smythe St E14 ....34 A2
Snarsgate St W10 .30 B4
Sneath Ave NW11 ...1 B4
Sneyd Rd NW2 .....9 B4
Snowberry Cl **11** ..19 C4
Snowbury Rd
SW6 ....166 B1
Snowden St
EC2 ....24 A1 98 A1
Snowe Ho SE27 ...75 A1
Snow Hill EC1 ....108 A3
Snowman Ho NW6 .78 B4
Snowsfields SE1 ..137 C4
Snowsfields Prim Sch
SE1 ....138 A4
Soames St SE15 ..64 B4
Soane Ct **30** NW1 .13 B1
Soane Ho SE17 ...151 C1
Soane Mus The*
WC2 ....106 C2
Soaphouse La
TW8 ....44 A3
SOHO 105 B1
Soho* W1 ....105 B2
Soho Parish CE Prim
Sch W1 ....119 B4
Soho Sq W1 ......105 B2
Soho St W1 ....105 B2
Sojourner-Truth Cl **11**
E8 ....17 A2

Solander Gdns
13 Shadwell E1 .....32 B2
Stepney E1 ....32 A2
Soldene Ct N7 ....14 B2
Solebay St E1 .....26 A1
Solent Ho **8** E1 ...33 A4
Solent Rd NW6 ....10 C3
Soley Mews WC1 ..95 B4
Solidarity Ho **5**
NW10 ....9 B2
Solna Ave SW15 ...57 B2
Solomon's Pas
SE15 ....65 A3
Solon New Rd
SW4 ....62 A3
Solon Rd SW2 .....62 A3
Solway Ho **12** E1 ..25 C1
Solway Rd SE22 ...64 C3
Somali Rd NW2 ...10 B3
Somborne Ho **11**
SW15 ....68 C4
Sombrook Ho
SE11 ....149 B3
Somer Ct SW6 ....155 B3
Somerfield Rd N4 ...6 A2
Somerfield St
SE16 ....40 C1
Somerford Gr N16 .16 B4
Somerford Grove Est
N16 ....16 B4
Somerford St E1 ..25 A1
Somerford Way
SE16 ....41 A4
Somerleyton Rd
SW9 ....62 C3
Somers Cl NW1 ...83 B2
Somers Cres W2 ..102 A1
Somerset Gdns
Highgate N6 ....3 C4
St Johns SE13 ....52 A1
Somerset Ho
WC2 ....121 A4
Somerset Ho
SW19 ....69 C1
Somerset Rd W13 .57 A3
Somerset Sq
W14 ....126 C2
Somers Pl SW2 ...74 B4
Somers Rd SW2 ...62 B1
SOMERS TOWN ...93 C4
Somers Town Est
NW1 ....83 A1
Somerton Ave
TW9 ....55 A4
Somerton Rd
Cricklewood NW2 ...1 A1
Nunhead SE15 ....65 A3
Somerville Ave
SW13 ....47 B4
Somerville Point
SE16 ....41 A4
Sonderburg Rd **13**
N7 ....5 B2
Sondes St SE17 ...48 C4
Sonia Gdns NW10 ..8 B4
Sonning Ho
E2 ....24 B2 98 C3
Sophia Cl N7 .....14 B2
Sophia Ho **10** W6 ..39 B1

Sophia Sq **14** SE16...33 A2
Sopwith Way
SW8 ....**160** A2
Sorrel La **7** E14.....34 C2
Sorrell Cl
Brixton SW9 ....**173** C2
SE14 ....5 A2
Soseki Mus★ SW4..**61** A4
Sotheby Rd N5 ......15 B4
Sotheran Cl **8**....28 C4
Sotheron Pl SW6.**156** B1
Soudan Rd SW11 ..**168** C3
Souldern Rd **10**
W14 ....39 C3
SOUTH ACTON 37 A3
South Acton Sta W3,
W4 ....37 B3
South Africa Rd
W12 ....30 A2
Southall St **1**..**137** B3
Southam Ho **9**
W10 ....23 A1
Southampton Bldgs
WC2 ....**107** B3
Southampton Pl
WC1 ....**106** B3
Southampton Rd
NW5 ....12 B3
Southampton Row
WC1 ....**106** B4
Southampton St
WC2 ....**120** B4
Southampton Way
SE5 ....49 A3
Southam St W10 ...23 A1
South Audley St
W1 ....**117** C2
South Ave SW14....44 C1
SOUTH BANK 120 C1
South Bank Bsns Ctr
SW8 ....**161** C3
Southbank
International Sch
NW3 ....11 B2
Southbank
International Sch
(Westminster
Campus) W1 .....**104** A4
Southbank Int Sch
W11 .....31 C2 **113** B3
South Bank Univ
London SW8....**171** C4
SE1 ....**136** A2
South Bermondsey
Sta SE16 ....40 B1
South Black Lion La
7 W6..............38 C1
South Bldg★ SW1.**133** A2
South Block **20** E1..32 B2
South Bolton Gdns
SW10 ....**142** B2
Southborough Ho
SE17 ....**152** B2
Southbourne Rd
E9 ....25 C4
SOUTH BROMLEY...34 C4
South Building★
SE10 ....52 C3
Southbury NW8...**79** A4
South Camden Com
Sch NW1 ....**83** B2
South Carriage Dr
SW1, SW7 ......**130** C4

South Chelsea Coll
SW9 ....62 B3
South Colonnade The
E14 ....**34** A1
Southcombe St
W14 ....**140** A4
Southcott Ho
8 Bromley E3 ......27 A2
W9 ....**89** A1
South Cres
Newham SW1 ....27 C1
WC1 ....**105** B3
South Ct **17** SW15...57 C1
Southdean Gdns
SW19 ....70 B2
Southdown N7 .....14 A2
South Eastern Univ
N7.......................5 B1
South Eaton Pl
SW1 ....**145** C4
South Edwardes Sq
W8 ....**127** B1
South End **8** W8..**128** B2
South End Cl NW3..12 A4
South End Gn
NW3 ....12 A4
South End Rd
NW3 ....12 A4
South End Row
W8 ....**128** B1
Southerngate Way
SE14 ....51 A3
Southern Gr E3 ....26 B1
Southern Row
W10 ....23 A1
Southern St N1 ....84 C2
Southern Way
SE10 ....43 B1
Southerton Rd
W6 ....39 B2
Southey Ho SE17 .**151** A2
Southey Mews
E16 ....35 C1
Southey Rd SW9 .**173** B4
Southfield Lo W4 ..37 C4
Southfield Prim Sch
W4 ....38 A4
Southfield Rd W4 ..37 C4
SOUTHFIELDS 71 A3
Southfields Com Coll
SW18 ....70 C3
Southfields Rd
SW18 ....58 C1
Southfields Sta
SW18 ....70 C4
Southgate Ct N1..15 C1
Southgate Gr N1..15 C1
Southgate Rd N1.**87** C4
South Gr N6..........3 C3
South Grove Ho N6..3 C3
SOUTH HACKNEY
...........................25 B4
SOUTH HAMPSTEAD
.........................11 B1
South Hampstead
High Sch NW3 ..11 C2
South Hampstead
High Sch Jun Dept
NW3 ....11 B1
South Hampstead
High Sch NW8 ..11 B1
South Hill Pk
NW3 ....12 A4
South Hill Pk Gdns
NW3 ....12 A4
Southill St E14 ....34 A3

South Island Pl
SW9 ....**163** B1
SOUTH KENSINGTON
...........................143 A3
South Kensington Sta
SW7 ....**143** B2
South Kensington
Station Arc SW7 **143** C4
SOUTH LAMBETH
........................**172** B3
South Lambeth Pl
SW8 ....**162** B4
South Lambeth Rd
SW8 ....**162** B2
Southlands Dr
SW19 ....69 C2
South Lo NW8......**89** B4
South London
Montessori Sch
SW11 ....**168** A3
Southmead Prim Sch
SW19 ....70 A3
Southmead Rd
SW19 ....70 A3
South Molton La
W1 ....**104** A1
South Molton Rd
E16 ....35 C3
South Molton St
W1 ....**104** A1
Southmoor Way
E9 ....18 B3
Southolm St
SW11 ....**170** B3
South Par W4........37 C2
South Parade
SW3 ....**143** C2
South Park Mews
SW6 ....59 A4
South Pl EC2......**109** C3
South Pl Mews
EC2 ....**109** C3
South Quay Plaza
E14 ....42 A4
South Quay Sta
E14 ....42 A4
South Row SE3.....53 B1
South Sea St SE16..41 B3
Southside N7.......13 C4
South Side W6.......38 B3
Southside Ind Est
SW8 ....**170** C4
Southside Quarter
SW11 ....**168** C2
Southside Sh Ctr
SW18 ....59 A1
South Sq WC1...**107** B3
South St W1 ......**117** C2
South Tenter St
E1 ....**111** A1
South Terr SW7 ..**144** A4
South Thames Coll
(Battersea Ctr)
SW11 ....**169** A3
South Thames Coll
(Putney Ctr)
SW15 ....57 C2
South Thames Coll
(Roehampton Ctr)
SW15 ....56 C1
South Thames Coll
(Wandsworth Ctr)
SW18 ....59 A1
Southvale Rd SE3..53 A1
Southview Ave
N10 ....8 B3

South Villas NW1...13 C2
Southville SW8...**171** C3
SOUTHWARK 40 B2
Southwark Bridge St
EC4 ....**123** A3
Southwark Bridge Rd
SE1 ....**123** A1
Southwark Cath★
SE1 ....**123** B2
Southwark Coll
SE1 ....**136** A4
Southwark Coll
(Blackfriars Ctr)
SE1 ....**122** A1
Southwark Coll
(Camberwell Ctr)
SE5 ....49 A3
Southwark Coll
(Grange Ctr)
SE1 ....**138** B1
Southwark Coll
(Surrey Docks Ctr)
SE16 ....40 C3
Southwark Park Est
11 SE16 ....40 A2
Southwark Park Prim
Sch SE16 ....40 A3
Southwark Park Rd
SE16 ....**153** B4
Southwark St
SE1 ....**122** C1
Southwater Cl **8**
E14 ....33 B3
Southway Cl **9**
W12 ....39 A4
Southwell Gdns
SW7 ....**142** C3
Southwell Ho
3 Bermondsey
SE16 ....40 A2
13 Stoke Newington
N16 ....16 A3
Southwell Rd SE5..63 B4
South Wharf Rd
W2 ....**101** C2
Southwick Mews
W2 ....**101** C2
Southwick Pl W2 .**102** A1
Southwick St W2 .**102** A2
Southwick Yd
W2 ....**102** A1
Southwold Mans
W9 ....23 C2
Southwood Ave N6..4 A4
Southwood Ct EC1..96 B3
Southwood Ho
W11 .....31 A2 **112** A4
Southwood Hospl
(Geriatric) N6 ....3 C4
Southwood Hts N6...4 A4
Southwood La N6....3 C4
Southwood Lawn Rd
N6.......................4 A4
Southwood Park
N6.......................3 C4
Southwood Smith Ho
4 E2..................25 A2
Southwood Smith St
N1.....................**86** A3
South Worple Ave
SW14 ....56 A4
Southwyck Ho
SW9 ....62 C3
South Yd EC1.....**109** B4
Sovereign Cl E1..**32** A2
Sovereign Cres
SE16 ....33 A2

Sovereign Ct
3 Richmond TW9 ..54 B3
13 Stepney E1 ....32 A2
Sovereign Ho **23**
E1 ....25 A1
Sovereign Mews **6**
E2 ....24 B3
Sovereign Pk
NW10 ....20 A1
Space Bsns Pk
NW10 ....20 A2
Spa Ct SE16 .....**139** B1
Spafield St EC1.....95 B2
Spalding Ho SE4...66 A2
Spanby Rd E3......26 C1
Spaniards Cl NW11..2 C3
Spaniards End
NW3 ....2 C3
Spaniards Rd NW3..2 B2
Spanish Pl W1 ...**103** C2
Spanish Rd SW18..59 B2
Spa Rd SE16 .....**139** A1
Sparke Terr **2**
E16 ....35 B3
Sparkford Ho
SW11 ....**167** C4
Sparks Cl W3 ......28 C3
Sparsholt Rd N19..5 B3
Sparta St SE10 ....52 B2
Spa Sch SE1 .....**153** B4
Spa View **16** SW16..74 B1
Speakers' Corner★
W1 ....**117** A4
Speakman Ho SE4..66 A4
Spear Mews SW5 **141** C3
Spears Rd N19 .....5 A3
Spectrum Ho
NW5 ....12 C4
Spedan Cl NW3 ....2 B1
Speechly Mews
E8 ....16 B3
Speed Ho EC2.....**109** B4
Speedwell St **5**
SE8 ....51 C3
Speedy Pl WC1...**94** A3
Speldhurst Rd
Bedford Pk W4.....37 C3
Homerton E9 ....17 C1
Spellbrook Wlk
N1.....................**87** A4
Spelman Ho E1 ...**111** B3
Spelman St E1 ...**111** B4
Spence Cl SE16 ....41 B4
Spencer Gdns
SW14 ....55 B2
Spencer Ho
Clapham SW8....**171** B1
12 Putney SW19 ..69 C3
Vale of Health NW3..2 C1
Wimbledon SW19..69 C1
Spencer House Mus★
SW1 ....**118** C1
Spencer Mews
Fulham W6 ....**154** A4
South Lambeth
SW9 ....**172** C3
Spencer Park Ct
SW18 ....59 C2
Spencer Pk SW18 .59 C2
Spencer Pl
18 Islington N1 ...15 A1
SW1 ....**133** A1
Spencer Rd
Acton W3 ....28 B1
Chiswick W4........45 B3
Wandsworth SW18..59 B2
Spencer Rise NW5..4 A1

Spencer St EC1 ... 96 A3
Spencer Wlk
28 Hampstead
NW3 .... 11 B4
Putney SW15 .... 57 C3
Spencer St SE3 .... 53 B1
Spenlow Ho SE16 139 C2
Spenser Gr N16 ... 15 C4
Spenser Mews
SE21 .... 75 C2
Spenser Rd SE24 . 63 A2
Spens Ho W1 .... 94 C1
Spensley Wlk N16 . 6 C1
Spert St E14 ...... 33 A2
Spey St E14 ...... 34 B4
Spezia Rd NW10 .. 21 C3
Spice Ct
10 Battersea
SW11 .... 59 B4
St George in t East
E1 .... 125 C2
Spice Quay Htss
SE1 .... 125 A1
Spicer Ct SE5, SW9. 48 A1
Spicer Ho
E2 .... 24 C2 99 B3
Spindrift Ave E14.. 42 A2
Spinnaker Ho 21
E14 .... 41 C4
Spinney The
Barnes SW13...... 47 A4
Streatham SW16 .. 73 C1
Spire Ct 10 TW10.. 54 A1
Spiro Ho W2 ..... 115 A4
Spirit Quay E1 .... 32 A1
SPITALFIELDS ... 111 A4
Spital St E1...... 110 B4
Spital St E1 ..... 111 B4
Spital Yd E1 ..... 110 B4
Splendour Wlk
SE16 .... 40 B1
Spode Ho 16 ... 135 B1
Spode Wlk NW3 ... 11 A3
Sporle Ct 6 SW11. 59 C4
Sprewell SW15 .... 58 A1
Spriggs Ho 14 N1 . 15 A1
Sprimont Pl SW3 . 144 C2
Springall St 9
SE15 .... 50 A3

Spring Gdns
Islington N5 ..... 15 B3
SW1 .... 120 A2
Spring Gr W4 .... 44 C4
Spring Grove Rd
TW10 .... 54 B2
Spring Hill E5 ..... 7 C2
Springhill Cl SE5 .. 63 C4
Spring Ho WC1 ... 95 B3
Spring Mews W1 103 A4
Springpark Dr N4 . 6 B3
Spring Pl NW5 .... 13 A3
Springrice Rd
SE13 .... 67 C1
Spring St W2 .... 101 B1
Spring Terr TW10.. 54 A2
Springtide Cl 10
SE15 .... 49 C2
Springvale Ave
TW8 .... 36 A1
Springvale Terr 5
W14 .... 39 C3
Springwater WC1 106 C4
Springwell Ave
NW10 .... 21 B4
Spring Wlk E1 ... 111 C4
Springwood Cl 8
E3 .... 26 C3
Spruce Ct W5 .... 36 A3
Spruce Ho 15
SE16 .... 40 C4
Sprules Rd SE4.... 51 A1
Spurgeon St SE1 . 137 B2
Spurling Rd SE22 . 64 B3
Spur Rd SE1 .... 135 B4
Spurstowe Rd E8.. 17 A2
Spurstowe Terr
E8 .... 17 A3
Square Rigger Row 7
SW11 .... 59 B4
Square The
Hammersmith W6.. 39 B1
SW6 .... 165 B3
Squarey St 71 B1
Squire Gdns NW8 . 89 B3
Squires St SW4 .. 172 B3
Squire's Mount
NW3 .... 2 C1
Squirrels The
SE13 .... 67 C4
Squirries St
E2 ...... 24 C2 99 C3
Stable Hu 9 SE16.. 40 B4
Stables Way SE11 149 B2
Stable Way W10... 30 B3
Stable Yd Rd
SW1 .... 133 A4
Stacey St
Highbury N7 ...... 5 C1
Soho WC2 ..... 105 C1
Stack Ho SW1 ... 145 C3
Stackhouse St
SW1 .... 130 C2
Stacy Path 15 SE5 63 A2
Stadium St SW10 157 A1
Stafford Cripps Ho
30 Bethnal Green
E2 .... 25 B2
SW6 .... 155 A3
Stafford Ct
Kensington W8.... 127 C2
South Lambeth
SW8 .... 172 A4
Stafford Ho 1 SE1 153 A2

Stafford Mans
13 Hammersmith
W14 .... 39 C3
10 Stockwell SW4 . 62 A3
SW1 .... 158 C1
Stafford Pl SW1 . 132 C2
Stafford Rd
Bow E3 .... 26 B3
Maida Vale NW6 .. 23 C2
Staffordshire St
Peckham SE15 ... 49 C2
Peckham SE15 ... 50 A2
Stafford St W1 ... 118 C2
Stafford Terr W8 . 127 B2
Stag La SW15 .... 68 B2
Stagshaw Ho 17
SE22 .... 64 A4
Stainer St SE1 ... 123 C1
Staining La EC2 . 109 A2
Stainsbury St 28
E2 .... 25 B3
Stainsby Rd E14 .. 33 C3
Stalbridge Flats
W1 .... 103 C1
Stalbridge Ho
NW1 .... 82 C1
Stalbridge St
NW1 .... 102 B4
Stalham St SE16 .. 40 A3
Stambourne Ho
SW8 .... 172 B4
Stamford Bridge
Stadium (Chelsea
FC) SW6 ..... 156 A2
Stamford Brook Ave
W6 .... 38 B3
Stamford Brook Gdns
1 W6 .... 38 B3
Stamford Brook Mans
2 W6 .... 38 B2
Stamford Brook Rd
W6 .... 38 B3
Stamford Brook Sta
W6 .... 38 B3
Stamford Cl 2
SW10 .... 156 B3
Stamford Cotts
SW10 .... 156 B3
Stamford Ct W6.. 38 C2
Stamford Gr E 1
N16 .... 7 C3
Stamford Gr W 4
N16 .... 7 C3
STAMFORD HILL .. 7 A3
Stamford Hill N16 .. 7 B3
Stamford Hill Mans 1
N16 .... 7 A4
Stamford Hill Sta
N16 .... 7 A4
Stamford Hospl
W6 .... 38 C2
Stamford Lo 2
N16 .... 7 A4
Stamford Mans 2
N16 .... 7 C3
Stamford Rd N1.. 16 A2
Stamford St SE1 . 121 C2
Stamp Pl E2 ..24 B2 99 A4
Stanard Ct N16..... 7 A4
Stanborough Ho 4
E3 .... 27 A1
Stanborough Pas
E8 .... 16 B2
Stanbridge Mans
SW15 .... 57 B4
Stanbridge Rd
SW15 .... 57 B4

Stanbrook Ct W1 . 118 C2
Stanbury Ct 18
NW3 .... 12 B2
Stanbury Rd
Nunhead SE15 ... 50 B1
Peckham SE15 ... 50 A1
Standard Pl
EC2 ..... 24 A2 98 B3
Standard Rd
NW10 .... 20 C1
Standen Rd SW18 . 70 C4
Standish Ho 6
W6 .... 38 C2
Standish Rd W6.. 38 C2
Stanesgate Ho 20
SE15 .... 49 C3
Stanfield Ho NW8 . 89 C2
Stanfield Rd 14
E3 .... 26 A3
Stanford Ct
Kensington W8.. 128 B1
Walham Green
SW6 .... 166 B3
Stanford Pl SE1 . 152 A3
Stanford Rd W8 . 128 B2
Stanford St SW1 . 147 B3
Stangate SE1 ... 135 A2
Stanhope Cl 28
SE16 .... 40 C4
Stanhope Gate
W1 .... 117 C2
Stanhope Gdns
SW7 .... 143 A4
Stanhope Ho
8 Putney SW15 .. 57 B2
SE8 .... 51 B3
Stanhope Mews E
SW7 .... 143 A4
Stanhope Mews S
SW7 .... 143 A3
Stanhope Mews W
SW7 .... 143 A4
Stanhope Par
NW1 .... 92 C4
Stanhope Pl W2 . 102 C1
Stanhope Row
W1 .... 118 A1
Stanhope St NW1 . 92 C3
Stanhope Terr
W2 .... 115 C4
Stanier Cl SW5 .. 141 A1
Stanlake Mews 7
W12 .... 30 B1
Stanlake Rd W12 . 30 B1
Stanlake Villas 8
W12 .... 30 B1
Stanley Bldgs
NW1 .... 84 B1
Stanley Cohen Ho
EC1 .... 96 C1
Stanley Cres
W11 ..... 31 B2 112 C4
Stanley Gdns
Bedford Pk W3.. 38 A4
Cricklewood NW2 .. 9 B3
W11 ..... 31 B2 112 C4
Stanley Gr SW11 . 169 C1
Stanley Ho
Clapham SW8 ... 171 B1
22 Poplar E14 ... 33 C3
Stanley Holloway Ct
E16 .... 35 C2
Stanley Mans
SW10 .... 157 A4

Stanley Mans continued
Upper Tooting
SW17 .... 72 B2
Stanley Rd
Acton Green W3 .. 37 B3
Mill Meads E15... 27 C4
Mortlake SW14 ... 55 A3
Stanley St SE14,
SE8 .... 51 B3
Stanley Studios
SW10 .... 157 A4
Stanley Terr 8
N19 .... 5 A2
Stanliff Ho 8 E14.. 41 C3
Stanmer St SW11. 168 B2
Stanmore Gdns
TW9 .... 54 B4
Stanmore Ho
SW8 .... 171 C2
Stanmore Pl NW1 . 82 B4
Stanmore Rd TW9. 54 B4
Stanmore St N1 .. 84 C4
Stannard Cotts 27
E1 .... 25 B1
Stannard Mews
E8 .... 16 C2
Stannard Rd E8 .. 16 C2
Stannary Pl SE11 . 149 C1
Stannary St SE11 . 149 C1
Stansbury Sq 3
W10 .... 23 A2
Stansfeld Ho SE1 . 153 A3
Stansfield Rd SW9 . 62 B4
Stanstead Ho E3 . 27 B1
Stansted Express
Terminal EC2.... 110 A3
Stanswood Gdns
SE5 .... 49 A3
Stanton Ho 6
SE10 .... 52 B4
Stanton Rd SW13.. 46 B1
Stanway Ct 33 N1. 24 A3
Stanway St N1 ... 24 A3
Stanwick Rd W14 140 C3
Stanworth St SE1 139 A3
Staplefield Cl 5
SW2 .... 74 A3
Staplefield Cl
SW19 .... 70 A4
Staplehurst Ho 10
E5 .... 17 A3
Staple Inn WC2.. 107 B3
Staple Inn Bldgs
WC2 .... 107 B3
Staples Cl SE16 .. 33 A1
Staple St SE1 ... 137 C3
Stapleton Hall N4 . 5 B4
Stapleton Hall Rd
N4 .... 5 B4
Stapleton Ho 19
E2 .... 25 A2
Stapleton Rd
SW17 .... 72 C1
Star Alley EC3.... 124 B4
Starboard Way
E14 .... 41 C3
Starcross St NW1 . 93 A3
Stardome 4 NW1 . 91 B1
Starfield Rd W12.. 38 C4
Star & Garter Mans
SW15 .... 57 C4
Starliner Ct N7.... 14 C2

Starling Ho NW8 . . . . . **80** A2
Star Pl E1 . . . . **125** C3
Star Rd W14 . . . . **140** C1
Star St W2 . . . . **102** A2
Star Works NW10 . . **21** C2
Star Yd WC2 . . . . **107** B2
Statham Ct N7 . . . . **5** A1
Statham Gr N16 . . . . . . **6** C1
Statham Ho SW8 . . **170** C4
Station App
  Dagenham NW10 . . . **21** B2
  Fulham SW6 . . . . **58** A4
  Richmond TW9 . . . . . **44** C2
Station Approach Rd
  W4 . . . . **45** B3
Station Ave
  5 Brixton SW9 . . . . **63** A4
  14 Richmond TW9 . . **44** C2
Station Cres SE3 . . . . **43** C1
Station Ct 5 SE15 . . **50** B1
Stationers Hall Ct
  EC4 . . . . **108** B1
Station Gdns W4 . . . . **45** B3
Station Mews Terr 4
  SE3 . . . . **43** C1
Station Par
  Cricklewood NW2 . . . . **9** B2
  Richmond TW9 . . . . . **44** C2
  4 Upper Tooting
  SW12 . . . . **72** C3
Station Pas SE15 . . **50** B2
Station Pl N4 . . . . **5** C2
Station Rd
  Barnes SW13 . . . . . . **46** B1
  Camden Town N19 . . . **4** B1
  Harlesden NW10 . . . **21** B3
  Lewisham SE13 . . . . **67** B4
Station Rise SE27 . . **75** A2
Station St E15 . . . . . **19** C1
Station Terr
  Camberwell SE5 . . . . **48** B2
  Kensal Rise NW10 . . **22** C3
Staunton Ho
  SE17 . . . . **152** A3
Staunton St SE8 . . . . **51** B4
Staveley NW1 . . . . . . **92** C4
Staveley Cl
  Hackney E9 . . . . **17** B3
  Lower Holloway N7 . . **14** A4
  New Cross Gate
  SE15 . . . . **50** A2
  8 Peckham SE15 . . **50** A2
Staveley Gdns W4 . . **45** C2
Staveley Ho SE4 . . . . **66** A2
Staveley Rd W4 . . . . . **45** C3
Stavers Ho 51 E3 . . . **26** B3
Staverton Rd NW2 . . **9** B1
Stave Yard Rd
  SE16 . . . . **33** A1
Stavordale Lo
  W14 . . . . **127** A2
Stavordale Rd N5 . . **15** A4
Stayner's Rd E1 . . . . **25** C1
Steadman Ct EC1 . . **97** A2
Stead St SE17 . . . . . **151** B3
Steal St E8 . . . . **24** B4
Stebbing Ho 8
  W11 . . . . **30** C1
Stebondale St E14 . . **42** B2
Stebon Prim Sch
  E14 . . . . **33** C3
Stedham Pl WC1 . . **106** A2
Steedman St
  SE17 . . . . **150** C3

Steele Rd
  Acton Green W4 . . . . **37** B3
  Becontree NW10 . . . . **20** B3
Steele's Mews N
  NW3 . . . . **12** B2
Steele's Mews S
  NW3 . . . . **12** B2
Steele's Rd NW3 . . . . **12** B2
Steel's La 23 E1 . . . **32** B3
Steen Way 7
  SE22 . . . . **64** A2
Steep Hill SW16 . . . . **73** C1
Steeple Cl SW6 . . . **164** B1
Steeple Ct 19 E1 . . . **25** A1
Steeple Wlk N1 . . . . **87** A4
Steerforth St
  SW18 . . . . **71** B2
Steers Way SE16 . . . **41** A4
Stelfax Ho WC1 . . . . **95** A4
Stellman Cl E5 . . . . . . **7** C1
Stephan Cl E8 . . . . . **24** C4
Stephen Ct 18
  SW19 . . . . **69** C3
Stephendale Rd
  SW6 . . . . **166** C2
Stephen Fox Ho 7
  W4 . . . . **38** A1
Stephen Hawking Sch
  E14 . . . . **33** A3
Stephen Mews
  W1 . . . . **105** B3
Stephen Pl SW4 . . . **61** B4
Stephen Saunders Ct
  SW11 . . . . **60** A2
Stephens Ct SE4 . . . **66** A4
Stephenson Ho
  21 Gospel Oak
  NW5 . . . . **13** A4
  8 Maitland Pk
  NW3 . . . . **12** B3
  Newington SE1 . . . **136** C2
Stephenson St
  Dagenham NW10 . . . **21** B2
  Newham E16 . . . . . . **35** A4
Stephenson Way
  NW1 . . . . **93** A2
Stephen St W1 . . . . **105** B3
STEPNEY **32** C4
Stepney City E1 . . . . **32** B4
Stepney Cswy E1 . . **32** C3
Stepney Gn E1 . . . . . **32** C4
Stepney Greencoat CE
  Prim Sch The
  E14 . . . . **33** B3
Stepney Green Ct 4
  E1 . . . . **32** C4
Stepney Green Sch
  E1 . . . . **32** C4
Stepney Green Sta
  E1 . . . . **25** C1
Stepney High St
  E1 . . . . **32** C4
Stepney Way E1 . . . **32** B4
Sterling Cl NW10 . . . **8** C1
Sterling Gdns
  SE14 . . . . **51** A4
Sterling Pl W5 . . . . . **36** A2
Sterling St SW7 . . . **130** B2
Sterndale Rd W14 . . **39** C3
Sterne St W12 . . . . . **39** C4
Sternhall La SE15 . . **64** C4
Sternhold Ave SW12,
  SW2 . . . . **73** C2
Sterry St SE1 . . . . . **137** B3
Steve Biko Ct
  W10 . . . . **22** C1
Steve Biko Rd N7 . . . **5** C1

Stevedore St 3
  E1 . . . . **32** A1
Stevenage Rd
  SW6 . . . . **47** C2
Stevens Ave E9 . . . . **17** B2
Stevenson Cres
  SE16 . . . . **40** A1
Stevenson Ho
  Battersea SW11 . . . **168** C1
  6 Clapham Pk
  SW2 . . . . **62** A2
  NW8 . . . . **78** C4
Stevens St SE1 . . . **138** B2
Steventon Rd W12 . . **29** B2
Stewart Headlam
  Prim Sch E1 . . . . . **25** A1
Stewart Ho SE1 . . . **138** A1
Stewart Rd E15 . . . . **19** C4
Stewart's Gr SW3 . . **144** A2
Stewart's Rd SW8 . . **170** C4
Stewart St E14 . . . . . **42** B4
Stew La EC4 . . . . . . **122** C4
Steyne Ho
  13 Acton W3 . . . . **28** A1
  11 Acton W3 . . . . **28** B1
Steyne Rd W3 . . . . . **28** A1
Stifford Ho E1 . . . . . **32** B4
Stile Hall Gdns
  W4 . . . . **36** C1
Stile Hall Par 6
  W4 . . . . **36** C1
Stileman Ho 4 E3 . . **33** B4
Stillingfleet Rd
  SW13 . . . . **46** C4
Stillington St
  SW1 . . . . **147** A4
Stillness Jun & Inf
  Schs SE23 . . . . . . **66** B1
Stillness Rd SE23 . . **66** B1
Stirling Ct
  Clerkenwell EC1 . . . **96** A2
  Strand WC2 . . . . . . **106** C1
Stirling Mans
  NW6 . . . . **11** B2
Stirling Rd
  South Acton W3 . . . . **37** A3
  Stockwell SW9 . . . . **172** B1
Stoatley Ho 10
  SW15 . . . . **68** C3
Stockbeck NW1 . . . . **83** A1
Stockfield Rd
  SW16 . . . . **74** B1
Stockholm Ho E1 . . **125** C4
Stockholm Rd
  SE16 . . . . **40** B1
Stockholm Way
  E1 . . . . **125** B2
Stockhurst Cl
  SW15 . . . . **47** C1
Stockleigh Hall
  NW8 . . . . **80** B2
Stock Orchard Cres
  N7 . . . . **14** B3
Stock Orchard St
  N7 . . . . **14** B3
Stocks Ct 5 E1 . . . . **25** C1
Stocks Pl 16 E14 . . **33** B2
Stockton Ho 6
  E2 . . . . **25** A2
STOCKWELL **62** A4
Stockwell Ave
  SW9 . . . . **62** B4
Stockwell Gdns
  SW9 . . . . **172** C3
Stockwell Gn
  SW9 . . . . **172** C1

Stockwell La
  SW9 . . . . **172** C1
Stockwell Park Cres
  SW9 . . . . **173** A3
Stockwell Park Rd
  SW9 . . . . **173** A3
Stockwell Park Sch
  SW9 . . . . **172** C3
Stockwell Park Wlk
  SW9 . . . . **62** C4
Stockwell Prim Sch
  SW9 . . . . **62** B4
Stockwell St SE10 . . **52** B4
Stockwell Sta
  SW4 . . . . **172** B2
Stockwell Terr
  SW9 . . . . **172** C3
Stoddart Ho SW8 . . **163** A3
Stodmarsh Ho
  SW9 . . . . **173** C4
Stoford Cl SW19 . . . **70** A4
Stokenchurch St
  SW6 . . . . **166** A3
STOKE NEWINGTON
  . . . . **7** A2
Stoke Newington
  Church St N16 . . . . **7** A2
Stoke Newington
  Comm N16 . . . . . . **7** B2
Stoke Newington
  High St N16 . . . . . . **7** B1
Stoke Newington Rd
  N16 . . . . **16** B4
Stoke Newington Sch
  N16 . . . . **7** A1
Stoke Newington Sta
  N16 . . . . **7** B2
Stoke Pl NW10 . . . . **21** B2
Stokesley St W12 . . **29** B3
Stondon Pk SE23 . . **66** A1
Stone Bldgs WC2 . . **107** A3
STONEBRIDGE **20** B4
Stonebridge Ctr 6
  NW10 . . . . **20** C4
Stonebridge Sch The
  NW10 . . . . **20** C4
Stone Cl SW4 . . . . . **171** A1
Stonecutter St
  EC4 . . . . **108** A2
Stonefield N4 . . . . . . **5** B2
Stonefield Mans
  N1 . . . . **85** B3
Stonefield St N1 . . . **85** C4
Stonegate 8
  NW5 . . . . **12** C2
Stonehill Cl SW14 . . **55** C2
Stonehill Rd
  Brentford W4 . . . . . . **36** C1
  Mortlake SW14 . . . . **55** C2
Stonehills Ct SE21 . . **76** A1
Stonehill's Mans 3
  SW16 . . . . **74** A1
Stonehouse NW1 . . **83** A3
Stonehouse Ct
  EC2 . . . . **110** B2
Stonehouse Ho 22
  W2 . . . . **31** C4
Stoneleigh Lo 13
  TW9 . . . . **44** B2
Stoneleigh Mews 18
  E3 . . . . **26** A3
Stoneleigh Pl
  W11 . . . . **30** C2
Stoneleigh St
  W11 . . . . **30** C2
Stoneleigh Terr
  N19 . . . . **4** A2

Stonell's Rd SW11 . . **60** B2
Stonenest St N4 . . . . **5** B3
Stones End St
  SE1 . . . . **136** C3
Stoneyard La E14 . . **34** A2
Stoney La E1 . . . . . **110** B2
Stoney St SE1 . . . . . **123** B2
Stonhouse St
  SW4 . . . . **61** C3
Stonor Rd W14 . . . . **140** C3
Stopes St SE15 . . . . **49** B3
Stopford Rd SE17 . . **150** B1
Stopher Ho SE1 . . . **136** B3
Storace Ho 8
  SW4 . . . . **62** A3
Storers Quay E14 . . **42** C2
Store St
  Bloomsbury WC1 . . . **105** B4
  Stratford New Town
  E15 . . . . **19** C3
Storey Ct NW8 . . . . **89** B3
Storey Ho 13 E14 . . **34** A2
Storey's Gate
  SW1 . . . . **133** C3
Stories Rd SE5 . . . . **64** A4
Storks Rd SE16 . . . **139** C1
Stormont House Sch
  E5 . . . . **17** A4
Stormont Rd
  Clapham SW11 . . . . **60** C3
  Highgate N6 . . . . **3** B4
Storrington WC1 . . . **94** B3
Story St N1 . . . . **14** B1
Stothard Ho 22 E1 . . **25** B1
Stothard Pl E1 . . . . **110** B4
Stothard St 8 E1 . . . **25** B1
Stott Cl SW18 . . . . . **59** C1
Stoughton Cl
  Roehampton SW15 . . **68** C3
  SE11 . . . . **149** A3
Stourcliffe Cl W1 . . **102** C2
Stourcliffe St W1 . . **102** C1
Stourhead Cl 6
  SW19 . . . . **69** C4
Stour Rd E3 . . . . **18** C1
Stowage SE8 . . . . . . **52** A4
Stowe Ho 11 N16 . . . . **6** C2
Stowe Rd W12 . . . . . **39** A4
Stracey Rd NW10 . . **20** C4
Stradbroke Rd N5 . . **15** B4
Stradella Rd SE24 . . **63** B1
Straffan Lo 8
  NW3 . . . . **11** C2
Stratford Ho 9
  SE8 . . . . **41** B1
Stratford Rd W3, . . **37** B4
Strafford Ho 8 SE8 . . **41** B1
Strafford St E14 . . . **41** C4
Strahan Rd E3 . . . . . **26** A2
Straightsmouth
  SE10 . . . . **52** B3
Straker's Rd SE15 . . **65** A3
Strale Ho 17 N1 . . . . **24** A4
STRAND **120** C4
Strand
  Strand WC2 . . . . . . **120** C4
  Strand WC2 . . . . . . **107** A1
Strand Dr TW9 . . . . . **45** A3
Strand La WC2 . . . . **121** A4
STRAND ON THE
  GREEN **44** C4
Strand-on-the-Green
  W4 . . . . **44** C4
Strand-on-the-Green
  Schs W4 . . . . **44** C4
Strang Ho N1 . . . . . . **86** C3
Strangways Terr
  W14 . . . . **126** C1

Stranraer Way N1 . . . . 14 A1
Strasburg Rd SW11 . . . . **170** A3
STRATFORD 19 B2
Stratford Bus Sta E15 . . . . 19 C1
Stratford Cir (Newham 6th Form Coll) E15 . . . . 19 C2
Stratford Gr SW15 . . . . 57 C3
Stratford International Sta E15 . . . . 19 B2
STRATFORD MARSH 27 A4
STRATFORD NEW TOWN 19 B3
Stratford Pl W1 . . . . **104** A1
Stratford Rd W8 . . . . **127** C1
Stratford Sh Ctr E15 . . . . 19 C1
Stratford Sta E15 . . . . 19 C1
Stratford Studios W8 . . . . **128** A1
Stratford Villas NW1 . . . . 13 C1
Stratford Workshops E15 . . . . 27 C4
Strathan Cl SW18 . . . . 58 A1
Strathblaine Rd SW11 . . . . 59 C3
Strathdon Dr SW17 . . . . 71 C1
Strathearn Ho W2 . . . . **116** A4
Strathearn Pl W2 . . . . **116** A4
Stratheden Par SE3 . . . . 53 C3
Stratheden Rd SE3 . . . . 53 C3
Strathleven Rd SW2 . . . . 62 A2
Strathmore Ct NW8 . . . . 90 A4
Strathmore Gdns W8 . . . . 31 C1 **113** C2
Strathmore Rd SW19 . . . . 70 C1
Strathray Gdns NW3 . . . . 12 A2
Strath Terr SW11 . . . . 60 A3
Strathville Rd SW18 . . . . 71 A2
Stratton Ct 4 N1 . . . . 16 A1
Strattondale St E14 . . . . 42 B3
Stratton St W1 . . . . **118** B2
Strauss Rd W4 . . . . 37 C4
Streamline Mews SE22 . . . . 76 C3
Streatham Ct SW16 . . . . 74 A2
Streatham & Clapham High Sch SW16 . . . . 73 C1
Streatham Ct SW16 . . . . 74 A1
STREATHAM HILL 74 A3
Streatham Hill SW2 . . . . 74 A3
Streatham Hill & Clapham High Sch SW2 . . . . 74 B3

Streatham Hill Sta SW2 . . . . 74 A2
Streatham Pl SW2 . . . . 74 A4
Streatham St WC1 . . . . **106** A2
Streathbourne Rd SW17 . . . . 72 C2
Streatham Wells Prim Sch SW2 . . . . 74 C2
Streatleigh Par 4 SW16 . . . . 74 A2
Streatley Pl 27 Hampstead NW3 . . . . 11 B4
Hampstead NW3 . . . . 11 C4
Streatley Rd NW6 . . . . 10 B1
Streimer Rd E15 . . . . 27 B3
Strelley Way W3 . . . . 29 A2
Stretton Mans 10 SE8 . . . . 51 C4
Strickland Ct SE15 . . . . 65 A4
Strickland Ho E2 . . . . 24 B2 **99** A3
Strickland Row SW18 . . . . 71 C4
Strickland St SE8 . . . . 51 C2
Stringer Hos 16 N1 . . . . 24 A4
Strode Ho 8 SW2 . . . . 74 C3
Strode Rd NW6 . . . . **154** A2
Willesden NW10 . . . . 8 C2
Strome Ho NW6 . . . . **78** A1
Stronsa Rd W12 . . . . 38 B4
Stroud Cres SW15 . . . . 68 C1
Stroud Green Prim Sch N4 . . . . 5 C3
Stroud Green Rd N4 . . . . 5 C3
Stroudley Ho SW8 . . . . **171** A4
Stroudley Wlk E3 . . . . 27 A2
Strout's Pl 2 E2 . . . . 24 B2 **98** C4
Strudwick Ct SW4 . . . . **172** B3
Strutton Ground SW1 . . . . **133** B1
Strype St E1 . . . . **110** C3
Stuart Ave W5 . . . . 36 B4
Stuart Ho Hammersmith W6 . . . . 39 B3
3 Homerton E9 . . . . 17 C1
5 Stockwell SW4 . . . . 62 A3
W14 . . . . **140** A4
Stuart Ho N1 . . . . **84** C1
Stuart Rd Acton W3 . . . . 28 B1
Maida Vale NW6 . . . . 23 C2
Nunhead SE15 . . . . 65 B3
Wimbledon SW19 . . . . 70 C1
Stubbs Ho Finsbury Pk N4 . . . . 5 B3
1 Globe Town E2 . . . . 25 C2
Stucley Pl 19 NW1 . . . . 13 A1
Studdridge St SW6 . . . . **165** C2
Studd St N1 . . . . **86** A4
Studholme Ct NW3 . . . . 10 C4
Studholme St SE15 . . . . 50 A3
Studio Pl SW1 . . . . **131** A3
Studios NW8 . . . . **78** C2

Studios The 4 Clapham SW4 . . . . **61** B3
SW8 . . . . **171** C3
Studland SE17 . . . . **151** B2
Studland Ho E14 . . . . 33 A3
Studland Rd W6 . . . . 39 A2
Studley Cl E5 . . . . 18 A3
Studley Ct 5 E14 . . . . 34 C2
Studley Rd SW4 . . . . **172** B2
Stukeley St WC2 . . . . **106** B2
Stunell Ho 28 SE14 . . . . 50 C4
Sturdee Ho 6 E2 . . . . 24 C3
Sturdy Ho 28 E3 . . . . 26 A3
Sturdy Rd SE15 . . . . 50 A1
Sturgeon Rd SE17 . . . . **150** C1
Sturge St SE1 . . . . **136** C4
Sturmer Way N7 . . . . 14 B3
Sturminster Ho SW8 . . . . **163** A1
Sturry St E14 . . . . 34 A3
Sturt St N1 . . . . **87** A1
Stutfield St E1 . . . . **111** C1
Stuttle Ho 6 E1 . . . . 24 C1 **99** B1
Styles Gdns SW9 . . . . 63 A4
Styles Ho SE1 . . . . **122** A1
Stylus Apartments 25 E1 . . . . 32 B3
Sudbourne Prim Sch SW2 . . . . 62 B2
Sudbourne Rd SW2 . . . . 62 B2
Sudbrooke Rd SW12 . . . . 60 C1
Sudbury Ct SW8 . . . . **171** C3
Sudbury Ho SW18 . . . . 59 A2
Sudeley St N1 . . . . **86** B1
Sudlow Rd SW18 . . . . 58 C2
Sudrey St SE1 . . . . **136** C3
Suffield Ho SE17 . . . . **150** B2
Suffolk Ho 6 NW5 . . . . 4 B1
Suffolk La EC4 . . . . **123** B4
Suffolk Pl SW1 . . . . **119** C2
Suffolk Rd Barnes SW13 . . . . 46 C3
Willesden NW10 . . . . 8 A1
Suffolk St SW1 . . . . **119** C2
Sugar House La E15 . . . . 27 B3
Sugar Loaf Wlk 6 E2 . . . . 25 B2
Sugden Rd SW11 . . . . 60 C3
Sulby Ho SE4 . . . . 66 A3
Sulgrave Gdns 11 W6 . . . . 39 B4
Sulgrave Rd W6 . . . . 39 B3
Sulina Rd SW2 . . . . 74 A4
Sulivan Ct SW6 . . . . **165** B1
Sulivan Ent Ctr SW6 . . . . 59 A4
Sulivan Prim Sch SW6 . . . . **165** B1
Sulivan Rd SW6 . . . . 58 C4
Sulkin Ho 11 E2 . . . . 25 C2
Sullivan Cl SW11 . . . . 60 A4
Sullivan Ct Stamford Hill N16 . . . . 7 B3
SW5 . . . . **141** C4
Sullivan Ho Chelsea SW1 . . . . **160** B4
Vauxhall SE11 . . . . **149** A3
Sultan St SE5 . . . . 48 B3
Sumatra Rd NW6 . . . . 10 C2

Sumburgh Rd SW12 . . . . 60 C1
Summercourt Rd E1 . . . . 32 B3
Summerfield Ave NW6 . . . . 23 A3
Summerhouse Rd N16 . . . . 7 A2
Summerlands Ave W3 . . . . 28 B2
Summerley St SW18 . . . . 71 A2
Summers St EC1 . . . . **95** B1
SUMMERSTOWN 71 B1
Summit Ct NW2 . . . . 10 A3
Summit Est N16 . . . . 7 C4
Sumner Ave SE15 . . . . 49 B2
Sumner Bldgs SE1 . . . . **122** C2
Sumner Ct SW8 . . . . **172** A4
Sumner Ho 6 E3 . . . . 34 A4
Sumner Pl SW7 . . . . **143** C3
Sumner Place Mews SW7 . . . . **143** C3
Sumner Rd SE15 . . . . 49 B3
Sumner St SE1 . . . . **122** C2
Sumpter Cl NW3 . . . . 11 B2
Sun Alley 6 TW9 . . . . 54 A3
Sun Alliance Ho WC2 . . . . **107** B2
Sunbeam Cres W10 . . . . 22 B1
Sunbeam Rd NW10 . . . . 20 C1
Sunbury Ave SW14 . . . . 55 C3
Sunbury Ct 6 SE14 . . . . 50 C4
Sunbury Ho 6 E2 . . . . 24 B2 **98** C3
Sunbury La SW11 . . . . **167** C4
Sunbury Workshops 6 E2 . . . . 24 B2 **98** C3
Sun Ct EC3 . . . . **109** C1
Sunderland Ct SE22 . . . . 76 C4
Sunderland Ho 28 W2 . . . . 31 C4
Sunderland Terr W2 . . . . **100** A2
Sundew Ave W12 . . . . 29 C2
Sundra Wlk 28 E1 . . . . 25 C1
Sundridge Ho 4 E9 . . . . 17 C2
Sunley Ho E1 . . . . **111** A3
Sunlight Sq 27 E2 . . . . 25 A2
Sunningdale Ave W3 . . . . 29 A2
Sunningdale Cl 22 SE16 . . . . 40 A1
Sunningdale Gdns W8 . . . . **127** C1
Sunninghill Ct 9 W3 . . . . 37 B4
Sunninghill Rd SE13 . . . . 52 A1
Sunnyhill Cl E5 . . . . 18 A4
Sunnymead Rd SW15 . . . . 57 A2
Sunnyside 6 NW2 . . . . 1 B1
Sunnyside Ho 6 NW2 . . . . 1 B1
Sunnyside Rd N19 . . . . 4 C4
Sun Pas SE16 . . . . **139** B2
Sunray Ave SE5, SE24 . . . . 63 C3

Sun Rd W14 . . . . **140** C1
Sun St Pas EC2 . . . . **110** A3
Sunset Rd SE5 . . . . 63 C3
Sun St EC2 . . . . **109** C4
Sunwell Cl SE15 . . . . 50 A2
Surcot Ho SW1 . . . . **171** C1
Surma Cl E1 . . . . 24 C1 **99** C1
Surrendale Pl W9 . . . . 23 C1
Surrey Canal Rd SE14, SE16, SE8 . . . . 50 C4
Surrey Cres 1 W4 . . . . 36 C1
Surrey Gr SE17 . . . . **152** A1
Surrey Ho 8 SE16 . . . . 32 C1
Surrey La SW11 . . . . **168** B3
Surrey Quays Rd SE16 . . . . 40 C3
Surrey Quays Sh Ctr SE16 . . . . 40 C3
Surrey Quays Sta SE16 . . . . 40 C2
Surrey Rd SE15 . . . . 65 C2
Surrey Row SE1 . . . . **136** B4
Surrey Sq SE17 . . . . **152** B2
Surrey Square Inf Sch SE17 . . . . **152** A2
Surrey Square Jun Sch SE17 . . . . **152** A2
Surrey St WC2 . . . . **121** A4
Surrey Terr SE17 . . . . **152** B2
Surrey Water Rd SE16 . . . . 32 C1
Surr St N7 . . . . 14 A3
Susan Constant Ct 18 E14 . . . . 34 C2
Susannah St E14 . . . . 34 B3
Sussex Cl N19 . . . . 5 A2
Sussex Ct 4 Barnes SW13 . . . . 46 B1
Greenwich SE10 . . . . 52 B4
Paddington W2 . . . . **101** B1
Sussex Gdns W2 . . . . **101** C1
Sussex Ho Hampstead NW3 . . . . 12 A2
Richmond TW9 . . . . 44 B1
Sussex House Sch SW3 . . . . **144** C4
Sussex Lo 2 W2 . . . . **101** C1
Sussex Mans South Kensington SW7 . . . . **143** B3
Strand WC2 . . . . **120** B4
Sussex Mews E W2 . . . . **101** C1
Sussex Mews W W2 . . . . **101** C1
Sussex Pl 22 Hammersmith W6 . . . . 39 B1
Lisson Gr NW1 . . . . **90** C2
Paddington W2 . . . . **101** C1
Sussex Sq W2 . . . . **115** C4
Sussex St SW1 . . . . **146** B2
Sussex Way Upper Holloway N7 . . . . 5 B1
Upper Holloway N7, N19 . . . . 5 A2
Upper Holloway N19 . . . . 4 C3
Sutherland Ave W9 . . . . **88** C2
Sutherland Ct 3 Paddington W9 . . . . 23 C1
Stoke Newington N16 . . . . 6 C1

Sutherland Gdns
SW14 .... 56 A4
Sutherland Gr SW18,
SW19 .... 70 B4
Sutherland Ho
Kensington W8 .... 128 A1
7 Putney SW15 .... 69 B4
3 South Hampstead
NW6 .... 11 B1
Sutherland Pl W2 .31 C3
Sutherland Rd
W4 .... 46 A4
Sutherland Row
SW1 .... 146 B2
Sutherland Sq
SE17 .... 150 C1
Sutherland St
SW1 .... 146 B2
Sutherland Wlk
SE17 .... 151 A1
Sutterton St N7 ...14 B2
Sutton Court Mans
W4 .... 45 B4
Sutton Court Rd
W4 .... 45 B4
Sutton Ct
Chiswick W4 .... 45 B4
3 Hackney E5 ...... 17 A4
Sutton Est SW3 . 144 B2
Sutton Est The **3**
W10 .... 30 C4
Sutton House★
E9 .... 17 B3
Sutton La EC1 ...... 96 B1
Sutton La N W4 ... 37 B1
Sutton La S W4 ... 45 B4
Sutton Pl E9 .... 17 B3
Sutton Row W1 .. 105 C2
Sutton Sq E9 .... 17 B3
Sutton St E1 .... 32 B3
Suttons Way EC1 . 97 A1
Sutton Way W10 .. 30 B4
Sutton Wlk SE1 .. 121 A1
Swaby Rd SW17,
SW18 .... 71 B2
Swaffield Prim Sch
SW18 .... 71 B4
Swaffield Rd
SW18 .... 71 B4
Swain's La N6 .... 4 A2
Swainson Ho N7 .14 C4
Swainson Rd W3 . 38 B4
Swains St NW8 .... 90 A2
Swallow Cl SE14 150 C2
Swallow Ct **3** W9 . 31 C4
Swallowfield NW1 . 92 B3
Swallow Ho NW8 . 80 A2
Swallow Pl
24 Poplar E14 ...... 33 B3
W1 .... 104 B1
Swallow St W1 ... 119 A3
Swanage Ct **5** N1 .16 A1
Swanage Ho SW8 162 C1
Swanage Rd SW18 .59 B1
Swanbourne
SE17 .... 150 C3
Swanbourne Ho
NW8 .... 90 A2
Swan Bsns Ctr **3**
W4 .... 37 C2
Swan Ct
Chelsea SW3 ..... 144 B1
Parsons Green
SW6 .... 155 B1
Poplar E14 .... 33 B3

Swan Ctr SW17 ...71 B1
Swandon Way
SW18 .... 59 A3
Swanfield St
E2 .... 24 B2 99 A3
Swan Ho N1 .... 15 C1
Swan La EC4 .... 123 C3
Swan Lane Pier
EC4 .... 123 B3
Swanlea Sec Sch
E1 .... 25 A1
Swanley Ho SE17 . 152 B2
Swan Mead SE1 .. 138 A1
Swan Mews
Stockwell SW9 ... 172 C2
SW6 .... 165 B4
Swanmore Ct
SW18 .... 59 B1
Swanne Ho **12**
SE10 .... 52 B3
Swan Pas E1 ...... 125 B3
Swan Pl SW13 ..... 46 B1
Swan Rd SE16 ..... 40 B4
Swanscombe Ho **11**
W11 .... 30 C1
Swanscombe Point **7**
E16 .... 35 B4
Swanscombe Rd
5 Chiswick W4 ... 38 A1
Shepherd's Bush
W11 .... 30 C2
Swan St SE1 ...... 137 A3
Swanton Gdns
SW19 .... 69 C3
Swanwick Cl
SW15 .... 68 B4
Swan Wlk SW3 .. 158 C4
Swan Yd N1 .... 15 A2
Swaton Rd E3 ...... 26 C1
Swaythling Ho
SW15 .... 56 B1
Swedenborg Gdns
E1 .... 32 A2
Sweden Gate
SE16 .... 41 A2
Swedish Quays
SE16 .... 41 A3
Swedish Sch The
SW13 .... 47 A4
Sweeney Cres
SE1 .... 139 A3
Sweyn Pl SE3 .... 53 C1
Swift Ho
16 Stepney E1 ...... 32 B3
15 Stoke Newington
N16 .... 7 A1
SW9 .... 163 C2
Swift St SW6 ...... 164 C4
Swinbrook Rd
W10 .... 31 A4
Swinburne Ct **4**
SE5 .... 63 C3
Swinburne Ho **12**
E2 .... 25 B2
Swinburne Rd
SW15 .... 56 C3
Swindon St W12 .. 30 B1
Swinford Gdns
SW9 .... 63 A4
Swingfield Ho **4**
E9 .... 25 B4
Swinley Ho NW1 . 92 B4
Swinnerton St E9 .18 A3
Swinton Ho
E2 .... 24 C2 99 B3
Swinton Pl WC1 .. 94 C4
Swinton St WC1 .. 94 C4

Swiss Cottage
NW3 .... 11 C1
Swiss Cottage Sch
South Hampstead
NW3 .... 11 C1
St John's Wood
NW8 .... 79 C4
Swiss Cottage Sta
NW3 .... 11 C1
Swiss Ct **8**
WC2 .... 119 C3
Swiss Re Building★
EC2 .... 110 B2
Swiss Terr **7**
NW3 .... 11 C1
Switch Ho **8** E14 . 34 C2
Sybil Phoenix Cl
SE8 .... 40 C1
Sybil Thorndike
Casson Ho SW5 . 141 C1
Sybil Thorndike Ho **9**
N1 .... 15 B2
Sycamore Ave E3 . 26 B4
Sycamore Cl W3 . 29 A1
Sycamore Ct
Kilburn NW6 .... 23 C4
Tufnell Pk N19 .... 4 C1
Sycamore Gdns W6,
W12 .... 39 A3
Sycamore Gr SE6 . 67 B1
Sycamore Ho
10 Maitland Pk
NW3 .... 12 B2
17 Rotherhithe
SE16 .... 40 C4
3 Shepherd's Bush
W6 .... 39 A4
2 Stoke Newington
N16 .... 6 C2
Sycamore Lo
SW15 .... 57 A4
Sycamore Mews **4**
SW4 .... 61 B4
Sycamore St EC1 .. 96 C1
Sycamore Wlk **1**
W10 .... 23 A2
Sydcote SE21 .... 75 B3
Sydenham Hill SE21,
SE22, SE23, SE26,
SE19 .... 76 C1
Sydenham Hill Sta
SE21 .... 76 B1
Sydner Mews N16 . 16 B4
Sydner Rd N16 .... 16 B4
Sydney Cl SW3 ... 143 C3
Sydney Ho **4** W4 . 38 A2
Sydney Mews
SW3 .... 143 C3
Sydney Pl SW7 ... 144 A3
Sydney Rd TW10,
TW9 .... 54 A3
Sydney St SW3 ... 144 A2
Sylva Cotts **3** SE8 .51 C2
Sylva Ct **3** SW15 . 69 C4
Sylvan Ct NW6 .... 78 A4
Sylvan Gr
Hampstead NW2 .... 9 C4
SE15 .... 50 A3
Sylvester Ho **7**
E8 .... 17 A2
Sylvester Path **8**
E8 .... 17 A2
Sylvester Rd E8 ... 17 A2
Sylvia Ct N1 .... 87 B1
Sylvia Pankhurst Ho
12 E2 .... 25 C2
Sylvia Young Theatre
Sch NW1 .... 90 B1

Symes Mews NW1 . 82 C2
Symington Ho
SE1 .... 137 B1
Symington Mews
E9 .... 17 C2
Symister Mews
N1 .... 24 A2 98 A3
Symons St SW3 .. 145 A3
Symphony Mews **15**
W10 .... 23 A2
Syringa Ho SE4 ... 66 B4

Tabard Ct **6** E14 .. 34 B3
Tabard Ho SE1 ... 137 C2
Tabard St SE1 .... 137 B2
Tabernacle St EC2 . 97 C2
Tableer Ave SW4 .. 61 C2
Tabley Rd N7 .... 14 A4
Tabor Rd W6 .... 39 A3
Tachbrook Est
SW1 .... 147 C1
Tachbrook Mews
SW1 .... 146 C4
Tachbrook St
SW1 .... 147 A3
Tack Mews SE4 ... 66 C4
Tadema Ho NW8 .. 89 C1
Tadema Rd SW10 157 A1
Tadmor St W12 .... 30 C1
Tadworth Ho SE1 136 A3
Taeping St E14 .... 42 A2
Taffrail Ho **2** E14 . 42 A1
Taft Way **6** E3 .... 27 A2
Tailworth St E1 .. 111 B3
Tait Ct
18 Old Ford E3 ...... 26 B4
SW8 .... 171 C4
Tait Ho SE1 .... 121 C1
2 Tufnell Pk N19 .. 13 B4
Takhar Mews
SW11 .... 168 B1
Talacre Rd NW5 .. 12 C2
Talbot Ct EC3 .... 123 C4
Talbot Grove Ho **10**
W11 .... 31 A3
Talbot Ho
Highbury N7 .... 5 C1
Poplar E14 .... 34 A3
Talbot Pl SE3 ...... 53 A1
Talbot Rd
Camberwell SE22 .. 64 A3
Notting Hill W2 .... 31 C3
Notting Hill W11 .. 31 B3
Talbot Sq W2 .... 101 B1
Talbot Wlk
Notting Hill W11 ... 31 A3
Willesden NW10 ... 8 A1
Talbot Yd SE1 .... 123 B1
Talcott Path **12**
SW2 .... 74 C3
Talfourd Pl SE15 .. 49 B2
Talfourd Rd SE15 . 49 B2
Talgarth Rd
Hammersmith W6 . 39 B1
W14 .... 140 B2
Talia Ho E14 .... 42 B3
Talina Ctr SW6 .. 166 C3
Talleyrand Ho SE5 . 48 B1
Tallis St EC4 ...... 121 C4
Talma Rd SW2 .... 62 C3
Talmud Torah Chaim
Meirim Sch N16 ... 7 B3

Talmud Torah
Machzikei Hadass
Sch E5 .... 7 C4
Talmud-Torah Yetev-
Lev N16 .... 7 C2
Talwin St E3 .... 27 A2
Tamar Cl **12** E3 .... 26 B4
Tamar Ho
10 Cubitt Town
E14 .... 42 B4
SE11 .... 149 C2
Tamarind **8**
W3 .... 28 B3
Tamarind Ho **4**
SE15 .... 49 C3
Tamarind Sq E1 . 125 C2
Tamarind Yd **3**
E1 .... 125 C2
Tamarisk Sq W12 . 29 B2
Tamworth N7 .... 14 A2
Tamworth St
SW6 .... 155 B3
Tangier Rd TW10 . 55 A4
Tangley Gr SW15 . 68 B4
Tangmere WC1 ... 94 C3
Tanhurst Ho **27**
SW2 .... 74 A4
Tankerton St WC1 . 94 B3
Tanner Ho SE1 ... 138 B3
Tanner's Hill SE8 . 51 C2
Tanners Mews
SE8 .... 51 B2
Tanner St SE1 .... 138 B3
Tanners Yd **33** E2 . 25 A3
Tannery Ho **1** E1 . 111 B4
Tannington Terr
N5 .... 5 C1
Tansley Cl N7 ...... 13 C3
Tanswell St SE1 . 135 B3
Tantallon Rd
SW12 .... 72 C3
Tant Ave E16 ...... 35 B3
Tanza Rd NW3 .... 12 B4
Tapley Ho SE1 ... 139 B3
Taplow NW3 .... 11 C1
Taplow Ho
E2 .... 24 B2 98 C3
Taplow St N1 .... 87 A1
Tappesfield Rd
SE15 .... 65 B4
Tapp St E1 .... 25 A1
Taranto Ho **14** E1 . 32 C4
Tarbert Rd SE22 .. 64 A2
Tarbert Wlk E1 .... 32 B2
Tarling Rd E16 ..... 35 B3
Tarling St E1 .... 32 B3
Tarnbrook Ct
SW1 .... 145 B3
Tarn St SE1 .... 136 C1
Tarns The NW1 .... 92 C4
Tarplett Ho **22**
SE14 .... 50 C4
Tarragon Cl SE14 . 51 A3
Tarranbrae NW6 .. 10 A1
Tarrant Ho E2 ...... 25 B2
Tarrant Pl W1 .... 102 C3
Tarrantt Ho W14 . 126 A2
Tarriff Cres SE8 ... 41 B2
Tarrington Cl
SW16 .... 73 C1
Tartan Ho **12** E14 . 34 B3
Tarver Rd SE17 .. 150 B2
Tarves Way SE10 . 52 A3
Tasker Ho **6** E14 . 33 B4
Tasker Lo W8 ..... 127 B4
Tasker Rd NW3 .... 12 B3
Tasman Ct **3** E14 . 42 A2
Tasman Ho **17** E1 . 32 A1
Tasman Rd SW9 .. 62 A4

Tasso Rd W6 ... 154 A4
Tasso Yd W6 ... 154 A3
Tatchbury Ho SW15 ... 56 B1
Tate Britain★ SW1 ... 148 A3
Tate Ho 11 E2 ... 25 C3
Tate Modern★ EC4 ... 122 B2
Tatham Ho NW8 ... 79 C2
Tatnell Rd SE23 ... 66 A1
Tatton Cres E5, N16 ... 7 B4
Tatum St SE17 ... 151 C3
Tauheed Cl N4 ... 6 B2
Taunton Ho W2 ... 100 C1
Taunton Mews NW1 ... 90 C1
Taunton Pl NW1 ... 90 C2
Tavern Cl SE1 ... 137 A1
Taverner Ho N16 ... 6 C1
Taverners Cl W11 ... 31 A1 112 A1
Taverner Sq 4 N5 ... 15 B4
Tavern La SW9 ... 173 C2
Tavistock Cl N16 ... 16 A3
Tavistock Cres W11 ... 31 B4
Tavistock Ct WC1 ... 93 C2
Tavistock Ho 3 W11 ... 31 B3
Tavistock Mews 3 W11 ... 31 B3
Tavistock Pl WC1 ... 94 A2
Tavistock Rd
  Dagenham NW10 ... 21 B3
  Notting Hill W11 ... 31 B4
Tavistock Sq WC1 ... 93 C2
Tavistock St WC2 ... 120 B4
Tavistock Terr N19 ... 4 C1
Tavistock Twr SE16 ... 41 A3
Tavy Cl SE11 ... 149 C2
Tawny Way SE16 ... 40 C2
Taybridge Rd SW11 ... 60 C3
Tayburn Cl E14 ... 34 B3
Tay Ho 10 E3 ... 26 B3
Tayler Ct NW8 ... 79 B4
Taylor Ave TW9 ... 45 A1
Taylor Cl SE8 ... 51 B4
Taylor Ct E15 ... 19 B3
Taylor Ho 10 SW2 ... 74 C3
Taylor's Gn W3 ... 29 A3
Taylor's La NW10 ... 8 A1
Tayport Cl N1 ... 14 A1
Tayside Ct 5 SE5 ... 63 C3
Teak Cl SE16 ... 33 A1
Tealby Ct N7 ... 14 B2
Teal Ct 30 SE8 ... 51 B4
Teale St E2 ... 24 C3
Teal St 1 SE10 ... 43 B3
Teather St 12 SE5 ... 49 A3
Tebbs Ho 18 SW2 ... 74 C4
Tedman Ct SE13 ... 67 B3
Ted Roberts Ho 3 E2 ... 25 A3
Tedworth Gdns SW3 ... 144 C1
Tedworth Sq SW3 ... 144 C1
Teesdale Cl E2 ... 25 A3
Teesdale St E2 ... 25 A3
Teesdale Yd 34 E2 ... 25 A3
Tee The W3 ... 29 A3

Teignmouth Cl 6 SW4 ... 61 C3
Teignmouth Rd NW2 ... 9 C2
Telegraph Hill NW3 ... 2 A1
Telegraph Pl E14 ... 42 A2
Telegraph Rd SW15 ... 69 B4
Telegraph St EC2 ... 109 B2
Telephone Pl SW6 ... 155 A4
Telfer Cl 4 W3 ... 37 B4
Telfer Ho EC1 ... 96 B3
Telferscot Prim Sch SW12 ... 73 C3
Telferscot Rd SW12 ... 73 C3
Telford Ave SW12, SW2 ... 74 A3
Telford Avenue Mans 7 SW2 ... 74 A3
Telford Ho 1
  8 Kensal Town W10 ... 31 A4
  SE1 ... 136 C2
Telford Parade Mans 6 SW2 ... 74 A3
Telford Rd W10 ... 31 A4
Telford Terr SW1 ... 146 C1
Telford Way W3 ... 29 A4
Tell Gr SE22 ... 64 B3
Telscombe Ho SW11 ... 169 B3
Temair Ho 1 SE10 ... 52 B3
Temeraire Pl TW8 ... 36 B1
Temeraire St SE16 ... 40 B4
Temperley Rd SW12 ... 72 C4
Templar Ho NW2 ... 10 B2
Templars Ho E15 ... 19 A3
Templar St SE5 ... 48 A1
Temple Ave EC4 ... 121 C4
Templecombe Rd E9 ... 25 B4
Temple Ct
  Stepney E1 ... 32 C4
  3 SW8 ... 162 A1
Temple Dwellings 7 E2 ... 25 A3
Temple Ho
  13 Battersea SW11 ... 60 A4
  4 Tufnell Pk N7 ... 4 B1
Templemead Cl W3 ... 29 A3
Templemead Ho E9 ... 18 A4
Temple Mill La E10, E15 ... 19 B4
Temple Mills Rd E9 ... 18 C4
Temple Pl WC2 ... 121 A4
Temple Rd
  Acton Green W4 ... 37 B3
  Richmond TW9 ... 54 B4
Temple Sheen SW14 ... 55 B2
Temple Sheen Rd SW14 ... 55 B3
Temple St E2 ... 25 A3
Temple Sta WC2 ... 121 B4
Templeton Cl 23

Templeton Pl SW5 ... 141 C3
Temple West Mews SE11 ... 136 A1
Templewood Ave NW3 ... 2 A1
Templewood Gdns NW3 ... 2 A1
Templewood Point NW2 ... 1 B2
Tenbury Ct SW12 ... 73 C3
Tenby Ho
  Islington N7 ... 14 C4
  W2 ... 100 C1
Tench St E1 ... 32 A1
Tendring Ho SW2 ... 62 C1
Tenham Ave SW2 ... 73 C2
Tenison Ct W1 ... 118 C4
Tenison Way SE1 ... 121 B1
Tenniel Cl W2 ... 114 B4
Tennis St SE1 ... 137 B4
Tennyson Ho SE17 ... 151 A2
Tennyson Rd NW6 ... 23 B4
Tennyson St SW8 ... 170 A1
Tensing Ho N1 ... 15 A2
Tenterden Ho SE17 ... 152 B2
Tenterden St W1 ... 104 B1
Tenter Ground E1 ... 110 C3
Tent St E1 ... 25 A1
Tequila Wharf E14 ... 33 A3
Terborch Way 6 SE22 ... 64 A2
Tercelet Terr NW3 ... 11 B4
Teredo St SE16 ... 40 C3
Terling Ho 9 W10 ... 30 B4
Terling Wlk N1 ... 86 C4
Tern Ho 8 SE15 ... 49 B2
Terrace Gdns SW13 ... 46 B1
Terrace La TW10 ... 54 A1
Terrace Rd E9 ... 17 B1
Terrace The
  Barnes SW13, SW14 ... 46 A1
  EC4 ... 107 C1
  Kilburn NW6 ... 23 C4
  10 Rotherhithe SE8 ... 41 B2
Terrano Ho 1 TW9 ... 45 A2
Terrapin Ct SW17 ... 73 A1
Terrapin Rd SW17 ... 73 A1
Terrick St W12 ... 30 A3
Territorial Ho SE11 ... 149 C3
Terry Ho SW2 ... 74 C3
Tersha St TW9 ... 54 B3
Tessa Sanderson Pl 6 SW8 ... 61 A4
Testerton Wlk 11 W11 ... 30 C2
Tetcott Rd SW10 ... 156 C1
Teversham La SW8 ... 172 B4
Teviot St E14 ... 34 B4
Teyham Ct SW11 ... 60 B1
Thackeray Ct
  Chelsea SW3 ... 144 C2
  West Kensington W14 ... 126 A1

Thackeray Ho
  College Pk NW10 ... 21 C2
  WC1 ... 94 A2
Thackeray Mews E8 ... 16 C2
Thackeray Rd SW8 ... 170 B1
Thackeray's Almshouses 5
Thackeray St W8 ... 128 B2
Thalia Cl SE10 ... 52 C4
Thame Rd SE16 ... 40 C4
Thames Ave SW10 ... 167 A4
Thames Bank SW14 ... 45 B1
Thames Christian Coll SW11 ... 59 C4
Thames Circ E14 ... 41 C2
Thames Cres W4 ... 46 A3
Thames Ct 10 SE15 ... 49 B3
Thames Hts SE1 ... 138 C4
Thameside Ctr TW8 ... 44 B4
Thames Link Ho 7 TW9 ... 54 A3
Thames Pl SW15 ... 57 C4
Thames Quay
  Millwall E14 ... 42 A4
  SW10 ... 167 A3
Thames Rd W4 ... 45 A4
Thames Reach W6 ... 47 B4
Thames Row TW9 ... 44 B4
Thames St SE10 ... 52 A4
Thames Village W4 ... 45 B2
Thames Wlk SW11 ... 158 A2
Thane Mans N7 ... 5 B1
Thanet Ho WC1 ... 94 A3
Thanet St WC1 ... 94 A3
Thane Villas N7 ... 5 B1
Thane Works N7 ... 5 B1
Thaxted Ct N1 ... 87 C1
Thaxted Ho SE16 ... 40 B2
Thaxton Rd W14 ... 155 A4
Thayer St W1 ... 103 C2
Theatre Sq E15 ... 19 C2
Theatre St SW11 ... 60 B4
Theed St SE1 ... 121 C1
Thelbridge Ho 28 E3 ... 27 A2
Theobalds Ct N4 ... 6 B2
Theobald's Rd WC1 ... 106 C4
Theobald St SE1 ... 137 B1
Theodore Ct SE13 ... 67 C1
Theodore Ho 1 SW15 ... 56 C2
Theodore Rd SE13 ... 67 C1
Therapia Rd SE22 ... 65 B1
Theresa Rd W6 ... 38 C2
Therfield Ct N4 ... 6 B2
Thermopylae Gate E14 ... 42 A2
Theseus Ho
  2 South Bromley E14 ... 34 C3

Thackeray Ho continued
  2 E14 ... 34 C3
Theseus Wlk N1 ... 86 B1
Thessaly Ho SW8 ... 160 C2
Thessaly Rd SW8 ... 171 A4
Thetford Ho SE1 ... 138 C2
Thetis Terr TW9 ... 44 C4
Third Ave
  East Acton W3 ... 29 B1
  West Kilburn W10 ... 23 A2
Thirleby Rd SW1 ... 133 A1
Thirlmere NW1 ... 92 B4
Thirlmere Ho 19 N16 ... 15 C4
Thirsk Rd SW11 ... 60 C3
Thistle Gr SW7 ... 143 A1
Thistle Ho 10 E14 ... 34 B3
Thistlewood Cl 3 N7 ... 5 B2
Thistly Ct SE8 ... 52 A4
Thomas Baines Rd SW11 ... 59 C4
Thomas Burt Ho 9 E2 ... 25 A2
Thomas Buxton Jun & Inf Sch E1 ... 24 C1 99 C1
Thomas Crowell Ct 27 N1 ... 16 A3
Thomas Doyle St SE1 ... 136 B2
Thomas Fairchild Com Sch N1 ... 87 A2
Thomas Ho
  3 Hackney E9 ... 17 B2
  4 Stockwell SW4 ... 62 A3
Thomas Hollywood Ho 8 E2 ... 25 B3
Thomas Jones Prim Sch W11 ... 31 A3
Thomas Milner Ho 5 SE15 ... 49 C3
Thomas More Ho EC2 ... 108 C3
Thomas More Sq E1 ... 125 B3
Thomas More St E1 ... 125 B3
Thomas North Terr 3 E16 ... 35 B4
Thomas Pl W8 ... 128 A3
Thomas Rd E14 ... 33 C4
Thomas Road Ind Est 2 E14 ... 33 C3
Thomas's London Day Sch SW11 ... 167 C3
Thomas's Prep Sch Clapham SW11 ... 60 B2
Thompson Ave
  Richmond TW9 ... 54 C4
  6 SE5 ... 48 B3
Thompson Ho
  11 Kensal Town W10 ... 23 A1
  SE14 ... 50 C4
Thompson Rd SE22 ... 64 B1
Thomson Ct 4 E8 ... 16 C2
Thomson Ho
  Pimlico SW1 ... 147 C1
  Walworth SE17 ... 152 A3
Thorburn Ho SW1 ... 131 B3
Thorburn Sq SE1 ... 153 B3
Thoresby Ho N16 ... 6 C1
Thoresby St N1 ... 97 A4

Thornaby Ho **15**
E2 . . . . .25 A2
Thornbill Ho **1**
SE16 . . . . .49 C3
Thornbury Cl N16 . .16 A3
Thornbury Ct
W11 . . . . .31 C2 **113** B4
Thornbury Ho N6 . . .4 B3
Thornbury Rd
SW2 . . . . .62 A1
Thornbury Sq N6 . . .4 B3
Thorncliffe Ct
SW2 . . . . .62 A1
Thorncliffe Rd
SW2 . . . . .62 A1
Thorncombe Rd
SE22 . . . . .64 A2
Thorncroft St
SW8 . . . . .162 A1
Thorndale Ho **10**
N16 . . . . .7 A3
Thorndean St
SW18 . . . . .71 B2
Thorndike Cl
SW10 . . . . .156 C2
Thorndike Ho
SW1 . . . . .147 B2
Thorndike Rd **21**
N1 . . . . .15 C2
Thorndike St
SW1 . . . . .147 B2
Thorne Cl E16 . . . . .35 C3
Thorne Ho
34 Bethnal Green
E2 . . . . .25 B2
4 Cubitt Town E14 . .42 B3
Thorne Pas **2**
SW13 . . . . .46 B1
Thorne Rd SW8 . .162 B1
Thorness Ct SW18 . .59 B1
Thorne St SW13,
SW14 . . . . .56 A4
Thornewill Ho **8**
E1 . . . . .32 B2
Thorney Cres
SW11 . . . . .157 C1
Thorneycroft Ho **11**
W4 . . . . .38 A1
Thorney Ct W8 . . .128 C3
Thorney Hedge Rd
W4 . . . . .37 A2
Thorney St SW1 . .148 A4
Thornfield Ho **5**
E14 . . . . .33 C2
Thornfield Rd
W12 . . . . .39 A4
Thornford Rd
SE13 . . . . .67 B2
Thorngate Rd W9 . .23 C1
Thornham Gr E15 . .19 C3
Thorn Ham Ho
SE1 . . . . .137 C2
Thornham St SE10 . .52 A4
Thornhaugh St
WC1 . . . . .93 C1
Thornhill Bridge
Wharf N1 . . . . .84 C3
Thornhill Cres N1 . .14 B1
Thornhill Gr N1 . . .14 C1
Thornhill Ho
12 Chiswick W4 . . . .38 A1
Islington N1 . . . . .14 C1
Thornhill Mews
SW15 . . . . .58 B3

Thornhill Prim Sch
N1 . . . . .14 C1
Thornhill Rd N1 . . .85 B4
Thornhill Sq N1 . . .14 B1
Thornicroft Ho
SW9 . . . . .173 A1
Thornley Pl **2**
SE10 . . . . .43 A1
Thornsett Rd
SW18 . . . . .71 A3
Thornton Ave
Chiswick W4 . . . . .38 A2
Streatham SW2 . . . . . .73 C3
Thornton Ct N7 . . .14 A3
Thornton Gdns
SW12 . . . . .73 C3
Thornton Ho
SE17 . . . . .152 A3
Thornton Pl W1 . . .103 A4
Thornton Rd
Mortlake SW14 . . . . . .55 C4
Streatham SW12,
SW2 . . . . .73 C3
Thornton St SW9 .173 B2
Thornville St SE8 . .51 C2
Thornwood Gdns
W8 . . . . .127 B4
Thornwood Lo
W8 . . . . .127 B4
Thornycroft Ct
TW9 . . . . .44 B1
Thorold Ho **1** SE1 . .136 C4
6 Streatham SW2 . . .74 A4
Thorparch Rd
SW8 . . . . .161 C1
Thorpebank Rd
W12 . . . . .29 C1
Thorpe Cl W10 . . . .31 A3
Thorpedale Rd N4. . .5 A3
Thorpe Ho N1 . . . .85 A3
Thorverton Rd
NW2 . . . . .1 A1
Thoydon Rd E3 . . . .26 A3
Thrale St SE1 . . . .123 A1
Thrasher Cl **20** E8 . .24 B4
Thrawl St E1 . . . . . .111 A3
Thrayle Ho **9**
SW9 . . . . .62 B4
Thredgold Ho **8**
N1 . . . . .15 C2
Threadneedle St EC2,
EC3 . . . . .109 C1
Three Colts La E2 . .25 A1
Three Colt St E14 . .33 B2
Three Cups Yd
WC1 . . . . .107 A3
Three Kings Yd
WC1 . . . . .118 A4
Three Mill La E3 . . .27 B2
Three Mills Studios
E14 . . . . .27 B2
Three Nun Ct EC2 .109 B2
Three Oak La SE1 .138 C4
Threshers Pl
W11 . . . . .31 A2 **112** A4
Thring Ho SW9 . . .172 C2
Throgmorton Ave
EC2 . . . . .109 C2
Throgmorton St
EC2 . . . . .109 C2
Thrush St SE17 . . .150 C2
Thurland Ho **3**
SE16 . . . . .40 A2
Thurland Rd SE16 .139 B2
Thurleigh Ave
SW12 . . . . .60 C1

Thurleigh Ct
SW12 . . . . .60 C1
Thurleigh Rd
SW12 . . . . .60 C1
Thurloe Cl SW7 . . .144 A3
Thurloe Ct SW3 . . .144 A3
Thurloe Pl SW7 . . .143 C4
Thurloe Place Mews
SW7 . . . . .143 C4
Thurloe Sq SW7 . . .144 A4
Thurloe St SW7 . . .143 C4
Thurlow Hill SE21 . .75 B2
Thurlow Ho **17**
SW16 . . . . .74 A1
Thurlow Park Rd SE21,
SE24 . . . . .75 B2
Thurlow Rd NW3 . . .11 C3
Thurlow St SE17 . .152 A1
Thurlow Terr
NW5 . . . . .12 C3
Thurlow Wlk
SE17 . . . . .152 A1
Thurnscoe NW1 . . .82 C3
Thursley Gdns
SW19 . . . . .69 C2
Thursley Ho **10**
SW2 . . . . .74 B4
Thurso Ho NW6 . . .78 A1
Thurston Ind Est
SE13 . . . . .67 A4
Thurston Rd SE8,
SE13 . . . . .52 A1
Thurtle Rd E2 . . . . .24 B3
Tibbatt's Rd E3 . . . .27 A1
Tibberton Sq N1 . . .86 C4
Tibbets Cl SW19 . . .69 C3
Tibbet's Corner
SW19 . . . . .69 C4
Tibbet's Ride
SW19 . . . . .69 C4
Tiber Cl **10** E3 . . . . . .26 C4
Tiber Gdns N1 . . . .84 C3
Tickford Ho NW8 . .90 A3
Tidal Basin Rd
E16 . . . . .35 B2
Tidbury Ct SW8 . . .160 C1
Tidemill Prim Sch
SE8 . . . . .51 C3
Tideswell **10** NW5 . .13 A4
Tideswell Rd
SW15 . . . . .57 B3
Tideway Ct **9**
SE16 . . . . .32 C1
Tideway Ho E14 . . .41 C4
Tideway Ind Est
SW8 . . . . .161 A3
Tideway Wharf
SW13 . . . . .46 A1
Tidey St E3 . . . . . . .33 C4
Tidworth Ho **13**
SE22 . . . . .64 A4
Tidworth Rd E3 . . .26 C1
Tierney Rd SW2 . . .74 A3
Tierney Terr SW2 . .74 A3
Tiger Ho WC1 . . . . .93 C3
Tiger Way E5 . . . . . .17 A4
Tignel Ct W3 . . . . .36 C4
Tilbury Cl **14** SE15 . .49 B3
Tilbury Ho **4**
SE14 . . . . .50 C4
Tildesley Rd SW15 . .57 B1
Tilehurst NW1 . . . .92 B3
Tilehurst Rd SW17,
SW18 . . . . .71 C3

Tile Kiln La N6 . . . . .4 B3
Tileyard Rd N7 . . . .14 A1
Tilford Gdns
SW19 . . . . .69 C2
Tilford Ho **8** SW2 . .74 B4
Tilia Rd E5 . . . . . . .17 A4
Tilia Wlk **2** SW9 . . .63 A3
Tiller Ho **16** N1 . . .24 A4
Tiller Rd E14 . . . . . .41 C3
Tillet Sq SE16 . . . . .41 A4
Tillet Way
E2 . . . . .24 C2 **99** B4
Tilling Ho **1** SE15 . .65 A4
Tillman Ho **2**
SW2 . . . . .74 B3
Tillman St E1 . . . . .32 A3
Tilloch St **9** N1 . . .14 B1
Tillotson Ct SW8 . .161 C1
Tilney Ct EC1 . . . .97 A2
Tilney Gdns **14** N1 . .15 C2
Tilney St W1 . . . . .117 C2
Tilson Ct **2** SE15 . .49 A3
Tilson Gdns SW2,
SW4 . . . . .74 A4
Tilson Ho SW2 . . . .74 A4
Tilton St SW6 . . . .154 B3
Tiltwood The W3 . .28 B2
Timberland Cl **18**
SE15 . . . . .49 C3
Timberland Rd E1 . .32 A3
Timber Mill Way
SW4 . . . . .61 C4
Timber Pond Rd
SE16 . . . . .40 C4
Timber St EC1 . . . .96 C2
Time Sq E8 . . . . . . .16 B3
Timothy Cl **1**
SW4 . . . . .61 B2
Timsbury Wlk
SW15 . . . . .68 C3
Tina Ct SW16 . . . . .74 C1
Tindal St SW9 . . . . .48 A2
Tinniswood Cl N5 . .14 C3
Tinsley Rd E1 . . . . .32 B4
Tintagel Cres
SE22 . . . . .64 B3
Tintagel Ct EC1 . . .96 A2
Tintern Cl
Belgravia SW1 . . . . .146 A3
Regent's Pk NW1 . . . .92 C4
Tintern St SW4 . . . .62 A3
Tinworth St SE11 . .148 B2
Tipthorpe Rd
SW11 . . . . .60 C4
Tiptree **7** NW1 . . . .13 A1
Tisbury Ct W1 . . . .119 B4
Tisdall Pl SE17 . . .151 C3
Tissington Ct **3**
SE16 . . . . .40 C2
Titan Bsns Est **3**
SE8 . . . . .51 C3
Titan Ct TW8 . . . . .36 B1
Titchborne Row
W2 . . . . .102 B1
Titchfield Rd NW8 . .80 C4
Titchwell Rd
SW18 . . . . .71 C3
Tite St SW3 . . . . . .158 C4
Titmuss St W12 . . .39 B4
Tiverton Rd NW6,
NW10 . . . . .22 C4
Tiverton St SE1 . . .136 C2
Tivoli Ct SE16 . . . .33 B1
Tobago St **12** E14 . .41 C4
Tobin Cl NW3 . . . . .12 A1
Toby La E1 . . . . . . .26 A1

Todber Ho W14 . . .126 A2
Todds Wlk N7 . . . . .5 B2
Tokenhouse Yd
EC2 . . . . .109 B2
Toland Sq SW15 . . .56 C2
Tolchurch **2** W11 . .31 C3
Toldos Yakov Yosef
sch N16 . . . . .7 A3
Tolhurst Dr **4**
W10 . . . . .23 A2
Tollbridge Cl W10 . .23 A1
Tollet St E1 . . . . . .25 C1
Tollgate Dr SE21 . . .76 A2
Tollgate Ho NW6 . .78 A2
Tollgate Rd E6,
E16 . . . . .35 C3
Tollhouse Way N19 . .4 B2
Tollington Ct N4 . . .5 B2
Tollington Ho **3**
N19 . . . . .5 A1
Tollington Pk N4 . . .5 B2
Tollington Pl N4 . . .5 B2
Tollington Rd N7 . .14 B4
Tollington Way N7 . .5 A1
Tolmers Sq NW1 . . .93 A2
Tolpaide Ho SE11 . .149 B3
Tolpuddle St N1 . . .85 B2
Tolsford Rd E5 . . . .17 A3
Tom Groves Cl
E15 . . . . .19 C3
Tom Hood Cl E15 . .19 C3
Tom Jenkinson Rd **5**
E16 . . . . .35 C1
Tomkyns Ho SE11 .149 B3
Tomline Ho SE1 . . .122 C1
Tomlin's Gr E3 . . . .26 C2
Tomlinson Cl
5 Gunnersbury
W4 . . . . .37 A1
Spitalfields
E2 . . . . .24 B2 **99** A3
Tomlin's Terr E14 . .33 A3
Tomlins Wlk **4** N7 . .5 B2
Tompion Ho EC1 . . .96 B2
Tompion St EC1 . . .96 B3
Tom Smith Cl
SE10 . . . . .53 A4
Tomson Ho SE1 . . .138 C2
Tom Williams Ho
SW6 . . . . .154 C3
Tonbridge Hos
WC1 . . . . .94 A3
Tonbridge St WC1 . .94 A3
Toneborough
NW8 . . . . .78 B3
Tonsley Hill SW18 . .59 A2
Tonsley Pl SW18 . . .59 A2
Tonsley Rd SW18 . .59 A2
Tonsley St SW18 . . .59 A2
Took's Ct EC4 . . . .107 B2
Tooley St SE1 . . . .124 A1
Tooting Bec Sta
SW17 . . . . .72 C2
Topham Ho **3**
SE10 . . . . .52 B3
Topham St EC1 . . . .95 B2
Topiary Sq TW9 . . .54 B4
Topmast Point **23**
E14 . . . . .41 C4
Torbay Ct **18** NW1 . .13 A1
Torbay Mans NW6 . .23 B4
Torbay Rd NW6 . . .10 B1
Torbay St **18** NW1 . .13 A1
Tor Ct W8 . . . . . . .127 C4
Tor Gdns W8 . . . . .127 B4
Tornay Ho
Hackney E9 . . . . . . .17 B1
N1 . . . . .84 C2
Torquay St W2 . . .100 A3

Torrence Ho **6**
N19 .... 4 B2
Torrens Ct SE5 .... 63 C4
Torrens Rd SW2 .... 62 B2
Torrens St EC1 .... 86 A1
Torres Sq E4 ...... 41 C1
Torriano Ave NW5 .. 13 C3
Torriano Cotts
NW5 .... 13 B3
Torriano Jun & Inf
Schs NW5 .... 13 C3
Torriano Mews
NW5 .... 13 B3
Torridge Gdns
SE15 .... 65 B3
Torridon Ho NW6 .. 78 A1
Torrington Ct
Bloomsbury WC1 ... 105 B4
St George in t East
E1 .... 125 C2
Torrington Sq
WC1 .... 93 C2
Tortington Ho **1**
SE15 .... 50 A3
Tothill Ho SW1 .... 147 C4
Tothill St SW1 .... 133 C3
Totland Ho SW18 .. 18 A3
Totnes Terr E1 .... 32 C3
Tottenhall **5**
NW1 .... 12 C1
Tottenham Court Rd
W1 .... 105 A4
Tottenham Court
Road Sta W1 .... 105 C2
Tottenham Mews
W1 .... 105 A4
Tottenham Rd N1 .. 16 A2
Tottenham St W1 .. 105 A4
Totteridge Ho
SW11 .... 167 C3
Touchard Ho N1 ... 97 C3
Toulmin St SE1 ... 136 C3
Toulon St SE5 .... 48 B3
Toulouse Ct **2**
SE16 .... 40 A1
Tounson Ct SW1 ... 147 C3
Tournay Rd SW6 .. 155 A2
Toussaint Wlk
SE16 .... 139 C2
Tovy Ho SE1 ...... 153 B1
Towcester Rd E3 .. 27 B1
Tower 42* EC2 .... 110 A2
Tower Bldgs **22**
E1 .... 32 A1
Tower Br App E1,
EC3 .... 124 C3
Tower Bridge* E1, EC3,
SE1 .... 124 C2
Tower Bridge Bsns
Complex SE16 ... 40 A3
Tower Bridge Bsns Sq
SE16 .... 40 A2
Tower Bridge Piazza
SE1 .... 124 C1
Tower Bridge Prim
Sch SE1 .... 138 C4
Tower Bridge Rd
SE1 .... 138 A3
Tower Bridge Sq
SE1 .... 138 C4
Tower CI NW3 .... 11 C3
Tower Ct
Brockley SE4 .... 66 A3
Stamford Hill E5 .. 7 B4
St Giles WC2 .... 106 A1

Tower Ct continued
St John's Wood
NW8 .... 80 B2
Towergate SE1 ... 152 A4
Towergate Ho **39**
E3 .... 27 B2
Tower Gateway Sta
EC3 .... 124 C4
TOWER HAMLETS 33 B4
Tower Hamlets Coll
Poplar E14 ...... 34 A2
Poplar E14 ...... 34 A3
Stepney E1 ...... 32 C3
Tower Hill EC3 ... 125 A3
Tower Hill Sta
EC3 .... 124 C4
Tower Mans SE1 .. 138 C1
Tower Mews E5 ... 18 A3
Tower Millennium
Pier E1 .... 124 B2
Tower Mill Rd **1**
SE15 .... 49 A3
Tower PI E EC3 ... 124 B3
Tower PI W EC3 ... 124 B3
Tower Rd NW10 ... 8 B1
Tower Rise TW9 ... 54 A4
Tower Royal EC4 .. 123 B4
Towers PI TW10 ... 54 A2
Tower St WC2 .... 106 A1
Towers The
Dartmouth Pk NW5 .. 4 A1
1 Richmond TW9 .. 54 B3
Tower Terr SE4 ... 66 A3
Tower* The EC3 ... 124 B3
Towerview SE13 ... 66 C2
Tower Wharf SE1 .. 138 C1
Tower Wlk SE1 ... 152 A4
Towncourt Path N4 .. 6 B3
Townhall Ave **3**
W4 .... 37 C1
Town Hall Rd
SW11 .... 60 B4
Town Ho EC1 ..... 96 B1
Townley Rd SE22 .. 64 A2
Townley St SE17 .. 151 C2
Townmead Bsns Ctr
SW6 .... 59 B4
Townmead Rd
Richmond TW9 ... 45 A1
Sands End SW6 .. 166 C1
Townsend Ho
SE1 .... 153 C3
Townsend Ind Est
NW10 .... 20 B3
Townsend Mews **3**
SW18 .... 71 B2
Townsend Prim Sch
SE17 .... 152 A4
Townsend St SE1,
SE17 .... 152 A4
Townsend Yd N6 .. 4 A3
Townshend Ct
NW8 .... 80 B2
Townshend Est
NW8 .... 80 A2
Townshend Ho
Primrose Hill NW8 .. 80 A3
Richmond TW9 ... 54 B3
Townshend Terr
TW9 .... 54 B3
Towns Ho **4** SW4 .. 61 C4
Towpath Wlk E9 ... 18 B3
Towton Rd SE27 ... 75 B2
Toxteth Ho N4 .... 6 B4
Toynbee St E1 .... 110 C3
Tracey Ave NW2 ... 9 B3

Tracy Ho **15** E3 ... 26 B2
Tradescant Ho **13**
E9 .... 17 B1
Tradescant Rd
SW8 .... 162 B1
Trade Twr **8**
SW11 .... 59 B4
Trade Winds Ct
E1 .... 125 C2
Trading Estate Rd
NW10 .... 20 B1
Traemore Ct
SW16 .... 74 C1
Trafalgar Ave
SE15 .... 49 B4
Trafalgar CI **6**
SE16 .... 41 A2
Trafalgar Gdns
Stepney E1 ...... 32 C4
1 E8 .... 16 C3
Trafalgar Gr SE10 .. 52 C4
Trafalgar Ho
SE17 .... 151 A2
Trafalgar Mews
E9 .... 18 B2
Trafalgar Point **2**
N1 .... 15 C1
Trafalgar Rd SE10 .. 43 A1
Trafalgar Sq*
SW1 .... 119 C2
Trafalgar St SE17 .. 151 C2
Trafalgar Way E14 .. 34 B1
Trafford CI E15 ... 19 A3
Trafford Ho N1 ... 87 C2
Tragail SW15 ..... 58 A2
Trahorn CI E1 .... 25 A1
Traitors Gate*
EC3 .... 124 C1
Tralee Ct **5** SE16 .. 40 A1
Tramway Ave E15 .. 19 C1
Trance Way W3 ... 36 C3
Tranmere Ho **7**
N7 .... 14 C3
Tranmere Rd SW17,
SW18 .... 71 B2
Tranquil Pas SE3 .. 53 B1
Tranquil Vale SE3 .. 53 A1
Transept St NW1 .. 102 B3
Transom CI SE16 .. 41 A2
Transom Sq E14 .. 42 A1
Tranton Rd SE16 .. 40 A3
Trappes Ho **5**
SE16 .... 40 A2
Travers Ho **6**
SE10 .... 52 C4
Travers Rd N7 .... 5 C1
Travis Ho SE10 ... 52 B2
Treadgold Ho **7**
W11 .... 30 C2
Treadgold St W11 .. 30 C2
Treadway St E2 ... 25 A3
Treasury Bldgs
SW1 .... 134 A4
Treaty St N1 ..... 84 C3
Trebeck St W1 .... 118 A1
Treborough Ho
W1 .... 103 B4
Trebovir Rd SW5 .. 141 C3
Treby St E3 ...... 26 B1
Trecastle Way **3**
N7 .... 13 C4
Tredegar Mews **10**
E3 .... 26 B2
Tredegar Rd E3 ... 26 B3
Tredegar Sq E3 ... 26 B2
Tredegar Terr E3 .. 26 B2
Trederwen Rd E8 .. 24 C4

Treen Ave SW13 ... 56 B4
Trees The N16 .... 6 C4
Trefil Wlk N7 .... 14 A4
Trefoil Rd SW18 .. 59 B2
Tregarvon Rd
SW11 .... 60 C3
Trego Rd E9 ...... 18 C1
Tregothnan Rd
SW9 .... 62 A4
Tregunter Rd
SW10 .... 142 C1
Treherne Ct SW9 .. 48 A2
Trehern Rd **12**
SW14 .... 55 C4
Trehurst St E5 ... 18 A3
Trelawney Est E9 .. 17 B2
Trelawney Ho
SE1 .... 136 C4
Trelawn Rd SW2 .. 62 C2
Trellis Sq **1** E3 .. 26 B2
Tremadoc Rd
SW4 .... 61 C3
Tremaine CI SE4 .. 51 C1
Trematon Ho
SE11 .... 149 C2
Tremlett Gr N19 .. 4 B1
Tremlett Mews N19 .. 4 B1
Trenchard St
SE10 .... 42 C1
Trenchold St
SW8 .... 162 A3
Trendell Ho **8**
E14 .... 33 C3
Trenmar Gdns
NW10 .... 22 A2
Trentham St W3 .. 28 C4
Trentham St
SW18 .... 70 C3
Trent Ho SE15 ... 65 B3
Trent Rd SW2 .... 62 B2
Treport St SW18 .. 71 A4
Tresco Ho SE11 .. 149 B2
Tresco Rd SE15 .. 65 A3
Tresham Cres
NW8 .... 90 A2
Tresham Wlk E9 .. 17 B3
Tressidder Ho **10**
SW4 .... 73 C4
Tressillian Cres
SE4 .... 66 C4
Tressillian Rd SE4 .. 66 C4
Trevanion Rd
W14 .... 140 B2
Trevelyan Gdns
NW10 .... 22 B4
Trevelyan Ho
18 Globe Town E2 .. 25 C2
SE5 .... 48 B3
Treveris St SE1 .. 122 B1
Treverton St W10 .. 22 C1
Treverton Twr
W10 .... 30 C4
Treves Ho
E1 .... 24 C1 99 C1
Treville St SW15 .. 69 A4
Trevithick Ho
13 Bermondsey
SE16 .... 40 A2
3 Gospel Oak
NW5 .... 13 A4
SW8 .... 171 B4
Trevithick St SE8 .. 51 C4
Trevor PI SW7 .... 130 B3
Trevor Roberts
Tutorial Coll
NW8 .... 11 C1
Trevor Sq SW7 .... 130 B3
Trevor St SW7 .... 130 B3
Trevose Ho SE11 .. 149 A2
Trewint St SW18 .. 71 B2
Triangle Ct SE1 .. 123 A1
Triangle Est The
SE11 .... 149 B1
Triangle Ho SE1 .. 138 C4
Triangle PI SW4 .. 61 C3
Triangle Rd **7** E8 .. 25 A4
Triangle The
Crouch End N19 .. 4 C4
EC1 .... 96 B2
Hackney E8 ..... 25 A4
Trident Ho **8** E14 .. 34 B3
Trident St SE16 .. 40 C2
Trieste Ct SW12 .. 72 B3
Trig La EC4 ...... 123 A4
Trigon Rd SW8 ... 163 A2
Trillington Ho
W12 .... 29 C1
Trimdon NW1 ..... 83 A3
Trimmer Wlk **11**
TW8 .... 44 A4
Trim St SE8 ...... 51 B4
Trinder Gdns N19 .. 5 A3
Trinder Rd N4, N19 .. 5 A3
Trinidad Ho **17**
E14 .... 33 B2
Trinidad St E14 .. 33 B2
Trinity Church Rd
SW13 .... 47 A4
Trinity Church Sq
SE1 .... 137 A2
Trinity CI
1 Clapham SW4 .. 61 B3
Lewisham SE13 .. 67 C3
Trinity Cotts TW9 .. 54 B4
Trinity Cres SW17 .. 72 C2
Trinity Ct
Finsbury WC1 ... 94 C2
2 Hoxton N1 ... 24 A4
Rotherhithe SE16 .. 41 A4
Willesden NW2 .. 9 B3
Trinity Gdns E16 .. 35 B4
Stockwell SW?
SW9 .... 62 B3
Trinity Gr **8** SE10 .. 52 B2
Trinity Ho SE1 ... 137 A2
Trinity Homes **14**
SW? 62 B3
Trinity Mews
SW18 .... 70 C3
Trinity PI EC3 .... 124 C3
Trinity Rd
Richmond TW9 ... 54 B4
Wandsworth SW17,
SW18 .... 72 A4
Trinity Rise SE24,
SW2 .... 75 A4
Trinity St Mary's CE
Prim Sch SW12 .. 72 C3
Trinity Sq EC3 ... 124 B3
Trinity St
9 Newham E16 .. 35 C4
SE1 .... 137 B2
Trinity Way W3 ... 29 B2
Trio PI SE1 ...... 137 B3
Tristan Ct **34** SE8 .. 51 B4
Triton Ct EC2 .... 97 C1
Triton Ho **2** E14 .. 42 A2
Triton Sq NW1 ... 92 C2
Triton Sq SE21,
SE27 .... 75 C1

Trocette Mans
SE1 . . . . **138** B2
Trojan Ct NW6 . . . . . . .10 A1
Trojan Ind Est
NW10 . . . . .8 B2
Troon Cl **5** SE16 . . . . .40 A1
Troon Ho **9** E14 . . . . .33 A3
Troon St E1 . . . . .33 A3
Tropical Ct **2**
W10 . . . . .22 C2
Trossachs Rd
SE22 . . . . .64 A2
Trothy Rd SE1 . . . . **153** C3
Trotman Ho **1**
SE14 . . . . .50 B2
Trott St SW11 . . . . **168** A3
Trotwood Ho **3**
SE16 . . . . .40 A4
Troubridge Ct **12**
W4 . . . . .37 B1
Troubridge Rd E9 . . **92** B3
Troutbeck NW1 . . . **92** B3
Troutbeck Rd
SE14 . . . . .51 A2
Trouville Rd SW4 . . .61 B1
Trowbridge Rd E9 . .18 B2
Trower Ho **5** E9 . . . .18 A2
Troy Ct W8 . . . . . . **127** B2
Troyes Ho NW3 . . . .12 B3
Troy Town SE15 . . . .64 C4
Troy Town Flats
SE15 . . . . .64 C4
Truman's Rd **24**
N16 . . . . .16 A3
Trump St EC2 . . . . **109** A1
Trundle St SE1 . . . **136** C4
Trundleys Rd SE8 . .51 A4
Trundley's Ter
SE8 . . . . .40 C2
Truro Ho **2** W2 . . . .31 C4
Truro St NW5 . . . . . .12 C2
Trussley Rd W6 . . . .39 B3
Trust Wlk SE21 . . . .75 A3
Tryon Cres E9 . . . . .25 B4
Tryon St SW3 . . . . **144** C2
Tubbs Rd NW10 . . . .21 B3
Tudor Cl
Crouch End N6 . . . . . . .4 B4
Hampstead NW3 . . . .12 A2
Tulse Hill SW2 . . . . .62 B1
Tudor Ct WC1 . . . . **94** A3
Tudor Ct
Kingsland N1 . . . . . .16 A2
5 Rotherhithe
SE16 . . . . .32 C1
South Acton W5 . . . .36 C4
Tudor East NW10 . . .20 A3
Tudor Gdns SW14 . .56 A4
Tudor Gr E9 . . . . . . .17 B1
Tudor Ho
Brook Green W14 . . .39 C2
34 Hackney E9 . . . .17 B1
Tudor Mews **2**
NW10 . . . . .8 C2
Tudor Rd E9 . . . . . . .25 A4
Tudor St EC4 . . . . **121** C4
Tudor Way W3 . . . . .36 C4
Tufnell Ct **6** E3 . . .26 B4
Tufnell Mans **2**
N7 . . . . .13 C4
TUFNELL PARK . .13 C4
Tufnell Park Mans **1**
N7 . . . . .5 A1
Tufnell Park Prim Sch
N7 . . . . .13 C4

Tufnell Park Rd N19,
N7 . . . . .13 C4
Tufnell Park Sta
N19 . . . . .13 B4
Tufton St SW1 . . . **134** A1
Tufton St SW1 . . . **134** A1
Tuke Sch SE15 . . . . .50 A2
Tullis Ho **12** E9 . . .17 B1
TULSE HILL 75 A4
Tulse Hill
Tulse Hill SW2 . . . . .74 C4
Tulse Hill SW27 . . . .75 A2
Tulse Hill Sta
SE27 . . . . .75 A2
Tulse Ho SW2 . . . . .62 C1
Tulsemere Rd SE21,
SE27 . . . . .75 B2
Tunbridge Ct **1**
SE26 . . . . .76 C1
Tunbridge Ho EC1 . .96 A4
Tunis Rd W12 . . . . . .30 A1
Tunley Gn **2** E14 . .33 B4
Tunley Rd
Dagenham NW10 . . . .21 A4
Upper Tooting SW12,
SW17 . . . . .72 C2
Tunnel Avenue Trad
Est SE10 . . . . .42 C4
Tunnel Rd SE16 . . . .40 B4
Tunstall Ct **6**
TW9 . . . . .44 B2
Tunstall Rd SW9 . . .62 B3
Tunstall Wlk **10**
TW8 . . . . .44 A4
Tunworth Cres
SW15 . . . . .56 B1
Tun Yd SW8 . . . . . . .61 A4
Tupman Ho **4**
SE16 . . . . **139** B3
Turberville Ho **1**
SW9 . . . . .62 B4
Turenne Cl SW18 . . .59 B3
Turin St **2** . . .24 C2 **99** B3
Turk's Head Yd
EC1 . . . . **108** A4
Turks Row SW3 . . **145** A2
Turle Rd N4 . . . . .5 B2
Turlewray Cl N4 . . . .5 B2
Turnagain La EC4 . **108** A2
Turnberry Cl **24**
SE16 . . . . .40 A1
Turnberry Quay **1**
E14 . . . . .42 A3
Turnbull Ho N1 . . . .86 B4
Turnchapel Mews **1**
SW4 . . . . .61 A4
Turner Cl **7** SW9 . .48 A2
Turner Ct
8 Herne Hill SE5 . .63 C3
2 Rotherhithe
SE16 . . . . .40 B4
Turner Ho
Finsbury Pk N4 . . . . .5 B3
22 Millwall E14 . . .41 C4
St John's Wood
NW8 . . . . .80 A2
Strand WC2 . . . . . **120** B3
Westminster SW1 . **147** C3
Turner Lo **10**
SW19 . . . . .69 C3
Turner Pl SW11 . . . .60 A2
Turners Ct E15 . . . . .19 B4
Turner's Rd E3 . . . . .33 B4
Turner St
Canning Town E16 . .35 B3
Stepney E1 . . . . .32 A4
Turneville Rd
W14 . . . . **154** C4

Turney Prim & Sec
Speci SE21 . . . . .75 B4
Turney Rd SE21 . . . .75 C4
Turnham Green Sta
W4 . . . . .38 A2
Turnham Green Terr
W4 . . . . .38 A2
Turnham Prim Sch
SE4 . . . . .66 A3
Turnham Rd SE4 . . .66 A3
Turnmill Ho **8**
SW2 . . . . .62 C2
Turnmill St EC1 . . **108** A4
Turnour Ho **31** E1 . .32 A3
Turnpike Cl SE8 . . . .51 B3
Turnpike Ho EC1 . . **96** B3
Turnpin La **3**
SE10 . . . . .52 B4
Turpentine La
SW1 . . . . **146** B1
Turpin Ho SW11 . . **170** A4
Turpin Way N19 . . . .4 C3
Turquand St SE17 **151** A3
Turret Gr SW4 . . . . .61 B4
Turville Ho NW8 . . **90** A2
Turville St
E2 . . . . .24 B1 **98** C2
Tuscan Ho **20** E2 . .25 B2
Tuskar St SE10 . . . . .43 A1
Tuttle Ho SW1 . . . **147** C1
Tweedale Ct E15 . . .19 B3
Tweed Ho E14 . . . . .34 B1
Tweezer's Alley
WC2 . . . . **121** B4
Twelvetrees Bsns Pk
E16 . . . . .27 C1
Twelvetrees Cres
E3 . . . . .27 B1
Twice Times
Montessori Sch
SW6 . . . . **165** C1
Twig Folly Cl **21**
E2 . . . . .25 C3
Twilley St SW18 . . . .71 A4
Twine Ct E1 . . . . . . .32 B2
Twisden Rd NW5 . . .13 A4
Twyford CE High Sch
W3 . . . . .28 A1
Twyford Ho N5 . . . . .6 A1
Twyford St N1 . . . . **84** C4
Twynholm Mans
SW6 . . . . **154** A2
Tyburn Tree (site
of) * W2 . . . . **116** C4
Tyburn Way W1 . . **117** A4
Tyer's Est SE1 . . . **138** A4
Tyers Gate SE1 . . . **138** A3
Tyers St SE11 . . . . **148** C2
Tyers Terr SE11 . . **149** A1
Tyler Cl E2 . . . . . . **24** B3
Tyler Ho SE3 . . . . . .52 C1
Tyler St
Greenwich SE10 . . . .43 A1
SE10 . . . . .53 A4
Tylney Ho **10** E1 . . .32 A3
Tymperley Ct
SW19 . . . . .70 A3
Tyndale La N1 . . . . .15 A1
Tyndale Mans N1 . . .15 A1
Tyndale Terr **13**
N1 . . . . .15 A1
Tyneham Cl **10**
SW11 . . . . .60 C4
Tyneham Rd
SW11 . . . . .60 C4

Tynemouth St
SW6 . . . . **166** C2
Tyne St E1 . . . . . . **111** A2
Tynsdale Rd NW10 . .8 A2
Tynte Ct SE9 . . . . . . .18 A3
Tynwald Ho **14**
SE26 . . . . .76 C1
Type St E2 . . . . .25 C3
Tyrawley Rd SW6 . **166** A4
Tyrells Ct **3** SE15 . .65 A4
Tyrrell Ho SW1 . . . **161** A4
Tyrrell Rd SE22 . . . .64 C3
Tyrwhitt Rd SE4 . . . .66 C4
Tysoe St EC1 . . . . . **95** C3
Tyssen Com Prim Sch
N16 . . . . .7 C3
Tyssen Rd N16 . . . . .7 B1
Tyssen St
Dalston E8 . . . . .16 B2
Hoxton N1 . . . . .24 A3
Tysson Ho E9 . . . . . .18 A1
Tytherton **20** E2 . . .25 B3
Tytherton Rd N19 . . .4 C1

U

Uamvar St E14 . . . . .34 A4
Udall St SW1 . . . . **147** A3
Udimore Ho **11**
W10 . . . . .30 B4
Uffington Rd
NW10 . . . . .22 A4
Ufford Rd SE1 . . . **135** C4
Ufton Gr N1 . . . . . . .15 C1
Ufton Rd N1 . . . . . . .16 A1
Uhura Sq **19** N16 . .7 A1
Ujima Ct N19 . . . . . .5 A3
Ullin St E14 . . . . . . .34 B4
Ullswater SW15 . . . .57 C1
Ullswater Ho SE15 . .50 B4
Ullswater Rd
Barnes SW13 . . . . . .46 C3
West Norwood SE27,
SW16 . . . . .75 A2
Ulster Pl NW1 . . . . **92** A1
Ulster Terr NW1 . . **92** A2
Ulundi Rd SE3 . . . . .53 A4
Ulva Rd SW15 . . . . .57 C2
Ulverscroft Rd
SE22 . . . . .64 C2
Ulverstone Rd
SE27 . . . . .75 A2
Ulysses Rd NW6 . . .10 B3
Umberston St E1 . . .32 A3
Umbria St SW15 . . . .56 C1
Una Ho **7** NW5 . . . .13 A2
Undercliff SE10 . . . .52 B2
Undercliff Rd
SE13 . . . . .67 A4
Underhill Ho **7**
E14 . . . . .33 C4
Underhill Pas
NW1 . . . . .82 B4
Underhill St NW1 . **82** B3
Undershaft EC3 . . **110** A1
Underwood Ho
W6 . . . . .39 A3
Underwood Rd
E1 . . . . .24 C1 **99** C1
Underwood Row
N1 . . . . .97 A4
Underwood St N1 . . **97** A4
Undine Rd E14 . . . . .42 A2
Unicorn Bldg **14**
E1 . . . . .32 C2
Unicorn Sch TW9 . .44 C1

Union Cl E11 . . . . . .19 C4
Union Ct
2B Paddington W2 . .31 C4
2 Richmond TW10 . .54 A2
South Lambeth
SW4 . . . . **172** A1
Union Dr E1 . . . . . . .26 A1
Union Gr SW8 . . . . **171** C2
Union Mews SW9 . **172** A1
Union Pk **11** SE10 . .43 B1
Union Rd SW8 . . . **171** C1
Union Sq N1 . . . . . **87** A3
Union St
Mill Meads E15 . . . . . .27 C4
SE1 . . . . **122** C1
Union Wharf N1 . . **87** A2
Union Wlk
E2 . . . . .24 A2 **98** B4
Union Yd W1 . . . . **104** B1
Unity Cl NW10 . . . . . .8 C2
Unity Mews NW1 . **83** B2
Univ Coll Jun Sch
NW3 . . . . .11 B4
Univ Coll London
Bloomsbury WC1 . . . . **93** B2
WC1 . . . . **94** B2
Univ Coll London
(Windeyer Inst)
W1 . . . . **105** A4
Univ Coll London
(Wolfson Ho)
NW1 . . . . **93** A3
Univ Coll Hospl
WC1 . . . . **93** A2
University Coll Sch
NW3 . . . . .11 B3
University Mans
SW15 . . . . .57 C4
University St WC1 . **93** A1
Univ of California
WC1 . . . . **105** C3
Univ of East London
(Duncan Ho) E15 . .27 C4
Univ of Greenwich
SE10 . . . . .52 C4
Univ of Greenwich
Rachel McmiIlan
Campus SE8 . . . . . .51 C4
Univ of London
WC1 . . . . **93** C1
Univ of London
(King's Coll Hall)
SE5 . . . . .63 C4
Univ of London
(Queen Mary &
Westfield Coll)
E1 . . . . .26 A1
Univ of Westminster
NW1 . . . . **92** C2
Univ of Westminster
(Cavendish Campus)
W1 . . . . **104** C3
Univ of Westminster
(Marylebone
Campus) W1 . . . **103** B4
Univ of Westminster
(Regent Campus)
W1 . . . . **104** C3
Univ of Westminster
(Regent Campus,
Univ HQ) W1 . . . **104** B2
Unwin Cl SE15 . . . . .49 C4
Unwin Rd SW7 . . **129** C2
Upbrook Mews
W2 . . . . **101** A1
Upcerne Rd
SW10 . . . . **157** A1

Upcott Ho
33 Bromley E3 .....27 A2
4 Hackney E9 .....17 B1
Upgrove Manor Way
12 SE24 .....74 C4
Upham Park Rd
W4 .....38 A2
Upland Rd SE22 .....64 C1
Uplands Cl SW14 .....55 A2
Upnall Ho 18 SE15 .....50 B4
Upnor Way SE17 .....152 B2
Upper Addison Gdns
W14 .....126 A4
Upper Bank St
E14 .....34 A1
Upper Bardsley Wlk 7
N1 .....15 B2
Upper Belgrave St
SW1 .....131 C2
Upper Berkeley St
W1 .....103 A1
Upper Brockley Rd
SE4 .....51 B1
Upper Brook St
W1 .....117 B4
Upper Caldy Wlk 18
 .....15 B2
Upper Camelford Wlk
14 W10 .....31 A3
Upper Cheyne Row
SW3 .....158 A4
Upper Clarendon Wlk
12 W11 .....31 A3
Upper Dengie Wlk
N1 .....86 C4
Upper Grosvenor St
W1 .....117 B3
Upper Ground
SE1 .....121 B2
Upper Gulland Wlk 20
N1 .....15 B2
Upper Hampstead
Wlk 20 NW3 .....11 B4
Upper Handa Wlk 2
N1 .....15 B2
Upper Harley St
NW1 .....91 C1
Upper Hawkwell Wlk
N1 .....87 A4
UPPER HOLLOWAY
 .....4 C2
Upper Holloway Sta
N19 .....4 C2
Upper James St
W1 .....119 A4
Upper John St
W1 .....119 A4
Upper Lismore Wlk 4
N1 .....15 B2
Upper Mall W6 .....39 A1
Upper Marsh SE1 .....135 A2
Upper Montague St
W1 .....102 C3
Upper North St E3,
E14 .....33 C4
Upper Park Rd
NW3 .....12 B3
Upper Phillimore
Gdns W8 .....127 B3
Upper Ramsey Wlk 15
N1 .....15 C2
Upper Rawreth Wlk
N1 .....87 A4
Upper Richmond Rd
SW15 .....57 B3

Upper Richmond Rd
W TW10, SW14,
SW15 .....55 B3
Upper St Martin's La
WC2 .....120 A4
Upper St N1 .....86 A3
Upper Tachbrook St
SW1 .....147 A4
Upper Talbot Wlk 7
W10 .....22 C1
Upper Terr NW3 .....2 B1
Upper Thames St
EC4 .....123 A4
Upper Tollington Pk
N4 .....5 C3
UPPER TOOTING 72 B1
Upper Tooting Park
Mans 17 SW17 .....72 C2
Upper Tooting Pk
SW17 .....72 B2
Upper Tooting Rd
SW17 .....72 B1
Upper Tulse Hill
SW2 .....74 B3
Upper Wimpole St
W1 .....103 C4
Upper Woburn Pl NW1,
WC1 .....93 C3
Upstall St SE5 .....48 A2
Upton Cl NW2 .....1 A1
Urban Mews N4 .....6 A4
Urlwin St SE5 .....48 B4
Urlwin Wlk 6 SW9 .....48 A1
Urmston Dr SW19 .....70 A3
Urmston Ho 4
E14 .....42 B2
Ursula Mews N4 .....6 B3
Ursula St SW11 .....168 A3
Urswick Rd E5, E9 .....17 B3
Usborne Mews
SW8 .....163 A2
Usher Rd E3 .....26 B3
Usk Rd SW11 .....59 B3
Usk St E2 .....25 C2
Utah Bldg 3 SE13 .....52 A2
Utopia Ho 3 NW2 .....8 C2
Utopia Village
NW1 .....81 B4
Uverdale Rd
SW10 .....157 A1
Uxbridge Rd W12 .....30 A1
Uxbridge St
W8 .....31 C1 113 B2

V

Vadnie Bish Ho
NW5 .....13 B2
Vaine Ho 4 E9 .....18 A2
Vale Cl W9 .....88 C3
Vale Ct
East Acton W3 .....29 B1
St John's Wood W9 .....88 C3
Vale End SE22 .....64 B3
Vale Est The W3 .....29 A1
Vale Fst The W3 .....29 A1
Vale Gr Acton W3 .....28 C1
Stoke Newington N4 .....6 B4
Valentia Pl SW9 .....62 C3
Valentine
1 Clapham Pk
SW4 .....61 B1
20 Old Ford E3 .....26 B4
Valentine Pl SE1 .....136 A4
Valens Ho 32 SW2 .....74 C3
Valentine Rd E9 .....17 C2

Valentine Row
SE1 .....136 A3
VALE OF HEALTH 2 C1
Vale of Health NW3 .....2 C1
Vale Rd N4 .....6 B4
Vale Rise NW11 .....1 B3
Vale Row N5 .....15 A4
Vale Royal N7 .....14 A1
Vale Sch The
SW7 .....128 C1
Vale The
Cricklewood NW11 .....1 A2
East Acton W3 .....29 A1
SW3 .....157 C4
Valetta Rd W3 .....38 B4
Valette Ho E9 .....17 B2
Valette St E8 .....17 A2
Valiant Ho
9 Cubitt Town
E14 .....42 B4
SW11 .....167 C3
Valliance Rd
E1 .....24 C1 99 C1
Vallier ce Rd NW10 .....21 C2
Val McKenzie Ave
N7 .....5 C2
Valmar Rd SE5 .....48 B2
Valmar Trad Est
SE5 .....48 B2
Valois Ho 2 SE1 .....138 C2
Valonia Gdns
SW18 .....58 B1
Vanbern Ho NW5 .....12 C2
Vanbrugh Ct
SE11 .....149 C3
Vanbrugh Fields
SE3 .....53 C3
Vanbrugh Hill SE10,
SE3 .....53 B4
Vanbrugh Ho 8
E9 .....17 B1
Vanbrugh Park Rd
SE3 .....53 B3
Vanbrugh Park Rd W
SE3 .....53 B3
Vanbrugh Pk SE3 .....53 B3
Vanbrugh Rd W4 .....37 C3
Vanbrugh Terr
SE3 .....53 B2
Vanburgh Ho E1 .....110 C4
Vancover Ho 33
E1 .....32 A1
Vanderbilt Rd
SW18 .....71 B3
Vanderbilt Villas 1
W12 .....39 C4
Vandon Ct SW1 .....133 A2
Vandon Pas SW1 .....133 A2
Vandon St SW1 .....133 A2
Vandyke Cl SW15 .....57 C1
Vandy St
EC2 .....24 A1 98 A1
Vane Cl NW3 .....11 C4
Vane St SW1 .....147 A4
Vange Ho 12 W10 .....30 B4
Van Gogh Ct E14 .....42 C3
Vanguard Bldg 6
E14 .....41 C4
Vanguard Ho 8
E8 .....17 A1
Vanguard St SE8 .....51 C2
Vanguard Trad Ctr
E15 .....27 B4
Vanneck Sq SW15 .....56 C2
Vanner Point 27
E9 .....17 C2

Vansittart St 7
SE14 .....51 A3
Vanston Pl SW6 .....155 C2
Vantage Mews 7
E14 .....34 B1
Vantage Pl W8 .....127 C1
Vantrey Ho SE11 .....149 B3
Varcoe Rd SE16 .....40 B1
Vardens Rd SW11 .....59 C3
Varden St E1 .....32 A3
Vardon Cl W3 .....29 A3
Vardon Ho SE10 .....52 B2
Varey Ho E1 .....26 A2
Varley Ho 5 NW6 .....23 C4
Varma Ct SE3 .....53 C2
Varna Rd SW6 .....154 C1
Varndell St NW1 .....92 C4
Varsity Row SW14 .....45 B1
Vascroft Est
NW10 .....20 A1
Vassall Ho 3 E3 .....26 A2
Vassall Rd SW9 .....163 C1
Vat Ho SW8 .....162 B2
Vauban Est SE16 .....139 A1
Vauban St SE16 .....139 A1
Vaudeville Ct N4 .....5 C2
Vaughan Ave W6 .....38 B2
Vaughan Est
E2 .....24 B2 98 C4
Vaughan Ho SE1 .....136 A4
Vaughan Rd SE5 .....63 B4
Vaughan St SE16 .....41 B4
Vaughan Way E1 .....125 C2
Vaughan Williams Cl
SE8 .....51 C3
VAUXHALL 148 B1
Vauxhall Bridge Rd
SW1 .....147 A3
Vauxhall Cross SE1,
SW8 .....148 B1
Vauxhall Gr SW8 .....162 C4
Vauxhall Prim Sch
SE11 .....149 A2
Vauxhall St SE11 .....149 A2
Vauxhall Sta
SE11 .....148 B1
Vauxhall Wlk
SE11 .....148 C2
Vawdrey Cl E1 .....25 B1
Vaynor Ho N7 .....14 A4
Vectis Ct SW18 .....59 A1
Veda Rd SE13 .....66 C3
Velde Way 1
SE22 .....64 A2
Vellacott Ho 3
W12 .....30 A3
Velletri Ho 21 E2 .....25 C3
Venables St NW8 .....101 C4
Vencourt Pl W6 .....38 C1
Venetian Rd SE5 .....48 B1
Venice Ct 16 SE5 .....48 B3
Venn Ho N1 .....85 A3
Venn St SW4 .....61 B3
Ventnor Rd SE14 .....50 C3
Ventura Ho 12
SW2 .....62 A3
Venue St E14 .....34 B4
Venus Ho
6 Millwall E14 .....41 C2
8 Old Ford E3 .....26 C4
Vera Ct W2 .....100 A2
Vera Rd SW6 .....164 B4
Verbena Gdns 4
W6 .....38 C1
Verdi Cres W10 .....23 B2
Verdun Rd SW13 .....46 C3
Vere Bank SW19 .....70 B3

Vereker Rd W14 .....140 B1
Vere St W1 .....104 A1
Verity Cl W11 .....31 A3
Verity Ho 20 E3 .....26 B2
Vermeer Ct E14 .....42 C3
Vermont Rd SW18 .....59 A1
Verne Ct 3 W3 .....37 B3
Verneer Gdns
SE15 .....65 B3
Verney Ho
Lisson Gr NW8 .....90 A2
South Kensington
SW10 .....156 C4
Verney Rd SE16 .....40 A1
Verney Way SE16 .....40 A1
Vernon Ct NW2 .....1 B1
Vernon Ho SE11 .....149 A1
Vernon Mews
W14 .....140 B3
Vernon Pl WC1 .....106 B3
Vernon Rd Bow E3 .....26 B3
Mortlake SW14 .....55 C4
Vernon Rise WC1 .....95 A4
Vernon Sq WC1 .....95 A4
Vernon St W14 .....140 B3
Vernon Yd
W11 .....31 B2 112 C4
Verona Ct
Chiswick W4 .....38 A1
19 SE14 .....50 C4
Veronica Ho
Brockley SE4 .....66 B4
46 Bromley E3 .....27 A2
Veronica Rd SW17 .....73 A2
Verran Rd SW12 .....73 A4
Verulam Bldgs
WC1 .....107 A4
Verulam Ho 1
W6 .....39 B4
Verulam St EC1 .....107 B4
Vervain Ho 2
SE15 .....49 C3
Verwood Ho SW8 .....163 A1
Verwood Lo 1
E14 .....42 C2
Vesage Ct EC1 .....107 C3
Vesey Path 18 E14 .....34 A3
Vespan Rd W12 .....38 C4
Vesta Ct SE1 .....138 A3
Vesta Ho 9 E3 .....26 C4
Vesta Rd SE4, SE14 .....51 A1
Vestry Mews 3
SE5 .....49 A2
Vestry Rd SE5 .....49 A2
Vestry St N1 .....97 B4
Viaduct Pl 22 E2 .....25 A2
Viaduct St E2 .....25 A2
Vian St SE13 .....67 A4
Vibart Gdns SW2 .....74 B4
Vibart Wlk N1 .....84 B4
Vicarage Ave SE3 .....53 C3
Vicarage Cres
SW11 .....167 C3
Vicarage Ct
7 Putney SW15 .....68 C4
W8 .....128 A4
Vicarage Dr SW14 .....55 C2
Vicarage Gate
W8 .....114 A1
Vicarage Gdns
Mortlake SW14 .....55 C2
W8 .....31 C1 113 C1
Vicarage Gr SE5 .....48 C2
Vicarage Rd SW14 .....55 C2

Vicarage Wlk
SW11...... 167 C4
Vicar's Cl E9...... 25 B4
Vicars Hill SE13...... 67 A3
Vicar's Rd NW5...... 12 C3
Viceroy Ct NW8...... 80 B2
Viceroy SW8...... 172 A4
Vic Johnson Ho 21
E3...... 26 B4
Vickery Ct EC1...... 97 A2
Vickery Ho 13
SW4...... 62 A3
Vickery's Wharf 3
E14...... 33 C3
Victor Cazalet Ho
N1...... 86 A4
Victoria & Albert
Mus★ SW7...... 129 C2
Victoria Arc SE1...... 132 B1
Victoria Ave EC2...... 110 B3
Victoria Bldgs 1
E8...... 25 A4
Victoria Chambers
EC2...... 24 A1 98 A2
Victoria Coach Sta
SW1...... 146 A3
Victoria Colls WC2...... 107 B2
Victoria Cotts
7 Richmond TW9...... 44 C2
Spitalfields E1...... 111 B4
Victoria Ct
5 Clapham Pk
SW4...... 61 C1
South Acton W3...... 36 C4
St George in t East
E1...... 125 B3
Victoria Dr SW19...... 69 C3
Victoria Emb
WC2...... 121 B3
Victoria Gdns
W11...... 31 C1 113 B2
Victoria Gr W8...... 128 C2
Victoria Gr Mews
W2...... 114 A3
Victoria Hall 16
E16...... 35 C1
Victoria Ho
6 Clapham Pk
SW4...... 61 C1
2 Shepherd's Bush
W12...... 38 C4
SW1...... 146 A2
Victoria Ind Est
W3...... 29 A4
Victoria Mans
8 Islington N7...... 14 C3
Willesden NW10...... 9 A1
Victoria Mews
Kilburn NW6...... 23 C4
Wandsworth SW18...... 71 B3
Victoria Mills 1
E15...... 19 C1
Victorian Gr N16...... 7 A1
Victorian Rd N16...... 7 B1
Victoria Park Ct 11
E9...... 17 B1
Victoria Park Ind Ctr
E9...... 19 A4
Victoria Park Lofts
E9...... 25 C4
Victoria Park Rd
E9...... 17 C1
Victoria Park Sq
E2...... 25 B2
Victoria Pas NW8...... 89 B2

Victoria Place Sh Ctr
SW1...... 146 B4
Victoria Rd
Finsbury Pk N4...... 5 B3
Kensington W8...... 128 C2
Kilburn NW6...... 23 B4
Mortlake SW14...... 55 C4
North Acton NW10...... 21 A3
Victoria Rise SW4...... 61 A4
Victoria Sq SW1...... 132 B2
Victoria St SW1...... 133 A1
Victoria Sta SW1...... 146 B4
Victoria Terr
Dagenham NW10...... 21 A1
Finsbury Pk N4...... 5 C3
Victoria
(Underground)
SW1...... 132 B1
Victoria Villas
TW9...... 54 B3
Victoria Wharf
E14...... 33 A2
Victoria Yd 1
E1...... 111 C1
Victor Rd NW10...... 22 A2
Victory Pl
6 Limehouse E14...... 33 A2
SE17...... 151 B4
Victory Sch SE17...... 151 B4
Victory Way SE16...... 41 A4
Victory Wlk SE8...... 51 C2
Video Ct N4...... 5 A4
View Cl N6...... 3 B4
Viewfield Rd
SW18...... 58 B1
Viewpoint 3 N5...... 15 A3
Vigo St W1...... 118 C3
Viking Cl 13 E3...... 26 A3
Viking Ho 8 SE5...... 48 B1
Viking Ct SW6...... 155 B3
Village Mount 11
NW3...... 11 B4
Village Sch The
NW3...... 12 B2
Village The SW11...... 60 A4
Village Way SE21...... 63 C1
Villa Rd SW9...... 62 C4
Villas On The Heath
NW3...... 2 B1
Villa St SE17...... 151 C1
Villiers Ct SW11...... 168 B4
Villiers Rd NW2...... 9 A2
Villiers St WC2...... 120 B2
Vince Ct N1...... 97 C3
Vincent Ct
Finsbury Pk N4...... 5 B4
Marylebone W1...... 102 C2
South Lambeth
SW9...... 173 A3
Vincent Mews 1
E3...... 26 C3
Vincent Rd W3...... 37 B3
Vincents Cl SE16...... 41 A4
Vincent Sq SW1...... 147 B4
Vincent St
Canning Town E16...... 35 B4
Westminster SW1...... 147 C4
Vincent Terr N1...... 86 B2
Vince St EC1...... 97 C3
Vine Ct E1...... 111 C3
Vinegar St E1...... 32 A1
Vinegar Yd SE1...... 138 A4
Vine Hill EC1...... 95 B1
Vine La SE1...... 124 B1
Vine Rd SW13...... 56 B4
Vine St Bridge
EC1...... 95 C1
Vine Sq W14...... 141 A1

Vines Sch The
SW11...... 60 C3
Vine St W1...... 119 A3
Whitechapel EC3...... 110 C1
Vineyard Path
SW14...... 55 C4
Vineyard Sch The
TW10...... 54 A1
Vineyard The
TW10...... 54 A2
Vineyard Wlk EC1...... 95 B2
Viney Ct 9 SW4...... 62 A3
Vine Yd SE1...... 137 A4
Viney Rd SE13...... 67 A4
Vining St SW9,...... 62 C3
Vinson Ho N1...... 87 C1
Vintners Ct EC4...... 123 A4
Viola Sq W12...... 29 B2
Violet Cl 5 SE8...... 51 A4
Violet Hill NW8...... 78 C1
Violet Hill Ho NW8...... 78 C1
Violet Rd E3...... 27 A1
Violet St 2 E2...... 25 A1
Virgil Pl W1...... 102 C3
Virgil St SE1...... 135 A2
Virginia Ct 7
SE16...... 40 A4
Virginia Ho 3 E14...... 34 B2
Virginia Prim Sch
E2...... 24 B2 98 C3
Virginia Rd
E2...... 24 B2 98 C3
Virginia St E1...... 125 C3
Virginia Wlk SW2...... 62 B1
Viscount Ct 9
W11...... 31 C3
Viscount St EC1...... 108 C4
Vista Bldgs 10 E3...... 26 B2
Vitae Apartments 7
W6...... 38 C3
Vittoria Ho N1...... 85 A3
Vittoria Prim Sch
N1...... 85 B3
Vivian Comma Cl 3
N4...... 6 A1
Vivian Ct NW6...... 78 A2
Vivian Ho N4...... 6 C4
Vivian Rd E3...... 26 A3
Vogans Mill SE1...... 139 A4
Vogler Ho 4 E1...... 32 B2
Vollasky Ho 9 E1...... 111 B4
Voltaire
2 Camberwell
SE5...... 49 B2
16 Richmond TW9...... 44 B2
Voltaire Rd SW11...... 169 C2
Voltaire Rd SW4...... 61 C4
Volt Ave NW10...... 21 A2
Vorley Rd N19...... 4 B2
Voss St E2...... 24 C2 99 C3
Voyager Bsns Est
SE16...... 139 B3
Vulcan Rd SE4...... 51 B1
Vulcan Sq E14...... 41 C2
Vulcan Terr SE4...... 51 B1
Vulcan Way N7...... 14 B2
Vyner Ct E5...... 7 C2
Vyner Rd W3...... 28 C2
Vyner St E2...... 25 A4

W

Wadcroft Ct SE4...... 66 B1
Wadding St SE17...... 151 B3
Waddington Rd
E15...... 19 C2
Waddington St
E15...... 19 C2
Wade Ho SE1...... 139 B3
Wadeson St E2...... 25 A3
Wade's Pl E14...... 34 A2
Wadham Gdns
NW3...... 80 A4
Wadham Rd SW15...... 58 A3
Wadhurst Rd W4...... 37 C3
Wager St E3...... 26 B1
Waghorn St SE15...... 64 C4
Wagner St SE15...... 50 B3
Wainford Cl SW19...... 69 C3
Wainwright Ho 3
E1...... 32 B1
Waite St SE15...... 49 B4
Waithman St EC4...... 108 A1
Wakefield Ho 6
SE15...... 49 C2
Wakefield Mews
WC1...... 94 B3
Wakefield St WC1...... 94 B3
Wakeford Cl SW4...... 61 B2
Wakeham St 3
N1...... 15 C2
Wakehurst Rd
SW11...... 60 B2
Wakeling Ho 6
SE27...... 75 A1
Wakeling St 11
E14...... 33 A3
Wakelin Ho 19 N1...... 15 A1
Wakeman Rd
NW10...... 22 C2
Wakley St EC1...... 96 A4
Walberswick St
SW8...... 162 B1
Walbrook EC4...... 123 B4
Walbrook Ct 32
N1...... 24 A3
Walbrook Wharf
EC4...... 123 B4
Walburgh St E1...... 32 A3
Walcorde Ave
SE17...... 151 A3
Walcot Gdns
SE11...... 149 B4
Walcot Ho 9
SE22...... 64 A4
Walcot Sq SE11...... 149 C4
Walcott St SW1...... 147 A4
Waldeck Gr SE27...... 75 A1
Waldeck Rd
Brentford W4...... 44 C4
Mortlake SW14...... 55 B4
Waldeck Terr
SW14...... 55 B4
Waldegrave Ho 5
SW15...... 57 B2
Waldemar Ave
SW6...... 164 B2
Waldemar Avenue
Mans SW6...... 164 A3
Walden Ct SW8...... 171 C4
Walden Ho
Clapham SW11...... 169 B2
SW1...... 145 C3
Walden St E1...... 32 A3
Waldo Cl SW4...... 61 B2
Waldo Rd NW10...... 22 A2

Waldron Ho 17
SW2...... 62 B2
Waldron Mews
SW3...... 157 C4
Waldron Rd SW18...... 71 B1
Walerand Rd SE13...... 52 B1
Waleran Flats
SE1...... 152 A4
Wales Cl SE15...... 50 A4
Wales Farm Rd
W3...... 28 C4
Waley St 1 E1...... 33 A4
Walford Ho 20 E1...... 32 A3
Walford Rd N16...... 16 A4
Walham Ct 19
NW3...... 12 B2
Walham Gr SW6...... 155 C2
WALHAM GREEN
...... 156 A1
Walham Green Arc
SW6...... 155 C2
Walham Yd SW6...... 155 C2
Walker Ho NW1...... 83 B1
Walker Mews 9
SW2...... 62 C2
Walkerscroft Mead
SE21...... 75 B3
Walker's Ct W1...... 119 B4
Walkers Lo 18 E14...... 42 B4
Walker's Pl SW15...... 58 A3
Walkinshaw Ct 9
N1...... 15 B1
Walkynscroft 1
SE15...... 50 A1
Wallace Collection★
...... 104 B2
Wallace Ct NW1...... 102 B3
Wallace Ho N7...... 14 B2
Wallace Lo N4...... 5 C3
Wallace Rd N1, N5...... 15 B2
Wallbutton Rd
SE4...... 51 A1
Wall Ct N4...... 5 B3
Waller Rd SE14...... 50 C1
Wallett Ct 11 NW1...... 13 B1
Wallflower St
W12...... 29 B2
Wallgrave Rd
SW5...... 142 A3
Wallingford Ave
W10...... 30 C3
Wallis Alley SE1...... 137 A4
Wallis Cl SW11...... 59 C4
Wallis Ho 5 SE14...... 51 A2
Wallis Rd E9...... 18 C2
Wallorton Gdns
SW14...... 55 C3
Wallside EC2...... 109 A3
Wall St N1...... 15 C2
Wallwood St E14...... 33 B4
Walm La NW2...... 9 B2
Walmer Ho 8
W10...... 30 C3
Walmer Pl W1...... 102 C4
Walmer Rd
North Kensington
W10...... 30 B3
W11...... 31 A2 112 A3
Walney Wlk 6 N1...... 15 B2
Walnut Cl SE8...... 51 B4
Walnut Ho 11 E3...... 26 B4
Walnut Tree Cl
SW13...... 46 B2
Walnut Tree Ho
SW10...... 156 B4
Walnut Tree Rd
Brentford TW8...... 44 A4

Walnut Tree Rd
continued
Greenwich SE10 . . . . . **43** A1
Walnut Tree Walk
Prim Sch SE11 . . . **149** B4
Walnut Tree Wlk
SE11 . . . . **149** B4
Walpole Ave TW9 . . **44** B1
Walpole Ct ⑦
 Hammersmith
 W14 . . . . **39** C3
 South Hampstead
 NW6 . . . . **11** B2
Walpole Gdns W4 . . **37** B1
Walpole Mews
NW8 . . . . **79** B3
Walpole St SW3 . . **145** A2
Walsham Cl N16 . . . . **7** C3
Walsham Ho
 New Cross Gate
 SE14 . . . . **50** C1
 SE17 . . . . **151** B2
Walsham Rd SE14 . . **50** C1
Walsingham NW8 . . **79** C4
Walsingham Lo
SW13 . . . . **46** C2
Walsingham Mans
SW6 . . . . **156** B2
Walsingham Pl SW11 . . . . **60** C1
Walsingham Rd E5 . . **7** C1
Walter Besant Ho ⑳
E1 . . . . **25** C2
Walter Ct ⑨ W3 . . **28** B3
Walter Green Ho
SE15 . . . . **50** B2
Walter Ho SW10 . . **157** B2
Walter Northcott Ho
② NW6 . . . . **10** C3
Walters Cl SE17 . . **151** A3
Walters Ho
 ③ *Camberwell*
 SE5 . . . . **49** A1
 Islington N1 . . . . . **86** B4
 ⑩ *Kennington*
 SE17 . . . . **48** A4
Walter Sickert Hall
N1 . . . . **86** C1
Walter St E2 . . . . . **25** C2
Walters Way SE23 . . **65** C1
Walter Taylor Ct
SE4 . . . . **66** B3
Walter Terr E1 . . . . **32** C3
Walterton Rd W9 . . **23** C1
Waltham Green Ct
SW6 . . . . **156** A1
Waltham Ho NW8 . . **78** C4
 Stockwell SW9 . . . **173** A1
Walton Cl SW8 . . . **162** B2
Walton Gdns W3 . . **28** A4
Walton Ho
E2 . . . . **24** B1
 Upper Holloway N7 . . **5** A1
 Wandsworth SW18 . **58** C1
Walton Pl SW3 . . . **130** C2
Walton St SW3 . . . **130** B1
Walton Way W3 . . . **28** A4
Walt Whitman Cl ⑥
SE24 . . . . **63** A3
WALWORTH **151** C2
Walworth Pl SE17 . **151** A1
Walworth Rd
SE17 . . . . **151** A2
Walworth Sch
SE17 . . . . **152** B1
Wanborough Dr
SW15 . . . . **69** A3

Wandle Ct ⑧ W12 . **38** A4
Wandle Ho NW8 . . **102** A4
 Wandsworth SW18 . **71** A4
Wandle Rd SW17 . . **72** A2
Wandle Way
SW18 . . . . **71** A3
Wandon Rd SW6 . . **156** B1
WANDSWORTH . . . **58** C1
Wandsworth Bridge
Rd SW6 . . . . **166** A3
Wandsworth Common
Sta SW12 . . . . **72** B4
Wandsworth Common
West Side SW18 . . . **59** B2
Wandsworth Gyratory
SW18 . . . . **59** A2
Wandsworth High St
SW18 . . . . **59** A2
Wandsworth Mus*
SW18 . . . . **59** A2
Wandsworth Plain
SW18 . . . . **59** A2
Wandsworth Rd
SW8 . . . . **162** A1
Wandsworth Road Sta
SW4 . . . . **171** A1
Wandsworth Town
Sta SW18 . . . . **59** A3
Wangford Ho ⑱
SW9 . . . . **63** A3
Wanless Rd SE24 . . **63** B3
Wanley Rd SE5 . . . . **63** C3
Wansbeck Rd E3,
E9 . . . . **18** B1
Wansdown Pl
SW6 . . . . **156** A2
Wansey St SE17 . . **151** A3
WAPPING **32** A1
Wapping Dock St ⑧
E1 . . . . **32** A1
Wapping High St
E1 . . . . **32** A1
Wapping La E1 . . . . **32** A1
Wapping Sta E1 . . . **32** B1
Wapping Wall E1 . . **32** B1
Warbeck Rd W12 . . **39** A4
Warburg Ho
E2 . . . . **24** C2
Warburton Cl ⑥
N1 . . . . **16** A2
Warburton Ho ⑤
E8 . . . . **25** A4
Warburton Rd ⑧
E8 . . . . **25** A4
Warburton St ⑥
E8 . . . . **25** A4
Wardalls Ho ⑫
SE8 . . . . **51** B4
Wardell Ho ⑦
SE10 . . . . **52** B4
Warden Rd NW5 . . . **12** C2
Wardens Gr SE1 . . **122** C1
Wardle St E9 . . . . . **17** C3
Wardley St SW18 . . **71** A4
Wardlow ⑦ NW5 . . **13** A4
Wardo Ave SW6 . . . **164** A4
Wardour Mews
W1 . . . . **105** A1
Wardour St W1 . . . **105** B1
Ward Point SE11 . . **149** B3
Ward Rd
 Camden Town N19 . . **4** B1
 Mill Meads E15 . . . **27** C4
Wardrobe Pl EC4 . . **108** B1

Wardrobe Terr
EC4 . . . . **122** B4
Wareham Ct ②
N1 . . . . **16** A1
Wareham Ho
SW8 . . . . **162** C2
Warfield Rd NW10 . **22** C2
Warfield Yd ⑥
NW10 . . . . **22** C2
Wargrave Ho
E2 . . . . **24** B2
Warham Rd N4 . . . . . **5** C4
Warham St SE5 . . . . **48** A3
Waring Ho
E2 . . . . **24** C2
Warley Ho N1 . . . . . **15** C2
Warley St E2 . . . . . **25** C2
Warlock Rd W9 . . . . **23** C1
Warlters Cl N7 . . . . **14** A4
Warlters Rd N7 . . . . **14** A4
Warltersville Mans
N19 . . . . **5** A4
Warltersville Rd N4, N8,
N19 . . . . **5** A4
War Meml Homes
W4 . . . . **45** C3
Warmington Rd
SE24 . . . . **63** B1
Warmsworth NW1 . **82** C4
Warndon St SE16 . . **40** B2
Warneford St E9 . . . **25** A4
Warner Ho
 ⑤ *Homerton* E9 . . **17** C2
 Lewisham SE13 . . . **52** A1
 NW8 . . . . **88** C4
Warner Pl
E2 . . . . **24** C2
Warner Rd SE5 . . . . **48** B2
Warner St EC1 . . . . **95** B1
Warner Yd EC1 . . . . **95** B1
Warnford Ho
SW15 . . . . **56** A1
Warnham WC1 . . . . **94** C3
Warnham Ho ⑥
SW2 . . . . **74** A4
Warple Mews W3 . . **38** A4
Warple Way W3,
W12 . . . . **38** A4
Warren Ave SW14,
TW10 . . . . **55** A3
Warren Cl SE21 . . . . **75** B4
Warren Ct N1 . . . . . **85** B2
Warrender Rd
N19 . . . . **13** B4
Warren Gdns E15 . . **19** C3
Warren Ho E14 . . . . **34** B3
Warren Mews W1 . . **92** C1
Warren St W1 . . . . . **92** C1
Warren Street Sta
NW1 . . . . **93** A2
Warriner Gdns
SW11 . . . . **169** B3
Warrington Cres
W9 . . . . **88** C2
Warrington Gdns
W9 . . . . **88** C1
Warspite Ho ③
E14 . . . . **42** A2
Warton Rd E15 . . . . **27** B4
Warwick W14 . . . . **141** A3
Warwick Ave W9 . . **88** C1
Warwick Avenue Sta
W9 . . . . **88** C1
Warwick Bldg
SW8 . . . . **160** A3
Warwick Chambers
W8 . . . . **127** B2

Warwick Cres
W2 . . . . **100** C4
Warwick Ct WC1 . . **107** A3
Warwick Dr SW15 . **57** A4
Warwick Gdns
W14 . . . . **141** A4
Warwick Ho
 Brixton SW9 . . . . **173** B1
 ⑪ *Putney* SW15 . . **69** B4
 Stoke Newington N4 . **6** B3
Warwick House St
SW1 . . . . **119** C2
Warwick La EC4 . . **108** B1
Warwick Lo NW2 . . **10** A3
Warwick Mans
SW5 . . . . **141** B4
Warwick Pas EC4 . **108** B2
Warwick Pl W9 . . . **100** C4
Warwick Pl N
SW1 . . . . **146** C3
Warwick Rd W14 . . . . **141** A4
Warwick Row
SW1 . . . . **132** B2
Warwickshire Path
SE8 . . . . **51** B3
Warwick Sq
 Holborn EC4 . . . . **108** B2
 Pimlico SW1 . . . . **146** C2
Warwick Sq Mews
SW1 . . . . **146** C3
Warwick St W1 . . . **119** A4
Warwick Way
SW1 . . . . **146** B4
Warwick Yd EC1 . . **97** A1
Wasdale NW1 . . . . . **92** B3
Washbrook Ho
SW2 . . . . **62** C1
Washington Bldg ①
SE13 . . . . **52** A2
Washington Cl ⑧
E3 . . . . **27** A2
Washington Ho
SW1 . . . . **130** C3
Washington Rd
SW13 . . . . **46** C3
Watchfield Ct ⑦
W4 . . . . **37** B1
Watcombe Cotts
TW9 . . . . **44** C4
Watercress Pl N1 . . **16** A1
Waterden Cres E9 . . **18** C3
Waterden Rd E15 . . **18** C2
Waterford Rd
SW6 . . . . **156** A1
Waterford Way
NW10 . . . . **8** C3
Water Gardens The
W2 . . . . **102** B2
Watergate EC4 . . . **122** A4
Watergate St SE8 . . **51** C4
Watergate Wlk
WC2 . . . . **120** B2
Waterhead NW1 . . . **92** C4
Waterhouse Cl
 Hammersmith W6 . . **39** C1
 Hampstead NW3 . . **11** C3
Wateridge Cl E14 . . **41** C3
Water La
 ⑯ *Camden Town*
 NW1 . . . . **13** A1
 SE14 . . . . **50** B3
Waterloo Bridge SE1,
WC2 . . . . **121** A3
Waterloo Cl E9 . . . . **17** B3
Waterloo East Sta
SE1 . . . . **121** C1

Waterloo Gdns
 ㉖ *Islington* N1 . . . **15** A1
 South Hackney E2 . . **25** B3
Waterloo Int Sta
SE1 . . . . **135** A4
Waterloo Pier
SE1 . . . . **134** C4
Waterloo Pl
 Kew TW9 . . . . **44** C4
 ⑨ *Richmond* TW9 . . **54** A3
 SW1 . . . . **119** B2
Waterloo Rd SE1 . . **135** C4
Waterloo Sta SE1 . **135** B4
Waterloo Terr N1 . . **15** A1
Waterlow Ct NW11 . . **2** A4
Waterlow Rd N19 . . . **4** B3
Waterman Bldg ②
E14 . . . . **41** C4
Watermans Ct ②
TW8 . . . . **44** A4
Waterman St
SW15 . . . . **57** C4
Waterman Way
E1 . . . . **32** A1
Watermead Ho E9 . . **18** B3
Watermeadow La
SW6 . . . . **166** C1
Water Mews SE15 . . **65** B3
Watermill Ct SE13 . **67** A4
Watermint Quay
N16 . . . . **7** C4
Water's Edge SW6 . . **47** B2
Waterside N1 . . . . . **86** C1
Waterside Cl
 Bermondsey SE16 . **139** C3
 Old Ford E3 . . . . . **26** B4
Waterside Ct SE13 . **67** C3
Waterside Pl NW1 . **81** C4
Waterside Point
SW11 . . . . **158** B2
Waterson St
E2 . . . . **24** B2
Waters Pl SW15 . . . . **47** B1
Water St WC2 . . . . **121** B4
Waterview Ho ④
E14 . . . . **33** A4
Waterworks Rd
SW2 . . . . **62** B1
Watford Cl SW11 . **168** B4
Watford Rd E16 . . . . **35** C4
Watkins Ho ⑪
E14 . . . . **42** B4
Watkinson Rd N7 . . **14** B2
Watling Ct EC4 . . . **109** A1
Watling Gdns
NW2 . . . . **10** A2
Watling St
 ④ *Camberwell*
 SE15 . . . . **49** A4
 City of London EC4 . **109** A1
Watney Cotts
SW14 . . . . **55** B4
Watney Mkt* E1 . . **32** A3
Watney Rd SW14 . . **55** B4
Watney St E1 . . . . . **32** A3
Watson Cl N16 . . . . **15** C3
Watson Ho ③
SW2 . . . . **74** A4
Watsons Mews
W1 . . . . **102** B3
Watson's St SE8 . . . **51** C3
Watts Gr E3 . . . . **34** A4
Watts Ho ⑥ W10 . . **31** A4
Watts St SE15 . . . . . **49** B2
 Wapping E1 . . . . . . **32** A1

Wat Tyler Rd SE10 . . . . . 52 C2	
Wavel Ct	
7 Streatham	
SW16 . . . . 74 A1	
3 Wapping E1 . . . . 32 B1	
Wavel Mews NW6 . . . 11 A1	
Wavendon Ho	
W4 . . . . 37 C1	
Waveney Ave	
SE15 . . . . 65 A3	
Waveney Cl E1 . . . . 125 C2	
Waveney Ho SE15 . . . . 65 A3	
Waverley Ct	
6 Brondesbury	
NW6 . . . . 10 A1	
W1 . . . . 103 C4	
Waverley Pl	
Finsbury Pk N4 . . . . 6 A3	
St John's Wood	
NW8 . . . . 79 B2	
Waverley Rd N8 . . . . . 5 A4	
Waverly Ct NW3 . . . 12 B2	
Waverton Ho **2**	
E3 . . . . 26 B4	
Waverton Rd	
SW18 . . . . 71 B4	
Waverton St W1 . . . 118 A2	
Wavertree Ct **9**	
SW2 . . . . 74 A3	
Wavertree Rd	
SW2 . . . . 74 B3	
Waxham NW5 . . . . . 12 B3	
Waxlow Rd NW10 . . 20 C3	
Wayford St SW11 . . 168 B1	
Wayland Ave E8 . . . . 16 C3	
Wayland Ho **2** SW9 . 173 B2	
Waylett Ho SE11 . . 149 B1	
Waylett Pl SE27 . . . . 75 A1	
Wayman Ct E8 . . . . . 17 A2	
Waynflete Sq	
18 North Kensington	
W10 . . . . 30 C3	
16 Shepherd's Bush	
W10 . . . . 30 C2	
Waynflete St	
SW18 . . . . 71 B2	
Wayside	
Golders Green	
NW11 . . . . 1 A3	
Mortlake SW14 . . . . . 55 B2	
Weald Cl **16** SE16 . . 40 A1	
Weardale Ho N4 . . . . 6 B4	
Weardale Rd SE13 . . 67 C3	
Wearmouth Ho **1**	
E3 . . . . 33 B4	
Wear Pl **18 2** E2 . . 25 A2	
Wearside Rd SE13 . . 67 A3	
Weatherbury **6**	
W2 . . . . 31 C3	
Weatherbury Ho **3**	
N19 . . . . 4 C1	
Weatherley Cl E3 . . 33 B4	
Weaver Ct **2** E2 . . 25 A1	
Weaver Ho	
E1 . . . . 24 C1 99 B1	
Weaver's La SE1 . . 124 B1	
Weaver St	
E1 . . . . 24 C1 99 B1	
Weavers Way	
6 Camden Town	
NW1 . . . . 13 C1	
NW1 . . . . 83 B4	
Webb Cl NW10 . . . . 22 B1	
Webb Ct W3 . . . . . . 37 A4	
Webber Row SE1 . . 136 A3

Webber St SE1 . . . . 136 A3	
Webb Est E5 . . . . . . 7 C4	
Webb Ho NW8 . . . . 161 C1	
Webb Pl NW10 . . . . 21 B2	
Webb Rd SE3 . . . . . . 53 B4	
Webb's Rd SW11 . . . 60 B2	
Webb's St SE1 . . . . 138 A1	
Webheath Ho 10	
N16 . . . . 16 A3	
Webster Rd SE16 . . 139 C1	
Weddell Ho **22** E1 . . 25 C1	
Wedderburn Rd	
NW3 . . . . 11 C3	
Wedgewood Ho	
SW1 . . . . 146 C1	
Wedgewood Mews	
W1 . . . . 105 C1	
Wedgewood Wlk	
NW3 . . . . 11 A3	
Wedgwood Ho	
17 Globe Town E2 . . 25 C2	
SE11 . . . . 135 B1	
Wedlake St W10 . . . 23 A1	
Wedmore Gdns	
N19 . . . . 4 C2	
Wedmore St N19 . . . 4 C1	
Weech Rd NW6 . . . . 10 C4	
Weedington Rd	
NW5 . . . . 12 C3	
Weedon Ho W12 . . . 29 C3	
Weekley Sq SW11 . . 59 C4	
Weighhouse St	
W1 . . . . 103 C1	
Weimar St SW15 . . . 58 A4	
Weir Ho **8** SW12 . . 73 A4	
Weir Rd	
Streatham SW12 . . . 73 B4	
Wimbledon SW19 . . .	
SW19 . . . . 71 A1	
Weir's Pas NW1 . . . . 93 C4	
Weiss Rd SW15 . . . . 57 C4	
Welbeck Ct W14 . . 140 C4	
Welbeck Mans 10	
NW6 . . . . 10 C3	
Welbeck St W1 . . . 104 A2	
Welbeck Way W1 . . 104 A2	
Welbury Ct E8 . . . . 16 A1	
Welby Ho N19 . . . . . 4 C4	
Welby St SE5 . . . . . 48 A2	
Weldon Ct SE1 . . . . 51 C1	
Welford Ct	
12 Camden Town	
NW1 . . . . 13 A1	
Clapham SW8 . . . . 170 C1	
Welland Ho SE15 . . 65 B3	
Welland Mews	
E1 . . . . 125 C2	
Welland St SE10 . . 52 B4	
Wellclose Sq E1 . . 125 C4	
Wellclose St **1** . . 125 C3	
Well Ct EC4 . . . . . . 109 A1	
Wellday Ho **2** E9 . 18 A2	
Welldon Ct 1	
SE21 . . . . 75 C2	
Weller Ho SE16 . . . 139 B3	
Weller St SE1 . . . . 136 C4	
Welles Ct **8** E14 . . 33 C2	
Wellesley Ave W6 . . 39 A3	
Wellesley Ho NW1 . . 93 B3	
Wellesley Pl	
Camden Town	
NW5 . . . . 12 C3	
NW1 . . . . 93 B3	
Wellesley Rd	
Gospel Oak NW5 . . . 12 C3

Wellesley Rd continued	
Gunnersbury W4 . . . 37 A1	
Wellesley St E1 . . . . 32 C4	
Wellesley Terr N1 . . 97 A4	
Wellfit St **5** SE24 . . 63 A4	
Wellgarth Rd NW11 . 2 A3	
Wellington Arch★	
SW1 . . . . 131 C4	
Wellington Bldgs	
1 Bow E3 . . . . 26 C2	
SW1 . . . . 145 C1	
Wellington Cl	
Kensington W11 . . . 31 C3	
New Cross Gate	
SE14 . . . . 50 C2	
Wellington Ct	
Knightsbridge	
SW1 . . . . 130 C3	
St John's Wood	
NW8 . . . . 79 C1	
Strand WC2 . . . . . . 120 A4	
Wandsworth SW18 . . 60 A2	
Wellington Gr	
SE10 . . . . 52 C3	
Wellington Ho 18	
NW3 . . . . 12 B3	
Wellington Hospl The	
NW8 . . . . 79 C1	
Wellington Mans	
N16 . . . . 16 B4	
Wellington Mews	
East Dulwich SE22 . . 64 C3	
3 Islington N7 . . . 14 B2	
Streatham SW16 . . . 73 C1	
Wellington Mons	
(Apsley Ho)★	
SW1 . . . . 131 C4	
Wellington Pl	
NW8 . . . . 89 C4	
Wellington Prim Sch	
E3 . . . . 26 C2	
Wellington Row	
E2 . . . . 24 C2 99 B4	
Wellington Sq	
SW3 . . . . 144 C2	
Wellington St	
WC2 . . . . 120 C4	
Wellington Terr **2**	
E1 . . . . 32 A1	
Wellington Way	
E3 . . . . 26 C2	
Well La SW14 . . . . . 55 B2	
Well Rd NW3 . . . . . . 2 C1	
Wells Ct	
2 Hampstead	
NW3 . . . . 11 B4	
1 Paddington NW6 . 23 C3	
Stoke Newington	
N1 . . . . 16 A3	
Wells Ho	
Finsbury EC1 . . . . . 96 A4	
12 Kensal Town	
W10 . . . . 23 A1	
New Cross Gate	
SE4 . . . . 51 A1	
3 Rotherhithe	
SE16 . . . . 40 B3	
Wells House Rd	
NW10 . . . . 29 A4

Wellside Gdns	
SW14 . . . . 55 B2	
Wells Mews W1 . . . 105 A2	
Wells Pl SW18 . . . . 71 B4	
Wells Rd W12 . . . . . 39 B4	
Wells Rise NW8 . . . . 80 C3	
Wells Sq WC1 . . . . . 95 A3	
Wells St W1 . . . . . . 105 A2	
Wells Terr N4 . . . . . 5 C2	
Wells Way	
Brompton SW7 . . . 129 B2	
Camberwell SE5 . . . 49 A4	
Well Wlk NW3 . . . . . 2 C1	
Wellwood Ct	
SW15 . . . . 57 B3	
Welmar Works	
SW4 . . . . 61 C3	
Welsford St SE1 . . . 153 B3	
Welsh Ho **14** E1 . . 32 A1	
Welshpool Ho **2**	
E8 . . . . 24 C4	
Welshpool St **1**	
E8 . . . . 25 A4	
Welstead Ho **29**	
E1 . . . . 32 A3	
Welstead Way W4 . . 38 B2	
Weltje Rd W6 . . . . . 38 C1	
Welton Ct SE5 . . . . . 49 A2	
Welton Ho E1 . . . . . 32 C4	
Welwyn St E2 . . . . . 25 B2	
Wembury Mews N6 . 4 B4	
Wembury Rd N6 . . . 4 A4	
Wemyss Rd SE3 . . . . 53 B1	
Wendell Park Prim	
Sch W12 . . . . 38 B4	
Wendell Rd W12 . . . 38 B4	
Wendle Ct SW8 . . . 162 A3	
Wendling NW5 . . . . 12 B3	
Wendon St E3 . . . . . 26 B4	
Wendover SE17 . . . 152 A1	
Wendover Ct	
Acton W3 . . . . 20 A1	
Becontree W3 . . . . . 20 B1	
4 Child's Hill NW2 . 1 C1	
W1 . . . . 103 B3	
Wendover Ho	
W1 . . . . 103 B3	
Wendover Rd	
NW10 . . . . 21 B3	
Wenham Ho	
SW8 . . . . 160 C1	
Wenlake Ho EC1 . . . 96 C2	
Wenlock Ct N1 . . . . 87 C1	
Wenlock Rd N1 . . . . 87 B1	
Wenlock St N1 . . . . 87 B1	
Wennington Rd	
E3 . . . . 25 C3	
Wensdale Ho E5 . . . 7 C2	
Wensleydale Ho 3	
SW3 . . . . 153 C3	
Wentworth Cres	
SE15 . . . . 49 C3	
Wentworth Ct	
W6 . . . . 154 A3	
Wandsworth SW18 . . 59 A1	
Wentworth Dwellings	
E1 . . . . 110 C2	
Wentworth Ho 4	
SE3 . . . . 53 C3	
Wentworth Mews	
E3 . . . . 26 B2	
Wentworth St E1 . . 111 A3	
Werrington St	
NW1 . . . . 83 A1	
Werter Rd SW15 . . . 58 A3	
Wesleyan Pl NW5 . . 13 A4

Wesley Ave NW10 . . 20 C2	
Wesley Cl	
Finsbury Pk N7 . . . . . 5 B2	
SE17 . . . . 150 B3	
Wesley Sq W11 . . . 103 C1	
Wesley Ho SE24 . . . 63 C1	
Wesley Rd NW10 . . 20 B4	
Wesley Sq W11 . . . 103 C3	
Wessex Ct SW15 . . . 57 C2	
Wessex Gardens Prim	
Sch NW11 . . . . . . 1 A3	
Wessex Gdns NW11 . 1 A3	
Wessex Ho SE1 . . . 153 A1	
4 Tufnell Pk N19 . . 5 A2	
Wessex St E2 . . . . . 25 B2	
Wessex Way NW11 . 1 A3	
West 12 Sh Ctr	
W12 . . . . 39 C4	
Westacott Cl N19 . . . 4 C3	
West Acton Prim Sch	
W3 . . . . 28 A3	
West Arbour St	
E1 . . . . 32 C3	
West Bank N16 . . . . 7 A4	
Westbere Rd NW2 . . 10 A3	
West Block **18** EC1 . 32 B2	
Westbourne Ave	
W3 . . . . 28 C3	
Westbourne Cres	
W2 . . . . 115 B4	
Westbourne Ct	
W2 . . . . 100 C2	
Westbourne Gdns	
W2 . . . . 100 A2	
Westbourne Gr	
Notting Hill W2,	
W11 . . . . 31 C3	
W2 . . . . 100 B1 113 C4	
Westbourne Gr Mews	
7 W11 . . . . 31 C3	
Westbourne Gr Terr	
W2 . . . . 100 A1	
Westbourne Ho	
SW1 . . . . 146 A2	
Westbourne Park Rd	
Notting Hill W11 . . . 31 B3	
Paddington W2, W11 . 31 C3	
Westbourne Park Sta	
W11 . . . . 31 B4	
Westbourne Park	
Villas W2 . . . . . 100 A3	
Westbourne Rd	
N7 . . . . 14 B2	
Westbourne St	
W2 . . . . 115 B4	
Westbourne Terr	
W2 . . . . 101 A2	
Westbourne Terrace	
Mews W2 . . . . . 100 C2	
Westbourne Terrace	
Rd W2 . . . . 100 C3	
Westbridge Cl	
W12 . . . . 29 C1	
Westbridge Prim Sch	
SW11 . . . . 168 A4	
Westbridge Rd	
SW11 . . . . 168 A4	
WEST BROMPTON . 156 A4	
West Brompton Sta	
SW5 . . . . 141 C1	
Westbrook Ho	
5 Bethnal Green	
E2 . . . . 25 B2

Westbrook Ho
continued
5 Clapham Pk
SW4 . . . . .61 B2
Westbury Ct SW4 . . .61 A1
Westbury Ho 6
NW10 . . . . .8 A1
Westbush Ct 1
W12 . . . . .39 A4
West Carriage Dr
W2 . . . . .116 A2
West Central St
WC1 . . . . .106 A2
Westchester Ho
W2 . . . . .102 C1
Westcliff Ho 13
N1 . . . . .87 C4
Westcombe Ct 1
SE3 . . . . .53 B3
Westcombe Hill SE3,
SE10 . . . . .53 C4
Westcombe Park Ho
SE3 . . . . .53 B3
Westcombe Park Sta
SE3 . . . . .43 C1
Westcott Ho 1
E14 . . . . .34 A2
Westcott Ho SE17 . .48 A4
West Cotts NW6 . . .10 C3
Westcroft Cl NW2 . .10 A4
Westcroft Ct 5
W6 . . . . .38 C2
Westcroft Sq W6 . . .38 C2
Westcroft Way
NW2 . . . . .10 A4
West Cromwell Rd
W14 . . . . .141 A2
West Cross Route W10,
W11 . . . . .30 C2
Westdean Cl
SW18 . . . . .59 A1
Westdown Rd E15 . .19 B4
WEST DULWICH . .75 B2
West Dulwich Sta
SE21 . . . . .75 C3
West Eaton Pl
SW1 . . . . .145 B4
West Eaton Pl Mews
SW1 . . . . .145 B4
West Ella Rd NW10 . .8 A1
West End Ct NW6 . .11 A1
West End La NW6 . .11 A2
westerdale Ct N5 . .15 A4
Westerdale Rd 2
SE10 . . . . .43 C1
Westerham NW1 . . .82 C3
Westerham Ho
SE1 . . . . .137 C2
Western Ave W3 . . .28 C3
Western Avenue Bsns
Pk W3 . . . . .20 A1
Western Beach Apts
E16 . . . . .35 C1
Western Ct
4 Dagenham W3 . . .28 C3
3 Kilburn W9 . . . . . .23 B3
Western Eye Hospl
The NW1 . . . . .102 C4
Western Gateway
E16 . . . . .35 C2
Western Ho 5
W9 . . . . .23 B1
Western La SW12 . . .72 C4
Western Mews
W9 . . . . .23 B1
Western Pl 19
SE16 . . . . .40 B4

Western Rd
Becontree NW10 . . .20 B1
Brixton SW9 . . . . .62 C4
Western Terr 3
W6 . . . . .38 C1
Western Wharf 2
SE15 . . . . .49 C4
Westferry Cir E14 . .33 C2
Westferry Rd E14 . .41 C3
Westferry Sta E14 . .33 C2
Westfield NW3 . . . . .10 C4
Westfield Cl
SW10 . . . . .156 C1
Westfield Ct 1
W10 . . . . .22 C2
Westfield Ho 6
SE16 . . . . .40 C2
Westfields SW13 . . .56 B4
Westfields Ave
SW13 . . . . .56 A4
Westfields Rd W3 . .28 A4
West Garden Pl
W2 . . . . .102 B1
Westgate Bsns Ctr
2 Kensal Town
W10 . . . . .23 A1
North Kensington
W10 . . . . .22 C1
Westgate Ct 15
SW9 . . . . .62 C4
Westgate St E8 . . . .25 A4
Westgate Terr
SW10 . . . . .156 B4
West Gdns E1 . . . . . .32 A2
West Gr SE10 . . . . . .52 C2
Westgrove La
SE10 . . . . .52 B2
West Halkin St
SW1 . . . . .131 B2
West Hall Rd TW9 . .45 A2
WEST HAMPSTEAD
. . . . .10 C4
West Hampstead
Mews NW6 . . . . . .11 A2
West Hampstead Sta
NW6 . . . . .10 C2
West Hampstead
Thameslink Sta
NW6 . . . . .10 C2
West Harding St
EC4 . . . . .107 C2
Westhay Gdns
SW14 . . . . .55 A2
West Heath Ave
NW11 . . . . .1 C3
West Heath Cl NW3 . .1 C1
West Heath Ct
NW11 . . . . .1 C3
West Heath Dr
NW11 . . . . .1 C3
West Heath Gdns
NW3 . . . . .1 C1
West Heath Rd
NW3 . . . . .2 A1
WEST HILL 58 B1
West Hill
Highgate N6 . . . . .3 C3
Putney SW15 . . . . . . .58 A1
West Hill Ct N6 . . . . .3 C1
West Hill Pk
Dartmouth Pk N6 . . .3 C2
Highgate N6 . . . . .3 B2
West Hill Prim Sch
SW18 . . . . .58 C2

West Hill Rd SW18 . .58 B1
West Ho 6 SW12 . . .73 B4
Westhope Ho
E2 . . . . .24 C2 99 C3
Westhorpe Rd
SW15 . . . . .57 B4
West House Cl
SW19 . . . . .70 A3
West India Ave
E14 . . . . .33 C2
West India Dock Rd
E14 . . . . .33 C2
West India Ho 1
E14 . . . . .33 C2
West India Quay Sta
E14 . . . . .33 C2
WEST KENSINGTON
. . . . .140 B3
West Kensington Ct
W14 . . . . .140 C3
West Kensington Mans
W14 . . . . .140 C2
West Kensington Sta
W14 . . . . .140 C3
WEST KILBURN . .23 A2
West La SE16 . . . . . . .40 A4
Westlake 12 SE16 . . .40 B2
Westland Pl N1 . . . .97 B4
Westlands Terr 3
SW12 . . . . .73 B4
Westleigh Ave
SW15 . . . . .57 B2
Westly Ct NW2 . . . . . .9 C2
Westmacott Ho
NW8 . . . . .89 C1
West Mall
W11 . . . . .31 C1 113 C2
Westmark Point 13
SW15 . . . . .69 A3
Westmead SW15 . . .57 A1
West Mews
SW1 . . . . .146 C3
Westmill Ct N4 . . . . . .6 B2
WESTMINSTER . . .133 A1
Westminster Abbey*
SW1 . . . . .133 C2
Westminster Abbey
Choir Sch SW1 . . .133 C2
Westminster Acad
W2 . . . . .102 A4
Westminster Acad
(Sch of English)
W1 . . . . .105 A2
Westminster Boating
Base SW1 . . . . .161 B4
Westminster Bridge
SE1, SW1 . . . . .134 C3
Westminster Bridge
Rd SE1 . . . . .134 C3
Westminster Cath
SW1 . . . . .132 C1
Westminster Cath
Choir Sch SW1 . . .147 A4
Westminster Cath RC
Prim Sch SW1 . . .133 A2
Westminster City Hall
SW1 . . . . .133 A2
Westminster City Sch
SW1 . . . . .133 A2
Westminster Ct
20 Rotherhithe
SE16 . . . . .32 C1
5 Wandsworth
SW18 . . . . .58 C2
Westminster Gdns
SW1 . . . . .148 A4

Westminster
Kingsway Coll
Battersea SW11 . . . .169 C4
St Pancras WC1 . . . . .94 C3
Westminster
Kingsway Coll
(Regent's Park Ctr)
NW1 . . . . .92 C3
Westminster Pier
SW1 . . . . .134 B3
Westminster Sch
SW1 . . . . .134 A2
Westminster Sta
SW1 . . . . .134 B3
Westminster Under
Sch SW1 . . . . .147 B3
Westmore Ct
SW15 . . . . .58 A2
Westmoreland Ho
NW10 . . . . .21 C2
Westmoreland Pl
SW1 . . . . .146 B1
Westmoreland Rd
Barnes SW13 . . . . . . .46 C2
Camberwell SE17 . . .48 C4
Westmoreland St
W1 . . . . .103 C3
Westmoreland Terr
SW1 . . . . .146 B1
WEST NORWOOD . .75 B1
West Norwood Sta
SE27 . . . . .75 A1
Westonbirt Ct 6
SE15 . . . . .49 B4
Weston Ct N4 . . . . . . .6 B1
Weston Ed Ctr The
SE5 . . . . .48 B1
West One Ho W1 . .104 C3
West One Sh Ctr
W1 . . . . .104 A1
Weston Ho
4 Brondesbury
NW6 . . . . .10 A1
8 South Hackney
E9 . . . . .25 B4
Weston Rise N1,
WC1 . . . . .95 A4
Weston St SE1 . .137 C2 138 A4
Weston Wlk 8 E8,
E9 . . . . .17 A1
Westover Ho 1 NW11 .1 C4
Westover Rd
SW18 . . . . .59 B1
West Park Ave
TW9 . . . . .45 A2
West Park Rd
TW9 . . . . .44 C2
West Parkside
Greenwich SE10 . . . .43 B3
Greenwich SE10 . . . .43 C2
West Plaza E14 . . . . .34 A1
Westpoint SW15 . . . .57 C1
West Point SE1 . . . .153 B2
Westpoint Trad Est
W3 . . . . .28 A4
Westport St E1 . . . . .32 C3
West Poultry Ave
EC1 . . . . .108 A3
West Quarters
W12 . . . . .29 C3
West Rd
Chelsea SW3 . . . . . .159 A4
Clapham Pk SW4 . . .61 C2
Westrow SW15 . . . . .57 B1

West Row W10 . . . . .23 A1
West Sheen Vale
TW9 . . . . .54 B3
Westside 11 W6 . . . .38 C3
Westside 5
W9 . . . . .23 B3
West Silvertown Sta
E16 . . . . .35 C1
West Smithfield
EC1 . . . . .108 B3
West Sq SE11 . . . . .136 A1
West St 50
2 Bethnal Green
E2 . . . . .25 A3
Soho WC2 . . . . .105 C1
West Temple Sheen
SW14 . . . . .55 A3
West Tenter St
E1 . . . . .111 A1
Westvale Mews
W3 . . . . .38 A4
Westview Cl
North Kensington
W10 . . . . .30 B3
Willesden NW10 . . . . .8 C3
Westville Rd W12 . . .38 C4
West Warwick Pl
SW1 . . . . .146 C3
Westway W10,
W12 . . . . .29 C3
Westway (Elevated
Rd) W10 . . . . .31 B4
Westway Lo 35
W2 . . . . .31 C4
Westwell 5 NW5 . . .12 C2
Westwick Gdns
W14 . . . . .39 C4
Westwood Bsns Ctr
NW10 . . . . .20 C1
Westwood Gdns
SW13 . . . . .56 B4
Westwood Ho
6 Shepherd's Bush
W12 . . . . .30 B1
5 Stoke Newington
N4 . . . . .6 C4
Westwood Park Trad
Est W3 . . . . .20 A1
Westwood Rd
SW13 . . . . .56 B4
Wetherby Gdns
SW5 . . . . .142 C3
Wetherby Mans
SW5 . . . . .142 A2
Wetherby Mews
SW5 . . . . .142 B2
Wetherby Pl SW7 . .143 A3
Wetherell Rd E9 . . . .25 C4
Wexco Wharf
SE15 . . . . .50 A4
Wexford Ho 11 E1 . .32 B4
Wexford Rd SW12 . .72 B4
Weybourne St
SW18 . . . . .71 B2
Weybridge Ct 19
SE16 . . . . .40 A1
Weybridge Ho N4 . . . .6 B4
Weybridge Point
SW11 . . . . .169 A2
Weydown Cl
SW19 . . . . .70 A3
Weyhill Ho 26 SE5 . .48 B1
Weyhill Rd E1 . . . . .111 C2
Wey Ho NW8 . . . . . . .89 C1

Weymouth Ct
- 5 Haggerston E2 ....24 B3
- 15 Streatham SW2 ..74 B4

Weymouth Ho
- Fitzrovia W1 ....104 B4
- South Lambeth
  SW8 ....162 C1

Weymouth Mews
- W1 ....104 A4

Weymouth St W1 104 A4

Weymouth Terr
- E2 ....24 B3

Whadcoat St N4....5 C2

Whaddon Ho
- 10 Camberwell
  SE5 ....64 A4
- SW11 ....131 A3

Wharfdale Rd N1...84 B2

Wharfedale St 5
- E5 ....17 C4

Wharfedale St
- SW10 ....142 A1

Wharf La 19 E14....33 B3

Wharf Pl E2 ....25 A4

Wharf Rd
- King's Cross NW1 ...83 C3
- Shoreditch N1 .....86 C1

Wharf Road NW1...84 A2

Wharfside Rd E16 ..35 A4

Wharf St E16 ....35 A4

Wharf View Ct 13
- E14 ....34 B3

Wharncliffe Ho 3
- SW15 ....57 B2

Wharton Cl NW10 ...8 A2

Wharton St WC1 .138 C2

Wharton St WC1....95 A3

Whateley Rd SE22 .64 B2

Whatman Ho 10
- E14 ....33 B3

Wheatland Ho 7
- SE22 ....64 A4

Wheatlands Rd
- SW17 ....72 C1

Wheatley Ho
- Gospel Oak NW5 ....13 A4
- 3 Putney SW15 ....68 C4

Wheatley St W1 ...103 C3

Wheat Sheaf Cl
- E14 ....42 A2

Wheatsheaf La
- Fulham SW6 ....47 B3
- SW8 ....162 A2

Wheatsheaf Terr
- SW6 ....155 A1

Wheatstone Ho 7
- W10 ....31 A4

Wheatstone Rd
- W10 ....31 A4

Wheeler Ct 8
- SW11 ....59 C4

Wheeler Gdns N1 ..84 B4

Wheeler La E1 .....110 C4

Wheelhouse The 4
- E14 ....42 A1

Wheelwright St
- N7 ....14 B1

Wheldon Ct SE1 ..138 C4

Wheler Ho
- E1 ....24 B1 98 C2

Wheler St
- E1 ....24 B1 98 C2

Whellock Rd W4 ...38 A3

Whetstone Park
- WC2 ....106 C2

Whewell Rd N19 ....5 A2

Whichcote St
- SE1 ....121 B1

Whidborne Bldgs
- WC1 ....94 A3

Whidborne Cl SE8 .51 C1

Whidborne St
- WC1 ....94 B3

Whippingham Ho 22
- E3 ....26 B2

Whiskin St EC1 .....96 A3

Whistler Mews 27
- SE15 ....49 B3

Whistlers Ave
- SW11 ....157 C1

Whistler St N5 .....15 A3

Whistler Twr
- SW10 ....156 C1

Whistler Wlk
- SW10 ....157 A2

Whiston Rd E2 ......24 C4

Whitbread Ct EC1 ..97 B1

Whitbread Rd SE4 .66 B3

Whitburn Rd SE13 .67 B3

Whitby Av NW10 ...20 A2

Whitby Ct 6 N7 ....14 A4

Whitby Ho NW8 ....78 C3

Whitby St
- E1 ....24 B1 98 C2

Whitcher Cl SE14 ..51 A4

Whitcher Pl NW1 ...13 B2

Whitchurch Ho 18
- W10 ....30 C3

Whitchurch Rd
- W11 ....30 C2

Whitcomb Ct W1 ..119 C3

Whitcomb St
- WC2 ....119 C3

Whitcome Mews
- TW9 ....45 A2

Whiteacre Mews
- SE11 ....149 C1

Whiteadder Way
- E14 ....42 A2

Whitear Wlk E15 ...19 C2

Whitebeam Cl
- SW9 ....163 A1

Whitebeam Ho 3
- NW3 ....12 B2

White Bear Pl 1
- NW3 ....11 C4

White Bear Yd
- EC1 ....95 B1

WHITECHAPEL ..110 C1

Whitechapel High St
- E1 ....111 A2

Whitechapel Mkt
- E1 ....111 A3

Whitechapel Rd
- E1 ....32 A4

Whitechapel Sta
- E1 ....32 A4

Whitechurch La
- E1 ....111 B2

Whitechurch Pas
- E1 ....111 B2

White City W10 ....30 B3

White City W12....30 B3

White City Est
- W12 ....30 A2

White City Rd
- W12 ....30 B2

White City Sta
- W12 ....30 B2

Whitecliff Ho
- SW18 ....59 A1

White Conduit St
- N1 ....85 C2

Whitecross Pl
- EC2 ....109 C4

Whitecross St EC1 .97 A1

White Cube The, The Art Gallery*
- N1 ....24 A2 98 A4

Whitfield Cl
- SE15 ....50 B3

Whitfield St
- EC4 ....107 C1

Whitehall SW1 ....134 A4

Whitehall Ct SW1 120 B1

Whitehall Gdns
- Chiswick W4 ....45 A4
- SW1 ....120 A1

Whitehall Mans 3
- N19 ....4 B3

Whitehall Park Rd
- W4 ....45 A4

Whitehall Pk N19 ...4 B3

Whitehall Pl WC2,
- SW1 ....120 A1

White Hart La
- Mortlake SW13 .....56 A4
- Willesden NW10 ...22 A4

White Hart St
- Holborn EC4 ....108 B2
- Kennington SE11 ..149 C2

White Hart Yd
- SE1 ....123 B1

Whitehaven St
- NW8 ....90 A1

Whitehead Cl
- SW18 ....71 B4

Whitehead Ho 8
- SW15 ....57 C2

Whitehead's Gr
- SW3 ....144 B3

Whitehorn Ho 6
- E1 ....32 B1

White Horse La
- E1 ....32 C4

Whitehorse Mews
- SE1 ....136 C2

Whitehorse Rd E1,3 33 A4

White Horse Rd
- E1 ....33 A3

White Horse St
- W1 ....118 B1

White Horse Yd
- EC2 ....109 B2

White Ho The
- NW1 ....92 B2

White Kennett St
- E1 ....110 B2

Whitelands Cres
- SW18 ....70 A4

Whitelands Ho
- SW3 ....145 A2

Whiteley Ho 9
- SW4 ....73 C4

Whiteleys Ctr W2 100 B1

White Lion Ct
- EC3 ....110 A1

White Lion Hill
- EC4 ....122 B4

White Lion St N1 ...85 C1

White Lion Yd 5
- W1 ....118 B3

White Lyon Ct
- EC2 ....108 C4

Whiteness Ho
- SW9 ....173 B4

White Post La E9...18 C2

White Post St SE14,
- SE15 ....50 B3

White's Grounds
- SE1 ....138 B4

White's Grounds Est
- SE1 ....138 B4

White's Row E1 ...110 C3

White's Sq SW4 ....61 C3

Whitestone La NW3 .2 B1

Whitestone Wlk
- NW3 ....2 B1

Whitethorn St E3 ..33 C4

Whitfield Ct SW4 ..172 A3

Whitfield Gdns
- W1 ....105 A4

Whitfield Ho NW8 ..90 A1

Whitfield Pl W1 .....93 A1

Whitfield St W1 ...105 A4

Whitgift Ho
- Battersea SW11 ...168 A4
- Lambeth SE11 .....148 C4

Whitgift St SE11 ..148 C4

Whitington Ave
- EC3 ....110 A1

Whitley Ho SW1 ...147 B4

Whitlock Dr SW19 .70 A4

Whitman Ho 20
- E2 ....25 B2

Whitman Rd E3 .....26 A1

Whitmore Gdns
- NW10 ....22 B2

Whitmore Ho 20
- E1 ....24 A4

Whitmore Prim Sch
- N1 ....87 C3

Whitmore Rd N1 ...24 A4

Whitnell Ct 7
- SW15 ....57 C2

Whitnell Way
- SW15 ....57 C2

Whitney Ho 6
- SE22 ....64 A4

Whitstable Ho 11
- W10 ....30 C3

Whitsters Ho SE1 138 C4

Whittaker Ct
- SW4 ....172 B3

Whittaker St SW1 145 B3

Whittaker Way
- SE1 ....153 C4

Whittingham Ct
- W4 ....46 A3

Whittingstall Mans
- SW6 ....165 A3

Whittingstall Rd
- SW6 ....165 A3

Whittington Hospl
- The N19 ....4 B2

Whittlebury Ho N4 ...6 B4

Whittlesey St SE1 121 C1

Whitton NW3 ....12 B1

Whitton Wlk E3 ....26 C2

Whitworth Ho
- SE1 ....137 A1

Whitworth St
- SE10 ....43 A1

Whorlton Rd SE15 .65 A4

Whyfaw Ho 10 E3 ..33 B4

Wicker St 24 E1 ....32 A3

Wickfield Ho
- SE16 ....139 C3

Wickford Ho 5
- E1 ....25 B1

Wickford St E1 .....25 B1

Wickham Cl E1.....32 B4

Wickham Gdns
- SE4 ....66 B4

Wickham Ho
- SW15 ....57 C1

Wickham Mews
- SE4 ....51 B1

Wickham Rd SE4 ...66 B4

Wickham St SE11 148 C2

Wick La
- Hackney E3 ....18 B1
- Stratford Marsh E3 .26 C4

Wicklow Ho N16 ....7 B3

Wicklow St WC1 ...94 C4

Wick Rd
- Hackney E9 ....17 C2
- Hackney E9 ....18 A2

Wickstead Ho
- TW8 ....36 B1

Wicksteed Ho
- SE1 ....137 A1

Wickway Ct 7
- SE15 ....49 B4

Wickwood St SE5 .48 A1

Widdenham Rd
- N7 ....14 B4

Widecombe Ho 32
- SE5 ....48 B1

Widegate St E1 ...110 B3

Widford 3 NW1 ....13 A2

Widford Ho N1 ......86 A1

Widley Rd W9 ......23 C1

Widnes Ho 6 N7 ...14 C3

Wigmore Hall*
- W1 ....104 A2

Wigmore Pl W1 ...104 A2

Wigmore St W1 ...103 C2

Wigram Ct SW11 ..168 A4

Wigram Ho 7
- E14 ....34 A2

Wigton Pl SE11 ...149 C1

Wilberforce Ho 4
- SW11 ....59 C4

Wilberforce Mews 9
- SW4 ....61 C3

Wilberforce Prim Sch
- W10 ....23 A2

Wilberforce Rd
- Finsbury Pk N4 ....6 A2
- Highbury N4, N5 .....6 B1

Wilbraham Ho
- SW8 ....162 A1

Wilbraham Pl
- SW1 ....145 B3

Wilby Mews
- W11 ....31 B1 113 A2

Wilcox Cl SW8 ....162 B2

Wilcox Ho 5 E3 ....33 B4

Wilcox Pl SW1 ....133 A1

Wilcox Rd SW8 ....162 A2

Wildcroft Manor
- SW15 ....69 B4

Wildcroft Rd
- SW15 ....69 B4

Wild Ct WC2 ....106 C2

Wilde Cl E8 ....24 C4

Wilde Pl SW18 .....71 C4

Wilderness Mews
- SW4 ....61 A3

Wilderton Rd N16 ...7 A4

Wild Goose Dr
- SE14 ....50 B2

Wilding Ho 17 E9 ..17 C2

Wild's Rents SE1 138 A2

Wild St WC2 ....106 C1

Wildwood Gr NW3 ...2 B3

Wildwood Rd NW11 .2 B4

Wildwood Rise
NW11 . . . . 2 B3
Wildwood Terr
NW3 . . . . 2 B3
Wilfred Fienburgh Ho
N7 . . . . .13 C4
Wilfred St SW1 . . . . . 132 C2
Wilfrid Gdns W3 . . . . . 28 B4
Wilkes Rd 3 TW8 . . . . 44 A4
Wilkes St E1 . . . . 111 A4
Wilkie Ho SW1 . . . . . 147 C2
Wilkins Ho SW1 . . . . 160 C4
Wilkinson Ho N1 . . . . . 87 C1
Wilkinson St SW8 . . . 162 C1
Wilkinson Way
W4 . . . . 37 C4
Wilks Pl N1 . . . . 24 A3
Willan Wall E16 . . . . . 35 B2
Willard St SW8 . . . . . . 61 A4
Wilbury Ho 4 N7 . .13 C3
Willcott Rd W3 . . . . . . 28 A1
Willenfield Rd
NW10 . . . . 20 B3
WILLESDEN 8 B1
Willesden Community
Hospl TW NW10 . . . . 8 C1
WILLESDEN GREEN
. . . . 22 A4
Willesden Green Sta
NW2 . . . . 9 B2
Willesden Junction
Sta NW10 . . . . 21 B2
Willesden La NW2,
NW6 . . . . 9 C2
Willes Rd NW5 . . . . . 13 A2
Willett Ho 7 . . . . 62 A4
William Banfield Ho
SW6 . . . . 164 C2
William Blake Ho 2
SE1 . . . . 49 C1
William Bonney Est SW
SW4 . . . . 61 C3
William Booth Meml
Training Coll SE5 . .48 C1
William Brown Ct
SE27 . . . . 75 A2
William Caslon Ho 28
E2 . . . . 25 A3
William Channing Ho
8 E2 . . . . 25 A2
William Cl SE13 . . . . . 67 B4
William Davis Prim
Sch E2 . . . . 24 C1 99 B2
William Dromey Ct
NW6 . . . . 10 B1
William Dunbar Ho
NW6 . . . . 23 B3
William Ellis Sch
NW5 . . . . 3 C1
William Ellis Way
SE16 . . . . 139 C1
William Evans Ho 9
SE8 . . . . 40 C2
William Gdns
SW15 . . . . 57 A2
William Guy Gdns 47
E3 . . . . 27 A2
William Harvey Ho 5
SW19 . . . . 70 A3
William Hogarth Prim
Sch The W4 . . . . . . 38 A1
William Hunt Mans
SW13 . . . . 47 B4
William IV St
WC2 . . . . 120 A3

William Margrie Cl 1
SE15 . . . . 49 C1
William Mews
SW1 . . . . 131 A3
William Morris Acad
W6 . . . . 39 C1
William Morris Ho
W6 . . . . 47 C3
William Morris Way
SW6 . . . . 166 C1
William Patten Prim
Sch N16 . . . . 7 B2
William Pl 2 E3 . . . . 26 B3
William Rathbone
Ho SE16 . . . . 153 B4
William Rushbrooke
Ho SE16 . . . . 153 B4
William Saville Ho 3
NW6 . . . . 23 B3
William's Bldgs 1
E2 . . . . 25 B1
Williams Cl SW6 . . . 154 B2
Williams Coll EC1 . . 107 C3
Williams Ho
10 Bow E3 . . . . 26 C2
7 Hackney E9 . . . . . 25 A4
14 Streatham SW2 . .74 C3
Williams La SW14 . . 45 B1
Williamson Cl
SE10 . . . . 43 B1
Williamson Ct
SE17 . . . . 150 C1
Williamson St N7 . .14 A4
William Sq 15
SE16 . . . . 33 A2
William St SW1 . . . . 131 A3
William Tyndale Prim
Sch N1 . . . . 15 A1
William Winter Ct 29
SW2 . . . . 74 C3
Willingham Cl 4
NW5 . . . . 13 B3
Willingham Terr
NW5 . . . . 13 B3
Willington Rd
SW9 . . . . 62 A4
Willis Ho 8 E14 . . . . 34 A3
Willis St E14 . . . . . . 34 A3
Willoughby Ho
EC2 . . . . 109 B3
34 Wapping E1 . . . . 32 A1
Willoughby Rd
NW3 . . . . 11 C4
Willoughby St
WC1 . . . . 106 A3
Willoughbys The
SW14 . . . . 56 A3
Willow Ave SW13 . .46 B1
Willowbank SW6 . . . 58 A4
Willowbank Rd
SE15 . . . . 49 B4
Willow Bridge Rd
N1 . . . . 15 B2
Willow Cotts TW9 . . 44 C4
Willow Ct
Brixton SW9 . . . . . 173 B3
Chiswick W4 . . . . . . 46 A3
EC2 . . . . . . 24 A1 98 A2
Islington N7 . . . . 14 B3
40 Paddington W2 . . 31 C4
3 Streatham SW16 . .74 C1
Willowdene
Highgate N6 . . . . 3 B4
1 Peckham SE15 . . . 49 C3
5 SE15 . . . . 50 A3

Willow Farm La
SW15 . . . . 57 A4
Willow Hall NW3 . .11 C4
Willow Ho
9 Maitland Pk
NW3 . . . . 12 B2
North Kensington
W10 . . . . 23 B2
Willow Lo
Fulham SW6 . . . . . . 47 C2
Putney SW15 . . . . . 57 A4
Willow Lodge 10
SW8 . . . . 61 A4
Willowmere SE13. . . . 67 A3
Willow Pl SW1 . . . . 147 A4
Willow Rd
Ealing W5 . . . . 36 A4
Hampstead NW3 . . . 11 C4
Willow St
EC2 . . . . . . 24 A1 98 A2
Willows Terr
NW10 . . . . 21 B3
Willow Tree Cl
10 Old Ford E3 . . . . 26 B4
Wandsworth SW18 . .71 A3
Willow Vale W12 . . . 29 C1
Willow Way 3
W11 . . . . 30 C2
Willow Wlk SE1 . . . 152 C4
Willsbridge Ct 1
SE15 . . . . 49 B4
Wilman Gr E8 . . . . . 16 C1
Wilmcote Ho W2 . . 100 A4
Wilmer Gdns 22
N1 . . . . 24 A4
Wilmer Ho 6 E3 . . . 26 A3
Wilmer Lea Cl
E15 . . . . 19 C1
Wilmer Pl N16 . . . . 7 B2
Wilmers Ct 5
NW10 . . . . 20 C4
Wilmington Ave
W4 . . . . 45 C3
Wilmington Sq
WC1 . . . . 95 B3
Wilmington St
WC1 . . . . 95 B3
Wilmot Cl SE15 . . . . 49 C3
Wilmot Pl NW1 . . . . 13 B1
Wilmot St E2 . . . . . . 25 A1
Wilna Rd SW18 . . . . 71 B4
Wilsham St
W11 . . . . . 31 A1 112 A2
Wilshaw Ho 10
SE8 . . . . 51 C3
Wilshaw St SE14 . . . 51 C2
Wilson Gr SE16 . . . . 40 A4
Wilson Ho
Clapham SW8 . . . . 171 B1
South Hampstead
NW6 . . . . 11 B1
Wilson Rd SE5 . . . . . 49 A2
Wilson's Pl E14 . . . . 33 B3
Wilson's Rd W6 . . . . 39 C1
Wilson St EC2 . . . . 109 C4
Wiltern Ct NW2 . . . . 10 A2
Wilton Ave W4 . . . . . 38 A1
Wilton Cres SW1 . . 131 B3
Wilton Ct
7 Richmond
TW10 . . . . 54 A2
3 Stepney E1 . . . . . 32 A3
Wilton Est E8 . . . . . . 16 C2
Wilton Ho 3 SE22 . . 64 A4
Wilton Mews
SW1 . . . . 131 C2
Wilton Pl SW1 . . . . 131 B3

Wilton Rd SW1 . . . . 146 C4
Wilton Row SW1 . . 131 B3
Wilton Sq N1 . . . . . . 87 B4
Wilton St SW1 . . . . 132 A2
Wilton Terr SW1 . . 131 B2
Wilton Villas N1 . . . . 87 B3
Wilton Way E8 . . . . . 16 C2
Wiltshire Cl SW3 . . 144 C3
Wiltshire Ct 2 N4 . . 5 B3
Wiltshire Rd SW9 . . 62 C4
Wiltshire Row N1 . . . 87 C3
Wimbart Rd SW2 . . . 74 B4
Wimbledon Lawn
Tennis Mus*
SW19 . . . . 70 C1
Wimbledon Park Ct
SW19 . . . . 70 B3
Wimbledon Park
Montessori Sch
SW18 . . . . 70 C2
Wimbledon Park Prim
Sch SW19 . . . . 71 A2
Wimbledon Park Rd
SW18, SW19 . . . . . 70 B3
Wimbledon Park Side
SW19 . . . . 69 C3
Wimbledon Park Sta
SW19 . . . . 70 C1
Wimbledon Stadium
Bsns Ctr SW17 . . . 71 C1
Wimbledon Windmill
Mus* SW19 . . . . . . 69 A1
Wimholt St
E2 . . . . 24 C2 99 B4
Wimborne Ho
Canning Town E16 . . 35 B2
Marylebone NW1 . . . 90 B1
South Lambeth
SW8 . . . . 163 A1
Upper Tooting
SW17 . . . . 73 B1
Wimborne Ct N1 . . . 87 B2
Wimborne Ho N1 . . . 87 B2
Wimpole Mews
W1 . . . . 104 A3
Wimpole St W1 . . . . 104 A2
Winans Wlk SW9 . . 173 B1
Winant Ho 10 E14 . . 34 A2
Wincanton Rd
SW18 . . . . 70 B4
Winchcombe Cl
SW15 . . . . 57 C2
Winchelsea Cl
SW15 . . . . 57 C2
Winchelsea Ho 10
SE16 . . . . 40 B4
Winchelsea Rd
NW10 . . . . 20 C4
Winchendon Rd
SW6 . . . . 165 A4
Winchester Ave
NW6 . . . . 10 A1
Winchester Cl
SE17 . . . . 150 B3
Winchester Ct
Richmond TW9 . . . . 54 B4
W8 . . . . 128 A4
Winchester Ho
Bayswater W2 . . . . 100 C1
Chelsea SW3 . . . . . 157 C3
22 Tower Hamlets
E3 . . . . 26 B2
Winchester Pal*
SE1 . . . . 123 B2
Winchester Pl
6 Dalston E8 . . . . . 16 B3
Highgate N6 . . . . 4 A3
Winchester Rd
Highgate N6 . . . . 4 A3

Winchester Rd
continued
South Hampstead
NW3 . . . . 11 C1
Winchester Sq
SE1 . . . . 123 B2
Winchester St
Acton W3 . . . . 37 B4
SW1 . . . . 146 B2
Winchester Wlk
SE1 . . . . 123 B2
Winchfield Ho
SW15 . . . . 56 B1
Winch Ho
Isle of Dogs E14 . . . 42 A3
SW10 . . . . 157 A2
Winchilsea Ho
NW8 . . . . 89 C3
Wincott St SE11 . . . 149 C3
Windermere NW1 . . . 92 B4
2 Putney SW15 . . . 57 C1
Windermere Ho
NW6 . . . . 23 A4
Windermere Ct
SW13 . . . . 46 B4
Windermere Ho
E3 . . . . 26 B1
Windermere Point 3
SE15 . . . . 50 B3
Windermere Rd
N19 . . . . 4 B2
Winders Rd SW11 . . 168 A2
Windham Rd TW9 . . 54 B4
Windlass Pl SE8 . . . . 41 A2
Windlesham Gr
SW19 . . . . 69 C3
Windmill WC1 . . . . 106 C4
Windmill Alley 7
W4 . . . . 38 A2
Windmill Cl
Bermondsey SE1 . . 153 C4
4 Lewisham SE13 . . 52 B1
Windmill Ct NW2 . . 10 A2
Windmill Dr
Clapham SW4 . . . . . 61 A2
Cricklewood NW2 . . 1 A1
Windmill Gdns
SW9 . . . . 60 B1
Windmill Hill
Hampstead NW3 . . . 2 B1
1 Hampstead NW3 . . 11 B4
Windmill Ho
4 Millwall E14 . . . . 41 C2
SE1 . . . . 121 C1
Windmill La E15 . . . 19 C2
Windmill Pas 9
W4 . . . . 38 A2
Windmill Rd
Chiswick W4 . . . . . . 38 A2
Roehampton SW19 . 69 A1
Wandsworth SW18 . 59 C1
Windmill Row
SE11 . . . . 149 B1
Windmill St W1 . . . 105 B3
Windmill Wlk
SE1 . . . . 135 C4
Windrush Cl
Battersea SW11 . . . . 59 C3
Chiswick W4 . . . . . . 45 B3
Windrush Ho
NW8 . . . . 101 C4
Windrush Rd
NW10 . . . . 20 C4

Windsock Cl ◨
SE16 . . . . 41 B2
Windsor Ct
Battersea SW11 . . **167** C2
Bayswater W2 . . . **114** A4
Chelsea SW3 . . . . **144** B1
☑ Clapham SW4 . . . 61 B3
Fulham SW6 . . . . . . 58 A4
⁰ Rotherhithe
SE16 . . . . 32 C1
☑ Wandsworth
SW18 . . . . 58 C2
West Hampstead
NW3 . . . . 10 C4
Windsor Gdns W9 . . 23 C1
Windsor Ho
☑ Acton Green
W4 . . . . 37 B1
Brondesbury NW2 . 10 A2
⁴ Globe Town E2 . . 25 C2
Regent's Pk NW1 . . 92 B4
Shoreditch N1 . . . . 97 A2
Stoke Newington N4 . . 6 B3
Windsor Pl SW1 . . **147** A4
Windsor Rd
Richmond TW9 . . . . 44 B1
Upper Holloway N7 . . 5 A1
Willesden NW2 . . . . 9 A2
Windsor St N1 . . . **86** B4
Windsor Terr N1 . . **97** A4
Windsor Way
W14 . . . . **140** A4
Windsor Wharf E9 . 18 B3
Windsor Wlk SE5 . . 48 C1
Windspoint Dr
SE15 . . . . 50 A4
Windus Rd N16 . . . . 7 B3
Windus Wlk N16 . . . 7 B3
Wine Cl E1 . . . . 32 B2
Wine Office Ct
EC4 . . . . **107** C2
Winfield Ho
SW11 . . . . **167** C2
Winford Ct ◨
SE15 . . . . 49 C2
Winforton St SE10 . 52 B2
Winfrith Rd SW18 . . 71 B3
Wingate Ho
⁰ Bromley E3 . . . . 27 A2
⁸ Stoke Newington
N16 . . . . 15 C4
Wingate Rd W6 . . . 39 A3
Wingfield Ct ◨
E14 . . . . 34 C2
Wingfield Ho
Paddington NW6 . . **78** A2
Spitalfields
E2 . . . . 24 B2 **98** C3
Wingfield Mews
SE15 . . . . 64 C4
Wingfield St SE15 . . 64 C4
Wingford Rd SW2 . . 62 A1
Wingham ⁸ NW5 . . 12 C2
Wingmore Rd
SE24 . . . . 63 B4
Wingrad Ho ◨ E1 . . 32 B4
Wingrave SE17 . . . **151** B3
Wingrave Rd W6 . . . 47 B4
Wingreen ⁷ NW8 . . **78** B4
Winicotte Ho W2 . **101** C4
Winifrede Paul Ho ☑
NW5 . . . . 13 A4
Winkley St ⁶ E2 . . . 25 A3

Winkworth Cotts ◨
E1 . . . . 25 B1
Winnett St W1 . . . **119** B4
Winnington Ho
⚹ Kensal Town
W10 . . . . 23 A1
⁸ SE5 . . . . 48 B3
Winscombe St N19 . . 4 B2
Winsham Gr
SW11 . . . . 60 C2
Winsham Ho NW1 . . **93** C4
Winslade Rd SW2 . . **62** A2
Winsland Mews
W2 . . . . **101** B3
Winsland St W2 . . . **101** B3
Winsley St W1 . . . **105** A2
Winslow SE17 . . . . **152** A1
Winslow Rd W6 . . . . 47 B4
Winstanley Rd
SW11 . . . . 59 C4
Winston Ho WC1 . . . **93** C2
Winston Rd N16 . . . 15 C4
Winston Wlk ☑
W4 . . . . 37 C2
Winterbourne Ho
W11 . . . . . . 31 A2 **112** A3
Winter Box Wlk
TW10 . . . . 54 B2
Winterbrook Rd
SE24 . . . . 63 B1
Winterfold Cl
SW19 . . . . 70 A2
Winterleys ⁷
NW6 . . . . 23 B3
Winter Lo SE16 . . . **153** C1
Winterslow Ho ⁴
SE5 . . . . 48 B1
Winterton Ho ◨
E1 . . . . 32 B3
Winterton Pl
SW10 . . . . **157** A4
Winterwell Rd
SW2 . . . . 62 A2
Winthorpe Rd
SW15 . . . . 58 A3
Winthrop Ho ◨
W12 . . . . 30 A2
Winthrop St E1 . . . . 32 A4
Winton Prim Sch
N1 . . . . **84** C1
Wirrall Ho ◨
SE26 . . . . 76 C1
Wisbech ⁵ N4 . . . . . . 5 B3
Wisden Ho SW8 . . . **163** A3
Wise Rd E15 . . . . . . 27 C4
Wiseton Rd SW17 . . 72 B3
Wisley Ho SW1 . . . **147** B2
Wisley Rd SW11 . . . 60 C2
Wisteria Ho SE4 . . . 66 A4
Wisteria Rd SE13 . . 67 C3
Wistow Ho ◨ E2 . . . 24 C4
Witanhurst La N6 . . . 3 C3
Witan St E2 . . . . . . 25 A2
Witchwood Ho ⁰
SW9 . . . . 62 C4
Witcombe Point ◨
SE15 . . . . 49 C2
Witham Ct SW17 . . . 72 B1
Witham Ho ⁸ SE5 . . 48 B1
Witherington Rd
N5 . . . . 14 C3
Withers Pl EC1 . . . . . 97 A3
Withycombe Rd
SW19 . . . . 69 C4
Withy Ho ⁴ E1 . . . . 25 C1
Witley Ct WC1 . . . . **94** A1
Witley Ho ☑ SW2 . . **74** B4

Witley Point ⁸
SW15 . . . . 69 A3
Witley Rd N19 . . . . . 4 B2
Wittering Ho
SW11 . . . . **169** A2
Wivenhoe Cl SE15 . . 65 A4
Wix Prim Sch
SW4 . . . . 61 A3
Wix's La SW4 . . . . . 61 A3
Woburn Ct
⁸² Bermondsey
SE16 . . . . 40 A1
Richmond TW9 . . . . 54 B4
Woburn Pl WC1 . . . . **94** A1
Woburn Sq WC1 . . . **93** C1
Woburn Wlk WC1 . . **93** C3
Wodehouse Gdns ◨
E1 . . . . 32 A4
Wodehouse Ave
SE15 . . . . 49 B2
Wodehouse Ct ◨
SW10 . . . . **157** A1
Woking Cl SW15 . . . 56 B3
Wolcot Ho NW1 . . . **83** A1
Wolfe Cres ⁴
SE16 . . . . 40 C4
Wolfe Ho ◨ W12 . . . 30 A2
Wolfson Ct
Golders Green
NW11 . . . . 1 A4
SE1 . . . . **139** A4
Wolftencroft Cl
SW11 . . . . 59 C4
Wollaston Cl SE1 . . **150** C4
Wollotan Ho N1 . . . **85** C2
Wolseley Ave SW18,
SW19 . . . . 70 C1
Wolseley Gdns
W4 . . . . 45 A4
Wolseley Rd W4 . . . 37 B2
Wolseley St SE1 . . . **139** A3
Wolsey Ho ⁸
NW5 . . . . 13 C2
Wolsey Mews
NW5 . . . . 13 C2
Wolsey Rd N1 . . . . . 15 C3
Wolsey St E1 . . . . . 32 B4
Wolverley St E2 . . . 25 A2
Wolverton SE17 . . . **152** A2
Wolverton Gdns
W6 . . . . 39 C2
Wontner Cl ⁵ N1 . . . 15 B1
Wontner Rd SW12,
SW17 . . . . 72 B2
Woodall Cl ◨ E14 . . 34 A2
Woodberry Down
N4 . . . . 6 B4
Woodberry Down
Com Prim Sch N4 . . 6 B4
Woodberry Gr N4 . . . 6 B4
Woodbine Terr ⁹ E9 . 17 B2
Woodborough Rd
SW15 . . . . 57 A3
Woodbourne Ave
SW16 . . . . 73 C1
Woodbourne Cl
SW16 . . . . 74 A1
Woodbridge Cl ◨
N7 . . . . 5 B2
Woodbridge Ct
N16 . . . . 6 C1
Woodbridge St
EC1 . . . . **96** A2
Woodchester Sq
W2 . . . . **100** A4

Woodchurch Ho
SW9 . . . . **173** B4
Woodchurch Rd
NW6 . . . . 11 A1
Wood Cl E2 . . 24 C1 **99** B2
Woodcock Ho ◨
E14 . . . . 33 C4
Woodcote Ho ⁴
SE8 . . . . 51 B4
Woodcott Ho ◨
SW15 . . . . 68 C4
Woodcroft Mews
SE8 . . . . 41 A2
Wood Dene ⁸
SE15 . . . . 50 A2
Woodfall Rd N4 . . . . 5 C2
Woodfall St SW3 . . **144** C1
Woodfarrs SE5 . . . . 63 C3
Wood Field NW3 . . . 12 B3
Woodfield Ave
SW16 . . . . 73 C1
Woodfield Ct
SW16 . . . . 73 C1
Woodfield Gr
SW16 . . . . 73 C1
Woodfield Pl W9 . . . 23 B1
Woodfield Rd W9 . . . 31 B4
Woodford Ct ◨
W12 . . . . 39 C4
Woodger Rd W12 . . . 39 B4
Woodhall ◨ NW1 . . **92** C3
Woodhall Dr SE21 . . 76 B1
Woodhall Ho ◨
SW18 . . . . 59 C1
Woodheyes Rd
NW10 . . . . 8 A3
Wood Ho
Clapham SW4 . . . **171** C2
☑ Paddington NW6 . 23 B3
Woodhurst Rd W3 . . 28 B2
Woodison St E3 . . . 26 A1
Wood La W12 . . . . 30 B2
Woodland Cres
◨ Rotherhithe
SE16 . . . . 40 C4
SE10 . . . . 52 C3
Woodland Gr
SE10 . . . . 43 A1
Woodland Hts
SE3 . . . . 53 A4
Woodland Mews
SW16 . . . . 74 A1
Woodlands SW4 . . . 61 A3
Woodlands Ave
W3 . . . . 28 A1
Woodlands Ct
NW10 . . . . 22 C4
Woodlands Gt
SW15 . . . . 58 B2
Woodlands Park Rd
SE10 . . . . 43 A1
Woodlands Rd
SW13 . . . . 56 B4
Woodland St ⁸
E8 . . . . 16 B2
Woodlands The
Highbury N5 . . . . . 15 B4
⁸² Hornsey N8 . . . . . 5 A4
Woodlands Way
SW15 . . . . 58 B2
Woodland Wlk
⁰ Greenwich
SE10 . . . . 43 A1
Hampstead NW3 . . 12 A3

Wood Lane High Sch
W12 . . . . 30 A3
Woodlawn Cl
SW15 . . . . 58 B2
Woodlawn Rd
SW6 . . . . 47 C2
Woodlea Rd N16 . . . 7 A1
Woodleigh Gdns
SW16 . . . . 74 A1
Woodman Mews
TW9 . . . . 45 A2
Woodmans Gr
NW10 . . . . 8 B3
Woodmans Mews
W12 . . . . 30 A4
Woodmere Cl ⁸
SW11 . . . . 60 C4
Woodpecker Mews
SE13 . . . . 67 C3
Woodpecker Rd ⁰
SE14 . . . . 51 A4
Wood Point ◨
E16 . . . . 35 C4
Woodquest Ave
SE24 . . . . 63 B2
Woodruff Ho ◨
SW2 . . . . 62 C1
Woodrush Cl ⁴
SE14 . . . . 51 A3
Woodseer St E1 . . . **111** B4
Woodsford SE17 . . . **151** B1
Woodsford Sq
W14 . . . . **126** B4
Woods Ho SW8 . . . **170** C4
Wood's Mews W1 . **117** B4
Woodsome Rd
NW5 . . . . 4 A1
Wood's Pl SE1 . . . . **138** B1
Woodspring Rd
SW19 . . . . 70 A2
Woods Rd SE15 . . . 50 A2
Wood St
Chiswick W4 . . . . . 38 A1
City of London EC2 **109** A2
Woodstar Ho ⁸
SE15 . . . . 49 C3
Woodstock Ave
NW11 . . . . 1 A4
Woodstock Ct
SE11 . . . . **149** A2
Woodstock Gr
W12 . . . . 39 C4
Woodstock Ho ⁸
SW15 . . . . 15 B4
Woodstock Mews
W1 . . . . **103** C3
Woodstock Rd
Bedford Pk W4 . . . . 38 A3
Finsbury Pk N4 . . . . 5 C3
Golders Green NW11 . 1 B3
Woodstock St
W1 . . . . **104** A1
Woodstock Studios ◨
W12 . . . . 39 C4
Woodstock Terr
E14 . . . . 34 A2
Woodthorpe Rd
SW15 . . . . 57 A3
Woodview Cl N4 . . . . 6 A4
Woodville Cl ⁸
SE10 . . . . 52 B2
Woodville Ho SE1 . **138** C2
Woodville Rd
Golders Green
NW11 . . . . 1 A4
Paddington NW6 . . 23 B3

Woodville Rd continued
Stoke Newington
N16 . . . . 16 A3
Woodwarde Rd
SE22 . . . . 64 A1
Woodwell St
SW18 . . . . 59 B2
Wood Wharf SE10 . . 52 B4
Woodyard CI NW5 . . 12 C3
Woodyard La
SE21 . . . . 76 A4
Woolcombes Ct ⁴
SE16 . . . . 32 C1
Wooler St SE17 . . 151 C2
Woolf CI ⁷ W3 . . . . 37 B3
Woolf Mews ⁴ 94 A2
Woolley Ho SW9 . . . 63 A4
Woollon Ho ⁸ E1 . . 32 B3
Woolmore Prim Sch
E14 . . . . 34 B2
Woolmore St E14 . . 34 B2
Woolneigh St
SW6 . . . . 166 A1
Woolpack Ho ⁸
E9 . . . . 17 B2
Woolridge Way
E9 . . . . 17 B1
Woolstaplers Way
SE16 . . . . 153 B4
Woolstone Ho ⁷
E2 . . . . 24 C4
Woolven Ho SE3 . . 53 B4
Wooster Gdns
E14 . . . . 34 C3
Wooster PI SE1 . . 152 A4
Wootton St SE1 . . 121 C1
Worcester Ct ⁴⁴
W2 . . . . 31 C4
Worcester Dr W4 . . 38 A4
Worcester Gdns
SW11 . . . . 60 B2
Worcester Ho:
Bayswater W2 . . . . 100 C1
⁸ Islington N1 . . . . . 15 B1
Lambeth SE11 . . . . 135 B1
⁹ Putney SW15 . . . . 69 B4
Worcester Mews ⁵
NW6 . . . . 11 A2
Wordsworth Ho
NW6 . . . . 23 C2
Wordsworth Ho ⁵⁸
NW5 . . . . 12 B3
Wordsworth Rd
Bermondsey SE1 . . 153 A3
Stoke Newington
N16 . . . . 16 A4
Worfield St SW11 . 158 B1
Worgan St:
Rotherhithe SE16 . . 40 C2
SE11 . . . . 148 C2
Working Men's Coll
The NW1 . . . . 83 A2
World's End Pas
SW10 . . . . 157 B2
World's End PI
SW10 . . . . 157 A2
World Trade Ctr
London E14 . . . . 42 A4
Worlidge St W6 . . . 39 B1
Worlingham Rd
SE22 . . . . 64 B3
Wormholt Park Prim
Sch W12 . . . . 29 C2

Wormholt Rd
W12 . . . . 29 C1
Wormwood St
EC2 . . . . 110 A2
Wornington Rd
W10 . . . . 31 A4
Woronzow Rd
NW8 . . . . 80 A3
Worple St SW14 . . . 55 C4
Worple Way TW10 . . 54 A3
Worship St
EC2 . . . . . . 24, 110 A4
Worsley Gr E5 . . . . 16 C4
Worsopp Dr SW4 . . 61 B2
Worth Gr SE17 . . . 151 B1
Worthington Ho
EC1 . . . . 95 C4
⁸ Streatham SW2 . . 74 C4
Wotton Ct ¹⁴ E14 . . 34 C2
Wotton Rd ¹⁸ SE8 . . 51 B4
Wouldham Rd E16 . . 35 B3
Wray Cres N4 . . . . . 5 B2
Wray Ct N4 . . . . 5 B2
Wray Ho ¹¹ SW2 . . . 74 A3
Wren Ave NW2 . . . . . 9 B4
Wren CI E16 . . . . . . 35 B3
Wren Ho:
⁸⁰ Bow E3 . . . . 26 A3
SW1 . . . . 147 B1
Wrenn Ho SW13 . . . 47 B4
Wren Rd SE5 . . . . . 48 C2
Wren St WC1 . . . . . 95 A2
Wrentham Ave
NW10 . . . . 22 C3
Wren View N6 . . . . . 4 B3
Wrestlers Ct EC3 . 110 A2
Wrexham Rd E3 . . . 26 C3
Wrigglesworth St
SE14 . . . . 50 C3
Wright CI SW13 . . . 47 A3
Wright Ho SW15 . . . 57 A2
Wright's Gn SW4 . . 61 C3
Wright's La W8 . . . 128 A2
Wright's Rd E3 . . . . 26 B3
Wrights Wlk
SW14 . . . . 55 C4
Wrotham Ho SE1 . . 137 C2
Wrotham Rd ⁸
NW1 . . . . 13 B1
Wrottesley Rd
NW10 . . . . 21 C3
Wroughton Rd
SW11 . . . . 60 B1
Wroxton Rd SE15 . . 50 B1
Wr Twr PI N1 . . . . . 86 A3
Wulfstan St W12 . . . 29 B3
Wyatt CI SE16 . . . . 41 B4
Wyatt Dr SW13 . . . . 47 A3
Wyatt Ho:
Blackheath Vale
SE3 . . . . 53 B1
NW8 . . . . 89 C1
Wyatt Park Mans ⁴
SW2 . . . . 74 A2
Wyatt Park Rd
SW2 . . . . 74 B2
Wyatt Rd N5 . . . . . . 6 B1
Wybert St NW1 . . . . 92 C2
Wycherley CI SE3 . . 53 B3
Wychwood End N6 . . 4 B4

Wychwood Ho N4 . . 6 B4
Wyclif Ct EC1 . . . . 96 A3
Wycliffe Ho ⁸
N16 . . . . 16 A4
Wyclif St EC1 . . . . 96 A3
Wycombe Ct SE3 . . 53 C3
Wycombe Gdns
NW11 . . . . 1 C2
Wycombe Ho NW8 . 90 A2
Wycombe PI
SW18 . . . . 59 B1
Wycombe Sq
W8 . . . . 31 C1 113 B1
Wyersdale Ho N4 . . . 6 B4
Wye St SW11 . . . . 167 C1
Wyfold Rd SW6 . . 154 A1
Wyke Rd E3 . . . . . . 18 C1
Wyldes CI NW11 . . . . 2 B3
Wyllen CI E1 . . . . . 25 B1
Wymering Mans ⁷
W9 . . . . 23 C2
Wymering Rd W9 . . 23 C2
Wymondham Ct
NW8 . . . . 79 C4
Wymond St SW15 . . 57 B4
Wynan Rd E14 . . . . 42 A1
Wyndham Cres N19 . 4 B1
Wyndham Deedes Ho
³⁰ E2 . . . . 24 C3
Wyndham Ho
SW1 . . . . 145 B3
Wyndham Mews
W1 . . . . 102 C3
Wyndham PI W1 . . 102 C3
Wyndham Rd SE5 . . 48 B3
Wyndhams Ct ⁴
E8 . . . . 16 B1
Wyndham St W1 . . 102 C4
Wyndham Yd W1 . . 102 C3
Wyneham Rd
SE24 . . . . 63 C2
Wynford Rd N1 . . . . 85 A2
Wynne Ho SE14 . . . 50 C2
Wynne Rd SW9 . . . 173 B1
Wynnstay Gdns
W8 . . . . 127 C2
Wynter Ho SW9 . . 173 A1
Wynter St SW11 . . . 59 B3
Wynton PI W3 . . . . 28 A3
Wynyard Ho SE11 . 149 A2
Wynyard Terr
SE11 . . . . 149 A2
Wynyatt Ho EC1 . . . 96 A4
Wynyatt St EC1 . . . 96 A4
Wytham Ho NW8 . . 89 C1
Wythburn Ct W1 . . 102 C2
Wythburn PI W1 . . 102 C2
Wyvil Prim Sch
SW8 . . . . 162 B2
Wyvil Rd SW8 . . . . 162 A2
Wyvis St E14 . . . . . 34 A4

Y

Yabsley St E14 . . . . 34 B1
Yaldam Ho SE1 . . . 152 A3
Yalding Ho ²⁰ E5 . . 17 A3
Yalding Rd SE16 . . 153 B4
Yale Ct NW6 . . . . . . 11 A3
Yardley St WC1 . . . 95 B3
Yard The N1 . . . . . . 84 B1
Yarmouth PI W1 . . 118 A1

Yarnfield Sq ¹⁵
SE15 . . . . 49 C2
Yarrow Ho:
¹² Cubitt Town
E14 . . . . 42 B3
¹⁶ North Kensington
W10 . . . . 30 B4
Yatesbury Ct E5 . . . 18 A3
Yates Ct NW2 . . . . . 9 C2
Yates Ho E2 . . 24 C2 99 C4
Yatton Ho ¹⁸ W10 . . 30 B4
Yeadon Ho ¹⁴
W10 . . . . 30 B4
Yearby Ho W10 . . . 22 B1
Yeate St N1 . . . . . . 15 C1
Yeats CI NW10 . . . . . 8 A2
Yeldham Ho W6 . . . 39 C1
Yeldham Rd W6 . . . 39 C1
Yelverton Rd
SW11 . . . . 167 C1
Yeoman Ct SE27 . . . 75 A1
Yeoman's Row
SW3 . . . . 130 B1
Yeoman St SE8 . . . 41 A2
Yeoman's Yd E1 . . 125 A4
Yeo St E3 . . . . 34 A4
Yeovil Ho:
Finsbury Pk N7 . . . . 5 B2
North Kensington
W10 . . . . 22 B1
Yerbury Prim Sch
N19 . . . . 4 C1
Yerbury Rd N19 . . . . 4 C1
Yeshivo Horomo
Talmudical Coll
N16 . . . . 6 C3
Yesodey Hatorah Sch
N16 . . . . 6 C3
Yet Lev Ct E5 . . . . . 7 C3
Yewfield Rd NW10 . . 8 B2
Yew Gr NW2 . . . . . . 9 C4
Yew Ho SE14 . . . . . 51 B1
Yew Tree CI ⁸
SE13 . . . . 67 B4
Yew Tree Ct ⁵
N16 . . . . 6 C2
Yew Tree Rd W12 . . 29 B2
Yoakley Rd N16 . . . . 7 A2
Yoke CI N7 . . . . . . 14 A2
Yonge Pk N4, N7 . . . 5 C1
York Ave
Mortlake SW14 . . . . 55 B2
Walworth SE17 . . . 151 A2
York Bldgs WC2 . . 120 B3
York Bridge NW1 . . 91 C2
York CI ¹⁷ SE5 . . . . 48 B1
York Gate NW1 . . . . 91 C1
York Gr SE15 . . . . . 50 B2
York Hill SE27 . . . . 75 A1
York Ho: Acton W3 . . 28 B2
Chelsea SW3 . . . . 145 A2
Islington N5 . . . . . 14 C3
Kensington W8 . . . 128 A4
¹¹ Kentish Town
N7 . . . . 13 C2
Kew TW9 . . . . 44 C2
Lambeth SE1 . . . . 135 A1
Marylebone W1 . . . 102 C4
Pentonville N1 . . . . 84 C1
Richmond TW10 . . . 54 C2
York House PI
W8 . . . . 128 A4

Yorkley Ho ³
W10 . . . . 22 B1
York Mans:
Battersea SW11 . . 169 C4
Marylebone W1 . . . 103 B4
Walworth SE17 . . . 151 A2
York Mews NW5 . . . 13 A3
York PI:
Battersea SW11 . . . 59 C4
WC2 . . . . 120 B3
York Place Mans
NW1 . . . . 103 A4
York Rd:
Battersea SW11,
SW18 . . . . 59 C4
Dagenham W3 . . . . 28 C3
⁴ Richmond TW10 . . 54 B2
SE1 . . . . 135 A4
York Rise NW5 . . . . . 4 A1
York Road Bsns Ctr
SW11 . . . . 167 B1
York St Chambers
W1 . . . . 102 C4
Yorkshire CI N16 . . . 7 A1
Yorkshire Grey PI ¹³
NW3 . . . . 11 B4
Yorkshire Grey Yd
WC1 . . . . 106 C3
Yorkshire Rd E14 . . 33 A3
York Sq ²⁸ E14 . . . . 33 A3
York St W1, ... 103 A4
York Terr E NW1 . . . 91 C1
York Terr W NW1 . . 91 B1
Yorkton St E2 . . . . 24 C3
York Way:
Barnsbury N1, N7,
N1 . . . . 14 A1
NL 84 B3
York Way Ct:
Islington N1 . . . . . 84 C3
Islington N1 . . . . . 84 B3
Young's Bldgs EC1 . 97 A2
Youngs Brewery
Visitor Ctr★
SW18 . . . . 59 A2
Youngs Ct SW11 . . 169 C3
Young St W8 . . . . . 128 A3
Yoxall Ho ⁷ W10 . . 22 B1
Yukon Rd SW12 . . . 73 A4

Z

Zampa Rd SE16 . . . 40 B1
Zander Ct
E2 . . . . 24 C2 99 C4
Zangwill Ho NW6 . . 23 B3
Zealand Ho ⁸
SE5 . . . . 48 B1
Zealand Rd E3 . . . . 26 A3
Zennor Rd SW12 . . 73 B3
Zetland Ho W8 . . . 128 A2
Zetland St E14 . . . . 34 B4
Zeus Ho N1 . . . . . . 97 B3
Zion Ho ⁶ E1 . . . . . 32 B3
Zoar St SE1 . . . . . 122 C2
Zodiac Ho ⁸ E3 . . . 26 C1
Zoffany St N19 . . . . . 4 C2

List of numbered locations

This atlas shows thousands more place names than any other London street atlas. In some busy areas it is impossible to fit the name of every place.

Where not all names will fit, some smaller places are shown by a number. If you wish to find out the name associated with a number, use this listing.

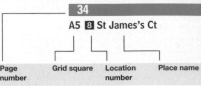

34			
A5	**8**	St James's Ct	
Page number	Grid square	Location number	Place name

1
- B1 **1** Mortimer Cl
- **2** Primrose Ct
- **3** Sunnyside Ho
- **4** Sunnyside
- **5** Prospect Pl
- B4 **1** Berkeley Ct
- **2** Exchange Mans
- **3** Beechcroft Ct
- **4** Nedahall Ct
- C1 **1** Portman Hts
- **2** Hermitage Ct
- **3** Moreland Ct
- **4** Wendover Ct

2
- B1 **1** Hampstead Sq
- **2** Stamford Ct
- **3** Mount Sq The

4
- B1 **1** Hunter Ho
- **2** Fisher Ho
- **3** Lang Ho
- **4** Temple Ho
- **5** Palmer Ho
- **6** Carlisle Ho
- **7** Durham Ho
- **8** Suffolk Ho
- **9** Lincoln Ho
- **10** Llewellyn Ho
- **11** Fell Ho
- **12** Aveling Ho
- **13** Merryweather Ho
- **14** Brennands Ct
- **15** St Christophers Ct
- **16** Francis Terrace Mews
- B2 **1** Flowers Mews
- **2** Archway Cl
- **3** Sandridge St
- **4** Bovingdon Cl
- **5** Cavell Ct
- **6** Torrence Ho
- **7** Rowan Wlk
- **8** Laurel Cl
- **9** Forest Way
- **10** Larch Cl
- **11** Pine Cl
- **12** Alder Mews
- **13** Aspen Cl
- B3 **1** Calvert Ct

3
- **2** Academy The
- **3** Whitehall Mans
- **4** Pauntley St
- **5** Archway Hts
- **6** Pauntley Ho
- C1 **1** Melchester Ho
- **2** Norcombe Ho
- **3** Weatherbury Ho
- **4** Wessex Ho
- **5** Archway Bsns Ctr
- **6** Harford Mews
- **7** Opera Ct
- **8** Rupert Ho
- **9** All Saints Church
- C2 **1** Bowerman Ct
- **2** Gresham Pl
- **3** Hargrave Mans
- **4** Church Garth
- **5** John King Ct
- **6** Ramsey Ct
- C3 **1** Louise White Ho
- **2** Levison Way
- **3** Sanders Way
- **4** Birbeck Ho
- **5** Scholars Ct
- C4 **1** Eleanor Rathbone Ho
- **2** Christopher Lo
- **3** Monkridge
- **4** Marbleford Ct
- **5** High London
- **6** Garton Ho
- **7** Hilltop Ho
- **8** Caroline Martyn Ho
- **9** Arthur Henderson Ho
- **10** Margaret Mcmillan Ho
- **11** Enid Stacy Ho
- **12** Mary McArthur Ho
- **13** Bruce Glasier Ho
- **14** John Wheatley Ho
- **15** Keir Hardie Ho
- **16** Monroe Ho
- **17** Iberia Ho
- **18** Lygoe Ho
- **19** Lambert Ho
- **20** Shelbourne Ho
- **21** Arkansas Ho
- **22** Lafitte Ho
- **23** Shreveport Ho
- **24** Packenham Ho
- **25** Orpheus Ho
- **26** Fayetville Ho
- **27** Bayon Ho

5
- A1 **1** Northview
- **2** Tufnell Park Mans
- **3** Fulford Mans
- **4** Tollington Ho
- A2 **1** Bracey Mews
- **2** Christie Ct
- **3** Ringmer Gdns
- **4** Kingsdown Rd
- **5** Cottenham Ho
- **6** St Paul's Ct
- **7** Rickthorne Rd
- **8** Stanley Terr
- **9** Arundel Lo
- **10** Landseer Ct
- A3 **1** Beeches The
- **2** Lambton Ct
- **3** Nugent Ct
- **4** Lambton Mews
- **5** Mews The
- A4 **1** Marie Lloyd Gdns
- **2** Edith Cavell Cl
- **3** Marie Stopes Ct
- **4** Jessie Blythe La
- **5** Barbara Rudolph Ct
- **6** Hetty Rees Ct
- **7** Leyden Mans
- **8** Brambledown
- **9** Lochbie
- **10** Lyngham Ct
- **11** High Mount
- **12** Woodlands The
- B2 **1** Berkeley Wlk
- **2** Lazar Wlk
- **3** Thistlewood Cl
- **4** Tomlins Wlk
- **5** Andover Ho
- **6** Barmouth Ho
- **7** Chard Ho
- **8** Methley Ho
- **9** Rainford Ho
- **10** Woodbridge Cl
- **11** Allerton Wlk
- **12** Falconer Wlk
- **13** Sonderburg Rd
- **14** St Mark's Mans
- **15** Athol Ct
- B3 **1** Lawson Ct

5 (cont.)
- **2** Wiltshire Ct
- **3** Fenstanton
- **4** Hutton Ct
- **5** Wisbech
- C2 **1** Brookfield
- **2** Churnfield

6
- A1 **1** Hurlock Ho
- **2** Blackstock Ho
- **3** Vivian Comma Cl
- **4** Monsell St
- B4 **1** Finmere Ho
- **2** Keynsham Ho
- **3** Kilpeck Ho
- **4** Knaresborough Ho
- **5** Leighfield Ho
- **6** Lonsdale Ho
- **7** Groveley Ho
- **8** Wensleydale Ho
- **9** Badminton Ho
- C2 **1** Chestnut Cl
- **2** Sycamore Ho
- **3** Lordship Ho
- **4** Clissold Ho
- **5** Beech Ho
- **6** Laburnum Ho
- **7** Ormond Ho
- **8** Yew Tree Ct
- **9** Oak Ho
- C4 **1** Selwood Ho
- **2** Mendip Ho
- **3** Ennerdale Ho
- **4** Delamere Ho
- **5** Westwood Ho
- **6** Bernwood Ho
- **7** Allerdale Ho
- **8** Chattenden Ho
- **9** Farningham Ho
- **10** Oakend Ho

7
- A1 **1** Gujarat Ho
- **2** Marton Rd
- **3** Painsthorpe Rd
- **4** Selkirk Ho
- **5** Defoe Ho
- **6** Edward Friend Ho
- **7** Sheridan Ho
- **8** Barrie Ho
- **9** Arnold Ho
- **10** MacAulay Ho

- **11** Stowe Ho
- **12** Carlyle Ho
- **13** Shaftesbury Ho
- **14** Lillian Cl
- **15** Swift Ho
- **16** Dryden Ho
- **17** Scott Ct
- **18** Kingsfield Ho
- **19** Uhura Sq
- **20** Hartopp Ct
- A3 **1** Godstone Ct
- **2** Farnham Ct
- **3** Milford Ct
- **4** Cranleigh Ct
- **5** Haslemere Ct
- **6** Belmont Ct
- **7** Hockworth Ho
- **8** Garratt Ho
- **9** Fairburn Ho
- **10** Thorndale Ho
- **11** Oakdene Ho
- **12** Briardale Ho
- B1 **1** Lawrence Bldgs
- **2** Cottage Wlk
- **3** Batley Pl
- B2 **1** Garnham St
- **2** Garnham Ho
- **3** Sanford La
- **4** Sanford Ho
- **5** Abney Gdns
- **6** Fleet Wood
- B3 **1** Stamford Hill Mans
- **2** Montefiore Ct
- **3** Berwyn Ho
- **4** Clent Ho
- **5** Chiltern Ho
- **6** Laindon Ho
- **7** Pentland Ho
- B4 **1** Regent Ct
- **2** Stamford Lo
- **3** Holmwood Ct
- C1 **1** Ravenscourt
- **2** Mellington Ct
- **3** Rendlesham Ho
- **4** Carroll Ct
- C2 **1** Cazenove Mans
- **2** Chedworth Ho
- **3** Aldergrove Ho
- **4** Abbotstone Ho
- **5** Briggeford Ct
- **6** Inglethorpe Ho
- **7** Ashdown Ho

8 (cont.)
- 6 Epping Ho
- 6 Cypress Cl
- C3 1 Stamford Gr E
- 2 Stamford Mans
- 3 Grove Mans
- 4 Stamford Gr W

8
- A1 1 Beveridge Rd
- 2 Purcell Mews
- 3 George Lansbury Ho
- 4 Charles Hobson Ho
- 5 Reade Wlk
- 6 Westbury Ho
- 7 Bridge Ct
- A4 1 Grange Ct
- 2 Green Ct
- C2 1 Regency Mews
- 2 Tudor Mews
- 3 Utopia Ho
- 4 Bell Flats
- 5 Angel Ct

9
- B2 1 Rutland Park Gdns
- 2 Rutland Park Mans
- 3 Queens Par
- 4 Harcourt Ho
- 5 Solidarity Ho
- 6 Electra Ct
- 7 Cassandra Ct
- 8 Carlton Ct
- C4 1 Oaklands Mews
- 2 Acer Ct
- 3 Maple Ct
- 4 Argyle Mans

10
- A1 1 Christ Church Ct
- 2 Paul Daisley Ct
- 3 Fountain Ho
- 4 Kingston Ho
- 5 Waverley Ct
- 6 Weston Ho
- 7 Mapes Ho
- 8 Athelstan Gdns
- 9 Leff Ho
- B1 1 Alma Birk Ho
- 2 Brooklands Ct
- 3 Brooklands Court Apartments
- 4 Cleveland Mans
- 5 Buckley Ct
- 6 Webheath
- C1 1 Linstead St
- 2 Embassy Ho
- 3 Acol Ct
- 4 Kings Wood Ct
- 5 Douglas Ct
- 6 King's Gdns
- 7 Carlton Mans
- 8 Smyrna Mans
- 9 New Priory Ct
- 10 Queensgate Pl
- 11 Brondesbury Mews
- C2 1 Dene Mans
- 2 Sandwell Cres
- 3 Sandwell Mans
- 4 Hampstead West
- 5 Redcroft
- C3 1 Orestes Mews
- 2 Walter Northcott Ho
- 3 Polperro Mans
- 4 Lyncroft Mans
- 5 Marlborough Mans
- 6 Alexandra Mans
- 7 Cumberland Mans
- 8 Cavendish Mans
- 9 Ambassador Ct
- 10 Welbeck Mans
- 11 Inglewood Mans
- 12 Dennington Park Mansions

11
- A2 1 Beswick Mews
- 2 Worcester Mews
- 3 Minton Mews
- 4 Doulton Mans
- 5 Laurel Ho
- 6 Sandalwood Ho
- 7 Iroko Ho
- 8 Banyan Ho
- 9 Rosewood Ho
- 10 Ebony Ho
- 11 Rosemont Mans
- 12 Exeter Mews
- B1 1 Harrold Ho
- 2 Glover Ho
- 3 Byron Ct
- 4 Nalton Ho
- B2 1 Petros Gdns
- 2 Heath Ct
- 3 Imperial Twrs
- 4 Fairhurst
- 5 St John's Ct
- 6 New College Ct
- 7 Chalford
- 8 Rosslyn Mans
- 9 Sutherland Ho
- B4 1 Windmill Hill
- 2 Highgrove Point
- 3 Gainsborough Ho
- 4 Holly Bush Hill
- 5 Pavilion Ct
- 6 Holly Bush Steps
- 7 New Campden Ct
- 8 Holly Berry La
- 9 Benham's Pl
- 10 Prospect Pl
- 11 Yorkshire Grey Pl
- 12 Gardnor Mans
- 13 Ellerdale Cl
- 14 Monro Ho
- 15 Prince Arthur Mews
- 16 Prince Arthur Ct
- 17 Village Mount
- 18 Perrin's Ct
- 19 Wells Ct
- 20 Bakers Pas
- 21 Spencer Wlk
- 22 Bird In Hand Yd
- 23 Kings Well
- 24 New Ct
- 25 Streatley Pl
- 26 Mansfield Pl
- 27 Upper Hampstead Wlk
- C1 1 New College Par
- 2 Northways Par
- 3 Noel Ho
- 4 Campden Ho
- 5 Centre Hts
- 6 Hickes Ho
- 7 Swiss Terr
- 8 Leitch Ho
- 9 Jevons Ho
- 10 Langhorne Ho
- 11 Park Lo
- 12 Avenue Lo
- C2 1 Belsize Park Mews
- 2 Baynes Mews
- 3 McCrone Mews
- C3 1 Belsize Court Garages
- 2 Roscommon Ho
- 3 Akenside Ct
- C4 1 White Bear Pl
- 2 Wells Ho The
- 3 Boades Mews
- 4 Flask Cotts
- 5 Coach House Yd
- 6 Pilgrim's Pl
- 7 Rosslyn Mews

12
- A2 1 Banff Ho
- 2 Glenloch Ct
- 3 Havercourt
- 4 Holmefield Ct
- 5 Gilling Ct
- 6 Howitt Cl
- 7 Manor Mans
- 8 Straffan Lo
- 9 Romney Ct
- 10 Lancaster Stables
- 11 Eton Garages
- B1 1 Hancock Nunn Ho
- 2 Higginson Ho
- 3 Duncan Ho
- 4 Mary Wharrie Ho
- 5 Rockstraw Ho
- 6 Cleaver Ho
- 7 Chamberlain St
- 8 Sharples Hall St
- 9 Primrose Mews
- 10 Rothwell St
- 11 St Georges Mews
- B2 1 Alder Ho
- 2 Hornbeam Ho
- 3 Whitebeam Ho
- 4 Aspen Ho
- 5 Kowan Ho
- 6 Beech Ho
- 7 Chestnut Ho
- 8 Oak Ho
- 9 Willow Ho
- 10 Sycamore Ho
- 11 Maple Ho
- 12 Hazel Ho
- 13 Elaine Ct
- 14 Falrcourt
- 15 Walham Ct
- 16 Stanbury Ct
- 17 Priory Mans
- 18 Wellington Ho
- 19 Grange The
- B3 1 Cayford Ho
- 2 Du Maurier Ho
- 3 Isokon Flats
- 4 Palgrave Ho
- 5 Garnett Ho
- 6 Stephenson Ho
- 7 Park Dwellings
- 8 Siddons Ho
- 9 Mall Studios
- 10 Park Hill Wlk
- 11 Wordsworth Pl
- 12 Fraser Regnart Ct
- 13 St Pancras Almshouses
- C1 1 Bridge Ho
- 2 Hardington
- 3 Mead Cl
- 4 Rugmere
- 5 Tottenhall
- 6 Beauvale
- 7 Broomfield
- 1 Silverbirch Wlk
- 2 Penshurst
- 3 Wingham
- 4 Westwell
- 5 Chislet
- 6 Burmarsh
- 7 Shipton Ho
- 8 Stonegate
- 9 Leysdown
- 10 Headcorn
- 11 Lenham
- 12 Halstow
- 13 Fordcombe
- 14 Cannington
- 15 Langridge
- 16 Athlone Ho
- 17 Pentland Ho
- 18 Beckington
- 19 Hawkridge
- 20 Edington

13
- A1 1 Ferdinand Ho
- 2 Harmood Ho
- 3 Hawley Rd
- 4 Hawley Mews
- 5 Leybourne St
- 6 Barling
- 7 Tiptree
- 8 Havering
- 9 Candida Ct
- 10 Lorraine Ct
- 11 Donnington Ct
- 12 Welford Ct
- 13 Torbay Ct
- 14 Bradfield Ct
- 15 Torbay St
- 16 Water La
- 17 Leybourne Rd
- 18 Haven St
- 19 Stucley Pl
- 20 Lawrence Ho
- A2 1 Ashington
- 2 Priestley Ho
- 3 Leonard Day Ho
- 4 Old Dairy Mews
- 5 Monmouth Ho
- 6 Alpha Ct
- 7 Una Ho
- 8 Widford
- 9 Heybridge
- 10 Roxwell
- 11 Hamstead Gates
- A4 1 Denyer Ho
- 2 Stephenson Ho
- 3 Trenthick Ho
- 4 Brunel Ho
- 5 Newcomen Ho
- 6 Faraday Ho
- 7 Winifrede Paul Ho
- 8 Wardlow
- 9 Fletcher Ct
- 10 Tideswell
- 11 Grangemill
- 12 Hambrook Ct
- 13 Calver
- B1 1 Cherry Tree Ct
- 2 Chichester Ct
- 3 Durdans Ho
- 4 Philia Ho
- 5 Bernard Shaw Ct
- 6 Foster Ct
- 7 Bessemer Ct
- 8 Hogarth Ct
- 9 Rochester Ct
- 10 Soane Ct
- 11 Wallett Ct
- 12 Inwood Ct
- 13 Wrotham Rd
- 14 St Thomas Ct
- 15 Caulfield Ct
- 16 Bruges Pl
- 17 Reachview Cl
- 18 Lawfords Wharf
- B3 1 Eleanor Ho
- 2 Falkland Pl
- 3 Kensington Ho
- 4 Willingham Cl
- 5 Kenbrook Ho
- 6 Aborfield
- 7 Great Field
- 8 Appleford
- 9 Forties The
- 10 Maud Wilkes Cl
- 11 Dunne Mews
- 12 Dowdeny Cl
- B4 1 Benson Ct
- 2 Tait Ho
- 3 Manorfield Cl
- 4 Greatfield Cl
- 5 Longley Ho
- 6 Lampson Ho
- 7 Davidson Ho
- 8 Palmer Ho
- 9 Lambourn Ct
- 10 Morris Ho
- 11 Owen Ho
- C1 1 Hillier Ho
- 2 Gairloch Ho
- 3 Cobham Mews
- 4 Bergholt Mews
- 5 Blakeney Cl
- 6 Weavers Way
- 7 Allensbury Pl
- C2 1 Rowstock
- 2 Peckwater Ho
- 3 Wolsey Ho
- 4 Pandian Way
- 5 Busby Mews
- 6 Caledonian Sq
- 7 Canal Bvd
- 8 Northpoint Sq
- 9 Lock Mews
- 10 Carters Cl
- 11 York Ho
- 12 Hungerford Rd
- 13 Cliff Road Studios
- 14 Cliff Ct
- 15 Camelot Ho
- 16 Church Studios
- 17 Camden Terr
- C3 1 Blake Ho
- 2 Quelch Ho
- 3 Lee Ho
- 4 Willbury Ho
- 5 Howell Ho
- 6 Holmsbury Ho
- 7 Leith Ho
- 8 Betchworth Ho
- 9 Rushmore Ho
- 10 Dugdale Ho
- 11 Horsendon Ho
- 12 Colley Ho
- 13 Coombe Ho
- 14 Ivinghoe Ho
- 15 Buckhurst Ho
- 16 Saxonbury Ct
- 17 Charlton Ho
- 18 Apollo Studios

20 Yalding Ho
21 Northbourne Ho
22 Monkton Ho
23 Milsted Ho
24 Athlone Cl
1 Clarence Pl
2 Gould Terr
3 Quested Ct
4 Brett Pas
5 Marcon Ct
6 Appleton Ct
A4 1 Ross Ct
2 Downs La
3 Gaviller Pl
4 Robert Owen Lo
5 Apprentice Way
6 Arrowe Ct
7 Gilwell Ct
8 Sutton Ct
9 St Andrews Mans
10 Kinnoull Mans
11 Rowhill Mans
12 Sladen Pl
13 Mothers Sq The
14 Richborough Ho
15 Sandgate Ho
16 Sheppey Ho
B1 1 Pitcairn Ho
2 Lyme Grove Ho
3 Shakespeare Ho
4 Upcott Ho
5 Loddiges Ho
6 Parkinson Ho
7 Sloane Ho
8 Vanbrugh Ho
9 Cambridge Pas
10 Lyttleton Ho
11 Victoria Park Ct
12 Tullis Ho
13 Fairchild Ho
14 Forsyth Ho
15 Tradescant Ho
16 Mason Ho
17 Capel Ho
18 Cordwainers Ct
19 Bridgeman Ho
20 St Thomas's Pl
21 Barclay Ho
22 Clayton Ho
23 Danby Ho
24 Sherard Ho
25 Catesby Ho
26 Petiver Cl
27 Leander Ct
28 Philip Turner Est
29 Grendon Ho
30 Shore Mews
31 Shore Bsns Ctr
32 Kendal Ho
33 Classic Mans
34 Tudor Ho
35 Enterprise Ho
36 Alpine Gr
37 Clarendon Cl
38 Rotheley Ho
39 Bernie Grant Ho
B2 1 Woolpack Ho
2 Elvin Ho
3 Thomas Ho
4 Hockley Ho
5 Retreat Ho
6 Butfield Ho
7 Brooksbank Ho
8 Cresset Ho
9 Brooksbank St
10 Lennox Ho

11 Milborne Ho
12 Collent Ho
13 Middlesex Pl
14 Elsdale Ho
15 Devonshire Hall
16 Brent Ho
C1 1 Stuart Ho
2 Gascoyne Ho
3 Chelsfield Point
4 Sundridge Ho
5 Banbury Ho
6 Lauriston Ho
C2 1 Musgrove Ho
2 Cheyney Ho
3 Haynes Ho
4 Warner Ho
5 Gilby Ho
6 Gadsden Ho
7 Risley Ho
8 Baycliffe Ho
9 Sheldon Ho
10 Offley Ho
11 Latimer Ho
12 Ribstone Ho
13 Salem Ho
14 Fieldwick Ho
15 Lever Ct
16 Matson Ho
17 Wilding Ho
18 Rennell Ho
19 Dycer Ho
20 Granard Ho
21 Whitelock Ho
22 Harrowgate Ho
23 Cass Ho
24 Lofts on the Park
25 Heathcote Point
26 Ravenscroft Point
27 Vanner Point
28 Hensley Point
29 San Ho
C4 1 Cromford Path
2 Longford Ct
3 Overbury Ho
4 Heanor Ct
5 Wharfedale Ct
6 Ladybower Ct
7 Ilkeston Ct
8 Derby Ct
9 Rushmore Cres
10 Blackwell Cl
11 Belper Ct

18
A2 1 Chigwell Ct
2 Wellday Ho
3 Selman Ho
4 Vaine Ho
5 Trower Ho
B2 1 Mallard Cl
2 Merriam Ave
3 Gainsborough St

19
C1 1 Service Route No 2
2 Service Route No 3
C4 1 Mulberry Ct
2 Rosewood Ct
3 Gean Ct
4 Blackthorn Ct
5 Cypress Ct

20
1 Carlyle Rd
2 Bernard Shaw Ho
3 Longlents Ho
4 Mordaunt Ho

5 Wilmers Ct
6 Stonebridge Ctr
7 Shakespeare Ave

21
A3 1 Futters Ct
2 Barrett Ct
3 Elms The
4 Fairlight Ct
B3 1 New Crescent Yd
2 Harlesden Plaza
3 St Josephs Ct
4 Jubilee Cl
5 Ellery Cl

22
B1 1 Princess Alice Ho
2 Yoxall Ho
3 Yorkley Ho
4 Northaw Ho
5 Oakham Ho
6 Markyate Ho
7 Letchmore Ho
8 Pagham Ho
9 Quendon Ho
10 Redbourn Ho
11 Ketton Ho
12 Hillman Dr
C2 1 Westfield Ct
2 Tropical Ct
3 Chamberlayne Mans
4 Quadrant The
5 Queens Park Ct
6 Warfield Yd
7 Regent St
8 Cherrytree Ho
9 Artisan Mews
10 Artisan Quarter

23
A1 1 Sycamore Wlk
2 Westgate Bsns Ctr
3 Buspace Studios
4 Bosworth Ho
5 Golborne Gdns
6 Appleford Ho
7 Adair Twr
8 Gadsden Ho
9 Southam Ho
10 Norman Butler Ho
11 Thompson Ho
12 Wells Ho
13 Paul Ho
14 Olive Blythe Ho
15 Katherine Ho
16 Breakwell Ct
17 Pepler Ho
18 Edward Kennedy Ho
19 Winnington Ho
A2 1 Selby Sq
2 Severn Ave
3 Stansbury Sq
4 Tolhurst Dr
5 John Fearon Wlk
6 Mundy Ho
7 Macfarren Ho
8 Bantock Ho
9 Banister Ho
10 Batten Ho
11 Croft Ho
12 Courtville Ho
13 Mounsey Ho
14 Bliss Mews
15 Symphony Mews
B1 1 Octavia Mews

2 Russell's Wharf
3 Western Ho
4 Kelly Mews
B2 1 Boyce Ho
2 Farnaby Ho
3 Danby Ho
4 Purday Ho
5 Naylor Ho
6 St Judes Ho
7 Leeve Ho
8 Longhurst Ho
9 Harrington Ct
10 Mulberry Ct
11 Kilburn Ho
B3 1 Claremont Ct
2 William Saville Ho
3 Western Ct
4 Bond Ho
5 Crone Ct
6 Wood Ho
7 Winterleys
8 Carlton Ho
9 Fiona Ct
C1 1 Westside Ct
2 Byron Mews
3 Sutherland Ct
4 Fleming Cl
5 Hermes Cl
C2 1 Pentland Rd
2 Nelson Cl
3 Pavilion Ct
4 Masefield Ho
5 Austen Ho
6 Fielding Ho
7 Argo Bsns Ctr
8 John Ratcliffe Ho
9 Wymering Mans
C3 1 Wells Ct
2 Cambridge Ct
3 Ely Ct
4 Durham Ct
5 Ryde Ho
6 Glengall Pass
7 Leith Yd
8 Daynor Ho
9 Varley Ho
10 Sandby Ho
11 Colas Mews
12 Bishopsdale Ho
13 Lorton Ho
14 Marshwood Ho
15 Ribblesdale Ho
16 Holmesdale Ho
17 Kilburn Vale Est
18 Kilburn Bridge

24
A3 1 Dracer Ho
2 Scorton Ho
3 Fern Cl
4 Macbeth Ho
5 Oberon Ho
6 Buckland Ct
7 Crondall Ct
8 Osric Path
9 Caliban Twr
10 Celia Ho
11 Juliet Ho
12 Bacchus Wlk
13 Malcolm Ho
14 Homefield St
15 Crondall Pl
16 Bianca Ho
17 Miranda Ho
18 Falstaff Ho
19 Charmian Ho
20 Myrtle Wlk

21 Arden Ho
22 Sebastian Ho
23 Stanway Ct
24 Jerrold St
25 Rosalind Ho
26 Cordelia Ho
27 Monteagle Ct
28 John Parry Ct
29 James Anderson Ct
30 Ben Jonson Ct
31 Sara Lane Ct
32 Walbrook Ct
A4 1 Portelet Ct
2 Trinity Ct
3 Rozel Ct
4 St Helier Ct
5 Corbiere Ho
6 Kenning Ho
7 Higgins Ho
8 Cavell Ho
9 Girling Ho
10 Fulcher Ho
11 Francis Ho
12 Norris Ho
13 Kempton Ho
14 Nesham Ho
15 Crossbow Ho
16 Catherine Ho
17 Strale Ho
18 Horner Hos
19 Stringer Hos
20 Whitmore Ho
21 Nightingale Ho
22 Wilmer Gdns
23 Arrow Ho
24 Archer Ho
25 Meriden Ho
26 Rover Ho
27 Bowyer Ho
28 Tiller Ho
29 Canalside Studios
30 Kleine Wharf
31 Benyon Wharf
32 Quebec Wharf
33 Belvedere Ct
34 Portfleet Pl
B3 1 Queensbridge Ct
2 Godwin Ho
3 Kent Ct
4 Brunswick Ho
5 Weymouth Ct
6 Sovereign Mews
7 Dunloe Ct
8 Cremer Bsns Ctr
9 James Hammett Ho
10 Allgood St
11 Horatio St
12 Cadell Ho
13 Horatio Ho
14 Shipton Ho
B4 1 Hilborough Ct
2 Scriven Ct
3 Livermere Ct
4 Angrave Ct
5 Angrave Pas
6 Benfleet Ct
7 Belford Ho
8 Orme Ho
9 Clemson Ho
10 Longman Ho
11 Lowther Ho
12 Lovelace Ho
13 Harlowe Ho

14 Pamela Ho
15 Samuel Ho
16 Acton Ho
17 Loanda Cl
18 Phoenix Cl
19 Richardson Ct
20 Thrasher Cl
21 Canal Path
22 Pear Tree Cl
23 Hebden Ct
24 Charlton Ct
25 Laburnum Ct
26 Mansfield Ct
28 Garden Pl
29 Amber Wharf
30 Haggerston Studios
C3 1 London Terr
2 Sturdee Ho
3 Maude Ho
4 Haig Ho
5 Jellicoe Ho
6 Ropley St
7 Guinness Trust Bldgs
8 Ion Ct
9 Columbia Rd
10 Moye Cl
11 Morrel Ct
12 Courtauld Ho
13 Drummond Ho
14 Gurney Ho
15 Atkinson Ho
16 Halley Ho
17 Goldsmith's Sq
18 Shajalal Ho
19 Ken Wilson Ho
20 April Ct
21 Crofts Ho
22 Sebright Ho
23 Beechwood Ho
24 Gillman Ho
25 Cheverell Ho
26 Besford Ho
27 Dinmont Ho
28 Elizabeth Mews
29 Sebright Pas
30 Wyndham Deedes Ho
31 Sheppard Ho
32 Mary James Ho
33 Hadrian Est
34 Blythendale Ho
35 George Vale Ho
36 Lion Mills
37 St Peter's Ave
38 Pritchard Ho
C4 1 Broke Wlk
2 Rochemont Wlk
3 Marlborough Ave
4 Rivington St
5 Magnin Cl
6 Gloucester Sq
7 Woolstone Ho
8 Marsworth Ho
9 Cheddington Ho
10 Linslade Ho
11 Cosgrove Ho
12 Blisworth Ho
13 Eleanor Ct
14 Wistow Ho
15 Muscott Ho
16 Boxmoor Ho
17 Linford Ho

18 Pendley Ho
19 Northchurch Ho
20 Debdale Ho
21 Broadway Market Mews
22 Welshpool Ho
23 Ada Ho

25

A1 1 Rochester Ct
2 Weaver Ct
3 Greenheath Bsns Ctr
4 Glass St
5 Herald St
6 Northsek Ho
7 Codrington St
8 Heathpool Ct
9 Mocatta Ho
10 Harvey Ho
11 Blackwood Ho
12 Rutherford Ho
13 Bullen Ho
14 Fremantle Ho
15 Pellew Ho
16 Ashington Ho
17 Dinnington Ho
18 Bartholomew Sq
19 Steeple Ct
20 Orion Ho
21 Fellbrigg St
22 Eagle Ho
23 Sovereign Ho
24 Redmill Ho
25 Berry Ho
26 Grindall Ho
27 Collingwood Ho
A2 1 Charles Dickens Ho
2 Adrian Bolt Ho
3 William Rathbone Ho
4 Southwood Smith Ho
5 Rushmead
6 William Channing Ho
7 John Cartwright Ho
8 Charles Darwin Ho
9 Thomas Burt Ho
10 John Fielden Ho
11 Gwilym Maries Ho
12 Joseph Priestley Ho
13 Wear Pl
14 John Nettleford Ho
15 Thornaby Ho
16 Stockton Ho
17 Barnard Ho
18 Gainford Ho
19 Stapleton Ho
20 James Middleton Ho
21 Kedleston Wlk
22 Queen Margaret Flats
23 Hollybush Ho
24 Horwood Ho
25 Norden Ho
26 Newcourt Ho
27 Seabright St
28 Viaduct Pl
29 Sunlight Sq
30 Providence Row Cl
A3 1 Dinmont St
2 Marian St
3 Claredale St
4 Keeling Ho

5 Maple St
6 Winkley St
7 Temple Dwellings
8 Argos Ho
9 Helen Ho
10 Lysander Ho
11 Antenor Ho
12 Paris Ho
13 Nestor Ho
14 Hector Ho
15 Ajax Ho
16 Achilles Ho
17 Priam Ho
18 Peabody Est
19 Felix St
20 Cambridge Cres
21 Peterley Bsns Ctr
22 Beckwith Ho
23 Brookfield Ho
24 Parminter Ind Est
25 Ted Roberts Ho
26 Cambridge St
27 Millennium Pl
28 William Caslon Ho
29 Hugh Platt Ho
30 West St
31 Mayfield Ho
32 Apollo Ho
33 Tanners Yd
34 Teesdale Yd
A4 1 Welshpool St
2 Broadway Ho
3 Regents Wharf
4 London Wharf
5 Warburton Ho
6 Warburton St
7 Triangle Rd
8 Warburton Rd
9 Williams Ho
10 Booth Cl
11 Albert Cl
12 King Edward Mans
13 Victoria Bldgs
14 Andrews Wharf
B1 1 William's Bldgs
2 Donegal Ho
3 Pelican Pas
4 Frederick Charrington Ho
5 Wickford Ho
6 Braintree Ho
7 Doveton Ho
8 Doveton St
9 Cephas Ho
10 Sceptre Ho
11 Bancroft Ho
12 Stothard St
13 Redclyf Ho
14 Winkworth Cotts
15 Amiel St
16 Hadleigh Ho
17 Hadleigh Cl
18 Ryder Ho
19 Mantus Cl
20 Kenton Ho
21 Colebert Ho
22 Ibbott St
23 Rickman Ho
24 Rickman St
25 Stothard Ho
26 Barbanel Ho
27 Stannard Cotts
28 St Peters Ct
29 Rennie Cotts
30 Pemell Cl
31 Pemell Ho
32 Leatherdale St

33 Gouldman Ho
34 Lamplighter Cl
35 Sherren Ho
36 Marlborough Lo
37 Hamilton Lo
38 Montgomery Lo
39 Cleveland Gr
40 Cromwell Lo
41 Bardsey Pl
42 Charrington Ho
43 Hayfield Yd
44 Allport Mews
45 Colin Winter Ho
B2 1 Mulberry Ho
2 Gretton Ho
3 Merceron Ho
4 Montfort Ho
5 Westbrook Ho
6 Sugar Loaf Wlk
7 Museum Ho
8 Burnham Est
9 Globe Terr
10 Moravian St
11 Shepton Hos
12 Mendip Hos
13 Academy Ct
14 Pepys Ho
15 Swinburne Ho
16 Moore Ho
17 Morris Ho
18 Burns Ho
19 Milton Ho
20 Whitman Ho
21 Shelley Ho
22 Keats Ho
23 Dawson Ho
24 Bradbeer Ho
25 Forber Ho
26 Hughes Ho
27 Silvester Ho
28 Rogers Est
29 Pavan Ct
30 Stafford Cripps Ho
31 Sidney Godley (VC) Ho
32 Butler Ho
33 Butler St
34 Thorne Ho
35 Bevin Ho
36 Tuscan Ho
B3 1 Evesham Ho
2 James Campbell Ho
3 Thomas Hollywood Ho
4 James Docherty Ho
5 Ebenezer Mussel Ho
6 Jameson Ct
7 Edinburgh Cl
8 Roger Dowley Ct
9 Sherbrooke Ho
10 Calcraft Ho
11 Burrard Ho
12 Dundas Ho
13 Ponsonby Ho
14 Barnes Ho
15 Paget Ho
16 Maitland Ho
17 Chesil Ct
18 Reynolds Ho
19 Cleland Ho
20 Goodrich Ho
21 Rosebery Ho
22 Sankey Ho
23 Cyprus Pl
24 Royston St

25 Stainsbury St
26 Hunslett St
27 Baildon
28 Brockweir
29 Tytherton
30 Malmesbury
31 Kingswood
32 Colville Ho
B4 1 Halkett Ho
2 Christchurch Sq
3 Helena Pl
4 Swingfield Ho
5 Greenham Ho
6 Dinmore Ho
7 Anstey Ho
8 Weston Ho
9 Carbroke Ho
10 Bluebell Cl
11 Cherry Tree Cl
12 Georgian Cl
13 Park Cl
14 Regency Cl
15 Norris Ho
C1 1 Raynham Ho
2 Pat Shaw Ho
3 Colmar Cl
4 Withy Ho
5 Stocks Ct
6 Downey Ho
7 Bay Ct
8 Sligo Ho
9 Pegasus Ho
10 Barents Ho
11 Biscay Ho
12 Solway Ho
13 Bantry Ho
14 Aral Ho
15 Pacific Ho
16 Magellan Ho
17 Levant Ho
18 Adriatic Ho
19 Genoa Ho
20 Hawke Ho
21 Palliser Ho
22 Ionian Ho
23 Weddell Ho
24 Carlyle Mews
25 Greencourt Ho
26 Sundra Wlk
C2 1 Stubbs Ho
2 Holman Ho
3 Clynes Ho
4 Windsor Ho
5 Gilbert Ho
6 Chater Ho
7 Ellen Wilkinson Ho
8 George Belt Ho
9 Ayrton Gould Ho
10 O'Brian Ho
11 Sulkin Ho
12 Jenkinson Ho
13 Bullards Pl
14 Sylvia Pankhurst Ho
15 Mary Macarthur Ho
16 Trevelyan Ho
17 Wedgwood Ho
18 Pemberton Ct
19 Leatherdale St
20 Walter Besant Ho
21 Barber Beaumont Ho
22 Brancaster Ho
23 Litcham Ho
C3 1 Kemp Ho
2 Piggott Ho
3 Mark Ho

4 Sidney Ho
5 Pomeroy Ho
6 Puteaux Ho
Doric Ho
5 Modling Ho
6 Longman Ho
10 Ames Ho
11 Alzette Ho
12 Offenbach Ho
13 Tate Ho
14 Norton Ho
15 St Gilles Ho
16 Harold Ho
17 Velletri Ho
18 Bridge Wharf
19 Gathorne St
20 Bow Brook The
21 Twig Folly Cl
22 Palmerston Ct
23 Lakeview
24 Peach Walk Mews
25 Caesar Ct

26
A1 **1** Formosa Ho
2 Galveston Ho
3 Arabian Ho
4 Greenland Ho
5 Coral Ho
6 Anson Ho
7 Cambay Ho
8 Lindop Ho
9 Moray Ho
10 Azov Ho
11 Sandalwood Cl
12 Broadford Ho
A2 **1** Imperial Ho
2 Newport Ho
3 Vassall Ho
4 Maurice Ct
5 Creed Ct
6 Christopher France Ho
7 Beaumont Ct
8 Pembroke Mews
A3 **1** Nightingale Mews
2 Bunsen Ho
3 Bunsen St
4 Beatrice Webb Ho
5 Margaret Bondfield Ho
6 Wilmer Ho
7 Sandall Ho
8 Butley Ct
9 Josseline Ho
10 Dalton Ho
11 Brine Ho
12 Ford Cl
13 Viking Cl
14 Stanfield Rd
15 Stoneleigh Mews
16 Ruth Ct
17 School Bell Cloisters
18 Schoolbell Mews
19 Medhurst Ho
20 Olga St
21 Conyer St
22 Diamond Ho
23 Daring Ho
24 Crane Ho
25 Exmoor Ho
26 Grenville Ho
27 Hyperion Ho
28 Sturdy Ho
29 Wren Ho
30 Ardent Ho

51 Senators Lo
2 Hooke Ho
3 Mohawk Ho
4 Ivanhoe Ho
55 Medway Mews
B2 **1** Trellis Sq
2 Sheffield Sq
3 Howcroft Ho
4 Astra Ho
5 Frye Ct
6 Byas Ho
7 George Lansbury Ho
8 Regal Ho
9 Coborn Mews
10 Tredegar Mews
11 Cavendish Terr
12 Lyn Mews
13 Buttermere Ho
14 Coniston Ho
15 Tracy Ho
16 Hanover Pl
17 St Clair Ho
18 Longthorne Ho
19 Vista Bldgs
20 Verity Ho
21 Icarus Ho
22 Whippingham Ho
23 Hamilton Ho
24 Winchester Ho
B3 **1** Roman Square Mkt
2 John Bond Ho
3 McKenna Ho
4 Dennis Ho
5 McAusland Ho
6 McBride Ho
7 Libra Rd
8 Dave Adams Ho
9 Regency Ct
10 Tay Ho
11 Sleat Ho
12 Brodick Ho
13 Ewart Pl
14 Lunan Ho
15 Cruden Ho
16 Anglo Rd
17 Mull Ho
18 Sinclairs Ho
19 Driftway Ho
20 Clayhall Ct
21 Berebinder Ho
22 Partridge Ho
23 Barford Ho
24 Gullane Ho
25 Gosford Ho
26 Dornoch Ho
27 Dunnet Ho
28 Enard Ho
29 Fraserburgh Ho
30 Forth Ho
31 Stavers Ho
32 Roscgate Ho
33 Crowngate Ho
34 Queensgate Ho
35 Ordell Ct
36 William Pl
B4 **1** Hampstead Wlk
2 Waverton Ho
3 Elton Ho
4 Locton Gn
5 Birtwhistle Ho
6 Clare Ho
7 Magpie Ho
8 Hornbeam Sq
9 Rowan Ho
10 Barge La

11 Walnut Ho
12 Birdsfield La
13 Atkins Ct
14 Willow Tree Cl
15 Jasmine Sq
16 Tait Ct
17 Ranwell Ho
18 Ranwell Cl
19 Tufnell Ct
20 Pulteney Cl
21 Vic Johnson Ho
22 Lea Sq
23 Iceni Ct
24 Tamar Ct
25 Roman Rd
26 Valentine Ho
C1 **1** Fairmont Ho
2 Healy Ho
3 Zodiac Ho
4 Buick Ho
5 Consul Ho
6 Bentley Ho
7 Cresta Ho
8 Daimler Ho
9 Riley Ho
10 Jensen Ho
11 Lagonda Ho
12 Ireton St
13 Navenby Wlk
14 Burwell Wlk
15 Leadenham Ct
16 Sleaford Ho
17 Bow Triangle Bsns Ctr
C2 **1** Bow Ho
2 Denmark Pl
3 Marsalis Ho
4 Lovette Ho
5 Drapers Almshouses
6 Mallard Point
7 Creswick Wlk
8 Bevin Ho
9 Huggins Ho
10 Williams Ho
11 Harris Ho
12 Marina Ct
13 Electric Ho
14 Matching Ct
15 Wellington Bldgs
16 Grafton Ho
17 Berkeley Ho
18 Columbia Ho
C3 **1** Vincent Mews
2 Menai Pl
3 Heathfield Ct
4 Redwood Cl
5 Acorn Ct
6 Primrose Cl
7 Briar Ct
8 Springwood Cl
C4 **1** Ironworks
2 Juno Ho
3 Chariot Cl
4 Saturn Ho
5 Hadrian Cl
6 Mercury Ho
7 Forum Cl
8 Venus Ho
9 Vesta Ho
10 Tiber Cl
11 Gemini Ho
12 Crown Close Bsns Ctr
13 Old Ford Trad Ctr

27
A1 **1** Broxbourne Ho

2 Roxford Ho
3 Biscott Ho
4 Stanborough Ho
5 Hillstone Ct
A2 **1** Bradley Ho
2 Prioress Ho
3 Alton Ho
4 Foxley Ho
5 Munden Ho
6 Canterbury Ho
7 Corbin Ho
8 Barton Ho
9 Jolles Ho
10 Rudstone Ho
11 Baxter Ho
12 Baker Ho
13 Insley Ho
14 Hardwicke Ho
15 Glebe Ct
16 Priory St
17 Sadler Ho
18 Ballinger Point
19 Henshall Point
20 Dorrington Point
21 Warren Ho
22 Fairlie Ct
23 Regent Sq
24 Hackworth Point
25 Priestman Point
26 Wingate Ho
27 Nethercott Ho
28 Thelbridge Ho
29 Bowden Ho
30 Kerscott Ho
31 Southcott Ho
32 Birchdown Ho
33 Upcott Ho
34 Langmead Ho
35 Limscott Ho
36 Northleigh Ho
37 Huntshaw Ho
38 Chagford Ho
39 Ashcombe Ho
40 Shillingford Ho
41 Patrick Connolly Gdns
42 Lester Ct
43 Franklin St
44 Taft Way
45 Washington Cl
46 Veronica Ho
47 William Guy Gdns
48 Denbury Ho
49 Holsworthy Ho
50 Padstone Ho
B2 **1** Miller's House Visitor Ctr
C1 **1** Crescent Court Bsns Ctr
2 Ashmead Bsns Ctr
3 Forward Bsns Ctr
C4 **1** Victoria Mills
2 Hallings Wharf Studios
3 Poland Ho
4 Peter Heathfield Ho
5 Burford Rd

28
A1 **1** Lantry Ct
2 Rosemount Ct
3 Moreton Twr
4 Acton Central Ind Est
5 Rufford Twr
6 Narrow St

7 Mount Pl
8 Sidney Miller Ct
9 Mill Hill Terr
10 Cheltenham Pl
11 Mill Hill Gr
12 Benjamin Ho
13 Arlington Ct
14 Lombard Ct
15 Steyne Ho
B1 **1** Rectory Rd
2 Derwentwater Mans
3 Market Pl
4 Hooper's Mews
5 Cromwell Ct
6 Locarno Rd
7 Edgecote Cl
8 Harleyford Manor
9 Coopers Ct
10 Avingdon Ct
11 Steyne Ho
B3 **1** Avon Ct
2 Bromley Lo
3 Walter Ct
4 Lynton Terr
5 Acton Ho
6 Fells Haugh
7 Springfield Ct
8 Tamarind Ct
9 Lynton Ct
10 Aspen Ct
11 Pegasus Ct
12 Friary Park Ct
C3 **1** Rosebank Gdns
2 Rosebank
3 Edinburgh Ho
4 Western Ct
5 Kilronan

30
A1 **1** Arlington Ho
2 Lugard Ho
3 Shabana Ct
4 Sitarey Ct
5 Oaklands Ho
6 Davenport Mews
A2 **1** Abercrombie Ho
2 Balmoral Ho
3 Brisbane Ho
4 Bantinck Ho
5 Ellenborough Ho
6 Lawrence Cl
7 Mackenzie Cl
8 Carteret Ho
9 Calvert Ho
10 Winthrop Ho
11 Auckland Ho
12 Blaxland Ho
13 Havelock Ct
14 Hargraves Ho
15 Hudson Ct
16 Phipps Ho
17 Lawson Ho
18 Hastings Ho
19 Wolfe Ho
20 Malabar Ct
21 Commonwealth Ave
22 Charnock Ho
23 Canning Ho
24 Cornwallis Ho
25 Commonwealth Ave
26 Champlain Ho

27 Grey Ho
28 Durban Ho
29 Baird Ho
30 Campbell Ho
31 Mitchell Ho
32 Denham Ho
33 Mackay Ho
34 Evans Ho
35 Davis Ho
36 Mandela Cl
A31 1 Holborn Ho
2 Clement Danes Ho
3 Vellacott Ho
4 O'Driscoll Ho
5 King Ho
6 Daley Ho
7 Selma Ho
8 Garrett Ho
B1 1 Linden Ct
2 Frithville Ct
3 Blomfield Mans
4 Poplar Mews
5 Hopgood St
6 Westwood Ho
7 Stanlake Mews
8 Stanlake Villas
9 Alexandra Mans
B3 1 Latimer Ind Est
2 Pankhurst Ho
3 Quadrangle The
4 Nightingale Ho
5 Gordon Ct
6 Ducane Cl
7 Browning Ho
8 Pavilion Terr
9 Ivebury Ct
10 Olympic Ho
B4 1 Galleywood Ho
2 Edgcott Ho
3 Cuffley Ho
4 Addlestone Ho
5 Hockliffe Ho
6 Sarratt Ho
7 Firle Ho
8 Sutton Est The
9 Terling Ho
10 Danes Ho
11 Udimore Ho
12 Vange Ho
13 Binbrook Ho
14 Yeadon Ho
15 Yatton Ho
16 Yarrow Ho
17 Clement Ho
18 Danebury
19 Coronation Ct
20 Calderon Pl
21 St Quintin Gdns
C1 1 St Katherine's Wlk
2 Dorrit Ho
3 Pickwick Ho
4 Dombey Ho
5 Carandly Villas
6 Mortimer Ho
7 Nickleby Ho
8 Stebbing Ho
9 Boxmoor Ho
10 Poynter Ho
11 Swanscombe Ho
12 Darnley Terr
13 Norland Ho
14 Hume Ho
15 Boundary Ho
16 Norland Rd

17 Helix Ct
C2 1 Frinstead Ho
2 Hurstway Wlk
3 Testerton Wlk
4 Grenfell Wlk
5 Grenfell Twr
6 Barandon Wlk
7 Treadgold Ho
8 St Clements Ct
9 Willow Way
10 Florence Ho
11 Dora Ho
12 Carton Ho
13 Agnes Ho
14 Marley Ho
15 Estella Ho
16 Waynflete Sq
17 Pippin Ho
18 Baseline Business Studios
C3 1 Kelfield Ct
2 Downing Ho
3 Crosfield Ct
4 Robinson Ho
5 Scampston Mews
6 Girton Villas
7 Ray Ho
8 Walmer Ho
9 Goodrich Ct
10 Arthur Ct
11 Whitstable Ho
12 Kingsnorth Ho
13 Bridge Cl
14 Prospect Ho
15 St Marks Rd
16 Whitchurch Ho
17 Blechynden Ho
18 Waynflete Sq
19 Bramley Ho
20 Dixon Ho

31
A3 1 Malton Mews
2 Lancaster Lo
3 Manning Ho
4 Galsworthy Ho
5 Hudson Ho
6 Cambourne Mews
7 Upper Talbot Wlk
8 Kingsdown Cl
9 Lower Clarendon Wlk
10 Talbot Grove Ho
11 Clarendon Wlk
12 Upper Clarendon Wlk
13 Camelford Wlk
14 Upper Camelford Wlk
15 Camelford Ct
A4 1 Murchison Ho
2 MacAulay Ho
3 Chesterton Ho
4 Chiltern Ho
5 Lionel Ho
6 Watts Ho
7 Wheatstone Ho
8 Telford Ho
9 Golborne Mews
10 Millwood St
11 St Columb's Ho
12 Norfolk Mews
13 Lionel Mews
B3 1 Silvester Ho
2 Golden Cross Mews
3 Tavistock Mews
4 Clydesdale Ho

5 Melchester
6 Pinehurst Ct
B4 1 Denbigh Ho
2 Blagrove Rd
3 All Saints Ho
4 Tavistock Ho
5 Leamington Ho
C3 1 Shottsford
2 Tolchurch
3 Casterbridge
4 Sandbourne
5 Anglebury
6 Weatherbury
7 Westbourne Gr Mews
8 Rosehart Mews
9 Viscount Ct
10 Hereford Mans
11 Hereford Mews
C4 1 Ascot Ho
2 Ashgrove Ct
3 Lockbridge Ct
4 Swallow Ct
5 Nightingale Lo
6 Hammond Lo
7 Penfield Lo
8 Harvey Lo
9 Hunter Lo
10 Barnard Lo
11 Falcon Lo
12 Johnson Lo
13 Livingstone Lo
14 Nuffield Lo
15 Finch Lo
16 Polesworth Ho
17 Oversley Ho
18 Derrycombe Ho
19 Buckshead Ho
20 Combe Ho
21 Culham Ho
22 Dainton Ho
23 Devonport Ho
24 Truro Ho
25 Sunderland Ho
26 Stonehouse Ho
27 Riverford Ho
28 Portishead Ho
29 Mickleton Ho
30 Keyham Ho
31 Moulsford Ho
32 Shrewsbury Mews
33 St Stephen's Mews
34 Westway Lo
35 Langley Ho
36 Brindley Ho
37 Radway Ho
38 Astley Ho
39 Willow Ct
40 Larch Ct
41 Elm Ct
42 Beech Ct
43 Worcester Ct
44 Union Ct
45 Leicester Ct
46 Kennet Ct
47 Oxford Ct
48 Fazerley Ct

32
A1 1 China Ct
2 Wellington Terr
3 Stevedore St
4 Portland Sq
5 Reardon Ho
6 Lowder Ho

7 Meeting House Alley
8 Farthing Fields
9 Oswell Ho
10 Park Lo
11 Doughty Ct
12 Inglefield Sq
13 Chopin's Ct
14 Welsh Ho
15 Hilliard Ho
16 Clegg St
17 Tasman Ho
18 Ross Ho
19 Wapping Dock St
20 Bridewell Pl
21 New Tower Bldgs
22 Tower Bldgs
23 Chimney Ct
24 Jackman Ho
25 Fenner Ho
26 Franklin Ho
27 Frobisher Ho
28 Flinders Ho
29 Chancellor Ho
30 Beechey Ho
31 Reardon Path
32 Parry Ho
33 Vancover Ho
34 Willoughby Ho
35 Sanctuary The
36 Dundee Ct
37 Pierhead Wharf
38 Scandrett St
39 St Johns Ct
A2 1 Newton Ho
2 Richard Neale Ho
3 Maddocks Ho
4 Cornwall St
5 Brockmer Ho
6 Dellow Ho
7 Bewley Ho
8 Artichoke Hill
9 Queen Anne Terr
10 King Henry Terr
11 King Charles Terr
12 Queen Victoria Terr
13 Sovereign Ct
14 Princes Court Bsns Ctr
15 Kingsley Mews
A3 1 Peter Best Ho
2 Mellish Ho
3 Porchester Ho
4 Dickson Ho
5 Joscoyne Ho
6 Silvester Ho
7 Wilton Ct
8 Sarah Ho
9 Bridgen Ho
10 Tylney Ho
11 Greenwich Ct
12 Damien Ct
13 Philson Mans
14 Siege Ho
15 Jacob Mans
16 Proud Ho
17 Sly St
18 Barnett St
19 Kinder St
20 Richard St
21 Hungerford St
22 Colstead Ho
23 Melwood Ho
24 Wicker St
25 Langdale St
26 Chapman Ho
27 Burwell Cl

28 Walford Ho
29 Welstead Ho
30 Norton Ho
31 Turnour Ho
32 Luke Ho
33 Dunch St
34 Sheridan St
35 Brinsley St
A4 1 Wodeham Gdns
2 Castlemaine St
3 Court St
B1 1 John Rennie Wlk
2 Malay Ho
3 Wainwright Ho
4 Riverside Mans
5 Shackleton Ho
6 Whitehorn Ho
7 Wavel Ct
8 Prusom's Island
B2 1 Shadwell Pl
2 Gosling Ho
3 Vogler Ho
4 Donovan Ho
5 Knowlden Ho
6 Chamberlain Ho
7 Moore Ho
8 Thornewill Ho
9 Fisher Ho
10 All Saints Ct
11 Coburg Dwellings
12 Lowood Ho
13 Solander Gdns
14 Chancery Bldgs
15 Ring Ho
16 Juniper St
17 Gordon Ho
18 West Block
19 North Block
20 South Block
21 Ikon Ho
B3 1 Woollon Ho
2 Dundalk Ho
3 Anne Goodman Ho
4 Newbold Cotts
5 Kerry Ho
6 Zion Ho
7 Longford Ho
8 Bromehead St
9 Athlone Ho
10 Jubilee Mans
11 Harriott Ho
12 Brayford Sq
13 Clearbrook Way
14 Rochelle Ct
15 Winterton Ho
16 Swift Ho
17 Brinsley Ho
18 Dean Ho
19 Foley Ho
20 Robert Sutton Ho
21 Montpelier Pl
22 Glastonbury Pl
23 Steel's La
24 Masters Lo
25 Stylus Apartments
26 Arta Ho
B4 1 Fulneck
2 Gracehill
3 Ockbrook
4 Fairfield
5 Dunstan Hos
6 Cressy Ct
7 Cressy Hos
8 Callahan Cotts
9 Lindley Ho
10 Mayo Ho
11 Wexford Ho

296   34 B3

6 Tabard Ct
7 Delta Bldg
8 Findhorn St
9 Kilbrennan Ho
10 Thistle Ho
11 Heather Ho
12 Tartan Ho
13 Sharman Ho
14 Trident Ho
15 Wharf View Ct
B4 1 Mills Gr
2 St Michaels Ct
3 Duncan Ct
C2 1 Quixley St
2 Romney Ho
3 Pumping Ho
4 Switch Ho
5 Wingfield Ct
6 Explorers Ct
7 Sexton Ct
8 Keel Ct
9 Bridge Ct
10 Sail Ct
11 Settlers Ct
12 Pilgrims Mews
13 Studley Ct
14 Wotton Ct
15 Cape Henry Ct
16 Bartholomew Ct
17 Adventurers Ct
18 Susan Constant Ct
19 Atlantic Ct
C3 1 Lansbury Gdns
2 Theseus Ho
3 Adams Ho
4 Jones Ho
5 Sam March Ho
6 Arapiles Ho
7 Athenia Ho
8 Julius Ho
9 Jervis Bay Ho
10 Helen Mackay Ho
11 Gaze Ho
12 Ritchie Ho
13 Blairgowrie Ct
14 Circle Ho
15 Dunkeld Ho
16 Rosemary Dr
17 Sorrel La
18 East India Dock
Road Tunnel

35

B3 1 Newton Point
2 Sparke Terr
3 Montesquieu Terr
4 Crawford Point
5 Rathbone Ho
6 George St
7 Emily St
8 Fendt Ct
9 Sabbarton St
10 Briary Ct
11 Shaftesbury Ho
B4 1 Radley Terr
2 Bernard Cassidy St
3 Rathbone Mkt
4 Thomas North Terr
5 Mary St
6 Hughes Terr
7 Swanscombe Point
8 Rawlinson Point
9 Kennedy Cox Ho
10 Cooper St

C1 1 Capulet Mews
2 Pepys Cres
3 De Quincey Mews
4 Hardy Ave
5 Tom Jenkinson Rd
6 Kennacraig Cl
7 Charles Flemwell
Mews
8 Gatcombe Rd
9 Badminton Mews
10 Holyrood Mews
11 Britannia Gate
12 Dalemain Mews
13 Bowes-Lyon Hall
14 Lancaster Hall
15 Victoria Hall
C2 1 Clements Ave
2 Martindale Ave
3 Balearic Apts
4 Marmara Apts
5 Baltic Apts
6 Coral Apts
7 Aegean Apts
8 Capital East Apts
C4 1 Odeon Ct
2 Edward Ct
3 Newhaven La
4 Ravenscroft Ct
5 Douglas Rd
6 Ferrier Point
7 Harvey Point
8 Wood Point
9 Trinity St
10 Pattinson Point
11 Clinch Ct
12 Mint Bsns Pk

36

A1 1 Burford Ho
2 Hope Cl
3 Centaur Ct
4 Phoenix Ct
C1 1 Surrey Cres
2 Forbes Ho
3 Haining Cl
4 Melville St
5 London Stile
6 Stile Hall Par
7 Priory Lo
8 Kew Bridge Ct
9 Meadowcroft
10 St James Ct
11 Rivers Ho

37

A1 1 Churchdale Ct
2 Cromwell Ct
3 Cambridge Rd S
4 Oxbridge Ct
5 Tomlinson Cl
6 Gunnersbury Mews
7 Grange The
8 Gunnersbury Cl
9 Bellgrave Lo
A4 1 Cheltenham Pl
2 Beaumaris Twr
3 Arundel Ho
4 Pevensey Ct
5 Jerome Twr
6 Anstey Ct
7 Bennett Ct
8 Gunnersbury Ct
9 Barrington Ct
10 Hope Gdns
11 Park Road E
B1 1 Arlington Park
Mans

2 Sandown Ho
3 Goodwood Ho
4 Windsor Ho
5 Lingfield Ho
6 Ascot Ho
7 Watchfield Ct
8 Belgrave Ct
9 Beverley Ct
10 Beaumont Ct
11 Harvard Rd
12 Troubridge Ct
13 Branden La
14 Fromow's Cnr
B2 1 Chiswick Green
Studios
2 Bell Ind Est
3 Fairlawn Ct
4 Dukes Gate
5 Dewsbury Ct
6 Chiswick Terr
7 Mortlake St
B3 1 Blackmore Twr
2 Bollo Ct
3 Kipling Twr
4 Lawrence Ct
5 Maugham Ct
6 Reade Ct
7 Woolf Ct
8 Shaw Ct
9 Verne Ct
10 Wodehouse Ct
11 Greenock Rd
12 Garden Ct
13 Barons Gate
14 Cleveland Rd
15 Carver Ct
16 Chapter Cl
17 Beauchamp Ct
18 Holmes Ct
19 Copper Mews
B4 1 Belgrave Ct
2 Buckland Wlk
3 Frampton Ct
4 Telfer Ct
5 Harlech Twr
6 Corfe Twr
7 Barwick Ho
8 Charles Hocking Ho
9 Sunninghill Ct
10 Salisbury St
11 Jameson Pl
12 Castle Ct
C1 1 Chatsworth Lo
2 Prospect Pl
3 Townhall Ave
4 Devonhurst Pl
5 Heathfield Ct
6 Horticultural Pl
7 Merlin Ho
8 Garth Rd
9 Autumn Rise
C2 1 Disraeli Ct
2 Winston Wlk
3 Rushall Mans
4 Bedford Park Mans
5 Essex Place Sq
6 Holly Rd
7 Homecross Ho
8 Swan Bsns Ctr
9 Jessop Ho

38

A1 1 Glebe Cl
2 Devonshire Mews
3 Binns Terr
4 Ingress St
5 Swanscombe Rd

6 Brackley Terr
7 Stephen Fox Ho
8 Manor Gdns
9 Coram Ho
10 Flaxman Ho
11 Thorneycroft Ho
12 Thornhill Ho
13 Kent Ho
14 Oldfield Ho
A2 1 Chestnut Ho
2 Bedford Ho
3 Bedford Cnr
4 Sydney Ho
5 Bedford Park Cnr
6 Priory Gdns
7 Windmill Alley
8 Castle Pl
9 Jonathan Ct
10 Windmill Pas
11 Chardin Rd
12 Gable Ho
A3 1 Fleet Ct
2 Ember Ct
3 Emlyn Gdns
4 Clone Ct
5 Brent Ct
6 Abbey Ct
7 Ormsby Lo
8 St Catherine's Ct
9 Lodge The
A4 1 Longford Ct
2 Mole Ct
3 Lea Ct
4 Wandle Ct
5 Beverley Ct
6 Roding Ct
7 Crane Ct
B1 1 Miller's Ct
2 British Grove Pas
3 British Grove S
4 Beresfede Rd
5 North Eyot Gdns
B2 1 Flanders Mans
2 Stamford Brook
Mans
3 Linkenholt Mans
4 Prebend Mans
5 Middlesex Ct
B3 1 Stamford Brook
Gdns
2 Hauteville Court
Gdns
3 Ranelagh Gdns
C1 1 Chisholm Ct
2 North Verbena
Gdns
3 Western Terr
4 Verbena Gdns
5 Montrose Villas
6 Hammersmith Terr
7 South Black Lion La
8 St Peter's Wharf
C2 1 Hamlet Ct
2 Derwent Ct
3 Westcroft Ct
4 Black Lion Mews
5 St Peter's Villas
6 Standish Ho
7 Chambon Pl
8 Court Mans
9 Longthorpe Ct
10 Charlotte Ct
11 Westside
12 Park Ct
13 London Ho
C3 1 Elizabeth Finn Ho
2 Ashchurch Ct

3 King's Par
4 Inver Ct
5 Ariel Ct
6 Pocklington Lo
7 Vitae Apartments
C4 1 Becklow Gdns
2 Victoria Ho
3 Lycett Pl
4 Kylemore Ct
5 Alexandra Ct
6 Lytten Ct
7 Becklow Mews
8 Northcroft Ct
9 Bailey Ct
10 Spring Cott
11 Landor Wlk
12 Laurence Mews
13 Hadyn Park Ct
14 Askew Mans
15 Malvern Ct

39

A1 1 Prince's Mews
2 Aspen Gdns
3 Hampshire Hog La
4 Blades Ct
A2 1 Albion Gdns
2 Flora Gdns
3 Lamington St
4 Felgate Mews
5 Galena Ho
6 Albion Mews
7 Albion Ct
8 King Street Clois-
ters
9 Dimes Pl
10 Clarence Ct
11 Hampshire Hog La
12 Marryat Ct
13 Ravenscourt Ho
A3 1 Ravenscourt Park
Mans
2 Paddenswick Ct
3 Ashbridge Ct
A4 1 Westbush Ct
2 Goldhawk Mews
3 Sycamore Ho
4 Shackleton Ct
5 Drake Ct
6 Scotts Ct
7 Raleigh Ct
8 Melville Court Flats
9 Southway Cl
B1 1 Bridge Avenue
Mans
2 Bridgeview
3 College Ct
4 Beatrice Ho
5 Amelia Ho
6 Edith Ho
7 Joanna Ho
8 Mary Ho
9 Adela Ho
10 Sophia Ho
11 Henrietta Ho
12 Charlotte Ho
13 Alexandra Ho
14 Bath Pl
15 Elizabeth Ho
16 Margaret Ho
17 Peabody Est
18 Eleanor Ho
19 Isabella Ho
20 Caroline Ho
21 Chancellors Wharf
22 Sussex Pl

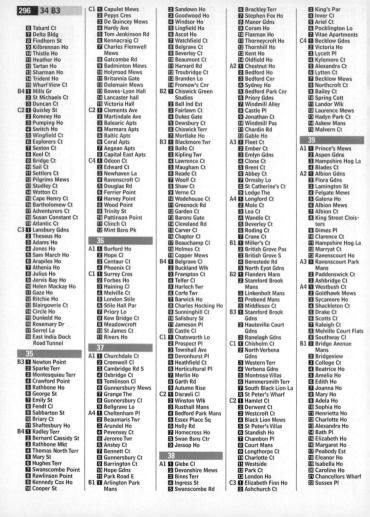

B2
1 Phoenix Lodge Mans
2 Samuel's Cl
3 Broadway Arc
4 Brook Ho
5 Hammersmith Broadway
6 Broadway Ctr The
7 Cambridge Ct
8 Ashcroft Sq
B4 1 Verulam Ho
2 Grove Mans
3 Frobisher Ct
4 Library Mans
5 Pennard Mans
6 New Shepherd's Bush Mkt
7 Kerrington Ct
8 Granville Mans
9 Romney Ct
10 Rayner Ct
11 Sulgrave Gdns
12 Bamborough Gdns
13 Hillary Ct
14 Market Studios
15 Lanark Mans
C3 1 Grosvenor Residences
2 Blythe Mews
3 Burnand Ho
4 Bradford Ho
5 Springvale Terr
6 Ceylon Rd
7 Walpole Ct
8 Bronte Ct
9 Boswell Ct
10 Southern Rd
11 Brook Green Flats
12 Haarlem Rd
13 Stafford Mans
14 Lionel Mans
15 Barradell Ho
C4 1 Vanderbilt Villas
2 Bodington Ct
3 Kingham Cl
4 Clearwater Terr
5 Lorne Gdns
6 Cameret Ct
7 Bush Ct
8 Shepherds Ct
9 Rockley Ct
10 Grampians The
11 Charcroft Ct
12 Addison Park Mans
13 Sinclair Mans
14 Fountain Ct
15 Woodford Ct
16 Roseford Ct
17 Woodstock Studios

40
A1 1 Hockney Ct
2 Toulouse Ct
3 Lowry Ct
4 Barry Ho
5 Lewis Ct
6 Gainsborough Ct
7 Renoir Ct
8 Blake Ct
9 Raphael Ct
10 Rembrandt Ct
11 Constable Ct
12 Da Vinci Ct
13 Gaugin Ct
14 Michelangelo Ct
15 Monet Ct
16 Weald Cl

17 Jasmin Lo
18 Birchmere Lo
19 Weybridge Ct
20 Florence Ho
21 Gleneagles Cl
22 Sunningdale Cl
23 Muirfield Cl
24 Turnberry Ct
25 St Andrews Cl
26 Kingsdown Cl
27 St Davids Cl
28 Galway Cl
29 Edenbridge Cl
30 Birkdale Cl
31 Tralee Ct
32 Woburn Ct
33 Belfry Cl
34 Troon Cl
35 Holywell Cl
A2 1 Market Pl
2 Trappes Ho
3 Thurland Ho
4 Ramsfort Ho
5 Hambley Ho
6 Holford Ho
7 Pope Ho
8 Southwell Ho
9 Mortain Ho
10 Radcliffe Ho
11 Southwark Park Est
12 Galleywall Road Trad Est
13 Trevithick Ho
14 Barlow Ho
15 Donkin Ho
16 Landmann Ho
17 Fitzmaurice Ho
18 Dodd Ho
A3 1 Perryn Rd
2 Chalfont Ho
3 Prestwood Ho
4 Farmer Ho
5 Gataker Ho
6 Gataker St
7 Cornick Ho
8 Glebe Ho
9 Matson Ho
10 Hickling Ho
11 St Andrews Ho
A4 1 Butterfield Cl
2 Janeway Pl
3 Trotwood Ho
4 Maylie Ho
5 Cranbourn Pas
6 Cranbourn Ho
7 Cherry Garden Ho
8 Burton Ho
9 Morriss Ho
10 Dixon's Alley
11 King Edward The Third Mews
12 Cathay St
13 Mission The
14 Millstream Ho
B2 1 Damory Ho
2 Antony Ho
3 Roderick Ho
4 Pedworth Gdns
5 Banner Ct
6 Rotherhithe Bsns Est
7 Beamish Ho
8 Corbetts Pas
9 Gillam Ho
10 Richard Ho
11 George Walter Ho
12 Westlake

18 Adron Ho
19 McIntosh Ho
B3 1 Blick Ho
2 Neptune Ho
3 Scotia Ct
4 Murdoch Ho
5 Edmonton Ct
6 Niagara Ct
7 Columbia Point
8 Ritchie Ho
9 Wells Ho
10 Helen Peele Cotts
11 Orchard Ho
12 Dock Offices
13 Landale Ho
14 Courthope Ho
15 Hithe Gr
16 China Hall Mews
B4 1 Mayflower St
2 St Mary's Est
3 Rupack St
4 Frank Whymark Ho
5 Adams Gardens Est
6 Hatteraick St
7 East India Ct
8 Bombay Ct
9 Stable Ho
10 Grannary The
11 Riverside
12 Cumberland Wharf
13 Seaford Ho
14 Hythe Ho
15 Sandwich Ho
16 Winchelsea Ho
17 Rye Ho
18 Kenning St
19 Western Pl
20 Ainsty St
21 Pine Ho
22 Beech Ho
23 Larch Ho
24 Turner Ct
25 Seth St
26 Risdon Ho
27 Risdon St
28 Aylton Est
29 Manitoba Ct
30 Calgary Ct
31 Irwell Est
32 St Olav's Sq
33 City Bsns Ctr
C2 1 John Kennedy Ho
2 Brydale Ho
3 Balman Ho
4 Tissington Ct
5 Harbord Ho
6 Westfield Ho
7 Albert Starr Ho
8 John Brent Ho
9 William Evans Ho
10 Raven Ho
11 Egret Ho
12 Fulmar Ho
13 Dunlin Ho
14 Siskin Ho
15 Sheldrake Ho
16 Buchanan Ct
17 Burrage Ho
18 Biddenham Ho
19 Ayston Ho
20 Empingham Ho
21 Deanshanger Ho
22 Codicote Ho
23 Buryfield Ct
C4 1 Schooner Cl
2 Dolphin Ct
3 Clipper Cl

4 Deauville Ct
5 Colette Ct
6 Coniston Ct
7 Virginia Ct
8 Derwent Ct
9 Grantham Ct
10 Serpentine Ct
11 Career Ct
12 Lacine Ct
13 Fairway Ct
14 Harold Ct
15 Spruce Ho
16 Cedar Ho
17 Sycamore Ho
18 Woodland Cres
19 Poplar Ho
20 Adelphi Ct
21 Basque Ct
22 Aberdale Ct
23 Quilting Ct
24 Chargrove Cl
25 Radley Ct
26 Greenacre Sq
27 Maple Leaf Sq
28 Stanhope Cl
29 Hawke Pl
30 Drake Cl
31 Brass Talley Alley
32 Monkton Ho
33 James Ho
34 Wolfe Cres

41
A2 1 Trafalgar Cl
2 Hornblower Cl
3 Cunard Wlk
4 Caronia Ct
5 Carinthia Ct
6 Freswick Ho
7 Graveley Ho
8 Husbourne Ho
9 Crofters Ct
10 Pomona Ho
11 Hazelwood Ho
12 Cannon Wharf Bsns Ctr
13 Bence Ho
14 Clement Ho
15 Pendennis Ho
16 Lighter Cl
17 Mast Ct
18 Rushcutters Ct
19 Boat Lifter Way
B1 1 Gransden Ho
2 Daubeney Ter
3 North Ho
4 Rochfort Ho
5 Keppel Ho
6 Camden Ho
7 Sanderson Ho
8 Berkeley Ho
9 Strafford Ho
10 Richman Ho
11 Hurleston Ho
12 Grafton Ho
13 Fulcher Ho
14 Citrus Ho
B2 1 Windsock Cl
2 St George's Mews
3 Linberry Wlk
4 Lanyard Ho
5 Golden Hind Pl
6 James Lind Ho
7 Harmon Ho
8 Pelican Ho
9 Bembridge Ho
10 Terrace The

11 George Beard Rd
12 Colonnade The
13 Pepys Ent Ctr
C1 1 Hudson Ct
2 Shackleton Ct
3 De Gama Pl
4 Mercator Pl
5 Maritime Quay
6 Perry Ct
7 Amundsen Ct
C2 1 Nova Bldg
2 Apollo Bldg
3 Gaverick Mews
4 Windmill Ho
5 Orion Point
6 Galaxy Bldg
7 Venus Ho
8 Olympian Ct
9 Poseidon Ct
10 Mercury Ct
11 Aphrodite Ct
12 Cyclops Mews
13 Neptune Ct
14 Artemis Ct
15 Hera Ct
16 Ares Ct
17 Ringwood Gdns
18 Dartmoor Wlk
19 Rothsay Wlk
20 Ashdown Wlk
21 Radnor Wlk
22 Ironmonger's Pl
23 Britannia Rd
24 Deptford Ferry Rd
25 Magellan Pl
26 Dockers Tanner Rd
C3 1 Bowsprit Point
2 St Hubert's Ho
3 John Tucker Ho
4 Broadway Wlk
5 Nash Ho
6 Fairlead Ho
7 Crosstrees Ho
8 Stanliff Ho
9 Keelson Ho
10 Clara Grant Ho
11 Gilbertson Ho
12 Scoulding Ho
13 Hibbert Ho
14 Cressall Ho
15 Alexander Ho
16 Kedge Ho
C4 1 Anchorage Point
2 Waterman Bldg
3 Jefferson Bldg
4 Pierpoint Bldg
5 Franklin Bldg
6 Vanguard Bldg
7 Edison Bldg
8 Seacon Twr
9 Naxos Bldg
10 Express Wharf
11 Hutching's Wharf
12 Tobago St
13 Bellamy Cl
14 Dowlen Ct
15 Cochrane Ho
16 Beatty Ho
17 Scott Ho
18 Laybourne Ho
19 Ensign Ho
20 Beaufort Ho
21 Spinnaker Ho
22 Bosun Cl

28 Topmast Point
29 Turner Ho
30 Constable Ho
31 Knighthead Point

42

A1 1 Slipway Ho
2 Taffrail Ho
3 Platehouse The
4 Wheelhouse The
5 Chart House The
6 Port House The
7 Beacon Ho
8 Blasker Wlk
9 Maconochies Rd
A2 1 Brassey Ho
2 Triton Ho
3 Warspite Ho
4 Rodney Ho
5 Conway Ho
6 Exmouth Ho
7 Akbar Ho
8 Arethusa Ho
9 Tasman Ct
10 Cutty Sark Ho
A3 1 Turnberry Quay
2 Balmoral Ho
3 Aegon Ho
4 Marina Point
B2 1 St John's Ho
2 Betty May Gray Ho
3 Urmston Ho
4 Salford Ho
5 Capstan Ho
6 Frigate Ho
7 Galleon Ho
8 Barons Lo
B3 1 Cardale St
2 Hickin St
3 John McDonald Ho
4 Thorne Ho
5 Skeggs Ho
6 St Bernard Ho
7 Kimberley Ho
8 Kingdon Ho
9 Killoran Ho
10 Alastor Ho
11 Lingard Ho
12 Yarrow Ho
13 Sandpiper Ct
14 Nightingale Ct
15 Robin Ct
16 Heron Ct
17 Ferndown Lo
18 Crosby Ho
B4 1 Llandovery Ho
2 Rugless Ho
3 Ash Ho
4 Elm Ho
5 Cedar Ho
6 Castalia Sq
7 Aspect Ho
8 Normandy Ho
9 Valiant Ho
10 Tamar Ho
11 Watkins Ho
12 Alice Shepherd Ho
13 Oak Ho
14 Ballin Ct
15 Martin Ct
16 Grebe Ct
17 Kingfisher Ct
18 Walkers Lo

10 Antilles Bay
C2 11 Verwood Lo
2 Fawley Lo
3 Lyndhurst La
4 Blyth Cl
5 Farnworth Ho
6 Francis Cl

43

A1 1 Bellot Gdns
2 Thornley Pl
3 King William La
4 Bolton Ho
5 Miles Ho
6 Mell St
7 Sam Manners Ho
8 Hatcliffe Alm-
shouses
9 Woodland Wlk
10 Earlswood Cl
B1 1 Baldrey Ho
2 Christie Ho
3 Dyson Ho
4 Cliffe Ho
5 Moore Ho
6 Collins Ho
7 Lockyer Ho
8 Halley Ho
9 Kepler Ho
10 Sailacre Ho
11 Union Pk
B3 1 Teal St
2 Maurer Ct
3 Mudlarks Blvd
4 Renaissance Wlk
5 Alamaro Lo
C1 1 Layfield Ho
2 Westerdale Rd
3 Mayston Mews
4 Station Mews Terr

44

A4 1 Ferry Sq
2 Watermans Ct
3 Wilkes Rd
4 Albany Par
5 Charlton Ho
6 Albany Ho
7 Alma Ho
8 Griffin Ct
9 Cressage Ho
10 Tunstall Wlk
11 Trimmer Wlk
12 Running Horse Yd
13 Mission Sq
14 Distillery Wlk
B2 1 Primrose Ho
2 Lawman Ct
3 Royston Ct
4 Garden Ct
5 Capel Lo
6 Devonshire Ct
7 Celia Ct
8 Rosslyn Ho
9 Branstone Ct
10 Lamerton Lo
11 Kew Lo
12 Dunraven Ho
13 Stoneleigh Lo
14 Tunstall Ct
15 Voltaire
C2 1 Clarendon Ct
2 Quintock Ho
3 Broome Ct
4 Lonsdale Mews
5 Elizabeth Cotts
6 Sandwys

7 Victoria Cotts
8 North Ave
9 Grovewood
10 Hamilton Ho
11 Melvin Ct
12 Royal Par
13 Power Ho
14 Station Ave
15 Blake Mews

45

A2 1 Terrano Ho
2 Oak Ho
3 Aura Ho
4 Maple Ho
5 Cedar Ho
6 Saffron Ho
7 Lime Ho
8 Lavender Ho
9 Juniper Ho

46

B1 1 Melrose Rd
2 Seaforth Lo
3 St John's Gr
4 Sussex Ct
5 Carmichael Ct
6 Hampshire Ct
7 Thorne Pas
8 Brunel Ct
9 Beverley Path

47

C4 1 Cobb's Hall
2 Dorset Mans
3 St Clements Mans
4 Bothwell St
5 Hawksmoor St

48

A1 1 Langport Ho
2 Iveagh Ho
3 Newark Ho
4 Edgehill Ho
5 Hopton Ho
6 Ashby Ho
7 Nevil Ho
A2 1 Fairbairn Gn
2 Hammelton Gn
3 Foxley Sq
4 Silverburn Ho
5 Butler Ho
6 Dalkeith Ho
7 Turner Cl
8 Bathgate Ho
9 Black Roof Ho
A4 1 Faunce Ho
2 Garbett Ho
3 Harvard Ho
4 Doddington Pl
5 Kean Ho
6 Jephson Ho
7 Cornish Ho
8 Bateman Ho
9 Molesworth Ho
10 Walters Ho
11 Cruden Ho
12 Brawne Ho
13 Prescott Ho
14 Chalmer's Wlk
15 Copley Ct
16 King Charles Ct
B1 1 Bergen Ho
2 Oslo Ho
3 Viking Ho
4 Jutland Ho
5 Norvic Ho

6 Odin Ho
7 Baltic Ho
8 Nobel Ho
9 Mercia Ho
10 Kenbury Gdns
11 Zealand Ho
12 Elsinore Ho
13 Norse Ho
14 Denmark Mans
15 Dane Ho
16 Canterbury Cl
17 York Cl
18 Kenbury Mans
19 Parade Mans
20 Winterslow Ho
21 Liliford Ho
22 Bartholomew Ho
23 Guildford Ho
24 Boston Ho
25 Hereford Ho
26 Weyhill Ho
27 Lichfield Ho
28 Lansdown Ho
29 Honiton Ho
30 Pinner Ho
31 Baldock Ho
32 Widecombe Ho
33 Nottingham Ho
34 Witham Ho
35 Barnet Ho
36 Empress Mews
B2 1 Bertha Neuberger
Ho
2 Mornington Mews
3 Badsworth Rd
4 Pearson Cl
5 Elm Tree Ct
6 Samuel Lewis Trust
Dwellings
7 Milkwell Yd
8 Keswick Ho
9 Mitcham Ho
B3 1 Boundary Ho
2 Day Ho
3 Burgess Ho
4 Carlyle Ho
5 Myers Ho
6 Thompson Ave
7 Palgrave Ho
8 Winnington Ho
9 Brantwood Ho
10 Lowell Ho
11 Jessie Duffett Ho
12 Otterburn Ho
13 Crossmount Ho
14 Venice Ct
15 Bowyer St
16 Livingstone Ho
17 Gothic Ct
18 Coniston Ho
19 Harlynwood
20 Carey Ct
21 Finley Ct
22 Grainger Ct
23 Hayes Ct
24 Moffat Ho
25 Marinel Ho
26 Hodister Cl
27 Arnot Ho
28 Lamb Ho
29 Kipling Ho
30 Keats Ho
31 Kenyon Ho
32 New Church Rd
33 Sir John Kirk Cl
C1 1 Selborne Ho
2 Hascombe Terr

C2 1 Joiners Arms Yd
2 Butterfly Wlk
3 Cuthill Wlk
4 Colonades The
5 Artichoke Mews
6 Peabody Bldgs
7 Brighton Ho
8 Park Ho
9 Peabody Ct
10 Lomond Ho
11 Lamb Ho
12 Kimpton Ct
13 Belham Wlk
14 Datchelor Pl
15 Harvey Rd
C3 1 Masterman Ho
2 Milton Ho
3 Pope Ho
4 Chester Ct
5 Marvel Ho
6 Flecker Ho
7 Landor Ho
8 Leslie Prince Ct
9 Evelina Mans
10 Langland Ho
11 Drinkwater Ho
12 Procter Ho
13 Shirley Ho
14 Drayton Ho
15 Bridges Ho
16 Cunningham Ho
17 Hood Ho
18 Herrick Ho
19 Dekker Ho
20 Houseman Way
21 Coleby Path
C4 1 Queens Ho
2 Arnside Ho
3 Horsley St
4 St Peter's Ho
5 St Johns Ho
6 St Marks Ho
7 St Stephens Ho
8 St Matthew's Ho
9 Red Lion Cl
10 Boyson Rd
11 Bradenham

49

A1 1 Springfield Ho
2 Craston Ho
3 Walters Ho
4 Edgecombe Ho
5 Fowler Ho
6 Rignold Ho
7 Chatham Ho
A2 1 Barnwell Ho
2 Brunswick Villas
3 St Giles Twr
4 Bentley Ho
5 Dawson Ho
6 Dryden Ho
7 Mayward Ho
8 Longleigh Ho
9 Fairwall Ho
10 Bodeney Ho
11 Sandby Ho
12 Vestry Mews
13 Netley
14 Lakanal
15 Racine
A3 1 Tower Mill Rd
2 Tilson Cl
3 Granville Sq
4 Edgar Wallace Cl
5 Potters Cl
6 Dorton Cl

7 Samuel Jones Ind Est	**9** Dunstall Ho	**10** Harry Lambourn Ho	**20** Greene Ct	**38** Eider Ct

7 Samuel Jones Ind Est
8 Dibden Ho
9 Marchwood Cl
10 Pilgrims Cloisters
11 Beacon Ho
12 Teather St
13 Stacy Path
14 Rumball Ho
15 Ballow Cl
16 Rill Ho
A4 1 Downend Ct
2 Andoversford Ct
3 Pearse St
4 Watling St
5 Gandolfi St
B2 1 Colbert
2 Voltaire
3 Finch Mews
4 Charles Coveney Rd
5 Bamber Rd
6 Crane St
7 Curlew Ho
8 Mallard Ho
9 Tern Ho
10 Crane Ho
11 Falcon Ho
12 Bryanston Ho
13 Basing Ct
14 Marcus Ho
15 Sheffield Ho
B3 1 Painswick Ho
2 Sharpness Ct
3 Mattingly Way
4 Hordle Prom N
5 Burcher Gale Gr
6 Calypso Cres
7 Hordle Prom S
8 Cinnamon Cl
9 Savannah Cl
10 Thames Cl
11 Shannon Ct
12 Amstel Ct
13 Danube Ct
14 Tilbury Cl
15 Hordle Prom E
16 Indus Ct
17 Oakcourt
18 Palm Ct
19 Rowan Ct
20 Blackthorn Ct
21 Pear Ct
22 Lidgate Rd
23 Whistler Mews
24 Boathouse Wlk
B4 1 Willsbridge Ct
2 Cam Ct
3 Quedgeley Ct
4 Saul Ct
5 Quenington Ct
6 Westonbirt Ct
7 Wickway Ct
C1 1 William Margrie Cl
2 William Blake Ho
3 Quantock Mews
4 Choumert Sq
5 Parkstone Rd
6 Atwell Rd
C2 1 Canal Head Public Sq
2 Angelina Ho
3 Jarvis Ho
4 Richland Ho
5 Honeywood Ho
6 Wakefield Ho
7 Primrose Ho
8 Hardcastle Ho

9 Dunstall Ho
10 Springdale Cl
11 Purdon Ho
12 Flamborough Ho
13 Lambrook Ho
14 Witcombe Point
15 Yarnfield Sq
16 Winford Ct
17 Portbury Cl
18 Robert Keen Cl
C3 1 Thornbill Ho
2 Vervain Ho
3 Woodstar Ho
4 Tamarind Ho
5 Hereford Retreat
6 Haymerle Ho
7 Furley Ho
8 Thomas Milner Ho
9 Applegarth Ho
10 Freda Corbett Cl
11 Rudbeck Ho
12 Henslow Ho
13 Lindley Ho
14 Collinson Ho
15 Sister Mabel's Way
16 Timberland Cl
17 Hastings Cl
18 Sidmouth Ho
19 Budleigh Ho
20 Stanesgate Ho
21 Breamore Ho
22 Ely Ho
23 Gisburn Ho
C4 1 Bowles Rd
2 Western Wharf
3 Northfield Ho
4 Millbrook Ho
5 Denstone Ho
6 Deerhurst Ho
7 Caversham Ho
8 Battle Ho
9 Cardiff Ho
10 Bridgnorth Ho
11 Exeter Ho
12 Grantham Ho
13 Aylesbury Ho
14 Royston Ho

50

A1 11 Walkynscroft
2 Ryegates
3 Hathorne Cl
4 Pilkington Rd
5 Russell Ct
6 Magdalene Cl
7 Iris Ct
A2 1 Willowdene
2 Pinedene
3 Oakdene
4 Beechdene
5 Hollydene
6 Wood Dene
7 Staveley Cl
8 Carnicot Ho
9 Martock Ct
10 Cherry Tree Ct
11 Kendrick Ct
A3 1 Tortington Ho
2 Credenhill Ho
3 Bromyard Ho
4 Hoyland Ct
5 Willowdene
6 Ashdene
7 Acorn Par
8 Havelock Ct
9 Springall St

10 Harry Lambourn Ho
11 Grenier Apartments
B1 1 Honiton Gdns
2 Selden Ho
3 Hathway Ho
4 Hathway Ho
5 Station Ct
B2 1 Trotman Ho
2 Boddington Ho
3 Heydon Ho
4 Boulter Ho
5 Astbury Bsns Pk
B3 1 Ambleside Point
2 Grasmere Point
3 Windermere Point
4 Roman Way
5 Laburnum Cl
6 Juniper Ho
7 Romney Cl
8 Hammersley Ho
9 Hutchinson Ho
10 Hammond Ho
11 Fir Tree Ho
12 Glastonbury Ct
13 Highbridge Ct
14 Filton Ct
15 Chiltern Ct
16 Cheviot Ct
B4 1 Penshurst Ho
2 Reculver Ho
3 Camber Ho
4 Chiham Ho
5 Otford Ho
6 Olive Tree Ho
7 Aspen Ho
8 Lewis Silkin Ho
9 Richborough Ho
10 Dover Ho
11 Eynsford Ho
12 Horton Ho
13 Lamberhurst Ho
14 Canterbury Ind Pk
15 Upnall Ho
16 Sissinghurst Ho
17 Rochester Ho
18 Saltwood Ho
19 Leybourne Ho
20 Lullingstone Ho
21 Royston Ho
C3 1 Richard Anderson Ct
2 Palm Tree Ho
3 Edward Robinson Ho
4 Antony Ho
5 Gerrard Ho
6 Palmer Ho
7 Pankhurst Cl
C4 1 Harrisons Ct
2 Grantley Ho
3 Sunbury Ct
4 Tilbury Ct
5 Graham Ct
6 Connell Ct
7 St Clements Ct
8 Henderson Ct
9 Jemotts Ct
10 Verona Ct
11 Heywood Ho
12 Francis Ct
13 Hind Ho
14 Donne Ho
15 Carew Ct
16 Burbage Ho
17 Newland Ho
18 Dobson Ho
19 Dalton Ho

20 Greene Ct
21 Redrup Ho
22 Tarplett Ho
23 Stunell Ho
24 Gasson Ho
25 Bryce Ho
26 Barnes Ho
27 Barkwith Ho
28 Bannister Ho
29 Apollo Ind Bsns Ctr

51

A2 1 Archer Ho
2 Browning Ho
3 Hardcastle Ho
4 Brooke Ho
5 Wallis Ho
A3 1 Batavia Ho
2 Marlowe Bsns Ctr
3 Batavia Mews
4 Woodrush Cl
5 Alexandra St
6 Primrose Wlk
7 Vansittart St
8 Granville Ct
9 Cottesbrook St
10 Ewen Henderson Ct
11 Fordham Ho
A4 1 Portland Ct
2 Phoenix Ct
3 Rainbow Ct
4 Hawke Twr
5 Chubworthy St
6 Woodpecker Rd
7 Hercules Ct
B3 1 Austin Ho
2 Exeter Way
3 Crossleigh Ct
4 Mornington Pl
5 Maple Ho
B4 1 Chester Ho
2 Lynch Wlk
3 Arlington Ho
4 Woodcote Ho
5 Cornbury Ho
6 Prospect Pl
7 Akintaro Ho
8 Mulberry Ho
9 Laurel Ho
10 Linden Ho
11 Ashford Ho
12 Wardalls Ho
13 Magnolia Ho
14 Howard Ho
15 Larch Cl
16 Ibis Ct
17 Merganser Ct
18 Wotton Rd
19 Kingfisher Sq
20 Sanderling Ct
21 Dolphin Twr
22 Mermaid Twr
23 Scoter Ct
24 Shearwater Ct
25 Brambling Ct
26 Kittiwake Ct
27 Diana Cl
28 Guillemot Ct
29 Marine Twr
30 Teal Ct
31 Lapwing Twr
32 Violet Ct
33 Skua Ct
34 Tristan Ct
35 Rosemary Ct
36 Cormorant Ct
37 Shelduck Ct

38 Eider Ct
39 Pintail Ct
C2 1 Admiralty Cl
2 Harton Lodge
3 Sylva Cotts
4 Pitman Ho
5 Heston Ho
6 Mereton Mans
7 Indiana Bldg
8 St John's Lodge
C3 1 Sandpiper Ct
2 Flamingo Ct
3 Titan Bsns Est
4 Rochdale Way
5 Speedwell St
6 Reginald Pl
7 Fletcher Path
8 Frankham Ho
9 Cremer Ho
10 Wilshaw Ho
11 Castell Ho
12 Holden Ho
13 Browne Ho
14 Resolution Way
15 Lady Florence Ctyd
16 Covell Ct
17 Albion Ho
C4 1 Dryfield Wlk
2 Blake Ho
3 Hawkins Ho
4 Grenville Ho
5 Langford Ho
6 Mandarin Ct
7 Bittern Ct
8 Lamerton St
9 Ravensbourne Mans
10 Armada St
11 Armada Ct
12 Benbow Ho
13 Oxenham Ho
14 Caravel Mews
15 Hughes Ho
16 Stretton Mans

52

A2 1 Washington Bldg
2 California Bldg
3 Utah Bldg
4 Montana Bldg
5 Oregon Bldg
6 Dakota bldg
7 Idaho Bldg
8 Atlanta Bldg
9 Colorado Bldg
10 Arizona Bldg
11 Nebraska Bldg
12 Alaska Bldg
13 Ohio Bldg
14 Charter Bldgs
15 Flamsteed Ct
16 Friendly Pl
17 Dover Ct
18 Robinscroft Mews
19 Doleman Ho
20 Plymouth Ho
A3 1 Finch Ho
2 Jubilee The
3 Maitland Cl
4 Ashburnham Retreat
B1 1 Ellison Ho
2 Pitmaston Ho
3 Aster Ho

52 B1 (continued)

4 Windmill Ho
5 Hermitage The
6 Burnett Ho
7 Lacey Ho
8 Darwin Ho
9 Pearmain Ho
B2 1 Penn Almshouses
2 Jervis Ct
3 Woodville Ct
4 Darnall Ho
5 Renbold Ho
6 Lindsell St
7 Plumbridge St
8 Trinity Gr
9 Hollymount Cl
10 Cade Tyler Ho
11 Robertson Ho
B3 1 Temair Ho
2 Royal Hill Ct
3 Prince of Orange La
4 Lambard Ho
5 St Marks Cl
6 Ada Kennedy Ct
7 Arlington Pl
8 Topham Ho
9 Darnell Ho
10 Hawks Mews
11 Royal Pl
12 Swanne Ho
13 Maribor
14 Serica Ct
15 Queen Elizabeth's Coll
B4 1 Crescent Arc
2 Greenwich Mkt
3 Turnpin La
4 Durnford St
5 Sexton's Ho
6 Bardsley Ho
7 Wardell Ho
8 Clavell St
9 Stanton Ho
10 Macey Ho
11 Boreman Ho
12 Clipper Appts
C4 1 Frobisher Ct
2 Hardy Cotts
3 Palliser Ho
4 Bernard Angell Ho
5 Corvette St
6 Travers Ho
7 Maze Hill Lodge
8 Park Place Ho

53

B3 1 Westcombe Ct
2 Kleffens Ct
3 Ferndale Ct
4 Combe Mews
5 Mandeville Ct
6 Pinelands Cl
C3 1 Mary Lawrenson Pl
2 Bradbury Ct
3 Dunstable Ct
4 Wentworth Ho
C4 1 Nethercombe Ho
2 Holywell Cl

54

A1 1 Lancaster Cotts
2 Lancaster Mews
3 Bromwich Ho
4 Priors Lo

5 Richmond Hill Ct
6 Glenmore Ho
7 Hillbrow
8 Heathshott
9 Friars Stile Pl
10 Spire Ct
11 Ridgeway
12 Matthias Ct
A2 1 Lichfield Terr
2 Union Ct
3 Carrington Lo
4 Wilton Ct
5 Egerton Ct
6 Beverley Lo
7 Bishop Duppa's Almshouses
8 Regency Wlk
9 Clear Water Ho
10 Onslow Avenue Mans
11 Michels Almshouses
12 Albany Pas
13 Salcombe Villas
A3 1 St John's Gr
2 Michel's Row
3 Michelsdale Dr
4 Blue Anchor Alley
5 Clarence St
6 Sun Alley
7 Thames Link Ho
8 Benns Wlk
9 Waterloo Pl
10 Northumbria Ct
C1 1 Chester Cl
2 Evesham Ct
3 Queen's Ct
4 Russell Wlk
5 Charlotte Sq
6 Jones Wlk
7 Hilditch Ho
8 Isabella Ct
9 Damer Ho
10 Eliot Ho
11 Fitzherbert Ho
12 Reynolds Pl
13 Chisholm Rd
B2 1 Alberta Ct
2 Beatrice Rd
3 Lorne Rd
4 York Rd
5 Connaught Rd
6 Albany Terr
7 Kingswood Ct
8 Selwyn Ct
9 Broadhurst Ct
B3 1 Towers The
2 Longs Ct
3 Sovereign Ct
4 Robinson Ct
5 Calvert Ct
6 Bedford Ct
7 Hickey's Almshouses
8 Church Estate Almshouses
9 Richmond International Bsns Ctr
10 Abercorn Mews

55

A3 1 Hershell Ct
2 Deanhill Ct
3 Park Sheen
4 Furness Lo
5 Merricks Ct
C4 1 Rann Ho

2 Craven Ho
3 John Dee Ho
4 Kindell Ho
5 Montgomery Ho
6 Avondale Ho
7 Addington Ct
8 Dovecote Gdns
9 Firmston Ho
10 Glendower Gdns
11 Chestnut Ave
12 Trehern Rd
13 Rock Ave

56

C2 1 Theodore Ho
2 Nicholas Ho
3 Bonner Ho
4 Downing Ho
5 Jansen Ho
6 Fairfax Ho
7 Devereux Ho
8 David Ho
9 Leigh Ho
10 Clipstone Ho
11 Mallet Ho
12 Arton Wilson Ho

57

B2 1 Inglis Ho
2 Ducie Ho
3 Wharncliffe Ho
4 Stanhope Ho
5 Waldegrave Ho
6 Mildmay Ho
7 Mullens Ho
C1 1 Balmoral Cl
2 Glenalmond Ho
3 Selwyn Ho
4 Keble Ho
5 Bede Ho
6 Gonville Ho
7 Magdalene Ho
8 Armstrong Ho
9 Newnham Ho
10 Somerville Ho
11 Balliol Ho
12 Windermere Ho
13 Little Combe Cl
14 Classinghall Ho
15 Chalford Ct
16 Garden Royal
17 South Ct
18 Anne Kerr Ct
19 Ewhurst
C2 1 Geneva Ct
2 Laurel Ct
3 Cambalt Ho
4 Langham Ct
5 Lower Pk
6 King's Keep
7 Whitnell Ct
8 Whitehead Ho
9 Halford Ho
10 Humphry Ho
11 Jellicoe Ho
C3 1 Olivette St
2 Mascotte Rd
3 Glegg Pl
4 Crown Ct
5 Charlwood Terr
6 Percy Laurie Ho

58

A2 1 Claremont
2 Downside
3 Cavendish Ct
4 Ashcombe Ct

5 Carltons The
6 Espirit Ho
7 Millbrooke Ct
8 Coysh Ct
9 Keswick Hts
10 Lincoln Ho
11 Avon Ct
B2 1 Keswick Broadway
2 Burlington Mews
3 Cambria Lo
4 St Stephen's Gdns
5 Atlantic Ho
6 Burton Lo
7 Manfred Ct
8 Meadow Bank
9 Hooper Ho
C2 1 Pembridge Pl
2 Adelaide Rd
3 London Ct
4 Windsor Ct
5 Westminster Ct
6 Fullers Ho
7 Bridge Pk
8 Lambeth Ct
9 Milton Ct
10 Norfolk Mans
11 Francis Snary Lo
12 Bush Cotts
13 Downbury Mews
14 Newton's Yd

59

A2 1 Fairfield Ct
2 Blackmore Ho
3 Lancaster Mews
4 Cricketers Mews
5 College Mews
6 Arndale Wlk
B4 1 Molasses Ho
2 Molasses Row
3 Cinnamon Row
4 Calico Ho
5 Calico Row
6 Port Ho
7 Square Rigger Row
8 Trade Twr
9 Ivory Ho
10 Spice Ct
11 Sherwood Ct
12 Mendip Ct
13 Chalmers Ho
14 Coral Row
15 Ivory Sq
16 Kingfisher Ho
C3 1 Burke Ho
2 Fox Ho
3 Buxton Ho
4 Pitt Ho
5 Ramsey Ho
6 Beverley Cl
7 Florence Ho
8 Linden Ct
9 Dorcas Ct
10 Johnson Ct
11 Agnes Ct
12 Hilltop Ct
13 Courtyard The
14 Old Laundry The
15 Oberstein Rd
16 Fineran Ct
17 Sangora Rd
18 Harvard Mans
19 Plough Mews
C4 1 Benham Cl
2 Milner Ho
3 McManus Ho

4 Wilberforce Ho
5 Wheeler Ct
6 Sporle Ct
7 Holliday Sq
8 John Parker Sq
9 Carmichael Ct
10 Fenner Sq
11 Clark Lawrence Ct
12 Shaw Ct
13 Sendall Ct
14 Livingstone Ho
15 Farrant Ho
16 Jackson Ho
17 Darien Ho
18 Shepard Ho
19 Ganley Ct
20 Arthur Newton Ho
21 Chesterton Ho
22 John Kirk Ho
23 Mantua St
24 Heaver Rd
25 Candlemakers

60

A4 1 Kiloh Ct
2 Lanner Ho
3 Griffon Ho
4 Kestrel Ho
5 Kite Ho
6 Peregrine Ho
7 Hawk Ho
8 Inkster Ho
9 Harrier Ho
10 Eagle Hts
11 Kingfisher Ct
12 Lavender Terr
13 Temple Ho
14 Ridley Ho
15 Eden Ho
16 Hertford Ct
17 Nepaul Rd
C1 1 Rayne Ho
2 St Anthony's Ct
3 Earlsthorpe Mews
4 Nightingale Mans
C4 1 Shaftesbury Park Chambers
2 Selborne
3 Rush Hill Mews
4 Marmion Mews
5 Crosland Pl
6 Craven Mews
7 Garfield Mews
8 Audley Cl
9 Basnett Rd
10 Tyneham Cl
11 Woodmere Cl

61

A4 1 Turnchapel Mews
2 Redwood Mews
3 Phil Brown Pl
4 Bev Callender Cl
5 Keith Connor Cl
6 Tessa Sanderson Pl
7 Daley Thompson Way
8 Rashleigh Ct
9 Abberley Mews
10 Willow Lodge
11 Beaufoy Rd
B1 1 Joseph Powell Cl
2 Cavendish Mans
3 Westlands Ct
4 Cubitt Ho
5 Hawkesworth Ho
6 Normanton Ho

7 Eastman Ho
8 Couchman Ho
9 Poynders Ct
10 Selby Ho
11 Valentine Ho
12 Gorham Ho
13 Deauville Mans
14 Deauville Ct
B2 1 Timothy Ct
2 Shaftesbury Mews
3 Brook Ho
4 Grover Ho
5 Westbrook Ho
6 Hewer Ho
7 Batten Ho
8 Mandeville Ho
9 George Beare Lo
B3 1 Polygon The
2 Windsor Ct
3 Trinity Cl
4 Studios The
5 Bourne Ho
B4 1 Clapham Manor Ct
2 Clarke Ho
3 Gables The
4 Sycamore Mews
5 Maritime Ho
6 Rectory Gdns
7 Floris Pl
C1 1 Parrington Ho
2 Savill Ho
3 Blackwell Ho
4 Bruce Ho
5 Victoria Ct
6 Victoria Ho
7 Belvedere Ct
8 Ingram Lo
9 Viney Ct
10 Bloomsbury Ho
11 Belgravia Ho
12 Barnsbury Ho
C3 1 Kendoa Rd
2 Felmersham Cl
3 Abbeville Mews
4 Saxon Ho
5 Gifford Ho
6 Teignmouth Cl
7 Holwood Pl
8 Oaklands Pl
9 Wilberforce Mews
10 William Bonney Est
C4 1 Chelsham Ho
2 Lynde Ho
3 Greener Ho
4 Towns Ho
5 Hugh Morgan Ho
6 Roy Ridley Ho
7 Lendal Terr
8 Slievemore Cl
9 Cadmus Cl
10 Clapham North Bsns Ctr

62
A2 1 King's Mews
2 Clapham Court Terr
3 Clapham Ct
4 Clapham Park Terr
5 Pembroke Ho
6 Stevenson Ho
7 Queenswood Ct
8 Oak Tree Ct
9 Park Lofts
10 Ashby Mews
A3 1 Morris Ho
2 Gye Ho
3 Clowes Ho

4 Thomas Ho
5 Stuart Ho
6 Storace Ho
7 Bedford Ho
8 Ascot Ct
9 Ascot Par
10 Ashmere Ho
11 Ashmere Gr
12 Ventura Ho
13 Vickery Ho
14 Stafford Mans
15 Beresford Ho
A4 1 Callingham Ho
2 Russell Pickering Ho
3 Ormrod Ho
4 Lopez Ho
5 Coachmaker Mews
B2 1 Beatrice Ho
2 Florence Ho
3 Evelyn Ho
4 Diana Ho
5 Brixton Hill Ct
6 Austin Ho
7 Manor Ct
8 Camsey Ho
9 Romer Ho
10 Gale Ho
11 Byrne Ho
12 Farnfield Ho
13 Marchant Ho
14 Rainsford Ho
15 Springett Ho
16 Mannering Ho
17 Waldron Ho
B3 1 Freemens Hos
2 Roger's Almshouses
3 Gresham Almshouses
4 Exbury Ho
5 Glasbury Ho
6 Dalbury Ho
7 Fosbury Ho
8 Chalbury Ho
9 Neilson-Terry Ct
10 Pavilion Mans
11 Daisy Dormer Ct
12 George Lashwood Ct
13 Marie Lloyd Ct
14 Trinity Homes
15 Lethaby Ho
16 Edmundsbury Ct Est
17 Regis Pl
18 Marlborough Mews
19 Alpha Ho
20 Beta Pl
21 Cedars Ho
B4 1 Turberville Ho
2 Thrayle Ho
3 Percheron Ct
4 Draymans Ct
C1 1 Eccleslun Ho
2 Scarsbrook Ho
3 Purser Ho
4 Rudhall Ho
5 Hardham Ho
6 Heywood Ho
7 Haworth Ho
8 Birch Ho
9 Lansdell Ho
10 Lomley Ho
11 Laughton Ho
12 Woodruff Ho
13 Bascome St

14 Dudley Mews
15 Herbert Mews
16 Blades Lo
17 Dick Shepherd Ct
18 Charman Ho
19 Morden Ho
20 Bishop Ct
21 Blackburn Ct
22 Leigh Ct
23 John Conwey Ho
C2 1 Crownstone Ct
2 Brockwell Ct
3 Nevena Ct
4 St George's Residences
5 Hanover Mans
6 Fleet Ho
7 Langbourne Ho
8 Turnmill Ho
9 Walker Mews
10 Cossar Mans
11 Carter Ho
C3 1 Electric Mans
2 Electric La
3 Connaught Mans
4 Clifton Mans
5 Hereford Ho
6 Chaplin Ho
7 Brixton Oval
8 Lord David Pitt Ho
9 Marcus Garvey Way
10 Montego Cl
11 Bob Marley Way
12 Leeson Rd
C4 1 Buckmaster Cl
2 Albemarle Ho
3 Goodwood Mans
4 Angell Park Gdns
5 Fyfield Rd
6 Howard Ho
7 Harris Ho
8 Broadoak Ct
9 Burgate Ct
10 Witchwood Ho
11 Blacktree Mews
12 Chartham Ct
13 Chilham Ct
14 Northgate Ct
15 Westgate Ct
16 Dover Mans

63
A3 1 Mahatma Gandhi Ind Est
2 Dylan Rd
3 Bessemer Park Ind Est
4 Pablo Neruda Cl
5 Langston Hughes Cl
6 Walt Whitman Cl
7 James Joyce Wlk
8 Alice Walker Cl
9 Louise Bennett Ct
10 Chadacre Ho
11 Burwood Ho
12 Pyrford Ho
13 Wangford Ho
14 Ashford Ho
15 Kenwood Ho
16 Moyne Ho
17 Elveden Ho
18 Carrara Cl
19 Broughton Dr
20 Angela Davis Ind Est

21 Tilia Wlk
22 County Ho
A4 1 Mallams Mews
2 Amberley Ct
3 Harper Ho
4 Leicester Ho
5 Station Ave
6 Wellfit St
7 Loughborough Ct
8 Belinda Rd
9 Higgs Ind Est
C3 1 Shaftesbury Ct
2 Mayhew Ct
3 Morris Ct
4 Swinburne Ct
5 Perth Ct
6 Tayside Ct
7 Matlock Ct
8 Hunter Ct
9 Turner Ct

64
A2 1 Velde Way
2 Delft Way
3 Arnhem Way
4 Isel Way
5 Kempis Way
6 Terborch Way
7 Steen Way
8 Deventer Cres
9 Nijmegen Way
10 Hilversum Cres
11 St Barnabas Cl
A4 1 Harfield Gdns
2 Karen Ct
3 Seavington Ho
4 Appleshaw Ho
5 Birdsall Ho
6 Whitney Ho
7 Wheatland Ho
8 Wilton Ho
9 Walcot Ho
10 Whaddon Ho
11 Melbreak Ho
12 Ledbury Ho
13 Tidworth Ho
14 Riseholme Ho
15 Ringmer Ho
16 Petworth Ho
17 Stagshaw Ho
18 Ivybridge Ho
19 Inwood Ho
20 Gatcombe Ho
21 Felbridge Ho
B3 1 Dulwich Mews
2 St James's Cloisters
C2 1 Dorothy Charrington Ho
2 Keswick Ho
3 Kendall Ct
4 Halliwell Ct

65
A4 1 Tilling Ho
2 Goodwin Ho
3 Tyrells Ct
4 Citron Terr
5 Basswood Cl
6 Cheam St
C3 1 Laxton Path
2 Barlings Ho
3 Bayfield Ho
4 Coston Wlk
5 Coverham Ho
6 Gateley Ho

7 Dereham Ho
8 Greenwood Ho
9 Hilton Ho
10 Goodall Ho
11 Horsley Ho
12 Jordan Ho

67
B4 1 Bankside Ave
2 Elder Wlk
3 Yew Tree Cl
4 Mill Ho

68
C3 1 Farnborough Ho
2 Rushmere Ho
3 Horndean Cl
4 Highcross Way
5 Timsbury Wlk
6 Foxcombe Rd
7 Ryefield Path
8 Greatham Wlk
9 Gosport Ho
10 Stoatley Ho
11 Milland Ho
12 Clanfield Ho
13 Fareham Ho
C4 1 Woodcott Ho
2 Lyndhurst Ho
3 Wheatley Ho
4 Allbrook Ho
5 Bordon Wlk
6 Chilcombe Ho
7 Vicarage Ct
8 Shawford Ct
9 Eastleigh Wlk
10 Kings Ct
11 Somborne Ho

69
A3 1 Ramsdean Ho
2 Purhrook Ho
3 Portsea Ho
4 Blendworth Point
5 Eashing Point
6 Hindhead Point
7 Hilsea Point
8 Witley Point
9 Buriton Ho
10 Grateley Ho
11 Hascombe Ho
12 Dunhill Point
13 Westmark Point
14 Longmoor Point
15 Cadnam Point
B4 1 Cumberland Ho
2 Devonshire Ho
3 Cornwall Ho
4 Norfolk Ho
5 Leicester Ho
6 Warwick Ho
7 Sutherland Ho
8 Carmarthen Ho
9 Worcester Ho
10 Rutland Ho
11 Paddock Way
C3 1 Sandringham Ho
2 Eastwick Ct
3 Oatlands Ct
4 Banning Ho
5 Grantley Ho
6 Caryl Ho
7 Duncombe Ho

8 Chilworth Ct
9 Kent Lo
10 Turner Ct
11 Marlborough
12 Parkland Gdns
13 Lewesdon Cl
14 Pines Ct
15 Ashtead Ct
16 Mynterne Ct
17 Arden
18 Stephen Ct
19 Marsham Ct
20 Doradus Ct
21 Acorns The
22 Heritage Ho
23 Conifer Ct
24 Spencer Ho
25 Chartwell
26 Blenheim
27 Chivelston
28 Greenfield Ho
29 Oakman Ho
30 Radley Lo
31 Simon Lo
32 Admirals Ct
C4 1 Brett Ho
2 Brett House Cl
3 Sylva Ct
4 Ross Ct
5 Potterne Ct
6 Stourhead Cl
7 Fleur Gates
8 Greenwood

70
A3 1 William Harvey Ho
2 Highview Ct
3 Cameron Ct
4 Galgate Cl
5 Green Ho The
6 King Charles Wlk
7 Florys Ct
8 Augustus Ct
9 Albert Ct
10 Hertford Lo
11 Mortimer Lo
12 Allenswood
13 Ambleside
14 Hansler Ct
15 Roosevelt Ct

71
B2 1 Beemans Row
2 St Andrew's Ct
3 Townsend Mews
4 Sheringham Mews

72
C2 1 Upper Tooting Park Mans
2 Cecil Mans
3 Marius Mans
4 Boulevard The
5 Elmfield Mans

6 Holdernesse Rd
7 Lumiere Ct
C3 1 Heslop Ct
2 St James's Terr
3 Boundaries Mans
4 Station Par
5 Old Dairy Mews
C4 1 Hollies Way
2 Endlesham Ct

73
A3 1 Holbeach Mews
2 Hildreth Street Mews
3 Coalbrook Mans
4 Hub Buildings The
5 Metropolis Apartments
A4 1 Meyer Ho
2 Faraday Ho
3 Hales Ho
4 Frankland Ho
5 Graham Ho
6 Gibbs Ho
7 Dalton Ho
8 Ainslie Wlk
9 Rokeby Ho
10 Caistor Ho
11 Ivanhoe Ho
12 Catherine Baird Ct
13 Marmion Ho
14 Devonshire Ct
15 Blueprint Apartments
B4 1 Limerick Ct
2 Homewoods
3 Jewell Ho
4 Glanville Ho
5 Dan Bryant Ho
6 Olding Ho
7 Quennel Ho
8 Weir Ho
9 West Ho
10 Neville Ct
11 Friday Grove Mews
C3 1 Sinclair Ho
2 MacGregor Ho
3 Ingle Ho
4 St Andrews Mews
C4 1 Riley Ho
2 Bennett Ho
3 White Ho
4 Rodgers Ho
5 Dumphreys Ho
6 Homan Ho
7 Prendergast Ho
8 Hutchins Ho
9 Whiteley Ho
10 Tressider Ho
11 Primrose Ct
12 Angus Ho
13 Currie Ho

74
A1 1 De Montfort Ct
2 Leigham Hall Par
3 Leigham Hall

4 Endsleigh Mans
5 John Kirk Ho
6 Raeburn Ct
7 Wavel Ct
8 Homeleigh Ct
9 Howland Ho
10 Beauclerk Ho
11 Bertrand Ho
12 Drew Ho
13 Dowes Ho
14 Dunton Ho
15 Raynald Ho
16 Sackville Ho
17 Thurlow Ho
18 Astoria Mans
A2 1 Wyatt Park Mans
2 Broadlands Mans
3 Stonehill's Mans
4 Streatleigh Par
5 Dorchester Ct
6 Picture Ho
A3 1 Beaumont Ho
2 Christchurch Ho
3 Staplefield Cl
4 Chipstead Ho
5 Coulsdon Ho
6 Conway Ho
7 Telford Avenue Mans
8 Telford Parade Mans
9 Wavertree Ct
10 Hartswood Ho
11 Wray Ho
A4 1 Picton Ho
2 Rigg Ho
3 Watson Ho
4 MacArthur Ho
5 Sandon Ho
6 Thorold Ho
7 Pearce Ho
8 Mudie Ho
9 Miller Ho
10 Lycett Ho
11 Lafone Ho
12 Lucraft Ho
13 Freeman Ho
14 New Park Par
15 Argyll Ct
16 Dumbarton Ct
17 Kintyre Ct
18 Cotton Ho
19 Crossman Hos
20 Cameford Ct
21 Parsons Ho
22 Brindley Ho
23 Arkwright Ho
24 Perry Ho
25 Brunel Ho
26 New Park Ct
27 Tanhurst Ho
28 Hawkshaw Cl
B1 1 Carisbrooke Ct
2 Pembroke Lo
3 Willow Ct
4 Poplar Ct
5 Mountview

6 Spa View
B3 1 Charlwood Ho
2 Earlswood Ho
3 Balcombe Ho
4 Claremont Ct
5 Holbrook Ho
6 Gwynne Ho
7 Kynaston Ho
8 Tillman Ho
9 Regents Lo
10 Hazelmere Ct
11 Dykes Ct
B4 1 Archbishop's Pl
2 Witley Ho
3 Outwood Ho
4 Dunsfold Ho
5 Deepdene Lo
6 Warnham Ho
7 Albury Lo
8 Tilford Ho
9 Elstead Ho
10 Thursley Ho
11 Brockham Ho
12 Capel Lo
13 Leith Ho
14 Fairview Ho
15 Weymouth Ct
16 Ascalon Ct
17 China Mews
18 Rush Common Mews
C3 1 Valens Ho
2 Loveday Ho
3 Strode Ho
4 Ethelworth Ct
5 Harbin Ho
6 Brooks Ho
7 Godolphin Ho
8 Sheppard Ho
9 McCormick Ho
10 Taylor Ho
11 Saunders Ho
12 Talcott Path
13 Derrick Ho
14 Williams Ho
15 Baldwin Ho
16 Churston Cl
17 Neil Wates Cres
18 Burnell Ho
19 Portland Ho
C4 1 Ellacombe Ho
2 Booth Ho
3 Hathersley Ho
4 Brereton Ho
5 Holdsworth Ho
6 Dearmer Ho
7 Cherry Cl
8 Greenleaf Cl
9 Longford Wlk
10 Scarlette Manor Wlk
11 Chandlers Way
12 Upgrove Manor Way
13 Ropers Wlk
14 Tebbs Ho
15 Bell Ho

16 Worthington Ho
17 Courier Ho
18 Mackie Ho
19 Hamers Ho
20 Kelyway Ho
21 Hurst Ho
22 Harriet Tubman Cl
23 Estoria Cl
24 Leckhampton Pl
25 Scotia Rd
26 Charles Haller St
27 Sidmouth Ho
28 Hunter Ct
29 Onslow Lo
30 William Winter Ct
31 Langthorne Lo

75
A1 1 Thanet Ho
2 Chapman Ho
3 Beaufoy Ho
4 Easton Ho
5 Roberts Ho
6 Lloyd Ct
7 Kershaw Ho
8 Wakeling Ho
9 Eldridge Ho
10 Jeston Ho
11 Lansdowne Wood Cl
12 Rotary Lo
C2 1 Welldon Ct
2 Coppedhall
3 Shackleton Ct
4 Bullfinch Ct
5 Gannet Ct
6 Fulmar Ct
7 Heron Ct
8 Petrel Ct
9 Falcon Ct
10 Eagle Ct
11 Dunnock Ct
12 Dunlin Ct
13 Cormorant Ct
14 Oak Lodge
15 Corfe Lodge

76
C1 1 Tunbridge Ct
2 Harrogate Ct
3 Bath Ct
4 Leamington Ct
5 Porlock Ho
6 Cissbury Ho
7 Eddisbury Ho
8 Dundry Ho
9 Silbury Ho
10 Homildon Ho
11 Highgate Ho
12 Richmond Ho
13 Pendle Ho
14 Tynwald Ho
15 Wirrall Ho
16 Greyfriars

www.philips-maps.co.uk

First published 2001 by

Philip's, a division of
Octopus Publishing Group Ltd
www.octopusbooks.co.uk
2–4 Heron Quays
London E14 4JP
An Hachette Livre UK Company

Third edition 2007
Second impression with revisions 2007

LONCB

© Philip's 2007

Spiral-bound
ISBN-10 0-540-09044-1
ISBN-13 978-0-540-09044-0

Perfect-bound
ISBN-10 0-540-09045-X
ISBN-13 978-0-540-09045-7

Hardback (navy)
ISBN-10 0-540-09107-3
ISBN-13 978-0-540-09107-2

Hardback (pink)
ISBN-10 0-540-09108-1
ISBN-13 978-0-540-09108-9

Hardback (red)
ISBN-10 0-540-09110-3
ISBN-13 978-0-540-09110-2

Hardback (grey)
ISBN-10 0-540 09111-1
ISBN-13 978-0-540 09111-9

Hardback (green)
ISBN-10 0-540-09113-8
ISBN-13 978-0-540-09113-3

Hardback (brown)
ISBN-10 0-540-09115-4
ISBN-13 978-0-540-09115-7

This product includes mapping data licensed from
Ordnance Survey®, with the permission of the
Controller of Her Majesty's Stationery Office.©
Crown copyright 2007. All rights reserved.
Licence number 100011710

To the best of the Publishers' knowledge, the
information in this atlas was correct at the time of
going to press. No responsibility can be accepted
for any errors or their consequences.

The representation in this atlas of a road, track
or path is no evidence of the existence of a right
of way.

Ordnance Survey and the OS symbol are
registered trademarks of Ordnance Survey, the
national mapping agency of Great Britain

This product contains driver restriction information
derived from Teleatlas ©TeleatlasDRI

The information for the speed camera locations
is used with permission of the London Safety
Camera Partnership and is correct at the time of
publishing. New sites will be installed by the LSCP,
for the latest list visit www.lscp.org.uk

Printed and bound in Spain
by Cayfosa-Quebecor

NOTES

NOTES

NOTES

NOTES

NOTES

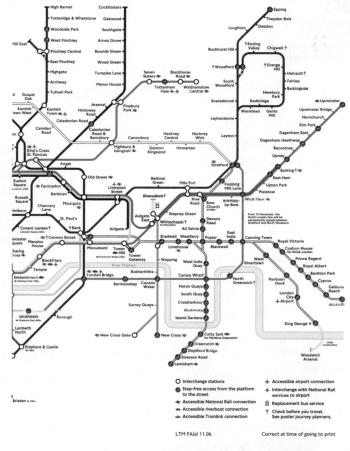

Transport for London

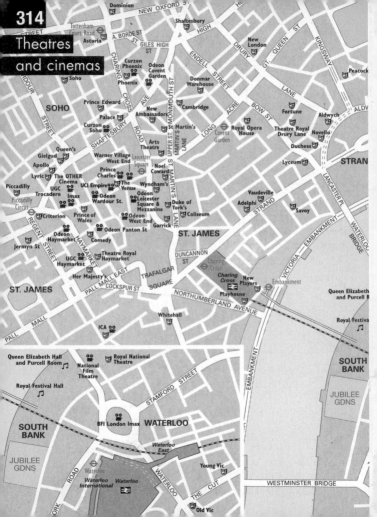

STREET

Dominion

NEW OXFORD ST

Tottenham
Court Road

Shaftesbury

A. BORDE ST

ST. GILES HIGH ST

Astoria

HIGH

DRURY

QUEEN ST

KINGSWAY

New
London

Peacock

Curzon
Phoenix

Odeon
Covent
Garden

ENDELL STREET

Soho

Phoenix

Donmar
Warehouse

LANE

SOHO

STREET

Prince Edward

Cambridge

ACRE

BOW ST

Fortune

Aldwych

ALDW

Palace

Curzon
Soho

New
Ambassadors

LONG

Royal Opera
House

Theatre Royal
Drury Lane

Novello

SHAFTESBURY

ST. MARTIN'S LANE

Covent
Garden

Duchess

Gielgud

Queen's

Arts
Theatre

UPPER ST MARTIN'S LANE

MONMOUTH ST

Lyceum

STRAN

Apollo

Warner Village
West End

Leicester
Square

ROAD

Noel
Coward

Lyric

Prince
Charles

The OTHER
Cinema

Piccadilly

UGC
Trocadero

UCI Empire

The
Venue

Wyndham's

Vaudeville

Imax

Odeon
Wardour St.

Odeon
Leicester
Square &
Mezzanine

Adelphi

STRAND

Savoy

Piccadilly
Circus

Odeon
West End

Duke of
York's

Criterion

Prince of
Wales

ST. MARTIN'S LANE

Coliseum

LANCASTER PL

WATERLOO

Odeon
Haymarket

Odeon Panton St

Garrick

ST. JAMES

REGENT STREET

Jermyn St

Comedy

DUNCANNON
ST

BRIDGE

UGC
Haymarket

HAYMARKET

Theatre Royal
Haymarket

Charing
Cross

Queen Elizabeth
and Purcell R

Her Majesty's

PALL MALL EAST

TRAFALGAR
SQUARE

Charing
Cross

New
Players

EMBANKMENT

Embankment

ST. JAMES

COCKSPUR ST

Playhouse

NORTHUMBERLAND AVENUE

VICTORIA

Royal Festiva

PALL MALL

Whitehall

ICA

Queen Elizabeth Hall
and Purcell Room

Royal National
Theatre

National
Film
Theatre

EMBANKMENT

SOUTH
BANK

Royal Festival Hall

STAMFORD STREET

JUBILEE
GDNS

BFI London Imax

WATERLOO

SOUTH
BANK

Waterloo
East

JUBILEE
GDNS

ORK

ROAD

Waterloo

Young Vic

Waterloo
International

Waterloo

WATERLOO

THE CUT

WESTMINSTER BRIDGE

Old Vic